# Dictionary of Russian Literature Since 1917

# Dictionary of Russian Literature Since 1917

## Wolfgang Kasack

Translated by Maria Carlson and Jane T. Hedges
Bibliographical Revision by Rebecca Atack

COLUMBIA UNIVERSITY PRESS

New York

1988

Acknowledgment is gratefully extended by the Press to Inter Nationes for a special grant supporting this publication.

Columbia University Press
New York      Guildford, Surrey

Translation of Wolfgang Kasack, Lexikon der russischen Literatur ab 1917, © 1976 Alfred Kröner Verlag, Stuttgart, and of Wolfgang Kasack, Lexikon der russischen Literatur ab 1917. Ergänzungsband (Arbeiten und Texte zur Slavistik, 38), published 1986 by Otto Sagner Verlag, Munich

Library of Congress Cataloging-in-Publication Data

Kasack, Wolfgang.
    Dictionary of Russian literature since 1917.

    Translation of: Lexikon der russischen Literatur ab 1917, and of Lexikon der russischen Literatur ab 1917, Ergänzungsband.
    Includes index.
    1. Russian literature—20th century—Bio-bibliography. 2. Authors, Russian—20th century—Biography—Dictionaries. I. Kasack, Wolfgang. Lexikon der russischen Literatur ab 1917. Ergänzungsband. English. 1988. II. Atack, Rebecca. III. Title.
Z2500.K3513 1988      891.7'09'004 [B]      87-20838
ISBN 0-231-05242-1 (alk. paper)

Book design by J. S. Roberts

Printed in the United States of America

# Preface

This dictionary of Russian literature since 1917 was first published in German in 1976. For this translation, all entries were updated and 153 entries were added. These additional entries were published as a supplementary volume to the German-language edition in 1986.[1] This English edition consists of 706 entries, 619 author and 87 subject entries.

The German edition was undertaken at the suggestion of the Alfred Kröner Verlag, based on their realization that we in the West have histories of modern Russian literature offering an extensive presentation of a few authors and some of their works, but not an up-to-date and comprehensive reference work encompassing many authors. *Kratkaya literaturnaya entsiklopediya*,[2] the Soviet work that comes closest to filling this informational gap, is politically one-sided, in its selection of authors as well as in its selection and presentation of the facts. During the six years occupied by the translating and editing of this dictionary, Victor Terras has edited his *Handbook of Russian Literature* and Harry B. Weber has completed eight volumes of his *Modern Encyclopedia of Russian and Soviet Literature*. Both of these publications contain considerably fewer authors from the period covered by this dictionary. When important supplementary material on the authors included here can be found in one of these

---

[1] W. Kasack, *Lexikon der russischen Literatur ab 1917* (Stuttgart: Alfred Kröner, 1976), 457 pages; idem, *Lexikon der russischen Literatur ab 1917: Ergänzungsband*, Arbeiten und Texte zur Slavistik, no. 38 (Munich: Otto Sagner, 1986), 225 pages.

[2] *Kratkaja literaturnaja enciklopedija*, 9 vols. (Moscow, 1962–78).

reference works, the bibliography will so indicate (using the abbreviations *HRL* and *MERSL*).[3]

This dictionary presents Russian literature as a unit; this is not a dictionary of "Soviet literature." Every literature is constituted above all on the basis of its language; political and geographic divisions are subordinate to criteria of language. For this reason, we must view Russian literature since 1917 as a single entity that, owing to political circumstances in the Soviet Union, has been split into a Soviet portion, which is accepted by the Soviet censor, and a non-Soviet portion, which is not, or has not been, so accepted. Membership in one group or the other has constantly shifted during the seven decades since 1917, reflecting the fluctuations in the policy of the Communist Party of the Soviet Union. There are authors who represent Soviet literature for a time and are then excluded (for example, V. Aksyonov, V. Nekrasov, A. Solzhenitsyn); there are also works that have met this fate. But there are also authors who have been excluded from Soviet literature for a while and who have then been rehabilitated and reincluded (for example, I. Babel, M. Bulgakov, M. Zoshchenko). The non-Soviet portion of Russian literature includes works that were printed in the Soviet Union and then forbidden, the authors who have been part of the three waves of emigration, and works that were written in the Soviet Union but published abroad because of censorship. Political developments have given even the term *Russian literature* a variety of meanings. In addition to works written in Russian by Russian authors, this term refers to books written in Russian by non-Russian authors (for example, G. Aygi or Ch. Aytmatov), and also to works by Russian authors who have built a bridge to another culture in emigration and who also write in the language of their host country (for example, V. Nabokov in English, W. Lindenberg in German). This work encompasses all these categories.

The selection of authors was undertaken with the informational needs of the reader clearly in mind. Thus, this work includes not only authors whom I personally consider "good writers"—an opinion that is usually confirmed by statements of others in works of criticism or histories of literature[4]—but also—especially in the field

---

[3] *Handbook of Russian Literature*, ed. V. Terras (New Haven, Conn.: Yale University Press, 1985); *The Modern Encyclopedia of Russian and Soviet Literature*, ed. Harry B. Weber (Gulf Breeze, Fla.: Academic International Press, 1977–).

[4] D. Brown, *Soviet Russian Literature since Stalin* (Cambridge–New York, 1978), E. Brown, *Russian Literature since the Revolution*, 2d ed. (New York, 1982); A. Eliasberg, *Russische Literaturgeschichte in Einzelporträts* (Munich, 1925); M. Geller, *Koncentracionnyj mir i so-*

of Soviet literature—authors whose recognition by Soviet official-
dom is based on purely political considerations (and who have thus
had greater possibilities for publication).[5] For such authors, the dictionary is envisioned as a resource offering an objective view of the
literary value of their work. Thus, all authors who have received
comprehensive treatment in the Soviet histories of literature of the
last decades and nearly all Russian-language recipients of the Lenin
and Stalin Prizes—first and second class—and a great number of recipients of the State Prizes are listed, even when their literary significance is nil. Readers of Soviet sources from various time periods
will encounter these names and should here find the possibility of
understanding the viewpoints of these sources. Whereas the most
important authors who are promoted by the Soviet authorities can
be fairly easily ascertained by statistical means, selecting among
Russian authors published abroad or published in the Soviet Union
but not canonized has been very difficult.

In 1974 when the first German edition was being prepared, V. Rasputin was a little-known author outside the Soviet Union; today
writers such as O. Chukhontsev, A. Kim, and V. Slavkin are among
those authors living in the Soviet Union who are appearing in a
Western reference book for the first time. The internationally most
recognized authors from the first emigration are, of course, included
in the dictionary. But this work also provides information on many
other authors from this period whose work deserves attention. The
second wave of Russian emigration (1941–45) had previously been
almost completely excluded from Slavic monographs and reference
books; this period provided much fertile soil. The third wave of emigration came into existence while this dictionary was being prepared. Many of these authors were included, regardless of whether
they were recognized authors before their departure from the Soviet
Union or whether they first began publishing in the West. Many au-

vetskaja literatura (London, 1974); J. Holthusen, Twentieth-Century Russian Literature: A Critical
Study (New York, 1972); J. Holthusen, Russische Literatur im 20. Jahrhundert (Munich, 1978);
E. Lo Gatto, Storia della letteratura russa contemporanea (Milan, 1958); Ju. Mal'cev, Vol'naja
russkaja literatura (Frankfurt am Main, 1976); Russkaja literatura v emigracii, ed. N. Polto-
rackij (Pittsburgh, 1972); H. B. Segel, Twentieth-Century Russian Drama: From Gorky to the
Present (New York, 1979); M. Slonim, Soviet Russian Literature: Writers and Problems 1917–
1977 (New York, 1977); G. Struve, Russian Literature under Lenin and Stalin 1917–1953
(London, 1971); G. Struve, Russkaja literatura v izgnanii (New York, 1956; 2d ed., Paris, 1984);
Petr Vajl', Aleksandr Genis, Sovremennaja russkaja proza (Ann Arbor, 1982).
  [5] Istorija russkoj sovetskoj literatury, 3 vols. (Moscow, 1958–61), 4 vols. (Moscow, 1967–
71); Istorija russkoj sovetskoj literatury, ed. P. S. Vykhodcev (Moscow, 1970; 2d ed., 1974; 3d
ed., 1979).

thors whose publications and whose position would have justified their inclusion will unavoidably be missing from this contemporary group. Just as editorial work on this dictionary was concluding, an anthology of contemporary Russian poetry of the third wave of emigration was published,[6] too late for consideration here. Contemporary literature is a developing phenomenon.

This dictionary contains only authors, not critics, literary scholars, or translators. The few exceptions, such as L. Grossman, M. Lozinsky, A. Lunacharsky, A. Voronsky, are critics who also did creative work in the fields of fiction, poetry, or drama. Thus the emphasis lies on this aspect of their work.

The subject entries describe the most important terms, associations, and journals of modern Russian literature. In the entries for journals, preference in listing members of the editorial board is given to those who have their own entry in the dictionary; a similar decision has been made for listing members of literary associations such as the Serapion Brothers. Extensive research was necessary to provide an overview of the literary prizes. In addition to the separate entry for this topic, individual prizes are mentioned in the entries for the authors in question; for the Stalin Prizes, the year to which the award refers and the year in which the award was distributed are distinguished and the class of the award is given for the first time. Similar new ground is covered by the entries for Writers Congresses and the Writers Union and by the information concerning the position individual authors held in the Union. For evaluating public activities and official recognition, the information concerning who has received prizes, been delegated to congresses, and held positions in the leadership is of considerable importance. The subject entries provide the necessary background. The entries for Censorship, Emigration, Gulag and Literature, Rehabilitation, Samizdat, and others open up areas that cannot be dealt with in Soviet works but that are essential for a comprehensive understanding of modern Russian literature.

In determining the length of individual author entries, conformity to the writer's literary significance has been the goal, yet this principle competed with the necessity of being more comprehensive for those authors who are not included in other reference works and for whom almost all particulars were assembled from scattered sources. Quotations from histories of literature are intended not only to pres-

[6] *Russkie poety na Zapade*, ed. A. Glezer, S. Petrunis (Paris–New York, 1986).

ent the opinion of the authors who wrote them but also to indicate that a more extensive discussion on a particular subject exists in the source mentioned. (Because these references are intended to refer to the work in general and because these works all have indexes, the specific bibliographic data for these quotations have not been included.)

The individual author entries are divided into a biographical portion and a portion evaluating the author's work. A selected bibliography follows. For Soviet Russian authors, the biographical data are often taken from Soviet reference works, but variations in official opinion and information concerning repression are also provided. For émigré authors, the biographical facts have been verified with the authors or their descendants as often as possible. The listing of secondary literature often includes articles by writers with their own entry in the dictionary for two reasons; first, because these are often among the best, and second, because the reader can expand his picture of many writers included in the dictionary by using the index to locate the articles of literary criticism written by an author of interest to him.

Every possible attempt has been made to include the following information in each author entry: last name, first name, and patronymic (with stress marked); mention of given name if the author uses a pseudonym; primary genre(s); date of birth (including the date according to the old calendar in brackets for those born before January 24, 1918); place of birth; date and place of death (if applicable); father's occupation; course of study; beginning of literary activity; membership in the Communist Party of the Soviet Union; lengthy tenure on the editorial board of literary journals; date of emigration (if applicable); position in the leading bodies of the Writers Unions; place of residence (at least as of 1986). The number of pseudonyms in contemporary Russian literature is quite high and often involves name alterations. A reference to the legal or original name is not necessary in many cases, because only the writer's chosen name is known. Providing precise dates of birth and death is often impossible, even for the compilers of Soviet reference works. Several discrepancies exist, for example, between the *Kratkaya literaturnaya entsiklopediya* and other reference works. Information from the various sources was compared, and when no other factors seemed significant, the data were taken from the most recently published source. Dates for those who died in prison should be given little credence, even when they have been included here.

In the text portion, the year that a work was first published in a journal is given, since it is important to present the works in their proper chronological order when discussing the author's biography and literary evolution. In the bibliography, the year given is most frequently that of first publication as a book. The titles of books and stories appear in italics; the titles of short poems appear in roman type and quotation marks. The titles of dramas are always in italics, regardless of whether they were published separately or not. The bibliography provides special details on the publication of dramas in journals since this information has not been included in any other source. The dictionary briefly describes individual works and provides aesthetic evaluations. As far as possible, the information was current as of 1986. In the biographical as well as in the evaluative section, I have tried, on the one hand, to include essential information based on the current level of research to the extent of space available and, on the other hand, to offer new, original material and views so that the two sources might complement each other.

The bibliographies are grouped under primary works and secondary literature. Titles in both groups are arranged chronologically. Collected works or volumes of selected works appear at the end of the primary literature section. In keeping with this principle, collections of dramas are not included here, since a work containing even two dramas would have to be taken out of chronological order and placed at the end. For poets, volumes of selected works have often been left in chronological order, since many a volume bearing the title *Izbrannoye* (Selected Works) represents a cross-section of a poet's creative work to a far less degree than would another volume with a specific title. Multivolume editions always appear at the end. To save space, the place of publication has been omitted from works published in Russia or the Soviet Union, but it has been included for all literature published in the West. Great importance has been attached to providing the reader with secondary literature. Since monographs exist for only a few authors and since a number of Russian journals and newspapers are easily available, many articles in periodicals have been listed. When an author appears in one or the other of two detailed bibliographies of Soviet prose writers and poets (*RSPP* or *RSPPo*), mention is always made of this fact.[7] The bibliographies for émigrés are more complete, since the possibilities for obtaining in-

---

[7] *Russkie sovetskie pisateli. Prozaiki*, 7 vols. (Leningrad, 1959–72); *Russkie sovetskie pisateli. Poety* (Moscow, 1977–).

formation on these authors are worse.[8] In general, I would like to refer readers to G. Wytrzens's bibliographies, which contain additional material in many cases.[9]

Literal translations of titles into English are supplied in the text, replaced by an English-language translation when known. English-language translations are also supplied, when known, for those original works listed only in the bibliographies. In certain instances, most often with authors whose works are more readily available in English, a separate section of translations is included in the bibliographies.

Cross-references within the dictionary (indicated by SMALL CAPITALS) are designed to increase the possibilities for obtaining additional information about a given subject. However, the system of cross-references would have been overburdened if every possible cross-reference had been made. Thus, reference is made to the majority of subject entries, but not to authors and journals included in this dictionary. As a rule, the reader will find that those mentioned have their own entry in the dictionary. The Writers Unions of the USSR and of the RSFSR and the literary prizes are mentioned so frequently that no cross-reference is made to these articles.

The transliteration system conforms to that used in the *Columbia Dictionary of Modern European Literature* and is different for the text and the bibliography. In the text the transliteration is phonetic (for example, Syomin, Shtorm, Zhitkov); in the bibliography, philologic (for example, Sëmin, Štorm, Žitkov); in both systems, the x is transcribed as *kh* (for example, Khodasevich, Khodasevič).

This dictionary could only be written because a number of scholars and student assistants at the Slavic Institute of the University of Cologne were avilable to assist me. These individuals helped collect statistical data and undertook bibliographic research, and they assisted in the practical tasks of obtaining the literature, typewriting, editing the manuscript, and reading proofs. I would like to thank Frau Monika Glaser, Frau Dr. Irmgard Lorenz, Frau Dr. Angela Martini-Wonde, and Frau Marianne Wiebe, M.A., for their cooperation and assistance. I also want to thank many students, especially Frau

[8] *Abstracts of Soviet and East European Emigré Periodical Literature* (Pacific Grove, Calif., 1981–); L. A. Foster, *Bibliography of Russian Emigré Literature 1918–1968*, 2 vols. (Boston, 1970); E. Štejn, *Poezija russkogo rassejanija 1920–1977* (Ashford, Conn., 1978).
[9] G. Wytrzens, *Bibliographie der russischen Autoren und anonymen Werke* (Frankfurt am Main, 1975); idem, *Bibliographie der russischen Autoren und anonymen Werke 1975–1980* (Frankfurt am Main, 1982).

Barbara Graf, Frau Astrid Grunewald, Frau Anette Fischbach, and Frau Schamma Schahadat.

The Writers Union of the USSR and VAAP provided me with biographical data and information. The Deutsche Forschungsgemeinschaft in Bonn, the Stiftung Volkswagenwerk in Hanover, and Inter Nationes in Bonn have all financially supported portions of the research for this project, and I am grateful to each of them. My thanks also go to the translators Maria Carlson and Jane T. Hedges, to Rebecca Atack for research on titles of works translated into English, as well as to Columbia University Press and its executive editor, William F. Bernhardt.

I remember with gratitude my first wife, Waltraut, née Schleuning, with whom, until her death in 1976, I discussed each entry. I am thankful to my second wife, Friederike, née Lagemann, M.A., with whom I worked closely on the conception and style of all new and revised entries.

WOLFGANG KASACK

*Cologne and Much, West Germany*
*June 1987*

# List of Abbreviations

ASSR = Autonomous Soviet Socialist Republic
b. = born
d. = died
Diss. = Dissertation
ed. = edition
Eng. tr. = English translation
enl. = enlarged
*HRL* = *Handbook of Russian Literature*
*Izbr.* = *Izbrannoe*
*Izbr. proizv.* = *Izbrannye proizvedenija*
*Izbr. soč.* = *Izbrannye sočinenija*
Komsomol = Kommunističeskij sojuz molodeži (Communist League of Youth)
Lit. = Literature, Literatura, Literaturnaja, Literaturnoe, Literaturnyj
*MERSL* = *Modern Encyclopedia of Russian and Soviet Literature*
NEP = New Economic Policy
orig. = originally
pov. = povest' or povesti
prov. = province
pseud. = pseudonym
rev. ed. = revised edition

ROSTA = Rossijskoe telegrafnoe agentstvo

RSDRP = Rossijskaja social-demokratičeskaja rabočaja partija (Russian Social-Democratic Workers Party)

RSFSR = Russian Soviet Federated Socialist Republic

RSPP = *Russkie sovetskie pisateli. Prozaiki*

RSPPo = *Russkie sovetskie pisateli. Poety*

*Sobr.* = *Sobranie*

*Sobr. soč.* = *Sobranie sočinenij*

*Soč.* = *Sočinenija, Sočinenij*

SSR = Soviet Socialist Republic

TASS = Telegrafnoe agentstvo Sovetskogo Sojuza (Soviet News Agency)

Univ. = University

USSR = Union of Soviet Socialist Republics

*Vestnik RKhD* = *Vestnik Russkogo Khristianskogo Dviženija*

vol. = volume

YugROSTA = Južnoe rossijskoe telegrafnoe agentstvo

# Changes in Place Names

The names of places in the dictionary are cited in accordance with the usage at the time in question. Subsequent changes in place names are indicated in the following list.

Akmolinsk, since 1961 Tselinograd

Bakhmut, since 1924 Artyomovsk

Dushambe, name changed to Stalinabad in 1929, since 1961 Dushanbe

Grushevsk, Aleksandrovsk-Grushevsky, since 1920 Shakhty (Rostovskaya oblast)

Kamenskaya (stanitsa), since 1927 Kamensk Shakhtinsky

Nikolayevsk, since 1918 Pugachovsk (Saratovskaya oblast)

Nizhny Novgorod, since 1932 Gorky

Novonikolayevsk, since 1925 Novosibirsk

Orenburg, name changed to Chkalov in 1938, since 1957 Orenburg

Perm, name changed to Molotov in 1940, since 1957 Perm

Pokrovsk, since 1931 Engelsk

Revel, since 1940 Tallinn

St. Petersburg, name changed to Petrograd in 1914, since 1924 Leningrad

Samara, since 1935 Kuybyshev

Sereda, since 1941 Furmanov

Simbirsk, since 1924 Ulyanovsk

Sulin, since 1926 Krasny Sulin (Rostovskaya oblast)

Tsaritsyn, name changed to Stalingrad in 1925, since 1961 Volgograd

Tsarskoye Selo, name changed to Detskoye Selo in 1918, since 1937 Pushkin

Tver, since 1931 Kalinin

Verkhneudinsk, since 1934 Ulan-Ude

Vladikavkaz, name changed to Ordzhonikidze in 1931 and to Dzaudzhikau in 1944, since 1954 Ordzhonikidze

Vyatka, since 1934 Kirov

Yekaterinburg, since 1924 Sverdlovsk

Yekaterinodar, since 1926 Dnepropetrovsk

Yelizavetgrad, since 1924 Kirovograd

Yuzovka, name changed to Stalino in 1924, since 1961 Donetsk

# Dictionary of Russian Literature Since 1917

# A

**Abrámov, Fyódor Aleksándrovich,** prose writer (b. Feb. 29, 1920, Verkola, oblast Arkhangelsk—d. May 14, 1983, Leningrad). Abramov was of peasant ancestry. In 1938 he began studying humanities at Leningrad University; during World War II he was a soldier, after 1945 a member of the Communist Party. In 1951 he completed his studies with a candidate's dissertation about M. Sholokhov; thereafter he worked as a college instructor. From 1956 to 1960 he held the chair for Soviet literature at Leningrad University; after 1960 he worked exclusively as a writer. He lived in Leningrad.

Abramov began publishing literary criticism in 1949. In 1954 his essay *Lyudi kolkhoznoy derevni v poslevoyennoy proze* (People in the Kolkhoz Village in Postwar Prose) created a great sensation and triggered a storm of indignation among the dogmatic critics (for example, A. Surkov). In this article, typical of the period immediately following Stalin's death, Abramov criticized the idealized, rose-colored portrayal of the Soviet village in Soviet literature that managed to sidestep the real problems. This article exceeded the permissible degree of criticism and was condemned by the Writers Union. In the essay written after the 22d Party Congress, *Vokrug da okolo* (1963; Eng. trs., *One Day in the "New Life,"* 1963; *The New Life,* 1963); Abramov spoke out in favor of greater participation in profits for the peasants and ridiculed, among other things, the refusal to grant the peasants internal passports. This criticism led to his exclusion from the editorial staff of the journal *Neva.* In his artistic prose, Abramov depicts life on the kolkhoz with the greatest possible candor. His first novel, *Bratya i syostry* (1958; Brothers and Sisters), which concerns life in a village in northern Russia during the war, was given a sequel in 1968 with *Dve zimy i tri leta* (Eng. tr., *Two Winters and Three Summers,* 1984) and initially concluded in 1973 with *Puti—pereputya* (Paths and Crossroads). In this work compiled under the title *Pryasliny* (1974; The Pryaslins) and expanded into a four-part series with the novel *Dom* (1978; The House), Abramov depicts honestly, though in a fashion somewhat diluted by the censor (see Ye. Klepikova), the difficult life of the Russian peasant population during the war, during the postwar period, and up to the present day. The plot, which spans decades, focuses on the village Pekashino in northern Russia. The work is sustained by a belief in the native power of rural life, a power that asserts itself in the face of external enemies as well as when confronted with the repressive measures of Party officials. In 1975 this work was awarded the State Prize of the USSR. In addition, Abramov published several short stories about village life in journals such as *Zvezda, Neva,* and *Novy mir.* "His prose is lean and precise, packed with vividly tangible, concrete details of ordinary village existence" (D. Brown). Characteristic is his predilection for open-ended conclusions and his avoidance of predictable and calculated denouements that detract from the literature he criticizes.

*Works: Ljudi kolkhoznoj derevni v poslevoennoj proze* (essay), in *Novyj mir* 1954:4; *Prjasliny* (novel-tetralogy): vol. 1: *Brat'ja i sëstry,* 1959, vol. 2: *Dve zimy i tri leta,* 1969 (see above), vol. 3: *Puti—pereput'ja,* 1973 (these three vols. as trilogy, 1974), vol. 4: *Dom,* 1979; *Bezotcovščina* (pov. and short stories), 1962; *Odin bog dlja vsekh* (play), in *Neva* 1962:8; *Vokrug da okolo* (essays), in *Neva* 1963:1 (see above); *Poslednjaja okhota* (pov. and short stories), 1973; *Derevjannye koni* (pov. and short stories), 1978; *Žarkim letom* (short stories), 1984.—*Izbr.,* 2 vols., 1975; *Sobr. soč.,* 3 vols., 1980–82.

*Secondary Lit.:* V. Lakšin, in *Novyj mir* 1961:5; L. Rakhmanov, in *Moskva* 1969:6; *RSPP* 7(1):1971; Ju. Andreev, in *Neva* 1973:3; B. Pankin, in *Lit. obozrenie* 1975:5 and in *Družba narodov* 1979:12; E. Klepikova, in *Vremja i my,* Tel Aviv–Paris–New York, 35:1978; I. Zolotusskij, in *Novyj mir* 1981:9 and in *Znamja* 1986:8; I. Dedkov, in *Voprosy lit.* 1982:7; K. Mehnert, in his *The Russians and Their Favorite Books,* Stanford, 1983; A. Ovčarenko, in *Naš sovremennik* 1984: 2, pp. 162–71; F. Kuznecov, in *Novyj mir* 1985:6.

**Acmeism** (Akmeízm), literary movement in Russian poetry that formed a counterweight to symbolism during the second decade of the 20th century. The leading theoretician was N. Gumilyov; the leading organizational center was TSEKH POETOV in St. Petersburg/Petrograd. Next to Gumilyov, the most important exponents were A. Akhmatova and O. Mandelshtam. The concept was taken from the Greek (akme = peak) and was meant to indicate the culminating achievement for which the artist was striving. The fundamental tendency was to emphasize primitive earthly elements and craftsmanship and to break away from the mystical qualities of symbolism. According to the symbolists' view, the acmeists' concentration on the concrete threatened to shift the focus away from the spiritual origin of the visible world. Other descriptions of the poetry of acmeism, such as "neoclassicism," "adamism," "klarizm," reveal its breadth. M. Kuzmin and I. Annensky are among its most important precursors. In contrast to FUTURISM, which also arose as a countermovement to symbolism, acmeism was based, not on a revolutionary change in versification, but rather on the most balanced, conscious, and unequivocal use of daily speech in the poetic sphere. In addition to the strong influence that its most important exponents had on Russian poetry of the 20th century in the Soviet Union and in emigration, acmeism, in contrast to symbolism and futurism, continued to be used to describe poetry written much later on.

Secondary Lit.: See AKHMATOVA, A.; GU-MILYOV, N.; MANDELSHTAM, O.; TSEKH POE-TOV. Antologija peterburgskoj poèzii èpokhi akmeizma, ed. and foreword by G. Ivask and H. W. Tjalsma, Munich, 1973; S. Driver, in Slavic and East European Journal 1968:2; R. D. Timenčik, in Russian Literature 7–8:1974; special issue of Russian Language Journal, 1975, ed. D. Mickiewicz; H. W. Tjalsma, in MERSL 1:1977; F. Rusinko, in Slavic Review 1982:3; J. G. Harris, in HRL 1985.

Adamóvich, Geórgy Víktorovich, poet, critic (b. April 19 [April 7], 1894, Moscow—d. Feb. 21, 1972, Nice). Adamovich studied history at St. Petersburg University. N. Gumilyov noted the influence of A. Akhmatova and I. Annensky on Adamovich's first volume of poetry, Oblaka (1916; Clouds). After the Revolution, Adamovich became a member of the acmeists. He emigrated in 1922 following the publication of his second volume of verse, Chistilishche (1922; Purgatory). As a contributor to numerous émigré journals (including Zveno

[1923–28] and Poslední novosti [1928–39]), Adamovich became a leading critic in Paris. His most important critical essays were published in the collections Odinochestvo i svoboda (1955; Solitude and Freedom) and Kommentarii (1967; Commentaries). At the same time he continued occasionally to write poetry, collected in the volumes Na zapade (1939; In the West) and Yedinstvo (1967; Unity).

Adamovich published only about 100 poems, but they establish him as a gifted if uneven poet. In addition to ascetically austere, compact, and musical verse, he also wrote verse of an expansive and declamatory nature. Many of his poems deal with the problem of émigré life and the inner peace that comes from the loss of material possessions, themes also dealt with in his essays. He called for the depiction in poetry of the basic themes of human existence—for example, love, suffering, and death—and he advocated the preservation of a classical simplicity in form. Under the term "Parisian Note," his stylistic patterns found a following in literary criticism. As a critic, Adamovich has considerable insight and intuition. He is impressionistic. Adamovich's comments on M. Tsvetayeva are among his more disastrous negative evaluations.

Works: Oblaka (poems), 1916; Čistilišče (poems), 1922; Na zapade (poems), Paris, 1939; L'autre patrie (essays), Paris, 1947; Odinočestvo i svoboda (essays), New York, 1955; Načalo povesti (short story), in Novyj žurnal, New York, 85:1966; O knigakh i avtorakh (essays), Munich-Paris, 1966; Edinstvo (poems), New York, 1967; Kommentarii (essays), Washington, 1967.
Secondary Lit.: G. Ivanov, in Novyj žurnal 43:1955; G. Struve, in Grani, Frankfurt am Main, 34–35:1957; Ju. Ivask, in Mosty, New York, 13–14:1968, in Novyj žurnal 106:1972 and 143:1979; I. Činnov, in Novyj žurnal 109:1972; V. Vejdle, in Russkaja mysl', Paris, March 2, 1972; R. M. Hagglund, in Novyj žurnal 108:1972, separate study, Ann Arbor, 1985, and bibliography, Ann Arbor, 1985; J. Glad, in MERSL 1:1977; Ju. Terapiano, in Russkaja mysl' May 18, 1978, p. 10.

Afinogénov, Aleksándr Nikoláyevich, playwright (b. April 4 [March 22], 1904, Skopin, prov. Ryazan—d. Oct. 29, 1941, Moscow). Afinogenov's father was a railroad official, later a writer who used the pseudonym N. Stepnoy. Afinogenov became a member of the Communist Party in 1922; in 1924 he completed his studies at the Moscow Institute of Journalism. He wrote his first drama in 1924; between 1927 and 1929 he was head of the literary section of the first Moscow Workers Theater of the PROLETKULT. In the early 1930s Afinogenov emerged as one of the leaders of RAPP on the basis of his theoretical articles on drama. When the Writers Union was formed in 1934, he was elected to the board and assumed the editorship of the journal *Teatr i dramaturgiya*. At the end of 1936 Afinogenov was exposed to acute political criticism and calumny and his plays were banned; in 1937 he was expelled from the Communist Party and from the Writers Union. He recorded his defense speech, which was never given, in his diary on May 16, 1937: "They took a peaceful man, a dramatist with nothing on his mind but a desire to write several dozen more good plays in the service of his country and his party—and they made this man into a pile of rubbish, a laughingstock." Physically unharmed but shunned by most people, Afinogenov lived in Peredelkino, where he forged a friendship with B. Pasternak and began a novel, *Tri goda* (Three Years). In 1938 he was rehabilitated. During World War II he was assigned to head the literary section of the Soviet Information Bureau. Just as he was to travel abroad in connection with his post, he lost his life in an air raid on Moscow while in the Central Committee building.

Afinogenov wrote 26 dramas; only a portion of them, however, are available in print. The earlier ones were essentially Proletkult propaganda plays. *Malinovoye vareniye* (1926; Raspberry Jam) is "a Communist melodrama, complete with bourgeois villains" and without artistic merit (Struve). Considerably more realistic and psychologically consistent is *Chudak* (1928; The Eccentric), a satire of bureaucracy, favoritism, and anti-Semitism. Afinogenov's next play, *Strakh* (1931; Eng. tr., *Fear*, 1934, and in *Six Soviet Plays*, ed. E. Lyons, 1934), was banned in its original version but was very successful in its second. Using as an example the problem of integrating the old intelligentsia into the new system, the play presents a remarkable criticism of the period: "We live in the epoch of great fear." "Fear does give voice to the legitimate apprehension of many intellectuals in Soviet society in the 1930s concerning the encroachment on science and scholarship by politics and the dangers inherent in a hasty proletarianization of culture" (Segel). Afinogenov's most critical play, *Lozh* (1933; The Lie), which spells out the consequences for the system of the lies inevitably told by lower Party officials, was censured by Stalin himself and banned

shortly after its performance. *Dalyokoye* (1935; Eng. trs., *A Distant Point*, 1941; *Far Taiga*, 1946) centers on death and the work for socialism in an unimportant, remote area. *Mashenka* (1940; Eng. adaptation, *Listen, Professor!*, 1944), which Pasternak admired, is a play about the development of the human element in human beings; it influenced later dramatists. The play reveals the structural features typical of Afinogenov's plays: its action takes place in a family circle, it is limited to a restricted space, and it occasionally employs indirect dialogue in the Chekhovian tradition. It was performed 3,036 times between 1960 and 1971. Afinogenov consciously opposes his traditional psychological and realistic drama to the type of drama called for by V. Vishnevsky and N. Pogodin, that is, loosely structured drama, arranged in scenes, that features many characters (the masses) and renounces personal destiny in favor of social circumstances.

*Works: Na perelome* (play), 1927; *Čudak* (play), 1930; *Tvorčeskij metod teatra* (articles), 1931; *Strakh* (play), 1931 (see above); *Lož'* (play), 1933, and in *Sovremennaja dramaturgija* 1982:1; *Dalëkoe* (play), 1935 (see above); *P'esy* (plays), 1935; *P'esy* (plays), 1940; *Vtorye puti* (play), 1940; *Mašen'ka* (play), 1941 (see above); *P'esy* (plays), 1956; *Dnevniki, Pis'ma. Vospominanija* (articles, diaries, letters), 1957; *Tri goda* (novel), in *Teatr* 1958:3; *Dnevniki i zapisnye knižki*, 1960; *Eë igra* (play) [1938], in *Teatr* 1984:6—*Izbr.*, 2 vols., 1977.

*Secondary Lit.:* A. O. Boguslavskij, 1952; A. Karaganov, 1957, 1964; M. Korjakov, in *Novyj žurnal*, New York, 56:1959; P. Markov, in *Teatr* 1967:4; S. Cimbal, in *Teatr* 1967:8; I. Černobrovov, in *Lit. obozrenie* 1978:11; M. Geller, in *Kontinent*, Paris, 16:1978; R. Korn, in *Teatr* 1983:3.

**Afónin, Vasíly Yegórovich,** prose writer (b. Sept. 3, 1939, Zhirnovka, oblast Novosibirsk). Afonin is of peasant descent. After completing a seven-year village school in 1955, Afonin worked at various practical trades. In 1966 he completed his ten-year education at night school and then studied law in Odessa until 1971. Immediately thereafter, Afonin began his literary career. His first prose work, *V tom krayu* (1972; In That Region), won recognition as an original contribution to VILLAGE PROSE: "a powerful, pure voice" (V. Lakshin). Since then, Afonin has regularly published in various journals and newspapers. In 1974 he moved to Tomsk; since 1975 his short stories and povesti have also appeared in book form. In 1976 Afonin became a member of the Writers Union of the USSR.

From the beginning, Afonin's prose has borne an autobiographical stamp. In V tom krayu he describes a summer in his native Siberian village of Yurga, where he visited his parents when he was a student. Scenes of working the land—mowing hay, tending cattle, gathering mushrooms, picking berries, fixing houses, hunting—link a realistic description of contemporary life with a humane vision. Pisma iz Yurgi (1973; Letters from Yurga) continues this episodic narrative style, using a different structure. The povest Klyukva yagoda (1979; Cranberries, previously published under the title Na bolotakh) forms a high point in Afonin's creative work. Against the background of harsh Soviet reality, Afonin provides insight into the way in which human fates are bound up with nature through the meeting of two brothers (the elder one understood the need to wait out World War I in a secure place in Siberia; the younger one was sent to a camp as soon as he returned from the front). The short story Tyotya Fenya (1979; Aunt Fenya) takes place in southern Russia and reveals Afonin's talent for creating graphic images of simple people and for analytically unveiling past history, using a slowly advancing contemporary plot.

Works: V tom kraju (pov.), in Naš sovremennik 1972:11; Pis'ma iz Jurgi (pov.), in Naš sovremennik 1973:11; V tom kraju (pov.), Novosibirsk, 1975; Poslednjaja osen' (pov. and short stories), 1976; Na bolotakh (pov.), in Junost' 1978:7; Kljukva jagoda (pov. and short stories), 1979; Tëtja Fenja (short story), in Družba narodov 1979:12; Večera (short story), in Avrora 1981:10; Igra v laptu (short stories), 1981; Žili-byli starik so starukhoj (pov.), in Sibirskie ogni 1983:1; Pis'ma iz Jurgi (five pov.), 1984; Večera (short stories and pov.), 1984; Taksist (pov. and short stories), 1985.
Secondary Lit.: V. Lakšin, in Junost' 1973:3; V. Kočetkov, in Moskva 1974:6; A. Kondratovič, in Lit. obozrenie 1976:10; I. Pitljar, in Novyj mir 1981:4; G. Pavlov, in Lit. Rossija June 10, 1983, p. 11; N. Nasedkin, in Lit. Rossija March 8, 1985, p. 11.

**Agápov, Borís Nikoláyevich**, prose writer (b. Feb. 19 [Feb. 7], 1899, Tbilisi—d. Oct. 6, 1973, Moscow). Agapov grew up in Tbilisi, where he completed his philological studies in 1922; in 1921–22 he was secretary of ROSTA's Caucasian Bureau. In 1922 he moved to Moscow to pursue his career in journalism. Agapov was a member of the literary group called constructivists (see CONSTRUCTIVISM), in whose anthologies he published several poems. After 1930 Agapov wrote aesthetically insignificant journalistic prose (ocherk) on the subject of socialist construction. His first major feature article in 1930 was about the newly built automobile plant in Nizhniy Novgorod (later Gorky). Between 1932 and 1947 he wrote feature articles based on journeys undertaken for the newspaper Izvestiya; their claim to literary status lies only in their use of dialogue. During World War II, Agapov's theme was reconstruction in the hinterlands. In the postwar period he toured the people's democracies and Japan in the service of the Studio of Documentary Films. His film scripts received Stalin Prizes for 1943–44 and 1947 (1st class). In 1959 his feature article about the Brussels World Fair was published in booklet form. For Agapov, art is "above all an instrument of communication" (Voprosy lit. 1967:11). For over 40 years Agapov played a role, acknowledged by the Writers Union, in popularizing economic and scientific current events in accordance with the Party line.

Works: Tekhničeskie rasskazy, 1936: Podvig novatorov, 1950; Poezdka v Brjussel', 1959; Šest' zagranic, 1974.
Translation: After the Battle: Stalingrad Watches, 1943.
Secondary Lit.: On Agapov's 70th birthday, in Lit. gazeta Feb. 19, 1969, p. 6; RSPP 7(1):1971; B. Volodin, in Lit. obozrenie 1974:7.

**Akhmadúlina, Bélla** (pseud. of Izabélla Akhátovna Akhmadúlina), poet (b. April 10, 1937, Moscow). Akhmadulina is descended from russified Italians and—on her father's side—from Tatars. She studied at the Gorky Literary Institute, completing her studies there in 1960. At the time her first poems were published in newspapers and journals, she already expressed a view of art that was unusual for the Soviet Union; art was "called not to bring joy to people, but to bring them sorrow" (Komsomolskaya pravda April 28, 1957). Her first volume of poetry, Struna (The String), appeared in 1962. Akhmadulina was Ye. Yevtushenko's first wife and was later married to Yu. Nagibin. The high acclaim of her apolitical, astoundingly perfect lyric led to the inclusion of some of her poems in the SAMIZDAT journal Sintaksis (1959–60) and to the publication of a book by the émigré publisher Posev (1968). The next year, her second volume of poetry was published in the Soviet Union, *Uroki muzyki* (Music Lessons). The verdict in the Soviet Union is divided: beside the highest praise stands the cautious reserve of the more dogmatic critics. Akhmadulina has a close relationship to Georgia. Her volume *Sny o Gruzii* (1979; Dreams of Georgia) contains, in addition to her own poems and essays, many translations of Georgian poetry. In 1979 Akhmadulina contributed to the collection *Metropol*. She lives in Moscow.

For Akhmadulina poetry is self-revelation, a conflict between her poetic being and the world of objects both new (tape recorder, airplane, traffic signal) and traditional (candle, a friend's house). Everything, even the most prosaic, can provide the impulse for her poetry; give wings to her wide-ranging fantasy for bold images or dreamy occurrences that span time; become, like every natural phenomenon, enlivened and ladened with symbols (*Skazka o dozhde* [1964; Fairy Tale about the Rain]). "The world begins with the word; language is not a means or a device but a self-contained essence, a new assemblage of words that has the magic power of creating a new reality" (Slonim). She expanded her vocabulary and syntax through recourse to old elements and then intertwined these with modern colloquial speech; the alienated use of individual words gives them their original meaning in context. Dynamics rather than statics determine the rhythm of her verse, whose "murderous speed" A. Voznesensky praises ("Nas mnogo . . . ," 1964). Bold, occasionally provocative assonances unite her verse (tselofane-tselovali, koroleva-kavalery, igrek-irod). At the beginning, the extent of the unusual surpassed most Russian lyric of her time; later her poetry became simpler, even narrative in form. In *Metropol* she published a piece of surrealist prose that was not cleared by the Soviet censor.

Works: *Struna* (poems), 1962; *Oznob* (poems), Frankfurt am Main, 1968; *Uroki muzyki* (poems), 1969; *Stikhi* (poems), 1975; *Metel'* (poems), 1977; *Sveča* (poems), 1977; *Sny o Gruzii* (poems, translations, essays), 1977, 2d ed., 1979; *Mnogo sobak i sobaka* (surrealistic prose), in *Metropol'*, 1979, pp. 21–47 (Eng. tr., "The Many Dogs and the Dog," in *Metropol*, pp. 6–29, 1982); *Tajna* (poems), 1983.

*Translations: Fever and Other New Poems*, 1969; poems, in *Three Russian Poets: Marga-*

rita Aliger, Yunna Moritz, Bella Akhmadulina, 1979, and in *Three Russian Women Poets, Anna Akhmatova, Marina Tsvetayeva, and Bella Akhmadulina*, 1983.

*Secondary Lit.*: A. Nejmirok, in *Grani*, Frankfurt am Main, 55:1964; L. Anninskij, in *Don* 1965:3; A. Mikhajlov, in *Den' poèzii*, Moscow, 1968; L. Rževskij, in *Vozdušnye puti*, New York, 5:1967, and in *Pročten'e tvorčeskogo slova*, New York, 1970; E. Evtušenko, in *Družba narodov* 1970:6; E. Ermilova, E. Sidorov, in *Lit. gazeta* Jan. 28, 1976, p. 7; C. Rydel, bibliography, in *10 Bibliographies of 20th Century Russian Literature*, Ann Arbor, 1977; RSPPo 2:1978; N. Condee, Diss., Yale Univ., 1978; Z. Papernyi, in *Oktjabr'* 1984:10; Yu. K., in *Grani* 131:1984; S. Lubenskaya, in *Russian Literature* 1985:2; R. Mustafin, in *Družba narodov* 1985:6.

**Akhmátova, Ánna Andréyevna** (pseud. of A. A. Gorénko), poet (b. June 23 [June 11], 1889, Bolshoy Fontan, near Odessa—d. March 5, 1966, Domodedovo, near Moscow). Akhmatova's father was an engineer in the merchant marine. Akhmatova spent her youth in Tsarskoye Selo near St. Petersburg. Beginning in 1907 she studied law in Kiev, then philology in St. Petersburg. Impressed by G. Derzhavin's classicism, Akhmatova wrote her first poems when she was 11; she began publishing in 1907. From 1910 to 1918 she was married to N. Gumilyov; in 1910–12 she traveled to Paris (where she formed a friendship with Amedeo Modigliani) and northern Italy; in 1910 Akhmatova, with Gumilyov, O. Mandelshtam, M. Zenkevich, V. Narbut, and others, formed the group of poets called Tsekh poetov, who differentiated themselves from symbolism and futurism. Akhmatova's very first volume of verse, *Vecher* (1912; Evening), led to her recognition as a poet; it was followed in 1913 by *Chyotki* (Rosary), which went through 11 printings. In spite of her critical attitude toward the Revolution, Akhmatova deliberately remained in Russia. She worked in the library of the Institute of Agronomy. She was married to the Ássyriologist and poet V. Shileyko from 1918 to 1921 and to N. Punin, the art historian, from about 1925 to 1938. After the appearance of Akhmatova's fifth volume of verse, *Anno Domini MCMXXI*, in 1922, neither her earlier nor her new poems were published for 18 years. Akhmatova worked intensively on A. Pushkin as well as on other topics. In 1940 she briefly resumed publishing with a volume of selected poems, *Iz shesti knig* (From Six

Books), which contained the new cycle *Iva* (The Willow). During World War II, Akhmatova was evacuated from the besieged city of Leningrad to Tashkent, where a volume of her selected poems appeared in 1943; she returned to Leningrad in June 1944. Three of her poems were published in *Pravda* during the war. In 1946 Akhmatova, together with the satirist M. Zoshchenko, was the victim of "the most unjustified and cruel attacks" (Tvardovsky) made as part of a campaign initiated by order of the Central Committee of the Communist Party in an effort to tighten its policy in the intellectual sphere (see PARTY RESOLUTIONS ON LITERATURE). Her works, "permeated by the spirit of pessimism," were judged "harmful to the education of our youth and not to be tolerated in Soviet literature"; she herself was abusively called "part nun, part whore" (Zhdanov) and expelled from the Writers Union. In this atmosphere she destroyed some of her prose of the postwar period and turned more and more to translation work. Forced poems about the struggle for peace sporadically appeared in *Ogonyok* in 1950; she had vainly hoped that they might ease the lot of her son, then suffering in the labor camps. She did not begin writing again until after the 20th Party Congress. Toward the end of her life, Akhmatova was allowed to travel to Italy and England to receive literary honors (Taormina, 1964; honorary doctorate from Oxford University, 1965). Although the Central Committee order of Aug. 14, 1946, was never rescinded, Akhmatova has been granted a place of honor in Soviet literature, even in official literary histories. On the other hand, the religious commitment of her work has been disavowed. Her last great poetical work, *Poema bez geroya* (Poem without a Hero), on which she worked from 1940 to 1962, "her spiritual testament, the 'acme' of her life and poetry" (Nag), has thus far been printed in full only in the West. Lidiya Chukovskaya, in her *Zapiski ob Anne Akhmatovoy* (1976, 1980), has presented the history of the writing of many of Akhmatova's poems and volumes of verse, the tragedy of her life, and its relation to the fate of the Russian intelligentsia.

Akhmatova is one of the most important Russian poets of the 20th century; she belongs, with her fellow acmeists, to those poets who "overcame symbolism" (Zhirmunsky), who consciously freed themselves from the mystical and sought to represent the external world in all its spiritual and emotional opulence. Clarity and concentration, along with great spiritual depth, have been the charac-

teristics of her verse from the beginning. Her verse is an expression of the personal; it has very seldom (as during the war) gone beyond this sphere, but there exists in it at all times a suprapersonal meaning, even in her cycle *Rekviem* (Munich, 1963; Requiem), composed between 1935 and 1943 in sorrow for her imprisoned son. A large part of her poetic testimony, which often tends toward epic expression, is devoted to the theme of love as seen from a woman's point of view: the presentiment and onset of love, its suffering, its loss and jealousy. Religious commitment and the motif of loneliness are combined, to some extent, with the subject of the poet's calling. Akhmatova belongs to the tradition of Pushkin; elements from ancient Oriental cultures, French classicism, and the Italian Renaissance, as well as from Russian folklore, may be found in her work. "A subtle sense of Russian nature, an ear perfectly attuned to the intonations of her native language, unerring psychological precision in the expression of spiritual dispositions, intricate simplicity, and the ease and freedom of intonation in her verse" are the special qualities that A. Tvardovsky stressed. Mandelshtam emphasized that she used "the traditional devices of Russian, and not only of Russian, but of all folk songs in general, with extraordinary persistence." Her style is characterized not by unexpected and frequent metaphors but by an "intensive and exhaustive use of a single domain of symbols," "a tendency toward the symbolism of a few semantic series" (Vinogradov, 1922, p. 137). Again and again the skillful use of the epithet, in frequently bold combinations, constitutes a fundamental characteristic of her musical verse.

*Works: Večer* (poems), 1912; *Četki* (poems), 1913; *Belaja staja* (poems), 1917; *Podorožnik* (poems), 1921; *U samogo morja* (poems), 1921; *Anno Domini MCMXXI* (poems), 1922 (reprinted, Letchworth, 1978); *Iz šesti knig* (poems), 1940; *Izbr.* (poems), 1943; *Izbr. stikhi* (poems), 1946; *Stikhotvorenija* (poems), 1946; *Izbr. stikhotvorenija* (poems), New York, 1952; *Stikhotvorenija* (poems), 1958; *Poèma bez geroja; triptikh* (narrative poem), in *Vozdušnye puti*, New York, 1:1960, separate ed., Ann Arbor, 1978; *Stikhotvorenija* (poems), 1961; *Rekviem* (poems), Munich, 1963, in *Oktjabr'* 1987:3; *Beg vremeni* (poems), 1965; *Stikhotvorenija* (poems), 1967; *Stikhotvorenija i poèmy* (lyric and narrative poems), 1976; *Stikhotvorenija* (poems), 1977; *Izbr. lirika* (poems), 1977; *Stikhi, perepiska, vospominanija, ikonografija* (poems, letters, memoirs),

Ann Arbor, 1977.—Soč., 3 vols., New York, Paris, 1967–83 (with detailed commentary and bibliography); *Izbr.*, 1974.

*Translations:* Forty-seven Love Poems, 1927; *Selected Poems,* 1969; *Poem without a Hero,* 1973, reprinted in *Selected Poems,* 1976; *Poems of Akhmatova,* 1973; *Tale without a Hero, and Twenty-two Poems by Anna Akhmatova,* 1973; *Moscow Trefoil and Other Versions of Poems from the Russian of Anna Akhmatova and Osip Mandelstam,* 1975; *Requiem,* in *Selected Poems,* 1976; *Requiem and Poem without a Hero,* 1976; *White Flock,* 1978; *Way of All the Earth,* 1979.

*Secondary Lit.:* B. Èjkhenbaum, 1923; V. Vinogradov, in *Lit. mysl'* 1 (1922), and 1925 (both reprinted, Munich, 1970); B. Filippov, in *Vozdušnye puti* 2:1961; A. Sinjavskij, in *Novyj mir* 1964:4; K. Čukovskij, in *Oxford Slavonic Papers,* 1965; A. I. Pavlovskij, 1966; A. Tvardovskij, in *Novyj mir* 1966:3; M. Nag, in *Scando-Slavica* 13:1967; E. Dobin, 1968; E. Bickert, Paris, 1970; K. Verheul, The Hague, 1971; V. M. Žirmunskij, 1973; M. Aliger, in *Moskva* 1974:12; bibliography for 1973–74, in *Cahiers du monde russe et soviétique* 1975:1 and 1976:4; T. V. Civ'jan, in *Russian Literature* 10–11:1975; L. Čukovskaja, 2 vols., Paris, 1976, 1980; A. Haight, New York, 1976; S. Driver, in *MERSL* 1:1977; M. Satin, Diss. Univ. of Pennsylvania, 1977; A. Hartmann, Diss., Univ. of Wisconsin–Madison, 1978; *RSPPo* 2:1978; V. Toporov, Berkeley, 1981; S. Leiter, Philadelphia, 1983; A. Bakhrakh, in *Novoe russkoe slovo,* New York, Dec. 4, 1983, p. 5; R. Orlova, L. Kopelev, in *Grani,* Frankfurt am Main, 131:1984; S. Ketchian, Munich, 1986.

**Aksyónov, Vasíly Pávlovich,** prose writer (b. Aug. 20, 1932, Kazan). Aksyonov's mother is Yevgeniya Ginzburg; he spent part of his childhood with her in Magadan, her place of exile. Aksyonov's father, a Party official, spent many years in a concentration camp, and for a long time was presumed dead. Aksyonov studied medicine in Leningrad until 1956; he worked as a doctor at various institutes in Leningrad and Moscow until 1960. In 1959 he began his literary activity by writing for the journal *Yunost,* where his first highly acclaimed prose work, *Kollegi* (Eng. tr., *Colleagues,* 1962), was published in 1960; Aksyonov's adaptations for the stage and screen have also been frequently staged or filmed. Aksyonov's prose of the next few years dealt especially with the concerns of youth. Around the novels *Zvyozdny bilet* (1961; Eng. trs., *A Starry Ticket,* 1962; *A Ticket to the Stars,* 1963) and *Apelsiny iz Marokko* (1963; Oranges from Morocco) a fierce controversy developed concerning not only the frankness of his plots but his search for new formal structures as well. After 1965 Aksyonov turned to other themes and sought to deepen his message through narrative means, through the inclusion of the irreal as well as the grotesque and absurd. From 1962 to 1969, Aksyonov, who was living in Moscow at that time, belonged to the editorial staff of the journal *Yunost.* He was a delegate to the congresses of the Writers Union only after 1965; in 1971 he served only in a nonvoting capacity. In 1977–78 Aksyonov published nonrealistic prose in the Soviet Union and in the United States. As one of the main publishers of the almanac METROPOL, he was sharply criticized; in December 1979 he withdrew from the Writers Union and was compelled to emigrate (July 22, 1980). He lives in the United States.

In the works dating from his first period as a writer, works that are much admired both at home and abroad, Aksyonov provides insight into the life of city-dwelling youth, using a form that is unusual for the Soviet Union. In *Zvyozdny bilet* he describes young people who view their world skeptically and with protest, who love Western literature and music, who attempt to comprehend abstract painting, and who thus contradict the Communist ideal. His thematic novelty corresponds to his experiments in form, in that he frequently changes the point of view in order to express democratic recognition of different opinions. "No contemporary Soviet writer, however, surpasses him in terms of formal inventiveness and exploratory daring" (D. Brown). Aksyonov incorporates the specific slang of his rebellious youth who stand far removed from the Communist ideal of the clear path into the future. The povest composed of eighteen different sketches written in the first person, *Apelsiny iz Marokko,* was toned down in this respect when it was reissued. In his other works (for example, *Zhal, chto vas ne bylo s nami* [1965; Wish You Were Here] and especially *Zatovarennaya bochkotara* [1968; Eng. tr., *Surplussed Barrelware,* 1985]), Aksyonov often departs from a strongly realistic form and tries to combine classical Russian narrative technique with the methods used by the literary avant-garde of the 1920s, especially A. Bely. *Vsegda v prodazhe* (Always for Sale), an unpublished play successfully produced at the Sovremennik at the end of the 1960s, combines grotesque reality and irreality into an effective critique of contemporary issues and compassionately features the opportunist. Aksyonov himself sees certain parallels to the unrest in France in 1968 in *Lyubov k elektrichestvu* (1971; The Love of Electricity)—a novel written for the series "Ardent Revolutionaries" and concerning the engineer and terrorist L. Krasin and the events between 1905 and 1908; this novel is distinguished by its description of the intelligentsia in general and of a particular individual actively engaged. *Moy dedushka— pamyatnik* (1972; My Grandfather Is a Monument) belongs to the genre of fantasy literature and, in its delineation of a superhero, reveals Aksyonov's talent for irony, parody, and multileveled statements, as well as for developing new artistic forms in the tradition of N. Gogol and M. Bulgakov. Aksyonov's last longer prose work published in the Soviet Union, *Poiski zhanra* (1978; In Search of a Genre), describes a car owner in search of adventure but lacks human concern. *Ozhog* (1980; Eng. tr., *The Burn*, 1984), his most comprehensive povest and one on which he worked for six years, is an ostensible "Chronicle of the 1960s and 1970s" only in its framework; formally it extends into the fantastic-symbolic and chronologically it reaches back into childhood. In *Metropol*, Aksyonov included a drama not published in the Soviet Union, *Chetyre temperamenta* (1979; The Four Temperaments), that poses the question of man's existence after death. *Ostrov Krym* (1981; Eng. tr., *The Island of Crimea*, 1985) deals with the contemporary political and human issues of emigration and of one's relationship to the Soviet homeland by using the fiction that the Crimea was not conquered by the Red Army in 1922 but developed freely as a Western country.

*Works:* Kollegi (pov.), 1961 (see above); *Zvëzdnyj bilet* (novel), in *Junost'* 1961:6–7 (see above); *Na polputi k lune* (short story), in *Novyj mir* 1962:7 (Eng. tr., "Halfway to the Moon," 1964); *Apel'siny iz Marokko* (pov.), in *Junost'* 1963:1; *Tovarišč Krasivyj Furažkin* (short story), in *Junost'* 1964:12; *Katapul'ta* (short stories and pov.), 1964; *Pora, moj drug, pora* (novel), 1965 (Eng. tr., *It's Time, My Friend, It's Time*, 1969); *Zatovarennaja bočkotara* (pov.), in *Junost'* 1968:3 (see above); *Žal' čto vas ne bylo s nami* (pov. and short stories), 1969; *Ljubov' k èlektričestvu, Povest' o Krasine* (two pov.), 1971; *Moj deduška—pamjatnik* (pov.), 1972; *Kruglye sutki non-stop* (impressions, thoughts, adventures), in *Novyj mir* 1976:8; *Stal'naja ptica* (short stories), in *Glagol*, Ann Arbor, 1:1977 (Eng. tr., *The Steel Bird and Other Stories*, 1979); *Poiski*

*žanra* (pov.), in *Novyj mir* 1978:1; *Zolotaja naša železka* (novel), Ann Arbor, 1980 (Eng. tr., *Our Golden Ironburg*, 1986); *Ožog* (autobiographical pov.), Ann Arbor, 1980 (see above); *Ostrov Krym* (novel), Ann Arbor, 1981 (see above); *Aristofaniana s ljaguškami* (play), Ann Arbor, 1981; *Bljuz s russkim akcentom* (film pov.), in *Grani*, Frankfurt am Main, 139:1986.

*Secondary Lit.:* Ju. Bondarev, in *Lit. gazeta* July 29, 1961, and Nov. 24, 1962; K. Čukovskij, in *Lit. gazeta* Aug 12, 1961; A. Borščagovskij, in *Moskva* 1962:12; A. Makarov, in *Znamja* 1966:7–9; St. Rassadin, in *Voprosy lit.* 1968:10; *RSPP* 7(1):1971; P. Meyer, Diss., Princeton Univ., 1971, and in *Russian Literature Triquarterly* 6:1973 (with extensive bibliography); L. Žak, in *Lit. gazeta* April 25, 1973, p. 5; A. Gromova, in *Lit. obozrenie* 1973:10; A. Naumov, in *Teatr* 1975:7; L. Anninskij and E. Evtušenko, in *Lit. obozrenie* 1978:7; Ju. Žediljagin, in *Grani* 124:1982; V. Tarsis, in *ZeitBild* Sept. 8, 1982; A. Gladilin, V. Nekrasov, S. Jur'enen, in *Novoe russkoe slovo*, New York, Aug. 22, 1982, p. 4; P. Dalgard, Arkona, 1982; V. Filipp, in *Novyj žurnal*, New York, 151:1983.

**Aldánov, Mark Aleksándrovich** (pseud. of M. A. Landáu), prose writer (b. Nov. 7 [Oct. 26], 1886, Kiev—d. Feb. 25, 1957, Nice). Aldanov completed his studies in physics, mathematics, and jurisprudence in Kiev and traveled all over the world before emigrating to Paris in April 1919 as a member of a small group of right-leaning socialists. There, beginning in 1921, he wrote numerous novels, both historical and set in the contemporary period. Translated into more than 20 languages, they resulted in worldwide, although not lasting, success. Between 1941 and 1947 Aldanov lived in the United States, where he and M. Tsetlin founded the journal *Novy zhurnal*.

Aldanov produced a voluminous body of novels that encompass Russian and European history between 1762 and 1948. Between 1923 and 1927 he published four novels about the French Revolution, combining them under the title *Myslitel* (The Thinker). *Istoki* (1950; sources; Eng. tr., *Before the Deluge*, 1947), one of Aldanov's best novels (Struve), focuses on the assassination of Aleksandr II; in the novel he investigates the history of the Russian Revolution of 1917, a subject handled in several of his novels: *Klyuch* (1930; Eng. tr., *The Key*, 1931), *Begstvo* (1932; Eng. tr., *The Escape*, 1950), and *Peshchera* (1934–36, The Cave). *Povest o smerti* (1953; A Story about

Death) is a novel about Balzac; *Nachalo kontsa* (1939; The Beginning of the End; Eng. tr., *The Fifth Seal*, 1943) concerns the immediate present of the prewar period; *Zhivi kak khochesh* (1952; Eng. tr., *To Live as We Wish*, 1952) deals with the postwar period. Aldanov's novels reveal the influence of A. France and L. Tolstoy. The major concern of his often ironic and skeptical presentation lies with people, with psychology and philosophy, not with historical events. Aldanov's skillfully structured (if considerably drawn-out) novels are interconnected to some extent by recurring characters; they contain numerous allusions to the present, to the Russian Revolution in particular, even when the action is not contemporary with that period. Significant are Aldanov's "philosophical fairy tales," such as *Desyataya simfoniya* (1931; Eng. tr., *The Tenth Symphony*, 1948), and his essays about historical and contemporary personalities, collected in *Sovremenniki* (1928; Contemporaries), *Portrety* (1931; Portraits), and *Zemli i lyudi* (1932; Lands and People). *Ulmskaya noch* (1953; Night in Ulm), a philosophical essay devoted to the role played by chance, is illuminating as Aldanov's own commentary to his novels.

*Works:* Lénine (essays), Paris, 1919 (Eng. tr., Lenin, 1922); *Zagadka Tolstogo*, Berlin, 1923 (reprinted, Providence, 1969); *Myslitel'* (tetralogy): (1) *Devjatoe termidora* (novel), Berlin, 1923 (Eng. tr., *The Ninth Thermidor*, 1926); (2) *Čortov most* (novel), Berlin, 1925 (Eng. tr., *The Devil's Bridge*, 1928); (3) *Zagovor* (novel), Berlin, 1927; (4) *Svjataja Elena, malen'kij ostrov* (novel), Berlin, 1923 (Eng. tr., *Saint Helena, Little Island*, 1924); *Sovremenniki* (essays), Berlin, 1928; *Ključ* (novel), Berlin, 1930 (see above); *Portrety* (essays), Berlin, 1931; *Desjataja simfonija* (philosophical tale), Paris, 1931 (see above); *Begstvo* (novel), Berlin, 1932 (see above); *Zemli i ljudi* (essays), Berlin, 1932; *Peščera* (novel), 2 vols., Berlin, 1934–36; *Načalo konca* (novel), Paris, 1939 (see above); *Istoki* (novel), 2 vols., Paris, 1950 (see above); *Živi kak khočeš'* (novel), 2 vols., New York, 1952 (see above); *Povest' o smerti* (novel, 1952–53), Frankfurt am Main, 1969; *Ul'mskaja noč'* (philosophical essay), New York, 1953; *Bred* (novel), in *Novyj žurnal*, New York, 38:1954–43:1957; *Samoubijstvo* (novel), New York, 1958, 2d ed., Paris, 1977; *Istrebitel'* (short story), Frankfurt am Main, 1967.

*Translation:* A Night at the Airport: Stories, 1949.

*Secondary Lit.:* N. Ul'janov, in *Novyj žurnal* 34:1953 and 62:1960; G. Struve, in *Books*

Abroad 28:1954; Y. S. Grabowski, Diss., Univ. of Toronto, 1969; C. N. Lee, The Hague, 1969, and in *MERSL* 1:1977; D. Cristesco and H. Cristesco, bibliography, 1976; M. Geller, in *Russkaja mysl'*, Paris, Feb. 24, 1977, p. 8; A. Bakhrakh, in *Novyj žurnal* 126:1977.

**Aldán-Semyónov, Andréy Ignátyevich** (pseud. of A. I. Semyonov), prose writer, poet (b. Oct. 27 [Oct. 14], 1908, Shungunur, prov. Vyatka— d. Dec. 8, 1985, Moscow). Aldan-Semyonov's father was a peasant. Aldan-Semyonov lived in an orphanage beginning in 1920; he studied at the Vyatka Pedagogical Institute without completing the degree. In 1926 he began a career in journalism; his first books appeared in 1931 in Alma-Ata (documentary prose) and in 1935–36 in Kazan (poetry). He devoted the years 1936 and 1937 to the collection and translation of Udmurt folk poetry. From 1935 to 1938 Aldan-Semyonov, as executive secretary, organized a section of the Writers Union in the Vyatka region. A victim of Stalin's despotism, he subsequently spent 15 years in Kolyma, a forced-labor camp in northeastern Siberia. His literary works appeared again in provincial publishing houses and periodical publications (in Khabarovsk, Alma-Ata, Magadan, among others) after 1954, and in Moscow, where he lived, after 1958.

Of his literary work, Aldan-Semyonov's short novel, *Barelyef na skale* (1964; Bas-relief on the Cliff), has attracted the greatest attention. The novel is one of a series of works depicting Stalin's prison camps; the tradition was begun by A. Solzhenitsyn in 1962 and was continued by such writers as E. Ginzburg and V. Shalamov, as well as by B. Dyakov in *Povest o perezhitom* (The Story of My Experience) and G. Shelest in *Kolymskiye zapisi* (Notes from Kolyma). Aldan-Semyonov's title alludes to a gigantic relief of Stalin that a prisoner in Kolyma was forced to carve out of a cliff. Impaired by literary defects in its handling of dialogue and in its clarity, this prose work makes its impression chiefly through its content. Although Aldan-Semyonov shows an idealized Communist hero among his prisoners, the work was not permitted to appear as a book. Aldan-Semyonov later turned more to historical prose, as in his biography of the geographer *Semyonov-Tyan-Shansky* (1965) and several novels about the Civil War. He incorporates the destinies of Larisa Reysner and M. Tukhachevsky, among others, into *Krasnye i belye* (1967–72; The Reds and the Whites); *Groza nad Rossiyey* (1980; Storm over Russia) is dedicated to M. Frunze, whose alleged assassination B. Pilnyak had depicted. Aldan-Semyonov's volume of poetry *Lyubov i zvyozdy* (1978; Love and Stars) includes poems from 1934 that largely concern the themes of the memory of love, yearning for love, and (weakened by the demands of censorship) the sorrows of the prison camp experience in the Arctic. Before 1938 and from 1954 on, Aldan-Semyonov periodically made translations from Tatar, Udmurt, and Kirghiz.

*Works: Belyj ostrov* (articles), 1931; *Kniga stikhov* (poems), 1935; *Zakon družby* (short stories), 1954; *Bukhta Želanija* (short stories), 1958; *Čerskij* (biography), 1962; *Metel' i solnce* (poems), 1963; *Barel'ef na skale* (pov.), in *Moskva* 1964:7; *Semënov-Tjan-Šanskij* (biography), 1965; *Saga o Severe* (pov.), 1968 (Eng. tr., *A Northern Saga*, in *Trailblazers*, 1973); *Krasnye i belye* (novel), 2 vols., 1970–74; *Bessonnica stranstvij* (poems), 1973; *Na kraju okeana* (novel), 1977; *Ljubov' i zvëzdy* (lyric and narrative poems), 1978; *Groza nad Rossiej* (pov.), 1980; *Dlja tebja, Rossija* (pov.), 1983.— *Izbr. proizv.*, 2 vols., 1983.

*Secondary Lit.:* P. Ščekotov, in *Zvezda* 1964:12; *RSPP* 7(1):1971; V. Cybin, in *Lit. Rossija* Oct. 30, 1968, p. 4; L. Žak, in *Lit. obozrenie* 1973:2; A. Filatova, in *Zvezda* 1980:11; A. Blinov, in *Oktjabr'* 1983:10; M. Kupčenko, in *Zvezda* 1985:1.

**Aleksandróvsky, Vasíly Dmítriyevich,** poet (b. Jan. 15 [Jan. 3], 1897, in the village of Baskakovo, prov. Smolensk—d. Nov. 13, 1934, Moscow). Aleksandrovsky's father was a peasant. Between 1908 and 1916 Aleksandrovsky worked as an errand boy and laborer in a leather factory; his first poems began appearing in proletarian newspapers in 1913. He joined the Communist Party in 1917; in 1918–19 he was an active member of the Moscow PROLETKULT, publishing numerous poems in their publications and three volumes of verse with the Proletkult publishing house: *Rabochiy posyolok* (1919; The Workers' Settlement), *Vosstaniye* (1919; The Uprising), and *Sever* (1919; The North). Along with other proletarian poets such as M. Gerasimov, S. Obradovich, and V. Kazin, Aleksandrovsky left the Proletkult and formed the writers' group KUZNITSA, which continued to strive for an independent proletarian art free of Party control; at first Aleksandrovsky played a leading role in this group. In common with many other poets who had been inspired by the Revolution, Aleksandrovsky was greatly disillusioned by NEP. His literary activity was limited to the years 1917 to 1925; in his last

years he suffered from alcoholism. Not until 23 years after his death did a volume of his poems appear again (1957).

Aleksandrovsky is among the most gifted of the Kuznitsa poets. Both his short and his longer poems reveal the influence of N. Nekrasov, S. Yesenin, A. Blok, and V. Mayakovsky. In addition to poems from the workers' milieu such as "Muskuly tyazhest prosyat" (1918; The Muscles Beg for Burdens) and passionate calls to revolution ("Slaves!/ Tear the royal purple/ With your teeth"), there appears repeatedly in Aleksandrovsky's work the theme of confrontation between the old Russia, by no means deserving only of condemnation, and the new Russia, on which all hopes are pinned despite serious immediate troubles: for example, "Dve Rossii" (1920; Two Russias); "Derevnya" (1921; The Village).

*Works: Rabočij posëlok* (poems), 1919; *Vosstanie* (poems), 1919; *Sever* (poems), 1919; *Utro* (poems), 1921; *Rossyp' ognej* (poems), 1922; *Zvon solnca* (poems), 1923; *Šagi* (poems), 1924; *Veter* (poems), 1925; *Podkovannye gody* (poems), 1926; *Kostër: Stikhi 1918–28* (poems), 1929; *Gody* (poems), 1932; *Stikhotvorenija i poèmy* (lyric and narrative poems), 1957; poems, in *Proletarskie poèty pervykh let sovetskoj èpokhi*, 1959.

*Secondary Lit.:* A. Voronskij, in his *Lit. portrety*, 1929; S. Rodov, in *Aleksandrovskij's Stikhotvorenija i poèmy*, 1957; Z. S. Papernyj, R. A. Šaceva, in *Proletarskie poèty pervykh let sovetskoj èpokhi*, 1959; A. Kovalenkov, in his *Khorošie, raznye*, 1962, 2d ed., 1966; *RSPPo* 1:1977.

**Alekséyev, Mikhaíl Nikoláyevich,** prose writer (b. May 4 [April 22], 1918, Monastyrskoye, prov. Saratov). Alekseyev's father was a peasant. After seven years at a technical boarding school, Alekseyev served in the army from 1938 to 1955 as a soldier, officer, and war correspondent and from 1950 to 1955 as an editor for the military publishing house. In 1942 he was admitted to the Communist Party. From 1955 to 1957 he was a student in the Advanced Literature Course at the Gorky Literary Institute. Alekseyev has been a member of the secretariat of the Writers Union of the RSFSR since 1965 and a member of the board of the Writers Union of the USSR since 1967. In 1968 he was appointed editor in chief of the journal *Moskva*; he lives in Moscow.

Alekseyev's first work, the immense novel *Soldaty* (1951; Soldiers), won early recognition because of its heroic presentation of the Soviet Army. Of his later prose, which stems from the same circle of experiences Alekseyev considers *Divizionka* (1959; The Division Newspaper; Eng. tr. of title story, "The Divvy," in *Men at War*, 1980)—a collection of "documentary" short stories—the most important. Alekseyev's second theme is the Russian village, which he portrays with evident political concern in, among others, the lengthy novel *Vishnyovy omut* (1961; Eng. tr. *Cherry Pool*, 1978): gloomy before the Revolution and blooming thereafter, freed through the struggle against the kulaks and through collectivization (Gorky Prize, 1966). *Ivushka neplakuchaya* (1970–74; The Willow That Did Not Weep) depicts the lives of Party functionaries during World War II and the following war-influenced decades (State Prize of the USSR, 1976).

*Works: Soldaty* (novel), 1951; *Naš lejtenant* (short stories), 1955; *Nasledniki* (pov.), 1957; *Divizionka* (short stories), 1960 (see above); *Višnëvyj omut* (novel), 1962; (see above); *Khleb—imja suščestvitel'noe* (novel), 1964; *Ivuška neplakučaja* (novel), in *Molodaja gvardija* 1970:1–2 (vol. 1), separate ed., 1970, and in 1974:10–12 (vol. 2), separate ed., 1975; *Amerikanskij dnevnik* (diary), 1971; *Dračuny* (novel), 1982.—*Izbr. proizv.*, 2 vols., 1972; 3 vols., 1981; *Sobr. soč.*, 6 vols, 1975–77.

*Secondary Lit.:* P. Skomorokhov, in *Znamja* 1951:11, *RSPP* 1:1959; V. Litvinov, in *Moskva* 1962:5; A. Sofronov, in *Moskva* 1964:8; N. Dalada, 1969; A. Dymšic, in his *Problemy i portrety*, 1972; M. Kolosov, in *Lit. gazeta* March 19, 1975, p. 5; A. Elkin, 1976; Dm. Moldavskij, in *Novyj mir* 1978:5; V. Surganov, in *Oktjabr'* 1982:7; S. Borzunov, 1983; A. Baygušev, in *Lit. Rossija* March 23, 1984, p. 8.

**Alekséyeva, Lídiya Alekséyevna** (pseud. of L. A. Ivánnikov, née Dével), poet (b. March 7 [Feb. 22], 1909, Dvinsk). Alekseyeva's father was descended from the Huguenots (Develle); he was a colonel with the General Staff. Alekseyeva grew up in Sevastopol; in November 1920 she emigrated with her parents to Belgrade via Constantinople (until mid–1922) and Bulgaria. After completing her studies in Slavic philology at the University of Belgrade, she taught Serbian language and literature at the Russian secondary school in Belgrade from 1934 to 1944. From 1937 to 1949 she was married to the prose writer M. Ivannikov. In October 1944 she fled from the Red Army, leaving her husband behind. After five years in a camp in Austria, she moved to New York in 1949. Using a pseudonym (formed from her father's name) with few exceptions, Alekse-

yeva began in 1949 to publish poetry regularly in journals such as *Vozrozhdeniye, Grani,* and *Novy zhurnal.*

*Lesnoye solntse* (1954; Forest Sun), was published in Frankfurt am Main ; by 1980 four other volumes had followed. Alekseyeva worked as a clerk for 11 years, then at the New York Public Library for 18 years. Her poems were well received. D. Klenovsky, whom Alekseyeva first met in 1972, thought very highly of her. Alekseyeva's translation of one of Ivan Gundulić's main works, the religious chant written in 1622, "Slezy bludnogo syna" (1965; Tears of a Lost Son), won high praise. Alekseyeva lives in New York.

The central theme of Alekseyeva's poetry is the willingness to accept this God-given life with its lack of security, its trials and sorrows. She perceives misfortune, her own and that of others, but does not view it with indifference; instead she focuses on the positive, the radiant, the pleasurable. Throughout her life Alekseyeva has found this positive aspect in nature, which she observes and describes with a frequency and precision that recalls K. Paustovsky and which she incorporates into her writing as comparison and metaphor. Love poems, verse on poetry, and reminiscences seldom appear. The search for the meaning of life governs her creative activity and remains an open question. With increasing age the motif of preparedness for death frequently appears, together with thankfulness for life as it is.

*Works: Malen'kie rasskazy* (short stories), in *Grani*, Frankfurt am Main, 20:1953; *Lesnoe solnce* (poems), Frankfurt am Main, 1954; *V puti* (poems), New York, 1959; *Prozračnyj sled* (poems), New York, 1964; *Vremja razluk* (poems), New York, 1971; *Stikhi* (poems), New York, 1980.

*Secondary Lit.:* O. Anstej, in *Grani* 23:1954 and in *Novyj žurnal*, New York, 81:1965 and 141:1980; Ju. Terapiano, in *Russkaja mysl'*, Paris, Feb. 6, 1960; Ja. Gorbov, in *Vozroždenie*, Paris, 158:1965; G. Zabežinskij, in *Novyj žurnal* 39:1954; Ju. Ofrosimov, in *Novyj žurnal* 63:1961 and 81:1965; I. Šakhovskoj (Strannik), in his *Perepiska s Klenovskim*, Paris, 1981; B. Filippov, in *Novoe russkoe slovo*, New York, Feb. 8, 1981, p. 5, and in *HRL* 1985; B. Narcissov, in *Novyj žurnal* 150:1983; O. Durić, in *Savremenik*, Belgrade, 1984:8–9.

**Aléksin, Anatóly Geórgiyevich,** prose writer, playwright (b. Aug. 3, 1924, Moscow). Aleksin's father was an official in the Communist Party of the Soviet Union. During World War

II, Aleksin was exempted from serving at the front and worked as a journalist reporting on industry. Aleksin began publishing in 1945; he completed his study of Oriental languages and literatures in 1950. His first book, *Tridtsat odna povest* (1950; Thirty-one Tales), was followed by collections of povesti and short stories about youth that appeared regularly—at least once every two years. Many were first published in the journal *Yunost*, where Aleksin has been a member of the editorial staff since 1969. At the end of the 1960s, Aleksin began to adapt some of his povesti into plays. Since 1970 he has been a member of the secretariat of the Writers Union of the RSFSR. In 1978 he received the State Prize of the USSR for *Pozavchera i poslezavtra* (1974; The Day before Yesterday and the Day after Tomorrow) and three other povesti. Thereafter he was able to publish his *Sobraniye sochineniy* (1979–81; Collected Works) with a print run of 300,000 copies; in the foreword to this volume, V. Kozhevnikov highlighted the "Communist morality" of Aleksin's literary work. Aleksin lives in Moscow.

Aleksin's works concern young people of many age groups and their problems with each other, but especially with adults. He addresses diverse themes but focuses his attention especially on ethical issues. A reasonable story line and pedagogical intent are clearly detectable in his works; Aleksin loves well-defined contrasts but knows how to present aptly chosen interpersonal conflicts in a psychologically penetrating fashion and without an obtrusive resolution.

*Works: Tridcat' odna povest'* (pov.), 1950; *Otrjad šagaet v nogu*, 1952; *Pogovorim o sovesti*, 1961; *Moj brat igraet na klarnete* (pov.), 1968; *Očen' strašnaja istorija, i drugie povesti*, 1969; *Pozavčera i poslezavtra* (pov.), 1974; *Dejstvujuščie lica i ispolniteli*, 1975; *Molodaja gvardija*, 1975; *Pojdëm v kino? . . .* (play), in *Teatr* 1977:7; *Tretij v pjatom rjadu* (pov.), 1981; *Zdorovye i bol'nye* (pov.), in *Naš sovremennik* 1982:2; *Moj brat igraet na klarnete, i drugie povesti*, 1983.—*Sobr. soč.*, 3 vols., 1979–81.

*Secondary Lit.*: V. Voronov, 1973, 2d ed., 1980, and in *Teatr* 1979:1; A. Karpov, in *Lit. obozrenie* 1976:6; I. Motjašov, in *Naš sovremennik* 1979:2; Yu. Smelkov, in *Lit. obozrenie* 1980:10; P. Ul'jašov, in *Lit. Rossija* April 9, 1982, p. 14; I. Šajtanov, in *Znamja* 1984:8.

**Aleshkóvsky, Yuz** (pseud. of Iósif Yefímovich), prose writer (b. Sept. 21, 1929, Krasno-

yarsk). As a result of World War II, Aleshkovsky was forced to interrupt his schooling in Moscow. After completing his military service with the navy, Aleshkovsky was sentenced to four years' imprisonment (1950–53) for breach of military discipline. After his release, he worked first as a truck driver and construction worker. In Moscow, after 1955, Aleshkovsky led a double life as a writer: officially he was an author of children's books and screenplays for film and television; unofficially he performed his own songs, including "Tovarishch Stalin, vy bolshoy uchony" (Comrade Stalin, You Are a Great Scholar), which was widely circulated. In 1970 Aleshkovsky wrote the povest *Nikolay Nikolayevich* (1980), which attained great popularity through SAMIZDAT. In his later satirical prose as well, Aleshkovsky refused to make even the slightest concessions that would have made publication in the Soviet Union possible. In 1979 he contributed some of his songs from the camps to the samizdat volume METROPOL. In February 1979, Aleshkovsky was allowed to emigrate to Vienna where he wrote the novel *Karusel* (1983; The Carousel). Later that year he accepted an invitation to move to the United States; he lives in Middletown, Connecticut.

Aleshkovsky lets his linguistically conscious novels speak with the voices of first-person narrators from the lower social strata. In addition, the satiric representation of Soviet reality is usually grotesquely mixed with the fantastic. From the viewpoint of a young thief who finds a job in a biological institute after his release from prison, *Nikolay Nikolayevich* reveals the absurdity of Trofim Lysenko's pseudoscience. *Kenguru* (1981; Eng. tr., *Kangaroo*, 1984), written in 1974–75, is a kind of modern picaresque novel in which an old thief recounts his numerous experiences during a show trial in the late Stalin period. Stalin himself is even personally involved in the events. *Maskirovka* (1980; The Camouflage), written in 1978, grotesquely portrays the entire reality of Soviet life as a camouflage. *Ruka* (1981; The Hand), written between 1977 and 1980, is a multilevel novel on the theme of "communism as the contemporary manifestation of absolute satanism"; the protagonist has worked his way up to the position of Stalin's bodyguard in order to revenge himself for his parents' murder as "kulaks." *Sinenkiy skromny platochek* (1982; Small Blue Kerchief), a monologue in the form of a letter written by a mentally ill war veteran, is set in the Brezhnev period. In *Karusel*, Aleshkovsky traces a Soviet worker's growing awareness that, in view of Soviet anti-Semitism, the only solution for Jews is to emigrate. Some of Aleshkovsky's books have been translated into English and French.

Works: *Dva bileta na električku* (children's short stories), 1965; *Kyš, dva portfelja i celaja nedelja* (children's pov.), 1970; songs, in *Metropol'*, Ann Arbor, 1979, and in *Kontinent*, Paris, 21:1979; *Nikolaj Nikolaevič. Maskirovka* (pov.), Ann Arbor, 1980; *Ruka* (novel), New York, 1980; *Kenguru* (novel), Ann Arbor, 1981 (see above); *Sinen'kij skromnyj platoček* (pov.), New York, 1982; *Karusel'* (novel), Northampton, 1983; interviews, in *Russkaja mysl'*, Paris, Sept. 1, 1983, p. 11, and March 29, 1984, p. 10; *Kniga poslednikh slov: 35 prestuplenij*, Benson, Vt., 1984; *Smert' v Moskve* (pov.), Benson, Vt., 1985.

Secondary Lit.: S. Jur'enen, in *Èkho*, Paris, 1979:1; Anon., in *Kontinent* 25:1980; F. Lewis, in *New York Times* Nov. 11, 1981; K. Sapgir, in *Kontinent* 28:1981; B. Paramonov, in *Russkaja mysl'* July 9, 1981, p. 11; L. Losev, in *Russkaja mysl'* Oct. 28, 1982, p. 10, and March 29, 1984, p. 10; Ju. Mal'cev, in *Kontinent* 33:1982; P. Meyer, in *Slavic and East European Journal* 1985:4; J. Glad, in *Washington Post* May 4, 1986; I. Brodskij (interview), in *Washington Post* May 4, 1986.

**Aligér, Margaríta Iósifovna,** poet (b. Oct. 7 [Sept. 24], 1915, Odessa). Aliger studied at the Gorky Literary Institute from 1934 to 1937. Her first poems appeared in 1933; her first collection, *God rozhdeniya* (The Year of Birth), in 1938. She joined the Communist Party in 1942. For the theme of her verse epic *Zoya* (1942), she chose the death of the partisan Zoya Kosmodemyanskaya; this work received a Stalin Prize (for 1942, 2d class). The form of the shorter verse epic also characterized her creative work in the following years. *Leninskiye gory* (1953; The Lenin Hills) is dedicated to the construction of Moscow University. At the Second Congress of the Writers Union in 1954, Aliger spoke out in favor of more generous treatment of those who deviate from the Party line. In 1956 she joined the editorial staff of the liberal almanac *Literaturnaya Moskva* but proffered a confession of remorse in the aftermath of the Party's criticism (*Lit. gazeta* Oct. 8, 1957). Aliger has participated in all congresses of the Writers Unions of the USSR and RSFSR since 1954 and has belonged to the board of the Writers Union of the USSR without interruption. Since 1958 she has undertaken numerous trips abroad, including to both parts of Germany,

England, Japan, and Chile. Her poems are regularly published. She lives in Moscow.

In her poetry, Aliger maintains a balance between the personal and the political, whereby even in her early verse epics the timely aspects are not obtrusive and in later ones the timeless elements predominate. Her poetry is close to prose, yet even in the verse epics or the poems inspired by her travels, her style is not narrative but rather descriptive and reflective. Her poetry is largely free of imagery, but taken as a whole it is often symbolic, as in "Iskusstvo sostavlyat bukety" (1963; The Art of Flower Arranging), where *ikebana* is used as a warning to retain only the essential in poetry.

Works: *God roždenija* (lyric and narrative poems), 1938; *Zoja* (narrative poem), 1942; *Skazka o pravde* (play in verse), 1945; *Leninskie gory* (poems), 1953; *Iz zapisnoj knižki* (poems), 1957; *Neskol'ko šagov* (poems), 1962; *Stikhotvorenija i poèmy* (lyric and narrative poems), 2 vols., 1970; *Zoja* (lyric and narrative poem), 1971; *V poslednij raz* (memoirs), in *Moskva* 1974:12; *Stikhi i proza* (poems and prose), 2 vols., 1975; *Tropinki vo rži* (essays), 1980; *Četvert' veka* (poems), 1981.—*Sobr. soč.*, 3 vols., 1984.

Secondary Lit.: K. Simonov, in *Novyj mir* 1947:1; A. Rybakov, in *Komsomol'skaja pravda* Oct. 7, 1965; P. Antokol'skij, in Aliger's *Stikhotvorenija i poèmy*, 1970; A. Turkov, in *Oktjabr'* 1975:2; I. Motjašov, in *Lit. obozrenie* 1976:5; RSPPo 1:1977; I. Metter, in *Novyj mir* 1981:3.

**All-USSR Writers Congresses.** See WRITERS CONGRESSES.

**Alyóshin, Samuíl Iósifovich** (pseud. of S. I. Kotlyar), playwright (b. July 21 [July 8], 1913, Zambrów, prov. Łomża, Poland). Alyoshin's father was a doctor; his mother, a teacher. In 1935 Alyoshin graduated from a military academy as a certified engineer. During World War II he was an officer and saw service in Stalingrad, where he wrote his first drama, *Mefistofel* (1942; Mephistopheles); it was printed in 1963. From 1941 to 1947 he published humorous short stories in *Krokodil* and *Ogonyok*. In 1946 Alyoshin defended his candidate dissertation; he worked in a research institute for the automotive industry until 1952. In 1950 his play *Direktor* (The Manager), a contribution to the officially required production theme, was first performed in Moscow. His drama *Odna* (1956; Eng. tr., *Alone*, in *The*

Year of Protest 1956, 1961), in which Alyoshin made use of the new opportunity created by the THAW to depict a marital problem and to leave it unresolved, drew attention. Tochka opory (1960; The Fulcrum) criticizes the Stalinist type of trade-union official. Alyoshin's highly regarded play Palata (1962; The Ward), which explores the problems of marriage and the attitude toward death along with those problems engendered by the substitution of political regimentation for responsible individual decision, contributed to the abolition of the spirit of dogmatism. In Diplomat (1967; The Diplomat), Alyoshin wrote a drama based on the early Soviet period; its central character is inspired by M. Litvinov and his activities in Copenhagen. In Drugaya (1968; The Other), Alyoshin once again takes up the problems of a man torn between two women and explores the mishandling of private problems when they are made public. In Lestnitsa (1976; The Staircase), he portrays physicists at a research institute confronted by everyday problems. The play Yesli . . . (1978; If . . .), set in the medical milieu Alyoshin so greatly admires, shows a woman whose anguish over a temporary separation from the man she loves leads to self-knowledge. People in love and their problems are also depicted in Tema s variatsiyami (1980; Theme and Variations). Alyoshin lives in Moscow; he participated in a congress of the Writers Union of the RSFSR for the first time in 1970.

A number of Alyoshin's dramas are devoted to historical and literary figures. Mefistofel, Togda v Sevilye (1947; Then in Seville [Don Juan]; first performed 1960), Gogol (1952), Chelovek iz Stratforda (1954; The Man from Stratford [Shakespeare]; first performed 1964). These plays are performed less frequently than Alyoshin's more topical works. Alyoshin's consciously composed plays contain numerous conflicts and abundant action; in them he adovcates uncompromising truth and demands total effort from the individual. Alyoshin is not fully successful in transforming rationally comprehended problems into characters who are internally motivated to act and speak convincingly.

Works: Direktor (play), 1951; P'esy (plays), 1958 (contains Direktor; Odna [see above]; Strogaja devuška; Gogol'; Čelovek iz Stratforda); P'esy (plays), 1962 (contains Vsë ostaëtsja ljudjam; Točka opory; Togda v Sevil'e); Mefistofel'. Palata (plays), 1963; Glavnaja rol' (play), 1964; 6 p'es (plays), 1968 (contains Mefistofel'; Togda v Sevil'e; Palata; Glavnaja

rol'; Každomu svoë; Diplomat); P'esy (plays), 1972 (contains Direktor; Odna; Vsë ostaëtsja ljudjam; Točka opory; Každomu svoë; Diplomat; Drugaja; Togda v Sevil'e; Čelovek iz Stratforda); Esli . . . i drugie p'esy (plays), 1978 (contains Graždanskoe delo; Lestnica; Beloe plat'e dlja grešnicy; Gogol'; Eë prevoskhoditel'stvo; Staruška; Esli . . . ; Točka opory); Tema s variacijami (play), in Teatr 1980:6; Vosemnadcatyj verbljud (play), in Teatr 1983:5; Sledstvie pokazalo . . . (play), in Teatr 1984:12.

Secondary Lit.: I. Kruti, in Teatr 1950:10; Z. Vladimirova, in Teatr 1962:10; N. Koževnikova, in Lit. Rossija Dec. 27, 1963, p. 5; L. Anninskij, in Znamja 1964:2; I. Višnevskaja, in Teatr 1967:10; L. Žukova, in Teatr 1972:8; A. Štejn, in Lit. gazeta June 20, 1979, p. 8.

**Amálrik, Andréy Alekséyevich,** playwright, prose writer, publicist (b. May 12, 1938, Moscow—d. Nov. 11, 1980, Guadalajara, Spain). Amalrik's father was a historian. At the age of 13 Amalrik built a puppet theater in which he performed plays he himself wrote. He studied history at Moscow University. In 1963 Amalrik was not allowed to continue his education when it was found that the views he adopted in a study on the Kievan state deviated from the official departmental position. Between 1963 and 1965 he wrote six plays that differed essentially in structure and content from the usual Soviet drama. Amalrik made his living by taking temporary jobs and assumed the care of his invalid father. He came to the attention of the civil police as a result of the interest American journalists showed in his friend, the nonconformist painter A. Zverev; in 1965 Amalrik was arrested for not holding a permanent job. A charge of disseminating anti-Soviet and pornographic writings, brought on the basis of the dramas found on the occasion of his arrest, was dropped, but like I. Brodsky, Amalrik was sentenced to two and a half years of exile in Siberia for "parasitism" (lack of regular employment). He worked on a kolkhoz in the oblast of Tomsk and in 1966 was allowed to return to Moscow before the expiration of his sentence. There he held various jobs, including one as journalist for the foreign press agency Novosti, where he worked until 1968. Amalrik wrote an autobiographical article, Nezhelannoye puteshestviye v Sibir (1970; Eng. tr., Involuntary Journey to Siberia, 1970), which was published in the United States. He acquired an international reputation when his treatise Prosushchestvuyet li Sovetskiy Soyuz do 1984 goda? (1969; Eng. tr., Will the Soviet Union Survive until 1984?, 1970, rev. ed., 1981), completed in 1969, likewise made it to the West through SAMIZDAT soon afterward. The treatise owes its effect to the dispassionate point of view from which Amalrik criticizes the system and living conditions in the Soviet Union. He was arrested again on May 20, 1970. On Nov. 12, 1970, in Sverdlovsk, Amalrik was sentenced to three years at hard labor; he served part of his sentence in Kolyma. In 1973, shortly before the completion of his sentence, a court in Magadan (Siberia) extended the sentence another three years. Protests against this "glaring injustice" (A. Sakharov) and petitions for clemency from all over the world (including one signed by 247 members of the PEN Club) resulted in the sentence being changed to exile in the district of Magadan. In May 1975 the sentence of exile was apparently revoked. In July 1976 Amalrik was allowed to leave the Soviet Union. Abroad he lectured at universities in Utrecht and Boston (Harvard) and actively championed human rights concessions in the Soviet Union. He died in an automobile accident.

Amalrik's literary talent, evident in the vivid, self-possessed article revealing conditions in the Soviet Union and discussing the time he spent in Siberia in 1965–66, is particularly obvious in his dramas. Amalrik belongs to the tradition of theater of the absurd; he was inspired by Eugene Ionesco and Samuel Beckett around 1963 and further developed the techniques employed by D. Kharms. Amalrik dispenses with a realistic plot; instead he connects, like interlocking links in a chain, conditionally independent plot units that, toward the end of the piece, often symbolically depict a random victim trapped by inhuman events. Such is the ending of Konformist li dyadya Dzhek? (1964; Eng. tr., Is Uncle Jack a Conformist?, in Nose! Nose? No-se! and Other Plays, 1973), in which one character is tied up, but at the same time those who are binding him become entangled themselves in the rope. Frequently Amalrik's characters are without names, being interchangeable, schematic figures representing the distrustful society of the time; none of them is an individual brought to the level of a type. The individual responses of the characters are nevertheless always realistic; such juxtapositioning produces a bizarre picture that is comic, alogical, ironic, and abstractly concentrated to a high degree. Between his exile and his eventually total separation from his own cultural sphere, Amalrik wrote Nos! Nos? No-s! (1968; Eng. tr., Nose! Nose? No-se!, 1973), a

play in 16 episodes, based on the grotesque world of N. Gogol's short story Nos; this play also demonstrates Amalrik's talent for the stage. "Taken as a whole, Amalrik's plays share with much absurdist drama a pessimistic view of the world which becomes the bleaker because of the contrasting surface nonsense" (H. Segel). A later drama, Vozzreniya gospozhi Lindy (1975; The Views of Mrs. Linda), is still unpublished.

Works: Prosuščestvuet li Sovetskij Sojuz do 1984 goda? (essay), Amsterdam, 1969 (see above); Neželannoe putešestvie v Sibir' (pov.), New York, 1970 (see above); P'esy (plays), Amsterdam, 1970 (contains Moja tётja živёt v Volokolamske; Vostokozapad; Čertyrnadcat' ljubovnikov nekrasivoj Meri-Enn; Skazka pro belogo byčka; Konformist li djadja Džek?; Nos! Nos? No-s!); Stat'i i pis'ma (essays and letters), Amsterdam, 1971; Neželannoe putešestvie v Kalugu (pov.), in Russkaja mysl', Paris, July 1, 8, 15, 1976; SSSR i Zapad v odnoj lodke (essays), London, 1978; Normanny i Kievskaja Rus' (scholarly work, 1960), Florence, 1979; Zapiski dissidenta (autobiography), Ann Arbor, 1982 (Eng. tr., Notes of a Revolutionary, 1982.

Translation: Nose! Nose? No-se! and Other Plays, 1973.

Secondary Lit.: E. Mettler, in Neue Zürcher Zeitung Jan. 18, 1970; M. Hayward, in Survey 74–75:1970; J. A. Armstrong, in Russian Review 1971:2; J. Keep, in Russian Review 1971:4; B. Litvinov, in Posev, Frankfurt am Main, 1971:7; K. Marko, Dogmatismus und Emanzipation in der Sowjetunion, Stuttgart, 1971; W. Kasack, in Neue Zürcher Zeitung July 18–19, 1976, p. 25; V. Malašin, in Russkaja mysl' July 5, 1979, p. 5; G. Nivat, Russkaja mysl' Nov. 20, 1980, p. 3; V. Čalidze, in Novoe russkoe slovo, New York, Nov. 16, 1980; K. Sapgir, in Russkaja mysl' March 5, 1981, p. 13; A. Gotzes, Mainz, 1986.


**Amfiteátrov, Aleksándr Valentínovich,** prose writer, playwright (b. Dec. 26 [Dec. 14], 1862, Kaluga—d. Feb. 26, 1938, Levanto, Italy). In 1885 Amfiteatrov completed his study of law in Moscow; for several decades he worked as a journalist, first for the conservative newspaper Novoye vremya (under the pseudonym "Old Gentleman"). In 1899, together with V. M. Doroshevich, he founded his own newspaper, Rossiya. Gospoda Obmanovy (1901; The Masters Obmanov [Deceivers]), a satire directed against the ruling Romanov family, caused the newspaper to be banned. In 1905

Amfiteatrov emigrated to Paris and created his own revolutionary organ called *Krasnoye znamya*. Starting in 1888 in St. Petersburg, he began publishing numerous novels and collections of shorter, usually satirical prose, such as a novel concerning prostitution and the current position of women in society—*Doch Viktorii Pavlovny* (1903; Victoria Pavlovna's Daughter)—and a series of wide-ranging novels about society, *Vosmidesyatniki* (1907–8; People of the Eighties), *Devyatidesyatniki* (1910; People of the Nineties). Thirty-four volumes of the planned 37-volume edition of his collected works were published in St. Petersburg between 1911 and 1916, the year of his return to Russia. Amfiteatrov's works were extraordinarily popular and wre reprinted in several, sometimes expanded, editions. After the Revolution, Amfiteatrov lived in Petrograd until the autumn of 1921; he then fled to Italy, where he continued with his literary work.

The respect shown Amfiteatrov as a writer was limited to his lifetime. His broad, realistic writing style bordered on the trivial. In addition to contemporary themes, Amfiteatrov also depicted historical events, such as the time of Nero's rule in *Zver iz bezdny* (1900; The Beast from the Abyss) or, through the use of *byliny*, life in Novgorod in the Middle Ages in the drama *Vasily Buslayev* (1922; Vasily Buslayev). Among his novels concerning the fate of women belongs *Dve Nadezhdy* (1936; The Two Nadezhdas), the short novel written in 1921 and translated into German, Czech, and Swedish, in which he depicts a woman offering herself in marriage to a commissar from the Cheka in order to save her brother. Yet, with his writing style, which is fluid but unidimensional and aimed at a broad section of the reading public, even this tragic situation that he himself experienced fails to attain a depth equal to the message.

Works: *Gospoda Obmanovy* (commentary), in *Rossija* Jan. 13, 1901; *Doč' Viktorii Pavlovny* (novel), 1903; *Vos'midesjatniki* (novel), 2 vols., 1907–8; *Devjatidesjatniki* (novel), 2 vols, 1910; *Začarovannaja step'*, Reval, 1921; *Sovremennye skazki*, New York, 1921; *Žarcvet* (tales), Berlin, 1922; *Vasilij Buslaev* (play), Reval, 1922; *Gorestnye zamety: Očerki Krasnogo Petrograda* (documentary prose), Berlin, 1922; *Sëstry* (novel), 2 vols., Berlin, 1923; *Znakomye muzy* (essays), Paris, 1928; *Včerašnie predki* (novel), 2 vols., Belgrade, 1928, 1931; *Liljaška* (novel), Riga, 1928; *Lit. v izgnanii*, Belgrade, 1929; *Oderžimaja Rus'* (pov.), Berlin, 1929; *Dve Nadeždy* (pov.), Shanghai,

1936.—*Soč.*, 37 vols. (vols. 1–30, 33–35, 37 were published), 1911–16.

Secondary Lit.: F. Ivanov, in *Spolokhi*, Berlin, 5:1922; B. K., in *Lit. ènciklopedija*, Moscow, 1929; Anon., in *MERSL* 1:1977.

**Aminádo, D.**, at first **Don-Aminádo** (pseud. of Aminád Petróvich Shpolyánsky), poet, prose writer (b. 1888, Novograd, prov. Kherson—d. 1957[?], Paris [?]). Aminado grew up in the small provincial town of Novograd, studied law in Odessa and Kiev, and, after completing his studies, began working in Moscow as a writer (regular contributor to the newspaper *Ranneye utro* and the journal *Satirikon*). During World War I, Aminado served as a soldier and published his first book, *Pesni voyny* (1915; Songs of War). Aminado emigrated, probably in 1919 via Constantinople, to Paris and regularly wrote feuilletons for P. Milyukov's newspaper *Posledniye novosti*. *Dym bez otechestva* (1921; Smoke without the Homeland), his first book published in emigration, contains satirical poems on contemporary themes; his second book, *Nasha malenkaya zhizn* (1927; Our Small Life), contains corresponding pieces of short prose. Frequently and enthusiastically read, Aminado also reached the French public with *Le rire dans la steppe* (1927; Laughter on the Steppe). He called his next volume, *Nakinuv plashch* (1928; The Thrown-on Raincoat), a "collection of poetic satire." In the following work, *Neskuchny sad* (1935; The Pleasure Garden), the titles he gave to some of the parts parodied, in a style typical for him, well-known titles from Russian literature: "Novy Kozma Prutkov" (New Kozma Prutkov), "Zapadny divan" (Western Divan), "Vechera na khutore bliz Bulonki" (Evenings on a Farm near Bulonka). After World War II, Aminado published (under the pseudonym D. Aminado) a volume of poetry, *V te basnoslovnye goda* (1951; In Those Legendary Years), and his memoirs, *Poezd na tretyem puti* (1954; The Train on Track 3).

Aminado is a linguistically highly talented writer who presents the typical situations of his time in an impressionistic style in his poetry and prose. His art is based on allusion to well-known facts from history, current events, and literature and on a succinct choice of words (often limited to nouns) that the reader expands upon to get the complete meaning. His basic attitude is ironic distance; his satire inclines to friendly, playful humor, yet behind the relaxed form his political seriousness and his human concern remain recognizable. In his memoirs he preserves an ironic distance even from himself and impressively recreates the atmosphere of literary life in Russia before 1919 and in emigration.

Works: Pesni vojny (poems), 1914, 2d ed., 1915; Vesna semnadcatogo goda, 1917; Dym bez otečestva (poems), Paris, 1921; Naša malen'kaja žizn' (short stories), Paris, 1927; Le rire dans la steppe (with Maurice Dekobra), Paris, 1927; Nakinuv plašč (poems), Paris, 1928; Neskučnyj sad (poems), Paris, 1935; Pointes de Feu, Paris, 1939; V te basnoslovnye goda (poems), Paris, 1951; Poezd na tret'em puti (memoirs), New York, 1954.

Secondary Lit.: A. Drozdov, in Russkaja kniga, Berlin, 1921:6; I. Bunin, in Sovremennye zapiski, Paris, 33:1927; M. Cetlin, in Sovremennye zapiski 37: 1928; A. Krajnij (Z. Gippius), in Sovremennye zapiski 58:1935; A. Sedykh, in Mosty, Munich, 7:1961 and in his Dalëkie, blizkie, New York, 1979; L. Zurov, in Novyj žurnal, New York, 90:1968.

**Amlínsky, Vladímir Ilyích,** prose writer (b. Aug. 22, 1935, Moscow). Amlinsky's father was a biologist. Amlinsky completed his studies at the State Institute of Cinematography (1958), then traveled extensively around the Soviet Union as a journalist. His first short story, Stantsiya pervoy lyubvi (1958; The Station of First Love), was introduced in the journal Yunost, in which Amlinsky published his later prose as well. His work first came out in book form in 1961; collections of his short stories have appeared frequently since 1966. With Tuchi nad gorodom vstali (1964; Clouds Gathered over the City), a povest praised by V. Aksyonov, Amlinsky turned to writing longer prose works. He has been a member of the editorial board of Yunost since 1969; and in 1970 he was selected as a delegate to a congress of the Writers Union for the first time; in 1976 he became a member of the board of the Writers Union of the USSR. He lives in Moscow.

Amlinsky's prose focuses on the figure of the new urban adolescent. Writing in the first person from the point of view of his 15-year-old narrator in Tuchi nad gorodom vstali, Amlinsky depicts life during the Siberian evacuation and addresses the problems that arise among school, paternal love, and the hardships caused by war. Quite possibly much of the material here is autobiographical. Amlinsky later strove for something more unusual in his prose works: in Zhizn Ernsta

Shatalova (1968; Eng. tr., The Life of Ernst Shatalov, 1971) he shows how a permanently bedridden young man overcomes his fate by working with his mind; in the novel Vozvrashcheniye brata (1973; The Brother's Return) he deals with the problem of a juvenile delinquent who is subject to weakness of will and who is exposed to endangering circumstances. In Neskuchny sad (1979; The Pleasure Garden), Amlinsky attempts to come to grips with the positive features of the decades from World War II to the 1970s by tracing the destinies of different children. His prose reveals a strong psychological interest; it is written in a flowing and lively manner.

Works: Stancija pervoj ljubvi (short stories), 1961; Tuči nad gorodom vstali (pov.), in Junost' 1964:10; Pervaja bessonnica (short stories), 1967; Žizn' Ernsta Šatalova (pov.), in Junost' 1968:12 (see above); Muzyka na vokzale (pov. and short stories), 1970; Vozvraščenie brata (novel), in Junost' 1973:3–4; Sredi ljudej (short stories), 1973; Na rassvete v načale dorogi (pov. and short stories), 1974; Den' i vecer (pov., novel, short stories, essays), 1976; Neskučnyj sad (pov., novel, short stories), 1979; Poltora časa dorogi (novel, pov., film script, short stories, essays), 1979; Nad rekoj Kizir (novel, pov., short stories, essays), 1981; Moskovskie stranicy (novel, pov., short stories), 1982; Bor'ka Nikitin (Remeslo), 1984; Opravdan budet každyj čas . . . (pov.), in Junost' 1986:10–11.

Secondary Lit.: Ju. Nagibin, in Znamja 1962:4; V. Aksënov, in Lit. Rossija Jan. 22, 1965, pp. 10–12; Ju. Trifonov, in Lit. gazeta March 16, 1965; K. Ščerbakov, in Novyj mir 1971:11 and in Lit. gazeta March 30, 1983; V. Gejdeko, in Lit. obozrenie 1973:9; M. Bremener, in Komsomol'skaja pravda Oct. 17, 1974; A. Vaksberg, in Lit. obozrenie 1975:1; E. Evtušenko, in Novyj mir 1980:7; N. Železnova, in Lit. obozrenie 1984:6; A. Gavrilov, in Novyj mir 1985:12; E. Sidorov, in Lit. gazeta Jan. 28, 1987, p. 4.

**Anányev** (pseud. Séversky), **Anatóly Andréyevich,** prose writer (b. July 18, 1925, Dzhambul, Kazakh SSR). Ananyev served as a soldier in World War II; in 1950 he joined the Communist Party. In 1957 he graduated in humanities from Alma Ata University. Ananyev began his career as a writer with short prose works that appeared in Alma-Ata in 1958. His war novel Tanki idut rombom (1963; The Tanks Move in a Rhombus) won recognition.

Additional prose works, such as the antireligious povest *Kozyri monakha Grigoriya* (1964; The Trumps of the Monk Grigory), appeared in Moscow. At the end of the 1960s, Ananyev himself moved to Moscow. In 1970 he became a member of the secretariat of the Writers Union of the RSFSR, in 1971 a member of the board of the Writers Union of the USSR. Following V. Kochetov's death, Ananyev was appointed editor in chief of the journal *Oktyabr* in 1974, and he improved its quality. For the novel *Vyorsty lyubvi* (1971; Levels of Love) he received the Gorky Prize in 1978.

*Tanki idut rombom* has as its theme the defense against the German tank attack at the Kursk Arc on July 4 and 5, 1943. Ananyev's representation won acclaim for his endeavors to incorporate his own experiences. Through glimpses into the past and the future, Ananyev also tries historically to position this episode, which is clearly limited both temporally and spatially. In later works the intricacy of his very slow-moving narrative style, which is overburdened with reflections, becomes more oppressively noticeable, as in *Mezha* (1969; The Boundary), a novel that attempts to penetrate psychologically and historically the boundaries still existing between the traditional and the new in the Russian village. This intricacy is reflected in overly long, complex constructions. His laborious style also detracts from *Vyorsty lyubvi*, in which he again gives form to the theme of war and the Russian peasant and criticizes the kulak mentality. In the novel *Gody bez voyny* (1975–81; Years without War), which portrays the effects of the war persisting after two decades, Ananyev raises serious concerns, including those of the influence of religion on youth and the success of small-scale private cultivation compared to the failure of kolkhoz agriculture.

*Works:* Vernenskie rasskazy (short stories), 1958; *Tanki idut rombom* (novel), 1963; *Malyj zaslon* (pov.), 1964; *Kozyri monakha Grigorija* (pov.), 1964; *Meža* (novel), 1970; *Vërsty ljubvi* (novel), 1972; *Zabyt' nel'zja* (novel, pov., short stories), 1972; *Gody bez vojny* (novel), vols. 1–4, in *Novyj mir* 1975:4–6, 1979:1–2, 1981:1–2, 1984:2–4, separate ed., 1982–85; *Tikhij sotrudnik* (play), in *Teatr* 1981:3.—*Izbr. proizv.*, 2 vols., 1977; *Sobr. soč.*, 4 vols., 1984–.

*Secondary Lit.:* F. Levin, in *Lit. Rossija* Feb. 21, 1964, p. 15; L. Krjačko, in *Lit. gazeta* Dec. 29, 1964; D. Dyčko, in *Lit. Rossija* Dec. 26, 1969, p. 8, and in *Lit. i sovremennost'* 10:1970; I. Grinberg, in *Moskva* 1973:2; Anon., in *Moskva* 1975:7; B. Filippov, in *Russkaja mysl'*,

Paris, Oct. 2, 1975, p. 10; V. Mikhal'skij, in *Družba narodov* 1979:2; V. Tarsis, in *ZeitBild*, Bern, 1979:10 and 1981:9; A. Bočarov, in *Znamja* 1981:7 and 1985:7; R. Kovalenko, 1985.

**Anchárov, Mikhaíl Leonídovich,** prose writer (b. March 28, 1923, Moscow). Ancharov was a soldier in World War II, graduated from the Foreign Language Institute of the Soviet Army in 1944, and joined the Communist Party in 1950. After the war, in 1954, he graduated from the Surikov Art Academy in Moscow and made his appearance as a writer with the short story *Vensky vals* (1964; Vienna Waltz), which L. Anninsky praised enthusiastically. His work is essentially philosophically oriented and religiously based; it can take on the external form of science fiction. His novel *Teoriya neveroyatnosti* (1965; The Theory of Improbability) was well received and was also staged. Ancharov wrote a series of screenplays for film and television, including a work he coauthored with V. Aksyonov, *Moy mladshy brat* (1962; My Younger Brother). He lives in Moscow.

Ancharov's creativity is focused by his belief in the spiritual foundation of human existence and in a truth that is not comprehensible through intellect alone. His first short story, *Vensky vals*, was based on a surprising reencounter. The next short story, *Zolotoy dozhd* (1965; The Golden Rain), derives from the Greek myth of Danaë and illustrates through the "golden rain" the light that art can give mankind and toward which, in the final analysis, human existence is directed. The novel *Etot siniy aprel* (1967; This Blue April) views the discovery of life as a miracle, the comprehension of the human being as a personal universe, and the recognition of good fortune as a transcendent experience. In the same sense, the protagonist of the novel *Teoriya neveroyatnosti* strives toward a metaphysical goal in his thoughts and actions; this attitude gives him room in which to accept the wonder and to perceive the divine totality of which this goal is composed. In the novel *Samshitovy les* (1979; The Boxwood Forest), which is especially loosely constructed without a strict plot line and thus leaves room for many reflections, the central focus is on a scientist who is seeking to become acquainted with reality in its spiritual dress. In this way, Ancharov includes here, as in his other works, the question concerning the status of art.

*Works:* Venskij val's (short story), in *Smena* 1964:21; *Zolotoj dožd'* (pov.), in *Moskva*

1965:5; *Teorija neverojatnosti* (novel), in *Junost'* 1965:8–9, separate ed., 1966; *Soda-solnce* (pov.), in *Fantastika* 1965:3, separate ed., 1968; *Golubaja žilka Afrodity* (pov.), in *Fantastika* 1966:3; *Ètot sinij aprel'* (novel), in *Moskva* 1967:5, separate ed., 1969; *Samšitovyj les* (novel), in *Novyj mir* 1979:9–10, separate ed., 1981; *Doroga čerez khaos* (pov.), 1983.
Secondary Lit.: L. Anninskij, in *Znamja* 1965:4; Ju. Tomaševskij, in *Moskva* 1966:1; F. Svetov, in *Novyj mir* 1967:5; M. Čudakova, in *Novyj mir* 1967:7; A. Jakubovskij, in *Teatr* 1971:8; V. Gejdeko, in *Lit. gazeta* July 21, 1971, p. 4; M. Lathouwers, in *Irénikon*, Chevetogne (Belgium), 1971:1 and in *Glaube in der 2. Welt* 1978:7–8; V. Tarsis, in *ZeitBild*, Bern, 1979:26; A. Rekemčuk, in *Znamja* 1980:2.

**Andrónikov, Irákly Luarsábovich** (pseud. of I. L. Andronikashvíli), literary scholar, prose writer (b. Sept. 28 [Sept. 15], 1908, St. Petersburg). Andronikov completed his study of philology at Leningrad University in 1930. As a literary scholar he specialized in M. Lermontov and remained active at home and abroad throughout his life in tracking down unknown material concerning Lermontov. This activity frequently found expression in narrative works. Starting in 1935, Andronikov began appearing as a master of vocal narration; with this skill he has captivated millions in the Soviet Union, at first only from the stage, then over the radio, and finally especially on television. In his one-man plays he has particularly developed the technique of portraiture, of playing the part of well-known writers (for example, A. Fadeyev, V. Shklovksy) and scientists. In 1949 Andronikov became a member of the Communist Party; in 1967 he was awarded the State Prize of the USSR for his book on Lermontov published in 1964, and in 1976 he received the Lenin Prize for several films for television in which he appears as narrator. He lives in Moscow.
The enthusiasm that Andronikov generates through his dramatic narration does not carry over to the written and published texts themselves. He prefers unusual, trenchant scenes in which he imitates the person being depicted. An example—Vsevolod Ivanov—can be found in K. Chukovsky's *Chukokkala* (1979, pp. 297–300). Andronikov's philological works also contain a narrative element that partly concerns the research work itself and partly involves the life of the author.

*Works: M. Lermontov* (scholarly articles), 1951, 4th ed., 1977; *Rasskazy literaturoveda* (short story), 1958, 6th ed., 1973; *Ja khoču rasskazat' vam . . .* (short stories), 1965, 3d ed., 1971.—*Izbr. proizv.*, 2 vols., 1975; *Sobr. soč.*, 3 vols., 1980–81.
Secondary Lit.: V. Ždanov, in *Novyj mir* 1964:10; Anon., in *MERSL* 1:1977; V. Lakšin, in *Lit. Rossija* Sept. 29, 1978, p. 9, and in *Oktjabr'* 1982:9; A. Gorlovskij, in *Novyj mir* 1983:5; E. Semunskaja, in *Lit. Rossija* Oct. 11, 1985, p. 9.

**Ánstey, Ólga Nikoláyevna**, poet (b. March 13 [Feb. 29], 1912, Kiev—d. May 30, 1985, New York). After graduating from the Foreign Language Institute in 1931, Anstey worked as a secretary and translator in the chemical industry. From childhood on, she wrote poems but never dared to attempt publication in the Soviet Union. In 1943 she left Kiev together with the poet I. Yelagin, whom she had married in 1937. Through Prague and Berlin she came to Munich around 1946. In this year, Anstey published her first poems in *Grani*; with *Dver v stene* (1949; A Door in the Wall), which was very well received, she published her only volume of poetry for a long while. Since then, her poems have appeared regularly in journals and almanacs. In May 1950, Anstey moved to New York, where she was divorced. From 1951 until 1972, Anstey worked at the United Nations, first as a secretary and after 1960 as a translator. She also worked at the Chekhov Press on B. Filippov's edition of N. Klyuyev's works (1954); she and Filippov were married for about a year. Together with her own poetry, Anstey published translations of poetry (including poems by Rainer Maria Rilke, Manfred Hausmann, G. K. Chesterton, and Tennyson and a short story by Stephen Vincent Benét, *The Devil and Daniel Webster*, in 1960). Her second volume of poetry, *Na yuru* (1976; In the Way), contains 66 poems carefully selected from her entire creative opus. Among her scholarly essays on literature, Anstey was most fond of *Mysli o Pasternake* (1951; Thoughts about Pasternak).
Anstey is a highly gifted poet who was successful in capturing the essence of what she observed and her own inner experiences in clear, balanced verse. For her "there is no painless joy on this earth," but she is able to perceive the beautiful and the valid beyond the suffering and the ugliness. Her fundamental belief, "We are in the hands of the living God," gives her the possibility not only of enduring but of recasting in a positive light the loneliness of the abandoned woman, the permanent loss of her homeland, and the vi-

ciousness of many people. She has a strong attachment to the incorporeal world and to the spiritual animation of the material world; among her religious poems are retellings of New Testament events, such as Christ's reappearance after death. Her poetry is descriptive, reminiscent, reflective, and uses repetitions and images economically.

Works: Dver' v stene (poems), Munich, 1949; Mysli o Pasternake (essay), condensed in Lit. sovremennik, Munich, 2:1951; Na juru (poems), New York, 1976.
Secondary Lit.: Ju. Bol'šukhin, in Lit. zarubež'e, Munich, 1958; F. Zverev (B. Filippov), in Russkaja literatura v èmigracii, ed. N. Poltorackij, Pittsburgh, 1972; V. Sinkevič, in Novoe russkoe slovo, New York, Sept. 11, 1977, p. 5; Anon., in Kontinent, Paris, 11:1977; W. Kasack, in Neue Zürcher Zeitung June 19, 1985, p. 39, and in Grani, Frankfurt am Main, 141:1986; T. Fesenko, in Novyj žurnal, New York, 161:1985; E. Tauber, in Novyj žurnal 163:1986.

**Antokólsky, Pável Grigóryevich**, poet (b. July 1 [June 19], 1896, St. Petersburg—d. Oct. 9, 1978). Antokolsky's father was a lawyer. Antokolsky moved to Moscow in 1904; between 1915 and 1917 he studied law at Moscow University. From 1919 to 1934 he worked as a director, first under E. Vakhtangov, then in the newly formed Vakhtangov Theater; in 1923 and 1928 he traveled abroad when the theater went on tour. During the same period Antokolsky wrote poetry (published from 1921 on). Historical themes, particularly the French Revolution, predominate in his neoclassical poetry of the 1920s and early 1930s. Themes based on contemporary Soviet reality, the Russian intellectual milieu, and his experience of the Caucasus, as well as translations from Armenian and Georgian, are frequently found in his poetry of the 1930s. Antokolsky put the pain he felt when his son was killed in World War II into the patriotic, pathos-laden narrative poem Syn (1943; My Son), which was highly regarded in the context both of his works and of Soviet war poetry in general (Stalin Prize for 1943–44, 2d class). He joined the Communist Party in 1943. When the liberal literature published after the 20th Party Congress and denouncing the despotism of the Stalinist period was attacked by the dogmatic faction in 1957, Antokolsky sided with the dogmatists (Lit. gazeta May 22, 1957); in 1966, however, he signed the petition supporting A. Sinyavsky and Yu. Daniel; he also

stood up for Yu. Galanskov. In Vysokoye napryazheniye (1962; High Tension), Antokolsky returned to the theme of European art, unbounded by country or historical period (Shakespeare, Michelangelo, Tsvetayeva, Picasso). In Chetvyortoye izmereniye (1964; The Fourth Dimension), he tries to approach more closely the true nature of time through creative lyrical composition; he describes "the image of time, irreversible, elusive, and fleeting, yet nevertheless leaving its mark on the world of three dimensions" (D. Samoylov). The volume also includes a short lyrical drama from the 1920s, Pozhar v teatre (Fire in the Theater), which is reminiscent of A. Blok. Antokolsky wrote prose as well: fairy tales, a travel documentary about Vietnam (1958), and numerous essays about poets, especially A. Pushkin.

Works: Stikhotvorenija (poems), 1922; Zapad (poems), 1926; Robesp'er i Gorgona (narrative poem), 1928; Kommuna 71 goda (narrative poem), 1931; Fransua Vijon (narrative poem), 1934; Bol'šie rasstojanija (poems), 1936; Puškinskij god (poems), 1938; Polgoda (poems), 1942; Syn (narrative poem), 1943; Okean (narrative poem), 1950; Poèty i vremja (essays), 1957; Masterskaja (poems), 1958; Sila V'etnama (short stories and poems), 1960; O Puškine (short stories and poems), 1960; Vysokoe naprjaženie (poems), 1962; Četvërtoe izmerenie (poems), 1964; Skazki vremeni, 1971; Vremja (lyric and narrative poems), 1973; Putevoj žurnal pisatelja, 1976; Konec veka (poems), 1977; Stikhi slednikh let (poems), in Neva 1981:2.—Izbr. soč., 2 vols., 1956; Izbr. proizv., 2 vols., 1961; Sobr. soč., 4 vols., 1971–73.
Secondary Lit.: A. Tarasenkov, in Znamja 1945:7; V. Lugovskoj, in his Razdum'e o poèzii, 1960; D. Samojlov, in Lit. gazeta Dec. 5, 1964; L. Levin, Četyre žizni, 1969; A. Urban, in Zvezda 1970:8; I. Bogomolov, 1976; RSPPo 1:1977; N. Bank, in Avrora 1982:5; A. Toom, in Lit. obozrenie 1986:1; I. Volgin, in Lit. gazeta July 30, 1986, p. 5.

**Antónov, Sergéy Petróvich**, prose writer (b. May 16 [May 3], 1915, Petrograd). Antonov's father was an engineer. In 1938 Antonov completed his studies at the Leningrad Institute of Highway Engineering. He worked initially as an engineer; he published his first poems in 1944 and his first prose after 1947. His first collection of short stories, Po dorogam idut mashiny (1950; Cars Travel on Roads), was awarded a Stalin Prize (for 1950, 3d class).

Antonov's short stories after 1951 stand out because they do not avoid dealing with genuine conflicts. B. Agapov attacked Antonov's *Dozhdi* (1951; The Rains) for its deviation from SOCIALIST REALISM, but post-Stalinist literary histories consider it to be the first example of the breakaway from the representational and idealizing trends in kolkhoz literature. After 1953 Antonov's longer stories adhered to the course set by the cautious criticism of that period. He turned several of his works into film scripts; moreover, he wrote several books about the short-story form for a general audience. Since 1954 Antonov has belonged to the board of the Writers Union of the USSR and he was a delegate to all congresses of the Writers Unions of the USSR and RSFSR. He lives in Moscow.

The major setting for action in Antonov's prose is the contemporary village. The restraint characteristic of his work distinguished it from the general body of published material even before 1953; K. Paustovsky's influence is visible in its lyrical tone. The povest *Delo bylo v Penkove* (1956; Eng. tr., *It Happened in Penkovo*, 1956), in which Antonov analyzes socioeconomic problems within the framework of a love story, generated a controversy: dogmatic critics were irritated that Antonov was writing about rural backwardness, liberal voices greeted his candor, and M. Shcheglov pointed out that Antonov, as in former times, idealized the conditions he presented, especially in his conclusions. Using a young enthusiast as his example, Antonov probes the problem of the development of human personality as influenced by character, environment, and the structure of the kolkhoz in *Razorvanny rubl* (1966; The Torn Ruble). His povest *Vaska* (Vaska) on the Moscow youth during the construction of the Metro in the early 1930s—which had been suppressed for many years—could be published only in the Gorbachev period of *glasnost*. He writes in a lively, vivid manner and with psychological integrity. Antonov collected his literary reflections on I. Turgenev, F. Dostoyevsky, M. Zoshchenko, and others in *Ot pervogo litsa* (1973; In the First Person).

*Works: Po dorogam idut mašiny* (short stories), 1950; *Doždi* (short story), in *Novyj mir* 1951:10; *Izbr.*, 1954; *Delo bylo v Pen'kove* (pov.), 1957 (see above); *Alënka* (pov.), 1960 (Eng. tr., *Alyona*, 1969); *Porožnij rejs* (pov.), 1960; (Povesti i rasskazy (pov. and short stories), 1961; *Razorvannyj rubl'* (pov.), in *Junost'* 1966:1; *Raznotrav'e* (short stories), 1968; *Carskij dvugrivennyj* (pov.), 1970; *Ja čitaju*

*rasskaz* (literary criticism), 1973; *Ot pervogo lica* (essays), 1973; *Povesti i rasskazy* (pov. and short stories), 1976, 1977; *Vas'ka* (pov.), in *Junost'* 1987:3.—*Izbr. proizv.*, 2 vols., 1979.

*Secondary Lit.:* M. Ščeglov, in *Družba narodov* 1956:11 and in his *Lit. kritika*, 1971; *RSPP* 1:1959; A. Marčenko, in *Voprosy lit.* 1961:8; A. Ognëv, 1968; S. Plekhanov, in *Voprosy lit.* 1975:2.

**Antonóvskaya, Ánna Arnóldovna,** prose writer (b. Jan. 12, 1886 [Dec. 31, 1885], Tbilisi—d. Oct. 21, 1967, Moscow). Antonovskaya's father was an engraver. Antonovskaya published several poems in acmeist publications in 1918–19; in 1921–22 she wrote political poems and plays for the Caucasian section of ROSTA. She moved to Moscow in 1922. From this time on, Antonovskaya essentially worked only on the historical novel *Veliky Mouravi* (The Great Mouravi), the first chapters of which were published in *Krasnaya nov* under the title "Georgy Saakadze" (1931) and the tenth and last part of which appeared in 1958. This work, 3,666 pages in length, is devoted to the history of Georgia during the late 16th and early 17th centuries; it centers on the struggle for unification under the leadership of the folk hero Saakadze and stresses the traditional friendship between Russia and Georgia in its pedagogical message. Antonovskaya received a Stalin Prize (for 1941, 2d class) for parts one through six. With B. Chorny, Antonovskaya wrote *Angely mira* (1945–46; Angels of Peace), a tendentious novel about military intervention in Georgia in 1918–19.

*Works: Velikij Mouravi* (novel), 1939–58; *Angely mira* (novel), in *Novyj mir* 1945:10– 12, 1946:1–2 (in collaboration with B. Čërnyj); *Didi Mouravi* (novel), 6 vols., 1960–61 (with B. Čërnyj); *Dokumental'nye rasskazy o Gruzii* (short stories), 1961 (with B. Čërnyj).

*Secondary Lit.:* G. Tavzišvili, 1958; *RSPP* 1:1959; Anon., in *Lit. gazeta* Jan. 18, 1966, p. 3; B. Čërnyj, in *Lit. Gruzija* 1971:3, 8–10.

**Arbúzov, Alekséy Nikoláyevich,** playwright (b. May 26 [May 13], 1908, Moscow—d. April 20, 1986, Moscow). Arbuzov studied at the Theater School in Leningrad. In 1923 he began working as an actor and in 1928 as a director at theaters in Leningrad and Moscow and wrote for the PROLETKULT theater. His first drama, *Klass* (Class), was performed in 1930. Since then he developed into one of the most important dramatists in the Soviet Union.

Until 1944 he ran a theater studio for soldiers at the front that he helped establish in 1939. Because of their "inadequate heroism" and his interest in experiments with form, his dramas were, to be sure, not always unreservedly welcomed by the critics, but they were unusually frequently performed. Some have also been performed in foreign countries. He lived in Moscow, was a delegate to all congresses of the Writers Unions of the USSR and of the RSFSR from 1954 on, and belonged to the review commission of the Writers Union of the USSR from 1954 on. In 1980 he was awarded the State Prize of the USSR "for his pieces of the last few years." "A multifaceted if not brilliant dramatist, Arbuzov has always been sensitive to the winds of change and willing to step out in new directions" (Segel).

Among his dramas of the early period, *Tanya* (1939; Eng. tr., in *Classic Soviet Plays*, 1979) is considered the most important. By 1956 it had been performed one thousand times. The passage of long periods of time between scenes helped Arbuzov illustrate the transformation of a female student in love into a responsible wife and doctor. The mature figure was insufficiently convincing, so Arbuzov reworked this drama in 1947, just as he extensively reworked many of his dramas. He wrote and performed *Gorod na zare* (1940; The City at Dawn) together with members of his studio (including A. Galich). *Irkutskaya istoriya* (1959; Eng. tr., *It Happened in Irkutsk*, in *Three Soviet Plays*, 1961), became one of the most important dramas of the post-Stalin period (in 1960, 4,202 performances; in 1961, 4,828). Against a backdrop of the construction of a tremendous hydroelectric power station in Siberia, and using the traditional paradigm of a woman positioned between two men, Arbuzov tries to present human relationships without false pathos and to unite these relationships to the growth of social consciousness. The inclusion of a form of the ancient chorus in this again epically structured work often slips into awkward commentary on the events. Some of Arbuzov's formal essays show the influence of Tennessee Williams and of John Osborne. *Moy bedny Marat* (1965; My Poor Marat; Eng. tr., *The Promise*, 1967), a play about the siege of Leningrad, shows the extension of time over many years that is typical of Arbuzov's work (1965–69, 3,253 performances). In *Skazki starogo Arbata* (1970; Tales of the Old Arbat District; Eng. tr., *Once Upon a Time*, in *Selected Plays*, 1982); performed 1,827 times from 1970 to 1973, Arbuzov places an artist of his own age onstage—the 60-year-old puppet maker. His love

affair with a 20-year-old woman and his relationship with his son and his friend serve somewhat abstractly to elucidate a philosophy of old age and of life. In the play *Zhestokiye igry* (1978; Eng. tr., *Cruel Games*, in *Selected Plays*, 1982), set contemporarily in a western Siberian oil field and in Moscow, the underlying concern is how each individual can inflict serious harm, both physical and ethical, on another person through thoughtlessness.

*Works: Tanja* (play), 1939 (see above); *Gody stranstvij* (play), 1954 (Eng. tr., *Years of Wandering*, in *Soviet Literature* 1954:9); *Gorod na zare* (play), in *Teatr* 1957:11; *P'esy* (plays), 1957; *Dvenadcatyj čas* (play), in *Teatr* 1959:8 (Eng. tr., *The Twelfth Hour*, in *Selected Plays*, 1982); *Irkutskaja istorija* (play), 1960 (see above); *Poterjannyj syn* (play), 1961; *Teatr* (play), 1961; *Nas gde-to ždut* (play), in *Teatr* 1963:1; *Moj bednyj Marat* (play), in *Teatr* 1965:1 (see above); *Nočnaja ispoved'* (play), in *Teatr* 1967:5 (Eng. tr., *Confession at Night*, 1971); *Sčastlivye dni nesčastlivogo čeloveka* (play), in *Teatr* 1968:4; *Dramy* (plays), 1969 (contains *Tanja; Gody stranstvij; Dvenadcatyj čas; Irkutskaja istorija; Poterjannyj syn; Moj bednyj Marat; Nočnaja ispoved; Sčastlivye dni nesčastlivogo čeloveka*); *Skazki starogo Arbata* (play), in *Teatr* 1970:9 (see above); *Vybor* (play), in *Novyj mir* 1971:9; *V ètom milom starom dome* (play), in *Teatr* 1972:2; *Moë zagljaden'e* (play), in *Moskva* 1972:5 (Eng. tr., *Lovely to Look At!*, in *Selected Plays*, 1982); *Staromodnaja komedija* (play), in *Teatr* 1975:6 (Eng. tr., *Do You Turn Somersaults?*, 1977, and revised tr., *Old-World*, 1977); *Vybor* (plays), 1976 (contains *Skazki starogo Arbata; Vybor; V ètom milom starom dome; Moë zagljaden'e; Večernij svet* [Eng. tr., *Evening Light*, in *Nine Modern Soviet Plays*, 1977]; *Staromodnaja komedija*); *Ožidanie* (play), in *Teatr* 1977:7; *Žestokie igry* (play), in *Teatr* 1978:4 (see above); *Vospominanie* (play), in *Teatr* 1981:5; *Pobeditel'nica* (play), in *Teatr* 1983:4; *Dramy*, 1983; *Vinovatye* (play), in *Teatr* 1984:12.—*Izbr.*, 2 vols., 1981.

*Secondary Lit.:* G. Vladimov, in *Teatr* 1954:12; N. Rabinjanc and V. Sergeev, in *Zvezda* 1955:8; K. Rudnickij, in *Teatr* 1957:4 and in his *Portrety dramaturgov*, 1961; V. M. Smirnov, in *Voprosy sovetskoj literatury*, vol. 8, 1959; I. Višnevskaja, 1971; T. Šakh-Azizova, in *Teatr* 1971:4; I. Vasilinina, in *Teatr* 1978:5 and 1983:6; A. Smith, Diss., Indiana Univ., 1981; E. Dangulova, in *Sovremennaja dramaturgija* 1982:1; A. Smeljanskij, in *Sovremennaja dramaturgija* 1982:2.

**Arkhángelsky, Aleksándr Grigóryevich,** poet (b. Nov. 16 [Nov. 4], 1889, Yeysk—d. Oct. 12, 1938, Moscow). Arkhangelsky's first volume of poetry was *Chornye oblaka* (1919; Black Clouds). Beginning in 1922 he worked on the editorial staff of the satirical journal *Krokodil* for ten years. For a while he also wrote satirical verse and journalistic prose. He then turned to writing parodies of the work of his writing colleagues (both poets and prose writers), in which he was successful in his hyperbolic reproduction of their typical thematic, syntactic, and semantic features. Arkhangelsky's parodies often took as their starting point actual literary works that were easy to recognize even in their satirical distortion, but they never lost sight of the whole writer. Arkhangelsky combined with his parodies the serious goal of exposing traits that threatened to become clichés. "He made the writer confront the issue of the need to reexamine his craftsmanship when it began to petrify" (Shklovsky). A volume of Arkhangelsky's selected parodies appeared during the THAW, 20 years after he died of tuberculosis, but Z. Paperny's call in 1964 for a more comprehensive edition of Arkhangelsky's work (based on his literary remains) came to nothing.

*Works: Černye oblaka* (poems), 1919; *Parodii* (parodies), 1927; *Derevenskie častuški* (poems), 1928; *O Babele, Gladkove, . . .* (parodies), 1930 (Eng. tr., *On Babel, Gladkov, Zharov, . . .* , 1976); *Izbr.: Parodii, èpigrammy, satira* (selected works), 1946; *Parodii* (parodies), 1958; *Iz nasledija . . .* , in *Lit. Rossija* Jan. 8, 1965, pp. 16–17; *Zabytye parodii i épigrammy* (parodies and epigrams), in *Voprosy lit.* 1976:2; *Parodii* (parodies), Jerusalem, 1982.

*Secondary Lit.:* F. Čelovekov (pseud. of A. Platonov), in *Lit. kritik* 1938:11; Z. Papernyj, in *Lit. Rossija* Nov. 6, 1964, pp. 18–19; A. Raskin, in *Lit. gazeta* Nov. 14, 1964, Feb. 7, 1968, p. 8, and Oct. 16, 1968, p. 16; G. Ryklin, in *Neva* 1967:4; RSPPo 1:1977.

**Arósev, Aleksándr Yákovlevich,** prose writer, Party official (b. May 25 [May 13], 1890, Kazan—d. Feb. 10, 1938 [?], while imprisoned). Arosev was of middle-class origin. From 1909 to 1911 he studied philology in Liège. He joined the RSDRP (Social Democrats) as a Bolshevik in 1907; in the years before the Revolution he worked in the political underground as one of its leading organizers, was arrested several times and exiled, and temporarily emigrated. During the October Rev-

olution he commanded the troops of the Moscow military revolutionary committee; in 1920 he served as presiding judge of the Supreme Court in the Ukraine; in 1922 he held high diplomatic posts in Lithuania and Czechoslovakia. Arosev began his literary career in 1916; supported by A. Voronsky, he published in *Krasnaya nov* and later in *Novy mir* as well. His short stories and novels continued to appear up to 1933. In 1934 Arosev was elected to the board of the Writers Union of the USSR and was named chairman of VOKS (All-Union Society for Cultural Relations with Foreign Countries). In the late 1930s Arosev perished in the mass purges. He was rehabilitated after 1956, but none of his works have been reprinted.

Arosev is the first writer in the Soviet Union to depict a Soviet official, trained in the underground, overcome by doubts as he sees the economic decline and the dangers associated with sudden and unexpected seizure of power during the Revolution. In his *Strada: Zapiski Terentiya Zabytogo* (1921; Toil: The Notes of Terentiy Zabyty), the main character, Derevtsov, takes his own life because of the weight of such doubts. In *Nedavniye dni* (1926; Recent Days), Arosev's theme is the subordination of personal relationships to political pressures: an official shoots his beloved wife because she is working for the Whites. Arosev writes realistically, without the stylistic experimentation characteristic of his time; he stands out not for his depiction of events or the development of his plot but for the profundity of his psychological penetration. Arosev was "the memoirist of the state of mind within the Party" (Voronsky).

*Works: Zapiski Terentija Zabytogo* (pov.), Berlin, 1922 (reprinted, in *Opal'nye povesti,* New York, 1955); *Belaja lestnica* (short stories), 1923; *Dve povesti* (pov.), 1923; *Nikita Šornev* (pov.), 1924; *Nedavnie dni* (pov.), 1926; *Farsitskaja legenda* (short stories), 1927; *Senskie berega* (novel), 1928; *Na boevykh putjakh,* in *Novyj mir* 1931:1–3.—*Sobr. soč.,* 2 vols., 1929.

*Secondary Lit.:* A Zonin, in *Na postu* 1923:2–3; A. Voronskij, *Lit. portrety,* vol. 2, 1929.

**Arsényev, Vladímir Klávdiyevich,** naturalist, prose writer (b. Sept. 10 [Aug. 29], 1872, St. Petersburg—d. Sept. 4, 1930, Vladivostok). Arsenyev graduated from the St. Petersburg Military Academy (Infantry), where, under the influence of the Central Asian explorer M. E. Grum-Grzhimaylo, he developed an interest in Asian geography. In 1899 he received a commission in the Soviet Far East and from 1902 on was able to accompany numerous expeditions from Vladivostok in the capacity of topographer. Arsenyev began publishing his travel notes in 1910. In 1927 he once again participated in a large expedition in the Khabarovsk region.

Arsenyev's descriptions, arranged as a series of individual, often perilous adventures, make vivid and absorbing reading; they contain scientifically significant and stylistically delightful observations of the world of plants and animals. Books such as his Po Ussuriyskomu krayu (1921; Through the Ussuri Region) rank among the most important, frequently reprinted works of Russian literature. Arsenyev's friendship with his regular Siberian guide, most strikingly reflected in Dersu Uzala (1923; Eng. trs., Dersu the Trapper, 1941; Dersu Uzala, 195?; and With Dersu the Hunter, 1965), conveys a sense of a primal, prescientific understanding of nature and a close human relationship.

Works: Po Ussurijskomu kraju (travel notes), 1921; Dersu Uzala (travel notes), 1923 (see above); V gorakh Sikhote-Alinja (travel notes), 1937; Vstreči v tajge (short stories), 1956.— Sobr. soč., 6 vols., 1947–49; 2 vols., 1986.

Secondary Lit.: N. Rogal', 1947; M. K. Azadovskij, 1956; V. Lidin, in his Ljudi i vstreči, 1957; RSPP 1:1959; M. Lomunova, in Lit. Rossija Sept. 8, 1972, p. 4.

**Artsybáshev, Mikhaíl Petróvich**, prose writer, playwright (b. Nov. 6 [Oct. 24], 1878, Akhtyrka, prov. Kharkov—d. March 3, 1927, Warsaw). Artsybashev came from the landed gentry; his father was a district police chief. At the age of 16, Artsybashev began publishing in newspapers. He studied painting and wanted to become a painter, but he first gained recognition as a writer with the povest Smert Lande (1904; Eng. tr., Ivan Lande, 1916). The numerous novels that followed until 1917—especially Sanin (1907; Eng. tr., Sanine, 1917), written in 1902 and later expanded—made Artsybashev into one of the most popular Russian authors. From 1913 to 1916 he wrote several plays and the more journalistic Zapiski pisatelya (1914; Notes of a Writer). In 1923 Artsybashev emigrated to Poland and, until his death, he spoke out, together with D. Filosofov, against Bolshevik power through the Warsaw newspaper that they jointly published, Za svobodu (For Freedom).

Artsybashev's comprehensive body of work is characterized by its negative heroes and approaches light fiction. In addition to lovely descriptions of nature, his work primarily provides insight into the topical problems of the intelligentsia of his time. At the center stand free love, power, egotism, murder, executions, suicides, the convulsions of death; his representation aims at a shocking effect. The frequently translated Sanin touched off worldwide discussions and pornography trials, and U posledney cherty (1914; Eng. tr., The Breaking Point, 1915) describes the suicides of seven different kinds of intellectuals. He labeled Dyavol (1925; The Devil), a work of prose in four acts and his last work, a "tragic farce."

Works: Smert' Lande (pov.), 1904 (see above); Sanin (novel), 1907 (reprinted, Letchworth, 1969) (see above); Čeloveceskaja volna (novel), 1907; Milliony (novel), 1909 (Eng. tr., The Millionaire, 1915); U poslednej čerty (novel), 1912 (see above); Vojna (play), 1913 (Eng. tr., War, 1916); Revnost' (play), 1914; Zapiski pisatelja (essays), 2 vols., 1914, Warsaw, 1925–27; Dikie (short story), Warsaw, 1923; D'javol (play), Warsaw, 1925 (reprinted, Letchworth, 1977).—Soč., 10 vols., 1905–17; Sobr. soč., 10 vols., 1912–16 (vol. 7 never published).

Translations: Tales of the Revolution, 1917; Jealousy, Enemies, the Law of the Savage, 1923.

Secondary Lit.: V. Vorovskij, Lit. očerki, 1923; A. Bagrij, in his Russkaja lit., Baku, 1926, pp. 291f.; K. Čukovskij, in his Sobr. soč., vol. 6, 1969, pp. 178–96; F. Sielicki, in Przegląd Humanistyczny 1974:6; Anon., in MERSL 1:1977; S. Nolda, in Zeitschrift für slavische Philologie 1983:2; N. Luker, in New Zealand Slavonic Journal 1985.

**Arzhák, Nikoláy** (pseud. of Yúliy Márkovich Daniél), prose writer, poet (b. Nov. 15, 1925, Moscow). Daniel's father was a Yiddish writer. In 1943–44 Daniel fought at the front and was discharged after being seriously wounded. He began his studies in 1946, first at Kharkov University, then in the Department of Philology at the pedagogical institute of the Moscow region. In 1950 he married Larisa Bogoraz. He completed his studies, probably in 1951, then worked as a teacher in Kaluga and Moscow (after 1954). Daniel began writing prose in 1952; his first povest, Begstvo (Flight), was printed by the Children's Publishing House in 1958; its sale, however, was prohibited. Beginning in 1957 he made his living as a translator; by 1965 he had translated some 40 volumes of verse from Yiddish, Slavic, and Caucasian languages. Between 1956 and 1961 he wrote four short stories that he allowed to be published outside the Soviet Union under the pseudonym Nikolay Arzhak. He was arrested on Sept. 12, 1965; on Feb. 12, 1966, he was sentenced (along with A. Sinyavsky [Terts]) to five years at hard labor for publishing "anti-Soviet short stories" abroad and circulating them among friends. In his closing speech Daniel convincingly demonstrated that the accusation, supported by the critic Z. Kedrina and the insignificant writer A. Vasilyev, was based on the identification of fictional events and statements of individual characters with the personal views of the author, on quotations taken out of context, and on other misrepresentations. A. Ginzburg compiled a transcript of the trial; this document was disseminated through SAMIZDAT and published in the West; its publication led to Ginzburg's being sentenced to five years at hard labor in 1968. Daniel's and Sinyavsky's conviction generated a universal protest: objections came from renowned Soviet writers as well as from leading representatives of Western writers' organizations and Communist parties. The two writers became the most famous Soviet prisoners. After M. Sholokhov abused them and their defenders and claimed their sentence was too mild at the 23d Party Congress in 1966, Lidiya Chukovskaya protested in an open letter: "One must confront ideas with ideas, not with camps and prisons." Daniel served out his sentence in prison camps near Potma. On Oct. 9, 1968, his wife (along with N. Gorbanevskaya) was arrested and sentenced to four years in exile for her part in the protest against the Soviet invasion of Czechoslovakia. After his release on Sept. 12, 1970, Daniel was not allowed to return to Moscow but was able to settle in Kaluga. The poems he had written in prison appeared in the West in 1971. Daniel continues to work as a translator but is able to publish only under a pseudonym.

Arzhak's first short story, Ruki (1956–58; Hands), is the story of a Red Army soldier who had been assigned to a GPU execution squad in the 1920s and who in carrying out his orders had experienced a shock that affected him for life. Govorit Moskva (1960–61; Eng. tr., in This Is Moscow Speaking and Other Stories, 1969) places the citizens of Moscow in a grotesque situation when a particular day is designated "Public Murder Day"; the story analyzes the psychology of the situation, which parallels the murders of the Stalin period. Iskupleniye (1963; Atonement)

explores the responsibility of the individual for the community, using the example of an innocent man, wrongly suspected of denouncing a friend, who becomes aware that he is nevertheless guilty because he neglected to protest when he should have. Arzhak's prose stems from an awareness of the politics of the 20th Party Congress; it warns of the dangers of a new cult of personality, has many parallels in Soviet literature, and is in no way anti-Soviet. His poems seldom touch upon actual prison-camp situations; rather, they deal with a heightened sense of human integrity.

*Works: Govorit Moskva* (pov.), Washington, 1962, 2d ed., New York, 1966 (also contains the following prose works) (see above); *Ruki. Čelovek iz MINAPa* (two short stories), Washington, 1963; *Iskuplenie* (pov.), New York, 1964; *Stikhi iz nevoli* (poems), Amsterdam, 1971 (Eng. tr., *Prison Poems*, 1972).

*Secondary Lit.:* Z. Kedrina, in *Lit. gazeta* Jan. 22, 1966, p. 2; B. Filippov, in *Grani*, Frankfurt am Main, 60:1966; *Belaja kniga po delu A. Sinjavskogo i Ju. Danielja*, compiled by A. Ginzburg, Frankfurt am Main, 1967 (Eng. tr., *On Trial: The Soviet State versus "Abram Tertz" and "Nikolai Arzhak,"* 1966); L. Tikos, in *Osteuropa* 1967:7; Z. Maurina, in her *Porträts russischer Schriftsteller*, Memmingen, 1968; *Literatur und Repression*, ed. H. von Ssachno and M. Grunert, Munich, 1970; C. Gerstenmaier, *Die Stimme der Stummen*, Stuttgart, 1971; biography, in *Grani* 80:1971; M. Dalton, Würzburg, 1973; A. Ginzburg, in *Russkaja mysl'*, Paris, Nov. 12, 1981, p. 2.

**Aséyev, Nikoláy Nikoláyevich**, poet (b. July 10 [June 28], 1889, Lgov, prov. Kursk—d. July 16, 1963, Moscow). Aseyev's father was an insurance agent. Aseyev was raised by his grandfather; he attended secondary school in Kursk until 1909, then studied in Moscow (he attended business school and Moscow University). His first poems were published in 1909, and from then on his poems, short stories, essays, and reviews appeared on a regular basis. His first volume of poems was entitled *Nochnaya fleyta* (1914; The Night Flute). From 1914 on, Aseyev, S. Bobrov, and B. Pasternak were the most important representatives of the futurist group "Tsentrifuga" (see FUTURISM). Despite intermittent military duty, Aseyev continued writing and publishing during World War I; his publications included *Oksana* (published by Tsentrifuga in 1916), a volume that also included those of his previous works Aseyev considered important.

After the Revolution, Aseyev was briefly engaged in cultural and political work in the Soviet Far East (with S. Tretyakov, D. Burlyuk, and N. Chuzhak); he returned to Moscow in 1922 and became a member of LEF, where he met and worked with V. Mayakovsky. Aseyev wrote numerous narrative poems, such as *Poema o Budyonnom* (1923; A Poem about Budyonny), a hymn to the successful Civil War cavalry general, in which Aseyev combines biography with an ideological depiction of revolutionary events. "Marsh Budyonnogo" (Budyonny's March), a song derived from Aseyev's narrative poem, became widely known. Aseyev shared his disappointment over NEP with many other poets who had been inspired by the Revolution; he expressed his disappointment in the narrative poem *Liricheskoye otstupleniye* (1924; Lyrical Digression), printed in *LEF*, vol. 2, in which he deplores the ideological concessions that had been made and critically highlights the controversion of the revolutionary idea by political reality. The OKTYABR critics attacked the work. Aseyev's *Poema o dvadtsati shesti bakinskikh kommisarakh* (1925; The Twenty-six Baku Commissars) is typical agitational poetry written in the style of Mayakovsky; in the poem, Aseyev—like S. Yesenin—responds to the Party appeal for a literary rendition of a scene from the conquest of the Caucasus by the Bolsheviks in 1918. In subsequent years Aseyev largely complied with the official demand for works on the theme of industrial construction. He received a Stalin Prize (for 1935–41, 1st class) for his extensive narrative poem *Mayakovksy nachinayetsya* (1937–40; Mayakovsky Begins); he expanded it in 1950; the section on V. Khlebnikov had to be deleted when the work was reprinted between 1948 and 1953. Aseyev's post-Stalinist poetry runs the gamut from publicistic poems addressing topics of the day ("Bezumye nad Reynom" [Madness above the Rhine]; "Za Kubu" [For Cuba]) to generally humanistic, contemplative poems. Aseyev turned to writing reflective poetry that searches for the meaning of life, as did other Soviet poets at this time; his new mood is expressed in the volume *Lad* (1961; Harmony) in particular. Aseyev also published several books on poetic theory.

The influence of the symbolist (A. Blok) as well as the acmeist (N. Gumilyov) and futurist movements is discernible in Aseyev's first lyrical works. "Many of Aseyev's poems are not only songlike, but are poetic recreations of songs, usually exuberant and full of abandon" (Markov). His work on Khlebnikov and his friendship with Mayakovsky left a futurist mark on Aseyev's poems even after the Revolution; in this connection, his intensive experiments with rhyme and neologisms (returning to Old Russian elements) were intermittently attacked as formalism. Over the years Aseyev, who published more than 70 volumes of verse, ceased to be revolutionary in form and content.

*Works: Nočnaja flejta* (poems), 1914; *Bomba* (poems), 1921; *Stal'noj solovej* (poems), 1922; *Liričeskoe otstuplenie* (narrative poem), 1924; *Oktjabr'skie pesni* (poems), 1925; *Vremja lučšikh* (poems), 1927; *Rabota nad stikhom* (essays), 1929; *Naša sila* (poems), 1939; *Majakovskij načinaetsja* (poems), 1940; *Izbr. stikhotvorenija i poèmy* (poems), 1947; *Razdum'ja* (poems), 1955; *Lad* (poems), 1961, 2d ed., 1963; *Stikhotvorenija i poèmy* (lyric and narrative poems), 1967; *O poetakh i poèzii* (essays and memoirs), 1985.—*Sobr. stikhotvorenij*, 3 vols., 1928–29, vol. 4 (supplementary vol.), 1930; 4 vols., 1931–32; 5 vols., 1963–64.

*Secondary Lit.:* N. Plisko, in *Novyj mir* 1941:4; S. Lesnevskij, in *Oktjabr'* 1959:6; A. Urban, in Aseev's *Stikhotvorenija i poèmy*, 1967; V. Markov, *Russian Futurism*, Berkeley, 1968; A. Mikhajlov, in *Lit. Rossija* July 11, 1969, pp. 8–9; B. Sarnov, in *Istorija russkoj sovetskoj lit.*, vol. 4, 1971; V. Mil'kov, 1973; S. Lesnevskij, in *MERSL* 1:1977; *RSPPo* 2:1978; O. Smola, 1980; R. Ivnev, in *Moskva* 1981:2; I. Šajtanov, in *Oktjabr'* 1982:6 and in *Voprosy lit.* 1984:1.

**Astáfyev, Víktor Petróvich,** prose writer (b. May 1, 1924, in the village Ovsyanka, Krasnoyarsk Territory, Siberia). Astafyev is the son of a peasant. He was seriously wounded in World War II. After 1945 he worked as a locksmith and part-time worker in Chusovo (Perm oblast), where his first stories were published in the local newspaper, *Chusovskoy rabochy*, from 1951 to 1955. In 1953 his first book was published in Perm, and after 1955 numerous others followed. From the autumn of 1959 until 1961, Astafyev studied literature at the Gorky Literary Institute. From that time on, his stories, which regularly appear in journals, have been published almost every year, not only by provincial publishers in the Urals (Perm, Sverdlovsk), but also by the central publishers in Moscow. In 1967 A. Tvardovsky accepted a story for *Novy mir* (7) for the first time. From 1969 to 1979 Astafyev lived in Vologda; in 1980 he moved to his hometown

Krasnoyarsk. Astafyev's *Tsar-ryba* (1976; Eng. tr., *Queen Fish*, 1982), an ethical work that is strongly tied to nature, was awarded the State Prize of the USSR in 1978. In the 1970s he also wrote his first dramas. His tale *Pechalny detektiv* (1986; The Sad Detective) turned out to be one of the most discussed literary works in the Soviet Union.

The focal point of Astafyev's literary activity lies in short prose, which he occasionally collects in a larger work. He writes short stories and povesti that express his attachment to the Russian village and that also appeal to children and adolescents. All of his prose is characterized by great human decency and by an honest effort, free from polemics and showiness, to write about unobtrusive people. Astafyev directs his attention to simple people and their not easy fates, to interpersonal relations in their ethical testing. The number of characters is generally not large; he chooses them from various age groups and from different professions; in the center often occurs a brief encounter between people who are traveling through the vast expanse of Russia, voluntarily or involuntarily. His most highly praised povest, *Krazha* (1966; The Theft), takes place in an orphanage at the end of the 1930s and reveals the life of the Old Believers in Siberia before the Revolution. Here and elsewhere he fashions danger from suffering and death, and shows the value of human life that becomes evident through these forces. *Posledniy poklon* (1968–75; Last Greeting), a work that came into being over a 20-year period, provides a glimpse of the difficult youth Astafyev experiences and reflects his thankfulness toward the people who raised him after he was orphaned in a Siberian village before the war. *Pastukh i pastushka* (1971; Shepherd and Shepherdess) concisely and movingly depicts the theme of love and death in war. Astafyev received the Gorky Prize in 1975 for these last three works. In *Tsar-ryba*, a large collection of numerous, often allegorical stories, Astafyev made an appreciable contribution to the ethical village prose of the 1970s. Using the example of his Yenisey homeland, he protests the intrusions of civilization that not only destroy nature, hundreds of years old, and her equilibrium but also morally poison people. The drama *Prosti menya* (1980; Pardon Me) retraces Astafyev's experiences during the war in its presentation of death and love in a military hospital. The publication of *Pechalny detektiv*, a portrayal of everyday crimes and materialistic brutalization in the Soviet Union, was made possible by the opportunity for open criticism afforded writers at the beginning of the Gorbachev era. Astafyev's preference is for lyrical short stories that stimulate thought and are artistic, humane, and modestly reticent.

*Works:* Do buduščej vesny (short stories), 1953; Pereval (pov.), 1959; Soldat i mat' (pov. and short stories), 1961; Kraža; Gde-to gremit vojna (pov.), 1968; Sinie sumerki (short stories), 1968; Poslednij poklon (pov.), 1968, continuation in Naš sovremennik 1974:5–6; Starodub (pov.), 1969; Pastukh i pastuška: Sovremennaja pastoral' (short story), in Naš sovremennik 1971:8; Zatesi (short stories), 1972; Car'-ryba (short-story cycle), in Naš sovremennik 1976:4–6 (see above), separate ed., 1978; Čeremukha (play), in Teatr 1978:8; Prosti menja (play), in Naš sovremennik 1980:5; Posokh pamjati (essays), 1980; Na dalekoj severnoj veršine (pov. and short stories), 1984; Žizn' prožit' (short story), in Novyj mir 1985:9; Pečal'nyj detektiv (pov.), in Oktjabr' 1986:1.— Sobr. soč., 4 vols., 1979–81.

*Translation:* The Horse with the Pink Mane and Other Siberian Stories, 1970.

*Secondary Lit.:* L. Fomenko, in Znamja 1966:5; A. Makarov, Vo glubine Rossii, 1969 (previously in Znamja 1967:5–6); I. Borisova, in Novyj mir 1970:1; RSPP 7(1):1971; V. Kožinov, in Lit. obozrenie 1973:1; V. Potanin, in Lit. Rossija Feb. 1, 1974, p. 14; A. Lanščikov, 1975; G. Goryšin, in Lit. obozrenie 1976:10; V. Kuratov, 1977; N. Shneidman, in Russian Language Journal 114:1979; A. Eršov, in Russkaja lit. 1984:1; E. Šklovskij, in Lit. obozrenie 1984:8; L. Lavlinskij, in Lit. obozrenie 1986:8; K. Ščerbakov, in Družba narodov 1986:6.

**Atárov, Nikoláy Sergéyevich,** prose writer (b. Aug. 25 [Aug. 12], 1907, Vladikavkaz—d. Sept. 12, 1978, Moscow). Atarov graduated from the Vladikavkaz Pedagogical Institute. In 1930 he became a journalist, writing for the magazine *Nashi dostizheniya;* he also began publishing literary works (mostly short fiction) in 1936. Atarov was a frontline correspondent during World War II; in 1947 he became a member of the Communist Party. From 1948 to 1956 Atarov was a member of the editorial staff of *Literaturnaya gazeta*. In 1957 he became the first editor in chief of the journal *Moskva;* he lost his position, however, after being criticized for deviating from the Party line (*Lit. gazeta* Aug. 8, 1957). Atarov is rarely mentioned in literary histories. He lived in Moscow.

A concern with psychology is discernible in Atarov's unobtrusive short stories, most of which take place in the present. His well-written *Povest o pervoy lyubvi* (1954; Eng. tr., *First Love*, in *Soviet Literature* 1:1957), in which he presents the purity of young love threatened by sordid, narrow-minded suspicion (on the part of the school administration and the Komsomol), triggered considerable polemics. By choosing love as the central theme of his story and by dispensing with positive heroes and lifeless optimism, Atarov contributed to the resuscitation of post-Stalinist Russian literature. In *A ya lyublyu loshad* (1970; But I Love a Horse), Atarov fashions his story from the point of view of a small-town child whose home life is unhappy and loveless and who finds consolation in his love for an animal. Atarov's contributions to literary criticism, which include articles on V. Grossman, I. Katayev, and K. Paustovsky, reveal a good eye for real literature.

*Works: Nastojaščee vremja* (short stories), 1939; *Magistral'naja gorka*, 1953; *Smert' pod psevdonimom* (novel), 1957; *Povest' o pervoj ljubvi*, 1959 (see above); *Ne khoču byt' malen'kim* (essays), 1967; *A ja ljublju lošad'* (pov. and short stories), 1970; *Tri versty berëzovoj allei* (short stories), 1971.—*Izbr.*, 2 vols., 1971, 1978.

*Secondary Lit.*: B. Brajnina, in *Novyj mir* 1955:9; F. Levin, in *Novyj mir* 1968:3; I. Varlamova, in *Novyj mir* 1971:9; G. Drobot, in *Lit. gazeta* March 12, 1975, p. 5; A. Borščagovskij, in *Lit. Rossija* Aug. 26, 1977, p. 11.

**Avdéyenko, Aleksandr Ostápovich,** prose writer (b. Aug. 21 [Aug. 8], 1908, Makeyevka, in the Donbas). Avdeyenko's father was a miner. As a child Avdeyenko was one of the *besprizornye* (homeless waifs). He worked as a laborer in the Donbas and Magnitogorsk. His first work, *Ya lyublyu* (Eng. tr., *I Love*, 1935), which describes his own transformation from one of the homeless children into a member of the collective, appeared in 1933. His next novel, *Sudba* (1935; Destiny), was unsuccessful because of its artistic defects, specifically its bad composition and its "striving for strong effects, regardless of their credibility" (Kolesnikova). In 1945 Avdeyenko became a member of the Communist Party. Post-Stalinist critics declared his novel *Trud* (1951; Labor), in which he returns to the Donbas theme of the 1930s, to be an example of the repression of human factors by technological concerns. In works printed in 1954 and 1955, Avdeyenko depicts the exploits of the Soviet security police against foreign spies. In 1963 he

chose the Hungarian Uprising of 1956, seen from the Soviet point of view, as the theme for a novel. In the novel *V pote litsa svoyego* . . . (1978; By the Sweat of His Brow), he combines the theme of industrial production with an autobiographical visit to his native region. Avdeyenko lives in Moscow; since 1958 he has occasionally been selected as a delegate to congresses of the Writers Union.

*Works: Ja ljublju* (novel), 1933 (see above); *Sud'ba* (novel), 1936; *Trud* (novel), 1951; *Nad Tisoj* (novel), 1954; *Gornaja vesna* (novel), 1955; *Čërnye kolokola* (novel), 1963; *Vsja krasota čelovečestva* (diary), 1970; *Sledopyt* (pov.), 1972; *Granica* (diary), 1977; *V pote lica svoego* . . . (novel), in *Novyj mir* 1978:1–3.

*Secondary Lit.*: G. Kolesnikova, in *Novyj mir* 1936:5; *RSPP* 1:1959; S. Zlobin, in *Junost'* 1960:2; L. Terakopjan, in *Naš sovremennik* 1969:7; G. Brovman, in *Lit. gazeta* July 19, 1978, p. 4.

**Avérchenko, Arkády Timoféyevich,** prose writer (b. March 18 [March 6], 1881, Sevastopol—d. March 12, 1925, Prague). Averchenko's father was a merchant. Averchenko worked initially as a bookkeeper. His first short story appeared in 1903 in a newspaper in Kharkov, where he was a contributor to the satirical journal *Shtyk* from 1905 to 1907. In early 1908 Averchenko moved to St. Petersburg. There he was one of the contributors to the satirical journal *Strekoza*, which he combined with his own journal *Satirikon* in 1908. As publisher and an author of *Satirikon* and (after 1913) *Novy satirikon*, Averchenko became one of the most important satirists of the late tsarist period. He wrote about the events of the day, including theatrical performances and concerts, using numerous pseudonyms (such as "Medusa," "Gorgona," "Falstaf," "Foma Opiskin," "Volk," "Ave"); his humorous short stories appeared under his own name. When the journal was banned in August 1918, Averchenko fled first to the Ukraine, then in 1919 to the Crimea (Sevastopol), where he wrote articles for newspapers and programs for theaters. On Nov. 15, 1920, he emigrated to Prague by way of Constantinople. As a touring comedian he visited many European cities. His short stories appeared in various cities, including Berlin, Prague, Paris, and Warsaw. In 1964 two volumes of Averchenko's selected works were published in Moscow.

Averchenko's satirical short stories and brief sketches often represent daily life in the big city; they are critical of common human weaknesses and, to a lesser extent, of specific political conditions. Life under the tsars is drawn just as satirically as life under the Bolsheviks or in emigration. Much of Averchenko's humor comes out in his alogical, multilayered dialogue.

*Works: Rasskazy (Jumorističeskie)* (short stories), 3 vols., 1910–11 (vol. 2 entitled *Zajčiki na stene*); *Vosem' odnoaktnykh p'es* (plays), 1911; *Čto im nužno . . .* (short stories), 1912; *Miniatjury i monologi dlja sceny* (short stories and short dramatic monologue), 1912; *Rasskazy dlja vyzdoravlivajuščikh* (short stories), 5th ed., 1913; *Čudesa v rešete* (short stories), 1915; *Zapiski prostodušnogo* (short stories), Constantinople, 1921, Berlin, 1923; *Djužina nožej v spinu revoljucii* (short stories), Paris, 1921; *Kipjaščij kotël* (short stories), Constantinople, 1922; *Deti* (short stories), Constantinople, 1922; *Dvenadcat' portretov*, Paris–Prague, 1923; *Čudaki na podmostkakh* (play), Sofia, 1924; *Otdykh na krapive* (short stories), Warsaw, 1924; *Rasskazy cinika* (short stories), Prague, 1925; *Šutka Mecenata* (novel), Prague, 1925; *Oskolki razbitogo vdrebezgi*, Leningrad, 1926; *Izbr.*, Washington, 1961; *Jumorističeskie rasskazy* (short stories), Moscow, 1964; *Okkul'tnye nauki* (short stories), Moscow, 1964; *Tri knigi* (short stories), New York, 1979; *Salat iz bulavok* (short stories), New York, 1982.— *Izbr. soč.*, 2 vols., Moscow, 1927; *Izbr. rasskazy*, 1985.

*Secondary Lit.:* O. Mikhajlov, in Averčenko's *Jumorističeskie rasskazy*, 1964; D. A. Levickij, Diss., Univ. of Pennsylvania, 1969, and Washington, 1973; B. Prjanišnikov, in *Novyj žurnal*, New York, 117:1974.

*Avróra* (Aurora), a literary journal, published monthly in Leningrad since July 1969, at first as the organ of the Central Committee of the Komsomol, of the Writers Union of the RSFSR, and of the Leningrad Writers Organization; starting in 1980, mention was no longer made of the last-named body. Editors in chief have been N. Kosareva initially; starting in 1973, V. Toporygin; briefly in 1977, A. Sharymov; then until 1982 the writer G. Goryshin, who was replaced by E. Shevelyov, apparently on account of the publication of the parable *Yubileynaya rech* (1981:12; The Jubilee Speech) alluding to L. Brezhnev. The following authors were members of the editorial staff for a varying number of years: O. Berggolts (1969–75), M. Dudin (1969–), A. Roshchin (1973–77), A. Samoylov (1973–79), G. Gorbovsky (1977–). *Avrora* emphasizes Leningrad as a

locality and youth as an age group, without limiting its appeal for authors or for its audience. Authors whose works are frequently published in *Avrora* include: V. Belov, A. Bitov, G. Gorbovsky, G. Goryshin, F. Iskander, A. Kushner, V. Shefner, V. Shukshin, V. Sosnora, A. and B. Strugatsky, S. Voronin. *Avrora* also published some of M. Bulgakov's short stories. A short story by a foreign author appears in almost every issue. Like *Yunost*, *Avrora* also regularly publishes reproductions of paintings by Soviet artists. The circulation climbed from 100,000 in 1970 to approximately 125,000 between 1976 and 1986; in 1987 it climbed up to 350,000.

*Secondary Lit.:* V. Razumnevič, in *Lit. Rossija* March 14, 1984, p. 10.

**Aygí, Gennády Nikoláyevich,** poet (b. Aug. 21, 1934, Shaymurzhino, Chuvash ASSR). Aygi's father was a teacher who translated A. Pushkin and other authors into Chuvash. At first Aygi wrote poems in the Chuvash language; from 1958 to 1980 he published five volumes of his poetry. From 1953 to 1959 he studied at the Gorky Literary Institute. On Dec. 10, 1958, A. Zharov denounced Aygi at the organizational meeting of the Writers Union of the RSFSR and deplored the fact that Aygi had not been expelled. At the suggestion of B. Pasternak and others, Aygi began writing in Russian in 1960; at first he translated his own poems, then also translated Russian poetry (for example, A. Tvardovsky's *Vasily Tyorkin* [1960]) into Chuvash. M. Svetlov, who considered Aygi to be his most original student at the Gorky Literary Institute, helped him to publish in *Literaturnaya gazeta* in 1961. No separate volume of his Russian poems has been printed in the Soviet Union; much of his work has been circulated among a small circle of friends. One of Aygi's close friends and admirers of his verse was Konstantin Bogatyryov (1925–76), the translator of Rainer Maria Rilke and Erich Kästner. Since 1962 translations of Aygi's poems have made his reputation abroad; his books have appeared in the following languages: Slovak (1967), Czech (1967), German (1971), Polish (1973), Hungarian (1974), and French (1976). From 1961 to 1971 Aygi earned his living as a consultant at the Mayakovsky Museum in Moscow. In 1968 the first anthology of French poetry into Chuvash, translated by Aygi and covering the 15th to 20th centuries, appeared in Cheboksary; it was highly praised for its outstanding preservation of the individual style of each of the 77 poets represented. The first book edition of his poems in Russian, *Stikhi 1954–71*, was prepared at Cologne University in 1975.

Aygi's poems are marked by extraordinary compactness, unusual word combinations, and a surprising power of imagery. For him, poetry is "a kind of sacred action," necessary "to disclose and to encourage kinship between the souls of men," for which he consciously utilizes "elements of 'metapoetry' and 'metagrammar.'" His poems are "a phenomenon of the utmost nonconformity," "the rebirth of sensitivity, which discreetly protests against an undiscriminating cult of matter and the masses as a sterile habit" (Dedecius). The conflict between the idea of an object and its embodiment, which Aygi often characterizes as a "doppelgänger," runs philosophically through his work. Aygi is a poet of abstract metaphors that are comprehensible only to a small circle and susceptible to differing individual interpretations. The images or thought fragments brought into confrontation are often limited to individual words and can only be interpreted in relation to several other poems. Aygi has devoted much time to the poets of FUTURISM and OBERIU; he belongs to their tradition. The unusual and the novel in Aygi's poetry is not a game of semantics but a serious quest for new, contemporary expression in the art of language, in opposition to everything that is heading toward empty functionalism and mechanistic debasement; to counter this trend, Aygi's poetry offers a spiritual resistance for the sake of true humanity.

*Works:* In Chuvash: In the Name of the Fathers (poems), 1958; Music for a Lifetime (poems), 1962; Step (poems), 1964; Poets of France, 15th to 20th Centuries: An Anthology, Čeboksary, 1968; Poems, 1980. In Russian: poems, in *Lit. gazeta* Sept. 26, 1961, in *Grani*, Frankfurt am Main, 74:1970, in *Kontinent*, Paris, 5:1975; *Stikhi 1954–71* (poems), Munich, 1975; *Poèt i vremja* (essay), in *Rossija*, Turin, 2:1975; "Poètu rozy poèta" (poems), in *Poèt-perevodčik Konstantin Bogatyrev*, Munich, 1982; *Otmečennaja zima* (poems), Paris, 1982.

*Secondary Lit.:* M. Svetlov, in *Lit. gazeta* Sept. 26, 1961; O. Točenyj, in *Lit. Rossija* Jan. 8, 1965, p. 9; A. Dmitriev, in *Lit. Rossija* Feb. 14, 1969, p. 17; D. Ivanova, in *Grani* 74:1970; K. Krolow, in *Der Tagesspiegel* April 11, 1971; K. Dedecius, foreword to Aygi's *Beginn der Lichtung*, Frankfurt am Main, 1971; W. Kasack, in *Osteuropa* 1976:2, in Aygi's *Stikhi*, Munich, 1975, and in *Neue Zürcher Zeitung*

March 11, 1987; V. Vorošil'skij, in *Vestnik RKhD* 118:1976; A. Martini, in *Literatur und Sprachentwicklung in Osteuropa im 20. Jahrhundert*, Berlin, 1982; A. Khuzangaj, in *Lit. obozrenie* 1983:8.

**Aytmátov, Chingíz Torekúlovich,** Kirghiz prose writer, writes in Russian (b. Dec. 12, 1928, Sheker). As a child living with his grandmother, Aytmatov experienced the primitive nomadic existence of the Kirghiz people; his parents, however, had received a Russian education. His father, a Party official since the October Revolution, fell victim to the Stalinist purges in 1937. Aytmatov grew up bilingually. In 1948 he graduated from a two-year veterinary training school and in 1953 from a college of agriculture. While working in a research institute for livestock breeding, he published a few short stories in local periodicals (starting in 1952). From 1956 to 1958 he participated in the Advanced Literature Course at the Gorky Literary Institute in Moscow; thereafter he worked as an editor for *Literaturny Kirgizstan* and as a journalist in Frunze. With the short story *Litsom k litsu* (in *Oktyabr* 1958:3; Face to Face), Aytmatov began to be favorably considered by Moscow journals; since 1958 he has belonged among the authors published in *Novy mir*. *Dzhamilya* (1958; Dzhamilya) earned him worldwide renown. In 1959 he joined the Communist Party. For the collection *Povesti gor i stepey* (Eng. tr., *Tales of the Mountains and Steppes*, 1969), he received the Lenin Prize in 1963. Since 1967 he has belonged to the editorial staffs of *Novy mir* and *Literaturnaya gazeta*. After several additional novels and short stories; Aytmatov, together with K. Mukhamedzhanov, wrote the drama *Voskhozhdeniye na Fudziyamu* (1973; Eng. tr., *The Ascent of Mount Fuji*, 1975), which was staged at the Sovremennik Theater in 1973. Aytmatov lives in Frunze. In 1981 he was a delegate to the 26th Party Congress of the Communist Party of the Soviet Union. In 1986 he became a member of the secretariat of the board of the Writers Union of the USSR; since 1966 he has been a member of the Supreme Soviet.

Aytmatov's prose is thematically bound up with his Kirghiz homeland. At the center stands the man who has experienced sorrow and been tested by fate. Aytmatov is successful at combining the magic of the Central Asian steppes with modern technology through the lives of tractor drivers, truck drivers, and kolkhoz workers; at transforming and integrating music and painting into language; and at allowing his characters, especially the feminine ones, to experience psychological events before they themselves begin to ponder them. Through the traditional form of a frame story and a fictional narrator (in Dzhamilya a 15-year-old boy), he adds depth to his exposition. In Proshchay, Gulsary (1966; Eng. tr., Farewell, Gulsary!, 1970) the severity of the protagonist's fate is the result not of the contrast between the traditional Kirghiz life-style and modern development but of Stalinist oppression. This povest was described as "more complex, broader, and more diverse than anything he has previously written" (Lebedeva) and was awarded the State Prize for 1968. With Bely parokhod (1970; Eng. tr., The White Steamship, 1972), Aytmatov allegorically incorporates mythical traditions into current events. The saga of the Horned Mother Deer, the embodiment of goodness and the divine, provides the focus for both the spiritual content and the narrative composition. In the contemporary plot, this goodness existing in the hearts of a seven-year-old boy and his grandfather perishes as a result of callous materialism. In Pegy pyos begushchiy krayem morya (1977; The Piebald Dog on the Seashore), Aytmatov transfers the action into the mythical days of yore and into the Sea of Okhotsk (Pacific Ocean). Sustained by a belief in the heavenly powers that guide everything on earth, grandfather, father, and another fisherman sacrifice themselves for a boy during a storm. The drama Voskhozhdeniye na Fudziyamu is more than just a contribution to attempts to come to terms with the past; it seizes upon the issue of complicity through silence by using the example of a victim of Stalinism who, to be sure, achieved REHABILITATION but was nevertheless destroyed as a person. Aytmatov's first novel, I dolshe veka dlitsya den (1980; Eng. tr., The Day Lasts More Than a Hundred Years, 1983), unites not only myth and the present day but also the reality of Central Asia and the science fiction of interplanetary contacts. Through this multidimensionality, Aytmatov poses basic ethical questions for modern civilization. For the novel Plakha (1986; The Block), Aytmatov chose the present-day topics of narcoticism, protection of the environment, and God-seekers in the USSR, and he included—in imitation of Bulgakov in Master i Margarita—a chapter about Christ and Pontius Pilate.

Works: Licom k licu (short stories), 1958; Rasskazy (short stories), 1958; Džamilja (short story), 1960; Povesti gor i stepej (short stories), 1962 (see above); Materinskoe pole (pov.), 1963;

Džamilja (pov.), 1965; Proščaj, Gul'sary (pov.), 1967 (see above); Otvetstvennost' pered duščim (essays), in Voprosy lit. 1967:9; Belyi parokhod (pov.), 1970 (see above); Povesti i rasskazy (short stories), 1970; (with K. Mukhamedžanov), Voskhoždenie na Fudzijamu (play), 1973 (see above); Rannie žuravli (pov.), 1975 (Eng. tr., The Cranes Fly Early, 1983); Pegij pës, beguščij kraem morja; Rannie žuravli (pov.), 1977; V soavtorstve s zemleju i vodoju (essays, talks, interview), 1978; I dol'še veka dlitsja den' (novel), in Novyj mir 1980:11 (see above); Plakha (novel), in Novyj mir 1986:6, 8–9.—Sobr. soč., 3 vols., 1982–84.

Secondary Lit.: M. Auèzov, in Lit. gazeta Oct. 23, 1958; K. Bobulov, in Lit. i sovremennost' 4:1963; L. Lebedeva, in Novyj mir 1966:9 and in Lit. i sovremennost' 7:1967; W. Kasack, in Osteuropa 1974:4 and in Die russische Novelle, Düsseldorf, 1982; V. Korkin, 1974; V. Voronov, 1976; N. Shneidman, in Russian Literature Triquarterly 16:1979; E. Sidorov, in Lit. gazeta Jan. 14, 1981, p. 4; V. Čubinskij, in Neva 1981:5; V. Iverni, in Russkaja mysl', Paris, June 24, 1982, p. 11; K. Mehnert, in his The Russians and Their Favorite Books, 1983; V. Levčenko, 1983; A. Archangel'skij, in Lit. obozrenie 1984:9; A. Ovčarenko, in Družba narodov 1984:11; A. Isenov, Alma-Ata, 1985.

**Azháyev, Vasíly Nikoláyevich,** prose writer (b. Feb. 12 [Jan. 30], 1915, in the village of Sotskoye, prov. Moscow—d. April 27, 1968, Moscow). Azhayev worked in the Soviet Far East for 15 years (from 1935); in 1944 he earned a degree from the Gorky Literary Institute in Moscow by correspondence. In 1937 he began writing short stories that, like Obyknovennaya pila (1946; A Common Saw), were difficult to read because of their artificial plot, obtrusive didacticism, and length. His major work, the novel Daleko ot Moskvy (1948; Eng. tr., Far from Moscow, 1950), appeared in Novy mir; it was edited by K. Simonov, who evidently made considerable stylistic revisions in the work. The novel received a Stalin Prize (for 1948, 1st class) and was intensively publicized. Azhayev belonged to the board of the Writers Union of the USSR from 1954 until his death.

Daleko ot Moskvy is a typical "production novel," a work intended to illustrate the heroic effort involved in industrial construction. For his plot, Azhayev chose the extremely rapid construction of a petroleum pipeline in Siberia at the start of World War II. The work is in complete accordance with the tenets of SOCIALIST REALISM in its interpretation of the period: the main characters are idealized in their function as positive heroes, the conflicts are artificial, and their positive outcome is predestined. The fusion of the novel's characters into a unified collective is illustrated by the fact that the most important technological ideas always occur to the various characters simultaneously. The characters are always shown in exceptional situations and the commentary on their actions always serves the author's own purposes. The fact that these pipelines were constructed by concentration-camp prisoners is of course passed over. After Stalin's death the glorification of this work, translated in its time into 20 languages, abated somewhat. Azhayev's second major prose work, *Predisloviye k zhizni* (Foreword to Life), was completed only in 1961. In this retrospective look at the period of the first Five-Year Plan, he remains true to the production theme with all its technological detail. His attempt to educate the reader in the ideas of the Party leads him to the point where (as Soviet critics have remarked), "as if fearing that the reader will not understand him, he formulates his thoughts in unnecessary detail" (Grudtsova).

*Works: Daleko ot Moskvy* (novel), 1948 (see above); *Beskonečnoe svidanie* (pov. and short fiction), 1971; *Predislovie k žizni* (pov. and short stories), 1972.

*Secondary Lit.: RSPP* 1:1959; O. Grudcova, in *Znamja* 1961:8; V. Sokolov, in *Novyj mir* 1961:10; F. Taurin, in *Lit. Rossija* May 9, 1968, p. 20; A. Mežirov, in *Lit. gazeta* Aug. 30, 1972, p. 5; V. Rosljakov, in *Lit. gazeta* Feb. 20, 1984, p. 7.

# B

**Babayévsky, Semyón Petróvich,** prose writer (b. June 6 [May 24], 1909, in the village Kunye prov. Kharov). Babayevsky was the son of a peasant. He grew up in the Kuban region and remained there; from 1930 to 1945 he worked as a journalist. In 1936 his first volume of short stories about kolkhoz life appeared. In 1939 he completed a correspondence course at the Gorky Literary Institute. Since 1939 he has been a member of the Communist Party; during World War II he was a war correspondent. With the novel *Kavaler zolotoy zvezdy* (1947–48; Eng. tr., *Cavalier of the Gold Star,* 1956) and its two-part sequel, *Svet nad zemlyoy* (1949 and 1950; Light over the Earth), Babayevsky moved into the ranks of the most highly praised Soviet writers of the Stalin era (he won three Stalin Prizes: for 1948 and 1949, 1st class; for 1950, 2d class). At that time, the protagonist of these novels was characterized as "an innovator, an educated, strong-willed person who was deeply attached to the people and capable of inspiring the masses" (V. Kozhevnikov, in *Novy mir* 1949:5, p. 247); after Stalin's death he became "a little angel on an Easter cake, strewn with glory as with colorful poppies" (V. Pomerantsev, in *Novy mir* 1953:12, p. 234). For a while, Babayevsky's novels became the incarnation of optimism in Soviet literature, of concealment or minimization of the true problems in the reorganization of agriculture after the war. Also in later novels such as *Synovny bunt* (1961; Revolt of the Sons), *Rodimy kray* (1967; The Home Territory), *Stanitsa* (1975–76; A Cossack Village), or *Privolye* (1978–79; The Open Space) Babayevsky remains deeply rooted in his theme of the socialist impetus given the kolkhoz of the Kuban region and in his hackneyed style of representation that dispenses with believability and with psychological consistency in favor of Party-influenced propaganda. Babayevsky lives in Moscow and has received conflicting reviews from Soviet literary critics.

*Works: Kavaler zolotoj zvezdy* (novel), 1948 (see above); *Svet nad zemlëj* (novel), 1950; *Synovnij bunt* (novel), 1961; *Rodimyj kraj* (novel), 1965; *Belyj svet* (novel), 2 vols., 1968–69; *Sovremenniki* (novel), 1974; *Stanica* (novel), 1977; *Privol'e* (novel), 1980; *Kak žit'?* (narrative poem), in *Moskva* 1984:9–10.—*Izbr. proizv.,* 2 vols., 1972; *Sobr. soč.,* 5 vols., 1979–81.

*Secondary Lit.:* A. Makarov, 1952; F. Abramov, in *Novyj mir* 1954:4; *RSPP* 1:1959; F. Svetov, in *Voprosy lit.* 1962:3; M. Zlobina, in *Novyj mir* 1968:9; V. Krasil'ščikov, in *Lit. Rossija* Sept. 5, 1980, p. 16; A. Hughes, in *Slavonic and East European Review* 1981:1.

**Bábel, Isaák Emmanuílovich,** prose writer (b. July 13 [July 1], 1894, Odessa—d. March 17, 1941[?], while imprisoned). Babel's father was a Jewish merchant. Babel witnessed the Jewish pogroms in Odessa in 1905; he received instruction in Hebrew, the Bible, and the Talmud. At the age of 15 he enrolled in business school; from 1911 to 1915 he studied at the Kiev Institute of Finance and Commerce and wrote his first short stories, in French. He was in St. Petersburg until 1917. Two of Babel's short stories were printed in M. Gorky's journal *Letopis* in 1916. Between 1917 and 1924 Babel was employed in various ways: he served as a soldier in World War I, held a position in the People's Commissariat for Education, took part in expeditions to requisition grain, and was a soldier in Budyonny's First Cavalry, a civil servant in Odessa, and a journalist in Petrograd and Tbilisi. In 1924 Babel settled in Moscow; his wife emigrated to Paris in 1925. Babel became suddenly famous in 1924 when several of his short stories were printed in *LEF*; these were later included in the two collections *Konarmiya* (1926; Eng. tr., *Red Cavalry*, 1929) and *Odesskiye rasskazy* (1931; Eng. tr., *Tales of Odessa*, in *The Collected Stories*, 1955), and were soon translated into more than 20 languages, making him universally famous. In addition to more stories, Babel wrote film scripts and plays, such as *Zakat* (1927; Eng. tr., *Sunset*, 1961), which premiered in Moscow in 1928, and *Mariya* (1935; Eng. tr., *Marya*, in *Three Soviet Plays*, 1966), which was not allowed to be performed. He spoke at the First Congress of the Writers Union in 1934; in 1938 he was vice chairman of the editorial advisory board of the State Publishing House for Literature. On May 15, 1939, Babel was arrested. His manuscripts were confiscated, and his name was purged from Russian literature. On Dec. 18, 1954, his conviction was reviewed by the Military Council of the Supreme Court of the USSR. In 1956 the date of his death was announced as March 17, 1941; place and cause were not named. The energetic efforts of K. Paustovsky opened the way for the acceptance of Babel after 1956. A carefully censored volume of his selected works appeared in 1957 with a foreword by I. Erenburg. Since then the attacks made in the 1920s and 1930s on Babel's too "subjective portrayal of the Civil War" have been revived; his REHABILITATION is considered restricted, his works not appearing in the USSR between 1967 and 1980.

The relatively limited extent of Babel's oeuvre (some 80 short stories and three theater pieces) cannot be attributed solely to Babel's arbitrary death at the age of 47. Babel was a writer who found it extraordinarily difficult to write and who often spent months revising his short stories. He relinquished *Lyubka Kazak* (1925) only after redrafting it

26 times. His prose achieves its effect by means of its succinct concentration, its compact language, and its powerful, striking images. Babel took Gustave Flaubert as his primary model. Cruelty, murder, violence, and obscenity are the dominant motifs in his stories about the Civil War, as they are in his Odessa tales. This exposure of human brutality is, however, countered with tender overtones and the description of ties to parents, homeland, literature, and music. "This play on disparities is the very foundation of Babel's style and art" (Slonim). In contrast to A. Chekhov's short stories, Babel's are dynamic and full of action. *Odesskiye rasskazy* preserves an untranslatable atmosphere through Babel's use of his native Odessa's particular dialect, which is saturated with Yiddish and Ukrainian elements and which Babel mixes with standard and elevated literary language.

*Works:* Konarmija (short stories), 1926 (see above); Odesskie rasskazy (short stories), 1931 (see above); Bluždajuščie zvёzdy (play), 1926 (reprinted, Ann Arbor, 1972); Evrejskie rasskazy (short stories), 1927; Zakat (play), 1928 (see above); Rasskazy (short stories), 1932; Marija (play), 1935 (see above); Izbr., 1957; excerpts from letters, in Vozdušnye puti, New York, 3:1963; Konarmija. Odesskie rasskazy. P'esy, 1957 (reprinted, Letchworth, 1965); Zabytye rasskazy. Iz pisem k druz'jam (stories and letters), Letchworth, 1965; Izbr., 1966; diary entries, in Lit. gazeta Nov. 3, 1971, pp. 6–7, supplement in Russkaja mysl', Paris, Jan. 22, 1976, p. 8; Zabytye proizv. (short stories), Ann Arbor, 1979; Detstvo i drugie rasskazy (short stories), Jerusalem, 1979; Rasskazy (short stories), Letchworth, 1980; Izbr., 1986.

*Translations:* Benya Krik, the Gangster, and Other Stories, 1948; The Collected Stories, 1955; Lyubka the Cossack, and Other Stories, 1963; The Lonely Years 1925–1939, 1964; You Must Know Everything: Stories 1915–1937, 1969; The Forgotten Babel, 1978.

*Secondary Lit.:* I. Babel': Stat'i i materialy, 1928; RSPP 1:1959; J. Stora-Sandor, Paris, 1968; H. Pross-Weerth, in Babel's Ein Abend bei der Kaiserin, 1970; P. Carden, Ithaca, N.Y., 1972; R. W. Hallett, Letchworth, 1972; F. Levin, 1972; Vospominanija sovremennikov, 1972; J. Salajczyk, Opole, 1973; J. E. Falen, Knoxville, Tenn., 1974; M. Jovanović, Belgrade, 1975; M. Cunningham, Diss., Northwestern Univ., 1976; C. D. Lynch, M. A. Diss., Belfast, 1977; C. Luplow and R. Luplow, in MERSL 2:1978; E. R. Sicher, Diss., Oxford Univ., 1979; R. Grøngaard, Århus, 1979; D. Mendelson, Ann Arbor, 1982; C. A. Luplow, Ann Arbor, 1982, and in *Russian Literature* 1984:3; S. Povarcov, in *Lit. gazeta* July 18, 1984.

**Bagrítsky, Eduárd Geórgiyevich** (pseud. of E. G. Dzyúbin), poet (b. Nov. 3 [Oct. 22], 1895, Odessa—d. Feb. 16, 1934, Moscow). Bagritsky's father was a Jewish merchant. Bagritsky graduated from a technical institute as a surveyor. He never worked at this trade. He began writing poems that were partially influenced by the acmeists and partially by the futurists and that appeared in various literary almanacs (*Serebranye truby, Avto v oblakakh*) in Odessa in 1915. During the revolutionary struggles, Bagritsky served temporarily with the Red Army (including the winter of 1917–18 on the Persian front, the summer of 1919 in a propaganda unit as the author of agitprop verses). From 1918 to 1920 he frequently occupied himself with English ballads. After the spring of 1920, Bagritsky again lived in Odessa and was active in the YugROSTA together with Yu. Olesha, V. Narbut, S. Bondarin, and V. Katayev. In 1925 he struck up a friendship with I. Babel that lasted throughout his life; he moved to Moscow when the diversity of literary life in Odessa subsided and, in accordance with his moderate political views, joined first the PEREVAL group in 1926, and after only a year the constructivists (see CONSTRUCTIVISM). In 1928 his first volume of poetry, *Yugo-zapad* (Southwest), appeared; these mostly unpolitical, heroic-emotional verses and narrative poems found many followers. Bagritsky, who was criticized for not being a Communist Party member, tried to strike up a deal with the powers that be in 1930 by joining RAPP and also wrote narrative poems that espoused the ideals of the Revolution. Bagritsky, who suffered severely from asthma, published two more collections: *Pobediteli* (1932; The Victors) and *Poslednyaya noch* (1932; The Last Night). Bagritsky's wife—V. Narbut's sister-in-law—and I. Babel were present at Bagritsky's death in 1934. Babel published a memorial volume in 1936. Bagritsky's wife, Babel, and Narbut were arrested after 1937; only Bagritsky's wife returned from Karaganda alive in 1956.

Together with M. Svetlov and N. Tikhonov, Bagritsky is considered one of the leading romantic poets of early Soviet literature. "Bagritsky possessed the astounding talent of being able to tug at one's heartstrings" (Slavin). The romantic world of this poet who was inspired by A. Grin was as attractive to many of his contemporaries as his personality was. Bagritsky was an active promoter of younger talents; many mention with pleasure having been influenced by him (for example, A. Galich). Bagritsky's early poems reveal the influence of N. Gumilyov's acmeist style through both the exoticism and heroism of their themes and the clarity of their language. Other poems from that period reflect the influence of the futurist works of I. Severyanin and V. Mayakovsky. In the later Odessa period, from 1918 to 1925, his poetry demonstrates an optimistic attitude and focuses on rebels, vagabonds, soldiers, sailors, revolutionaries, and smugglers, "all seeking adventure, freedom and happiness" (Kowalski). In *Yugo-zapad*, which together with the kind of poem just mentioned also contains translations of the English romantics, Bagritsky included as the only narrative poem about the Revolution *Duma pro Opanasa* (1926; Song of Opanas). Here, with humane compassion, he portrays a peasant deserter from the Red Army, who as a Makhno-anarchist must shoot his former commissar. With respect to form he recalls Ukrainian folk songs and T. Shevchenko's "Haidamaki." In the second volume, *Pobediteli*, the message is personal and the tone pessimistic. The title is void of any clear reference and, compared to the officious mode of expression of those years, points more toward an ironic distance. The three narrative poems in the last volume, *Poslednyaya noch*, reflect his inner dispute with the ideals of the Revolution. In *Smert pionerki* (The Death of the Young Pioneer), the mother stands at her daughter's deathbed among the detachments of Young Pioneers who embody the Marxist extinction of the individual in favor of the survival of the masses. Intermingled are a personal awareness of guilt, a heroic recollection of the Revolution, and the Christian cross. Bagritsky's last narrative poem, *Fevral* (1933–34; February), which was posthumously published with N. Khardzhiyev's help and is seldom reprinted, depicts, probably autobiographically, the conflict between the shy Jewish youth of schooltime and wartime and the revolutionary of the February Revolution enjoying equal rights even as a Jew; in his latter guise, as a result of his suddenly acquired power, he takes by force a girl who rejects him. Bagritsky's poetry is usually narrative in form but only episodically chronological. The illustrated events and images often permit a broad range of interpretations. The linguistic and metrical variety is more closely united through rhyme in his early works than in his later ones.

*Works: Jugo-zapad* (poems), 1928; *Pobediteli* (poems), 1932; *Poslednjaja noč'* (narrative poems), 1932; *Sobr. soč.*, 2 vols., 1938 (only vol. 1 was published); *Stikhotvorenija* (poems), 1956; *Stikhotvorenija i poèmy* (lyric and narrative poems), 1964 (contains *Fevral'*); *Dnevniki, Pis'ma, Stikhi* (diary, letters, poems), 1964; *Izbr.*, 1975.

*Secondary Lit.*: Al'manakh E. B., ed. V. Narbut, 1936; I. Grinberg, 1940; A. Sinjavskij, in *Istorija russkoj sovetskoj lit.* (3 vols.), vol. 1, 1958; S. Bondarin, in *Novyj mir* 1961:4; E. Ljubareva, 1964; L. Slavin, in his *Portrety i zapiski*, 1965; I. Roždestvenskaja, 1967; *E. B. Vospominanija sovremennikov*, 1973; L. H. Kowalski, in *Russian Literature Triquarterly* 8:1974; N. V. Fridman, in *Russkaja lit.* 1976:2; W. A. Rosslyn, London, 1977, and in *MERSL* 2:1978; *RSPPo* 2:1978; V. Azarov, in *Lit. Rossija* Nov. 11, 1985, p. 15.

**Bakhmétyev, Vladímir Matvéyevich**, prose writer (b. Aug. 14 [Aug. 2], 1885, Zemlyansk, prov. Voronezh—d. Oct. 16, 1963, Moscow). Bakhmetyev, who joined the Communist Party in 1909, was active in the revolutionary movement in Voronezh until 1917 and later in Siberia. In 1921 he moved to Moscow; in 1923 he joined KUZNITSA; in 1934 he served as a member of the first board of the Writers Union. Bakhmetyev published short stories about the emergence of revolutionary consciousness among Siberian peasants in the period after 1910. *Prestupleniye Martyna* (1928; Martyn's Crime), his novel about the development of a Party official during the Civil War, generated a discussion in the press; a revised version of the book appeared in 1947. Bakhmetyev's planned trilogy, likewise devoted to the theme of revolutionary struggle, remained unfinished; its first part, *Nastupleniye* (The Attack), appeared in 1934; other parts and revised versions of the work were published only at rare intervals.

*Works: Na zemle* (short stories), 1924; *Prestuplenie Martyna* (novel), 1932; *Nastuplenie* (novel), 1938; *U poroga* (novel), 1941.—*Sobr soč.*, 3 vols., 1926–28; 3 vols., 1930; *Izbr.*, 1947; *Izbr.*, 1953; *Izbr. proizv.* 2 vols., 1957.

*Secondary Lit.*: G. Kolesnikova, in *Oktjabr'* 1947:3; *RSPP* 1:1959; G. Pavlov, in *Zvezda* 1960:11; obituary, in *Lit. gazeta* Oct. 19, 1963; P. Vorob'ëv, in *Lit. Rossija* Aug. 13, 1965, p. 11; Ju. Lukin, in *Lit. gazeta* Sept. 25, 1985, p. 6.

**Baklánov, Grigóry Yákovlevich** (pseud. of G. Ya. Frídman), prose writer (b. Sept. 11, 1923,

Voronezh). Baklanov finished school in the summer of 1941 and went to work in a factory. During World War II he served at the front as a soldier and officer; he has been a member of the Communist Party since 1942. From 1946 to 1951 Baklanov studied at the Gorky Literary Institute. His first short stories of 1950–55 are about life on the kolkhoz. He made his reputation after 1958 with several *povesti* in which he gave an unvarnished version of experiences at the front during the war. Baklanov also wrote film scripts; in 1962 he collaborated with Yu. Bondarev and V. Tendryakov on *49 dney* (49 Days). In 1986 he became a member of the buro of the secretariat of the Writers Union of the USSR and editor of the journal *Znamya*. He lives in Moscow.

Baklanov's short stories based on kolkhoz life are among the first works of post-Stalinist literature critical of society to present genuine conflicts. His war books, above all *Pyad zemli* (1959; Eng. tr., *The Foothold*, 1962), were the source of intense polemics in the Soviet Union; conservative critics felt that Baklanov's frank writing manner, which did not deny the horror and the fear of war, the so-called truth of the trenches, was, historically and politically speaking, insufficiently in line with the official position. Baklanov's works are an example of the literary revisionism in the depiction of World War II that became possible only after the 20th Party Congress and that is directed against the pseudodocumentary and heroic war literature of the Stalin era. *Myortvye sramu ne imut* (1961; The Dead Should Not Be Shamed) deals with the problem of frontline egotism and cowardice, as well as guilt about the dead. In his novel *Iyul 1941 goda* (1965; July 1941), which no longer limits itself to a presentation of only a small sector of the front, Baklanov attempts a historical and political interpretation of the war. In *Druzya* (1975; Friends) he contrasts two architects who are friends: the one places personal advancement above all else, the other serves the cause alone, both in his professional and in his private life. Baklanov's *Kanada* (1976; Canada) reflects his experiences on a trip abroad. In *Naveki—devyatnadtsatiletniye* (1979; Nineteen Years Old Forever) he returns once more to the theme of the war and the war dead.

*Works: V. Snegirjakh* (short stories), 1955; *Južnee glavnogo udara* (pov.), 1958 (Eng. tr., *South of the Main Offensive*, 1963); *Pjad' zemli* (pov.), 1960 (see above); *Mërtvye sramu ne imut* (pov.), 1962; *49 dnej* (film script, written in collaboration with Ju. Bondarev and V.

Tendrjakov), 1962; *Ijul' 41 goda* (novel), 1965; *Karpukhin* (pov. and short stories), 1967; *Byl mesjac maj* . . . (film script), 1971; *Temp večnoj pogoni* (travel notes), 1972; *O našem prizvanii* (essays), 1972; *Druz'ja* (novel), 1976; *Čem ljudi živy* (play), in *Teatr* 1976:9; *Kanada* (diary), in *Oktjabr'* 1976:7–8; *Naveki—devjatnadcatiletnie* (pov.), in *Oktjabr'* 1979:5; *Men'šij sredi brat'ev* (pov.), in *Družba narodov* 1981:6.—*Izbr.*, 1974; *Izbr. proizv.*, 2 vols., 1979–80.

*Secondary Lit.*: I. Kozlov, in *Moskva* 1960:1; A. Bočarov, in *Znamja* 1965:5; V. Sokolov, in *Novyj mir* 1968:4; *RSPP* 7(1):1971; V. Bykov, in *Lit. Rossija* Sept. 14, 1973, p. 6; A. Nikul'kov, in *Lit. gazeta* July 9, 1975, p. 4; V. Oskockij, in *Lit. obozrenie* 1980:1; L. Anninskij, in *Lit. obozrenie* 1981:11; I. Dedkov, in *Novyj mir* 1983:5.

**Balmónt, Konstantín Dmítriyevich,** poet (b. June 15 [June 3], 1867, Gumnishchi, prov. Vladimir—d. Dec. 24, 1942, Noisy-le-Grand, near Paris). Balmont's father was a noble landowner. Balmont studied law at Moscow University in 1886 but did not graduate. With the publication of volumes such as *Budem kak solntse* (1903; Let Us Be Like the Sun) from 1898 to 1903, Balmont quickly became one of the central figures of the early symbolist movement, a pioneer of "modernity" or "decadence," a public idol. For political reasons, he spent many years between 1905 and 1913 in foreign countries; he lived temporarily in Paris, and his lengthy trips (then and later, until 1917) to all corners of the world found an echo in numerous volumes of poetry. His work, which was no longer considered of such trailblazing significance, repeatedly appeared in collected editions (for example, 1908–13, ten volumes). Balmont welcomed the February Revolution of 1917 but rejected the October Revolution as an act of violence and the oppression of individuality. On June 25, 1920, he left Russia legally but remained in Paris as an émigré. There, too, Balmont wrote many poems that were perfect in form and in addition translated from at least 30 languages; he was, however, published less often and gradually little noticed. From 1927 on, Balmont lived in Capbreton on the Atlantic coast; after 1932 he suffered from a mental disorder. He died in poverty.

Balmont's early lyric poetry collected in *Pod severnym nebom* (1894; Under the Northern Sky), demonstrates the influence of poets like Mikhail Lermontov, Afanasy Fet, Semyon Nadson, and Edgar Allan Poe. The volume *Tishina* (1898; Silence) is above all a literary expression of Balmont's preoccupation with theosophy, especially the writings of Helena Blavatsky. After V. Bryusov praised *Budem kak solntse* as the culmination of Balmont's creative work in 1903, Balmont's later lyric poetry barely received notice. In a collection of 225 sonnets, *Sonety solntsa, myoda i luny* (1917; Sonnets of the Sun, Honey, and Moon), Balmont consciously confronted his critics with his talent undiminished and at its highest perfection of form. In a late volume, *V razdvinutoy dali* (1929; In the Extended Distance), memories of Russia and his childhood predominate; avowals of previous existences evince his early preoccupation with theosophy. Balmont's lyric poetry, which is perfect in form, gets its life from emotion and sound and is entirely determined by what is musical. For him, poetry is "inner music, externally expressed in metric speech" (1914). N. Gumilyov called his talent "as proud as the thought of a European, as beautiful as a southern fairy tale, as contemplative as a Slavic soul." Balmont wrote extraordinarily easily and prolifically. His poetry is extravagant in its oscillation between the demonic and the earthly, in its historical and geographical grasp of world events. A yearning for the infinite, pride in the great mission of the poet, and the cult of individualism are frequent themes of his poetry, which always experienced wide fluctuations in quality but which, throughout his life, reflected the spirit of symbolist expression he created to oppose realistic and rational trends. As a prolific translator, he also left the stamp of his individual genius on his free adaptations. Worthy of note are Balmont's essays on Western European and Russian literary culture.

*Works: Sbornik stikhotvorenij* (poems), 1890; *Pod severnym nebom* (poems), 1894; *Tišina* (poems), 1898; *Budem kak solnce* (poems), 1903; *Tol'ko ljubov'* (poems), 1903; *Liturgija krasoty* (poems), 1905; *Pesni mstitelja* (poems), Paris, 1907; *Žar-ptica. Svirel' slavjanina* (poems), 1907; *Zelënyj vertograd* (poems), 1909; *Poèzija kak volšebstvo* (essays), 1915 (reprinted, Letchworth, 1973); *Sonety solnca, mëda i luny* (poems), Berlin, 1917; *Marevo* (poems), Paris, 1922; *Pesnja rabočego molota* (poems), 1922; *Moe-ej. Rossija* (poems), Prague, 1924; *V razdvinutoj dali* (poems), Belgrade, 1929; *Severnoe sijanie* (poems), Paris, 1931; *Stikhotvorenija* (poems), Leningrad, 1969; *Izbr.* (poems), Munich, 1975; *Izbr.* (poems, translations, essays), 1980.—*Sobr. stikhov*, 2 vols., 1904–5; *Polnoe sobr. stikhov*, 10 vols., 1908–

13; *Sobr. liriki*, 6 vols., 1917 (vols. 1, 2, 4, 6 were published).
Secondary Lit.: A. Blok, in *Voprosy žizni* 1905:3 (reprinted in his *Sobr. soč.*, vol. 5, 1962); N. Gumilëv, in *Vesna* 1908:10 (reprinted in his *Sobr. soč.* vol. 4, Washington, 1968); Ju. Ajkhenval'd, in his *Siluèty russkikh pisatelej*, 1913; A. Sedykh, in *Novyj žurnal*, New York, 55:1958; V. Markov, in *Slavic Review* 1969:2; R. L. Patterson, Diss., Univ. of California, Los Angeles, 1969, and in *MERSL* 2:1978; H. Schneider, Diss., Munich, 1970; S. Althaus-Schönbucher, Bern, 1975.

**Bálter, Borís Isaákovich**, prose writer (b. July 6, 1919, Samarkand—d. June 8, 1974, Moscow). After he finished school in Yevpatoria, Balter was sent in 1936 to the military academy in Leningrad; in 1938 he transferred to the academy in Kiev. He served as a frontline officer in the Finnish-Russian War and in World War II; in 1944 he joined the Communist Party. From 1948 to 1953 Balter studied at the Gorky Literary Institute; his work there included a seminar taught by K. Paustovsky, with whom he subsequently remained friends (*Yunost* 1967:5). After 1953 Balter headed the literary section of the Khakassian Research Institute for Language, Literature, and History in Abakan (Siberia) for several years; in 1955 and 1958 he made translations of Khakass (a Turkic language) fairly tales. Balter was the initiator of the liberal collection *Tarusskiye stranitsy* (Eng. tr., *Pages from Tarusa*, 1964), which Paustovsky published in 1961; his own most important work, the largely autobiographical novel *Troye iz odnogo goroda* (Three from One Town) (later renamed *Do svidaniya, malchiki!* [Eng. tr., *Good-by, Boys!*, 1967], was published in that anthology. Balter's short story *O chom molchat kamni* (1964; What the Stones Are Silent About) is based on his research into the Khakass past. Balter was never selected as a delegate to a congress of the Writers Union; his name is missing from Soviet literary histories. He lived in Moscow; in 1968 he was expelled from the Party after signing a letter in support of Yu. Galanskov and A. Ginzburg. Balter continued to work on translations from Uzbek and Tadzhik literature to the end of his life.

In *Do svidaniya, malchiki!* Balter presents, from the politically freer point of view that was possible at the time of the novel's writing, the life of 18-year-old boys and girls in June 1936; his was the first substantial work about the youth of those who were born after the Revolution. The work's first-person narrative structure, with its occasional reflections, aids in the critical coming to terms with the past; its allusions to the death of one character in the war and of another while imprisoned in 1952 create an awareness of the Stalinist persecutions and of the war even though this period is not depicted in the novel. Balter's clear, unconstrained, very seriously written prose in this work was well received by the critics.

Works: *Pervye dni* (short stories), 1953; *Troe iz odnogo goroda* (pov.), in *Tarusskie stranicy*, 1961, rev. ed., *Do svidanija, mal'čiki!*, 1963, 1978 (see above); *O čëm molčat kamni* (pov.), 1964; *Proezdom* (pov.), in *Junost'* 1965:10.
Secondary Lit.: K. Paustovskij, in *Lit. gazeta* Feb. 7, 1961; E. Starikova, in *Novyj mir* 1963:1; B. Sarnov, in *Voprosy lit.* 1964:7; V. Voronov, in *Voprosy lit.* 1966:2; *RSPP* 7(1):1971; V. Vojnovič, in *Russkaja mysl'*, Paris, July 19, 1984, pp. 8–9.

**Baránskaya, Natálya Vladímirovna**, prose writer (b. Dec. 31 [Dec. 18], 1908, St. Petersburg). Baranskaya's father was a physician. In 1930 Baranskaya graduated in ethnology from Moscow University. She participated in the establishment of a new Pushkin Museum in Moscow (1958–66). In 1968 she published her first short stories in *Novy mir* and became well known at home and abroad for her povest concerning the daily life of an educated woman in the Soviet Union, *Nedelya kak nedelya* (1969; Eng. tr., "A Week Like Any Other," in *The Massachusetts Review* 15:1974). Baranskaya generally publishes brief short stories focusing on similar issues; she was able to publish her first collection, *Otritsatelnaya Zhizel* (The Negative Giselle), only in 1977. Her research on Aleksandr Pushkin conducted in connection with her museum work provided the impetus for several historical short stories during the 1970s; the most comprehensive of these, *Tsvet temnogo medu* (1977; Dark Honey-colored), draws a balanced portrait of Pushkin's wife during the years after his death. She compiled all these texts in *Portret, podarenny drugu* (1982; Portrait Given to a Friend). Baranskaya has been overlooked in Soviet histories of literature; she lives in Moscow.

The sociologically incontestably correct accusation concerning the condition of women in the Soviet Union contained in *Nedelya kak nedelya* has led to frequent Soviet criticism of Baranskaya. She describes one woman's typical week—rushing from her job at a chemical laboratory to her home where she cares for her husband and children—and her inability, despite all good intentions, to fulfill all her responsibilities in any one area. In briefer short stories Baranskaya especially deals with the ethical questions of daily Soviet life. In *Lyubka* (1977) she depicts the inhumanity and injustice of public courts of arbitration in the Soviet Union. In her prose, through psychological precision and prudent realism, Baranskaya is able to make brief periods of time (days or hours)—in the lives of women and children especially—allegorically reflect conditions in the Soviet Union. Through a narrative perspective that changes from chapter to chapter, *Tsvet temnogo medu* reveals her capacity for compassionate empathy with her various characters.

*Works: Nedelja kak nedelja* (pov.), in *Novyj mir* 1969:11, separate ed., Copenhagen, 1973 (see above); *Čemu raven iks?"* (short story), in *Junost'* 1974:5, and *Koldovstvo* (short story), in *Junost'* 1976:7, separate eds., Munich, 1980; *Cvet tëmnogo mëdu* (pov.), in *Sibir'* 1977:3; *Otricatel'naja Žizel'* (pov. and short stories), 1977 (also contains *Ljubka*); *Ženščina s zontikom* (pov. and short stories), 1981; *Portret, podarennyj drugu: Očerki i rasskazy o Puškine; Povest'* (short stories and pov.), 1982.

*Secondary Lit.:* Ja. Èl'sberg, in *Lit. gazeta* Dec. 11, 1968; N. Denisova, in *Lit. obozrenie* 1978:1; D. D. Blagoj, T. G. Cjavlovskaja, et al., in *Sibir'* 1979:2; W. Kasack, in *Osteuropa* 1981:3; I. Vladimirova, in *Neva* 1981:8; O. Murav'ëva, in *Neva* 1984:5.

**Bartó, Ágniya Lvóvna,** poet (b. Feb. 17 [Feb. 4], 1906, Moscow—d. April 1, 1981, Moscow). Barto's father was a veterinarian. Barto published her first poems for children in 1925 while she was still attending drama school. From that time on, the simple verses she wrote kept her continuously involved in the sphere of Communist children's education. She was a recipient of the Stalin Prize (for 1949, 2d class) and the Lenin Prize (in 1972). Barto also collaborated on film scripts. By 1962 more than 20 million copies of her books had appeared in over 400 printings. She lived in Moscow.

Barto's primitive rhymes are directed primarily at little children; they relate harmless incidents from a child's life. Her volume *Bratishki* (1928; Little Brothers) is meant to promote friendship among nations; *Petya risuyet* (1951; Petya Draws) is a deprecatory, black-and-white sketch that gives the impression that the United States is a country of exploitation, murder, and capitalism, where "everyone is against peace." Most of Barto's poems are limited to one idea; they promote modesty, politeness, cleanliness, respect for work, and love for the Soviet Union.

*Works: Bratiški* (poems), 1928; *Devuška-revuška* (poems), 1930; *Stikhi detjam* (poems), 1949; *Petja risuet* (poems), 1951; *Tvoi stikhi* (poems), 1960 (Eng. tr., selections in *Merry Rhymes*, 1976); *Stikhi* (poems), 1960; *Najti čeloveka* (memoirs), 1969; *Za cvetami v zimnij les* (poems), 1970; *Zapiski detskogo poèta*, 1976; *U nas pod krylom* (poems), 1981.— *Sobr. soč.*, 3 vols., 1969; 4 vols., 1981–84.

*Secondary Lit.:* V. Dmitrieva, 1953; B. Solov'ëv, in his *Poèzija i žizn'*, 1955, and separate ed., 1967; E. Pel'son, in *Lit. Rossija* Feb. 12, 1965, pp. 14–15, and in *Detskaja lit.* 1966 (1967); I. Motjašov, in *Moskva* 1976:2; Ju. Jakovlev, in *Novyj mir* 1979:9 and in *Lit. Rossija* Feb. 27, 1981, p. 20.

**Barúzdin, Sergéy Alekséyevich,** prose writer (b. July 22, 1926, Moscow). In 1938 his first short stories appeared in the youth journal *Pioner*. In 1943 he served as a soldier. Since 1947 he has written simple children's poems and, since 1951, prose. In 1949 he became a member of the Communist Party. He graduated from the Gorky Literary Institute in 1958. By 1963, more than 12 million copies of Baruzdin's children's books had been published in the Soviet Union, and they had been translated into more than 30 languages of the USSR and other countries. Since 1966 Baruzdin has been editor in chief of the journal *Druzhba narodov*, in which he has published much good literature. Since 1967 he has been a member of the secretariat of the Writers Union of the USSR, and since 1958 he has belonged to the board of the Writers Union of the RSFSR. He lives in Moscow.

Among his best-known children's stories are *Ravi i Shashi* (1956; Ravi and Shashi), the story of two baby elephants who, as Jawaharlal Nehru's gift to Soviet children, must make a long journey by sea, and *Kak Snezhok v Indiyu popal* (1957; How Snowflake Found Itself in India), the story of the Soviet reciprocal gift, a small polar bear. One series of short stories was united for more than 12 years by the central figure, Svetlana. Because of Baruzdin's significant contribution to the education of Communist children through sensible child psychology, the story *Novye* dvoriki (1961; New Little Courts) was much praised in the Soviet Union. With *Novy adres Niny Streshnevoy* (1962; The New Address of Nine Streshneva), Baruzdin made a more blatant contribution to the atheistic education of children. In his poems for children, he adapts himself somewhat to Russian folk poetry. In the povest *Samo soboy* (1980; From Self), Baruzdin attempts to depict the fate of a painter born in 1917, but the poetically unmastered intent remains isolated in individual episodes and impressionistic reflections, and the experience of the war predominates. The poems of *Indiyskiye stikhi* (1980; Poems from India) are narrowly nationalistic and simple in form and in content. In *Lyudi i knigi* (1978; People and Books), Baruzdin relates his autobiographical experiences with 44 Soviet—primarily non-Russian—authors.

*Works: Kto postroil ètot dom* (poems), 1950; *Pro Svetlanu* (short stories), 1951; *Kto segodnja učitsja* (poems), 1955; *Ravi i Šaši* (short story), 1956; *Kak Snežok v Indiju popal* (short story), 1957; *Lastočkin mladšij i Lastočkin staršij* (short story), 1957; *Novye dvoriki* (short story), 1961; *Novyj adres Niny Strešnevoj* (short story), 1962; *Povtorenie projdennogo* (novel), 1964; *Povesti o ženščinakh* (pov.), 1967; *Ja ljublju našu ulicu . . .* (short stories and pov.), 1969, 1972; *Ot semi do desjati* (short stories and pov.), 1969; *Stikhi* (poems), 1973; *Ljudi i knigi* (literary notes), 1978, 2d enl. ed., 1982; *Samo soboj: Iz žizni Alekseja Gorskogo* (pov.), in *Moskva* 1980:8, separate ed., 1980; *Indijskie stikhi*, in *Družba narodov* 1980:8; *Stikhi bez nazvanija*, 1980; *A pamjat' vsë zovët* (novel and pov.), 1981.—*Izbr. proizv.*, 2 vols., 1977.

*Secondary Lit.*: A. Aleksin, in *Znamja* 1961:2; V. Šišov, in *Naš sovremennik* 1963:3; N. Bavina, in *Lit. gazeta* Aug. 27, 1975, p. 6; D. Orlov, 1976; A. Kondratovič, in *Lit. gazeta* Nov. 26, 1980, p. 6; G. Kuklis, in *Lit. Rossija* March 27, 1981, p. 14; V. Dubrovin, in *Moskva* 1982:10; L. Lekhtina, in *Lit. Rossija* Dec. 9, 1983, p. 9; D. Kholendro, in *Oktjabr'* 1985:4.

**Bazhóv, Pável Petróvich,** prose writer (b. Jan. 27 [Jan. 15], 1879, Sysertsky Zavod, near Yekaterinburg, in the Urals—d. Dec. 3, 1950, Moscow). After he completed his studies at the theological seminary in Perm, Bazhov worked as a teacher from 1899 to 1917. He was very interested in the folklore of the Urals and collected folk poetry. In 1918 he volunteered for the Red Army and joined the Communist Party. Beginning in 1923 he lived in

Sverdlovsk, working on the editorial staff of the newspaper *Krestyanskaya gazeta* (until 1929). His first book, *Uralskiye byli* (True Happenings in the Urals), which contained memoirs of the pre-Revolutionary period, appeared in 1924; it was followed by historical and journalistic prose about Siberian partisans and Red Army battles. Bazhov found his natural literary form in 1939 in a collection of folkloristic, fairy-tale-like short stories, *Malakhitovaya shkatulka* (Eng. tr., *The Malachite Casket: Tales from the Urals*, 1944), which he expanded in the following years. The collection received a Stalin Prize (for 1942, 2d class) in 1943. Bazhov characterized his short stories as *skazy*, a term that originally referred to a literary style, popularized by M. Gogol and N. Leskov, that uses a fictitious narrator with a characteristic speech style but that otherwise harks back to the "secret *skazy*," the oral tradition of the Ural miners. From these legends Bazhov adopted a mixture of fairy-tale and folkloric elements. He emphasizes the theme of work and workers.

*Works: Ural'skie byli* (short stories), 1924; *Malakhitovaja škatulka* (short stories), 1939 (see above).—*Soč.*, 3 vols., 1952; *Izbr. proizv.*, 2 vols., 1964.

*Secondary Lit.*: L. Skorino, 1947, and in *Novyj mir* 1944:6–7; RSPP 1:1959; M. Batin, 2d ed., 1963, 1976; E. Permjak, in *Lit. gazeta* Dec. 13, 1972, p. 6; D. Moldavskij, in *Neva* 1979:1; A. Platonov (1940), in his *Razmyšlenija čitatelja*, 1980.

**Bédny, Demyán** (pseud. of Efím Alekséyevich Pridvórov), poet (b. April 13 [April 1], 1883, Gubovka, prov. Kherson—d. May 25, 1945, Moscow). Bedny's father was a peasant. From 1896 to 1900 Bedny trained as an army surgeon; from 1904 to 1908 he studied philology at St. Petersburg University. His first poem appeared in 1899. Bedny joined the Bolshevik faction of the Social Democrats in 1912 and from then on published in *Pravda*. His *Basni* (Fables), written in imitation of I. Krylov, appeared in 1913. Bedny wrote political doggerel in a folk style; during the Revolutionary period his poetry acquired a pointedly agitational character. Its primitive content and easily accessible form made it known to broad sections of the public. After the Revolution, Bedny actively contributed to antireligious propaganda. His prominent position as a friend of high-ranking Party leaders was diminished in 1930 because he persisted in using a coarse, inflammatory style in spite of the changing political situation (Stalin's letter of Dec. 12, 1930); nevertheless, in 1934 he became a member of the presidium of the board of the Writers Union. Soon afterward, his libretto for the comic opera *Bogatyri* (1936; Epic Heroes) was sharply criticized for traducing Russian history and satirically distorting Russia's conversion to Christianity; the incident led to Bedny's expulsion from the Communist Party in 1938. During World War II, Bedny composed anti-German fables and lampoons, but was unable completely to regain his original favored position. The Party Resolution of Feb. 24, 1952 (see PARTY RESOLUTIONS ON LITERATURE), sharply denounced the 1950 and 1951 editions of his work for their "crude political misrepresentations," a result of the inclusion of earlier versions of Bedny's works rather than the later, politically modified versions. On the whole, however, Soviet literary historians still assign Bedny a high place of honor.

*Works: Polnoe sobr. soč.*, 19 vols., 1925–33; *Sobr. soč.*, 5 vols., 1953–54; 8 vols., 1963–65; *Stikhotvorenija i poèmy* (lyric and narrative poems), 1965; *Stikhi, basni* (poems and fables), 1973.
*Secondary Lit.:* I. Èventov, 1953; V. A. Cybenko, 1961; A. Monastyrskij, in *Voprosy lit.* 1963:4; *Vospominanija o D. B.*, 1966; I. Èventov, 1967, 1968, 1972, and in *Zvezda* 1983:4; *RSPPo* 2:1978; D. Moldavskij, in *Voprosy lit.* 1984:2.

**Bek, Aleksándr Alfrédovich,** prose writer (b. Jan. 3, 1903 [Dec. 21, 1902], Saratov—d. Nov. 2, 1972, Moscow). Bek's father was a military doctor. At the age of 16 Bek volunteered for the Red Army and worked for the army newspapers; he subsequently embarked on a career in journalism. His first prose work (1934) was inspired by his assignment to the industrial construction district of Kuznetsk. From 1941 to 1945 Bek was a correspondent in World War II; after the war he transformed his war experiences into fiction. In 1956 he was coeditor of *Literaturnaya Moskva*. Bek lived in Moscow; he was a delegate to some but not all congresses of the Writers Union.

Two themes dominate Bek's work: the steel and iron industry, with its motif of technological progress, and the war. Bek became known primarily for his war povest, *Volokolamskoye shosse* (1943–44; The Volokolamsk Highway; Eng. tr. of Part 1, *On the Forward Fringe*, 1945), which skirts primitive, idealized chauvinism and still conforms to official

requirements in just the right degree to have met with approval in the Soviet Union ever since its appearance. His first-person narrative structure is unusual; it transforms the narrator, Momysh-Uly, into a historical figure from whose point of view the engagement of Panfilov's army (which included Central Asian units) near Moscow in 1941 is reflected and various military and ethical aspects (for example, the justice of the death sentence) are considered. In 1960 Bek again took up this theme for the last time in the povesti *Neskolko dney* (Several Days) and *Rezerv generala Panfilova* (General Panfilov's Reserves). The creative individual in the industrial sphere occupies the center of Bek's best "production prose." In his first povest, *Kurako* (*Znamya* 1934:5; written in collaboration with G. Grigoryev), Bek elevates the achievements of a historical figure—a miner revolutionary, and pioneer of Kuznetsk—to the level of legend. *Novy profil* (1951; A New Profile) contains much that is typical of the late Stalin period in the sense of its being artificial and encumbered with technical details. In the novel he started before the war, *Zhizn Berezhkova* (1956; Eng. tr., *Berezhkov, the Story of an Inventor*, 1958), Bek again attempts to illuminate the state of mind of a historical figure (an airplane engine builder, in this case) by using the first-person narrative structure. *Novoye naznacheniye* (A New Assignment), a roman à clef completed in 1965, is about the longtime minister of metallurgical engineering during the time of Stalin, I. Tevosyan; although the publication of the novel had been announced in *Novy mir* (1965:11), it first appeared in Frankfurt am Main in 1972 and only in 1986 (*Znamya* 10 and 11) in the Soviet Union. The printing ban in the Soviet Union, incidentally, was due not to any anti-Stalinist content but to the intervention of Tevosyan's widow.

*Works: Kurako* (pov.), in *Znamja* 1934:5, separate ed., 1939, rev. ed., 1953; *Volokolamskoe šosse* (pov.), 1945 (see above); *Domenščiki* (pov.), 1946; *Timofej—otkrytoe serdce* (pov.), 1948; *Novyj profil'* (pov.), in *Novyj mir* 1951:10; *Žizn' Berežkova* (novel), 1956 (see above); *Rezerv generala Panfilova* (pov.), in *Novyj mir* 1960:12, separate ed., 1961; *Moi geroi* (pov.), 1967; *Počtovaja proza* (memoirs, essays, letters), 1968; *Novoe naznačenie* (novel), Frankfurt am Main, 1972; *V poslednij čas* (short stories and pov.), 1972; *Na svoem veku* (novel), 1975; *Novoe naznačenie* (novel), in *Znamja* 1986:10–11.—*Sobr. soč.*, 4 vols., 1974–76.
*Secondary Lit.:* T. Khmel'nickaja, in *Zvezda*

1945:3; I. Pitljar, in Znamja 1956:8; RSPP 1:1959; O. Grudcova, 1967; N. Štejn, in Novyj mir 1967:10 N. Bank, in Neva 1973:6; D. Ivanov, in Oktjabr' 1975:8; E. Vorob'ëv, in Lit. gazeta Feb. 16, 1983, p. 4.

**Belinkóv, Arkády Víktorovich** prose writer, literary scholar (b. Sept. 29, 1921, Moscow—d. May 14, 1970, New Haven, Conn.). Belinkov came from a family of Jewish intellectuals; in the early 1940s he studied at the Gorky Literary Institute with V. Shklovsky and M. Zoshchenko, among others, and at Moscow University. During World War II he was a part-time TASS correspondent and a member of the commission investigating the historical monuments destroyed by the Germans. During this time he wrote the novel Chernovik chuvstv, antisovetsky roman (A Rough Draft of Feelings: An Antisoviet Novel). After this was read privately, he was denounced and arrested, condemned to death after 22 months, and, thanks to A. Tolstoy's and V. Shklovsky's intercession on his behalf, granted a reprieve to eight years in a GULAG. While still in prison—where he was given leadership of the camp theater owing to health reasons—he was sentenced to an additional 25 years. In the fall of 1956 he was granted amnesty. Briefly, he was allowed to teach at the Gorky Literary Institute; then he worked as a literary scholar, writing numerous contributions for the KRATKAYA LITERATURNAYA ENTSIKLOPEDIYA, for example, the article on A. Blok. A biographical, analytical work, Yury Tynyanov (1961), was so enthusiastically received (for example, by Shklovsky) that two editions appeared in a short period of time. Only two chapters from a book about Yu. Olesha were published. In 1968 Belinkov made use of a trip to Hungary with his wife to flee via Yugoslavia. He settled in the United States and taught at several universities. Belinkov became a member of the PEN Club. His prose is lost; his book about Olesha, Sdacha i gibel sovetskogo intelligenta (1976; Surrender and Fall of a Soviet Intellectual), for which he already had a publication contract in the Soviet Union, appeared posthumously.

Belinkov's gift as a writer was suppressed by the Soviet regime. Like the first book, which sent him to the camps, his other literary works, which he wrote in the camps, have not been preserved. His works of literary scholarship are written in a literary style. The intriguing feature of his book about Tynyanov is his gift for making the historical an allegory for the present. In Olesha, Belinkov sees a writer who was unable to resist the pressure of the system and was therefore ruined as an artist. He sarcastically paints his portrait against the backdrop of the literary development of the Soviet Union. "In order to bypass Soviet censorship, Belinkov mixed several styles—journalistic, scientific and literary" (Belinkova).

Works: Jurij Tynjanov (literary criticism), 1961, 2d ed., 1965; Poèt i Tolstjak (literary criticism), in Bajkal 1968:1–2; Sdača i gibel' sovetskogo intelligenta: Jurij Oleša (literary criticism), Madrid, 1976.

Secondary Lit.: V. Šklovskij, in Lit. gazeta April 8, 1961; L. Levickij, in Novyj mir 1961:7; V. Erlich, in Slavic Review 1970:3; R. Gul', in Odvukon', New York, 1973, pp. 219–25; M. Friedberg, in Slavic Review 1977:2; N. Belinkova, V. Dunham, in MERSL 2:1978.

**Belóv, Vasíly Ivánovich,** prose writer (b. Oct. 23, 1932, Timonikha, oblast Vologda). Belov attended a village school and worked as a farmhand and carpenter. From 1952 to 1955 he served in the military; since 1956 he has been a member of the Communist Party. Between 1956 and 1958 he wrote for provincial newspapers (short prose and poems). From 1959 to 1964 he studied at the Gorky Literary Institute. Since 1964 Belov has lived in Vologda, but he returns to the village Timonikha as often as possible. The longer short story Derevnya Berdyayka (The Village Berdyayka), published in Nash sovremennik (1961:3), first attracted the critics' attention; since 1968, Belov's short stories have also been published in Novy mir. In 1981 Belov received the State Prize of the USSR for his prose works "of the last few years."

Belov's literary creativity centers on the life of the simple kolkhoz peasant. His faithfulness to truth is not the result of a dispute with the insincere literature of the Stalin period, as is the case with older authors; the critical element does not predominate in his realism. His attention is drawn to the peasant as an individual, in his suffering and in his joy and with his often bitter fate. In Ivan Afrikanovich, the protagonist of his povest Privychnoye delo (1966; A Customary Affair), Belov created a peasant who has become typical for Russian village liierature and accepts the difficult living conditions on the kolkhoz as predestined and manages to fight his way through somehow. "It is a tale about the life of a man who is portrayed in relation to general values, not about a 'victim' or a man treated as a 'function' by the people in an established system" (Lipelis). In *Plotnitskiye rasskazy* (1968; A Carpenter's Tales), he depicts an argument between two neighbors that is as interminable as it is senseless. Several later short stories are also built around the protagonist Konstantin Zorin; these reflect the tension between urban and rural life-styles. In *Vospitaniye po doktoru Spoku* (1978; Childrearing According to Dr. Spock), he examines the unfortunate situation of a child in a loveless marriage. With *Kanuny* (1972–76; The Eves) Belov composed a "chronicle" about a northern Russian village—a healthy community before destructive forced collectivization was imposed—that forms a "chronicle of the 1920s." He wants to continue the story up to 1930. In *Lad: Ocherki o narodnoy estetike* (1979–81; Harmony: Sketches on Folk Aesthetics), Belov compiled his short, encyclopedic observations on old peasant observances: the seasons, trades, plants, customs. Uniting them is a reminder of the lost integrity of peasant life and of its deep roots in the harmony of nature. In the play *Nad svetloy vodoy* (1973; On Light Water), which was successfully performed for several years, he criticizes the indefensible dissolution, in economic and human terms, of the ancient villages. Belov's works are characterized by a profound seriousness, a natural tie to peasant life, and healthy psychological reasoning. In the dialogue he puts into the peasants' mouths, as well as in narrative passages, he preserves the ornamental style of peasant speech with its words and idioms not usually found in written Russian. The stream of consciousness he creates for his characters in this fashion becomes the natural mirror of their thoughts. The critics' high regard (E. Dorosh: "This is good Russian literature") derives from the depth of his message and from his attachment to tradition arising from his deep involvement in the contemporary world.

Works: *Derevnja Berdjajka* (short story), in *Naš sovremennik* 1961:3; *Dereven'ka moja lesnaja* (poems), 1961; *Znojnoe leto* (short stories), 1963; *Rečnye izluki* (pov. and short stories), 1964; *Tiša da Griša* (pov. and short stories), 1966; *Za tremja volokami* (pov. and short stories), 1968; *Plotnickie rasskazy* (short stories), 1968; *Sel'skie povesti*, 1971; *Kholmy* (pov. and short stories), 1973; *Celujutsja zori . . .* (pov. and short stories), 1975; *Kanuny* (novel), 1976; *Gudjat provoda* (short stories), 1978; *Vospitanie po doktoru Spoku* (prose collection), 1978; *Lad: Očerki o narodnoj estetike* (documentary prose), in *Naš sovremennik* 1979:10 and 12, 1980:3, 1981:1, 5–7, sep-

arate ed., 1982; *Rajonnye sceny* (play), in *Moskva* 1980:8; *Vse vperedi* (novel), in *Naš sovremennik* 1986:7–8.

Secondary Lit.: I. Borisova, in *Novyj mir* 1964:6; E. Doroš, in *Novyj mir* 1966:8; A. Marčenko, in *Voprosy lit.* 1969:4; *RSPP* 7(1):1971; S. Zalygin, in *Lit. i sovremennost'* 11:1972; Ju. Surovcev, in *Lit. obozrenie* 1973:2; A. Pistunova, in *Lit. Rossija* Aug. 24, 1973, p. 13; L. Antopol'skij, in *Junost'* 1974:8; Ju. Seleznev, in *Naš sovremennik* 1974:11; V. Solov'ëv, in *Lit. obozrenie* 1975:10; I. Lipelis, in *MERSL* 2:1978; V. Oboturov, in *Naš sovremennik* 1979:10; G. Hosking, in his *Beyond Socialist Realism*, New York, 1980; Ju. Seleznev, in *Moskva* 1981:10; P. S. Vykhodcev, in *Russkaja lit.* 1982:1; N. Agiševa, in *Teatr* 1982:8; K. Mehnert, in his *The Russians and Their Favorite Books*, 1983; A. Pankov, in *Moskva* 1984:2; R. Polčaninov, in *Novoe russkoe slovo*, New York, June 16, 1985, p. 6; N. Rubcov, in *Lit. obozrenie* 1987:1.

**Bély, Andréy** (pseud. of Borís Nikoláyevich Bugáyev), poet, prose writer (b. Oct. 26, [Oct. 14], 1880, Moscow—d. Jan. 8, 1934, Moscow). Bely's father was a professor of mathematics at Moscow University. Bely was first inspired by German culture (Goethe, Heine, Beethoven); after 1897 he delved intensively into the works of Dostoyevsky and Ibsen as well as modern French and Belgian poetry. After graduating from secondary school in 1899 he was attracted to Vladimir Solovyov and Nietzsche. His favorite composers were Grieg and Wagner. His interest in the natural sciences complemented his love of philosophy and music and found an outlet in his study of mathematics at Moscow University; he completed this course of study in 1903 but continued to study the humanities (until 1906). Around 1903 he met A. Blok and K. Balmont, joined the circle of St. Petersburg symbolists gathered around D. Merezhkovsky and Z. Gippius, and worked on the journal *Vesy* until 1909. Bely's numerous publications begin with a piece of rhythmic prose, *Simfonia* (1902; Symphony), which was acclaimed for its unusual linguistic and intellectual features. Bely collected his early poems in the volume *Zoloto v lazuri* (1904; Gold in Azure); this was later followed by *Pepel* (1908; Ashes) and *Urna* (1909; The Urn); these titles reflect his foregoing phase of disillusionment. Bely published his first novel, *Serebryany golub* (1909; Eng. tr., The Silver Dove, 1974), in *Vesy*. A new phase of his philosophically oriented literary work began in 1910 and lasted until about 1920. In 1910–11 Bely traveled to Italy, Tunisia, Egypt, and Palestine. From 1912 to 1916 he spent most of his time in Western Europe; for a while he lived in Dornach with Rudolf Steiner, whose anthroposophy strongly influenced him. In Germany he made friends with Christian Morgenstern. In 1916 he returned to Russia, published his second long novel, *Peterburg* (1916; Eng. tr., *Petersburg* 1978), and joined the literary group "Scythians" (with R. Ivanov-Razumnik and Blok). Bely viewed the October Revolution mystically as the beginning of a religious and spiritual rebirth of mankind. At first he taught theory of verse and prose at PROLETKULT studios. In 1921 Bely emigrated to Berlin where he published numerous volumes of poetry, prose, and theoretical writings. In 1923 he returned to Russia. His subsequent works are primarily autobiographical. They remain in the tradition of symbolism and thus stand apart from the mainstream of Soviet literature, but their quality is not equal to his earlier work.

In the fields of philosophy, the theory of poetry, the lyric, and prose, Bely is one of the leading Russian symbolists, one of the pioneers of modern Russian literature. His art is strongly characterized by mystical experience and strives for renewal in all spheres. His four early *Simfonii* (1902–8) combine the goal of fusing poetry and music with a striving to renew syntax and the rhythmic structure of the language, to "free" language from its "state of exhaustion." *Zoloto v lazuri*, Bely's early collection of poetry, bears the mark of the "apocalyptic" phase of Russian symbolism and of the experience of a large city. The later recollections more closely reflect Russian reality and remain true to his magical conception of the word. Bely's concern with the occult is evident in the theme of his novel *Serebryany golub*, in which he deals with the old cultural-philosophical problem of Russia's position between East and West by using the example of a man from the civilized West who is drawn to the occult powers of the East. Bely is interested in descriptive techniques, imagery, the musical principles of repetition, and the structure of rhythm. Bely draws on Gogolian forms of the grotesque. *Peterburg* arose from the same complex of tensions between Eastern and Western thought yet is tied to anthroposophy and to the father-son conflict through a senator and his son who has fallen under the influence of terrorists; it "exhausts itself with its depiction of consciousness, but this consciousness is grotesquely distorted and broken up into individual seg-ments" (Holthusen). In both macro- and microstructure, Bely destroys the unity of form present in traditional style. His mystical world view also found expression in the equation of revolutionary activity and the Christian doctrine of salvation as revealed in the verse epic written in April 1918, *Khristos voskres* (Christ Is Risen). Bely's stylized prose reaches its climax in his extensively autobiographical novel, *Kotik Letayev* (1922; Eng. tr., 1971); written in 1917, this is a representation of the consciousness of a child on the border between space and time, reality and myth, a work that is "an anticipation of Joyce's most daring experiments in technique" (Struve). Equating people with mythological figures is only one of the ways of intensifying his exposition philosophically and antirationally—in an anthroposophical sense. Memoirs from the years 1929 to 1933 remain stylistically brilliant but are historically unreliable. Bely's experimental style influenced early Soviet ornamental prose in various ways; his philological experiments affected the FORMALIST SCHOOL.

*Works: Simfonija* (lyrical prose), 1902; *Četyre simfonii*, 1902–8 (reprinted, Munich, 1971); *Zoloto v lazuri* (poems), 1904; *Lug zelënyj* (essays), 1910 (reprinted, New York–London, 1969); *Serebrjanyj golub'* (novel), 1910, Berlin, 1922 (reprinted, Munich, 1967) (see above); *Simvolizm* (essays), 1910 (reprinted, Munich, 1969); *Arabeski* (essays), 1911 (reprinted, Munich, 1969); *Peterburg* (novel), 1916, 2d ed., 1922, 1928 (reprinted, Munich, 1967) (see above); *Khristos voskres* (narrative poem), in *Naš put'* 1918:2; *Pervoe svidanie* (narrative poem), 1921 (reprinted, Munich, 1972) (Eng. tr., *The First Encounter*, 1979); *Kotik Letaev* (pov.), 1922 (reprinted, Munich, 1964) (see above); *Vospominanija ob A. A. Bloke* (essays), 1922–23 (reprinted, Munich, 1969); *Zapiski čudaka*, Berlin, 1923; *Moskva* (novel), 2 vols.: vol. 1.1: *Moskovskij čudak*, vol. 1.2: *Moskva pod udarom*, vol. 2: *Maski*, 1926–32 (reprinted, Munich, 1968); *Na rubeže dvukh stoletij* (memoirs, part 1), 1930 (reprinted, Letchworth, 1966); *Načalo veka* (memoirs, part 2), 1933 (reprinted, Chicago, 1967); *Masterstvo Gogolja* (scholarly articles), 1934 (reprinted, Munich, 1969); *Meždu dvukh revoljucij* (memoirs, part 3), 1935 (reprinted, Chicago, 1967); *Stikhotvorenija i poèmy* (lyric and narrative poems), 1966; *Vospominanija o Štejnere* (memoirs), Paris, 1982; *Stikhotvorenija* (poems), 4 vols., Munich, 1982–84 (3 vols. published).

*Translation: Complete Short Stories*, 1979.

Secondary Lit.: R. Ivanov-Ruzumnik, Veršiny, 1923; Lit. nasledstvo 27–28:1937; K. Močul'skij, Paris, 1955; J. Holthusen, Studien zur Ásthetik und Poetik des russischen Symbolismus, Göttingen, 1957, and in Russian Literature 5:1973; A. Hönig, Munich, 1965; K. Bugaeva, in Novyj žurnal, New York, 108:1972, and Berkeley, 1981; S. Cioran, The Hague–Paris, 1973; G. Nivat, in Cahiers du monde russe et soviétique 15:1974, pp. 7–146; A. Kovac, Bern, 1976; B. Christa, Amsterdam, 1977; G. Janecek, in MERSL 2:1978; A Belyj: A Critical Review, ed. G. Janecek, Lexington, 1978; R. A. DiCarlo, Diss., Brown Univ., 1979, and Ann Arbor, 1981; A. Steinberg, Cambridge, 1981; M. Deppermann, Munich, 1982; M. Ljunggren, Stockholm, 1982; F. C. Kozlik, Frankfurt am Main, 1983; J. D. Elsworth, London, 1983; D. Burkhart, Frankfurt am Main, 1984; E. Schmidt, Munich, 1986.

**Belyáyev, Aleksándr Románovich,** prose writer (b. March 16 [March 4], 1884, Smolensk—d. Jan. 6, 1942, Pushkin, oblast Leningrad). Belyayev's father was a priest. Belyayev studied law and the violin (the latter at the Moscow Conservatory); he traveled to Germany, Austria, Italy, and France. Before 1925, when he devoted himself exclusively to literature, Belyayev held many jobs, including those of legal adviser, librarian, and private tutor. In 1916 he developed tuberculosis of the bone, which for many years confined him to his bed; he never completely recovered. In 1928 Belyayev moved from Moscow to Leningrad, then to Kiev in 1929; after 1931 he lived in Tsarskoye Selo (later renamed Pushkin). Influenced by Jules Verne, Belyayev became the first significant Soviet writer of science-fiction novels and short stories. His thrilling, psychologically consistent plots present futuristic problems from the realms of biology, medicine, physics, and technology. Rocket technology, interplanetary flight, organ transplants, exploration of the ocean's depths, and control of atomic energy are only a few of the scientific themes popularized in his adventure books. The popularity of his novels and short stories contradicts the opinion of dogmatic criticism, which had predicted that the Soviet science-fiction novel would confine itself to describing what science could achieve in the near future instead of developing into ultrafuturistic, often incredible fantasy. Consequently, only some of the more than 50 novels and short stories that appeared in various journals during Belyayev's lifetime were ever published in book form; his work was not printed at all between 1942 and 1956. Since then it has again become a part of Soviet literature, and Belyayev is recognized as "the father of Soviet science fiction."

Works: Golova professora Douèlja (short story), 1926, substantially revised version, 1938 (Eng. tr., Professor Dowell's Head, 1980); Ostrov pogibšikh korablej (novel), 1927, 1929, 1958; Čelovek-amfibija (novel), 1928 (Eng. tr., The Amphibian, 1950); Vlastelin mira (novel), 1929, 1958; Pryžok v ničto (novel), 1933; Zvezda KÈC (novel) 1940, 1958; Fantastika, 1976.—Izbr. naučno-fantastičeskie proizv., 2 vols., 1956; 3 vols., 1957, 2d ed., 1958, 3d ed., 1959; Sobr. soč., 8 vols., 1963–64; 5 vols., 1983–85.

Secondary Lit.: S. Poltavskij, in Zvezda 1958:2; RSPP 1:1959; B. V. Ljapunov and R. Nudel'man, 1967, and foreword to the eds. of 1956, 1958, 1963; J. Glad, in MERSL 2:1978; S. Beljaeva, in Avrora 1982:9.

**Belýkh, Grigóry Geórgiyevich,** prose writer (b. Aug. 20 [Aug. 7], 1906—d. Aug. 14 [?], 1938, while imprisoned). After the Revolution, Belykh, who was one of the "homeless waifs" (besprizornye), was institutionalized at Shkid (Shkola sotsialno-individualnogo vospitaniya im. F. Dostoyevskogo [Dostoyevsky School for Social-Individual Education]). There he became friends with L. Panteleyev. After their release (presumably after 1924) both of them lived in Leningrad, became journalists, and, encouraged by S. Marshak, wrote the book Respublika Shkid (1927; The Republic of Shkid). This lively report, based on their own experiences, made the two authors well known; it was later criticized by A. Makarenko. In addition to Respublika Shkid, Belykh published on his own two little short stories and a povest for children, Dom vesyolykh nishchikh (1930; The House of Happy Beggars), which showed him to be very knowledgeable about the workers' districts in Petrograd before and during the Revolution. About 1937 Belykh became a victim of the government purges. In 1958 L. Chukovskaya recommended a new printing of his works; it appeared in 1962, without, however, bringing Belykh or Panteleyev back into the mainstream of Soviet literature.

Works: Respublika Škid (in collaboration with L. Panteleev), 1927; Lapti (short story), 1929; Belogvardeec (short story), 1930; Dom vesëlykh niščikh (pov.), 1930, 3d ed., 1962.
Secondary Lit.: see PANTELEYEV, L.

**Berbérova, Nína Nikoláyevna,** prose writer (b. Aug. 8 [July 26], 1901, St. Petersburg). Berbérova's father was an American who worked in the Ministry of Finance; her mother was descended from Russian landowners. Berberova studied in Rostov-on-Don (1919–20). Her first poems appeared in 1921 in St. Petersburg where she was in contact with circles of poets; in June 1922 she legally emigrated from Soviet Russia with V. Khodasevich. Until they both settled in Paris as émigrés in 1925, they lived with M. Gorky in Berlin and in Italy. For 15 years in Paris Berberova was a constant contributor to *Posledniye novosti*, in which *Biankurskiye prazdniki* (Holidays in Villancourt), her first artistic prose work, appeared in installments (no book publication). Her three novels, *Posledniye i pervye* (1930; The Last and the First), *Povelitelnitsa* (1932; Your Majesty), and *Bez zakata* (1938; Without Sunset), received a cool reception. Her short stories that appeared in *Sovremennye zapiski* from 1934 to 1941 and were collected in the volume *Oblegcheniye uchasti* (1949; Relieving Fate) received greater acclaim. Her book *Chaykovsky* (1936) was especially successful; it was repeatedly translated. In 1932 Berberova divorced Khodasevich and in 1947 she divorced her second husband, N. V. Makeyev, after having remained in the German-occupied part of France during World War II. In 1950 she moved to the United States and worked at various universities as a lecturer. From 1958 to 1968, while living in the United States, she belonged to the editorial staff of the almanac MOSTY. In addition to criticism, she published poems and short stories. Her masterpiece is her autobiography, *Kursiv moy* (1972; Eng. tr., The Italics Are Mine, 1969), which sparked sharp personal and substantive criticism, by R. Gul among others, in reaction to her subjective judgments about numerous émigrés. *Zheleznaya zhenshchina* (1981; The Iron Lady) is the biography of M. I. Zakrevskaya-Benkendorf-Budberg, who was the mistress of Gorky before sharing H. G. Wells's life and whose role as a double agent is now well known.

Berberova's main contribution, beginning with her earliest works, lies in her having focused on the fate of Russians in emigration. In *Posledniye i pervye*, the supporting framework for the plot is the desire of a Russian émigré working in a Paris factory to move to the south of France. The ambitious, multilevel structure and Dostoyevsky's influence no longer weigh down the succeeding novels based on love-related problems. In the center of the short story *Akkompaniatorsha* (1935;

The Accompanist on the Piano) stands a young woman disadvantaged by fate—first in St. Petersburg, then in Moscow, and finally in Paris. A good depiction of the female psyche is—as is often the case with Berberova—impaired by her manipulation of the subject, which makes her intention too obvious. *Pamyati Shlimana* (1958; In Commemoration of Schliemann) is a short story set in the year 1984 that tends toward the grotesque in its portrayal of people who are dependent on machines and suffocated by civilization and overpopulation. A predominance of the negative in her work reflects Berberova's own assertion that "the transcendent does not interest me."

Works: *Poslednie i pervye; roman iz èmigrantskoj žizni* (novel), Paris, 1930; *Povelitel'nica* (novel), Berlin, 1936; *Čajkovskij, istorija odinokoj žizni* (biography), Berlin, 1936; *Borodin* (biography), Berlin, 1938; *Bez zakata* (novel), Paris, 1938; *Akkompaniatorša* (short story), in *Sovremennye zapiski* 58:1935; *Oblegčenie učasti* (short stories), Paris, 1949; *Mys bur'* (novel), in *Novyj žurnal,* New York, 24:1950–27:1951; *Pamjati Šlimana* (short story), in *Mosty,* Munich, 1:1958; *Malen'kaja devočka* (short story), in *Mosty* 9:1962; *Kursiv moj* (autobiography), Munich, 1972 (see above), rev. and enl. ed., New York, 1983; *Železnaja ženščina* (biography), New York, 1981; *Stikhi 1921–83* (poems), New York, 1984.

Secondary Lit.: E. Bakunina, in *Čisla,* Paris, 6:1932; L. Savel'ev, in *Sovremennye zapiski* 67:1938; D. Knut, in *Russkie zapiski* 10:1938; G. Struve, in *Russkaja literatura v izgnanii,* New York, 1956, pp. 292–94; R. Gul', in *Novyj žurnal* 99:1970; M. Barker, in *MERSL* 2:1978.

**Berezóvsky, Feoktíst Alekséyevich,** prose writer (b. Jan. 13 [Jan. 1], 1877, Omsk—d. April 6, 1952, Moscow). Berezovsky came from a family of workers and himself worked in a factory, in a printing shop, and as a telegraph operator for the Siberian railroad; he became a member of the Social Democratic Party in 1904 and participated in revolutionary activities; from 1918 on, he was engaged in Party work and journalism in Siberia. In 1924 Berezovsky moved to Moscow and pursued his literary career. In 1934 he became permanent chairman of the Appeals Commission of the Writers Union of the USSR.

Berezovsky's first prose appeared in 1900 in an Omsk newspaper. In his povest *Mat* (1923; Mother) he presents the fate of a Russian woman in the underground movement caught in the conflict between personal ties and revolutionary responsibilities. Further short stories and the novel *Babyi tropy* (1928; Paths of Country Women), which takes place in Siberia before and after the Revolution, are similarly motivated. Berezovsky wrote very little prose after 1930.

*Works: Mat'* (pov.), 1925, 2d enl. ed., 1925; *Varvara* (short story), 1926; *Taëžnye zastrel'ščiki* (memoirs), 1926, 1955; *Bab'i tropy* (novel), 5th ed., 1930, 1957.—*Sobr. soč.*, 5 vols. (only vols. 1 and 3 published), 1928–30. *Secondary Lit.:* P. P. Migreckij, in Berezovskij's *Sobr. soč.*, 1928; A. Šafir, in *Novyj mir* 1928:7; A. Necvetaeva, 1958; *RSPP* 1:1959; A. Begaev, in *Sibirskie ogni* 1967:3; *F.A.B.: K 100-letiju so dnja roždenija,* 1976 (contains bibliography).

**Berggólts, Ólga Fyódorovna,** poet (b. May 16 [May 3], 1910, St. Petersburg—d. Nov. 13, 1975, Leningrad). Her father was a doctor. During the Civil War, Berggolts was evacuated to Uglich; she returned to Petrograd in 1921. In 1925 she belonged to the literary group "Smena"; there she met her first husband, the poet Boris Kornilov, who died in custody in 1938. In 1930 Berggolts completed her studies in philology at Leningrad University and married her second husband, the literary scholar Nikolay Molchanov. She subsequently worked as a journalist in Kazakhstan and Leningrad. The publication of several children's books (after 1929) and collections of journalistic articles (after 1932) was followed by the appearance of Berggolts's first volumes of poetry in 1934 and 1936; both part of the demand for Five-Year Plan literature. Berggolts was admitted to the Communist Party in the early 1930s. She was arrested on Dec. 13, 1938, and dismissed from the Party; on July 3, 1939, she was released and achieved REHABILITATION and in 1940 was readmitted to the Party. During the blockade of Leningrad in World War II, Berggolts worked for the local radio; in poems such as "Fevralsky dnevnik" (1942; February Diary) she depicted the suffering of the besieged Leningraders and their will to survive. Her second husband was among those who died of starvation during the blockade (Jan. 1942). A short trip to Sevastopol on Party business was reflected in *Vernost* (1946–54; Loyalty), a tragedy in verse. Berggolts was awarded a Stalin Prize (for 1950, 3d class) for *Pervorossiysk* (1950), a verse epic on the subject of construction. Her subsequent work is based mostly on past events in her life; in addition to poetry, she wrote an autobio-

graphical, lyrical prose work, *Dnevnye zvyozdy* (1959; Daytime Stars), the second part of which remained unpublished. Berggolts, who called for liberalization at the beginning of the THAW, was among the regular participants in the congresses of the Writers Union of the USSR (with the exception of 1959) and the Writers Union of the RSFSR. She lived in Leningrad.

Berggolts has a highly developed feeling for the suffering of people, including children, which she is able to transpose into seminarrative, semireflective verse that is "laconic, precise, bare, resembling graphic art rather than painting" (Sinyavsky). Her forceful depiction of starvation, cold, and death during the horrror of the Leningrad blockade and their conquest by faith in victory is based on personal experience. The structure of *Vernost* is an unusual blend of tragedy and elevated narrative verse; its goal is the harmonization of truth derived from experience with Party truth. The discrepancy between Berggolts's actual way of thinking and her published works is illustrated by the exerpts from her diaries from 1932 to 1975, published outside the USSR in 1980 together with several poems from the period she spent in custody. The diaries themselves were confiscated after her death.

*Works: Stikhotvorenija* (poems), 1934; *Dnevnye zvëzdy* (memoirs), 1960, 1971; *Stikhi i proza* (poems, memoirs, publicistic prose), 1961; *Uzel* (poems), 1965; *Vernost'* (lyrical play), 1970; *Pamjat'* (lyric and narrative poems), 1972; *Stikhi i poèmy* (lyric and narrative poems), 1979; *Iz dnevnikov* (memoirs), in *Vremja i my,* Tel Aviv, 57:1980.—*Soč.,* 2 vols., 1958; *Izbr. soč.,* 2 vols., 1967; *Sobr. soč.,* 3 vols., 1972–73; *Izbr. proizv.,* 1983.

*Secondary Lit.:* T. Khmel'nickaja, in *Zvezda* 1951:2; A. Sinjavskij, in *Novyj mir* 1960:5 and in *Lit. i sovremennost'* 2:1961; N. Bank, 1962; A. Pavlovskij, 1962; L. Levickij, in *Novyj mir* 1966:1; M. Roščin, in *Novyj mir* 1967:10; E. M. Fiedler, Munich, 1977; D. Khrenkov, 1979 and 1982; *Vspominaja O. B.,* 1979; *BSPPo* 3(1):1979; L. Gendlin, in *Russkaja mysl',* Paris, March 22, 1979, pp. 10–11; S. Babenyševa, E. Ètkind, in *Vremja i my* 57:1980; L. Levin, in *Novyi mir* 1984:12; A. Ar'ev, in *Zvezda* 1985:5.

**Beryózko, Geórgy Sergéyevich,** prose writer (b. Sept. 7 [Aug. 25], 1905, Vilnius—d. Nov. 22, 1982, Moscow). Beryozko's father was a teacher. At the age of 14 Beryozko joined the Red Army as a volunteer. He published his first poems in 1925. In 1927 he completed his studies in ethnology at Moscow University and worked as an art teacher, an editor at a publishing house, and an assistant director of several military films. During World War II, Beryozko saw action. His war experiences were the source of his first prose works (short stories and povesti) in 1942, as well as of newspaper articles; the attention they attracted permitted him to become a professional writer. His works are of little literary value. He lived in Moscow.

Beryozko's themes are war and the military. In Mirny gorod (1952–54; Peaceful City), a novel of excessive length and schematic characterization, he deals with the reversal near Tula in 1942. When a work about the Soviet Army in peacetime was required, he described the training of a paratroop unit, using a title intended to illustrate the strength of an ideological position: Silneye atoma (1952; More Powerful Than the Atom). The novel's much-debated chapter endings, written in rhythmic prose, burden the novel with their commentary instead of enriching it stylistically. In his novel Prisutstviye neobychaynogo (1980; The Presence of the Extraordinary), Beryozko has attempted to free himself from the military theme and to write a didactic detective novel. In addition to a dozen film scripts, he has also written dramas based on the themes of his major works, but they have not been successful.

Works: Krasnaja raketa (short story), Komandir divizii (pov.), 1945; Noč' polkovodca (pov.), 1947, dramatic adaptation, Mužestvo, 1948; Mirnyj gorod (novel), 1952–54; Izbr. povesti i rasskazy (pov. and short stories), 1957; Silnee atoma (novel), 1959; Ljubit' i ne ljubit' (kinopov.), in Moskva 1963:1; Neskol'ko neobjazatel'nykh sovetov, in Voprosy lit. 1973:1, 4, separate ed., 1974; Dom učitel'ja (novel), 1973; Prisutstvie neobyčajnogo (novel), in Moskva 1980:1–2.—Izbr. proizv., 2 vols., 1972.

Secondary Lit.: Ju. Nagibin, in Znamja 1958:6; RSPP 1:1959; S. Nel's, in Molodaja gvardija 1960:7; I. Kozlov, in Lit. obozrenie 1973:11, in Lit. gazeta Jan. 14, 1976, p. 6, and in Lit. Rossija May 13, 1985, p. 8; N. Bukhancev, in Lit. gazeta April 23, 1980, p. 6.

**Betáki, Vasíly Pávlovich,** poet (b. Sept. 29, 1930, Rostov-on-Don). Betaki grew up in Leningrad as the son of a futurist whom V. Mayakovsky protected from arrest and who was a set designer for films. In 1950, to avoid arrest, Betaki was forced to break off his study of Iranian language and literature at Leningrad University. Until 1955 he lived in the south of Russia. From 1953 to 1960 he studied at the Gorky Literary Institute as a correspondence student. After returning to Leningrad he worked from 1956 to 1961 as the deputy scientific director of the museum in the palace at Pavlovsk. Betaki's poems appeared occasionally in almanacs. (Den poezii, Leningrad) and journals; his only book published in the Soviet Union, Zemnoye plamya (1965; The Earthly Flame), led to his acceptance into the Writers Union of the USSR but also to the cessation of his publishing in journals. Betaki earned a living by translating numerous works and by reading poetry. In 1972 Betaki was expelled from the Writers Union. In 1973 he was allowed to emigrate from Leningrad to Paris. There he and his wife, V. Iverni, are regular reviewers for the journal Kontinent. His poems have been published in journals and in three small collections: Zamykaniye vremeni (1974; Short Circuit of Time), Yevropa-ostrov (1981; The Island Europe), and Pyaty vsadnik (1985; The Fifth Horseman).

Betaki writes poems that are rich in metaphors and capable of various meanings. Starting from a direct experience—for example, from images of the city and the countryside but also from political events of the present and the past—they hint at interpretations. Betaki, who is very talented in his use of form, can write witty, playful rhymes. A large section of his narrative poem Plyaski istorii (1974; Dancing Stories), his first work published in the West, discusses V. Betaki, his ancestor who was exiled for being a Decembrist. For the poems in the cycle Étyen Falkone (1972–82; Etienne Falconet) concerning the sculptor of the St. Petersburg statue of Peter the Great, Betaki uses different 18th-century verse structures. The authors whose works Betaki has translated include Byron, Scott, Kipling, Poe, Shakespeare, Goethe, and Seifert.

Works: Zemnoe plamja (poems), 1965; Pljaski istorii (narrative poem), in Grani, Frankfurt am Main, 91:1974; Zamykanie vremeni (poems), Paris, 1974; Evropa-ostrov (poems), Paris, 1981; Pjatyj vsadnik (poems), Paris, 1985 (also contains Ét'en Fal'kone).

Secondary Lit.: V. Vejdle, foreword to Betaki's Zamykanie vremeni, 1974; A. Rannit, in Kontinent, Paris, 33:1982.

**Bezyménsky, Aleksándr Ilyích,** poet, literary official (b. Jan. 19 [Jan. 7], 1898, Zhitomir, prov. Volhynia—d. June 26, 1973, Moscow). Bezymensky graduated from a gymnasium in Vladimir in 1916; for a short time he attended a commercial school in Kiev. He was admitted to the Communist Party in 1916. In 1917 Bezymensky participated in the October Revolution in Petrograd, after which he worked for the Komsomol and the Party. His first publications appeared in 1918. In 1922 Bezymensky was one of the founding members of the literary groups MOLODAYA GVARDIYA and OKTYABR, and he bears a share of the responsibility for the intolerant and aggressive course pursued by these institutions, which remained close to the Party. After 1924 he became one of the dogmatic officials of VAPP. Bezymensky was named to the board of the Writers Union of the USSR in 1934; he was appointed a delegate to all Writers Union congresses held in 1954 and after but was never again elected to the ranks of the leadership. He lived in Moscow.

As a poet Bezymensky wrote tendentious poems on current problems of the day, consistent with the Party line of the time; his work manifested a joyful optimism. As a result, "much of his poetry is mere rhymed journalism" (Struve). Bezymensky's satirical drama in verse, Vystrel (1930; The Shot), a feeble imitation of V. Mayakovsky's satires, was attacked by his colleagues at RAPP. For support Bezymensky turned to Stalin, who on March 19, 1930, "attested that there was nothing inimical to the Party" in the work and that it could be counted among "the prototypes of revolutionary proletarian art." In his subsequent poems and epics in verse Bezymensky propagandized, among other topics, collectivization and the Five-Year Plans; in 1949 he collaborated on the anti-American campaign.

Works: Lučšie stroki (poems), 1932; Vystrel (play), 1930; Tragedijnaja noč' (narrative poem), 1966; Partbilet No. 224332 (poems and memoirs), 1968; Komsomolija (poems), 1972.— Izbr. proizv., 2 vols., 1958.

Secondary Lit.: B. Solov'ëv, in Zvezda 1926:4; A. Selivanovskij, V literaturnykh bojakh, 1959; O. Presnjakov, 1964; L. Terekhin, in Lit. gazeta Oct. 30, 1968, pp. 4–5; L. Bezymenskij, in Lit. gazeta Jan. 25, 1978, p. 7; RSPPo 3(1):1979.

Biánki, Vitály Valentínovich, prose writer (b. Feb. 11 [Jan. 30], 1894, St. Petersburg—d. June 10, 1959, Leningrad). Bianki's father was a biologist and served as consultant to the Zo-

ological Museum of the Academy of Sciences. Bianki studied biology and art history in St. Petersburg. He participated in expeditions to the Urals and the Altai and for a short time worked as a teacher and director of the local museum in the Altai. Bianki began to write animal stories for children in Petrograd in 1922. Year after year, beginning in 1924, he published books about the world of nature for children and young people. Altogether Bianki wrote over 300 short stories, fairy tales, povesti, and articles that reached a total publication of some 40 million copies in 120 separate editions. His works were translated into many languages, both within and outside the USSR.

Bianki is a talented and popular children's writer. His works depict mammals, birds, insects, and plants, sometimes by themselves, sometimes with human beings. Bianki combines zoological and biological information with a talent for pedagogy and artistic inspiration. His rendering of the animal world makes intelligent use of the lack of distinction between instinct and reason that is characteristic of the juvenile psyche (Shcheglov). The real world and the fabulous, enchanted world merge into each other. Many of Bianki's fairy tales, such as Lyulya (1934), which tells the story of a small bird that sacrifices itself for the other animals and is then no longer able to find a niche for itself on the very earth it saved, have the power of effective symbols. Odinets (1927; The Loner), one of Bianki's longer stories, is about the fate of an old elk that lives in silent friendship with a grouse on an island in a swamp and about a student who wants to shoot the elk but who, through his prolonged encounter with nature, becomes at last mature enough not to fire the fatal shot as the elk flees across the water. Lesnaya gazeta na kazhdy god (1923–58; A Forest Newspaper for Every Year), a work that occupies a special place in Bianki's oeuvre, is based on a suggestion made by S. Marshak. Its short stories and concise observations constitute, in narrative form, an encyclopedic survey of the flora and fauna of the forests and steppes, mountains and seas, over the course of a year. For the first two years of its publication, parts of Lesnaya gazeta appeared regularly in the children's journal Vorobey (after 1924, Novy Robinson); ten expanded editions of the work (with N. M. Pavlova as consultant after 1949) were published between 1928 and 1957.

Works: Kto čem poët? (short story), 1924; Na velikom morskom puti (pov.), 1924; Murzuk (pov.), 1925; Po sledam (short stories), 1926; Odinec (pov.), 1927; Askyr (pov.), 1927; Lesnaja gazeta na každyj god (short stories), 1928, 11th ed., 1969; Konec zemli (short stories), 1933; Skazki (fairy tales), 1945; Rasskazy i skazki (short stories and fairy tales), 1949; Povesti i rasskazy (pov. and short stories), 1956.—Sobr. soč., 4 vols., 1972–75.

Translations: Tales of an Old Siberian Trapper, 1946; Galinka, the Wild Goose, 1963; Peek the Piper, 1964; The Fox and the Mouse, 1967; How I Wanted to Pour Salt on a Rabbit's Tail and Other Stories, 1967; Humphrey Goes Hunting, 1967; The First Hunt, 1978; Forest Homes, 1978.

Secondary Lit.: G. Grodenskij, 1954, 2d ed., 1966; L. Kassil', in Ogonëk 1954:7, p. 22; I. Sokolov-Mikitov, in Lit. gazeta March 18, 1954; T. Khmel'nickaja, in Leningradskie pisateli—detjam, 1954; M. Ščeglov, in Novyj mir 1954:7; V. Anikin, in Russkij fol'klor 1958; Žizn' i tvorčestvo V. Bianki, 1967; B. Semënov, in Neva 1978:6; V. Korpenko, in Prostor 1981:7; S. Sakharnov, in Avrora 1983:12.

**Bill-Belotserkóvsky, Vladímir Naúmovich** (pseud. of V. N. Bill), playwright (b. Jan. 9, 1885 [Dec. 28, 1884], Aleksandriya, Ukraine—d. March 1, 1970, Moscow). In his youth Bill-Belotserkovsky was a sailor; he lived in the United States for six and a half years until 1917, when he was motivated by the Revolution to return to Russia. He joined the Communist Party in 1917 and took part in the Civil War; he began publishing in 1918. A member of the PROLETKULT and later of the KUZNITSA group, Bill-Belotserkovsky was an active Communist cultural functionary. In 1929 he denounced M. Bulgakov and the Moscow Art Theater to Stalin for failure to assume a properly Soviet position. He wrote primarily political plays and is best known for only one, Shtorm (1925; The Storm). In 1934 Bill-Belotserkovsky was a member of the board of the Writers Union of the USSR. He lived in Moscow.

Bill-Belotserkovsky's plays Ekho (1924; Echo) and Levo rulya (1925; Steer to the Left) illustrate the oppression of the working class under capitalism and are marked by the agitational character of the period. Shtorm, which propagandizes the victorious struggle of the Bolshevik Party, belongs to the classical repertoire of the Soviet stage; the play was repeatedly revised after 1935. Bill-Belotserkovsky juxtaposes series of scenes from the birth of the Soviet state, such as a session of a district soviet or the struggle against sabotage;

his episodic structuring of character types and plot situations and his incorporation of mass scenes establish a link with early revolutionary drama. Active political involvement also characterizes his later dramas, such as Luna sleva (1927; Moon on the Left), a comedy about the conflict between love and revolutionary duty that polemicizes with S. Malashkin. Zhizn zovyot (1933; Eng. tr., Life Is Calling, 1938) is an artistically inadequate attempt at writing a psychological drama about the intelligentsia under the new regime. With his last play, Tsvet kozhi (1948; Skin Color; also known by the title Vokrug ringa [Around the Ring]), Bill-Belotserkovsky placed himself in the service of anti-American and anticosmopolitan propaganda (see COSMOPOLITANISM).

Works: Smekh skvoz' slëzy (short stories), 1919; Bifšteks s krov'ju (play), 1919; P'esy (plays), 1940; Izbr., 1954; P'esy (plays), 1955; Put' žizni (short stories), 1959; Rasskazy i očerki (short stories and publicistic prose), 1965.—Izbr. proizv., 2 vols., 1962; 2 vols., 1976.

Secondary Lit.: N. Pogodin, in Lit. gazeta Jan. 8, 1955; Ju. Zavadskij, in Lit. gazeta Jan. 9, 1960, Jan. 14, 1965, Jan. 15, 1975, p. 8; K. Rudnickij, Portrety dramaturgov, 1961; S. Amert, in MERSL 3:1979.

**Bítov, Andréy Geórgiyevich**, prose writer (b. May 27, 1937, Leningrad). Bitov's father was an architect. Bitov grew up in Leningrad after returning from the evacuation in 1944. His studies at the Leningrad Institute of Mining from 1955 to 1962 were interrupted by military service from 1957 to 1958; thereafter he served as the drilling master on geological expeditions. His first short stories were published in journals in 1959. Since the appearance of his first collection of short stories, Bolshoy shar (1963; The Big Balloon), Bitov's prose has been highly acclaimed; his absolute commitment to candor and his search for new narrative structures made him an important representative of the new trend in literature that became viable after the 20th Party Congress in 1956. He lives in Moscow; he was appointed a delegate to the Third Congress of the Writers Union of the RSFSR in 1970. The novel Pushkinsky dom (1978; The Pushkin House), which appeared in segments in Soviet journals, was published as a complete novel only in the United States. In 1979 Bitov was among the contributors to METROPOL.

In the foreword to Bitov's third book, Dachnaya mestnost (1967; A Country Place), V.

Panova emphasized "his keen way of thinking, his artistic care, and his passionate interest in man's inner life." His sixth volume, *Obraz zhizni* (1972; Way of Life), which was the first not bearing the title of one of the short stories included, confirmed the independence of his talent, which consciously rejected the required pedagogic intent. Conservative critics noted the absence of social commentary and of a clear statement and accused him of abstract psychologizing and of acknowledging ethical principles as not being subordinate to social principles. The book *Dni cheloveka* (1976; Man's Days), which consists of individual short stories, revolves around the question of self-recognition and, in the section called "Rol" (The Role), also deals with the issue of the role that a person plays, wants to play, and has to play. *Sem puteshestviy* (1976; Seven Trips) combines travel sketches written between 1959 and 1973 in which the observing traveler with his analytic reflections is more important than the particular object he observes. Bitov makes his most comprehensive claim to giving shape to the world of experience of people in the USSR in the novel *Pushkinsky dom*, which is also dedicated to the theme of preserving the Russian literary tradition. Influenced by Western Europe, Bitov looks for a renewal of narrative technique and for a verification of Russian traditions in his work. He has a predilection for depicting the thinking process, especially the inconsistent stream of consciousness held captive by the smallest details. He seizes and reflects upon not the unusual but the commonplace, the trivial; travel frequently serves as the stage for his psychological observations; the weak or distracted person is depicted in a relentless, open, moralistic self-trial; interpersonal relationships are psychologically probed from a single point of view to a depth that the reader can scarcely tolerate, without admitting a definitive resolution. Bitov searches for a fragmentary narrative form that can provide a loose association between the chapters of a novel at the same time that, as a product of these fragmentary prose units, it can capture the immensity of life—even its transcendental aspects.

*Works:* Bol'šoj šar (pov.), 1963; Takoe dolgoe detstvo (short stories), 1965; Dačnaja mestnost' (pov.), 1967; Aptekarskij ostrov (short stories and pov.), 1968; Granicy žanra (essays), in Voprosy lit. 1969:7; Obraz žizni (pov.), 1972; Čto bylo, čto est', čto budet . . . (pov.), in Avrora 1975:1; Dni čeloveka (pov.), 1976; Sem' putešestvij (pov.), 1976; Puškinskij dom

(novel), Ann Arbor, 1978; Proščal'nye den'ki (short stories) in Metropol', Ann Arbor, 1979; Voskresnyj den' (short stories, pov., and travel sketches), 1980; Vospominanie o Puškine (essay), in Znamja 1985:12; Predpoloženie žit' (essay), in Zvezda 1986:1.

*Translation:* Life in Windy Weather: Short Stories, 1986.

*Secondary Lit.:* L. Ivanova, in Moskva 1965:8; L. Anninskij, in Lit. gazeta April 17, 1968, p. 5; V. Ivaščenko, in Junost' 1968:5; V. Turbin, in Novyj mir 1972:4; A. Urban, in Zvezda 1973:7; G. Trefilova, in Lit. obozrenie 1973:10; Ju. Karabčievskij, in Grani, Frankfurt am Main, 106:1977; M. Epštejn, in Družba narodov 1978:8; P. Meyer, in MERSL 3:1979; W. Schmid, in Wiener Slawistischer Almanach 4:1979 and 5:1980 (includes valuable bibliography); K. Sapgir, in Grani 132:1984.

**Blok, Aleksándr Aleksándrovich,** poet (b. Nov. 28 [Nov. 16], 1880, St. Petersburg—d. Aug. 7, 1921, Petrograd). Blok's great-great-grandfather was the German personal physician to the Empress Elizabeth and belonged to the Mecklenburg nobility. Blok's father was a professor of constitutional law at the University of Warsaw; his mother was a translator of belles lettres. Blok spent his youth with his grandfather, the rector of St. Petersburg University. In 1898–1901 Blok studied law, then humanities (graduating in 1906) at St. Petersburg University. In 1902 Blok, who had written poems since childhood, entered the circle of St. Petersburg symbolists that included D. Merezhkovsky and Z. Gippius, who in 1903 were the first to publish Blok's poems in their journal, Novy put. Blok found his first admirers in Moscow in the circle of the "Argonauts" around A. Bely, with whom Blok had a temporary friendship. In 1903 Blok married Lyubov Dmitriyevna Mendeleyeva, the addressee and ideal of his first symbolist cycle of poems written in 1901–2, Stikhi o Prekrasnoy Dame (1904; Poems about the Beautiful Lady). This first book and the additional collections of poetry of the next few years were noticed by a narrow circle only. However, his play Balaganchik (1906; Eng. tr., The Puppet Show, 1963) aroused considerable discussion; V. Meyerhold staged the premiere in the Kommissarzhevskaya Theater on Dec. 30, 1906, emphasizing its disillusioned character. Two further lyric dramas and numerous cycles of poems, such as Snezhnaya maska (1907; The Snow Mask), established his reputation, so that he was the only symbolist writer popular in wider circles in 1910. Regular trips to Western Europe—Italy, France, Belgium, the Netherlands, and his special favorite, Germany—belonged to his customary life-style and found varying echoes in his poetry. With *Roza i krest* (1913; Eng. tr., *The Rose and the Cross*, 1936), Blok returned once again to drama. In July 1916, Blok was inducted into the armed services but not sent to the front. Following the February Revolution he worked as one of the editors on the Extraordinary Investigative Commission examining the political offenses of the tsarist government. He envisioned the Bolshevik seizure of power being mystically transfigured into a cosmic revolution. The revolutionary events found an echo in one of Blok's most important poems, the much interpreted and interpretable narrative poem *Dvenadtsat* (1918; Eng. tr., *The Twelve*, 1920). A few days later he gave form to his experience of the end of the old world and his view of the future of Europe and Asia in the great narrative poem *Skify* (1918; Eng. tr., "The Scythians," 1921). In the post-Revolutionary period, Blok grew silent as a poet. He was active in the cultural organizations of the new regime and wrote some essays. Physically and spiritually not up to the anguish, horror, and disruption of these years, Blok died at the age of 40.

Blok was the idol of the young Russian intelligentsia during the second decade of the 20th century; he is Russia's greatest symbolist. Within Russian symbolism he belongs to the second generation. His early work reveals the influence of romantic poets such as V. Zhukovsky and M. Lermontov and of later representatives of pure lyric such as Ya. Polonsky and A. Fet. The Sophianism of Vladimir Solovyov and the mystical ideas of the St. Petersburg symbolists shaped his first published cycle of poems, *Stikhi o Prekrasnoy Dame*. Blok sees divine wisdom and the Virgin Mary mystically transcended in the beautiful lady Sophia. The "desired friend," the "white sovereign," the "incomparable woman" becomes the eternally feminine. The next volume of poetry, *Nechayannaya radost* (1906; The Unexpected Joy), emphasizes the religiously reverent through the name of a Russian icon of Mary chosen for the title, but it has a similarly ambivalent erotic-demonic character. The poem "Neznakomka" (1906; Eng. tr., "The Unknown Woman," 1921) is contained in the cycle *Gorod* (1901–8; The City), in which Blok, influenced by V. Bryusov, turns toward the phenomenon of people in a large city. "Neznakomka" blends the visionary with the earthly, mixing images of ladies in a metropolis and streetwalkers, and leads up to *Snezh-*

*naya maska*, the effect of which derives from the dynamic development and intersection of bold metaphors. Blok is a poet of instantaneous, real, and visionary impressions that are modeled colorfully and picturesquely from a musical perception of the totality. *Balaganchik* drags all allegories of the eternally feminine into ridiculous banality and is simultaneously an inner controversy and a disillusioned game. Blok expanded this short drama into a trilogy with *Korol na ploshchadi* (1906; Eng. tr., *The King in the Square*, 1934) and *Neznakomka* (based in part on the poem of the same title). In Blok's later lyric poetry, poems about Russia stand out; these were collected and published at the beginning of World War I in *Stikhi o Rossii* (1915; Poems about Russia). From his work with medieval French poetry arose the romantic, symbolist drama *Roza i krest*, a renewed antirealistic platform for expressing his disagreement with the contemporary theater; in this play Blok lets the historical and imaginary levels continually overlap. He tried in vain to schedule a performance during the war. The narrative poem *Dvenadtsat* reports in its rhythmically and contextually independent twelve parts on twelve Red Army soldiers marching through Petrograd, unites the departure from the old world, the chaos of the Revolution, and a solemn appeal to the future, and in the end places Christ at the head of the revolutionary expedition with a red banner and white roses. Blok is a poet with a great sensitivity to form whose verses exercise an unusual suggestive power. His departure from a system of tonic syllables, in favor of a system of pure tonics, had an enduring effect on future Russian poetry.

*Works: Stikhi o Prekrasnoj Dame* (poems), 1904; *Nečajannaja radost'* (poems), 1906; *Balagančik* (play), 1906 (see above); *Korol' na ploščadi* (play), 1906 (see above); *Neznakomka* (play), 1906 (see above); *Snežnaja maska* (poems), 1907; *Zemlja v snegu* (poems), 1908; *Nočnye časy* (poems), 1911; *Roza i krest* (play), 1913 (see above); *Skazki* (fairy tales), 1913; *Stikhi o Rossii* (poems), 1915; *Dvenadcat'* (narrative poem), 1918 (see above); *Skify* (narrative poem), 1918 (see above); *Rossija i intelligencija* (essays), 1918; *Jamby* (poems), 1919; *Za gran'ju prošlykh dnej* (poems), 1920.—*Sobr. stikhotvorenij*, 3 vols., 1911–12; *Polnoe sobr. stikhotvorenij*, 2 vols., 1946; *Sobr. soč.*, 12 vols., 1932–36; 8 vols., 1960–63; 6 vols., 1971.

*Translations: The Spirit of Music* (essays), 1946 (includes essays from *Rossija i intelli-*

gencija); The Twelve and Other Poems, tr. J.
Stallworthy and P. France, 1970, and under
the title Selected Poems of Aleksandr Blok,
1974; The Twelve and Other Poems, tr. A.
Hollo, 1971; Selected Poems, 1981.
Secondary Lit.: V. Žirmunskij, 1922; K. Ču-
kovskij, Berlin, 1922 (reprinted, Paris, 1976);
M. A. Beketova, 1930; S. Bonneau, Paris, 1946;
N. Berberova, Paris, 1947; J. v. Guenther,
Munich, 1948; K. Močul'skij, Paris, 1948 (Eng.
tr., 1983); E. Mayr, Diss., Vienna, 1950; V.
Orlov, 1956, 1980; C. Kisch, London, 1960; F.
D. Reeve, New York, 1962; N. Vengrov, 1963;
R. Kemball, The Hague, 1965; R.-D. Kluge,
Munich, 1967; I. T. Kruk, 1970; I. Masing,
Stockholm, 1970; D. Wörn, Munich, 1974; S.
Hackel, Oxford, 1975; D. Maksimov, 1975; G.
Pirog, Diss., Yale Univ., 1975; M. Banjanin
and E. K. Bristow, in MERSL 3:1979; RSPPo
3(2):1980; A. B. Novye materialy i issledo-
vanija, 3 vols., 1980–82 (published as part of
series, Lit. nasledstvo, vol. 92, parts 1–3); D.
Bergstraesser, Heidelberg, 1982.

**Bobróv, Sergéy Pávlovich**, poet (b. Nov. 8
[Oct. 27], 1889, Moscow—d. Feb. 1, 1971,
Moscow). Bobrov's father was a civil servant.
In 1913 Bobrov completed his studies at the
Moscow Archaeological Institute. Bobrov,
whose poems were first published in 1911,
belonged to the poets and theoreticians associated with FUTURISM. Initially he played a
leading role in the neosymbolist group "Lirika" (1913–14), whose first publication was
Bobrov's volume of verse Vertogradari nad
lozami (1913; Gardeners at the Vines). With
N. Aseyev and B. Pasternak, who were also
members of "Lirika," Bobrov formed the futurist group "Tsentrifuga" in 1914. In addition to his own poetry he published theoretical and polemical articles, the basic ideas of
which are to be found in Liricheskaya tema
(1914; A Lyrical Theme). Using nine pseudonyms, Bobrov contributed approximately
one-third of the poems to the futurist anthology Vtoroy sbornik Tsentrifugi (Tsentrifuga's
Second Collection) in 1916. In the early 1920s
he published several social-utopian novels.
Bobrov also wrote popular-science books for
young people, such as Volshebny dvurog (1949;
The Magic Diceros), which is based on the
history of mathematics and its place in man's
life. The liberal almanac Literaturnaya Moskva
(2:1956) reminded readers of his work by including two of his poems. Toward the end of
his long life Bobrov depicted some episodes
from his own childhood in the "lyrical povest" Malchik (1966; The Boy); other thoughts

on art and genius were incorporated into a
16-part verse epic written in a balanced, classical language, Evgeny Delakrua (1970–71;
Eugène Delacroix), in which Bobrov includes
comparisons and portraits of the great artists
of the world, such as Pushkin, Bach, Michelangelo, and Rembrandt. During the entire Soviet period Bobrov lived a retiring life; he
earned his living by doing translations and
was almost completely ignored.

Works: Vertogradari nad lozami (poems),
1913; Liričeskaja tema (essays), 1914 (reprinted, in Manifesty i programmy russkikh
futuristov, Munich, 1967); Zapiski stikho-
tvorca (essays), vols. 1–2, 1916–23; Alma-
znye lesa (poems), 1917; Lira lir (poems), 1917;
Vosstanie mizantropov (novel), 1922; Speci-
fikacija idotola (novel), 1923; Našedsij so-
krovišče (novel), 1931 (pseud. A. Jurlov); Volšebnyj dvurog (book for young people), 1949;
Arkhimedovo leto, 2 vols., 1959–62; Mal'čik
(novel), 1966, 2d enl. ed., 1976; Russkij toni-
českij stikh . . . (article), in Russkaja lit. 1967:1
and 1968:2; Evgenij Delakrua, živopisec (narrative poem), 1971, excerpt in Lit. Rossija July
24, 1970, p. 21.
Secondary Lit.: V. Markov, Russian Futurism, Berkeley, 1968; L. Ozerov, in Detskaja
lit. 1972:6; A. A. Sidorov, in Lit. Rossija July
21, 1972, p. 17.

**Bóbyshev, Dimítry Vasílyevich**, poet (b. April
11, 1936, Mariupol). Bobyshev grew up in
Leningrad; his father died there during the
blockade, and Bobyshev was adopted by his
stepfather after World War II. In 1959 Bobyshev completed his training as a chemical
equipment engineer at the Leningrad Technological Institute and began working at this
trade. For seven years starting in the late 1960s,
Bobyshev worked for the Leningrad television
broadcasting station as an editor in the technical division. Bobyshev's first poems date
from the mid-1950s; they were first published
in the SAMIZDAT journal Sintaksis (1959–60)
reprinted in Grani 58:1965). At the end of the
1960s a few poems were published in Soviet
periodicals (in Yunost and Leningrad almanacs). Since the 1970s, Bobyshev's poems have
only been published in the West. A transcendental experience in 1972 prompted Bobyshev to join the Russian Orthodox Church.
At the end of 1979, in the same year that
Ziyaniya (1979; Gaping Ravines), his first volume of poetry, appeared in Paris, Bobyshev
was allowed to emigrate to the United States;
he lives in Milwaukee, Wisconsin, and com-

bines his work as an engineer with his calling as a poet.

The most significant event in Bobyshev's life that contributed to his development as a poet was his encounter with Anna Akhmatova in 1960 (she dedicated her poem "Pyataya roza" to him). Bobyshev considers Rainer Maria Rilke's poems an essential spiritual and literary source. Among the émigré poets, Yury Ivask is the best versed in Bobyshev's work. Bobyshev writes poetry that expresses spiritual events, visions, experiences. In its quest for meaning and beauty, for the divine in the earthly, his philosophically searching poetry consistently incorporates the transcendental world into its portrayal of the material. In addition to general philosophical poems, he writes love poems and poems on the writing of poetry. At certain intervals Bobyshev compiles his poems, which he only reworks during his first, inspired phase, into cycles. The poems "Russkiye tertsiny" (1982; Russian Terza Rima), written between 1977 and 1981 and consisting of 90 stanzas, outlines his critical analysis of the Soviet present, Russian history, and the emigration. Bobyshev's poetry is rich in imagery and associations; the search for meaning accords with a conscious, often unusual, choice or creation of words, as well as with his delight in the reciprocal elucidation that similar sounding words lend each other.

*Works:* "Traurnye oktavy" (poem cycle), in *Pamjati Anny Achmatovoj,* Paris, 1974; "Triždy—Tjul'panov" (poems), in *Kontinent,* Paris, 12:1977; *Zijanija* (poems), Paris, 1979; "Russkie terciny" (poem), in *Kontinent,* Paris, 31:1982.

*Secondary Lit.:* N. Gorbanevskaja, in *Kontinent* 22:1980; Ju. Ivask, in *Russkaja mysl',* Paris, Sept. 25, 1980, and in *Vestnik RKhD,* Paris, 134:1981; K. Sapgir, in *Russkaja mysl'* March 6, 1980, p. 12; K. Filips-Juzwigg, in *Russkaja mysl'* May 20, 1982, p. 10; S. Jur'ev, in *Russkaja mysl'* Sept. 9, 1982, p. 12, and Aug. 15, 1986, p. 10.

**Bogdánov, Nikoláy Vladímirovich,** prose writer (b. March 5, [Feb. 20], 1906, Kandoma prov. Ryazan). Bogdanov is the son of a country doctor. From 1921 on, he worked as an official in the Komsomol; from there he was given a temporary assignment at the Bryusov Institute of Literature and Art in Moscow. From 1923 on, he belonged to the group of Komsomol writers, MOLODAYA GVARDIYA. Within the field of Komsomol literature that

arose at the end of the 1920s, his first novel, *Pervaya devushka* (1928; The First Girl), found the greatest acclaim. He reports on the first female member of a district branch during the Civil War. In conformity with changing moral principles, the tragedy of her life derives from the initial propagandism in favor of free love. Other prose works of the 1930s have the same focus. Bogdanov's reports from the front were published in book form before World War II was over. In 1952 in *Oktyabr* he published Legends from the Wise Mao, which were told in a childlike fashion. In 1958 he published the revised version of his first novel. In *Odin iz pervykh* (1961; One of the First) Bogdanov also remained within the realm of his youthful experiences, here describing the first attempt to establish a Young Pioneer cell in his village. This work is directed toward young people, as is most of what Bogdanov has written. In *Gvardii ryadovoy* (1978; The Soldier of the Guard) he collected nine of his short stories about the war. Bogdanov lives in Moscow.

*Works: Zvëzdnyj probeg* (short stories), 1927; *Pionerskij pokhod* (short stories), 1927; *Pervaja devuška* (novel), 1928, rev. ed., 1958; *Plenum druzej* (novel), 1934; *Zapiski voennogo korrespondenta* (war reports), 2 vols., 1941–42; *O smelykh i umelykh* (short stories), 1956; *Odin iz pervykh* (novel), 1961; *Kogda ja byl vožatym,* 1961; *Čudesniki* (pov.), 1967; *Gvardii rjadovoj* (short stories), 1978.—*Izbr.,* 2 vols., 1966.

*Secondary Lit.:* B. Grossman, in *Novyj mir* 1929:3; RSPP 1:1959; G. Pavlov, in *Oktjabr'* 1962:6; A. Vysockij, *I pust' nastupit utro,* 1967; "N. V. Bogdanovu—75 let," in *Lit. gazeta* April 15, 1981, p. 5.

**Bogomólov, Vladímir Ósipovich,** prose writer (b. July 3, 1926, Kirillovo, oblast Moscow). Bogomolov is of peasant ancestry. Bogomolov was still a schoolboy when he went in 1941 to the front, where he was wounded; in 1958 he completed his studies in journalism at the Party Institute; he lives in a home for seriously disabled veterans in Moscow. His volume of children's poetry, which appeared in Stalingrad in 1955, went unnoticed. However, his first war prose, the short story *Ivan* (1958; Eng. tr., "Ivan," in *The Third Flare,* 1958), made Bogomolov suddenly famous; his work won recognition as an example of an honest war literature. The short story was translated into 30 languages and was also an international success in the film version by A. Tarkovsky in 1962 (*Detstvo Ivana* [Ivan's Child-hood]). For reasons of health, Bogomolov wrote little in the following years; at first he produced more short stories, such as *Pervaya lyubov* (1958; First Love), *Serdtsa moyego bol* (1965; My Heartache), and *Zosya* (1965); finally he wrote *V avguste sorok chetvyortogo* (1974; In August 1944), a novel about the activity of Russian counterespionage (Smersh), which, despite its falsification of Polish underground activities, makes an interesting contribution to Russian war literature, exposing Stalin's role.

All of Bogomolov's prose is based on the events of war. It owes its reputation to its honest description of experiences and to its profound penetration into the psychology of men at war. It refrains from idealizing and making heroes of the people it depicts and does not try artificially to integrate segments into a historical context. The plot is unobtrusive but nevertheless holds the parts together and in its candor produces an impression that extends beyond the limits of the narrative. *Ivan* tells the story of a 12-year-old boy at the front who is cheated of his childhood by the tragedy and horror of war; *Zosya* is about a sensitive 19-year-old officer who, after a rigorous 800-kilometer advance, is unable to demonstrate his feelings of budding love during three days of leave in Poland. It is likely that the first-person narrative form that Bogomolov prefers has an autobiographical basis.

*Works:* Ivan (short story), 1959 (see above); Zosja (short story), in Znamja 1965:1; Serdca moego bol' (short stories), 1965, 2d ed., 1976; Rasskazy (short stories), 1970; V avguste sorok četvërtogo (novel), 1974; Moment istiny. Izbr., 1981; Serdca moego bol' (pov., short stories, and the novel Moment istiny), 1985.

*Secondary Lit.:* A. Černov, in Naš sovremennik 1966:4; L. Vol'pe, in Don 1966:5; V. O. Prikhod'ko, in Don 1971:4; V. Grubin, in Zvezda 1975:5; A. Drawicz, in Zapis, London, 1977:1; V. Galanov, in Znamja 1979:5.

**Bogoraz, Vladimir Germanovich.** See TAN, V. G.

**Bókov, Víktor Fyódorovich,** poet (b. Sept. 19 [Sept. 6], 1914, Yazvitsky, prov. Moscow). Bokov was of peasant ancestry. He worked as a turner; he attended the Gorky Literary Institute from 1934 to 1938. He was arrested and spent years in camps and in internal exile. In 1950 he published *Russkaya chastushka,* a folklore collection of Russian humorous songs. His own poetry, based on village life and nature, has been published since 1958. He lives in Moscow.

Bokov's poetry, which M. Prishvin first acknowledged prior to 1930, is always associated with nature. Bokov believes in nature's originality and life-giving power; he describes incidents from kolkhoz life or natural phenomena. His poetry is inspired by a strong faith in life and nature; it constantly varies this theme without imparting any particular profundity to it. Rhyme and rhythm are simple, although they are occasionally thrust aside by feeling, and make the reader constantly aware of Bokov's background in folk poetry. Because they forgo the pseudolyrical, his miniatures in prose, *Nad rekoy Istermoy: Zapiski poeta* (1960; Above the Isterma River: Notes of a Poet), attracted some attention from Soviet critics, but they, too, remain on the level of external observation: nature, the kolkhoz farmers, and the unusual word. "Many of his verses have become popular songs" (D. Brown).

*Works:* Russkaja častuska (compiled by Bokov), 1950; Jar-khmel' (poems), 1958; Zastrugi (poems), 1958; Nad rekoj Istermoj (short prose), 1960; Vesna Viktorovna (poems), 1961; Lirika (poems), 1964; U polja, u morja, u rek (poems), 1965; Leto-mjata (poems), 1966; Izbr., 1970; Stikhotvorenija i pesni (poems and songs), 1973; Poklon Rossii (lyric and narrative poems), 1976; Stežki—dorožki (poems), 1985.—Izbr. proizv., 2 vols., 1975.

*Secondary Lit.:* A. Platonov (1939), in his Razmyšlenija čitatelja, 1980; S. Surtakov, in Lit. gazeta May 20, 1961; N. Gubko, in Zvezda 1962:8; L. Bezrukov, in Moskva 1964:9; M. L'vov, in Znamja 1964:12; D. Kovalëv, in Lit. obozrenie 1975:3; I. Grinberg, in Bokov's Izbr. proizv., 2 vols., 1975; RSPPo 4:1981; A. Bobrov, in Lit. Rossija Dec. 27, 1985, p. 14; A. P'janov, in Lit. gazeta Feb. 19, 1986, p. 4.

**Bóndarev, Yúry Vasílyevich,** prose writer (b. March 15, 1924, Orsk, Orenburg region). Bondarev's father worked for the civil service. Bondarev moved to Moscow in 1931. In World War II he was an artillery officer; in 1944 he joined the Communist Party. In 1945 he wrote his first unpublished poems, which were influenced by S. Yesenin, A. Blok, and A. Tvardovsky. From 1946 to 1951 he studied at the Gorky Literary Institute (with K. Paustovsky, among others). In 1949 his first short story was published, followed by his first collection in 1953. Bondarev's narrative talent blossomed only after the 20th Party Congress in 1956 when he was able to make his candid depiction of the war and postwar period the theme of his longer prose works. Together with other authors (for example, G. Baklanov and V. Tendryakov), Bondarev wrote screenplays. Since 1967 he has been a member of the board of the Writers Union of the USSR and since 1971 one of the leading members of the secretariat there. In 1981 he was a delegate to the 26th Party Congress of the Communist Party of the Soviet Union. He lives in Moscow.

Bondarev made his first contribution to the new literature about the war that is based on the "truth of the trenches" and opposes the heroic adulteration of the Stalinist period with the povest *Batalyony prosyat ognya* (1957; The Battalions Are Asking for Fire), which depicts the sacrifice of battalions of soldiers by using the example of an event that occurred along the Dnieper in October 1943. *Posledniye zalpy* (1959; Eng. tr., *The Last Shots*, 1961) concerns responsibility for others, confirmation of humanity, and fear of death. "By his microscopic method of looking intently at a small group in a single incident, Bondarev produces a distinctly superior war novel" (D. Brown). Bondarev's novel *Tishina* (1962; Eng. tr., *Silence*, 1965), together with its sequel *Dvoye* (1964; The Two), belongs among the most significant books on the late Stalinist period and provoked considerable controversy in the Soviet Union. Using the example of a former officer at the front who is expelled from the university after his father, a victim of oppression, is arrested in a movingly depicted scene, "he reminds us with sharp and bitter power of what must not be allowed to be forgotten: of the period of the cult of personality, of the years of frightful unhappiness for the entire nation that our country paid for with many human victims" (K. Paustovsky). For *Goryachy sneg* (1970; Eng. tr., *The Hot Snow*, 1971), Bondarev chose the decisive moment in the battle for Stalingrad; here he repeatedly describes the same event from various perspectives. *Bereg* (1975; The Shore) combines two time periods: the end of the war and the contemporary present, including a trip the protagonist, a writer, makes to Hamburg. He was awarded the State Prize of the USSR in 1977. In *Vybor* (1980; Eng. tr., *The Choice*, 1983; State Prize of the USSR, 1983), Bondarev again opposes wartime and the present day, contrasting the fates of two comrades at the front: one becomes a well-recognized Soviet painter; the other chooses

to emigrate in 1945. In 1985 Bondarev published the novel *Igra* (Play), which, together with the novels *Bereg* and *Vybor*, forms a trilogy.

*Works: Na bol'šoj reke* (short stories), 1953; *Junost' komandirov* (pov.), 1956; *Baltal'ony prosjat ognja* (pov.), 1957; *Poslednie zalpy* (pov.), 1959 (see above); *Tišina* (novel), 1962 (see above); *Pozdnim večerom* (short stories), 1962; *Dvoe* (novel), 1964; *Gorjačij sneg* (novel), 1970 (see above); *Vzgljad v biografiju* (essays), 1971; *Bereg* (novel), in *Naš sovremennik* 1975:3; *Mgnovenija* (notes), 1979; *Čelovek nesët v sebe mir* (essays), 1980; *Vybor* (novel), 1981 (see above); *Igra* (novel), in *Novyj mir* 1985:1 and 2.—*Sobr. soč.*, 4 vols., 1973–74; *Izbr. proizv.*, 2 vols., 1977; *Sobr. soč.*, 6 vols., 1984–86.

*Secondary Lit.*: G. Baklanov, in *Novyi mir* 1959:7; I. Kozlov, in *Moskva* 1960:1 and in *Lit. gazeta* July 2, 1975, p. 4; K. Paustovskij, in *Izvestija* Nov. 28, 1962; *RSPP* 7(1):1971; A. Elkin, in *Moskva* 1973:2; O. Mikhajlov, 1976; V. Amlinskij, in *Novyj mir* 1980:4; Ju. Idaškin, 1980; and in *Lit. Rossija* June 6, 1984, p. 14; E. Gorbunova, 1981; F. Čapčakhov, in *Lit. gazeta* Jan. 1, 1981, p. 5; K. Mehnert, in his *The Russians and Their Favorite Books*, 1983; G. Semënov, in *Lit. gazeta* Feb. 27, 1985, p. 4; I. Dedkov, in *Voprosy lit.* 1986:7; A. Lanščikov, in *Moskva* 1986:12.

**Bondárin, Sergéy Aleksándrovich,** prose writer (b. Jan. 27 [Jan. 14], 1903, Odessa—d. Sept. 25, 1978, Moscow). Bondarin's father worked for the civil service. Bondarin grew up in Odessa; at the beginning of the 1920s he belonged to the local circle of writers there and was in particular a friend of E. Bagritsky. In 1929 Bondarin completed his study of law at the Institute of Political Economy in Odessa. Bondarin wrote poems, short stories, and journalistic articles. These suggest that he traveled extensively throughout the country, as does his first book intended for children, *Dyndyp iz doliny Durgun-Khotok* (1931; Dyndyp from the Valley of Durgun-Khotok), which is set in Mongolia. Protests about the lack of attention shown him, including those by V. Shklovsky and L. Slavin (*Lit. gazeta* Oct. 24, 1934), led to his first collection of prose works, *Pyat let* (1935; Five Years). Thereafter, Bondarin's works occasionally appeared in *Krasnaya nov*, including folkloric sketches based on personal experience, *Balkarskiye rasskazy* (1936; Balkar Tales). From 1940 until 1955 Bondarin's name vanished from the literary scene; he was in internal exile at the very least. During World War II he served with the Black Sea fleet, but his war stories appeared only after 1955; in the liberal almanac *Literaturnaya Moskva* (1956:2) he is represented with a brief short story on a religious topic. *Nash sovremennik* published, from 1961 to 1963, Bondarin's reminiscences about Bagritsky, Yu. Olesha, A. Vesyoly, I. Ilf, and I. Babel that are impressive for their human decency, expressiveness, and excellent eye for literary quality. The single somewhat longer prose work, *Malchik s kotomkoy* (1963; The Youth with Knapsack), describes with human warmth the fate of exiles in a taiga settlement using the example of a single day. In *Grozd vinograda* (1964; A Cluster of Grapes), Bondarin collected this prose work, his literary reminiscences, and some early short stories; after that he occasionally published similar books; in a reminiscence about Babel he speaks of the "spiritual martyrdom of the silent ones of art, always honest whether their silence be brief or long." This reference is also the key to understanding the fate of this scarcely noticed author. Bondarin lived in Moscow.

*Works: Dyndyp iz doliny Durgun-Khotok* (children's lit.), 1931; *Pjat' let* (short stories), 1935; *Balkarskie raskazy* (short stories), in *Krasnaja nov'* 1936:3; *Liričeskie rasskazy* (short stories), 1957; *Eduard Bagrickij* (essays), in *Novyj mir* 1961:4; *Nikola-na-vodakh* (short story), in *Naš sovremennik* 1961:3; *Razgovor so sverstnikom* (short stories), in *Naš sovremennik* 1962:5; *Mal'čik s kotomkoj* (pov.), in *Naš sovremennik* 1963:1; *Grozd' vinograda* (short stories and essays), 1964; *Povest' dlja syna* (pov., memoirs, short stories), 1967; *Zlataja cep'* (short stories), 1971; *Prikosnovenie k čeloveku* (short stories), 1973.

*Secondary Lit.:* V. Šklovskij and L. Slavin, in *Lit. gazeta* Oct. 24, 1934; A. Selivanovskij, in *Lit. kritik* 1935:10; I. Motjašov, in *Lit. Rossija* Oct. 11, 1963, pp. 10–11; N. Bannikov, in *Lit. Rossija* Sept. 11, 1964, pp. 14–15; M. Čudakova, in *Novyj mir* 1965:6; S. Grigor'janc, in *Družba narodov* 1968:3; V. Nikolaev, in *Lit. gazeta* Sept. 8, 1971, p. 7.

**Borísov, Leoníd Ilyích**, prose writer (b. June 5 [May 24], 1897, St. Petersburg—d. Dec. 4, 1972, Leningrad). Borisov's father was a tailor; his mother was in service to Professor Sharleman of the Academy of Arts. Borisov graduated from a gymnasium in 1915, then saw active duty in World War I, and had his first poem published; in 1919 he served with the Red Army, then worked for various Soviet institutions. Borisov began his literary career by writing poetry; he first gained popularity in 1927 with *Khod konyom* (Knight's Move), a novel that was translated into several languages. It tells the story of an intellectual who cannot find a niche for himself under Soviet conditions. During the Stalin period Borisov published only short prose works, which were criticized for their romantic tone. After the Party Resolution of Aug. 14, 1946 (see PARTY RESOLUTIONS ON LITERATURE), Borisov's povest about A. Grin, *Volshebnik iz Gel-Gyu* (1945; The Wizard from Gel-Gyu), earned him a negative characterization; he was nevertheless able to continue publishing. In 1955 he wrote a novel about Jules Verne that made it clear that Borisov, like Verne, was inclined toward unusual plot structures; in 1957 he wrote a novel about Robert Louis Stevenson. Borisov's prose frequently concerns itself with Russian writers and composers; in 1963, for instance, he used Sergey Rakhmaninov as the central figure of a rather sentimental, anti-Western story. These works are based not on research but on Borisov's own personal impressions and imagination. Toward the end of his life, Borisov wrote predominantly memoirs.

*Works: Khod koněm* (novel), 1927; *Nezakatnoe solnce* (short stories), 1940; *Volšebnik iz Gel'-G'ju* (pov.), 1945; *Žjul' Vern* (novel), 1955; *Pod flagom Katriony* (novel), 1957; *V toske i slave* (pov.), in *Zvezda* 1963:8–9; *Sčedryj rycar'. Cvety i slëzy* (pov.), 1964; *Svoi po serdcu* (novel and short stories), 1966; *Roditeli, nastavniki, poèty . . . Kniga v moej žizni* (memoirs), 1967, 1972; *Za kruglym stolom prošlogo* (memoirs), 1971.—*Izbr.*, 1957; *Izbr. proizv.*, 2 vols., 1968.

*Secondary Lit.:* E. Brandis, in *Zvezda* 1959:1; *RSPP* 1:1959; G. Filippov, in *Zvezda* 1967:8; S. Tkhorževskij, in *Prostor* 1973:2.

**Borísov, Trofím Mikháylovich**, prose writer (b. 1882 [exact date unknown], Guryev—d. Sept. 15, 1941, Tashkent). Borisov's father was a fisherman. Borisov served as a soldier in the Russo-Japanese War, then worked as a caviar fisherman with his father. After the Revolution he was manager of the fishing trust "Dalryba." In the last years of his life Borisov was a professional staff member of the Far Eastern Research Institute of Fishing Management and Oceanography.

Borisov wrote literary nonfiction in addition to well-received technical articles on fishing techniques. V. Lidin places him in the same category with V. Arsenyev as a "bard of the Far East," one primarily depicting the life of the fishermen of the Siberian rivers and the Pacific Ocean. Borisov is associated with Arsenyev not only by ties of personal friendship but also by his inner relationship to the Soviet Far Eastern landscape and his skill in recording his observations and experiences in beautiful Russian. Borisov attracted M. Gorky's attention in 1927 with his povest *Tayna malenkoy rechki* (The Secret of the Small River). Toward the end of his life Borisov wrote several books about life on the Amur and in Kamchatka.

*Works: Tajna malen'koj rečki* (pov.), 1927; *Po širokim plesam Amura* (articles), 1938; *Na beregakh Kamčatki* (articles), 1939; *Syn orla* (novel), 1939.—*Izbr. proizv.*, 1940; *Izbr.*, 2 vols., 1948; *Izbr. proizv.*, 2 vols., 1968.
*Secondary Lit.:* V. Lidin, in *Novyj mir* 1949:9 and in his *Ljudi i vstreči*, 1957; G. Gor, in *Zvezda* 1950:3; RSPP 1:1959.

**Borodín, Leoníd Ivánovich,** prose writer (b. April 14, 1938, Irkutsk). Borodin's father was a teacher. Borodin was expelled from Irkutsk University for his work with a student group, "Svobodnoye slovo" (The Free Word); in 1962, however, he was able to complete his studies at the pedagogical institute as a nonresident student. Borodin became the director of a school in the Leningrad region. In 1967 he was sentenced to six years of hard labor in the GULAG for being a member of VSKhSON (Vsesoyuzny Sotsial-khristiansky Soyuz Osvobozhdeniya Naroda [All-Union Social Christian Union for the Liberation of the People]). Borodin began writing poetry in prison; after his release in 1973 he shifted to prose. His texts reached the West through SAMIZDAT and were frequently published in the journal *Grani*. His first collection, *Povest strannogo vremeni* (1978; Tale of a Strange Time), was published in Frankfurt am Main; three povesti followed: *God chuda i pechali* (1981; Eng. tr., *The Year of Miracle and Grief,* 1984), *Tretya pravda* (1981; The Third Truth), and *Gologor* (1982; Gologor). In addition to his underground activity as a writer, Borodin was a coworker on the samizdat journal *Veche* and, after this journal was broken up by the KGB, he published a samizdat almanac, *Moskovsky sbornik* (Moscow Anthology), that espoused a religious and nationalistic Russian attitude. After being arrested again in May 1982, Borodin was sentenced to ten years of hard labor

and five years of internal exile in 1983. He was released in 1987 and lives in Moscow. In 1983 the French PEN Club awarded him its Peace Prize.

Borodin's prose recounts unusual incidents from Soviet daily life. It reveals a clear Christian faith and a Russian-Siberian feeling of national identity. Borodin supports his specific message with a narrative rich in contrasts. *Povest strannogo vremeni* shows a family tragically ruined by the father's sentencing to a labor camp. *Tretya pravda* describes the fates of Russians in Siberia and reveals faith as the only valid truth. In *Gologor*, a Moscow woman is transplanted into the raw, coarse life of Siberian fur hunters. In *God chuda i pechali,* a 12-year-old living in the Soviet period comes face to face with legendary figures from Lake Baikal.

*Works: O russkoj intelligencii* (scholarly articles), in *Grani*, Frankfurt am Main, 96:1975; *Stikhi* (poems), in *Grani* 105:1977; *Povest' strannogo vremeni* (short stories), Frankfurt am Main, 1978; *God čuda i pečali* (pov.), Frankfurt am Main, 1981 (see above); *Gologor* (pov.), in *Grani* 124:1982; *Rasstavanie* (novel), Frankfurt am Main, 1984; *Tret'ja pravda* (pov.), Frankfurt am Main, 1984; *Pravily igry* (pov.), in *Grani* 140:1986.
*Secondary Lit.:* Ju. Mal'cev. *Freie Russische Literatur 1955–80,* Frankfurt am Main–Berlin, 1981, pp. 281–83; Ju. Voznesenskaja, in *Russkaja mysl'*, Paris, June 23, 1983, p. 7.

**Borodín, Sergéy Petróvich** (pseud. until 1941, Amir Sargidzhan), prose writer (b. Oct. 8 [Sept. 25], 1902, Moscow—d. June 22, 1974, Tashkent). Borodin attended secondary school in Belevo (prov. Tula) from 1913 to 1920, then participated in the work of the local PROLETKULT studio. He took part in ethnographic expeditions to Bukhara in 1923 and to Samarkand in 1925–26. In 1926 he completed studies at the Bryusov Institute of Literature and Art (specialty: folklorism). Borodin spent a considerable period of time in the Soviet Far East (1928), Kazakhstan (1929), Tadzhikistan (1931), and Armenia (1933). In 1931 he broke with PEREVAL, to which group he had belonged for some time. He became a member of the Communist Party in 1943. Borodin moved to Tashkent in 1951.

Borodin published his first poems and essays in 1915. In the 1930s he wrote short novels and stories based on his stays in remote regions of the USSR. His natural talent lay in the historical novel. His first, *Dmitry*

Donskoy (1941; Eng. tr., Dmitri Donskoi, 1944), is set in the period of Mongol domination; it is one of the many novels about Russian historical figures written at the time, the result of the changed attitude of the Communist Party toward its own history (Stalin Prize for 1941, 2d class). His second historical work, a trilogy entitled Zvyozdy nad Samarkandom (1953–73; The Stars above Samarkand), paints a vivid picture of Central Asia and the Transcaucasus in the 14th and 15th centuries, with Tamerlane as its central figure. The trilogy's third part, Bely kon (1974; The White Horse), is incomplete; it consists of a few isolated chapters. Borodin also translated works from Tadzhik, Uzbek, and Chuvash.

Works: Poslednjaja Bukhara (novel), 1932; Egiptjanin (novel), 1933, 1969; Master ptic (short stories), 1934; Dmitrij Donskoj (novel), 1941, 1974 (see above); Zvëzdy nad Samarkandom (novel-trilogy), 1955–73, vol. 1 of which is Khromoj Timur, 1955; Molnienosnyj Bajazet (novel), 1973 (advance publication in Lit. Rossija Sept. 9, 1966, pp. 12–14, and Družba narodov 1972:3, 1973:2); Belyj kon' (chapters from an unfinished novel), in Družba narodov 1977:9.—Sobr. soč., 5 vols., 1958–60; 6 vols., 1973–77.

Secondary Lit.: E. Starikova, in Novyj mir 1956:7; G. Vladimirov, Poèzija pravdy, Taškent, 1959, and foreword to Borodin's Sobr. soč., 1958; RSPP 1:1959; V. Akimov, Taškent, 1972; N. Bannikov, in Lit. Rossija Sept. 29, 1972, p. 11, and June 28, 1974, p. 14; L. Mil', foreword to Borodin's Sobr. soč., 1973–77; V. Osockij, in Znamja 1980:9.

**Borshchagóvsky, Aleksándr Mikháylovich,** prose writer (b. Oct. 14, [Oct. 1], 1913, Belaya Tserkov). Borshchagovsky's father was a journalist. Borshchagovsky completed his studies at the Kiev Theater Institute in 1935 and was admitted to the Communist Party in 1940. Between 1946 and 1948 he published several works about Ukrainian dramatists. He was sharply attacked for his criticism of the pseudoconflict, obligatory in Soviet literary works, "between the good and the better" (see COSMOPOLITANISM; THEORY OF CONFLICTLESSNESS); in late 1948 he lost his position on the editorial staff of Novy mir. Borshchagovsky began writing fiction in 1953. He lives in Moscow.

Borshchagovsky's literary career begins with the historical novel Russky flag (1953; The Russian Flag), which has as its subject a relatively unknown episode from the Crimean War, the defense of Petropavlovsk (on the Kamchatka Peninsula) against the Anglo-French fleet. Minutely researched, the novel, with its large number of historical and fictional characters, suffers from an unbalanced narrative flow, not least of all because of Borshchagovsky's dependence on numerous documents. Borshchagovsky gave up his original plan to write additional historical works associated with the Kamchatka Peninsula, opting instead for topical povesti about his experiences there. His Propali bez vesti (1955; Missing, Presumed Dead), the true story of six Soviet seamen who were rescued off the coast of Kamchatka after being shipwrecked for 82 days, attracted particular attention. The limitations of Borshchagovsky's literary adaptation of this incident from early 1954 are evident in the degree to which he fails to generate suspense, to distinguish the individual characters from each other, or to illustrate their psychological states. His drama Medvezhya shkura (1958; The Bear Skin), about the pioneers who first opened up the Soviet Far East in modern times, is likewise set in the Kamchatka area. In his short stories, assembled in such collected volumes as Ne chuzhiye (1978; Not Strangers), Borshchagovsky presents everyday experiences while touching on ethical and interpersonal problems. Primarily in several short stories from the 1960s, he advocates candor and courage in dealing with the petty problems of everyday life, which is consistent with his appreciation of K. Paustovsky's work. Like Yu. Trifonov, V. Aksyonov, and B. Okudzhava, Borshchagovsky contributed to the series "Ardent Revolutionaries" by writing Sechen: Povest ob Ivane Babushkine (1978; January: The Story of Ivan Babushkin).

Works: Russkij flag (novel), 1953, 1971; Propali bez vesti (pov.), 1955; Sedaja čajka (pov.), 1958 (Eng. tr., "The Grey Sea-Gull," in Soviet Literature 1957:10); Ostrov vsekh nadežd (pov.), 1962; Noev kovčeg (short stories), 1968; Mlečnyj put' (novel), 1970; Gde poselitsja kuznec (novel), in Sibirskie ogni 1974:11–12, 1975:1–2, separate ed., 1976; Tri topolja (novel and short stories), 1974; Ne čužie (short stories), 1978; Sečen': Povest' ob Ivane Babuškine (pov.), 1978; Damskij portnoj (play), in Teatr 1980:10; Byla pečal' (pov.), in Oktjabr' 1981:9; Portret po pamjati, in Oktjabr' 1984:3.—Izbr. proizv., 2 vols., 1982.

Secondary Lit.: R. Messer, in Zvezda 1954:3; N. Panov. in Lit. gazeta Sept. 3, 1955; V. Sokolov, in Novyj mir 1968:8; V. Surganov, in Voprosy lit. 1971:8; R. Podol'nyj, in Lit.

*obozrenie* 1975:6; G. Štorm, in *Lit. gazeta* Jan. 28, 1975, p. 4; L. Kanunova, in *Zvezda* 1979:11; E. Galanova, in *Lit. Rossija* Dec. 17, 1982; *I. Pitljar*, in *Novyj mir* 1984:12.

**Bragínsky, Emíl** (pseud. of Emmanuél) **Veniamínovich**, and **Ryazánov, Eldár Aleksándrovich**, collaborating playwrights (Braginsky b. Nov. 19, 1921, Moscow; Ryazanov b. Nov. 18, 1927, Samara). Braginsky completed his study of law at Moscow University in 1953; Ryazanov graduated from the Faculty of Directors at the All-Union Film Institute (VGIK) in 1950 and worked successfully as a film director after 1956. For several years, Braginsky wrote for film and theater independently; he joined with Ryazanov for the first time on the *povest Beregis avtomobilya* (1964; Beware of the Car). In 1966 they reworked this into a script for a film that Yu. Smelkov in 1978 still called "the best comedy film of the postwar period." In addition to other film scripts that they published in the collection *Smeshnye nevesyolye istorii* (1979; Ridiculous, Unhappy Stories) after reworking them and expanding them around the figure of a storyteller, they wrote several comedies that enjoyed quite exceptional popularity with the public. *S lyogkim parom!* (1969; Have Fun in the Steam Bath!) was performed 5,398 times in 1970, and with 7,030 performances in 128 theaters in 1972–73 *Sosluzhivtsy* (1971; Fellow Employees) attained a performance maximum unsurpassed by any other theater piece. These plays were followed by *Rodstvenniki* (1973; Relatives), *Pritvorshchiki* (1975; Pretenders), *Garazh* (1977; Garage), and *Amoralnaya istoriya* (1977; An Amoral Story), which they collected in the volume *Ironiya sudby, ili S lyogkim parom!* (1983; The Irony of Fate; or, Have Fun in the Steam Bath!). In 1977 Braginsky and Ryazanov were awarded the State Prize of the USSR for the title play in this volume. They live in Moscow.

The writer Braginsky and the experienced film director Ryazanov form a team of authors who have, with great adroitness, pledged their allegiance to the genre of popular entertainment. Their plays are based on an unusual occurrence, are set amidst the reality of Soviet life, seize upon the grievances of daily life (for example, shortage of apartments, inadequacy of hotels, attempted bribery, uniform construction, deficiencies in supplies, purchases from abroad, standing in line) using harmlessly comic satire in the dialogue, and confine the plot to interpersonal relations to a great extent. Their mastery of the scene of action determines the success of their plays and films. With the reliable artifice of a comedy of errors, *S lyogkim parom!* brings a man into the wrong apartment on the evening before his wedding. *Sosluzhivtsy* illustrates the human dynamics existing among six people in a Soviet office. *Pritvorshchiki* combines a flirtation and the pangs of love with professional concerns in the field of Soviet film and shows pretenders in all walks of life.

*Works* (with E. Rjazanov): *Beregis' avtomobilja!* (pov.), in *Molodaja gvardija* 1964:10; *Zigzag udači* (pov.), in *Naš sovremennik* 1968:4; *Sosluživcy* (play), in *Teatr* 1971:9; *Stariki—razbojniki* (film script), in *Iskusstvo kino* 1972:1–2; *Pritvorščiki* (play), in *Teatr* 1976:12; *Smešnye nesvesëlye istorii* (film script), 1979; *Ironija sud'by, ili S lëgkim parom!* (play), 1983 (also contains *Pritvorščiki*; *Sosluživcy*; *Garaž*; *Amoral'naja istorija*; *Rodstvenniki*).

*Works* (by Braginskij alone): *Pjat' turistskikh rasskazov* (short stories), in *Molodaja gvardija* 1965:10; *Počti smešnaja istorija* (film script), in *Iskusstvo kino* 1976:11; *Sueta suet*; *Učitel' penija* (film script), 1979; *Igra voobraženija* (play), in *Teatr* 1980:8; *Rabotaju v neprestižnom žanre* (essays), in *Teatr* 1982:11; *Radovat'sja nado umet'* (essays), in *Sovremennaja dramaturgija* 1983:2; *Avantjuristka (Takoj neponjatnyj vizit)* (play), in *Teatr* 1984:9.

*Secondary Lit.*: E. Baumann, in *Iskusstvo kino* 1969:1; N. Zorkaja, in *Iskusstvo kino* 1971:11; R. Krečetova, in *Teatr* 1972:2; V. Mikhalkovič, in *Iskusstvo kino* 1976:6; Ju. Smelkov, in *Lit. obozrenie* 1978:8; I. Vasilinina, in *Teatr* 1982:9 and 1985:11.

**Braun, Nikoláy Leopóldovich**, poet (b. Jan. 15 [Jan. 2], 1902, Parakhino, prov. Tula—d. Feb. 12, 1975, Leningrad). Braun's father was a teacher. Braun spent his childhood in central Russia, attended school in Oryol, then went on to study in Leningrad, where his first volume of poetry appeared in 1926. He finished his studies in literary criticism and theory at the Leningrad Pedagogical Institute in 1931. Braun then worked as a teacher and a contributor to various journals in Leningrad. During World War II he served with the navy; he was later assigned to the besieged city of Leningrad as a frontline reporter. Between 1934 and 1970 Braun participated in all congresses of the Writers Unions of the USSR and the RSFSR, but occupied no posts. He lived in Leningrad.

Braun's early poetry is influenced by

B. Pasternak, O. Mandelshtam, and N. Ti-khonov; it strives to achieve a defamiliarizing effect and delights in experimentation, without ever equaling its models. In the course of time Braun's verse became realistic. It is more descriptive and visual than narrative, and, in his later work, retrospective. Much of it belongs to nature poetry; occasionally it has a patriotic touch. There are also numerous poems that address very different poets, such as A. Pushkin and N. Nekrasov, A. Akhmatova, M. Tsvetayeva, and A. Fadeyev. Without descending to cheap propaganda, Braun dealt with current topics in all of his creative periods as well; his work was always published and recognized by the critics.

Works: Mir i master (poems), 1926; Novyj krug (poems), 1928; Vylazka v buduščee (poems), 1931; Vernost' (poems), 1936; Zven'ja (poems), 1937; Morskaja slava (poems), 1945; Doliny Rodiny moej (poems), 1947; Zemlja v svetu (poems), 1955; Stikhotvorenija (poems), 1958; Novaja lirika (poems), 1958; Živopis' (poems), 1963; Tol'ko o žizni (poems), 1972.— Izbr., 2 vols., 1972.

Secondary Lit.: V. Roždestvenskij, in Zvezda 1959:7; V. Kuznecov, in Oktjabr' 1968:10 and in Lit. i sovremennost' 9:1968; B. Solov'ëv, in Neva 1973:5; I. Samojlov, in Zvezda 1977:1; G. Filippov, 1981; RSPPo 4:1981.

**Brémener, Maks Solomónovich,** prose writer (b. Nov. 16, 1926, Moscow—d. Jan. 23, 1983, Moscow). Bremener's father was a doctor. Bremener studied at the Gorky Literary Institute, completing the course in 1949; one of his teachers, K. Paustovsky, subsequently became a personal friend. Bremener's first stories for children appeared in 1947; his first collection was published in 1955. Bremener's short stories consistently served the cause of honesty in the presentation of life. He frequently wrote about children between the ages of ten and fifteen. Because Bremener's prose pieces (such as Pervaja stupen [1957; The First Step]) did not idealize their subjects, they were not accepted without criticism. Bremener published from time to time collections of his short stories, such as Chur, ne igra! (1962; Hey, This Is No Game!). He also wrote literary criticism. He lived in Moscow.

Bremener's careful prose presents the problems of children in a psychologically astute and often humorous manner. It reveals a talent for observation and a refined sensitivity to the pain of growing up. In Pust ne soshlos s otvetom (1956; So What if the Answers Don't Tally), Bremener advocates honesty in education and attacks an essential evil inherent in ideological tactics: the method of inflating small mistakes into monstrous crimes in order to create a hostile image of the enemy and make a pretense of one's own vigilance. "Tebe posvyashchayetsya . . ." (1965; "Dedicated to You . . .") addresses the problem of unpunished and inexpiable guilt in daily school life. The povest Prisutstviye dukha (1969; The Presence of the Spirit) deals with ethical problems in an occupied area during World War II. Bremener's work attempts realistically to expose wrong behavior in everyday situations.

Works: Slučaj so Stepnym (short stories), 1955; Pust' ne sošlos' s otvetom! (pov.), in Junost' 1956:10; Peredača vedětsja iz klassa (pov.), 1959; Tolja—Trilli (short stories), 1960; Čur, ne igra! (short stories), 1962; "Tebe posvjaščaetsja . . ." (pov. and short stories), 1965; Prisutstvie dukha (pov.), 1969; Grenadskaja volost' (short stories), 1978.

Secondary Lit.: A. Šarov, in Lit. gazeta Dec. 3, 1955; I. Dik, in Lit. gazeta Nov. 15, 1956; E. Gal'perina, in Novyj mir 1956:12; I. Mačulin, in Lit. gazeta Sept. 14, 1957; V. Dmitrievskij, in Teatr 1966:2; P. Borisov, in V mire knig 1970:5; "M. S. Bremeneru—50 let," in Lit. gazeta Dec. 1, 1976, p. 4; I. Andreeva, in Detskaja lit. 1980:1.

**Brézhnev, Leoníd Ilyích,** Party official, bearer of the Lenin Prize for Literature, 1979 (b. Dec. 19 [Dec. 6], 1906, Kamenskoye—d. Nov. 10, 1982, Moscow). Brezhnev completed his training at an agricultural technical school in 1927 and joined the Communist Party in 1931. During World War II he was head of the political division of an army. Until 1952, when Brezhnev was appointed one of the secretaries of the Central Committee of the Party, he occupied various positions of political leadership in the Ukraine and in the Moldavian Republic. After Stalin's death, Brezhnev was removed from his position as secretary of the Central Committee and made deputy head of the Main Political Administration of the army and navy. Favored by Khrushchev, Brezhnev was sent to the Virgin Lands in Kazakhstan as a Party leader after 1954; in 1956 he regained his position as a secretary of the Central Committee. After Khrushchev's fall in 1964, Brezhnev assumed the leadership of the Communist Party of the Soviet Union and held this position until his death. In 1978, Brezhnev, who by then also occupied the highest governmental and military posts, published his memoirs in three thin booklets followed by an additional booklet in 1981. These memoirs, which are completely without literary value, were published in print runs of several million copies and were extolled as political and literary trend-setting works, awarded the highest literary prize, and propagated through opera, drama, and film. Brezhnev was not known to be a member of the Writers Union of the USSR.

Brezhnev's writings describe his work in the military, in the development of Ukrainian industry, and in the Virgin Lands, stressing his own accomplishments. *Tselina* (1978; Eng. tr., *The Virgin Lands*, 1979) is the first Party document in a long time to mention Khrushchev's name again, even if disparagingly.

*Works: Malaja zemlja* (memoirs), 1978 (Eng. tr., *Little Land*, 1978); *Vozroždenie* (memoirs), 1978 (Eng. tr., *Rebirth*, in his *Trilogy*, 1980); *Celina* (memoirs), 1978 (see above); *Vospominanija* (memoirs), 1981 (Eng. tr., *Memoirs*, 1982).

*Secondary Lit.:* E. Ètkind, in *Vremja i my*, Tel Aviv, 30:1978; L. Rojtman, in *Russkaja mysl'*, Paris, Jan. 4, 1979, p. 10; F. Ph. Ingold, in *Schweizer Monatshefte* 1979:2; *Leonid Il'ič Brežnev: Kratkij biografičeskij očerk*, 3d ed., 1982; V. Aksënov, V. Nekrasov, V. Vojnovič, et al., in *Russkaja mysl'* Nov. 18, 1982, pp. 4–5.

**Bródsky, Iósif Aleksándrovich,** poet (b. May 24, 1940, Leningrad). Brodsky's father was a photographer. Brodsky's first poems date from 1958; he considers himself a member of the " 'Generation of 1956,' the generation whose first primal scream was the Hungarian Uprising. Pain, turmoil, grief, shame at our helplessness" (in *Die Zeit* Nov. 24, 1972). Very few of his poems were published in Soviet almanacs; some appeared in 1959–60 in the SAMIZDAT journal *Sintaksis*. Brodsky was not a member of the Writers Union, only of the Writers Trade Union, and he earned a living translating from English, Spanish, Polish, and Serbo-Croatian. On Feb. 18, 1964, Brodsky was sentenced to five years of forced labor for "parasitism," that is, the failure to be engaged in socially recognized work. After massive protests by writers such as A. Akhmatova, K.ʼ Chukovsky, K. Paustovsky, and S. Marshak and the outrage expressed by the world media at his trial, Brodsky was released after approximately one and one-half years. F. Vigdorova stenographically recorded the course of the court session. This material was distributed as a white paper in samizdat and was published in New York. In June 1972 Brodsky was forced to leave the Soviet Union within the scope of the policy permitting Jewish emigration. On June 4, 1972, he wrote: "Poets always return, either personally or on paper." Brodsky lives in New York. In Leningrad between 1972 and 1974 V. Maramzin compiled a five-volume (2,000 pages) typewritten collection of Brodsky's poems and translations.

Brodsky's poetry, which met with the early acclaim of A. Akhmatova, was published in Russian in the United States as early as 1965 and 1970. After his emigration, Brodsky also began writing poetry in English. Brodsky's poetry, which enjoys an excellent reputation in emigration, is characterized by a tragic frame of mind and is essentially apolitical, never anti-Soviet, often religiously bound up with the Old Testament; many verses revolve around the issue of death. Brodsky's poems are metaphysical, with a strong consciousness of words and letters that extends into the playful. The highly acclaimed "Bolshaya elegiya Dzhonnu Donnu" (1963; Great Elegy to John Donne) reveals, together with a penchant for metaphysics, the narrative element present in several of his poems. He also wrote personal confessional and contemplative poetry. Brodsky's poems are rich in imagery and diverse in structure. He remains true to the classical form and in so doing reveals his delight in the wealth of linguistic structures. In 1987 Brodsky was awarded the Nobel Prize.

*Works:* Poems, in *Grani*, Frankfurt am Main, 56, 68, 70, 72, 76:1964–70 and regularly in *Kontinent*, Paris, beginning with 1:1974; *Stikhotvorenija i poèmy* (lyric and narrative poems), New York, 1965; *Pamjati T. S. Èliota* (poems), in *Den' poèzii*, Leningrad, 1967; *Ostanovka v pustyne* (poems), New York, 1970; *Blick zurück ohne Zorn* (essay), in *Die Zeit* Nov. 24, 1972; *20 sonetov k Marii Stjuart* (poems), in *Russian Literature Triquarterly* 11:1975; *Čast' reči* (poems), Ann Arbor (Eng. tr., *A Part of Speech*, 1980); *Konec prekrasnoj èpokhi* (poems), Ann Arbor, 1977; *Rimskie elegii* (poems), New York, 1982; *Novye stansy k Avguste* (poems), Ann Arbor, 1983; *Mramor* (play), Ann Arbor, 1984; *Less Than One: Selected Essays*, New York, 1986.

*Translations: Elegy to John Donne and Other Poems*, 1967; *Selected Poems*, 1973.

*Secondary Lit.:* E. Rajs, in *Grani* 59:1965; report on his trial, in *Vozdušnye puti*, New York, 4:1965; Ju. Ivask, in *Novyj žurnal*, New York, 79:1965, 102:1971, and in *Mosty*, New

York, 12:1966; N. Bethell, in *J. B. Elegy to John Donne . . . ,* London, 1967; G. Kline, in *Russian Literature Triquarterly* 1:1971 and in *10 Bibliographies of 20th Century Russian Literature,* Ann Arbor, 1977, and with R. D. Sylvester, in *MERSL* 3:1979; K. Verheul, in *Russian Literature Triquarterly* 6:1973 and in *Dutch Contributions to the Seventh International Congress of Slavists,* 1973; A. Losev, in *Kontinent* 14:1977; J. E. Knox, Diss., Univ. of Texas at Austin, 1978; E. Ezerskaja, in *Vremja i my,* Jerusalem, 63:1981; T. Venclova, in *Sintaksis* 10:1982; M. Kreps, Ann Arbor, 1984; V. Polukhina, in *Wiener Slawistischer Almanach* 17:1986; *Poètika Brodskogo,* Tenafly, N.J., 1986.

**Bryúsov, Valéry Yákovlevich,** poet, prose writer, literary scholar (b. Dec. 13 [Dec. 1], 1873, Moscow—d. Oct. 9, 1924, Moscow). Bryusov's father was a merchant. In 1892 Bruysov began studying history at Moscow University (graduated 1899). He remained active as a critic and scholar throughout his life; for example, he edited A. Pushkin's letters in 1903, and in *Dalyokiye i blizkiye* (1912; Far and Near) he compiled essays on Russian poets from F. Tyutchev to his own contemporaries. Bryusov, who began writing poems as a child, was impressed by modern French poetry as a student and published three small collections, *Russkiye simvolisty* (1894–95; Russian Symbolists), of primarily his own poems bearing the influence of Charles Baudelaire, Paul Verlaine, and Stéphane Mallarmé. The following volumes, *Chefs d'oeuvre* (1895), *Me eum esse* (1897), *Tertia vigilia* (1900), and *Urbi et orbi* (1903), reveal in their titles and contents his predisposition to Western European classicism and his great scientifically grounded interest in foreign and ancient cultures. From 1904 to 1909 he managed the most important symbolist journal, *Vesy* (The Scales), and became a leading figure among the Moscow symbolists. *Stephanos* (1906), his fifth volume of poetry, contributed considerably to his renown. Bryusov continued to publish much of his own poetry and to translate from many languages but also shifted to prose and wrote short stories with exuberantly adventurous and exotic plots as well as historical novels such as *Ognenny angel* (1908; Eng. tr., *The Fiery Angel,* 1930) and *Altar pobedy* (1911–12; The Altar of Victory). His sixth volume of poetry, *Vse napevy* (1909; All Melodies), reveals the further development of his experiments with rhyme and linguistic structuring. Bryusov often made trips to Western Europe. An edition of his works in 25 volumes was initiated in 1913–14. During World War I, Bryusov worked as an editor and translator from the Armenian. After the Revolution, Bryusov joined the Communist government, becoming in 1920 the only symbolist poet who did not emigrate to join the Communist Party, and held positions in cultural institutions. In 1921 he founded the academy for literature and art that was later named for him. In addition to these activities, Bryusov continued to work as an author and literary scholar.

A high degree of cool deliberateness marks Bryusov's creative work. His first volumes were designed to promote symbolism in Russia. His major concern was not a symbolist world view but a new order of aesthetic criteria. The mastery of problems of form with great discipline and precision is characteristic of his work. "In his usage, the Russian language has a steely sound, like classical Latin" (Eliasberg). This highly educated poet also often worked with classical motifs; historical and mythological themes determine a large part of his work that has neither national nor social ties. Bryusov is enthused about the heroic and views love rationally, even as cruel and sadistic. Under the influence of Emile Verhaeren he also gave form to the theme of the large city at the beginning of this century; in "Kon bled" (1903–4; The Pale Horse) he mixed this theme with an apocalyptic vision. "He made a great contribution as a pioneer in the shift from the strict meters of syllabo-tonic verse, which Bloc in particular developed further" (Lewis). Bryusov's early prose work presents people who are anarchically uninhibited because they are hopelessly ruined; their most consummate depiction probably appears in the utopian short story *Respublika Yuzhnogo Kresta* 1905; Eng. tr. in *The Republic of the Southern Cross and Other Stories,* 1918). His later work reflects his preference for historical, even ancient, material and runs parallel to the work of D. Merezhkovsky. *Ognenny angel* takes place in 16th-century Germany and, together with autobiographical elements, especially reveals a profound preoccupation with the occult. *Altar pobedy* is set in 4th-century Rome and reflects Bryusov's interest in religious questions. Both are characterized by cultural-historical precision and a cool, cleverly chosen narrative perspective. A sequel to *Altar pobedy* that deals with the final Christianization of Rome, *Yupiter poverzhenny* (Jupiter Overthrown), remained incomplete at his death and only appeared in 1934. His most important literary work preceded World War I. After this poet—whose view of life was primarily rational and scientific—had joined the new regime, he shifted to more administrative activities. In the view of Soviet émigré and Western critics, the new poems he wrote between 1917 and 1924 are below his earlier level.

Works: Russkie simvolisty (ed. by Brjusov, mostly his own poems), 3 vols. 1894–95; Chefs d'oeuvre (poems), 1895; Me eum esse (poems), 1897; Tertia vigilia (poems), 1900; Urbi et orbi (poems), 1903; Respublika Južnogo Kresta (short story), in Vesy 1905:12 (see above); Stephanos. Venok (poems), 1906; Ognennyj angel (pov.), 1908, 2d enl. ed., 1909 (reprinted, Munich, 1971) (see above); Puti i pereput'ja (poems), 3 vols, 1908–9; Vse napevy (poems), 1909; Zerkalo tenej (poems), 1912; Dalëkie i blizkie (essays), 1912 (reprinted, Letchworth, 1973); Al'tar pobedy (pov.), 1913 (reprinted, Munich, 1969); Stikhi Nelli (poems), 1913; Poslednie mečty (poems), 1920; Mig (poems), 1922; Dali (poems), 1922; Mea! (poems), 1924; Osnovy stikhovedenija (scholarly articles), 1924 (reprinted, Letchworth, 1971); Dnevniki 1891–1900 (diary), 1927 (reprinted, Letchworth, 1973); Moj Puškin (scholarly articles), 1929 (reprinted, Munich, 1970); Neizdannaja proza (various prose), 1934; Stikhotvorenija i poèmy (lyric and narrative poems), 1961.—Polnoe sobr. soč. i perevodov 1–4, 12, 13, 15, 21, 1913–14; Izbr. proizv., 3 vols., 1926; Izbr. soč., 2 vols., 1955; 1 vol., 1959; Sobr. soč., 7 vols., 1973–75.

Secondary Lit.: V. Žirmunskij, 1921; D. E. Maksimov, 1940, 1969; K. Močul'skij, Paris, 1962; A. Schmidt, V. B's Beitrag zur Lit. Theorie, Munich, 1963; T. I. Binyon, Bibliography . . . , in Oxford Slavonic Papers, 1965; R. Zayni, Diss., Vienna, 1972; M. P. Rice, Ann Arbor, 1975; D. B. Arthur, Diss., Univ. of Texas at Austin, 1976; B. Flickinger, Munich, 1976; Bibliografija, ed. E. S. Danieljan, 1976; Lit. nasledstvo 85:1976; S. S. Grečiškin, A. V. Lavrov, in Wiener Slawistischer Almanach 1–2:1978: S. Gindin, in Voprosy lit. 1978:7; K. Lewis, in MERSL 3:1979.

**Bubennóv, Mikhaíl Semyónovich,** prose writer (b. Nov. 21 [Nov. 8], 1909, Vtoroye Polomoshnevo, Altai region—d. Oct. 3, 1983). Bubennov was of peasant descent. After nine years of schooling he became a village schoolteacher in 1927 and began publishing at the same time. He was admitted to the Communist Party in 1951. Bubennov belonged to the board of the Writers Union of the RSFSR from 1965 to 1975; he lived in Moscow.

Bubennov's short story Bessmertiye (1940; Eng. tr., "Immortality," in Soviet Literature 1957:6) was written with the aim of glorifying the heroism of the Bolsheviks in the Civil War. It was attacked for its sketchiness of character, its lack of convincingness in the characters' behavior, and its inflated style. Bubennov's major work is the war novel Belaya beryoza (1947; Eng. tr., The White Birch, 1949), the first part of which received a Stalin Prize (for 1947, 1st class). The second part (1952), which, in the context of the cult of personality, characterized Stalin not only as a brilliant army commander but also, as Mayakovsky expressed it, as "the most earthly of all the people who have ever walked the earth," no longer met with approval after 1956 because it had been written under the influence of the THEORY OF CONFLICTLESSNESS. Bubennov abandoned its sequel and chose instead to write novels on the Party-advocated themes of "the heroism of youth in the struggle for land reclamation" (Orlinaya step [1959; Eagle Steppe]) and contemporary industrial construction in Siberia (Stremnina [1971; The Rapids]). In his book Zarnitsy krasnogo leta (1977; Lightning of the Red Summer), Bubennov subordinates the depiction of his own childhood to the work's propagandistic message.

Works: Bessmertie (short stories), 1940 (see above); Belaja berëza (novel), 1947 (see above); Orlinaja step' (novel), in Oktjabr' 1959:7–10, separate ed., 1964; Stremnina (novel), 1971; Zarnicy krasnogo leta, in Molodaja gvardija 1977:1–2; Svetlaja dal' junosti (pov.), in Moskva 1983:5.—Izbr. proizv. 2 vols., 1973; Sobr. soč., 4 vols., 1981–82.

Secondary Lit.: M. Kornev, in Novyj mir 1941:1; A. Barsuk, K. Sekušina, in Zvezda 1952:9; N. Kalustova, 1956; RSPP 1:1959; E. Osetrov, in Naš sovremennik 1972:11 and foreword to Bubennov's Izbr. proizv., 1973; M. Lapšin, in Moskva 1979:11.

**Budántsev, Sergéy Fyódorovich,** prose writer (b. Dec. 10 [Nov. 28], 1896, Glebkovo, prov. Ryazan—d. Feb. 6, 1940 [?], while imprisoned). Budantsev's father was an estate manager. Budantsev studied philology at Moscow University in 1915–16. Between 1916 and 1918 he was in Persia; afterward he worked as a journalist in the Caucasus and central Russia. Budantsev began his literary career in 1910; he achieved recognition with his novel *Myatezh* (1922; The Revolt), which reflects the conflict between the Bolsheviks and the Socialist Revolutionaries and their differing interpretations of the Revolution. Budantsev emphasized the experimental nature of his imagery-rich style by using different type-faces. After coming to an agreement with D. Furmanov, who had also written a novel with the same title, Budantsev changed the title of his novel to *Komandarm* (The Army Commander) in 1927. His novel *Sarancha* (The Locust), which appeared in *Krasnaya nov* (1927:9), shows the desolation in Turkestan after the Revolution; it was criticized for not presenting the typical. Budantsev's strong interest in psychology is particularly apparent in *Povest o stradaniyakh uma* (1929; A Tale of the Sufferings of Mind), "an altogther unusual work in Soviet literature" (Struve); the work is set in the previous century and centers on the two suicide attempts of a scholar who sees his personal problems in a conscious opposition to society. Budantsev, who lived in poor economic conditions, was a friend of A. Platonov. A concise survey of Budantsev's heterogeneous and critical works (he is supposed to have written some 50 short stories) is not yet possible. About 1937 he became a victim of the government purges. After his REHABILITATION around 1957, two books came out simultaneously in 1959, one of them his novel *Pisatelnitsa* (The Woman Writer), written in 1933–36. Budantsev attracts little attention today.

Works: *Mjatež* (novel), 1923, under the title *Komandarm*, 1927; *Saranča* (novel), 1927; *Japonskaja duèl'* (short stories), 1927; *Rasskazy* (short stories), 1929; *Povest' o stradanijakh uma* (novel), 1929; *Zenit* (short stories), 1934; *Kollekcija mednykh monet* (play), in *Ljubov' k žizni*, 1935, 2d ed., 1959; *Pisatel'nica* (novel), 1959.—*Sobr. soč.*, 3 vols., 1928–29; *Izbr.*, 1936.

Secondary Lit.: A. Palej, in *Novyj mir* 1928:2; A. Glagolev, in *Novyj mir* 1931:7; V. Percov, in *Krasnaja nov'* 1935:2; E. Mindlin, in his *Neobyknovennye sobesedniki*, 1968; M. Kalantarova, in *Russkaja lit.* 1978:3.

**Bulgákov, Mikhaíl Afanásyevich,** playwright, prose writer (b. May 14 [May 2], 1891, Kiev— d. March 10, 1940, Moscow). Bulgakov's father was a professor at the Kiev Seminary. From 1909 to 1916 Bulgakov studied medicine at Kiev University; thereafter he worked

as a physician in the countryside near Smolensk and in Kiev. In 1919 he switched to literary work and in 1920–21 lived in Vladikavkaz. In 1921 he moved to Moscow and worked for many newspapers and journals. From 1922 to 1924 he wrote for, among others, the newspaper *Nakanune*, which was published in Berlin and was friendly toward the Soviet Union. Bulgakov regularly published in the railroad newspaper *Gudok*, which brought him together with I. Babel, V. Katayev, I. Ilf, Ye. Petrov, Yu. Olesha, and K. Paustovsky. These early comments and sketches, which throw a lot of light on his later work, were first published in book form more than 50 years later in Cologne. The publication of his first novel, *Belaya gvardiya* (1924; Eng. tr., *The White Guard*, 1969), in *Rossiya* led to the journal being forced to cease publication. A volume with five satiric short stories, *Dyavoliada* (1925; Eng. tr., *Diaboliad*, 1972), remained his only published book. At the instigation of the Moscow Art Theater and based on *Belaya gvardiya*, Bulgakov wrote a play—*Dni Turbinykh* (1926; Eng. tr., *Days of the Turbins*, 1934)—that was performed after considerable difficulties. Despite the crass attacks by RAPP, which banned the play between 1929 and 1932, it continued to be successfully produced until 1941 (987 performances). Bulgakov's first satirical contemporary play, *Zoykina kvartira* (1926; Eng. tr., *Zoya's Apartment*, 1972), was performed in 1926 and 1927 but published for the first time in the Soviet Union in 1982. Another satire, *Bagrovy ostrov* (1927; Eng. tr., *The Crimson Island*, 1972), did not get beyond a few performances. Bulgakov's second drama about the Revolution, *Beg* (1926–28; Eng. tr., *Flight*, 1972), was banned immediately before its premiere. Numerous epic and dramatic works remained unpublished; critics only endeavored to defame him. From July 1929 to March 1930, after none of his plays were being performed and not a line from his pen was being published, Bulgakov began writing letters to influential people such as M. Gorky and to Stalin requesting that he be allowed to emigrate or at least to earn money working at the theater. Stalin personally responded by telephone on April 18, 1930 (four days after V. Mayakovsky's suicide), and Bulgakov was allowed to work at the Moscow Art Theater as assistant producer from 1930 to 1936. His play about the conflict between a poet of genius and the state, *Kabala svyatosh (Molyer)* (Eng. tr., *A Cabal of Hypocrites*, 1972), written between 1930 and 1936, was adulterated in the staging and was removed from performance after a short while; only his adaptation of N. Gogol's Myortvye dushi (Dead Souls) continued to be performed after 1932. Bulgakov switched to the Bolshoy Theater in 1936 and kept body and soul together by working as an opera libretist and translator. His literary works remained in manuscript. As a blind man on his deathbed he was still dictating corrections to his prose masterpiece Master i Margarita (1928–40; Eng. tr., The Master and Margarita, 1967). In Leningrad and Moscow in 1941, Don Kikhot (Don Quixote), written in 1938, was briefly performed. Bulgakov's play about A. Pushkin, Posledniye dni (The Last Days), written in 1934–35, was staged between 1943 and 1948. Bulgakov continued to be excluded from histories of literature and publishers' lists. Yelena Sergeyevna Bulgakova preserved his literary remains. Starting in 1955, Bulgakov's works were allowed to be published and performed again thanks to the active intervention of V. Kaverin and K. Paustovsky. The first to appear were Dni Turbinykh and Posledniye dni in 1955; a volume of selected works published in 1962 included the previously unpublished Beg, Kabala svyatosh, and Don Kikhot. However, Bulgakov's satirical plays were only published in the West. From an apparent total of 30 plays, the texts of only 12 are known to date. The publication in Novy mir in 1965 of Teatralny roman (A Theatrical Novel; Eng. tr., Black Snow, 1967), written in 1936–37, paved the way for the limited inclusion of his prose in Russian literature, 25 years after his death. Master i Margarita appeared in 1966–67 with a considerable number of passages deleted; these were restored in a new edition published in 1973 after the complete text had been published in the West. Bulgakov's return to the literary scene in the Soviet Union initiated a spate of research in the West. Many texts have not yet been published in the Soviet Union; the commission handling his legacy has had the goal of publishing a four-volume edition of his selected works since 1981.

Bulgakov is one of the most important Russian writers of this century. The leading position he occupies as a satirist stands in logical opposition to the minimal appreciation shown him in Soviet histories of literature. Four thematic areas stand out. In Belaya gvardiya, Dni Turbinykh, and Beg, he deviates from the accepted pattern by depicting the Whites' patriotic and idealistic motives. From his work as a doctor comes first Zapiski yunogo vracha (Eng. tr., A Country Doctor's Notebook, 1975), written between 1925 and

1927 and first published in 1963, and then the povest Sobachye serdtse (Eng. tr., The Heart of a Dog, 1968), written in 1925, published in the West in 1968, and only in 1987 in the Soviet Union; alienation that is grotesque and sharply critical characterizes this povest, which reveals Bulgakov's early technical narrative experiments with an adroit mixture of first- and third-person narrative. His comedies are amusing and biting satires of Russia during the 1920s. Through its exclusively negative characters, Zoykina Kvartira provides an image of the criminal side of NEP in Moscow. Many characters in these early comedies reappear in later works. The central theme of his historical dramas about Molière and Pushkin is the dependence of a genius on the despotic state and its administrative agencies. This theme links the extensively autobiographical Teatralny roman (about the fate of Dni Turbinykh) with Master i Margarita. This last-named work, multilevel and structurally complex, features the devil's appearance in Moscow in the 1930s and an author whose unpublished novel about Pontius Pilate is interwoven as a story within a story; the book reveals Bulgakov's unusual artistic imagination and philosophically grounded topical criticism, as well as the suffering that creative people exerience in the absence of freedom and in the presence of the impervious attitude of despots.

Works: D'javoliada (short stories), 1925 (reprinted, Letchworth, 1970) (see above); Sbornik rasskazov (short stories), New York, 1952; Dni Turbinykh (see above), Poslednie dni (plays), 1955; P'esy (plays), 1962 (contains Dni Turbinykh; Beg [see above]; Kabala svjatoš [see above]; Poslednie dni; Don Kikhot); Ivan Vasil'evič, Mërtvye duši (comedies), Munich, 1964; Teatral'nyj roman (novel), in Novyj mir 1965:8 (reprinted, Letchworth, 1972) (see above); Dramy i komedii (plays and comedies), (contains Dni Turbinykh; Beg; Kabala svjatoš; Poloumnyj Žurden; Poslednie dni; Ivan Vasil'evič; Don Kikhot), 1965; Blaženstvo (1934; play), in Zvezda Vostoka 1966:7 and in Grani, Frankfurt am Main, 85:1972; Izbr. proza (selected prose), 1966; Pis'mo Sovetskomu pravitel'stvu (letter), in Grani 66:1967; Master i Margarita (novel), in Moskva 1966:11, 1967:1, Paris, 1968, complete version, Frankfurt am Main, 1969 (see above); Belaja gvardija (novel), London, 1969 (see above); Zojkina kvartira (1926 ed.), in Novyj žurnal, New York, 97–98:1969–70, 1935 ed., Ann Arbor, 1971, and in Sovremennaja dramaturgija 1982:2 (see above); Sobač'e serdce (pov.), in

Grani 69:1968, separate ed., Paris, 1969, in Znamja 1987:6 (see above); Zapiski na man-žetakh (short stories), some stories published in Grani 77:1970 and in Teatr 1987:6; Zapiski junogo vrača (short stories), Letchworth, 1970 (see above); P'esy (plays), Paris, 1971 (contains Adam i Eva; Bagrovyj ostrov [see above]; Zojkina kvartira); Belaja gvardija. Teatral'nyj roman. Master i Margarita (novels), 1973; Rannjaja neizdannaja proza (short stories), Munich, 1976; Neizdannyj Bulgakov (short stories), Ann Arbor, 1977; Rannjaja nesobrannaja proza (short stories), Munich, 1978; Rannjaja neizvestnaja proza (short stories), Munich, 1981; Belaja gvardija: Vtoraja redakcija p'esy "Dni Turbinykh" (play), Munich, 1983; Zabytoe: Rannjaja proza (short stories), Munich, 1983; Glava iz romana (Belaja gvardija) i pis'ma, in Novyj mir 1987:2.—Sobr. soč., 10 vols., Ann Arbor, 1982– (only vols. 1–3 published to date).

Secondary Lit.: V. Kaverin, in Teatr 1956:10 and in his Sobr. soč., vol. 6, 1966; K. Paustovskij, in Teatral'naja žizn 1962:14 and in his Sobr. soč., vol. 8, 1970; V. Lakšin, in Novyj mir 1968:6; E. Stenbock-Fermor, in Slavic and East European Journal 1969:3; R. Beermann, in Osteuropa 1970:3; Y. Hamant, bibliography, in Cahiers du monde russe et soviétique 1970:12; E. Proffer, in Russian Literature Triquarterly 1, 3, 6, 7:1971–73, and Ann Arbor, 1984; D. G. Piper, in Forum for Modern Language Studies 1971:7; M. Čudakova, in Voprosy lit. 1973:7, 1976:1; A. Drawicz, in his Zaproszenie do podróży, Kraców, 1974; V. Levin, Munich, 1975; E. N. Maklow, New York, 1975; S. A. Gutry, Diss., Princeton Univ., 1976; L. Milne, Birmingham, 1977; A. C. Wright, Toronto–Buffalo–London, 1978; all articles in Russian Literature Triquarterly 15:1978; L. E. Belozerskaja-Bulgakova, Ann Arbor, 1979; H. Riggenbach, Bern, 1979; G. El'baum, Ann Arbor, 1981; L. Janovskaja, 1983; A. Zerkalov, Ann Arbor, 1984; M. Kaganskaja and Z. Bar-Zella. Tel Aviv, 1984; M. Kreps, Ann Arbor, 1984; N. Natov, Boston, 1985.

**Búnin, Iván Alekséyevich,** prose writer, poet (b. Oct. 22 [Oct. 10], 1870, Voronezh—d. Nov. 8, 1953, Paris). Bunin's father was a landowner. From 1889 to 1895 Bunin worked as a journalist in Oryol and as a librarian in Poltava. As a writer, Bunin began by publishing poetry; his first poem appeared in 1887 and his first collection in 1891. One of the subsequent collections, Listopad (1901; The Falling of the Leaves), was awarded the Pushkin Prize. Bunin's first short story appeared

in 1893. His acquaintance with M. Gorky in 1899 led him to the circle of realist authors associated with the publisher Znaniye. In 1909 Bunin became an honorary member of the Academy of Sciences of the USSR. At that time he traveled to Greece, Turkey, Palestine, Egypt, and India. Bunin viewed the October Revolution disparagingly; he first fled to the Crimea and emigrated to France in January 1920. His literary work remained thematically bound up with Russia and attained great heights, bringing him acclaim as the best writer of the first Russian emigration. In 1933 he was awarded the Nobel Prize. Bunin remained creative to an advanced age; he continued to keep abreast of Russian literature appearing in the Soviet Union and occasionally commented on it (K. Paustovsky, A. Tvardovsky). Toward the end of his life his Vospominaniya (1955; Memoirs) appeared with articles about A. Blok, V. Bryusov, A. Tolstoy; a book left incomplete at his death, Chekhov (1955), appeared posthumously. He died in poverty. Soviet critics view Bunin's work, especially that written in emigration, coolly. However, since the Second Congress of the Writers Union in 1954 he has been accepted and his works are published.

Bunin is one of the most important prose writers in Russian literature. His earliest prose is reportage in a journalistic style. Before the turn of the century he had achieved narrative perfection; especially productive was the period from 1910 to 1916. His central theme for a long time involved the decline of aristocratic culture and the effects of the changing environment. In Sukhodol (1912; Eng. tr., Dry Valley, 1935), Bunin chronicles the gradual dissolution of a so-called manor. Through a consistent narrative perspective, Bunin combines the independent units into a well-rounded image. In this way "the border between 'real' and symbolic reality is kept consciously fluid" (Holthusen). The form of a longer short story is typical for Bunin. In Derevnya (1910; Eng. tr., The Village, 1923), he depicts the appalling backwardness in the countryside by describing the fate of two brothers. Bunin's short stories about the issue of death, such as Gospodin iz San Frantsisko (1916; Eng. tr., The Gentleman from San Francisco, 1922), are extraordinarily powerful; they are equal to his short stories about love, such as Mitina lyubov (1925; Eng. tr., Mitya's Love, 1926). His personal criticism of the Bolsheviks' use of force and their antispirituality appears in his diary of the revolutionary period, Okayannye dni (1925; The Cursed Days). Part of his works written in emigration have an autobiographical character. *Zhizn Arsenyeva* (1927–39; The Life of Arsenyev; Eng. tr. of 1927 ed., *The Well of Days*, 1933), the most famous of these, depicts his own youth and the social conditions in Russia of that time without a closely knit plot but with a connection to lyrical, narrative, descriptive, and philosophic elements. Bunin's prose follows in the tradition of I. Turgenev, I. Goncharov, and L. Tolstoy; but he never elected to work with the literary form of the novel. Economical and effective use of artistic means, deepening of his exposition through special narrative perspectives, vividness, and psychological depth are only some of the characteristics of his style. In their perfection of form, several of his novellas belong to the best of world literature. Bunin's poetry is close to his prose in its clear structure, but it is less well known and less appreciated. Paustovsky said that the ring of Bunin's language stretches "from a ceremoniousness that resounds like copper to the transparency of flowing spring water, from a measured imprint to an intonation of astonishing softness, from a light melody to the slow roar of thunder."

*Works:* Pod otkrytym nebom (poems), 1898; *Listopad* (poems), 1901; *Derevnja* (pov.), 1910 (see above); *Sukhodol* (pov. and short stories), 1912 (see above); *Gospodin iz San Francisko* (pov.), 1916 (see above); *Roza Ierikhovna* (short stories and poems), Berlin, 1924; *Mitina ljubov'* (short story and poems), Paris, 1925 (see above); *Solnečnyj udar* (short stories), Paris, 1927; *Grammatika ljubvi* (short stories), Belgrade, 1929 (Eng. tr., *Grammar of Love*, 1934); *Žizn' Arsen'eva* (pov.), 2 vols.: vol. 1: *Istoki dnej*, Paris, 1930; vols. 2: *Lika*, Paris, 1939, both vols., New York, 1952 (see above); *Tëmnye allei* (short stories), New York, 1943, 2d ed., 1946 (Eng. tr., *Dark Avenues*, 1949); *Vospominanija* (memoirs), Paris, 1950 Eng. tr., *Memories and Portraits*, 1951; *O Čekhove* (biography), New York, 1955; *Stikhotvorenija* (poems), Leningrad, 1956; *Stikhotvorenija* (poems), Leningrad, 1961; *Okajannye dni* (memoirs), Berlin, 1935, London, Canada, 1973; *Iz dnevnikov* (diary), in *Novyj žurnal*, New York, 108–16:1972–74; *Ustami Buninykh* (diary and archival material), 3 vols., Frankfurt am Main, 1977–82.—*Sobr. soč.*, 1902–9; *Polnoe sobr. soč.*, 6 vols., 1915; *Sobr. soč.*, 12 vols., Berlin, 1934–39; 5 vols., 1956; 9 vols., 1965–67.

*Translations:* The Dreams of Chang and Other Stories, 1923; The Gentleman from San Francisco and Other Stories, 1933; The Elaghin Affair and Other Stories, 1935; Stories and

Poems, 1979; *Long Ago: Fourteen Stories*, 1984. *Secondary Lit.:* G. Struve, in *Slavonic and East European Review*, 1933; B. Zajcev, Paris, 1934; V. N. Muromceva-Bunina, Paris, 1959; V. N. Afanas'ev, 1966; A. K. Baboreko, 1967; G. Kuznecova, *Grasskij dnevnik*, Washington, 1967; O. N. Mikhajlov, 1967; B. Kirchner, Diss., Tübingen, 1968; A. A. Volkov, 1969; S. Kryzytski, The Hague, 1971, and in *MERSL* 3:1979; J. A. Berzups, Diss., Georgetown Univ., 1976; N. M. Cvetanovič, Diss., Ohio State Univ., 1976; M. L. Spain, Diss., Stanford Univ., 1978; J. B. Woodward, Chapel Hill, 1980.

**Buríkhin, Ígor Nikoláyevich,** poet (b. Oct. 3, 1943, Troitskoye, oblast Vologda). Burikhin, who took his last name and patronymic from his stepfather, a teacher, grew up mainly in Staraya Russa and around Novgorod. In 1959 he moved to Leningrad to begin his studies; in 1974 he completed his study of German language and literature at the Institute for Theater Studies. In the same year he was not allowed to defend his completed candidate's dissertation on Bertolt Brecht for political reasons (among other articles, Burikhin had written one on I. Brodsky for V. Maramzin's five-volume SAMIZDAT collection). Around this time, Burikhin, who had been baptized as a child, found his way back to the Orthodox faith and began to travel throughout the USSR (Central Asia, Siberia, and elsewhere) as a pilgrim or an assistant on geological expeditions. On June 21, 1979, Burikhin was permitted to emigrate to Vienna. Since 1979 he has lived in Lindlar near Cologne. Burikhin gathered his poetry written between 1964 and 1983, none of which has been published in the USSR, and organized it into four collections. From the first collection (unpublished as a whole), *Opyty soyedineniya stikhov posredstvom stikhov* (1964–73; Attempts at Uniting Verses through Verses), the cycle *Kon Rek* (1974; The Horse of the Rivers) was published in M. Shemyakin's anthology, *Apollon '77* (published in Paris); another cycle appeared in *Vremya i my* (26:1978). Various émigré journals, such as *Kontinent* (8:1976) and *Grani* (103:1977), also published excerpts from the second collection of poems, *Rossiya budet moyey* (1974–76; Russia Will Be Mine). In addition, Burikhin's first book, *Moy dom slovo* (1978; My House Is the Word), which was published in Paris, found its origins in this second collection. Excerpts from Burikhin's third collection of poems, *Prevrashcheniya na vozdushnykh putyakh* (1981; Conversion to Aerial Paths), which included poems from 1977–78, were published in journals before the book edition appeared. Burikhin completed the manuscript of the fourth collection, *Prigotovleniya k absolyutno belomu* (Preparation for the Absolute White), in 1983; from this collection, the narrative poem *Telo-pokayanny psalom* (The Body Is an Atonement Psalm), was published.

As the titles of his collections show, Burikhin seeks to free the poetic word from accepted tradition by using discordant references. Paradoxical confrontations and unusual metaphors characterize his poems. Burikhin sharpens the sense of the semantics of words by occasionally using new words to convey traditional common connotations. In this way, the domains of dreams, of darkness, of the cosmos are smoothly integrated into the world of animated subjects and of everyday reality. The totality remains a fixed conjunction of sound fragments, continues to be chaos seeking order, and does not present a harmonious universe. Burikhin's poetry is a never-ending critical analysis of himself and of his flight, undertaken in the knowledge that on earth there is no refuge.

*Works*: Poems, in *Kontinent*, Paris, 8:1976, 27:1981, 45:1985; in *Vestnik RkhD*, Paris, 123:1977; in *Apollon '77*, Paris, 1977; in *Grani*, Frankfurt am Main, 103:1977; in *Vremja i my*, Tel Aviv, 26:1978, 42:1979; in *NRL: Neue russische Literatur*, Salzburg, 1978; in *Èkho*, Paris, 1979:1; in *Gnosis*, New York, 5–6:1979; in *Russkij al'manakh*, Paris, 1981; in *Sternenfall* (German and Russian), Zurich, 1981. *Moj dom slovo* (poems), Paris, 1978; *Prevraščenie na vozdušnykh putjakh* (poems), Paris, 1981.

*Secondary Lit.*: V. Maramzin, in *Apollon '77*, 1977.

**Burlyúk, Davíd Davídovich**, poet, painter (b. July 22 [July 9], 1882, Semirotoshchina, near Kharkov—d. Jan. 15, 1967, Southhampton, Long Island, New York). Burlyuk's father was an estate manager. Burlyuk began to study painting in 1898 in Kazan, Odessa, and Moscow; he studied in Munich in 1902–3 and in Paris in 1904. He exhibited at home and abroad, including with the "Blue Rider" group. From 1910 to 1913 Burlyuk lived in Moscow, met V. Mayakovsky, and with him and A. Kruchonykh signed the Futurist Manifesto in 1913 (see FUTURISM); he organized readings, edited futurist works for publication, and became a very enterprising champion of futurist poets and abstract art. After the Revolution, Burlyuk organized exhibits of his own

work in Siberia, was active in the far eastern branch of the futurist movement with N. Aseyev and S. Tretyakov, and published his first collection of poetry. From Vladivostok Burlyuk moved to Japan in August 1920, then to the United States in September 1922. In New York Burlyuk's attempts to gain recognition as the "Father of Russian Futurism" included participation in pro-Soviet groups and the composition of a poetic work in honor of the tenth anniversary of the October Revolution in 1928. In 1930–31 he published two books written about him by Russian writers; in 1932 he brought out a selection of his own poetry, *1/2 veka* (1/2 Century), in honor of his 50th birthday. In 1930 he began (and continued for decades) the private publication of a journal, *Color and Rhyme*, written partly in English and partly in Russian, containing from four to 100 pages, and including his own illustrations, poetry, memoirs, letters, and reviews, as well as reproductions of futurist works. In 1956 Burlyuk traveled to the Soviet Union as a tourist.

Burlyuk indeed had talent as a painter and, moreover, as an organizer of the "cubo-futurist" movement. His own poetry is eclectic and hardly significant. Several poems attract attention as something unusual by their abbreviated syntax and their disinclination to use prepositions, but the majority are straightforward, without depth, and stylistically unremarkable. Burlyuk's self-representations of the émigré period border on the embarrasing.

*Works*: "Die Wilden Russlands," in *Der Blaue Reiter*, Munich, 1912; *Burljuk požimaet ruku Vul'vort Bil'dingu* (poems), New York, 1924; *Marusja san* (poems), New York, 1925; *Novelly*, New York, 1929; *Entelekhizm: Teorija, kritika, stikhi, kartiny 1907–30* (poems and articles), New York, 1930; *1/2 veka* (poems), 1932; *Color and Rhyme* (journal; contains poems, prose, memoirs, etc.), vols. 1–60, New York, 1930–66.

*Secondary Lit.*: I. Postupal'skij, New York, 1931; K. Dreier, New York, 1944; V. Zavališin, in *Novoe russkoe slovo*, New York, Jan. 28, 1967, and June 13, 1982, p. 5; V. Markov, in his *Russian Futurism*, Berkeley, 1968; H. Ladurner, in *Wiener Slawistischer Almanach* 1:1978; J. E. Bowlt, in *MERSL* 3:1979; X. Werner, in *Wiener Slawistischer Almanach* 17:1986.

**Býkov, Vasíly Vladímirovich** (Vasil Bykau), Belorussian prose writer who translates most of his works into Russian himself (b. June 19,

1924, Cherenovshchina, oblast Vitebsk). Bykov's father was a peasant. As a student at the
art academy in Vitebsk, Bykov volunteered to
go to the front in 1941; by the end of the war
he was an officer in Austria, and he remained
in the army for ten more years. Bykov's literary activity began in 1955 with short stories
about the war, Smert cheloveka (The Death of
a Man) and Oboznik (The Driver of the Transport Train). When his povest Tretya raketa
(1962; Eng. tr., The Third Flare, 1963) appeared in Russian, Bykov found great acclaim
as one of the most honest portrayers of wartime experiences. Bykov's unsparing critical
realism in Mertvym ne bolno (1966; The Dead
Feel No Pain) evoked the Party's criticism.
Bykov, for whom "art is not the fancy of the
artist, not the planned product of society, but
the soul of society" (1966), remained true to
his theme: human reliability and failure at the
front or with the partisans. After 1972 he also
wrote plays. In 1974 he received the State
Prize for two longer stories, Obelisk (1972)
and Dozhit do rassveta (1973; Eng. tr., Live
until Dawn, 1981); and in 1986 he was awarded
the Lenin Prize for his povest Znak bedy. He
lives in Minsk, and his works are regularly
published in Novy mir. In 1986 he became a
member of the buro of the secretariat of the
Writers Union of the USSR.

Bykov belongs to the tradition that opposes
the pseudoheroism of Viktor Nekrasov's novels about Stalingrad. His central focus is on
daily life during the war with its grayness,
with hunger and cold, with helpfulness and
meanness in one's own ranks. Bykov generally portrays soldiers in seemingly hopeless
situations in which they are faced with essentially moral decisions; he dares, for example
in Alpiyskaya ballada (1964; Eng. tr., Alpine
Ballad, 1966), to protest against the official
view that guilt rather than bad luck causes
one to be taken prisoner. In Sotnikov (1970;
Eng. tr., The Ordeal, 1972) he succeeds in
depicting the problem of sacrificial death in
a psychologically meticulous and moving
manner. In Obelisk, a story about a teacher's
voluntary death in the partisan battle, he leaves

essential aspects of the interpretation up to
the reader by using a frame story and declining to include the protagonist's thoughts. The
povest Poyti i ne vernutsya (1978; To Go and
Never to Return), which was also staged in
1980, takes place in the fall of 1942 in the
Belorussian backcountry and analyzes the
problem that constantly moves Bykov: people's moral stability in times of grave danger.
Conscious shifting of the storyteller's point of
view characterizes Bykov's work, for which
he chooses short spans of time, lets the action
move forward slowly and descriptively, and
periodically expands upon the plot by using
flashbacks to his characters' past.

*Works:* Žuravlinyj krik (pov. and short stories), 1961; Tret'ja raketa (pov. and short stories), 1963 (see above); Frontovaja stranica
(pov.), in Oktjabr' 1963:9; Al'pijskaja ballada
(pov.), in Ogonëk 1964:12–16, separate ed.,
1964 (see above); Reč' na s"ezde Sojuza pisatelej Belorussii (speech), in Grani, Frankfurt
am Main, 61:1966; Mërtvym ne bol'no (pov.),
in Novyj mir 1966:1–2; Ataka s khodu (pov.),
in Novyj mir 1968:5; Krugljanskij most (pov.),
in Novyj mir 1969:3; Sotnikov (pov.), 1970
see above); Obelisk (pov.), 1973; Dožit' do
rassveta. Obelisk (pov.), 1973 (see above);
Kogda khočetsja žit' (play), 1974; Volč'ja staja
(pov.), 1975 (Eng. trs., "The Wolf Pack," in
Soviet Literature 1975:5; Pack of Wolves, New
York, 1981); Pojti i ne vernut'sja (pov.), 1980;
Znak bedy (pov.), in Družba narodov 1983:3;
Kar'er (pov.), in Družba narodov 1986:4–5.—
Sobr. soč., 4 vols., 1985–86.

*Secondary Lit.:* G. Baklanov, in Lit. gazeta
March 1, 1962; L. Lazarev, in Novyj mir 1963:6
and 1986:11 in Družba narodov 1980:5, and
1979; I. Kozlov, in Znamja 1965:3 and in Lit.
i sovremennost' 6:1965; S. Hoppe, in Zeit-
schrift für Slawistik 1974:5; I. Buzylev, in
Oktjabr' 1975:2; M. Sedykh, in Teatr 1975:5;
N. Gubko, in Zvezda 1975:6; I. Štokman, in
Družba narodov 1978:4 and in Oktjabr'
1986:10; A. B. McMillin, in MERSL 3:1979; I.
Dedkov, 1980, and in Novyj mir 1983:10; A.
Ovčarenko, in Družba narodov 1983:11.

# C

**Censorship** (tsenzúra). In the field of literature
in the Soviet Union, censorship refers to the
practices of censorship per se as well as to
the authorities charged with (1) the actual
enforcement of the principles of PARTY SPIRIT

(partiynost) and of SOCIALIST REALISM and (2)
the safeguarding of state secrets. Censorship
encompasses the production and distribution
of all printed materials and the distribution
of information through the mass media. Offi-

cially the sole admission is that "state supervision has been established" (Gos. kontrol unstanovlen; *Bolshaya sovetskaya entsiklopediya*, 3d ed., vol. 28, col. 1457), but the institutions responsible are not named. The supreme censorship authority in the Soviet Union is the Central Committee of the Communist Party, especially its Department of Ideology and Propaganda. Immediately after the October Revolution, on Nov. 7, 1917, censorship, which had been abolished following the February Revolution, was reintroduced with the Decree Concerning the Press. The special board of censors still existing today, the Central Administration for Matters of Literature and Publishing (Glavnoye upravleniye po delam literatury i izdatelstv), was established on June 6, 1922. The abbreviation *Glavlit* has remained in use even though the name of the organization has been changed (Central Administration for Safeguarding Military and State Secrets in the Press [Glavnoye upravleniye po okhrane voyennykh i gosudarstvennykh tayn v pechati]). Glavlit is formally subordinate to the Committee for the Press of the Council of Ministers of the USSR. In addition to the central office in Moscow, a broadly branching network of lower-level offices exists. In the publishing houses as well as in most of the editorial offices of newspapers and journals throughout the entire Soviet Union, representatives of the board of censors have their own offices. The Communist Party exercises a second type of direct censorship independently of Glavlit through permanent representatives in all editorial councils that come under local Party committees (Departments of Agitation and Propaganda and Departments of Culture). In addition to these two forms of general censorship, there are special boards of censors, for example, in the military, in the KGB, in the Ministry of Foreign Affairs, and so forth. These censorship authorities work together with the editors, not with the authors. Moreover, editors also practice direct censorship. They decide which institutions, in addition to Glavlit, should be included in the inspection. Additional censorship occurs in trade with foreign countries. MEZHDUNARODNAYA KNIGA supervises book exports and imports. The control of all translations to be published abroad lies in the hands of VAAP.

In the Russian Empire, censorship was first established under Catherine II, and the first Censorship Statute *(Tsenzurny ustav)* was enacted in 1804. Nicholas I personally acted as A. Pushkin's censor. In 1865 all original works longer than ten signatures, all translations longer than twenty signatures, and all periodicals in the capital cities were exempted from prepublication censorship (in accordance with an authorization from the Ministry of the Interior). All prepublication censorship was rescinded in 1905–6. In addition, starting in 1862, all censored works were publicly listed (see *Brokgauz-Efron. Entsiklopedichesky slovar,* "Tsenzurnye vzyskaniya"). In the Soviet Union, censorship has progressively and continuously intensified. Censorship practices, as well as the organization and procedures of the censor, remain secret. At present all printed materials must undergo a three-part prepublication censorship that is repeated for a new edition; furthermore, they are subject to an unlimited postpublication censorship that can lead to changes decades after publication and to the prohibition of books that were initially passed by the censor. Prepublication censorship affects the manuscript, the galley proofs, and a preprint *(signalny eksemplar)*. The censor gives the editor orders relating to factual secrecy and, as a rule, suggestions concerning ideological issues. Changing "ideologically not fully valuable [content]" *(ideyno nepolnotsennoye)* or expunging "useless specifics" *(nenuzhnye utochneniya)* is left to the editor and the author, but the author is not permitted to see the orders and suggestions made by the censor. In addition to the editor directly responsible, other members of the editorial staff— the editor in chief and the director of the publishing house—participate in the editorial decision-making process. They stand between the board of censors and the author and can contribute toward modifying but also toward preserving the author's intent. A manuscript is released from the board of censors with the stamp "Free of Military or State Secrets" (Razglasheniya voyennoy ili gosudarstvennoy tayny net); galley proofs, with the stamp "Authorized for Publication" (Razreshaetsya v svet). Authors often first learn of changes when they receive their proof copy. In the Soviet Union, literary works usually appear first in a journal, then as a book. The book can be either closer to the author's original text, owing to the restitution of changed or deleted passages, or further away from it, owing to renewed interventions by the board of censors. What happens depends on the reaction of the critics, on general political developments, as well as on the disposition of the new editors and censors.

The standards of censorship change in accordance with the Party line (under Stalin, they also changed according to the personal taste of the dictator). They are regularly re-drawn, especially in the annual secret "Cata-logue of Materials and Information Forbidden to Be Published in the Public Press" (Per-echen materialov i svedeniy zapreshchon-nykh k opublikovaniyu v otkrytoy pechati). These standards give the censor a large mea-sure of responsibility, and he can be called to account for an insufficiently strict interpreta-tion. A continuous tightening of censorship is revealed, for example, in the provision con-cerning references to émigré and persecuted authors. In the 1920s, such references were still possible, but today mentioning any au-thor from the second or third wave of emigra-tion is totally prohibited. In 1947 the board of censors began modifying all works in a Russian-chauvinist manner to accord with the struggle against COSMOPOLITANISM. During the THAW (1953–63), censorship was more lib-eral, contributing to a flourishing of literature. During the last few decades, distinguished authors highly regarded abroad have been given more ideological freedom than less well known authors have.

From the experience of many authors in the Soviet Union, some principles can be de-duced that are applied by the censors with varying intensity. Life in the Soviet Union is to be depicted in an essentially positive light, social conflicts are to be concealed (for ex-ample, between privileged members of the nomenclatura and common citizens, between Russians and other nationalities, between city and country, between propaganda and real-ity). Taboo are depictions of personal experi-ences in the past and present that contradict the desired image of state and society; of pos-itive religious, transcendental experiences; and not only of any sexual joy and sorrow but also of the physiological realm of human existence per se. Forbidden are critical depictions of high-level state functionaries or artists; for-bidden is the concern with their private life; forbidden is the reference to peoples and in-dividuals who fall under the Party's disfavor; forbidden is the critical treatment of the So-viet military, the police, the Party; forbidden is a depiction of foreign countries or of an individual foreigner if the superiority of the Soviet Union in every respect is not illus-trated thereby; forbidden (by a secret Glavlit circular sent to publishers in 1971) are refer-ences to the year 1937—that is, Stalin's mur-ders—to prisons in the Soviet Union, to pol-lution. Every exception must be depicted as a highly individual case. For each of these categories, exceptions can be found for certain authors at a specific time in a few passages,

but these do not call into question the basic tendency; instead they are merely to be viewed as tactical measures.

Censorship first engenders a self-censor-ship, an "internal censorship," that affects every author's writing as he checks to see whether all his thoughts, all his images, all his words will pass the censor. The practices of external censorship relate to deleting or changing individual words, paragraphs, or chapters, but also to the prohibition of entire books. Consequently, for no writer of the So-viet period does a complete edition of his works exist (not even for M. Gorky or V. Mayakovsky). For authors with a good inter-national reputation but little attachment to socialist ideology, such as V. Khlebnikov, N. Klyuyev, O. Mandelshtam, B. Pilnyak, or M. Voloshin, editions are published, after de-cades of neglect, but in print runs so small that for all practical purposes they are only for foreign countries and for a few libraries in the Soviet Union; thus access remains con-trolled. Changes in the Party line are the rea-son for the variants in many frequently re-printed works. About 1950, A. Fadeyev, V. Katayev, and M. Sholokhov had to rewrite prominent novels to falsify historical facts, and in P. Vershigora's documentary novel Lyudi s chistoy sovestyu, the partisans' posi-tion toward the Communist Party was trans-formed into its opposite. After 1954 Stalin's name was temporarily eliminated, which led to a complete transformation of the content of many works (for example, N. Pogodin).

Censorship measures against individual au-thors do not end with the prohibition of spe-cific works but extend through the prohibition to publish collected works or to publish books at all, up to the total silencing of an author. In L. Timofeyev's history of literature pub-lished in 1951, not only are all the writers who died in the purges, such as I. Babel, O. Mandelshtam, B. Pilnyak, or A. Voronsky, missing but writers such as M. Bulgakov, Yu. Olesha, B. Pasternak, or A. Platonov are also absent; many, such as K. Paustovsky or M. Svetlov, only appear in lists. In the history of literature that P. Vykhodtsev published in 1979 for institutes and academies, these authors are all mentioned—having been rehabilitated by that time—but highly respected authors such as V. Aksyonov, V. Nekrasov, A. Solzheni-tsyn, G. Vladimov, and V. Voynovich are ab-sent. The falsification of the history of litera-ture goes so far that the index to the Kratkaya literaturnaya entsiklopediya (vol. 9, 1978) omits such authors, even if preceding vol-umes included entries on them.

Censorship also applies to the literature of the 19th century. For decades the works of certain authors were not reissued (F. Dostoyevsky, N. Leskov), and some works, especially religious ones, were completely suppressed. In all Soviet editions, the word *Bog* (God) is inaccurately spelled with a lowercase *B*. Alterations in the text have even been ascertained in editions of letters (A. Chekhov, F. Dostoyevsky).

The translated works of foreign authors are also subject to censorship. During the Stalin period, with the exception of a few politically chosen authors (such as James Aldridge, Louis Aragon, Paul Eluard, Howard Fast), no belles lettres from Western countries were translated. Currently, belles lettres from the socialist countries are given preference. With some works, deletions as well as changes and additions are undertaken. Heinrich Böll's *Gruppenbild mit Dame* (Group Portrait with Lady), published in Russian in 1973, was altered in 150 places (500 lines). Ernest Hemingway's *For Whom the Bell Tolls*, published in Russian in 1968, was tampered with in more than 20 places. James Jones's *From Here to Eternity* was cut by one-third; Arthur Miller's play *The Crucible* was so transfigured that the topical criticism was made to apply only to the West. Distortions have also been ascertained in the translated works of other authors, including Samuel Beckett, Günter Grass, Graham Greene, Hermann Kasack, John Steinbeck, and Carl Zuckmayer.

The constriction of literature through censorship has only occasionally provoked public or semipublic reaction in the Soviet Union. In general, SAMIZDAT and TAMIZDAT are consequences of censorship. In 1967, at the Fourth Congress of the Writers Union, A. Solzhenitsyn protested, in an open letter, against Glavlit as an organization that was not provided for by the constitution and that harbored literary incompetents who were allowed to practice oppression against writers. His attempt at least to stimulate a discussion of censorship succeeded only outside the framework of the formal speeches. In front of the delegates, only O. Gonchar attacked the board of censors as "invisible men with colored pencils in their tightly clutched hands." G. Svirsky was expelled from the Communist Party for his speech on Jan. 16, 1968, in defense of Solzhenitsyn's position, in which he leveled weighty attacks on Glavlit. The volume that came into being by partially evading Glavlit, *Tarusskiye stranitsy* (1961), and the abortive legal attempt to publish the volume METROPOL in 1979 without Glavlit's interfer-

ence are efforts at protest against censorship.

For Russian literature, the consequences of the suppression caused by censorship are considerable. Many authors have not published their consequential works for decades and have often no longer been able to write at all. Much of what was written has disappeared: either the authors have destroyed it out of fear or the security service has confiscated it. Nevertheless, artistic creativity cannot be suppressed, and for some authors the need to keep an eye on the censor has led to a metaphoric and Aesopian style and, in some cases, to a greater multiplicity of levels. In the Soviet Union important, often internationally highly acclaimed works are temporarily or permanently withheld from the reader (for example, the novels of M. Bulgakov, I. Bunin, D. Merezhkovsky, V. Nabokov, B. Pasternak, I. Shmelyov, A. Solzhenitsyn, or the experimental poetry of V. Khlebnikov, D. Kharms, A. Vvedensky, G. Aygi, and others). Although many of the works published outside the Soviet Union make their way into the hands of some authors, the impoverishment censorship inflicts on Russian literature, in a spiritual as well as a formal sense, is immeasurable. For every literary work published in the Soviet Union one must wonder whether it reflects the author's true intent. No history of Russian literature published in the Soviet Union escapes distortion, and the disavowal of religious content and the silence regarding the intellectual creativity of writers living abroad are only especially blatant examples. To be sure, in nearly seventy years, the formidable censorship apparatus has not been successful in forcing Russian literature in the Soviet Union to conform to the ideas of the Communist Party without exception, yet this is little consolation in view of the extensive impoverishment of literary productivity in the USSR.

*Secondary Lit.*: (On censorship in general): *Dejstvujuščee zakonodatel'stvo o pečati*, ed. L. Fogelevič, 1931; R. Gul', in *Sovremennye zapiski*, Paris, 66:1938, in *Novyj žurnal*, New York, 106:1972, and in his *Odvukon'*, New York, 1973; M. Friedberg, in *Problems of Communism*, Washington, 1954:1, in *Literature and Revolution in Soviet Russia 1917–1962*, London, 1963, also in his *A Decade of Euphoria*, Bloomington, Ind., 1977; M. Fainsod, in *Problems of Communism* 1956:2; S. Štut, in *Novyj mir* 1956:9; "Glavlit," in *Posev*, Frankfurt am Main, 1968:7; P. Hübner, in *Osteuropa* 1972:1; *The Soviet Censorship*, ed. M. Dewhirst, R. Farrell, New York, 1973 (with extensive bibliography); A. Solženicyn, *Pis'mo*

IV s"ezdu Sojuza sovetskikh pisatelej, in his Bodalsja telënok s dubom, Paris, 1975; E. Ètkind, in his Zapiski nezagovorščika, London, 1977 (esp. pp. 319ff.), and in Sintaksis, Paris, 9:1981; G. Walker, Soviet Book Publishing Policy, Cambridge, 1978; G. Svirskij, Na lobnom meste, London, 1979, (pp. 404f. and note 81); L. Losev, in Russkaja mysl', Paris, June 16, 1983, and in his Zakrytyj raspredelitel', Ann Arbor, 1984, and On the Beneficence of Censorship, Munich, 1984; M. Jakobson, in Strelec, Montgeron–Jersey City, N.J., 1984:5; W. Kasack, in Osteuropa 1985:2.

(On individual authors): G. Struve, in Slavonic and East European Review 1955:2 (Čekhov); L. Twarog, in American Slavic and East European Review 1955:3 (Kostylev); D. Goldstein, in American Slavic and East European Review 1961:2 (Dostoevskij); G. Ermolaev, in Mosty, Munich, 12:1966 (Šolokhov); L. Rževskij, in Novyj žurnal 90:1968 (Bulgakov); F. Scholz, in L. Leonov, Vor (reprinted, Munich, 1975); H.-J. Dreyer, Munich, 1976 (Veršigora); Ju. Telesin, in Encounter 1976:6 and in Vremja i my, Jerusalem, 75:1984 (Hemingway); H. Glade (with P. Bruhn), Heinrich Böll in der Sowjetunion, Berlin, 1980; L. Milne, in M. Bulgakov, Belaja gvardija, P'esa v četyrëkh dejstvijakh, Munich, 1983.

**Chakóvsky, Aleksándr Borísovich,** prose writer, literary official (b. Aug. 26 [Aug. 13], 1913, St. Petersburg). Chakovsky's father was a doctor. Chakovsky graduated from the Gorky Literary Institute in 1938. He first worked as a critic, then he wrote biographies of writers (Henri Barbusse, Heinrich Heine, Martin Andersen Nexö). In 1941 he joined the Communist Party. During World War II he was a reporter at the front. From then on, Chakovsky was a writer within the narrow circle of SOCIALIST REALISM. His works fully reflect the principle of PARTY SPIRIT. In 1954 he was elected to the board of the Writers Union of the USSR, in 1958 to that of the Writers Union of the RSFSR. In 1967 he became a member of the secretariat of the Writers Union of the USSR; in 1971 and 1976 he was given a place in the buro of the secretariat. In 1950–55 he belonged to the editorial staff of the journal Znamya, then he became editor in chief of the journal Inostrannaya literatura until 1963; since the end of 1962 he has been in charge of Literatura gazeta. He is a deputy to the Supreme Soviet and lives in Moscow.

He describes his experiences during the war and the postwar period in the trilogy Eto bylo v Leningrade (1944–47; That Was in Lenin-

grad). For U nas uzhe utro (1949; Here It Is Already Morning), his novel about Soviet construction work in South Sakhalin, the area Japan had to cede to the Soviet Union after the war, Chakovsky received a Stalin Prize (for 1949, 3d class). Topical ideological questions provide the focus for his later novels. In Svet dalyokoy zvezdy (1962; Eng. tr., The Light of a Distant Star, 1965), he illustrates the controversy that arose in 1956 from the Party's dogmatic standpoint: the years after 1937 may not be viewed solely as the era of the cult of personality; not one's personal conscience but the Party's truth is decisive for one's actions. He strengthened his political message through the traditional division into positive and negative characters and through artless commentaries on the action. In the novel Blokada (1969–79; Blockade), which concerns the war in Leningrad, he turns away from the politics of the 20th and 22d Party Congresses and reintroduces Stalin into literature (Lenin Prize, 1978). The novel Pobeda (1978–81; Victory), which is expressly described as "political," concentrates on the summer of 1945.

Works: Èto bylo v Leningrade (novel), 1945, as a trilogy, 1948; U nas uže utro (novel), 1950; Tridcat' dnej v Pariže (articles), 1955; God žizni (novel), 1956 (Eng. tr., A Year of Life, 1958); Dorogi, kotorye my vybiraem (novel), 1960; Svet dalëkoj zvezdy (pov.), 1963 (see above); Blokada (novel), 1969–79; Pobeda (political novel), 2 vols., 1980–81; Neokončennyj portret (novel), in Znamja 1983:9, 1984:7–8; Njurnbergskie prizraki (novel), in Oktjabr' 1987:1.—Sobr. soč., 6 vols., 1974–77.

Secondary Lit.: A. Makarov, in Novyj mir 1946:4–5; K. Mehnert, in Osteuropa 2:1952; G. Mitin, in Znamja 1963:2; RSPP 6(1):1969; A. Èl'jaševič, in Lit. i sovremennost' 10:1970; I. Kozlov, in Oktjabr' 1974:11; V. Pankov, in Oktjabr' 1975:7; I. Kozlov, 1979; M. Sinel'nikov, in Novyj mir 1982:11; D. Moldavskij, in Zvezda 1984:1; A. Novikov, in Zvezda 1985:5.

**Chapýgin, Alekséy Pávlovich,** prose writer (b. Oct. 17 [Oct. 5], 1870, in the village of Bolshoy Ugol, prov. Olonets—d. Oct. 21, 1937, Leningrad). Chapygin was of peasant descent. In 1883 he began training as a scene painter in St. Petersburg; his first prose work was published in 1903; his first collection came out in 1912. In his early stories, written under the influence of N. K. Mikhaylovsky and V. G. Korolenko, Chapygin describes life in the peasant milieu of his northern Russian homeland, as in *Bely skit* (1913; The White Hermitage). Chapygin is known in Soviet literature primarily for his 1,000-page historical novel, *Razin Stepan* (1926; Eng. tr., *Stepan Razin*, 1946), which met with M. Gorky's approbation and is still being reprinted today. In a barely shorter novel, *Gulyashchiye lyudi* (1934–37; Itinerant People), Chapygin addressed the urban insurrections of the 17th century.

*Razin Stepan* is one of the first historical novels written in the Soviet period; it depicts the peasant rebellions of 1667–71 with an emphasis on the role of the common people. Chapygin endowed the Cossack hero of the title with modern motivations: for instance, Razin's contrived atheistic and antitsarist attitudes. Period coloring is limited to the use of archaic language, the effect of which tends to be burdensome. S. Zlobin and V. Shukshin dealt with the same topic in their novels of 1951 and 1974, respectively.

*Works:* Neljudimye (short stories), 1912; *Belyj skit* (pov.), 1914; *Razin Stepan* (novel), 1926–27 (see above); *Guljaščie ljudi* (novel), 1935–37.—*Sobr. soč.*, 7 vols., 1928; 5 vols., 1967–69.

*Secondary Lit.:* B. Val'be, 1935, 2d ed., 1959; P. Artjukhov, 1955; RSPP 6(1):1969; V. Semënov, 1974; T. Atanov, in *Russkaja lit.* 1984:12.

**Chayánov, Aleksándr Vasílyevich,** prose writer (b. Jan. 29 [Jan. 17], 1888, Moscow—d. March 20, 1939 [?], Alma Ata, while imprisoned). Chayanov's father was a merchant (of peasant descent). Chayanov studied at the Moscow Agricultural Institute (1906–10); between 1908 and 1912 he undertook several trips to Western Europe for professional reasons. In 1910, as an agricultural economist, he began teaching and conducting research at Moscow universities and institutes and began publishing extensively. As a historian, Chayanov was also recognized as a specialist on the history of Moscow and combined his own passion for collecting antiquities (engravings, icons, books, porcelain) with scholarly publications. After 1906 he also worked as a writer of dramas (1906, 1921), poems (published in 1911), and prose rich in fantasy. He published five povesti in separate editions between 1918 and 1928 (written under the pseudonym "Botanik X" or "Moskovsky Botanik")—for example, *Yuliya ili Vstrechi pod Novodevichem* (1928; Julia; or, The Meeting at Novodevichy Monastery). In addition to these, his utopian novel,

*Puteshestviye moego brata Alekseya v stranu krestyanskoy utopii* (1920: My Brother Aleksey's Trip to the Land of Peasant Utopia), written under the pseudonym "Iv. Kremnyov," was allowed to be published thanks to personal instructions from Lenin. Chayanov traveled to London, Heidelberg, and Berlin in 1922–23; to Berlin and Paris in 1927–28. In July 1929 Chayanov was arrested in connection with the breakup of the Timiryazev Academy; in 1930 he was sentenced to five years in prison. In Alma-Ata where he was later sent into exile, he was arrested again in 1938 and probably shot in 1939. In 1967 an eight-volume collection of his articles on economics was reprinted in Paris; around 1980 his literary works were reissued in the United States.

Chayanov's novellas combine his historical aesthetic interest with a preference for E. T. A. Hoffmann and V. F. Odoyevsky. The style of his novellas is that of romantic short stories; they also use the fairy-tale motifs of romanticism; for example, the novella published in Berlin, *Venetsianskoye zerkalo ili Dikovinnye pokhozhdeniya steklyannogo cheloveka* (1923; The Venetian Mirror; or, The Wonderful Adventure of the Glass Man), uses the doppelgänger motif. *Puteshestviye moego brata Alekseya v stranu krestyanskoy utopii* is a Utopian novel set in the year 1984 (without reference to George Orwell) in a cooperatively organized Russian peasant state in which the considerably scaled-down cities and the proletariat play a subordinate role, manual labor takes precedence over work with machines, and elements of popular art from the 1920s are mingled with theosophical elements in artistic life. This utopian image of Russia's future also contains numerous allusions to events contemporary with its writing.

*Works:* Istorija parikmakherskoj kukly, ili Poslednjaja ljubov' Moskovskogo arkhitektora M. (pov.), 1918; *Obmanščiki* (play), 1921; *Venediktov, ili Dostopamjatnye sobytija žizni moej* (pov.), 1921; *Venecianskoe zerkalo, ili Dikovinnye pokhoždenija stekljannogo čeloveka* (pov.), Berlin, 1923; *Neobyčajnye, no istinnye priključenija grafa Fëdora Mikhajloviča Buturlina* (pov.), 1924; *Julija, ili Vstreči pod Novodevičem* (pov.), 1928; all six texts reprinted in *Istorija parikmakherskoj kukly i drugie sočinenija Botanika X*, New York, 1982; *Putešestvie moego brata Alekseja v stranu krest'janskoj utopii* (novel), 1920 (reprinted, New York, 1981); *Oeuvres choisies* (selected works), 8 vols., Paris, 1967 (reprint of the Russian eds., contains also *Putešestvie . . .*).

*Secondary Lit.:* N. D. Shaw, in *Slavic and*

East European Journal 1963:3; B. Kerblay, in Cahiers du monde russe et soviétique 1964:4, B. Filippov, in Russkaja mysl', Paris, Sept. 2, 1971, and in Novoe russkoe slovo, New York, May 16, 1982; M. Geller, in Russkaja mysl' Nov. 27, 1975; L. Čertkov, foreword in Chayanov's Putešestvie moego brata Alelseja v stranu krest'janskoj utopii, New York, 1981; N. Pervušin, in Novyj žurnal, New York, 149:1982; Ja. Tel'nov, in Novyj žurnal 158:1985.

**Chepúrin, Yúly Petróvich,** playwright (b. May 10 [April 27], 1914, Saratov). Chepurin's father was an icon painter. Chepurin worked at many jobs, including musician, shoemaker, tractor driver, and circus acrobat; he later graduated from a four-year drama school. He served as a frontline reporter during the Finnish-Russian War and on the Stalingrad front during World War II. In 1942 he joined the Communist Party and became involved in Party work. Chepurin's first play, Stalingradtsy (The Stalingraders), was performed in 1944 on the anniversary of the liberation of Stalingrad. Chepurin expanded it into a trilogy, adding the two plays Posledniye rubezhi (1948; The Last Borders) and Sovest (1949; Conscience). As a response to the Stakhanovite workers' appeal to dramatists "to show the wealth of thought and feeling of the people of the Stalin era," Sovest was awarded a Stalin Prize (for 1950, 3d class). The pseudoconflict of the play consists in the solving of the problem of whether a model industrial plant can eliminate the last percentage of shoddy production by Party appeal to the workers' conscience, or whether stronger control measures will be necessary. After 1953 Sovest was viewed critically, while Stalingradtsy, because of the scenes featuring the masses, was viewed more positively. Chepurin's subsequent dramas center on the problems of industrial construction. He is frequently unsuccessful in transposing his intentions into dramatic form and at the same time maintaining credibility. Khozyayeva zhizni (1962; Masters of Life) was criticized for its "obvious violations of the characters' logic" (Dymshits). Zapakh zemli (1966; The Smell of Earth) was intended as a contribution to the battle against rural flight to the cities; Snega (1970; Snows) is Chepurin's Lenin drama. He lives in Moscow and served on the Appeals Commission of the Writers Union of the RSFSR from 1965 to 1975.

Works: Stalingradcy (play), 1944; Vesennij potok (play), 1954; P'esy (plays), 1954;

Khozjaeva žizni (play), in Teatr 1962:6, separate ed., 1964; Dramy (plays), 1964 (contains Est' na Volge utës . . . ; Poslednie rubeži; Sovest'; Vesennij potok; Meč i zvëzdy; Kogda nam bylo semnadcat'; Tjažëloe ranenie; Khozjaeva žizni); Moë serdce s toboj (play), 1967; Naperekor (play), 1969; Vesëlyj samoubijca (play), 1971; Snega (play), in Teatr 1971:4, Snega (plays), 1973 (contains Snega; Stalingradcy; Tjažëloe ranenie; Meč i zvëzdy; Moë serdce s toboj; Vesëlyj samoubijca).
Secondary Lit.: A. Mackin, in Teatr 1951:4; S. Preobraženskij, in Vydajuščiesja proizvedenija sovetskoj lit. 1950 g., 1952; A. Dymšic, in Lit. i žizn' Aug. 1, 1962; I. Višnevskaja, in Teatr 1967:10; I. Nazarov, in Lit. gazeta June 18, 1975, p. 8.

**Chervínskaya, Lídiya Davýdovna,** poet (b. 1907). Chervinskaya belongs to the first wave of EMIGRATION and must have moved to Paris around 1922. Starting in 1930, her poems and reviews began appearing in various journals and were regularly included in anthologies. Her first collection of 37 poems, Priblizheniya (1934; Approachings), was published by N. Otsup in his Chisla publishing house and was followed by a similar second volume dedicated to G. Adamovich, Rassvety (1937; Dawns). The third volume, Dvenadtsat mesyatsev (1956; Twelve Months), was published by S. Makovsky in his poetry series at the Rifma publishing house. In 1985 Chervinskaya was living in Paris.
Chervinskaya's poetry emphasizes emotion and revolves around the motifs of love, longing, tearfulness, and doubt. She gives poetic expression to such contrasts as the ideal and reality, hope and disillusionment, past and present, emigration and Russia. Her verses are musical and take on elements of comprehensibility and entreaty through repetition and anaphora. She loves the skeptical, rhetorical question. In the later poems, her melancholy also encompasses her memories of war and of lost friends.

Works: Približenija (poems), Paris, 1934; Rassvety (poems), Paris, 1937; Dvenadcat' mesjacev (poems), Paris, 1956.
Secondary Lit.: N. Ocup, in Čisla, Paris, 10:1934; E. Tauber, in Grani, Frankfurt am Main, 31:1956; K. Pomerancev, in Vozroždenie, Paris, 59:1956.

**Chínnov, Ígor Vladímirovich,** poet (b. Sept. 25 [Sept. 12], 1909, Riga) Chinnov was the son of a lawyer. Chinnov, who had lived with his parents in Russia from 1914 to 1922, studied law in Riga and worked there as a legal adviser to business enterprises. He left Latvia in 1944 and lived first in Germany (until 1947), then in Paris (until 1953), returned to Germany, and then moved to the United States in 1962, where he was professor of Slavic languages and literatures at the University of Kansas until 1968 and at Vanderbilt University in Nashville until 1976. Chinnov lives in Daytona Beach, Florida.

Chinnov's first poems came out in Chisla in 1933–34; he published his first volume of 42 poems, Monolog, in Paris in 1950. Since then Chinnov's poems have been regularly published by Novy zhurnal, Grani, and other émigré journals. The title of his second volume, Linii (1960; Lines), a reference to the lines of fate in palmistry, emphasizes the intellectual focal point of Chinnov's verse. Chinnov included a selection from his first volume in the fifth, Kompozitsiya (1972; Composition); the entire second volume was included in the sixth, Pastorali (1976; Pastorals). Chinnov's verse emanates from his despair at the grief, dreariness, and horror in the world. The subject matter of his work is not his personal fate but doubt about the larger meaning of human existence. Occasionally the beauties of nature give him pause; these evoke very rare reminiscences about his native land. The idea of death as a horror and an enigma is found throughout his entire oeuvre. Pastorali is lighter in tone; here, too, Chinnov's numerous journeys provide a stimulus for rather more autobiographical verse. In his later work Chinnov takes refuge in irony and in fantastic, grotesque estrangement. This is apparent above all in Antiteza (1979; Antithesis), a collection of poems that assume a position "antithetical" to the transcendent, to the seriousness of the search for the meaning of life, death, and poetry. Chinnov's verse is clear, especially in the early volumes; his use of rhyme (which he abandoned later) is unpretentious. The poetic power of his verse comes primarily from its musical rhythm, changing meter, and multifarious repetition.

Works: Monolog (poems), Paris, 1950; Linii (poems), Paris, 1960; Metafory (poems), New York, 1968; Smotrite-stikhi (essays), in Novyj žurnal, New York, 92:1968; Partitura (poems), New York, 1970; Kompozicija (poems), Paris, 1972; Pastorali (poems), Paris, 1976; Antiteza (poems), College Park, Md., 1979; Avtograf, Holyoke, 1984.

Secondary Lit.: S. Makovskij, in Opyty, New York, 1:1953; E. Rajs, in Grani, Frankfurt am Main, 47:1960; Ju. Ivask, in Russkaja literatura v èmigracii, ed. N. Poltorackij, Pittsburgh, 1972, and in Novyj žurnal 138:1980; B. Narcissov, in Novyj žurnal 118:1975; V. Vejdle, in Novyj žurnal 123:1976; A. Bakhrakh, in Russkaja mysl', Paris, Feb. 16, 1978; J. Glad, V. Terras, in Činnov's Antiteza, 1979 (with bibliography); Z. Šakhovskaja, in Russkaja mysl' Nov. 15, 1979, and April 4, 1985; W. Kasack, in Osteuropa 1981:4; J. Glad, in MERSL 4:1981; T. Fesenko, in Novyj žurnal 161:1986.

Chísla (Numbers) a journal of literature, art, and philosophy. Altogether, ten issues (250 to 300 pp. each) of Chisla appeared in Paris between 1930 and 1934. This privately supported journal was aesthetically perhaps one of the most beautiful literary journals of the first emigration. Its editor was Nikolay Avdeyevich Otsup; the first four issues were coedited by Irma V. de Marciarli and, through her, the editorial board of the theosophical journal Cahiers de l'Etoile. The bulk of the literary contributions came from authors of the younger generation of émigrés, those who first began to write abroad (I. Chinnov, G. Gazdanov, A. Ginger, I. Odoyevtseva, B. Poplavsky, S. Sharshun, et al.). The authors whose reputations had been established prior to emigration were represented above all by Z. Gippius, D. Merezhkovsky, A. Remizov, and B. Zaytsev. The journal not only reported important new publications in Russian literature published abroad and in the Soviet Union but also commented on cultural life in Western Europe. The twenty-odd illustrations that appeared in each issue included works by M. Chagall, N. Goncharova, A. Jakovlev, M. Larionov, and I. Pougny, as well as Eugène Delacroix, André Derain, and Maurice de Vlaminck. Semyon Frank and Lev Shestov contributed articles on philosophy and religion. As a general rule the journal did not accept political articles. Despite the individualism of its literary and critical contributions and essays, Chisla was unified by its aloofness from formal experimentation and its respect for the intellectual basis of all art. The journal was printed in editions of 1000 and 1200 copies.

Secondary Lit.: M. Osorgin, in Sovremennye zapiski, Paris, 46:1931; B. Poplavskij, in Čisla, Paris, 10:1934; G. Struve, in his Russkaja literatura v izgnanii, New York, 1956, pp. 213–18; M. Bargman, in MERSL 4:1981; N. Ocup, in his Sovremenniki, Paris, 1961.

**Chórny, Sásha** (pseud. of Aleksándr Mikháylovich Glíkberg), poet, prose writer (b. Oct. 13 [Oct. 1], 1880, Odessa—d. Aug. 5, 1932, La Lavandou). Glikberg's father was the manager of a pharmacy. Glikberg spent his youth in Belaya Tserkov and his school years in Zhitomir. He worked for the customs service from 1902 to 1905, published journalistic articles in Zhitomir in 1904, and moved to St. Petersburg in 1905. There he also published political satires in journals, including Zritel. He studied in Heidelberg for one year (1906–7). In 1908 he returned to St. Petersburg and acquired unusual renown and acclaim within a few weeks for his satires in Satirikon, for which he had chosen the pseudonym Sasha Chorny. The first collection of his poems sarcastically exposing human weaknesses appeared under the title Satiry (1910; Satires); a second collection, Satiry i lirika (Satires and Lyric), was published in 1911. New and partially enlarged editions of both collections have appeared. In 1911 Chorny severed his ties to Satirikon and worked for various journals. He also began to write prose; to translate from German (including Heinrich Heine, Richard Dehmel); and at K. Chukovsky's request, to write children's books. In St. Petersburg he became friends with L. Andreyev and A. Kuprin. A narrative poem, Noy (1914; Noah), reveals his hopeless view of the future, a view that did not foresee improvement even as the result of a social revolution. From 1914 to 1917 Chorny was mobilized and was sent, as a soldier, to a field hospital, an experience that found an echo in poems and fairy tales published later. In 1920 Chorny emigrated to Vilnius, then to Kaunas, and then further to Berlin where he changed his pseudonym to A. Chorny and published extensively. Together with new editions of his two volumes of poetry he compiled a third, Zhazda (1923; Longing); edited the works of A. Chekhov, V. Zhukovsky, and I. Turgenev for children's editions; and wrote his own children's books. In 1924, as the private tutor of L. Andreyev's children, he moved to Rome with Andreyev's widow and finally settled in Paris at the end of 1924. Together with additional children's books he wrote Soldatskiye skazki (1933; Soldiers' Fairy Tales), a work that ensured him a permanent place in Russian literature. His travesty of N. Nekrasov, the narrative poem Komu v emigratsii zhit khorosho (1931–32; Who Is Happy in Emigration?), makes obvious the pessimistic undercurrents in this often so lighthearted narrative poet. A few months after moving to Provence, Chorny died by overexerting his heart while trying to extinguish a fire. In 1960, for the first time since his emigration, a comprehensive collection of his poetry appeared in the series "Biblioteka poeta" (Poet's Library). Several volumes were reprinted in Paris in 1978.

Chorny is a diverse and frequently read writer whose literary work can be mainly divided into his occasionally satiric poetry, his poetry for children, and his Soldatskiye skazki. After writing political satire for a brief period, he turned to a form of social satire in which he ridicules the pettiness, superficiality, and bourgeois attitude of the urban upper class, partially from behind an ironic mask. His satires are often narrative in form, always full of imagery, and effective through their unusual and pointed epithets. To a great degree this consciousness of words distinguishes Soldatskiye skazki, for there he makes generous and humorous use of the Russian vernacular. The hero is often the simple Russian soldier who, thanks to his peasant shrewdness, amusingly masters difficult or dangerous encounters with his superiors or with spirits. From 1911 on, Chorny published approximately 25 books for children; his own poetry, short stories, and dramas as well as editions of others' works and translations. They are directed at preschool-age and older children and have been enthusiastically received, first in tsarist Russia and later in emigration. Some were even published in the Soviet Union until 1930.

*Works:* Satiry (poems), 1910, 6th ed., Berlin, 1922, 7th ed., Paris, 1978; Satiry i lirika (poems), 1911, 1913, 4th ed., Berlin, 1922, 5th ed., Paris, 1978; Živaja azbuka (children's verses), 1913, 3d ed., Berlin, 1922; Detskij ostrov (poems), Danzig, 1921; Žažda (poems), Berlin, 1923; Rumjanaja knižka (children's short stories), Belgrade, 1929 (reprinted, Paris, 1978); Trubočist (children's verses), 1930; Soldatskie skazki (tales), Paris, 1933 (reprinted, Paris, 1978); Izbr. skazki (tales), Monterey, Calif., 1964; Stikhotvorenija (poems), 1960; Stikhotvorenija (poems), 1962.

*Secondary Lit.:* K. Čukovskij, in Černyj's Stikhotvorenija, 1960 and 1962; E. Evstigneeva, in Černyj's Stikhotvorenija, 1960 and 1962; Z. Papernyj, in Novyj mir 1960:9; E. Kannak, in Russkaja mysl', Paris, Aug. 10, 1978, p. 10; V. Andreev, in Russkaja mysl' Oct. 19, 1978, p. 10; W. Kasack, in Osteuropa 1981:8.

**Chukhóntsev, Olég Grigóryevich,** poet (b. March 8, 1938, Pavlovsky Posad, oblast Moscow). Chukhontsev's father was a leading economic official. In 1962 Chukhontsev graduated in humanities from the teachers college for the Moscow region. Since 1958 he has published poems in journals such as *Yunost* or *Molodaya gvardiya*; in addition, his poems were occasionally included in the anthologies *Den poezii*. His poem "Povestvovaniye o Kurbskom" (*Yunost* 1968:1) touched off several years of officious criticism. N. Korzhavin attributes the scandal solely to the poem's coincidence with the writer A. Belinkov's sensational escape to the United States (1968) rather than to Chukhontsev's accusation that a tyrant himself brings about treason and emigration through his own subversive behavior. Acknowledged by many as one of the most significant poets in the Soviet Union, Chukhontsev was allowed to publish his first slender volume of poetry, *Iz tryokh tetradey* (1976; From Three Notebooks), only at the age of 38. This volume was well received. An additional volume, *Slukhovoye okno* (Rooftop Window), was published in 1983 with many new poems. Chukhontsev also works as a translator and literary critic. In 1986 he was charged with the leadership of the poetry section in the journal *Novy mir*. He lives in Moscow.

Chukhontsev has characterized the ability "to listen to oneself" as "perhaps the principal prerequisite for the development of a poet" (*Druzhba narodov* 1982:5). Listening to his own voice and rendering what he hears in original images and associations is the distinguishing feature of Chukhontsev's poetry. He has a deep understanding of the pain and suffering of human beings and a great regard for the poor and persecuted, the Job-figures of this world. He perceives that one of the responsibilities of artists is to offer resistance to earthly evil and he understands the spiritual and religious basis of all art. He searches for the unusual and for the valid revealed in nature and in the commonplace and makes them visible to the receptive reader. He draws on historical situations and illustrates their spiritual and historical relevance but, through his poetic vision, he also lends them a universality that encompasses the present. Chukhontsev's language is founded in tradition and does not flaunt a consciousness of words. Images of cemeteries, crosses, belfries, and cloisters often serve to illustrate loneliness and silence, and the necessity of overcoming them.

Works: Poems, in *Junost'* 1962:10, 1965:3, 1966:6, 1968:1, and 1974:8; in *Molodaja gvardija* 1962:12, 1964:4, and 1965:9, in *Novyj*

*mir* 1970:6 and 1971:5; and in *Družba narodov* 1973:4 and 1982:10. *Iz trëkh tetradej* (poems), 1976; *Slukhovnoe okno* (poems), 1983.

Secondary Lit.: G. A. Novickij, in *Lit. gazeta* Feb. 7, 1968; N. Koržavin, in *Kontinent*, Paris, 17:1978; I. Andreeva, in *Družba narodov* 1978:2; B. Sarnov, in *Lit. obozrenie* 1978:12; I. Rodnjanskaja, in *Novyj mir* 1982:10; W. Kasack, in *Neue Zürcher Zeitung* Dec. 22/23, 1984; I. Šajtanov, in *Lit. obozrenie* 1985:2; L. Anninskij, in *Junost'* 1985:3; L. Vinokurova, in *Oktjabr'* 1985:3.

**Chukóvskaya, Lídiya Kornéyevna,** prose writer, critic (b. March 24 [March 11], 1907, Helsinki). Chukovskaya's father was the writer K. I. Chukovsky. Chukovskaya studied philology in Leningrad. For years she worked in publishing houses as an editor of children's literature. Using the pseudonym A. Uglov, she published her first short story, *Leningrad-Odessa*, in 1928 and later published in the field of literary criticism. Chukovskaya's husband was a victim of the Stalinist purges. In 1955 Chukovskaya published short monographs on S. Georgiyevskaya and B. Zhitkov. Her contribution to the liberal almanac *Literaturnaya Moskva* (1956:2) was *Rabochiy razgovor*, a piece about attitudes and abuses that exist in the process of editing belles lettres; she later expanded this work into the book *V laboratorii redaktora* (1960; In the Editor's Laboratory). Her own prose, which serves to present the truth about the Stalinist period and the sad consequences it had for many, could only be published in the West: her *Sofya Petrovna* was published under the title *Opustely dom* (1965; Eng. tr., The Deserted House, 1967); *Spusk pod vodu* (1972; Eng. tr., Going Under, 1972, 1976) uses the diary form to provide a moving, well-written insight into the position of writers in 1949. Chukovskaya addressed M. A. Sholokhov in an open letter written in April 1966, following his attacks on the convicted writers A. Sinyavsky and Yu. Daniel before the 23d Party Congress. "Literature is not subject to penal law. One must confront ideas with ideas, not with camps and prisons." In the same spirit she took up a position in favor of the protection of human rights and against the increasing number of cases of the suppression of information concerning the terror under Stalin (for example, A. Solzhenitsyn and A. Sakharov). On Jan. 9, 1974, Chukovskaya was expelled from the Writers Union, an event described as a typical case in her book *Protsess isklyucheniya* (1979; Process of Elimination). Between 1938 and

1941 and again between 1952 and 1956 Chukovskaya kept a detailed diary of her conversations with Anna Akhmatova. Appending extensive notes and commentary, she published this document, a highly significant comment on the spiritual state of the USSR in general, in Paris: *Zapiski ob Anne Akhmatovoy* (1976–80; Notes on Anna Akhmatova). Verse, which Chukovskaya wrote occasionally between 1936 and 1976, was also published in Paris in *Po etu storonu smerti* (1978; On This Side of Death); it reveals, in addition to her personal suffering from different forms of persecution, her love for her husband and her sorrow for the fate of Russia in view of the emigrations and exiles of the 1970s. Chukovskaya lives in Moscow and Peredelkino.

*Works:* Under the pseud. A. Uglov: *Leningrad-Odessa* (short story), 1929; *Povest' o Tarase Ševčenko* (pov.), 1930; *Na Volge* (pov.), 1931. Under her own name: *Istorija odnogo vosstanija* (short story), 1940; *Boris Žitkov* (literary criticism), 1955; *Susanna Georgievskaja* (literary criticism), 1955; *Rabočij razgovor* (essay), in *Lit. Moskva* 1956:2; *V laboratorii redaktora* (essay), 1960, 2d ed., 1963; *Opustelyj dom* (pov.), Paris, 1965; *Otvetstvennost' pisatelja i bezotvetstvennost' "Literaturnoj gazety"* (essay), in *Novyj žurnal*, New York, 93:1968; *Spusk pod vodu* (pov.), Paris, 1972; *Frida Abramovna Vigdorova* (literary criticism), in *Russian Literature Triquarterly* 5:1973; *Gnev naroda. Otkrytoe pis'mo* (open letter), in *Russkaja mysl'*, Paris, Nov. 1, 1973, p. 5; *Proryv nemoty* (literary criticism), in A. Solženicyn, *Bodalsja telёnok s dubom*, Paris, 1975; *Otkrytoe slovo* (documentary texts, contains among others the letters concerning Šolokhov and Solženicyn), New York, 1976; *Zapiski ob Anne Akhmatovoj* (diary), 2 vols., Paris, 1976, 1980; *Po ètu storonu smerti* (diary), Paris, 1978; *Process isključenija* (essay), Paris, 1979; *Pamjati detstva*, New York, 1983.

*Secondary Lit.:* G. Makagonenko, in *Lit. obozrenie* 1940:23; D. Bregova, in *Novyj mir* 1955:10; A. Turkov, in *Novyj mir* 1961:4; S. Kryžickij, in *Novyj žurnal* 109:1972; E. Brejtbart, in *Grani*, Frankfurt am Main, 104:1977; A. Klimoff, in *MERSL* 4:1981; E. Ètkind, in *Vremja i my*, Tel Aviv, 66:1982; A. Bakhrakh, in *Novoe russkoe slovo*, New York, Nov. 20, 1984, p. 5; W. Kasack, in *Die Welt* March 24, 1987.

**Chukóvsky, Kornéy Ivánovich** (pseud. of Nikoláy Vasílyevich Korneychukóv), poet, literary historian (b. March 31 [March 19], 1882, St. Petersburg—d. Oct. 28, 1969, Kuntsevo). Chukovsky is the father of the writers Lidiya Chukovskaya and Nikolay Chukovsky. He attended secondary school in Odessa and Nikolayev. In 1903–5 he worked as the London correspondent for the *Odesskiye novosti*, thereafter in St. Petersburg as the publisher of the satiric journal *Signal* and as a literary critic. He was friends with many renowned writers. From 1912 to 1917 Chukovsky lived in Kuokkala, a Finnish village. From 1916 to 1927 he wrote numerous children's books that combine both English and Russian influences. Later his children's poetry was sharply condemned by RAPP and the dogmatic pedagogues. Since that time, these children's fairy tales in verse form, such as *Moydodyr* (1923; Eng. tr., *Wash 'Em Clean*, 1969), have been published in millions of copies. "Already the fifth generation of children has grown up with these entertaining, enchanting books full of colors, music, fantasy, and joie de vivre" (V. Panova). In the book *Ot dvukh do pyati* (1933; Eng. tr., *From Two to Five*, 1963, rev. ed., 1971), Chukovsky demonstrates his fine comprehension of the psychological and linguistic-theoretical aspects of this first stage of childhood. After 1918 Chukovsky directed the Anglo-American division of the publisher Vsemirnaya literatura (World Literature) and translated many English works of belles lettres. After 1927 Chukovsky primarily occupied himself with translations concerning the history of literature and with translation theory; for his book about N. Nekrasov, *Masterstvo Nekrasova* (1952; Nekrasov's Literary Creativity), he received his doctorate in 1957 and the Lenin Prize in 1962. In 1962 Oxford University awarded him an honorary doctorate. Chukovsky, who moved to Moscow in 1938, also actively defended the cause of the purity of the Russian language, especially after 1954.

In his verse fairy tales for small children that were inspired by his loving, perceptive appreciation of such tales, Chukovsky developed a dynamic fable contrasting the bright and the dark sides of existence. The tales "immediately acquired immense popularity" (L. Chukovskaya). They allow the child to coexist with animals and animated objects; their effect is strongly dependent on folksong-like verses that have internal rhyme, repetitions, and many interjections.

*Works: PrikIučenija Krokodila Krokodiloviča* (fairy tales for children), 1919 (Eng. trs., *Crocodile*, 1931 and 1964); *Mojdodyr* (children's book), 1923 (see above); *Malen'kie deti* (treatise), 1928, 3d rev. ed. under the title *Ot dvukh do pjati*, 1933 (see above); *Skazki* (fairy tales for children), 1935; *Čudo-derevo* (fairy tales), 1943; *Masterstvo Nekrasova* (treatise), 1952; *Čukokkala. Rukopisnyj al'manach K. Č.* (visitors' book with commentary), 1979.—*Sobr. soč.*, 6 vols., 1965–69.

*Translations: Chekhov the Man*, 1945; *Baltic Skies*, 1957; *The Stolen Sun*, 1965; *Limpopo*, 1966; *Wonder Tales*, 1973; *The Silver Crest: My Russian Boyhood*, 1976; *The Poet and the Hangman (Nekrasov and Muravyov)*, 1977; *Alexander Blok as Man and Poet*, 1982; *The Art of Translation: Kornei Chukovsky's A High Art*, 1983.

*Secondary Lit.:* Ju. Tynjanov, in *Detskaja lit.* 1939:4; M. Petrovskij, 1966; S. T. Rassadin, in *Novyj mir* 1967:7; V. Panova, in her *Zametki literatora*, 1972, pp. 124–29; M. Slonimskij, in *Zvezda* 1972:8; *Žizn' i tvorčestvo K. Č.* (collection), 1978; L. Čukovskaja, in *MERSL* 4:1981; Z. Papernyj, in *Oktjabr'* 1982:3; L. Kopelev, R. Orlova, in *Russkaja mysl'*, Paris, April 1, 8, and 15, 1982.

**Chukóvsky, Nikoláy Kornéyevich**, prose writer, translator (b. June 2 [May 20], 1904, Odessa—d. Nov. 4, 1965, Moscow). Chukovsky was the son of the writer K. I. Chukovsky. Chukovsky grew up and went to school in St. Petersburg. He embarked on his career as a writer in 1922 by writing poems; he also wrote children's stories in the early 1920s. His novels about the Civil War appeared in the 1930s; of these, the most significant is *Yaroslavl* (1938, 3d ed., 1957). Chukovsky served as a frontline reporter during the Finnish-Russian War (1939–40) and World War II (in Leningrad). After the war he lived in Moscow, where between 1946 and 1954 he worked on his novel *Baltiyskoye nebo* (Eng. tr., *Baltic Skies*, 1959), a meticulously composed work, rich in action, about the defense of Leningrad. Chukovsky is the author of numerous short stories, one of which, *Brodyaga* (The Vagabond), was included in *Literaturnaya Moskva* (1956:2), an anthology heavily criticized by the dogmatic critics. The melancholy and hopeless tone of this short story (written originally in 1932) sharply distinguishes it from the literature of SOCIALIST REALISM of the preceding years, as well as from Chukovsky's own war novel with its positive characters. Chukovsky collected the most important works of his 30-year writing career in a volume of selected works in 1963. His whole life he was active as a translator of works from many languages (including those of Jack London,

Ernest Thompson Seton, Robert Louis Stevenson, Mark Twain, Sandor Petöfi). Chukovsky was a member of the editorial board of the journal *Znamya* from 1955 to 1962, and belonged to the boards of the Writers Unions of the USSR and the RSFSR. He was head of the translation section.

*Works: Tantalena* (pov.), 1925; *Russkaja Amerika* (pov.), 1928, 3d ed.; *Skvoz' dikij raj* (poems), 1928; *Knjažij ugol* (novel), 1937; *Jaroslavl'* (novel), 1938, 2d ed., 1949, 3d ed., 1957; *Voditeli fregatov* (novel), 1941; *Baltijskoe nebo* (novel), 1955, 9th ed., 1965 (see above); *Brodjaga* (novel), in *Lit. Moskva* 1956:2; *Izbr.*, 1963; *Pjatyj den'* (pov.), 1967; *Morskoj okhotnik* (pov. and short stories), 1972.—*Izbr. proizv.*, 2 vols., 1977.

*Secondary Lit.:* V. Vil'činskij, in *Zvezda* 1955:1; G. Trefilova, in *Novyj mir* 1963:12; *RSPP* 6(1):1969; M. Slonimskij, in *Neva* 1980:2; M. Aliger, in *Lit. gazeta* Aug. 15, 1984, p. 6.

**Chulkóv, Geórgy Ivánovich**, poet, prose writer (b. Feb. 1 [Jan. 20], 1879, Moscow—d. Jan. 1, 1939, Moscow). Chulkov was of noble descent. In 1899 he was expelled from university for his political activities; in 1902–4 he lived in exile in Siberia, thereafter in St. Petersburg, where he published his first poems in 1904 and a lyrical drama in 1907. Chulkov published the almanacs *Fakely* (1906–8) and *Belye nochi* (1907) and became editor in chief of *Zolotoye runo* (1908–10). His aspiration to unite "mystical anarchism" (of which he was the chief advocate) with symbolism met with considerable opposition from A. Bely. As a critic, Chulkov was on the staff of the journals *Novy put* and *Vesy*. Two novels, *Satana* (1915; Satan) and *Metel* (1917; The Blizzard), reveal the influence of F. Dostoyevsky in their psychological methodology. *Salto mortale ili povest o molodom volnodumtse Pyere Volkhovskom* (1930; Salto mortale; or, The Tale of the Young Freethinker Pierre Volkovsky) is a historical novel about the Decembrist period that takes liberties with historical facts. After the Revolution, Chulkov continued as a prose writer and literary publicist. A collection of essays, *Nashi sputniki* (1922; Our Fellow Travelers), and the memoirs *Gody stranstvij* (1930; Years of Travel) give his personal view of the symbolist period; they were criticized for their exaggerated emphasis of Chulkov's personal role and his alleged revolutionary attitude (M. Rabinovich). In 1933 he published a bio-bibliographic documentary study of F. Tyutchev; a work on Dostoyevsky, the value of which lies in its accumulation of material, was published posthumously. Chulkov's publicistic contribution to construction literature was *Putevye zametki* (1935; Travel Notes), an account of a journey to the Caucasus.

*Works: O mističeskom anarkhizme* (essay), 1906 (reprinted, Letchworth, 1971); *Satana* (novel), 1915; *Metel'* (novel), 1917; *Naši sputniki* (essays from 1912–22), 1922; *Stikhotvorenija* (poems), 1922; *Mjatežniki 1825 goda* (novel), 1926; *Gody stranstvij* (memoirs), 1930; *Salto mortale ili povest' o molodom vol'nodumce P'ere Volkhovskom* (novel), 1930; *Letopis' žizni i tvorčestva F. I. Tjutčeva* (scholarly study), 1933; *Putevye zametki* (publicistic prose), in *Novyj mir* 1935:12; *Kak rabotal Dostoevskij* (scholarly articles), 1939.—*Sobr. soč.*, 6 vols., 1911–12.

*Secondary Lit.:* Avrelij (pseud. of V. Ja. Brjusov), in *Vesy* 1906:8; A. Belyj, in *Arabeski* 1911, pp. 335–42; M. Rabinovič, in *Novyj mir* 1930:8–9; M. Poljakova, in *Novyj mir* 1939:9; W. H. Richardson, in *MERSL* 4:1981.

**Chumándrin, Mikhaíl Fyódorovich,** prose writer (b. 1905 [exact date unknown], Tula—d. Feb. 4, 1940, killed in action during the Finnish-Russian War). Chumandrin's father was a stoker. Chumandrin grew up in a children's home and also became a stoker. In 1923 he began a political career in Leningrad; in 1925 he also started a literary career; in 1927 he became a member of the Communist Party. As an official of LAPP (see RAPP), Chumandrin was on the editorial boards of various journals. In 1936–37 he headed the repertory department of the Gorky Theater. In 1937 his works, praised at one time, were attacked for giving too prominent a place to "leftist Communists" (*Lit. gazeta* Aug. 15, 1937). By admitting the error of his ways and accusing other writers (for example, Yu. Libedinsky), Chumandrin managed to save himself from further persecution (E. Brown).

Between 1926 and 1935 Chumandrin wrote several novels based on the lives of workers. *Fabrika Rable* (1928; The Rablé Factory) became the best known because of its subject, the private factory in the Soviet Union during the NEP period. The novel's aesthetic shortcomings, in terms of plot development, psychology, and verbal expression, were sharply attacked (Mashbits-Verov). Chumandrin published his impressions of his trip to Germany in 1931–32 in the account *Germaniya* (1933; Germany). He made several attempts to write plays inspired by his lengthy stay in the Soviet Far East (1935–36).

*Works: Rodnja* (pov.), 1927; *Fabrika Rable* (novel), 1928; *Leningrad* (novel), 1931; *Germanija* (articles), 1933, excerpted in *Novyj mir* 1933:1; *God roždenija 1905* (autobiographical novel), 1936; *Bikin vpadaet v Ussuri. Stojbišče Mitacheza* (plays), 1940.—*Izbr.*, 1958.

*Secondary Lit.:* I. Mašbic-Verov, in *Novyj mir* 1928:12; A. Štejn, in *Zvezda* 1940:12; E. Brown, *The Proletarian Episode in Russian Literature*, New York, 1953; *RSPP* 6(1):1969; A. Štejn, in *Moskva* 1980:1.

**Constructivism,** LTsK (Literatúrny Tséntr Konstruktivístov [Literary Center of the Constructivists]). In 1924 the LTsK, an independent, form-conscious literary group, was established; its members drew upon the "constructivist" tendencies in painting and architecture (Vladímir Tatlin, Naum Gabo, Antoine Pevsner) that were closely connected to FUTURISM and were prevalent at the beginning of the 1920s. The primary exponents were I. Selvinsky, K. Zelinsky (as theoretician), V. Lugovskoy, E. Bagritsky, V. Inber, B. Agapov, and Ye. Gabrilovich. Constructivism saw itself as a rational, Marxist movement in modern literature. In response to the dominant role of technology, a work of art should be thoroughly organized and perfectly constructed technically, and its separate parts should exhibit maximum functionalism. Constructivism established the ideal of "local semantics": images, metaphors, and rhymes should be subordinated to the central theme. "A love of numbers, of objective speech, of quotes from documents, of facts, of the description of an event—all these are characteristics of constructivism" (K. Zelinsky, 1928). Constructivism saw its social task as helping the proletariat—culturally the most backward class—to find their link to the developed cultural superstructure as quickly as possible. In their art, the exponents of constructivism, some of whom were important figures, adopted a position that was quite independent of the declaration they published in *LEF* (1925:3). As a result of the unification of intellectual life, the LTsK disbanded in the spring of 1930; some members—such as Bagritsky, who had previously been a member of PEREVAL—joined RAPP.

*Works: Gosplan literatury* (collection), 1925. *Secondary Lit.:* K. Zelinskij, in *Čitatel' i pisatel'* 1928:3 and in *Lit. manifesty* (see below); *Lit. manifesty,* 2d ed., 1929 (reprinted, Munich, 1969); H. Ermolayev, *Soviet Literary Theories 1917–1934,* Berkeley, 1963; *Kulturpolitik der SU,* Stuttgart, 1973; R. Grübler, *Russischer Konstruktivismus,* Wiesbaden, 1981.

**Cosmopolitanism** *(Kosmopolitízm),* a term introduced in 1947 to defame a positive attitude toward the intellectual achievements of the non-Communist West that did not correspond to the Party line. Diverging from the positive tradition associated with the term, the semiofficial philosophical journal *Voprosy filosofii* provided the following definition in 1948: "Cosmopolitanism is a reactionary ideology that preaches renunciation of national traditions, contempt for the distinctive features in the national development of each people, and renunciation of the feelings of national dignity and national pride. . . . The ideology of cosmopolitanism is hostile to, and in radical contradiction with, Soviet patriotism—the basic feature that characterizes the world outlook of Soviet man." Through the slogan "Campaign against Cosmopolitanism" or "Anti-Cosmopolitanism," literature and the humanities were drawn into the Soviet Union's anti-American and anti-English foreign policy during the period following World War II. The "Campaign against Rootless Cosmopolitans" forms the most embarrassing chapter in the centuries-old spiritual controversy over the relationship of art in Russia to art in Europe, a controversy that culminated in the struggle between the "Westerners" and the "Slavophiles" in the 19th century. The campaign against cosmopolitanism in literature was launched through the Party Resolution of 1946 (see PARTY RESOLUTIONS ON LITERATURE) in which the inclusion of any aspect of Western intellectual culture is proscribed as "kowtowing to the West." In the spring of 1947, A. Fadeyev mounted a campaign, whose tone and scope can scarcely be imagined, directed against highly regarded literary scholars and critics (for example, A. Dolinin, B. Eykhenbaum, V. Propp, A. Veselovsky,

V. Zhirmunsky) who had written about the influence Western European literature has had on Russian literature, through classicism or the use of fairy-tale motifs, for example. To some extent the campaign bore anti-Semitic traits. The attack was especially directed against the theater, among others against A. Borshchagovsky and L. Malyugin who had criticized cheap Party plays (by N. Virta, A. Sofronov, B. Romashov). Writers were called upon to illustrate the perniciousness of cosmopolitanism according to the Party line. Works in this style by Ye. Dolmatovsky, G. Fish, B. Lavrenyov, S. Mikhalkov, A. Shteyn, K. Simonov, A. Sofronov, A. Surkov, and A. Surov written between 1947 and 1949 are constructed according to the pattern of villainous Americans and isolated conscienceless Russian admirers of things foreign who are contrasted with nationally proud, patriotic Soviet Russians and isolated respectable Communist foreigners. The insincerity, schematism, and primitiveness of these works can scarcely be surpassed. After 1956, Soviet literary scholarship distanced itself from the works of this period to a great extent and labeled them dogmatic; nevertheless, Soviet patriotism remains as much an ideal today as it did before.

*Secondary Lit.:* V. Kirpotin, in *Oktjabr'* 1947:9 and 1949:3; *Protiv buržuaznoj ideologii kosmopolitizma,* in *Voprosy filosofii* 1948:2; A. Tarasenkov, in *Novyj mir* 1948:2 and in *Znamja* 1950:1; N. Gribačëv, in *Znamja* 1949:1 and in *Pravda* Feb. 16, 1949; K. Simonov, in *Pravda* Feb. 28, 1949, and in *Novyj mir* 1949:3; A. Sofronov, in *Znamja* 1949:2; P. Izmest'ev, in *Oktjabr'* 1949:3; A. Fadeev, in *Znamja* 1949:8; Ju. Žukov, in *Novyj mir* 1950:3; G. Struve, *Russian Literature under Lenin and Stalin 1917–1953,* London, 1972; P. Hübner, in *Kulturpolitik der SU,* Stuttgart, 1973.

**Country prose.** See VILLAGE PROSE.

**Cubo-futurism.** See FUTURISM.

# D

**Daniel, Yuliy Markovich.** See ARZHAK, NI-KOLAY.

**Davýdov, Yúry Vladímirovich,** prose writer (b. Nov. 20, 1924, Moscow). Davydov served with the navy from 1942 to 1949; he became a member of the Communist Party in 1947. He emerged as a writer for the first time in 1945; his first published collection of short stories was V moryakh i stranstviyakh (1949; At Sea and Abroad). Davydov is best known for his novel Glukhaya pora listopada (1968–70; The Silent Fall of Leaves). He lives in Moscow.

Two thematic spheres stand out in Davydov's literature: the first is the world of seafarers and discoverers, the second is the "Narodnaya volya" (people's will) movement of the period around 1880. Supported by primary archival research, Davydov captures the romanticism surrounding an unknown Russian explorer of 1815 in Vizhu bereg (1964; Land Ahoy); his Sudba Usoltseva (1973; Usoltsev's Fate) is a popularized presentation of the failure of Russian colonization in Africa. Mart (1959; March) is a novel about the attempts to assassinate Aleksandr II. Glukhaya pora listopada, which depicts especially well the psychological disintegration of the agent Degayev, who has sold out to the police, is inspired by the same historical sphere of the Narodnaya volya. In two subsequent povesti, Zaveshchayu Vam, bratya (1975; I Bequeath to You, Brothers) and Na Skakovom pole, okolo boyni (1978; On Skakovo Field, Near the Slaughterhouse), Davydov returns to the thematic sphere of the Narodnaya volya.

Works: V morjakh i stranstvijakh (short stories), 1949, 1956; Južnyj krest (pov.), 1957; Idi polnym vetrom (pov.), 1961; O druz'jakh tvoikh, Afrika (short stories), 1962; Mart (novel), 1964; Vižu bereg (pov.), 1964; Glukhaja pora listopada (novel), 1970; Sud'ba Usol'ceva (short stories and pov.), 1973; Zaveščaju Vam, brat'ja . . . (pov.), 1975; Na Skakovom pole, okolo bojni (pov.), 1978; Dve svjazki pisem (novel), in Družba narodov 1982:8–9; Karžavin Fëdor, volonter svobody (pov.), in Družba narodov 1986:10.—Izbr., 1985.

Secondary Lit.: V. Tvardovskaja, in Novyj mir 1959:12; S. Rassadin, in Junost' 1969:1

and in Voprosy lit. 1985:5; M. Korallov, in Novyj mir 1974:6; V. Kardin, in Lit. obozrenie 1976:9; A. Gladilin, in Novoe russkoe slovo, New York, Dec. 19, 1982, p. 5; S. Eremina, V. Piskunov, in Lit. obozrenie 1983:3.

**Deméntyev, Nikoláy Stepánovich,** prose writer (b. Feb. 17, 1927, Leningrad). After completing his studies in water transport engineering, Dementyev worked in Siberia. He began his literary career by writing short stories that were published in the journal Sibirskiye ogni from 1952 on and in separate collections in 1954 and 1955. His first major prose work, the povest Kubanets (1958; The Man from the Kuban), is set among students. Dementyev became known principally for Moi dorogi (1958; My Roads), a povest set in Siberia that deals with the growth of an institute graduate while he is doing practical work in the collective. Its sequel, Prekrasnaya zima v Sibiri (1960; A Wonderful Winter in Siberia), again shows Dementyev's interest in the maturation of a young man's character by success and failure, but above all by the fortifying power of work. The then-current theme of the connection between work and scientific research is resolved in Dementyev's writing in accordance with the official point of view. Dementyev sets the perspective and attempts to depict the creative process of scientific work, using the first-person narrative structure he favors. He selected the blockade of Leningrad as the subject of his povest Chuzhiye bliznetsi (1962; Unknown Twins). Dementyev lives in Leningrad. For a while he belonged to the board of the Writers Union and the RSFSR after its formation in 1958; from 1963 to 1967 he was a member of the editorial board of the journal Neva.

Works: Pervoe pis'mo (short stories), 1954; Sëstry (short stories), 1955; Moi dorogi (pov.), 1958, 1972; Prekrasnaja zima v Sibiri (pov.), in Zvezda 1960:11–12; Idu v žizn' (pov. and short stories), 1961; Zamužestvo Tat'jany Belovoj (novel), in Neva 1963:12, separate ed., 1964; Čužie bliznecy (pov.), 1965; Kakogo cveta nebo (pov.), 1969; Vo imja čeloveka (novel and pov.), 1975; Ljudi, prostite menja (pov.), in Neva 1983:3.

Secondary Lit.: G. Curikova, in Novyj mir 1959:5; V. Baskakov, in Voprosy lit. 1959:5;

V. Litvinov, in *Lit. gazeta* Jan. 24, 1961; N. Janovskij, in *Moskva* 1964:7; Ju. Rjurikov, in *Voprosy lit.* 1965:8; Ja. Nazarenko, in *Lit. obozrenie* 1976:8.

**Dikóvsky, Sergéy Vladímirovich,** prose writer (b. March 14 [March 1], 1907, Moscow—d. Jan. 6, 1940, during the Finnish-Russian War). Dikovsky's father was an art teacher. Dikovsky grew up in the Ukraine. He changed jobs several times after completing school; beginning in 1925 he worked as a journalist. In 1928–29 he saw service in the Red Army and took part in the border fighting in the Soviet Far East. In 1930 Dikovsky began a program of Japanese studies in Vladivostok but returned to his journalism career that very same year. He traveled extensively within the Soviet Union and briefly to Japan on assignment for *Komsomolskaya Pravda* and *Pravda* (after 1934). Most of Dikovsky's works, which consist primarily of short stories, are set in the Soviet Far East and deal with border guards and fishermen. *Gospozha Sliva* (1935; Madame Plum), a concentrated work about the tragic life of a Japanese woman, is one of his best stories. His *povest Patrioty* (1937; The Patriots), praised by S. Gekht for its extraordinary landscape descriptions and its masterful double-layered composition, was highly regarded. In 1939 his short story *Komendant Ptichyego ostrova* (Eng. tr., in *The Commandant of Bird Island*, 1947) was made into a film. Dikovsky's early death put an end to plans for a novel and a drama.

*Works: Zastava N* (short stories), 1933; *Gospoža Sliva* (short story), 1935; *Patrioty* (pov.), 1937; *Konec "Sago Maru"* (short stories), 1938; *Komendant Ptič'ego ostrova* (short story), 1939 (see above); *Priključenija katera "Smelyj"* (short stories), 1940; *Izbr.*, 1948; *Izbr. proizv.*, 1956; *Patrioty* (pov. and short stories), 1962. *Translation: The Commandant of Bird Island* (contains the title story, "Patriots," "The End of the 'Sago Maru'," "Beri-Beri," and "Above All—Don't Lose Your Temper"), 1947. *Secondary Lit.:* S. Gekht, in *Novyj mir* 1940:6; A. Makarov, in *Znamja* 1956:7; *RSPP* 1:1959; O. Kučkina, in *Molodaja gvardija* 1963:4.

**Dmítriyev, Víktor Aleksándrovich,** prose writer (b. Nov. 5 [Oct. 23], 1905, Paris—d. Oct. 22, 1930, Moscow). Dmitriyev fought with the Bolsheviks in the Civil War. He studied in the Department of Indian Studies at the Leningrad Institute of Oriental Studies. From 1924 to 1927 he worked as a journalist, writing primarily for the journal *Molodoy bolshevik*. Dmitriyev's actual literary career was limited to the two-year period from 1928 to 1930. He wrote several short stories, such as *Stranniki* (1929; The Wanderers), and a novel, *Druzhba* (1930; Friendship). Dmitriyev was attacked in *Na literaturnom postu* as a slanderer of Soviet reality (because of his story *Syn* [Son]) and was expelled from RAPP. He rebutted this crude criticism and pointed out that he himself was the first writer in Soviet literature to draw attention to the dangers associated with a particular character type. He never completed a study of contemporary affairs, *K voprosu ob industrializatsii SSSR* (1930; On the Problem of Industrialization in the USSR). Dmitriyev took his own life. L. Slavin undertook to bring out an edition of his works in 1932; Dmitriyev was subsequently forgotten. The *Kratkaya literaturnaya entsiklopediya* (The Short Encyclopedia of Literature) did include his name in 1964; in 1970 V. Kaverin examined Dmitriyev's works closely and called for a new edition.

Dmitriyev's journalism is polemical, presumably modeled on that of D. Pisarev, and rich in irony. His literary prose is consciously based on that of Yu. Olesha; he signed his prose piece *Semya* (The Family) with the pseudonym "Kavalerov." Olesha's concreteness, as well as his juxtaposition of practical people and dreamers, can be found in Dmitriyev's work. *Druzhba*, "a novel about unrealized glory and betrayed trust" (Kaverin), is largely autobiographical in character.

*Works: Rasskazy* (short stories), 1930; *Sem'ja* (pov.), 1930; *Povesti i rasskazy* (pov. and short stories), 1932. *Secondary Lit.:* A. Efremin, in *Tridcat' dnej* 1929:10; M. Serebrjanskij, in *Na literaturnom posty* 1930:10; V. Kaverin, in his *Sobesednik*, 1973.

**Dobrovólsky, Vladímir Anatólyevich,** prose writer (b. April 17, 1918, Kharkov). Dobrovolsky completed his philological studies in 1941. He became a member of the Communist Party in 1948. Dobrovolsky began his literary career in 1938 but attracted no attention until the publication of his novel *Troye v serykh shinelyakh* (1948; Three Men in Gray Overcoats), for which he received a Stalin Prize (for 1948, 3d class). Working with Ya. Smolyak, he adapted the novel for the stage: the play *Yablonevaya vetka* (The Apple Branch) was performed in 1951. Dobrovolsky published several novels after 1957, including *Bosikom po luzham* (1965; Barefoot through the Puddles), which draws on the experience of his own youth. Dobrovolsky lives in Kharkov; he has never been selected as a delegate to any of the congresses of the Writers Union and is not mentioned in literary histories. Dobrovolsky's novels are devoted primarily to the theme of youth. His novel Troye v serykh shinelyakh, the title of which alludes to J. B. Priestley's Three Men in New Suits (1945), depicts the day-to-day life of students during the reconstruction period that followed World War II. Dom v tupike (1959; The House in the Cul-de-sac) shows young people in 1931 caught in the conflict, political as well as personal, between home and school. Dobrovolsky's next work takes place in a scientific milieu; its title, Avgust, padayut zvyozdy (1964; August, Stars Are Falling), has a double meaning and alludes to the downfall of a criminal. In Bosikom po luzham, Dobrovolsky returns to the central character of his novel of the 1930s. Za nedelyu do otpuska (1976; A Week before Vacation) pursues the problems faced by an engineer who has caused a fatal accident and who is divided between his need to confess his guilt and his desire to take advantage of the situation. Tekushchiye dela (1978; Current Affairs) also takes place in the world of industry. Dobrovolsky's style is lively; there is an abundance of action, with several interlocking, carefully laid-out plot lines. Occasionally, mostly in the conclusions, he becomes schematic and inadequately realizes his purpose. Dobrovolsky's works provide an instructive insight into everyday Soviet life.

*Works: Troe v serykh šineljakh* (novel), 1948; Ženja Maslova (novel), 1950; Na vsju žizn' (novel), 1957; Dom v tupike (novel), 1959; Uglovaja komnata (pov.), 1962; Avgust, padajut zvëzdy (pov.), 1964; Bosikom po lužam (novel), 1965; I dukh naš molod (novel), 1971; Za nedelju do otpuska (pov.), 1977; Tekuščie dela (novel), in Zvezda 1978:11–12, separate ed., 1980; Mera presečenija (pov.), in Zvezda 1981:9–10; Krymskie persiki (pov.), in Zvezda 1984:6.

*Secondary Lit.:* G. Lenobl', in Novyj mir 1949:7; E. Ljubarëva, in Oktjabr' 1950:6 and in Lit. gazeta Dec. 28, 1965; V. Brjuggen, in Lit. gazeta Nov. 3, 1964, in Novyj mir 1966:6, and in Raduga 1973:2; K. Lasta, in Oktjabr' 1977:3; M. Sinel'nikov, in Lit. gazeta May 16, 1979, p. 4.

**Dolmatóvsky, Yevgény Arónovich,** poet (b. May 5 [April 22], 1915, Moscow). Dolmatovsky's father was a lawyer. In 1933–34 Dol-

matovsky, a Komsomol member, worked on the building of the Moscow subway; in 1934 he completed his studies at the Gorky Literary Institute. His first publication was in 1934; he became a member of the Communist Party in 1941; he was a Stalin Prize winner (for 1949, 3d class). Dolmatovsky has belonged to the boards of the Writers Unions of the USSR and the RSFSR since 1958. He lives in Moscow.

Dolmatovsky is one of the much-printed poets of the Stalin period who turned against the anti-Stalinists even after 1956: "Not only executioners and victims/ Existed at that time." His poems are publicistic; their subject matter is always topical: the Spanish War, the Finnish-Russian War, World War II, the building of the Volga-Don Canal, COSMOPOLITANISM, colonialism, the Hungarian Uprising, the Vietnam War, travels to East Germany, Africa, and India were all reflected in his poems. In Bylo (2 vols., 1975, 1979; It Happened), Dolmatovsky published reminiscences and sketches of his life. His poems are narrative in form, understandable on the first reading, and have only one level of meaning; they are limited to one subject and intended for a broad reading public. Many have been set to music. Dolmatovsky is an experienced writer of verses that flow easily in smooth rhythm; he selects easy, usually grammatical rhymes. "Many resounding words have I said of the Party"—indeed, he has placed his poetic talent in the Party's service.

*Works: Slovo o zavtrašnem dne* (poems), 1949; Stikhi o nas (poems), 1964; Vsadniki, pesni, dorogi, 1973; Nadeždy, trevogi . . . (poems), 1977; Bylo. Zapiski poeta (sketches), 2 vols., 1975, 1979; Zelënaja brama (essays), in Oktjabr' 1987:7 and 1982:6; Interstikh, 1982.—Izbr. proizv., 1959; 2 vols., 1971; Sobr. soč., 3 vols., 1978–79.

*Secondary Lit.:* E. Troščenko, in Novyj mir 1943:10–11; B. Solov'ev, in Moskva 1963:10; A. Sinjavskij, in Novyj mir 1965:3; G. Stepanidin, in Oktjabr' 1973:12; M. Sinel'nikov, in Lit. gazeta April 16, 1980, p. 5; I. Vasjučenko, in Oktjabr' 1985:5.

**Dombróvsky, Yúry Ósipovich,** prose writer (b. May 12 [April 29], 1909, Moscow—d. May 29, 1978). Dombrovsky's father was a lawyer. From 1926 to 1932 Dombrovsky was a student in the Advanced Literature Courses in Moscow. He later earned a living as an academic employee in a museum in Alma-Ata. He began his literary work in 1937 by writing poems; his first, unnoticed novel, Derzhavin, appeared in Alma-Ata in 1939. Around this time he was apprehended, a victim of the atmosphere of mistrust, and he spent almost 20 years in prisons, labor camps, and exile. From 1943 to 1958 he wrote the novel *Obezyana prikhodit za svoim cherepom* (1959; The Ape Is Coming to Pick Up His Skull). Dombrovsky then moved to Moscow. With *Khranitel drevnosti* (1964; Eng. tr., The Keeper of Antiquities, 1969), a work based on his own experiences, Dombrovsky created one of the best works on the Stalin period. Only the abridged version of the novel was published in the Soviet Union. The novel written between 1964 and 1975, *Fakultet nenuzhnykh veshchey* (1978; The Faculty of Superfluous Things), was only published abroad. Dombrovsky translated from Kazakh (novels by I. Yesenberlin) and occasionally published shorter prose works. He signed the petition for A. Sinyavsky and Yu. Daniel in 1966 but otherwise remained outside literary life; he is seldom mentioned in reference books. He lived in Moscow.

*Obezyana prikhodit za svoim cherepom* is a traditionally written novel concerning the German occupation of Western Europe that symbolically depicts the conflict with brutal force. In *Khranitel drevnosti*, Dombrovsky illustrates the individual intellectual's surrender to mistrust and force in the 1930s by using grotesquerie, irony, and historical analogies. The novel *Fakultet nenuzhnykh veshchey*, whose title alludes to the failure to apply rights and law in the Soviet Union, provides realistic, literarily significant insight into the senselessness of interrogations and human degradation in a totalitarian system, using the example of the leader of an archaeological expedition for gold in Kazakhstan in 1937. Dombrovsky's later prose also uses historical references (for example, Shakespeare's time) to elucidate the present. Dombrovsky writes clearly and vividly; *Khudozhnik Kalmykov* (1970; The Painter Kalmykov) shows his respect for the irrational in art; his theoretical contributions reflect his conscious relationship to language.

Works: Deržavin (novel), 1939; Obez'jana prikhodit za svoim čerepom (novel), 1959; Khranitel' drevnosti (novel), in Novyj mir 1964:7–8, separate ed., 1966 (see above), complete ed., Paris, 1978; Literatura i jazyk (inquiry), in Voprosy lit. 1967:6; Smuglaja ledi (three pov.), 1969; Khudožnik Kalmykov, in Prostor 1970:9; "Daže v pekle nadežda zavoditsja . . ." (poem) ["Iz konclagernoj poèzii"], in Grani, Frankfurt am Main, 85:1972; Derevjannyj dom na ulice Gogolja, in Prostor 1973:11; Ledi Makbet (short story), in Sel'skaja molodëž' 1974:1; Fakel (short stories), 1974; Ja by mog . . . (essay), in Novyj mir 1975:12; Fakul'tet nenužnykh veščej (novel), Paris, 1978; Pis'mo k Sergeju Antonovu, in Grani 111–12:1979.

Secondary Lit.: I. Mikhajlov, in Neva 1960:9; A. Flaker, in Československa rusistiká 1966:11; F. Svetov, in Prostor 1969:7; M. Čudakova, in Lit. obozrenie 1974:8; V. Vladimirov, in Lit. obozrenie 1975:4; E. Cvetkov, in Vremja i my, Tel Aviv, 30:1978; A. Malumjan, in Kontinent, Paris, 20:1979; I. Šenfel'd, in Grani 111–12:1979; Ju. Gastev, in Russkaja mysl', Paris, June 3, 1982, pp. 6–7.

**Don-Aminado.** See AMINADO, D.

**Dorónin, Iván Ivánovich,** poet (b. Aug. 15 [Aug. 2], 1900, Sloboda, prov. Tula—d. Nov. 9, 1978, Moscow). Doronin was of peasant descent. Doronin worked as a horticulturalist until 1915 and as a factory worker in Tula until 1920. His first poems date from 1919. In 1920 he became a member of the Communist Party. Doronin attended the writing classes at the PROLETKULT and the Bryusov Institute of Literature and Art. In 1922 he joined the literary association of proletarian writers "Rabochaya vesna," and later, OKTYABR. *Granitny lug* (The Granite Meadow), his first volume of verse, appeared in 1922. The influence of M. Koltsov (evident in Doronin's ties to nature and his use of a manner imitative of folk songs), coupled with the basic stance of a Komsomol poet and an awareness of being a proletarian, is a characteristic of Doronin's verse. A. Lunacharsky, who described Doronin's *Traktorny pakhar* (1926; Plowman with a Tractor) as "a collection of striking and talented material for a genuine poem about the city and the country," lent Doronin his support because of the poet's ability to give concrete form to, and to describe the fusion of, proletarian and peasant elements. Doronin's reputation declined at the end of the 1920s; the few things he wrote subsequently were paraphrases of his earlier poems. Doronin, who lived in Moscow, participated in neither the First Congress of the Writers Union of the USSR nor in any that took place after 1954. He appears not to have written any more original verse but instead collected large quantities of recorded Soviet folk poetry as it appeared in provincial papers and wall newspapers or was presented in amateur theaters. An extensive selection of this material, O chom

*poyot narod Otchizny* (Of What the Fatherland Sings), appeared in 1968.

Works: *Granitnyj lug* (poems), 1922; *Pesni
sovetskikh polej* (poems), 1924; *Lesnoe Komsomol'e* (poems), 1925; *Izbr. stikhi* (poems),
1925; *Traktornyj pachar'* (narrative poem),
1926; *Otvet* (poems), 1927; *Stikhi* (poems),
1937; *Moja doroga* (poems), 1937; *Družinnica
Nataša* (narrative poem), 1942; *O čëm poët
narod Otčizny* (collected folklore), 1968; *Rodniki narodnye* (collected folklore), 1973.
Secondary *Lit.*: A. V. Lunačarskij, in *Oktjabr'*
1924:3 and in his *Stat'i o sovetskoj literature*,
1958, 2d ed., 1971; V. Krasil'nikov, in *Novyj
mir* 1925:12; N. Sergovancev, in *Oktjabr'*
1963:9; obituary, in *Lit. gazeta* Nov. 17 and
22, 1978; RSPPo 7:1984; R. Doronina, in *Lit.
Rossija* Aug. 16, 1985, p. 19.

**Dórosh, Yefím Yákovlevich** (pseud. of Ye.
Ya. Gólberg), prose writer (b. Dec. 25 [Dec.
12], 1908, Yelizavetgrad, prov. Kherson—d.
Aug. 20, 1972, Moscow). In the early 1920s
Dorosh led a hand-to-mouth existence in
Odessa; in 1924 he moved to Moscow. He
studied art history until 1931; at the same
time he was the director of an amateur theater
group for which he wrote one-act plays. In
1939 and 1941 he collected into two small
volumes some of the short stories he had been
publishing separately since 1931. Dorosh was
a frontline reporter during World War II; he
subsequently became a correspondent for *Literaturnaya gazeta*. He was admitted to the
Communist Party in 1945. In the mid-1940s
Dorosh selected life on the kolkhoz as the
major theme of his short stories and documentary prose. His work achieved its full potential only after the 20th Party Congress. He
lived in Moscow and was a member of the
editorial boards of the journals *Znamya* (1954–
56), *Moskva* (1957–58), and *Novy mir* (1967–
70); in 1966 he came out in support of
A. Sinyavsky and Yu. Daniel. Dorosh was
selected as a delegate only to the congresses
of the Writers Union of the RSFSR held in
1965 and 1970.
    Most of Dorosh's short stories develop
themes established in his *Derevensky dnevnik*
(1963; A Village Diary), which he continued
on a regular basis. Every year for 20 years he
traveled to the area around Rostov Veliky and
recorded his careful observations of the changes
in the people and their way of life in his
articles. Dorosh's attempt to achieve a convincing degree of realism determined his consistent preference for the first-person narrative

structure; in this way his narrator shares the
experiences of the present and reports those
of the past. In this manner also Dorosh exposes abuses, primarily those that result from
bureaucratic directives issued by a central
management divorced from reality. "Better
than any other writer of countryside sketches,
Dorosh combines an understanding of Russian peasants as a class with a profound respect for them as individuals, each with his
own personality, desires, and ambitions. He
finds them more interesting and wholesome
than city dwellers" (D. Brown). In the late
1960s Dorosh began to include the thematic
complex of the preservation of the cultural
values of the past in his work. The concise
and vivid style and the convincing dialogue
of Dorosh's prose place it among the best work
of contemporary Russian literature.

Works: *Maršal'skie zvëzdy* (short stories),
1939; *Voennoe pole* (short stories), 1941;
*S novym khlebom* (short stories), 1952; *Rasskazy* (short stories), 1954; *Derevenskij dnevnik* (short stories), 1958, enl. ed., 1963; *Dožd'
popolam s solncem* (short stories), 1965, enl.
ed., 1973; *Živoe derevo iskusstva* (essays),
1967, enl. ed., 1970; *Ivan Fedoseevič ukhodit
na pensiju* (pov.), 1971; archival materials, in
*Voprosy lit.* 1975:7 and *Novyj mir* 1975:7.
Secondary *Lit.*: N. Atarov, in *Oktjabr'* 1955:6;
RSPP 1:1959; V. Lakšin, in *Novyj mir* 1966:3;
G. Žekulin, in *Canadian Slavic Studies* 1967:1
and in *Russian and Slavic Literature*, Ann
Arbor, 1976; V. Surganov, in *Znamja* 1971:2;
E. Klepikova, in *Zvezda* 1972:1; M. Kuz'min,
in *Slavia Orientalis* 1973; A. Turkov, in *Lit.
gazeta* Jan. 30, 1974, p. 5; C. Theimer Ne-
pomnyashchy, in MERSL 5:1981.

**Dovlátov, Sergéy Donátovich**, prose writer
(b. Sept. 3, 1941, Ufa). Dovlatov's father, a
Jew, was a stage director; his mother, an Armenian, was an actress. Born during the evacuation, Dovlatov grew up in Leningrad after
1944. In 1959 he began studying Finnish philology at Leningrad University but was forced
to cut his studies short after two and a half
years. Dovlatov was then drafted into the military and served as a guard at a penal camp
in the north of the Komi ASSR from 1962 to
1965. After returning to Leningrad, Dovlatov
resumed his studies (Faculty of Journalism).
He worked as a journalist and began writing
short stories but was able to publish only a
few insignificant reviews and essays in Leningrad journals. He was a member of the Leningrad writers' circle Gorozhane (The Towns-

DOVZHÉNKO 88

people), a circle that also included the authors V. Maramzin, I. Yefimov, and B. Vakhtin; the mother of the last-named, V. Panova, gave Dovlatov a position as secretary and thus protected him from prosecution. In 1974 Dovlatov withdrew to Tallinn (Estonia) but had to return to Leningrad in 1976. After the late 1960s, Dovlatov's short stories circulated in SAMIZDAT; in 1977–78 the first ones appeared in TAMIZDAT (*Kontinent* [11:1977], *Vremya i my* [14, 27, 28:1978]). He was harassed for these publications; in August 1978 he was allowed to emigrate with his family. He moved to New York where, within a short period of time, he published numerous short stories in various émigré journals. *Nevidimaya kniga* (1978; Eng. tr., *The Invisible Book*, 1979) published before he emigrated. By 1986 eight additional books had followed; parts of the works included in these volumes had previously been published in journals. These books are *Solo na undervude* (1980; Solo for Underwood), *Kompromiss* (1981; Eng. tr., *The Compromise*, 1983), *Zona* (1982; Eng. tr., *The Zone*, 1985), *Marsh odinokikh* (1983; The March of the Lonely), *Zapovednik* (1983; The Preserve [that is, the Pushkin Museum near Pskov]), *Nashi* (1983; Our People), *Remeslo* (1985; Craft), *Chemodan* (1986; The Suitcase).

*Zona*, Dovlatov's first written work of prose, differs from other literature about the camps in the time period depicted (end of the Khrushchev era), in the point of view (that of a soldier guard), and finally in its psychological awareness that the prisoners and guards, the victims and executioners, begin to resemble one another in their behavioral norms. In *Kompromiss* he recounts his experiences as a journalist in Estonia and provides realistic accounts of the life of the Soviet intelligentsia. *Solo na undervude* is a compilation from his diaries with an aphoristic character. Through the ironic distancing in the blend of realistic reports, documents, and quotes from the subsequently published *Solo na undervude*, *Nevidimaya kniga* reveals Dovlatov's truly bizarre struggle to get his prose published in the face of opposition from the establishment of Soviet writers. *Marsh odinokikh* brings together Dovlatov's editorials from *Novy Amerikanets*, the newspaper he cofounded. *Zapovednik* describes his experiences as a tour guide at A. Pushkin's estate (1976–77). *Nashi* is the story of his family. Dovlatov knows how to make the reader immediately feel a part of the depicted situation; his writing is smooth and lively. Using striking incidents from his own experience, he provides a reli-

able image of life in the Soviet Union during the 1960s and 1970s.

*Works:* Short stories, in *Kontinent*, Paris, 11:1977; in *Vremja i my*, Tel Aviv, 14:1977, 28:1978, 36:1978, 38:1979, 40:1979; in *Ėkho*, Paris, 1979:1–3; in *Tret'ja volna*, Montgeron, 7–8:1979, 10:1980; in *Čast' reči*, New York, 1:1980; in *Russica*, Paris, 1981; in *Grani*, Frankfurt am Main, 135:1985. *Nevidimaja kniga* (pov.), Ann Arbor, 1978 (see above); *Solo na undervude* (aphoristic notes), Paris, 1980, 2d ed., Holyoke, 1983; *Kompromiss* (pov.), New York, 1981 (see above); *Zona* (pov.), Ann Arbor, 1982 (see above); *Zapovednik* (pov.), Ann Arbor, 1983; *Naši* (pov.), Ann Arbor, 1983; *Marš odinokikh* (essays), Holyoke, 1983; *Remeslo* (pov.), Ann Arbor, 1985; *Lišnij* (short story), in *Grani* 135:1985; *Rasskazy iz čemodana* (short stories), in *Grani* 137:1985; *Čemodan* (short stories), Tenafly, N.J., 1986.

*Secondary Lit.:* E. Schoen, in *New York Times* Sept. 7, 1980; Anon., in *Kontinent* 24:1980; L. Loseff, in *MERSL* 5:1981; D. M. Fiene, in *Slavic and East European Journal* 1983:2; W. Goodman, in *New York Times* Aug. 30, 1983; M. Taranov, in *Kontinent* 36:1983; K. Rosenberg, in *The Nation* Nov. 5, 1983; A. H. Karriker, in *World Literature Today* Autumn 1983; S. Mydans, in *New York Times* Sept. 23, 1984; I. Serman, in *Grani* 136:1985; E. Tudorovskaja, in *Grani* 140:1986.

**Dovzhénko, Aleksándr Petróvich,** Ukrainian script writer, playwright, prose writer (b. Sept. 11 [Aug. 30], 1894, Sosnitsa, prov. Chernigov—d. Nov. 25, 1956, Moscow). Dovzhenko was of peasant descent. After 1917 Dovzhenko studied at various institutions, including the Kiev School of Business and Kiev University; in 1921–22 he served in the diplomatic corps in Warsaw and Berlin; he studied art in Berlin until 1923. From 1923 to 1926 he was an illustrator for a newspaper in Kharkov. After 1926 he worked in Ukrainian film studios as director and scenarist of his own films: *Zvenigora* (1927), *Arsenal* (1928), *Zemlya* (1930; Eng. tr., *Earth*), in *Two Russian Film Classics*, 1973), and *Ivan* (1932). Demyan Bedny launched an extremist political attack on Dovzhenko's film *Zemlya in Izvestiya*. Dovzhenko's opportunities to work were severely curtailed; his film *Ivan*, produced in 12 days as instructed, was torn apart in the Party press. Dovzhenko, labeled a fascist, moved to Moscow in 1932. There at Mosfilm he was able to film a series of his screenplays; he received a Stalin Prize (for 1935–40, 1st class) for his direction of the film *Shchors*. In 1944, however, Stalin personally reprimanded Dovzhenko (his diary entry for July 27, 1945, reads: "Comrade Stalin . . . why have you turned my life into torment?"). Up to the THAW, he was unable to film any of the scripts he wrote after 1948. Dovzhenko wrote a series of short stories and, partly after curtailment of his work with film, recast his screenplays in independent literary form; in 1948 he reworked his script of *Michurin* (Stalin Prize for 1948, 2d class) into a play: *Zhizn v tsvetu* (Life in Bloom). K. Paustovsky valued Dovzhenko's great gift for oral narration and his artistic versatility (1956). In 1955 Dovzhenko was once again able to realize his artistic goals, which were primarily of an ethical nature, in the screenplay *Zacharovannaya Desna* (Eng. tr., *The Enchanted Desna*, 1979), which was filmed in 1957 only after his death. Following his death, his wife and former assistant, Yu. P. Solntseva-Dovzhenko, implemented many of his ideas. In 1959 Dovzhenko was posthumously awarded the Lenin Prize for the film *Poema o more* (A Song of the Sea).

*Works:* Ščors (film script), in *Izbr. scenarii sovetskogo kino*, vol. 3, 1949; Mičurin (film script), in *Izbr. scenarii sovetskogo kino*, vol. 6, 1950; *Izbr.: Sbornik scenariev, rasskazov, statej* (film scripts, short stories, articles), 1957; *Iz zapisnykh knižek* (diary excerpts), in *Iskusstvo kino* 1963:1–2, 4–5; *Začarovannaja Desna. Iz zapisnykh knižek* (film script, diary excerpts), 1964 (see above); *Ja prinadležu k lagerju poetičeskomu* . . . (essays, speeches, notes), 1967.—*Sobr. soč.*, 4 vols., 1966–69.

*Secondary Lit.:* P. Juren'ev, 1959; I. Račuk, *Poetika D.*, 1964; Ju. Barabaš, in *Družba narodov* 1964:9 and separate study, 1968; V. Percov, in *Znamja* 1964:10; L. Schnitzer and J. Schnitzer, Paris, 1966; S. Gerasimov and M. Ryl'skij, foreword to Dovženko's *Sobr. soč.*, 1966–69; A. Alinin, in *Moskva* 1977:2; R. Sobolev, 1980; L. Onyshkevych, in *MERSL* 5:1981; O. Gončar, in *Lit. gazeta* Sept. 12, 1984, p. 8.

**Drúskin, Lev Savélyevich,** poet (b. Feb. 8, 1921, Petrograd). Druskin's father and mother were pharmacists. Druskin grew up in Leningrad; he is confined to a wheelchair owing to an early case of polio. He discontinued his studies after the first year. During World War II, Druskin was evacuated to Tashkent. After 1957 he was able to publish six volumes of poetry that received recognition mainly from Leningrad newspapers and journals. Druskin has translated into Russian much of the poetry of other peoples in the Soviet Union using interlinear translations. On July 10, 1980, after several years of being kept under surveillance, Druskin's home was searched. Because of the diary that was confiscated at that time, he was expelled from the Writers Union of the USSR and forced to emigrate (Dec. 21, 1980). In Germany, Druskin first published a volume of his poetry translated into German, *Mein Garten ist zerstört* (1983; Razoren moy sad [My Garden Is Destroyed]), then a bilingual edition, *Am Abend ging ich fort* (1984; A vecherom ya ukhodil [In the Evening I Departed]). In England he was able to publish his diary under the title *Spasyonnaya kniga* (1984; The Rescued Book), and in the United States he published his first representative collection of poems, *U neba na vidu* (1986; In Sight of Heaven). He lives in Tübingen, West Germany.

Among Druskin's models of a poet, S. Marshak holds a central position. Druskin writes clear, linguistically unpretentious, often narrative poetry. The routine events of life, as they intrude upon him in his room, find expression through his account of them and their union with the underlying questions of life. "For the poet, the encounter with nature always becomes a meeting with himself" (Kay Borowsky). Numerous religious poems written with an honesty that is typical of Druskin have as a central theme the search for God. *Spasyonnaya kniga* fashions his own life in prose and poetry. It contains valuable portraits of writers such as A. Akhmatova, O. Berggolts, D. Granin, S. Marshak, and V. Shklovsky, provides insight into the lives of writers in Koktebel and Komarovo, and captures in a documentary style the inhumane behavior of the state authorities from the time his house was searched until his emigration. Especially valuable are his short stories (often less than one page in length) that illustrate typical situations in the Soviet Union in a manner that could not be depicted in censored literature.

*Works:* Ledokhod (lyric and narrative poems), 1961; *Stikhi* (poems), 1964; *Stikhi* (poems), 1967; *Stikhotvorenija* (poems), 1970; *Prikosnovenie* (poems), 1974; *Mein Garten ist zerstört* (poems), Tübingen, 1983; *Spasённaja kniga. Vospominanija leningradskogo poeta* (diary), London, 1984; *Am Abend ging ich fort. A večerom ja ukhodil tuda* (poems), Tübingen, 1984. Other poems in *Kontinent*, Paris, 30:1981, 33:1982; *Vremja i my*, Tel Aviv, 61:1981; *Grani*, Frankfurt am Main, 126:1982; *Russkaja mysl'*, Paris, March 31, 1983, p. 9, July 14, 1983, Jan. 5, 1984, p. 11; *U neba na vidu* (poems), Tenafly, N.J., 1986.

*Secondary Lit.:* G. Adler, in *Oktjabr'* 1962:8; L. Anninskij, in *Lit. gazeta* April 14, 1968, p. 5; V. Betaki, in *Russkaja mysl'* Aug. 5, 1982, p. 10; A. Krasnov-Levitin, in *Russkaja mysl'* June 2, 1983, p. 12, and in *Glaube in der Zweiten Welt* 1983:6; G. Ziegler, in *Stuttgarter Zeitung* Nov. 8, 1983; K. Borowsky, afterword to Druskin's *Mein Garten ist zerstört*, 1983; B. Khazanov, in *Grani* 137:1985; W. Kasack, in *Neue Zürcher Zeitung* July 7, 1986, p. 35; A. Radaškevič, in *Russkaja mysl'* Aug. 1, 1986, p. 10.

**Drútse, Ión Panteléyevich,** prose writer, playwright, writes in Moldavian and Russian (Rumanian spelling of his name is Druţă) (b. Sept. 13, 1928, Horodişte, Ataki District, Rumania). Drutse is of peasant ancestry; after the annexation of Bessarabia by the USSR (1940), he held various positions including that of secretary of the village soviet. From 1947 to 1951 he served in the military. At first (after 1950), Drutse wrote in Moldavian and published volumes of short stories such as *La noi in sat* (1953; At Home in the Village), which was followed by other volumes in 1954 and 1959. After completing the Advanced Literature Courses at the Gorky Literary Institute in Moscow in 1957, Drutse became well known in the Soviet Union through the translation of his povest *Listya grusti* (1958; Leaves of Sadness), also published under the title *George, vdoviy syn* (George, Widow's Son). This was soon followed by another volume of diverse prose whose title expresses the author's underlying human concern: *Chelovek—tvoyo pervoye imya* (1960; Man, Your First Name). At the beginning of the 1960s under pressure from the constant criticism of the Communist Party of the Moldavian Republic, Drutse moved to Moscow; from then on, he translated his works himself in part or wrote directly in Russian. Of his principal prose work to date, *Bremya nashey dobroty* (1968; The Burden of Our Kindness), the first, still somewhat episodically structured part appeared in 1963 under the title *Stepnye ballady* (Ballades of the Steppe). In addition to film scripts, Drutse has also written a number of plays—such as *Ptitsy nashey molodosti* (1971; Eng. tr., *The Birds of Our Youth*, in *Nine Modern Soviet Plays*, 1977), *Svyataya svyatykh* (1977; Holy of Holies), *Imenem zemli i solntsa* (1978; In the Name of the Earth and the Sun)—that have also won recognition abroad. Drutse translated classic Russian writers such as Anton Chekhov into Moldavian. He was awarded the State Prize of the Moldavian SSR in 1967 for the novel *Stepnye ballady*, for the povest *Posledniy mesyats oseni* (The Last Month of Autumn), and for the play *Kasa mare* (1965; Eng. tr., *Casa Mare*, in *Moldavian Autumn*, 1970).

Drutse's works reflect his great love for his Moldavian homeland, especially for his native village. They are characterized by a high ethical and religious consciousness. *Bremya nashey dobroty*, a novel whose plot covers the 40 years from the end of World War II to the beginning of the Soviet period for Moldavia, emphasizes the goodness of the village tradition and was therefore attacked, especially by the Moldavian Party critics. The play *Kasa mare*, which features a Moldavian peasant woman, has its roots in the Rumanian peasant tradition. Its title serves an ethically symbolic function. *Svyataya svyatykh*, in which Drutse depicts the superiority of friendship and love over the incivility of Soviet reality, illustrates his great ability to construct a scene by combining real dialogue and a surrealistic exchange of thoughts. Drutse turned to historical themes in *Vozvrashcheniye na krugi svoya* (1978; Return to One's Own Circles), a play based on a povest written in 1972 that deals with Lev Tolstoy's last days, and in *Belaya tserkov* (1982; The White Church), a novel set in the reign of Catherine II in which he contrasts the circle surrounding the empress to that surrounding a Moldavian peasant woman whose life is focused on the building of a village church.

*Works: George, vdovij syn* (pov.), in *Dnestr* 1957:6–7; *Čelovek—tvoë pervoe imja* (short stories), 1959; *Stepnye ballady* (novel), in *Družba narodov* 1963:3, separate ed., 1963; *List'ja grusti* (pov. and short stories), 1965; *Nenast'e i naždy* (novel), 1965; *Kasa mare* (play), 1965 (see above); *Bremja našej dobroty* (novel), 1968; *Dojna* (play), in *Teatr* 1971:6; *Vozvraščenie na krugi svoja* (pov.), in *Družba narodov* 1972:2, and as a play, 1978; *Zapakh speloj ajvy* (pov.), in *Junost'* 1973:9; *Svjataja svjatykh* (play), in *Teatr* 1977:8; *Imenem zemli i solntsa* (plays), 1977 (contains *Kasa mare*; *Dojna*; *Pticy našej molodosti* [see above]; *Vozvraščenie na krugi svoja*; *Imenem zemli i solntsa*; *Svjataja svjatykh*); *Belaja cerkov'* (novel), in *Novyj mir* 1982:6–7, separate ed., 1983; *Obretenie* (play), in *Sovremennaja dra-*

maturgija 1984:2; Svjataja svjatykh (plays), 1984 (contains Kasa mare; Dojna; Pticy našej molodosti; Khorija; Vozvraščenie na krugi svoja; Obretenie).—Izbr., 2 vols., 1984. Translation: Moldavian Autumn (short stories and play), 1977.
Secondary Lit.: A. Val'ceva, in Družba narodov 1958:2; A. Lebedev, in Družba narodov 1960:3; M. Turovskaja, in Teatr 1961:8; I. Pitljar, in Novyj mir 1963:5; A. Borščagovskij, in Družba narodov 1966:3; L. Anninskij, in Molodaja gvardija 1973:1; N. Velekhova; in Teatr 1978:11; V. Maksimova, in Sovremennaja dramaturgija 1982:4; M. Bruchis, in MERSL 6:1982; V. Turbin, in Lit. gazeta Jan. 26, 1983, p. 4; A. Mikhajlov, in Naš sovremennik 1984:1; B. Ljubimov, in Lit. obozrenie 1986:2.

**Drúzhba naródov** (Friendship of Peoples), a literary journal, published in Moscow since 1939, at first irregularly as an almanac, then every two months starting in 1949, and monthly since 1955. Druzhba narodov assists in popularizing the literary works of non-Russian peoples in the USSR through Russian translation. In addition, it includes articles on literature, culture, and art of these peoples. Editors in chief have been A. Surkov (1958–59, a member of the editorial staff until 1964), Vas. Smirnov (1960–65, a member of the editorial staff until 1970), and since 1966 S. Baruzdin (a member of the editorial staff since 1964). The following writers belonged to the large editorial collective or advisory council for a period of several years: P. Antokolsky (1955–64), E. Grin (1958–64), Ya. Smelyakov (1958–72), Ch. Aytmatov (1964–69), M. Lukonin (1970–76). Druzhba narodov's importance is enhanced by the fact that for non-Russian authors in the USSR the path onto the world literary scene leads almost exclusively through a translation into Russian. Several of the leading non-Russian authors in the Soviet Union write in Russian (for example, G. Aygi, Ch. Aytmatov, V. Bykov, M. Ibragimbekov, F. Iskander, A. Kim, O. Suleymenov), but they are not typical authors of Druzhba narodov. Approximately one third of the works published in Druzhba narodov are written by Russians. The journal has published the prose of V. Baklanov, V. Belov, A. Bitov, B. Mozhayev, B. Okudzhava, A. Rybakov, V. Syomin, V. Tendryakov, Yu. Trifonov, and S. Zalygin, as well as the poetry of G. Gorbovsky, A. Kushner, L. Martynov, D. Samoylov, B. Slutsky, and K. Vanshenkin. Circulation climbed from 190,000 in 1975 to 240,000 in 1982, then dropped to 160,000 at the beginning of 1983, and to 153,000 in 1984.
Secondary Lit.: A. Bočarov, in Znamja 1958:11 and in Lit. gazeta Dec. 14, 1961; O. Mikhajlov, in Novyj mir 1959:11; Z. Kedrina, in Lit. obozrenie 1975:9; I. Corten, in MERSL 6:1982; Anon., in Lit. gazeta March 24, 1982, p. 6.

**Dúbov, Nikoláy Ivánovich**, prose writer (b. Nov. 4 [Oct. 22], 1910, Omsk—d. May 24, 1983, Kiev). Dubov was born into a family of workers. Initially he worked in a ship repair yard; in 1929 he embarked on a career in journalism and literature, achieving some local success with his plays in 1948 and 1950. Since the 1950s Dubov essentially wrote stories of some length for and about young people. He lived in Kiev.
Dubov's particular interest lies in the maturation of children and the influence of proper and improper education. He places his young characters in situations with strong conflicts. The same central character appears in his povesti Sirota (1955; The Orphan) and Zhostkaya proba (1960; The Difficult Test); Dubov shows this character first in conflict with adults who have taken the place of parents, then as an apprentice associated with dishonest workmen. In his later povesti as well, for example, in Beglets (1966; Eng. tr., The Fugitive, 1977), he portrays people in borderline situations and shows how they take care of themselves or fail, how they mature through necessity. In 1967 Dubov published the two povesti Sirota and Zhostkaya proba together as a novel entitled Gore odnomu (It's Hard to Be on One's Own), for which he received the State Prize in 1970. In his novel Koleso Fortuny (1977; Wheel of Fortune), Dubov combines two levels of time: the present, featuring an incident involving a mockingly depicted American tourist at a Ukrainian kolkhoz, and the past, containing a sarcastic portrait of Empress Catherine II. "Dubov has a clear-eyed comprehension of life" (D. Brown). "He seeks ethical lessons in history" (Razgon).

Works: Ogni na reke (pov.), 1953 (Eng. tr., Lights on the River, 1954); Sirota (pov.), 1955; Povesti, 1960; Žёstkaja proba (pov.), 1961; Mal'čik u morja (pov.), 1964 (Eng. tr., A Boy by the Sea, 1974); Beglec (pov.), 1966 (see above); U otdel'no stojaščego dereva (pov.), 1966; Gore odnomu (novel), 1967; Koleso Fortuny (novel), 1980; Rodnye i blizkie (pov.), in

Naš sovremennik 1980:1.—Sobr. soč., 3 vols., 1970–71.

Secondary Lit.: O. Vojtinskaja, in Moskva 1961:11; L. E. Razgon, Mir v kotorom deti—ne gosti, 1969; and in Lit. obozrenie 1978:1; A. Turkov, in Sem'ja i škola 1970:5; M. Petrovskij, in Novyj mir 1970:8; I. Mikhajlova, in Zvezda 1973:4; E. S. Pomerantseva, in MERSL 6:1982.

**Dúdin, Mikhaíl Aleksándrovich,** poet (b. Nov. 20 [Nov. 7], 1916, Klevnevo, prov. Ivanovo). Dudin's father was a peasant. Dudin attended a factory school, then worked on the editorial staff of a provincial newspaper and took evening courses at the Ivanovo Pedagogical Institute. From 1939 to 1945 he was a soldier; he took part in the Finnish-Russian War and the defense of Leningrad. From 1942 on, he was a frontline reporter. Dudin wrote his first poems in the late 1930s; a small collection was published in Ivanovo in 1940. He became known for his war poetry. His poems, which range from intimate lyrics to publicistic rhymes, have appeared in many journals and books (some 55 by 1974). Dudin became a member of the Communist Party in 1951. He has been a member of the board of the Writers Union of the RSFSR since 1958 and of the board of the Writers Union of the USSR since 1967. At the Fourth Congress of the Writers Union of the USSR in 1967 Dudin delivered the keynote address on Soviet poetry; in 1972 he was awarded the Gorky Prize. Dudin lives in Leningrad and was chairman of the local section of the Writers Union around 1970.

The combination of a dispassionate look at sorrow and bravery and a sensitive feeling for the beauty of nature is characteristic of the war poetry that made Dudin popular. His most famous poem, "Solovyi" (1942; The Nightingales), juxtaposes dying soldiers and nature in the springtime. Landscapes exercise a determining influence over his better poetry later on as well. In addition to topical subjects such as postwar reconstruction and the struggle for peace, reminders of the front and of the Leningrad blockade, written in memory of the dead, run through his work; even the imagery is often determined by these themes. Dudin loves to address his characters with the lyrical "I" and uses authorial commentary to illustrate their essential nature, while the plot plays a diminished role even in his narrative poems. One senses that some poems owe their genesis to chance rather than to inner necessity. L. Ozerov justifiably criticizes Dudin's diffuseness and L. Lavlinsky comments on his increasingly direct didacticism in the early 1970s.

Works: Liven' (poems), 1940; Voennaja Neva (poems), 1943; Sčitajte menja kommunistom (poems), 1950; Izbr. (poems), 1951; Rodnik (poems), 1952; Stikhotvorenija. Poèmy (poems), 1956; Sosny i veter (poems), 1957; Mosty. Stikhi iz Evropy (poems), 1958; Do vostrebovanija (poems), 1963; Stikhotvorenija (poems), 2 vols., 1966; Vremja (poems), 1969; Solov'i (lyric and narrative poems), 1972; Tatarnik (poems), 1973; Gosti (poems), 1974; Poèmy (narrative poems), 1975; Sto stikhotvorenij (poems), 1979; Pole pritjaženija (poems), 1981, 1984.—Sobr. soč., 3 vols., 1976–77.

Secondary Lit.: T. Khmel'nickaja, in Zvezda 1944:7–8; V. Nazarenko, in Novyj mir 1955:9; N. Rylenkov, in Lit. i žizn' Nov. 14, 1962; V. Grečnev, in Zvezda 1966:11; L. Ozerov, in Voprosy lit. 1970:3 and in Lit. i sovremennost' 10:1970; L. Lavlinskij, in Lit. gazeta April 12, 1972, p. 6, and in Naš sovremennik 1974:9; S. Davydov, in Lit. gazeta Dec. 12, 1973, p. 5; D. Moldavskij, in Lit. gazeta Feb. 12, 1975, p. 7; V. Lavrov, 1976; N. Bank, in Neva 1976:10; M. Lisjanskij, in Neva 1981:7; RSPPo 7:1984; V. Šošin, in Znamja 1985:2; S. Strašnov, in Naš sovremennik 1986:11.

**Dúdintsev, Vladímir Dmítriyevich,** prose writer (b. July 29, 1918, Kupyansk, oblast Kharkov). In 1940, after completing his law studies in Moscow, Dudintsev fulfilled his military obligation; during World War II he was an officer at the front until he was wounded in 1942; afterward he served on a Siberian military tribunal. From 1946 to 1951 he was a correspondent for Komsomolskaya pravda. Dudintsev's first volume of short stories, U semi bogatyrey (With Seven Heroes), was published in 1952. In 1956 Novy mir published his novel Ne khlebom yedinym (Eng. tr., Not by Bread Alone, 1957), which became the most widely discussed Soviet work both in the USSR and abroad in 1956–57. Dudintsev subsequently wrote only short prose; his allegorical story, Novogodnaya skazka (1960; Eng. tr., A New Year's Tale, 1960), attracted some attention. Dudintsev lives in Moscow; he publishes reviews of important Soviet literary works and translations of non-Russian Soviet literature.

Ne khlebom yedinym is a novel about an inventor during the Stalin years who struggles desperately against the power of superiors and mediocre bureaucrats until he is gotten rid of by slander. The significance of the novel lies not in any particular literary quality but in the frank depiction of the gap that exists between the isolated ruling class and the common people. After an initially positive critical assessment, the novel was sharply condemned by orthodox critics at the end of 1956. On Oct. 22, 1956, K. Paustovsky defended the novel as showing "merciless truth, the only thing that the people need for the difficult business of building a new society." He emphasized the typicalness of the negative character in the novel, Drozdov: "This new class of exploiters and dictators have nothing to do with the Revolution. . . with socialism. . . . Their weapons are treachery, slander, moral character assassination, and actual murder" (*Moskovsky literator* Nov. 3, 1956; *Lit. gazeta* Oct. 27, 1956; *L'Express* March 29, 1957). In March 1957 the two fronts again clashed with force before the plenum of the Writers Union of the USSR (*Lit. gazeta* March 19, 1957). The novel was allowed to be published in book form in 1957. Vsevolod Kochetov responded by writing an "anti-Dudintsev novel" (K. Mehnert; see Steininger, p. 85), *Bratya Yershovy* (1958; The Brothers Yershov). Dudintsev's second novel, *Belye odezhdy* (White Raiment), was not allowed to be printed for about 20 years. This book, which tries to present the truth about the situation in Soviet biology around 1948, only in 1987 was to appear in the journal *Neva*.

*Works: U semi bogatyrej* (short stories), 1952; *Ne khlebom edinym* (novel), in *Novyj mir* 1956:8–10, separate ed., Munich, 1957, Moscow, 1957, 1968 (see above); *Povesti i rasskazy* (pov. and short stories), 1959; *Novogodnaja skazka* (short story), 1960 (see above); *Rasskazy* (short stories), 1963; *Belye odeždy* (novel), in *Neva* 1987:1–4.
*Translation: Nina and Other Stories*, 1954.
*Secondary Lit.:* S. Smirnov, in *Novyj mir* 1952:12; N. Ždanov, in *Trud* Oct. 31, 1956; D. Erëmin, in *Oktjabr'* 1956:12; H. Hamm, in *Ost-Probleme* 1957:14; B. Tich, in *Grani*, Frankfurt am Main, 33:1957; G. Avis, in *Journal of Russian Studies* 18:1969; Ju. Kuz'menko, in *Novyj mir* 1970:10; M. Pursglove, in *MERSL* 6:1982.

*Dvádtsat dva* (Twenty-two), a "sociopolitical and literary journal of the Jewish intelligentsia from the USSR in Israel," published six times a year in Tel Aviv and containing about 240 pages. This cultural-political journal arises from the Jewish emigration from the Soviet Union and is a publication of the cultural fund "Moscow-Jerusalem." Since its establishment in 1978, the editor in chief has been Rafail Nudelman; nine other editors belong to the editorial staff (as of issue no. 35 [1984]). The title alludes to the 22 letters of the Hebrew alphabet, on the one hand, and to the journal *Tsion*, which this journal replaced with issue no. 22, on the other. *Dvadtsat dva* provides a platform, especially but not exclusively, for Russian Jews living in Israel: prose writers, poets, playwrights, journalists, philosophers, historians, and art historians. In addition to literary works, numerous journalistic essays and reviews are published. Its authors include E. Kuznetsov, D. Markish, Yu. Miloslavsky, F. Roziner, L. Vladimirova; works by D. Bobyshev, I. Brodsky, S. Dovlatov, N. Gorbanevskaya, F. Gorensteyn, Yelena Shvarts, and S. Sokolov have also appeared in *Dvadtsat dva*. The journal also includes modern Western authors in Russian translation in its publishing program, and texts by Friedrich Dürrenmatt (5:1979), Jurek Becker (15:1980), Stefan Zweig (22:1981), and James Joyce (29:1983) have appeared. *Dvadtsat dva* is illustrated and publishes photos of modern art.

*Secondary Lit.:* G. Andreev, in *Russkaja mysl'*, Paris, Aug. 26, 1982, p. 10; March 17, 1983, p. 10; July 21, 1983, p. 12; Jan. 12, 1984, p. 12; April 12, 1984, p. 12; Oct. 25, 1984, p. 12; Nov. 14, 1986, p. 11.

**Dýmov, Ósip** (pseud. of Ósip Isidórovich Perelmán), prose writer, playwright (b. Feb. 16 [Feb. 4], 1878, Białystok—d. Feb. 1, 1959, New York). In 1902 Dymov completed his studies at the St. Petersburg forestry institute. From 1892 on, Dymov was active as a contributor to numerous journals, such as *Teatr i iskusstvo* (1900–4), *Signal* (1905–6), *Satirikon* (1908). By 1915, several other plays had followed his first, *Golos krovi* (1903; The Voice of Blood). Dymov's short stories and novels enjoyed wide popularity. Dymov emigrated to the United States, probably in 1913; for a while he lived in Germany (Berlin), where he became well known through several translations.
Illness, psychological analysis of self and others, eroticism, melancholy—these are the essential elements of Dymov's creativity. In the novel *Tomleniye dukha* (1912; Languor of the Spirit) he depicts the senseless workings of the Petersburg "intelligentsia." In *Vlas* (1909; Vlas) he relates the story of a precocious youth who grows up in unresponsive surroundings. His short stories, characterized by fragmen-

tary episodes, incompletely pronounced words and sentences, parts of experiences, and effective combinations of words, are impressionistic miniatures. The drama Nyu (1908; Eng. tr., Nju: An Everyday Tragedy, 1917) is a marital drama about a woman caught between a husband she does not love and a young poet who ultimately disappoints her. Not knowing which man is the father of her unborn child, she commits suicide. This play consists of a series of poetic scenes with high emotional content. Ten of Dymov's plays were performed in Germany between 1908 and 1932. They enjoyed relatively limited success, however. Dymov also wrote works in Yiddish.

Works: Golos krovi (play), 1903; Solncevorot (short stories), 1905; Kain (play), 1906; Slušaj Izrail' (play), 1907; Nju (also under the titles of Každyj den' and Tragedija každogo dnja) (play), Berlin, 1908 (see above); Zemlja cvetët (short stories), 1908; Vlas (pov.), in Apollon 1–3:1909; Vesëlaja pečal' (short stories), 1910; Razzkazy (short stories), 1910; Beguščie kresta (novel), Berlin, 1911 (Eng. tr., The Flight from the Cross, 1916); Tomlenie dukha (novel), in Al'manakh Šipovnik 17:1912; Večnyj strannik (play), 1914; Novye golosa (short stories), 2d ed., 1915.

Secondary Lit.: N. Petrovskaja, in Vesy 1905:7; K. Čukovskij, in his Ot Čekhova do našikh dnej, 1908; M. Geršenzon, in Krit. obozrenie 1908:1; V. Gofman, in Russkaja mysl', Paris, 1908:4; V. Kranikhfel'd, in Sovremennyj mir 1912:4; A. Polgar, in Die Schaubühne, Berlin, 1913, vol. 1, pp. 229ff.; A. Luther, Geschichte der russischen Lit., Leipzig, 1924; H.-H. Krause, Die vorrevolutionären russischen Dramen auf der deutschen Bühne, Emsdetten, 1972; S. L. Simovskij, in MERSL 6:1982.

# E

Édlis, Yúliu Filíppovich, playwright (b. July 3, 1929, Bendery, Rumania [annexed by the Soviet Union after World War II]). In 1949 Edlis completed acting school (Advanced Theater Studio) in Tbilisi, Georgia. He then studied at the college of humanities of the Moldavian Pedagogical Institute in Kishinyov (graduated 1956). His first publications appeared in 1952. His first drama, Pokoy nam tolko snitsya (1955; We Only Dream of Rest), remained unnoticed; critics noted the influence of Italian neorealism in his second drama, Moy bely gorod (1959; My White City). In 1968 Edlis again chose this title for the first collection of his dramas. By that time the plays Volnolom (1961; The Breakwater), Argonavty (1962; The Argonauts), Kaplya v more (1962; A Drop in the Sea), and Serebryany bor (1964; The Silver Thief) had been frequently and successfully performed, and Gde tvoy brat, Avel? (1965; Abel, Where Is Your Brother?) had aroused considerable political discussion as a play as well as in its frequent television productions. A new play by Edlis was performed almost annually for several years: Vyzyvayutsya svideteli (1968; The Witnesses Will Be Summoned); Proyezdom (1969; Passing Through); Iyun, nachalo leta (1970; June—the Beginning of Summer)—with 973 performances in 19 theaters in 1972, this drama attained the highest performance record of all of Edlis's plays—and Solomennaya storozhka (1973; The Watchman's Hut with the Thatched Roof). The literature about Edlis is minimal considering his performance record. He is completely absent from histories of literature. Edlis lives in Moscow.

Edlis sees in literature the conscience and confession of his time and positions his dramatic work in the tradition of Anton Chekhov with his composure, succinctness, and deep social concern. He considers A. Arbuzov, M. Bulgakov, V. Rozov, and A. Volodin the Soviet playwrights closest to himself. In Volnolom, a young harbor engineer conquers the passivity of his inferiors. Argonavty presents people who are willing to stand up for their ideals and thereby reveals the spiritual tenderness behind many a hard exterior. Gde tvoy brat, Avel?, written for two people—"I" and "He"—deals with the problem of guilt, that is, its cancellation owing to the passage of time, through the meeting of two Russian former prisoners of war—the politruk (political instructor) and the Vlasov soldier. Edlis's solution, to leave the guilty one to his conscience, which has been awakened through conversation, was heavily criticized. The question of guilt also plays a central role in Vyzyvayutsya svideteli, but the play takes place in ordinary everyday life, as does Iyun, nachalo leta, which psychologically exposes the dangers of daily life by using the example of a divorce. In Messa po Deve (1972; A Mass for the Maid of Orleans), Edlis recounts the legend of Joan of Arc's survival and opposes the typical course of history to the one-time action of an individual. In *Zhazhda nad ruchyom* (1975; Thirst at the Brook), a play about François Villon, Edlis describes with timeless validity the poet of genius who will not subordinate himself to either aesthetic fashion or public demand. As a playwright in the period following the 20th Party Congress, Edlis writes plays that are indebted to truth, that doubt heroism, that attempt to grasp the contradictions in life, and that, by being open in content and form, permit multiple interpretations.

*Works: Moj belyj gorod* (play), in *Sovremennaja dramaturgija* 16:1959; *Argonavty* (play), 1962; *Gde tvoj brat, Avel'?* (play), in *Teatr* 1965:6; "Otvetstvennost' khudožnika" (reply to inquiry), in *Voprosy lit.* 1966:1; *Kaplja v more* (play), 1966; *Serebrjanyj bor* (play), 1967; *Moj belyj gorod* (plays), 1968 (contains Argonavty; Volnolom; Moj belyj gorod); *Ijun, načalo leta* (play), in *Teatr* 1971:8; *Oproverženie* (pov.), 1976; *Žažda nad ruč'ёm* (plays), 1977 (contains Serebrjanyj bor; Proezdom; Gde tvoj brat, Avel'?; Mir bez menja; Messa po Deve; Žažda nad ruč'ёm; Pokhmel'e); *Polnolunie* (play), in *Teatr* 1978:5; *Naberežnaja* (play), in *Sovremennaja dramaturgija* 1983:4; Jugo-zapad (pov.), 1983, *Žizneopisanie* (short story), in *Novyj mir* 1983:5; *Izbr.* (plays), 1983 (contains Gde tvoj brat', Avel'?; Mir bez menja; Messa po Deve; Žažda nad ruč'ёm; Igra tenej; Solomennaja storožka; Polnolunie); *Antrakt* (novel), in *Novyj mir* 1986:4–5.

*Secondary Lit.*: A. Černova, in *Teatr* 1963:7; K. Ščerbakov, in *Molodaja gvardija* 1963:11; L. Bulgak, in *Teatr* 1965:9; Anon., in *Pravda* July 8, 1965; E. Kentler, in *Teatr* 1970:3; A. Injakhin, in *Teatr* 1982:4; N. Ivanova, in *Lit. gazeta* July 23, 1986, p. 4.

**Efremov, Ivan Antonovich.** See YEFREMOV, IVAN ANTONOVICH.

**Ego-futurism.** See FUTURISM.

*Ékho* (Echo), a literary journal of the third emigration published quarterly since 1978 under the editorship of V. Maramzin and A. Khvostenko by their own publishing house. After 12 issues the journal ceased publication with the fourth issue for 1980, but resumed publication in 1984 with issue 13 (issue 14

appeared in 1986). In the issues published to date, *Ekho* has demonstrated its uniqueness as a literary journal. As Maramzin announced in the first issue, *Ekho* "is not especially devoted to politics, but nevertheless it never forgets the fateful date 1917." *Ekho* recognizes no boundary between Russian literature written in Russia and that written abroad but publishes more texts from Leningrad than from other regions of Russia. *Ekho* is especially a forum for texts divorced from the realistic tradition and searching for formal innovation. *Ekho* has published short stories, poems, essays, and other works by M. Armalinsky, I. Brodsky, I. Burikhin, S. Dovlatov, A. Khvostenko, V. Krivulin, Ye. Limonov, A. Losev, Yu. Mamleyev, V. Maramzin, Yelena Shvarts, V. Sosnora, and B. Vakhtin. *Ekho* occasionally publishes older texts, for example those of G. Gorbovsky (early poems from SAMIZDAT), Georgy Peskov, A. Vvedensky, and A. Platonov; a detailed bibliography concerning the literary work of the last-named was spread among several issues. Some reviews and illustrations (mostly photos of authors) complete this journal whose primary concern is literary quality.

*Secondary Lit.*: Index of issues 1–12 (1978, no. 1, to 1980, no. 4), in *Ékho* 1980:4; R. Petrov, in *Grani*, Frankfurt am Main, 111–12:1979; K. Sapgir, in *Russkaja mysl'*, Paris, Aug. 23, 1979, p. 13, and Oct. 15, 1981, p. 13; E. Kogan, in *Russkaja mysl'* March 26, 1981, p. 16; Ju. K., in *Russkaja mysl'* March 15, 1984, p. 12.

**Elágin** (pronounced Yelágin), **Iván Venedíktovich** (pseud. of I. V. Matvéyev), poet (b. Dec. 1, 1918, Vladivostok—d. Feb. 8, 1987, Pittsburgh). Elagin's father was a poet (Venedikt Mart). The outbreak of World War II prevented Elagin from completing his medical studies. In 1943 he used the wartime to leave Kiev with his wife, the poetess Olga Anstey, and went to Germany. After the war he lived in Munich, where he published two volumes of poems, some written in the Soviet Union, some in emigration: *Po doroge ottuda* (1947; On the Way from There) and *Ty, moyo stoletiye* (1948; You, My Century). In 1950 Elagin moved to the United States, where in 1953 all his poems written prior to that time were published under the title of his first collection. In 1959 an emigrant group in Munich published the political satires in verse he wrote between 1952 and 1959. In the United States Elagin was publishing poems in *Novy zhurnal*

(New York) since 1949; they appeared in nearly every issue since 1961. The journal also collected his poems in *Otsvety nochnye* (1963; Nocturnal Reflections) and *Kosoy polyot* (1967; Oblique Flight). He included 150 poems from his earlier volumes in *Pod sozvezdiyem Topora* (1976; Beneath the Constellation of the Adze). Elagin translated a great deal of American poetry into Russian; his most ambitious translation was of S. V. Benét's *John Brown's Body*, the first part of which appeared in February 1970 in *Amerika*, a U.S. State Department magazine intended for distribution in the Soviet Union. Elagin received the Ph.D. degree in 1970 and was a professor of Russian literature at the University of Pittsburgh.

Elagin's poems are varied. On the one hand, he writes witty political verse, such as "Pesenka o kollektivnom rukovodstve" (A Little Song about Collective Leadership), which, modeled on "Ten Little Indians," deals with the removal of seven Party leaders—Beriya, Shepilov, Malenkov, Kaganovich, Molotov, Zhukov, Bulganin—until only Khrushchev is left. On the other hand, there are poems that have grown out of the isolation of a genuine talent, poems that develop eternal human themes, or contain reflections about poetry and the poet's place in today's world, or explore modern themes, such as the threat of civilization. In the narrative poem *Pamyat* (1979; Memory), he describes specific encounters from his younger years in the Soviet Union, principally with writers such as B. Pilnyak, D. Kharms, and A. Akhmatova. Elagin loves word games, clever rhymes, and sound parallels.

*Works: Po doroge ottuda* (poems), Munich, 1947; *Ty, moë stoletie* (poems), Munich, 1948; *Portret madmuazel' Tarži* (comedy), Munich, 1949; *Po doroge ottuda* (poems), New York, 1953; *Politiceskie fel'etony v stikhakh 1952–1959* (poems), Munich, 1959; *Otsvety nočnye* (poems), New York, 1963; *Kosoj polët* (poems), New York, 1967; *Drakon na kryše* (poems), New York, 1973; *Pod sozvezdiem Topora* (poems), Frankfurt am Main, 1976; *Pamjat'* (narrative poem), in *Grani*, Frankfurt am Main, 116:1980; *V zale Vselennoj* (poems), Ann Arbor, 1982.
*Translation into Russian:* S. Bene. *Telo Džona Brauna*, Ann Arbor, 1973.
*Secondary Lit.:* E. Raič, in *Novyj žurnal*, New York, 23:1950; R. Gul', in *Novyj žurnal* 36:1954; Ju. Ivask, in *Novyj žurnal* 74:1963; G. Glinka, in *Novyj žurnal* 88:1967; F. Zverev, "Poèty 'novoj' èmigracii," in *Russkaja lit. v. èmigracii*, ed. N. Poltorackij, Pittsburgh, 1972;

V. Betaki, in *Grani* 103:1977; L. Rževskij, in *Novyj žurnal* 126:1977 and in *Novoe russkoe slovo*, New York, Dec. 12, 1982, p. 5; T. Fesenko, in *MERSL* 6:1982; V. Sinkevič, in *Posev*, Frankfurt am Main, 1987:4.

**Emigration.** The emigration of a large number of often quite prominent Russian authors is a phenomenon that distinguishes the development of Russian literature since 1917 as much as does the attempt by the Communist Party of the Soviet Union to force literary life within its sphere of influence to serve a useful political function. There are three waves of emigration: the first was a direct result of the Civil War and reached its height in 1920. The second followed from the opportunity of Soviet citizens to leave their homeland under the protection of the German troops in 1943–44. The third is a consequence of the disappointment the intellectual and artistic elite experienced at the brevity of the THAW after Stalin's death and at the reversal of liberal advances, but especially as a result of the actively critical protest lodged by these artists and intellectuals whom the Soviet leadership tried to control by expelling individuals, by granting permission to emigrate, as well as by persecuting people in the USSR. This wave reached its climax to date in the 1970s.

The total number of Russians who left their homeland during the first emigration is estimated at between 1 and 2 million. Well-known writers include: G. Adamovich, L. Alekseyeva, A. Amfiteatrov, D. Aminado, L. Andreyev, A. Averchenko, K. Balmont, A. Bely, N. Berberova, D. Boborykin, I. Bunin, D. Burlyuk, L. Chervinskaya, I. Chinnov, S. Chorny, O. Dymov, Yu. Felzen, G. Gazdanov, A. Ginger, Z. Gippius, M. Gorky, M. Gorlin, G. Grebenshchikov, R. Gul, M. Ivannikov, G. V. Ivanov, V. I. Ivanov, Yu. Ivask, V. Khodasevich, I. Knorring, D. Knut, V. Korvin-Piotrovsky, V. Krymov, A. Kuprin, G. Kuznetsova, A. Ladinsky, V. Lindenberg, L. Lunts, S. Makovsky, Yu. Mandelshtam, Mat Mariya, D. Merezhkovsky, N. Minsky, S. Mintslov, V. Nabokov (Sirin), B. Nartsissov, I. Novgorod-Seversky, Yu. Odarchenko, I. Odoyevtseva, M. Osorgin, N. Otsup, V. Pereleshin, G. Peskov, B. Poplavsky, A. Prismanova, S. Rafalsky, A. Rakhmanova, G. Rayevsky, A. Remizov, V. Ropshin (Savinkov), A. Sedykh, I. Severyanin, V. Shklovsky, I. Shmelyov, A. Shteyger, V. Smolensky, E. Tauber, N. Teffi, Yu. Terapiano, A. Tolstoy, M. Tsvetayeva, V. Varshavsky, T. Velichkovskaya, A. Velichkovsky, I. Yassen, N. Yevreinov, Ye. Zamyatin, B. Zaytsev, V. Zlobin. This naturally incomplete list features the so-called older generation, writers who had made a name for themselves in Russia before 1917, as well as the younger generation who only began to write in emigration. Emigration occurred in part as a flight from mortal danger, in part within the framework of the evacuation through the Crimea in 1920, in part legally with an exit visa. Constantinople was the short-term haven for those evacuated from the Crimea. For others, the first places of refuge were Berlin, Paris, Prague, Belgrade, Riga, Tallinn, Harbin, and Shanghai. Until 1924, Berlin was the literary center of the emigration. From Berlin contact with Soviet authors was regularly maintained; for a while the indecisive writers who later returned to the Soviet Union, such as A. Bely, I. Erenburg, M. Gorky, V. Shklovsky, and A. Tolstoy, lived there. German foreign policy favoring the Soviet Union (Rapallo Treaty) and economic developments caused the literary center of the emigration to be shifted to Paris where Z. Gippius and D. Merezhkovsky, among others, ran a literary salon. The occupation of Paris by German troops led to the further emigration to the United States of part of the Russian colony in Paris.

The second emigration includes far fewer writers. The most famous were G. Andreyev (G. Khomyakov), O. Anstey, I. Chinnov, Yu. Ivask, D. Klenovsky, Alla Ktorova (Viktoria Kochurova), S. Maksimov, N. Morshen (N. Marchenko), N. Narokov, L. Rzhevsky, B. Shiryayev, V. Sinkevich, I. Yelagin, and V. Yurasov (V. Zhabinsky). Of necessity this group, too, went first to Germany, where they developed centers in Munich and Frankfurt for their own cultural and religious life. In 1945 the Soviet government endeavored to persuade these émigrés, together with those of the first emigration, to return to the USSR. The émigrés of 1917–20 were offered Soviet passports until Nov. 1, 1946; émigrés from 1943–44 were sometimes forcibly repatriated. Many of the "displaced persons" emigrated from Europe to the United States around 1950.

The third emigration began in 1958 when, at the height of the campaign against him, B. Pasternak was encouraged to emigrate. Only by petitioning was he able to avoid exile. The first Soviet author for whom an exit visa was granted for the purposes of exile was V. Tarsis (1966). In the 1970s the Soviet government relaxed its strict prohibition against emigration with respect to Jews wishing to go to Israel and prominent members of the intelligentsia. Among the best-known authors who have been part of the third wave of emigration

are: V. Aksyonov, Yu. Aleshkovsky, A. Amalrik, A. Belinkov, V. Betaki, D. Bobyshev, I. Brodsky, I. Burikhin, S. Dovlatov, L. Druskin, A. Galich, Yu. Galperin, A. Gladilin, N. Gorbanevskaya, F. Gorenshteyn, F. Kandel, L. Kopelev, N. Korzhavin, Yu. Kublanovsky, A. Kuznetsov, E. Limonov, A. Lvov, Vl. Maksimov, Yu. Mamleyev, Vl. Maramzin, D. Markish, V. Nekrasov, V. Rybakov, Ye. Sevela, B. Shapiro, S. Sokolov, A. Solzhenitsyn, V. Tarsis, Ye. Ternovsky, A. Terts (A. Sinyavsky), A. Tsvetkov, L. Vladimirova, G. Vladimov, A. Volokhonsky, V. Voynovich, S. Yuryenen, and A. Zinovyev. A few of the persons named obtained permission to emigrate because they married a citizen of a Western country (for example, Yu. Galperin, A. Ktorova, B. Shapiro, S. Sokolov, S. Yuryenen). The majority of these émigrés first occupied a place of recognition in Soviet literature, some of them as members of the Communist Party. They came into conflict with the representatives of the political system because they depicted self-experienced truth in their works instead of the desired propaganda and because they opposed the suppression of human rights. Their works not sanctioned by the censor circulated in SAMIZDAT to some extent. The third emigration is spread across the Western world: some live in Israel; larger groups are in Paris and the United States; several authors have settled in the Federal Republic of Germany.

Each of the groups of émigrés has established its own journals, newspapers, and publishing houses (see LITERARY JOURNALS). From the first emigration the Parisian Sovremennye zapiski, Vestnik Russkogo Khristianskogo Dvizheniya, and Chisla are especially well known. Representatives of this group created Novy zhurnal after they moved to the United States and undertook the newspaper Novoye russkoye slovo, founded in 1910. With Grani the second emigration founded an enduring journal, and with Russkaya mysl they have a newspaper that is published weekly with regular, extensive articles on literature. With Mosty and Vozdushnye puti they established important almanacs that appeared for about a decade. In the late 1970s and early 1980s the third emigration published about 100 journals, of which Kontinent, Strelets, Vremya i my, Ekho, Tretya volna, Vstrechi, Gnosis, and Sintaksis enjoy the strongest acclaim. Kontinent also goes beyond the boundaries of the Russian language and includes works by authors exiled from all countries within the Soviet sphere of influence.

In its underlying concerns, Russian émigré literature is similar to literature throughout the world; it is concerned with the literary representation of man's physical and spiritual existence, with the meaning of life and death, with love and interpersonal relationships in general. But the forms of expression for all of these issues are freer than those found in Soviet literature where the Communist, atheist ideology virtually prohibits adopting a metaphysical approach. Russian literature in exile and Soviet-censored literature differ markedly in their depiction of contemporary and often historical phenomena. Thus the early stages of the first emigration include documentary reports on the horrors of the Civil War; the second emigration afforded unadulterated images of Soviet forced labor camps and the reality of war; and the third emigration, together with the literature written in the Soviet Union but published elsewhere, has provided the complete truth about the history of the Soviet Union and about daily life there as well as information on the inhumane conditions in the camps and in internal exile. The theme of Russia itself, especially in its traditional connection with Orthodox Christianity, plays a major role in the works of the first emigration; the themes of life in a new environment and of the reciprocal relationships with another culture begin after several years abroad in most cases. Scarcely any Russian authors have fallen silent abroad; many of the third wave brought completed works with them; many have been able to develop their talents fully only in exile. Some have adapted to their new cultural milieu to such an extent that their works are written partly, or entirely in the language of their host country (V. Nabokov, V. Lindenberg [Chelishchev], I. Brodsky, B. Shapiro). The awarding of the Nobel Prize to I. Bunin in 1933 gave a great impetus to émigré literature; the corresponding honoring of B. Pasternak in 1958 and A. Solzhenitsyn in 1970—before his exile—made it evident that the honest depiction of contemporary life in the Soviet Union can only be published outside the USSR and that in this regard the author's place of residence (whether in the USSR or in exile) is not relevant.

*Anthologies: Na Zapade: Antologija zarubežnoj poèzii*, ed. Ju. Ivask, New York, 1953; *Literaturnoe zarubež'e*, Munich, 1958; *Muza diaspory: Izbrannye stikhi zarubežnykh poètov 1920–1960*, ed. Ju. Terapiano, Frankfurt am Main, 1960; *Modern Russian Poetry* (Russian/English), ed. and trans. Vl. Markov and M. Sparks, Indianapolis–New York, 1966; *Russkij al'manakh*, ed. Z. Šakhovskaja, R. Guerra, and E. Ternovskij, Paris, 1981; *A Rus-*

*sian Cultural Revival: A Critical Anthology of Emigré Literature before 1939*, ed. T. Pachmuss, Knoxville, Tenn., 1981; *Russica-81*, ed. A. Sumerkin, New York, 1982; *Russkie poèty na Zapade*, ed. A. Glezer, Paris–New York, 1986.

*Secondary Lit.*: H. von Rimscha, *Russland jenseits der Grenzen 1921–1926*, Jena, 1927; J. Delage, *La Russie en exil*, Paris, 1930; W. C. Huntington, *The Homesick Million: Russia-out-of-Russia*, Boston, 1933; N. Lidin, in *Russkie zapiski*, Paris, 1937:1 and 2; N. Ul'janov, in *Novyj žurnal*, New York, 28:1952; Ju. Terapiano, *Vstreči*, New York, 1953; V. Varšavskij, *Nezamečennoe pokolenye*, New York, 1956; G. Struve, *Russkaja literatura v izgnanii*, New York, 1956, 2d ed., 1984; I. Okuncov, *Russkaja èmigracija v Severnoj i Južnoj Amerike*, Buenos Aires, 1967; L. Foster, *A Bibliography of Russian Emigré Literature 1918–1968*, Boston, 1971; M. Beyssac, *La vie culturelle de l'émigration russe en France: Chronique 1920–1930*, Paris, 1971; *Russkaja literatura v èmigracii: Sbornik statej*, ed. N. Poltorackij, Pittsburgh, 1972; Z. Šakhovskaja, *Otraženija*, Paris, 1975; *L'émigration russe en Europe: Catalogue collectif des périodiques en langue russe 1855–1940*, ed. T. Ossorguine-Bakounine, Paris, 1976; . . . *1940–1979*, ed. A. Volkoff, Paris, 1981; Ju. Mal'cev, *Vol'naja russkaja literatura*, Frankfurt am Main, 1976; *The Bitter Air of Exile: Russian Writers in the West 1922–1972*, ed. S. Karlinsky and A. Appel, Berkeley, 1977; M. Geller (on his expulsion in 1922), in *Vestnik RKhD* 127:1978; G. Svirskij, *Na lobnom meste*, London, 1979; L. Dienes, L. Rževskij, L. Losev, in *MERSL* 6:1982; O. Djurić, *Ruski emigrantski književni kružoci u Beogradu (1920–40)*, in *Savremenik*, Belgrade, 1984:8–9.

**Érdman, Nikoláy Robértovich,** playwright (b. Nov. 16 [Nov. 3], 1902, Moscow—d. Aug. 10, 1970, Moscow). Erdman was of russified Baltic German descent. He was initially associated with the imagists through his brother Boris (1899–1960). His "Avtoportret" (1922; Self-Portrait), "a poem with Moscow as its background, is plainly Imaginist in its eroticism and urbanism" (V. Markov). Erdman began his dramatic career by writing topical parodistic interludes for D. Lensky's *Lev Gurych Sinichkin*, which his brother Boris staged at the Vakhtangov Theater in Moscow in 1924. In 1924 Erdman also contributed to a comic revue, *Moskva s tochki zreniya* (Moscow from a Point of View), written for the opening of the Theater of Satire. Erdman's first full-length comedy, *Mandat* (1924; Eng. tr., *The Mandate*, 1975), was staged with great success by V. Meyerhold on April 20, 1925 (the play's 100th performance was given March 26, 1926), and it was performed in many cities of the Soviet Union. In 1927 the play was staged in Berlin. Erdman's second play, *Samoubiytsa* (1928; Eng. tr., *The Suicide*, 1975), was in rehearsal at Meyerhold's theater and at the Moscow Art Theater when both companies were obliged to cancel performances in 1932. In 1927 Erdman began to coauthor and occasionally to author numerous film scripts, writing in collaboration with the imagists V. Shershenevich and A. Mariengof after 1928. In 1934 and 1938 he figured as a film-script writer with V. Mass and G. Aleksandrov. It was presumably at some time during this period that Erdman wrote a third, unknown play, *Zasedaniye o smekhe* (Conference on Laughter), which ostensibly led to his arrest. For three years Erdman lived in exile in Yeniseysk and Tomsk; afterward he was permitted to settle only in Kalinin. M. Bulgakov wrote to Stalin (the text of his letter appeared in *Novy zhurnal* 111:1973, p. 159) in order to facilitate Erdman's return to Moscow and to literary work. Erdman remained unnoticed as far as the literary critics were concerned for yet some time. It was later learned that after 1942 he had once again worked in film. In 1943 he wrote *Prints i nishchiy*, a film script based on Mark Twain's *The Prince and the Pauper*; Erdman collaborated with M. Volpin on several subsequent film scripts, and together they received a Stalin Prize (for 1950, 2d class). The film script for one of Erdman's numerous animated cartoons, *Bratya Lyu* (1952; The Brothers Lyu), appeared in an anthology of filmed fairy tales. The point at which Erdman was permitted to return to Moscow is not known (he was registered as a member of the Writers Union in 1959). In 1956 *Mandat* was once again performed at the Film Actors Studio Theater in Moscow; an adaptation of Dostoyevsky by Erdman was staged in 1957. His comedies were for a long time suppressed in the Soviet Union, but in the Gorbachev era *Samoubiytsa* was staged and published (1987).

In *Mandat* Meyerhold saw a satire in the tradition of N. Gogol and A. Sukhovo-Kobylin. Erdman grotesquely distorts the problems of his time resulting from the privileges accorded to persons with secret Party authorization (mandate) and to proletarians; from the unworldliness of many opponents of the regime; and from the fear of arrest. *Samoubiytsa*, the story of how a planned fake suicide is used by the "suicide" himself and by those

around him for personal advantage, goes deeper, disclosing a tragic hopelessness of existence in the Soviet Union lying beneath the comic element and for which there is only one solution: suicide. Erdman writes brilliant dialogue; he makes use of the pun (based on topical vocabulary) as well as situation comedy, and readily builds a complex plot structure using the traditional comedy of errors.

*Works:* Mandat (1924), Munich, 1976; *Samoubijca* (1928), in *Novyj žu..nal*, New York, 112–14:1973–74 and in *Sovremennaja dramaturgija* 1987:2, Eng. tr. in *Russian Literature Triquarterly* 7:1973 (Eng. tr., *Two Plays:* "The Suicide" and "The Mandate", Ann Arbor, 1975); *Brat'ja Lju* (film script), in *Fil'my-Skazki* 1952; poems, in *Russian Imagism 1919–1924*, ed. V. Markov, Giessen, 1980.

*Secondary Lit.:* I. Solov'ëva, in *Teatr* 1957:3; K. Rudnickij, *Režissër Mejerkhol'd*, 1959; M. Hoover, in *Russian Literature Triquarterly* 2:1972; W. Kasack, foreword to *Mandat*, Munich, 1976; V. Markov, *Russian Imagism 1919–1924*, Giessen, 1980; V. Zavališin, in *Russkaja mysl'*, Paris, Jan. 1, 1981; M. L. Hoover, in *MERSL* 7:1984; J. Freedman, in *Slavic and East European Journal* 1985:4.

**Erenbúrg, Ilyá Grigóryevich**, prose writer (b. Jan. 27 [Jan. 15], 1891, Kiev—d. Aug. 31, 1967, Moscow). Erenburg spent his youth in Moscow, where his father was the manager of a brewery. He became involved in revolutionary activities and was arrested, then emigrated to Paris in 1908. His first volume of verse appeared there in 1910; in 1913 he began his career as a journalist by writing for Russian newspapers even though he was living abroad. His wartime articles were later collected in *Lik voyny* (1920; The Face of War). In 1917 Erenburg returned to Russia, where his attitude toward the Revolution was ambivalent. Between 1921 and 1941 Erenburg served for long periods of time in missions abroad, of an increasingly official nature, initially in Berlin, then in Paris, Spain (1936–37), and occupied Paris (1940–41). During World War II, Erenburg was one of the most energetic propaganda writers. Having published numerous novels since 1921, in most cases abroad first, he received a Stalin Prize (for 1941, 1st class) for *Padeniye Parizha* (1942; Eng. tr., *The Fall of Paris*, 1943, 1962); he received a second Stalin Prize (for 1947, 1st class) for his novel *Burya* (1947; Eng. tr., *The Storm*, 1949), which, generally speaking, is thematically associated with *Padeniye Parizha*. He was active as a "fighter for peace." After Stalin's death, Erenburg was among the first to speak out in favor of the revision of literary policy, both as a journalist, in his essay *O rabote pisatelya* (1953; On the Writer's Job), and as a writer of literature, in his povest *Ottepel* (1954, expanded ed., 1956; Eng. tr., *The Thaw*, 1955); from the latter work came the name by which that period has become commonly known in the West (*see* THAW). Like V. Kaverin, K. Paustovsky, and others, Erenburg worked for the REHABILITATION of persecuted and silenced writers, above all M. Tsvetayeva and I. Babel. His memoirs, *Lyudi, gody, zhizn* (1960–65; Eng. tr., *People and Life: Memoirs of 1891–1917*, 1961; *Memoirs 1921–1941*, 1964), are devoted to reestablishing an accurate picture of cultural life in the first half of the 20th century; A. Tvardovsky called them Erenburg's "most significant work." After the ambivalence of his position in the 1920s and the skillful maneuvering to assure himself a position of advantage during the Stalin years, Erenburg was repeatedly attacked by conservative elements in the post-Stalin period; on the other hand, he was elected to the board of the Writers Union of the USSR at all of the congresses of the Writers Union held between 1934 and 1967. In literary histories, *Ottepel* is discussed negatively, and *Lyudi, gody, zhizn* is mentioned very guardedly.

The line that separates Erenburg the journalist from Erenburg the literary artist is fluid; his poetry is of little importance. The attention that he attracted during his lifetime both at home and abroad is based on his prose. "At its best his writing is fictionalized reportage," writes Marc Slonim. "He has his own easily recognizable style, a combination of irony and sentimentality, couched in taut sentences and explosive, aphoristic similes." His first novel, *Neobychaynye pokhozhdeniya Khulio Khurenito* (1922; Eng. trs., *The Extraordinary Adventures of Julio Jurenito and His Disciples*, 1930; *Julio Jurenito*, 1958, 1963), which he never renounced even in later years, is considered to be his best; it is "primarily a ruthless, satirical indictment of modern European civilization, in which no country, no nationality, and no aspect of that civilization is spared" (Struve). Among his many later novels, the satires of the NEP period—*Rvach* (1925; The Grabber), *Leto 1925 goda* (1926; The Summer of 1925), and above all *Burnaya zhizn Lazika Roytshvanetsa* (1928; Eng. trs., *The Stormy Life of Lazik Roitschwantz*, 1960; *The Stormy Life of Laz Roitshvants*, 1965), a delightful narrative, full of Jewish humor, about the life of a small tailor in Russia and abroad—

stand out from the rest. Erenburg's contribution to the literature of the Five-Year Plan was *Den vtoroy* (1934; The Second Day; Eng. tr., *Out of Chaos*, 1934). His war novels, written in the form of chronicles, also fall in with the Party line; such is *Devyaty val* (1951; Eng. tr., *The Ninth Wave*, 1955), about the period of the anti-American and anti–West European campaigns of 1948–52. Erenburg's *Ottepel* is significant not as a work of art but as an indicator of the direction in which literature was heading after 1954. "He is a polemicist, an excellent foreign correspondent, and a gifted writer who reflects in his hybrid work the literary, political, and sometimes intellectual stimuli and fashions of his times" (Slonim). V. Shklovsky's judgment in 1922 was prophetic: "He is not only a newspaperman who knows how to gather other people's thoughts into a novel but almost an artist who senses the contradictions between the old culture of humanism and the new world now being built by machine" (from *ZOO; or, Letters Not about Love*).

Works: *Stikhi* (poems), Paris, 1910; *Lik vojny* (articles), Sofia, 1920; *Neobyčajnye pokhoždenija Khulio Khurenito . . .* (novel), 1922 (see above); *Portrety russkikh poètov* (essays), Berlin, 1922 (reprinted, Munich, 1972); *Žizn' i gibel' Nikolaja Kurbova* (novel), Berlin, 1923; *Trest D.E.* (novel), Berlin, 1923; *Trinadcat' trubok* (short stories), 1923; *Ljubov' Žanny Nej* (novel), 1924 (Eng. tr., *The Love of Jeanne Ney*, 1929); *Rvač* (novel), 1925; *Leto 1925 goda* (novel), 1926; *V Protočnom pereulke* (novel), in *Tridcat' dnej* 1927:1–3 (Eng. tr., *A Street in Moscow*, 1932); *Burnaja žizn' Lazika Rojtšvaneca* (novel), Paris, 1928 (see above); *Zagovor ravnykh* (historical novel), Berlin, 1928; *10 l.s.* (novel), Berlin, 1929 (Eng. tr., *The Life of the Automobile*, 1976); *Moskva slëzam ne verit* (novel), 1933; *Den' vtoroj* (novel), 1934 (see above); *Ne perevodja dykhanija* (novel), 1935; *Padenie Pariža* (novel), 1942 (see above); *Burja* (novel), 1948 (see above); *Devjatyj val* (novel), 1951 (see above); *O rabote pisatelja* (essay), in *Znamja* 1953:10; *Ottepel'* (pov.), 1954, expanded to 2 vols. in 1956 (see above); *Francuzskie tetradi* (articles), 1958; *Stikhi 1938–58* (poems), 1959; *Ljudi, gody, žizn'* (memoirs), 3 vols., 1961–66 (see above); *Stikhotvorenija* (poems), 1977; (with A. Tolstoj), *Rubaška Blanš* (play), in *Sovremennaja dramaturgija* 1982:4; *Ispanskie reportaži, 1931–1939*, 1986.—*Polnoe sobr. soč.*, 8 vols., 1927–28; *Soč.*, 5 vols., 1952–54; *Sobr. soč.*, 9 vols., 1962–66.

Secondary Lit.: T. Trifonova, 1952; V. Erlich, in *Problems of Communism* 12:1963 and

14:1965; RSPP 6(2):1969; H. Oulanoff, in Canadian Slavonic Papers 1969:2; J. Laychuk, in Canadian Slavonic Papers 1970:4 and 1977:1; E. Ujvary-Meier, Diss., Zurich, 1970; Vospominanija ob I. E., 1975; P. C. Stupples, 1978; A. Goldberg, London, 1984; L. B. Turkevich, in MERSL 7:1984; L. Lazarev, in Znamja 1987:2.

Erofeyev, Venedikt. See YEROFEYEV, VENEDIKT.

Esenin, Sergey Aleksandrovich. See YESENIN, SERGEY ALEKSANDROVICH.

Evdokimov, Ivan Vasilyevich. See YEVDOKIMOV, IVAN VASILYEVICH.

Evdokimov, Nikolay Semyonovich. See YEVDOKIMOV, NIKOLAY SEMYONOVICH.

Evreinov, Nikolay Nikolayevich. See YEVREINOV, NIKOLAY NIKOLAYEVICH.

Evtushenko, Yevgeny Aleksandrovich. See YEVTUSHENKO, YEVGENY ALEKSANDROVICH.

# F

Fadéyev, Aleksándr Aleksándrovich, prose writer, literary official (b. Dec. 24 [Dec. 11], 1901, Kimry, prov. Tver—d. May 13, 1956, Moscow). Fadeyev's father was a peasant, later a village schoolteacher. Fadeyev was raised in the Soviet Far East by his stepfather; from 1912 to 1919 he attended a business school in Vladivostok. He became a member of the Communist Party in 1918 and took part in the Civil War. In 1921–22 Fadeyev studied at the Institute of Mining in Moscow. His first publication, a short story, came out in 1923. Between 1924 and 1926 Fadeyev was engaged in Party work in Krasnodar and Rostov-on-Don. From 1926 to 1932, as one of the leaders of RAPP, he played an influential role in the regimentation of literature. Fadeyev remained in a position of political control over Soviet literature until Stalin's death: from 1934 on, as a member of the board of the Writers Union of the USSR; from 1939 to 1944, as secretary of the Writers Union; from 1946 (following the Party Resolution of Aug. 14) to 1954 (the Second Congress of the Writers Union), as general secretary and chairman of the board of the Writers Union; from 1954 to 1956, as a member of the secretariat of the Writers Union; and from 1939 to 1956, as a member of the Central Committee of the Communist Party. As a writer Fadeyev became famous with his novel of the Civil War, Razgrom (1925–26; Eng. trs., The Nineteen, 1929; The Rout, 1956). During World War II he was a correspondent for Pravda. His novel about young partisans, Molodaya gvardiya (1945; Eng. tr., The Young Guard, 1958), received a Stalin Prize (for 1945, 1st class); in 1947, however, the novel was

criticized for underemphasizing the leading role of the Party. Fadeyev revised it accordingly in 1951. As a leading dogmatic Stalinist who shared the responsibility for the tragic fates of many, Fadeyev lost his power when the dictator died in 1953; at the 20th Party Congress, M. Sholokhov censured Fadeyev, referring to him as the "power-hungry general secretary" (Pravda Feb. 21, 1956). Fadeyev committed suicide. With the establishment of the Fadeyev Medal in 1974, the Soviet regime acknowledged a return to his literary policies.

Fadeyev, the theoretical champion of Communist education through literature, completed only two novels. The first, Razgrom, is about partisan fighting in the Soviet Far East; continuing the tradition of psychological realism in the manner of L. Tolstoy, it exerted a strong formal influence on Soviet literature. The novel is compulsory reading in the schools, as is also Fadeyev's second novel, Molodaya gvardiya, a tendentious idealization of youthful heroism during World War II written in accordance with the principles of SOCIALIST REALISM. Fadeyev again took up the theme of the Civil War more broadly in Posledniy iz udege (1930–40; The Last of the Udege), a novel that, after severe criticism, remained unfinished; the same fate befell Fadeyev's attempt to write a production novel, Chornaya metallurgiya (1951–56; The Iron Industry). In this case reality and the conception of PARTY SPIRIT changed too greatly over the course of the novel's writing for it to be completed. The enormous volume of Soviet secondary literature about Fadeyev is the result of ideological considerations.

Works: Razliv (pov.), 1924; Razgrom (novel), 1927 (see above); Poslednij iz udège (novel), 1929–56; Molodaja gvardija (novel), 1946, 2d ed., 1951 (see above); Za tridcat' let (essays, speeches, and letters about literature), 1957, 2d ed., 1959; Pis'ma 1916–56 (letters), 2d ed, 1973.—Sobr. soč., 5 vols, 1959–61; 7 vols., 1969–71; 4 vols., 1979.
Secondary Lit.: V. G. Boborykin, 1968 and 1979; RSPP 5:1968; A. Bušmin, 1971; S. Zaika, 1972, and in Russkaya lit. 1981:4; S. U. Šešukov, 2d ed., 1973; A. Fadeev: Materialy i issledovanija, 1977; S. N. Preobraženskij, 1981; J. Sih, in MERSL 7:1984; I. Žukov, in Lit. obozrenie 1985:11.

**A. A. Fadeyev Medal.** See LITERARY PRIZES.

**Faykó, Alekséy Mikháylovich,** playwright (b. Sept. 19 [Sept. 7], 1893, Moscow—d. Jan. 25, 1978, Moscow). Fayko was of aristocratic descent. In 1917 he completed his studies in history at Moscow University. Following his first literary efforts during his student days, Fayko turned to drama after the Revolution; one of his jobs was stage director at Studio Two of the Moscow Art Theater. He began his career as a dramatist in 1921, writing comedies. Success came with Ozero Lyul (1923; Lake Lyul), an effectively staged detective play set in an abstract country and containing many ironic allusions to capitalists and revolutionaries. Uchitel Bubus (1925; Bubus the Teacher), which V. Meyerhold staged at his theater using 46 musical pieces by Liszt and Chopin, and Yevgraf, iskatel priklyucheniy (1926; Yevgraf, the Seeker of Adventure) combine the element of adventure and contemporary satire of Soviet reality. The very effective staging of Fayko's Chelovek s portfelem (1928; The Man with the Briefcase), a period piece with detective overtones about a ruthless Soviet scientist who carves a career for himself out of the new social structure at the expense of those around him, kept the play running until the mid-1940s. Fayko combines his satire of successful people of the Stalinist stamp with the serious problem of the intelligentsia's adjustment to the new system and the overcoming of the non-Communist past. "In its melodramatic aspect Fayko's The Man with the Briefcase recalls, in some respects, Sukhovo-Kobylin's trilogy" (Segel). After a 13-year hiatus the play was again staged in 1957. Fayko continued his creative career, with long intervals; in 1948 and 1949 he worked only as a coauthor with the Party-

approved writers G. Fish and C. Solodar. Fayko's last drama, Ne sotvori sebe kumira (1956; Thou Shalt Not Make Unto Thee Any Graven Image), had mixed reviews. He lived in Moscow.

Works: Učitel' Bubus (play), 1925; Evgraf, iskatel' priključenij (play, first performed 1926), 1963; Čelovek s portfelem (play), 1929 (reprinted, Letchworth, 1979); P'esy (plays), 1935 (contains Ozero Ljul'; Evgraf, iskatel' priključenij; Čelovek s portfelem; Neblagodarnaja rol'); Koncert (play), 1936; Ne sotvori sebe kumira (play), in Teatr 1956:12; Dramy i komedii (plays), 1958 (contains Ozero Ljul'; Čelovek s portfelem; V setjakh dobrodeteli; Ne sotvori sebe kumira); Teatr, P'esy, Vospominanija (plays, articles, memoirs), 1971 (contains Ozero Ljul'; Učitel' Bubus; Evgraf, iskatel' priključenij; Čelovek s portfelem; Koncert); Zapiski starogo teatral'ščika (memoirs), in Teatr 1975:6–7, 9, and 1978.
Secondary Lit.: P. Markov, in Novyj mir 1927:1 and 1933:1; E. Surkov, in Teatr 1957:6; V. Frolov, in Oktjabr' 1958:6; N. Vojtkevič, in Teatr 1973:2, 11; S. Ovčinnikova, in Novyj mir 1979:4.

**Fédin, Konstantín Aleksándrovich,** prose writer, literary official (b. Feb. 24 [Feb. 12], 1892, Saratov—d. July 15, 1977, Moscow). Fedin's father was a merchant of peasant descent; his mother was of noble descent. Fedin grew up in Saratov. From 1911 to 1914 he studied at the Moscow Institute of Commerce; his first literary publications date from 1913–14. In 1914 Fedin traveled to Germany where, interned as a civilian during World War I, he was able to work in various cities; his jobs included acting. After his return to Russia, Fedin worked as a newspaper editor from 1919 to 1921, initially in Syzran (Volga), then with the Red Army. He joined the Communist Party in 1919, but nevertheless quit in 1921. In 1921 Fedin became a member of the SERAPION BROTHERS in Petrograd. After Pustyr (1923; Wasteland), his first volume of short stories, Fedin turned to the longer epic form and published six contemporary historical novels at great intervals between 1924 and 1967. Pervye radosti (1945; Eng. tr., Early Joys, 1948) and Neobyknovennoye leto (1948; Eng. tr., No Ordinary Summer, 1950) received a Stalin Prize (for 1948, 1st class). When the Writers Union of the USSR was founded in 1934, Fedin was elected to the board; from then on he continually held leading positions. In 1959 he was given, as first secretary, the leadership of the Union; from 1971 until his death he was chairman of the board. Fedin also belonged to the board of the Writers Union of the RSFSR from 1958 on. He was a member of the Academy of Sciences of the USSR and served several times as deputy of the Supreme Soviets of the RSFSR and USSR. Up to 1958 Fedin's theoretical statements contain a recognizable artistic message in addition to the obvious Party line. When the altercation regarding the publication of A. Solzhenitsyn's Cancer Ward occurred in 1968, the novel was banned on Fedin's recommendation. In response, A. Tvardovsky and V. Kaverin expressed their devastating opinion of Fedin in open letters (circulated in SAMIZDAT and in the West) and revealed the consequences of his decision for the development of Russian literature.

Fedin's early short stories, such as Sad (1920; Eng. tr., "The Orchard," in Great Soviet Short Stories, 1962), sympathetically describe the problem of breaking away from the pre-Revolutionary mode of life; they are influenced by the traditional models of A. Chekhov and I. Bunin. Fedin's novel Goroda i gody (1924; Eng. tr., Cities and Years, 1962), which explores the problem of the intellectual in the Revolution both in Germany and in Russia, "owes more to modern European narrative forms than to the predominantly antipsychological Russian trends of that time" (Holthusen). Fedin's next novel, Bratya (1927–28, The Brothers), is the last to contain the experimental element, consisting of a nonchronological narrative manner; the novel deals with the attitude of the artist vis-à-vis the political demands of the Revolution and is influenced by F. Dostoyevsky. While this work does not yet offer an unequivocal solution to the problem posed, all of Fedin's subsequent work is clearly in accord with the demands of the principle of PARTY SPIRIT. Pokhishcheniye Yevropy (1933–35; The Rape of Europe) compares the economic decline of Europe to the aspirations of the Soviet Union; "it is disjointed, its plot is slim, its motley episodes are not well integrated, and the characters lack depth" (Slonim). Even the "Magic Mountain" theme that Fedin depicts from personal experience in Sanatoriy Arktur (1940; Eng. tr., Sanatorium Arktur, 1957) serves to propagandize the healthy Soviet Union as opposed to the moribund capitalist West. During World War II, Fedin wrote war communiqués and began a trilogy that, in imitation of L. Tolstoy's War and Peace, was intended to portray the origin and growth of Soviet power by portraying the fate of individual, "typical"

characters. Pervye radosti takes place in 1910, apparently in Saratov; Neobyknovennoye leto is set in 1919 (here Fedin, serving the cult of personality, brings Stalin onto the stage); Kostyor (1961–65; Eng. tr., The Conflagration, 1968) begins in 1941 and is unifinished. In addition to handling an extensive chronology, Fedin, in imitation of Tolstoy, also manages a form containing many plot lines, historical commentaries, and the psychologically realistic rendering of ideas. As a conformist, however, Fedin is not committed to objective truth but serves, in the context of SOCIALIST REALISM, only the preconceived notions of the Communist Party.

Works: Sad (short story), 1922 (see above); Pustyr' (short stories), 1923; Goroda i gody (novel), 1924 (see above); Transvaal (pov.), 1926; Brat'ja (novel), 1928; Pokhiščenie Evropy (novel), 2 vols., 1933–35; Sanatorij Arktur (novel), 1940 (see above); Gor'kij sredi nas (memoirs), 1941–44; Pervye radosti (novel), 1945 (see above); Neobyknovennoe leto (novel), 2 vols., 1947–48 (see above); Pisatel', iskusstvo, vremja (articles), 1957, 2d ed., 1961; Kostër (novel), 1967 (see above).—Sobr. soč., 4 vols., 1927–28; 6 vols., 1952–54; 9 vols., 1959–62; 10 vols., 1969–73.

Secondary Lit.: E. Simmons, Russian Fiction and Soviet Ideology, New York, 1958; B. Brajnina, 5th ed., 1962, and 1980; J. M. Blum, The Hague–Paris, 1967; RSPP 5:1968; M. M. Kuznecov, 1969 and 1973; A. Tvardovskij and V. Kaverin, in Literatur und Repression, Munich, 1970; I. V. Strakhov, 1979; Vospominanija o K. F., 1981; P. A. Bugaenko, 1981; D. Lewis, in MERSL 7:1984; Ju. Oklajanskij, in Lit. obozrenie 1984:7, and 1986; A. Starkov, 1985.

**Fellow travelers** (popútchiki), a term—developed by A. Lunacharsky in 1920 and promoted by Trotsky after 1923—designating non-Communist writers who accepted the Revolution or who actively supported its ideals. The term, which played an essential role in the literary-political controversies of the 1920s, was vague and essentially encompassed all writers who were not members of the Communist Party or of proletarian origin (KUZNITSA). Typical fellow travelers included B. Pilnyak, M. Prishvin, I. Babel, K. Paustovsky, I. Erenburg, A. Tolstoy, L. Leonov; as well as members of the SERAPION BROTHERS, such as V. Kaverin, N. Tikhonov, M. Slonimsky, K. Fedin, Vs. Ivanov, M. Zoshchenko; of the imagists (see IMAGISM), such as S. Yesenin; and also of PEREVAL, a group that included Party members who did not sympathize with the aggressive politics of OKTYABR. The fellow travelers were actively supported by the Marxist critic A. Voronsky, who recognized that these were some of the most significant literary talents of the time and enlisted their cooperation in *Krasnaya nov*. Beginning in 1923, the fellow travelers were sharply attacked by the Communist literary officials in the group Oktyabr *(napostovtsy)*. The Party Resolution of 1925 (see PARTY RESOLUTIONS ON LITERATURE) did not yet grant these officials the proletarian dictatorship over literature they coveted; instead it granted the fellow travelers temporary sufferance in the hope that they could be ideologically influenced. The struggle accelerated through VAPP's platform in 1927 and through that of RAPP in 1928; these groups also attacked V. Mayakovsky and M. Gorky as fellow travelers. When RAPP attained total domination in 1930, the fellow travelers were, practically speaking, either crowded out or forced into complete ideological conformity. Through the Party Resolution of 1932 and the formation of a single Writers Union of the USSR, the concept was abolished; thereafter writers either participated in the development of Soviet literature or stood outside it; and even Party members were sometimes branded outsiders.

*Secondary Lit.*: See RAPP. A Lunačarskij, *Literatura i revoljucija* (1920), in his *Sobr. soč.*, vol. 7, 1967; L. Trockij, *Literatura i revoljucija*, 1923 (Eng. tr., *Literature and Revolution*, 1968); B. Ol'khovyj, in *Pečat' i revoljucija* 1929:5–6.

**Félzen, Yúry** (pseud. of Nikoláy Bernárdovich Freydenshtéyn, prose writer [b. Oct. 22 [Oct. 10], 1895, St. Petersburg—d. 1943 [?], while imprisoned in Germany). Félzen's father was a physician in St. Petersburg, where Felzen attended secondary school and, in 1912, completed his study of law. After the Bolsheviks seized power, Felzen emigrated first to Riga with his parents and siblings, then, about 1922, to Berlin and, probably in 1924, to Paris. There he worked as a banker and lived in his sister's house. His first novel, *Obman* (1930; Deceit), appeared in Paris; his next, *Schastye* (1932; Happiness), in Berlin; his last book, *Pisma o Lermontove* (1936; Letters about Lermontov), which he began writing before his first book, was again published in Paris. Felzen also published shorter prose texts and reviews in *Sovremennye zapiski, Chisla, Krug,*

and other periodicals of Russian émigré literature. In 1935 he was elected chairman of the Association of Poets and Writers (Obyedineniye poetov i pisateley). After Paris was occupied by German troops in 1940, Felzen initially remained there. In 1942, as he attempted to escape to his sister in Switzerland, he was taken prisoner by a German patrol, held in a camp in Paris, and taken to Germany at the beginning of 1943. He probably died in a German concentration camp.

Felzen was a very refined man of literature, a great admirer of Marcel Proust; he adopted from Proust the representation of the stream of consciousness as the primary stylistic technique of his predominantly autobiographical prose. Neither of his two novels nor *Pisma o Lermontove* has a plot, so the three works can scarcely be distinguished from each other. They are sketches from the diary of an "I" and his beloved, in which past, present, and future behavior is psychologically examined in minute detail. The pervasive theme is love, an agonizing unsuccessful love plagued by jealousy. The attempt to portray inner life as honestly and completely as possible leads, in Felzen's extensively revised prose, to an excess of adjectives and to burdensome length, but nevertheless the fascination of his work does not get lost. Felzen was justly considered a writer for the literati rather than for the public at large. His works were favorably reviewed. In 1940 V. Nabokov wrote: "This is true literature, pure and honest." Even in his observations about M. Lermontov he examines his own psychological concerns and leaves Lermontov's fundamental religiosity untouched. *Kompozitsiya* (1939; Composition), a short story, has a different—reportorial—narrative structure, but this work is also marked by the love theme that is characteristic of Felzen: reminiscences of the meetings with his first, unrequited, love during the period from 1910 to 1927.

*Works: Obman* (novel), Paris, 1930; *Pis'ma o Lermontove* (novel), in *Čisla*, Paris, 4:1930–31, 7–8;1933, 9:1933, separate ed., Paris, 1936; *Sčast'e* (novel), Berlin, 1932; *Probuždenie* (autobiography), in *Sovremennye zapiski*, Paris, 53:1933; *Umiranie iskusstva* (short story), in *Krug*, Paris, 2:1937; *Povtorenie projdennogo* (fragment of a novel), in *Krug* 3:1938; *Kompozicija* (short story), in *Sovremennye zapiski* 68:1939.
*Secondary Lit.*: A. Novik, in *Sovremennye zapiski* 46:1931 and in *Volja Rossii*, Prague, 1–2:1931; Ju. Terapiano, in *Čisla* 7–8:1933 and in his *Vstreči*, New York, 1953; S. Sa-

vel'ev, in *Sovremennye zapiski* 62:1936; V. Sirin (Nabokov), in *Sovremennye zapiski* 70:1940; G. Adamovič, in his *Odinočestvo i svoboda*, New York, 1955; A. Bakhrakh, in *Novoe russkoe slovo*, New York, July 15, 1979; V. Janovskij, in *Gnosis*, New York, 5–6:1979; L. Dienes, in *MERSL* 7:1984.

**Filíppov, Borís Andréyevich** (formerly B.A. Filistínsky), prose writer, poet, literary scholar (b. Aug. 6 [July 24], 1905, Stavropol, Caucasus). Filippov's father was an officer who fell in 1914 during World War I; his mother was a dentist. After completing his course of studies at the Oriental Institute in Leningrad (1924–28), where he studied Mongolian philology and became interested in Buddhism and Hinduism, he completed a course at the Leningrad Evening Institute of Industrial Construction (1929–33) and worked from 1928 to 1936 as an engineer for production planning in Leningrad. He spent the years from 1936 to 1941 in the camps of the GULAG. He was released to Novgorod and, as a result of the German conquests at the beginning of World War II, ended up in Germany in 1944. His first poems, which were published later, date from this period. Filippov lived near Kassel and then near Munich until 1950. In Munich he began his impressive work in literature, literary criticism, and editorship that was to stretch over decades. *Grani, Novy zhurnal, Novoye russkoye slovo, Russkaya mysl,* and *Vozrozhdenie* are the major periodicals in which his short stories, poems, essays, and critical writings appear. In 1950 Filippov moved to the United States; he lived in New York until 1954, thereafter in Washington, D.C. He served as an adviser for scholarly institutions, wrote for the Voice of America, and lectured at universities (including the American University, 1968–78). By 1985 Filippov had published 28 books and brochures: 22 with poems and short stories, 6 with collections of his essays and criticism of Russian literature. Among the most important collections edited by Filippov—which he often compiled in cooperation with other scholars, especially Gleb Struve and Yevgeniya Zhiglevich—are the collected works of A. Akhmatova, N. Gumilyov, N. Klyuyev, O. Mandelshtam, B. Pasternak, M. Shkapskaya, M. Voloshin, N. Zabolotsky, and Ye. Zamyatin. In addition, he edited individual works, including those by G. Adamovich, N. Arzhak, O. Forsh, K. Leontyev, B. Nartsissov, A. Remizov, Yu. Terapiano, A. Terts, and M. Zoshchenko.

The content of Filippov's short stories is determined by what he experienced and observed. Vivid tales of unusual but essentially commonplace and typical events, enlivened through dialogue or the use of a fictitious storyteller, characterize his works. Thus, his thematic realm is extensive; from daily life in the Soviet Union before 1941 up to the living conditions of émigrés in Germany and the United States. He always depicts people as they confront the tension between inner experiences and external events over which the individual has no control. In Filippov's poetry, which strongly relies on sound and rhythm, the themes of music and architecture form the bridges to other fields of art that are also important to the author. His legends and his book *Leningradsky Peterburg* (1973; The Leningrad Petersburg) stand apart; in them he combines his own reflections with fragments of poetry and prose by Russian writers whose subject is the longtime capital city.

*Works:* Kresty i perekrëstki (short stories), Munich, 1957; Pyl'noe solnce (short stories), Washington, 1961; Muzykal'naja škatulka (short stories), Washington, 1963; Živoe prošloe (essays), 2 vols., Washington, 1965, 1973; Predan'ja stariny glubokoj (short stories and poems), Washington, 1971; Za tridcat' let (poems), Washington, 1971; Leningradskij Peterburg v russkoj poèzii i proze (anthology), Paris, 1973, 2d ed., 1974; Skvoz' tuči (pov.), Washington, 1975; Škatulka s dvojnym dnom (essays), Washington, 1977; Mysli naraspašku (articles on literary criticism), 2 vols., Washington, 1979, 1982; Stat'i o literature (literary criticism), London, 1981; Izbr. (short stories), London, 1984.

*Secondary Lit.:* B. Narcissov, in *Novoe russkoe slovo*, New York, Oct. 6, 1952; Oct. 19, 1973; July 7, 1974; Jan. 18, 1976; E. Rajs, in *Grani*, Frankfurt am Main, 45:1960; S. Rafal'skij, in *Novoe russkoe slovo* Oct. 25, 1961; Ju. Bol'šukhin, in *Novoe russkoe slovo* Dec. 18, 1963; April 11, 1964; Aug. 24, 1969; Jan. 29, 1971; Feb. 6, 1972; O. Emel'janova, in *Grani* 75:1970; A. Rannit, in *Slavic and East European Review* 1970:3; A. Sedykh, in *Novoe russkoe slovo* Nov. 3, 1974; Aug. 3, 1980, p. 5; G. Stammler, in *Russian Review* 1980:4; V. Sinkevič, in *Novoe russkoe slovo* June 21, 1981, pp. 5 and 10, and in *MERSL* 7:1984; bibliography in Filippov's *Izbr.*, 1984; N. Poltorackij, in *HRL* 1985.

**Finn, Konstantín Yákovlevich** (pseud. of K. Ya. Finn-Khálfin), playwright (b. June 1 [May

19], 1904, Moscow—d. Jan. 3, 1975, Moscow). From 1926 to 1929 Finn attended the State Higher Courses in Literature. His first prose work was published in 1926; after 1930 he wrote predominantly drama. Finn served as a frontline reporter for *Izvestiya* during World War II. He became a member of the Communist Party in 1961 and lived in Moscow. Finn wrote more than 40 dramas that have been in performance since 1932. The primitive construction, superficial psychology, sprawling, artificial plots, and overt didacticism of his plays mark them as trivial literature in which officially prompted themes are readily identifiable. Literary histories written between 1958 and 1970 list his best-known dramas, *Synovya* (1937; The Sons) and *Chestnost* (1950; Honesty), as examples of the THEORY OF CONFLICTLESSNESS and as "lacquered reality"; *Pyotr Krymov* (1942) is cited as an example of the propagation of undemocratic, dictatorial behavior among senior officials. *Oshibka Anny* (1955; Anna's Mistake) illustrates the perniciousness of alcohol; *Nachalo zhizni* (1958; Life's Beginning) shows youthful enthusiasm for reclamation of the Virgin Lands in Kazakhstan; and *Dnevnik zhenshchiny* (1962; Diary of a Woman) illustrates ideal technical and human achievements in bridge building. "The action of the principal characters is nothing other than constant competition in unselfishness and nobility" (Yu. Volchek).

*Works: Ošibka Anny* (play), in *Novyj mir* 1955:10; *Dramy i komedii* (plays), 1957 (contains V odnom dome; *Ošibka Anny; Rodilsja čelovek; Ličnaja žizn'; Veročka; Sekret krasoty; Ne ot mira sego); Načalo žizni* (play), in *Moskva* 1959:6; *Dnevnik ženščiny* (play), in *Teatr* 1962:7; *Trevožnoe sčast'e* (play), in *Teatr* 1964:9; *P'esy* (plays), 1965; *Sëstry razbojnicy* (play), in *Teatr* 1965:7; *Nočnaja Moskva* (play), in *Moskva* 1967:8; *Ženščina bez vozrasta* (play), in *Teatr* 1969:11; *Rasskazy i povesti mnogikh let* (short stories), 1969; *P'esy* (plays), 1972.

*Secondary Lit.:* V. Ozerov, in *Oktjabr'* 1956:6; Ju. Vol'ček, in *Novyj mir* 1962:10; V. Pimenov, in *Ogonëk* 1964:24; S. Babaevskij, in *Lit. gazeta* June 12, 1974.

**Fish, Gennády Semyónovich,** prose writer (b. April 10 [March 28], 1903, Odessa—d. July 6, 1971, Moscow). Fish's father was a civil engineer. Fish moved to Leningrad in 1905; in 1925 he completed his philological studies at Leningrad University and studied art history.

He began his career in journalism and literature in 1922 (writing poems, short stories, reviews). Fish published several volumes of verse between 1926 and 1933; from then on, he wrote publicistic prose. In 1936 he moved to Moscow. Fish worked as a frontline reporter during the Finnish-Russian War and World War II. In 1943 he joined the Communist Party; around 1960 he made several trips to northern Europe. He lived in Moscow and was a delegate to the congresses of the Writers Union of the RSFSR between 1958 and 1970.

Fish's prose is based on his personal experiences and on his literary studies; it contains no fictional events, no poetic intuition. Three thematic complexes stand out in his work: first, the Karelian-Finnish complex, which in his early prose appears in association with the Civil War (*Padeniye Kimas-ozera* [1932; The Fall of Lake Kimas]), with socialist construction, then with war experiences; second (from 1939 on), biological science in its relation to socialist agriculture, the special cause that Fish promoted even in the late Stalin period; and third, educational-political travel notes about Denmark, Finland, Norway, and Sweden, for which he received honorary awards from the Soviet Peace Committee. Several of Fish's film scripts were produced between 1937 and 1941.

*Works: Padenie Kimas-ozera* (pov.), 1933; *My vernëmsja, Suomi!* (novel), 1934; *Jalguba* (pov.), 1936; *Pervaja vintovka*, 1939; *Kamennyj Bor* (novel), 1947; *Sovetskaja byl' i amerikanskie skazki* (publicistic prose), 1948; *Zdravstvuj, Danija!* (travel notes), 1959; *Po doroge v Segežu* (pov.), 1960; *Vstreči v Suomi* (travel notes), 1960; *Norvegija rjadom* (travel notes), 1963; *U pisatelej Švecii* (travel notes), in *Novyj mir* 1965:12; *U švedov* (travel notes), 1966; *Skandinavija v trëkh licakh* (travel notes), 2 vols., 1969; *Posle ijulja v semnadcatom. Nevydumannye povesti* (pov.), 1970; *Snova v Skandinavii* (travel notes), 1973.—*Izbr.*, 1965; 2 vols., 1976.

*Secondary Lit.:* V. Goffenšefer, in *Lit. kritik* 1936:8; G. Vladimov, in *Novyj mir* 1959:7; B. Galanov, in *Novyj mir* 1964:2; *RSPP* 5:1968; V. Baranov, in *Novyj mir* 1971:7; A. Gorelov, in *Zvezda* 1973:9; L. Žak, 1976; T. Nikol'skaja, in *MERSL* 7:1984.

**Foménko, Vladímir Dmítriyevich,** prose writer (b. Sept. 29 [Sept. 16], 1911, Chernigov). Fomenko's father was an office worker: his mother, a teacher. Fomenko grew up in Rostov-on-Don, where he worked as a laborer after 1927. After completing his military service in the Red Army, he studied literature at the Rostov Pedagogical Institute (1935–41). He served as an artillery officer during World War II. Fomenko was admitted to the Communist Party in 1942. In 1946–47 he spent two years in the Virgin Lands. He lives in Rostov.

Fomenko's literary career began in 1946 with the publication of some poems and a volume of articles from the war and postwar period. His short stories about the kolkhoz began to appear in 1951. His major work is a two-part novel, *Pamyat zemli* (1961 and 1970; The Earth's Memory), first published in *Novy mir*. As his theme Fomenko chose the building of the Volga-Don Canal in the early 1950s; the construction of the canal forced the inhabitants of many traditional villages to abandon their homes to make room for the "Tsimlyanskoye more" reservoir. In using this example Fomenko attempts, in conscious contrast to the simplification and misrepresentation of actual difficulties that are typical of the literature of the Stalinist period, to present an accurate picture of the problems of that time. He contrasts the Stalinist Party leader, who considers command and obedience to be proper procedural methods, with the "Leninist" type, who chooses the way of patient persuasion and takes into consideration not only the requirements of national policy but also the small concerns of the individual. A leisurely development of plot with many episodes, detailed dialogue interspersed with reconstructions of the characters' thoughts, and a critical view of each of the many characters make it apparent that Fomenko's goal is to master the problem of the consequences of the "cult of personality." The novel received good reviews.

*Works: Delo česti* (articles), 1946; *Čelovek v stepi* (articles), 1949, enl. ed., 1954; *Rasskazy* (short stories), 1952, 2d ed., 1954; *Pamjat' zemli* (novel), vol. 1, 1961, vol. 2, 1971, in 2 vols., 1972.

*Secondary Lit.:* A. Turkov, in *Lit. gazeta* Aug. 31, 1961, and Oct. 3, 1973, p. 4; G. Brovman, in *Lit. i sovremennost'* 3:1962; *RSPP* 5:1968; V. Surganov, in *Voprosy lit.* 1971:8 and in *Moskva* 1974:1; E. Džičoeva, in *Lit. Rossija* Oct. 2, 1981.

**Formalist school,** a movement within literary criticism that took hold in the Soviet Union in the 1920s and was analogous to the corresponding Western European trend toward studying what is inherent in the work of art. The formalist school dates from the Moscow Circle of Linguists, a study group founded in 1915 that included R. Jakobson, G. Vinokur, and O. Brik, and from the Society for the Study of Poetic Language (OPOYAZ), which was closely related to FUTURISM and was formed in Petrograd in 1916 by V. Shklovsky, B. Eykhenbaum, Yu. Tynyanov, L. Yakubinsky, S. Bernshteyn, and E. Polivanov. The formalist school arose in opposition to the historical, biographical, and sociological approach to literature prevalent throughout the 19th century; it insisted that aesthetic analysis be the focal point of a scholarly investigation of a work of art. The primary subject of inquiry should not be literature viewed as the sum total of artistic works but the aesthetic function of language. Proceeding from the realization that a literary work is something "made," Russian formalists provided an essential and lasting contribution through their philologically precise description of the great works of Russian literature. Shklovsky's concepts of *priyom* (stratagem) and *ostraneniye* (alienation) played an important role in this connection. The literary work was viewed as the sum of its devices, later as a system of devices, and the goal was to define the structure of this system. The exponents of the formalist school regarded form and content as a single entity, but they started with an analysis of form; they were opposed by the Marxists, whose approach was oriented toward a strict sociological method. Because the Marxists denied that "formalist esthetics are descriptive rather than metaphysical" (Erlich, p. 7), they reproached the formalists for their "l'art pour l'art" tendencies. The increasing politicization of intellectual life led to the demise of the formalist school around 1930 after its prime during the years between 1921 and 1926. The ideas of the formalist school persisted through the Prague Circle of Linguists and were then incorporated into the general European movement of structuralism. In the Soviet Union, the term *formalism* serves to characterize an objectionable attitude on the part of an artist, an attitude that deviates from the norms of SOCIALIST REALISM.

*Secondary Lit.:* B. M. Engel'gardt, *Formal'nyj metod v istorii literatury,* 1927; *Russian Formalist Criticism: Four Essays,* trans. and ed. L. T. Lemon and M. J. Reis, Lincoln, Nebraska, 1965; *Texte der russischen Formalisten,* 2 vols., Munich, 1969, 1972; Frederic Jameson, *The Prison-House of Language,* Princeton, 1972; *Russian Formalism: A Col-*

lection of Articles and Texts in Translation, ed. S. Bann and J. E. Bowlt, Edinburgh, 1973; Formalism: History, Comparison, Genre, ed. L. M. O'Toole and A. Shukman, Oxford, 1977; A. A. Hansen-Löve, Vienna, 1978, and in Wiener Slavistisches Jahrbuch 24:1978; V. Erlich, Russian Formalism: History, Doctrine, 4th ed., The Hague–New York, 1980; C. Mailand-Hansen, in Scando-Slavica 29:1983; P. Steiner, Ithaca, N.Y., 1984.

**Forsh, Ólga Dmítriyevna**, prose writer (b. May 28 [May 16], 1873, Gunib, Dagestan—d. July 17, 1961, Leningrad). Forsh was the daughter of General D. V. Komarov. Educated at a boarding school for young ladies, she received instruction in art, in which she later gave lessons. Forsh began her literary career at the start of the century, writing under such pseudonyms as A. Terek. Odety kamnem (Eng. tr., Palace and Prison, 1958), her first historical novel about a 19th-century revolutionary, was published in 1924–25. Forsh maintained a lifelong attachment to the historical novel. The attitude of Soviet critics and literary historians toward her work is positive but qualified, since her historical point of view deviates from official interpretations in varying degrees.

N. Gogol and his friend, the painter A. Ivanov, are the central figures in Sovremenniki (1926; The Contemporaries). Sumasshedshiy korabl (1931; The Mad Ship) portrays the early 1920s in Petrograd; as a novel, it has additional documentary significance. Simvolisty (1933; The Symbolists) depicts the period of Russian symbolism, with V. Rozanov, A. Remizov, Vyach. Ivanov, and M. Kuzmin. These last two works, which are exceptional in that they reflect a period personally experienced by the author, were sharply criticized and are missing from later editions of her collected works. Forsh returned to the theme of the revolutionary in her trilogy Radishchev (1932–39), which she followed with her presentation of the Decembrist movement, Perventsy svobody (1950–53; Eng. tr., Pioneers of Freedom, 1954). "Her thrilling and colorful work always maintained a good literary standard, combining exciting plots with solid historical background. Her genuine revolutionary feelings allowed her to link the biographical with the politically inspired historical novel" (Slonim).

Works: Čto komu nravitsja (short stories), 1914; Obyvateli (short stories), 1923; Odety kamnem (novel), 1924–25 (see above); Sovre-

menniki (novel), 1926; Sumasšedšij korabl' (pov.), 1931 (reprinted, Washington, 1964); Radiščev (novel-triology), 1932–39; Voron (retitled ed. of Simvolisty; novel), 1934; Pervency svobody (novel), 1950–53 (see above); Odety kamnem. Mikhajlovskij zamok (novels), 1980.—Sobr. soč., 7 vols., 1928–30; 8 vols., 1962–64; Izbr. proizv., 2 vols., 1972.

Secondary Lit.: N. Lugovcov, 1964; R. Messer, 1965; RSPP 5:1968; O. F. v vospominanijakh sovremennikov, 1974; A. Tamarčenko, 2d ed., 1974; G. Curikova, foreword to Forsh's Odety kamnem. Mikhajlovskij zamok, 1980; L. G. Muratov, in Russkaja lit. 1982:4; K. B. Lewis, in MERSL 8:1987.

**Frayermán, Ruvím Isáyevich**, prose writer (b. Sept. 22 [Sept. 10] 1891, Mogilev—d. March 28, 1972, Moscow). Frayerman came from a poor Jewish family. Between 1914 and 1917 he studied at the Institute of Technology in Kharkov; in the following years he held various jobs (as fisherman, teacher, bookkeeper) in the Caucasus and then in the Soviet Far East, where he fought with the partisans during the Civil War. Frayerman gradually worked his way into a career in journalism in Yakutsk, Omsk, Batum, and Moscow. His first literary work, the povest Ognevka, appeared in Sibirskiye ogni in 1924. For a long time Frayerman combined careers in literature and journalism. Most of his short stories and povesti, such as Buran 1926; The Snowstorm), Vaska-gilyak (1929; Vaska the Gilyak), and Nikichen (1932), are set in the Soviet Far East and are aimed principally at children. A volume of his publicistic articles about tractor stations appeared in 1931 under the title 22 × 36. His friendship (dating back to the 1930s) with K. Paustovsky, A. Gaydar, M. Loskutov, S. Gekht, and A. Roskin frequently took him, together with these writers, into the central Russian woodland and lake area of Meshchora. During World War II, Frayerman was a soldier and frontline reporter for a time; in the late Stalin period his works were attacked for their sentimentalism and "detachment from SOCIALIST REALISM" (B. Solovyov). Paustovsky's essay about Frayerman, written in 1948, could not be published until 1956. Frayerman lived outside the literary establishment in Moscow.

Paustovsky called Frayerman "a good and pure talent," one who "communicates to the reader his most profound belief that freedom and love for man are the most important goals toward which we must strive always." A. Tolstoy described Frayerman's povest Dikaya sobaka Dingo, ili Povest o pervoy lyubvi (1939;

Wild Dog Dingo; or, A Story about First Love; Eng. tr., The Dingo, 1959, 1974) as one of the best that Frayerman ever published, "fresh, permeated by the most subtle, innocent fragrance of love"; the story reveals Frayerman's psychological and poetic strengths.

Works: Vtoraja vesna (pov.), 1932; Nikičen (pov.), 1933; Sobolja (short stories), 1935; Dikaja sobaka Dingo, ili Povest' o pervoj ljubvi (pov.), in Krasnaja nov' 1939:7 (see above); Rasskazy (short stories), 1939; Dal'nee plavanie (pov.), 1946; Povesti i rasskazy (pov. and short stories), 1949; Naš Gajdar (essay), in Žizn' i tvorčestvo A. P. Gajdara, ed. R. Fraerman, 1951, 3d ed., 1964; Žizn' i neobyknovennye priključenija kapitana-lejtenanta Golovnina, putešestvennika i morekhodca (pov.), 1953 (in collaboration with P. Zajkin); Povesti i rasskazy (pov. and short stories), 1954; Izbr., 1958; Naš Paustovskij (essay), in Izvestija May 31, 1976; Povesti (pov.), 1975; Povesti i rasskazy (pov. and short stories), 1976.

Secondary Lit.: E. Taratuta, in Molodaja gvardija 1933:7, in Detskaja lit. 1936:6, and in Komsomol'skaja pravda Sept. 17, 1954; B. Solovëv, in Zvezda 1948:10; V. Dudincev, in Komsomol'skaja pravda Sept. 28, 1950; K. Paustovskij, in his Sobr. soč., vol. 5, 1958; M. M. Blinkova, 1959; A. Ivič, in his Vospitanie pokolenij, 4th ed., 1969; V. Nikolaev, in Lit. Rossija Feb. 25, 1972, p. 11; obituary, in Lit. gazeta April 5, 1972, p. 5; L. P. Jakimova, in Sibirskie ogni 1972:1; A. Injakhin, in Teatr 1985:5.

**Fúrmanov, Dmítry Andréyevich,** prose writer (b. Nov. 7 [Oct. 26], 1891, Sereda, prov. Kostroma—d. March 15, 1926, Moscow). Furmanov was of peasant descent. He attended school until 1908, first in Ivanovo-Voznesensk, then in Kishinyov. He studied in Moscow from 1912 to 1914; during World War I he was a medical orderly until 1916. Furmanov's sympathies during the Revolution lay at first with the Socialist Revolutionaries, then with the anarchists until he joined the Bolshevik Party in 1918. During the Civil War he served as political commissar with the partisan leader Chapayev's 25th Division, then as head of the political section on the Turkestan front, and finally with the army in the Kuban. Furmanov lived in Moscow from 1921 on, belonged to the leadership of VAPP, and was secretary of MAPP. After writing newspaper articles between 1916 and 1921, Furmanov embarked on a literary career in Moscow. His

povest Krasny desant (1921; The Red Landing Party), about an engagement of the army in the Kuban, is reportage that maintains a first-person narrative structure. Furmanov incorporated his experiences in the southeastern steppes beyond the Volga into his semidocumentary novel Chapayev (1923; Eng. tr., 1935, 1959), in which he himself served as the model for Klychkov, the political commissar who disciplined the primitive folk hero Chapayev. Using the same mixture of quotations from primary documents and reportage conforming to the Party position and rejecting the ornamental narrative techniques characteristic of his contemporaries (for example, I. Babel, whom he admired), Furmanov depicts the struggle of Soviet forces against rebellious units in Central Asia in his third work, Myatezh (1925; The Revolt). By 1964 his novel Chapayev was in its 71st printing and had been made into a film; it is now considered a standard work of Soviet literature. Furmanov's hometown today bears his name.

Works: Krasnyj desant (pov.), 1921; Čapaev (novel), 1923 (see above); Mjatež (novel), 1925; Za kommunizm (play), in Lit. nasledstvo, vol. 74, 1965; Zametki o literature, 1979.—Sobr. soč., 4 vols., 1926–27; 5 vols., 1928; 4 vols., 1960–61.

Secondary Lit.: V. Ozerov, 1953; K. Kasper, Halle, 1962; G. Gorbunov, 1965; P. Kuprijanovskij, 1967, and in Lit. Rossija Nov. 18, 1983, p. 9; RSPP 5:1968; M. Sotskova, 1969; Furmanovskij sbornik, 1973; H. M. Pilgrim, Diss., Exeter, 1981; H. Stephan, in MERSL 8:1987.

**Futurism,** an avant-garde, heterogeneous literary movement that existed between 1910 and 1920. Russian futurism is an independent part of the European revolution in art whose relationships to Italian futurism is varyingly viewed. The initial impetus for this movement, which grew out of symbolism and impressionism, was the revolution in form, especially in literary language. The most important group were the cubo-futurists, organized in 1910, whose members included V. Khlebnikov, David and Nikolay Burlyuk, and A. Kruchonykh. Their primary concern was the "autonomy and freedom of the word"; the element of form and sound, the "word as such," as more important than the meaning. This principle led to an attempt to develop a metalanguage—zaum. Other experiments concerned syntax (for example, D. Burlyuk's rejection of prepositions), neologisms, the verse and rhyme system. The provocative element revealed itself in the manifesto of 1912, *Poshchochina obshchestvennomu vkusu* (A Slap in the Face of Public Taste), which rejected all preceding literature. The cubo-futurists welcomed the Revolution as a possible forum in which they could realize their radical conceptions of art. In 1922 K. Chukovsky noted three tendencies: one urban, emphasizing the technical and industrial; a second primal, rejecting culture; and a third anarchic in a way that was almost unconsciously typically Russian and that surged forward toward the destruction of all laws and values. The group of ego-futurists founded by Igor Severyanin in 1911 in St. Petersburg and led by Ivan Ignatyev between 1912 and 1914 adopted the designation *futurist* and must be distinguished from other futurist groups. Taking egoism as the guiding principle of life, ego-futurism advocated individualism and promoted the abrogation of ethical and moral limits in art. Some members of the short-lived group, such as R. Ivnev and V. Shershenevich, later formed the imagists (see IMAGISM). Closer to the views of the cubo-futurists was the literary group "Tsentrifuga" (Centrifuge), which existed in Moscow between 1914 and 1922 and championed especially the revival of the lyrical and its metaphors and imagery in general. With S. Bobrov, B. Pasternak, and N. Aseyev this group formed "perhaps the most broadminded and cultivated futurist group" (Markov). In addition to the three central trends within futurism, there existed numerous other liaisons: for example, G. Petnikov and N. Aseyev, with their publishing house Liren in Kharkov, who worked together with Khlebnikov; or "Mezonin Poezii" (Mezzanine of Poetry), a Moscow group affiliated with ego-futurism that existed for four months in 1913. In spite of the futurists' (especially V. Mayakovsky's) positive attitude toward the Revolution, the Soviet regime opposed futurism, as well as LEF, a group that grew out of futurism, and OBERIU, a Leningrad association that was influenced by futurism. The views of OKTYABR and RAPP, which fought against these opponents of bourgeois culture and these revolutionaries in the field of art because of their original paths, are still current today. Futurism is considered bourgeois and decadent.

*Secondary Lit.*: K. Čukovskij, *Futuristy*, 1922; *Lit. manifesty*, 2d ed., 1929 (reprinted, Munich, 1969); D. Tschižewskij, *Die Anfänge des russ. Futurismus*, Heidelberg, 1963; *Manifesty i programmy russkikh futuristov*, Munich, 1967; V. Markov, *Russian Futurism*, Berkeley,

1968; R. Ziegler, *Die Manifeste, Programme und theoretischen Schriften der Kubofuturisten*, Diss., Vienna, 1971; V. D. Barooshian, *Russian Cubo-Futurism 1910–1930*, The Hague, 1974, and Ann Arbor, 1981; K. B. Jensen, *Russian Futurism, Urbanism and Elena Guro*, Århus, 1977; S. P. Compton, *The World Backwards: Russian Futurist Books 1912–1916*, London, 1978; Z. Folejewski, *Futurism and Its Place in the Development of Modern Poetry*, Ottawa, 1980; *The Ardis Anthology of Russian Futurism*, Ann Arbor, 1980; R. D. B. Thomson, in *MERSL* 8:1987.

**Fyódorov, Vasíly Dmítriyevich**, poet (b. Feb 23, 1918, Kemerovo—d. April 19, 1984, Moscow). Fyodorov's father was a mason. Fyodorov grew up in a village; he spent two years on a kolkhoz after finishing six years of schooling. In 1938 he completed a technical school for aircraft construction in Novosibirsk and subsequently worked in aircraft factories in Siberia until 1947. In 1945 he was admitted to the Communist Party. In 1939 his first poems were published in factory newspapers; in 1947 his first book came out in Novosibirsk. Fyodorov studied at the Gorky Literary Institute until 1950. His second volume of verse appeared in 1955; from then on, his works were published on a regular basis in Moscow, where he also lived and where he was a member of the editorial board of the journal *Molodaya gvardiya* from 1959 on.

Fyodorov's poetry, which literary critics and historians have treated as a good example of topical verse, is frequently narrative in character. Particular attention was attracted by his narrative poems *Belaya roshcha* (1956; The White Grove), which tells the story of a tractor driver who becomes acclimated to life in the Virgin Lands; *Prodannaya Venera* (1959; The Sold Venus), about the sacrifices that had to be made at the time of the first Five-Year Plan for the present moment; and *Sedmoye nebo* (1959–60; Seventh Heaven). In this partly autobiographical poem Fyodorov attempts to cover the development of the USSR over a period of decades; the poem's subject, typical of Fyodorov's work, is the striven-for goal (Gorky Prize, 1968). His narrative poem *Zhenitba Donzhuana* (1977; The Marriage of Don Juan) uses the literary image to depict the immediate present. In *Sny poeta* (1979; A Poet's Dreams) Fyodorov reports and comments upon his own dreams from childhood on. In rhythmic, progressive verses with an unfixed number of stresses and unpretentious rhymes, Fyodorov speaks his mind fully; next to the light he shows the shadow, although he still leaves little to the imagination. Fyodorov was awarded the State Prize of the USSR in 1979.

*Works:* Liričeskaja trilogija (poems), 1947; Lesnye rodniki (poems), 1955; Mar'evskie zvëzdy (poems), 1955; Belaja rošča (narrative poems), 1958; Dikij mëd (poems), 1958; Zolotaja žila (narrative poems), 1959; Ne levee serdca (poems), 1960; Sed'moe nebo (narrative poem), 1968; Tret'i petuchi. Sed'moe nebo (lyric and narrative poems), 1970; Kryl'ja na polden' (poems), 1971; Naše vremja takoe . . . O poèzii i poètakh (essays), 1973; Stikhi (poems), 1978; Ženit'ba Donžuana (narrative

poem), 1977 (also in Moskva 1978:1–3; Sny poèta (stort stories), in Moskva 1979:8–10; I togda pridut slova . . . (interview), in Moskva 1984:12; Sny poèta (short stories), in Naš sovremennik 1985:4.—Stikhotvorenija i poèmy (lyric and narrative poems), 2 vols, 1970; Sobr. soc., 3 vols., 1975–76.

*Secondary Lit.:* E. Sučkov, in Lit. i sovremennost' 3:1962; M. Lapšin and L. Ivanov, in Naš sovremennik 1963:2; V. Erëmin, 1969; V. Pankov, in Lit. i sovremennost' 10:1970; I. Denisova, 1971; G. Gorlanov, in Oktjabr' 1973:12; M. Lapšin, in his Ličnost' v literature, 1973, and in Moskva 1977:5; A. Šagalov, in Znamja 1980:3; V. Cybin, in Lit. Rossija April 27, 1984, p. 11.

# G

**Gabrilóvich, Yevgény Iósifovich,** screenplay writer (b. Sept. 29 [Sept. 11], 1899, Voronezh). Gabrilovich published his first short prose in 1921 and belonged to the Literary Center of the Constructivists (see CONSTRUCTIVISM), disbanded in 1920. In the 1930s he wrote publicistic prose about industrial construction and collectivization. Aside from short stories written during World War II, Gabrilovich's literary work lies in the area of the cinema. His first screenplay, Poslednyaya noch (1937; The Last Night), deals with Lenin's last days. During the war, when he wrote the texts for the films Mashenka (1942), Mechta (1943; The Dream), and Dva boytsa (1943; Two Warriors), he received a Stalin Prize (for 1942, 2d class). Gabrilovich was highly regarded for his film Kommunist (1958; The Communist), which, in a manner characteristic of his work, illustrates historical events by focusing on an unobtrusive, psychologically credible, representative individual (in this case, a worker in the camps). After the 20th Party Congress, Gabrilovich advocated a simpler and more human image of Lenin in film; however, influenced by the critics, he did not completely realize his intentions in the films Rasskazy o Lenine (1958; Stories of Lenin) and Lenin v Polshe (1965; Lenin in Poland). In 1960–62 Gabrilovich wrote a screenplay based on L. Tolstoy's novel Voskreseniye (Resurrection). Gabrilovich, who has written numerous essays on cinematic dramaturgy, received the State Prize in 1967 and again in 1983. In Chetyre chetverti (1975; Four Fourths) he attempts to depict his own life in four segments;

his later short stories are likewise turned toward events from decades long past. Gabrilovich lives in Moscow.

*Works:* Tikhij Brovkin (pov.), in Krasnaja nov' 1936:1–2; Kniga scenariev (film scripts), 1959; Zametki kinodramaturga (essay), in Mosfil'm 1:1959; Lenin v Pol'še (film script), in Oktjabr' 1962:1; O tom, čto prošlo (memoirs), 1967; Tvoj sovremennik (film script, in collaboration with Ju. Rajzman), 1969; V ogne broda net. Načalo (film scripts, in collaboration with G. Panfilov), 1972; Četyre četverti (autobiography), 1975; Roždenie veka (short stories), 1978; Dialog za kinoèkran (with S. Jutkevič), in Avrora 1984:7.

*Secondary Lit.:* A. Kapler, in Lit. gazeta Dec. 24, 1959; I. Bereza, in Zvezda 1959:12; S. Štut, in Voprosy lit. 1960:7, pp. 42–46; D. Ostrovskij, in Lit. gazeta Sept. 23, 1970, p. 8; Z. Vladimirova, in Teatr 1981:5.

**Galanskóv, Yúry Timoféyevich,** poet (b. June 19, 1939, Moscow—d. Nov. 4, 1972 [?], while imprisoned, Baransevo, Mordovian ASSR). Galanskov was the son of a worker. Galanskov's "independent views" were the cause of his expulsion from Moscow University after two semesters of studying law. In 1961 he was one of the editor-publishers of the SAMIZDAT publication Feniks No. 1, in which his poems "Chelovechesky manifest" (The Human Manifesto) and "Proletarii vsekh stran, soyedinyaytes" (Proletarians of All Lands, Unite) appeared. Galanskov personally signed the volume Feniks No. 2 (or Feniks—66) as editor-publisher, and created a significant samizdat document by printing A. Sinyavsky's *Chto takoye sotsialistichesky realizm?* and his own poetic and publicistic contributions to democracy and pacifism. On Jan. 19, 1967, Galanskov was arrested; on Jan. 12, 1968, he was sentenced to seven years at hard labor along with A. Ginzburg, whom he had helped to put out the Sinyavsky-Daniel white paper. After June 1969 Galanskov was treated several times in camp hospitals for a duodenal ulcer; he died of blood poisoning following an operation. His obituary notice, signed by N. Gorbanevskaya, V. Maksimov, and A. Sinyavsky, read: "Galanskov ended up in the camps because he was an honest poet and an honest man. His poems and articles never found a place on the pages of official publications. . . . Galanskov was an implacable and fearless foe of any and all coercion, hypocrisy, and outrage against human dignity." This definition covers the essence of Galanskov's political verse, which in powerful imagery, often similar to rhythmic prose, cries out from deepest despair and frees itself from oppressive visions of authority. "Prolog iz poemy dlya detey" (Prologue from a Poem for Children) reveals the poet's delicate sensitivity in a genre in which he himself was unable to develop his potential.

*Works: Ju. T. Galanskov, Poet i čelovek* (poems), Frankfurt am Main, 1973 (in German in *Russ. Samizdat: Stimmen aus dem anderen Russland*, vol. 6, Bern, 1974; Eng. tr., *Poet and Man: In Memory of Yuri Galanskov*, 1973); *Pis'ma rodnym i druz'jam* (letters), in *Grani*, Frankfurt am Main, 94:1974; *Jurij Galanskov* [Sbornik], Frankfurt am Main, 1980.

*Secondary Lit.:* A. Čakovskij, in *Lit. gazeta* March 27, 1968, p. 13; biography, in *Grani* 80:1971; C. Gerstenmaier, *Die Stimme der Stummen*, Stuttgart, 1971; various articles in *Jurij Galanskov*, 1980; J. Deutsch, in *MERSL* 8:1987.

**Gálich, Aleksándr Arkádyevich,** playwright, poet (b. Oct. 19, 1919, Yekaterinoslav—d. Dec. 15, 1977, Paris). Galich attended the acting academy and the Gorky Literary Institute in Moscow. His early poetic endeavors reveal E. Bagritsky's influence. Galich appeared in the play he wrote with others, *Gorod na zare* (1941; The City at Dawn), as a member of the Moscow Theater Studio led by A. Arbuzov and V. Pluchek. During World War II, Galich worked in a theater at the front. During the Stalin period, some plays were performed in which he is named as coauthor. "There were also enthusiastic and talentedly written plays that never saw the limelight, and others excessively well received at the beginning that were later scathingly criticized without sufficient reason" (Pluchek). Between 1954 and 1960 some of the plays he wrote independently became famous, such as *Pokhodny marsh/Za chas do rassveta* (1957; Field March/ An Hour before Dawn) or *Parokhod zovut "Orlyonok"* (1958; The Steamboat Is Called "Orlyonok"). Numerous of his screenplays were made into movies. After the mid-1960s, Galich increasingly dissociated himself from the requirements of conformity and devoted himself more and more to writing candid, accusatory poetry that had a songlike character and that found wide circulation in SAMIZDAT when tape-recorded with a guitar accompaniment. His poetry is critical of society and is anti-Stalinist, speaks out for the victims of labor camps, and remembers the persecuted such as A. Akhmatova, D. Kharms, O. Mandelshtam. It unites the religious with the political (for example, in "Poema o Staline") and combines sober reflections with irony and satire. Galich fights unconditionally for the "freedom of self-realization," even when this occurs at the price of imprisonment. Thus, in the verse epic *Kadish,* Janusz Kortszak, who voluntarily accompanies the Jewish children entrusted to his care into the gas chamber at Treblinka, is one of his most important images. Galich was not allowed to appear in public after 1968; his poems were published abroad, and he was expelled from the Writers Union of the USSR and from the Litfond on Dec. 29, 1971. In June 1974 he received an exit visa; he went first to Norway and then to Munich where he settled. In Frankfurt, where *Pesni* (1969; Songs), the first collection of his poems, had already been published, he published a new collection, *Pokoleniye obrechonnykh* (1972, 2d ed., 1974; The Generation of the Damned). In *Generalnaya repetitsiya* (1974; The Final Dress Rehearsal) he presents the story of the forbidden performance of a play, *Matrosskaya tishina* (Sailor's Silence), and offers, together with the text of the drama, a glimpse into Soviet theater life and the management of literature.

*Works:* (with K. F. Isaev) *Vas vyzyvaet Tajmur* (play), in *Ogonëk* 1948:22; (with G. Munblit) *Položenie objazyvaet* (play), 1949; *Pokhodnyj marš* (play), in *Teatr* 1957:3; (with A. Arbuzov et al.) *Gorod na zare* (play), in *Teatr* 1957:11; *Parokhod zovut "Orlënok"* (play), in *Sovremennaja dramaturgija* 6:1958;

Triždy voskresšij (film script), in Iskusstvo kino 1958:8; (with S. Rostockij) Na semi verakh (film script), in Iskusstvo kino 1961:6; Pesni (poems), Frankfurt am Main, 1969; Pokolenie obrečënnykh (poems), Frankfurt am Main, 1972, 2d ed., 1974; General'naja repeticija (documentary prose), Frankfurt am Main, 1974; Stikhi (poems), in Kontinent, Paris, 2:1975; Blošinyj rynok (novel) in Vremja i my, Tel Aviv, 24–25:1977–78; Kogda ja vernus' (poems), Frankfurt am Main, 1977, enl. ed., 1981.
    Translation: Songs and Poems, Ann Arbor, 1983.
    Secondary Lit.: V. Pluček, in Teatr 1957:3; S. Mežinskij, in Izvestija Aug. 28, 1957; biography, in Grani, Frankfurt am Main, 83:1972; G. Smith, in Index 3:1974; E. Ètkind, in Kontinent 5:1975; A. Sinjavskij, in Vremja i my, Tel Aviv, 4:1977; L. Kopelev, in Kontinent 16:1978; R. Orlova, in Vremja i my 51:1980; N. Gorbanevskaja et al., in Russkaja mysl', Paris, Dec. 16, 1982; V. Aksënov, in Novoe russkoe slovo, New York, Dec. 25, 1983; V. Frumkin, in Obozrenie, Paris, 9:1984; D. Boss, Diss., Munich, 1985; G. S. Smith, in MERSL 8:1987.

**Gálin, Aleksándr Mikháylovich,** playwright (b. Sept. 10, 1947, Alekseyevka, Matveye-Kurgansk District, oblast Rostov). Galin worked in a factory as a milling-machine operator, in provincial theaters as an actor, and at the studio theater of Leningrad University as production director. In 1974 Galin graduated from the Leningrad Academy of Culture. Since 1975 he has been writing plays and film scripts. Galin became famous overnight with his first play, Retro (1980; Retro). In 1981 this play premiered at the Maly Theater in Moscow, and until 1983 it was the most frequently staged comedy in the RSFSR (Teatr 1985:11). In 1984 a translation of this play was broadcast on television in the Federal Republic of Germany. Galin's second play, Vostochnaya tribuna (1982; The Eastern Stage), received its premiere at the Sovremennik Theater in Moscow in 1983; his third play, Navazhdeniye (1983; Delusion), premiered at the Theater on the Malaya Bronnaya in Moscow in 1983. Galin lives in Moscow.
    Retro depicts a widowed 72-year-old pensioner whose daughter tries to interfere in his life, with good intentions but without understanding. Tragic and comic aspects intermingle in the confrontation among three potential new wives. In Vostochnaya tribuna, an elderly orchestral violinist returns for a few

hours to his hometown, where he meets five women with whom he was close at one time during his youth. The analytically structured drama gradually reveals these past events and also includes contemporary problems, such as black-market dealings in foreign clothing. In Navazhdeniye Galin again focuses on a pensioner in his search for human warmth.

    Works: Retro (play), 1980; Vostočnaja tribuna (play), in Sovremennaja dramaturgija 1982:3.
    Secondary Lit.: K. Ščerbakov, in Lit. obozrenie 1983:9; N. Agiševa, in Pravda April 21, 1983.

**Galpérin, Yúry Aleksándrovich,** prose writer (b. July 12, 1947, Leningrad). Galperin grew up in Leningrad as the son of a musician, wrote his first short story in 1964, and began his studies at the Leningrad Electrotechnical Institute in the same year. When he abandoned his studies of his own accord, he was drafted into the military and spent three years (1966–68) in the polar region. There Galperin continued to write, but with difficulty. In 1970 he began studying history at Leningrad University; in 1976 he completed his exams. After his first publications in local newspapers, Galperin was able to publish only two short stories in the almanac Molodoy Leningrad in 1971. In 1971–72, under the assumed name of K. Begalin, Galperin, together with the young philologist V. Belodubrovsky, wrote a serious play, Shol malchishke 13-y god (1972; The Youth Was Twelve Years Old), which was performed by the Leningrad Youth Theater in 1972. In 1978 Galperin married a Swiss woman; in 1979 he emigrated to Bern, where since 1980 he has worked at the historical museum. Since 1980 Galperin has published his short stories written in the Soviet Union and in Switzerland in Kontinent, Russkaya mysl, and other periodicals. Some of these stories have been translated into German and French. He won recognition with Most cherez Letu (1982; Bridge over Lethe), the povest written in Leningrad in 1975 and published in London. For this he was awarded the Vladimir Dal Prize in Paris in 1981. His second book was the povest written at the end of 1974, Igrayem bljuz (1983; Play the Blues). A novel written between 1979 and 1983, Russky variant (The Russian Variant), was published at the end of 1986 in the journal Strelets.
    Most cherez Letu, with the subtitle Praktika prozy (The Praxis of Prose), is a literary description of the reality of fictional creation; of

the reciprocal penetration and conditionality of reality, the representation of reality, and the literary creation of a new reality; and of the depiction of this unity. The plot—meeting, love, and accidental death—is reduced to a minimum to give room to the analytic, reflective narrative told from changing perspectives in which the boundaries between time, space, life, and death vanish. *Igrayem bljuz* reveals a spiritually similar approach and deals with a musician whose love of music causes him to lose touch with his material existence, even in its essential forms. Galperin's short stories reveal the spiritual depth of individuals in situations that border on the tragic, and he cleverly interweaves the chronological progression of events and the analytical uncovering of antecedents and connections.

*Works:* Short stories, in *Kontinent*, Paris, 26 1980, 32:1982, 36:1983, 41:1984; in *Èkho*, Paris, 1980:3; in *Russkaja mysl'*, Paris, May 14 and June 4, 1981; April 15, April 22, and Oct. 7, 1982; Jan. 13, May 26, July 27, and Aug. 11, 1983; April 12, April 29, May 31, Nov. 8, and Nov. 15, 1984; May 31, 1985; July 25 and Oct. 3, 1986; in *Strelec*, Montgeron–Jersey City, N.J., 1984:12. *Most čerez Letu* (pov.), London, 1982; *Igraem bljuz* (pov.), Paris, 1983; interview, in *Russkaja mysl'* May 31, 1984, pp. 8–9; *Russkij variant* (novel), in *Strelec* 1986:8–12.

*Secondary Lit.:* K. Sapgir, in *Novoe russkoe slovo*, New York, Oct. 10, 1982, p. 2, and *Russkaja mysl'* Sept. 15, 1983, p. 10; N. Gorbanevskaja, in *Russkaja mysl'* Aug. 12, 1982, p. 12; V. Iverni, in *Kontinent* 34:1982; A. Glezer, in *Novoe russkoe slovo* July 10, 1983, p. 5; R. Porter, in *World Literature Today* 1983:2.

**Gástev, Alekséy Kapitónovich,** poet (b. Oct. 8 [Sept. 26], 1882, Suzdal—d. 1941 [?], while imprisoned). Gastev was the son of a teacher. Gastev's education as a teacher in Moscow was curtailed in 1902 by his involvement in revolutionary activity; as a professional revolutionary, he spent part of his time in emigration (in Paris) and part in Russia. The first of his expressive prose poems appeared in 1913. In 1918 he participated in the work of the PROLETKULT; with them he published the volume *Poeziya rabochego udara* (Poetry of the Working-Class Attack), reprinted six times by 1926. Most of Gastev's poems were written between 1913 and 1917; the last he wrote between 1917 and 1919. In 1920 he became head of the Central Institute of Labor, which he founded, and wrote only publicistic arti-

cles about the organization of labor. He was admitted to the Communist Party in 1931. Gastev was arrested in 1938; the exact date of his death is unknown. He was rehabilitated around 1957.

Gastev's poetry tends more toward anthem-style prose than toward unrhymed or unmetrical verse. It frequently lacks even an organizing rhythm. It consists of poems about the laboring masses or about the worker as symbol in which realistic details are mixed with bold metaphors and principles of action bordering on the fantastic. Thus: "In the veins flows new, iron blood. . . . and I will shout out my iron 'We will win!' " ("My rastyom iz zheleza" [1914; We Grow Out of Iron]); or, on the relationship of men to machines, "We are their levers, we are their breath, their intention" ("Vorota" [between 1913 and 1917; Gates]). Gastev believes in the unification of the proletarians of the world in order to end individualism and to achieve "mechanized collectivism," where "there are expressionless faces, a soul free of lyricism, sensation that will be measured not by a cry or by laughter but by pressure gauge and taximeter." V. Khlebnikov called Gastev "an ecclesiastical painter of labor, who replaces the word 'God' with the word 'I' in the old prayers."

*Works: Poèzija rabočego udara* (poems), 1918, 6th ed., 1926, 7th ed., 1964, 1971; *Pačka orderov* (poems), 1921.

*Secondary Lit.:* V. Percov, in *Lit. gazeta* Oct. 9, 1962, and in his *Ot svidetelja sčastlivogo . . .*, 1977; Z. Papernyj, in *Gastev's Poèzija rabočego udara*, 1964; N. Os'makov, in *Lit. gazeta* Oct. 25, 1972, p. 5; *RSPPo* 5:1982; K. Johansson, Stockholm, 1983; H. Stephan, in *MERSL* 8:1987.

**Gaydár, Arkády Petróvich** (pseud. of A. P. Gólikov), prose writer (b. Jan. 22 [Jan. 9], 1904, Lgov, prov. Kursk—d. Oct. 26, 1941, near Kanev, Ukraine). Gaydar's father was a teacher. At the age of 14 Gaydar volunteered for the Red Army, in which he served until 1924. His first literary attempts in 1925–26 did not as yet reveal talent, but the stories, both short and long, for young readers that he wrote later brought him lasting success. In 1941 he became a war correspondent for *Komsomolskaya pravda*; he died in battle. K. Paustovsky, who (like R. Frayerman) was a friend of Gaydar's, called him a "genuine and great man," one who was "distinguished in every action and every word."

Largely autobiographical, Gaydar's first po-rest, Shkola (1930; The School), traces the development into a convinced Bolshevik of a child who lives through World War I, the Revolution, and the Civil War. His best short stories, such as Golubaya chashka (1936; The Blue Cup) and Chuk i Gek (1939; Eng. tr., Chuck and Geck, 1953), are also permeated by a generally humane and concretely political pedagogical message. A gripping plot, one of the characteristic features of Gaydar's prose, forms the basis of his most important book for young readers, Timur i ego komanda (1940; Eng. trs., Timur and His Gang, 1943; Timur and His Squad, 1948, 1960); it tells the story of a young Pioneer who establishes a secret organization to aid the families of soldiers at the front. The enormous success among Soviet youth of Gaydar's frequently printed prose is also based on the psychological shrewdness with which he conveys "the similarity between juvenile and adult consciousness" (Kaverin) and on his clear and lyrical style, which is oriented toward fairy tales and colloquial speech. Many of his works have been filmed and dramatized.

*Works:* Škola (pov.), 1930; Dal'nie strany (pov.), 1931; Golubaja čaška (short story), 1936; Čuk i Gek (short story), 1939 (see above); Timur i ego komanda (pov.), 1941 (see above).—Sobr. soč., 4 vols., 1964–65; 4 vols., 1971–73.

*Secondary Lit.:* Žizn' i tvorčestvo, compiled by R. Fraerman, 1954; V. Smirnova, 1961, 2d ed., 1972; B. Kamov, 1963 and 1979; L. Kassil', in the foreword to Gajdar's Sobr. soč., 1964 and 1971; A. Ivič, in his Vospitanie pokolenij, 1969; N. N. Orlova, 1974; I. Rozanov, 1979; M. Fedosjuk, in Russkaja reč 1984:1; L. Loseff, in MERSL 8:1987.

**Gazdánov, Gaytó Ivánovich,** prose writer (b. Dec. 6 [Nov. 23], 1903, St. Petersburg—d. Dec. 5, 1971, Munich). Gazdanov's father was a forester. Owing to frequent trips and his father's transfers, Gazdanov became acquainted with quite a few regions of Russia as a child. He attended secondary school in Kharkov from 1912 to 1919, fought against the Bolsheviks for a year, and was evacuated through the Crimea to Constantinople with Wrangel's troops in 1920. There (1922) and in Bulgaria (1923) he completed his education. In the winter of 1923 Gazdanov moved to Paris; he scraped through in great need until, from 1928 to 1952, he was able to earn a living by working as a taxi driver at night. Between 1926 and 1931 Gazdanov intermittently studied at the Sorbonne. Between 1927 and 1929 Gaz-

danov's first short stories were published in the Prague journal Volya Rossii; thereafter his works regularly appeared in Sovremennye zapiski. The publication of the novel Vecher u Kler (1930; Eng. tr., An Evening with Claire, 1984) brought him the highest acclaim from all the leading Russian critics; his name was frequently mentioned together with that of V. Nabokov. He sustained a very productive creative phase until 1940: he wrote 4 of his 9 novels, and 28 of his 37 short stories. In 1932, influenced by M. Osorgin, Gazdanov joined a Masonic lodge in Paris where he made a good name for himself through his philosophical and religious talks. During the German occupation, Gazdanov was active in the resistance movement despite his anti-Soviet attitude (see his book Je m'engage à défendre [1946]). In 1953 Gazdanov was offered a permanent position with Radio Liberty in Munich. He worked there until his death (1959–67 as a correspondent in Paris), intermittently as head of the Russian desk.

At the beginning of Gazdanov's writing career, many critics felt they recognized Marcel Proust's influence. Gazdanov's representation of the stream of consciousness, "journeys to the depth of one's own memory," arose, however, from his own literary searching (only later did he read and admire Proust) and confirms (as with Nabokov) his well-grounded position within Western European literature. Gazdanov's writings are esentially autobiographical, not the ramblings of an unencumbered imagination. Gazdanov's first novels are loose, episodically structured. Vecher u Kler uses his first night of love with a French woman as the framework for reminiscences and reflections about his school years, his tank platoon in the Civil War, and his first love. Among Gazdanov's short stories, Schastye (1932; Happiness) and Osvobozhdeniye (1933; Liberation) have earned recognition— the first for its view, typical of Gazdanov, of the bonds uniting man and his fate, and the second for its quarrel with death. The novel Istoriya odnogo puteshestviya (1935; The Story of a Journey)—"in some regards perhaps his best" (Dienes)—depicts a series of psychological trips into the depth of consciousness and feeling as these are revealed in the visible world (for example, during the months in Constantinople). Nochnye dorogi (Night Paths), completed in 1941 and published in a revised and enlarged edition in 1952, illustrates Gazdanov's experiences with the lowest class of Parisians as a taxi driver. Prizrak Aleksandra Volfa (1944–48; Eng. tr., The Specter of Alexander Wolf, 1950) combines Gazdanov's psychological searching with an exciting fictional plot: Gazdanov explores the question of the immutability of fate by using the meeting between an alleged murderer and his supposed victim, whom he then indeed kills. As one of the youngest writers of the first emigration, Gazdanov provides, in his prose works, an amalgamation of everyday life during the years of upheaval in Russia and during his early emigration, in a modern Western European narrative style bordering on the Kafkaesque.

Works: Povest' o trekh neudačakh (pov.), in Volja Rossii, Prague, 1927:2; Večer u Klèr (novel), Paris, 1930 (reprinted, Ann Arbor, 1979) (see above); Vodjanaja tjur'ma (short story), in Čisla, Paris, 1:1930; Sčast'e (short story), in Sovremennye zapiski, Paris, 49:1932; Istorija odnogo puteštvija (novel), in Sovremennye zapiski 67–70:1934–35; Osvoboždenie (short story), in Sovremennye zapiski 60:1936; Nočnaja doroga (novel), in Sovremennye zapiski 67–70:1939–40, separate ed. as Nočnye dorogi, New York, 1952; Je m'engage à défendre, Paris, 1946; Prizrak Aleksandra Vol'fa (novel), in Novyj žurnal, New York, 16–18:1947–48 (see above); Vozvraščenie Buddy (novel), in Novyj žurnal 33–36:1953–54 (Eng. tr., Buddha's Return, 1951); Probuždenie (novel), in Novyj žurnal 78–82:1965–66; Èvelina i eë druz'ja (novel), in Novyj žurnal 92, 94–102, 104–5:1968–71.

Secondary Lit.: M. Slonim, in Volja Rossii 1929:10–11 and 1930:5–6; N. Ocup, in Čisla 1:1930; V. Vejdle, in Vozroždenie, Paris, June 19, 1930; V. Varšavskij, in Sovremennye zapiski 61:1936; G. Adamovič, in Novoe russkoe slovo, New York, Dec. 11, 1971 (reprinted in Russkaja mysl', Paris, Dec. 30, 1971); Ju. Terapiano, in Russkaja mysl' Jan. 27, 1972; L. Dienes, Munich, 1982, bibliography, Paris, 1982, and in MERSL 8:1987; Ju. Ivask, in Russkaja mysl' April 28, 1983, p. 12.

**Gekht, Semyón Grigórevich,** prose writer (b. March 27 [March 14], 1903, Odessa—d. June 10, 1963, Moscow). After six years of schooling (1916–22), Gekht worked as an errand boy and unskilled laborer until E. Bagritsky discovered his literary talent and Gekht's first short stories were published. I. Babel included him in a volume of Odessa writers, planned in 1923, which also included K. Paustovsky, L. Slavin, and I. Ilf. In 1923 Gekht, together with Yu. Olesha, M. Bulgakov, Ilf, and Paustovsky, was a member of the staff of the journal Gudok in Moscow; he wrote short stories, povesti, and novels. In the 1930s he also wrote publicistic prose for the journal

Nashi dostizheniya. While Gekht's novel Pouchitelnaya istoriya (1939; An Instructive Story) was received positively, his novel Vmeste (1941; Together) encountered sharp criticism; in an unpublished review A. Fadeyev termed it "a slander of Soviet reality." Gekht spent many years in the north of Russia as a victim of Stalinist despotism; his name did not reappear in literature until 1955. Budka Solovya (1957; Solovey's Cabin), a first-person povest that recounts incidents taken from the life of woodcutters in the marshy region of the north, was presumably based on Gekht's own experiences. The last of the four books that he was able to publish after his REHABILITATION appeared immediately preceding his premature death, which resulted from the hardships he had suffered.

In Pouchitelnaya istoriya Gekht tells the story of a young Jew who becomes an engineer. Several of his books are aimed directly at children; the time of the search for missing persons after World War II unifies his last collection of short stories, Dolgi serdtsa (1963; Duties of the Heart). With its gradual development, exceptional handling of action, and penetrating psychology, the short story Uzkaya koleya (1938; The Narrow Track) serves as a representative example of Gekht's fine narrative skill. K. Paustovsky, who emphasized Gekht's contribution to the development of Soviet literature in Odessa, as well as his human dignity and integrity, wrote an obituary characterizing Gekht as "the purest man on earth" (Lit. gazeta June 13, 1963).

Works: Čelovek, kotoryj zabyl svoju žizn' (short story), 1930; Istorija pereselencev Budlerov (short story), 1930; Syn sapožnika (short story), 1931; Vesëloe otročestvo (pov.), 1932; Parokhod idët v Jaffu i obratno (novel), 1936; Uzkaja koleja (short story), in Novyj mir 1938:8; Poučitel'naja istorija (novel), 1939; Vmeste, in Lit. sovremennik 1941:1; Budka Solov'ja (pov.), 1957; Tri plova (short stories), 1959; V gost'jakh u molodëži (memoirs), 1960; Dolgi serdca (short stories), 1963; Prostoj rasskaz o mertvecakh (short stories), Jerusalem, 1983.

Secondary Lit.: K. Paustovskij, in Lit. gazeta June 26, 1939, and June 13, 1963; F. Levin, in Znamja 1963:10.

**Gélman, Aleksándr Isáakovich,** playwright (b. Oct. 25, 1933, Dondyushany, Moldavian SSR). Gelman worked first as a locksmith, joined the Communist Party in 1956, and studied at Kishinyov University from 1960 to 1963. Gelman was well known for his journalistic plays, which were among the most frequently performed of any plays in the USSR. He generally wrote a play every two years (*Yunost* 1981:6, p. 98). *Protokol odnogo zasedaniya* (1974; Protocol of a Meeting) was successfully performed in Moscow and Leningrad in 1975, and it was filmed under the title *Premiya* (The Prize). For this work, Gelman was awarded the State Prize of the USSR in 1976. In the same realm of the tension concerning a plan, the report of its successful completion, and reality lie his following plays: *Obratnaya svyaz* (1976; Back Coupling), *My, nizhepodpisavshiyesya* (1979; We, the Undersigned), and *Nayedine so vsemi* (1982; Alone with Everyone). In *Skameyka* (1983; The Park Bench), Gelman shifts entirely to the realm of interpersonal relations. *Zinulya* (1984; Zinulya) is again set in a large industrial plant. Gelman also wrote screenplays together with T. Kaletskaya. He lives in Moscow.

In his plays, Gelman attacks the ethical problem of the continual lies about successes in the Soviet planned economy, but without making it clear that these are caused by the system itself. In *Protokol odnogo zasedaniya* a brigade leader delivers an analysis of the deficiencies within his firm, of the delays that are not his fault, and of the untruthful reports. In *My, nizhepodpisavshiyesya*, Gelman illustrates how a fradulent building inspection of a train is conducted after the fact; in *Nayedine so vsemi*, he emphasizes the tragic consequences for the personal life of a Soviet industrial manager who is forced into deceit. *Skameyka*, which is like *Nayedine so vsemi*, limited to two characters, is dedicated entirely to the theme of love by using the setting of a tension-filled meeting after many years between a married woman and a married man. Gelman is a skillful playwright who presents contemporary Soviet problems in a manner that respects the bounds of censorship. He combines a tension that is resolved in the end together with the gradual disclosure of the background of the story and he can create believable positive figures. With increasing clarity his plays reveal the human tragedy that is a product of the compulsive lie.

Works: *Protokol odnogo zasedanija* (play), in *Teatr* 1976:2; *Obratnaja svjaz'* (play), 1977; *My, nižepodpisavšiesja* (play), in *Teatr* 1979:7; interview, in *Lit. gazeta* Dec. 12, 1979, p. 8; *Mysli o publicistike* (essays), in *Lit. učёba* 1980:1; *Naedine so vsemi* (play), in *Teatr* 1982:3; *Skamejka* (play), in *Sovremennaja dramaturgija* 1983:2; *Zinulja* (play), in *Teatr* 1984:10; *P'esy* (plays), 1985 (contains *Proto-*

*kol odnogo zasedanija; Obratnaja svjaz'; My, nižepodpisavšiesja; Naedine so vsemi; Ska-mejka).*

Secondary Lit: Ju. Volček, in *Teatr* 1976:6; G. Citrinjak, in *Lit. gazeta* Oct. 5, 1977, p. 8; Ju. Kuz'menko, in *Oktjabr'* 1979:2; A. Radov, in *Lit. gazeta* March 25, 1981, p. 8; V. Rozov, in *Lit. gazeta* Feb. 10, 1982, p. 8; I. Višnevskaja, in *Teatr* 1982:4; K. Ščerbakov, in *Lit. gazeta* Nov. 21, 1984, p. 8; A. Law, in *Osteuropa* 1984:4, p. 238, and 1985:4, p. 276; L. Anninskij, in *Sovremennaja dramaturgija* 1986:4.

**Geórgiyevskaya, Susánna Mikháylovna**, prose writer (b. May 23 [May 10], 1916, Odessa—d. Nov. 27, 1974, Moscow). Georgiyevskaya's family moved to Leningrad in 1930. She completed her philological studies in 1936 and worked as an actress, translator, and journalist. Her first prose piece, *Petrushka*, was published in the children's magazine *Chizh* in 1939. Georgiyevskaya served as a volunteer at the front during World War II, then continued her writing career afterward. She was selected as a delegate to a writers congress (without voting rights) only once, to the Second Congress of the Writers Union of the USSR in 1954. She lived in Moscow.

Georgiyevskaya's literary work consists predominantly of short stories and povesti based on the lives of children. They are aimed in part at children, in part at adults, with the purpose of strengthening the reader's understanding of a child's sensitive emotional life. *Otrochestvo* (1953; Adolescence) considers the period when childhood ends; *Tarasik* (1959; Little Taras) combines penetration into the psyche of a five-year-old child with a depiction of a parental crisis; *Zhemchuzhny ostrov* (1961; Pearl Island) serves as a typical example of Georgiyevskaya's work in its reflection of the richness of experience in the life of a child and in its mixture of realistic and fairy-tale elements. The lyricism of her prose, attacked by many Soviet critics for pathos and "superficial poetization," is also expressed in the depiction of nature and love in *Serebryanoe slovo* (1955; The Silver Word), a povest about the work of a librarian in the Siberian region of Tuva. In the povest *Monolog* (1975; The Monologue), published posthumously by G. Semyonov and F. Iskander, Georgiyevskaya combines a discussion of war experiences with a report about a journey to East Germany. Her style is characteristically concise, often limited to main clauses, and is additively structured; the result is that her povesti are "permeated by a bright, somewhat disquieting light that shines out from [their] very depths" (Rutko).

Works: Galina mama (short story), 1947; Babuškino more (short story), 1949; Otročestvo (pov.) 1954; Povesti i rasskazy (pov. and short stories), 1954; Serebrjanoe slovo (pov.), in Novyj mir 1955:9, separate ed., 1963 (also contains Žemčužnyj ostrov); Tri povesti (pov.), 1957; Tarasik (pov.), 1959; Svetlye goroda (pov.), 1964; Dvaždy dva—četyre (pov.), 1966; Lgun'ja (pov.), 1969; Rodilsja čelovek (pov.), 1970; Ljubov' i kibernetika (pov.) 1972; Povesti o ljubvi (pov.) 1975; Monolog (pov.) in Novyj mir 1975:6; Starosti ne byvaet (pov.), 1976; Kolokola (pov.), 1983.
Secondary Lit.: L. Čukovskaja, 1955; E. Starikova, in Znamja 1956:3; M. Ščeglov, in Družba narodov 1965:2 and in his Lit. kritika, 1971; B. Sarnov, in Lit. i. žizn' April 5, 1961; A. Rut'ko, in Lit. Rossija March 19, 1965, p. 10; A. Vislov, in Lit. Rossija Jan. 15, 1971, p. 11; D. N. Ignashev, in MERSL 8:1987.

**Gerásimov, Mikhaíl Prokófyevich,** poet (b. Oct. 12 [Sept. 30], 1889, near Buguruslan, prov. Samara—d. 1939[?], while imprisoned). Gerasimov's father was a railway worker. In 1905 Gerasimov became a member of the Social Democratic Party; he was arrested for his revolutionary activities and spent nine years in emigration. In Paris he came in contact with a circle of proletarian writers, including A. K. Gastev and A. V. Lunacharsky. Gerasimov's first poems appeared in Bolshevik publications in 1913; from 1917 on, he published numerous collections of poems and contributed to almost all important proletarian journals and anthologies. He was deputy chairman of VAPP. In 1918, in addition to other political positions, he held the office of chairman of the PROLETKULT in Samara. In 1920 Gerasimov was one of the founders, together with V. Aleksandrovsky, S. Obradovich, and V. Kazin, among others, of the writers' organization KUZNITSA, which continued to fight for an independent proletarian literature not subservient to Party propaganda. Like other writers inspired by the Revolution, he was disillusioned by the conservative nature of NEP and resigned from the Party in 1921. Between 1927 and 1930 his new poems adhered to the general theme of socialist construction. A final collection appeared in 1936. In 1937 Gerasimov fell victim to Stalin's repressive measures; the exact date of his death in 1939 is unknown. His REHABILITATION took place around 1957.

In his poetry Gerasimov glorifies workers of all times and countries ("We laid the stones of the Parthenon, and of the gigantic pyramids" [written in 1917]). The imagery of heavy industry dominates Gerasimov's work as it does the works of other proletarian writers of his time. His frequent use of biblical terminology and the combination of industrial and natural imagery are striking; he titles one volume of verse Zheleznye tsvety (1919; Iron Flowers), and speaks of "a garden of iron and granite" and of "the steely neighing and stamping of factories and machine tools." The Revolution is comprehended abstractly rather than as a concretely emotional event. Gerasimov's form remains rooted in tradition. V. Kazin and G. Sannikov, who were founders of the Kuznitsa group together with Gerasimov, wrote the introduction to a volume of his selected works, which were again allowed to appear in print 20 years after Gerasimov's arbitrary death.

Works: Vešnie zovy (poems), 1917; Monna Liza (poems), 1919; Zavod vesennij (poems), 1919, Železnye cvety (poems), 1919; Železnoe cveten'e (poems), 1923; Pčëlka, (pov.), in Novyj mir 1925:5; Bodroe utro (poems), 1928; K sorevnovaniju (poems), 1930; Zarjad: Stikhi 1910–1930 (poems), 1933; Stikhi (poems), 1936; Stikhotvorenija (poems), 1958; Stikhotvorenija (poems), 1959.
Secondary Lit.: V. Kazin and G. Sannikov, in Gerasimov's Stikhotvorenija, 1958; F. Levin, in Gerasimov's Stikhotvorenija, 1958; B. Papernyj, R. A. Šaceva, in Proletarskie poèty pervykh let sovetskoj èpokhi, 1959; K. Zelinskij, in his Na rubeže dvukh epokh, 1960; RSPPo 5:1982; Z. Samojlov, in MERSL 8:1987.

**Gerásimova, Valériya Anatólyevna,** prose writer (b. April 27 [April 14], 1903, Saratov—d. June 2, 1970, Moscow). Gerasimova's father was a journalist. Gerasimova grew up in Siberia; she attended school in Yekaterinburg, then studied at Moscow University (Department of Pedagogy), from which she graduated in 1925. She was an active member of the Komsomol and worked as a teacher; she joined the Communist Party in 1926. From 1923 on, Gerasimova published short stories and povesti infrequently but regularly; she also wrote literary criticism. She lived in Moscow.
Gerasimova began by writing about the Komsomol. It is featured in one of her best povesti, Khitrye glaza (1938; Cunning Eyes), in which parents who belong to the old intelligentsia gradually come to understand their daughter's membership in the Komsomol.

Gerasimova's literary output consists of "variations on themes, images, and motifs inwardly close and of poignant interest to the writer" (Pitlyar). Her prose is structured according to an abstract plan and places contrasting figures in a situation of conflict and struggle; each part is subordinated to the resolution of this conflict.

Works: *Pancir' i zabralo* (short stories), 1931; *Žalost'* (pov.), 1934; *Khitrye glaza* (pov.), 1938; *Sverstniki* (pov. and short stories), 1948; *Prostaja familija* (pov.), 1955; *Glazami pravdy* (pov.), 1965; *Byt' soboj* (pov. and short stories), 1970.—*Izbr.*, 1935; *Izbr. proizv.*, 1958.
Secondary *Lit.*: I. Pitljar, in *Novyj mir* 1958:7 and in *Lit. gazeta* March 18, 1961; *RSPP* 1:1959; O. Grudcova, in *Lit. gazeta* Feb. 11, 1970, p. 6.

**Gérman, Yúry Pávlovich,** prose writer (b. April 4 [March 22], 1910, Riga—d. Jan. 16, 1967, Leningrad). German began working as a journalist in 1926. His novel *Vstupleniye* (1931; The Beginning) describes the intellectual transformation of a bourgeois scientist. German devoted other early novels to Komsomol members during the NEP period and to the decadence of Germany in the 1920s. He repeats the theme of the individual's evolution into a valuable member of the new society in subsequent novels, which are frequently set in the world of the secret police. In 1947, after the Party Revolution against M. Zoshchenko and A. Akhmatova was issued (see PARTY RESOLUTIONS ON LITERATURE), German became a member of the Zvezda editorial board that remained in office until 1951; he was again a member of that board from 1966 until his death. He received a Stalin Prize (for 1947, 2d class) for the screenplay he wrote for the film *Pirogov*. German's novels, imbued with the principle of PARTY SPIRIT, were always reviewed positively. In 1958 German was simultaneously accepted into the Communist Party and elected to the board of the Writers Union of the RSFSR. He lived in Leningrad.
In 1960 German reworked two of his povesti about the secret police, *Lapshin* and *Aleksey Zhmakin* (1937–38; Eng. tr., *Alexei the Gangster*, 1940), into the novel *Odin god* (One Year) to conform to the newly revised interpretation of the 1930s. In *Rossiya molodaya* (1952; Young Russia), the long-winded novel about the time of Peter I that he wrote after 1944, German conformed to the new patriotic trend and emphasized the crucial role played by the common people. In his trilogy, *Delo, kotoromu ty sluzhish* (1957; Eng. tr., *The Cause*

*You Serve*, 1961), *Dorogoy moy chelovek* (1961; My Dear Man; Eng. tr., *The Staunch and the True*, 1967), and *Ya otvechayu za vsyo* (1965; I Answer for Everything; Eng. tr., *Eternal Battle*, 1967), German attempted to trace, from the 1930s to the present, the fate of an individual who never loses his faith in the Communist ideal despite all objections.

Works: *Raffael' iz parikmakherskoj* (novel), 1931; *Bednyj Genrikh* (novel), 1934; *Naši znakomye* (novel), 1936 (Eng. tr., *Antonina*, 1937; *Tonia*, 1938); *Lapšin* (pov.), 1937; *Aleksej Žmakin* (pov.), 1938 (see above); *Rasskazy o Felikse Dzeržinskom* (short stories), 1947; *Pirogov* (film script), in *Izbr. scenarii sovetskogo kino* 6:1950; *Rossija molodaja* (novel), 1952; *Podpolkovnik medicinskoj služby* (novel), 1956; *Delo, kotoromu ty služiš'* (novel), 1957; *Odin god* (novel), 1960; *Dorogoj moj čelovek* (novel), 1961; *Ja otvečaju za vsë* (novel), 1965; *Vospominanija* (memoirs), 1968; *Zdravstvujte, Marija Nikolaevna!* (pov.), in *Zvezda* 1980:5.—*Sobr. soč.*, 6 vols., 1975–77.
Secondary *Lit.*: *RSPP* 1:1959; L. Fomenko, in *Lit. i žizn'* Sept. 5, 1962; R. Messer, in *Zvezda* 1963:4; A. Pervencev, in *Lit. Rossija* Jan. 20, 1967, p. 4; R. Fajnberg, 2d ed., 1970; A. Forostenko, Diss. Bryn Mawr College, 1972; L. Levin, in *Zvezda* 1981:6–7 and separate, ed., 1981; M. Kuznecova, in *Lit. Rossija* Feb. 3, 1984, p. 7; L. Lazarev, in *MĚRSL* 8:1987.

**Gilyaróvsky, Vladímir Alekséyevich,** prose writer (b. Dec. 8 [Nov. 26], 1853, in prov. Vologda—d. Oct. 1, 1935, Moscow). Gilyarovsky's father was an assistant estate manager for Count Olsufyev; his mother was of Kuban Cossack descent. Beginning in 1871 Gilyarovsky spent ten years wandering throughout Russia; he worked as a barge hauler, factory laborer, and firefighter, he broke in wild horses, fought as a volunteer in the Russo-Turkish War (1877–78), and was an actor. In 1873 he began publishing occasional articles based on his many and varied experiences. In 1881 he came to Moscow and remained there as a journalist. His first collection of prose, *Trushchobnye lyudi* (1887; People of the Slums), was confiscated by the censor; it was not reprinted until 1957. Poems and short stories also appeared occasionally between 1894 and 1912; his poem *Stenka Razin* appeared in 1926. Gilyarovsky's best-known work is his collection of sketches, *Moskva i Moskvichi* (1926; Moscow and Muscovites), from which emerges a many-sided, vivid, concise, and fascinating cultural and historical picture of life in Moscow in the 1880s and 1890s as lived in the markets and slums, among policemen and swindlers, officials and merchants, in bookshops and the baths, even in the sewers of the Neglinnaya. V. Lidin called Gilyarovsky, who was acquainted with A. Chekhov, A. Kuprin, and I. Bunin, "the living memory of Moscow"; K. Paustovsky described "Uncle Gilyay" in his introduction to the reprint of Moskva i Moskvichi (1955): "Everything about him was picturesque—his biography, his appearance, his style of speaking, his ingenuousness, his many-sided and impetuous talents. . . . Gilyarovsky had the soul, and the appearance, too, of a Zaporozhye cossack. Not without reason did Repin use him as a model for one of the cossacks writing a letter to the Turkish sultan. . . . None of our writers knew the many-sided and brilliant aspects of Moscow better than Gilyarovsky."

*Works*: Byli, Rasskazy (short stories), 1909; Stenka Razin (narrative poem), 1926; Moskva i Moskviči (memoirs), 1926; Moi skitanija (memoirs), 1928.—Izbr., 3 vols., 1960; Soč., 4 vols., 1967.

*Secondary Lit.*: N. Ašukin, in Novyj mir 1926:4; K. Paustovskij, introduction to Giljarovskij's Moskva i Moskviči, 1955, 1981; V. G. Lidin, Ljudi i vstreči, 1957; N. I. Morozov, 1963; V. Lobanov, 1972; E. Kiselëva, in Naš sovremennik 1978:12.

**Gínger, Aleksándr Samsónovich,** poet (b. 1897—d. Aug. 26, 1965, Paris). Ginger belongs to the second generation of the first wave of EMIGRATION and probably arrived in Paris in 1921. There he joined "Palata poetov" (Chamber of Poets) in 1922—D. Knut was also a member—and published his first collection of poems with their publishing house: Svora vernykh (1922; The Leash of the Faithful). Before regular publication in journals such as Chisla began in 1926, he published his second book, Predannost' (1925; Devotion), with 35 poems. The next, Zhaloba i torzhestvo (1939; Complaints and Triumph), which had a print run of 200 copies, contained only 23 poems. Despite the great danger to him as a Jew, Ginger remained steadfastly in Paris with his wife, the poet A. Prismanova, during the German occupation. His strong belief in fate was confirmed by his escaping arrest four times by being away from the house at the appropriate time. In 1946, Ginger and his wife were among those émigrés who accepted Soviet passports. For his fourth volume of poetry, Vest (1957; Message), Ginger selected only 13 poems from the years 1939 to 1955. In the fifth volume, Serdtse (1965; Heart), in the knowledge of his impending death, he collected 36 poems (from 1917 to 1964). G. Gazdanov, who had known Ginger for more than 40 years and who wrote his obituary, was not the only one to call Ginger an unusual man—in his behavior, dress, speech, and literary accomplishments; according to Gazdanov, Ginger had described himself as a Buddhist.

Ginger was considered an excellent judge of Russian and French poetry; he weighed his own poems carefully and considered only a few worthy of publication. They are an expression of deliverance from the suffering of the world, from loneliness, from the silence that greets the speaker. His poems could be prayers or calls to prayer; they admonish one to be undemanding and to accept earthly fate and its inclusion in the course of time; they direct one's view to the change from generation to generation. He summons everyone to be thankful for each new day and to the awareness that we are living toward our own death. His ideal is not heroism but the spirit of sacrifice. The language of his poetry is clear, does not shun the rhetorical, and includes older linguistic forms.

*Works*: Svora vernykh (poems), Paris, 1921; Predannost' (poems), Paris, 1925; Večer na vokzale (short story), in Čisla, Paris, 2–3:1930; Žaloba i toržestvo (poems), Paris, 1939; Vest' (poems), Paris, 1957; Serdce (poems), Paris, 1965.

*Secondary Lit.*: S. Osokin, in Russkie zapiski, Paris, 18:1939; Ju. Trubeckoj, in Novyj žurnal, New York, 50:1957; V. Rudinskij, in Vozroždenie, Paris, 66:1957; N. Tatiščev, in Vozroždenie 168:1965; Ju. Terapinao, in Russkaja mysl', Paris, Aug. 7 and Sept. 11, 1965; G. Gazdanov, in Novyj žurnal 82:1966; G. Adamovič, in Mosty, Munich, 12:1966; A. Bakhrakh, in Russkaja mysl' July 12, 1979, pp. 8–9; K. Pomerancev, in Russkaja mysl' Nov. 29, 1985, pp. 8–9.

**Gínzburg, Lev Vladímirovich,** prose writer, translator (b. Oct. 24, 1921, Moscow—d. Sept. 17, 1980, Moscow). Ginzburg graduated from Moscow University in 1950. He was a highly gifted, active translator of German poetry from the earliest periods to the present; moreover, he was one of the most important Soviet journalists in the sphere of Soviet-German relations and described in print his numerous trips to both East and West Germany. The posthumously published Razbilos lish serdtse moyo (1981; It's Only My Heart That's Broken) combines the memoirs of a translator with political pamphleteering. Ginzburg lived in Moscow and headed the translation section of the Writers Union.

Half of Ginzburg's Tsena pepla (1962; The Price of Ashes) is concerned with literary questions. Bezdna (1965; The Abyss) uses documents from a war crimes trial to reconstruct the horrible murder of an SS unit. In 1966 Ginzburg translated Die Ermittlung, Peter Weiss's play about the Auschwitz trial. In Potustoronniye vstrechi (1969; Meetings on the Other Side) he reproduces conversations with former leaders of the Third Reich Baldur von Schirach, Albert Speer, and Hjalmar Schacht. Ginzburg's picture of the Federal Republic of Germany ascribes to the problem of the continuing influence of the Nazi spirit a significance out of proportion to the political reality of the 1960s; retrospectively, crimes are unilaterally blamed only on the Germans; the contrast between the two Germanies corresponds to the demands of the principle of PARTY SPIRIT and consequently is consciously tendentious. Ginzburg's translations are significant, but his publicistic work is important only for understanding the distortion of the image of Germany in the USSR.

Works: Dudka Krysolova (publicistic prose), 1960; Cena pepla (publicistic prose), 1962; Slova skorbi i utešenija (publicistic prose), 1963; Bezdna (publicistic prose), 1966; Potustoronnie vstreči (publicistic prose), in Novyj mir 1969:10–11; Dviženie vremeni (article), in Lit. gazeta May 1, 1972, pp. 9, 14, and May 9, 1972, pp. 9, 14; Razbilos' liš' serdce moë (essayistic novel), in Novyj mir 1981:8.—Izbr., 1985.

Secondary Lit.: I. Fradkin, in Voprosy lit. 1963:4; E. Ètkind, in his Poèzija i perevod, 1963; S. L'vov, in Lit. Rossija March 3, 1972, p. 23; E. Vinokurov, in Lit. gazeta Sept. 12, 1979, p. 15; V. Mil'čina, in Lit. obozrenie 1982:7; G. Mitin, in Družba narodov 1984:10.

**Gínzburg, Yevgéniya Semyónovna,** prose writer (b. Dec. 20 [Dec. 7], 1906—d. May 25, 1977, Moscow). Ginzburg was of Jewish descent. She and her husband were among the first Komsomol and Communist Party members to work for the expansion of Soviet power in the settlement area of the Tatars, primarily in Kazan, immediately following the Revolution. During the 1920s Ginzburg worked there as a teacher, college instructor, and journalist. She was arrested in Kazan in 1937 and, after 730 days in solitary confinement, was sent to a forced labor camp in the Kolyma region. She was released in 1947, remaining in exile in Magadan, where she lived for a short time with her son, Vasily (later the writer Aksyonov). In 1951 she was again sent to the camps; her REHABILITATION came in 1956. Ginzburg then turned to writing her memoirs. Her account of her experiences as a teacher in Kazan during the 1920s, Tak nachinalos . . . (1963; Thus It Began . . .), was first published in the Soviet Union; it was followed by further descriptions of that period, printed in Yunost between 1965 and 1967. Novy mir printed reviews and accepted for examination her extensive description of the camp years, Krutoy marshrut (vol. 1, 1967, vol. 2, 1980; Eng. trs., vol. 1, Journey into the Whirlwind, 1967; Precipitous Journey, 1967; vol. 2, Within the Whirlwind, 1981). The work was not approved for publication in the Soviet Union; it nevertheless circulated in SAMIZDAT. In 1967 the first part appeared in Italian in Milan and in Russian in Frankfurt am Main; it was quickly recognized in Western Europe as one of the best books written about the camps. Ginzburg, who apparently was not a member of the Writers Union, was consequently no longer able to publish. She lived in Moscow.

Ginzburg's first book, in spite of its fictional structure, is just as autobiographical as her later prose. A vivid account of the 1920s from the point of view of a faithful Communist who continued to idealize the movement, her work at the same time erects a memorial to the numerous victims of the government purges. Krutoy marshrut stands beside the works of M. Buber-Neumann as the first description of the camp experience from the point of view of a Russian woman. It is Ginzburg's record of her shock at the injustice of the events leading to her imprisonment (1934–37) and of the 18 agonizing years spent in custody, forced labor, and exile. The role of poetry that the prisoners knew by heart as a source of inner strength, the experience of being at the mercy of a despotic authority, and the sense of purification and profound understanding of human existence that results from suffering—all are portrayed with a vividness and a lifelike dialogue that have an artistic power above and beyond Ginzburg's historically accurate testimony. Because her works were banned from publication, Ginzburg's hope that her work would help her countrymen overcome a guilt-ridden past remains unfulfilled.

Works: Tak načinalos' . . . (articles), Kazan', 1963; Edinaja trudovaja . . . (memoirs),

in *Junost'* 1965:11; *Studenty dvadcatykh go-*
*dov* (memoirs), in *Junost'* 1966:8; *Junoša* (documentary pov.), in *Junost'* 1967:9; *Krutoj*
*maršrut* (memoirs), vol. 1, Frankfurt am Main,
1967, vol. 2, Milan, 1979 (see above).
*Secondary Lit.:* B. Nevskaja, in *Družba na-*
*rodov* 1964:12; F. Meichsner, in *Die Welt* March
23–24, 1967; H. Pross-Weerth, in *Frankfurter*
*Allgemeine Zeitung* Nov. 28, 1967; M. K., in
*Grani*, Frankfurt am Main, 110:1978; K. Pomerancev, in *Russkaja mysl'*, Paris, Dec. 13,
1979, p. 9; H. Böll, foreword to the German
trans. of *Krutoj maršrut*, vol. 2, 1980, in Russian in *Sintaksis*, Paris, 8:1980; L. Kopelev,
R. Orlova, in *Vremja i my*, Tel Aviv, 49:1980;
D. Lowe, in *Slavic and East European Journal*
1983:2.

**Gíppius** (Hippius), **Zinaída Nikoláyevna**, poet,
critic, prose writer (b. Nov. 20 [Nov. 8], 1869,
Belyov, prov. Tula—d. Sept. 9, 1945, Paris).
Gippius's ancestors were German aristocrats
who emigrated to Moscow in 1515. She spent
her childhood intermittently in St. Petersburg,
where she lived for the 30 years between her
marriage to D. Merezhkovsky in 1889 and her
emigration. This marriage was a special relationship in that it furthered the mutual intellectual enhancement of two significant figures
of world literature. Gippius wrote her first
poems when she was seven; she began publishing verse in 1888; her first short story
came out soon after. She published numerous
volumes of verse, novels, short-story collections, and dramas before the October Revolution. From 1903 to 1909 she was associated
with the editorial board of the religio-philo-
sophical journal *Novy put* and published noted
literary criticism there and in other journals
under the pseudonym. "Anton Krayny" (Anton the Extreme). From 1905 to 1917 she hosted
a salon in St. Petersburg that became a meeting place of the symbolists. Gippius condemned the October Revolution as an act directed against freedom and human dignity. In
1919 she and Merezhkovsky succeeded in emigrating to Paris. There Gippius became an
important émigré poet. Her volume *Stikhi*
(1922; Verses) appeared in Berlin; a second
volume, *Siyaniya* (1938; Radiance), came out
in Paris. Her publicistic works, primarily the
collection *Zhivye litsa* (1925; Living Portraits), attracted appreciable attention. Her book
about her husband, *Dmitry Merezhkovsky*
(1951), appeared posthumously. Gippius's
work since the Revolution has not been published in the Soviet Union; in the early 1970s
a number of new editions were reprinted in
Munich.

Gippius's polished verse is profoundly contemplative and religious. Her origins go back
to the symbolists, for whom literature is part
of a comprehensive cultural context and an
expression of a higher spiritual reality. Man,
love, and death are the central themes around
which Gippius's verse revolves. For her, poetry is spiritual discovery and constant philosophical and psychological conflict with oneself and the imperfection of earthly existence.
In her poetry Gippius combines intellectual
brilliance and lyrical sensitivity. Her prose
fiction, influenced by F. Dostoyevsky, tends
to depict people in extreme situations. It is
held together by a religious view that is less
mystical than Merezhkovsky's. Gippius's
publicistic work (both her diaries and, above
all, the very personal portraits of A. Blok, V.
Bryusov, and V. Rozanov, among others) is of
a high quality. Like much of her verse, it is
sharply anti-Bolshevik and testifies to her high
regard for freedom, human dignity, and the
Russian cultural tradition.

*Works: Novye ljudi* (short stories), 1896, 2d
ed., 1907 (reprinted, Munich, 1973); *Zerkala*
(short stories), 1898; *Pobediteli* (novel), 1898
(reprinted, Munich, 1973), *Sobr. stikhov*
(poems), 2 vols., 1904–10; *Lit. dnevnik* (diary), 1908 (reprinted, Munich, 1970); *Makov*
*cvet* (play), 1908; *Čortova kukla* (novel), 1911;
*Roman-carevič* (novel), 1913 (reprinted, with
*Čortova kukla*, Munich, 1972); *Zelënoe kol'co*
(play), 1916 (Eng. tr., *The Green Ring*, 1920);
*Poslednie stikhi* (poems), 1918; *Nebesnye slova*
(short stories), Paris, 1921; *Stikhi* (poems),
Berlin, 1922; *Živye lica* (essays), 2 vols., Prague,
1925 (reprinted, Munich, 1971); *Sinjaja kniga*
(diary), Belgrade, 1929; *Sijanija* (poems), Paris,
1938; *Dmitrij Merežkovskij* (biography), Paris,
1951; *P'esy* (plays) (contains *Svjataja krov'*;
*Makov cvet; Zelënoe kol'co*), Munich, 1972;
*Stikhotvorenija i poèmy* (lyric and narrative
poems), 2 vols., Munich, 1972 (reprint of collected volumes of verse with additional material); *Intellect and Ideas in Action: Selected*
*Correspondence of Zinaida Hippius*, Munich,
1972; *Between Paris and St. Petersburg: Se-*
*lected Diaries of Zinaida Hippius*, Urbana,
1975.

*Translations: Selected Works of Zinaida*
*Hippius*, 1972; "The Door," "The Mad
Woman," and "An Ordinary Event," in *Women*
*Writers in Russian Modernism*, 1978.

*Secondary Lit.:* V. Zlobin, in *Novyj žurnal*,
New York, 31:1952 and 86:1967, Washington,
1970, and Berkeley, 1980; J. Bayley, Diss.,
Harvard Univ., 1965; T. Pachmuss, in *Cana-*
*dian Slavonic Papers* 1965:7 and Carbondale,
1971, materials in reprints of Gippius's works,

1971–73; O. Matich, Munich, 1972; W. E.
Napier, Diss., Univ. of Illinois, Urbana, 1975;
D. R. Schaffer, Diss., Univ. of Wisconsin–
Madison, 1979; S. Karlinsky, in V. Zlobin,
1980.

**Gladílin, Anatóly Tíkhonovich,** prose writer
(b. Aug. 21, 1935, Moscow). After completing
school in 1953, Gladilin worked as an electrician in a research institute; from 1954 to 1958
he studied at the Gorky Literary Institute. His
first povest, *Khronika vremyon Viktora Pod-
gurskogo* (The Chronicle of the Time of Victor
Podgursky), appeared in *Yunost* (1956:9).
Gladilin writes about unformed young people.
He stayed with this theme in later years as
well. Gladilin was not a delegate to the congresses of the Writers Unions. He lived in
Moscow and emigrated in April 1976 to Paris,
where his works are regularly published in
émigré journals.

Gladilin's prose occupies a certain place
within the literature of the THAW. His characters concern themselves with the question,
"How can we continue our fathers' work
without repeating their mistakes?" (*Yunost*
1963:2, p. 47). His povest *Yevangeliye ot
Robespyera* (1970; The Gospel According to
Robespierre) belongs to the revival of literature about historical revolutions that occurred
at the end of the 1960s. In 1972 his novel
*Prognoz na zavtra* (Forecast for Tomorrow)
made it abroad and was published in Frankfurt am Main. As his protagonist, Gladilin
again chose a person of his own age with his
personal and financial difficulties. From his
first prose works on, Gladilin has ventured
along new formal paths, mixed fiction with
fictitious diary entries, and shifted the point
of view through several first-person narrators,
as V. Aksyonov does. In *Repetitsiya v pyat-
nitsu* (1978; Rehearsal on Friday), he combines four stories written between 1965 and
1976, among which *Tigr perekhodit ulitsu* (A
Tiger Crosses the Street) demonstrates his narrative ability through its satiric-ironic detachment. *Parizhskaya yarmarka* (1980; Paris Fair)
is a collection of ironic comments, travel
sketches, Parisian scenes, and literary portraits written in emigration. Gladilin's exposition of the literary scene in the 1960s, *The
Making and Unmaking of a Soviet Writer*
(1979), appeared only in English.

Works: *Khronika vremën Viktora Podgur-
skogo* (pov.), 1958; *Brigantina podnimaet parusa* (pov.), 1959; *Večnaja komandirovka*
(pov.), 1962; *Iduščij vperedi* (short stories and
pov.), 1962; *Pervyj den' Novogo goda* (pov.

and short stories), 1965; *Istorija odnoj kom-
panii* (novel), in *Junost'* 1965:9–10; *Evangelie
ot Robesp'era* (pov.), 1970; *Prognoz na zavtra*
(novel), Frankfurt am Main, 1972; *Dva goda
do vesny* (novel and short stories), 1975; *Tigr
perekhodit ulicu* (short story), in *Kontinent*,
Paris, 7:1976; *Repeticija v. pjatnicu* (pov. and
short stories), Paris, 1978; *The Making and
Unmaking of a Soviet Writer*, Ann Arbor, 1979;
*Parižskaja jarmarka* (travel commentary and
literary portraits), Paris–Tel Aviv, 1980; *Bol'šoj
begovoj den'*, Ann Arbor, 1983; *FSSR. Fran-
cuzskaja Sovetskaja Socialističeskaja Respublika* (pov.), New York, 1985.

Secondary Lit.: V. Oskockij, in *Moskva*
1960:4; I. Solov'ëva, in *Novyj mir* 1963:4; L.
Krjačko, in *Oktjabr'* 1966:2; *RSPP* 7(1):1971;
I. Basova, in *Grani*, Frankfurt am Main,
135:1985.

**Gladkóv, Fyódor Vasílyevich,** prose writer (b.
June 21 [June 9], 1883, Chernavka, prov. Saratov—d. Dec. 20, 1958, Moscow). Gladkov
was of peasant descent. His family were Old
Believers. He was trained, and beginning in
1902 worked, as an elementary-school teacher.
He became involved in revolutionary activity
in 1905; in 1906 he joined the Russian Social
Democratic Party. Gladkov lived in internal
exile from 1906 to 1909, after which he worked
as a teacher in Novorossiysk. He began to
publish occasionally in newspapers in 1900.
During the Civil War, Gladkov sided with the
Bolsheviks; he became a member of the Communist Party in 1920 and worked as a newspaper editor in Novorossiysk. In 1921 he moved
to Moscow, where he became affiliated with
the proletarian writers' association KUZNITSA
in 1923. Gladkov's novel propagandizing the
industrial reconstruction of the NEP period,
*Tsement* (1925; Eng. tr., *Cement*, 1929), brought
him official recognitions a prominent Soviet
writer. From 1932 to 1940 Gladkov belonged
to the editorial board of the journal *Novy mir*.
During World War II he was a correspondent
for *Pravda* and *Izvestiya* in the Urals; between
1945 and 1948 he served as director of the
Gorky Literary Institute. He described his youth
from the point of view of the class struggle in
an autobiographical trilogy, consisting of *Povest o detstve* (1949; A Tale of Childhood),
which received a Stalin Prize (for 1949, 2d
class), *Volnitsa* (1950; The Free Gang), also a
Stalin Prize winner (for 1950, 1st class), and
*Likhaya godina* (1954; Hard Times). An additional part, *Myatezhnaya Yunost* (Eng. tr.,
*Restless Youth*, 1959), was never completed.
Gladkov, who was also a deputy of the Supreme Soviet of the RSFSR and a member of

the board of the Writers Union of the USSR, published articles on A. S. Neverov, P. P. Bazhov, A. G. Malyshkin, and A. S. Serafimovich, in addition to his contributions to literary politics.

The version of *Tsement* that has become the standard work known to Soviet schoolchildren as the first construction novel reproduces very little of the novel's original artificially stylized form. Gladkov revised it several times in order to make it conform to the demands of SOCIALIST REALISM. In the Soviet Union the novel's "urgency of theme, brightness of the image of the Bolshevik, enthusiasm about construction, and ardent Party spirit" were praised (Seyfullina), while its stylistic inadequacies, its "incongruous mixture of old-fashioned realism, naturalism, and ill-digested modernism" (Slonim) were overlooked. *Tsement* "established a pattern that had nothing to do with literary perfection: the most important thing for fiction of Communist persuasion was to express faith and to show the triumph of hope" (Slonim). Gladkov's contribution to the literature of the Five-Year Plan, not very highly regarded even in the USSR, was *Energiya* (1933; Energy), a novel about the construction of the Dneproges, a power plant on the Dnepr River; like *Tsement*, it was revised several times. Gladkov called his povest *Beryozovaya roshcha* (1941; The Birch Grove) "one of my favorite works."

*Works: Cement* (novel), in *Krasnaja nov'* 1925:1–2, 5–6, first published in book form as vol. 3 of *Sobr. soč.*, 3 vols., 1926; radically revised versions in vol. 2 of *Sobr. soč.*, 3 vols., 1929–30, and in *Izbr.*, 1944 (see above); *Ènergija* (novel), 1933; *Berëzovaja rošča* (pov.), in *Novyj mir* 1941:3; *Povest' o detstve* (novel), 1949; *Vol'nica* (novel), 1950; *Likhaja godina* (pov.), 1954.—*Sobr. soč.*, 3 vols., 1926; 3 vols., 1928; 3 vols., 1929–30; 5 vols., 1950–51; 8 vols., 1958–59.

*Secondary Lit.:* I. P. Ukhanov, 1953; B. Ja. Brajnina, 1957; *RSPP* 1:1959; F. *Gladkov: Vospominanija sovremennikov*, 1965; L. N. Ul'rich, 1968; A. P. Voloženin, 1969; *Vospominanija o F. Gladkove*, 2d ed., 1978; R. L. Busch, in *Slavic and East European Journal* 1978:3; D. Blagov and B. Leonov, in *Russian Language Journal* 129–30:1984.

**Glavlít.** See CENSORSHIP.

**Golódny, Mikhaíl Semyónovich** (pseud. of M. S. Épshteyn), poet (b. Dec. 24 [Dec. 11],

1903, Bakhmut, prov. Yekaterinoslav, Ukraine—d. Jan. 20, 1949, Moscow). Golodny came from a family of Jewish laborers. At the age of 12 he was working in a factory. His first poems were published in 1920; in 1922 his collection *Svayi* (The Stakes) came out in Kharkov. Golodny studied at the Bryusov Institute of Literature and Art in Moscow. A typical Komsomol poet, Golodny was initially affiliated with the editorial staffs of *Na postu* and *Molodaya gvardiya*, but then went over to *Krasnaya nov.* He was a member of PEREVAL until 1927; later he joined the orthodox VAPP. During this time the critics attacked him for his pessimism. In the 1930s Golodny became popular as the author of several new Civil War songs, such as "Pesnya o Shchorse" (1935; A Song of Shchors) and "Partizan Zheleznyak" (1936; A Song of Shchors) and "Partizan Zheleznyak" (1936; Zheleznyak the Partisan). He became a member of the Communist Party in 1939. In 1942 Golodny appropriately published *Pesni i ballady Otechestvennoy voyny* (Songs and Ballads of the War for the Fatherland). He also translated from Ukrainian, Polish, and White Russian.

As a poet of the Communist youth movement, to which he belonged until 1928, Golodny wrote poems about the Revolution, the land of the Soviets, and the struggle for a better world. According to A. Voronsky, his collection *Zemnoye* (1924; Earthly) nevertheless "stands out to advantage from the drumbeating, from the studied, the rote-learned," without his poetic persona becoming overdefined (1929). In his ballads and songs, which are broad, easily understood, and often written in primitive rhyme. Golodny remained true to revolutionary enthusiasm in the context of the principle of PARTY SPIRIT.

*Works: Svai* (poems), 1922; *Zemnoe* (poems), 1924; *Novye stikhotvorenija* (poems), 1928; *Stikhi i pesni* (poems), 1930; *Pesni i ballady Otečestvennoj vojny* (poems), 1942; *Izbr.* 1949; *Izbr.* 1956; *Stikhotvorenija. Ballady* (poems), 1959.

*Secondary Lit.:* M. Zenkevič, in *Novyj mir* 1928:3; A. Voronskij, *Lit. portrety*, vol. 2, 1929; Ja. Khelemskij, in *Oktjabr'* 1947:10; *RSPPo* 6:1983.

**Gólubov, Sergéy Nikoláyevich,** prose writer (b. June 20 [June 8], 1894, Saratov—d. Feb. 8, 1962, Moscow). Golubov's father was in government administration. Golubov studied law at Moscow University; he served as a cavalry officer in World War I and as a regimental commander with the Red Army during the Civil War. After 1922 he worked as a Soviet government official in the area of labor efficiency. Golubov first found his way into literature in the mid-1930s by publishing historical biographies of artists (V. Bazhenov, A. Bestuzhev-Marlinsky). In compliance with the newly positive attitude toward Russian history introduced in the late 1930s, he turned to writing novels about military history. He continued to write on this topic, which he saw primarily from the point of view of military and political training, all through the Stalin years. His depiction of the patriotic impulse during the War of 1812 in *Bagration* (1943; Eng. tr., *Bagrattion, the Honour and Glory of 1812*, 1945; *No Easy Victories*, 1945) met with approval during World War II. He had previously written about the Decembrists; he later wrote about the final days of the tsarist regime. In 1950–53 Golubov described the fate of the Brest Fortress between 1914 and 1945 in *Kogda kreposti ne sdayutsya* (1953; When Fortresses Do Not Surrender); in this case, his account of World War II includes the unreal situations, the cheap sketches in black and white, and the clichéd motif of heroic death that are characteristic of the period in which he began writing the work. The central character of his last novel, *Ptitsy letyat iz gnyozd* (1958; Birds Leave Their Nests), is a Bulgarian revolutionary.

*Works: Bestužev (Marlinskij)* (biography), 1938, 1960; *Iz iskry—plamja* (novel), 1940, 2d ed., 1950; *Soldatskaja slava* (novel), 1941; *Bagration* (pov.), 1943, 1960 (see above); *Sotvorenie veka* (novel), 1947; *Kogda kreposti ne sdajutsja* (novel), 1953, 4th ed., 1958; *Pticy letjat iz gnëzd* (novel), 1958; *Snimem, tovarišči, šapki* (pov.), 1961.—*Izbr. proizv.*, 2 vols., 1958.

*Secondary Lit.:* A. Derman, in *Novyj mir* 1943:9; V. Genovska, in *Lit. gazeta* Sept. 9, 1958; *RSPP* 1:1959; obituary, in *Novyj mir* 1962:3.

**Gor, Gennády** (pseud. of Gdály Samúilovich Gor), prose writer (b. Jan. 28 [Jan. 15], 1907, Verkhneudinsk—d. Jan. 6, 1981, Leningrad). Gor moved to Leningrad in 1923; he began publishing in 1925. In 1930 he completed his studies in ethnography at Leningrad University, then was engaged in scientific research until 1936. Gor lived in Leningrad; from 1967 to 1980 he belonged to the editorial staff of *Neva*.

Gor's first volume of short stories, *Zhivopis*

(1933; Painting), was attacked for its "eccentric form" and "pompous language." His *povesti* and short stories of the 1930s and 1940s depicted the life and folklore of the peoples of northern Siberia. After describing war experiences in *Dom na Mokhovoy* (1945; The House on Mokhovaya Street), Gor turned to the subject of the scientist and scientific integrity. The lives of a theoretical physicist, a chemist of synthetics, and an agronomic biologist are intricately intertwined in his novel *Universitetskaya naberezhnaya* (1959; The University Embankment). During this time Gor also wrote popular-science books. In the 1960s he turned to the realm of scientific utopias. *Dokuchlivy sobesednik* (1961; The Tiresome Interlocutor) combines the subject of the discovery of inhabited stars with robot doppelgängers, philosophy, cybernetics, and biology; the work mixes a realistic level with a utopian level and contains a novel within a novel. With this novel *Izvayaniye* (1972; The Sculpture) Gor again tackled the problem of the philosophy of art, using the form of science fiction. His story *Risunok Darotkana* (1972; Darotkan's Sketch) makes use of many biographical elements from the first ten years of Gor's life in a similar context. *Geometrichesky les* (1973; The Geometric Forest) also combines science fiction with the philsophy of art—the painted forest becomes palpable reality, art becomes a doorway into past and future. The juxtaposition of a painter such as K. Petrov-Vodkin and a writer with the autobiographical features of Gor, and the exploration of the relationship between an artist's style and his biography, constitute the basic themes of Gor's *povest Pyat uglov* (1977; Five Corners).

*Works: Živopis'* (short stories), 1933; *Lanžero* (pov. and short stories), 1938; *Bol'šie pikhtovye lesa* (short stories), 1940; *Pankov* (pov.), in *Lit. sovremennik* 1940:7; *Dom na Mokhovoj* (pov.), 1945; *Ostrov budet otkryt* (pov.), 1946; *Junoša s dalekoj reki* (novel), 1953; *Ošibka professora Oročeva* (pov.), 1955 (Eng. tr., *Professor Orochev's Delusion*, 1957); *Vasilij Ivanovič Surikov* (biography), 1955; *Universitetskaja naberežnaja* (novel), 1960; *Dokučlivyj sobesednik* (pov.), 1961; *Kumbi* (pov.), 1963; *Gosti s Uazy* (pov.), 1963; *Glinjanyj papuas* (science-fiction pov.), 1966; *Kumbi* (science-fiction pov. and short stories), 1968; *Neneckij khudožnik K. Pankov* (scholarly articles), 1968 (Eng. tr., *Konstantin Pankov: Nenets Painter*, 1973); *Fantastičeskie povesti i rasskazy* (science fiction), 1970; *Izvajanie* (science fiction), 1972; *Risunok Dar-*

otkana (pov.), in Zvezda 1972:4; Pjat' uglov (pov.), in Neva 1977:6, separate ed., 1983; Volšebnaja doroga (novel, pov., and short stories), 1978; Sinee okno Feokrita (pov.), 1980. Secondary Lit.: G. Munblit, in Lit. kritik 1933:6; D. Moldavskij, in Zvezda 1958:10; RSPP 1:1959; I. Pitljar, in Novyj mir 1960:7; E. Val'dman, in Novyj mir 1963:7; A. Urban, in Zvezda 1967:2 and in Avrora 1974:10; S. Kara and S. Lur'e, in Lit. obozrenie 1973:3 and in Neva 1980:3; "G. S. Goru—70 let," in Lit. gazeta March 9, 1977, p. 5.

**Gorbanévskaya, Natálya Yevgényevna,** poet (b. May 26, 1936, Moscow). Gorbanevskaya began her philological studies in Moscow in 1953 and continued, with interruptions, until 1963, when she completed her studies at Leningrad University by correspondence; she then worked as a technical translator and bibliographer. Several of her poems, written between 1956 and 1961, were collected for the first time in the SAMIZDAT publication Feniks 1961 (Phoenix). She has rejected a portion of her poems from that collection, as well as from two additional samizdat anthologies. She subsequently considered only the later compilations Poteryanny ray (1965; Paradise Lost), Temnota (1966; Darkness), and Angel derevyanny (1967; Wooden Angel) to constitute a lasting poetic statement. The samizdat editions of this period appeared in Frankfurt am Main under the title Stikhi (1969; Poems). Nine of Gorbanevskaya's poems were published in the Soviet Union between 1965 and 1968. In 1968 she became active in the dissident movement. On Feb. 5, 1968, she headed the petition drive on behalf of Yu. Galanskov and A. Ginzburg; she was among the founders of the samizdat newspaper Khronika tekushchikh sobytiy (No. 1, April 30, 1968); on Aug. 25, 1968, she was one of the seven demonstrators who protested the entry of Soviet troops into Czechoslovakia. The documentary report she compiled about this event circulated abroad as Polden (1970; Eng. tr., Red Square at Noon, 1972). On Dec. 24, 1969, Gorbanevskaya was again arrested and forcibly committed to a special psychiatric asylum in Kazan. Her release on Feb. 24, 1972, was followed by the publication in Ann Arbor of Poberezhye (1972; The Seacoast), a volume of personally selected poems expanded by the addition of verse written during the period of her imprisonment. Of the three samizdat editions that contain her poems from the years 1972 to 1974, one stands out: Dozhdi, i zasukha, i novye dozhdi (1973: Rains, and

Drought, and New Rains) is dedicated to her imprisoned fellow fighter for intellectual freedom, Gabriel Superfin. These poems were subsequently published in the West in Tri tetradi stikhotvoreniy (1975; Three Notebooks of Poems). Gorbanevskaya and her two children were allowed to leave the Soviet Union on Dec. 17, 1975. She has lived in Paris since Feb. 1, 1976. She published new poems in the collections Pereletaya snezhnuyu granitu (1979; Flying across the Snowy Border), Chuzhiye kamni (1983; Strange Stones), Peremennaya oblachnost (1985; Variable Clouds), and Gde i kogda (1985; Where and When), as well as in Angel derevyanny (1982), which included earlier poems. She is now on the editorial board of the journal Kontinent. Besides her own poetical work, she often translates, especially from the Polish.

Gorbanevskaya's poetry is the expression of a tormented, despairing soul. It is marked by personal, inner experience; it barely narrates, and does not describe. Traditional images of darkness, frost and snow, clouds and dust correspond naturally to the cry that is born of personal grief. Occasionally the poems, prayerlike, become an appeal to God. They are dominated, as Gorbanevskaya writes in one of her three poems to Iosif Brodsky, by "torment instead of music." Formally, her poetry is unpretentious, neither experimental nor exceptionally concentrated; it reveals, primarily in its alliteration, its conscious design.

Works: Poems, in Znamja 1966:6; poems, in Zvezda Vostoka 1968:1; poems, in Grani, Frankfurt am Main, 69:1968, 70:1969, 76:1970; Stikhi (poems), Frankfurt am Main, 1969; Polden': Delo o demonstracii 25 avgusta 1968 goda na Krasnoj ploščadi (documentary report), Frankfurt am Main, 1970 (see above); Poberež'e (poems), Ann Arbor, 1973; poems, in Russian Literature Triquarterly 9:1974; Tri tetradi stikhotvorenij (poems), Bremen, 1975; Probleski nadeždy (interview), in Russkaja mysl', Paris, March 25, 1976, p. 8; Pereletaja snežnuju granicu (poems), 1979; Angel derevjannyj (poems), Ann Arbor, 1982; Čužie kamni (poems), New York, 1983; Peremennaja oblačnost' (poems), Paris, 1985; Gde i kogda (poems), Paris, 1985. Translation: Selected Poems, 1972. Secondary Lit.: O. Možajskaja, in Grani 78:1970; C. Gerstenmaier, in her Die Stimme der Stummen, Stuttgart, 1971; editorial, in Russkaja mysl' Feb. 5, 1976, p. 1, March 11, 1976, p. 14; N. Borisov, in Russkaja mysl' March 25, 1976, p. 3; W. Kasack, in Neue Zürcher Zeitung April 9, 1976; V. Alloj, in

Kontinent, Paris, 11:1977; N. Djuževa, in Kontinent 26:1980; C. A. Rydel, in Russian Language Journal 123–24:1982; Ju. Kubljanovskij, in Russkaja mysl' Oct. 29, 1983, p. 10; L. Losev, in Russkaja mysl' July 7, 1984, p. 10; A. Radaškevic, in Russkaja mysl' Nov. 11, 1985, p. 10.

**Gorbátov, Borís Leóntyevich,** prose writer (b. July 15 [July 2], 1908, Petromaryevsky rudnik, Donbas—d. Jan. 20, 1954, Moscow). Gorbatov's father was in government administration. As a representative of Zaboy, the Donbas writers' association he helped organize, Gorbatov became part of the VAPP leadership in 1926 and moved to Moscow. After several attempts at writing both prose (1922) and poetry, he established himself as a writer of longer prose with his povest about the Komsomol, Yacheyka (1928; The Cell). He joined the Communist Party in 1930. Gorbatov wrote travel articles for Pravda and novels that, in compliance with the principle of PARTY SPIRIT, dealt with immediate problems, primarily those of the Donbas region.

Gorbatov's novel Moyo pokoleniye (1933; My Generation) met with general approval. Using many elements from his first povest, the novel treats the Five-Year Plan; Gorbatov uses emotionality rather than characterization to express socialist enthusiasm. Gorbatov's experiences as a correspondent for Pravda in the Arctic were reflected in various articles. The personal tone, lyrical pathos, and rhetorical repetition of his Pisma k tovarishchu (1941–44; Letters to a Comrade) distinguish it from other literary works of World War II ("the pinnacle of wartime publicism" [K. Simonov]). Gorbatov's povest about occupied Donbas, Nopokoryonnye (1943; Eng. tr., Taras' family, 1946), published in Pravda, received a Stalin Prize (for 1943–44, 2d class); the work vividly propagandizes the workers' resistance under Party leadership. Gorbatov never completed a planned multivolume novel, Donbass (vol. 1, 1951; Eng. tr., Donbas, 1953), which returns to the theme of the 1930s and the Stakhanovite movement.

Works: Jačejka (pov.), 1928; Naš gorod (novel), 1930; Moë pokolenie (novel), 1933; Obyknovennaja Arktika (short stories), 1940; Pis'ma k tovarišču (publicistic letters), 1941–44; Nepokorënnye (pov.), 1944 (see above); Donbass (novel), 1951 (see above).—Sobr. soč., 5 vols., 1955–56.

Secondary Lit.: G. Kolesnikova, 1957; RSPP 1:1959; V. Karpova, Čuvstvo vremeni, 2d ed.,

1970; I. Frenkel', in Lit. gazeta July 26, 1978, p. 7.

**Gorbóvsky, Gleb Yákovlevich,** poet (b. Oct. 4, 1931, Leningrad). Gorbovsky worked in Siberia as a lumberman and raftsman and participated in geologic expeditions; he lives in Leningrad. His first poems appeared in 1954. The titles of the first four volumes of poetry (disregarding his writings for children)—Poiski tepla (1960; Search for Warmth), Spasibo, zemlya (1964; Thank You, Earth), Kosye suchya (Slanted Branches), and Tishina (1968; Silence)—point to two essential qualities of his work: the search for security and the commitment to nature. Gorbovsky's verses have a beautiful musicality and are consciously simple in word choice and rhyme (see "Moi rifmy obychny" [My Rhymes Are Common]; in Molodoy Leningrad, 1964) but profound in the expanse of their vision and the unconventionality of their associations. Gorbovsky is possessed with the primal search for the meaning behind the appearances of life; his loneliness seeks consolation; the tensions between time and eternity, reality and fairy tales, man and the universe, are depicted in images that are ever new. Gorbovsky shows people in their responsibility for themselves, for others, and for fate and is able to transform everyday images from the Soviet present into a vital symbology of such basic issues. A poem such as "Ne plach ty osen bezuteshno" (Autumn, Don't Cry Inconsolably; in Neva 1973:11) is typical because of its animated manner and the tension between solitude and security, between the unhappy present and a longed-for better time that is suggested by the image of nature. In the poem "Dostuchatsya do zvyozd" (1974; On the Stars I Would Like to Knock), the yearning tends toward the transcendental. Occasionally ironic and humorous elements appear. Gorbovsky also published fine children's poems (for example, in Neva 1973:9) that, like everything he writes, are free from political didacticism but that are more playful than his poetry proper, which stems from true inspiration. His first volume of collected prose, Vokzal (1980; Railroad Station), reflects serious ethical concerns, as does his poetry.

Works: Poiski tepla (poems), 1960; Spasibo, zemlja (poems), 1964; Kto na čëm edet (children's poems), 1965; Kosye suč'ja (poems), 1966; Tišina (poems), 1968; Novoe leto (poems), 1971; Raznye istorii (children's poems), 1972; Vozvraščenie v dom (poems),

1974; *Vetka šipovnika* (pov.), in *Avrora* 1974:7–8; *Dolina* (poems), 1975; *Monolog* (poems), 1977; *Videnija na kholmakh* (poems), 1977; *Pesni* (poems) in *Èkho*, Paris, 1978:3; *Krepost'*: *Novye stikhi* (poems), 1979; *Vokzal* (pov.), 1980; *Izbr.*, 1981; *Jav'* (poems), 1981; *Čerty lica* (poems), 1982; *Pervye protaliny* (pov.), in *Zvezda* 1983:4–5; *Pod muzyku doždja* (pov.), in *Zvezda* 1984:8–9.

*Secondary Lit.*: E. Vinokurov, in *Lit. gazeta* Aug. 4, 1960; I. Mikhajlov, in *Neva* 1961:9 and in *Zvezda* 1965:4; A. Èljaševič, in *Zvezda* 1965:11 and in his *Poèty, Stikhi, Poèzija*, 1966; A. Urban, in *Zvezda* 1972:8 and in *Avrora* 1981:11; I. Kuz'mičev, in *Zvezda* 1974:12; E. Evtušenko, in *Lit. gazeta* June 30, 1975, p. 6; A. Polovnikov, in *Neva* 1976:1; N. Bank, in *Neva* 1978:8 and 1981:2; V. Klimov, in *Oktjabr'* 1983:8; *RSPPo* 6:1983; S. Pedenko, in *Lit. Rossija* Dec. 7, 1984, p. 11; S. Gozias, in *Novyj žurnal*, New York, 162:1986.

**Gordéychev, Vladímir Grigóryevich,** poet (b. March 5, 1930, Kastornoye, oblast Kursk). From 1948 to 1950 Gordeychev taught in a village school, then attended a pedagogical institute. In 1957 he completed his studies at the Gorky Literary Institute and was admitted to the Communist Party. Gordeychev, whose poems first began appearing in 1950, has published volumes of verse on a regular basis since 1957. He lives in Voronezh and has been a delegate to all congresses of the Writers Union of the RSFSR since 1958.

Gordeychev's poems show his ties to the nature of his native region, in which he is able to find the beautiful even in the unprepossessing. The world of plants and animals serves him as a metaphor for his ethical messages. He is in favor of acting in accordance with one's conscience, he admires human purity and resolution and he fights against the abdication of responsibility. He admonishes his readers to respect natural forces instead of trusting exclusively in science. Publicistic rhetoric is as foreign to him as experimentation with form. Gordeychev professes to follow in the tradition of A. Tvardovsky, V. Lugovskoy, and B. Kornilov; he has found general recognition as a writer since V. Soloukhin's favorable review of his first volume.

*Works: Nikitiny kamen'ja* (poems), 1957; *Zemnaja tjaga* (poems), 1959; *U linii priboja* (poems), 1960; *Bespokojstvo* (poems), 1961; *Zrelost'* (poems), 1962; (on his own work), in *Voprosy lit.* 1962:9; *Svoimi slovami* (poems), 1964; *Okopy ètikh let* (poems), 1964; *Glavnoe svojstvo* (poems), 1966; *Pora čerëmukh*, 1971; *Puti-dorogi. Stikhi i poèma "V zvone žavoronka"* (lyric and narrative poems), 1973; *Svet v okne* (poems), 1975; *Soizmeren'ja* (lyric and narrative poems), 1976; *Vremja okrylennykh* (lyric and narrative poems), 1977; *Izbr.*, 1980; *Dar polej* (poems), 1983.

*Secondary Lit.*: V. Soloukhin, in *Oktjabr'* 1958:7; A. Marčenko, in *Voprosy lit.* 1960:6; A. Abramov, in *Zvezda* 1965:4; A. Baeva, in *Lit. Rossija* July 26, 1968, p. 9; Al. Mikhajlov, in *Znamja* 1970:8; L. Dement'eva, in *Lit. obozrenie* 1973:11; Dm. Moldavskij, in *Lit. obozrenie* 1977:6; I. Fedorov, in *Znamja* 1978:10 and in *Moskva* 1982:1; A. Makhov, in *Lit. obozrenie* 1984:8.

**Gorenshtéyn, Frídrikh Naúmovich,** prose writer (b. March 18, 1932, Kiev). Gorenshteyn's father was a professor of economics; as a leading official in the Communist Party he was arrested in 1935 and died in custody. Gorenshteyn's mother, an educator who worked with juvenile delinquents, hid to escape execution. Gorenshteyn grew up in the Ukraine and, during World War II, in the Caucasus in children's homes and with relatives. In 1949 he was a construction worker. From 1950 to 1955 he studied at the Mining Institute in Dnepopetrovsk; he worked as a mining engineer until 1958 and then until 1961 as a civil engineer in Kiev. At the same time he wrote several short stories but more especially film scripts for film and television. (None were produced.) As a result, in 1961 he was admitted into the Academy Courses for Scriptwriters of the Writers Union and of the Film Association, where he studied with V. Rozov among others. After completing the course in 1963 he remained in Moscow and by 1980 had written 16 film scripts, five of which were filmed and produced. Gorenshteyn wrote short stories and novels, but only in 1964 was a short prose work published in the journal *Yunost*. In 1977 Gorenshteyn decided to send his prose to the West; several works appeared in journals and a few were translated. In 1979 Gorenshteyn was among the contributors to the almanac METROPOL. In September 1980 he emigrated, first to Vienna; he now lives in Berlin.

Gorenshteyn's first short story, *Dom s bashenkoy* (1964; The House with the Tower), portrays a brave youth in the backcountry during the war whose mother died on a transport train. *Zima 53-go goda* (1978; Winter of

1953) recalls his own experiences as a mining engineer. *Iskupleniye* (1979; Atonement) takes place in 1946 in the territory previously occupied by the Germans and depicts human failure during the war and postwar period. *Stupeni* (1979; Eng. tr., *Steps*, 1982), the longest *povest* in *Metropol*, illustrates the conscious and unconscious religious quest in the Soviet Union. The short story *Tri vstrechi s M. Yu. Lermontovym* (1979; Three Meetings with M. Yu. Lermontov) reveals an astonishing ability to capture the spirit of a historical period. The novel *Psalom* (The Psalm), written in 1974–75 and first published in French in 1984, combines the religious problem of judgment with that of political development in the USSR in five spatially and chronologically independent parts (covering the 1930s to the 1970s). *Mesto* (The Place), Gorenshteyn's main work, a comprehensive novel written between 1969 and 1976, concerns the position that a person occupies in society and among his fellowmen. It has not been published. Gorenshteyn writes fluidly and relatively diffusively, and his writing is sustained by a humane concern. The issues of Judaism, anti-Semitism, Russian chauvinism, and Christian religiosity appear in most of his works.

*Works: Dom s bašenkoj* (short story), in *Junost'* 1964:6; *Zima 53-go goda* (pov.), in *Kontinent*, Paris, 17:1978 and 18:1979; *Iskuplenie* (novel), in *Vremja i my*, Jerusalem, 42:1979; *Stupeni* (pov.), in *Metropol'*, Ann Arbor, 1979 (see above); *Berdičev* (play), in *Vremja i my* 50–51:1980; *Kontrèvoljucioner* and *Tri vstreči s M. Yu. Lermontovym* (short stories), in *NRL: Neue russische Literatur*, Salzburg, Almanach 2–3:1979–80; *Moj Čekhov oseni i zimy 1968 goda*, in *Vremja i my* 55:1980; *Razgovor* (short story), in *Vremja i my* 59:1981; *Jakov Kaša* (pov.), in *Kontinent* 29:1981; *Čekhov i "mysljaščij proletarij"* (essay), in *Russkaja mysl'*, Paris, Aug. 6, 1981; *Tri rasskazy: Tri vstreči s M. Yu. Lermontovym; Kontrèvoljucioner; Archeologičeskie strasti* (short stories), in *Vremja i my* 68:1982; *Košeločka* (short story), in *Sintaksis*, Paris, 10:1982; *Mukha i kapli čaja* (pov.), in *Kontinent* 35–36:1983; *Počemu ja pišu* (essay), in *Strana i mir*, Munich, 1985:5; *Ulica Krasnykh Zor'* (pov.), in *Grani*, Frankfurt am Main, 137:1985; *Psalom* (novel), Munich, 1986.

*Secondary Lit.:* E. Ètkind, in *Vremja i my* 42:1979; W. Kasack, in *Neue Zürcher Zeitung*, Fernausgabe Nr. 284, Dec. 7, 1979; N. Koržavin, in *Russkaja mysl'* June 5, 1980, pp. 7, 10;

E. Reichmann, in *Le Monde* Sept. 21, 1984, p. 24; M. Muravnik, in *Kontinent* 47:1986; B. Khazanov, in *Strana i mir* 1986:9; D. Milivojevic, in *MERSL* 8:1987.

**Górky, Maksím** (pseud. of Alekséy Maksímovich Peshkóv), prose writer, playwright (b. March 28 [March 16], 1868, Nizhniy Novgorod—d. June 18, 1936, Gorky, near Moscow). Gorky's father was a cabinetmaker. As a child, Gorky lived with his grandfather and spent only a few months in school. After the age of 12, he worked as a messenger and kitchenboy, among other jobs. In Kazan after 1884, he continued his education by himself; he came into contact with revolutionary circles. After 1888 he traveled extensively throughout Russia. In Tiflis in 1892 he published his first short story, *Makar Chudra* (Eng. tr., in *Selected Short Stories*, vol. 1, 1954), under the alternate pseudonym "The Bitter One," alluding to his own fate and to that of his characters. From then on, he worked as a writer and journalist in Nizhniy Novgorod and Samara. In 1898 his first two-volume collection appeared and was welcomed with unusual acclaim both at home and abroad. The novels *Foma Gordeyev* (1899; two Eng. trs., 1901, 1906) and *Troye* (1900; Eng. tr., *Three of Them*, 1902; *The Three*, 1953) followed. *Pesnya o burevestnike* (1901; Eng. tr., "The Song of the Stormy Petrel," in *Sewanee Review* 44:1936), a revolutionary prose poem, made Gorky, who had joined Lenin's "Iskra," widely known. During this time Gorky wrote his first dramas, including *Na dne* (1902; Eng. trs., *Night's Lodging*, 1905; *The Lower Depths*, 1912; *At the Bottom*, 1930); in performance at the Moscow Art Theater and in Max Reinhardt's staging in Berlin in 1903 this play, with its new characters from the lumpen proletariat, made an impression that his later dramas never again attained. With Gorky's collaboration, the first legal Bolshevik newspaper, *Novaya zhizn*, was founded in 1905. Gorky met Lenin in 1905, and a lifelong but unstable relationship developed. Because of his support of the revolutionaries, Gorky was forced into exile at the very beginning of 1906; via Berlin and Paris he went to the United States, where he wrote several pieces including the novel *Mat* (Eng. tr., *Mother*, 1907), and then settled in Capri from the autumn of 1906 until 1913. Under A. Bogdanov's influence he strove to connect Russian images of divinity with revolutionary thoughts and gave form to this striving in *Ispoved* (1908; Eng. tr., *The Confes-*

*sion*, 1916). As a result of the amnesty, Gorky returned to Russia in 1913, published *Pervy sbornik proletarskikh pisateley* (First Anthology of Proletarian Authors) in 1914, and in 1915 established the journal *Letopis*, which was Bolshevik but did not conform to Party doctrine. During this period Gorky began an autobiographical trilogy with the publication of *Detstvo* (1913–14; Eng. trs., *My Childhood*, 1915; *Childhood*, 1954) and *V lyudyakh* (1915–16; Eng. trs., *In the World*, 1917; *My Apprenticeship*, 1957). Before the October Revolution, considerable tensions developed between him and Lenin, and these found expression in, among other writings, his journalistic contributions in 1917–18 to the newspaper *Novaya zhizn*, which was banned in July 1918. These articles were later collected in *Nesvoyevremennye mysli* (Eng. tr., *Untimely Thoughts*, 1968). Gorky enthusiastically championed the preservation of Russia's cultural heritage, tried to help young writers (see SERAPION BROTHERS), founded the publishing house Vsemirnaya literatura (World Literature), which provided a livelihood for many writers, and endeavored to protect authors from the Red terror. In 1921 Lenin persuaded Gorky to accept exile again, only partially for reasons of health. Until 1924 Gorky lived in Germany and in Czechoslovakia; in Berlin he founded the journal *Beseda*, which combined the works of Soviet writers and émigrés. In 1924, after Lenin's death, Gorky continued in exile in Sorrento. His relationship to the Soviet Union remained confused. Gorky, who completed his autobiographical trilogy in 1922 with *Moi universitety* (Eng. trs., *My University Days*, 1923; *My Universities*, 1949), wrote other novels including *Delo Artamonovykh* (1925; Eng. trs., *Decadence*, 1927; *The Artamonov Business*, 1948) and *Zhizn Klima Samgina* (1925–26; Eng. tr. of part 1, *Bystander*, 1930; part 2, *The Magnet*, 1931; part 3, *Other Fires*, 1933; part 4, *The Specter*, 1938; the last part remained incomplete at his death. In 1928 and 1929 he visited the Soviet Union; in 1931 he returned to live there. Gorky, whose right to be considered a "proletarian writer" was extensively discussed by the Communist Academy in 1927, was given a leading and honored position in literary-political matters, especially as chairman of the Writers Union of the USSR, established in 1934; he was in personal contact with Stalin. He professed his loyalty to the established system and even defended the horrible forced labor camps (quotes by A. Solzhenitsyn, *Gulag Archipelago*, vol. 2, Paris, 1974, pp. 61–85). The circumstances surrounding his death are puzzling. The official Soviet announcement of March 3, 1938—that he was murdered at the direction of Genrikh Yagoda, the head of the Cheka—does not preclude the possibility, although it has since been denied, that Gorky was a victim of Stalin's tyranny, like Sergei Kirov whose body lies next to his in the Kremlin wall.

In the Soviet Union, Gorky is considered the founder of Soviet literature, although his works depict pre-Revolutionary Russia. *Mat* is called the first work of SOCIALIST REALISM, a style that was introduced 26 years later. Gorky has a "predilection for unusual characters" (Struve); in portraying them, Gorky persecutes them in a kind of hate-love relationship. *Bosyaki* (vagabond peasants), criminals, merchants, representatives of antirevolutionaries, and the willingly conforming intelligentsia are typical figures in his extensive works. During neither his first nor his second exile did Gorky integrate his new environment into his writing, and he learned no foreign languages. His works written during the Soviet period seize again upon the mostly autobiographical material of his experience in Russia. These prose works, as well as the dramas, reveal his basic epic talent, which is bound up with the countryside along the Volga. In *Zhizn Klima Samgina*, Gorky tries to describe the historical events of the four decades preceding the October Revolution from the point of view of a petit-bourgeois Russian intellectual to whom he contrasts the ardent Bolsheviks. The frequently revised, long-winded work, the fourth part of which was compiled from sketches left behind at his death, is additively structured as a "chronicle novel" and has literary significance only in the characterizations within individual episodes. Gorky views all the exploration with form that occurred at the beginning of the 20th century without understanding; his romantic, pathos-laden realism leads from the 19th century to the literature of socialist realism.

*Works: Nesvoevremennye mysli* (essays, 1917–18), Paris, 1971 (see above).—*Sobr. soč.*, 22 vols., 1923–28; 25 vols., 1933–34; *Archiv A. M. G.*, 1939– (vol. 14 appeared in 1972); *Sobr. soč.*, 30 vols., 1949–55; 18 vols., 1960–62; 16 vols., 1979.

*Works and Lit.: G. i sovetskie pisateli, Lit. nasledstvo* 70:1963.

*Translations: Collected Works*, 10 vols., 1978–82. For individual titles, see these bibliographies: *Proizv. A. M. G. v perevodakh na inostrannye jazyki (otdel'nye zarubežnye iz-*

*danija 1900–1955)*, Moscow, 1958; R. Lewanski, *The Slavic Literatures*, New York, 1967 (vol. 2 of *The Literatures of the World in English Translation: A Bibliography*); G. Gibian, *Soviet Russian Literature in English*, Ithaca, N.Y., 1967.

Secondary Lit.: N. Gourfinkel, Hamburg, 1958; *RSPP* 1:1959; F. M. Borras, 1967; B. A. Kaleps, Diss., Heidelberg, 1969; F. Sielicki, Warsaw, 1971; H. Imendörffer, Berlin–Wiesbaden, 1973; G. Gerling-Brudzinskij, in *Kontinent*, Paris, 8:1976; W. Pailer, Munich, 1978; K. Muratova, *M. G. Seminarij*, 1981; W. Baumann, Frankfurt–Bern, 1982; M. Bryld, in *Scando-Slavica* 28:1982.

**Gorky Prize.** See LITERARY PRIZES.

**Górlin, Mikhaíl Génrikhovich,** poet (b. June 11, 1909, St. Petersburg—d. April 1944 [?], while imprisoned in Germany). Gorlin's father earned a doctoral degree in Heidelberg and was a wealthy Jewish merchant. Through private tutoring, Gorlin attained a profound literary education. In 1919 he emigrated with his parents via Vilnius and London to Berlin (1922). There he studied Slavic philology with M. Vasmer from 1927 to 1931 and wrote a dissertation entitled "N. V. Gogol and E. T. A. Hoffman" (1933). Gorlin, who had written poems since his youth, published as his first work a volume that he himself translated into German under the pseudonym D. Mirayev: *Märchen und Städte* (1930; Fairy Tales and Cities). Each year from 1931 to 1933 he edited anonymously a volume that included some of his own poems in Russian: *Sbornik berlinskikh poetov* (Collection of Berlin Poets). With the poet Raisa Blokh, later his wife, he emigrated in 1933 to Paris where he became an assistant to A. Mazon at the Institut d'Etudes slaves. From 1931 to 1936 he published probably only 14 poems in periodicals and a few scholarly articles on Russian literature. His only volume of Russian poetry, *Puteshestviya* (1936; Travels), contained some of the same poems that had appeared in German in the book published in 1930. On May 14, 1941, Gorlin was arrested as a Jew and deported to Germany. His wife was also arrested while attempting to escape to Switzerland and also died in Germany. Their friends arranged for a memorial volume for the two of them, *Izbrannye stikhotvoreniya* (1959; Selected Poems).

Closely attached to romanticism and its fairytale world, Gorlin camouflaged his bilingual (Russian-German) status as a poet through the creation of a doppelgänger, Mirayev. Gorlin's "neoromanticism . . . makes one laugh and smile, is coquettish and captivating like a precocious silent film" (Kreuzer). The fairytale elements in his works live in the present with its modern cities, means of transportation, and other acquisitions of civilization. His poetry is religously grounded and can attain the form of prayer. It is clear, rhythmic, multileveled, and delightfully playful.

Works: *Märchen und Städte* (poems), Berlin, 1930 (partially reprinted, Siegen, 1985); *Die philosophisch-politischen Strömungen in der russischen Emigration*, in *Osteuropa* 8:1932–33, pp. 279–94; *Putešestvija* (poems), Berlin, 1936; (with Raisa Blokh) *Izbr. stikhotvorenija* (poems), Paris, 1959.

Secondary Lit.: M. Cetlin, in *Sovremennye zapiski*, Paris, 62:1936; A. Mazon, in *Revue des Etudes slaves*, 1946, pp. 289–91; E. Kannak, in *Novyj žurnal*, New York, 57:1959; L. Alekseeva, in *Grani*, Frankfurt am Main, 45:1960; H. Kreuzer, in Gorlin's *Märchen und Städte*, 1985.

**Gorodétsky, Sergéy Mitrofánovich,** poet, opera librettist (b. Jan. 17 [Jan. 5], 1884, St. Petersburg—d. June 8, 1967, Moscow). Gorodetsky's father was an ethnographer. Gorodetsky studied philology in St. Petersburg between 1902 and 1912 without completing the course of study. His first volume of verse, *Yar* (1907; Frenzy), was welcomed by A. Blok, V. Bryusov, M. Voloshin, and K. Chukovsky. In 1912 Gorodetsky, along with N. Gumilyov, was one of the founders of the acmeist literary group. After meeting S. Yesenin in 1915, he was briefly involved with the "peasant poets" S. Klychkov, N. Klyuyev, and A. Shiryayevets. Gorodetsky spent World War I and the Revolutionary years in the Caucasus. He joined the Red Army immediately and held cultural-political posts in the Caucasus, Petrograd, and (after 1921) in Moscow. Until 1924 Gorodetsky was with the Theater of the Revolution; he worked for the literary section of *Izvestiya* until 1932. After 1924 Gorodetsky wrote numerous opera libretti, for example, *Proryv* (The Breakthrough), a libretto about the Civil War for an opera by S. I. Pototsky; furthermore, he translated the texts of such world-famous operas as *Fidelio* and *Die Meistersinger von Nürnberg* into Russian. He adapted M. Glinka's opera *A Life for the Tsar* under the title *Ivan Susanin*. During World War II, Gorodetsky was evacuated to Tashkent; afterward, he worked primarily as a translator and taught at the Gorky Literary Institute.

Gorodetsky's early verse was influenced by the symbolists, above all by K. Balmont; it also harks back to motifs from pagan Slavic mythology and revolves around the theme of the primordial power of nature-related elements. After the Revolution, Gorodetsky wrote political verse, ranging from agitational poetry of the Civil War period, salutatory poems on the proletarian poets (1921), the Party Congresses (1931, 1958), and the cosmonauts (1962), to a cantata, "Pesn o partii" (Song of the Party).

Works: Jar' (poems), 1907; Perun (poems), 1907; Kladbišče strastej (short stories), vol. 1, 1909 (reprinted, Letchworth, 1980); Sobr. stikhov (poems), 2 vols., 1910–16; Stikhotvorenija (poems), 1956; Ivan Susanin (libretto), 2d ed., 1964; Stikhi (poems), 1966; Stikhotvorenija i poèmy (lyric and narrative poems), 1974.

Secondary Lit.: A. V. Lunačarskij (1929), in Lit. nasledstvo 74:1965; D. Moldavskij, in Zvezda 1957:4; S. I. Mašinskij, foreword to Gorodeckij's Stikhotvorenija . . . . , 1974; RSPPo 6:1983; N. Bogomolov, in Lit. obozrenie 1987:1.

**Gorýshin, Gleb Aleksándrovich**, prose writer (b. March 15, 1931, Leningrad). Goryshin's father worked for the civil service. From 1949 to 1954 Goryshin studied journalism at Leningrad University; thereafter he worked for the newspaper Molodyozh Altaya in Barnaul; in 1957 he returned to Leningrad. Goryshin frequently spent time in Siberia, not only as a journalist but also as a participant in geological expeditions, as a lumberman, and as a hunter, among other occupations. Goryshin views his short story Luchshiy lotsman (1957; The Best Pilot) as the transition between his work as a journalist and that as a writer. Since then, his short stories and povesti have regularly been published individually and in collections such as Sneg v oktyabre (1966; Snow in October). Goryshin has been a member of the board of the Writers Union of the RSFSR since 1965. From 1977 until April 1982 he was editor in chief of the journal Avrora; his work there was probably terminated as a reaction to the ironic parable Yubileynaya rech (1981:12; The Jubilee Speech) alluding to Brezhnev's 75th birthday.

The theme of Goryshin's prose concerns the superiority that the man who is attached to nature enjoys over the townsman and is close to the attitude expressed by M. Prishvin, K. Paustovsky, and I. Sokolov-Mikitov. His prose is autobiographical to a great degree, has minimal plot, and depicts isolated experiences with often laconic succinctness. The emphasis on humanity in his poetic message links it with the concern expressed by his contemporaries who also began writing after the 20th Party Congress. The collection Star i mlad (1978; Old and Young) illustrates his geographic breadth, the diversity of his characters, and his stylistic variety, which ranges from sketches rich in data to lyrical contemplation.

Works: Lučšij locman (short stories), 1957; Khleb i sol' (short stories), 1958; V tridcat' let (pov. and short stories), 1961; Fiord Od'ba (short stories), 1961; Sinee oko (pov. and short stories), 1963; Sneg v oktjabre (short stories), 1966; Blizko more (short stories), 1967; Kto sidit u kostra (short stories), 1968; Do poludnja (pov.), 1968; Lica Vstrečnykh (pov. and short stories), 1971; Vodopad (pov. and short stories), 1971; Den'-denskoj (pov. and short stories), 1972; Star i mlad (pov., short stories, and essays), 1978; Zapon' (pov., short stories, and essays), 1980; Vesennjaja okhota na borovuju dic' (pov. and short stories), 1986.—Izbr., 1981.

Secondary Lit.: L. Anninskij, in Moskva 1962:1; S. Tkhorževskij, in Zvezda 1966:8; RSPP 7(1):1971; S. Voronin, in Neva 1973:6; V. Kurbatov, in Lit. obozrenie 1973:9; Ju. Petrovskij, in Zvezda 1981:3; I. Kuvšinov, in Oktjabr' 1982:9; A. Urban, in Moskva 1985:1; V. Kavtorin, in Neva 1986:10.

**Gráni** (Facets; an almost untranslatable title, it refers to the polished edge of a glass or crystal and applies this image to the spiritual sphere), a journal for literature, art, science, and social thought, published since 1946 by the Posev Publishing House in Frankfurt am Main up to four times a year; no. 143 was issued in 1987. Grani was established by members of the second emigration who were interested in literature and who came to West Germany from the Soviet Union during World War II. From 1946 to 1961 (nos. 1–50) the editor in chief was Ye. Romanov; from 1962 to 1982 it was N. Tarasova, who also worked with an editorial staff of which she herself had been a member since 1953. She was followed by R. Redlikh (until 1983). From 1983 to 1986 the editor in chief was G. Vladimov, followed by E. A. Breytbart-Samsonova. At first Grani attracted literary figures from among

# 133                                                    GRÁNIN

the "displaced persons" in Germany and France; for example, a work by I. Yelagin was published in no. 2. The literary critics B. Filippov, V. Markov, L. Rzhevsky, V. Zavalishin, and others belonged among the early contributors. In a second phase, the journal developed ties to the older emigration; this allowed the prose of I. Bunin and B. Zaytsev to be included. In its third phase in the mid-1950s, the journal began publishing works from the Soviet Union, usually those that were forbidden by the censor and were thus circulated through SAMIZDAT; of necessity these were generally reprinted without the author's knowledge. For example, the underground journals *Feniks* (1961), *Sintaksis* (1–3:1959–60), and *Sfinksy* (1965) were reprinted as were the works of almost all the important writers who later emigrated, such as I. Brodsky, A. Galich, N. Gorbanevskaya, N. Korzhavin, V. Maksimov, A. Sinyavksy, A. Solzhenitsyn, G. Vladimov, and V. Voynovich. Numerous works by representatives of the third emigration were first published in *Grani*; for example, L. Druskin, A. Gladilin, F. Kandel, D. Markish, Vl. Rybakov, K. Sapgir, Ye. Ternovsky, Yu. Voznesenskaya. *Grani* also published works by authors living in the Soviet Union (some of whom have since died), such as A. Akhmatova, G. Aygi, Yu. Daniel, Yu. Dombrovsky, Yu. Galanskov, Ye. Ginzburg, V. Grossman, Vl. Kornilov, M. Naritsa, B. Okudzhava, B. Pasternak, V. Shalamov, V. Soloukhin, V. Sosnora, A. and B. Strugatsky. To a lesser extent, *Grani* also tries to preserve forgotten literature, such as the work of the OBERIU members D. Kharms and A. Vvedensky, in addition to works by M. Bulgakov and A. Platonov, and works by émigrés such as M. Tsvetayeva and Z. Gippius. Yu. Terapiano compiled a brief anthology of émigré poetry from 1920 to 1960 (no. 44); Ye. Rays complemented this with a survey of the history of Russian poetry published in the USSR during the same period (nos. 49–51). Some of the longer works of literature first reprinted in *Grani* were later published in book form by the Posev Publishing House.

*Secondary Lit.*: V. Zavališin, in *Russkaja literatura v èmigracii*, ed. N. Poltorackij, Pittsburgh, 1972; A. P. Majewicz, Birmingham, 1980; G. Andreev, in *Russkaja mysl'*, Paris, May 13, 1982, p. 11; Feb. 3, 1983, p. 10; April 8, 1983, p. 12; Aug. 13, 1984, p. 12; June 14, 1985, p. 12; and Nov. 1, 1985, p. 10; G. Vladimov, *Neobkhodimoe ob"jasnenie*, in *Grani* 140:1986; *Vynuždennyj otvet [izdatel'stva Posev]*, in *Grani* 140:1986.

**Gránin, Daniíl Aleksándrovich** (pseud. of D. A. Gérman), prose writer (b. Jan. 1, 1919, Volyn). Granin's father was a forest ranger. In 1940 Granin completed his studies in electromechanics at the Polytechnical Institute in Leningrad. He joined the Communist Party in 1942; until 1950 he worked as an engineer in industry and research. Granin, who has published works of literature since 1949, became famous for his topical prose both at home and abroad after 1954. Since 1954 he has been on the board of the Writers Union of the USSR, and since the establishment of the Writers Union of the RSFSR in 1958 he has been a member of the board of that organization; since 1965, one of the secretaries there. From 1954 to 1969 Granin was one of the secretaries of the Leningrad branch of the Writers Union. Granin has been a member of the editorial staff of the journal *Neva* since 1967. In 1978 he was awarded the State Prize of the USSR for his povest about World War II, *Klavdiya Vilor* (1976; Claudius Vilor). He lives in Moscow.

Beginning with his first prose works, Granin chose the field of industrial research. The povest *Spor cherez okean* (1949; Fight over the Ocean) conforms to the general theme of that time: the Soviet Union's superiority over the United States. In a successful novel from 1954, *Iskateli* (Eng. tr., *Those Who Seek*, 1957), the protagonist represents the ideal union between a true Soviet man and the engineer of genius (A. Steininger); through many secondary characters, Granin reveals the negative consequences of the Stalin era (fear of responsibility, a desire to protect oneself, indifference). Granin was criticized at first for his parable of a deceitful Soviet technocrat, *Sobstvennoye mneniye* (1956; One's Own Opinion). His next novel, *Posle svadby* (1958; After the Wedding), about a backward kolkhoz, also brought polemics to the fore. In 1962 he returned to the theme of the technological intelligentsia with *Idu na grozu* (Eng. tr., *Into the Storm*, 1965) and provided insight into topical problems that have arisen since the 20th and 22d Party Congresses (exploratory research, abstract art, jazz, the return of forbidden literature, among others). In *Prekrasnaya Uta* (1970; The Lovely Uta [from Naumburg]) Granin deals with the issue of meetings between Germans and Russians 20 years after the war through a free association of reflection and autobiographical commentary. In his povesti he frequently depicts the ethical and psychological problems scientists face: *Kto-to dolzhen* (1970; One Must Indeed) examines the contrasts between certain success and a thorny, risky venture, between performance of one's duty and sacrificing oneself for the cause. *Eta strannaya zhizn* (1974; This Strange Life) builds on documentary material about a botanist who was thoroughly devoted to science and formally gains in appeal by combining various storytelling genres (including autobiographical lyricism). *Odnofamilets* (1975; Namesake) also portrays an engineer's confrontation with himself, as one who was unjustly criticized in his youth. Numerous trips abroad found an echo in reports rich in reflections and observations. *Glavy iz blokadnoy knigi* (1977, 1981; Chapters in the Blockade Book) is the product of interviews with survivors of the Leningrad blockade and is enriched with contemporary commentaries. Granin's novel *Kartina* (1980; Picture) is set in a small town with its controversy about preserving tradition or encouraging industrial development.

*Works: Pobeda inženera Korsakova (Spor čerez okean)* (pov.), 1950; *Jaroslav Dombrovskij* (novel), 1951; *Iskateli* (novel), 1954 (see above); *Sobstvennoe mnenie* (short story), in *Novyj mir* 1956:8; *Posle svad'by* (novel), 1958; *Idu na grozu* (novel), 1962 (see above); *Mesjac vverkh nogami* (articles), 1966; *Naš kombat* (pov.), in *Sever* 1968:4; *Kto-to dolžen* (pov. and short stories), 1970; *Neožidannoe utro* (travel commentary), 1970 (also contains *Prekrasnaja Uta*); *Sad kamnej* (pov.), 1972; *Do poezda ostavalos' tri časa* (pov. and short stories); *Èta strannaja zizn'* (pov.), 1974; (jointly with A. Adamovič) *Glavy iz blokadnoj knigi* (memoirs), in *Novyj mir* 1977:12 and 1981:11, separate ed. as *Blokadnaja kniga*, 1982; *Obratnyj bilet* (pov.), 1978; *Klavdija Vilor* (pov.), 1980; *Kartina* (novel), 1980; *Dva kryla*, 1983; *Tridnadcat' stupenek* (pov.), 1984; *Zubr* (pov.), in *Novyj mir* 1987:1–2.—*Sobr. soč.*, 4 vols., 1978–80.

*Secondary Lit.: RSPP* 1:1959; F. Levin, in *Voprosy lit.* 1959:10 and in *Novyj mir* 1968:6; V. Survillo, in *Novyj mir* 1963:3; O. Vojtinskaja, 1966; E. Šubin, in *Zvezda* 1969:1; V. Gorbačëv, in *Oktjabr'* 1969:6; E. Kholševnikova, in *Zvezda* 1973:11; S. Tutorskaja, in *Oktjabr'* 1974:10; V. Percovskij, in *Novyj mir* 1975:11; L. Plotkin, 1975; A. Pavlovskij, in *Neva* 1981:1; A. Starkov, 1981; I. Grekova, in *Zvezda* 1981:1; N. Kuznecova, in *Grani*, Frankfurt am Main, 131:1984; L. Fink, in *Zvezda* 1986:7.

**Grebénshchikov, Geórgy Dmítriyevich,** prose writer (b. May 6 [April 24], 1883, Nikolayevsky rudnik, prov. Tomsk—d. Jan. 11, 1964,

Lakeland, Florida). Grebenshchikov was of peasant heritage. From 1906 on, he was a journalist and was literarily active. In 1912–13 he was editor of the newspaper *Zhizn Altaya* in Barnaul. Grebenshchikov published his first collection of short stories, *V prostorakh Sibiri* (2 vols., 1913–15; In the Openness of Siberia), in St. Petersburg. This collection was followed by several other books. In 1920 Grebenshchikov emigrated to Paris, where his previous and current prose was published in a six-volume edition of collected works in 1922–23. In *Sovremennye zapiski* (1921–22, nos. 5–10), he began *Churayevy* (The Churayevs), a serialized novel advertised as a twelvepart "epic poem." After Grebenshchikov emigrated to the United States, the third volume of this novel was published by Alatas, his own publishing house (located first in New York, later in Southbury, Connecticut), in 1925. Grebenshchikov brought his novel as far as the sixth volume in 1937, but he also published numerous other books. In 1943–44 he published in *Novy zhurnal*.

In his prose, Grebenshchikov concentrates on Siberia; he is conscious of tradition and is closely attached to his homeland, but his broadly ranging style, rich in descriptive epithets, has a trivializing effect. His plans exceed his artistic capabilities. Nevertheless, he has his readers, and he was celebrated as the "bard" of Siberia on the occasion of the fiftieth anniversary of his literary career.

*Works: V prostorakh Sibiri* (short stories), 2 vols., 1913–15; *Zmej Gorynyč* (short stories), 1916; *Step' da nebo* (short stories), 1917; *Čuraevy* (novel), 6 vols. New York, 1922–37; *Bylina o Mikule Bujanoviče* (novel), New York, 1924 (Eng. tr., *The Turbulent Giant*, 1940); *Radonega, Skazanie o Sv. Sergii* (novel), Southbury, 1938, 2d ed., 1954; *Zlatoglav* (narrative poem), Southbury, 1939; *Egorkina žizn'* (autobiographical short story), in *Vozrождenie*, Paris, 29:1953 and 61:1957.—*Sobr. soč.*, 6 vols., Paris, 1922–23.

*Secondary Lit.: V. Pravdukhin, in *Sibirskie ogni* 1922:5; G. V. Alekseev, in *Novaja russkaja kniga*, Berlin, 1922:9; F. Ivanov, in *Novaja russkaja kniga* 1923:3; A. Žernakova-Nikolaeva, in *Vozrождenie* 52:1956; V. Maevskij, in *Vozrождenie* 58:1956.

**Grékova, Irína Nikoláyevna** (pseud. of Eléna Sergéyevna Vénttsel), prose writer (b. March 21 [March 8], 1907, Reval). In 1929 Grekova graduated from Leningrad University in mathematics. In 1954 she earned a doctorate in the technical sciences; in 1955 she was appointed professor. Grekova seems to have held leading positions in scientific research institutes of the air force for a long time and was probably evacuated during World War II. As a writer she became famous at home and abroad for her short story Za prokhodnoy (1962; Eng. tr., "Beyond the Gates," in The Young Russians, 1972). By 1967 Novyj mir had published three more short stories that also touched off conservative polemics. She collected some of these in her first published book, Pod fonaryom (1966; Under the Lamp). In 1967 she was accepted into the Writers Union of the USSR. Grekova's second book, Kafedra (1980; The Professorship), is a collection of three povesti from the 1970s. Grekova lives in Moscow.

Grekova, who is rarely mentioned in Soviet histories of literature but frequently discussed in journal articles, first deserves consideration because of the peculiarity of her subject matter. From the experiences of her own life, she portrays scientists in their enthusiasm for their professions and in the concerns of their daily lives. Deming Brown, who takes into consideration the autobiographical aspects of her work, praises "her intelligent and ingenious social satire, her honesty and humanity, and her deep concern over problems of personal integrity." Za prokhodnoy takes place in a secret institute; in Pod fonaryom a woman scientist reviews her life as she thinks about a personal decision. Damsky master (1963; Eng. trs., "The Lady's Hairdresser," in The Ardis Anthology of Recent Russian Literature, 1975; "Ladies' Hairdresser," in Russian Women, 1983), one of her best short stories, presents an objective and critical portrait of a half-educated young man who would like to get ahead in Soviet society. Na ispytaniyakh (1967; On the Testing Ground) revives the atmosphere of mistrust of the late Stalin period in the field of military research. Malenky Garusov (1970; Little Garusov) describes the spiritual trauma of a person who is not fully mature physically and psychologically as a result of having suffered through the Leningrad blockade as a child. In Kafedra she explores the human problems that arise within a circle of colleagues when a professorship changes hands. Grekova writes extremely economically, with psychological depth and a critical realism. She knows how to make detail as typical as her characters, who, by focusing on the essential, gain a significance beyond themselves.

Works: Za prokhodnoj (short story), in Novyj mir 1962:7 (see above); Damskij master (short story), in Novyj mir 1963:11 (see above); Letom v gorode (short story), in Novyj mir 1965:4; Pod fonarëm (short story), in Zvezda 1965:12, and published separately together with other short stories, 1966; Na ispytanijakh (pov.), in Novyj mir 1967:7; Malen'kij Garusov (pov.), in Zvezda 1970:9; Khozjajka gostinicy (pov.), in Zvezda 1976:9 (Eng. tr., "The Hotel Manager," in Russian Women, 1983); Kafedra (pov.), in Novyj mir 1978:9, separate ed., 1981 (with Khozjajka gostinicy and Malen'kij Garusov); Vdovij parokhod (pov.), in Novyj mir 1981:5, separate ed., Paris, 1983; Porogi, in Oktjabr' 1984:10–11.

Secondary Lit.: S. Melešin et al., in Lit. Rossija June 26, 1964, pp. 10–11; V. Lakšin, in Novyj mir 1965:4; A. Ninov, in Zvezda 1967:7; B. Leonov, in Moskva 1969:5; V. Percovskij, in Voprosy lit. 1971:10; V. Oskockij, in Družba narodov 1977:4; L. Popov, in Neva 1979:5; T. Khmel'nickaja in Neva 1982:2.

Gribachóv, Nikolái Matvéyevich, poet, prose writer (b. Dec. 19 [Dec. 6], 1910, Lopush, prov. Oryol). Gribachov is of peasant descent. In 1932 Gribachov completed technical school, where he studied water conservation, and began working as a journalist in Petrozavodsk and Smolensk. He was a frontline reporter during the 1939 Finnish-Russian War and World War II; he joined the Communist Party in 1943. Gribachov received Stalin prizes (for 1947, 1st class, and for 1948, 2d class) for his narrative poems Kolkhoz "Bolshevik" (1947) and Vesna v "Pobede" (1948; Spring at the "Victory" Kolkhoz). From 1950 to 1954 and again after 1956 he was editor in chief of the journal Sovetsky Soyuz. Gribachov accompanied Khrushchev on his visit to the United States in 1959; in 1960 he received the Lenin Prize for coauthoring Litsom k litsu s Amerikoy (1960; Face to Face with America). Since 1954 Gribachov has been a member of the board of the Writers Union of the USSR, and since 1959 a member of the secretariat of the board; he has been a member of the board of the Writers Union of the RSFSR since 1958 and a candidate for the Central Committee of the Communist Party since 1961. In 1980 he was named chairman of the Supreme Soviet of the RSFSR. Gribachov lives in Moscow.

At all times Gribachov sees his literary activity first and foremost as a political mission. Verse and prose serve the interests of the Communist Party in much the same way that publicistic writing does. The epics in verse for which he received Stalin Prizes and in which he intended to proclaim a genuinely socialistic, optimistic attitude toward postwar kolkhoz labor are typical of the "varnishing of reality" that characterizes the period of the cult of personality. Gribachov illustrates the respective Party standpoints in a declamatory manner (see PARTY SPIRIT) in his subsequent work as well. He praises Communist achievements in the people's democracies and is polemically anti-Western. "He is not afraid to be tendentious; on the contrary, he strives to be tendentious. . . . He is always on the offensive" (Ilyin).

Works: Kolkhoz "Bolševik" (narrative poem), 1948, Vesna v "Pobede" (narrative poem), 1949; Stikhotvorenija i poèmy (lyric and narrative poems), 1951, 2d ed., 2 vols., 1958; Licom k licu s Amerikoj (in collaboration with Adžubej et al.; travel notes), 1960; Lirika (poems), 1973; O žizni, o doroge, o ljubvi (poems), 1980.—Izbr. proizv., 3 vols., 1960; Sobr. soč., 5 vols., 1971–73.
Secondary Lit.: B. Privalov, 1962; V. Il'in, 1968; A. Murav'ëv, in Znamja 1973:8; V. Privalov, in Moskva 1980:12; RSPP 6:1983; S. Lipkin, in Dekada, New York, 1983 (chap. 13).

**Grin, Alekśandr Stepánovich** (pseud. of A. S. Grinyévsky), prose writer (b. Aug. 23 [Aug. 11], 1880, Slobodskoy, prov. Vyatka—d. July 8, 1932; Stary Krym). Grin's father was a Polish bookkeeper, exiled in 1883. After four years of school, Grin embarked on an adventurous life as a vagabond in 1896 (he was a sailor, gold prospector, soldier and exile). His first volume of short stories appeared in 1908; after 1912 he lived in St. Petersburg in impoverished circumstances. He was drafted into the Red Army in 1919–20. In 1924 he moved to Feodosiya on the Black Sea, and in 1930, to Stary Krym. Grin was a popular writer even before the Revolution. His fantastic stories, free of any political reference, continued to be popular; the dogmatic critics, however, attacked him with increasing asperity. The planned 15-volume edition of his collected works was terminated in 1929 after the appearance of only 8 volumes. His work was not reprinted after 1941, and in 1950 he was posthumously accused of bourgeois COSMOPOLITANISM. With the help of K. Paustovsky, Yu. Olesha, and others, Grin's works reappeared in 1956; since then millions of copies have been published.

Grin's adventure stories and novels, influenced to some extent by Edgar Allan Poe, Robert Louis Stevenson, and Joseph Conrad, are hardly popular because of their high literary value but rather because of their unique position in Soviet literature. Grin retained the romantic, exotic local color characteristic of many works in the early 1920s. His "Grinland" is an imaginary place, his reality is always interspersed with the fabulous, and his belief in the goodness of man (as in Alye parusa [1923; Eng. tr., Scarlet Sails, 1967]) stands apart from all slogans of SOCIALIST REALISM.

Works: Šapka nevidimka (short stories), 1908; Alye parusa (pov.), 1923 (see above); Blistajuščij mir (novel), 1924; Avtobiografičeskaja povest' (autobiographical pov.), 1932; Izbr. (short stories), 1941; Rasskazy (short stories), 1956.—Sobr. soč., 3 vols., 1913; Polnoe sobr. soč., 15 vols. (of which vols. 2, 5, 6, 8, 11–14 appeared), 1927–29; Sobr. soč., 6 vols., 1965; 6 vols., 1980.
Translations: Echo: Short Stories, 1964; The Seeker of Adventure: Selected Short Stories, 1978; Selected Short Stories, 1985.
Secondary Lit.: V. Važdaev, in Novyj mir 1950:1; M. Ščeglov, in Novyj mir 1956:10; RSPP 1:1959; C. Frioux, in Cahiers du monde russe et soviétique 1962:4; V. Kovskij, in Novyj mir 1966:6, in his Romantičeskij mir A. Grina, 1969, and in Voprosy lit. 1981:10; L. Mikhajlova, 1972; Vospominanija ob A. Grine, 1972; N. J. L. Luker, London, 1973, in Russian Literature Triquarterly 8:1974, bibliography, in 10 Bibliographies of 20th Century Russian Literature, Ann Arbor, 1977, and Newtonville, Mass., 1980; B. Scherr, in Slavic and East European Journal 1976:4; C. G. Thomas, Diss., Manchester, 1977; V. Šklovskij, in Oktjabr' 1980:8; N. Medvedeva, in Filologičeskie nauki 1984:2.

**Grin, Elmár** (pseud. of Aleksándr Vasílyevich Yakímov), prose writer (b. June 15 [June 2], 1909, Kivennapa, prov. Vyborg). Grin comes from a peasant family. After the early death of his parents, Grin was raised in orphanages. From 1922 to 1929 he traveled across Russia working as a farmhand; then he spent five years with the Baltic Sea fleet and worked from 1935 to 1939 as a wireless operator in Leningrad and environs. His first short story appeared in 1937. Starting in 1939, Grin was in the military and served as a war correspondent at the front at the end of World War II. In 1943 he was accepted into the Communist Party. From 1958 to 1965 he was a member of the board of the Writers Union of the RSFSR and belonged to the review commission of the Writers Union of the USSR from 1959 to 1981. He lives in Leningrad.

Grin's entire work is dedicated to the places

he lived as a child—Estonia, Karelia, and Finland. The first short stories (1939) concern the lives of Estonian peasants living in Soviet territory as seen through the themes of class struggle and collectivization. The povest *Veter s yuga* (1946; Eng. tr., *Wind from the South*, 1948, 1951), which takes place in Finland from 1939 to 1946, was awarded a Stalin Prize (for 1946, 1st class). The following novel, *Drugoy put* (1956; Another Way), covers half a century of life in Finland; the next one, *V strane Ivana* (1962–67; In the Land of Ivan), also written in the first person, recounts a homeless Finnish farmhand's path to political maturity in the Soviet Union. In the 1970s Grin published almost nothing new. Grin has accommodated his journalistic and literary work to the ideological theme of international brotherhood.

*Works:* Rasskazy (short stories), 1939; *Veter s juga* (pov.), 1946 (see above); *Izbr.* (pov. and short stories), 1948; *Drugoj put'* (novel), vol. 1, 1956, vols. 1–2, 1963; *V strane Ivana* (novel), in *Zvezda* 1962:10–12, 1967:11–12, separate ed., 1969; *Projdënnye bolota* (short stories and pov.), 1966; *Žil-byl Matti* (autobiographical pov.), 1981.

*Secondary Lit.:* S. Nemirovskij, in *Novyj mir* 1941:2; *RSPP* 1:1959; A. Rubaškin, in *Zvezda* 1962:4; M. Školenko, in *Oktjabr'* 1963:5; R. Messer, in *Neva* 1968:4; A. Kolpakov, in *Oktjabr'* 1968:10; A. Pavlovskij, 1960; Ju. Petrovskij, in *Zvezda* 1979:6.

**Grónsky, Nikoláy Pávlovich,** poet (b. July 24 [July 11], 1909, Finland—d. Nov. 21, 1934, Paris). Gronsky emigrated with his parents to Paris in 1920; he studied in Brussels, where he wrote a dissertation on G. Derzhavin. M. Tsvetayeva, who published a lengthy and highly commendatory article about him following his accidental death in the Paris subway, discussed his poems written in the years 1928–29. Before his death, he himself compiled his only volume of poetry, *Stikhi i poemy* (1936; Lyric and Narrative Poems).

Gronsky, whose poetry is rooted in the 18th century, stood apart from the "Parisian Note" group influenced by G. Adamovich. He wrote elevated, metaphysically grounded, thematically rich, formal, somewhat uneven poems. His narrative poem *Belladonna* (1934; Belledonne [name of a mountain range in the Alpes du Dauphiné]) provides a point of departure for ethical and religious concerns against a backdrop of his passion for, and wealth of experiences in, mountain climbing. Tsveta-

yeva recognized in his work the proof that there were impressive, original talents within the second generation of the first wave of emigration.

*Works: Belladonna: Al'pijskaja poèma* (narrative poem), in *Poslednie novosti* Dec. 9, 1934, and in *Vozdušnye puti*, New York, 5:1967; *Stikhi i poèmy* (poems), Paris, 1936; *Stikhi* (poems), in *Na Zapade*, New York, 1953.

*Secondary Lit.:* Ju. Ivask, in *Žurnal sodružestva*, Vyborg, 1935:9; M. Cvetaeva, in *Sovremennye zapiski*, Paris, 36:1961 and in *Vozdušnye puti* 5:1967 (both titles also in M. Cvetaeva's *Izbr. proza*, 2 vols., New York, 1979, vol. 2); V. Blinov, in *HRL*, 1985.

**Gróssman, Leoníd Petróvich,** literary scholar, prose writer (b. Jan. 24 [Jan. 12], 1888, Odessa—d. Dec. 15, 1965, Moscow). Grossman's father was a doctor. Grossman completed his law studies at Odessa University in 1911. From 1921 on, he taught at various institutions, including the Bryusov Institute of Literature and Art in Moscow; he subsequently worked in publishing. Grossman's publications in the 1920s included monographs of F. Dostoyevsky, A. Pushkin, I. Turgenev, and A. Sukhovo-Kobylin; a highly erudite scholar, he was close to the FORMALIST SCHOOL. Grossman's academic research led not only to purely philological publications and biographies of writers but also, in the early 1930s, to the writing of historical novels. Because of his European spirit and his numerous comparisons of Russian trends to Western and Oriental literature, Grossman (who had already been attacked often before) was among those scholars accused of rootless COSMOPOLITANISM in 1948. His scholarly studies and popular works again found an audience after 1954.

Grossman wrote three literary works: *Zapiski D'Arshiaka* (1930; d'Archiac's Notes; Eng. tr. *Death of a Poet*, 1945), the fictitious memoirs of the Vicomte d'Archiac, who was d'Anthès's second in the latter's duel with Pushkin; *Ruletenburg* (1932; Roulettenburg), a novel, set in Germany, about Dostoyevsky's passion for gambling; and *Barkhatny diktator* (1933; The Velvet Dictator), a novel-cycle about M. Loris-Melikov and Aleksandr II, V. Pleve, K. Pobedonostsev, V. Garshin, and others. A comprehensive knowledge of the respective historical periods and the lives of the individual figures enabled Grossman to write historical novels that are essentially based on historical events and characters but that dispense with the traditional method of using fictitious action, such as love intrigues, set against a detailed historical background. Grossman's focus on the tragic events in an artist's life enabled him to present vivid, psychologically accurate, and moving descriptions of Pushkin's duel, Dostoyevsky's reprieve on the scaffold, and Garshin's experience of Mlodetsky's execution and his own path through insanity to suicide.

*Works: Zapiski D'Aršiaka* (novel), 1930 (see above); *Aprel'skie buntari: Glavy iz romana o Dostoevskom*, in *Novyj mir* 1931:11; *Ruletenburg* (novel), 1932; *Barkhatnyj diktator* (pov.), 1933; bibliography of scholarly works, in *Kratkaja lit. ènciklopedija*, vol. 2, 1964.— *Sobr. soč.*, 4 vols., 1928.

*Secondary Lit.:* I. Sergievskij, in *Novyj mir* 1929:7; obituary, in *Lit. gazeta* Dec. 21, 1965.

**Gróssman, Vasíly Semyónovich,** prose writer (b. Dec. 12 [Nov. 29], 1905, Berdichev, prov. Kiev—d. Sept. 14, 1964, Moscow). Grossman's father was a chemist. Grossman completed his studies in chemistry at Moscow University in 1929, worked as a chemist in the Donbas until 1932, and then moved to Moscow. There in 1934 he embarked on a writing career that spanned 30 years. During the Stalin period Grossman was intermittently fully acknowledged and then stiffly criticized; from 1954 until his death he belonged to the board of the Writers Union of the USSR, but in secret he wrote works so mercilessly critical of the system (in the manner later made famous primarily by A. Solzhenitsyn) that they could be published only in the West.

In 1934 Grossman began writing short stories and published the povest *Glyukauf* (Glückauf), based on the life of miners in the Donbas after the Revolution. In his first novel, *Stepan Kolchugin* (parts 1–3, 1937–40; Eng. tr., *Kolchugin's Youth*, 1946), Grossman described a young, pre-Revolutionary worker's growth into a fellow fighter of the Bolsheviks. Between 1941 and 1945 Grossman was a frontline reporter for *Krasnaya zvezda*. As his first literary presentation of World War II experiences and "one of the best" (Slonim) of this period, Grossman's povest *Narod bessmerten* (1942; Eng. trs., *The People Immortal*, 1943; *No Beautiful Nights*, 1944) attracted widespread attention. *Yesli verit Pifagoreytsam* (If You Believe the Pythagoreans), a drama written before the war and published in 1946 before literary politics became more rigid, was denounced as a "harmful play" (Yermilov)

because it showed the inevitable recurrence of similar conflicts in different periods of history, a notion incompatible with historical materialism. Written in the Tolstoyan tradition, Grossman's *Za pravoye delo* (1952; For a Just Cause) is a diffuse novel with numerous characters about the battle for Stalingrad and World War II; the work had to be revised after polemical criticism from the Party (for example, M. Bubennov, in *Pravda* Feb. 13, 1953). Grossman owes his later positive classification in Russian literature to the efforts of V. Kaverin (1954) and others. During the post-Stalinist period Grossman was able to publish only short stories, in addition to the corrected version of *Za pravoye delo*, in the Soviet Union. Its sequel, titled *Zhizn i sudba* (1980; Eng. tr., *Life and Fate*, 1986), on which Grossman had worked for many years, was confiscated in 1961 because it was ideologically unacceptable; nevertheless, the work was preserved and began appearing in *Kontinent* in 1975. In it Grossman highlights the correspondences between Soviet socialism and German national socialism through the fates of individuals and through authorial reflections. After 1955 Grossman worked coextensively on the novel *Vsyo techot* (Eng. tr., *Forever Flowing*, 1972), which combines literary and essayistic elements; the novel is a deeply felt, painfully endured indictment of the Communist system, providing insight into the world of spying and denunciation, the extermination of population segments (the persecution of the kulaks), and the surrender of the individual to the power of the State. The work was confiscated in 1961 but appeared in SAMIZDAT in a version completed in 1963 and was published in Frankfurt am Main in 1970.

*Works: Gljukauf* (novel), 1934; *Stepan Kol'čugin* (novel), parts 1–3, 1937–40 (see above), parts 1–4, 1947; *Narod bessmerten* (pov.), 1942 (see above); *Stalingrad* (articles), 1943; *Gody vojny* (short stories and articles), 1945; *Esli verit' Pifagorejcam* (play), in *Znamja* 1946:7; *Za pravoe delo* (novel), in *Novyj mir* 1952:7–10, rev. ed., 1954; *Povesti, Rasskazy, Očerki* (pov. and short stories), 1958; *Staryj učitel'* (pov. and short stories), 1962; *Dobro vam!* (short stories), 1967; *Vsë tecët . . .* (novel), Frankfurt am Main, 1970 (see above); *Žizn' i sud'ba* (novel), Lausanne, 1980 (see above).

*Translations: Stalingrad Hits Back*, 1942; *The Inferno of Treblinka*, 1945; *With the Red Army in Poland and Byelorussia*, 1945; *The Years of War (1941–1945)*, 1946; *The Black Book*, ed. with Ilya Ehrenburg, 1981.

Secondary Lit.: V. Percov. in Znamja 1945:9; RSPP 1:1959; A Bočarov, 1970, and in Lit. i sovremennost' 10:1970; A. Drawicz, in his Zaproszenie do podróży, Kraków, 1974; B. Jampol'skij, in Kontinent, Paris, 8:1976; D. Šturman, in Vremja i my, Tel Aviv, 42:1979; E. Ètkind, in Vremja i my 45:1979; B. Zaks, in Kontinent 26:1980; S. Lubensky, in Slavic and East European Journal 1982:2; G. Nivat, in Russkaja mysl', Paris, Aug. 30, 1984, p. 10; S. Lipkin, in Vremja i my, Jerusalem, 83:1985, and Ann Arbor, 1986; G. Svirskij, in Grani, Frankfurt am Main, 136:1986; Ju. Kublanovskij, in Grani 141:1986.

**Gúber, Borís Andréyevich,** prose writer, critic (b. July 9 [June 26], 1903, Kamenka, prov. Kiev—d. 1937 [?], while imprisoned). Guber's father was an estate manager. Guber never finished school; in 1920 he served as a volunteer in the Civil War. He became a member of the literary organization PEREVAL in 1925. Before the critics of RAPP launched a major attack against Pereval in 1930, Guber managed to publish four books that contained realistic short stories and povesti about the Civil War, the period of NEP, and the early years of collectivization. They reveal the influence of I. Bunin. In 1931 Guber complied with the demand for documentary literature about Soviet construction and published articles with no artistic merit about a collective farm in the Kuban. In 1936 he defended the system of denunciation and the concentration camps in his short story Druzhba (Friendship). In 1937 he became a victim of the Stalinist purges because of his association with Pereval; the exact date of his death is unknown. Guber's REHABILITATION took place after 1955.

Works: Šaraškina kontora (short stories), 1926; Sosedi (short stories), 1926; Izvestnaja Šurka Šapkina (short stories), 1927; Prostaja pričina (short story), 1928; Upravdel (short story), in Novyj mir 1928:7; Èšelon opazdyvaet (short story), 1931 (in collaboration with G. Glinka); Nespjaščie (feature articles), 1931; Bab'e leto (pov.), 1935; Družba (short story), 1936; Bab'e leto (pov. and short stories), 1959.
Secondary Lit.: M. Guščin, in Zvezda 1935:6; G. Glinka, Na perevale, New York, 1954.

**Gudzénko, Semyón Petróvich,** poet (b. March 5, 1922, Kiev—d. Feb. 12, 1953, Moscow). Gudzenko studied at the Moscow Institute of Philosophy, Literature, and History from 1939 to 1941. During World War II he served as a

soldier until he was severely wounded in 1942, after which he was a frontline reporter in Rumania, Hungary, Czechoslovakia, and Germany. Gudzenko's first poems appeared in 1941 in army newspapers; I. Erenburg took notice of his first volume of poetry, Odnopolchane (1944; Fellow Soldiers). After the war Gudzenko traveled within the Soviet Union. He died as a result of his war wounds.

Gudzenko's poetry originated directly from the experience of war; it is "the echo of what has just been lived through, a shorthand record of faltering speech, a cardiogram of a racing heart, not yet calmed" (P. Antokolsky). The language of his poems is firm and terse; his presentation of war experiences is reliable and matter-of-fact, as is the horror and fear; his frequent theme is that of the young man who is matured by war and danger. Gudzenko's posthumously published Armeyskiye zapisnye knizhki (1962; Army Notebooks) makes clear this war volunteer's protest against the pseudoheroism of a writer such as V. Lebedev Kumach. His postwar works, such as Zakarpatskiye stikhi (1948; Trans-Carpathian Poems) and Poyezdka v Tuvu (1949; Journey to Tuva), reveal his predilection for narrative poetry and ballads, for N. Tikhonov and A. Tvardovsky; however, influenced by the dogmatic criticism of those years, his postwar poems are substantially weaker than his war poems, which in their turn were no longer highly regarded by the end of 1946. For all that, Gudzenko's Dalniy garnizon (1950; The Distant Garrison), a narrative poem about the daily life and training of soldiers in Turkestan, still stands above the other poetry of the period, in which "poems were frequently as didactic as resolutions and as apathetic as circulars" (P. Antokolsky).

Works: Odnopolčane (poems), 1944; Stikhi i ballady (poems), 1945; Posle marša (poems), 1947; Zakarpatskie stikhi (poems), 1948; Bitva (poems), 1948; Poezdka v Tuvu (poems), 1949; Dal'nyj garnizon (narrative poem), 1950, 1985; Novye kraja (poems), 1953; Stikhi i poèmy 1942–1952 (poems), 1956; Izbr. (poems), 1957; Stikhi (poems), 1961; Armejskie zapisnye knižki (diary), 1962; Izbr. (lyric and narrative poems), 1977.
Secondary Lit.: I. Èrenburg, in Znamja 1944:5–6; B. Runin, in Novyj mir 1947:12; P. Antokol'skij, in Lit. gazeta Aug. 30, 1956; A. Leont'ev, in Novyj mir 1962:12; L. Lazarev, foreword to Gudzenko's Izbr., 1977; S. Golovanivskij, in Lit. gazeta March 10, 1982, p. 5; RSPPo 6:1983; A. Aronov, in Lit. obozrenie 1985:5.

**Gul, Román Borísovich,** prose writer, critic (b. Aug. 1 [July 21], 1896, Penza—d. June 30, 1986, New York). Gul's father was a notary and a landowner. Gul studied law at Moscow University between 1914 and 1916; he served in the army during World War I. His participation in the Civil War in the Don region in 1917–18 with the White Army was reflected in *Ledyanoy pokhod* (1921; Campaign of Ice), a book that was also published in Moscow in 1923. In late 1918 Gul was expelled from the Ukraine and went to Berlin, where his jobs included working on the editorial staff of the pro-Soviet journal *Nakanune.* For the Moscow State Publishing House, Gul wrote a conformist view of the émigré community in German in *Zhizn na fuksa* (1927; A Life on Good Luck) and served as a correspondent for Leningrad newspapers (1927–28). In addition to literary criticism, Gul wrote his first historical novel, *General Bo* (Eng. tr., *General B. O.*, 1931; *Provocateur*, 1932), in 1929; it was followed by four more published by Berlin émigré houses. Gul was briefly detained after the Nazis came to power; in September 1933 he was allowed to emigrate to Paris, where his publications included *Oranienburg* (1937), an account of the 21 days he spent in a concentration camp. After February 1950 Gul lived in the United States, where he worked as coeditor (from 1959 on) and as editor (from 1966 on) of the journal *Novy zhurnal* in New York. From 1946 on, this journal published many of Gul's articles about contemporary Russian literature, the most important of which were collected and published under the title *Odvukon* (1973, 1982; Relay Rider).

Gul depicted the Revolution and the first few years of emigration repeatedly and with great diversity. The novel *V rasseyanii sushchiye* (1923; The Dispersed Community) handles the question of returning to post-Revolutionary Russia in a politically neutral way. The autobiographical *Zhizn na fuksa* gives the Soviet reader a negative picture of the years of emigration in Berlin. *Kon ryzhiy* (1946–48; The Chestnut-colored Steed), an autobiography covering the period from the Revolution to his arrival in Paris, mentions the murders carried out by the Cheka in Kiev and depicts deportation as a life-saving measure. The revolutionary became Gul's literary theme. As his first revolutionary, he selected the terrorist B. Savinkov as the protagonist in his noted novel *General Bo*, which in its third edition in 1959 was renamed *Azef* (Eng. tr., *Asef*, 1962), after its second major character. In 1974 Gul brought out the work, which had

been translated eight times by 1933, in a revised edition and adapted it, with V. Trivas, for the stage as *Tovarishch Ivan* (1968; Eng. tr., *Comrade Ivan*, 1969), a drama about the psychology of terrorism and provocation. In his novel *Skif* (1931; The Scythian), Gul depicts the figure of the nihilist Mikhail Bakunin against a background of the revolutionary events of 1848–49; he later revised the work under the title *Skif v Yevrope* (1958; The Scythian in Europe) and included a dedication to those who fell in the Hungarian Uprising of 1956, emphasizing the novel's reference to the present. Gul describes the October Revolution primarily through portraits of individual revolutionaries, such as Budyonny, Blyukher (Blücher), Dzerzhinsky, and in his autobiographical *Kon ryzhiy*, which briefly discusses the emigration as well. Gul describes his years as an émigré in detail in *Ya unyos Rossiyu* (1981, 1984; I Carried Russia Away with Me), the first two volumes of which had been published before Gul died. A third volume is being published in *Novy zhurnal.*

*Works: General Bo* (novel), Berlin, 1920 (see above), 3d ed. under the title *Azef*, New York, 1959 (see above), 4th ed., New York, 1974; *Ledjanoj pokhod* (documentary prose), Berlin, 1921, 2d ed., Moscow, 1923; *V rassejanii suščie* (pov.), Berlin, 1923; *Žizn' na fuksa* (novel), 1927; *Skif* (novel), 2 vols., Berlin, 1931, 2d ed. under the title *Skif v Evrope*, New York, 1958, 3d ed. under the title *Bakunin*, New York, 1974; *Krasnye maršaly*, Berlin, 1933; *Dzeržinskij* (novel), Paris, 1936, 2d ed., 1974; *Oranienburg* (articles), Paris, 1937; *Tovarišč Ivan* (play), in *Novyj žurnal*, New York, 92:1968 (see above); *Odvukon'* (literary criticism), New York, 1973; *Kon' ryžij* (autobiography), New York, 1952, 2d ed., New York, 1975; *A. Solženicyn v SSSR i na Zapade* (essay), in *Novyj žurnal* 120:1975; *Ja unës Rossiju: Apologija emigracii* (projected trilogy): vol. 1, *Rossija v Germanii*, New York, 1981; vol. 2, *Rossija v Francii*, New York, 1984; vol 3, *Rossija v Amerike*, in *Novyj žurnal* 158–61:1985. *Odvukon' dva* (articles), New York, 1982.

*Secondary Lit.:* G. Ivanov, in *Novyj žurnal* 34:1953; D. Anin, in *Novyj žurnal* 52:1958; N. Ul'janov, in *Novyj žurnal* 95:1969; B. Narcissov, in *Novyj žurnal* 113:1973; Ja. Gorbov, in *Vozroždenie*, Paris, 243:1974; L. Rževskij, in *Novyj žurnal* 119:1975; V. Vejdle, in *Novyj žurnal* 119:1975; N. Andreev, in *Russkaya mysl'*, Paris, Oct. 15, 1981, p. 11; Ju. Troll', in *Novyj žurnal* 146:1982 and 148:1982; B. Filippov, in *Novyj žurnal* 162:1986.

Gulag and literature. GULag (Glávnoye upravléniye lageréy [Central Administration of the Camps]) has become an internationally known term for the Soviet forced labor camps, prison camps, and places of exile through A. Solzhenitsyn's book Arkhipelag GULag (1973–75; Eng. tr., The Gulag Archipelago, 3 vols., 1974–78). The gulag came into being at the beginning of the 1930s when the Soviet concentration camps were relabeled "work improvement camps." Since an artist's truly creative work is individual and gives expression to his unique feelings and experiences, an unavoidable tension arises between the totalitarian state, which claims the right to organize intellectual life in a uniform fashion, and serious, inspired writers. The Bolshevik, later Soviet, government has, from the beginning, been prepared to ensure its control with force when necessary (for other methods, see PARTY RESOLUTIONS ON LITERATURE). Thus, a large number of well-known authors have spent time in the gulag; many have died there from malnutrition, mistreatment, lack of medical attention, and other causes. Among those Russian writers (that is, not including those from the Baltic states, the Caucasus, etc.) who have been executed or have died in the gulag are A. Arosev, I. Babel, G. Belykh, S. Budantsev, A. Chayanov, A. Gastev, M. Gerasimov, B. Guber, N. Gumilyov, I. Kasatkin, I. Katayev, D. Kharms, V. Kin, V. Kirillov, V. Kirshon, S. Klychkov, N. Klyuyev, V. Knyazev, S. Kolbasyev, M. Koltsov, B. Kornilov, M. Loskutov, I. Makarov, O. Mandelshtam, V. Narbut, G. Nikiforov, N. Oleynikov, P. Oreshin, B. Pilnyak, V. Pravdukhin, V. Ropshin, A. Tarasov-Rodionov, S. Tretyakov, P. Vasilyev, A. Vesyoly, A. Voronsky, A. Vvedensky, B. Yasensky, N. Zarudin, and V. Zazubrin. The number of writers who have lived through a period of detention in a gulag is also large. The following writers (some of whom are still being detained) belong to this group: A. Afinogenov, A. Aldan-Semyonov, Yu. Aleshkovsky, A. Amalrik, N. Arzhak, A. Belinkov, O. Berggolts, N. Bogdanov, L. Borodin, I. Brodsky, Yu. Dombrovsky, I. Dvoretsky, N. Erdman, B. Filippov, S. Gekht, Ye. Ginzburg, N. Gorbanevskaya, F. Kandel, L. Konson, L. Kopelev, N. Korzhavin, S. Maksimov, V. Maksimov, D. Markish, M. Naritsa, N. Narokov, G. Obolduyev, L. Panteleyev, I. Ratushinskaya, B. Ruchyov, G. Serebryakova, V. Shalamov, B. Shiryayev, P. Slyotov, A. Solzhenitsyn, V. Syomin, V. Tarsis, A. Terts, Ya. Volchek, V. Yurasov, N. Zabolotsky, and A. Zhigulin. These lists do not include directors such as V. Meyerhold; literary scholars such as M. Bakhtin, Yu. Oksman, or F. Shiller; translators such as K. Bogatyryov; or family members of those exiled such as O. Mandelshtam's wife, Nadezhda; Ye. Ginzburg's son, V. Aksyonov, who spent part of his childhood in the gulag region of Magadan; M. Tsvetayeva's daughter, A. Efron; N. Gumilyov's and A. Akhmatova's son, Lev Gumilyov; B. Pasternak's girl friend O. Ivinskaya. And this list includes only a few, those connected with literature in some way. During the early days of the gulag, some authors celebrated the gulag system. In doing so, they followed the lead of M. Gorky, who, together with 35 other authors, wrote an apology for forced labor (Belomorsko-Baltiysky kanal im. Stalina, Moscow, 1934). Although this book was banned in 1937 owing to the participation of the head of the GPU, Genrikh Yagoda, works by G. Belykh/L. Panteleyev, A. Makarenko, and N. Pogodin retained semiofficial acclaim. As a result of the second wave of EMIGRATION, some authors who had survived their stay in the gulag were able to depict its horror in their writing. B. Shiryayev reported on the first large-scale Leninist camp on the monastery island of Solovki. N. Narokov explored the psychology of the Chekists. The works of V. Yurasov and S. Maksimov describe arrests, trials, and the reality of the gulag. During the THAW after Stalin's death, as the Party acknowledged the injustices of the mass terror, numerous works concerning the gulag appeared in censored Soviet literature. At the top stands A. Solzhenitsyn's Odin den Ivana Denisovicha (1962; Eng. tr., One Day in the Life of Ivan Denisovich, 1963, rev. tr., 1971); worthy of note also are V. Kaverin's novels and V. Rozov's plays. However, most of the works on this topic were distributed through SAMIZDAT at home and TAMIZDAT abroad, as were Solzhenitsyn's later works. Among the most artistically and informationally significant works of this type are those by A. Akhmatova (on a mother's suffering), Yuz Aleshkovsky (on the creation of guilt), A. Amalrik (on the desolation of exile), L. Chukovskaya (on the process of recognizing betrayal), Yu. Dombrovsky (on the abandonment of the intelligentsia), A. Efron (letters to Pasternak from exile), V. Grossman (on the gulag in comparison to German concentration camps), F. Kandel and L. Konson (impressionistic scenes of life in the camps), L. Kopelev (on the special camps), V. Maksimov (on the disillusionment of the workers), V. Shalamov (on daily life in the gulag), A. Terts and G. Vladimov (on the training of the guards).

In Soviet, that is to say, censored, literature from the 1970s on, passages concerning the horrors of the gulags of the Stalinist period appear only rarely and usually in the works of very well known authors (for example Ch. Aytmatov and Yu. Trifonov); the current reality of the camps from Khrushchev to Gorbachev is not discussed. The immeasurable suffering that has been and continues to be inflicted on people in the gulag under the Bolshevik/Communist system has been recorded in literature as a horrible experience. But these works also document the preservation of compassion in adversity and suffering, of ethical growth in affliction, and of the strength that the humiliated and dishonored found in their faith.

*Secondary Lit.*: M. Geller, *Koncentracionnyj mir i sovetskaja literatura*, London, 1974; A. Solženicyn, *Arkhipelag GULag*, 3 vols., Paris, 1973–77 (see above); J. Rossi, *Spravočnik po Gulagu*, London, 1987.

**Gumilyóv, Nikoláy Stepánovich,** poet (b. April 15 [April 3], 1886, Kronstadt—d. Aug. 24, 1921, Petrograd). Gumilyov's father was a navy doctor. Gumilyov began publishing in 1902. From 1907 to 1914 he studied philology in Paris and St. Petersburg; at the same time he traveled extensively abroad, visiting Italy, the Near East, and Africa. He was married to Anna Akhmatova from 1910 to 1918; Akhmatova, Gumilyov, and Osip Mandelshtam belonged to the ACMEIST literary group, which they founded together in 1911. Between 1914 and 1917 Gumilyov was at the front as a volunteer (he received the Cross of St. George), then served on the staff of the Russian Expeditionary Corps in Paris. Early in 1918 he returned to Russia through London and Murmansk. In Petrograd, M. Gorky included him on the editorial board of the publishing house Vsemirnaya literatura. Gumilyov lectured at various institutions, including PROLETKULT, Dom iskusstv (The House of the Arts), and Institut Zhivogo Slova (Institute of the Living Word). In Russia in 1918 Gumilyov published his sixth volume of verse, an "African Poem," and poetry translated from the Chinese; in the following year he published his translation of the Gilgamesh epic. An attempt by Gumilyov, N. Otsup, G. Ivanov, and G. Adamovich to revive the acmeist "TSEKH POETOV" (Guild of Poets) as a literary association of writers unaffiliated with the Party was unsuccessful. Gumilyov, who made no secret of his negative attitude toward the Bolshevik system, was arrested on Aug. 3, 1921; he and 60 other persons were accused of counterrevolutionary activity and shot on Aug. 24. A few volumes of his poetry continued to appear through 1923; in 1938 his name was deleted from literature. Since the early 1960s Gumilyov has been mentioned occasionally in the USSR; a comprehensive entry (written by A. D. Sinyavsky) about him appears in the *Kratkaya literaturnaya entsiklopediya* (1964). Not a single volume of his poems was published in the Soviet Union from 1923 to 1986. In 1986 he was literarily rehabilitated (see *Ogonyok* 1986:17 and 36). For 1987 an edition of his poems was planned.

As a consequence of his execution in 1921, the bulk of Gumilyov's literary career lay before the Revolution; it was of an essentially lyrical nature. The early volume *Zhemchuga* (1910; Pearls) embraces a wide range of themes from American exoticism and classical mythology to European Christian experience. Later volumes, such as *Kostyor* (1918; The Bonfire), *Shatyor* (1921; The Tent), and *Ognenny stolp* (1921; Pillar of Fire), indicate a turn toward spiritual problems such as death, reincarnation, and the interpenetration of the earthly and the transcendental. Gumilyov also wrote six dramas "of a romantic-escapist character" (Segel) and prose; he achieved the position of the most significant theoretician of acmeism and was known as a literary critic. His exuberant personality and his distant journeys find their reflection in various spheres of his work: in the world-embracing subject matter of his West European–influenced verse, geographically and temporally speaking; in the combination of legendary, religious, neoromantic, and dispassionately realistic elements (above all, in *Zapiski kavalerista* [1915–16; Notes of a Cavalryman]); and in his myth of the strong man. In the protests of the acmeists against excesses of the symbolists, Gumilyov seeks clarity and strength in poetry, but nevertheless remains close to the symbolists in many ways. His notion of poetry as craft is expressed by the great importance he attached to verse technique. His verse "is saturated, at times oversaturated, with colors, images, and sounds" (N. Otsup).

*Works: Put' konkvistadorov* (poems), 1905; *Romantičeskie cvety* (poems), 1908; *Žemčuga* (poems), 1910; *Čužoe nebo* (poems), 1912; *Kolčan* (poems), 1916; *Kostër* (poems), 1918 (reprinted, Ann Arbor, 1979); *Farforovyj pavil'on, Kitajskie stikhi* (poems), 1918; *Mik. Afrikanskaja poema* (poem), 1918; *Šatër* (poems), 1921; *Ognennyj stolp* (poems), 1921 (reprinted, Letchworth, 1978); *Stikhotvorenija* (poems), 1923; *Izbr.*, Paris, 1959; *Neizdannye stikhi i pis'ma* (poems and letters), Paris, 1980; *Otravlennaja tunika* (play), in *Sovremennaja dramaturgija* 1986:3; *Neizdannoe i nesobrannoe*, Paris, 1986; *Stikhi* (poems), in *Ogonëk* 1986:17, in *Lit. Rossija* April 11, 1986, and in *Znamja* 1986:10.—*Sobr. soč.*, 4 vols., Washington, 1962–68.

Translations: *The Abinger Garland: Poems Translated from the Russian by Yakov Hornstein*, 1945; *Selected Works of Nikolai S. Gumilev*, 1972; *On Russian Poetry*, 1977.

Secondary Lit.: N. Minskij, in *Novaja russkaja kniga* 1922:1; S. Makovskij, in *Grani*, Frankfurt am Main, 36:1957; N. Ocup, in *Gumilëv's Izbr.*, 1959; G. Struve, V. Sečkarëv, V. Vejdle, in *Gumilëv's Sobr. soč.*, Washington, 1962–68; M. Maline, Brussels, 1964; V. Orlov, in *Voprosy lit.* 1966:10; V. Zavališin, in *Novyj žurnal*, New York, 94:1969; E. Sampson, in *Russian Literature Triquarterly* 1:1971 (bibliography) and Boston, 1978; N. E. Rusinko, Diss., Brown Univ., 1976; G. Cheron, in *Wiener Slawistischer Almanach* 9:1982; *Gumilëvskie čtenija*, Vienna, 1984; Ju. Kuznecov, V. Bondarenko, in *Sovremennaja dramaturgija* 1986:3; A. Pavlovskij, in *Voprosy lit.* 1986:10.

**Gúsev, Víktor Mikháylovich**, poet, playwright (b. Jan. 30 [Jan. 17], 1909, Moscow— d. Jan. 23, 1944, Moscow). Gusev attended acting school in 1925–26; from 1926 to 1929 he was enrolled in the State Higher Courses in Literature; he attended Moscow University until 1931. Gusev began publishing his poetry in *Pravda* in 1933; in 1935 he turned to writing drama. He received Stalin Prizes for his screenplays (for 1941, 2d class; for 1943–44, 1st class). During World War II, Gusev headed the literary section of the Union Radio Committee.

Gusev's poetry is political and patriotic. The artificial form of his early verse developed into a fashionable style that was based on the emotions aroused by nationalism and that utilized the elements of folk poetry. His poetry was inspired by journeys made with writers' brigades to industrial construction sites in the Urals (1931) and to Turkmenistan and Uzbekistan (1932–33). Gusev responded to political, economic, and military events of the day with "rough, swiftly drawn lines" (Gorky). His song lyrics (he wrote about a hundred) made him popular; the Red Army Chorus made his "cavalry song of the steppes," "Polyushko-pole" (1934; O Field, Little Field), world-famous. His drama *Slava* (1936; Glory), written in verse that approximates colloquial speech, was frequently performed. In his lyrical comedy *Vesna v Moskve* (1941; Spring in Moscow), he sets his exposition of the theme "criticism and self-criticism" in a scientific milieu. In *Synovya tryokh rek* (1944; Sons of Three Rivers), Gusev even brings the rivers Volga, Seine, and Elbe onstage as symbolic characters that function as the embodiment of the three nations.

Works: *Pokhod veščej* (poems), 1929; *Slava* (play), 1936; *Vesna v Moskve* (comedy), 1941; *Svinarka i pastukh* (film script), 1941; *V šest' časov večera posle vojny* (film script), 1944; *Synov'ja trëkh rek* (play), 1944; *Izbr.* 1948; *Soč.*, 2 vols., 1955; *Stikhi* (poems), 1957; *P'esy* (plays), 1959.

Secondary Lit.: M. Zenkevič, in *Novyj mir* 1930:2, pp. 231–32; N. Krjukov, in *Gusev's Soč.*, 1955; A. Tarasenkov, in his *Stat'i o lit.*, vol. 1, 1958; K. Finn, in *Lit. Rossija* Jan. 31, 1969, p. 9; *RSPPo* 6:1983.

# H

**Hippius, Zinaida Nikolayevna.** See GIPPIUS, ZINAIDA NIKOLAYEVNA.

# I

**Ibragimbékov** (proper pronunciation: Ibrahimbekov), **Maksúd** (pseud. of Maksud Mamed Ibragim ogly), prose writer and playwright. Ibragimbekov is an Azerbaijani who writes in Russian (b. May 11, 1935, Baku). In 1959 in Baku, Ibragimbekov completed a technical course of study and worked for several years as a civil engineer. Then he began to study at the Institute for Scriptwriters and Directors in Moscow and wrote several film scripts, such as *Glavnoye intervyu* (1970; The Main Interview), that were also filmed. His first prose work appeared in Baku in 1960. With *Fistashkovoye derevo* (1965; The Pistachio Tree), a story first published in *Yunost*, Ibragimbekov gradually became known as a writer in the Soviet Union. Further stories followed in *Yunost* and in *Literaturny Azerbaydzhan*. He collected some of them in *Nemnogo vesennego prazdnika* (1973; A Little Spring Holiday). The povest already published in *Novy mir*, *I ne bylo luchshe brata* (1973; Eng. tr., *There Was Never a Better Brother*, 1982), attracted great attention in this collection. The second Moscow collection, *Neznakomaya pesnya* (1974; The Unknown Song), followed. In 1969 Ibragimbekov and his brother Rustam wrote a drama that was performed in Moscow, *Kto priydyot v polnoch* (He Who Comes at Midnight); an independently written play, *Mezozoyskaya istoriya* (1974; Tales from the Mesozoic), which takes place partly at a floating petroleum drilling station, received the first prize in a competition for works about the working class. He lives in Baku and has worked since 1967 for the state television and radio broadcasting stations.

Ibragimbekov has considerable writing talent. In a restrained narrative style, he exposes his characters to unusual and commonplace events and penetrates deeply into the realm of the soul. *I ne bylo luchshe brata* unites Oriental ethical norms—which can also have the ability to destroy through the traditional power of personal ties (here brotherly love)— with general human uncertainties. The realistic narrative style that expresses joy in primal physical events (love, fights, death) is emphasized through a circumspect symbolism. *Za vsyo khorosheye—smert* (1974; For All Goodness—Death) incorporates a tense plot set in the present—the mortal danger of four youths trapped in a cave—with flashbacks to a personal and political past, and in a similarly forceful way reveals Ibragimbekov's ability to create a psychologically absorbing, lively, and mutable, yet guarded, exposition.

*Works: Katastrofa* (short stories), 1963; *Fistaškovoe derevo* (short stories), 1965; *Glavnoe interv'ju* (film script), in *Lit. Azerbajdžan* 1970:5; *I ne bylo lučše brata* (pov.), in *Novyj mir* 1973:10 (see above), later under the title *Ssora: Nemnogo vesennego prazdnika* (pov. and short stories), 1973; *Mezozojskaja istorija* (play), in *Lit. Azerbajdžan* 1974:10; *Neznakomaja pesnja* (pov.), 1974; *Pust' on ostanetsja s nami* (pov.), 1976 (Eng. tr., "Let Him Stay with Us," in *Soviet Literature* 1979:6); *Za vsë khorošee—smert'* (pov.), 1978; *V odin prekrasnyj den'* (short stories and pov.), 1980; *interview*, in *Lit. gazeta* Feb. 2, 1983, p. 6; *Istorija s blagopolučnym koncom* (pov. and play), 1983; *Neskol'ko pričin dlja razvoda* (pov.), 1985.

*Secondary Lit.:* N. Ignat'eva, in *Iskusstvo kino* 1972:2; A. Marčenko, in *Lit. gazeta* Dec. 26, 1973, p. 5 and in *Voprosy lit.* 1974:8; V. Oskockij, in *Lit. obozrenie* 1974:8; Vl. Solov'ëv, in *Avrora* 1975:12; W. Kasack, in *Slavistische Studien zum VIII. Intern. Slavistenkongress*, Cologne, 1978.

**Ilf, Ilyá** (pseud. of Ilyá Arnóldovich Faynsílberg), prose writer who wrote his principal works in collaboration with Yevgeny Petrov (b. Oct. 15 [Oct. 3], 1897, Odessa—d. April 13, 1937, Moscow). Ilf's father was a bank clerk. In 1913 Ilf completed technical school in Odessa, where he worked as a draftsman, telephone operator, and factory laborer, among other tasks, and finally as a journalist (for YugROSTA, the journal *Moryak*, and the journal *Sindetikon*). In 1923 he moved to Moscow; there he was on the editorial staff of *Gudok*; he published short satirical prose, articles, and film reviews in various journals. In 1925 Ilf journeyed to Central Asia. He began his literary collaboration with Petrov in 1927 on the initiative of Valentin Katayev, Petrov's brother. In addition to short prose, published in *Literaturnaya gazeta*, *Pravda*, and other papers, the two also collaborated on the novels *Dvenadtsat stulyev* (1928; Eng. trs., *Diamonds to Sit On*, 1930; *The Twelve Chairs*, 1961) and *Zolotoy telyonok* (1931; Eng. trs., *The Little Golden Calf*, 1932; *The*

# 145 ILYÍN

*Golden Calf*, 1962, 1964), which became famous as humorous satires of the NEP period. In the winter of 1933–34 they traveled in Europe; in 1935–36 they undertook a six-month automobile tour across the United States. These trips abroad were reflected in their publicistic works, which were supplemented by Ilf's subsequently published notebooks. Ilf died of tuberculosis in 1937.

*Dvenadtsat stulyev* is a satirical picaresque novel; its conventional plot (inspired by V. Katayev)—the search for a treasure hidden in one of twelve chairs scattered over Russia—"is only the external motivation for a portrait of the customs and the age, in which Soviet life during the NEP period appears in all its bewildering contradiction" (Holthusen). The novel is consciously placed in the tradition of N. Gogol's *Dead Souls* and has a similar epic structure of accumulated incidents, with each episode being largely independent. The central character, Ostap Bender, is killed off in the conclusion (after the authors drew lots to decide his fate), but is resurrected for the next novel, *Zolotoy telyonok* which, in its more elementally structured plot about a clandestine millionaire in the Soviet Union, continues the seemingly endless number of observations on which the satiric picture of the period is built. Soon after Ilf's death, the satiric works were handled by the critics with great restraint and disparaged as a "distortion of reality" for some 15 years. After 1956 they were again printed several times.

*Works:* (with Petrov): *Dvenadcat' stul'ev* (novel), 1928, 6th ed., 1934 (see above); *Odnaždy letom* (film script), in *Krasnaja nov'* 1932:8; *Zolotoj telënok* (novel), 1933 (see above); *Kak sozdavalsja Robinzon* (short stories), 1933 (reprinted, Letchworth, 1968); *Odnoètažnaja Amerika* (articles), 1937 (Eng. tr., *Little Golden America*, 1937); *Fel'etony i rasskazy* (short stories), 1957; *Ostorožno, ovejano vekami!* (publicistic prose), 1963.—*Sobr. soč.*, 4 vols., 1938–39; 5 vols., 1961. *Il'f's Works: Zapisnye knižki* (diaries), 1939, 2d enl. ed., 1957; *Rannie očerki i fel'etony: Pis'ma iz Ameriki* (sketches, satirical commentaries, letters), 1961; *Amerikanskij dnevnik 1935–1936*, in *Lit. nasledstvo* 74:1965.

*Secondary Lit.:* V. Šklovskij, in *Lit. gazeta* Jan. 5, 1933; B. Gorbatov, in *Novyj mir* 1949:10; A. Vulis, 1960; B. Galanov, 1961; *Vospominanija ob I. I. i E. P.*, 1963; *RSPP* 2:1964; D. Nikolaev, in *Voprosy lit.* 1964:1; L. M. Janovskaja, 2d ed., 1969; K. Reitermajer, Diss., Vienna, 1971; U. M. Zehrer, Giessen, 1975; D. Moldavskij, in his *Tovarišč smekh*, 1981.

**Ilyénkov, Vasíly Pávlovich,** prose writer (b. March 24 [March 12], 1897, Shilovo-Uspenskoye, prov. Smolensk—d. Jan. 15, 1967, Moscow). Ilyenkov's father was a priest. Ilyenkov completed four years of study at the Theological Academy in Smolensk; from 1915 to 1917 he was a student in the Department of History and Philology at Yuryev University (he did not graduate). In 1917 Ilyenkov served as a soldier; in 1918 he was admitted to the Communist Party, then worked as a Party official. He moved to Moscow in 1930. He was organizational secretary for RAPP until 1932. Ilyenkov began publishing in 1929; his work consists of short stories and three novels.

Ilyenkov's first two novels responded to the Party's appeal for literature depicting socialist construction in its beginning stages. His novel *Vedushchaya os* (1932; Eng. tr., *Driving Axle*, 1933) was at the center of an intense polemic; *Solnechny gorod* (1935; City of the Sun) presents the theme of the transformation of the USSR from an agrarian to an industrial state, using the Kursk Ironworks as a case in point. Written in accordance with the THEORY OF CONFLICTLESSNESS, Ilyenkov's *Bolshaya doroga* (1949; The Highway) presents the obligatory problem between the good and the better by using "a collective farm worth millions" in 1941 as an example (Stalin Prize for 1949, 3d class). The novel's conclusion, which seemed pessimistic in light of Ilyenkov's description of the German invasion, had to be rewritten for the book edition. After the 20th Party Congress, Ilyenkov's short stories were reprinted and praised for their rejection of artificial plots and strained effects and for their fine descriptions of the countryside and their well-developed dialogue.

*Works: Konskij cekh* (short stories), 1931; *Veduščaja os'* (novel), 1932 (see above); *Solnečnyj gorod* (novel), 1935; *Ličnost'* (short stories), 1938; *Bol'šaja doroga* (novel), 1949; *Rasskazy* (short stories), 1955; *Mirskoe serdce* (short stories), 1964.

*Secondary Lit.:* M. Šaginjan, in *Novyj mir* 1939:6; A. Čakovskij, in *Novyj mir* 1950:2; M. Čarnyj, in *Novyj mir* 1956:11 and in *Lit. Rossija* March 24, 1972, pp. 11–12; *RSPP* 2:1964.

**Ilyín, Mikhaíl** (pseud. of Ilyá Yákovlevich Marshák), prose writer (b. Jan. 10, 1896 [Dec. 29, 1895], Bakhmut—d. Nov. 15, 1953, Moscow). Ilyin was the brother of S. Ya. Marshak. In 1925 he completed engineering school in Leningrad; he worked as an engineer until

1929. Ilyin began his literary career in 1924 as a contributor to various children's magazines.

Ilyin's literary work served to popularize scientific and technological phenomena, both historical and modern, as well as objects used in everyday life. Originally intended for children, his work was by no means limited only to this circle of readers. His book *Kotory chas?* (1927; What Time Is It?) tells the story of the measurement of time; *Chornym po belomu* (1928; Black on White) is about the development of the art of writing. Ilyin's style is easy to understand and abounds in rhetorical questions, paradoxes, and metaphors: old cars become grandmothers, "monsters with samovar spouts and little legs," and machine tools have many more hands than a human being. His *Rasskaz o velikom plane* (1930; The Story of a Great Plan) was a much-translated work popularizing the first Five-Year Plan; it radiates the optimistic drive to conquer nature and the belief in happiness made possible by technology. Ilyin's history of mankind from the Paleolithic period to the Middle Ages, *Kak chelovek stal velikanom* (Eng. tr., in three vols.: *How Man Became a Giant* 1942; *Giant at the Crossroads*, 1948; and *The Giant Widens His World*, 1949), written in collaboration with his wife, E. Segal, between 1940 and 1946, is the story of glorious and continuous forward progress, guided by man alone.

*Works: Solnce na stole* (short story), 1927; *Kotoryj čas?* (short story), 1927; *Černym po belomu* (short story), 1928; *Sto tysjač počemu* (short story), 1929; *Rasskaz o velikom plane* (short story), 1930; *Rasskazy o veščakh* (short stories), 1936; *Kak čelovek stal velikanom*, 1946 (in collaboration with E. Segal) (see above); *Putešestvie v atom*, 1948.—*Izbr. proizv.* 3 vols., 1962.
*Secondary Lit.*: B. Ljapunov, 1955; A. Ivič, 1956; S. Maršak, in *Voprosy lit.* 1961:9 and in Il'in's *Izbr. proizv.*, 1962; I. Solov'ëva and V. Šitova, in *Novyj mir* 1962:11.

**Imagism** *(Imazhinízm)*, a form-conscious movement in literature dating from the beginning of the 1920s. Imagism placed imagery at the center of its poetics. In Moscow the group of imagists came together at the end of 1918 under the leadership of the ego-futurist V. Shershenevich (see FUTURISM). The most important exponent of imagism was S. Yesenin, but the group included N. Erdman, I. Gruzinov, R. Ivnev, A. Kusikov, A. Mariyengof, and M. Royzman. One of the imagists' first declarations was published in the newspaper *So-*

*vetskaya strana* on Feb. 10, 1919. In 1920 anthologies such as *Plavilnya slov* (Foundry of Words) appeared. The imagist poets published numerous volumes of poetry in a kind of illegal self-publishing house called Imazhinisty. Between 1922 and 1924 four issues of their own newspaper *Gostinitsa dlya puteshestvuyushchikh v prekrasnom* (The Inn for Travelers in the Beautiful) appeared. The imagists continued the discussion concerning the regeneration of the form poetry should take that the symbolists had begun, with somewhat different accents than those adopted by the futurists. They were opposed to ideology in art, a position attributable in part to their disillusionment with their own idealistic conceptions of the Revolution. Shershenevich, who spoke of the image itself as the sole aim of poetry *(obraz kak samotsel)*, gave his poems titles that reveal the rational intent, for example, "Catalogue of Images" *(Katalog obrazov)* or "Lyrical Construction" *(Liricheskaya konstruktsiya)*. In the forefront stood their demand that comparisons and metaphors be new, original, and concrete. The tendency to shock, which was achieved through the use of coarse, crude, and obscene images, found its parallel in their dissolute, antibourgeois, bohemian life-style. Political developments, which gave preference to unlyrical, publicistic verses and regarded shortlived propaganda rhymes as poetry, prevented the imagists from further pursuing their goal: the deeper penetration into the poet's stock of images and words, into the expression of the essential in the poetic image. In 1924 the group fell apart; in 1927 it was disbanded. Looking back on the imagists in 1928, V. Shershenevich called A. Mariyengof's *Buyan-ostrov* (1920; The Island Buyan), S. Yesenin's *Klyuchi Marii* (1919; The Sources of Mary), and his own *Dvazhdy dva pyat* (1920; $2 \times 2 = 5$) the imagists' most important contributions to the analysis of the word and the image.

*Secondary Lit.*: S. Esenin, *Ključi Marii* (essays), 1920 (also in *Lit. manifesty*, see below); A. Mariengof, *Bujan-ostrov: Imažinizm* (essays), 1920; V. Šeršenevič, $2 \times 2 = 5$: *Listy imažinista* (essavs). 1920; V. Šeršenevič, *Komu ja žmu ruku* (essays), 1921; V. Šeršenevič, *Suščestvujut li imažinisty* (essays), in *Čitatel' i pisatel'* 1928:3 and in *Lit. manifesty* (see below); I. Gruzinov, *Imažinizma osnovnoe* (essays), 1921; R. Ivnev, *Četyre vystrela v Esenina, Kusikova, Mariyengofa, Šeršeneviča* (essays), 1921; V. L'vov-Rogačevskij, *Imažinizm i ego obraznost'*, 1921; I. Sokolov, *Imažinistika*, 1921; *Lit. manifesty*, 2d ed., 1929 (reprinted, Munich, 1969); N. Å. Nilsson, *The*

Russian Imaginists, Stockholm, 1970; V. Markov, Russian Imagism 1919–1924, 2 vols., Giessen, 1980 (with texts).

Ínber, Véra Mikháylovna, poet (b. July 10 [June 28], 1890, Odessa—d. Nov. 11, 1972, Leningrad). Inber's father was the owner of a scientific publishing house. She studied in Odessa. From 1910 to 1914 she was in Paris, where she published her first volume of verse, Pechalnoye vino (1914; Sad Wine), at her own expense. She experienced the Revolution in Moscow, the Civil War years in Odessa. In 1922 she moved to Moscow, where she later joined the Literary Center of the Constructivists. In her attempt to conform to the ruling ideology, Inber also worked as a journalist; she lived in Paris, Brussels, and Berlin as a correspondent from 1924 to 1926; she turned more to writing prose, attracting attention at home and abroad by her ironically distanced point of view. In 1938 she wrote her first narrative poem, Putevoy dnevnik (Travel Diary), a travel feature about Georgia consisting of 984 verses. With her husband, a doctor, she went to Leningrad at the start of World War II and there lived through the blockade. Inber received a Stalin Prize (for 1945, 2d class) for her narrative poem Pulkovsky meridian (1942; The Pulkovo Meridian) and her prose work Pochti tri goda: Leningradsky dnevnik (1946; Eng. tr., Leningrad Diary, 1971). Inber, who was admitted to the Communist Party in 1943, was from this time on an officially recognized writer. After the war she returned to the subject of socialist construction. In 1960 she published Aprel (April), along with poems about Lenin written after 1954. Inber lived in Moscow.

In her early poems, Inber began by "imitating Anna Akhmatova but lacking Akhmatova's sincerity and depth" (Struve). The constructivist striving for conciseness and concentration (see CONSTRUCTIVISM) is apparent in her work only in its simplicity of syntax and content. "Synu, kotorogo net" (1927; To the Son Who Does Not Exist), the title poem of a volume of verse, remains an imperfect paraphrase of M. Lermontov's "Cossack's Cradle Song." Her unpretentiously rhymed verse is determined by reason, not by emotion; also, in poems about Pushkin, Stalin, and Lenin, it has a narrative character. Uniformity, length, and a low level of originality characterize those of Inber's narrative poems devoted to topical themes.

Works: Pečal'noe vino (poems), 1914; Synu, kotorogo net (poems), 1927; Mesto pod solncem (novel), 1928; Putevoj dnevnik (narrative poem), 1938; Pulkovskij meridian (narrative poem), 1942; Počti tri goda (diary and essay), 1946 (see above); Aprel' (poems), 1960; Za mnogo let (essays and memoirs), 1964.—Izbr. proizv., 3 vols., 1958; Sobr. soč., 4 vols., 1965–66; Izbr. proza, 1971.

Secondary Lit.: E. F. Usievič, in Znamja 1945:12; A. Tarasenkov, in Izbr. proizv., 1954; I. Grinberg, in Znamja 1960:9 and 1961; G. Kondrašov, in Zvezda 1965:1; Večnaja molodost' serdca, in Znamja 1980:7.

Isakóvsky, Mikhaíl Vasílyevich, poet (b. Jan. 19 [Jan. 7], 1900, Glotovka, Elnya district, prov. Smolensk—d. July 20, 1973, Moscow). Isakovsky was of peasant descent. He became a member of the Communist Party in 1918; from 1921 to 1931 he worked as a journalist in Smolensk. Isakovsky considered 1924 to mark the start of his literary career, irrespective of earlier attempts to write poetry. His first important volume of verse, Provoda v solome (1927; Electric Wires in the Thatch), had a mixed reception. Soon after he moved to Moscow (1931), however, Isakovsky asserted himself as one of the best-established poets of the collectivized village, a poet who reached a wide audience primarily with his popular songs and to whom literary criticism and literary scholarship devoted a good deal of space. Isakovsky received a Stalin Prize (for 1942, 1st class) for the song lyrics of "I kto yego znayet" (1938; Who Really Knows?), "Katyusha" (1938), "Shol so sluzhby pogranichnik" (1939; The Borderguard Came from His Post), and others. During World War II he wrote many soldiers' songs (Stalin Prize for 1948, 1st class). Isakovsky composed only a few new poems after 1953. In 1954 he became a member of the board of the Writers Union of the USSR and was on the presidia of all congresses of the Writers Union from then on.

The number of poems written by Isakovsky is not great; the basic body of poems is repeated in the most frequent editions. Isakovsky's poems are mostly narrative in form and have much in common with the poetics of folk songs. Thematically speaking, this is particularly true of his love poems, which use the traditional motifs of meeting at the well, separation, and hope; formally speaking, the description is applicable to nearly his entire output. Isakovsky contrasts the poverty of the earlier period with the happiness of the present; it is not the problems of life that resound in his songs but faith in goodness, touched at most by a light pain. A. Tvardovsky attests: "He is sincere and true when he welcomes in happy song what was new in the Soviet village at its very beginnings." Toward the end of his life Isakovsky completed a lengthy autobiographical memoir, *Na Yelninskoy zemle* (1973; In the Elnya Region).

*Works: Provoda v solome* (poems), 1927; *Stikhi i pesni* (poems), 1949, 1966; *Stikhotvorenija* (poems), 1965; *O poetakh, o stikhakh, o pesnjakh* (literary criticism), 1968, 2d ed., 1972; *Na El'ninskoj zemle: Avtobiografičeskie stranicy* (memoirs), 1972; *Iz perepiski dvukh poetov: A. T. Tvardovskij—M. V. Isakovskij* (letters), in *Družba narodov* 1976:7–9; *Dva goda v Čistopole* (letters), in *Voprosy lit.* 1982:5.—*Soč.*, 2 vols., 1956; 2 vols., 1959; 2 vols., 1961; *Sobr. soč.*, 4 vols., 1968–69.

*Secondary Lit.:* A. Tvardovskij, in *Lit. gazeta* July 5, 1938, in *Novyj mir* 1967:8, and separate study, 1969; V. Aleksandrov, 1950; E. Litvin, in *Zvezda* 1955:3; A. Urban, in *Družba narodov* 1972:10; E. Osetrov, in *Oktjabr'* 1975:1 and in *Naš sovremennik* 1980:1; N. Kotovčikhina, in *Russkaja lit.* 1985:4.

**Isáyev, Yegór** (orig. Geórgy) **Aleksándrovich**, poet (b. May 2, 1926, Korshevo, oblast Voronezh). Isayev's father was a village schoolteacher. Isayev entered the army at the end of World War II; he subsequently served in Germany and Austria. He began publishing in 1945 and completed his studies at the Gorky Literary Institute in 1955. From 1963 to the present Isayev has been a member of the editorial board of the newspaper *Literaturnaya Rossiya*. He has belonged to the board of the Writers Union of the RSFSR since 1965; in 1981 he became a member of the secretariat of the board of the Writers Union of the USSR. He lives in Moscow.

Isayev writes political narrative poems in the manner of A. Tvardovsky. His only works to attract attention were *Sud pamyati* (1963; Eng. tr., *The Verdict of Memory*, 1981) and *Dal pamyati* (Memory's Distance), narrative poems composed in elevated stanzas between 1955 and 1977, for which Isayev received the Lenin Prize in 1980. The first tells the story of three former German soldiers in a stereotypically militaristic and fascistic West Germany. Isayev's superficial message reminds the individual of his personal responsibility for the fate of his countrymen.

*Works: Sud pamjati* (narrative poem), in *Oktjabr'* 1962:6, separate ed., 1963 (see above); *Atmosfera stikha* (essay), in *Voprosy lit.* 1967:4;

*Dal' pamjati* (narrative poem), in *Moskva* 1976:1, 1977;11, separate ed., 1977; *Žizn' prožit'* . . . (narrative poems), 1979; *Dvadcat' pjatyj čas* (poem), in *Moskva* 1985:1.

*Secondary Lit.:* V. Dement'ev, in *Neva* 1963:3 and in *Lit. i sovremennost'* 4:1963; V. A. Zajcev, in *Vestnik MGU, Filologija i žurnalistika* 1964:5; A. Elkin, in *Moskva* 1972:3; A. Pavlovskij, in *Zvezda* 1980:12; A. Dement'ev, in *Znamja* 1985:1.

**Iskandér, Fazíl Abdúlovich,** Abkhasian poet and prose writer who writes in Russian (b. March 6, 1929, Sukhum, into a family of artisans). Iskander attended school in Abkhasia, then was trained as a librarian. He graduated from the Gorky Literary Institute in Moscow in 1954; then he worked as a journalist in Kursk and Bryansk and as an editor in the Abkhasian State Publishing House in 1959. Iskander's first volumes of poetry, *Gornye tropy* (1957; Mountain Paths) and *Dobrota zemli* (1959; The Good of the Earth), which were published in Russian in Sukhum, met with a positive response in leading periodicals; several poems seemed to reflect the influence of B. Pasternak, E. Bagritsky, N. Tikhonov (Sarnov). These were followed by additional volumes of poetry and, after 1962, by prose in the journals *Yunost* and *Novy mir* as well; this prose was collected for the first time in *Zapretny plod* (1966; Eng. tr., *Forbidden Fruit and Other Stories*, 1972). Iskander lives in Moscow.

Iskander's poetry is characterized by its vivid language and its ties to the Caucasus with its mountains, animals, and the sea, all of which often serve as the image of human fortitude. The poignancy of his poetry includes both a historical perspective that departs from Marxist topicality (*Novy mir* 1966:12) and the story of Christ (*Novy mir* 1968:11). In his prose, Iskander reveals himself to be a lengthy and willingly digressive narrator whose first-person structure rarely disguises his own voice and who enjoys inserting humorous contemporary criticism into his subtle observations. N. Atarov speaks of the "Rembrandt-like expressive force of his details," of a "humor of meaninglessness from behind which a deeper import peers." In *Sozvezdiye kozlotura* (1966; Eng. tr., *The Goatibex Constellation*, 1975), he ridicules the "campaigns" in agriculture and the ease with which public opinion is manipulated in the USSR. In *Letnim dnyom* (1969; On a Summer's Day), he transforms the story of a German who, seized with panic, manages to avoid being forced to become a

spy for the Gestapo into a fundamental exploration of the recruitment of agents. *Den Chika*
(1971; Chik's Day) is one of his treasured
children's stories, beloved also for its musical
language. *Sandro iz Chegema* (1973; Eng. tr.,
*Sandro of Chegem*, 1983) combined novellas
about a character who is closely associated
with Abkhasian folklore, old Uncle Sandro
from a village in the Caucasus, into a kind of
modern picaresque novel without a continuous plot that ironically depicts episodes from
pre-Revolutionary times up until the present
day. The Soviet censors cut the Soviet edition
by more than 50 percent; the American edition is complete. Iskander submitted a masterful satire, *Malenky gigant bolshogo seksa*
(1979; Eng. tr., "A Very Sexy Little Giant,"
1981), to METROPOL; in individual accounts
of love affairs, one of which is even set in
Beria's private life, he attacks human and
social deficiencies in the USSR.

*Works:* Gornye tropy (poems), 1957; Dobrota zemli (poems), 1959; Zelënyj dožd'
(poems), 1960; Molodost' morja (poems), 1964;
Sozvezdie kozlotura (pov.), in Novyj mir 1966:8
(see above); Zapretnyj plod (short stories),
1966 (see above); Kolčerukij (short story), in
Novyj mir 1967:4; Letnij les (poems), 1969;
Letnim dnëm (short story), in Novyj mir 1969:5;
Derevo detstva (short stories), 1970; Den' Čika
(short story), in Junost' 1971:10; Pervoe delo
(short stories), 1972; Vremja sčastlivykh na-
khodok (short stories and pov.), 1973; Sandro
iz Čegema (novel), in Novyj mir 1973:8–11,
separate ed., 1977 (abridged), and Ann Arbor,
1979 (see above); Pod sen'ju greckogo orekha
(pov.), 1979; Malen'kij gigant bol'šogo seksa
(pov.), in Metropol', Ann Arbor, 1979; Ko-
rotko, no ne koroče istiny (interviews), in Lit.
obozrenie 1985:11; Čegemskaja Karmen; Bar-
men Adgur (short stories), in Znamja 1986:12.
*Secondary Lit.:* M. Ivanova, in Lit. gazeta
Aug. 20, 1957; B. Sarnov, in Novyj mir 1958:5;
E. Vinokurov, in Lit. gazeta July 24, 1962; L.
Lenč, in Lit. gazeta Oct. 14, 1966, p. 9; N.
Atarov, in Novyj mir 1969:1; I. Varlamova, in
Lit. obozrenie 1974:4; Ja. Èl'sberg, in Lit.
obozrenie 1975:9; C. N. Packard, Diss., Ohio
State Univ., 1975; H. P. Burlingame, in Rus-
sian Literature Triquarterly 14:1976; B. Sar-
nov, in Voprosy lit. 1978:7; P. Vajl and A.
Genis, in Vremja i my, Tel Aviv, 42:1979; A.
Lebedev, in Lit. obozrenie 1984:10; B. Briker
and P. Dal'gor, in Scando-Slavica 30:1984.

**Ivánnikov, Mikhaíl Dmítriyevich,** prose writer
(b. Sept. 19 [Sept. 6], 1904, Georgiyevsk, Cau-

casus—d. Sept. 7, 1968, Belgrade). Ivannikov
emigrated with his parents, probably in 1920,
going first to Constantinople and finally in
Belgrade, Yugoslavia. In 1922 he moved to
Czechoslovakia and completed secondary
school there. He studied at the Faculty of
Agriculture in Brno, Czechoslovakia, and at
the Faculty of Law in Prague. For a time he
lived in a small Russian Orthodox monastery
in Slovakia, then he studied at the theological
institutes of the Russian Orthodox Church in
Paris and Belgrade. Ivannikov did not complete his studies and lived by doing odd jobs,
including working as a projectionist. He first
occupied himself with literature in the Prague
group "Scythian" *(Skif).* In Belgrade he belonged to the unions Book Circle *(Knizhny
kruzhok),* Literary Surroundings *(Literaturnaya sreda),* and Union of Russian Writers
and Journalists *(Soyuz russkikh pisateley i
zhurnalistov).* Ivannikov made his first appearance as a writer in the Parisian newspaper
*Posledniye novosti* with the animal story Lord
(1931; Lord), which was followed by three
other short stories in the journal Sovremennye
zapiski before World War II. From 1936 to
1938 he wrote satires for the Belgrade newspaper published by M. Kuzmin, Russkoye delo.
In Belgrade, Ivannikov was friends with the
poet E. Tauber and was married to L. Alekseyeva. She left Yugoslavia in October 1944,
and they were divorced in 1949. After the war
he worked as a cameraman for film and television and published four more short stories
from 1955 to 1969; the publication of a book
never came about.

Ivannikov's work consists of eight short stories of varying length that reveal his considerable talent. To these must be added the
longer, incomplete short story Schastye (Happiness), only excerpts of which were published in Novoye russkoye slovo after his death.
He focuses on people, especially on their inner lives, their thoughts and feelings. Contemporary external events, such as the Bolshevik
seizure of power or the émigré situation in
Yugoslavia, form only the background. In
Sashka (1935; Sashka) he depicts a young
man caught among sexuality, love, family dis-
cord, and disintegrating ethical norms; in Doroga (1937; The Way) he creates a monument
to his Orthodox teacher from Slovakia, Vitaly
Ustinov. In Pravila igry (1955; Rules of the
Game) he describes a Russian émigré on a
psychological teeter-totter, feeling himself
persecuted while himself persecuting others.
In Chempionat (1969; The Championship) he
portrays a tragic fate at the circus. Ivannikov
admired I. Bunin, A. Chekhov, and L. Tolstoy

but viewed F. Dostoyevsky with reserve. He always placed great value on exposing the human psyche and on narrative style as such, and he underscored meaning by using linguistic-rhythmic aspects.

Works: Lord (short story), in *Poslednie novosti*, Paris, 1931 (reprinted in *Novyj žurnal*, New York, 67:1962); *Saška* (short story), in *Sovremennye zapiski*, Paris, 57:1935; *Aviorasskaz* (short story), in *Sovremennye zapiski* 61:1936; *Doroga* (pov.), in *Sovremennye zapiski* 65:1937; *Pravila igry* (short story), in *Novyj žurnal* 44:1955; *Zagovor* (short story), in *Novyj žurnal* 46:1956; *Iskus* (short story), in *Novyj žurnal* 74–75:1963–64; *Čempionat* (short story), in *Novyj žurnal* 96:1969.

Secondary Lit.: A. Adamovič, in *Russkaja mysl'*, Paris, July 5, 1956; E. Tauber, in *Novyj žurnal* 96:1969; O. Djurić, in *Savremenik*, Belgrade, 1948:8–9.

**Ivanóv, Anatóly Stepánovich,** prose writer (b. May 5, 1928, Shemonaikha, East Kazakhstan). From 1946 to 1950 Ivanov studied journalism at Alma-Ata University. He worked as a journalist, first for provincial newspapers in Central Asia and Siberia and then in the army (1951–53). Since 1952 he has been a member of the Communist Party. From 1958 to 1964 he was nominal editor in chief of the journal *Sibirskiye ogni*. Ivanov has published short stories since 1954; the first volume, *Alkiny pesni* (Alkin's Songs), appeared in 1956; his first novel, *Povitel* (Lesser Bindweed), appered in 1958 and the second, *Teni ischezayut v polden* (The Shadows Disappear at Midday), in 1963. At the end of the 1960s he moved from Novosibirsk to Moscow. For *Vechny zov* (1970–76; Eng. tr., *The Eternal Call*, 1978) he was awarded the Gorky Prize (for the novel) in 1971 and the State Prize of the USSR (for the television script) in 1979. Ivanov has been a member of the board of the Writers Union of the RSFSR since 1965 and a member of the board of the Writers Union of the USSR since 1971; since 1981 he has been one of the secretaries of the latter organization. Since 1972 he has been the editor in chief of the journal *Molodaya gvardiya*.

Ivanov, who has often chosen the Siberian village as his scene of action, says that he has "set himself the goal of showing how Soviet reality cleanses people of the dirty remains of capitalism" (in *Moskva* 1959:10). In the family saga *Povitel*, which covers the period from World War II to the present, Ivanov especially attacks private property; his second novel

makes an active contribution to the Party's campaign of atheism under Khrushchev by equating Christians with gangsters. *Vechny zov* attempts to portray the Communist development of Siberia during the course of 60 years. Only a "true Party passion" (Ognyov) remains of Ivanov's untalented narrative style with its simple, optimistic conclusions.

Works: *Alkiny pesni* (short stories), 1956; *Povitel'* (novel), 1958; *Teni isčezajut v polden'* (novel), 1963; *Večnyj zov* (novel), 1971, vol. 2 in *Moskva* 1976:7–10, separate ed., 1977 (see above); *Žizn' na grešnoj zemle, Izbr.*, 1971; *Vražda* (pov.), 1980; *Pečal' polej* (pov.), 1983.—*Izbr. proizv.*, 2 vols., 1974; *Sobr. soč.*, 5 vols., 1979–81.

Secondary Lit.: D. Nagiškin, in *Novyj mir* 1959:5; O. Vojtinskaja, in *Moskva* 1959:10; *RSPP* 2:1964; A. Ognëv, in *Sibirskie ogni* 1967:2; N. Sergovancev, in *Lit. Rossija* April 19, 1974, pp. 10–11; D. Žukov, in *Naš sovremennik* 1978:5; V. Gorbačëv, in *Znamja* 1981:6; N. Pavlov, in *Lit. obozrenie* 1984:10; V. Apukhtina, in *Oktjabr'* 1984:8.

**Ivánov, Geórgy Vladímirovich,** poet (b. Nov. 10 [Oct. 29], 1894, Kovno—d. Aug. 27, 1958, Hyères, France). Ivanov was of noble descent; his father was in the military. Ivanov graduated from the St. Petersburg cadet corps in 1910. His first poems were connected with ego-futurism (see FUTURISM). His first volume of poetry, *Otplytiye na o. Tsiteru* (1912; Embarquement pour l'ile de Cythère—from a painting by Watteau), won recognition from, among others, I. Severyanin and N. Gumilyov, who, together with M. Kuzmin, influenced Ivanov. Ivanov became a regular contributor to the journal *Apollon*, and his volume of poetry *Veresk* (1916; Heather) preserves the spirit of ACMEISM. In 1923 he emigrated together with his wife, the poet Irina Odoyevtseva, to Paris where he became one of the most famous representatives of the old emigration and worked on many journals as poet and critic. During World War II he fled to Biarritz (1943–46). He spent his last years in a home for the aged. Four collections of poetry appeared in Paris, Berlin, and New York. Remembrances of his youth, *Peterburgskiye zimy* (1928; Petersburg Winters), are controversial because of their subjectivity. Since 1975 his entire lyric work has been accessible thanks to an edition by V. Setchkarev and M. Dalton.

In his first ego-futuristic volume of poetry, Ivanov stands amid the wave of decadence fashionable at the time. The second, *Gornitsa*

(1914; Living Room), continues this style and again reflects Kuzmin's influence. *Pamyatnik slavy* (1915; Monument of Glory) is patriotic and governed by World War I. With *Veresk* and *Sady* (1921; Gardens) Ivanov's lyric poetry gained its stamp of individuality, became more musical (for example, through parallel constructions and repetitions), more conscious of form, and showed a predilection for detail. The contemplative lyric poetry of his first foreign-published collection, *Rozy* (1931; Roses), which even met with the approval of his opponents, includes, as new aspects of his style, elements of A. Blok, as well as subtle themes from Paris and from remembered Russia. His postwar volume, *Portret bez skhodstva* (1950; A Portrait without Resemblance), is characterized by poems about the essence of art. He incorporated parts in the volume published shortly before his death, *1943–1958. Stikhi* (1958; 1943–1958. Poems), which, as a whole, is defined by his pessimistic ideas about life. Ivanov's lyric poetry is clear and polarized in its thought pattern. Marked by an increasing negativity, it is emphatically antireligious. It is the expression of a metaphysical emptiness that exhausts itself in the negation of oneself, of human existence, of nature, and of art. It is typical of that Russian intellectual who has broken away from the religious ties of the Russian people.

*Works: Otplytie na o. Citeru* (poems), 1912; *Gornica* (poems), 1914; *Pamjatnik slavy* (poems), 1915; *Veresk* (poems), 1916, 2d ed., Berlin, 1923; *Sady* (poems), 1921, 2d ed., Berlin, 1922; *Lampada* (poems), 1922; *Peterburgskie zimy* (memoirs), Paris, 1928, 2d ed., New York, 1952; *Tretij Rim* (novel), vol. 1 in *Sovremennye zapiski*, Paris, 39–40:1929, extracts from vol. 2 in *Čisla*, Paris, 2–3:1930; *Rozy* (poems), Paris, 1931; *Otplytie na ostrov Citeru* (selected poems), Berlin, 1937; *Raspad atoma* (essays), Paris, 1938; *Portret bez skhodstva* (poems), Paris, 1950; *1943–1958 Stikhi* (poems), New York, 1958; *Sobr. stikhotvorenij*, Würzburg, 1975 (reprint of all collected poems and supplements); *Izbr. stikhi*, (poems), Paris, 1980.

*Secondary Lit.*: R. Gul', in *Novyj žurnal*, New York, 42:1955; G. Struve, in *Russkaja literatura v izgnanii*, New York, 1956, and obituary in *Novyj žurnal* 54:1958; I. G. Agushi, Cambridge, Mass., 1970; Ju. Ivask, in *Novyj žurnal* 98:1970; K. Pomerancev, in *Russkaja mysl'*, Paris, May 20, 1976, Nov. 27, Dec. 12, 1980, and Nov. 27, 1984, pp. 8–9; Vl. Markov, in *The Bitter Air of Exile: Russian Writers in the West 1922–1972*, ed. S. Karlinsky and A.

Appel, Berkeley, 1977; V. Vejdle, in *Kontinent*, Paris, 11:1977; Ju. Terapiano, in *Russkaja mysl'* Sept. 28, 1978; V. Krejd, in *Novyj žurnal* 160:1985; U. Michalowski, in *Zeitschrift für slavische Philologie* 1986:2.

**Iványov, Vsévolod Vyacheslávovich**, prose writer (b. Feb. 24 [Feb. 12], 1895, Lebyazhye, prov. Semipalatinsk—d. Aug. 15, 1963, Moscow). Ivanov's father was a teacher. Ivanov spent his youth in western Siberia. He did not complete his education, but was forced to earn his living at an early age; his various occupations included typesetter, sailor, and circus clown. He began to publish his literary work in 1915. Under M. Gorky's influence Ivanov did a great deal of reading in the following years. During the Revolution he was politically indifferent, siding initially with the Whites, then with the Reds. In 1921 he moved to Petrograd and became a member of the KOSMISTS, a proletarian writers' group from which he was expelled in 1922 for affiliating himself with the SERAPION BROTHERS. The first and most important post-Revolutionary literary journal, *Krasnaya nov*, was launched in 1921 with Ivanov's *Partizany* (The Partisans). In 1922 the same journal carried *Bronepoyezd No. 14–69* (Eng. tr., *Armoured Train 14–69*, 1933), Ivanov's best-known *povest* about partisan activity. Ivanov moved to Moscow and wrote a great deal in the following decades. In the late 1920s the critics of RAPP attacked him harshly; in the early 1930s Ivanov found himself in the mainstream of construction literature and achieved lasting recognition. In accord with the spirit of the times, Ivanov returned to the subject of the Civil War in 1938–39 with his novel *Parkhomenko*. As a correspondent for *Izvestiya* during World War II, Ivanov went all the way to Berlin. In the late Stalinist period he published works that steered away from topical problems, such as *Vstrechi s Maksimom Gorkim* (1947; Meetings with Maksim Gorky) or the drama *Lomonosov* (1949–53). Substantial portions of his work (novels and povesti) remained unpublished. Ivanov completely altered the form of his autobiographical novel *Pokhozhdeniya fakira* (1934–35; Eng. tr., *The Adventures of a Fakir*, 1935) to produce *My idyom v Indiyu* (1960; We Are Going to India). From 1934 on, Ivanov belonged to the board, but not the secretariat, of the Writers Union of the USSR.

From the very beginning Ivanov was considered to be one of the most talented of the Serapion Brothers. His "legends of the steppes, or actually, the incidents that have been transformed into the legends of the steppes" (Gorbov) are narrated in "the spicy, ornamental language, full of dialecticisms" (Struve) that is typical of the early 1920s, and he deals with unusual, frequently horrible incidents. "The special thing about Ivanov's art of presentation is that he does not project a picture of political or historical perspective, but seeks all of the human being's motives in his local environment" (Holthusen). Ivanov revised his works frequently. *Bronepoyezd No. 14–69* strongly emphasizes the role of the Communist Party only in its dramatic version (1927). Ivanov changed the prose version so fundamentally that it was not included in the 1968 edition of his works (*Novyj mir* 1970:2, p. 224). He subsequently rewrote many of his works from the Stalinist period, such as *Parkhomenko*. Some of his early prose was reprinted in the Soviet Union, some in the West. The allegorical short story *Sizif, syn Eola* (Eng. tr., "Sisyphus, the Son of Aeolus," in *View from Another Shore*, 1973), which V. Kaverin suggested was an illustration of Ivanov's dire fate during Stalin's dictatorship, is a model in miniature of Ivanov's conflict with his time, as expressed in larger, subsequently published works such as *Vulkan* (Vulcan), *Agasfer* (Ahasuerus), and *Uzhginsky Kreml* (The Kremlin of Uzhga), or ones unpublished in the Soviet Union such as *U*.

*Works: Partizany* (pov.), 1921; *Bronepoezd No. 14–69* (pov.), 1922 (see above); *Ditë* (Eng. tr., "The Child," in *Great Soviet Short Stories*, 1962). *Loga* (two short stories), 1922; *Cvetnye vetra* (pov.), 1922; *Vozvraščenie Buddy* (pov.), 1923; *Pokhoždenija fakira* (novel), 1934–35 (see above); *Parkhomenko* (novel), 1939; *Vstreči s Maksimom Gor'kim* (memoirs), 1947; *My idem v Indiju* (novel), 1960; *Èdesskaja svjatynja* (novel), 1965; *P'esy* (plays), 1979; *Užginskij Kreml'* (novel), 1981; *U* (novel), Lausanne, 1982; *Mednaja lampa* (short stories and novels), 1984.—*Sobr. soč.*, 7 vols., 1928–31; 8 vols., 1958–60; *Izbr. proizv.*, 2 vols., 1968 (contains, among others, *Vulkan* and *Agasfer*); 8 vols., 1973–78.

*Secondary Lit.:* D. Gorbov, in *Novyj mir* 1925:12; M. Ščeglov, in his *Lit.-kritičeskie stat'i*, 1958; *RSPP* 2:1964; A. Kron, in his *Večnaja problema*, 1969; I. Solov'ëva, in *Novyj mir* 1970:2; *Vsevolod Ivanov—pisatel' i čelovek*, 1970; L. A. Gladkovskaja, 1972; E. Cejtlin, 1977 and 1983; M. C. Smith, Diss., Univ. of Pennsylvania, 1978; F. S. F. Snyder, Diss., Univ. of Michigan, 1979; E. A. Krasnoščekova, 1980; V. Dement'ev, in *Lit. Rossija* Feb. 22, 1985, p. 11.

**Ivánov, Vyácheslav Ivánovich,** poet, historian (b. Feb. 28 [Feb. 16], 1866, Moscow—d. July 16, 1949, Rome). Ivanov's father was a surveyor. Ivanov began studying history at Moscow University in 1884 and Roman history and classical philosophy at Berlin University in 1886. After 1891, when he went to Paris, Ivanov occupied himself especially with the study of ancient miracle plays, Friedrich Nietzsche, and the cult of Dionysus. In 1896 Magnus Hirschfeld and Theodor Mommsen accepted his dissertation, but Ivanov did not take the oral examinations for his doctorate. In 1902 he traveled to Greece, Egypt, and Palestine. Ivanov wrote poems even as a child; his first poem was published in 1898, and the first collections appeared during his stay abroad: *Kormchiye zvyozdy* (1903; Lodestars) and *Prozrachnost* (1904; Transparency). In 1905 he settled in St. Petersburg, where his apartment in the "Tower" in the Tauride Garden became the regular meeting place for poets, artists, and scientists until about 1910. Ivanov published numerous essays in *Zolotoye runo*, in *Vesy*, or in his own books; these essays are characterized by mystical religious thought and show Ivanov to be "one of the most cultivated Russian poets" (Eliasberg). After a renewed stay abroad (1912–13), Ivanov settled in Moscow. During the February Revolution he was at the Black Sea. From 1920 to 1924 he worked as a college teacher in Baku; in 1921 he defended his dissertation on the cult of Dionysus. In 1924 Ivanov traveled with permission to Rome and remained in Italy to the end of his life. In 1926 he converted to Catholicism. He held a teaching position for Russian language and literature at the University of Pavia (1926–34); he later taught at the Papal Institute for Eastern Studies (1934–43). Publication of a planned six-volume edition of his works began in Brussels in 1971. In the Soviet Union, a volume of selected poems appeared in the series "Biblioteka poeta (malaya seriya)" in 1976 after a 55-year absence of his works.

Ivanov occupies an exceptional position among the symbolists. His poems are suffused with themes from Greek mythology, accompanied by elements of early Christianity. He tries to justify the presence of the Dionysian principle in Christian reinterpretation as a religious revelation. Ivanov's lyric poetry is extraordinarily difficult to understand because of its symbolic code. His language is of "overly great philologic elaborateness" (Blok), ornate and dramatic, rich in Old Church Slavonic and neologisms from European languages. Through unusual compound epithets and new abstract nouns, and through poetic allusions to the most remote concepts, Ivanov tries to allow his intended meaning to be perceived intuitively. Ivanov also wrote two tragedies, *Tantal* (1903; Tantalus) and *Prometey* (1919; Prometheus), in which he gives form to his religious-philosophic and abstract poetic views. To his most important achievements as an essayist belongs the "correspondence" with M. Gershenzon, *Perepiska iz dvukh uglov* (1920; Correspondence between Two Corners). At his death he left behind, among other things, a volume of deeply spiritual poems in simple, clear language.

Works: *Kormčie zvëzdy* (poems), 1903; *Prozračnost'* (poems), 1904 (reprinted, Munich, 1967); *Tantal* (tragedy), 1905; *Èros* (poems), 1907; *Po zvëzdam* (poems), 1909 (reprinted, Letchworth, 1971); *Cor ardens* (poems), 2 vols., 1911–12; *Nežnaja tajna* (poems), 1912; *Borozdy i meži* (essays), 1916 (reprinted, Letchworth, 1971); *Krizis gumanizma* (essays), 1918; *Prometej* (tragedy), 1919 (reprinted, Paris, 1967); *Perepiska iz dvukh uglov* (essays), 1921 (reprinted, Ann Arbor, 1980); *Čelovek* (poems), Paris, 1939; *Das alte Wahre* (essays), Berlin, 1959; *Svet večernij* (selected poems), Oxford, 1962; *Stikhotvorenija i poèmy* (lyric and narrative poems), 1976.— *Sobr. soč.*, 6 vols. (vols. 1–4 have appeared), Brussels, 1971–.

Secondary Lit.: A. Belyj, in *Poèzija slova*, 1922; O. Chor-Dechartes, in *Oxford Slavonic Papers*, 1954, 1957, and foreword to *Sobr. soč.*, 1971; F. Stepun, in *Die Welt der Slaven* 1963:8; J. Holthusen, foreword to the reprint of *Prometej*, 1967; T. Tschöpl, Munich, 1968; J. West, *Russian Symbolism*, London, 1970; A. Hetzer, Munich, 1972; V. Markov, in *Russkaja mysl'*, Paris, Nos. 2884, 2886, and 2887, 1972; S. Averincev, in *Voprosy lit.* 1975:8; S. M. Olson, Diss., Univ. of Illinois at Urbana-Champaign, 1976; E. Ternovskij, in *Russkaja mysl'* Jan. 8, 1981; L. Ivanova, in *Novyj žurnal*, New York, 147–50:1982–83; I. Baskina, in *Russkaja mysl'* Oct. 7, 1986, p. 12.

**Ívask, Yúry Pávlovich,** poet, literary critic (b. Sept. 14 [Sept. 1], 1907, Moscow—d. Feb. 13, 1986, Amherst, Mass.). Ivask's father was a manufacturer of Estonian-German descent; his mother was a Russian from an old Moscow merchant family. In 1920 Ivask's family moved to Estonia, where, in 1932, Ivask graduated with a degree in law from Dorpat University. In 1930 Ivask began to publish literary criticism and poetry in Russian émigré journals.

His first volume of poetry, *Severny bereg* (1938; Northern Shore), appeared in Warsaw. In 1944 Ivask fled to Germany; from 1946 to 1949 he studied Slavic languages and literatures in Hamburg. In 1949 he moved to the United States where he earned a Ph.D. at Harvard University in 1954 with a dissertation about Pyotr Vyazemsky. His second volume of poetry, *Tsarskaya Osen* (1953; Tsar's Autumn), was published in Paris; in New York he concurrently published an anthology of Russian poetry written abroad, *Na Zapade* (1953; In the West), a distinguished union of the first and second emigration. Ivask taught at several universities until he was appointed professor at the University of Massachusetts (Amherst) in 1969 (1977 professor emeritus). Ivask combined his work as a critic with that of a poet. He edited the works of G. P. Fedotov (1952) and V. Rozanov (1956); wrote essays about I. Bunin, M. Tsvetaeva, O. Mandelshtam, and others and a book about Konstantin Leontyev (1974); published poems—often lightly revised—in numerous periodicals; and collected his poetry in *Khvala* (1967; Praise) and *Zolushka* (1970; Cinderella). His most extensive poetic work, *Igrayushchiy chelovek* (1973; Homo Ludens), and a selection of poems were published in Moscow in 1978 as a SAMIZDAT publication (500 pages). At the end of the 1970s and beginning of the 1980s, Ivask published excerpts from his autobiographical prose.

Ivask's lyricism grows out of his experience of poetry, poets, and art on many trips to Greece, Italy, and Portugal, among other places. He considers Gavrila Derzhavin his Russian forefather; his first volume of poetry begins with a poem to Evgeny Baratynsky. His encounter with the religious culture of ancient Mexico in 1956 was the central spiritual experience of his life and was deepened through six later visits. The title of his third volume of poetry, *Khvala*, reflects a positive attitude toward life, one that is grounded in religion and that recognizes an eternally valid order beyond that of earthly life. *Igrayushchiy chelovek* is a longer verse poem that unites autobiographical, chronologically constructed stages of life and portraits of poets with thoughts about the fundamental questions of life. Together with Russian poets and Mexican art, English metaphysical lyric serves as one of the essential points of departure of this episodically structured work. A wealth of imagery, linguistic games (from 18th-century Russian up to the Oberiuts), biographical and literary allusions (partially explained in notes), and a neobaroque sensibility characterize the intellectual, historical, and formal variety of his poetry. "Ivask's poetry represents an experiment in transfiguring the poet's images, visions, his entire sensibility into play and poetry, or a playful poetry whose very serious intent is to become an object for his—and by extension, everyone's—paradise" (Dienes).

Works: *Severnyj bereg* (poems), Warsaw, 1938; *O poslevoennoj èmigrantskoj poèzii* (essay), in *Novyj žurnal*, New York, 23:1950; *Carskaja osen'* (poems), Paris, 1953; *Pokhvala rossijskoj poèzii* (essay), in *Mosty* Munich, 5:1960; *Khvala* (poems), Washington, 1967; *Zoluška* (poems), 1970; *Pis'mo o man'erizme (manifesto neo-baročnoj poèzii)* (essay), in *Mosty*, New York, 15:1970; *Poèzija staroj èmigracii* (essay), in *Russkaja literatura v èmigracii*, Pittsburgh, 1972; *Igrajuščij čelovek* (narrative poem), in *Vozroždenie*, Paris, 240–42:1973; *Konstantin Leont'ev* (treatise), Bern, 1974; *Povest' o stikhakh* (memoirs), in *Novoe russkoe slovo*, New York, Aug. 28 and Sept. 4, 1977, in *Russkaja mysl'*, Paris, June 24, July 17, Oct. 9, Oct. 16, 1980, and Nov. 18, 1982; *Esli by ne bylo revoljucii* (novel), extracts in *Russkaja mysl'* Dec. 11, 1980, Jan. 22, Jan. 29, March 12, March 19, June 25, 1981; interview, in *Russkaya mysl'* March 21, 1985; *Zavoevanie Meksiki* (poems), 1986. Other essays also in *Novyj žurnal* 60:1960, 99:1970, 102:1971, 128:1977, 150:1983 and in *Vestnik RKhD* 106:1972.

Secondary Lit.: P. Bicilli, in *Sovremennye zapiski*, Paris, 66:1938; A. Nejmirok, in *Grani*, Frankfurt am Main, 19:1953, 67:1968; G. Adamovič, in *Novyj žurnal* 88:1967; J. Bailey, in *Journal of Slavic Linguistics and Poetics* 13:1970; V. Vejdle, in *Novoe russkoe slovo*, New York, Sept. 18 and Oct. 21, 1973; V. Evdokimov, in *Vestnik RKhD* 127:1978; L. Dienes, in *World Literature Today* 53(2):1979; A. Kopejkin, in *Russkaja mysl'* Aug. 16, 1984, p. 10; D. Bobyšev, V. Blinov, in *Russkaja mysl'* March 14, 1986, pp. 10–11; D. Bobyšev, V. Blinov, V. Perelešin, in *Novyj žurnal* 163:1986.

**Ívnev, Ryúrik** (pseud. of Mikhaíl Aleksándrovich Kovalyóv), poet, prose writer (b. Feb. 23 [Feb. 11], 1891, Tbilisi—d. Feb. 20, 1981, Moscow). Ivnev's father was a military lawyer. Ivnev completed his studies in law at Moscow University in 1912. He published his first poems in 1909 and his first volume of verse, *Samosozhzheniye* (Self-Immolation), in 1913. From 1913 to 1916 Ivnev was a member of the ego-futurists (see FUTURISM) and lived in Petrograd. Immediately after the Revolution he put himself at the service of the Bolsheviks, became secretary to A. Lunacharsky, and moved to Moscow. In 1919 Ivnev, V. Shershenevich, A. Mariyengof, and S. Yesenin formed a group called the imagists (see IMAGISM), but Ivnev never really became a representative of their ideas. His volume of verse from this period, *Solntse v grobe* (1921; The Sun in Its Grave), includes 25 poems selected by Yesenin, with "themes and motifs [such] as abandonment of God, attraction to death, suffering, pain, guilty conscience, madness, blood, Christ, crucifixion" (Markov, p. 45). Ivnev, who had written a novel under the influence of A. Bely in 1917, published three novels about Bohemian life under the Soviet regime between 1925 and 1928; they were negatively received. Ivnev lived by translating from the Caucasian languages into Russian. Between 1942 and 1945 two collections of his verse and three small children's books were published in Tbilisi. After 1965 he published poems and autobiographical prose from time to time; two books were published as late as 1978. Ivnev lived in Moscow. He entered Soviet literature in the shadow of the imagists. He is not particularly significant either as a poet or as a prose writer.

Works: *Samosožženie* (poems), 3 vols., 1913–15; *Plamja pyšet* (poems), 1913; *Zoloto smerti* (poems), 1916; *Samosožženie* (poems), 1917; *Nesčastnyj angel* (novel), 1917; *Solnce v grobe* (poems), 1921; *Četyre vystrela v Esenina, Kusikova, Mariengofa, Šeršeneviča* (essays), 1921; *Osada monastyrja* (poems), 1925; *Ljubov' bez ljubvi* (novel), 1925; *Otkrytyj dom* (novel), 1927; *Geroj romana* (novel), 1928; *Izbr. stikhi* (poems), 1965; *Pravda i mify o Sergee Esenine* (memoirs), in *Volga* 1967:5; *Pamjat' i vremja* (poems), 1969; *U podnožija Mtacmindy. Memuary. Novelly raznykh let. Povest'* (memoirs), 1973; *Izbr. stikhotvorenija* (poems), 1974; *Čas i golosa* (poems and memoirs), 1978; *Tëplye list'ja* (poems), 1978.—*Izbr. 1907–1981* (poems), 1985.

Secondary Lit.: P. Žurov, in *Krasnaja nov'* 1927:2; K. Zelinskij, foreword to Ivnev's *Izbr. stikhi*, 1965; I. Mikhajlov, in *Lit. Rossija* Aug. 21, 1970, p. 17; Anon., in *Lit. Rossija* Feb. 26, 1971, p. 17; V. Pokrovskij, in *Lit. Azerbajdžan* 1972:1; M. Šapovalov, in *Volga* 1974:8; Anon., in *Lit. gazeta* March 10, 1976, p. 7; V. Markov, *Russian Imagism 1919–1924*, 2 vols., Giessen, 1980; A. Cvetaeva, in *Znamja* 1986:10.

# J

Jasieński (Russian: Yasénsky), **Brúno**, Polish prose writer, wrote in Russian after 1931 (b. July 17, 1901, Klimontów, Sandomierz district, Poland—d. Oct. 20, 1941 [?], while imprisoned). Jasieński's father was a doctor. Jasieński attended school in Warsaw and studied in Kraków after 1918. His first futurist poems appeared in 1919. In the early 1920s Jasieński joined the Communist movement and worked as a journalist. In Paris, where he emigrated in 1925, he published a narrative poem written in his early phase and of particular importance to him, *Słowo o Jakóbie Szeli* (1926; The Story of Jakob Szela), about the uprising of the Polish peasants in 1846–48. Jasieński joined the French Communist Party; in 1927 he organized a workers' theater in Paris and wrote his first major prose work, *Palę Paryż* (1928; French: *Je brûle Paris*, in L'Humanité 1928), a utopian revolutionary novel and polemic directed against Paul Morand's *Je brûle Moscou*. In that same year it appeared in Moscow as *Ya zhgu Parizh* (I Set Fire to Paris). Expelled from France in 1929 because of his Communist propaganda, Jasieński went to Moscow by way of Germany and Belgium. In the Soviet Union his work as a journalist included the editorship of a Polish cultural magazine. He was admitted to the Communist Party in 1930. Jasieński first wrote a fantastic, satirical play polemicizing against Western social democracy, *Bal manekenov* (1931; The Mannequins' Ball), and adapted *Słowo o Jakóbie Szeli* (translated by E. Bagritsky, N. Aseyev, and D. Brodsky) for the stage. His two trips to Tadzhikistan in 1930 and 1931 were reflected in a novel, *Chelovek menyayet kozhu* (1932; Eng. tr., *Man Changes His Skin*, 1935), which until 1937 went through numerous printings every year and was enormously successful. In 1934 Jasieński was elected to the board of the Writers Union of the USSR. A novel begun in 1936, *Zagovor ravnodushnykh* (Conspiracy of the Indifferent), remained in fragmentary form, since Jasieński was arrested early in 1937 and liquidated as a "Trotskyite." After his REHABILITATION in 1956, *Novy mir* published the novel fragment, prepared for publication by Jasieński's widow. His other prose works were also reprinted.

Jasieński writes smooth, action-packed, and vivid prose that serves to propagandize the Communist idea. The influence of the futurist tendencies present in his earlier Polish verse is also evident. His Five-Year Plan novel, *Chelovek menyayet kozhu*, with its "well-organized plot" (Struve), is clothed in the form of an American engineer's journey to Tadzhikistan. In other works also Jasieński includes the West, applying an obvious ideological interpretation.

*Works: But w butonierce*, Warsaw, 1921; *Nogi Izoldy Morgan* (pov.), L'vov, 1923; *Słowo o Jakóbie Szeli*, Paris, 1926, Warsaw, 1956; *Je brûle Paris* (novel), 1928, in Russian: *Ja žgu Pariž*, 1928; *Palę Paryż* (novel), Warsaw, 1929, 3d ed., 1957; *Bal manekenov* (play), 1931; *Galicijskaja žakerija* (*Slovo o Jakove Šele*) (play), 1931; *Čelovek menjaet kožu* (novel), 1932–33, 1969 (see above); *Nos* (pov.), 1936; *Zagovor ravnodušnykh* (novel), in *Novyj mir* 1956:5–7; *Utvory poetyckie, manifesty, szkice* (essays), Warsaw, 1972.—*Izbr. proizv.* (also autobiography), 2 vols., 1957.

*Secondary Lit.:* E. Tager, in *Lit. kritik* 1933:4; Vl. Lidin, in *Lit. gazeta* Aug. 4, 1956; V. Kardin, in *Družba narodov* 1959:9; E. Balcerzan, Warsaw, 1968; A. Stern, Warsaw, 1969; *RSPP* 7(2):1972; J. Dziarnowska, Warsaw, 1978; A. Erokhin, in *Lit. Rossija* Feb. 26, 1982, p. 14; N. Kolesnikoff, Waterloo, Ont., 1982.

# K

**Kabó, Lyubóv Rafaílovna**, prose writer (b. Aug. 4, 1917, Moscow). Kabo completed her studies at the Moscow Pedagogical Institute in 1940 and worked as a teacher in Bessarabia; she became a member of the Communist Party in 1945. After Stalin's death, Kabo revised her first novel, *Za Dnestrom* (1950; Beyond the Dnestr), a description of the basic problems of her teaching profession, and retitled it *Druzya iz Levkauts* (1955; Friends from Levkauts). She is best known for her povest *V trudnom pokhode* (1956; A Difficult Campaign), in which she exposes errors in the field of primary education and the activities of Komsomol officials reduced to the level of self-centered routine during the Stalin years, contrasting them with new ideas. Although the critics confirmed that Kabo was objectively correct, her work was nevertheless criticized precisely because it insufficiently emphasized the role of the Party and was not as a whole tendentiously oriented. In Povest o Borise Bekleshove (1962; A Tale of Boris Bekleshov), Kabo used primary material to present a geographer, distinguished neither by position nor by professional achievement, who exposed unjust accusations, lived for others, and, to a great extent, "expressed himself in others" (Orlova) during the Stalin period. Kabo only rarely went beyond the thematic realm of the school, as she did, for example, in her possibly autobiographical short story V tot den (1969; On That Day), based on the familiar milieu of Bessarabian kinship groups. Kabo lives in Moscow.

Works: Za Dnestrom (novel), 1950; Druz'ja iz Levkauc (novel), 1955; V trudnom pokhode (pov.), in Novyj mir 1956:11–12; Povest' o Borise Beklešove (pov.), 1962; Ostorožno: Škola!, 1962; V tot den' (short story), in Novyj mir 1969:10; Žil na svete učitel', 1970; Sladčajšee naše bremja, 1971; Kino v èstetičeskom i nravstvennom vospitanii detej (essays), 1978; . . . I ne zabyvaj, čto ja tebja ljublju (pov.), in Oktjabr' 1984:7.

Secondary Lit.: V. Ljubimova, in Lit. gazeta May 9, 1957; M. Gus, in Lit. gazeta June 26, 1958; R. Orlova, in Moskva 1963:9; L. Rybak, in Iskusstvo kino 1966:8; R. Litvinov, in Sovetskaja pedagogika 1972:3.

**Kalínin, Anatóly Veniamínovich**, prose writer (b. Aug. 22 [Aug. 9], 1916, Kamenskaya, oblast Don). Kalinin's father was a teacher. After finishing school, Kalinin briefly attended a technical college; he began working as a journalist in 1932. Influenced by M. Sholokhov, Kalinin's first novel, Kurgany (1941; Burial Mounds), describes the collectivization of the Don region at the end of 1933 and the Party's victory in the class war in the countryside. During World War II, Kalinin was a correspondent for Komsomolskaya pravda. He reworked two war novels, published in Novy mir in 1944 and 1946, into a single new work, Krasnoye znamya (1951; Red Banner). Kalinin was admitted to the Communist Party in 1946. After the war he lived in a village near Rostov,

where in addition to literary work he wrote publicistic prose about kolkhoz life; during the post-Stalinist years, this prose was aimed at a critical illumination of the past in the manner of V. Ovechkin. Kalinin's novel Surovoye pole (1958; The Rugged Field), in which he takes up the thorny subject of the across-the-board condemnation of all Soviet prisoners of war, in particular those who had temporarily served in German forces (the Vlasov army), and calls for reestablishing the trust in people that had been lost during the Stalin years, was the source of a sharp polemical controversy. Human problems also lie at the center of Zapretnaya zona (1962; Restricted Area), a novel about the construction of the gigantic reservoir on the Don. Kalinin wrote essays about M. Sholokhov. In 1973 he received the Gorky Prize for his povesti Ekho voyny (1963; Eng. tr., Echoes of the War, 1966) and Vozvrata net (1972; No Return). Kalinin's novels and povesti are closely related to each other through their geography and, to a great extent, through their characters. Kalinin has been a member of the boards of the Writers Unions of the RSFSR and the USSR since 1965 and 1967, respectively. He lives in a village near Rostov.

Works: Kurgany (novel), 1941; Na juge (novel), 1944 (Eng. tr., In the South, 1946); Tovarišči (novel), 1945; Tikhie verby (short stories and play), 1950; Krasnoe znamja (novel), 1951; Neumirajuščie korni (short stories), 1955; Surovoe pole (novel), 1958, 2d ed., 1962; Zapretnaja zona (novel), 1962; Ekho vojny (see above). Cygan (pov.), (Eng. tr., The Gypsy, 1966), 1963; Granatovyj sok (articles and short stories), 1968; Vozvrata net (pov.), 1972; Zemlja i grozd'ja, 1972; Ekho vojny (pov. and novel), 1975; Dve tetradi, 1979; Vremja "Tikhogo Dona," 1979.—Izbr. proizv., 2 vols., 1976; Sobr. soč., 4 vols., 1982–83.

Secondary Lit.: S. Rozanov, in Novyj mir 1952:1; S. Zlobin, in Novyj mir 1959:7, A. Dement'ev, in Novyj mir 1959:7; I. Šekhovcov, in Naš sovremennik 1962:2; M. Lobanov, in Moskva 1963:3; RSPP 2:1964; N. Dalada, 1965; V. Karpova, 1973; B. Primerov, in Naš sovremennik 1976:8; V. Sidorov, in Lit. obozrenie 1980:4; V. Voronov, in Don 1984:9.

**Kaménsky, Vasíly Vasílyevich**, poet (b. April 17 [April 5], 1884, Perm—d. Nov. 11, 1961, Moscow). Kamensky spent his youth in the Urals, where his father worked in the gold-mining industry. Under the influence of V.

Meyerhold, Kamensky began his literary career in 1904. In 1907 he passed his university entrance examinations in St. Petersburg and went on to study agricultural science. With his friends D. Burlyuk and V. Khlebnikov, he formed the group of cubo-futurists (see FUTURISM). In 1911 he went abroad (to Berlin and Paris) for training as a pilot; returning (by way of London and Vienna) to Russia, he served briefly as one of the first Russian fliers. In 1913–14 Kamensky traveled with Burlyuk and V. Mayakovsky through Russia and the Caucasus on a lecture tour; later he continued to give readings of his futurist poetry. In 1916 he published Stenka Razin, a lyrical novel that he subsequently revised several times. The October Revolution aroused great enthusiasm in Kamensky; he undertook, among other things, to do cultural work in the Red Army. In the 1920s Kamensky turned increasingly to drama. As the regime departed from the ideals of the Revolution, curbed the revolutionary impulse, and checked experimentation in the arts, Kamensky lost his influence. From the 1930s on, his talents were given no room in which to develop further. He died after an illness that lasted for 13 years.

In its antiurban orientation Kamensky's futurist poetry is close to that of Khlebnikov and S. Gorodetsky. Kamensky glorifies nature, the primitive, and the elemental. His poetry is rich in neologisms, word play, and sound parallels that give structure to his verse. His novel Stenka Razin (written in 1914–15) is not a historical novel but a combination exalted by lyrical prose with poetry. Kamensky praises the restlessness and rebelliousness of the Russian people; he portrays Razin as a gusli player and bard (with autobiographical features). Kamensky not only revised the novel extensively but also wrote his best narrative poem, Serdtse narodnoe—Stenka Razin (1918; The Heart of the People—Stenka Razin), on the basis of this novel. His 1919 stage production of Stenka Razin linked the play's conclusion to the revolutionary present. Several of his dramas were performed up to 1927; the majority, however, remained in manuscript. Two later narrative poems draw from the same thematic sphere as the first: Yemelyan Pugachov (1931) and Ivan Bolotnikov (1934); they contain more historical elements and are artistically weaker. This is also true of the poems Kamensky wrote on contemporary themes. Of his realistic prose, Leto na Kamenke (1927; Summer on the Kamenka) deserves attention for its fine portrayal of nature in Kamensky's native area, the Ural-Kama region. Kamensky also wrote memoirs about the futurist period, including Zhizn s Mayakovskim (1940; Life with Mayakovsky).

Works: Zemljanka (lyrical short stories), 1911; Tango s korovami: Železobetonnye poèmy (poems), 1914; Sten'ka Razin (novel), 1916, 2d ed. under the title Stepan Razin, 1918; Zvučal vesnejanki (poems), 1918; Serdce narodnoe—Sten'ka Razin (narrative poem), 1918; Sten'ka Razin (play), 1919; 27 priklju-čenij-Kharta Džojsa (novel), 1924; Sbornik p'es (collected plays), 1925; Puškin i Dantes (novel), 1928; Izbr. stikhi (selected poems), 1934; Tri poèmy (narrative poems), 1935; Rodina sča-st'ja (poems), 1937; Žizn' s Majakovskim (memoirs), 1940 (reprinted, Munich, 1974); Izbr., 1958; Poèmy (narrative poems), 1958; Leto na Kamenke (novel and short stories), 1961; Stikhotvorenija i poèmy (lyric and narrative poems), 1966; Stikhi (poems), 1977.

Secondary Lit.: K. Čukovskij, Futuristy, 1922; S. Gorodeckij, in Lit. gazeta Nov. 16, 1961; E. Večtomova, in Zvezda 1962:8; N. L. Stepanov, in Stikhotvorenija i poèmy, 1966; A. Kašina-Evreinova, in Russkaja mysl' Paris, Jan. 20, 1972, p. 8; S. Ginc, Perm', 1974; B. Sluckij, in Stikhi, 1977; V. Bubrin, Diss., Univ. of Toronto, 1982; N. Zinov'ev, in Lit. gazeta April 18, 1984, p. 5.

**Kándel, Féliks Solomónovich,** prose writer (b. Oct. 21, 1932, Moscow). From 1950 to 1956 Kandel completed his studies at the Moscow Institute for Aviation; until 1962 he built thermojets. In 1963 he began working primarily as a writer using the pseudonym F. Kamov. Kandel became especially well known as a scriptwriter of animated films; the film and television series he helped create, "Nu pogodi!" (Now, Wait a Minute!), enjoyed great popularity in the Soviet Union. After 1973, Kandel fought to gain permission for himself and other Jews to emigrate to Israel; he was finally granted permission in the fall of 1977. In Israel, under his own name, Kandel published books about life in the Soviet Union that he had written there without hope of publication. He first published his third book, Zona otdykha (1979; The Region of Rest), written in 1976–77, then the fourth, Vrata iskhoda nashego (1980; The Gate of Our Exodus), written from 1974 to 1978 partly in Moscow and partly in Jerusalem. Following these works about the experiences of a Jew wishing to emigrate, he published previously written novels: Koridor (1981; The Corridor), written between 1967 and 1969, *Pervy etazh* (1982; The Ground Floor), written from 1971 to 1973, and *Na noch glyadya* (1985; Casting a Look on Night), written from 1974 to 1976. Kandel lives in Jerusalem and works as a journalist for Israeli radio.

Kandel's often satiric and ironic prose gains poetic force through its lyrical and musical descriptive style. *Koridor* depicts life in a Soviet communal apartment and sheds light on the fate of many. *Pervy etazh* and *Na noch glyadya* form a pair, in which Kandel depicts the lives of two brothers who had come from a village to Moscow. One of them remains on the ground floor of life, the other is able to reach the higher floors of power. The affliction of the poorest, the dependence of the drunkard, the helplessness of the clergy, the endangerment of female taxi drivers—with human compassion, Kandel provides unsparing insight into these aspects of life. *Zona otdykha* is the report of his 15 days in prison with other Jewish demonstrators, a testament to human fellowship under the degrading conditions of imprisonment in the Soviet Union during the 1970s. *Vrata iskhoda nashego* deals with the difficulties Jews have in emigrating from the USSR and, in its analysis of anti-Semitism, begins with the history of the destruction of the Jewish theater during the struggle against COSMOPOLITANISM. *Ljudi mimoyezzhiye* (1984–85; People Passing By), a journey both realistic and surrealistic through the Russia of today, shows Kandel as a satirist full of humor who is able to describe people in their relationships vividly. Kandel's works have no well-developed plot but they are unified through other aspects of form and content. Furthermore, Kandel is a master at creating detail, dialogue, and musical, rhythmical representation.

*Works:* Ja—*malen'kij* (short story), in *Novyj mir* 1966:10; *Koridor* (novel), excerpts in *Grani*, Frankfurt am Main, 102:1976, 105:1977, separate ed., Jerusalem, 1981; short stories, in *Kontinent*, Paris, 11:1977, 16:1978, and in *Vremja i my*, Tel Aviv, 29:1978; *Zona otdykha* (pov.), excerpts in *Kontinent* 20:1979, separate ed., Jerusalem, 1979; *Vrata iskhoda našego* (pov.), Tel Aviv, 1980; *Pervyj ètaž* (novel), London, 1982; interview, in *Russkaja mysl'*, Paris, Oct. 28, 1982, p. 7; *Ljudi mimoezžie* (travel articles), in *Kontinent* 41–43:1984–85, separate ed., Jerusalem, 1986; *Na noč' gljadja* (novel), Frankfurt am Main, 1985.

*Secondary Lit.:* V. Maksimov et al., in *Kontinent* 10:1976; K. Sapgir, in *Kontinent* 23:1980 and in *Russkaja mysl'* Dec. 31, 1981, p. 10;

Anon., in *Kontinent* 25:1980; N. Gorbanevskaja, in Kandel's *Pervyj ètaž*, 1982; M. Khejfec, in *Kontinent* 34:1982; Anon., in *Kontinent* 48:1986.

**Karav.yeva, Ánna Aleksándrovna,** prose writer (b. Dec. 27 [Dec. 15], 1893, Perm—d. May 21, 1979, Moscow). Karavayeva taught from 1911 to 1913 after completing her studies at the local gymnasium; she was a student in the Department of History and Philology at the Bestuzhev Institute in St. Petersburg until 1916; after the Revolution she held various teaching posts, including one at a Party school in Barnaul in the Altai. Karavayeva began her literary career in 1922; in 1926 she joined the Communist Party; she moved to Moscow in 1928, where she associated herself with VAPP after briefly belonging to PEREVAL. From 1931 to 1938 she was editor of the journal *Molodaya gvardiya*, where her friendship with N. Ostrovsky began. During World War II, Karavayeva lived in the Urals and worked as a correspondent for *Pravda*. Her trilogy *Rodina* (1950; Homeland), based on personal experiences, complies with the principle of PARTY SPIRIT (the novel received a Stalin Prize for 1950, 3d class). Karavayeva lived in Moscow and was a member of the board of the Writers Union of the USSR from 1934 on.

For her early short fiction Karavayeva selected the common subject of the transformation of the Russian village by revolutionary forces; she advocated the unity of the working and the farming classes. Her stay in Barnaul also resulted in a historical *povest* about serf workers in the gold mines in the period of Catherine the Great, *Zolotoy klyuv* (1925; The Golden Beak). Karavayeva's first novel, *Lesozavod* (1928; The Timber Mill), belongs, with F. Gladkov's *Tsement*, to the body of early literature about industrial reconstruction; it illustrates the leading role of the Party in the economic sector as well as in the cultivation of a collective consciousness. On the 20th anniversary of the Komsomol in 1938, Karavayeva dedicated a book to the role of young people in the struggle for Soviet power. The three novels constituting *Rodina*, written between 1943 and 1950, are based on *Stalinskiye mastera* (1943; Stalin's Craftsmen), Karavayeva's journalistic articles about the work being done in relocated armament plants. In the post-Stalinist period she published memoirs and articles about her journeys as a delegate abroad. Karavayeva, who saw herself as a tireless fighter for communism, followed in such a narrow sense the Party dictum that literature should educate the reader that her conflicts were criticized for being contrived and, among other things, her dialogue was criticized for lacking credibility.

Works: Medvežatnoe (pov.), 1926; Lesozavod (novel), 1928; Dvor (pov.), 1929; Lena iz Žuravlinoj rošči (novel), 1938, 1970; Zolotoj kljuv (pov.), 1939, 1968; Stalinskie mastera (articles), 1943 (title later changed to Ural'skie mastera); Ogni (novel), 1944; Razbeg (novel), 1948; Rodnoj dom (novel), 1950; Rodina (novel-trilogy, consisting of Ogni; Razbeg; Rodnoj dom), 1951; Po dorogam žizni (memoirs), 1957; Grani žizni (novel), 1963; Zvëzdnaja stolica. Zapiski i vospominanija sovremennika (essays and memoirs), 1968.—Sobr. soč., 6 vols., 1927–29; 5 vols. (of which only vols. 1–3, 5 were published), 1930; 5 vols., 1957–58; Izbr. proizv., 1967; 2 vols., 1973.

Secondary Lit.: N. Zamoškin, in Novyj mir 1926:7; L. Krupenikov, in Novyj mir 1947:10; L. Skorino, in her Sem' portretov, 1956; Ju. Pukhov, in Moskva 1958:12; RSPP 2:1964; I. Kozlov, in Lit. Rossija Dec. 21, 1973, p. 5, and June 10, 1983, p. 16; obituary, in Lit. gazeta May 30, 1979, p. 2; Šenfel'd, in Russkaja mysl', Paris, June 28, 1979, p. 9; V. Karavaeva, in Moskva 1983:12.

**Kasátkin, Iván Mikháylovich,** prose writer (b. April 11 [March 30], 1880, Baranovitsy, prov. Kostroma—d. May 13, 1938 [?], while imprisoned). Kasatkin's father was a peasant; later, a day laborer. Kasatkin had a hard childhood and was forced to earn his own living; he learned to read at the age of 13. In the late 1890s he moved to St. Petersburg; in 1902 he joined the Social Democrats and was arrested and exiled several times for being a revolutionary. Kasatkin's first publication, a short story, appeared in 1907; in 1916 his first volume of collected stories, Lesnaya byl (A Forest Tale), was published. After the Revolution, Kasatkin helped to organize the peasant writers. From 1925 to 1935 he edited various journals (Krasnaya niva, Kolkhoznik) and worked as an editor for the State Publishing House for Literature in Moscow. His pre-Revolutionary short stories and several new ones appeared in numerous editions up to 1937. In 1938 Kasatkin became a victim of the government purges; not until his REHABILITATION some 20 years later did his name reappear in print.

Kasatkin's short stories, taken from the peasant milieu to which he confined his work, have extraordinary verbal power. He was able convincingly to depict his deep inner bond with the peasants' lot and his real knowledge of their way of life. His skillfully composed stories are very simply structured. The plot, rich in vivid details, advances slowly; the individual sentences, rich in epithets, develop in the same leisurely manner. The dialogue reflects folk speech in its choice of vocabulary and the peasant way of thinking in its structure, without ever appearing artificial. Compared to the high esteem in which the short stories Kasatkin wrote before the Revolution were held, the new stories written during the Soviet period were criticized for offering only an objectively correct picture of the backward village, not "the germ cells of real ideals" (Divilkovsky). In the judgment of V. Ivanov, Kasatkin's death in GULAG cut off his talent just as it was gradually concentrating itself into "a great, perhaps an epic work."

Works: Lesnaja byl' (short stories), 1916, new eds. with different contents: 2d, 1919, 3d, 1923, 4th, 1925; Derevenskie rasskazy (short stories), 1925; Galčata (short stories), 1930; Tak bylo (short stories), 1935; Pered rassvetom (short stories), 1977.—Sobr. soč., 3 vols., 1928–29; Izbr. rasskazy, 1933, 1937, 1957.

Secondary Lit.: L. G., in Novyj mir 1925:9; A. Divil'kovskij, in Novyj mir 1926:7; N. Zamoškin, in Novyj mir 1927:7; V. Ivanov, foreword to Kasatkin's Izbr. rasskazy, 1957, and in his own Sobr. soč., vol. 8, pp. 397–406; RSPP 2:1964; V. Meškov, in Lit. Rossija April 11, 1980, p. 19.

**Kassíl, Lev Abrámovich,** author of books for children and young people, prose writer (b. July 10 [June 27], 1905, Pokrovskaya, prov. Samara—d. June 21, 1970, Moscow). Kassil's father was a doctor; his mother, a music teacher. Kassil moved to Moscow in 1923; he studied mathematics but did not complete the degree. He began his career in literature and journalism in 1925. Kassil was introduced as a writer of children's literature by V. Mayakovsky in the journal Novy LEF in 1927. Based on autobiographical material, his two most important works, Konduit (1930; The Grade. Book) and Shvambraniya (1933; Eng. tr., The Land of Shvambrania, 1935), deal with school life before the Revolution. With Vratar Respubliki (1938; Goalkeeper of the Republic) and Cheremysh, brat geroya (1938; Eng. tr., The Hero's Brother, 1957), Kassil wrote the first Soviet sports novels. His subsequent books, which he planned in great detail, are also dedicated to current topics and serve to educate young people in the spirit of communism. Several of his works from the Stalin period were criticized for their artificial romanticism and his later war stories were accused of false heroism. Kassil received a Stalin Prize (for 1950, 3d class) for *Ulitsa mladshego syna* (1949; The Street of the Youngest Son), a povest written in collaboration with the journalist M. Polyanovsky that glorifies a student's activity as a partisan. Of Kassil's post-Stalinist children's literature, the best known is his publicistic work *Pro zhizn sovsem khoroshuyu* (1959; All About a Really Great Life), which, written in the form of a dialogue, popularized the Communist ideal in connection with the 21st Party Congress; S. Baruzdin rated it as equal in importance to M. Ilyin's *Rasskaz o velikom plane* (1930).

*Works:* Konduit (pov.), 1930; Švambranija (pov.), 1933 (see above) (later combined with Konduit into one povest); Vratar' Respubliki (novel), 1938; Čeremyš, brat geroja (pov.), 1938 (see above); Velikoe protivostojanie (novel), vol. 1, 1941, vols. 1–2, 1947; Dorogie moi mal'čiški (pov.), 1944; Ulica mladšego syna (pov.), 1949; Rannij voskhod (pov.), 1953 (Eng. tr., Early Dawn, 1956); Povesti, 1955; Pro žizn' sovsem khorošuju, 1959; Bud'te gotovy, Vaše vysočestvo! (pov.), 1964; Sportivnye rasskazy (short stories), 1967; Tri strany, kotorykh net na karte (publicistic prose), 1970.—Sobr. soč., 5 vols., 1965–66.

*Secondary Lit.:* I. Svirskaja, Tvorčestvo L. A. K., 1955; I. Krotova, postscript to Kassil''s Povesti, 1955; S. Baruzdin, in Moskva 1960:5 and in Lit. gazeta July 1, 1970, p. 3; V. Nikolaev, Dorogami mečty i poiska, 1965; A. Ivič, in his Vospitanie pokolenij, 4th ed., 1969; S. M. Lojter, 1973; Ju. Jakovlev, in Oktjabr' 1975:11; Žizn' i tvorčestvo L. K., 1979; M. Priležaeva, in Lit. gazeta July 23, 1980, p. 6.

**Katáyev, Iván Ivánovich,** prose writer (b. May 27 [May 14], 1902, Moscow—d. May 2, 1939 [?], while imprisoned). Katayev's father was a history professor. Katayev attended the gymnasium in Moscow and Suzdal. In 1919 he volunteered for the Red Army and became a member of the Communist Party; beginning in 1921 he studied economics at Moscow University. Katayev worked as a journalist until 1927. In 1923 he joined RAPP; in 1926 he became one of the most important members of the writers' group PEREVAL. Katayev pursued his literary career from 1927 to 1937; he wrote mostly short stories that appeared in the publications of Pereval and in Krasnaya

nov, Nashi dostizheniya, 30 dney, Prozhektor, and others. His first book was published in 1928; in 1930 he was sent on assignment to gather material for the literary propagandization of collectivization; in 1932 he became a member of the organizational committee of the Writers Union of the USSR; in 1934 he joined the board of the Writers Union. In 1937 Katayev became a victim of Stalinist repression because of his previous membership in Pereval. His REHABILITATION took place in 1955.

Katayev wrote only short prose that was often poetically structured: for example, Poet (1928; The Poet), Serdtse (1928; The Heart), Zhena (1927; The Wife), and Moloko (1930; Milk; written 1929). This last short story, which addresses the theme of collectivization, triggered Party criticism because of its humane and conciliatory position with regard to the persecuted peasants (kulaks). Katayev prefers a first-person narrative structure; in Moloko he additionally uses the literary device of stylizing the speech mannerisms of his fictional narrator. His fine descriptive gift is evident in the picture of the city of Moscow that he sketches in Leningradskoye shosse (1933; The Leningrad Highway). Katayev's prose from the period of the first Five-Year Plan approaches objective reportage but is nevertheless artistically appealing; it is as rich in lyrical elements as his short stories. His last prose work, Pod chistymi zvyozdami (1936; Beneath the Clear Stars), was not permitted to appear until 20 years after it was written (in Lit. Moskva 1956:2); during those two decades Katayev's name was expunged from literature.

*Works:* Serdce (short stories), 1928 (includes title story, Poèt, Žena); Žena (short story), 1930; Moloko (short story), in Rovesniki 7:1930; Dviženie. Janvar' i fevral' 1930 na Kubani (short stories), 1932; Leningradskoe šosse (short story), in Krasnaja nov' 1933:11; Čelovek na gore (short stories), 1934; Otečestvo (short stories), 1935; Izbr., 1957; Pod čistymi zvëzdami (short stories), 1969; Serdce (pov. and short stories), 1980.

*Secondary Lit.:* N. Zamoškin, in Novyj mir 1928:12; N. Atarov, in Moskva 1957:1; V. Goffenšefer, foreword to Kataev's Izbr., 1957; RSPP 2:1964; E. Mindlin, in his Neobyknovennye sobesedniki, 1968; Vospominanija ob I. K., 1970.

**Katáyev, Valentín Petróvich,** prose writer, playwright (b. Jan. 28 [Jan. 16], 1897, Odessa— d. April 12, 1986, Moscow). Katayev's father was a teacher. Katayev's first poems were published during his school years (after 1910); he served as an officer in World War I: after 1919 he wrote journalistic propaganda and did political agitation for ROSTA in Odessa; in 1921 he worked in Kharkov with the YugROSTA; after 1922 he worked in Moscow, first as a journalist (Gudok), later as a writer. During World War II he worked as a correspondent for Pravda and Krasnaya zvezda, periodically at the front. For his povest about the war, Syn polka (1945; The Son of the Regiment), he won a Stalin Prize (for 1945, 2d class). From 1946 to 1954 he worked on the editorial staff of Novy mir. In 1955 he founded and until 1962 served as the editor in chief for the journal Yunost. He promoted young talents such as V. Aksyonov. From 1958 on, he was a member of the Communist Party. Katayev belonged to the board of the Writers Union of the USSR from 1934 on and lived in Moscow and Peredelkino. He conducted himself in accordance with Party dictates by refusing to sign the petition for A. Sinyavsky and Yu. Daniel and by signing the letter against A. Solzhenitsyn (Aug. 31, 1973).

After his first attempts at lyric poetry, Katayev wrote short stories set during World War I and the Civil War. At the beginning of the 1920s, complexly structured adventure stories with the theme of world revolution followed. Katayev became especially well known for his satirical novel Rastratchiki (1926; Eng. trs., The Embezzlers, 1929; Embezzlers, 1975), an amusing caricature of the NEP period. His comedy about mistaken identity, Kvadratura kruga (1928; Eng. tr., Squaring the Circle, 1936), is theatrically effective both at home and abroad to this day, owing less to its critical insight into the apartment shortage and student marriages than to its masterful dramatic construction. Katayev responded to the Party appeal for descriptions of industrial development during the first Five-Year Plan in Vremya vperyod (1932; Eng. tr., Time Forward!, 1933), a "chronicle povest" about enthusiastic overfulfillment of quotas in Magnitogorsk that with "its cinematographic style of flashbacks, rapidly shifting scenes, terse dialogue, and black-and-white character portrayal projected against roughly sketched backgrounds is definitely a departure from psychological realism and is somewhat reminiscent of American expressionists, particularly of the early Dos Passos" (Slonim). Beleyet parus odinoky (1936; Eng. trs., Lonely White Sail; or, Peace Is Where the Tempests Blow, 1937; A White Sail Gleams, 1954), a widely acclaimed, strongly autobiographical novel set in Odessa, became, through the in-

clusion of the 1905 Revolution, the starting point for the four-part series written over a 25-year period, Volny Chornogo morya (1961; Black Sea Waves).

The second part, Khutorok v stepi (1956; Eng. tr., The Small Farm in the Steppe, 1958), takes place from 1910 to 1912; the next one, Zimny veter (1960; Winter Wind), is set during the Civil War. The fourth part, Katakomby (1961; Catacombs), dedicated to Odessa's fate during World War II, was first published in 1949. Katayev reworked the novel at that time in response to M. Bubennov's sharp criticism of his failure to consider the Communist Party (Za vlast Sovetov [1951; For the Powers of the Soviets]). With the publication in 1965 of Svyatoy kolodets (Eng. tr., The Holy Well, 1967), which was well received both at home and abroad, Katayev shifted from a chronologically coherent narrative to a new style that harkened back to his own early experiments with form (Ser Genri i chort [1920; Sir Henry and the Devil]; Zheleznoye koltso [1923; The Iron ring]) and associatively linked the half-realistic with the half-fantasy-like in the depiction of his American experiences. In doing so he partially strives to depict an incoherent way of thinking and partially, as author, playfully uses his artistic media. Recollections of I. Bunin, his literary mentor, and of V. Mayakovsky, as well as thoughts about Russian literature, form the main body of the similarly loosely constructed book Trava zabveniya (1967; Eng. tr., The Grass of Oblivion, 1969). In Kubik (1969; Brick), Katayev depicts the fragility of the world in the alternation between an impersonal, third-person narrator and the first-person narratives of various fictitious "I"s. In Razbitaya zhizn ili volshebny rog Oberona (1972; Eng. tr., A Mosaic of Life; or, The Magic Horn of Oberon: Memoirs of a Russian Childhood, 1976), a collection of approximately 250 childhood memories in unchronological order, the memories become almost secondary to the process of remembering. Similarly in Almazny moy venets (1978; My Diamond Wreath), Katayev associatively combines memories of the 1920s with reflections without mentioning the names of the authors concerned.

Works: Ser Genri i čёrt (short stories), Berlin, 1923; Železnoe kol'co (short story), in Nakanune, Berlin, May 27, 1923; Ostrov Èrendorf (novel), 1924; Rastratčiki (pov. and short stories), 1927 (see above); Otec (short stories and poems), 1928; Kvadratura kruga (play), in Krasnaja nov' 1928:5 (see above); Vremja vperëd (pov.), 1932 (see above); Beleet parus odinokij (novel), 1936 (see above); Ja—

syn trudovogo naroda (novel), 1937; Žena (pov.), 1944 (Eng. tr., The Wife, 1946); Syn polka (pov.), 1945; Za vlast' Sovetov (novel), 1949, new ed., 1951, 2d new ed. under the title Katakomby, as vol. 4 of Volny Černogo morja, 1961; Khutorok v stepi (novel), 1956 (see above); Zimnij veter (novel), 1960; Volny Černogo morja (novel in four parts), 1961; Počti dnevnik (diary), 1962, 2d ed., considerably revised, 1978; Svjatoj kolodec (novel), 1965 (see above); Trava zabvenija (pov.), 1967 (see above); Kubik (pov.), in Novyj mir 1969:2; Raznoe (short stories), 1970; Razbitaja žizn' ili volšebnyj rog Oberona (memoirs), in Novyj mir 1972:7–8; separate ed., 1973 (see above); Fialka (play), in Teatr 1974:12; Kladbišče v skulinakh (novel), in Novyj mir 1975:10; Almaznyj moj venec (pov.), 1979; Junošeskij roman moego starogo druga Saši Pčëlkina rasskazannyj im samim (novel), in Novyj mir 1982:10–11.—Sobr. soč., 5 vols., 1956–57; 9 vols., 1968–72; 10 vols., 1983–86.

Secondary Lit.: T. Sidel'nikova, 1957; B. Brajnina, 1960; RSPP 2:1964; L. Skorino, 1965; A. P. Reilly, America in Contemporary Soviet Literature, New York, 1971; M. Priležaeva, in Lit. gazeta Jan. 26, 1972, p. 3; E. A. Val'burov, in Russkaja lit. 1973:2; A. Drawicz, in his Zaproszenie do podróży, Kraców, 1974; V. Iverni, in Kontinent, Paris, 7:1976; P. M. Johnson, Diss., Cornell Univ., 1976; W. Cukierman, in Russian Language Journal 111:1978; D. Kiziria, Diss., Indiana Univ., 1979; R. Russell, Diss., Edinburgh Univ., 1979, B. Galanov, 1982; Ju. Karpenko, in Russkaja reč' 1984:4; E. Tudorovskaja, in Grani, Frankfurt am Main, 140:1986.

**Kavérin, Veniamín Aleksándrovich** (until 1930 pseud. of V. A. Zilber), prose writer (b. April 19 [April 6], 1902, Pskov). Kaverin's father was a musician. Kaverin grew up in Pskov, completed secondary school in Moscow in 1919, and there began to study at the university. In 1920 he moved to Petrograd, completed his course in Arabic languages and literatures in 1923, and defended his doctoral dissertation in Russian philology in 1929. In 1920 Kaverin began to write short stories and became a member of the SERAPION BROTHERS. In 1923 his first collection of fantastic, plot-intensive stories met with success. Starting with his first novel, Konets khazy (1925; The End of a Gang), which was also successful, be began to include current events in his writing. Khudozhnik neizvesten (1931; Eng. tr., The Unknown Artist, 1947), like Konets khazy, also takes place in Leningrad and describes a

spiritual conflict in the late 1920s—the increasing exclusion of artists by politically thinking officials with no appreciation for art. Kaverin was sharply attacked by RAPP for everything that he wrote during that time. His novel Ispolneniye zhelaniy (1935–36; Eng. tr., The Larger View, 1938) treats ethical problems in the field of humanities; it was substantially revised for a new edition in 1973. During World War II, Kaverin worked as a correspondent for Izvestiya. His novel Dva kapitana (1938–44; Eng. trs., Two Captains, 1942, 1957) was his only work to win lasting recognition from the official critics (Stalin Prize for 1943–44, 2d class). In 1966 Kaverin, who was maliciously defamed in the phase following the Party Resolution of 1946 (see PARTY RESOLUTIONS ON LITERATURE), wrote about these times: "I, too, was deceived, guilty without guilt, punished with humiliation and fear. I, too, believed and believed not and worked sullenly." Before the Second Congress of the Writers Union of the USSR in 1954, no one expressed writers' hopes for a free Russian literature that would be allowed to develop without guardianship as validly as Kaverin. From that time on, he never tired of intervening for true poetry and liberal literary policy. Together with K. Paustovsky and others, Kaverin published the almanac Literaturnaya Moskva (1956) in which his novel Poiski i nadezhdy (Searches and Hopes) was included. His title characterizes this epoch of Soviet literature just as the title of I. Erenburg's work Ottepel does (see THAW). Kaverin provided for the literary REHABILITATION of Yu. Tynyanov and M. Bulgakov. He contributed to the exposition of the truth about the actual remaining danger from Stalinists with his novel Dvoynoy portret (1966; Double Portrait). In essays he fought for the candid inclusion of the Serapion Brothers in the history of literature. He signed the petition for the condemned A. Sinyavsky and Yu. Daniel. For artistic reasons, he featured A. Solzhenitsyn, together with K. Paustovsky and M. Bulgakov, in Nasushchnye voprosy literatury (1967; Essential Questions of Literature), a talk written for the Fourth Congress of the Writers Union of the USSR that was suppressed in the Soviet Union but was published in Frankfurt am Main in 1971. In 1968, in an open letter, Kaverin broke with K. Fedin when the latter withheld Solzhenitsyn's Rakovy korpus from Russian readers. Through his memoirs, V starom dome (1971; In the Old House), he contributed to the return of OBERIU members D. Kharms and A. Vvedensky and of many other persecuted writers to he literary scene. As a late literary work, his novel based on original letters, Pered zerkalom (1971; In Front of the Mirror), is very valuable. The Academy of Sciences of the USSR granted Kaverin barely one of the 2,900 pages in its four-volume history of literature n 1967–71. He lives in Moscow. In 1930 Kaverin adopted his pen name as his real name.

Kaverin is one of the most important Russian novelists writing plot-intensive, artistically arranged novels that are often absorbing detective stories. Starting with Konets khazy, whose allure also lay in its inclusion of thieves' cant, Kaverin worked with several plot lines. Khudozhnik neizvesten, one of the last and most significant experiments with form in early Soviet literature, contains the act of writing hat novel as one of its own story lines. Ispolneniye zhelaniy, dedicated to the joy of philologic research and the danger of early fame, was tightened by its later revision, whereas Konets khazy, probably truncated by the censor, has the charm of a topical satire only in its earliest version. In Otkrytaya kniga (1949–56; incomplete Eng. tr., Open Book, 1955), a trilogy ending with Poiski i nadezhdy, Kaverin solves a psychological and narrative problem by letting a woman narrator recount in the first person the story that encompasses 35 years. In Dvoynoy portret, the novel about a dismissed scholar who is sent to a prison camp because a pseudoscientist denounces him, not only is Kaverin's frequent knack of contrasting two figures absolutely essential to the story, but his return to the technique of describing the origins of the novel itself is also functional, for it deepens the desired image of both the difficulties of coming to terms with the Stalinist past and the limits in attempting to do so. In Pered zerkalom Kaverin reveals the fate, especially in emigration, of a Russian woman painter during the period from 1910 to 1932 by cautiously incorporating original evidence in fictional form. Osveshchonnye okna (1974–76; Illuminated Windows) and Dvukhchasovaya progulka (1978; A Two-Hour Walk) are examples of his poetic treatment of his own childhood and youth, whereas in Verlioka (1982) he resumes the thread of earlier fairy tales. The high literary sense expressed through the changing structure of his own prose also characterizes Kaverin's numerous essays about literature.

Works: Mastera i podmaster'ja (short stories), 1923; Konec khazy (novel), 1926; Devjat' desjatykh sud'by (novel), 1926; Khudožnik neizvesten (novel), 1931 (see above); Ispolnenie želanij (novel), 1935–36 (see above), revised in Izbr., 1973; Dva kapitana (novel), 1940 (see above); Otkrytaja kniga (novel-trilogy), 1953–56: (1) Junost'; (2) Doktor Vlasenkova, in one vol., 1953 (see above); (3) Poiski i nadezdy, in Lit. Moskva 1956:2; "Zdravstvuj, brat. Pisat' očen' trudno . . .": Portrety, pis'ma o lit., vospominanija, 1965; Dvojnoj portret (novel), 1967; Otkrytoe pis'mo Konstantinu Fedinu, in Zarubež'e, Munich, 1968:2 (Eng. tr., "An Open Letter to Konstantin Fedin," in Survey 68:1968); V starom dome (memoirs), in Zvezda 1971:9–10; Nasuščnye voprosy literatury (essay), in Posev, Frankfurt am Main, 1971:10; Pered zerkalom (novel), 1972; Sobesednik (essays), 1973; Osveščonnye okna (novel), 1976; Petrogradskij student (novel), 1976; (coauthored with V. Savčenko) Éksperiment (play), in Teatr 1977:2; Dvukhčasovaja progulka (novel and pov.), 1979; Večernij den' (letters, encounters, portraits), 1980; Verlioka (pov.), in Novyj mir 1982:1; Khudožnik neizvesten i drugie proizv., Jerusalem, 1982; Nauka rasstavanija (novel), 1983; Zagadka (pov.), in Oktjabr' 1984:1; Pis'mennyj stol (memoirs, letters), in Oktjabr' 1984:9.— Izbr., 1973; Izbr. proizv., 2 vols., 1977; Sobr. soč., 8 vols., 1980–83.

Secondary Lit.: N. Maslin, in Novyj mir 1948:4; RSSP 2:1964; T. Khmel'nickaja, in Novyj mir 1967:1; W. Kasack, epilogues to the translations into German, Das Ende einer Bande, 1973, and Das doppelte Porträt, 1973; A. Urban, in Zvezda 1973:12; T. Khlopljankina, in Lit. obozrenie 1974:9; Ju. Krutogorov, in Lit. obozrenie 1975:4; H. Oulanoff, Ann Arbor, 1976; V. Gusev, M. Zolotonosov, in Lit. obozrenie 1979:8; E. K. Beaujour, in Slavic and East European Journal 1980:3; A. I. Forman, Diss., Brown Univ., 1982; L. Sobolev, in Lit. obozrenie 1984:10; D. Šturman, in Russkaja mysl', Paris, May 10, 1984, p. 10; O. Novikova, V. Novikov, in Novyj mir 1985:3; E. Gessen, in Grani, Frankfurt am Main, 136:1985.

**Kazakévich, Emmanuíl Génrikhovich,** prose writer (b. Feb. 24 [Feb. 11], 1913, Kremenchug, prov. Poltava—d. Sept. 22, 1962, Moscow). Kazakévich's father was a teacher and journalist. In 1930 Kazakevich completed engineering school in Kharkov; between 1931 and 1938 he was in the Soviet Far East, serving in the Jewish autonomous regions of Birobidzhan as cultural official, kolkhoz director, journalist, and director of the Birobidzhan theater. Between 1932 and 1941 Kazakevich published various literary works, primarily lyrical and narrative poetry in Yiddish, including translations from Russian. In 1938 he moved to Moscow. During World War II, Kazakevich saw combat duty; he rose from the rank of soldier to head of an army reconnaissance detachment at the conquest of Berlin. He was a member of the Communist Party from 1944. His prose in Russian, for which Kazakevich suddenly became famous in 1947, generated intense polemics; two of his works received Stalin Prizes in 1948 and 1950, while others were condemned from the ideological point of view. As the coeditor of *Literaturnaya Moskva*, in 1956 Kazakevich was actively involved in the regeneration of Russian literature; for him "the building of communism was inseparable from the exposure of Stalin and his methods" (*Voprosy lit.* 1962:5). "The sharpness and boldness of his thought, his free and intelligent talent, his profound integrity, the brilliance of his imagination, and that impetuous, human charm that instantly subjugates everyone made him one of the first and best people of our time," wrote K. Paustovsky of Kazakevich. From 1954 on, Kazakevich was a member of the board of the Writers Union of the USSR; he lived in Moscow.

*Zvezda* (1947; Eng. tr., *Star*, 1950), Kazakevich's first war story and the recipient of a Stalin Prize (for 1947, 2d class), is about the successful mission and the inescapable destruction of a reconnaissance unit behind enemy lines; it avoids heroic embellishments. His second war story, *Dvoye v stepi* (1948; Eng. tr., *Two Men in the Steppe*, in *Selected Works*, 1978), uses the example of a Soviet officer, who is facing the death sentence, and his guard, who dies in battle, to deal with the problem of mistrust during the Stalin years and to explore the existential questions of guilt, the fear of death, and the liberation that results from a willingness to die. The immediate and sharp condemnation of this work by dogmatic critics (for example, B. Solovyov), an attitude that persisted even after Stalin's death (K. Simonov, in *Pravda* Dec. 17, 1954), prevented the publication of Kazakevich's povest in book form until 1962. His novel about the last phase of the war, *Vesna na Odere* (1949; Eng. tr., *Spring on the Oder*, 1953), which received a Stalin Prize in 1950 (for 1949, 2d class), was weakened by its adherence to the principle of SOCIALIST REALISM requiring that the Party point of view be shown. *Serdtse druga* (1953; Eng. tr., *Heart of a Friend*, 1955) stresses the human problems of the individual caught in war; it was

defended by V. Kaverin against A. Fadeyev' attacks at the Second Congress of the Writer Union in 1954. *Dom na ploshchadi* (195( Eng. Tr., *The House on the Square*, 1957), novel about the first period of the occupatio of Germany, "is inclined, despite certain p( lemical, antidogmatic aspects, to the simpli fication of the difficult problem of postwa Germany" (Drawicz). After writing a poves about Lenin, *Sinyaya tetrad* (1961; Eng. tr *The Blue Notebook*, 1962), Kazakevich turne again to the theme of war in *Pri svete dny* (1961; Eng. tr., "By the Light of Day," i) *Selected Works*, 1978), a short story that use double perspective to make a particularly pro found psychological impact. Period criticisr and the problem of alienation are evoked i) *Priyezd ottsa v gosti k synu* (1962; A Fathe Visits His Son), a short story with a relativel innocuous plot. Kazakevich's later works ar "distinguished by an abundance of master fully developed psychological detail, a re lentlessly unsentimental treatment of huma nature and, at the same time, a remarkabl( understanding of the human heart" (D. Brown)

Works: *Zvezda* (pov.), 1947 (see above); *Dvo(* *v stepi (pov.), in Znamja* 1948:5 (see above) *Vesna na Odere* (novel), 1950 (see above) *Serdce druga* (pov.), in *Novyj mir* 1953:1 1954 (see above); *Vengerskie vstreči* (articles) 1955; *Dom na ploščadi* (novel), 1956 (se( above); *Pri svete dnja* (short story), 1961 (se( above); *Sinjaja tetrad'* (pov.), 1961 (see above) *Povesti: Zvezda, Dvoe v stepi, Serdce drug(* (pov.), 1962; *Priezd otca v gosti k synu* (shor story), 1962.—*Soč.*, 2 vols., 1963; *Izbr. proizv.* 2 vols., 1974; *Sobr. soč.*, 3 vols., 1985–.

Secondary Lit.: B. Solov'ëv, in *Novyj mi.* 1948:10; L. Slavin, in *Lit. gazeta* March 8 1951; S. L'vov, in *Novyj mir* 1956:9; Z. Ke drina, in her *Lit.-kritičeskie stat'i*, 1956; V. Sur villo, in *Novyj mir* 1961:10 and 1966:1; K Paustovskij, in *Novyj mir* 1962:10; *RSPI* 2:1964; A. Bočarov, 1965, 1967, 1970; A. Med nikov, in *Novyj mir* 1968:8; S. Bytovoj, i) *Neva* 1970:8; A. Kron, in *Voprosy lit.* 1978:11 *Vospominanija o E. K.*, 1979.

**Kazakóv, Vladímir,** prose writer (b. Aug. 29( 1938, Moscow). Kazakov is of Russian, Ar menian, and Polish extraction. He was expellec from military school in 1956 and from th( Department of Humanities at university ir 1958. Between 1959 and 1962 he was a laborer (gold washer, stoker, lumberjack, among oth ers) in Kolyma. In 1965 he began writing absurdist literature that was not published in the Soviet Union. In 1966 he met the former futurist A. Kruchonykh, who advised him to write prose instead of poetry. In July 1972 Kazakov was baptized in the Russian Orthodox faith. Since 1972 his books have appeared in Germany, and additional individual texts have come out in journals there. Kazakov lives in Moscow.

Kazakov's first book, a collection of short prose and scenes written in 1967–68, *Moi vstrechi s Vladimirom Kazakovym* (1972; My Encounters with Vladimir Kazakov), reveals, in its scenes and dialogue both from everyday life and with historical personages, a conscious tie to FUTURISM and in particular to the Leningrad group OBERIU, which was being gradually rediscovered in those years. By removing logical referents Kazakov illustrates human isolation and the soulless cruelty of rational normality. The novel *Oshibka zhivykh* (1976; The Error of the Living), written in 1970, is a loose series of narrative units bearing a strong absurdist stamp. The title is an allusion to V. Khlebnikov's *Oshibka smerti* (1916; The Error of Death). The work as a whole is connected not by a continuous plot but by recurring names, by constantly repeated absurdist techniques (for example, reversal of subject and object, animation of objects), and by the frequent use of word complexes, such as *mirror, clock*, and *streetlamp*. His third volume, *Sluchayny voin* (1978; The Accidental Warrior), includes all the poems written between 1961 and 1976, six short dramas written between 1970 and 1974 (in which logical connections are abolished to an even greater extent than in Western absurdist drama), and a 1972 essay, *Zudesnik*, about Kruchonykh. His next two publications—*Zhizn prozy* (1982; The Life of Prose) and *Ot golovy do zvyozd* (1982; From Head to Stars), written between 1972 and 1974—reveal a similar structure: absence of plot; prevalence of scenes, thoughts, plays on words; an inclination toward the antithetical; and the later abrogation of previous statements. The titles of subsequent, as yet unknown books are *Prodolzheniye vozdukha* (1972; The Continuation of Air) and *V chest vremeni* (1973; In Honor of Time). Kazakov's short prose is very dense and word-conscious. It is a reaction against a system that believes that the world can be logically comprehended and that denies the existence of the transcendental.

*Works: Moi vstreči s Vladimirom Kazakovym. Proza. Sceny. Istoričeskie sceny*, Munich, 1972; *Ošibka živykh* (novel), Munich, 1976; *Slučajnyj voin. Stikhotvorenija*

*1961–76. Poemy—Dramy—Očerk "Zudesnik"* (poems, plays, essays), Munich, 1978; poems, in NRL: *Neue russische Literatur*, Almanach 2–3, 1979–80; *Klejmenaja noč'* (narrative poem), in *Wiener Slawistischer Almanach* 6:1980; *Žizn' prozy*, Munich, 1982; *Ot golovy do zvëzd* (novel), Munich, 1982.

*Secondary Lit.:* P. Urban, afterword in Kazakov's *Moi vstreči . . .* , 1972; W. Kasack, in *Neue Zürcher Zeitung* Aug. 15, 1974, p. 39, and in *Osteuropa* 1984:3; p. 229; A. Kostin, in *Russkaja mysl'*, Paris, July 22, 1976; Bertram Müller, Munich, 1978, and foreword in Kazakov's *Slučajnyj voin*, 1978; Vl. Markov, in *Fiction and Drama in Eastern and Southeastern Europe*, Columbus, Ohio, 1980.

**Kazakóv, Yúry Pávlovich**, prose writer (b. Aug. 8, 1927, Moscow—d. Nov. 29, 1982). Kazakov's father was a worker. In 1944 Kazakov entered a technical institute for architecture; from 1946 to 1951 he attended an academy of music; thereafter he worked as a musician in orchestras. In 1953 his first short story was published. From 1953 to 1958 he studied at the Gorky Literary Institute and published numerous short stories in journals as well as the collections *Arktur—gonchiy pyos* (1957; Eng. tr., *Arcturus: The Hunting Hound and Other Stories*, 1968) and *Manka* (1958). Kazakov continued to work with the short prose form, which brought him recognition at home and abroad, especially in connection with the next collections: *Na polustanke* (1959; At a Small Station) and *Po doroge* (1961; On the Way). Kazakov, who lived in Moscow, also worked as a translator. He was a delegate to the congresses of the Writers Union from 1965 to 1975 but was not allowed to vote in 1971.

Kazakov's short stories follow in the tradition of I. Bunin, A. Chekhov, and K. Paustovsky and are "possibly the best that were written in Russia in the fifties and sixties" (D. Brown). His prose is lyrical, closely tied to nature, marked by musical rhythm, and removed from dogmatism and contemporary politics, features that have caused conservative critics to denounce its decadence. The focal point of his short stories lies not in unusual occurrences but in the penetration of the commonplace that achieves poetic force through his delivery. Typical for him is the character "who has isolated himself from the normal flow of life about him, from ordinary social intercourse" (Kramer). "These and similar stories of solitude and defeat form the main bulk of Kazakov's work" (Slonim). "There are writers with an individuality so strongly marked that anything to which they have set their hand proclaims their authorship" (Gibian).

*Works: Teddi* (short story), 1957; *Arktur— gončij pës* (short stories), 1958 (see above); *Man'ka* (short stories), 1958; *Na polustanke* (short stories), 1959; *Po doroge* (short stories), 1961; *Goluboe in zelënoe* (short stories), 1963; *Dvoe v dekabre* (short stories), 1966; *Osen' v dubovykh lesakh* (short stories), 1969 (Eng. tr., *Autumn in the Oak Woods*, 1970); *Severnyj dnevnik* (diary), 1973; *Vo sne ty gor'ko plakal* (short stories), 1977: *Olen' i roga* (short stories), 1980; *Izbr.* (short stories), 1985.

*Translations: Selected Short Stories*, with introduction by G. Gibian, 1963; *Going to Town and Other Stories*, 1964; *The Smell of Bread and Other Stories*, 1965.

*Secondary Lit.:* K. D. Kramer, in *Slavic and East European Journal*, 1966; A. Bitov, in *Voprosy lit.* 1969:7; RSPP 7(1):1971; A. Ninov, in *Lit. gazeta* March 13, 1974, p. 4; E. Klepikova, in *Novyj mir* 1974:7; L. Mikhajlova, in *Lit. obozrenie* 1975:4; S. F. Orth, in *Russian Language Journal* 112:1978 and 118:1980; G. Goryšin, in *Naš sovremennik* 1986:12.

**Kazakóva, Rímma Fyódorovna**, poet (b. Jan. 27, 1932, Sevastopol). In 1954 Kazakova completed her studies in history at Leningrad University. Her first poems were published in 1955. For seven years she lived in the Soviet Far East and worked as a reader and editor in Khabarovsk. Her first volume of poetry, *Vstretimsya na Vostoke* (We Will Meet in the East), was published there in 1958. Other volumes followed every two or three years. In the early 1960s she moved to Moscow, where she evidently earns a living by translating from numerous languages. Kazakova, one of the talented poets who in the early post-Stalinist period made a name for herself, published a large selection from her five most important volumes (1955–78) in 1979. She was a member of the secretariat of the Writers Union of the USSR only from 1976 to 1981.

Kazakova's lyric poetry is rich with images and careful in word choice. From her childhood experience of World War II and of the difficulty of daily life in the Soviet Far East has grown her understanding of the value of sorrow. Her work is characterized by a search for human decency that was typical of the late 1950s and an aversion to pathos and propaganda. She writes contemplative lyric poems

in which nature occasionally reveals its symbolic power at the end. She also writes lyrical love poems with delicate empathy. Especially in her early poetry, the word is used as an expression of the experienced and is formed with a great awareness of responsibility. Later, much of her poetry is narrative in form and not very concise. On occasion, unusual metaphors may stand in too great a contrast to their context; however, a humane earnestness always underlies her poetry.

*Works: Vstretimsja na Vostoke* (poems), Khabarovsk, 1958; *Tam, gde ty* (poems), 1960; *Stikhi* (poems), 1962; *Izbrannaja lirika* (poems), 1964; *Pjatnicy* (poems), 1965; *V tajge ne plačut* (poems), Khabarovsk, 1965; *Poverit' snegu* (poems), Taškent, 1967; *Ëlki Zelënye* (poems), 1969; *Snežnaja baba* (poems), 1972; *Pomnju: Stikhi raznykh let* (poems), 1974; *Nabelo* (poems), 1977; *Ruslo; Izbrannye stikhotvorenija* (poems), 1979; *Strana ljubov'* (poems), 1980; *Probnyj kamen': Novaja kniga stikhov* (poems), 1982; *Sojdi s kholma* (poems), 1984.—*Izbr. proizv.*, 2 vols., 1985.

*Secondary Lit.:* S. Rassadin, in *Lit. gazeta* Aug. 11, 1960; M. Lapšin, in *Naš sovremennik* 1966:6 and in *Ogonëk* 1966:9; A. Mežirov, in *Lit. gazeta* March 8, 1966; A. Mikhajlov, in *Znamja* 1970:8; M. Nogteva and G. Kubat'jan, in *Lit. obozrenie* 1973:7; T. Žirmunskaja, in *Lit. gazeta* Aug. 1, 1973, p. 5; V. Korkija, in *Lit. obozrenie* 1978:6; I. Fonjakov, in *Lit. gazeta* March 3, 1982, p. 5.

**Kazántsev, Aleksándr Petróvich**, prose writer (b. Sept. 2 [Aug. 20], 1906, Akmolinsk). Kazantsev's father worked for the civil service. In 1930 Kazantsev graduated from a technical college in Tomsk and then worked for ten years in Moscow as an engineer in factories and research institutes. His report on the New York World's Fair (in *Novyj mir* 1939:12), where he was employed as chief engineer of the industrial division of the Soviet pavilion, ushered in his journalistic activity. In 1940 his first novel was published. After fighting in World War II, he became a professional writer in 1946; he belongs to the editorial staffs of popular scientific journals. Kazantsev joined the Communist Party in 1954. He lives in Moscow.

Kazantsev's first novel, *Pylayushchiy ostrov* (1940; The Flaming Island), concerns science fiction, as does a large portion of his work. This novel has been repeatedly reprinted since 1956. Kazantsev's utopian prose revolves around the topics of opening up the Arctic Ocean, conquering space, and the landing on earth of inhabitants of other planets. Kazantsev has been criticized for his arbitrary handling of scientific data, as well as for his trite and schematic plot development. Kazantsev is also active in popularizing technical knowledge, especially where agricultural machinery is concerned: *Mashiny poley kommunizma* (1953; Machines on the Fields of Communism). In the novel *Kupol nadezhdy* (1980; Dome of Hope), he develops a fanciful, idealistic image of the work done by people in Antarctica.

*Works: Pylajuščij ostrov* (novel), 1941, 1966; *Arktičeskij most* (novel), 1946; *Protiv vetra* (short stories), 1950 (Eng. tr., *Against the Wind*, 195?); *Mašiny polej kommunizma* (short stories), 1953; *Poljarnaja mečta* (novel), 1956; *Gost' iz kozmosa* (pov.), 1958; *Vnuki Marsa* (pov.), 1963; *L'dy vozvraščajutsja* (novel), 1964; *Sil'nee vremeni* (novel), 1973; *Kupol nadeždy* (novel), in *Molodaja gvardija* 1980:3–6, separate ed., 1980.—*Sobr. soč.*, 3 vols., 1977–78.

*Secondary Lit.*: A. Ivič, in *Novyj mir* 1955:11; S. Smuglyj, in *Naš sovremennik* 1960:6; V. Revič, in *Novyj mir* 1965:6; *RSPP* 7(1):1971; A. Filippov, in *Oktjabr'* 1973:6; M. Škerin, in *Lit. gazeta* Jan. 28, 1981, p. 5.

**Kázin, Vasíly Vasílyevich,** poet (b. Aug. 6 [July 25], 1898, Moscow—d. Oct. 1, 1981, Moscow). Kazin's father was a craftsman of peasant descent. Kazin completed secondary school in Moscow in 1918. His first poems date from 1914; from 1918 to 1920 he was an auditor at the Literary Studio of the Moscow PROLETKULT, published in proletarian journals, and worked on the editorial board of the Literary Section of the People's Commissariat for Education. In 1920 he became one of the cofounders of KUZNITSA. The poems assembled in Kazin's first volume of verse, *Rabochiy may* (1922; Working May), and his narrative poem *Lisya shuba i lyubov* (1926; Fox Fur and Love) brought Kazin recognition as one of the best of the proletarian poets; later he was accused of being bourgeois and was no longer considered to be a proletarian writer. From 1931 to 1940 Kazin was an editor of belles lettres for the State Publishing House. Between 1938 and 1953 his own work was hardly published at all. Kazin reestablished his reputation with the narrative poem *Veliky pochin* (1954; The Great Initiative), which glorified the introduction, on May 10, 1920,

of voluntary labor on nonworking days *(Subbotnik)* and in which Lenin himself appears. Kazin lived in Moscow.

Kazin's early poems deal with the joy of labor. In his "Kamenshchik" (1919; Eng. tr., "The Bricklayer," in *A Book of Russian Verse,* 1943), "the apron sings a red song of bricks to the descendants." The subject of craftsmanship and the association with nature and village life endow his poems with their own special quality within the proletarian poetic tradition. Kazin's later poems are of a naïve Communist character; for example, he describes the salutary effect of forced labor in *Belomorskaya poema* (1936–62; Poem of the White Sea Canal), praises the Agricultural Exhibit ("VSKhV," 1954), is surprised that B. Pasternak "stands apart from great concerns" ("Borisu Pasternaku," 1934), or rejoices that Lenin had one of Kazin's volumes of verse in his private library ("V biblioteke Lenina," 1969). This same mixture of a basic hymnlike attitude and simple form is found in Kazin's nonpolitical poems as well; for example, he venerates a dead mother or takes consolation in the poems of A. Pushkin.

*Works: Rabočij maj* (poems), 1922; *Izbr. stikhi* (poems), 1925; *Lis'ja šuba i ljubov'* (narrative poem), 1926; *Priznanija* (poems), 1928; *Stikhotvorenija* (poems), 1937; *Velikij počin* (narrative poem), 1956; *Stikhotvorenija i poèmy* (lyric and narrative poems), 1957; *Lirika* (poems), 1960; *Izbr.,* 1972; *Tri poèmy* (*Lis'ja šuba i ljubov'; Belomorskaja poema; Velikij počin*; narrative poems), 1974; *Izbr.,* 1978.

*Secondary Lit.*: B. Solovëv, in *Lit. gazeta* Jan. 26, 1957; B. Borovič, in *Moskva* 1957:4; P. Bogdanov, in *Oktjabr'* 1973:2; L. Poljakova, 1977; E. Vinokurov, in *Lit. gazeta* Oct. 7, 1981, p. 3.

**Kédrin, Dmítry Borísovich,** poet (b. Feb. 17 [Feb. 4], 1907, Donbas, Bogodukhovski Mine, now Shcheglovka—d. Sept. 18, 1945, Tarasovka, oblast Moscow). From 1922 to 1924 Kedrin studied communications at a technical school in Dnepropetrovsk, then worked as a journalist; during this time he published his first poems. In 1931 he moved to Moscow, where he earned his living first as a contributor to a factory newspaper, then as literary consultant to the publishing house Molodaya gvardiya. Kedrin's historically independent and tragic verse went largely unnoticed. His only volume of poems, *Svideteli* (The Witnesses), appeared in 1940. Kedrin became a

# KETLÍNSKAYA

frontline reporter in 1943. Soviet sources describe his death as "tragic"; in reality he was pushed from a train in a deliberate plot to eliminate him. After his death, a long silence was imposed on Kedrin's work; S. Shchipachov protested this state of affairs at the Second Congress of the Writers Union in 1954.

Kedrin was a poet known only to a few specialists until he was included in the "Biblioteka poeta" (Poet's Library) series in 1974. Narrative poetry, often historical and encompassing elements of song, nature, public affairs, and satire, predominates in his work. In clear, graphic verses that in moderate tones evoke the spirit and language of the past, Kedrin illustrates the suffering and attainments of the Russian people and the cruelty, baseness, and despotism of autocratic rule. One of his best-known ballads, "Zodchiye" (1938; The Master Builders), presents the legend of the blinding of the builder of St. Basil's Cathedral on Red Square by Ivan the Terrible, ending with a bitterly ironic allusion to the clandestine songs "about the Tsar's terrible favor." In 1953 this ballad was banned from inclusion in a volume of selected works. Kedrin's war poems do not present frontline experiences but vividly grasp the pain of war from an inner distance. Kedrin's greatest work, the verse tragedy Rembrandt (1938), is devoted to the subject of the gifted artist who lives in poverty but is unwilling to bow to the wishes of the buyer against the dictates of his own conscience. Kedrin's poems are in themselves self-contained historical portraits even without the allusions to, or commentaries on, contemporary events; their symbolic dimension, however, is attested to by those who banned his work. Kedrin's poetic prophecy of the poet who will achieve fame only after death (in "Pridanoye" [1935; The Dowry]) and of the tyrant who vainly wishes to perpetuate his fame through the works commissioned to honor him (in "Piramida" [1940; The Pyramid]) has since been substantiated.

Works: Svideteli (poems), 1940; Rembrandt (play), in Oktjabr' 1940:4–7; Izbr., 1947, 1953, 1957; Stikhotvorenija i poèmy (lyric and narrative poems), 1959; Krasota (poems), 1965; Izbr. proizv., 1974, 1978; Zodčie (poem), 1980; Stikhotvorenija. Poèmy, 1982.

Secondary Lit.: V. Ognëv, in Lit. gazeta Nov. 27, 1956; V. Lugovskoj (1957), in his Sobr. soč., vol. 3, 1971; I. Sel'vinskij, in Novyj mir 1957:8; P. Tartakovskij, 1963; L. Kedrina, in Lit. Rossija Feb. 17, 1967, pp. 12–13; K. Kuliev, in Den' poèzii, Moscow, 1967; A. Urban, in Zvezda 1975:1; W. Kasack, in Osteu-

ropa 1975:11; G. Krasukhin, 1976; E. Evtušenko, in Lit. Rossija Aug. 4, 1978, p. 18; I Losievskij, in Moskva 1982:2; A. Znatnov, in Lit. Rossija Jan. 30, 1987, p. 18.

**Ketlínskaya, Véra Kazimírovna**, prose writer (b. May 11 [April 28], 1906, Sevastopol—d April 23, 1976, Leningrad). Ketlinskaya was the daughter of a rear admiral in the tsarist navy who was killed by the Whites after he went over to the Red Army. Ketlinskaya became an active Komsomol official in 1920 and was admitted to the Communist Party in 1927 In 1923 she moved to Leningrad, where she worked in factories until 1926. Her first literary work was published in 1928, while she was working as an editor for the State Publishing House. She later combined careers in journalism and literature. Ketlinskaya's prose works of the 1920s and 1930s are set in the milieu of the Komsomol and among young workers. Her novel Muzhestvo (1938; Eng. tr., Fortitude, 1975), about the contribution of the Komsomol to the building of the city of Komsomolsk in the Far Eastern taiga, drew the greatest notice among her works. The novel's intention, to portray the genesis of the new man, is expressed less by the plot itself and more by the author's commentaries on values; the use of dialogue is psychologically weak and unconvincing. Ketlinskaya received a Stalin Prize (for 1947, 3d class) for V osade (1947; Besieged), her war novel about the defense of Leningrad. She selected contemporary themes, mostly connected with industry and Party life, for her subsequent novels as well; in 1952 she described industrial reconstruction, in 1958 a journey to China. In her novel Inache zhit ne stoit (1960; The Only Life Worth Living), Ketlinskaya is concerned with the candid depiction of the despotic acts of the Stalinist period in the sphere of industrial research in 1937. She based Vecher, okna, lyudi (1972; Evening, Windows, People) on five decades of her own experience. Ketlinskaya periodically wrote articles on literary politics and criticism.

Works: Natka Mičurina (pov.), 1929; Rost (novel), 1934; Mužestvo (novel), 1938 (see above); Rasskazy o leningradcakh (short stories), 1944; V osade (novel), 1948; Dni našej žizni (novel), 1953 (Eng. tr., Days of Our Life, 1955); Kitaj segodnja i zavtra (articles), 1958; Inače žit' ne stoit (novel), 1961; Den' prožityj dvaždy (short stories), 1964; Večer, okna, ljudi (memoirs), 1974.—Sobr. soč., 4 vols., 1978–80.

Secondary Lit.: A. Kondratovič, in Novyj
ıir 1952:12; E. Rapoport, 1958; V. Starikova,
ı Lit. i žizn' Dec. 16, 1960; RSPP 2:1964;
, Kozlov, in Naš sovremennik 1966:2; N.
'odzorova, in Lit. gazeta Jan. 17, 1973, p.
».

**\harms, Daniíl Ivánovich** (pseud. of D. I.
Ґuvachóv), poet, playwright, prose writer (b.
)ec. 30 [Dec. 17], 1905, St. Petersburg—d.
'eb. 2, 1942 [?], Leningrad, while impris-
ıned). Kharms, whose most frequently used
ıseudonym probably derives from the English
vord harm, made his appearance as a writer
ıt the end of 1925 with A. Vvedensky in
ıerformances of the group "Levy flang" in
.eningrad. In 1926 and 1927 three of his poems
vere published in almanacs; the book manu-
ıcript that was completed in 1927, Upravle-
ıiye veshchey: Stikhi malodostupnye (The
Management of Things: Barely Accessible
Ɔoems), could not be published. Kharms be-
onged to the initiators and main representa-
ives of the futuristic-surrealistic group OBE-
ʀIU. His primary literary activity between 1928
ınd 1930 lay in joint recitation with other
Ɔberiuts. In addition, many of his poems cir-
ːulated in manuscript form. The drama writ-
ien in December 1927, Yelizaveta Bam, was
ıharply criticized after it was performed in
1928. After an Oberiu performance in April
1930, this form of literary exposition of life
was virtually banned. Kharms, whose assistance in writing children's literature both S.
Marshak and A. Vvedensky had sought in the
spring of 1927, published a few short children's books; one, Vo-pervykh i vo-vtorykh
(1929; Firstly and Secondly), was illustrated
by V. Tatlin. After his arrest on Aug. 23, 1941,
Kharms was removed from the literary scene.
His REHABILITATION occurred in 1956. With
Ḷ. Chukovskaya's help, he gradually gained
literary recognition after 1960. In 1962 his
slender children's book Igra (Game) was reprinted, and additional short books followed
in 1967, 1972, and 1973. Yelizaveta Bam was
performed in Warsaw in 1966. G. Gibian arranged for publication in Würzburg in 1974
of a first edition of those of Kharms's works
that had been published in various places and
kept in manuscript form. M. Meylakh and V.
Erl began publishing an edition based on a
private archive in Leningrad in 1978. With
Mikhail Levitin's performance of a collage
based on Kharms's works and biography in
Moscow in 1986–87, Kharms's absurdist art
was acknowledged for the first time following
his condemnation in 1930.

Yelizaveta Bam and an earlier play, Komediya goroda Peterburga (1927; Comedy of
the City of Petersburg), were consciously kept
fragmentary; these fragments dispense with
consistency to a great extent, interchange the
roles of characters, and abolish the traditional
concept of time; they represent attempts "to
make the canonized structures [and] tricks
less automatic" (Martini). In Komediya goroda Peterburga, Nikolas II, Griboyedov's
character Famusov, and a pseudomember of
the Komsomol appear. Other scenes that could
be parts of such plays were performed in
isolation. The prose cycle Sluchai (1936–39;
Incidents) brings together the briefest of stories that, from behind their grotesque structure, reveal the automated, casual cruelty and
the estrangement of people. Kharms is seldom
concretely critical of his time as in Istoriya
(A Story), the tale of a blind disabled worker
who feeds himself from garbage cans because
his pension is insufficient; even here he ends
optimistically, using the artistic device of parody that is typical of his style. In a similar
way, Kharms abstracts events in his poems,
leads his thoughts to the most fantastically
veiled conclusion, abolishes logic and psychology. "Alienation techniques, which one
could especially describe as dissolution, inversion, displacement, covering up, negation
of logical linguistic and poetological processes and contexts, are, among other qualities, characteristic of Kharms's poetry" (Ziegler). The "anti-event," the automation of
commonplace events that is symbolized
through repetition, and depersonalized language are even present in his children's poetry
to some extent. Comedy often arises through
the playful addition of unequal components,
through the gradual abolition of original as-
sertions, and through alogical, trite closing
sentences. Deeper examination reveals the despair at the brutality, the prevalence of lies,
and the tedium of the uniformity of daily life
that underlies his entire literary work.

Works: Ozornaja probka (children's lit.),
1928; Teatr, 1928; Vo-pervykh i vo-votorykh
(children's lit.), 1929; Igra (children's verses),
1930, 1962; Million, 1931; Lisa i zajac (children's lit.), 1940; Čto èto bylo (children's
verses), 1967; Dvenadcat' povarov (children's
verses), 1972; Ivan Ivanovič Samovar (children's verses), 1973; Jumorističeskie para-
doksy (children's lit.), in Voprosy lit. 1973:11;
Izbr. (also contains Elizaveta Bam [play]),
Würzburg, 1974; Stikhi (children's verses),
1981.—Sobr. proizv., 3 vols., Bremen, 1978–
80.

Secondary Lit.: See OBERIU. A. Aleksandrov, in Den poèzii, Leningrad, 1965, and in Lit. gazeta Jan. 28, 1981; B. Sluckij, in Junost' 1968:9; D. Flaker, in Československa rusistika 1969:2; P. Urban, in D. Kh. Fälle, 1970; G. Gibian, in Izbrannoe, 1974; W. Kasack, in Die Welt der Slaven 1976:1; B. Semënov, in Avrora 1977:4; R. Ziegler, in Wiener Slawistischer Almanach 7:1981; A. Martini, in Zeitschrift für slavische Philologie 1981:1; A. Stone-Nakhimovsky, Vienna, 1982; E. Chances and J. Stelleman, in Russian Literature 1985:4; J.-Ph. Jaccard, in Cahiers du monde russe et soviétique 1985:3–4.

**Khatsrévin, Zakhár Lvóvich,** prose writer (b. Sept. 5, 1903, Vitebsk—d. Sept. 1941, near Kiev). Khatsrevin began writing in collaboration with B. Lapin in 1932. He was a student of Oriental studies (Iranian studies) in Moscow and Leningrad from 1919 to 1925. Khatsrevin was then employed in Tehran; using a first-person narrative structure, he recorded his experiences there in Tegeran (1933; Tehran), the most important work he wrote without a collaborator. Khatsrevin wrote very little prose on his own after his journey with Lapin to Mongolia (and other places). In his collaborative work his major contribution was to the emotional and musical side through his fertile imagination and "a sort of absolute ear for literature" (L. Slavin). Khatsrevin was an epileptic; according to I. Erenburg, in 1941 he suffered a seizure while serving as a war correspondent at the front. Lapin stood by to help him, and both men were unable to escape the pocket in which they were trapped.

Works: Tegeran (short stories), 1933; short stories in collaboration with Lapin and Slavin: Leto v Mongolii, 1939; with Lapin: Rasskazy i portrety, 1939. For additional works, see LAPIN, B.

**Khlébnikov, Velimír** (pseud, of Víktor Vladimírovich Khlébnikov), poet (b. Nov. 9 [Oct. 28], 1885, Malye Derbety, prov. Astrakham—d. June 28, 1922, Santalovo, prov. Novgorod). Khlebnikov's father was an ornithologist. In 1903 Khlebnikov began studying mathematics and the natural sciences at Kazan University, in 1908 at St. Petersburg University—both without receiving a degree. Khlebnikov, who had written poems since the beginning of his university studies and whose poems had appeared in various anthologies since 1908, quickly came into the avant-garde literary circles in St. Petersburg. Khlebnikov belongs among the founders of Russian FUTURISM. D Burlyuk and A. Kruchonykh published his first three brief separate collections of poetry in 1913–14. These were followed by only a few independent books, such as the grotesque-absurd dramatic sketch Oshibka smert (1916; The Error of Death), the narrative poem Noch v okope (1921; A Night in the Trench) and, immediately before his death, Zangez (1922), in addition to numerous publications in journals, almanacs, and anthologies. Khlebnikov led an unsettled life: 1912–15 in Moscow, 1918–20 in the Ukraine, 1921–22 with the Red Army in Persia, 1922 in Moscow. Before his death Khlebnikov prepared the three parts of his historical-mathematical writings for publication, Doski sudby (1922–23; Tablets of Fate). A volume of poetry, half of which he himself had selected, was published in 1923 from the abundant and scattered works that remained behind at his death; from 1928 to 1933 Yu. Tynyanov and N. Stepanov oversaw the "Collected Works." A "Group of Khlebnikov's Friends," including N. Aseyev, O. Brik, V. Mayakovsky, S. Kirsanov, B. Pasternak, Yu. Tynyanov, I. Selvinsky, V. Shklovsky, V. Katayev, and Yu. Olesha, published, at the same time, the mimeographed collection Neizdanny Khlebnikov (The Unpublished Khlebnikov). For 20 years, a selection N. Stepanov made for the series "Biblioteka poeta (malaya seriya)"—Stikhotvoreniya (1940; Poems)—together with Neizdannye proizvedeniya (1940; Unpublished Works), a carefully annotated edition overseen by N. Khardzhiyev, the expert on futurism, remained Khlebnikov's last books. The conservatives always had an unfavorable opinion of Khlebnikov; in 1951 (in Znamya 1951:1) V. Sayanov declared: "In Soviet poetics there is no place for Khlebnikov." The influence of Khlebnikov's experimental lyric poetry can be detected in N. Zabolotsky, D. Kharms, A. Vvedensky, and N. Tikhonov; in spite of infrequent publication, his influence is also marked later on, and not only among avant-garde poets such as G. Aygi and V. Kazakov. A large reprint edition edited by V. Markov (Munich, 1968–71) has made it possible to use Khlebnikov's work in Western academic research. In the Soviet Union a comprehensive edition—Tvoreniya (1986; Works)—was published for his 100th anniversary.

In his understanding of the spiritual context of creation, Khlebnikov is a highly important, poetically and academically talented man who was far ahead of his time. He looked for new sources in ancient Slavic, ancient Oriental, nd Central Asian myths, developed a transational language (zaumny yazyk) for his potic expression, and invented "strongly expressive 'neologisms' from the original spirit of the language in sympathetic imitation of he actually existing vocabulary" (Holthusen). Elements of various cultures, such as the Chinese, Mexican, Indian, or Arabic, occur in Khlebnikov's Ka (eight editions) written in 1915; a surrealistic short story about the shadow of a soul (ka means "soul" in Egyptian) and the transmigration of souls, Ka is a series of dreams in which adventure and fanastic visions are united while time is suspended. Here his language is mathematically clear. In his late narrative poem, Noch v okope, which is also not linguistically experimental, he mythically presents the struggle between he Whites and the Reds of his own time, measuring the historical moment against the supertemporal perspective of pre-Christian statues of "stony female recluses" who accommodate to world affairs the victory gained at the price of a tremendous number of casualties, and also prophesying the demise of the Red Army. Zangezi, a sverkh-povest (superpovest) written before his death, is a poetic union of the linguistic, mythological, historical, and mathematical quests of his life. In dramatic dialogue, Khlebnikov speaks through Zangezi, the figure of a prophetic sage and poet, about the cultural and historical principles that move him, such as the destruction of driving forces and the omnipotence of the 'language of the stars" that is founded on algebraic conceptions, and about the return of science, poetry, and language to a mythical original state. "Khlebnikov wrote neither verse nor verse epics but a powerful all-Russian image-prayer book from which all those who are not too indolent will draw for centuries and centuries. . . . He has hinted at paths of language development, at transitional paths, at a way station, and this historically unprecedented path taken by the fate of the Russian language—which has only been realized in Khlebnikov—is fixed in its transrational language, which represents nothing but a transitional form that did not manage to become covered with the layer of meaning of a language developing properly and regularly" (O. Mandelshtam).

*Works: Rjav! Perčatki 1908–14* (poems), 1913; *Izbornik stikhov 1907–14* (poems), 1914; *Tvorenija 1906–8* (poems), 1914; *Ošibka smerti* (play), 1916; *Noč' v okope* (narrative poem), 1921; *Zangezi* (pov.), 1922 (reprinted, Ann Arbor, 1978); *Stikhi* (poems), 1923; *Neizdan-*

nyj Khlebnikov, 1928–33; *Izbr. proizv.* (selection), 1936; *Neizdannye proizv.* (poems), 1940 (reprinted, see below); *Stikhotvorenija* (poems), 1940; *Stikhotvorenija i poèmy* (lyric and narrative poems), 1960; *Ladomir* (poems), 1985; *Stikhotvorenija i poèmy*, 1985; *Stikhotvorenija, poèmy, dramy, proza* (poems, narrative poems, plays, prose-texts), 1986.—*Sobr. proizv.*, 5 vols., 1928–33 (reprinted, see below); *Sobr. soč.*, 4 vols. (reprint of *Sobr. proizv.*, 1928–33, and of *Neizdannye proizv.*, 1940, with supplementary material), Munich, 1968–71; *Tvorenija* (selection), 1986.
*Translation: Snake Train: Poetry and Prose*, 1976.

*Secondary Lit.:* R. Jakobson, *Novejšaja russkaja poèzija*, Prague, 1921; V. Majakovskij, in *Krasnaja nov'* 1922:4 and in his *Polnoe sobr. soč.*, vol. 12, 1959; O. Mandel'štam, in *Russkoe iskusstvo* 1923:1–2 and in his *Sobr. soč.*, vol. 2, Washington, 2d ed., 1971, pp. 260–65, 348–49; Ju. Tynjanov, in Khlebnikov's *Sobr. proizv.*, 1928; Vl. Markov, in *Grani*, Frankfurt am Main, 22:1954, in *Russian Review* 1960, separate ed., Berkeley, 1962, and in Khlebnikov's *Sobr. soč.*, vols. 1 and 3, 1968, 1972; K. Zelinskij, in *Znamja* 1957:12; V. Percov, in *Voprosy lit.* 1966:7; Vj. Ivanov, in *Učënye zapiski Tartusk. univ.* 198:1967; A. M. Ripellino, Turin, 1968; A. Drawicz, in *Poezja*, Warsaw, 1971:7; S. Mirsky, Munich, 1975; N. Khardžiev, in *Russian Literature* 9:1975; B. A. Uspensky, in *Russian Literature* 9:1975; R. F. Cooke, in *Russian Literature Triquarterly* 12:1975; R. Vroon, in *Russian Literature Triquarterly* 12:1975 and Ann Arbor, 1983; N. Stepanov, 1975; H. Baran, Diss., Harvard Univ., 1976, and in *Slavic and East European Journal* 1978:1; B. Lönnqvist, Stockholm, 1979; seven articles in *Russian Literature* 1981:1; W. Weststejn, Amsterdam, 1983; V. Grigor'ev, 1983; P. Vykhodcev, in *Russkaja lit.* 1983:2; A. Urban, in *Zvezda* 1983:4; Ju. Nagibin, in *Novyj mir* 1983:5; V. *Khlebnikov: A Stockholm Symposium*, ed. N. A. Nilsson, Stockholm, 1985; P. Tartakovskij, 1986.

**Khodasévich, Vladisláv Felitsiánovich**, poet (b. May 28 [May 16], 1886, Moscow—d. June 14, 1939, Billancourt, near Paris). Khodasevich's father was a Polish painter; his mother was Jewish, but converted to Catholicism. Khodasevich was educated in Moscow. His first volumes of verse, *Molodost* (1908; Youth) and *Schastlivy domik* (1914; The Happy House), attracted the attention of N. Gumilyov, particularly by their composition. Khodasevich, who affiliated himself with neither the symbolists nor the acmeists, found no wider response to his work. He wrote literary criticism. In 1918–19 Khodasevich taught at the PROLETKULT in Moscow. From 1920 to 1922 he lived in Petrograd. *Putyom zerna* (1920; The Way of the Seed), the most important of his works published in Russia, reveals his hope for the renascence of Russia following the destruction occasioned by the Revolution. After publishing a significant little collection of poems, *Tyazholaya lira* (1922; The Heavy Lyre), in 1922 Khodasevich emigrated with N. Berberova to Berlin; there he brought out an anthology of Hebrew poetry he himself had translated and a second edition of *Tyazholaya lira* (1923). Khodasevich went next to Paris. He brought together his latest lyrics, 26 poems written between 1922 and 1926, under the title *Yevropeyskaya noch* (1927; European Night) and included it in *Sobraniye stikhov* (1927; A Collection of Poems), the only collection of his verse to be published in Paris. In 1927 Khodasevich became the leading critic for the journal *Vozrozhdeniye* and engaged, with cautious skepticism, in considerable polemical controversies with other émigré critics, such as G. Adamovich. He wrote only a very few poems after 1927. Some of his work may have been lost during the German occupation when his second wife, who was Jewish, was arrested and his papers were confiscated. His wife died in a concentration camp. Prior to 1986, only in 1963 were a few of Khodasevich's poems published in the Soviet Union, whose political system he strictly rejected; however, Khodasevich's poetry circulated there in SAMIZDAT copies. In 1986 and 1987 several poems and essays appeared in Soviet journals.

Khodasevich is a significant poet whose style is schooled in the classical mode of A. Pushkin. "He is one of the most thrifty and self-disciplined poets in Russian literature" (Struve). Some of his poems and epics in verse are about the poverty and famine of the revolutionary years; on the whole, however, Khodasevich does not react directly to experiences and phenomena of this world. For him, the world is the confining, alien, "quiet hell" in which the soul, originally free, suffers. He sees earthly existence as part of a cycle of human reincarnation (probably under the influence of anthroposophy, an influence that was also important to A. Bely, M. Voloshin, and D. Klenovsky). Analysis of his own self and of his poetic being is a frequent motif in Khodasevich's few but important poems, on which Bely had already bestowed the highest accolades by 1923.

*Works: Molodost'* (poems), 1908; *Sčastlivy domik* (poems), 1914; *Putëm zerna* (poems) 1920; *Iz evrejskikh poètov* (poems translate by Khodasevič), Berlin, 1922 (reprinted, Ann Arbor, 1983); *Stat'i o russkoj poèzii* (literar criticism), 1922 (reprinted, Letchworth, 1971 *Tjažëlaja lira* (poems), 1922, Berlin, 1923 (re printed, Ann Arbor, 1975); *Sobr. stikhov* (con tains *Putëm zerna; Tjažëlaja lira; Evropej skaja noč'*; poems), Paris, 1927 (reprinted, Nev York, 1978); *Deržavin* (biography), Paris, 193 (reprinted, Munich, 1975); *Nekropol'* (mem oirs), Brussels, 1939 (reprinted, Paris, 1976) *Evropejskaja noč'* (poems; excerpts), in *Moskv* 1963:1; *Mladenčestvo* (autobiographical es says), in *Vozdušnye puti*, New York, 4:1965 *Iz černovikov* (rough drafts), in *Vozdušny puti* 4:1965; *Stikhi* (poems), in *Ogonë* 1986:48.—*Izbr. proza*, New York, 1982; *Sobr stikhov*, 2 vols., Paris, 1983; *Sobr. soč.*, 5 vols. Ann Arbor, 1981– (vol. 1 has appeared).

*Secondary Lit.:* A. Belyj, in *Sovremenny zapiski*, Paris, 15:1923; V. Vejdle, *Sovremen nye zapiski* 34:1928 and separately in 1928 also in *Novyj žurnal*, New York, 66:1961; D Klenovskij, in *Grani*, Frankfurt am Main 20:1953; B. Filippov, in *Grani* 49:1961; F Radley, Diss., Harvard Univ., 1964; V. Kho dasevič, in *Novyj mir* 1969:7; N. Berberova *Kursiv moj*, 1972; W. S. Schmid, Diss., Vi enna, 1973; R. P. Hughes, in *The Bitter Air o Exile: Russian Writers in the West 1922–1972* ed. S. Karlinsky and A. Appel, Berkeley, 1977 N. Struve, in *Vestnik RKhD* 127:1978; M Sixsmith, in *Vestnik RKhD* 130:1979; G. S Smith, in *Slavic and East European Journa* 1980:1; J.-A. Miller, Diss., Univ. of Michigan 1981; David M. Bethea, 1983; Z. Šakhovskaja in *Novoe russkoe slovo*, New York, Feb. 20 1983, p. 5; Ju. Levin, in *Wiener Slawistische Almanach* 17:1986; A. Voznesenskij, in *Ogo nëk* 1986:48.

**Khólopov, Geórgy Konstantínovich**, pros writer (b. Nov. 9 [Oct. 27], 1914, Shemakha Azerbaijan). Kholopov's father was a peasant Kholopov finished his schooling in Baku i 1931, moved to Leningrad, and worked as mechanic. His journalistic activity first bega on factory newspapers in 1932; his short pros pieces appeared in *Rezets*. Kholopov's firs povest, *Bratya* (1936; The Brothers), based o the life of the Old Believers, appeared in *Zvezda*. In 1939–40 the editorship of thi journal was in his hands. During World Wa II, Kholopov was a frontline correspondent in 1948 he became a member of the Commu nist Party. Since the end of the war he ha published novels and short stories. He has been editor in chief of Zvezda since 1957; he has been a member of the board of the Writers Union of the USSR since 1967. In the early 1970s he was named head of the Leningrad section of the Writers Union of the USSR.

Kholopov chose the figure of the Leningrad Party secretary S. M. Kirov as his central subject. In his novel Ogni v bukhte (1946; Fire in the Bay) he presents Kirov as the organizer of post-Revolutionary reconstruction in Baku, and in Grozny god (1954; The Terrible Year), as the leader of the Communists during the Civil War in Astrakhan. Kholopov's subsequent novels are more autobiographical: Grenada (1961; Granada) describes the years 1922–26 in Baku from a boy's point of view; its title, taken from M. Svetlov's most popular poem, is intended to reflect the universality of the Communist idea; its sequel, Doker (1965; The Dock Worker), continues the story into the early 1930s. In the 1970s Kholopov chose to set his work in the eastern Carpathian region. His prose has a documentary rather than a literary character; it is burdened by superficiality and is often implausible, especially in its portrayal of negative characters, as a result of its strict compliance with the principle of PARTY SPIRIT.

Works: Brat'ja (pov.), in Zvezda 1936:9; Ogni v bukhte (novel), 1947; Groznyj god (novel), 1955; Nevydumannye rasskazy o vojne (short stories), 1960; Grenada (novel), 1962; Doker (novel), 1965; Vengerskaja povest' (pov.), in Zvezda 1970:4; Malen'kaja povest' i bol'šie rasskazy (pov. and short stories), 1970; Mozaika (short stories), 1973; Desjat' let raboty (article), in Zvezda 1974:9; Putešestvie v Burkut (travel notes), in Zvezda 1977:6; Ivanov den' (pov. and short stories), 1977.—Izbr. proizv., 2 vols., 1974; Izbr., 2 vols., 1982.

Secondary Lit.: A. Šagalov, in Zvezda 1955:8; V. Ditc, in Neva 1964:12; RSPP 7(2):1972; D. Moldavskij, in Neva 1974:11; R. Messer, foreword to Kholopov's Izbr. proizv., 1974; N. Lugovcov, 1979; V. Kosolapov, in Novyj mir 1982:8; O. Ljubin, in Moskva 1984:1.

**Kim, Anatóly Andréyevich**, Russian prose writer of Korean ancestry (b. June 15, 1939, Sergiyevka, Tyulkubas Region, Kasakhstan SSR). Kim's parents were apparently sent into internal exile. His father was a teacher; his ancestors immigrated to Russia in the 19th century. Kim began studying painting at a Moscow school of art. After three years of military service, he devoted himself to writing. He graduated from the Gorky Literary Institute in 1971; his first published collection of short stories was Goluboy ostrov (1976; The Blue Island). This was followed by Chetyre ispovedi (1978; Four Confessions) and Solovinoye ekho (1980; The Nightingale's Echo), by other collections that were favorably reviewed by the critics, and by the povest Lotos (1980; The Lotus Flower), the peak of his first period of creative work. This work unleashed both enthusiastic approval and sharp rejection because of his antimaterialist, unambiguously spiritual position. Kim's first novel was Belka (1984; The Squirrel). He lives in Moscow.

Kim belongs among the leading authors of Russian literature who made their debuts in the mid-1970s. In his early short stories it was not only the exotic quality of the past and present fates of his Korean landsmen on Sakhalin Island that attracted attention to him but also his lively style and his spiritual concern. In Lotos Kim takes the meeting between a dying mother and her adult son as the point of departure for a clear avowal of the continuation of man's individual existence after physical death. In surrealistic passages, Kim—a great admirer of V. Khlebnikov—illuminates the dissolution of time from the established perspective of the eternal. Changing viewpoints (impersonal and personal from various first-person perspectives) enrich the work. Nefritovy poyas (1981; The Nephrite Belt) depicts the conquering of the fear of death. Belka is an attempt to translate the polyphony of the world into a polyphonic novel based on J. S. Bach's musical structures. In all his creative works Kim tries to grasp reality as the history of spirit from a higher point of view.

Works: Poklon oduvančiku (pov.), in Avrora 1975:5–6; Goluboj ostrov' (short stories), 1976; Četyre ispovedi (pov.), 1978; Solov'inoe ekho (short stories and pov.), 1980; Lotos (pov.), in Družba narodov 1980:10; Nefritovyj pojas (pov.), 1981; Sobirateli trav (pov.), 1983; Belka (novel), 1984; Plač' kukuški (play), in Sovremennaja dramaturgija 1984:4; Vkus tërna na rassvete, Priključenija (short stories), in Oktjabr' 1985:8; Prošlo dvesti let (play), in Sovremennaja dramaturgija 1986:2.

Secondary Lit.: E. Šklovskij, in Lit. obozrenie 1978:11; E. Kholševnikova, in Avrora 1979:3; A. Pikač and N. Cyganova, in Zvezda 1979:7; A. Goršenin, in Oktjabr' 1980:10; S. Elkin, in Moskva 1981:10; A. Mikhajlov, in Voprosy lit. 1981:4; E. Jukina, in Novyj mir 1984:12; V. Novikov and V. Surganov, in Lit. gazeta Feb. 13, 1985, p. 4; A. Nemzer and L. Anninskij, in *Lit. obozrenie* 1985:8; M. Vol'pe, in *Moskva* 1986:8.

**Kim, Román Nikoláyevich,** prose writer (b. Aug. 1 [July 20], 1899, Vladivostok—d. May 14, 1967, Moscow). Of Korean descent, Kim spent his youth in Japan and was educated in Tokyo (1907–17). In 1923 he graduated in Oriental studies at Vladivostok University and went on to teach Chinese and Japanese literature at various institutions of higher education in Moscow (1923–30). The field of Oriental literature also served as the source of the various nonscholarly and journalistic publications that Kim wrote before World War II. Nothing is known of his activities during the war years, but after the war he emerged as a writer of espionage and detective thrillers, such as *Tetrad, naydennaya v Sunchone* (1951; Notebook Found in Sunchon). Written in the form of a Japanese spy's report during the Korean War, the novel is markedly anti-Western in its portrayal of Americans as stupid, criminal, cowardly, and treacherous. The detective novels that subsequently appeared are also pointedly political, having to do with the events of the war (Pearl Harbor, for example, in *Po prochtenii szhech* [1962; Burn after Reading]) or with current political topics (*Kto ukral Punnakana* [1963; Who Stole Punnakan?]). Kim's novels are smoothly written, gripping, and rich in local color (set primarily in the East); politically, they are one-sidedly aggressive. The development of the action is not always psychologically credible. Kim's novels were frequently translated. Kim, of whom L. Slavin spoke highly as a person, lived in Moscow. He did not participate in any of the congresses of the Writers Union after 1954.

*Works:* Nogi k zmee (travel commentary), in Boris Pil'njak, *Korni japonskogo solnca*, 1927; *Tetrad', najdennaja v Sunčone* (pov.), in *Novyj mir* 1951:5, separate ed., 1951; *Devuška iz Khirošimy* (pov.), in *Oktjabr'* 1954:8–9; *Agent osobogo naznačenija. Kobra pod poduškoj* (pov.), 1962; *Po pročtenii sžeč'* (pov.), in *Naš sovremennik* 1962:1–2; *Kto ukral Punnakana* (pov.), in *Oktjabr'* 1963:10; *Škola prizrakov* (pov.), in *Naš sovremennik* 1965:8–10, separate ed., 1965; *Delo ob ubijstve Šerloka Kholmsa* (short story), in *Naš sovremennik* 1966:4; *Tajna ul'timatuma* (pov. and short stories), 1969.
*Secondary Lit.:* A. Palladin, in *Znamja* 1952:2; L. Slavin, in *Lit. gazeta* July 12, 1962; A. Gromova, in *Lit. Rossija* July 10, 1964, p. 18; V. Travinskij, in *Zvezda* 1964:3.

**Kin, Víktor Pávlovich** (pseud, of V. K. Surovíkin), prose writer (b. Jan. 14 [Jan. 1], 1903 Novokhopersk, prov. Voronezh—d. Nov. o˕ Dec. 1937 [?], while imprisoned). Kin was the son of a locomotive engineer. He became a member of the Komsomol in 1918 and joined the Communist Party in 1920, becoming active in Party work; at the end of 1921 he was dispatched by the Party to the Far Eastern Republic to work in the underground. He became a Party official and journalist in Sverdlovsk in 1923; he moved to Moscow in 1924 where he studied in the literary section of the Institute of Red Professors (1928–30). Kin became known as a writer with the publication of his novel *Po tu storonu* (1928; Eng. trs. *Over the Border*, 1932; *Across the Lines*, 1960) As a correspondent for TASS, he was sent to Rome and then to Paris (1931–36); in 1937 he assumed the editorship of the propaganda newspaper *Le Journal de Moscou*. Kin was arrested as an "enemy of the people" on Nov. 3, 1937; his death allegedly occurred later that same year. His REHABILITATION took place some time around 1956.

Kin's one major literary work, *Po tu storonu*, is based on his own experiences during Party missions in the Soviet Far East (1921–23). "An expressive conciseness is one of the greatest virtues of Kin's novels" (Slavin). The book was reprinted periodically up to 1937 and again after 1956, filmed twice, and twice adapted for the stage. In 1937 the NKVD confiscated a novel that was three-quarters completed about the period of World War I, *Lill* (Lille), and an unfinished povest about the life of a journalist, along with Kin's entire literary papers. Short fragments and notebooks, which survived by accident, point to Kin's painstaking method of writing; these were published after 1956.

*Works:* Rasskazy Vas'ki Zybina (short stories), 1925; *Po tu storonu* (novel), 1928 (see above) (excerpt from dramatized version, *Naša molodost'*, in K. Mehnert, *Amerikanische und russische Jugend um 1930*, Stuttgart, 1973, pp. 196–201); *Nezakončennyj roman o žurnalistakh*, in *Novyj mir* 1959:1; *Lill': Iz nezakončennogo romana. . .* , in *Novyj mir* 1963:1; Izbr., 1965.
*Secondary Lit.:* L. Slavin, in his *Portrety i zapiski*, 1965; *Vsegda po ètu storonu: Vospominanija. . .* , ed. S. Ljandres, 1966; M. Čarnyj, in his *Ušedšie gody*, 1967; S. Kin, in *Novyj mir* 1969:5–6; RSPP 7(1):1971.

**Kiríllov, Vladímir Timoféyevich,** poet (b. Oct. 14 [Oct. 2], 1890, in the village of Kharino, prov. Smolensk—d. Dec. 18, 1943 [?], while imprisoned). Kirillov's father was a bookstore manager in Smolensk. In 1903 Kirillov became a cabin boy in the Black Sea fleet; by 1905 he was an active revolutionary. While in internal exile (1906–9), he steeped himself in the poetry of F. Tyutchev, A. Fet, and the symbolists. Kirillov lived in St. Petersburg until 1914. His first poems were published in 1913 by a workers' press. He served as a soldier in World War I; during the Revolution he was at the head of an insurgent regiment. In 1917–18 he served as Bolshevik Party secretary in one of the Moscow districts. In 1918 Kirillov became a member of the Petrograd PROLETKULT; in late 1918 and early 1919 he joined the Tambov Proletkult, and at the end of 1919, the Moscow Proletkult; his poems "My" (1917; We) and "Zhelezny messiya" (1918; The Iron Messiah) were widely disseminated at the time. In 1920 Kirillov transferred to the Moscow writers' association KUZNITSA, which continued to support the principle of an independent proletarian poetry, free of Party regimentation; he served as the first chairman of VAPP. Kirillov was a friend of M. P. Gerasimov; both men saw the introduction of NEP in 1921 as a betrayal of the Revolution and left the Party; their subsequent poetry reflected their disillusionment, and Kirillov was sharply criticized. Between 1929 and 1937 he traveled throughout the Soviet Union. In 1937 Kirillov fell victim to the Stalinist purges; he died in 1943, presumably in a concentration camp.

Kirillov's poetry reflects the fervor typical of the proletarian revolutionary poets. Not only is it traditional in its form (for which V. Mayakovsky criticized it), but its religious imagery ("Zhelezny messiya") points to its symbolist heritage. In "My" Kirillov heralds the rejection by the "Legion of Labor" of all tradition ("In the name of our Tomorrow we will burn the Raphaels, raze the museums, and trample the flowers of art"). After his break with the Party, Kirillov's now pessimistic poems acknowledged that the idea of the Revolution being a unique event was an illusion, recognized the "inhumanity, the mechanism of a world of machines," and criticized his own Proletkult work. Kirillov was rehabilitated in 1957, and in 1958 the first collection of his work in 25 years was published.

Works: Stikhotvorenija (poems), 1918; Parusa (poems), 1921; Železnyj messija (poems), 1921; Otplytie (poems), 1923; Stikhotvorenija: Kniga 1-ja 1913–23 (poems), 1924; Izbr. stikhi (poems), 1926; Golubaja strana: 2-ja kniga stikhov (poems), 1927; Izbr. stikhi 1917–32

(poems), 1933; Stikhotvorenija (poems), 1958; Stikhotvorenija i poèmy (lyric and narrative poems), 1970.

Secondary Lit.: K. Zelinskij, in Stikhotvorenija, 1958; Z. S. Papernyj and R. A. Šaceva, in Proletarskie poèty pervykh let sovetskoj èpokhi, 1959; G. Kratz, Die Geschichte der "Kuznica," 1978.

Kirsánov, Semyón Isaákovich, poet (b. Sept. 18 [Sept. 5], 1906, Odessa—d. Dec. 10, 1972, Moscow). Kirsanov was the son of a tailor. He spent the years of the Revolution in Odessa; he wrote avant-garde agitational poetry in the style of V. Mayakovsky, which the latter printed in LEF after his visit to Odessa in 1924. After completing his studies in philology at the Odessa Institute for Public Education, Kirsanov moved to Moscow in 1925 and took part in Mayakovsky's political-literary work for the general public, including joint lecture tours. After a period of engaging almost exclusively in publicistic affairs ("I believed that poetry helped mine coal and built factories"), at the end of the 1930s Kirsanov returned to writing poetry; because of its experimental character, however, it was sharply attacked as formalistic. During World War II, Kirsanov served at the front as a news reporter. The influence of Goethe's Faust, Part II, is apparent in his narrative poem Nebo nad Rodinoy (1947; The Sky above the Homeland), where Kirsanov combines war motifs (a pilot who dive-bombs an enemy tank) with personified nature (talking clouds) to create "a suggestive, symphonic image" (Drawicz). In 1950 Kirsanov contributed to the development of the Stakhanovite movement with his narrative poem Makar Mazay (Stalin prize, 1950, 3d class). At the Second Congress of the Writers Union in 1954 he made a liberal speech advocating the right of poetry to explore an inner world and to make use of fantasy. After the 20th Party Congress, Kirsanov came to be regarded as a noted writer of the THAW with his narrative poem Sem dney nedeli (1956; The Seven Days of the Week), a protest against bureaucrats with "hearts of stone." In 1967 he was able to publish poems that had not been printed for decades in Iskaniya (Quests). Kirsanov was a member of the board of the Writers Union from 1954 on; he lived in Moscow.

As a follower of Mayakovsky, Kirsanov held fast to the search for new form and experimentation with language. Poetry remained something of a craft for him his whole life long. In his "Poema poetov" (1939; A Poets' Poem), he presents five stylistically different fictional poets. Kirsanov's poetry is often allegorical, combining contemporary politics with philosophy and history and playful humor with a serious message. In his last poems Kirsanov compellingly expressed his recognition of the threat posed to humanity by the rationalist Marxist system and his perception of the necessity of uniting human destiny with that of the natural world.

Works: *Pricel* (poems), 1926; *Moja imeninnaja* (narrative poem), 1928; *Zoluška* (narrative poem), 1935; *Tri poèmy* (narrative poems), 1937; *Nebo nad Rodinoj* (narrative poem), in *Oktjabr'* 1947:8; *Makar Mazaj* (narrative poem), 1951; *Tovarišči stikhi* (poems), 1953; *Sem' dnej nedeli* (narrative poem), in *Novyj mir* 1956:9; *Odnaždy zavtra* (lyric and narrative poems), 1964; *Kniga liriki* (poems), 1965; *Iskanija* (lyric and narrative poems), 1967; *Zerkala* (poems), 1970, 2d ed., 1972—*Soč.*, 2 vols., 1954; *Izbr. proizv.*, 2 vols., 1961; *Sobr. soč.*, 4 vols., 1974–76.

Secondary Lit.: S. Tregub, in *Novyj mir* 1941:2 and in *Oktjabr'* 1947:3; M. Isakovskij, in *Znamja* 1949:8; V. Nazarenko, in *Zvezda* 1955: 5; I. Grinberg, in *Lit. gazeta* Nov. 15, 1967, p. 5; E. Evtušenko, in *Lit. gazeta* July 15, 1970, p. 5; P. Antokol'skij, in *Lit. Rossija* Sept. 24, 1976, p. 15; Ju. Mineralov, in his *Poèzija. Poètika. Poèt*, 1984.


**Kirshón, Vladímir Mikháylovich,** playwright, literary official (b. Aug. 19 [Aug. 6], 1902, Nalchik—d. July 28, 1938 [?], while imprisoned). Kirshon's father was a lawyer. Kirshon spent his youth in St. Petersburg and Kislovodsk; during the Civil War he fought with the Bolsheviks. He became a member of the Communist Party in 1920 and worked as a Party official in Rostov-on-Don (he was head of the instructional section of the Party Institute). Kirshon organized proletarian writers' associations in Rostov-on-Don and the northern Caucasus; in 1925 he became one of the secretaries of RAPP in Moscow. Kirshon began his career as a dramatist in 1920 by first writing agitational plays "without artistic individuality" (Altman) for amateur theatricals. Helped by his play *Konstantin Teryokhin* (1926; Eng. tr., *Red Rust*, 1930), written in collaboration with A. Uspensky, Kirshon embarked on an independent dramatic career with *Relsy gudyat* (1927; The Rails Are Humming). In this play he presents the proletarian as director of a large factory in the struggle for socialist construction and the creation of the new man. From the very beginning, the play's artistic level was held to be low. His

subsequent plays—*Gorod vetrov* (1928; City of Winds), about the frequently used theme of the 26 commissars in Baku; *Khleb* (1930; Eng. tr., *Bread*, in *Six Soviet Plays*, 1934), about collectivization; and *Sud* (1933; The Trial), about the German Communists—always present a schematic political message transposed into dramatic form. Kirshon's best work is considered to be his comedy *Chudesny splav* (1934; The Wonderful Alloy), the title of which alludes simultaneously to the research being done in an institute of the aircraft industry and to the formation of a young collective. After 1956 this play, despite having been written by an author who was arrested in 1937 and liquidated in 1938, was again performed frequently. Kirshon's literary papers were presumably destroyed in 1937. He was an advocate of the classical, self-contained drama and in defense of his views engaged in polemics against V. Vishnevsky and N. Pogodin.

Works: *Sergej Esenin* (essays), 1926; *Konstantin Terëkhin* (play), 1927 (see above); *Rel'sy gudjat* (play), 1928; *Gorod vetrov* (play), 1931; *Khleb* (play), 1931 (reprinted Letchworth, 1980) (see above); *Sud* (play), 1933; *Dramatičeskie proizv.* (plays), 1933; *Čudesnyj splav* (play), 1934 (also in *Novyj mir* 1934:5); *Bol'šoj den'* (play), 1936 (also in *Novyj mir* 1937:2; reprinted, Letchworth, 1980); *Dramatičeskie proizv.* (plays), 1957; *Izbr.*, 1958; *Stat'i i reči o dramaturgii, teatre i kino* (essays), 1962; *O literature i iskusstve* (essays), 1967.

Secondary Lit.: I. Al'tman, in *Lit. kritik* 1934:2; E. Gorbunova, in *Teatr* 1962:8; O. K. Borodina, 1964; L. Tamašin, 1965; A. Sofronov, in *Lit. Rossija* Aug. 18, 1972, p. 11; A. Naumov, in *Teatr* 1977:9; R. Korn, in *Teatr* 1980:9; I. Višnevskaja, in *Lit. gazeta* May 8, 1982, p. 8.


**Klenóvsky, Dmítry Iósifovich** (pseud. of D. I. Krachkóvsky), poet (b. Oct. 6 [Sept. 24], 1893, St. Petersburg—d. Dec. 26, 1976, Traunstein). Klenóvsky's father, Iosif Yevgeniyevich Krachkovsky, was a painter and a member of the Academy. From 1904 to 1911 Klenovsky attended secondary school in Tsarskoye Selo and made numerous trips to Italy and also to France with his parents. From 1911 to 1913 he lived in Switzerland for reasons of health. In 1913–17 he studied at St. Petersburg University (law and humanities). He performed his military service in the years 1917–20 by working in the administration, in Moscow 1918–20. Klenovsky, who had already be-

come interested in anthroposophy while at
the university, attended lectures (including
those of A. Bely and M. Voloshin) given by
the Society for Comparative Religious Research (=Anthroposophy). He published
poems in Petersburg journals after 1914; his
first volume, *Palitra* (Palette), appeared in 1917.
A second volume, *Podgorye* (Foothills), which
was more closely related to acmeist poetry,
could not be published because of the Revolution. In 1921–22 Klenovsky worked as a
journalist; after 1922 he worked in the Ukrainian news service and in Kharkov as a translator. His complete rejection of the Communist regime for religious and general ethical
reasons caused his poetic talent to be silenced. In 1942 he and his wife fled via Austria to Germany, and he began to write poems
again while he was still in a refugee camp.
They appeared under the pseudonym of Klenovsky in *Novy zhurnal* (New York) after
1947 and in *Grani* (Frankfurt) and other periodicals after 1950. From 1950 to 1977 Klenovsky published 11 volumes, each with new
poems; the titles of the first few volumes express his relationship to the religious-spiritual
world: *Navstrechu nebu* (1952; Against
Heaven), *Neulovimy sputnik* (1956; The Elusive Companion), and *Prikosnovenye* (1959;
Touch). He collected the poems written between 1945 and 1964 that were most important to him in the volume *Stikhi* (1967; Poems).
Klenovsky occasionally also wrote essays on
Russian literature. The most important,
*Okkultnye motivy v russkoy poezii nashego
veka* (1953; Occult Motifs in Russian Poetry
of This Century), offers essential insights into
the creative work of poets such as V. Khodasevich, N. Gumilyov, and M. Voloshin that
differ from the usual interpretations of these
poets. Klenovsky lived a withdrawn life in
Traunstein, Bavaria.

Two sources nourish Klenovsky's poetry:
the spiritual riches of Russian Orthodoxy and
of anthroposophy and the acmeist perception
of language. His poetry also reveals his independent religious experiences (the broadest
experience of angels in Russian literature) and
his own individual linguistic imprint. N.
Gumilyov, whom Klenovsky revered as an
older student in secondary school in Tsarskoye Selo and as a victim of Bolshevik force,
became Klenovsky's spiritual model through
his late poetic cycles, such as "Kostyor." Klenovsky views earthly life as a stage in the true
spiritual existence of man, from which he
emerges and to which he returns in death.
Just like A. Bely, Khodasevich, Gumilyov, A.
Voloshin, and W. Lindenberg, Klenovsky has

no doubt about multiple reincarnations that
serve man's further development. Thus his
poetry reveals not a fear of death but indeed
a clear awareness that the giving and the recognition of meaning in earthly life come
through death. Joy in nature, professions of
the meaning that love of, and service to, one's
fellowman give to life, occasional remembrances of Tsarkoye Selo and Italy, are further
motifs in his poetry, which begins to gain a
greater maturity in 1945 as a result of his age
and his fate and which reaches its acme in
the 1967 collection. His linguistic clarity and
modesty combine with an economical use of
imagery and neologisms.

*Works: Palitra* (poems), 1917; *Sled žizni*
(poems), Frankfurt am Main, 1950; *Navstreču
nebu* (poems), Frankfurt am Main, 1952;
*Okkul'tyne motivy v russkoj poèzii našego
veka* (essay), in *Grani*, Frankfurt am Main,
20:1953; *Kaznënnye molčaniem* (essay), in
*Grani* 23:1953; *Neulovimyj sputnik* (poems),
Frankfurt am Main, 1956; *Prikosnoven'e*
(poems), Munich, 1959; *Ukhodjaščie parusa*
(poems), Munich, 1962; *Razroznennaja tajna*
(poems), Munich, 1965; *Stikhi: Izbr. iz šesti
knig i novye stikhi 1965–66* (poems), Munich,
1967; *Pevučaja noša* (poems), Munich, 1969;
*Počerkom poèta* (poems), Munich, 1971; *Të-
plyj večer* (poems), Munich, 1975; *Poslednee*
(poems), Munich, 1977; I. Šakhovskoj, *Perepiska s Klenovskim* (letters), Paris, 1981.—
*Sobr. stikhov,* in 2 vols., vol. 1, Paris, 1980.

*Secondary Lit.:* N. Berberova, in Klenovsky's *Sled žizni,* 1950, and in *Novyj žurnal,*
New York, 31:1952; L. Rževskij, in *Grani* 9
and 15:1950; Ju. Ivask, in *Novyj žurnal* 24:1950;
G. Struve, in *Novyj žurnal* 47:1956; B. Širjaev,
in his *Religioznye motivy v russkoj poèzii,*
Brussels, 1960; E. Bobrova, in *Novyj žurnal*
138:1980: W. Kasack, in *Osteuropa* 1982:2
and in *Communicatio Fidei: Festschrift für
Eugen Biser,* Regensburg, 1983.

**Klychkóv, Sergéy Antónovich** (pseud. of
S. A. Leshónkov), poet, prose writer (b. July
13 [July 1], 1889, Dubrovki, prov. Tver—d.
Jan. 21, 1940 [?], while imprisoned). Klychkov's father was a shoemaker of peasant descent. After completing his studies at a science gymnasium in 1908, Klychkov traveled
to Italy; he served as a soldier in World War
I. Klychkov's friends already valued him as a
poet by 1905. He began publishing short stories as well as poems in 1907, but subsequently wrote verse predominantly until 1925.
After the Revolution, Klychkov lived in Mos-

cow and belonged to the "peasant poets"; he was the only one of them to turn to prose. His three novels, Sakharny nemets (1925; The Saccharine German), Chertukhinsky balakir (1926; The Pitcher from Chertukhino), and Knyaz Mira (1928; Prince of Peace), did indeed attract attention with their linguistic structure, but were sharply criticized as archreactionary for their orientation toward the pre-Revolutionary village with its mythic associations. An abridged and revised version of Sakharny nemets appeared under the title Posledny Lel (1927; The Last Lel). After 1927 Klychkov was attacked as a representative of "kulak" literature together with N. Klyuyev and, to a great extent, S. Yesenin and P. Oreshin. In 1934 Klychkov was ostensibly sentenced to internal exile; only his literary adaptations in the folkloric tradition continued to be published. He was arrested in 1937 and his name was deleted from literary studies. Around 1956 the illegality of the proceedings against Klychkov was conceded and a date of death (but not place of death) was published. Since then Klychkov has been mentioned in literary histories, but his books were not reissued before 1985.

Klychkov's verse is associated with folklore; it seeks solace from nature. At first it was mostly descriptive; it never contained revolutionary elements; later it was characterized by pantheistic and pessimistic thought. Klychkov's prose combines a primary relationship to traditional peasantry and the peasant world of demons with the literary influence of N. Gogol, N. Leskov, and A. Remizov. Sakharny nemets focuses on the emotional experiences of a Russian soldier who in wartime shoots down a German while the latter is fetching water and cannot rid himself of the murder. Klychkov's novels consist of associated scenes, rich in imagery but with little plot, that hover among reality, dream, and the spirit world, and that are narrated in a broad and rambling manner by a fictitious peasant narrator, often in beautiful, rhythmic prose. For Klychkov, who is tied to the metaphysical world of village and forest, the city, machines, iron, and factory smokestacks, symbols of the proletarian revolution, are Satanic elements.

Works: Pesni (poems), 1911; Potaënnyj sad (poems), 1913, 2d ed., 1918; Dubravna (poems), 1918; Gost' čudesnyj (poems), 1923; Domašnie pesni (poems), 1923; Sakharnyj nemec (novel), 1925, 2d ed., 1929 (reprinted, Paris, 1982); Čertukhinskij balakir' (novel), 1926; Poslednij Lel' (novel), 1927; Talisman (poems), 1927; Knjaz' mira (novel) 1928 (reprinted, Paris,

1985); V gostjakh u žuravlej (poems), 1930 (reprinted, Moscow, 1985); Saraspan, Obrabotki fol'klora i perevody (folklore), 1936; Stikhotvorenija (poems), Paris, 1985.

Secondary Lit.: D. Gorbov, in Novyj mir 1925:12; A. Divil'kovskij, in Novyj mir 1926:7–9; L. G. Lelevič, in Novyj mir 1926:1; M. Zenkevič, in Novyj mir 1928:3; G. Zabežinskij, in Novyj žurnal, New York, 29:1952; M. Stepanenko, Rockville, 1973; M. Niqueux, in Cahiers du monde russe et soviétique 1977:1–2 and introduction to S. Klytchkov, Le livre de la vie et de la mort, Lausanne, 1981; A. Radaškevič, in Russkaja mysl', Paris, Oct. 10, 1985, p. 10; K. Ju., in Grani, Frankfurt am Main, 138:1985.

**Klyúyev, Nikoláy Alekséyevich,** poet (b. Oct. 10 [Sept. 27], 1884, Koštug, a small village near Vytegra, prov. Olonetsk—d. Aug. 1937 [?], while imprisoned). Klyuyev was of peasant descent (sectarian). His mother was a bylina singer. When a child, Klyuyev lived for a time at the Solovetsky Monastery; in 1906–7 he traveled to Baku on behalf of the Flagellants (Khlysty). A few poems from this period have survived. In 1907 Klyuyev turned to A. Blok, who, impressed by the poet's yearning for spiritual expression and the poetic strength of his poems, himself saw to the publication of Klyuyev's first works and maintained a correspondence with him. Around 1908, Klyuyev made a second long trip for the Flagellants, this time to India, Persia, and the Near East. From 1911 on, Klyuyev traveled occasionally to Moscow and St. Petersburg; in 1912 he published his first collection of verse, Sosen perezvon (The Chimes of the Pines), which attracted considerable attention from the symbolists (V. Bryusov wrote the foreword). It was followed by some older poems in Bratskiye pesni (1912; Fraternal Songs), and then by Lesnye byli (1913; Forest Tales) and Mirskiye dumy (1916; Secular Ballads), which completely won over the ACMEISTS. Through S. Gorodetsky, Klyuyev met S. Yesenin, whom he then introduced to Blok. Klyuyev's attitude toward the Revolution was at first positive; he saw it as an expression of the peasants' life of freedom, interpreted in a mystico-religious manner; Klyuyev was also associated with the group "Skify" (Scythians), as were the left Socialist Revolutionaries R. Ivanov-Razumnik, A. Bely, Yesenin, S. Klychkov, and P. Oreshin; in a neonationalist manner, the group expected salvation to come from the peasantry. The Berlin publishing house Skify published three volumes of Klyuyev's poetry between 1920 and 1922; a two-volume anthology, *Pesnoslov* (Hymnologue), came out in Petrograd in 1919. After enduring several years of famine, Klyuyev returned to Petrograd and Moscow around 1922; his new books, however, were sharply criticized and taken off the market. Not even a 1924 volume of poems devoted to Lenin improved Klyuyev's catastrophic financial position. After Yesenin's suicide, Klyuyev wrote "Plach o Yesenine" (1926; Lament for Yesenin), which was quickly banned when it appeared in book form in 1927. Klyuyev's disappointment with post-Revolutionary developments found expression in (among other works) the poem and the verse epic "Pogorelshchina" (Eng. tr., "The Burning Bush"), which he read in private circles and which he gave to the Italian Slavicist E. Lo Gatto for posthumous publication. *Izba i pole* (1928; The Cottage and the Field) was the last collection of Klyuyev's poetry to appear in the Soviet Union during his lifetime. He was arrested in 1933 and exiled to the Narym region; M. Gorky's intercession on his behalf allowed Klyuyev to travel to Tomsk in mid-1934, where he was arrested again. The circumstances of Klyuyev's death have never been completely cleared up, and his work remained banned in the Soviet Union. His literary remains are thought to be lost. Although his REHABILITATION took place in 1957, Klyuyev's name is seldom mentioned. In 1977, after 49 years of suppression, a first volume of his selected poems appeared in Leningrad.

Klyuyev's is an unusually great literary talent, often ranked above Yesenin's; the roots of his creativity are to be found in folk poetry and in a centuries-old religious impulse. A life firmly rooted in the primitive strength of the peasant and a striving for poetic expression were united in Klyuyev with an initially instinctive, and later politically conscious, rejection of urban civilization and Bolshevik technocracy; this was paralleled in the development of his poetic form, which initially resembled folk poetry and then went on, under the influence of the symbolists, to more conscious structures. N. Gumilyov praised Klyuyev's "sonorous and clear verse, saturated with content." Poems in the spirit of old laments mingle with poems that suggest biblical psalms; the style is exceedingly ornamental. An intensity of inner, at times prophetic, vision is manifest in the richness of the imagery. Klyuyev's poetry, incomprehensible even to Russians without a gloss for the folk-speech elements, has been an object of serious research only since the publication of

the second edition of the collected works outside the Soviet Union in 1969.

*Works: Sosen perezvon* (poems), 1912, 2d ed., 1913; *Bratskie pesni* (poems), 1912; *Lesnye byli* (poems), 1913; *Mirskie dumy* (poems), 1916; *Mednyi kit* (poems), 1919; *Pesnoslov* (poems), 2 vols., 1919; *Pesn' Solncenosca. Zemlja i železo* (poems), Berlin, 1920; *Izbr. pesni*, Berlin, 1920; *L'vinyj khleb* (poems), 1922, 2d ed., Berlin, 1922; *Četvërtyj Rim* (poems), 1922 (reprinted, 1974); *Mat'—Subbota* (poems), 1922; *Lenin* (poems), 1924, 2d ed., 1924, 3d ed., 1924; (with P. N. Medvedev) *Sergej Esenin* (contains "Plač o Esenine"; poems), 1927, 2d ed., New York, 1954; *Izba i pole* (poems), 1928; *Polnoe sobr. soč.*, 2 vols., New York, 1954; *Soč.*, 2 vols., Munich, 1969; *Stikhotvorenija i poèmy* (lyric and narrative poems), 1977.—*Izbr.* (selected poems), 1981.

*Translation: Poems*, 1977.

*Secondary Lit.:* N. Gumilëv, in *Apollon* 1912:1 and in Gumilëv's *Sobr. soč.*, vol. 4, Washington, 1968, pp. 281–83; B. Filippov, in *Novyj žurnal*, New York, 19:1948, foreword to *Polnoe sobr. soč.*, 1954 and to *Soč.*, 1969, with comprehensive bibliography, and in *Vestnik RkhD* 143:1984, pp. 119–27; R. Menskij, in *Novyj žurnal* 32:1953; E. Lo Gatto, in *Novyj žurnal* 35:1953; N. Khomčuk, in *Russkaja lit.* 1958:2; E. Rajs, Paris, 1964; V. Orlov, in *Lit. Rossija* Nov. 25, 1966, pp. 16–17; E. Breidert, Diss., Bonn, and in *Zeitschrift für slavische Philologie* 1973; J. Davies, in *New Zealand Slavonic Journal* 2:1974; K. M. Azadovskij, in *Russkaja lit.* 1975:3; V. G. Bazanov, in *Stikhotvorenija i poèmy*, 1977, and in *Russkaja lit.* 1979:1; S. Subbotin, in *Russkaja lit.* 1984:4; G. McVay, in *Slavonic and East European Review* 1985:4.

**Knórre, Fyódor Fyódorovich**, playwright, prose writer (b. April 15 [April 2], 1903, St. Petersburg). At the age of 16 Knorre volunteered for the Red Army; he subsequently worked in the theater as actor and director, initially in Leningrad, in Moscow from the 1930s on. After 1926 Knorre wrote some 20 film scripts and several theater pieces, such as *Trevoga* (1931; Alarm) and *Vstrecha v temnote* (1944; Encounter in the Darkness), which attracted no particular attention and never appeared in book form. Knorre has been writing prose since 1938. His 1948 collection, *Tvoya bolshaya sudba* (Your Great Destiny), was attacked by narrow-minded critics of the time for its "passion for presenting mental and physical suffering." After the appearance of his collection of 17 short stories in 1953, his *Zhena polkovodtsa* (The Colonel's Wife) was reviewed positively as a presentation of a tragic wartime reunion in which sorrow and death are taken into consideration. Knorre's true-to-life prose is frequently constructed from the serious links in the chain of human destiny; such is the case in *Kamenny venok* (1973; the Stone Wreath), the story of a woman who convinces herself to give up plans for her own life in order to take care of her deceased sister's family. Knorre lives in Moscow and has published regularly since 1964 (often children's books). He has not been a delegate to any congresses of the Writers Union since 1954 and the critics have paid little attention to his work. Many of Knorre's works have been filmed.

*Works: Tvoja bol'šaja sud'ba* (short stories), 1948; *Mat'* (short stories), 1951; *Rasskazy* (short stories), 1953; *Sëstry* (play), in *Teatr* 1957:8; *Navsegda* (novel), 1960; *Povesti i rasskazy* (short stories), 1964; *Solënyj pës* (children's stories), 1965; *Kapitan Krokus* (fairy tales and pov.), 1966; *Khobotok i Lenora* (pov.), 1969; *Šorokh sukhikh list'ev* (pov. and short stories), 1969; *Kamennyi venok* (pov.), 1973; *Vesennjaja putëvka* (pov. and short stories), 1976; *Rassvet v dekabre* (pov. and short stories), 1979; *Izbr. proizv.*, 2 vols., 1984.

*Secondary Lit.:* A Kotljar, in *Novyj mir* 1948:8; O. Ziv, in *Lit. gazeta* Feb. 18, 1954; S. L'vov, in *Znamja* 1954:4; S. Baruzdin, in *Lit. Rossija* Oct. 20, 1965, p. 11, and in *Družba narodov* 1983:8; I. Zav'jalova, in *Lit. obozrenie* 1973:9

**Knórring, Irína Nikoláyevna,** poet (b. May 4 [April 21], 1906, on her parents' estate in prov. Samara—d. Jan. 23, 1943, Paris). Knorring grew up in Kharkov. In 1920 she emigrated with her family via Simferopol to Bizerte (Tunisia) where she completed secondary school. In 1925 she moved to Paris, studied at the French-Russian Institute, and married the poet Yu. Sofiyev in 1928. In 1927 Knorring became ill with diabetes, an event that reoriented her thinking and writing toward death. During her lifetime, Knorring published two volumes of poetry: *Stikhi o sebe* (1931; Poems about Myself), which included 43 poems, and *Okna na sever* (1939; Window toward the North), which included 46 poems. Her mother published the poems remaining unpublished at her death in *Posle vsego* (1949; After Everything), which included 49 poems written from 1924 to 1942.

Knorring's poetry has a personal character and is marked by the themes of love and death. She uses biblical images but is unable to integrate her own anticipated death into an encompassing spiritual existence. She gives voice to the significance of ethical questions, to the necessity of accepting one's fate, and always returns to her love for her son and husband. Somewhat apart stands her "Ballada o dvadtsatom gode" (1924; Ballad about the Year 1920), a poetic depiction of the horror of the Revolution experienced by a 14-year-old. Her soft, melancholic poetry shaped itself within her mind and was written down without needing further reworking.

*Works: Stikhi o sebe* (poems), Paris, 1931; *Okna na sever* (poems), Paris, 1939; *Posle vsego* (poems), Paris, 1949.

*Secondary Lit.:* N. Ocup, in *Čisla*, Paris, 5:1939; Ju. Sotiev, in *Novyj žurnal*, New York, 8:1943; M. Cetlin, in *Novyj žurnal* 32:1949; N. Knorring, in I. Knorring's *Posle vsego*, 1949; Ju. Terapiano, in his *Vstreči*, New York, 1953; N. Stanjukovič, in *Vozroždenie*, Paris, 57:1956.

**Knút, Dóvid** (pseud. of Davíd Mirónovich Fíksman), poet (b. 1900, Kishinyov—d. Feb. 14, 1955, Tel Aviv). Knut's father owned a small shop in Kishinyov; Knut settled in Paris in 1920. He studied chemistry in Cannes and, during the 1920s, ran an inn in the Latin Quarter in Paris with his siblings. Later he earned his living as a fabric painter. For his poetry, he chose his mother's name. In the spring of 1922 he established the group of poets called "Palata poetov" (Chamber of Poets) (see *Novaya russkaya kniga* 1922:2) with B. Poplavsky, A. Ginger, and other representatives of the younger generation of the first EMIGRATION. In 1925 he joined the "Soyuz molodykh poetov" (Union of Young Poets). Following the publication of his first book of poetry, *Moikh tysyacheletiy* (1925; Of My Millennia), which was acclaimed by V. Khodasevich, his poems were regularly published in such journals as *Sovremennye zapiski*. With N. Berberova—his longtime friend—Yu. Terapiano, and V. Fokht, he published three issues of the literary journal *Novy dom* during 1926 and 1927. Of the three following volumes of his own poetry, *Vtoraya kniga stikhov* (1928; Second Book of Poetry), *Parizhskiye nochi* (1932; Parisian Nights), and *Nasushchnaya lyubov* (1938; Vital Love), Terapiano considered the one published in 1932 to be his best. A trip to Palestine, probably in 1937, found expression in the report *Albom puteshestvennika* (1938; Album of a Traveler) and in the cycle of poems called *Prarodina* (The

Ancestral Homeland). During World War II, Knut fought in the Jewish group of the French resistance movement. In 1944 his second wife, a daughter of the composer Aleksandr Skryabin, was arrested and killed by the Gestapo in Toulouse; Knut was able to escape to Switzerland. Before the volume *Izbrannye stikhi* (1949; Selected Poems)—a compilation of 87 poems selected from his entire creative opus—could be published, Knut moved to Israel with his children from both marriages. His poems are a permanent feature of anthologies of Russian poetry.

Knut is a consciously Jewish poet who gets his creative inspiration from a historical and spiritual tradition thousands of years old. His poetry seeks the permanent, valid, and essential that hides behind the earthly evanescent. His poetry is religious and approaches the quality of prayer. In the three-part poem written in 1926–27, *Ispytaniye* (The Ordeal), he describes God's call to himself and the vocation of the poet, which is bound up with material sacrifice for spiritual gain. Knut contrasts the lonely man in the "frightful world" to eternity and succeeds in creating the true vision of life as seen through death and through an enlightened state of mind. His poetry is musical, inclining toward rhythmic anaphoric repetition, conscious of word choice, seldom narrative; in the especially well known poem "Kishinyovskiye pokhorony" (Funerals in Kishinyov), for example, his writing is economical and dense.

*Works: Moikh tysjačeletij* (poems), Paris, 1925; *Vtoraja kniga stikhov* (poems), Paris, 1928; *Parižskie noči* (poems), Paris, 1932; *Kruglogolov i kompanija* (short story), in *Vstreči*, Paris, 1:1934; *Nasuščnaja ljubov'* (poems), Paris, 1938; *Al'bom putešestvennika* (travel sketches), in *Russkie zapiski*, Paris, 5 and 7:1938; *Izbr. stikhi*, Paris, 1949 (also contains *Prarodina*).

*Secondary Lit.:* M. Cetlin, in *Sovremennye zapiski*, Paris, 35:1928; P. Bicilli, in *Čisla*, Paris, 6:1932, and in *Sovremennye zapiski* 67:1938; Ju. Terapiano, in *Sovremennye zapiski* 51:1933, in *Opyty*, Paris, 5:1955, and in *Grani*, Frankfurt am Main, 44:1959; N. Berberova, in *Russkie zapiski* 10:1938, and in her *Kursiv moj*, New York, 1983; A. Sedykh, in his *Dalëkie, blizkie*, New York, 1962; G. Shapiro, in *Cahiers du monde russe et soviétique* 1986:2.

**Knyázev, Vasíly Vasílyevich,** poet (b. Jan. 18 [Jan. 6], 1887, Tyumen, prov. Tobolsk—d. Nov. 10, 1937, or March 1938 [?], while impris-

oned). Knyazev came from a family of wealthy Siberian merchants. He attended the gymnasium in Yekaterinburg; in 1904–5 he attended a St. Petersburg teachers college, from which he was expelled for political activities. In 1905 Knyazev embarked on an active literary career by publishing his work in various satiric journals (he used the pseudonyms "V. K.," "V-K-V," "Vasily," "Vasya," "Vysotsky," and so on); he also pursued his interests in folklore, collecting proverbs and short songs (*chastushki*). Knyazev went over to the revolutionary camp shortly after the October Revolution; as a "proletarian poet" he regularly wrote agitational poetry for *Krasnaya gazeta* (Red Gazette), using various pseudonyms such as "Krasny zvonar" (Red Bellringer) and "Krasny poet" (Red Poet). During the Civil War, Knyazev traveled to the front with an agitational train sponsored by the PROLETKULT. With the introduction of NEP, Knyazev gave up writing political and satiric verse. In the 1920s he published several collections of *chastushki*, followed by a volume of Russian proverbs (*Kniga poslovits* [1930]). His last book appeared in 1935. Knyazev became a victim of Stalinist despotism in 1937 and was rehabilitated around 1957.

Knyazev's poetry stands somewhat apart from other proletarian revolutionary verse (V. Aleksandrovsky, M. Gerasimov, V. Kirillov) with its enthusiasm for the international workers' movement; his poems reflect the influence of Demyan Bedny, are cleverly written, and aggressively call for the destruction of the enemy.

*Works: Satiričeskie pesni* (poems), 1910; *Krasnoe Evangelie* (poems), 1918; *Pesni krasnogo zvonarja* (poems), 1919; *Deti goroda* (poems), 1919; *Pervaja kniga stikhov (1905–1916)* (poems), 1919; *Kaplja krovi Il'iča* (poems), 1924; *Kniga izbrannykh stikhotvorenij* (poems), 1930; *Poslednjaja kniga stikhov (1918–1930)* (poems), 1933; *Za četvert' veka (1905–1930)* (poems), 1935; *Izbr.*, 1959.

*Secondary Lit.:* V. Sajanov, in *Knjazev's Izbr.*, 1959; R. A. Šaceva, in *Proletarskie poèty pervykh let sovetskoj èpokhi*, 1959; L. Evstigneeva, in *Poèty "Satirikona,"* 1966.

**Kóchetov, Vsévolod Anísimovich,** literary official, prose writer (b. Feb. 4 [Jan. 22], 1912, Novgorod—d. Nov. 4, 1973, Moscow). Kochetov's father was a peasant. Kochetov began working as an agronomist on sovkhoz farms in 1931 after completing an agricultural technical school; in 1938 he became a journalist; in 1944 he joined the Communist Party. He began publishing in 1946. Kochetov's assiduous campaign against all post-Stalinist liberal tendencies in Soviet literature began with the ideological controversy engendered by V. Panova's Vremena goda. From 1953 to 1955 Kochetov served as secretary of the Leningrad section of the Writers Union; in 1954 he became a member of the board of the Writers Union and moved to Moscow. From 1955 to 1959 he was the editor in chief of Literaturnaya gazeta; from 1961 to 1973, of the journal Oktyabr. Kochetov was a member of the Central Appeals Commission of the Central Committee of the Communist Party.

Kochetov was "one of the leading administrative figures of literary orthodoxy" (von Ssachno, p. 143). His Stalinist family novel, Zhurbiny (1952; Eng. tr., The Zhurbins, 1953), and all of his subsequent works resort to the simple-minded division of characters into positive embodiments of Party attitudes and negative figures. Bratya Yershovy (1958; The Yershov Brothers), his attempt to write an anti-Dudintsev novel and to discredit the literary THAW, was itself criticized by Pravda (Sept. 25, 1958) for exaggeration. In Chego zhe ty khochesh? (1969; Just What Is It You Want?), Kochetov not only ridiculed I. Babel, M. Tsvetayeva, and O. Mandelshtam for being victims of Stalinism but also attacked the spread of SAMIZDAT and even the reading of Western Communist newspapers. Kochetov's lack of literary ability, clearly visible in the pseudodisputations in all his works, is further underlined by his narrow-minded comments on writers' views and intentions.

Works: Predmest'e (pov.), 1948; Čerty kharaktera (short stories), 1949; Tovarišč agronom (novel), 1952; Žurbiny (novel), 1952 (see above); Molodost' s nami (novel), 1954, 1972; Brat'ja Eršovy (novel), 1958, 1965; Ruki naroda. Iz kitajskogo dnevnika (articles), 1961; Sekretar' obkoma (novel), 1961; Ugol padenija (novel), 1970; Čego že ty khočeš'? (novel), 1970; Publicistika. Vospominanija sovremennikov (journalistic prose), 1977.—Izbr. soč., 3 vols., 1962; Sobr. soč., 6 vols., 1973–76.

Secondary Lit.: L. Mikhajlova, in Novyj mir 1952:5; E. Surkov, in Lit. gazeta Dec. 16, 1961; A. Mar'jamov, in Novyj mir 1962:1; V. Druzin, in Moskva 1962:2; RSPP 2:1964; N. Velengurin, 1970; N. Sergovancev, in Moskva 1972:2; A. D. Okorukov, in Molodaja gvardija 1974:2; A. Grebenščikov, in Zvezda 1977:11; J. Glad, in Russian Language Journal 32:1978; S. Babaevskij, in Lit. Rossija Feb. 5, 1982, pp. 8–9; V. Pekšev, in Oktjabr' 1984:2; Ju. Idaškin, in Lit. Rossija May 12, 1985, pp. 10–11.

Kógan, Pável Davýdovich, poet (b. July 4, 1918, Kiev—d. Sept. 23, 1942, in action, near Novorossiysk). Kogan spent his childhood, from 1922 on, in Moscow. In 1936 he began his studies at the Moscow Institute of Philosophy, Literature, and History; in addition, in 1939 he entered the Gorky Literary Institute, where his studies included I. Selvinsky's seminar, which he attended along with A. Yashin. Like M. Kulchitsky, Kogan was considered to be a promising talent. A sojourn in Karelia found expression in poems. In 1941 his participation in a geological expedition was interrupted by World War II. Kogan, whose earliest poems are dated 1934, did not publish a single line during his lifetime. His pirate ballad "Brigantina" (1937; Brigatine) was popular in student circles. His poems were first published in the late 1950s; a collection of his verse, Groza (1960; The Storm), brought a selection of his remaining work together in one volume.

Kogan's poems, many of which have been lost, reflect the influence of E. Bagritsky, who had great prestige during Kogan's youth. Revolutionary enthusiasm mingles with patriotism and with the theme of the threat of war. Bitterness and a search for meaning in the surrounding world are discernible in some of his nonpolitical poems, but in general they reveal deep inner conflict. Kogan strives for a narratively engrossing, rhythmic style.

Works: Groza (poems), 1960; poems, in Sovetskie poèty, pavšie na Velikoj Otečestvennoj vojne, 1965; Stikhi (poems), 1966.

Secondary Lit.: S. Narovčatov, in Kogan's Groza, 1960; A. Jašin, in Lit. gazeta Aug. 25, 1960; V. Pankov, in Lit. i žizn' Sept. 21, 1960.

Kolbásyev, Sergéy Adámovich, prose writer (b. March 17 [March 5], 1898, St. Petersburg—d. Oct. 30, 1942 [?], while imprisoned). Kolbasyev's father was an assistant court judge. Kolbasyev attended the school of the Navy Cadet Corps; in 1917 he became an officer in the Red Fleet in the Baltic Sea and the Sea of Azov; for some time he commanded a minesweeper. In 1921 he returned to Petrograd and, with N. Tikhonov and K. Vaginov, became a member of the literary group "Ostroviityane"; his first five poems came out in its publication. Between 1923 and 1928 Kolbasyev worked for the diplomatic service as translator at the Soviet missions in Kabul and Helsinki. After his return to Leningrad he devoted himself exclusively to literature and joined the military writers' association LOKAF.

The adventures of the Red Fleet from the time of the Civil War to the first Five-Year Plan constitute the sole theme of his short stories, three collections of which appeared between 1930 and 1936. I. Rakhtanov reports that Kolbasyev owned an extraordinarily large collection of jazz records, and that Tikhonov attributed Kolbasyev's influential encounter with the works of Rudyard Kipling to his proficiency in foreign languages. Around 1930 Kolbasyev also wrote popular-science books about radio for young people. In 1937 he was arrested and his name was passed over in silence for the next 20 years; his death was disclosed only after his REHABILITATION. a volume of Kolbasyev's selected works, with a foreword by Tikhonov, appeared in 1958; Salazhonok (1931), his short story about one of the "homeless waifs" *(besprizorniki)* cut adrift by the Revolution who eventually becomes a naval officer, was reprinted in 1960.

Kolbasyev describes various events at sea with a concern for technical procedures. His mostly autobiographical prose is lively but not weighty; he likes to use surprise effects and to add animation through direct dialogue. In 1937 he was reproached with "being more a sailor than a Red Fleet man," that is, with neglecting the political aspect of events.

*Works: Otkrytoe more* (poems), 1922; *Povorot vsë vdrug* (short stories), 1930; *Salažonok* (short story), 1931, 2d ed., 1960; *Pravila sovmestnogo plavanija* (short stories), 1935; *Voennomorskie povesti* (short stories), 1936; *Povesti i rasskazy (pov. and short stories),* 1958; *Povorot vsë vdrug* (pov. and short stories), 1978; *Dva rasskaza* (short stories), in *Avrora* 1984:12.

*Secondary Lit.:* A. Žukov in *Lit. učëba* 1937:3; N. Tikhonov, foreword to Kolbas'ev's *Povesti i rasskazy,* 1958; I. Rakhtanov, in his *Na širotakh vremeni,* 1973, pp. 433–44.

**Kollontáy, Aleksándra Mikháylovna,** née Domontovich, prose writer, political figure (b. March 31 [March 19], 1872, St. Petersburg—d. March 9, 1952, Moscow). Kollontay was the daughter of a tsarist general. She studied privately at home, passing her university entrance examinations in 1888. She was married to V. Kollontay from 1893 to 1898. In 1898–99 she studied political economy in Zurich. In her struggle for equal rights for women, she allied herself with the Marxists in 1899; in 1908 she sided with the Mensheviks, but from 1915 on her allegiance lay with the Bolsheviks. Valued by Lenin as a brilliant speaker

and publicist, Kollontay took part in revolutionary activities in exile between 1908 and 1917; from November 1917 to March 1918 she was People's Commissar for Social Welfare. From 1922 to 1945 she served in the diplomatic corps, as ambassador to Norway, Mexico, and Sweden. In addition to her memoirs, only fragments of which were ever published, Kollontay also wrote fiction. *Lyubov pchol trudovykh* (1923; Eng. trs., *A Great Love,* 1929, 1982; *Love of Worker Bees,* 1978), as well as the other two povesti included in the volume (*Lyubov tryokh pokoleniy* [The Love of Three Generations] and *Vasilisa Malygina*), is dedicated to the theme of the sexual emancipation of women; it was translated into seven languages. *Zhenshchina na perelome* 1923; Woman in Crisis) contains three more povesti that depict, in fictional form, the priority of work and personal choice over love and marriage. Because of her liberal attitude toward sexual relationships, Kollontay was attacked by orthodox critics even at the time. Her literary works were not reprinted after 1927.

*Works: Ljubov' pčël trudovykh* (three pov.), 1923 (see above); *Položenie ženščiny v èvoljucii khozjajstva* (essays), 1923; *Ženščina na perelome* (three pov.), 1923; *Bol'šaja ljubov'* (novel), 1927 (Eng. tr., *Red Love,* 1927); *Vasilisa Malygina* (pov.), 1927; "Ziel und Wert meines Lebens," in *Führende Frauen Europas,* July 1926; *Autobiographie einer sexuell emanzipierten Kommunistin,* Munich, 1970 (Eng. tr., *The Autobiography of a Sexually Emancipated Communist Woman,* 1971); *Izbr. stat'i i reči* (articles and speeches), 1972; *Iz moej žizni i raboty* (memoirs and diaries), 1974.

*Secondary Lit.:* F. Budnev, in *Na postu* 1924:1; K. Bailes, in *Cahiers du monde russe et soviétique* 1965:4; H. Lenczyk, in *Cahiers du monde russe et soviétique* 1973:1–2 (contains detailed bibliography); S. Breslav, in *Neva* 1973:4 and 1974; R. McNeal, in *Slavic Review* 1982:2; È. Šejnis, in *Novyj mir* 1982:4–5.

**Koltsóv, Mikhaíl Yefímovich** (pseud. of M. Ye. Frídlyand), prose writer (b. June 12 [May 31], 1898, Kiev—d. April 4, 1942 [?], while imprisoned). Koltsov's father was an artisan. In 1915 Koltsov studied at the Psychoneurological Institute in Petrograd; he began his career as a publicist in 1916. Koltsov joined the Communist Party in 1918; in 1919 he served with the Red Army in Kiev. His work as a journalist in Moscow beginning in 1920 included being a regular contributor to *Pravda*

(1922–38). Koltsov was editor of *Ogonyok* from 1923—when the journal was founded—to 1938, of the satirical journal *Chudak* from 1928 to 1930, and of *Krokodil* from 1934 to 1938; he coedited *Za rubezhom* with M. Gorky from 1932 to 1938. Koltsov was frequently dispatched abroad as a correspondent; his postings included a prolonged assignment to Spain during the Civil War (1936–37). In 1938 he became a delegate to the Supreme Soviet of the RSFSR and corresponding member of the Academy of Sciences of the USSR. Koltsov was chairman of the Foreign Commission of the Writers Union. In December 1938 he became a victim of the government purges; he was rehabilitated after 1956.

Koltsov, "the first journalist of his age" (K. Chukovsky), had already been acknowledged as a writer in his own lifetime (V. Shklovsky); in 1967 the Academy history of literature devoted an entire chapter to him. Koltsov wrote some 2,000 newspaper articles about current foreign and domestic political events, a chronicle, as it were, of the period from the Revolution to the end of the 1930s. In these articles he showed himself a master of satirical commentary, commanding a graphic, terse, exciting style capable of brilliantly intensifying his political message through irony, paradox, and hyperbole. Koltsov composed effortlessly, dictated everything into a machine, and revised little. His short prose always uses the first-person narrative form, never crosses the line separating journalism from fiction, and is predominantly structured by the mere addition of small units of text. Three multivolume editions of Koltsov's works were published between 1928 and 1936, as well as numerous other collections; of the latter, only *Ispansky dnevnik* (1938; Spanish Diary) is thematically consistent.

*Works: Pervyj krug* (journalistic prose), 1922; *Ispanskij dnevnik* (diary), 1938; *Fel'etony i očerki* (journalistic prose), 1956; *Pisatel' v gazete* (journalistic prose), 1961.—*Sobr. soč.*, 4 vols. (only vols. 1–3 published), 1928–29; 3 vols. (only vols. 2–3 published), 1933–34; 6 vols. (only vols. 1–2, 4–6 published), 1935–36; *Izbr. proizv.*, 3 vols., 1957.

*Secondary Lit.:* N. Kružkov, in *Novyj mir* 1938:6; L. Slavin, in *Lit. gazeta* July 21, 1956 and in his *Lit portrety*, 1965; D. Zaslavskij, in Kol'cov's *Izbr. proizv.*, 1957; B. E. Efimov (Kol'cov's brother), in *Sovetskie pisateli, avtobiografii* 1:1959 and in *Lit. gazeta* June 15, 1963; *RSPP* 2:1964; M. K., *kakim on byl: Vospominanija*, 1965; A. Rubaškin, 1971, and in *Zvezda* 1968:2; B. Verevkin, 1977.

**Konétsky, Víktor Víktorovich,** prose writer (b. June 6, 1929, Leningrad). Konetsky's father was an examining magistrate. Konetsky spent the winter of 1941–42 in besieged Leningrad. In 1952 he graduated from the Naval Military Institute, then served as helmsman and captain on military and civilian vessels, particularly in the Arctic; he never completely gave up his naval profession even after beginning a literary career. Konetsky was admitted to the Communist Party in 1953. He began publishing his literary works in 1956. Konetsky has attended the congresses of the Writers Union of the RSFSR and has been a member of the Union's Appeals Commission since 1965. He lives in Leningrad.

Konetsky became a writer as a result of his own experiences as a sailor and under the influence of the books of K. Paustovsky, which served as his "one and only safety valve" in the postwar period, when the "air of social life became heavier" (*Novy mir* 1969:3). His short stories and povesti are more or less associated with sea travel; his real concern, however, is the realm of the human spirit. His accounts of the thoughts of lonely people, accompanied by numerous digressions into the past, determine the character of his prose; his stories frequently deal with "the conflicts of heroes with themselves" (Holthusen). His concern with the question of the meaning of life connects his work with the best prose of the early 1960s. The problem of people's trials in difficult situations runs through his work and arouses the reader's sympathy; questions are raised rather than resolved. His povest *Zavtrashniye zaboty* (1961; Tomorrow's Concerns) evoked contradictory reactions from Soviet critics. *Kto smotrit na oblaka* (1967; He Who Looks at Clouds) combines ten independent narrative units, referring to separate years between 1942 and 1966, into an artistic whole. The parts, such as a 16-year-old girl's encounter in 1942 with death and doubt, or an exiled captain's sorrow in the postwar period, were seen as the milestones of a quarter century. Konetsky himself described *Solyony lyod* (1969; Salty Ice), based on his own experience at sea, as a prose work that stands outside literary genres. Like G. Vladimov, Konetsky eschews the romanticism of sailing; he emphasizes the dullness, harshness, and boredom of the sailor's day-to-day life. Occasionally assuming an ironic stance, Konetsky remains at the border between two sides, both of which have their right to be heard. His next publication, *Sredi mifov i rifov* (1972; Between Myths and Reefs), maintains the form and basic orientation of his sailing narratives. Self-reflections and thoughts about manner of presentation, found in the sailing narrative *Vcherashniye zaboty* (1979; Leave Your Worries Behind), appeared more frequently in his work during the 1970s. Konetsky also writes film scripts.

*Works: Zaindevelye provoda* (short stories), 1957; *Skvoznjak* (short stories), 1957; *Kamni pod vodoj* (short stories), 1959; *Zavtrašnie zaboty* (pov.), 1961; *Luna dnëm* (pov. and short stories), 1963; *Nad belym perekrëstkom* (short stories), 1966; *Kto smotrit na oblaka* (novel), 1967; *Solënyj lëd* (travel notes), 1969; *Povesti i rasskazy* (short stories), 1970; *Sredi mifov i rifov* (travel notes), 1972; *210 sutok na okeanskoj orbite* (travel notes), in *Zvezda* 1972:7–8; *Morskie sny* (travel notes), 1975; *Za dobroj nadeždoj* (novel), 1977; *Solënyj khleb* (selections), 1979; *Včerašnie zaboty* (pov.), 1979; *Tretij lišnij* (pov.), in *Zvezda* 1982:8.

*Secondary Lit.:* V. Lakšin, in *Novyj mir* 1961:8; I. Kuz'mičev, in *Zvezda* 1969:3; I. Gitovič, in *Novyj mir* 1969:3; L. Anninskij, in *Junost'* 1970:6; RSPP 7(1):1971; R. Messer, in *Avrora* 1973:8; R. Fajnberg, 1980; A. Laskina, in *Lit. gazeta* Jan. 1, 1983, p. 6.

**Konoválov, Grigóry Ivánovich,** prose writer (b. Oct. 1 [Sept. 18], 1908, Bogolyubovka, prov. Samara). Konovalov was of peasant descent. Konovalov worked as a farmhand; from 1928 to 1931 he studied at a school for workers in Perm. He joined the Communist Party in 1930; in 1936 he completed his studies at the pedagogical institute in Perm and was further educated at the Institute of Red Professors at Moscow. In 1940–41 and after World War II (he served in the Pacific fleet), Konovalov taught Russian literature at the pedagogical institute in Ulyanovsk until 1957. Konovalov, who began his literary career in 1927, wrote novels of no literary value, but as prescribed by the principle of PARTY SPIRIT. He is a member of the boards of the Writers Unions of the RSFSR (1958–65 and since 1970) and the USSR (since 1971). Konovalov lives in Saratov.

Konovalov's first novel, *Universitet* (1947; The University), is typical of the struggle against COSMOPOLITANISM in its denial of foreign achievements and its glorification of the Stalin period. Konovalov's inability to translate the Party-approved message into "a somewhat serious level" of literature was criticized even then (Golubov). Konovalov selected the kolkhoz as the subject of *Stepnoy mayak* (1949; Beacon of the Steppes). "But 'good moments'

are not really enough, there must be a full-valued artistic resolution," stated M. Kuznetsov (*Sovetsky roman,* 1963, p. 269), speaking of Konovalov's *Istoki* (1959; Sources), part 1 of a family history planned as a trilogy. The award of a Gorky Prize for the first two parts in 1969 identifies *Istoki* as a recognized work of SOCIALIST REALISM.

*Works: Universitet* (novel), 1947; *Stepnoj majak* (novel), 1950 (revised as *Večnyj rodnik,* 1955); *Istoki* (novel), 1959, 2 vols., 1969; *Bylinka v pole* (novel), 1970; *Predel* (novel), in *Moskva* 1973:3–4, separate ed., 1975.—*Sobr. soč.,* 5 vols., 1977–80.

*Secondary Lit.:* E. Usievič, in *Lit. kritik* 1938:11; S. Golubov, in *Novyj mir* 1948:1; V. Nazarenko, in *Lit. i žizn'* March 25, 1960; RSPP 2:1964; Ja. Javčunovskij, Saratov, 1969; A. Elkin, in *Lit. Rossija* July 5, 1974, p. 14; V. Čalmaev, in *Lit. obozrenie* 1974:9 and in *Moskva* 1978:10; N. Mašovec, in *Moskva* 1976:10; L. Gerasimova, in *Lit. Rossija* April 23, 1982, p. 11; S. Betkin, in *Lit. Rossija* April 1, 1983, p. 14.

**Kontinént,** a literary journal of the third emigration, published quarterly since 1974 under the editorship of V. Maksimov (Paris) at the journal's own publishing house (located in Berlin). At different times the narrow circle of editors has included N. Gorbanevskaya, V. Iverni, V. Nekrasov, and Ye. Ternovsky. The extensive editorial staff has included V. Aksyonov, I. Brodsky, Vl. Bukovsky, A. Galich, P. Grigorenko, N. Korzhavin, and A. Sakharov, as well as Western writers and journalists. Extracts from the journal have been published in German, French, English, Dutch, Italian, and Greek. *Kontinent* publishes works by Russians who emigrated after 1970, as well as translated articles and works not published in the USSR because of censorship. Emphasis is given to literary works. These are complemented by literary criticism, essays on the fine arts, contemporary documentation, analyses, religious contemplations. Contributions by authors from the countries in the Soviet sphere of influence are also included. Issues 1 to 48 (1986) included contributions, by, among others, V. Aksyonov, Yuz Aleshkovsky, G. Aygi, V. Betaki, S. Bobyshev, I. Brodsky, I. Burikhin, S. Dovlatov, L. Druskin, A. Galich, A. Gladilin, A. Glezer, N. Gorbanevskaya, F. Gorenshteyn, V. Grossman, F. Kandel, V. Kornilov, N. Korzhavin, Yu. Kublanovsky, I. Lisnyanskaya, L. Losev, V. Lyon, V. Maksimov, Yu. Mamleev, M. Maramzin, V.

Nekrasov, I. Ratushinskaya, L. Rhzevsky, Vl. Rybakov, A. Solzhenitsyn, A. Terts, L. Vladimirova, V. Voynovich, I. Yelagin, and V. Yerofeyev.

Secondary Lit.: V porjadke diskussii: Dukhovnye pereput'ja "Kontinenta," in Vestnik RKhD 115:1975; S. Artamonov, in Russkaja mysl', Paris, March 4, 1976; W. Kasack, in Osteuropa 1976:12; Konferencija "Kontinenta" v Russkaja mysl' Nov. 24, 1977; G. Andreev, in Russkaja mysl' June 24, Sept. 16, and Dec. 16, 1982; April 21, June 23, and Sept. 1, 1983; Aug. 2, and Oct. 4, 1984; April 25 and Sept. 6, 1985; Jan. 9, 1987, p. 10; I. Kosinskij, in Novoe russkoe slovo, New York, May 27, 1984, p. 6; L. Losev, in Novoe russkoe slovo July 8, 1984, p. 8; Kontinentu—10 let, in Russkaja mysl' July 12, 1984, pp. 10–11.

**Kópelev, Lev Zinóvyevich,** prose writer, scholar of German literature (b. April 9 [March 27], 1912, Kiev). Kopelev's father was an agronomist. Kopelev learned German from his parents, received only a seven-year education as a result of the Revolution, and combined work in industry with political and journalistic activity. In 1933 he began to study German language and literature in Kharkov; he continued his studies in Moscow in 1935, where he came into close contact with the German Communist émigré community. In 1941 he completed the requirements for a candidate's degree with a work on Friedrich von Schiller's dramas and the problems of the bourgeois French Revolution. As a member of the Communist Party he worked in the propaganda department during World War II. In early 1945 Kopelev was arrested and sentenced to ten years in a camp. Until 1950 he and A. Solzhenitsyn were together in the same special camp; Solzhenitsyn has captured some of Kopelev's characteristic features in the character Lev Rubin (in V kruge pervom). After his REHABILITATION in 1956 (in 1957 he was even reinstated as a Party member), Kopelev was especially active as a translator and scholar of German literature. Some of his articles were collected in Serdtse vsegda sleva (1960; The Heart Is Always Left). Popular scholarly books about Goethe's Faust (1962) and about Bertolt Brecht (1966) were disparaged by the conservative critics. The departure from the policy of the THAW led to Kopelev's support for numerous dissidents such as Yu. Daniel, A. Sinyavsky, A. Solzhenitsyn, Yu. Galanskov, L. Chukovskaya, P. Grigorenko, and especially

A. Sakharov. In 1968, after he published the essay "Ist eine Rehabilitierung Stalins möglich?" (Is Stalin's Rehabilitation Possible?) in the Viennese Communist journal Tagebuch, he was dismissed from the Moscow Research Institute for Art History and expelled from the Party. At that point he also broke with Marxism. After 1971 Kopelev began publishing regularly in the West; his autobiography covering the years 1945–47, Khranit vechno (1975; Eng. tr., To Be Preserved Forever, 1977), made him world famous in its ten generally condensed versions in translation. In November 1980 Kopelev was given permission to emigrate together with his wife, R. Orlova. In 1981 Kopelev was awarded the Peace Prize of the German Book Trade. He lives in Cologne.

Kopelev works as an author, as a scholar of German literature, and as a journalist writing on political and ethical questions. He has written a three-part autobiography. I sotvoril sebe kumira (1978; And I Created for Myself an Idol; Eng. tr., The Education of a True Believer, 1980) covers his childhood and youth; the Russian title alludes to his recognition of his own guilt. Khranit vechno describes the end of the war and his first arrest. Utoli moya pechali (1981; Eng. tr., Ease My Sorrows, 1983) has as its title the earlier name of the church converted into a special camp where Kopelev was imprisoned. A perception of the humane in an inhumane system is the quality that unites and distinguishes his books. A poetic biography of Heinrich Heine completed in 1968—Ein Dichter kam vom Rhein (1981; A Poet Came from the Rhine; "Povest o poete," Russian unpublished),—and Svyatoy doktor Fyodor Petrovich (1985; The Holy Doctor Fyodor Petrovich), the history of F. J. Haass, a German doctor in Russia, link up with his books on Goethe and Brecht in their popular scholarly style. As a scholar of German literature, Kopelev viewed contemporary German literature as essentially one entity, even while he was still in the Soviet Union; he particularly wrote about Heinrich Böll, Erwin Strittmatter, Max Frisch, Wolfgang Koeppen, and Brecht, promoted Konstantin Bogatyrev as a translator of poetry, and, after emigrating, embarked on a project to explore German-Russian literary connections. A collection of his journalistic work, Verbietet die Verbote (1977; Prohibit the Prohibitions; in German only), containing letters, speeches, and essays from 1962 to 1975, is characterized by his concern for individuals and for Russia.

Works: Genrich Mann (bio-bibliography), 1957; Jaroslav Gašek i ego Švejk (essay), 1958;

Serdce vsegda sleva (essays), 1960; (with R. Orlova) Bez prošlogo i buduščego . . . (essays), 1960; "Faust" Géte (treatise), 1962; Leonard Frank (bio-bibliography), 1965; Brecht (poetic biography), 1966; "Ist eine Rehabilitierung Stalins möglich?" (essay), in Tagebuch, Vienna, Feb., 1968; "Rilke in Russland" (essay), in Die Zeit April 21, 1972; Zwei Epochen d.-russ. Literaturbeziehungen, Frankfurt am Main, 1973; Khranit' večno (memoirs), Ann Arbor, 1975 (see above, 2d rev. ed. 1978; Verwandt und verfremdet (essays), Frankfurt am Main, 1976; I sotvoril sebe kumira . . . (memoirs), Ann Arbor, 1978 (see above); Utoli moja pečali (memoirs), Ann Arbor, 1981 (see above); (jointly with H. Böll) Warum haben wir aufeinander geschossen? (essays), Bornheim, 1981; Na krutykh povorotakh korotkoj dorogi (pov. and short stories), New York, 1982; Deržava i narod (essays), Ann Arbor, 1982; (with R. Orlova) Vstreča s Annoj Akhmatovoj (essay), in Grani, Frankfurt am Main, 131:1984; Svatoj doktor Fédor Petrovič (poetic biography), London, 1985.

Secondary Lit.: N. Vil'mont, in Novyj mir 1961:3; G. Mitin, in Oktjabr' 1963:7; A. Dymšic, in Znamja 1966:9; H. Böll, in Die Zeit May 10, 1968, and in Frankfurter Allgemeine Zeitung Oct. 17, 1981; M. Dönhoff, in Die Zeit Feb. 6, 1976; A. Galič, in Kontinent, Paris, 12:1977; W. Kasack, in Börsenblatt für den Deutschen Buchhandel 37, Frankfurt am Main, Sept. 14, 1981; J. B. Dunlop, in Slavic Review 1982:3.

**Koptélov, Afanásy Lázarevich,** prose writer (b. Nov. 6 [Oct. 24], 1903, Shatunovo, in the Altai). Koptelov is descended from peasants who belonged to the Kerzhenets Old Believers; he had little schooling. After the Revolution he was actively involved in the campaign against illiteracy, served as chairman of a commune, and, as a journalist, wrote on agricultural questions. He began his literary career in 1924. In his short stories from the 1920s, Koptelov attempted to depict the life of the Kerzhenets Old Believers, whom P. I. Melnikov-Pechersky had described in his novels written about 1880. Koptelov's novel Svetlaya krov (1931; Bright Blood), an unliterary account of the construction of the Turksib railroad line, was his contribution to the literature of the Five-Year Plan. The major subject of Koptelov's total oeuvre is the Altai, its folklore, its history, and the transformation of the local nomads after the Revolution. The merit of his work lies far more in its accu-

mulation of materials than in its actual composition, as his novel Velikoye kochevye (1935; The Great Nomadic Territory) proves; later he continually revised this work. His articles, collected in Forposty sotsializma (1931; Outposts of Socialism) had already been criticized for lacking in essentials, for "false folklore," and for "consciously distorted and crude language." In 1944 Koptelov became a member of the Communist Party. Sad (1955; The Garden), a novel propagandizing the agricultural push in Siberia, is smothered by superfluous material and marred by obviously cheap idealization. Bolshoy zachin (1963; The Great Beginning), Vozgoritsya plamya (1966; The Flame Will Be Kindled), and Tochka opory (1977; The Fulcrum) compose a Lenin trilogy; in 1979 Koptelov was awarded the State Prize of the USSR for its third part. He lives in Novosibirsk.

Works: Antichristovo vremja (short story), in Sibirskie ogni 1925:4–5; Forposty sotsializma (articles), 1931; Svetlaja krov' (novel), 1933; Pervyj rejs (short story), in Sibirskie ogni 1931:1; Velikoe kočev'e (novel), 1935, subsequently revised eds., 1940, 1949, 1952, 1954, 1964; Naši zemljaki (articles), 1944; Sad (novel), 1956, subsequently revised eds., 1959, 1962; Bol'šoj začin (novel), 1963; Vozgoritsja plamja (novel), 1966, 1969; Točka opory (novel), in Sibirskie ogni 1977:1–2, separate ed., 1979; Minuvšee i blizkoe, 1983; Sobr. soč., 5 vols., 1978–82.

Secondary Lit.: B. Grossman, in Novyj mir 1931:12; N. Narvekov, in Lit. kritik 1935:10; A. Dement'ev, in Lit. gazeta June 19, 1955; V. N. Kuprejanova, 1956; I. Kozlov, in Znamja 1964:2; RSPP 2:1964; A. Dremov, in Oktjabr' 1966:11; N. Janovskij, 1966, and in Lit. Rossija July 3, 1985, p. 16; V. Khmara, in Pravda Aug. 19, 1970; G. Ermakova, in Zvezda 1980:4; G. Kolesnikova, in Lit. obozrenie 1984:8.

**Koptyáyeva, Antonína Dmítriyevna,** prose writer (b. Nov. 7 [Oct. 25], 1909, Yuzhny, Eastern Siberia). Koptyayeva began working as an office clerk for the mining industry in 1926. In 1932 she accompanied her husband to Kolyma, where she became administrative director of the gold mines. Her first short story came out in 1935. She enrolled at the Gorky Literary Institute in 1939, interrupted her studies to work in a military hospital during World War II, and completed her degree in 1947. Koptyayeva's first novel, Fart (1940; Striking It Lucky), is set in the gold-mining milieu; her second novel, Tovarishch Anna

(1946; Comrade Anna), which deals with the marriage problems of a female mining engineer, she substantially revised in 1947 after the novel was accused of being apolitical. In 1950 Koptyayeva received a Stalin Prize (for 1949, 3d class) for *Ivan Ivanovich* (1949; Eng. tr., 1952), the first part of her trilogy about a neurosurgeon. Part 1 is based on the early prose she wrote in Kolyma; the second part, *Druzhba* (1954; Friendship), is set during wartime; and the third part, *Derzaniye* (1958: Daring), takes place after the war. Some 1,500 pages long, the work met with little approval because of its great length, frequent medical descriptions, and poor psychological penetration. *Dar zemli* (1963; Gift of the Earth) fits into the context of her earlier work by combining the theme of the extraction of raw materials—in this case petroleum—with the theme of minority nationalities. For more than ten years she worked on her novel *Na Uralereke* (1971–78; On the Ural River), in which she turns to the events of the Civil War, with particular emphasis on Lenin's activities in Orenburg. Koptyayeva has been a member of the board of the Writers Union of the RSFSR since 1958 and of the board of the Writers Union the USSR since 1971. She lives in Moscow.

*Works:* Kolymskoe zoloto (pov.), 1936 (under pseud. A. Zejte); *Fart* (novel), 1941; *Tovarišč Anna* (novel), 1946; *Ivan Ivanovič* (novel), 1950 (see above); *Družba* (novel), 1954; *Derzanie* (novel), 1958; *Dar zemli* (novel), 1965; *Na Urale-reke* (novel), 1971, part 2 in *Molodaja gvardija* 1978:2–5, separate ed., 1979.— *Sobr. soč.*, 6 vols., 1972–75.

*Secondary Lit.:* B. Jakovlev, in *Novyj mir* 1948:3; E. Koval'čik, in *Novyj mir* 1950:1; A. Èl'jaševič, in *Lit. gazeta* Dec. 2, 1958; Ju. Konstantinov, in *Novyj mir* 1959:10; *RSPP* 2:1964; A. Vlasenko, in *Lit. Rossija* Oct. 31, 1969, p. 11; B. Brajnina, in *Lit. Rossija* Nov. 23, 1973, p. 14; L. Junina, in *Znamja* 1978:11.

**Kor   nílov, Borís Petróvich**, poet (b. July 29 [July 16], 1907, Pokrovskoye, prov. Nizhniy Novgorod—d. Nov. 21, 1938 [?], while imprisoned). Kornilov's father, a village schoolteacher of peasant descent, was intent on furthering his son's education. In 1922 the family moved to Semyonovo, where Kornilov became an active member of the Komsomol. He went to Leningrad at the end of 1925, intending to show his first poems to S. Yesenin, but Yesenin was by then dead. Through V. Sayanov, Kornilov joined the "Smena" group, to

which Olga Berggolts (later his wife) also belonged. The title of his second volume of poems, *Pervaya kniga* (1931; First Book), indicates a fundamental break with his first volume, *Molodost* (1928; Youth). These books were followed, during the years up to 1935, by nine more collections of lyric and narrative verse, which in spite of considerable criticism led gradually to recognition, even on the official level, for Kornilov. The official attitude toward Kornilov changed in 1936; in October he was expelled from the Writers Union of the USSR and was subsequently arrested (probably in 1937). His papers (which included a completed verse drama written for the theater of V. Meyerhold, who held him in high esteem) were destroyed; for 20 years, until the revision of this arbitrary action, his name was deleted from literary studies.

Kornilov's poetry is often considered to have been influenced by Yesenin and E. Bagritsky. He is regarded as one of the "Komsomol poets"; he wrote some of the first song lyrics with highly political content, such as "Pesnya o vstrechnom" (1932; A Song of Encounter), which Dmitri Shostakovich set to music. The song was so popular that during the period of Kornilov's official "nonexistence" it was published with the words "folk text" (*slova narodnye*) appended to it. In its natural simplicity Kornilov's verse has something elemental about it. When he turned to the officially prescribed theme of the denunciation of independent farmers as kulaks, intimations of Kornilov's original ties to the village nevertheless persisted. Kornilov began writing narrative poetry with a lyrical reworking of I. Babel's "Sol," *Tripolye* (1933), which recounts a tragic episode from the Civil War. It is probably his best work in this genre. The international revolutionary stance of *Moya Afrika* (1933–34; My Africa), a mixture of fantasy and reality about a black man's struggle and death in revolutionary Petrograd, inspired Romain Rolland (*Pravda* Dec. 6, 1935).

*Works:* Molodost' (poems), 1928; *Pervaja kniga* (poems), 1931; *Stikhi i poèmy* (lyric and narrative poems), 1933; *Novoe* (narrative poem), 1935; *Tripol'e* (narrative poem), first complete printing in *Zvezda* 1935:1; *Moja Afrika* (narrative poem), in *Novyj mir* 1935:3; *Stikhotvorenija i poèmy* (lyric and narrative poems), 1957, 2d ed., 1960; *Stikhotvorenija i poèmy* (lyric and narrative poems), 1966; *Agent ugolovnogo rozyska* (narrative poem), in *Lit. gazeta* Oct. 4, 1968, pp. 12–14; *Prodolženie žizni* (poems), 1972; *Izbr.* (lyric and narrative poems), Gor'kij, 1977.

Secondary Lit.: M. Lukonin, in Novyj mir 1959:1; O. Berggol'c, in Kornilov's Stikhotvorenija i poèmy, 1960; G. Curikova, 1963; Ja. Smeljakov, in Moskva 1963:12; L. Anninskij, in Kornilov's Stikhotvorenija i poèmy, 1966; A. Urban, in Zvezda 1977:8; K. Pozdnjaev, 1978, and in Moskva 1982:7.

**Kornílov, Vladímir Nikoláyevich**, poet (b. June 29, 1928, Dnepropetrovsk). Kornilov's father was a construction engineer who was evacuated to Siberia during World War II. Kornilov studied at the Gorky Literary Institute from 1945 to 1950. Kornilov, who began publishing his poems in 1953, was honored in 1961 when his narrative poem Shofyor (The Driver) was included in the liberal anthology coedited by K. Paustovsky, Tarusskiye stranitsy. Only in 1964 did Kornilov publish his first volume of verse, Pristan (A Haven), a selection of poetry written after 1948 to which serious critics responded favorably. He subsequently published occasional poems in Novy mir, Yunost, Prostor, and other journals. Soon after he completed his studies, two small volumes of his prose were published in Kuybyshev; they later circulated in SAMIZDAT. His povest Devochki i damochki (written 1968; Little Girls and Little Ladies) was banned by the censors after the editorial board of Novy mir had accepted it for publication in late 1971. The povest appeared in the West in 1974 (as all of Kornilov's subsequent work did up to 1986). Kornilov also works as a translator of poetry. In 1966 he was one of the supporters of A. Sinyavsky and Yu. Daniel; in 1977 he was expelled from the Writers Union. Kornilov lives in Moscow.

Kornilov's poems are, so to speak, letters to himself. A highly developed consciousness of responsibility to life and a serious search for the meaning of existence speak out from his verses about childhood, military service, love, and art. Accordingly, he limits his message to the essential, writes economically and concretely, and combines pleasure in alliteration and sound with a painstaking avoidance of the superfluous. His image of a leafless tree, an image emphasizing only the essential, serves as a metaphor for his work, in which "he strives to penetrate to the heart of a given phenomenon" (Vanshenkin). The melancholy element in his poems seeks consolation in light and goodness. Kornilov's prose reproduces everyday Soviet reality in a matter-of-fact, realistic manner, although it is somewhat short on plot. Devochki i damochki shows women, working as sappers outside Moscow

in 1941, at the mercy of total disorganization. Bez ruk, bez nog (1974–75; Armless and Legless) draws a picture of life shortly after World War II, with all its distress and insincerity, from the point of view of an adolescent. In his novel Demobilizatsiya (1976; Demobilization), written between 1969 and 1971, Kornilov describes the life of the Moscow intelligentsia in the mid-1950s and living conditions in the army. The novel "Kamenshchik, kamenshchik" (1980; "Stonemason, Stonemason") is a record of day-to-day Russian life from the end of the last century to the Brezhnev era. Kornilov's central character in the novel is a man living in internal exile who works at not serving the vicious system that surrounds him.

Works: Šofër (narrative poem), in Tarusskie stranicy, 1961; Pristan' (poems), 1964; poems, in Novyj mir 1964:12, 1965:8, 12, 1966:7, in Junost' 1965:12, 1971:8; Vozrast (poems), 1967; Skazat' ne želaju (pov.), 1973; Devočki i damočki (pov.), in Grani, Frankfurt am Main, 94:1974; Bez ruk, bez nog (pov.), in Kontinent, Paris, 1:1974 and 2:1975; Demobilizacija (novel), Frankfurt am Main, 1976; "Kamenščik, kamenščik . . ." (novel), Frankfurt am Main, 1980; Nadežda (poems), in Znamja 1986:11.

Secondary Lit.: L. Levin, in Den' poèzii, Moscow, 1964; K. Vanšenkin, in Moskva 1964:10; Z. Papernyj, in Trud Dec. 23, 1964; S. Babënyševa, in Znamja 1965:1; V. Iverni, in Kontinent 9:1976.

**Kórvin-Piotróvsky, Vladímir Lvóvich**, poet, playwright (b. 1891, Belaya Tserkov—d. April 2, 1966, Los Angeles). Korvin-Piotrovsky was descended from ancient nobility and could trace the first part of his last name back to the Hungarian royal family. He was an officer in the artillery and fought against the Bolsheviks in the Civil War. He emigrated to Berlin, probably in 1920, where he earned a living by working at different jobs, among others as a chauffeur, and published articles in many Russian newspapers and journals under the name of Piotrovsky. In the journal Spolokhi (Lightening, nos. 1–21, Nov. 1921–July 1923) published in Berlin, he supervised the poetry section and published his own poems. Out of the six volumes of poetry that he published before World War II, he later acknowledged the reworked version of only a few poems. His later acknowledgment also extended to the drama Beatriche (1929; Beatrice) and three dramatic sequences in the style of A. Pushkin.

In 1939 Korvin-Piotrovsky moved to Paris where he was active in the resistance movement; he spent ten months in the Gestapo's prison. Just as he survived being shot in the Civil War, he here escaped the death sentence. After the war he was overcome by a wave of patriotism for a short while, but he did not allow himself to be repatriated. From then on he used his full name, Korvin-Piotrovsky; in the collection *Vosdushny zmey* (1950; The Paper Dragon), he published lyric poetry that he composed (and learned by heart) in prison in 1944 and poems written from 1937 to 1949. His longer narrative poems and a few later lyric poems that also described experiences in Russia were compiled in *Porazheniye* (1960; The Defeat). A regular contributor to *Novy zhurnal* from 1953 on, Korvin-Piotrovsky moved to Los Angeles. *Pozdniy gost* (1968–69; A Late Guest), a two-volume collection of his partially rewritten lyric poetry and dramas, edited by Tatyana Fesenko and with eight essays about him, was published posthumously.

In 1966 Korvin-Piotrovsky began a short autobiography by calling himself an officer in the artillery. In accordance with this view, his poetry, what he acknowledged of it since the 1950s, is marked by a spirit of military and aristocratic terseness. His early lyric poetry is different: *Zvezdnoy tropoyu* (1921; On the Path to the Stars), a long narrative poem about Mary of Egypt and her path from whore to saint, is without rhyme, emotional, and religious and antireligious at the same time. His later poetry is almost classical, rhyming, clear and hard, and gives preference to iambic tetrameter. Only seldom, as in the poems written in prison, does his poetry relate directly to the present; more frequently it places the reader in another century, as in his "Plach Yaroslavny" (Yaroslav Lament). Military events, usually related to horses; cosmic imagery; and a medieval world of motifs marked by night, fog, autumn, and winter penetrate his quaint creative work. It depicts a timeless spiritual condition, touches on metaphysics, but is not borne along by faith. Korvin-Piotrovsky's drama *Beatriche*, which he wrote from 1926 to 1928 and reworked toward the end of his life, is set in Rome in 1598. The same considerable artistic power of positioning oneself completely in another time and another cultural world is demonstrated in his short dramas consciously modeled after Pushkin: *Noch* (Night), originally called *Pered duelyu* (Before the Duel), which shows Pushkin experiencing the messenger of death; *Smert' Don Zhuana* (1929; The Death of Don Juan),

which follows from Pushkin's *Kamenny gost*; *Korol* (1929; The King), which is set in the Middle Ages in Western Europe and depicts the problem of crime and revenge; and *Brodyaga Glyuk* (The Vagabond Gluck), dedicated to the theme of creative freedom. Korvin-Piotrovsky occupies an exceptional position as a poet and playwright in the tradition of Russian romanticism.

*Works: Polyn' i zvëzdy* (poems), Berlin, 1923; *Svjatogor-skit* (poems), Berlin, 1923; (with G. Rosimov) *Vesëlye bezdelki* (poems), Berlin, 1924; *Kamennaja ljubov'* (poems), Berlin, 1925; *Beatriče* (play), Berlin, 1929 (also contains *Korol'*; *Smert' Don Žuana*; *Pered duèl'ju*); *Vozdušnyj zmej* (poems), Paris, 1950; *Poraženie* (lyric and narrative poems), Paris, 1960; *Pozdnij gost'* (lyric and narrative poems), 2 vols., Washington, 1968–69.

*Secondary Lit.*: G. Rosimov, in *Novaja russkaja kniga*, Berlin, 1923:2; P. Tverskoj (N. Andreev), in *Grani*, Frankfurt am Main, 12:1951; K. Vil'čkovskij, in *Vozroždenie*, Paris, 53:1956; G. Adamovič, in *Novoe russkoe slovo*, New York, April 10, 1960; Ju. Ofrosimov, in *Novyj žurnal*, New York, 61:1960, 84:1966; K. Pomerancev, in *Mosty*, Munich, 4:1960, and in *Russkaja mysl'*, Paris, June 9, 1966; T. Fesenko, in *Novoe russkoe slovo* April 15, 1966; G. Struve, in *Russkaja mysl'* June 11, 1966; R. Gul', in *Novyj žurnal* 83:1966; V. Blinov, in *Novyj žurnal* 138:1980 and in HRL 1985.

**Korzhávin, Naúm** (pseud. of Naúm Moiséyevich Mándel), poet (b. Oct. 14, 1925, Kiev). Korzhavin is the grandson of a Zaddik Jew. After World War II ended in 1945, Korzhavin enrolled in the Gorky Literary Institute, where "he was considered to be one of the most gifted students" (Soloukhin). On Dec. 20, 1947, Korzhavin was arrested, incarcerated in the Lubyanka Prison for eight months, and exiled from Moscow for three years. He was assigned to live in the village of Chumakovo (Mikhaylovsky district, Novosibirsk oblast) in Siberia until 1951. Subsequently Korzhavin was forced to live in Karaganda, where in 1953 he completed mining school as a pit foreman. In 1954 he was granted amnesty and returned to Moscow, where he earned his living by doing translations. His REHABILITATION followed in 1956. Korzhavin completed his studies at the Gorky Literary Institute in 1959. His poems were occasionally printed in various journals. His first major publication, 16 poems, took place in the liberal anthology *Tarusskiye* *stranitsy* (1961). Only once (in the year he was admitted to the Writers Union) was a volume of his verse approved for publication: *Gody* (1963; Years) brings together, under the editorship of E. Vinokurov, 54 poems written between 1941 and 1961. Much of Korzhavin's work circulates in SAMIZDAT. His articles on literary theory and his reviews in *Novy mir* prove him to be an astute critic. In 1967 the Stanislavsky Theater performed his drama *Odnazhdy v dvadtsatom* (Once in 1920), which was immensely successful despite considerable intereference by the censors. Korzhavin attracted attention with his unequivocally liberal opinions; he signed the appeals supporting Yu. Daniel and A. Sinyavsky in 1966, favored the discussion of A. Solzhenitsyn's letter at the Fourth Congress of the Writers Union in 1967, and supported Yu. Galanskov and Ye. Ginzburg in 1967, but did not otherwise assume a dissident role. In 1973 Korzhavin applied for permission to leave the Soviet Union "for lack of air to breathe" and settled in the United States in Boston. Since 1974 he has belonged to the editorial staff of *Kontinent;* his poetry has attracted as much attention as his essays, which contribute to an understanding of the intellectual situation in the Soviet Union. A large selection of his early and later poetic works is contained in the volumes *Vremena* (1976; Times) and *Spleteniya* (1981; Interweavings), both published in Frankfurt am Main. Korzhavin writes austere, contemplative verse; he is "an advocate of exactness, of precision, of the serious element of ethical clarity that extracts from history the rational core needed by the present" (Drawicz). The historical poems that appeared in the Soviet Union refer symbolically to Stalin and the present (see "Borodino"). Instead of retelling the hackneyed story of the Decembrists' wives who followed their husbands into exile, Korzhavin uses this historical situation to communicate the suffering of loved ones forcibly separated in the Soviet period. "The Children of Auschwitz" ("Men tormented children. Cleverly. Deliberately. Skillfully"), written with the "austere, almost ascetic pathos" (Urban) typical of Korzhavin, becomes a memorial against all ideologically determined action. Korzhavin's compact, imagery-poor, abstractly political and ethical verse arises out of his experience of meanness and darkness, yet it retains a knowledge of decency and light. His first publications after emigration clarify Korzhavin's religious position. In his *Poema grekha* (1974; Poem of Sin), he questions, in connection with Russian history during and after Stalin's time, the

purpose and source of the Soviet system's constant lie and its urge toward the forcible expansion of power. Korzhavin's literary criticism and essays place the relevant subject matter in a larger context. His *Opyt poeticheskoy biografii* (Toward a Poetic Biography), written in 1968, uses Korzhavin's personal fate to give the reader an idea of how those who think independently in the Soviet Union are muzzled. In the essay *Sudba Yaroslava Smelyakova* (Yaroslav Smelyakov's Fate), written in 1972–73, Korzhavin uses the example of an author who degenerates from gifted writer to conformist hack to give a psychological history of Russian society over a period of several decades.

*Works:* 16 poems, in *Tarusskie stranicy,* 1961; *V zaščitu banal'nykh istin* (essay), in *Novyj mir* 1961:3; poems in *Novyj mir* 1961:7, in *Junost'* 1962:4, 1965:9, in *Den' poèzii,* Moscow, 1965, 1966, 1969, 1970, in *Grani,* Frankfurt am Main, 80:1971, in *Novyj žurnal,* New York, 113:1973; *Roždenie veka* (narrative poem), in *Molodaja gvardija* 1962:8; *Gody* (poems), 1963; *Lirika Maršaka* (essay), in *Novyj mir* 1963:3; *Poezija A. K. Tolstogo,* in *Voprosy lit.* 1967:4; *Odnaždy v dvadcatom* (in Polish trans.), in *Dialog,* Warsaw, 1969:11; *Sud'ba Jaroslava Smeljakova* (essay), in *Grani* 91:1974; *Poèma grekha* (narrative poem), in *Novyj žurnal* 116:1974; *Opyt poètičeskoj biografii* (essay), in *Kontinent,* Paris, 2:1975; *Igra s d'javolom* (essay), in *Grani* 95:1975; *Vremena* (poems), Frankfurt am Main, 1976; *Psikhologija sovremennogo entuziazma* (essay), in *Kontinent* 8:1976 and 9:1976; *Spletenija* (poems), Frankfurt am Main, 1981; *A byl li Stalin-to* (essay), in *Kontinent* 39–40:1984.

*Secondary Lit.:* V. Soloukhin, in *Novyj mir* 1964:1; A. Urban, in *Voprosy lit.* 1964:1; L. Lazarev, in *Junost'* 1964:2; I. Mikhajlov, in *Zvezda* 1964:4; Ju. Ajchenval'd, in *Teatr* 1968:4; W. Kasack, in *Osteuropa* 1976:2; Z. Zinik, in *Kontinent* 11:1977; M. Morgulis, in *Novoe russkoe slovo,* New York, Oct. 18, 1983, p. 5; V. Vojnovič, in *Russkaja mysl',* Paris, Oct. 18, 1985, p. 10.

**Kosmíst,** a literary association of proletarian writers analogous to the Moscow group KUZNITSA that was founded in 1920 by former members of the PROLETKULT such as A. Gastev and V. Kazin. This group approached politics and art in the same way as Kuznitsa; the designation *Kosmist* emphasizes the internationality of their revolutionary concerns and the cosmic, hyperbolic quality of their imagery. After the leading role had been transferred to the Party-oriented group OKTYABR (1922), Kosmist was disbanded in June 1923.

*Secondary Lit.:* See KUZNITSA; PROLETKULT.

**Kóstylev, Valentín Ivánovich,** prose writer (b. March 15 [March 3], 1884, Moscow—d. Aug. 29, 1950, Moscow). Kostylev had three years of formal education; he began writing occasionally in 1903. After the October Revolution he was a journalist and official, working in Nizhniy Novgorod (present-day Gorky) from 1922 on. Beginning in 1935 Kostylev published several historical novels. He became a member of the Communist Party in 1944. His first novel, *Khvoyny shtorm* (1935; The Conifer Storm), dramatizes revolutionary events in the Volga region; his next novel, *Pitirim* (1936), takes place in the reign of Peter the Great; *Zhretsy* (1937; The Priests) is also linked to historical events. *Kozma Minin* (1939) is set in the early 17th century. The best known of Kostylev's novels is the trilogy *Ivan Grozny* (1943–47; Ivan the Terrible). The trilogy's presentation of Ivan the Terrible's conquest of the Baltic countries (along with similar efforts by A. N. Tolstoy, I. Selvinsky, V. A. Solovyov, and S. Eisenstein) provided a historical basis for the Soviet annexation of the Baltic regon in 1940. The novel primitively idealizes the despot, whom Stalin admired; it justifies tyranny in the interests of national policy, minimizes the significance of cruelty and atrocities, and presents the Russian soldiers as liberators of the Lithuanians, Latvians, and Estonians from German bondage (Stalin Prize for 1947, 2d class). Post-Stalinist textbooks acknowledged the novel's historical falsifications.

*Works: Khvojnyj štorm* (novel), 1935, revised under the title *Sčastlivaja vstreča,* 1947; *Pitirim* (novel), 1936, rev. ed., 1948; *Žrecy* (novel), 1937; *Koz'ma Minin* (novel), 1939; *Ivan Groznyj* (novel-trilogy), 1943–47.—*Izbr. soč.,* 6 vols., 1951–52.
*Secondary Lit.:* I. Makarov, in *Novyj mir* 1946:5; L. I. Twarog, in *American Slavic and East European Review* 1955:3; *RSPP* 2:1964; M. Korallov, in *Voprosy lit.* 1965:9.

**Kovchég** (The Ark), a literary journal edited by Nikolay Bokov, published irregularly in Paris since 1978 (no. 6, 1981). (An anthology by the same name was published in New York in 1942 by the Union of Russian Writers in New York [Obyedineniye russkikh pisateley v Nyu Yorke] with contributions from M. Aldanov, I. Bunin, Yu. Ivask, Yu. Terapiano, A. Shteyger, and others.) Issues 1 to 4 were published by N. Bokov and A. Kron; issues 5 and 6 are signed only by Bokov, who, however, names the following advisers: L. Bokova (New York), I. Burikhin (Cologne), M. Grobman (Jerusalem), A. Kron (Paris), K. Kuzminsky (Texas), Yu. Lekht (Los Angeles), Yu. Maltsev (Bergamo), Ye. Mnatsakanova (Vienna), I. Pomerantsev (Lahnstein), A. Rabinovich (Geneva), L. Sheliya (Paris), Ye. Vagin (Rome). The journal is emphatically avant-garde. In form and content, those texts that distinguish themselves from the traditional canon of Russian literature are given preference. The journal takes advantage of the freedom to be surrealistic, erotic, or provocative that is granted literature out of the reach of Soviet CENSORSHIP. Among the contributing authors—some of whom live in emigration, some in the Soviet Union—are G. Aygi, L. Chertkov, V. Kazakov, E. Limonov, Yelena Shvarts.

**Kozakóv, Mikhaíl Emmanuílovich,** prose writer (b. Aug. 23 [Aug. 11], 1897, Romodan, prov. Poltava—d. Dec. 16, 1954, Moscow). After a brief period of study in Kiev, Kozakov was caught up in the Civil War, fighting on the side of the Bolsheviks. In 1921 he went to Petrograd, where he finished his law studies in 1922. His career as a writer grew out of his profession as a journalist. Kozakov's first collection of short stories, *Popugayevo schastye* (Parrot's Happiness), appeared in 1924. The influence of A. Remizov's delight in narrative devices, such as interference in narrative flow, unusual metaphors, and syntactic defamiliarization, is stronger in the stories of *Popugayevo schastye* than in Kozakov's first longer work, *Meshchanin Adameyko* (1927; The Petit Bourgeois Adameyko), a detective story in the manner of F. Dostoyevsky's *Crime and Punishment;* its theme is disillusionment with the Revolution. Kozakov was attacked sharply when official criticism subsequently censured all experimentation in literature as formalistic. His major work is the novel *Krusheniye imperii* (1956; The Downfall of the [Russian] Empire), the first parts of which, published between 1929 and 1937 under the title *Devyat tochek* (The Nine Points), went practically unnoticed by the critics. This far-ranging novel, combining both documentary and fictitious elements from the period 1913 to 1917, was first published in its complete and revised form only after Kozakov's death. "Kozakov's novel, on ideological-social and historical levels, is based on the Leninist interpretation of the events of the February Revolution" (Fedin).

Works: Popugaevo sčast'e (short stories), 1924; Čelovečja zakuta (short stories), 1926; Meščanin Adamejko (pov.), 1927; Čelovek, padajuščij nic (short stories), 1930 (reprinted, Tel-Aviv, ca. 1981); Tri povesti, 1934 (reprinted, 1979); Žiteli ètogo goroda (novel), 1955; Krušenie imperii (novel), 1956.—Izbr. soč., 4 vols., 1929–31.

Secondary Lit.: A. Ležnev, in Novyj mir 1929:5; K. Fedin, foreword to Žiteli ètogo goroda, 1955, and in his Sobr. soč., vol. 9, 1962; RSPP 2:1964.

**Kozhévnikov, Alekséy Venedíktovich,** prose writer (b. March 18 [March 6], 1891, Khabazy, prov. Vyatka—d. Jan. 5, 1980, Moscow). Kozhevnikov's father was a peasant. Before the Revolution, Kozhevnikov taught in a village school; during the Civil War he served in the Red Army. In 1923 he attended the Bryusov Institute of Literature and Art in Moscow. Kozhevnikov began his literary career in 1924; he was a member of KUZNITSA. He made extended trips from Moscow throughout the Soviet Union, to the Volga and Ural regions, Siberia, Central Asia, and the Khakass Autonomous Region, to gather material for his books. Kozhevnikov sought to depict the changes that took place in various areas as the result of the October Revolution and socialist construction. Many of his publications were aimed at young readers. Seven retrospective stories integrated into the text of Veniki (1928; Twig Brooms), an early povest about the Volga raftsmen, make this work technically interesting. His novel Zdravstvuy, put! (1934; Greetings, Train Tracks!) glorifies the builders of the Turkistan-Siberia Railroad. Kozhevnikov selected a colorful appellation for the Yenisey River, Brat okeana (1939; The Ocean's Brother), as the title of his novel about the construction of the city of Igarka. He received a Stalin Prize (for 1950, 3d class) for his novel Zhivaya voda (1950; Eng. tr., Living Water, 1954), a standard work of SOCIALIST REALISM, with unflawed positive heroes at its center, that depicts the successful overcoming of pseudo-obstacles in order to implement a new irrigation system in the Khakass Autonomous Region. The novel promotes the Communist Party decree "On the Improvement of Agriculture in the Post-war Period" and prepares the way for the implementation of this irrigation system. In his last

novel, Na velikoy letnoy trope (1980; On the Great Summer Path), Kozhevnikov deals with the years of revolutionary unrest (1905–17), a prevalent theme in Soviet literature.

Works: Špana. Iz žizni besprizornykh (short stories), 1925, 2d enl. ed., 1929; Čelovek-pesnja (novel for young people), 1927; Veniki (pov.), 1928; Magistral' (novel), 1934 (rev. version: Zdravstvuj, put'!, 1936); Brat okeana (novel), 1939; Živaja voda (novel), 1950 (see above); Dobrye vskhody (pov., short stories, and articles), 1960; Solnce ezdit na olenjakh (novel), 1972; Vozdušnyj desant (novel), 1972; Na velikoj letnoj trope (novel), 1980.—Sobr. soč., 4 vols., 1977–79.

Secondary Lit.: N. Zamoškin, in Novyj mir 1929:3; F. Levin, in Lit. kritik 1939:7; I. Aramilev, in Oktjabr' 1950:8; RSPP 2:1964; I. Sokolov, in Lit. gazeta June 27, 1973, p. 4; Ju. Lukin, in Lit. gazeta April 1, 1981, p. 6.

**Kozhévnikov, Vadím Mikháylovich,** prose writer (b. April 22 [April 9], 1909, Narym, Siberia—d. Oct. 20, 1984, Moscow). Kozhevnikov's father was a doctor. in 1925 Kozhevnikov moved to Moscow; from 1929 to 1933 he was a student in the Department of Literature and Ethnology at Moscow University; he began working as a journalist in 1933. In 1939 Kozhevnikov's first volume of short stories was published. He worked as a war correspondent from 1941 to 1945 (from 1943 on, for Pravda); in 1943 he was admitted to the Communist Party. In 1947–48 Kozhevnikov was editor of the Literature and Art section of Pravda; from 1949 until his death he was editor in chief of the journal Znamya. Kozhevnikov began writing longer prose works in 1956. He held numerous high offices in the literary administration, was a member of the boards of the Writers Unions of the USSR and the RSFSR and, from 1967 and 1970 respectively, of their secretariats as well. In 1981 he was a delegate to the 26th Communist Party Congress. Kozhevnikov lived in Moscow.

Kozhevnikov's prose primarily endeavors to carry out the intentions of the Party and to create the new Communist man. His war stories serve the cult of personality totally: an idealized super-hero completes his assignments super-quickly and super-well; armed only with a little hatchet, invulnerable, he attacks an enemy armed with submachine guns (Most [1943; The Bridge]). The sugary image of war presented in the trivial legends that were constantly being reprinted even in the post-Stalinist period detracted from the actual achievements of the Red Army. More than ten years after their publication, such falsifications elicited fictional counterresponses from G. Baklanov, V. Nekrasov, B. Okudzhava, and others. Kozhevnikov's short stories about China (1952–55) correspondingly revolve around a Chinese superman. His novel *Zare navstrechu* (1956–57; Toward the Dawn) combines autobiographical elements with an idealized picture of Russian revolutionaries during the Civil War in Siberia. *Znakomtes, Baluyev* (1960; Allow Me to Introduce Baluyev), a povest about the construction of a natural gas pipeline in Siberia, serves to propagandize the Party idea of the early realization of communism. This work about the men of the future gave rise to a discussion that continued for years; the povest was indicted by such sober writers as S. Antonov because Baluyev's concern was "not for people" but only "for people at machines"; it was greeted favorably by dogmatic advocates such as I. Kozlov because it implemented "the principle of the superelevation of the positive." Kozhevnikov fought for the ideal figure of the "positive hero" as demanded in the early years of SOCIALIST REALISM in theoretical articles as well: "It is difficult to imagine a genuine heroic image of a contemporary man that would be exhausted by the present—there must always be traits of the future in him" (*Lit. gazeta* July 20, 1961). Kozhevnikov's return to the war novel in *Shchit i mech* (1965; Eng. tr., *Shield and Sword*, 1970) went practically unremarked. In his povest *Osoboye podrazdeleniye* (1969; Special Unit), which is also set partially during World War I, Kozhevnikov tries to create an ideal image of the Soviet worker (a factory hand who receives an engineering degree by correspondence and ultimately becomes a Party official). Kozhevnikov received the State Prize of the USSR for this work in 1971. Kozhevnikov's *Korni i krona* (1981–82; Roots and Crown) is a production novel that poses artificial problems.

Works: *Nočnoj razgovor* (short stories), 1939; *Mart-aprel'* (short stories), 1942; *V velikom narodnom Kitae* (articles), 1952; *Zare navstreču* (novel), 1956–57; *Znakomtes', Baluev* (pov.), 1960; *Šturm veršin* (essay), in *Lit. gazeta* July 20, 1961; *Ščit i meč* (novel), 1965 (see above); *Osoboe podrazdelenie* (pov. and short stories), 1969, 1970; *V polden' na solnečnoj storone*, 1973; *Lilas' reka* (short stories), 1980; *Korni i krona* (novel), in *Znamja* 1981:9–10, 1982:1–2.—*Sobr. soč.*, 6 vols., 1968–71.

Secondary Lit.: E. Knipovič, in *Novyj mir* 1956:6 and foreword to Koževnikov's *Sobr. soč.*, 1968; I. Kozlov, in *Lit. gazeta* April 25,

1959, and in *Lit. i sovremennost'* 2:1961; W. Horst, in *Süddeutsche Zeitung* July 9, 1960; S. Antonov, in *Lit. gazeta* March 4, 1961, and in *Naš sovremennik* 1963:1; *RSPP* 2:1964; N. Gej, V. Piskunov, in *Novyj mir* 1966:4; L. Krjačko, in *Moskva* 1970:6; I. Grinberg, 1972; E. Kriger, in *Lit. gazeta* Nov. 29 1972, p. 5; M. Sinel'nikov, in *Moskva* 1979:4 and in *Znamja* 1985:1; B. Rakhmanin, in *Lit. gazeta* Jan. 21, 1981, p. 4; G. Brovman, in *Novyj mir* 1982:12; M. Sinel'nikov, in *Znamja* 1985:1.

**Kozlóv, Iván Andréyevich,** publicist, prose writer (b. July 6 [June 24], 1888, Sandyri, prov. Moscow—d. March 27, 1957, Moscow). Kozlov was the son of a peasant. He became a member of the RSDRP (Social Democrats) in 1905. A professional revolutionary, he worked in the Ukrainian underground in 1918–19; from 1923 to 1925 he attended the Bryusov Institute of Literature and Art. From 1920 on, Kozlov combined Party work with his literary career. At the start of World War II he was Party secretary of the Crimean underground movement.

Kozlov's first literary work, *Podpolye* (1920; The Underground), was a little-noted drama about underground activities at the time of the Civil War. Kozlov first achieved recognition with his documentary provest *V Krymskom podpolye* (1947; In the Crimean Underground), on account of his Party work and partisan activities. The work received a Stalin Prize, 3d class, in 1947. Only the first part of his memoirs, *Zhizn v borbe* (1955; A Life in the Struggle), written mostly before World War II, was published during his lifetime; it deals with the period of preparation for the 1905 Revolution. Kozlov's goal was "to show the development of the world view and the character of rank and file Party workers and to serve in the cause of educating our Soviet youth in high ideological principles."

Works: *Podpol'e* (play), 1920 (reprinted, in *Pervye sovetskie p'esy*, 1958); *V Krymskom podpol'e* (pov.), 1947; *V gorode russkoj slavy* (pov.), 1950; *Žizn' v borbe* (memoirs), 1955; *Ni vremja, ni rasstojanie* (vol. 2 of his memoirs), 1966; *Naš poslednij i rešitel'nyj* (vol. 3 of his memoirs), 1969.

Secondary Lit.: A. Kosticyn, in *Novyj mir* 1951:3; F. Levin, in *Zvezda* 1956:2; A. Ilupina, in *Novyj mir* 1959:3.

**Krásnaya nov** (Red Virgin Soil), a literary journal that appeared in Moscow from 1921 to 1942, at first every two months and then

)

monthly. As the first "thick" literary journal, edited by A. Voronsky, *Krasnaya nov* held the leading role among literary journals, uniting especially the good young talents among the FELLOW TRAVELERS and publishing important works of new literature. *Krasnaya nov* was increasingly attacked by OKTYABR; in 1925 the Central Committee placed two MAPP representatives on the editorial board; in 1927 Voronsky—who had been accused of Trotskyism—was driven out. A. Fadeyev was one of the later, frequently changing, editors who extensively altered the spirit of the journal. In 1923, when *Krasnaya nov* was in its prime, its authors included: V. Aleksandrovsky, A. Arosev, D. Bedny, S. Bobrov, V. Bryusov, I. Erenburg, K. Fedin, O. Forsh, M. Gerasimov, F. Gladkov, M. Gorky, S. Gorodetsky, Vs. Ivanov, V. Kazin, V. Kirillov, S. Klychkov, N. Lyashko, O. Mandelshtam, A. Mariyengof, V. Mayakovsky, V. Narbut, A. Neverov, N. Nikitin, P. Nizovoy, S. Obradovich, P. Oreshin, B. Pasternak, B. Pilnyak, S. Podyachev, N. Poletayev, Ye. Polonskaya, L. Reysner, S. Semyonov, S. Sergeyev-Tsensky, M. Shaginyan, N. Tikhonov, A. Tolstoy, K. Trenyov, V. Veresayev, A. Vesyoly, M. Voloshin, S. Yesenin, M. Zoshchenko. Later *Krasnaya nov* published important works by I. Babel, V. Katayev, Yu. Olesha, A. Platonov, M. Prishvin, and L. Seyfullina, among others. The circulation climbed from about 15,000 (1921) to 22,000 (1932) and again to 45,000 (1941), but the number of pages in the journal decreased.

*Secondary Lit.*: See VORONSKY, A.; Ju. Mandel'štam, in *Čisla*, Paris, 1:1930; H. McLean, in *American Slavic and East European Review* 1949, pp. 185–200; Pis'mo . . . , in *Novyj mir* 1964:12; M. Kuznecov, in *Očerki istorii russkoj sovetskoj žurnalistiki*, 1966; R. Maguire, *Red Virgin Soil*, Princeton, 1968.

**Krátkaya literatúrnaya entsiklopédiya** (*KLE*; Short Encyclopedia of Literature), a Soviet literary encyclopedia edited by A. A. Surkov and published in Moscow in eight volumes (1962–75) and one supplemental volume (9:1978). The *KLE* is the most comprehensive literary reference work in the USSR. In more than twelve thousand signed entries, it presents authors from Russian and world literature, literary terms, movements, groups, journals, and newspapers. Some entries describe separate national literatures. The *KLE* came into being during a relatively liberal phase of Soviet literary policy; thus, although the principle of PARTY SPIRIT is recognizable throughout, it is not overly confining. The scope of the entries for individual authors, and whether or not the entry includes a photo, depends first on politics, then on literature; however, in addition to all the important Soviet authors, this work includes persecuted ones such as N. Gumilyov and authors belonging to the first wave of emigration, such as V. Khodasevich, V. Nabokov, and B. Zaytsev. Authors belonging to the second wave of emigration, such as O. Anstey, N. Morshen, I. Yelagin, are completely ignored. For authors who were killed during the purges, such as V. Kirshon or V. Zazubrin, mention is usually made that they were "illegally repressed, posthumously rehabilitated"; for O. Mandelshtam it is only noted that he was "repressed." In volume 9, mention of suppression and REHABILITATION is missing for those additionally included authors who also fell victim to the purges (for example, G. Belykh, S. Budantsev). Volume 9 includes authors whose renown came only during the period in which volumes 1 to 8 were being issued (such as B. Akhmadulina, A. Ananyev, V. Astafyev, V. Belov, A. Vampilov) or authors whom the censors now allow to be mentioned (such as K. Vaginov or A. Vvedensky) or émigrés (such as G. Adamovich, D. Aminado, or N. Yevreinov). Volume 9 contains an index to all volumes, but all the names of émigrés from the 1970s are missing, even those of V. Maksimov and V. Nekrasov for whom detailed entries exist. *KLE* is a carefully compiled Soviet reference work, but owing to the limitations imposed by CENSORSHIP, it should never be used as an exclusive source.

**Kratt, Iván Fyódorovich,** prose writer (b. Aug. 29 [Aug. 17], 1899, Olshany, prov. Chernigov—d. May 19, 1950, Leningrad). Kratt was the son of an office worker. From 1920 to 1923 he studied at the Institute of Political Economy in Kiev; from 1924 to 1930 he held various minor positions with the railroad. In 1930 Kratt moved to Leningrad, where he worked in the administration of the transportation system and began his literary career by writing three plays. A journey to Kolyma in 1936–37 inspired some journalistic articles, which were collected and published under the title *Moya zemlya* (1938; My Land). Journeys to the North, the Soviet Far East, and Siberia provided material for a novel, *Zoloto* (1939; Gold), and some short stories. Kratt served as a soldier in besieged Leningrad during World War II. Afterward, he published two historical novels based on the life of Russian settlers in North America around 1800, *Ostrov Baranova* (1945; Baranov's Island) and *Koloniya Ross* (1950; The Ross Colony).

Kratt's early short stories depict the integration of smaller national minorities into the Soviet system. His later war stories received little attention. Kratt's two historical novels, combined under the title *Veliky okean* (1950; The Great Ocean), are considered to be his major work. A contribution to the battle against COSMOPOLITANISM, the work presents the Russian colonization of North America as if it had been implemented solely in friendship with the Indians and sabotaged by American spies and hired killers.

*Works: Moja zemlja* (feature articles), 1938; *Zoloto* (novel), 1940; *Velikij okean* (novel in 2 parts; 1. *Ostrov Baranova*, 2. *Kolonija Ross*), 1950; *Vesennee solnce* (short stories), 1961.— *Izbr.*, 1951.

*Secondary Lit.*: R. Messer, in *Zvezda* 1950:6; *RSPP* 2:1964.

**Kron, Aleksándr Aleksándrovich** (pseud. of A. A. Kreyn), playwright (b. July 13 [June 30], 1909, Moscow—d. Feb. 24, 1983, Moscow). Kron's father was a composer. Kron spent the Civil War years in a youth camp near Moscow. He completed his studies in philology at Moscow University in 1930. His first drama, *Vintovka No. 492116* (1929; Rifle No. 492116), written in 20 days while Kron was at university, was successfully staged in Leningrad in 1930. In 1930–31 Kron worked in Baku. His subsequent plays were variously received. He became a member of the Communist Party in 1939. During World War II he was an officer with the Baltic fleet; he served both at sea and in besieged Leningrad. As a teacher at the Gorky Literary Institute during the post-Stalinist period, Kron was one of the discoverers of V. Rozov. Kron's *Zametki pisatelya* (1956; Observations of a Writer), in which he denounced abuses in the theater (such as prescription of subject matter, interference from editors [censorship], and bureaucratic suppression of creative initiative), provoked sharp criticism from the Party. He himself wrote no more plays, but changed his focus primarily to articles about theater arts and autobiographical prose, such as *Vechnaya problema* (1969; The Eternal Problem) and the novels *Dom i korabl* (1964; House and Ship) and *Bessonnitsa* (1977; Insomnia). Kron lived in Moscow.

*Vintovka No. 492116* records the experiences of two months of student military training aimed at disciplining "homeless waifs" (*besprizornye*). The underlying themes of this play, which was still being staged 40 years later (129 performances in 1962), are educa-tion, self-education, and fitting in to the community; these themes pervade Kron's subsequent work. *Trus* (1935; The Coward) centers on obedience to the Party of the revolutionaries of 1905; *Nashe oruzhiye* (1936; Our Weapons), which Kron considered to be his weakest work, is a commissioned sequel to his first drama. *Glubokaya razvedka* (written in 1937–40; Exploratory Drilling) became popular as an attempt to expand psychologically the assignment of writing a production novel. Kron's musical comedy, *Raskinulos more shiroko . . .* (1942; Wide Spread the Spacious Sea . . .), written in collaboration with V. Vishnevsky and V. Azarov in besieged Leningrad, was staged some 150 times a year between 1964 and 1969 and in 1972. Kron's war play, *Ofitser flota* (1943; Officer of the Fleet), was sharply criticized by N. Pogodin and B. Lavrenyov, among others, because of its emphasis on the discussion of honor, duty and decency by an independent-thinking superior officer; only later did the play achieve recognition. *Vtoroye dykhaniye* (1945; Second Wind), which likewise is set in the world of officers, could not be performed until 1956. *Kandidat partii* (1950; Candidate for the Party), a play about human integrity in the Party milieu, was revised twice in 1953 and 1969 under the influence of the changing Party line. In his plays Kron places major emphasis on psychological depth and dramatically effective, intelligible structuring of conflict; he does not experiment with form. His novel *Bessonnitsa*, which, as it were, is based on the autobiographical notes of his doppelgänger, defends the variety of ethical, historical, and ideological positions of 1957 against rigid Party dogma, using human conflicts among scientists as its example. Kron's *Zametki pisatelya* (1956) has lasting validity for the understanding of Soviet literature.

*Works: Kandidat partii* (play), in *Novyj mir* 1950:10; *P'esy* (plays), 1955; *Zametki pisatelja*, in *Lit. Moskva*, 1956:2; *Dramatičeskie proizvedenija* (plays), 1958; *Na khodu i na jakore* (articles), 1961; *Dom i korabl'* (novel), 1965; *Večnaja problema* (essays), 1969; *Teatr* (plays), 1971 (contains *Vintovka No. 492116*; *Trus*; *Naše oružie*; *Glubokaja razvedka*; *Oficer flota*; *Vtoroe dykhanie*; *Kandidat partii*); *Izbr.*, 1972; *Bessonnica* (novel), in *Novyj mir* 1977:4–6, separate ed., 1980; *Izbr.*, 1978; *P'esy i stat'i o teatre* (plays and essays), 1980; *Izbr. proizv.*, 2 vols., 1980; *Kapitan dal'nego plavanija* (pov.), in *Novyi mir* 1983:2.

*Secondary Lit.*: L. Maljugin, in *Moskva* 1957:5; B. Zubavin, in *Lit. gazeta* Feb. 2, 1961; V. Ketlinskaja, in *Lit. gazeta* Nov. 28, 1964;

V. Survillo, in *Novyj mir* 1965:2; L. Plotkin, in *Neva* 1965:10; A. Latynina, in *Lit. obozrenie* 1977:9; V. Tarsis, in *ZeitBild*, Bern, 1977:14–16; I. Grekova, in *Novyj mir* 1981:7; L. Lazarev, in *Družba narodov* 1984:1; I. Metter, in *Voprosy lit.* 1986:8.

**Kruchónykh, Alekséy Yeliséyevich**, poet (b. Feb. 21 [Feb. 9], 1886, Olevka, prov. Kherson—d. June 17, 1968, Moscow). Kruchonykh was of peasant descent. He finished his studies at the School of Arts in Odessa in 1906. He became one of the most important poets and theoreticians of Russian FUTURISM and the Moscow cubo-futurists; he and V. Khlebnikov published together in 1912–13. In his revolt against tradition, Kruchonykh went so far as to create an artificial poetic language that grew out of his poem "Dyr bul shchyl" (1912) and was composed of word fragments, grammatical endings, and meaningless combinations of sounds and signs. In *Slovo kak takovoye* (1913; The Word as Such), he gave this language the name by which it is widely known, *zaumny yazyk*, or *zaum* ("transsense," metalogical language). Kruchonykh's "productions," as he called his futurist works that were in part composed in this metalanguage, were not published in journals except LEF; initially they were printed in small pamphlets by various publishers, later (sometime after 1923) they were privately printed by the author, occasionally being duplicated by hand or machine. Between 1916 and 1919 Kruchonykh lived in Tbilisi with other futurists. One of their last publications appears to be *Iro-niada* (1930), produced in 150 hectographed copies. According to V. Markov, Kruchonykh published 236 "productions," only some of which have been located. From 1930 on, Kruchonykh was ostracized as "formalist" (see FORMALIST SCHOOL); thereafter he made only rare appearances as critic or bibliographer. He lived in Moscow as a member of the Writers Union.

Kruchonykh's work has never been reprinted in the Soviet Union. A first volume of his selected writings appeared in Munich in 1973. Of all the cubo-futurists, Kruchonykh pushed the tendency toward the absurd and toward play with sound, word fragments, and signs the furthest. In addition to metalogical poetry, he inclines to chaotic coarseness, repulsiveness, disharmony, to antiaestheticism in general. The effect achieved by unusual graphic layouts, for which he used different typefaces and eccentric typographical design and in which he incorporated his own and borrowed sketches (for example, from Kazimir

Malevich), was always an essential part of his work. This form of poetry, the absurd and alogical elements of which influenced Vladimir Kazakov in the 1960s, was complemented by prose and polemical literary criticism (S. Yesenin, V. Mayakovsky).

*Works: Igra v adu* (narrative poem written with V. Khlebnikov), 1912, 1913; *Slovo kak takovoe* (short stories and poems written with V. Khlebnikov), 1913; *Troe* (written with E. Guro and V. Khlebnikov), 1913; *Vzorval'*, 1913; *Pobeda nad solncem* (play), 1913 or 1914 (reprinted, ed. G. Erbslöh, Munich, 1976); *Go-lodnjak* (poems), 1922; *Zudesnik. Zudutnye zudesa*, 1922; *Faktura slova* (short stories), 1922; *Fonetika teatra* (poems and short stories), 1923; *500 novykh ostrot i kalamburov Puškina* (essay), 1924; *Van'ka-Kain i Son'ka-Manikjuršćica* (narrative poem), 1925; *Esenin i Moskva kabackaja* (short stories), 1926; *Če-tyre fonetičeskikh romana* (narrative poems), 1927; *Novoe v pisatel'skoj tekhnike* (essays), 1927; *Ironiada* (poems), 1930; letters, in *Wiener Slawistischer Almanach* 1:1978.—*Izbr.*, Munich, 1973.

*Secondary Lit.:* I. Terent'ev, Tbilisi, 1919 (reprinted, in Kručënykh's *Izbr.*, 1973); K. Čukovskij, *Futuristy*, 1922; V. Markov, *Russian Futurism*, Berkeley, 1968, and in Kručënykh's *Izbr.*, 1973; Ju. Ivask, in *Novyj žurnal*, New York, 117:1974; C. Douglas, in *Russian Literature Triquarterly* 12:1975; R. Ziegler, in *Wiener Slavistisches Jahrbuch* 1978 and 1981; S. Sukhoparov, Kherson, 1986.

**Krupín, Vladímir Nikoláyevich**, prose writer (b. Sept. 7, 1941, Kilmez, oblast Kirov). Krupin is of peasant ancestry; his father was a forester. In 1957 Krupin completed his schooling and worked for up to three years to fulfill his military obligations for a district (rayon) newspaper and as a craftsman. Since he was not admitted into the Gorky Literary Institute, he studied Russian philology at the pedagogical institute of the Moscow region (graduating in 1967). Then he worked as a Russian teacher and as an editor for the publisher Sovremennik, a position he later lost owing to the publication of G. Vladimov's *Tri minuty molchaniya* (1977). Krupin is a member of the Communist Party. His first book, *Zerna* (1974; Grain), includes both povesti and short stories and revealed his talent as an original exponent of VILLAGE PROSE. After his next volume, *Do vecherney zvezdy* (1977; Until the Evening Star), the work that contributed most to the considerable and quite diverse attention paid him was the povest

Zhivaya voda (1980; The Water of Life), published in Novy mir. The documentary povest Sorokovoy den (1981; The Fortieth Day) unleashed official Party criticism for its truthful and unvarnished account of conditions in the contemporary Soviet village. This povest was published in the journal Nash sovremennik and caused the dismissal of its first deputy editor in chief, Yu. Seleznev. In 1982 Krupin was allowed to publish Zhivaya voda as a book, together with other works. Krupin has not yet been mentioned in histories of literature and reference works; he lives in Moscow.

In his attachment to the peasant tradition, with its piety and folklore, in his love of pristine nature, his respect for people who live off the land, and his concern for forests, fields, and meadows, Krupin is a typical writer of Soviet village prose. The geographic area of his expertise is the region around Vyatka (now Kirov). One of the povesti in Zerna—"Varvara" (Barbara)—depicts the difficult fate of a kolkhoz peasant woman during World War II and the postwar period. In Zhivaya voda his protagonist is simple man, a watchman and groom who has fallen under the spell of alcohol. His close encounter with death precipitates his transformation and his search for the meaning of life. Krupin's narrative style is extremely loose, often comical, occasionally tending toward the fantastic. It is also symbolic and allegorical and alludes to fundamental human and religious concerns in an Aesopian style whereby the protagonist acquires some of the traits of a wise old Russian village fool. In its mixture of realistic-prosaic and ironic styles—in the form of fourteen letters from a journalist-author to his wife—Sorokovoy den reveals the complete absence of commentary that is typical of Krupin. The bare facts of ruined fields, destroyed roads, the peasant population that is not even supplied with sufficient foodstuffs, and widespread alcoholism are, to be sure, well known at home and abroad, but Krupin makes the human consequences of these conditions especially evident. He contrasts the destructive centralism of the kolkhoz and sovkhoz system to the positive experiences of the decentralized age-old Russian system of independent rural communities.

Works: Zerna (short stories and pov.), 1974; Do večernej zvezdy (essays and pov.), 1977; Živaja voda (pov.), in Novyj mir 1980:8, separate ed., 1982 (also contains Na dnjakh ili ran'še: Jamščickaja povest'); Sorokovoj den' (pov.), in Naš sovremennik 1981:11; Slovo, obraz, mysl' (essay), in Lit. gazeta May 18,

1983, p. 5; Povesti i rasskazy, 1985; Prosti, proščaj . . . (pov.), in Novyj mir 1986:11.

Secondary Lit.: V. Korobov, in Oktjabr' 1974:12 and in Lit. gazeta Feb. 4, 1981, p. 5; V. Tendrjakov, in Komsomol'skaja pravda Oct. 27, 1976; G. Nikolaev, in Zvezda 1978:6; I. Zolotusskij, in Lit. gazeta Feb. 4, 1981, p. 5; A. Latynina, in Lit. obozrenie 1981:9; S. Zalygin et al., in Lit. gazeta May 26, 1982, p. 5.

**Krupskaya Prize.** See LITERARY PRIZES.

**Krutílin, Sergéy Andréyevich,** prose writer (b. Oct. 2, 1921, Delekhovo, prov. Ryazan—d. Feb. 28, 1985, Moscow). Krutilin was of peasant descent. In 1940 Krutilin finished technical-vocational school and worked on building sites in the Soviet Far East. He fought in World War II. In 1945 he was admitted to the Communist Party; in 1947 he completed his philological studies at Moscow University. He then embarked on a career in literature and wrote numerous novels of varying length in accord with the principle of PARTY SPIRIT. Krutilin was a member of the boards of the Writers Unions of the RSFSR and the USSR since 1965 and 1981, respectively. He was a member of the editorial board of the journal Moskva from 1967 on. Krutilin lived in Moscow.

The focal points of Krutilin's loose, rambling works are life in the countryside and the war. His first major prose work, Podsnezhniki (1961; Snowdrops), describes the reclamation of the Virgin Lands in Kazakhstan and propagandizes the new, ideal type of Party leader. His extensive, fictionalized "Sketches of a Village Schoolteacher," Lipyagi (1963–65; The Village of Lipyagi), attracted great attention. In 15 independent chapters, expanded and transposed in the course of revision for several new editions, Krutilin deals with the destinies of various families from a village in the Ryazan area; he portrays collectivization as the basis of their ascent and describes their decline in the course of extensive government interference and bad management during the Stalinist period. Krutilin allows the work to strike an emphatically optimistic note. It remains publicistic prose; the individual parts of its voluminous material are not connected together into a novel-like experience (Gorky Prize, 1967). Based on Krutilin's own experiences, his trilogy Apraksin bor (1968–76; Apraksin's Woods) deals with World War II, especially its early part, and focuses particular attention on the role played by Party officials. *Proshchalny uzhin* (1977; The Farewell Party) combines an account of the rebuilding of Tashkent after the 1966 earthquake with a love story.

*Works: Rodniki* (pov.), 1953; *Za povorotom* (short stories), 1961; *Podsnežniki* (novel), 1961; *Lipjagi* (pov.), 1965; *Kosoj dožd'* (pov.), 1970; *Lejtenant Artjukhov*, 1970; *Pustošel'* (pov.), in *Družba narodov* 1973:1–2; *Kresty* (novel), in *Moskva* 1975:7–8; *Okruženie* (novel), in *Naš sovremennik* 1976:12; *Proščal'nyj užin* (pov.), in *Družba narodov* 1977:10; *Apraksin bor* (novel in 3 books): (1) *Lejtenant Artjukhov*, (2) *Kresty*, (3) *Okruženie*, 1978; *Grekhi naši tjažkie* (novel), 1982; *Sobr. soč.*, 3 vols. 1984.

*Secondary Lit.*: Z. Kedrina, in *Lit. gazeta* Dec. 3, 1953; V. Matveev, in *Lit. gazeta* April 11, 1962; I. Pitljar, in *Novyj mir* 1965:3; V. Surganov, in *Moskva* 1971:10 and 1974:1; M. Kolesnikov, in *Lit. gazeta* Feb. 6, 1974, p. 6; I. Kozlov, in *Lit. Rossija* May 12, 1979, p. 15; M. Lomunova, in *Lit. Rossija* Oct. 1, 1982, p. 14.

**Krýmov, Vladímir Pímenovich**, prose writer (b. 1878—d. 1968, Paris [?]). Krymov came from a family of Old Believers and was proud to count the archpriest Avvakum among his ancestors. He completed his studies at Moscow University in 1908. Krymov was considered a talented journalist who enjoyed reporting on his trips abroad and who published the illustrated journal *Stolitsa i Usadba* (The Capital and the Country Estate). Krymov published his first four books between 1909 and 1917. After the Revolution Krymov emigrated and, following a trip around the world (Japan and the United States), settled in Berlin, where his first publication concerned his travel experiences: *Bogomoly v korobochke* (1921; The Pilgrim in a Box). After publishing nine other books, Krymov won special appreciation (even in English translation) for his trilogy *Za millionami* (1933; Eng. tr., *Out for a Million*, 1935), which begins in provincial Russia at the end of the 19th century and ends in emigration. In 1933 Krymov moved to Paris. There he published seven additional novels and several works on literature.

Krymov knows how to captivate the reader with a fluid, vivid, and exciting prose style. According to an inquiry conducted by N. Knorring in 1933, he stood in second place in terms of readership in the Turgenev Library in Paris with 225 borrowers for his books (S. Mintslov 251; I. Bunin 124, A. Kuprin and M. Osorgin 99 each, A. Chekhov 89, N. Gogol 39,

I. Babel 21; see *Vstrechi*, 1934, p. 176). *Sidorovo ucheniye* (Sidor's Teaching), the first part of his trilogy, reveals how a wealthy Old Believer teaches his nephew to earn money; *Khorosho zhili v Peterburge* (They Lived Well in Petersburg; Eng. tr., *He's Got a Million*, 1936) gives a negative picture of the world of businessmen in the Russian capital before and during World War I; *Dyavolyonok pod stolom* (1933; The Little Devil under the Table; Eng. tr., *End of the Imp*, 1937) continues the plot in emigration. *Fuga* (1935; Fugue), a novel with a double plot, has the same protagonist and supplements the trilogy. *Pokhozhdeniya grafa Azar* (1938; The Adventures of Count Azar) is a detective story; *V tsarstve durakov* (1939; In the Kingdom of Fools) is science fiction; *Fenka* (1945; Eng. tr., *Fienka*, 1949) concerns the life of an Old Believer and is a novel that was especially praised by I. Tkhorzhevsky. *Iz kladovoy pisatelya* (1951; From the Treasure Chamber of the Writer) combines remembrances of famous authors. *Anatas* (1960; Natas), a short story from the realm of parapsychology, proves his first-rate knowledge of the subject as well as his ability to entice the reader by including elements of mystery.

*Works: Zdes'*, 1909; *O pročem*, 1914; *Bogomoly v korobočke* (essays), Berlin, 1921; *Bog i den'gi* (novel), 2 vols., Berlin, 1926; *Ljudi v pautine* (novel), Berlin, 1930; *Za millionami* (novel-trilogy), (1) *Sidorovo učenie*, (2) *Khorošo žili v Peterburge*, (3) *D'javolënok pod stolom,*), Berlin, 1933 (see above); *Fuga* (novel), Paris, 1935; *Pokhoždenija grafa Azara* (novel), Paris, 1938; *V carstve durakov* (novel), Paris, 1939; *Sensacija grafa Azara* (novel), Paris, 1940 (Eng. tr., *Count Azar*, 1938); *Fen'ka* (novel), Paris, 1945 (reprinted, Paris, 1973) (see above); *Iz kladovoj pisatelja* (essays), Paris, 1951; *Zaveščanie Murova* (novel), New York, 1960; *Anatas* (short story), in *Mosty*, Munich, 5: 1960; *Golosa gornoj peščery* (novel), Buenos Aires, 1966.

*Secondary Lit.*: I. Tkhorževskij, *Russkaja lit.*, Paris, 1950, pp. 550f.; A. Slizskoi, in *Vozroždenie*, Paris, 23:1953; Èffi, in *Vozroždenie* 60:1956; N. Klimenko, in *Vozroždenie* 110:1961; K. Pomerancev, in *Russkaja mysl'*, Paris, May 23, 1985, p. 8.

**Krýmov, Yúry Solomónovich** (pseud. of Yu. S. Beklemíshev), prose writer (b. Jan. 19 [Jan. 6], 1908, St. Petersburg—d. Sept. 20, 1941, in action, near Bogodukhovka, oblast Cherkassk). Krymov's father, Solomon Yulyevich

Kopelman, ran the publishing house Shipovnik; his mother, Vera Yevgenyevna Beklemisheva (1881–1944), was a writer and literary critic. Krymov's pseudonym stems from two summer vacations spent in the Crimea as a cabin boy and a hired hand on a fishing boat. After studying radio engineering at Moscow University (1925–30), Krymov worked as an engineer on the Caspian Sea and elsewhere. It was Yu. Libedinsky who first discovered Krymov's literary abilities; with his help, Krymov's highly regarded novel Tanker "Derbent" was published in Krasnaya nov in 1938 (Eng. tr., Tanker "Derbent," 1940). The events of the novel take place in 1935 and are based on the theme of the collective: the need to overcome egoism in a spirit of solidarity and self-sacrifice. Krymov became a member of the Communist Party in 1941. In his povest Inzhener (1941; The Engineer), Krymov once again combines human problems with those of industrial production; the story is a negative portrayal of a man who does his duty throughout but who is unable to take the initiative and transcend mere duty on his own. Krymov's first povest, Podvig (A Heroic Deed), was not published until 1961 (in K. Paustovsky's Tarusskiye stranitsy); it is the story of an airplane pilot who, after he is fatally wounded in a crash, seeks a way out in suicide. "This voice in defense of man's right to his weakness and to his own decisions was too unusual to evoke a profound response, considering the situation in those days" (Drawicz). Krymov's tragic death and the resulting loss of a promising literary talent explain the tremendous amount of attention that Soviet literary criticism accords his work.

Works: Tanker "Derbent" (novel), 1938 (see above); Inžener (pov.), 1941; Povesti, 1944; Podvig (pov.), in Tarusskie stranicy, 1961; Iz pisem, in Voprosy lit. 1986:10.
Secondary Lit.: N. Semičev, in Lit. kritik 1938:7; A. Kron and N. Otten, in Novyj mir 1941:4; Ju. Libedinskij, foreword to Krymov's Povesti, 1944; M. Kuznecov, 1951; P. Gromov, 1956; N. Otten, foreword to Krymov's Podvig, 1961; RSPP 2:1964; A. Janov, in Lit. i sovremennost' 11:1972; A. Platonov, in his Razmyšlenija čitatelja, 1980.

Którova, Álla (pseud. of Viktóriya Ivánovna Sándor, née Kochúrova), prose writer (b. Dec. 29, 1926, Moscow). In 1954 Ktorova completed a course of study in English at the Moscow Pedagogical Institute for Foreign Languages and then worked as an English teacher. She married an American citizen in 1957 and was allowed to emigrate to the United States in March 1958. In the United States she has worked as a Russian instructor, from 1962 to 1986 at George Washington University, Washington, D.C. Since 1960 she has been writing prose based on her experiences in Moscow and publishing these works—such as Domrabyni (1960; The Female House Slaves) or Yurin Pereulok (1963; Yury's Alley)—in émigré periodicals. Her most comprehensive work, Litso Zhar-Ptitsy (1964; The Face of the Firebird), which she calls "fragments of an unfinished antinovel," was published as a book in the United States after appearing in the journal Grani. This was followed by three volumes of collected works: Eksponat molchashchiy (1974; The Silent Exhibit); Krapivny otryad: Dom s rozovymi steklami (1978; The Stinging-Nettle Detachment: The House with the Rose-Colored Windows); and Melky zhemchug (1986; Seed-Pearls). Ktorova has regularly visited the Soviet Union since she became an American citizen in 1969. She lives in Rockville, Maryland.

Ktorova's prose is like a sketch, composed of very short, loosely united segments that freely depict her own experience. Litso Zhar-Ptitsy revolves around the love a Russian woman, an interpreter, feels toward a foreigner and her final successful emigration. An impressionistic mosaic of people and their fates is considered characteristic of her style. In her works, Ktorova concentrates almost entirely on women's private lives, especially on their acquaintances and friendships; the reader scarcely learns anything about the heroines' professional activities or political loyalties. Plot is of minor importance in her composition; often the events do not even appear to fall into scenes. In Krapivny otryad, Ktorova describes the appeal cemeteries hold for her; usually, however, religious activity and spiritual searching are not her concern. The satirical-comical tone of her work and the diversity of her linguistic expression are praised by the critics.

Works: Domrabyni (short story), in Mosty, Munich, 7:1961; Jurin pereulok (short story), in Grani, Frankfurt am Main, 53:1963; (additional original publications in Grani 55 and 56:1964, 59:1965, 67:1968; in Novyj žurnal, New York, 63:1961, 74:1963; in Vozroždenie, Paris, 200:1968, 223:1970; in Mosty, New York, 15:1970; in Sovremennik, Toronto, 26–27:1974); Lico Žar-Pticy (novel), Washington,

1969; *Jazyk i vremja* (essays), in *Novoe russkoe slovo*, New York, June 10, Nov. 18, and Dec. 16, 1973, and April 21, 1974; *Ėksponat molčaščij* (short stories), Munich, 1974; *Krapivnyj otrjad: Dom s rozovymi stëklami* (short stories), Washington, 1978; *Melkij žemčug* (pov.), Rockville, 1986.
*Secondary Lit.*: Ja. Gorbov, in *Vozroždenie* 140:1963 and 146:1964; O. Hughes, in *Triquarterly*, 1973, and in *The Bitter Air of Exile: Russian Writers in the West 1922–1972*, ed. S. Karlinsky and A. Appel, Berkeley, 1977; B. Filippov, in Ktorova's *Ėksponat molčaščij*, 1974; Ju. Bol'šuchin, in *Grani* 99:1976; Z. Šakhovskaja, in *Russkaja mysl'*, Paris, Feb. 22, 1979, p. 7; N. Belinkova, in *Vremja i my*, Tel Aviv, 38:1979.

**Kublanóvsky, Yúry Mikháylovich**, poet (b. April 30, 1947, Rybinsk). Kublanovsky's father was an actor and director. In Rybinsk, Kublanovsky attended school for seven years, studied at a technical secondary school for two years, and in 1964 passed the equivalency exam for the ten-year school as a nonresident. In 1964 Kublanovsky moved to Moscow; he studied art history at Moscow University (exams 1970). Kublanovsky's inner ties to ancient, Orthodox Russia found external expression in his work as a guide and museum employee in the monasteries of Solovki, Kirillo-Belozersk, and others. With two exceptions, his own poetry has not been published in the Soviet Union. An open letter written in 1976 on the occasion of the second anniversary of the expulsion of A. Solzhenitsyn, who had become for Kublanovsky the central figure in Russian life over the previous decade, touched off the state security service's harassment of him. He lost all possibilities of pursuing a career in keeping with his education and found a job as the sexton of a church that provided him with only a miserable existence but left him with his inner freedom. His poems were regularly published in *Vestnik Russkogo Khristianskogo Dvizheniya* and in other journals in the West. In 1979, eight poems were included in the almanac METROPOL. The first volume of his poetry, *Izbrannoye* (1981; Selection), overseen by I. Brodsky and published in the United States, represents a high point of his recognition in the West. Kublanovsky was forced to emigrate on Oct. 3, 1982. He lives in Paris. In *S poslednim solntsem* (1983; With the Last Sun), Kublanovsky offered deep insight into his poetic work during the preceding decades. In his collection of 1985, *Ottisk* (Imprint), which to a high degree rests on Western material, he attempts to create a wholly poetical book with a unity of composition and showing variations on the theme of Europe and Russia.

For Kublanovsky, "Poetry is a miracle that enables the expression of a perception of the world forged from life" (*Russkaya mysl* Nov. 18, 1982). The primary focus of his creative imagination is Russian history, whose tragedy he grasps. From the Rus of Suzdal through the tsarist period up to Wrangel and the Cheka, Kublanovsky combines various epochs, using the leitmotifs of a despairing love of Russia and of an exposition, based on religious conviction, of the evil embodied in Communist despotism. Kublanovsky speaks out in favor of a poetry that will fight for the spiritual regeneration of his Russian homeland. His poetry is filled with facts, connects images and scenes, favors description over direct, rational assertion the message of which derives from what remains unsaid. V. Betaki emphasizes the "ambiguity" of his conception of history. L. Losev elaborates: "Kublanovsky's approach to history and geography is through irony." I. Brodsky ascertains that "he possesses perhaps the richest vocabulary since Pasternak."

*Works*: *Ko vsem nam* (essays), in *Russkaja mysl'*, Paris, July 8, 1976; poems, in *Den' poèzii*, 1970, and in *Leninskie gory* [university almanac], 1977; poems, in *Metropol'*, Ann Arbor, 1979; *Izbr.* (poems), Ann Arbor, 1981; interview, in *Russkaja mysl'* Nov. 18, 1982; *S poslednim solncem* (poems), Paris, 1983; *Pisatel' i absoljutnoe zlo* (essavs), in *Russkaja mysl'* June 8, 1983; *Ottisk* (poems), Paris, 1985; essay, in *Grani* 144:1987.
*Secondary Lit.*: L. Losev, in *Russkaja mysl'* Oct. 3, 1982, and in *Kontinent*, Paris, 37:1983; V. Betaki, in *Kontinent* 32:1982; I. Brodsky, in Kublanovsky's *S poslednim solncem*, 1983; Ju. Miloslavskij, in *Grani*, Frankfurt am Main, 133:1984; A. Radaškevič, in *Russkaja mysl'* May 23, 1985; P. Šmidt, in *Grani* 138:1986; D. Bobyšev, in *Novyj žurnal*, New York, 162:1986.

**Kulchítsky, Mikhaíl Valentínovich**, poet (b. Aug. 19, 1919, Kharkov—d. Jan. 19, 1943, near Stalingrad). Kulchitsky's father was a tsarist officer, lawyer, and writer. Kulchitsky studied philology, first at Kharkov University (1937–39) and then at the Gorky Literary Institute (1939–42), after which he went into military service. A few of his poems found their way into various journals, and after 1958 his poetry was included in anthologies of poets who had died in World War II. The first collection of his poems was published in Kharkov in 1966.

Kulchitsky, who was one of B. Slutsky's friends from student days, was prized by him early on as a great talent. As a schoolboy, Kulchitsky had already sought to express himself in poetry; he grew up with the poetry of Bagritsky, Gumilyov, Akhmatova, Mayakovsky, Khlebnikov, and Yesenin; he studied under I. Selvinsky. His earlier poems reflect a romantic Komsomol enthusiasm for revolutionary events, embodied for Kulchitsky particularly in the figure of Nikolay Shchors (who was killed on the poet's birthday). Kulchitsky endeavored to maintain a revolutionary turbulence. The poems he wrote at the front have not survived; his other poems deal with the theme of readiness for war and hint at the gradual development of a somber seriousness. Kulchitsky's poetry combines a youthful readiness for self-sacrifice with faith in one's own poetic word. Even as a 20-year-old poet, Kulchitsky knew the critical importance of the formative moment in the creative process; from that point on, further revision only harms the work of art ("Tvorchestvo," 1940; Creativity). He wrote in his diary (entry for March 14, 1940): "What is wanted now is 'Forward! Hurrah!! The red dawn!!!' In God's name, I cannot write that sort of thing." His comments about altercations with literary bureaucrats and editors over the preservation of his original meaning indicate Kulchitsky's early conflicts with the censors.

*Works:* Poems, included in *Sovetskie poèty, pavšie na Velikoj Otečestvennoj vojne,* 1965; *Samoe takoe* (poems), Kharkov, 1966; *Živoj golos vremeni* (diary excerpts), in *Voprosy lit.* 1967:10; *Rubež* (poems), 1973.

*Secondary Lit.:* G. Levin, in *Lit. gazeta* Dec. 17, 1960, and in *Den' poèzii,* Moscow, 1966; V. Kardin, *Lit. kritičeskie stat'i,* 1962; M. L'vov, in *Lit. gazeta* April 10, 1985, p. 3.

**Kuprín, Aleksándr Ivánovich,** prose writer (b. Sept. 7 [Aug. 26], 1870, Narovchat, prov. Penza—d. Aug. 25, 1938, Leningrad). Kuprin's father was a minor official. Kuprin grew up in Moscow; from 1880 to 1890 he was educated at military schools and served as a career officer in the province of Podolsk until 1894. After several attempts at writing poetry,

Kuprin published his first short story in 1889. In 1894 he left military service, became a freelance writer, and moved at first to Kiev. At that time he worked at many different jobs (factory worker, singer in a chorus, moving man, hunter, fisherman, journalist) and traveled extensively. From 1903 to 1907 he was close to M. Gorky's "Znaniye" group; his novel *Poyedinok* (1905; Eng. tr., *The Duel,* 1916), which soon made him famous, was published in Znaniye's sixth collection. From 1905 to 1917 Kuprin's wide variety of realistic prose appealed successfully to a broad reading public; his work was collected and published in a 12-volume edition between 1910 and 1916. As an opponent of the Bolshevik regime, Kuprin left the Soviet Union in 1919 and lived in Paris. Being uprooted from his homeland had a very adverse effect on his work; only a few passages from the autobiographical novels written in Paris exhibit anything like his original narrative power. Seriously ill, he was granted permission to return to the Soviet Union in 1937; he died there a year later. Kuprin is recognized by Soviet literary critics, but with certain reservations.

Kuprin is a good realistic narrator, primarily in his ability to weave into his narrative diversity of descriptive material without presenting philosophical complexities. His very first major prose work, *Molokh* (1896; Eng. tr., *Moloch,* 1917), accommodated contemporary public taste in its criticism of early capitalist industrialization. *Poyedinok,* a portrayal of the vacuity and dull monotony of military service at a small garrison, in which Kuprin regrets the mistakes of his service as a career officer, achieved a lasting success as an antimilitaristic novel. In *Yama* (1909–15; Eng. trs., *Yama: The Pit,* 1929; *Yama, the Hell-Hole,* 1952) he portrays, in his own vivid manner, a bordello in Odessa but weakens the work artistically by his moralistic interpolations. He wrote a great number of short stories; these reflect both upper- and lower-class milieus, and are set both in large cities and small towns; they often have sensational plots and focus on incidents involving men and animals. Kuprin likes to feature physically strong men (for example, in the circus) but is also inclined to portray those wronged by fate. Two of his best-known short stories are *Gambrinus* (1907), about a harbor tavern in Odessa and the Jewish fiddler there, and *Granatovy braslet* (1911; Eng. tr., in *The Bracelet of Garnets and Other Stories,* 1917). In the latter, Kuprin elaborately develops the story of a tragic love whose depth and fateful inevitability the woman comprehends completely only after the suicide of her admirer. Kuprin's most ambitious work undertaken in emigration, the novel *Yunkera* (1933; The Cadets), is devoted to his reminiscences about his own youth at cadet college. Parts of the work had appeared in the Soviet Union by 1947.

*Works: Molokh* (pov.), in *Russkoe bogatstvo* 1896:12 (see above); *Olesja* (pov.), in *Kievljanin* 1898, pp. 300–18, separate ed., 1905; *Poedinok* (novel), 1906 (see above); *Gambrinus* (short story), in *Sovremennyj mir* 1907:2; *Izumrud* (short story), in *Šipovnik* 1907:3; *Sulamif'* (short story), in *Zemlja* 1:1908; *Jama* 'pov.), in *Zemlja* 3:1909, 15:1914, 16:1915 see above); *Granatovyj braslet* (short story), in *Zemlja* 6:1911 (see above); *Zvezda Solomona* (short stories), Helsinki, 1920; *Koleso vremeni* (novel), Belgrade, 1930; *Junkera* 'novel), Paris, 1933.—*Polnoe sobr. soč.*, 12 vols., 1910–16; 12 vols., 1921–25; *Izbr. soč.*, 1947; *Sobr. soč.*, 6 vols., 1957–58; 9 vols., 1964; 9 vols., 1970–73.

*Translations: In Honour's Name*, 1907; *A Slav Soul and Other Stories*, 1916; *The River of Life and Other Stories*, 1916; *The Duel*, 1916, 1961; *The Bracelet of Garnets and Other Stories*, 1917; *Sasha and Other Stories*, 1920; *Shulamith*, 1923; *Gambrinus and Other Stories*, 1925; *Yama; The Pit*, 1929; *Yama, the Hell-Hole*, 1952; *Sentimental Romance*, 1969; *Tales*, 1969; *The Garnet Bracelet*, 1976.

*Secondary Lit.:* C. Ledré, *Trois romanciers russes*, Paris, 1935; P. N. Berkov, 1956; V. N. Afanas'ev, 1960; A. A. Volkov, 1962; K. Čukovskij, in his *Sovremenniki*, 1963; A. Dynnik, East Lansing, Mich., 1969; L. V. Krutikova, 1971; C. Thompson, bibliography, in *Russian Language Journal* 105:1976; N. Luker, in *10 Bibliographies of 20th Century Russian Literature*, ed. F. Moody, Ann Arbor, 1977, and separate study, Boston, 1978; K. A. Kurina, 1979.

**Kúshner, Aleksándr Semyónovich**, poet (b. Sept. 14, 1936, Leningrad). Kushner graduated in humanities from the Herzen Pedagogical Institute in Leningrad in 1959 and worked as a teacher for ten years. His first volume of poetry, *Pervoye vpechatleniye* (1962; The First Impression), which identified him as an apolitical, well-read, and sensitive poet, generated controversy among the critics. Kushner joined the Writers Union of the USSR before 1965 but has never participated in its congresses. Additional volumes—*Nochnoy*

*dozor* (1966; The Nightwatch), *Primety* (1969; Signs), *Pismo* (1974; Letter), and *Pryamaya rech* (1975; Direct Speech)—substantiate his great talent. Poems occasionally appear in *Yunost, Neva, Avrora*, and in the anthologies *Den poezii*. He lives in Leningrad.

Kushner's poetry originates from the concrete events of his immediate surroundings, from interiors and from nature, from his personal experiences. "He writes as a quiet and observant city dweller, noticing the way people behave in the streets" (D. Brown). He does not recount events but compresses what he observes and raises it to the level of allegory. Contrasts clarify his astonishment at the unique that is revealed in the apparently commonplace. Kushner's poetry belongs to the realm of the serious contemplative lyric, which includes the poems of V. Shefner, A. Tarkovsky, K. Vanshenkin, and Ye. Vinokurov. His lyricism is carried along by a primitive fear of disquietude, evil, and danger; in his poetry he searches for beauty and harmony and, despite his love for geometry and for the simple architectural style of the 1920s, he recognizes the goodness of life in the fact "that no system, but a soul, lies within it." Sometimes "he trusts the word, his creative and sanctioning power, his possibilities for ordering" (Drawicz); sometimes distress resounds in view of the superiority of the unspiritual and of the cold indifference that makes the hands stiffen and does not allow music to be heard any more. Kushner's poems have a modest, prose-like simplicity, the artistry of which first becomes evident through a calm inspection, such as that with which he opens up the world for himself.

*Works: Pervoe vpečatlenie* (poems), 1962; *Nočnoj dozor* (poems), 1966; *Primety* (poems), 1969; *Zavetnoe želanie* (poems), 1973; *Pis'mo* (poems), 1974; *Prjamaja reč'* (poems), 1975; *Gorod v podarok* (poems), 1976; *Golos* (poems), 1978; *Kanva. Iz šesti knig* (poems), 1981; *Zametki na poljakh* (poems and letters), in *Voprosy lit.* 1981:10; *Vtoraja real'nost'*, in *Lit. gazeta* Aug. 29, 1984; *Tavričeskij sad. Sed'-maja kniga*, 1984; *Stikhotvorenija* (poems) 1986; *Dnevnye sny* (poems), 1986.

*Secondary Lit.:* A. Asarkan, in *Novyj mir* 1963:3; A. Marčenko, in *Lit. Rossija* Oct. 22, 1965, pp. 8–9, and in *Voprosy lit.* 1966:11; E. Evtušenko, in *Lit. Rossija* Aug. 9, 1974, p. 11; Vl. Solov'ëv, in *Lit. obozrenie* 1975:2; S. Čuprinin, in *Oktjabr'* 1979:12; M. P'janykh, in *Neva* 1982:2 and 1985:3; A. Tatarinov, in *Russkaja mysl'*, Paris, July 26, 1985, p. 10; D.

Likhačëv, in *Lit. obozrenie* 1985:11; V. Baevskij, in *Novyj mir* 1986:11.

**Kúsikov, Aleksándr Borísovich** (pseud. of A.
B. Kusikyán), poet (b. Sept. 17, 1896, Arma-
vir—d. July 20, 1977, Paris). In 1915 Kusikov
went to the front as a soldier; at the time of
the February Revolution he served as a military commissar in Anapa (on the Black Sea);
in 1917 he moved to Moscow. Kusikov began
writing poetry as a schoolboy. The closeness
of his work to FUTURISM is apparent in his
first collection of poems, *Zerkalo Allakha*
(1918; Allah's Mirror). In 1919 Kusikov and
V. Shershenevich founded a group that called
itself the imagists (see IMAGISM); their press,
Chikhi-Pikhi, published several chapbooks.
Kusikov wrote *Zvyozdny byk*, (1921; Starry
Bull) in collaboration with S. Yesenin. Supported by A. Lunacharsky, Kusikov traveled
to Berlin in 1921; there he worked in the
editorial offices of the pro-Soviet journal *Nakanune*. Kusikov's own work, such as the narrative poem *Iskander Name* (1921) and the
collection of poems written between 1917 and
1921, *Ptitsa bezymyannaya* (1922; The Nameless Bird), continued to appear up through
1922. In 1926 he abandoned his literary career
and moved to Paris, where he lived until his
death.

A fundamental pessimism and a sense of
isolation characterize Kusikov's poetry. His
poems attempt to transcend the chaos of the
world, which particularly reveals itself in,
and emanates from, the large city, by turning
to the religious sphere and to the landscape
of Kusikov's native Caucasus. The title of his
collection of poems *Koyevangelyeran* (1920)
indicates, by fusing the Russian words for
"Koran" and "Evangel," the two sources of
Kusikov's creativity, which he attempted to
synthesize.

*Works: Zerkalo Alakha* (poems), 1918; *Sumerki* (poems), 1919; *Poèma poèm* (narrative
poem), 1919, 2d ed., 1920; *Al'-Barrak* (narrative verse), 1920; *Koevangelieran* (poems),
1920; *V nikuda* (poems), 1920; *Al'kadr* (narrative poem), 1920; *Iskander Namè* (narrative
poem), Berlin, 1921; *Aljaf-Ljam—mim* (poems),
1921; *Džul' Fikar* (narrative poem), 1921;
*Zvëzdnyj byk* (poems; in collaboration with
S. Esenin), 1921; *Ptica bezymjannaja* (selected poems), Berlin, 1922; autobiography,
in *Novaja russkaja kniga* 1922:3.
*Translations: Poems, in Russian Imagism
1919–1924*, 2 vols., ed. V. Markov, Giessen,
1980.

*Secondary Lit.*: See IMAGISM; I. È., in *Novaja russkaja kniga* 1922:1; G. Nivat, in
*Cahiers du monde russe et soviètique* 1974:
1–2.

**Kuzmín, Mikhaíl Alekséyevich**, poet, prose
writer, playwright (b. Oct. 5 [Sept. 23], 1872
Yaroslavl—d. March 3, 1936, Leningrad).
Kuzmin was of aristocratic descent. He grew
up in Saratov and St. Petersburg (after 1885),
where he was a student in Nikolai Rimsky-
Korsakov's composition class at the conserva
tory. His journeys to Italy and Egypt and to
the settlements of the Old Believers in north
ern Russia were reflected in his later writings
Kuzmin began publishing in 1905; he was an
active contributor to the journals *Vesy* and
*Apollon*, in the latter of which he published
his programmatic article *O prekrasnoy yas
nosti* (On Beautiful Clarity) in 1910. In break
ing with symbolism, Kuzmin's article advo
cated the rational creation of the work of ar
by means of what he called *klarizm* (that is
clarity). His goal, however, was not to estab
lish a new literary school but to focus greate
attention on the writer's individuality. Al
three literary genres are presesnt in Kuzmin'
work from the very beginning: his first povest
*Krylya* (1907; Wings), was followed by the
soon-confiscated *Tri pyesy* (1907; Three Plays
and a volume of verse, *Seti* (1908; Nets). Kuz
min's works were often reprinted. After the
Revolution he remained in Petrograd but kep
aloof from political developments. A few o
Kuzmin's books were still published in the
early 1920s, but after 1924 he was excluded
from literary life. He worked almost exclu
sively as a translator. During this time he wa
associated with the OBERIU group. Not a sin
gle book of his was published after 1929
Kuzmin died destitute and impoverished.

In his work Kuzmin initially looked to Al
exandrian culture, late Rome, and France and
Italy of the 18th century; he loved the rococo
period and the music of Mozart. Kuzmin'
post-Revolutionary poems are influenced by
Gnostic thought. Different stylistic levels blen
together in his last volume of verse, *Fore
razbivayet lyod* (1929; The Trout Breaks the
Ice), which marks "the beginning of a new
period of fundamental stylistic transforma
tion" in his work (Markov, vol. 3, p. 392)
Concreteness and corporeality, in an eroti
sense as well, characterize his verse. In thi
sense, Kuzmin's homosexual poems grasp the
fundamentals of love to such a degree tha
biographical identifications become meaning
lessly reductive. Kuzmin is extraordinaril

conscious of form and enjoys elaborate poetic games. In *Priklyucheniya Eme-Lebefa* (1907; The Adventures of Aimé Leboeuf), Kuzmin takes up the tradition of the picaresque novel. "The distinctive characteristics of M. Kuzmin's prose are the definiteness of his plot, its smooth development, and a special purity of thought, characteristic possibly of him alone in contemporary literature, which does not tolerate passionate interest in any aim that is alien to the art of the word. . . . M. Kuzmin's language is steady, stringent, and clear, I would even say: hyaline" (Gumilyov).

*Works: Kryl'ja* (pov.), 1907, 2d ed., 1923 (reprinted, Ann Arbor, 1979); *Priključenija Eme-Lebefa* (pov.), 1907; *Komedija o Martiniane* (play), 1908 (reprinted, Letchworth, 1970); *Komedija o Evdokii iz Geliopolja* (play), 1908 (reprinted, Letchworth, 1970); *Komedija o Aleksee, čeloveke bož'em* (play), 1908 (reprinted, Letchworth, 1970); *Podvigi velikogo Aleksandra* (novel), 1908; *Seti* (poems), 1908; *Tri p'esy* (plays), 1909 (reprinted, Letchworth, 1970); *Nežnyj Iosif* (short story), 1909; *O prekrasnoj jasnosti* (essay), in *Apollon* 1910:4; *Putešestvie sera Džona Firfaksa po Turcii* (novel), 1910; *Kuranty ljubvi* (poems, with music by Kuzmin), 1911; *Voennye rasskazy* (short stories), 1915; *Zelënyj solovej* (short stories), 1915; *Čudesnaja žizn' Iosifa Bal'zamo, grafa Kaliostro* (novel), 3 vols., 1919 (reprinted, New York, 1982); *Aleksandrijskie pesni* (poems), 1921; *Paraboly* (poems), Berlin, 1923 (reprinted, Letchworth, 1978); *Novyj Gul'* (poems), 1924; *Tikhij straž* (novel), 1924; *Forel' razbivaet lëd* (poems), 1929 (reprinted, Ann Arbor, 1979). —*Soč.*, 9 vols., 1914–18; *Sobr. stikhov*, 3 vols., Munich, 1977; *Proza*, 10 vols., 1984– (seven vols. had been published by 1987).
*Translations: Wings: Prose and Poetry*, 1972; *Selected Prose and Poetry*, 1980.
*Secondary Lit.*: A. Blok, in his *Sobr. soč.*, vol. 5, pp. 182–86; N. Gumilëv, in *Apollon* 1910:5, 1912:8, and in his *Sobr. soč.*, vol. 4, Washington, 1968, pp. 305–7, 413–14; A. Field, in *Russian Review* 1964; V. Orlov, in *Voprosy lit.* 1966:10; N. Stivenson, in *Novyj žurnal*, New York, 106:1972; J. Malmstad, in *Slavic Review* 1975:1 and in Kuzmin's *Sobr. stikhov*, 1977; V. Markov, in Kuzmin's *Sobr. stikhov*, 1977; W. Kasack, in *Welt der Slaven* 23:1978; S. Karlinsky, in *Slavic Review* 38:1979; Ju. Ivask, in *Russian Language Journal* 117:1980; J. Barnstead, in *Canadian Slavonic Papers* 1982:1; R. Ivnev, in *Zvezda* 1982:5; G. Cheron, in *Wiener Slawistischer Almanach* 12:1983; V. Petrov, in *Novyj žurnal* 163:1986.

**Kuznetsóv, Anatóly Vasílyevich,** prose writer (b. Aug. 18, 1929, Kiev—d. June 13, 1979, London). As a child Kuznetsov lived through the German occupation of the Ukraine. In 1952 he was a worker in the long-term mobilization of labor for the building of the "Novaya Kokhovka" power station. He was admitted to the Communist Party in 1955. In 1960 he completed his studies at the Gorky Literary Institute. While engaged in his studies in 1956 he worked as a mixer of concrete on the building of the Irkutsk power station, an experience reflected in his successful povest for young readers, *Prodolzheniye legendy* (1957; Eng. tr., *Sequel to a Legend*, 1959). After publication of several other prose works, including *U sebya doma* (1964; At Home), Kuznetsov's novel *Babiy Yar* 1966; Eng. tr., *Babi Yar*, 1967), about the murder of Jews near Kiev, attracted considerable attention. On July 30, 1969, Kuznetsov took advantage of an official trip to London to defect to the West. He admitted that as an informant for the secret service (KGB) he had calumniated writers such as Ye. Yevtushenko during the previous six months in order to facilitate his own defection. Not only was Kuznetsov expelled from the Writers Union of the USSR as a traitor, but he was also morally condemned by the dissident A. Amalrik. Using the pseudonym A. Anatoly, Kuznetsov published a new edition of *Babiy Yar* in 1969 (Eng. tr., *Babi Yar*, 1970), emphasizing those portions deleted by Soviet censors and adding further materials that had remained unwritten because they would never have passed censorship. Kuznetsov lived in London.
*Prodolzheniye legendy* describes the conflict of a young man, raised during the Stalin years, who is faced with the contradictions of reality. This fictional diary was translated into many languages. *Babiy Yar* combines an indictment of the SS's murder of the Jews by the SS with an indictment of the Soviet authorities, particularly because they blew up Kiev's main street, the Kreshchatik, and failed to pay any tribute to the murdered Jews. As in Kuznetsov's earlier prose, the effect is produced by the work's unusual content, not by its literary form.

*Works: Juveliry. Pošekhonskaja nov'* (publicistic prose), 1957; *Prodolženie legendy* (pov.), 1962 (see above); *Avgustovskij den'* (short stories), 1962, also in *Novyj žurnal*, New York, 112:1973; *U sebja doma* (pov.), in *Novyj mir* 1964:1; *Babij Jar* (novel), in *Junost'* 1966:8–10, rev. ed. in *Novyj žurnal* 97:1969, separate ed., Frankfurt am Main, 1970 (see above); *Artist mimansa* (short story), in *Novyj mir* 1968:4, rev. ed. in *Novyj žurnal* 100:1970; *Ogon'* (novel), in *Junost'* 1969:3–4.

*Secondary Lit.:* A. Berzer, in *Novyj mir* 1960:11; L. Anninskij, in *Novyj mir* 1961:8; L. Terakopjan, in *Lit. Rossija* April 25, 1969, pp. 8–9; B. Polevoj, in *Lit. gazeta* Aug. 6, 1969, p. 3; A. Amal'rik, in *Survey* 74–75:1970; A. Rothberg, *The Heirs of Stalin*, Ithaca, N.Y., 1972, pp. 251–67; Z. Vatnikova-Prizel, in *Russian Literature Triquarterly* 106:1976; A. Gladilin, in *Russkaja mysl'*, Paris, June 28, 1979, p. 3.

**Kuznetsóva, Galína Nikoláyevna** prose writer, poet (b. 1902, Kiev—d. Feb. 8, 1976, Munich). Kuznetsova emigrated in 1920 via Constantinople, going first to Prague and then settling in France, where she lived with Ivan Bunin's family in Paris and Grasse from 1927 to 1942. In 1922 she began publishing poems and short stories in various periodicals. Her collection of 12 short stories, *Utro* (1930; Morning), won high praise from G. Adamovich; her only novel, *Prolog* (1933; Prologue), won P. Bitsilli's recognition. She collected her poetry from the years 1923 to 1929 in the volume *Olivkovy sad* (1937; The Olive Garden). In 1949 she moved to the United States and worked eight years in the Russian publications division of the United Nations. She published notes from her days in Paris with Bunin—after prepublication in *Novy zhurnal*—as *Grassky dnevnik* (1967; The Diary from Grasse).

Her closeness to Bunin colored Kuznetsova's poetry and prose, as well as her position in Russian literature. Her quite homogeneous poems concern nature and express her melancholia in addition to providing clear and beautiful descriptions. Her prose is short on plot and is reflective and reminiscent. Interpersonal relations from the early post-Revolutionary period and from emigration are captured with a fine psychological feel. Her last short story, *Potseluy svidaniya* (1954; The Rendezvous Kiss), which concerns the ecstatic love a married man feels for a woman who is not his wife, reveals her gift for reserved, spiritually revealing description. Her novel consists of imaginary recollections. Despite the subjectivity of her view, her *Grassky dnevnik* is of enduring significance, not only for the study of I. Bunin it offers, but generally for the atmosphere of the Parisian émigré community it creates.

*Works:* Poems in, among others, *Sovremennye zapiski*, Paris, 33:1927, 36:1928, 38:1929, 63:1937, 65:1937; in *Novyj žurnal*, New York, 18:1948, 27:1951, 80:1965; in *Mosty*, Munich, 12:1966. *Utro* (short stories), Paris, 1930; *Prolog* (novel), Paris, 1933; *Olivkovyj sad* (poems), Paris, 1937; *Poceluj svidanija* (short story), in *Novyj žurnal* 36:1954; *Grasskij dnevnik* (diary), Washington, 1967 (preprint in *Vozdušnye puti*, New York, 3:1963, 4:1965 and *Novyj žurnal* 74:1963, 76:1964).

*Secondary Lit.:* G. Adamovič, in *Sovremennye zapiski* 42:1930; L. Červinskaja, in *Čisla*, Paris, 2–3:1930; P. Bicilli, in *Sovremennye zapiski* 53:1933; M. Cetlin, in *Sovremennye zapiski* 65:1967; R. Gul', in *Novyj žurnal* 92:1968; L. Brom, Diss., Univ. of Colorado, 1970; L. Dienes, in *HRL* 1985.

**Kúznitsa** (The Smithy), a literary association of proletarian writers established in Moscow in 1920. Kuznitsa consisted of a group of poets (V. Aleksandrovsky, M. Gerasimov, S. Obradovich, G. Sannikov, later V. Kirillov) who withdrew from the PROLETKULT in early 1920 (*Pravda* Feb. 5, 1920), founded the journal *Kuznitsa* in May (which lasted until 1922), and chose the title of the jourrnal as the name of their association in December 1920. KOSMIST arose concurrently in Petrograd. Despite the controversies with the Proletkult over the freedom of artistic means, among other issues, the members of Kuznitsa rejected Party control of cultural development just as the Proletkult did. NEP, which was proclaimed in 1921, with its attempt to rescue the political economy that had been destroyed during the Revolution by promoting private agriculture, was rejected by the members of Kuznitsa as a betrayal of the principles of world revolution. Aleksandrovsky, Gerasimov, and Kirillov withdrew; the last two also withdrew from the Communist Party. After 1923, Kuznitsa which claimed a leading role in the creation of new proletarian art and whose initiative was responsible for the associations of proletarian writers, lost significance owing to the formation of the group OKTYABR (1922); in 1928 Kuznitsa became a member of the All-Union Organization of Associations of Proletarian Writers (VOAPP); internal divisions followed, and Kuznitsa was ultimately disbanded by the Party Resolution of 1932 (see PARTY RESOLUTIONS ON LITERATURE). Kuznitsa never had a lot of members; V. Bakhmetyev, F. Berezovsky, F. Gladkov, M. Lyashko, A. Neverov, G. Nikiforov, P. Nizovoy, A. Novikov-Priboy were members for a while. The social composition was given as 80 percent workers, 15 percent peasants, and 5 percent intelligentsia; politically, 50 percent of Kuznitsa's members were also members of the

Party. The idealization of work and of the proletariat, of metals and the machine, characterizes the poetry of Kuznitsa members written primarily during the period of the Proletkult. Their prose is less uniform than their poetry, but it is also not particularly noteworthy.

*Secondary Lit.:* See PROLETKULT; A. Voronskij, "Prozaiki i poèty 'Kuznicy'," in his *Lit. portrety,* vol. 2, 1929; *Lit. manifesty,* 2d ed., 1929 (reprinted, Munich, 1969); G. Kratz, Giessen, 1979.

# L

**Ladínsky, Antonín Petróvich,** poet, prose writer (b. Jan. 31 [Jan. 19], 1896, Obshcheye Pole, oblast Pskov—d. June 4, 1961, Moscow). Ladinsky's study of law at Petrograd University was interrupted by World War I. During the Civil War, Ladinsky served as an officer in the White Army and emigrated via Egypt to France in 1920. In 1926 Ladinsky began publishing poems in newspapers; from 1931 to 1938 he published four volumes of poetry. After lengthy travels through Europe and the Near East, one of which he described in *Puteshestviye v Palestinu* (1937; Trip to Palestine), he shifted over to the genre of the historical novel. In 1946 Ladinsky accepted Soviet citizenship, worked for the newspaper *Sovetsky patriot,* and served as a correspondent for *Pravda.* After the Soyuz Sovetskikh Patriotov (Union of Soviet Patriots) was prohibited, Ladinsky was expelled from France on Sept. 5, 1950. He lived in Dresden (East Germany) and returned to the Soviet Union in March 1955. His poems continued to be published by émigré publishers; after 1959 in Moscow he published two of his older and two of his new historical novels. In 1961 he was accepted into the Writers Union of the USSR.

Ladinsky's poems are usually limited to a central thought that is presented in a narrative or reflective way. They are full of images, and he both uses comparisons and metaphors frequently and conceives poems as parables. Themes from history, from his travels, and from his longing for Russia mix with man's fundamental questions about the past and the present, life and death, heaven and earth. After the novel based on Roman history of the second century, *XV legion* (1937; The Fifteenth Legion), which was reissued in Moscow in 1961 under the title *V dni Karakally* (At the Time of Caracalla), he turned to the oldest period of Russian history (989–1125) and to Russia's changing relationship with Byzantium and Western Europe. The trilogy that began with *Golub nad Pontom* (1938; The Dove over Pontus)—the Soviet edition was called *Kogda pal Khersones* (1959; When the Chersonese Fell)—and was completed in Moscow in 1960 is, despite its considerable detail, neither correct in its historical facts nor even partially accurate in its reflection of the spirit of this chosen epoch. The Soviet publisher laments: "Ladinsky views the religious discussions, which at that time constituted the focal point of the spiritual life of the society, with the disdainful grin of a Voltairean" (A. Kazhdan).

*Works:* Čërnoe i goluboe (poems), Paris, 1931; Severnoe serdce (poems), Paris, 1931; Stikhi o Evrope (poems), Paris, 1937; Putešestvie v Palestinu (travel articles), Tallinn, 1937; XV legion (novel), Tallinn, 1937, 2d ed. under the title V dni Karakally, Moscow, 1961; Pjat' čuvstv (poems), Paris, 1938; Golub' nad Pontom (novel), Tallinn, 1938, 2d ed. under the title Kogda pal Khersones, Moscow, 1959; Roza i čuma (poems), Paris, 1950; Poslednij put' Vladimira Monomakha (novel), 1966; (trilogy) Kogda pal Khersones, Anna Jaroslavna— Koroleva Francii, Poslednij put' Vladimira Monomakha, Moscow, 1973; Istoričeskie romany, 1984.

*Secondary Lit.:* K. Močul'skij, in Čisla, Paris, 5:1931; M. Cetlin, in Sovremennye zapiski, Paris, 45:1931 and 65:1937; G. Fedoseev, in Sovremennye zapiski, 63:1937; V. Vejdle, in Russkie zapiski, Paris, 11:1938 and in Sovremennye zapiski 68:1939; G. Fedotov, in Sovremennye zapiski 69:1939; Ju. Ivask, in Novyj žurnal, New York, 25:1951; V. Inber, in Lit. gazeta June 16, 1960; A. Každan, in Ladinsky's Poslednij put' Vladimira Monomakha, 1966; A. Nemirovskij, in Lit. obozrenie 1968:8.

**Lápin, Borís Matvéyevich,** prose writer (b. May 30 [May 17], 1905, Moscow—d. Sept. 1941, near Kiev). Lapin's father was a doctor. Lapin completed his studies at the Bryusov Institute of Literature and Art in 1924; through independent study he achieved a proficiency in various foreign languages and expanded his knowledge in the field of Oriental studies. An eagerness for knowledge, rather than adventurousness, prompted Lapin to make long trips to remote areas in connection with his work; after 1925 he traveled in the Karakum desert, with an Academy of Sciences expedition, in the Pamirs, among the fur-breeders of Chukotka, and in Japan. As a sailor, he visited many ports in Europe and Asia. Lapin began his literary career in 1920 by writing poetry. Inspired by his travels, he turned to writing documentary fiction; the first such book-length work, *Povest o strane Pamir* (A Tale of the Land of Pamir), was published in 1929. Lapin met Z. Khatsrevin in 1932 and subsequently collaborated with him on some of his books; Lapin also wrote two film scripts (the first in collaboration with L. Slavin) based on a trip he made to Mongolia. Early in World War II both Lapin and Khatsrevin were trapped in a pocket and killed in battle near Kiev.

L. Slavin called Lapin's early expressionistic poems a "curious mixture of Karamzin and Khlebnikov"; they reflect the experimental tendencies of their time. Lapin's prose affords more than just documentary, journalistic reporting; in his prose he attempted "to abolish the line between dry reportage and fiction" (Erenburg); his fictional amplifications met with more approval than disapprobation from the critics. *Stalinabadsky arkhiv* (1932; The Stalinabad Archives), the first major work that Lapin and Khatsrevin wrote together, supplements the journalistic and fictional levels by the inclusion of translated Tadzhik fiction; in general, the focal point of their episodically constructed books of distant lands lies in the sphere of culture rather than of economics, and in the shaping of individual human destiny.

Works: *Molnijanin* (poems), 1922; *1922-ja kniga stikhov* (poems), 1923; *Povest' o strane Pamir* (pov.), 1929; *Tikhookeanskij dnevnik* (short stories), 1929; *Žurnalist na granice* (short stories), 1930; *Podvig* (pov.), 1933, 1966; *Izbr.*, 1947; *Izbr.*, 1958.
Works in collaboration with Khacrevin: *Amerika graničit s nami* (short stories), 1932; *Stalinabadskij arkhiv* (short stories), 1932; *Dal'nevostočnye rasskazy* (short stories), 1935; *Priključenija khrabrogo mongola* (short stories), 1937; *Putešestvie* (short stories), 1937; *Leto v Mongolii* (collected articles), 1939; *Rasskazy i portrety* (short stories), 1939; *Pis'ma s fronta* (short stories), 1947, 2d ed., 1958; *Ego zovut Sukhè-Bator* (film script), in *Izbr. scenarii sovetskogo kino* 5:1950.

Secondary Lit.: V. Gol'cev, in *Novyj mir* 1929:7 and 1930:2; A. Selivanovskij, in *Novyj mir* 1933:3; L. Slavin, in *Novyj mir* 1947:1 and in his *Portrety i zapiski*, 1965; I. Èrenburg, *Ljudi, gody, zizn'*, in *Novyj mir* 1962:5, pp. 148–51, and 1963:1, pp. 74–77; *RSPP* 2:1964; Ja. Gordon, *Otkryvateli nekhoženykh trop*, 1973.

**LAPP** (Leningrádskaya assotsiátsiya proletárskikh pisáteley). See RAPP.

**Lavrenyóv, Borís Andréyevich,** playwright, prose writer (b. July 17 [July 5], 1891, Kherson—d. Jan. 7, 1959, Moscow). Lavrenyov's father was a teacher. Lavrenyov studied law at Moscow University from 1909 to 1915. He served as an officer during World War I. Between 1918 and 1923 he fought both in the Ukraine and in Turkistan as a Red Army volunteer. Lavrenyov, who belonged to the egofuturists (see FUTURISM) and published his first poems in 1911, settled in Leningrad in late 1923 and published short stories in various journals. His first drama, *Dym (Myatezh)* (Smoke [The Revolt]), was performed in 1925. Lavrenyov's *Razlom* (1927; The Breakup), first performed on the tenth anniversary of the Revolution, became one of the most highly regarded Soviet plays about that event; in 1944 he revised the play to conform to the Party position. From 1930 to 1932 Lavrenyov belonged to LOKAF. During the Finnish-Russian War and World War II, Lavrenyov, who had already secretly been to sea as a schoolboy, became a frontline correspondent attached to the navy. His war plays are set in this milieu; *Za tekh, kto v more* (1945; For Those at Sea) was awarded a Stalin Prize (for 1945, 1t class). His play *Golos Ameriki* (1949; Voice of America), commissioned as part of the postwar anti-American propaganda campaign, was similarly rewarded (Stalin Prize for 1949, 2d class). Lavrenyov, who was chairman of the Drama Section of the Writers Union of the USSR for many years, was named to the board of the Writers Union of the USSR in 1954.

The distinguishing characteristics of Lavrenyov's early stories, such as *Veter* (1924; Wind) and *Sorok pervy* (1924; The Forty-first), include "quick, dynamic action; plenty of incident; unusual situations; tense, romantically heightened collisions" (Struve). Later he supplemented his stories with various other prose genres. Lavrenyov's dramas are most often set in the military sphere and conform to the Party line. Razlom combines the problem of the intelligentsia's adaptation to the dictatorship of the proletariat and the Aurora incident during the October Revolution. On the whole, Lavrenyov's characters are just as schematic and the drama's tendentious purpose is just as apparent as in later propaganda plays.

Works: Veter (short stories), 1924; Sorok pervyj (short story), in Zvezda, 1924:6, separate ed., 1927; Razlom (play), in Voennyj vestnik 1928; Za tekh, kto v more (play), in Zvezda 1945:12; Golos Ameriki (play), in Zvezda 1949:8; Lermontov (play), in Teatr 1953:4; Bessmertnaja vakhta (journalistic prose), 1973; P'esy (plays), 1974; Služil delu realizma (letters), in Teatr 1981:10.—Izbr. proizv., 2 vols., 1958, 1972; Sobr. soč., 5 vols., 1931; 6 vols., 1963–65.

Translations: Story of a Simple Thing, 1934; White Death, 193?; Stout Heart and Other Stories, 1943; The Forty-first, 1958.

Secondary Lit.: I. Èventov, 1951; I. Višnevskaja, 1962; V. Pimenov, in Teatr 1966:5; V. Michailovich, in Russian Language Journal 113:1978; C. Solodar', in Teatr 1980:6; V. Kardin, 1981; B. Filippov, in Lit. Rossija Feb. 18, 1983.

**Lébedev-Kumách, Vasíly Ivánovich** (pseud. of V. I. Lébedev), poet (b. Aug. 8 [July 27], 1898, Moscow—d. Feb. 20, 1949, Moscow). Lebedev-Kumach began publishing his propagandistic pieces in prose and verse in Bolshevik newspapers and journals at the time of the Revolution. From 1922 to 1934 he worked on the satirical journal Krokodil as a contributor and a member of the editorial staff. After 1934 he was known primarily as a writer of lyrics for political songs that were then widely disseminated by the Komsomol, schools, films, and radio. Beginning in 1938 Lebedev-Kumach served as a delegate to the Supreme Soviet several times (even there he gave his speeches in verse); in 1939 he received a post on the board of the Writers Union of the USSR; he became a member of the Communist Party in 1940. In 1941 Lebedev-Kumach received a Stalin Prize (for 1935–41, 2d class). Between 1938 and 1948, more than 20 collections of his poems and songs were published; some of the individual songs, such as "Pesnya o rodine" (1935; Song of My Homeland)—"Shiroka strana moja rodnaja . . ." ("Wide is my native land, . . . I know of no other land where a man might breathe as freely")—reached editions of more than 20 million copies. The opening notes of "Pesnya o rodine" have served as the identifying signal of Radio Moscow for decades.

Lebedev-Kumach's secular hymns are characterized by their link to the Party slogans of the day, their Soviet patriotism, tendentious optimism, and tawdry idealization. Their vocabulary and predominantly grammatical rhyme schemes are primitive, their content is often banal, and they employ empty epithets ("gray fog," "golden sunbeams").

Works: Kniga pesen (song lyrics), 1938; Pesni i stikhotvorenija (song lyrics and poems), 1960.

Secondary Lit.: I. Rozanov, in Novyj mir 1938:5; S. Vasil'ev, in Oktjabr' 1947:1; M. Čarnyj, in Moskva 1959:3; S. Ivanov, in Lit. Rossija Aug. 10, 1973, pp. 12–13; E. Sergeev, in Lit. Rossija Aug. 4, 1978, p. 15; L. Ošanin, in Lit. gazeta May 1, 1985, p. 3.

**LEF** (Lévy front iskússtva [Left Front of Art]), a Marxist literary group that arose in Moscow at the end of 1922 essentially from the former adherents of FUTURISM. LEF saw itself as the only correct advocate of revolutionary art and was attacked by the proletarian groups OKTYABR and VAPP. The group and its journal of the same name (1923–25) were led by V. Mayakovsky; its members included B. Arvatov, N. Aseyev, O. Brik, N. Chuzhak, V. Kamensky, A. Kruchonykh, B. Kushner, B. Pasternak (at the beginning), V. Pertsov, and S. Tretyakov. LEF was a rational movement characterized by a belief in progress, technology, science, and organization whose theoreticians aspired to a union between art and production. However, LEF opposed the attaining of this union by reducing art to the level of "elementary understandability" and demanded "the dictatorship of taste." In music O. Brik supported jazz; in drama LEF was closely connected to V. Meyerhold's biomechanics; in the visual arts the tendency ran toward depicting commodities and toward photography; in film (S. Eisenstein, Dziga Vertov) the documentary took precedence over the feature film. The continuation of their journal published under the title Novy LEF (New LEF), first by Mayakovsky and after 1928 by Tretyakov, promulgated the rejection of fictional art in favor of reportage and documentation by using the slogan literatura fakta (literature of fact), criticized FELLOW TRAVELERS as well as Communists (for example, A. Fadeyev and F. Gladkov), and championed the autobiographical works of V. Arsenyev, D. Furmanov, and V. Shklovsky (who had joined

LEF and formed a bridge to the FORMALIST SCHOOL). At the end of 1928 LEF disbanded, shaken by internal tensions following the resignation of Mayakovsky and Brik in September 1928. Mayakovsky's attempt to infuse new life into the movement by creating REF (Revolyutsionny front [Revolutionary Front]) collapsed in 1929 during the period when groups with divergent views were definitely liquidated by RAPP. Mayakovsky and Aseyev joined RAPP in 1930.

Secondary Lit.: LEF 1–7:1923–25; Novyj LEF 1927–28 (reprinted, Munich, 1970); Lit. manifesty, 2d ed., 1929 (reprinted, Munich, 1969); Literatura fakta (collection), ed. N. Čužak, 1929 (reprinted, Munich, 1972); H. Ermolayev, Soviet Literary Theories 1917–1934, Berkeley, 1963; L. K. Švecova, in Očerki istorii russkoj sovetskoj žurnalistiki, 1966; G. Wilbert, Entstehung und Entwicklung des Programms der "Linken" Kunst . . . , Giessen, 1976; H. K. Stephan, "LEF" and the Left Front of the Arts, Munich, 1981; K istorii vykhoda pervogo nomera žurnala "LEF," in Voprosy lit. 1983:7.

**Lench, Leoníd Sergéyevich,** (pseud. of L. S. Popóv), prose writer (b. Aug. 2 [July 20], 1905, Morozovka, prov. Smolensk). Lench completed his studies in economics at the University of Rostov-on-Don in 1925. He turned early to the literary genre that characterizes his oeuvre, the topical, humorous short story with a single line of development. From 1929 to 1934 Lench was a regular contributor to the journal Chudak, following which Mikhail Koltsov brought him over to Krokodil. Lench's stories were published regularly in collections from 1936 on; even during the Stalin years their conformity to the desired line brought them complete recognition. Lench's satire remains superficial, his conflicts do not penetrate to the heart of genuine human problems; at times his "positive humor" was even regarded as an expression of the THEORY OF CONFLICTLESSNESS. Lench was admitted to the Communist Party in 1954; he became a member of the board of the Writers Union of the RSFSR in 1965. He has also written several humorous dramas that attracted limited attention. His povest Chornye pogony (1961; Black Epaulets) is about the postwar years. Lench lives in Moscow; he was a member of the editorial board of the newspaper Literaturnaya Rossija from 1963 until 1973.

Works: Pervaja ulybka (short stories), 1936; Ukroščenie stroptivykh (short stories), 1939;

Osinovyj kol (short stories), 1942; Jumorističeskie rasskazy (short stories), 1951; Dorogie gosti (short stories), 1954; Komedii, scenki, šutki (comedies and short stories), 1961; Čërnye pogony (pov.), 1962; Trudnaja služba (short stories), 1967; Rečnoe kino (short stories), 1973; Duševnaja travma. Rasskazy o tekh, kto rjadom, i o sebe samom (short stories), 1974; Izbr., 1975; Dušespasitel'naja beseda (short stories and essays), 1977; Okazyvaetsja, suščestvuet (short stories), 1977; Iz roda Karaevykh (pov.), in Moskva 1980:12, separate ed., 1982; Izbr. proizv., 2 vols., 1982; Trudnyj starik, 1984; Načnem snačala! (plays), 1986.

Secondary Lit.: S. Vasil'ev, in Oktjabr' 1951:7; N. Leont'ev, in Neva 1958:11; L. Plotkin, in Lit. i žizn' July 3, 1960; B. Privalov, in Lit. Rossija July 30, 1965, p. 11, and in Lit. obozrenie 1976:1; G. Gulia, in Lit. gazeta June 25, 1975, p. 5; A. Khort, in Lit. obozrenie 1978:5; G. Gorin, in Novyj mir 1983:7; A. Ašplatov, in Lit. gazeta Aug. 8, 1983, p. 4; S. Anan'in in Moskva 1985:8.

**Lenin Prize.** See LITERARY PRIZES.

**Leningrád,** a literary journal that appeared biweekly as the organ of the Leningrad branch of the Writers Union from 1940 to 1946. This journal replaced the more publicistic Rezets (1924–39). The only well-known writer to serve as editor in chief was V. Sayanov (1942–44). The Party Resolution of Aug. 14, 1946 (see PARTY RESOLUTIONS ON LITERATURE) called for the journal's proscription as a result of its publication of A. Akhmatova's poems and M. Zoshchenko's short stories.

Secondary Lit.: See PARTY RESOLUTIONS ON LITERATURE; ZVEZDA.

**Leónov, Leoníd Maksímovich,** prose writer, playwright (b. May 31 [May 19], 1899, Polukhino, near Moscow). Leónov's father was a peasant and a journalist. Leonov attended a gymnasium in Moscow and began writing poems and short prose in 1915. Between 1920 and 1922 he served in the Red Army. Leonov's early stories, such as Buryga (1922; Eng. tr., in Slavonic Review 17:1938–39) and Tuatamur (1924; Eng. tr., 1935), place him in the mainstream of post-Revolutionary prose in search of new forms. His recognition as a major Russian writer came with the novels Barsuki (1924; Eng. tr., The Badgers, 1947) and Vor (1927; Eng. tr., The Thief, 1931, 1960).

In 1926 he also began writing dramas based in part on his prose works. Leonov, whose first novels appeared in Krasnaya nov, was considered to be a FELLOW TRAVELER; in 1929 he was named chairman of the All-Russian Writers Association, an organization of minor importance in the development of Soviet literary politics. In 1934 Leonov was given a position on the board of the Executive Committee of the newly formed Writers Union. After writing two Five-Year Plan novels, Sot (1930; Eng. tr., Soviet River, 1931) and Skutarevsky (1932; Eng. tr., 1936), Leonov concentrated on dramatic writing. Polovchanskiye sady (1938; Eng. tr., The Orchards of Polovchansk, in Seven Soviet Plays, 1946), a play that attempts to juxtapose a positive Soviet orchard against A. Chekhov's Cherry Orchard, is "a paradigm of the acrobatics—and compromises—of revision in which Leonov had to engage" (Segel). During World War II, Leonov achieved official recognition in the dramatic genre as well with his plays Nashestviye (1942; Eng. tr., The Invasion, in Four Soviet War Plays, 1943), (Stalin Prize for 1942, 1st class) and Lyonushka (1943). His lengthy novel Russky les (1953; Eng. tr., The Russian Forest, 1966), written between 1948 and 1955, was likewise awarded the first Lenin Prize (after the revision of the LITERARY PRIZES). During the THAW Leonov rewrote several early works, intending to restore the versions that were unpublishable under Stalin. From 1946 to 1958 Leonov was a deputy of the Supreme Soviet. He has been a member of the board of the Writers Union of the USSR since 1934 and a member of its secretariat since 1958; he belongs to the board of the Writers Union of the RSFSR and has been a delegate to all congresses of the Writers Union. He lives in Moscow.

Leonov's early prose, in its breadth of content (it even includes Oriental themes) and in its artificial stylistic experimentation in the tradition of N. Gogol, N. Leskov, A. Remizov, A. Bely, Ye. Zamyatin, and B. Pilnyak, displays the typical features of the avant-garde literature of its time without being imitative; in this sense, "foreground reality and the irrational world of dreams blend seamlessly into each other" (F. Scholz). The povest Konets melkogo cheloveka (1924; The End of a Petty Man) treats the collapse of the uprooted intelligentsia, gripped by the horror caused by the excesses of the Revolution, with intelligent skepticism. (A 1960 version of this work has been idealized to conform to the Party line.) The novel Barsuki, an action-packed exposition of the fate of two brothers, centers on the contrast between the city as the starting point of communism and the village as the preserver of tradition. An inserted episode, the story of the furious Kalafat, serves as an early allegory of Soviet bureaucracy, that is, it exposes the common illusion that human life can be totally controlled. Leonov himself considers his most important work to be Vor, a novel set in the Moscow criminal world during the NEP period. The work has numerous, sprawling levels of action; it shows Leonov's admiration for F. Dostoyevsky even with regard to the psychological penetration of human events. He brought out a new version in 1959. Among works of Five-Year Plan literature, Sot stands out in a positive way for its treatment of the problem of technology's invasion of the organically developed world of nature and for its rich linguistic features. With Nashestviye, Leonov wrote an accepted play somewhat outside the usual pattern of representing war; the work's original aim, to allow a released political prisoner to become a defender of the fatherland, ready to sacrifice himself, first became apparent in the version of 1964. Leonov's growing conformity to the principles of SOCIALIST REALISM reaches its highest point in Russky les, a novel that combines many of Leonov's earlier themes and devices, but the psychological direction of which often lacks credibility. In Evgenia Ivanovna (1963; Eng. tr., "Eugenia Ivanovna," in Soviet Literature 1964:5), too, a povest he started in 1938 about the fate of an émigré, Leonov is unable to achieve the great artistic power of his early prose.

Works: Buryga (short story), in Šipovnik 1:1922 (see above); Derevjannaja koroleva (short stories), 1923; Zapisi nekotorykh èpizodov, sdelannye v gorode Goguleve Andreem Petrovičem Kovjakinym (pov.), in Russkij sovremennik 1924:1–2; Tuatamur (short story), 1924 (see above); Konec melkogo čeloveka (pov.), 1924; Barsuki (novel), 1925, rev. ed., 1950 (see above); Vor (novel), 1928 (reprinted, Munich, 1974), rev. ed., 1959 (see above); Untilovsk (play), in Novyj mir 1928:3; Sot' (novel), 1931 (see above); Skutarevskij (novel), 1932 (see above); Doroga na okean (novel), 1936 (Eng. tr., Road to the Ocean, 1944); Našestvie (play), 1942 (see above); Lënuška (tragedy), 1943; Vzjatie Velikošumska (pov.), 1944 (Eng. tr., Chariot of Wrath, 1946); Zolotaja kareta (play), 1946, rev. ed., 1957; Russkij les (novel), 1954, rev. ed., 1961 (see above); Evgenia Ivanovna (pov.), 1963 (see above); Rannie rasskazy (short stories), Munich, 1972 (reprint of 1923 and 1926 vols.)— Sobr. soč., 5 vols., 1928–30; 6 vols., 1953–55; 9 vols., 1960–62; 10 vols., 1969–72.

Secondary Lit.: M. Nusinov, 1935; F. Vlasov, Poèzija žizni, 1961, Èpos mužestva, 2d ed., 1973; V. Kovalëv, 1962, Realizm L. Leonova, 1969, Ètjudy o L. Leonove, 1974, 2d ed., 1978; RSPP 2:1964; R. B. D. Thomson, bibliography in Slavic and East European Journal 1972:4 and in Canadian Slavonic Papers 1974; J. Sałajczyk, Teatr L. Leonova, Wrocław, 1967; Chr. Brümmer, Munich, 1971; E. Starikova, 1972; F. Scholz, in the reprints of 1972 and 1974; L. L. Mihalap, Diss., Univ. of North Carolina, 1973; M. L. Iwanchuk-Schnoes, Diss., Univ. of Wisconsin, 1975; Mirovoe značenie tvorčestva L. Leonova (collected articles), 1981.

**Lévin, Borís Mikháylovich**, prose writer (b. Jan. 5, 1899 [Dec. 24, 1898], Zagorodino, prov. Vitebsk—d. Jan. 6, 1940, during the Finnish-Russian War). Levin served in the Red Army from 1918 to 1922; one of his posts was regimental commissar. From 1923 on, he worked as a journalist and writer, contributing initially to various humor magazines, such as Krokodil; he subsequently worked for Izvestiya (1927–32) and Pravda (1932–39). His short stories were published in various pamphlets beginning in 1926. Levin's povest Zhili dva tovarishcha (1931; There Were Once Two Comrades) and his novel Yunosha (1932–33; The Youth) were strongly attacked by the critics of RAPP; in 1936 and 1940, however, there were several comprehensive articles devoted to him. Yakov Sverdlov, a film script that he wrote in 1939 in collaboration with P. A. Pavlenko, was filmed in 1940. Levin's work received little attention; his novel was not reprinted until 1957; since then only occasional reprints of his other work in journals and magazines have appeared.

Levin portrays the fates of intellectual Komsomol and Party members whose lives are dislocated by the constantly changing Party line. He avoids oversimplified friend-or-foe clichés and attempts to comprehend the difficulties of those who stand apart from the uniform aspirations of the crowd. His novel Yunosha, which introduces the world of artists who live outside the proletarian-socialist ideal, and which is centered on a negative hero, is loosely structured. Levin writes very concisely, leads immediately into the plot, and sustains the vigorous pace of the action not only at the high points but throughout the work.

Works: Žili dva tovarišča (pov.), 1931; Junoša (novel), 1933, 2d ed., 1957; Doktor (short story), in Krasnaja nov' 1934:9; Rodina (play), 1936; Izbr., 1946; Jakov Sverdlov (film script;

in collaboration with P. Pavlenko), 1940, in Izbr. scenarii sovetskogo kino 3:1949; Khrasturija (comedy), in Sovremennaja dramaturgija 14:1959.
Secondary Lit.: F. Levin, in Lit. kritik 1934:2; A. Karavaeva, in Novyj mir 1940:9; T. Khmel'-nickaja, in Zvezda 1947:5; RSPP 2:1964.

**Lévin, Dóyvber** (pseud. of Borís Mikháylovich Lévin), prose writer (b. 1904, Lyady, prov. Mogilyov—d. Dec. 17, 1942, in battle near Leningrad). Levin spoke Yiddish and White Russian as a child; he learned Russian while studying in Petrograd from 1921 on (first at the university, then after 1922 in the theater department at the Institute of Art History). At the end of the 1920s Levin belonged to the OBERIU group. His Pokhozhdeniye Feokrita (The Adventures of Theocritus), an early prose work evidently written in the absurdist manner, was not preserved. Influenced by S. Marshak and D. Kharms, Levin became a contributor to the journals Yozh and Chizh; he wrote Polyot gerr Dumkopfa (1930; The Flight of Herr Dummkopf), a short children's book about engineering inventions. In Desyat vagonov (1931; The Ten Wagons), Levin deals with the theme of neglected youth in a series of stories about Jewish children in a Leningrad children's home. Ulitsa sapozhnikov (1932; Shoemaker Street), a novel that treats the conventional theme of a proletarian child's path to revolutionary thought, went through three editions. Other works likewise dealt with the topic of the Civil War. After his death, Levin's works were no longer reprinted. Critical attention was drawn to Levin's work by the research done on the Oberiu group in the 1960s and 1970s.

Works: Polët gerr Dumkopfa (children's lit.), 1930; Desjat' vagonov (pov.), 1931; Ulica sapožnikov (novel), 1932, 2d ed., rev., 1935; Vol'nye štaty Slaviči (pov.), 1932; Likhovo (novel), 1934; Fed'ka (film script), 1936; Fed'ka (pov.), 1939; Amur-reka (play), 1939.
Secondary Lit.: R. Vikhirëva, in Detskaja lit. 1935:11; Sovetskie detskie pisateli, biobibl. slovar', 1961. I. Rakhtanov, in his Na širotakh vremeni, 1973, pp. 424–32; for additional information, see OBERIU.

**Levitánsky, Yúry Davýdovich**, poet (b. Jan. 21, 1922, Kiev). Levitansky finished his schooling in Stalino in 1939 and went on to study at the Moscow Institute of Philosophy, Literature, and History. In 1941 he became a soldier, then an officer and a frontline reporter. Levitansky published his first volume of verse, *Soldatskaya doroga* (1948; A Soldier's Road), in Irkutsk; additional volumes followed regularly. In 1957 Levitansky completed the Advanced Literature Courses of the Writers Union of the USSR in Moscow. His earlier collections, published in the provinces, remained unnoticed; A. Yashin drew attention to *Zemnoye nebo* (1963; Earthly Sky). In 1966 Levitansky was one of the signers of the petition in support of A. Sinyavsky and Yu. Daniel. *Kinematograf* (1970; The Cinematographer), externally structured according to the order of the seasons, reveals Levitansky's severance from convention and his search for new poetic forms. Levitansky lives in Moscow; he has not been a delegate to congresses of the Writers Union and occupies no posts. He also works as a translator.

Levitansky is an intellectual poet who puts into verse his distanced, individual observations and thoughts. His verse is relatively broad; it repeats and varies the same formulations, revealing technical ability without extravagance. Levitansky loves irony: he has even composed a series of parodies on contemporary poets *(Den poezii*, Moscow, 1963). A profound concern lies at the root of his proselike, occasionally expansive poems, which never touch upon political topics; their creative naturalness, which comes from within, is less obvious. "To be 'as worthy as possible'—this is the poet's credo" (Chuprinin). Up to now Levitansky's significance has for the most part been underestimated.

*Works:* Soldatskaja doroga (poems), 1949; Naši dni (poems), 1952; Storony sveta (poems), 1959; Zemnoe nebo (poems), 1963; Tečenie let (poems), 1969; Kinematograf (poems), 1970; Vospominanie o Krasnom snege (poems), 1975; Dva vremeni (poems), 1980; Pis'ma Katerine, ili, progulka s Faustom (poems), 1981.—Izbr., 1982.

*Secondary Lit.:* A. Jašin, in Lit. gazeta May 23, 1964; F. Svetov, in Den' poèzii, Moscow, 1964; E. Sidorov, in Lit. gazeta Aug. 19, 1970, p. 6; A. Latynina, in Lit. Rossija April 14, 1972, p. 15; G. Kubat'jan, in Lit. obozrenie 1977:1; S. Čuprinin, in Novyj mir 1981:12; Ju. Boldyrev, in Levitansky's Izbr., 1982; M. Pozdujaev, in Lit. gazeta Dec. 14, 1983, p. 6.

**Libedínsky, Yúry Nikoláyevich,** prose writer (b. Dec. 10 [Nov. 28], 1898, Odessa—d. Nov. 24, 1959, Moscow). Libedinsky's father was a doctor. Libedinsky spent his childhood in the Urals; in 1918 he completed his studies in the gymnasium in Chelyabinsk. He joined the Communist Party in 1920, served as a political commissar in the Red Army, and worked as a political instructor in a Moscow army institute (1921–23). His povest *Nedelya* (1922; Eng. tr., A Week, 1923), which was hailed by A. Voronsky, established Libedinsky's position as a writer. Libedinsky became an active official in the Communist writers' associations OKTYABR and MAPP; he was one of the leaders of RAPP. Like A. Fadeyev, he survived the period of the purges, and from 1934 until his death he served (probably without interruption) as chairman of the Central Appeals Commission of the Writers Union of the USSR.

Libedinsky attracted attention as a writer in the early 1920s. In *Nedelya* he attempted in vain to imitate the style of A. Bely and tried to portray "average communists shown in connection with their party work" (Struve); this he also attempted in *Komissary* (1925; The Commissars) and in the politically criticized povest *Zavtra* (1923; Tomorrow), which reveals Libedinsky's disillusionment with NEP. His novel *Rozhdeniye geroya* (1930; Birth of a Hero) was initially praised for its presentation of the then-current theme of "living people," but later, as a consequence of RAPP's internal altercations, the novel became a target of considerable criticism for its failure to idealize the character of the Party official. Libedinsky's later lengthy novels about socialist construction and the period of the Revolution in the Caucasus, *Gory i lyudi* (1939–47; Mountains and People), *Zarevo* (1952; The Glow), and *Utro Sovetov* (1957; Morning of Soviets), are lesser contributions to standardized Soviet literature.

*Works:* Nedelja (pov.), 1923 (see above); Zavtra (pov.), 1924; Komissary (pov.), 1926; Roždenie geroja (novel), 1930; Gory i ljudi (novel), 1947; Zarevo (novel), 1952; Utro Sovetov (novel), 1957; Svjaz' vremën (memoirs, short stories, sketches), 1962; Zelënaja lampa (memoirs), 1966.—Sobr. soč., 2 vols., 1930; Izbr. proizv., 2 vols., 1958; Izbr. 2 vols., 1972.

*Secondary Lit.:* D. Gorbov, in Novyj mir 1925:12 Ju. Suščev, in Čisla, Paris, 4:1930–31; A. Karavaeva, in Znamja 1953:12 and in Voprosy lit. 1962:5; G. Fiš, in Novyj mir 1957:11; RSPP 2:1964; A. Šmakov, in Lit. Rossija Dec. 13, 1968, p. 8; W. J. Weeks, Diss., Brown Univ., 1971.

**Lichútin, Vladímir Vladímirovich,** prose writer (b. March 13, 1940, Mezen, oblast Arkhangelsk). In 1962 Lichutin completed his studies at the Faculty of Journalism of Leningrad University and in 1975 graduated from the Advanced Literature Courses at the Gorky Literary Institute. Lichutin's first collection of povesti and reportage, Belaya gornitsa (1973; The White Chamber), was published in Arkhangelsk and followed initial publication in journals such as Sever beginning in 1970. Lichutin won rapid acclaim as a tradition-conscious writer of prose about the Russian village who expressed ethical concerns. His second book, Vremya svadeb (1975; Time of Weddings), appeared in Moscow. Since then he has regularly published prose in central journals and with central publishers. Lichutin was a delegate to a congress of the Writers Union in 1980 for the first time. He lives in Moscow.

Lichutin is an exponent of Russian VILLAGE PROSE; all his works concern his homeland, a village on the shore of the White Sea. His texts benefit from his personal experiences in his native region, as well as from the knowledge he attained on folkloristic expeditions. Lichutin's prose is loosely structured. He combines isolated, often unusual and dramatic, events and favors the theme of a visitor to the village who has various encounters. The geographic concentration and the connection of many texts through reappearing characters contrasts with a temporal expansiveness ranging from the present day back into the past of many generations ago. Dolgy otdykh (1974; Lengthy Rest) takes place at the beginning of the 19th century; Iona i Aleksandra (1973; John and Alexandra), after World War II; Dusha gorit (1976; The Soul Burns) and Posledniy koldun (1979; The Last Sorcerer), in the present day. In Belaya gornitsa, written at the beginning of his career as a writer, he turned to the difficult theme of the village before forced collectivization. Vdova Nyura (1978; The Widow Nyura) illustrates especially clearly his humane concern through his depiction of a woman buffeted by fate who takes hold of her life in her complete isolation. "Lichutin's heros are usually people who strive to make their lives an act of conscious spiritual choice" (I. Vinogradov).

Works: Iona i Aleksandra (pov.), in Sever 1973:2; Belaja gornica (pov. and essays), 1973; Dolgij otdykh (novel), in Sever 1974:10–12 separate ed., 1977; Vremja svadeb (pov.), 1975; Zolotoe dno (pov.), 1976; Babuški i djaduški (pov.), in Družba narodov 1976:6; Duša gorit (pov.), 1978 (contains Vdova Njura); Poslednij koldun (pov.), 1980; povesti, 1980; interview, in Lit. gazeta May 25, 1983, p. 6; Domašnij filosof (pov.), 1983; Povesti o ljubvi, 1985; Divis'-gora (essays), 1986.
Secondary Lit.: A. Jakhontov, in Lit.

obozrenie 1973:4; V. Kamjanov, in Družba narodov 1975:7 and in Novyj mir 1977:4; I Vinogradov, in Družba narodov, 1980:2; G. Cvetov, in Zvezda 1980:8; I. Dedkov, in Družba narodov 1981:3; A. Kondratovič and Ju. Smelkov, in Lit. obozrenie 1981:1; N. Pavlov, in Lit. obozrenie 1984:2.

**Lídin, Vladímir Gérmanovich** (pseud. of V. G. Gómberg), prose writer (b. Feb. 15 [Feb. 3], 1894, Moscow—d. Sept. 27, 1979, Moscow). Lidin's father was a merchant. Lidin specialized in Oriental studies and law (he graduated from Moscow University in 1915). During the Civil War he saw action with the Red Army in Siberia and elsewhere. He began publishing prose pieces while still a student; his first short-story collection appeared in 1916. In the years immediately following the Revolution, Lidin was able to make several journeys to Western Europe and the Near East. He published either a volume of stories or a novel almost every year beginning in 1922; only in the 1940s were there breaks of up to three years. Despite the fact that his works were to a certain extent linked to topics of the day, Lidin was long attacked by orthodox critics, who accused him of being a bourgeois writer; L. Timofeyev's 1951 history of literature omitted his name altogether. Lidin, who was not associated with any literary groupings, was well acquainted with many writers who were outside the official literary establishment and wrote about them in Lyudi i vstrechi (1957, 1961, 1965; People and Encounters). He lived in Moscow, where he taught at the Gorky Literary Institute for over 30 years.

Lidin's "regular problem novel" (Struve), Otstupnik (1927; Eng. tr., The Apostate, 1931, and The Price of Life, American ed., 1932), uses a student's fate to depict the dangers people faced during the NEP period; the novel's plot development is not always convincing. Lidin did his best work in his short stories, which are reminiscent not only of A. Chekhov and I. Bunin but also of B. Pilnyak in the 1920s and K. Paustovsky in the 1960s. Goluboye runo (1926; The Blue Fleece) showcases his talent for impressionistic characterization while at the same time maintaining epic objectivity. Until the very end of his life he continued to write and publish new collections of short stories. They have the same unbroken power to portray, with human warmth, difficult lives by using nature-related narrative and realistic dialogue.

Works: Nord (short stories), 1925; Goluboe runo (short story), in Ogonëk 1926:6; Otstup-

*nik* (novel), in *Novyj mir* 1927:4–8 and in *Sobr. soč.*, vol. 3, 1928 (see above); *Iskateli* (novel), 1930; *Izbr. rasskazy* (short stories), 1935; *Zima 1941 goda* (short stories), 1942; *Dve žizni* (novel), 1950; *Dal'nevostočnye povesti* (pov.), 1954; *Ljudi i vstreči* (memoirs), 1957, 2d ed., 1961, 3d ed., 1965; *Nočnye poezda* (short stories), 1959; *Vse časy vremeni* (short stories), 1972; *Otraženija zvëzd: Rasskazy 1974–1976* (short stories), 1978.— *Sobr. soc.*, 6 vols., 1928–29; 3 vols., 1973–74.

Secondary Lit.: G. Fedoseev, in *Novyj mir* 1936:10; *RSPP* 2:1964; A. Anosov, in *Sever* 1968:5; S. Mašinskij, in his *Slovo i vremja*, 1975; I. Šenfel'd, in *Russkaja mysl'*, Paris, Dec. 6, 1979, p. 13; V. Pimenov, in *Oktjabr'* 1982:8.

**Likhodéyev, Leoníd Izrailévich** (pseud. of L. I. Lídes), prose writer (b. April 14, 1921, Yuzovka, prov. Yekaterinoslavsk). Likhodeyev became a member of the Communist Party in 1942. After World War II he studied at the Gorky Literary Institute in Moscow, where he also lives. He holds no posts in the Writers Union and has not participated in its congresses. Likhodeyev began his literary career as a poet. His collections published between 1953 and 1957 contain satirical verse in imitation of V. Mayakovsky and reportage in verse. In 1957 Likhodeyev began writing prose and became famous for satirical glosses that frequently appeared in *Literaturnaya gazeta* and other publications. *Istoriya odnoy poyezdki, povestvuyushchaya o puteshestvii na rechnom parokhode . . .* (1957; The History of a Journey, Telling of a Trip Aboard a River Steamboat . . .), his first major prose work, reveals the distinctive characteristics of his style: irony and wit, in part humorous, in part sarcastic, portraits of people, pleasure in comic formulations and in speech rhythms. The lively and vividly narrated observations, conversations, and reflections make no claim to any particular profundity, but they are psychologically consistent, entertaining, and amusing. Likhodeyev retains the formal device of the journey: *Poyezdka v Tofalariyu* (1958; Journey to Tofalariya) tells of a visit to a barely known people in eastern Siberia; *Volga vpadayet v Kaspiyskoye more* (1959; The Volga Falls into the Caspian) chooses B. Pilnyak's old title for a modern journey managed by tourist guides and directs its ridicule against general human weaknesses or specific, petty Soviet abuses. *Chetyre glavy iz zhizni Maryi Nikolayevny* (1978; Four Chapters from the Life of Marya Nikolayevna) constitutes a short novel dealing with interpersonal, day-to-day problems during a vacation.

Works: *Pokorenie pustyni* (poems), 1953; *Svoimi glazami* (poems), 1955; *Otkrytoe okno* (poems), 1957; *Poezdka v Tofalariju* (pov.), 1959; *Volga vpadaet v Kaspijskoe more* (pov.), 1960; *Fel'etony* (essays), 1961; *Murlo meščanina* (essays), 1962; *Istorija odnoj poezdki* (pov.), 1964; *Četyre glavy iz zizni Mar'i Nikolaevny* (novel), 1965; *Ukazat' na nedopustimost'* (glosses), 1967; *Ja i moj avtomobil'* (novel), 1972; *Četyre glavy iz zizni Mar'i Nikolaevny* (novel), in *Don* 1978:1–2; *Sentimental'naja istorija* (novel), in *Novyj mir* 1984:7–9.

Secondary Lit.: L. Lenč, in *Znamja* 1959:7; D. Moldavskij, in *Neva* 1959:11; E. Klepikova and V. Solov'ëv, in *Neva* 1966:8; V. Kardin, in *Novyj mir* 1970:3; Z. Dičarov, in *Lit. gazeta* May 31, 1972, p. 6.

**Likhonósov, Víktor Ivánovich,** prose writer (b. April 30, 1936, Topki, oblast Kemerovo, Siberia). Likhonosov's father, a peasant from Voronezh, eventually became an unskilled laborer; he fell near Zaporozhye in 1943. Likhonosov grew up in Krivoshchekovo on the Ob and attended school in Novosibirsk. From 1956 to 1961 he studied in the Department of History and Philology at the Krasnodar Pedagogical Institute. He was subsequently employed as a village schoolteacher for some time, then he returned to Krasnodar and has lived there since. He began to write short stories in 1963; *Bryanskie* (1963; The People of Bryansk) was the first to be published in *Novy mir.* Under A. Tvardovsky's editorship three more of Likhonosov's works appeared in that journal; since 1969 his emphatically Russian short stories have been published in *Nash sovremennik.* Likhonosov's nonpolitical prose quickly found considerable recognition, but it regularly also provoked critics who demanded superficial social and political commitment. Beginning in 1966 he published several anthologies of short stories and one more or less autobiographical povest, *Na dolguyu pamyat* (1969; In Remembrance). In 1984 he edited a first collection of his prose in two volumes. Likhonosov has been a delegate to congresses of the Writers Union only since · 1970.

Likhonosov is a very talented narrator who concentrates on the forms taken by psychological occurrences in everyday situations, not on the development and resolution of plot lines. The realm of logic and intellect is secondary to the world of the spirit and the irrational in his work. His positively depicted characters live according to the heart, not the mind. Likhonosov's work, which belongs to VILLAGE PROSE, is inspired by a yearning for the expanses of nature and silence; it recognizes the disturbing influence of the means of mass communication and technology without denying reality. It is directed against the inhumanity that springs from soullessness. Yu. Kazakov, in his introduction to Likhonosov's third volume, calls the latter's characters "wanderers in the highest sense," people in search of the harmony of life. Likhonosov has a traditional, natural narrative manner; he gradually distills the character of his figures from a limited plot line that scrupulously captures details, from realistic dialogue, and from frequent accounts of a character's thoughts. He retreats as the author even in first-person narratives. The same attitude of mind gave birth to his first novel, *Kogda zhe my vstretimsya?* (1978; When Will We Meet?), in which Likhonosov develops the opposition between the city and the countryside; he makes his point by presenting two friends separated by fate and emphasizes the lasting yearning for the original village.

*Works:* Brjanskie (short story), in *Novyj mir* 1963:11; Večera (short stories), 1966; Čto-to budet (short stories), 1966; Golos v tišine (short stories), 1967; Na dolguju pamjat' (pov.), 1969; Osen' v Tamani (short stories), 1972; Čistye glaza (short stories), 1973; Èlegija (pov. and short stories), 1976; Kogda že my vstretimsja? (novel), 1978; Rodnye (pov. and short stories), 1980; Na dolguju pamjat' (pov. and short stories), 1980; Izbr. proizv., 2 vols., 1984.

*Secondary Lit.:* O. Mikhajlov, in *Naš sovremennik* 1971:9; O. Kučkina, in *Lit. obozrenie* 1973:8; Ju. Seleznev, in *Moskva* 1974:4; D. Žukov, in *Naš sovremennik* 1974:4; N. Bukhancev, in *Moskva* 1980:7; N. Kuzin, in *Don* 1983:11; V. Potanin, in *Lit. Rossija* May 2, 1986, p. 11.

**Líndenberg, Vladímir (Aleksándrovich),** prose writer (b. May 16 [May 3], 1902, Moscow). Lindenberg is descended from the Chelishchevs, a Russian noble family that can be traced back to Wilhelm of Lüneburg who fled to Russia in 1237. Lindenberg's father, Aleksandr Chelishchev, was a composer and pianist. Lindenberg was brought up by his mother and stepfather, Carl Lindenberg, in a feudal country seat in Gireyevo near Moscow. In 1915 he spent two months with his father doing meditation exercises in Eremitage near Rybinsk, a castle for meditation belonging to

the Russian Rosicrucians and built in the middle of the 18th century by his ancestors. In 1917 he avoided execution and in 1918 he was able to emigrate to Germany with his stepfather. In 1920 Lindenberg wrote his first autobiographical work, *Tri doma* (The Three Houses); it was published in 1985. He studied medicine in Bonn from 1921 until 1927 and now works as a neurologist and specialist in the treatment of brain injuries. Arrested in 1936, Lindenberg was a political prisoner in a concentration camp from 1937 to 1941. Since 1947 he has combined his work as a physician with the profession of writer in German; by 1986 he had published 32 books whose total combined print run exceeded 500,000 copies. After writing several medical books, he wrote six autobiographical works between 1961 and 1973. Concurrently, he wrote books such as *Mysterium der Begegnung* (1959; Mystery of Encounter), *Yoga mit den Augen eines Arztes* (1960; Yoga with the Eyes of a Doctor), and *Mit Freude Leben* (1979; Live with Joy) that were grounded in a rich Study of world religions and that explore religious and ethical questions and occasionally weave in some of his own experiences. Since 1941 Lindenberg has lived in Berlin.

Lindenberg is an ethical writer who supplements his own experience with many quotations from metaphysical and religious literature. Each of his autobiographical and ethical works mentions his Russian origins, presents examples of the role the Chelishchevs played in Russian history, and illustrates the power of Russian Orthodox beliefs. His autobiographical books create a lively picture of life in the circles of Russian nobility before 1915 (*Marionetten in Gottes Hand* [1961; Marionettes in God's Hand]); of the daily horror of the Revolution (*Bobik im Feuerofen* [1964; Bobik in the Oven of Fire]); of trips to the Orient and to Western Europe as well as his personal experienes in the Rosicrucian castle (*Bobik begegnet der Welt* [1969; Bobik Meets the World]); of the problems of integration faced by an émigré in the 1920s (*Bobik in der Fremde* [1971; Bobik in Foreign Countries]); of his encounters with Africa (1930–31), among other places, as a ship's doctor (*Wolodja* [1973; Volodya]); and of his experiences as an internal émigré and concentration-camp prisoner under Nazism (*Himmel in der Hölle* [1983; Heaven in Hell]). By alternating quotes, observations, and narration, Lindenberg's ethical books examine the significance of fateful providence (*Geheimnisvolle Kräfte um uns* [1974; Spiritual Forces Around Us]), of meditation and prayer (*Die Menschheit betet* [1956;

Eng. tr., *Meditation and Mankind*, 1959)), or of death as a transition to spiritual existence and life as a link in a chain of reincarnations striving toward perfection (*Über die Schwelle* [1972; *Across the Threshold*]). In *Der unversiegbare Strom* (1982; The Inexhaustible Stream), Lindenberg wrote about the sources of strength in Russian Orthodox faith by using the examples of the *startsy*, the saints, and the victims of Bolshevism. Through its striking depiction of the ruination of a noble family during the horrors of the Revolution, *Tri doma* reveals the 18-year-old author's excellent command of poetic language. From 1948 on, the language of his country of residence became for him the medium for his creative work.

*Works: Tragik und Triumph grosser Ärzte*, Ulm, 1948; *Die Unvollendeten*, Hamburg, 1948 (reprinted under the title *Frühvollendete*, Munich, 1966); *Die Menschheit betet*, Munich, 1956 (see above); *Training der positiven Lebenskräfte*, Büdingen-Geltenbach, 1957; *Mysterium der Begegnung*, Munich, 1959; *Yoga mit den Augen eines Arztes*, Berlin, 1960; *Marionetten in Gottes Hand*, Munich, 1961; *Schicksalsgefährte sein . . .* , Munich, 1964; *Bobik im Feuerofen*, Munich, 1964; *Gottes Boten unter uns*, Munich, 1967; *Bobik begegnet der Welt*, Munich, 1969; *Jenseits der Fünfzig*, Munich, 1970; *Bobik in der Fremde*, Munich, 1971; *Über die Schwelle*, Munich, 1972; *Wolodja*, Munich, 1973; *Geheimnisvolle Kräfte um uns*, Munich, 1974; *Tag um Tag ist guter Tag*, Munich, 1976; *Riten und Stufen der Einweihung*, Freiburg, 1978; *Mit Freude leben*, Munich, 1979; *Der unversiegbare Strom*, Munich, 1982; *Himmel in der Hölle*, Munich, 1983; *Lob der Gelassenheit*, Freiburg, 1984; *Tri doma*, Munich, 1985.

*Secondary Lit.:* N. A. Čeliščev, *Sbornik materialov dlja istorii roda Čeliščevykh*, St. Petersburg, 1893; articles concerning the Čeliščevs, in *Russkij biografičeskij slovar'*, vol. 22, St. Petersburg, 1905; W. Kasack, in *Universitas*, Stuttgart, 1985:2, in Lindenberg's *Tri doma*, 1985, in *Festschrift für Herbert Bräuer*, Cologne, 1986, pp. 175–92, and Munich, 1987

**Lipátov, Vil Vladímirovich**, prose writer (b. April 10, 1927, Chita, Eastern Siberia—d. May 1, 1979, Moscow). Lipatov's father was a journalist; his mother, a teacher. Lipatov finished his studies at the Tomsk Pedagogical Institute in 1952 and went to work as a journalist. He started publishing in 1951; his short stories

began appearing in 1956. He was admitted to the Communist Party in 1957. From 1964 to 1966 he worked as a correspondent for the newspaper *Sovetskaya Rossiya*. In 1967 Lipatov moved to Moscow. He was a member of the secretariat of the board of the Writers Union of the RSFSR from 1970 on and of the board of the Writers Union of the USSR from 1971 on. Like most of his narratives, Lipatov's first major *povest*, *Shestero* (1958; The Six), takes place in his Siberian homeland; it sketches portraits of individuals linked to each other through work. In *Glukhaya Myata* (1960; Wild Mint), Lipatov describes life in a brigade of lumberjacks, with its tensions between the collective and the individual. *Derevensky detektiv* (1967; Eng. tr., *A Village Detective*, 1970) is a narrative cycle of criminal investigations undertaken by a village policeman. *Lida Varaksina* (1968) illustrates the internal strain experienced when a semiliterate peasant girl become the village cultural officer. *Seraya mysh* (1970; The Gray Mouse) very candidly discusses the problem of alcoholism in Russia as Lipatov describes a quartet of drinkers on a Sunday and follows up their destinies using flashbacks. In *I eto vsyo o nyom . . .* (1974; And That's All About Him . . .), Lipatov's first novel, he very broadly asks basic questions about the proper kind of human existence, to which he links two destinies, but he does this—for which he was often reproached—without smoothing over adverse circumstances or ignoring incompetence and baseness. In his novel *Igor Savvovich* (1977) he deals with the threat to man posed by material well-being without maturity of mind and combined with the discrepancy between leadership and ability. Lipatov sees the soulless "consumer type" who serves materialism as the major menace of our times.

*Works:* Šestero (pov.), 1958; *Glukhaja Mjata* (pov.), 1960; Strežen' (pov.), 1961; Černyj jar. Čužoj (pov.), 1965; Derevenskij detektiv (short stories and pov.), 1968 (see above); *Lida Varaksina* (pov.), in Znamja 1968:12; Skazanie o direktore Prončatove (pov.), in Znamja 1969:1–2; Povesti, 1970; Seraja myš' (pov.), in Znamja 1970:12; Eščë do vojny (pov.), in Znamja 1971:9–10; I èto vsë o nëm . . . (novel), 1975; Samolëtnyj kočegar (short stories), 1975; Igor' Savvovič (novel), 1978; Povest' bez nazvanija, sjužeta i konca . . . (pov.), in Novyj mir 1978:4–6; Žitie Vanjuški Murzina, ili ljubov' v Staro-Korotkine (short story), in Znamja 1978:8–9.—Sobr. soč., 4 vols., 1982–85.

*Secondary Lit.:* V. Dudincev, in *Lit. gazeta*

May 21, 1964; I. Rodnjanskaja, in *Novyj mir* 1968:12; *RSPP* 7(1):1971; V. Rosljakov, in *Lit. gazeta* Feb. 3, 1971, p. 4; N. Podzorova, in *Lit. gazeta* Aug. 15, 1973, p. 6, and May 21, 1975, p. 5; I. Rakša, in *Lit. obozrenie* 1978:3.

**Lípkin, Semyón Izráilovich,** poet, translator (b. Sept. 19 [Sept. 6], 1911, Odessa). Lipkin's father was a worker. Lipkin moved to Moscow in 1929 and began publishing his poems in newspapers and journals. When his verse was no longer published after 1931, he learned Persian and concentrated instead on translation. In 1937 he completed his studies at the Institute of Economic Engineering in Moscow. Lipkin became known primarily as a translator of Oriental languages; he translated epics and folk poetry from Kalmuk, Kirghiz, Kabardin, and Uzbek, as well as Firdausi's *Shah Namah*. Lipkin also wrote prose paraphrases of verse epics: *Priklyucheniya bogatyrya Shovshura* (1947; The Adventures of the Hero Shovshura), *Manas Velikodushny* (1948; Manas the Magnanimous), and *Tsarevna iz goroda Tmy* (1961; The Tsar's Daughter from the City of Darkness). Only two collections of Lipkin's own verse, which is far removed from any political emotionalism, have been published in the Soviet Union: *Ochevidets* (1967; Eyewitness) and *Vechny den* (1975; Eternal Day); otherwise, his poems appeared in anthologies such as *Den poezii*. Lipkin lives in Moscow and has seldom been a delegate to congresses of the Writers Union; he is held in great esteem, however, in the Central Asian republics whose literature he has translated into Russian. The publication of several of his poems in METROPOL (1979; Eng. tr., 1982) led to considerable sanctions against him. Lipkin resigned from the Writers Union, of which he had been a member since 1934. He now publishes regularly in the West. His poems have appeared in the émigré journal *Vremya i my*. *Volya* (1981: Will), a volume of collected verse that came out in the United States, contains the poems that for decades Lipkin was able to write only for his desk drawer. In October 1986 he again became a member of the Writers Union of the USSR.

Lipkin is an extraordinarily gifted translator who has been praised because, among other things, he has neither modernizes ancient Oriental literature nor homogenizes different poets. His enormous command of language and verse and his rich vocabulary can also be felt in his own verse. This is frequently based on a description of an isolated phenomenon of nature or of everyday life, which Lipkin then elevates to a universal experience by associative reflection. Lipkin speaks of the thrush, whose individual voice can be heard even above the river ("Drozd" [1966; The Thursh]); of the conjunction "i" (and), without which the language cannot exist any more than humanity can exist without those people whose names begin with the letter *I* ("Soyuz" [1968; The Conjunction]); of a newborn Jewish infant and its mother shot in a mass grave, recalling the icon of the Mother of God ("Bogoroditsa" [1962; Mother of God]). Lipkin loves to oppose images and words, present and past, and only hints at their syntheses. The poems that first became known in 1981 reveal from the very start Lipkin's basically religious position; they include war poems that condemn all killing and reflect the author's constant struggle never to become insensitive but continually to serve humanity. Lipkin's first novel, *Dekada* (1983, written 1979–80; The Decade), is the first reflection in Russian literature of Stalin's cruel nationality policy and the human consequences it had on the fate of an exiled Caucasian people.

*Works: Očevidec* (poems), 1967, 2d ed., Èlista, 1974; poems, in *Den poèzii*, Moscow, 1963–71; *Večnyj den'* (poems), 1975; *Tetrad' bytija. Stikhi i perevody* (poems), Dušanbe, 1977; poems, in *Metropol'*, Ann Arbor, 1979 (see above); *Volja* (poems), Ann Arbor, 1981; *Dekada* (novel), New York, 1983; *Stikhi raznykh let* (poems), in *Grani*, Frankfurt am Main, 131:1984; *Kočevoj ogon'* (poems), Ann Arbor, 1984; *Kartiny i golosa* (dramatic prose), London, 1986.

*Lipkin's Translations: Kabardinskaja èpičeskaja poèzija*, 1956; *Golosa šesti stoletij*, 1960; *Stranicy tadžikskoj poèzii*, 1961; *Stroki mudrykh*, 1961; *Poèty Tadžikistana*, 1972; *Slovo i kamen'. Izbr. perevody iz uzbekskoj poèzii* (poems), 1977.

*Lipkin's Paraphrases: Priključenie bogatyrja Šovšura, prozvannogo Lotosom*, 1947; *Manas Velikodušnyj*, 1948; *Carevna iz Goroda T'my*, 1961; *Povesti o bogatyrjakh, umel'cakh i volšebnikakh*, 1963 (contains *Priključenie bogatyrja Šovšura* and *Carevna iz Goroda T'my*).

*Secondary Lit.*: N. Čukovskij, in *Znamja* 1948:6; A. Kešokov, in *Novyj mir* 1957:5; A. Lejtes, in *Lit. gazeta* Sept. 21, 1961; V. Ognëv, in *Družba narodov* 1963:1; K. Kuliev, in *Novyj mir* 1967:12; D. Kugul'tinov, in *Lit. Rossija* Nov. 19, 1971, p. 13; L. Šereševskij, in *Lit. obozrenie* 1976:11; V. Nekrasov, in *Novoe russkoe slovo*, New York, June 12, 1983, p. 5; R. Orlova, in *Grani* 135:1985.

**Lisnyánskaya, Ínna Lvóvna,** poet (b. June 24, 1928, Baku). Lisnyanskaya did not complete a higher education degree. Her first poems appeared in 1948 in Baku, where she was also able to publish a small volume, *Eto bylo so mnoyu* (1957; It Happened to Me). She was admitted to the Writers Union, Moscow's leading journals and newspapers accepted her poems, and in 1960 she was able to move to Moscow, where her next three volumes of verse were published: *Vernost* (1958; Loyalty), *Ne prosto lyubov* (1963; Not Simply Love), and *Iz pervykh ust* (1966; At First Hand). The poems were favorably received. The considerable censorship problems with her fourth book, resulting in abridgments and disfigurations, initiated a wide-scale suppression of her work. Lisnyanskaya translated a large body of poetry from Azerbaijani. Only after more than a decade had passed was she able to publish her fifth volume, *Vinogradny svet* (1978; Grape Light). After seven of her poems were included in the suppressed anthology *Metropol* (1979; Eng. tr., 1982), Lisnyanskaya was completely prohibited from publishing (even translations). With V. Aksyonov and S. Lipkin, her husband, she resigned from the Writers Union, a step that led to her expulsion even from the Litfond, and consequently deprived her of her right to social security. Since 1980 her poems have appeared in Russian émigré journals such as *Vremya i my* and *Kontinent*. Her volume *Dozhdi i zerkalo* (1983; Rain and Mirrors), which was published in Paris, finally shows Lisnyanskaya's real personality. She lives in Moscow with her husband.

Lisnyanskaya writes lucid, nonnarrative, contemplative poetry. Those poems published in the Soviet Union convey the impression of a poet devoted to timeless ethical problems; the uncensored publications after 1980 indicate that this impression is false. Lisnyanskaya is a religious writer who, with a fine instinct for immediate, even politically caused suffering, manages to combine the temporal and the timeless. She is "under the spell of time and eternity" (Etkind). The themes of freedom, treason, fear, and loneliness recur frequently. Out of her faith and her poetic being springs her admirable strength to deal with a difficult fate: "If we are sent away, we won't go; if we are killed, we won't die."

*Works:* Èto bylo so mnoju (poems), Baku, 1957; Vernost' (poems), 1958; Ne prosto ljubov' (poems), 1963; Iz pervykh ust (poems), 1966; Vinogradnyj svet (poems), 1978; Doždi i zerkala (poems), Paris, 1983; Na opuške sna (poems), Ann Arbor, 1985; poems, in *Metropol'* 1979, in *Kontinent*, Paris, 23:1980, 26:1980, 31:1982, 34:1982, 38:1983, in *Vremja i my*, Tel Aviv, 49:1979, 50:1980, 52:1980.

*Secondary Lit.:* A. Dymšic, in *Znamja* 1963:7; M. Šekhter, in *Lit. Rossija* Aug. 30, 1963, p. 14; E. Ètkind, in *Vremja i my* 49:1979; A. Radaškevič, in *Russkaja myst'*, Paris, July 5, 1985, p. 10; L. Druskin, in *Grani*, Frankfurt am Main, 138:1985.

**Literary Center of the Constructivists.** See CONSTRUCTIVISM.

**Literary journals.** To a greater extent than in many other countries, Russian literary journals form a mirror reflecting literary life, since most works of literature appear first in a journal before being published as a book. With literarily weak works or those later deemed politically unacceptable (see PARTY SPIRIT and SOCIALIST REALISM), independent publication as a book never occurs. With the literary works of especially talented writers, a translation may be published before the Russian book edition. Not infrequently the journal publication differs from the book edition, either because the author revised his work or because the censor intervened. Some journals have preserved a specific character over long periods of time: in the early 1920s, *Krasnaya nov* was the leading literary organ that served especially to unify the FELLOW TRAVELERS; the Prague journal *Volya Rossii* was under the editiorial direction of the Socialist Revolutionaries; *Oktyabr*—under V. Kochetov's direction—perpetuated its narrowly dogmatic literary policy even after 1956; whereas *Novy mir*—under A. Tvardovsky—published a great number of frank and valuable works. *Sovremennye zapiski* is considered the best literary journal of the first EMIGRATION; *Kontinent* offers a focal point for the emigration of the 1970s. This dictionary provides entries for the following literary journals, almanacs, and newspapers: *Avrora, Chisla, Druzhba narodov, Dvadtsat dva, Ekho, Grani, Kontinent, Kovcheg, Krasnaya nov, Leningrad, Literatura i zhizn, Literaturnaya gazeta, Literaturnaya Rossiya, Literaturnoye obozreniye, Literaturny sovremennik, Metropol, Molodaya gvardiya, Moskva, Mosty, Nash sovremennik, Neva, Novy mir, Novy zhurnal, Oktyabr, Opyty, Pechat i revolyutsiya, Russkiye zapiski, Sintaksis, Sovremennye zapiski, Strelets, Teatr, Tretya volna, Vestnik RKhD, Volya Rossii, Voprosy literatury, Vozdushnye puti,*

Vozrozhdeniye, Vremya i my, Vstrechi, Yunost, Znamya, Zvezda.

**Literary prizes** (Literatúrnye prémii). Literary prizes have been awarded in the Soviet Union since 1941; literary awards are usually established and conferred together with prizes for scholarly or artistic accomplishments in other fields (music, fine arts, theater, film). With their large endowments they represent an unusual material incentive, an award not least of all for political work.

The first prize to become well known in the cultural sphere was the Stalin Prize established on Dec. 20, 1939; the Lenin Prize established on June 23, 1925, preceded it but did not include awards for literature. Stalin Prizes for literature were first awarded on March 15, 1941: three 1st-class prizes (100,000 rubles each) and an approximately equal number of 2d-class prizes (50,000 rubles) distributed among the genres of prose, poetry, and drama as well as literary criticism. The first Stalin Prizes went to works written between 1935 and 1941. In following years, the award went to works written in the preceding year; in 1944 and 1945 no awards were made because of World War II; these were awarded later—on Jan. 26, 1946, for 1943–44 and on June 26, 1946, for 1945. The years given in published works on Soviet literature are inconsistent: sometimes the year in which the award was conferred is provided, sometimes the year to which the award refers. (In this dictionary, the year to which the award refers and the class of the award are consistently provided.) Stalin Prizes for music, painting, sculpture, architecture, opera, ballet, and film were also awarded. In 1943 it became possible to receive the Stalin Prize "for several years of outstanding achievements." In 1948, for 1947, seven 3d-class prizes (25,000 rubles) were conferred for the first time. The last award was made in 1952 for 1951 (Pravda March 15, 1952). Numerous recipients of the Stalin Prize received the prize more than once (for example, I. Erenburg, K. Simonov, A. Tolstoy). In the final years in which this prize was awarded, the number of prizewinners increased; the total number of Russian writers honored with a Stalin Prize is about 220. Among the prizewinners are excellent writers such as V. Kaverin, V. Nekrasov, M. Lozinsky, and A. Tvardovsky as well as literarily very weak authors such as S. Babayevsky, N. Biryukov, V. Popov, and A. Surov, who is no longer mentioned in any Soviet history of literature. Signaling official recognition, the

bestowal of a Stalin Prize often initiated favorable reviews. Its receipt guaranteed large print runs and after 1945 ensured translation into the languages of the countries within the Soviet sphere of influence. After Stalin's death, the errors made in bestowing the prizes were openly acknowledged (for example, by Khrushchev in Pravda Aug. 28, 1957). The system of awarding prizes was revised after the 20th Party Congress during the period of de-Stalinization (see Pravda Sept. 8, 1956). Whereas the Stalin Peace Prize was renamed the Lenin Peace Prize, Stalin's name was simply deleted from the Stalin State Prize (its complete title). Since then, Soviet publications have only referred to this prize as the State Prize of the USSR, even when discussing its award during Stalin's lifetime.

On Aug. 15, 1956, the Lenin Prize established in 1925 was revived by government and Party decree (see Pravda Sept. 8, 1956); from a total of 50 prizes (75,000 rubles each, 7,500 rubles after the currency reform), 8 were earmarked for the fields of literature and art. In October 1966 the total number of Lenin Prizes was reduced to 30, the number designated for literature and art was reduced to 5, the endowment raised to 10,000 rubles (Lit. Rossiya Oct. 7, 1966). Lenin Prizes are awarded on April 22, Lenin's birthday. Candidates may be proposed by, among others, the board of the Writers Union, publishers, and the editorial staffs of journals; the decision is made by a committee of important figures involved in the cultural and political life of the Soviet Union whose number ranges between 108 (1963) and 62 (1971). In the field of literature, between 1 and 4 prizes are awarded for individual works; about half of these go to authors writing in Russian. From 1957 to 1967 prizes were awarded annually. No prizes were awarded in 1958 or 1966. Since 1967 prizes have been awarded every two years (no awards in either 1968 or 1969). Among the recipients of the Lenin Prize are: L. Leonov (1957), A. Tvardovsky (1961), Ch. Aytmatov (1963), S. Marshak (1963), V. Peskov (1964), M. Svetlov (1967, posthumously), S. Mikhalkov (1970), K. Simonov (1974), G. Markov (1976), L. Brezhnev (1979), V. Bykov (1986).

As the number of Lenin Prizes decreased and the endowment increased, the State Prize of the USSR was revived on Sept. 9, 1966 (Lit. Rossiya Oct. 7, 1966); from a total of 60 prizes, 10 are designated for literature and art. Since 1976, 2 or more of these 10 have been awarded to writers either for a single work or for several works. The endowment of 5,000 rubles corresponds to the former Stalin Prize, 2d class. Awards are made annually on November 6 to commemorate the anniversary of the October Revolution. The decision lies in the hands of the same committee that awards the Lenin Prizes. Among the recipients of the State Prize of the USSR are: Ya. Smelyakov (1967), V. Kozhevnikov (1971), M. Lukonin (1973), L. Martynov (1974), F. Abramov and G. Troyepolsky (1975), Ch. Aytmatov (1977 and 1983), V. Rasputin (1977), V. Astafyev (1978), A. Arbuzov (1980), V. Belov (1981), G. Baklanov (1982), A. Chakovsky and Yu. Bondarev (1983), Ye. Yevtushenko (1984), K. Vanshenkin (1985).

On Feb. 16, 1965 (*Lit. Rossiya* Feb. 26, 1965), the *State Prize of the RSFSR* was established for the Russian Republic. For literature, this prize is called the *Gorky Prize*; every year 3 or 4 prizes are earmarked for outstanding works of poetry or prose (endowment, 2,500 rubles). For dramatic works and achievement in the field of theater, the Stanislavsky Prize was created; in addition there is a Glinka Prize for musicians and a Repin Prize for the fine arts; since 1967 there has also been an architectural award; authors can share in the Brothers Vasilyev Prize for film. In April 1969 an additional prize, the *Krupskaya Prize* for children's and young people's literature, was established. The committee responsible for awarding all these prizes consisted of 111 people in 1966. Prizes are awarded at the end of the year for works published by the middle of the same year. Some of the prizewinners are so insignificant in a literary sense that major Soviet histories of literature barely mention them.

On March 18, 1966 (*Lit. gazeta* May 19, 1966), a *Prize of the Leninist Komsomol* was established for works of literature and art (endowment, 5,000 rubles). Awards are conferred (annually since 1975) more or less on the anniversary of the founding of the Komsomol on Oct. 29. Prizewinners include: O. Suleymenov (1967), Ya. Smelyakov (1968), V. Firsov (1968), R. Rozhdestvensky (1972), A. Likhanov (1976), V. Amlinsky (1980), as well as posthumously—a peculiarity of this prize—N. Ostrovsky (1966), V. Mayakovsky (1968), A. Fadeyev (1969–70), M. Svetlov (1972), B. Gorbatov (1978).

On Jan. 17, 1972, the Council of Ministers of the USSR established an *A. A. Fadeyev Medal* that is awarded annually in gold and silver for literary works depicting the past and present of the Soviet military. The prizewinners are agreed upon by both the secretariat of the Writers Union of the USSR and the main political administration of the Soviet

Army and Navy. The first recipients (for 1973) of this medal, named for the central literary official of the Stalin period, were M. Sholokhov (gold), A. Surkov (gold), A. Ananyev (silver). Later recipients include (gold medal): Yu. Bondarev (1974), G. Beryozko (1975), N. Tikhonov (1976), M. Dudin (1978), V. Kozhevnikov (1980), S. Baruzdin (1981).

In addition to the above-mentioned literary prizes, there are numerous others awarded by institutions, especially prizes of the Ministry of Defense of the USSR (established in 1966, awards made every two years), of the Writers Union of the USSR (established in 1978, awards made annually), and of the State Security Service—the KGB (established in 1979); A. Avdeyenko (1979) is among the recipients of the last-named award. There are also prizes awarded by individual editorial staffs such as those of *Druzhba narodov*, *Nash sovremennik*, and *Literaturnaya Rossiya*; whether or not these prizes are awarded regularly is unknown. Finally, the Union Republics also bestow literary prizes that are occasionally received by Russian authors who have made a contribution through translations.

The number of literary prizes in the Soviet Union is quite high. Political considerations always play a decisive role in these awards: works that, in conformity with the Party line, spoke out against COSMOPOLITANISM received awards at the end of the 1940s, and A. Solzhenitsyn, who was among the finalists in 1964, did not receive the Lenin Prize. The prevailing Party policy with regard to literature can be inferred from the names of the prizewinners and of the prizewinning works for any given year.

*Secondary Lit.*: I. Ignat'ev, in *Russkaja mysl'*, Paris, Feb. 1, 1979, p. 8; *Pisateli-laureaty premij SSSR i sojuznykh respublik*, 1980, 2d ed., 1982.

*Literatúra i zhizn* (Literature and Life), a literary newspaper, the organ of the board of the Writers Union of the RSFSR, that was published in Moscow three times a week between April 6, 1958, and the end of 1962. When the decision was made to establish a WRITERS UNION of the RSFSR, *Literatura i zhizn* was created, first as the official organ of the organizing committee (until issue no. 109) and then of the board. In addition to information similar to that appearing in *Literaturnaya gazeta*, this newspaper also published prose, journalistic prose, poetry, and literary criticism. Editors in chief were V. Poltoratsky

(1958–61) and K. Pozdnyayev (1961–62), who then assumed the editorship of its successor, LITERATURNAYA ROSSIYA.

*Secondary Lit.:* O *gazete "Literatura i žizn":* Postanovlenie Bjuro CK KPSS po RSFSR 4 dekabrja 1957 g., in O *literature i iskusstve,* 2d ed., 1960, pp. 139–40; L. Sobolev, in *Lit. i žizn'* April 6, 1958.

**Literatúrnaya entsiklopédiya** (Literary Encyclopedia), the first Soviet literary encyclopedia, of which volumes 1 to 9 (A-*roman*) and 11 *(Stantsy-forma)* were published in Moscow from 1929 to 1939. This work, whose first 8 volumes were published by the Communist Academy (Seriya literatury, iskusstva i yazyka), reflects through its changing staff of editors and contributors, as well as in its shifting political outlook, the reorientation of cultural policy in the USSR on the path toward a totalitarian state. The editor responsible for volumes 1 to 3 was V. M. Friche (who held this position until his death). He was followed by A. V. Lunacharsky (until volume 7, which begins with his obituary); E. N. Mikhaylov signed volumes 7–9 and 11 as scholarly secretary. *Literaturnaya entsiklopediya* was the most comprehensive literary reference work in the USSR until KRATKAYA LITERATURNAYA ENTSIKLOPEDIYA was published (1962 to 1978). Several thousand signed entries, some of which are recognized for their scholarship, describe authors from Russian and world literature, literary terminology, movements, groups, journals, newspapers, and so forth. As the "first attempt to create a Marxist literary encyclopedia," this work differs in substance from the *Kratkaya literaturnaya entsiklopediya.* For example, the term *Soviet literature* can only be found in isolated usage in the last volumes, whereas *proletarian literature* is still considered the ideal concept of Party-oriented writing. There is still an entry for CENSORSHIP under "Glavlit" (vol. 2, 1929); volume 5 (1931) contains a 19-column entry on "Cain" in which N. Nusimov deals with the use of this religious motif in world literature. The *Kratkaya literaturnaya entsiklopediya* has no entries for either "Cain" or "Glavlit," but in contrast to *Literaturnaya entsiklopediya* it has an entry "Partiynost v literature" (the Party spirit in literature; see PARTY SPIRIT). Although V. Pereverzev is named as coworker for methodological entries in the first volume (1929), he is later sharply criticized for being a Menshevik. Numerous coworkers and authors who were described favorably fell victim to the purges around 1937 or during the battle against

so-called COSMOPOLITANISM. *Literaturnaya entsiklopediya* is a carefully compiled Soviet reference work that, despite its intrinsic ideological limits, provides information on many people and issues that later became taboo.

**Literatúrnaya gazéta** (Literary Gazette), the organ of the board of the Writers Union of the USSR that was established in 1929 and has been published weekly in a 16-page format since 1967. The first issue was published on April 22, 1929. *Literaturnaya gazeta* was the organ of the Federation of the Association of Soviet Writers (Federatsiya obyedineniy sovetskikh pisateley [FOSP]) from 1929 to 1932; the editorial staff included representatives of RAPP, PEREVAL, the constructivists (see CONSTRUCTIVISM), and the All-Union Union of Writers (Vsesoyuzny soyuz pisateley [VSP]). Free competition among various literary groups, the principle of *Literaturnaya gazeta* that was in line with the party resolution of 1925 (see PARTY RESOLUTIONS ON LITERATURE), gave way to the promotion of the hegemony of RAPP in 1930. Following the Party Resolution of 1932, *Literaturnaya gazeta* became an "organ of the Organizing Committees of the Writers Union of the USSR and RSFSR" and, following the First WRITERS CONGRESS in 1934, a weekly organ of the board of the Writers Union of the USSR. After January 1942, *Literaturnaya gazeta* was combined with the newspaper *Sovetskoye iskusstvo* (Soviet Art) under the title *Literatura i iskusstvo* (Literature and Art). Editorial control was in the hands of A. Fadeyev. After November 1944, the newspaper reappeared as *Literaturnaya gazeta,* once a week at first, twice a week after September 1947, and three times a week from July 1950 to December 1966. During this period the editors in chief were A. Surkov (1944–46), V. Yermilov (1946–50), K. Simonov (1950–53), B. Ryurikov (1953–55), V. Kochetov (1955–59), S. S. Smirnov (1959–60), V. Kosolapov (1960–62), A. Chakovsky (1962–). *Literaturnaya gazeta* reflects and defines the official literary-political line in the USSR. It reports on the Writers Congresses, provides information on the bestowal of LITERARY PRIZES, publishes congratulatory messages and obituaries (the length of these announcements is a clear indication of a writer's place in the literary-political hierarchy). *Literaturnaya gazeta* publishes prose, poetry, journalistic prose, reviews, and interviews with writers. Official visits by foreign authors are reported on, as are the official trips abroad undertaken by Soviet writers. Many contributions have a purely political character; these are complemented by articles on art, science, and sport. In 1973 the circulation was 1.550 million; in 1984, 3.100 million.

Secondary Lit.: Editorials, in Novyj mir 1935:6, pp. 237–40; in Krasnaja nov' 1935:3, pp. 254–56, and 1935:4, pp. 254–56; and in Lit. gazeta May 11, 1949; S. S. Smirnov, in Lit. gazeta May 26, 1959; A. Čakovskij, in Lit. gazeta Oct. 6, 1966, and in Lit. Rossija April 27, 1979, p. 4; L. Švecova, in Očerki istorii russkoj sovetskoj žurnalistiki, 1968; B. Filippov, in Novoe russkoe slovo, New York, June 17, 1984, p. 5, and Aug. 25, 1985, p. 4; V. Vojnovič, in Novoe russkoe slovo Aug. 5, 1984, p. 3.

**Literatúrnaya Rossíya** (Literary Russia), weekly literary newspaper founded in 1963 as the organ of the board of the Writers Union of the RSFSR and the Moscow branch of the Writers Union of the RSFSR. Literaturnaya Rossiya replaced the newspaper Literatura i zhizn (Literature and Life), which was published from April 1958 until 1962. The editors in chief have been K. Pozdnyayev (1963–73), Yu. Gribov (1973–82), M. Kolosov (1982–). Like Literaturnaya gazeta, Literaturnaya Rossiya promotes the official literary-political line, and both periodicals contain the same information. Literaturnaya Rossiya publishes prose, poetry, journalistic prose, reviews, and occasional portraits of authors. In 1973 the circulation was 100,000.

Secondary Lit.: Editorials, in Lit. gazeta Jan. 1, 1963, and Oct. 1, 1963; in Lit. Rossija Oct. 4, 1963, p. 4, and Nov. 29, 1968, p. 14; and in Sovetskaja Rossija Dec. 8, 1968; N. Rodičev, in Lit. Rossija Nov. 26, 1968, p. 3.

**Literatúrnoye obozréniye** (Literary Review), a monthly journal for literary criticism that has been published in Moscow since 1973 as an organ of the Writers Union of the USSR. This journal is a direct result of the Party Resolution of 1972 concerning literary criticism (see PARTY RESOLUTIONS ON LITERATURE). From 1973 to 1977 the editor in chief was Yu. Surovtsev; he was followed by L. Lavlinsky. Each year Literaturnoye obozreniye contains about 40 survey articles and approximately 350 reviews of new works. In addition to reviews of individual books, the journal includes portraits of authors, essays, articles contrasting differing points of view, criticism of criticism, reports from librarians,

and so forth. In 1976 the circulation was 30,000; in 1984, about 24,000; in 1987, about 21,000.

Secondary Lit.: Otkryvaja nomer, editorials from each issue of Lit. obozrenie.

**Literatúrny sovreménnik** (The Literary Contemporary), a literary journal, the organ of the branch of the Writers Union in Leningrad, that was published monthly from 1933 to 1941. Literaturny sovremennik replaced a journal called Leningrad (1930–32). N. Braun, G. Gor, M. Kozakov, A. Prokofyev, Yu. Tynyanov, and M. Zoshchenko were all members of the editorial staff for a time. Together with the works of these authors, Literaturny sovremennik also published novels by V. Kaverin, A. Chapygin, Yu. German, V. Sayanov, and V. Shishkov; povesti by V. Belyayev and I. Metter; short stories by A. Kuprin, L. Borisov, and N. Nikitin; plays by Ye. Shvarts, V. Katayev, and O. Forsh; and poems by B. Kornilov, N. Zabolotsky, E. Bagritsky, V. Shefner, and O. Berggolts. During the 1930s Literaturny sovremennik was the most important literary journal for Leningraders.

**LOKAF** (Literaturnoye obyedineniye Krasnoy Armii i Flota [Literary Association of the Red Army and Navy]). LOKAF was founded on Aug. 29, 1930. The founders included N. Aseyev, D. Bedny, A. Bezymensky, Yu. Libedinsky, A. Surkov, and V. Vishnevsky. LOKAF united more than 120 writers and more than 2,500 members of the literary circles of the Red Army and journalists and writers working for the military. LOKAF had branches in Leningrad (where L. Sobolev was the secretary), Moscow, the Ukraine, the northern Caucasus, the Volga region, Central Asia, Belorussia, and with the Black Sea fleet. LOKAF issued its own publications, called Lokaf in Moscow and Zalp, renamed Znamya in 1933, in Leningrad. As a result of the Party Resolution of 1932 (see PARTY RESOLUTIONS ON LITERATURE), which decreed the establishment of a single Writers Union of the USSR, LOKAF was disbanded.

Secondary Lit.: L. Sobolev, in Lit. gazeta Sept. 4, 1930; N. Svirin, in Lokaf 1931:12; V. Surganov and L. Sobolev, in Oktjabr' 1958:7.

**Lóskutov, Mikhaíl Petróvich,** prose writer (b. Sept. 24 [Sept. 11], 1906, Kursk—d. 1940 [?], while imprisoned). Loskutov was a journalist; in 1929–30 he published three volumes of collected articles. Between 1930 and 1932 he worked in Central Asia, at the radio station in Tashkent, and made numerous journeys into the barely accessible Karakum Desert. After returning to Moscow, where he belonged to K. Paustovsky's and R. Frayerman's circle, he reworked his notes into the book *Trinadtsaty karavan* (1933; The Thirteenth Caravan). The immediacy and freshness with which the book depicts the "incorporation of the desert into the world" raises it above the usual documentary prose about the start of socialist construction. Loskutov's own personal and often adventurous experiences are enriched by his retelling of stories from the history of the desert tribes. His participation in the first automobile expedition from Moscow to the Karakum and back provided Loskutov with material for further works on Central Asia. Loskutov's literary career was forcibly terminated just as he began to turn from journalistic prose to fiction. He was arrested about 1937 and his work was suppressed. After his REHABILITATION around 1956, he was at first thought to have died in 1943. The "Foreword" in the first reprinting of his work in 1957 was written by Paustovsky, who characterized Loskutov as an exceedingly gifted writer with an original point of view and a laconic sense of humor.

*Works:* Konec meščanskogo pereulka (articles), 1928; Trinadcatyj karavan (articles), 1935, 2d ed., 1958; Rasskazy o dorogakh (short stories), 1935; Belyj slon (articles and short stories), 1958; Sledy na peske (articles and short stories), 1959; Nemnogo v storonu (articles and short stories), 1968, enl. ed., 1971.

*Secondary Lit.:* K. Paustovskij, in his Sobr. soč., vol. 5, 1958; E. Rževskaja, in Novyj mir 1959:1; N. Atarov, in Lit. gazeta July 7, 1959; A. Sergeev, in Novyj mir 1970:1; I. Rakhtanov, in Detskaja lit. 1971:2 and in his Na širotakh vremeni, 1973.


**Lozínsky, Mikhaíl Leonídovich,** translator, poet (b. July 20 [July 8], 1886, St. Petersburg—d. Feb. 1, 1955, Leningrad). Lozinsky received his degree in law in 1908 and his degree in philology in 1913 from St. Petersburg University. The poems he had written between 1906 and 1913 were published in 1916 in the volume *Gorny klyuch* (The Mountain Spring). From 1914 to 1937 Lozinsky worked in the Public Library in Leningrad. For several years, beginning in 1918, he was a staff member of the Vsemirnaya literatura publishing house and edited numerous poetry translations. With

the exception of a few occasional poems, Lozinsky worked exclusively as a translator from this time on; in 35 years he translated 80,000 stanzas of poetry and 500 printed sheets of prose from various Western European languages. Lozinsky received a Stalin Prize (for 1943–44, 1st class) for his most ambitious work, a translation of Dante's *Divine Comedy,* on which he worked from 1936 to 1943, in part during his evacuation to Yelabuga in World War II.

As a poet, Lozinsky is closely connected with the ACMEISTS. As a translator, he combines a refined literary sense with a broad philological education and a great mastery of languages. He gave the works of Shakespeare, Cervantes, Molière, Corneille, Goethe, Schiller, Heine, and Lope de Vega an effective Russian form. "He saw the meaning of his existence in being a guardian of culture, in conquering for us those trophies of Western poetry that seemed to him its most precious fruits" (Etkind).

*Works:* Gornyj ključ (poems), 1916; three poems from 1916–19, in Antologija Peterburgskoj poèzii èpokhi akmeizma, Munich, 1973; Mysli o perevode (essay), in Leningradskij al'manakh 1955:10; Iskusstvo stikhotvornogo perevoda (article), in Družba narodov 1955:7 and in Bagrovoe svetilo, 1974.

*Lozinsky's Translations:* Servantes, 1962; Šekspir, Gamlet, 1964; Dante, 1967; Bagrovoe svetilo (assorted verse), 1974.

*Secondary Lit.:* E. Ètkind, in Inostrannaja lit. 1956:3 and in Bagrovoe svetilo, 1974; A. Akhmatova, in her Soč., vol. 2, 1968, pp. 188–90; I. Ivanovskij, in Den' poèzii, Leningrad, 1972; V. Grebenščikov, in Russian Language Journal 108:1977; D. Segal, in Russian Literature 1938:4; A. Lavrov, R. Timenčik, in Lit. gazeta July 30, 1986, p. 5; I. Tolstoj, in Zvezda 1986:7.


**Lugovskóy, Vladímir Aleksándrovich,** poet (b. July 1 [June 18], 1901, Moscow—d. June 5, 1957, Yalta). Lugovskoy's father was a literature teacher in a gymnasium; his mother, a singer. After the Revolution, Lugovskoy attended Moscow University for a short time, then served in the Red Army until 1924; there he studied at the Military Teachers Institute (1919–21) and took part in action at the front and worked in the Kremlin. Lugovskoy's first poem appeared in Novy mir in 1925; it was followed by a small volume of verse, Spolokhi (1926; Sheet Lightning). In 1926 Lugovskoy became friends with P. Antokolsky. From 1926 to 1930 he was a member of the constructivists (see CONSTRUCTIVISM) and became their most consistent spokesperson. In 1930 he joined RAPP. His participation in a writers' journey to Turkmenia in 1930 marked for him the start of a period of travel to Central Asia, the Caucasus, and twice briefly to Europe; his travels were reflected in his numerous and generally longer poems. His poetry had until then found a varying reception, but on April 26, 1937, Literaturnaya gazeta published a resolution of the board of the Writers Union of the USSR condemning several of his poems as politically harmful. Lugovskoy remained free after acknowledging his error (Znamya 1937:6), but despite his several publications he was ignored until after Stalin's death. Lugovskoy suffered from severe depression and spent the World War II years ill in Tashkent. The improvement of the literary and political climate during the THAW led to an extraordinarily prolific creative period in his life. Lugovskoy wrote two poetry cycles. Solntsevorot (1956; The Sun's Course) and the almost-completed Sinyaya vesna (1958; The Blue Spring). In Seredina veka (1958; The Middle of the Century) he produced a completely revised version of a lyrical narrative work conceived in 1942 and consisting of 25 long poems. Although he published 36 books during his lifetime, Lugovskoy achieved complete recognition, as demonstrated by new editions of his work and by the interest of literary critics and scholars, only after his death.

As a poet of the 1920s, Lugovskoy wrote enthusiastic poems that ranged widely over space and time, affirmations of his support for the Revolution and the Civil War. His volume Muskul (1929; Muscle), written in his constructivist period, is inspired by a reasonable enthuasism for self-denial for the sake of the masses. His volume of publicistic verse, Yevropa (1932; Europe), displays the typical lack of independence that characterizes tendentious poetry. The genuine love lyrics of Kaspiyskoye more (1936; The Caspian Sea) raise it above such poetry in support of construction as his Bolshevikam pustyni i vesny (1931, 1933, 1948; To the Bolsheviks of Wilderness and Spring). Justifiably, Lugovskoy considered his last three books to be his most essential works. Written "in a single breath," the cycle Solntsevorot is an attempt to comprehend the constant transformation of life in the new present; it pits the criterion of truth against the earlier theme of faith and confession. Sinyaya vesna turns more to the past and seeks to give expression to the quintessence of the heart. Seredina veka explores

post-Revolutionary historical and personal development in connection with common human problems, such as chance versus the lawful regularity of nature or the position of the individual with regard to the state. The loose structure of this epic, written in blank verse, is characteristic of Lugovskoy's work: he uses mosaiclike series rather than chronological narration, he replaces the realistic depiction of concrete conditions with abstraction, reflection, metaphoric association, and emotional confession. A note of deep despair is heard occasionally, as in "Zhestokoye probuzhdenie" (1929; Cruel Awakening), a poem that was attacked in 1937, but it is outweighed, as in all of Lugovskoy's work, by an optimistic insistence, prompted by a yearning faith, on "happiness for all."

Works: Spolokhi (poems), 1926; Muskul (poems), 1929; Stradanija moikh druzej (poems), 1930; Evropa (poems), 1932; Žizn' (narrative poem), 1933; Kaspijskoe more (poems), 1936; Pustynja i vesna (Bol'ševikam pustyni i vesny) (poems), 1931–52, 1953; Lirika (poems), 1955; Solncevorot (poems), 1956; Izbr. soč., 1956; Seredina veka (narrative poetry), 1958; Sinjaja vesna (poems), 1958; Razdum'e o poèzii, 1960; Materialy k tvorčeskoj istorii knigi "Seredina veka," in Lit. nasledstvo 74:1965; Stikhotvorenija i poèmy (lyric and narrative poems), 1966.—Sobr. soč., 3 vols., 1971.

Secondary Lit.: A Turkov, 1958; Stranicy vospominanij o V. A. L., 1962; L. Levin, 1963, 2d ed., 1972; V. Ognëv, in Lugovskoj's Stikhotvorenija i poèmy, 1966; Ju. Moric, in Zvezda vostoka 1968:6; I. Grinberg, in Lugovskoj's Sobr. soč., 1971; È. Solovej, 1977; Stranicy vospominanij o Lugovskom, 1981; E. Bykova and M. Nogteva, in Voprosy lit. 1981:7; E. Bykova, in Teatr 1982:4.

**Luknítsky, Pável Nikoláyevich,** prose writer (b. Oct. 12 [Sept. 29], 1900, St. Petersburg— d. June 23, 1973, Moscow). Luknitsky's father was an army engineer. Luknitsky studied philology in Tashkent and Petrograd (1921–25); beginning in 1922 he focused his attention on poetry. Between 1925 and 1929 he traveled to the Crimea, the Caucasus, and Turkmenistan. Beginning in 1930, Luknitsky took part in numerous expeditions to the Pamir region of Tadzhikistan, which from that time on became his specialty. During World War II he worked in besieged Leningrad as a correspondent for TASS. After that time, he resided in Moscow, spending a part of each year traveling in Central Asia; he belonged to the Appeals Commission of the Writers Union of the RSFSR from 1958 until his death.

Luknitsky's early poems were influenced by the modern efforts characteristic of the second decade of the 20th century. His second and final volume of poetry, *Perekhod* (1931; Transition), already evokes an impression of the Soviet Far East. Luknitsky's participation in expeditions to the uncharted mountainous world of the Pamirs was reflected in numerous journalistic works in the 1930s and afterward. These range from a mixture of what he experienced and heard concerning the present and the past in *Vsadniki i peshekhody* (1934; Riders and Walkers), to novels such as *Nisso* (1946; Eng. tr., 1949, 1953), based on the life of the mountain people; from popularized general accounts such as *Tadzhikstan* (1951; Eng. tr., *Soviet Tajikistan*, 1954), to diaries of the years 1930–32, *Puteshestviya po Pamiru* (1955; Travels in the Pamirs). Luknitsky's presentation is rather general and does not have the poetic strength of V. Arsenyev's; nevertheless, its directness makes it thoroughly effective. His major work of the last decade is *Leningrad deystvuyet . . . Frontovoy dnevnik* (1961–68, 3 vols.; Leningrad in Action . . . A Diary from the Front); rich in material, Luknitsky's presentation of World War II, and of the siege of Leningrad in particular, limits itself to eyewitness reports and avoids generalizations.

*Works: Volčec* (poems), 1927; *Mojra* (novel), 1930; *Perekhod* (poems), 1931; *Za sinim pamirskim kamnem* (pov., short stories, sketches), in *Novyj mir* 1932:2; *Vsadniki i pešekhody* (articles and short stories), 1934; *Zemlja molodosti* (novel), 1936; *Solnce vsë vyše* (pov. and short stories), 1939; *Nisso* (novel), 1946, 2d ed., 1963 (see above); *Tadžikistan*, 1951 (see above); *Putešestvija po Pamiru* (diary), 1955; *Leningrad dejstvuet . . . Frontovoj dnevnik* (diary), 3 vols., 1961–68, 2d ed., 1971; *Izbr.*, 1972.

*Secondary Lit.*: D. Moldavskij, in *Zvezda* 1952:6; Anon., in *Lit. i žizn'* Oct. 12, 1960; A. Zyrin, in *Zvezda* 1961:5; *RSPP* 2:1964; V. Šošin, in *Zvezda Vostoka* 1978:2.

**Lukónin, Mikhaíl Kuzmích**, poet (b. Oct. 29, 1918, Astrakhan—d. Aug. 4, 1976, Moscow). Lukonin spent his youth in village on the Volga; he worked in a Stalingrad tractor factory. In 1937 he completed teachers college in Stalingrad and studied intermittently at the Gorky Literary Institute. In 1939–40 he was a soldier in the Finnish-Russian War. Lukonin

considered this to mark the "starting point of his path" as a poet. In 1942 he became a member of the Communist Party. His poems from World War II, in which he was a correspondent at the front, constitute his first published volume, *Serdtsebiyenie* (1947; Heartbeat). In the narrative poem *Rabochiy den* (1948; The Working Day), for which he received a Stalin Prize (for 1948, 2d class), each day is conceived as a stage in the development of Soviet society. *Priznaniye v lyubvi* (1960; Declaration of Love), is like almost all of Lukonin's works, a patriotic confession; it combines personal recollection with crucial political moments in Soviet history. After 1961 he published his reminiscences of other poets, entitled *Tovarishch poeziya* (Comrade Poetry). Lukonin became a member of the boards of the Writers Unions of the RSFSR (in 1970) and the USSR (in 1971). He lived in Moscow.

Lukonin's verse is occasionally modeled on V. Mayakovsky's in the graphic arrangement of its lines. Now and then his love lyrics reveal poetic power, but they lack a sense of rhythm. Even during the Stalinist period his verse was recognized more for intention than for actual achievement; Soviet critics later criticized it for its awkwardness and for its lack of concentration and artistic complexity. Lukonin's collection *Neobkhodimost* (1973; Necessity), however, found the limited recognition of a State Prize in 1973. Lukonin's death was followed by many positive evaluations of his work.

*Works: Serdcebienie* (poems), 1947; *Rabočij den'* (poems), 1948; *Doroga k miru* (poems), 1951; *Stikhi dal'nego sledovanija* (poems), 1956; *Priznanie v ljubvi* (narrative poem), in *Lit. i žizn'* Feb. 14, 1960, p. 3, separate ed., 1972; *Kljatva* (poems), 1962; *Tovarišč poèzija* (essays), 1963, 2d ed., 1972; *Peredovaja* (lyric and narrative poems), 1973; *Stikhotvorenija i poèmy* (lyric and narrative poems), 1985.— *Izbr. proizv.*, 2 vols., 1969; 1 vol., 1973; *Sobr. soč.*, 3 vols., 1978–79.

*Translation: Selected Poems*, 1980.

*Secondary Lit.*: B. Solov'ëv, in *Zvezda* 1951:3; I. Denisova, 1968; V. Percov, in *Znamja* 1969:8 and in *Lit. i sovremennost'* 10:1970; A. Kireeva, 1970, 2d ed., 1980; K. Selikhov, in *Lit. obozrenie* 1973:10; K. Vanšenkin, in his *Lica i golosa*, 1978; L. Anninskij, in *Novyj mir* 1980:3 and separate ed., 1982; *Vospominanija o M.L.*, 1982.

**Lunachársky, Anatóly Vasílyevich**, political figure, critic, playwright (b. Nov. 23 [Nov. 11], 1875, Poltava—d. Dec. 26, 1933, Menton,

France). Lunacharsky's father was a civil servant. Lunacharsky became interested in Marxism when he was 15; in 1892 he joined a social-democratic organization. He studied philosophy and natural science in Zurich (1895–97) and in Russia (1897–1906). In 1903 he allied himself with the Bolsheviks; he spent the years between 1906 and 1917 in emigration. Together, Lunacharsky and A. Bogdanov formed "Vperyod," a group that cut away from the Bolsheviks in 1909 and ran its own party school in Bologna and Capri. During this period Lunacharsky wrote numerous scholarly, critical, and philosophical articles on European literature and art. In 1917 he returned to Russia and was readmitted to the Bolshevik Party. Lunacharsky became the People's Commissar for Education in 1917. He differed from Lenin in his positive attitude toward the PROLETKULT. In opposition to the futurists (see FUTURISM) and some of the Proletkult officials, Lunacharsky advocated the continuity of cultural tradition; furthermore, he wanted to include FELLOW TRAVELERS in the building of post-Revolutionary culture and favored the existence of different literary tendencies. Between 1918 and 1927 Lunacharsky, who had published his first drama, Korolevsky bradobrey (The King's Barber), in 1906, wrote 18 dramas, among them several historical-philosophical tragedies about the nature of the Revolution. Lunacharsky was dismissed from his position as People's Commissar in 1929; he continued on the editorial boards of Novy mir (1925–31) and Krasnaya niva (1923–30). He was named director of the Literary Institute of the Communist Academy and became a member of the Academy of Sciences of the USSR in 1930. Lunacharsky's expulsion from literary and cultural life culminated in his designation as ambassador to Spain. He died en route.

Several of Lunacharsky's plays, such as Magi (1919; Eng. tr., The Magi, 1923), Vasilisa Premudraya (1920; Eng. tr., Vasilisa the Wise, 1923), and Ivan v rayu (1920; Ivan in Paradise), are close in spirit to neoromantic fairy tales. His historical tragedies depict problems posed by the Revolution by using examples from history, since he considered the concept to be more important than historical accuracy. In Oliver Kromvel (1920; Oliver Cromwell) he presents the champion of the new as he is forced by circumstances to compromise, plagued by doubts as to whether such enormous sacrifices are justifiable. Lunacharsky completed Parts 1 (Narod [1920; The People]) and 2 (Gertsog [1922; The Duke]) and the first act of Part 3 (Solntse [The Sun]) of Foma Campanella (Tommaso Campanella), a trilogy

set in 17th-century Italy; in the trilogy's romantically embellished Renaissance atmosphere, the early Italian utopian socialist falls victim to the Jesuits but preserves a moral victory. In Osvobozhdyonny Don Kikhot (1922; An Emancipated Don Quixote), Lunacharsky selects the title character as a figure symbolizing the revolutionary who does not accept the necessity of terrorism. Lunacharsky's dramas were criticized by supporters of the Proletkult (P. Kerzhentsev) for lacking agitational and inflammatory character. Collections of his work appeared only in 1912, 1923, and 1963.

Works: Korolevskij bradobrej (play), 1906; Pjat' farsov dlja ljubitelej (play), 1907; Vavilonskaja paločka (play), 1912; Idei v maskakh (play and short stories), 1912, 2d ed., 1924; Faust i gorod (play), 1918; Komedii (comedies), 1919; Magi (play), 1919 (see above); Vasilisa Premudraja (play), 1920 (see above); Ivan v raju (play), 1920; Oliver Kromvel' (play), 1920; Skazanie o tom, kak Ivan-durak umnym stal (play), 1920; Foma Kampanella (trilogy: Narod, 1920; Gercog, 1922; Solnce [fragment]); Kancler i slesar' (play), 1921; Iskušenie (play), 1922; Osvoboždënnyj Don Kikhot (play), 1922; Bomba (play), 1923; Dramatičeskie proizv. (plays), 2 vols., 1923; Medvež'ja svad'ba (play; after Merimée), 1924; Podžigateli (play), 1924; Jad (play), 1926; Barkhat i lokhmot'ja (play; after E. Stucken), 1927; O teatre i dramaturgii, 2 vols., 1958; P'esy (plays), 1963 (contains Korolevskij bradobrej; Faust i gorod; Oliver Kromvel'; Kancler i slesar'; Osvoboždënnyj Don Kikhot; Jad); Neizdannye materialy (articles), in Lit. nasledstvo 82:1970; Stat'i o sovetskoj literature (articles), 2d ed., 1971; Literatura novogo mira (essays), 1982.— Sobr. soč., 8 vols., 1963–67.

Translations: Three Plays of A. V. Lunacharski: Faust and the City, Vasilisa the Wise, The Magi, 1923; The Bear's Wedding, 1926; On Literature and Art, 1965, 2d rev. ed., 1973; Revolutionary Silhouettes, 1968.

Secondary Lit.: V. Brjusov, in Pečat' i revoljucija 1921:1; V. Vol'kenštejn, in Pečat' i revoljucija 1923:5; K. E. Bailes, in Cahiers du monde russe et soviétique 1967:2; A. Lebedev, 2d ed., 1969; M. Čerkezova, in Russkaja lit. 1971:4; A. L. Tait, Diss., Cambridge Univ., 1972; N. Trifonov, 1974; A. V. L.: Ukazatel' trudov, 2 vols., 1975–79 (bibliography); N. Generalova, in Russkaja lit. 1983:1; I. Lunačarskaja, in Novyj mir 1985:1.

**Lunts, Lev Natánovich,** playwright, prose writer (b. May 2 [April 19], 1901, St. Petersburg—d. May 10, 1924, Hamburg). In 1922

Lunts completed his studies in Romance languages and literatures at Petrograd University and was offered a career in scholarship. He was among the founders of the literary group the SERAPION BROTHERS in 1921 and became their leading theoretician, formulating in his essays a creed of the autonomy of art and the freedom of political conviction; he refused to tolerate the misuse of literature for the purposes of propaganda. To Lunts fell the "lion's share in championing the freedom of art on behalf of the Serapions" (Struve). As a close friend of V. Kaverin, Lunts looked toward Western European trends in his reflections on the formal renewal of Russian prose and drama in *Na Zapad* (1923; To the West); above all he demanded aesthetically sophisticated plot development. Lunts published his writings on literary theory, such as *Pochemu my Serapionovy bratya* (1922; Why We Are Serapion Brothers), and his own literary work in various Petrograd journals and in *Beseda*, a journal published in Berlin by M. Gorky, V. Khodasevich, and A. Bely. Suffering in 1923 from malnutrition and exhaustion, Lunts sought medical care in Germany, where his parents had emigrated. He died of a brain embolism. His play *Vne zakona* (1921; Eng. tr., *The Outlaw*, n.d.), already prepared for performance, was forbidden before its opening; nor were his friends able to carry out their plans after his death to publish one volume of his writings (four plays and three short stories) and another of contributions by Ye. Zamyatin, K. Chukovsky, V. Shklovsky, Gorky, and 11 of the Serapion Brothers. Lunts has never been reprinted in the Soviet Union. In 1967 the Writers Union of the USSR appointed a commission for the purpose of reviewing his literary estate.

In 1924 Chukovsky wrote that Zamyatin had considered Lunts the most talented of the Serapion Brothers. Above all, he singled out *Vne zakona* for praise; the drama is about revolutionary events "in an algebraic Spain": in the name of freedom for the people, a stonemason overthrows the ruling duke, only to become a tyrant himself. The tragedy was performed in Berlin, Vienna, and Prague. *Gorod pravdy* (1924; Eng. tr., *The City of Truth*, 1929), blends images of a post-Revolutionary reality with those of an ideal Communist state in the future, reminiscent of Zamyatin's *My* in its inhumanity. The expressionistic imagery of *V pustyne* (1922; In the Desert) shows the people of Israel at the mercy of an obscure and mysterious ruling power; the allegorical parallel to events in Russia after the Revolution readily suggests itself.

*Works: Vne zakona* (tragedy), in *Beseda*, Berlin, 1:1921 (reprinted, Würzburg, 1972 (see above); *Obez'jany idut!* (play), 1921, in *Vesëlyj al'manakh* 1923; *V pustyne* (short story), in *Serapionovy brat'ja*, Berlin, 1922 (reprinted, Munich, 1973); *Iskhodjaščaja No. 37* (short story), in *Rossija* 1922:1; *Počemu my Serapionovy brat'ja* (essays), in *Lit. zapiski* 1922:3; *Nenormal'noe javlenie* (short story), in *Peterburg* 1922:3; *Obol'stitel'. V vagone* (short stories), in *Mukhomor* 1922:9; *Vernaja žena* (short story), in *Mukhomor* 1922:10; *Bertran de Born* (play), in *Gorod* 1923 (Eng. tr., 1970); *Rodina* (pov.), in *Evrejskij al'manakh* 1923; *Na Zapad* (essays), in *Beseda* 2:1923; *Patriot* (short story), in *Krasnyj voron* 1923:33; *Poslednjaja stat'ja* (essay), 1923, in *Novyj žurnal*, New York, 81:1965; *Vosstanie veščej* (film script), 1923, in *Novyj žurnal* 79:1965; *Gorod pravdy* (play), in *Beseda* 5:1924 (see above); *Putešestvie na bol'ničnoj kojke* (short story), 1924, in *Novyj žurnal* 90:1968; correspondence, in *Opyty*, New York, 1:1953; in *Novyj žurnal* 82–83:1966, 97:1969; in *Russian Literature Triquarterly* 15:1978; *Rodina* (pov.), short stories, plays, essays; Jerusalem, 1981; *Zaveščanie carja* (film script), essays, short stories), Munich, 1983.

*Secondary Lit.:* M. Gor'kij, in *Beseda* 5:1924; K. Fedin, in *Zizn' iskusstva* 1924:22; V. Kaverin, in *Novyj mir* 1965:9, pp. 153–54; H. Kern, Diss., Princeton Univ., 1969, and in *Russian Literature Triquarterly* 2:1972; J. Day, in *Die Welt der Slaven* 1972; A. A. Hansen-Löve, in *Wiener Slawistischer Almanach* 1:1978; B. Filippov, in *Russkaja mysl'*, Paris, Dec. 7, 1978, p. 8; W. Schrieck, in *Die Welt der Slaven* 1984:1.

**Lvóv, Arkády Lvóvich**, prose writer (b. March 9, 1927, near Odessa). Lvov's father was both a laborer and a white-collar worker. Lvov grew up in Odessa. Starting in 1943, he studied modern history at Odessa University; after he was expelled in 1946, he continued his studies illegally at Chernovitsy University until 1949; in 1951 he completed his exams in Odessa. Lvov worked as a teacher in the western Ukraine and returned to Odessa in 1968. From 1965 to 1973 his short stories were published in Soviet journals. From 1966 to 1972 Lvov was able to publish six books. Absurd allegations of Zionist activity led to interrogations by the KGB in 1970 and 1973. After endeavoring to emigrate for one and one-half years, he obtained permission in June 1976, and since Oct. 21, 1976, he has lived in New York. Lvov's greatest work, the novel

*Dvor* (1981; The Courtyard), which was written in the Soviet Union from 1968 to 1972, found its first success in French translation (1979). Lvov published the Russian edition more or less simultaneously with the short stories also written in Odessa, *Bolshoye solntse Odessy* (1981; The Large Sun of Odessa), only half of which he had been able to publish in Moscow in 1968. In *Biznesmen iz Odessy* (1981; Businessman from Odessa), he compiled the stories written in the West; in *Utoleniye pechalyu* (1984; Consolation in Mourning), he published six essays about Russian Jewish writers such as I. Babel, E. Bagritsky, M. Svetlov; two similar collections are to follow. Translations of his shorter prose into English have appeared since 1979 in journals such as *Midstream*; a translation of his novel was planned for 1986.

Lvov is an observant writer who realistically recounts the life of a broad segment of the population and consistently rejects any commentary from the narrator's perspective (even through the use of adjectives). In more than 800 pages, *Dvor* depicts the variable, intersecting lives of some simple people in the courtyard of an apartment house in Odessa from 1936 to 1953; only the first half was written with the intention of publishing it in the Soviet Union. Two additional volumes concerning the Khrushchev and the Brezhnev–Andropov periods are planned. Lvov concentrates on people who are severely hampered by the propaganda that permeates information. Conflicts over living space, fear of imprisonment, and dependence on functionaries are typical motifs. Thinking and action are suffocated by mataerial concerns. Lvov's short stories set in Odessa are similar; the theme of the stories collected in *Biznesmen iz Odessy* is the first impressions on émigrés of life in the United States. Here Lvov also emphasizes the reporting of external worldly events or of the physical, in sexual passages, and does not include spiritual, reflective behavior. Lvov is planning to write a novel parallel to *Dvor* in which the point of intersection of people's fates is to be a skyscraper in Manhattan.

*Works: Krakh patenta* (short stories), Odessa, 1966; *Bul'var Celakantus* (pov. and short stories), 1967; *Bol'šoe solnce Odessy* (short stories), 1968, complete ed., Munich, 1981; *Dve smerti Cezare Rossolino* (pov.), Odessa, 1969; *V Odesse leto* (pov. and short stories), 1970; *Skaži sebe, kto ty* (short stories), 1972; *Biznesmen iz Odessy* (short stories), Munich, 1981; *Dvor* (novel), 2 vols., Munich, 1981–82;

*Utolenie pečal'ju* (essays), New York, 1984. *Secondary Lit.:* Ju. Troll', in *Novoe russkoe slovo*, New York, Aug. 7, 1983, p. 5; S. Mydans, in *New York Times* Aug. 23, 1984.

**Lyashkó, Nikoláy Nikoláyevich** (pseud. of N. N. Lyáshchenko), prose writer (b. Nov. 19 [Nov. 7], 1884, Lebedin, prov. Kharkov—d. Aug. 26, 1953, Moscow). Lyashko's father was a soldier; his mother, a peasant. From 1895 on, Lyashko was employed in Kharkov; in 1899 he began working as a novice lathe operator in factories, continuing his studies at the same time. Between 1901 and 1914 Lyashko was involved in politics; he was exiled after 1903 for being a member of the RSDRP (Social Democrats), where he belonged to the Menshevik faction. Lyashko began publishing his fiction in 1905. He was casually associated with PROLETKULT (1918–19) and later joined KUZNITSA (1920), where he was acknowledged by A. Voronsky as Kuznitsa's most gifted prose writer. Lyashko shared M. Gerasimov's and V. Kirillov's disillusionment over the betrayal of revolutionary ideals during NEP; nevertheless, he increasingly adapted himself to the Communist Party line. He joined the Party in 1928. As a writer, Lyashko remained active and popular to the end of the 1920s. A seven-volume edition of his collected works appeared between 1926 and 1928. In the following 25 years, Lyashko published only occasionally. A second, three-volume, edition of his works was published in 1955.

Lyashko won a place in Soviet literature above all with his povest *Domennaya pech* (1925–26; The Blast Furnace), in which he depicts factories standing idle as a result of the Revolution and the attempt to get them working again; he tackled this theme before F. Gladkov and dealt with it in a substantially more matter-of-fact manner. *Zheleznaya tishina* (1921; The Iron Silence), "the best thing that he has ever written" (Voronsky), is in the same vein. In the spirit of the Kuznitsa poets, *Krepnushchiye krylya* (1922; Wings Growing in Strength) relies on the metaphor of iron to represent solitude. In *V razlom* (1924; The Break), he depicts the breaking up of an exiled family as the result of differing political convictions. His ties to his home village can be seen in *S otaroy* (1926; With the Flock). Lyashko is influenced by V. Korolenko; he writes dense prose and is more interested in psychology than in plot development.

*Works: Rasskazy II*, 1922–23; *Železnaja tišina* (short stories), 1922; *Krepnuščie kryl'ja* (short story), 1922; Vorova mat' (short story), 1922; Rasskazy, 1925; S otaroj (pov.), 1927; Skazki, 1930; Kamen' u morja (short stories), 1939; Nikola iz Lebedina (short stories), 1951; Vtoroe roždenie (short stories), 1958—Sobr. soč., 6 vols., 1926–27; Izbr., 1933, 1949, 1950; Soč., 3 vols., 1955.

Secondary Lit.: V. Krasil'nikov, in Novyj mir 1927:4 and 1927:8; A. Voronskij, Lit. portrety, vol. 2, 1929, pp. 150–56, 193–98; M. Serebrjanskij, 1931; L. Eršov, in Voprosy sovetskoj lit. 1958:7; RSPP 2:1964; G. Sannikov, in Oktjabr' 1964:12; V. Čalmaev, in Lit. gazeta Dec. 11, 1974, p. 3; A. Filatov, in Lit. Rossija Nov. 30, 1984, p. 16; A. Vlasenko, in Lit. gazeta Dec. 12, 1984, p. 7.

**Lyubímova, Valentína Aleksándrovna,** playwright (b. Nov. 16 [Nov. 4], 1895, Shchurovo, prov. Ryazan—d. May 26, 1968, Moscow). Lyubimova's father was a priest. She worked as a teacher until 1924. Her first book of children's verse was published in 1926; her first play, Kak babushka Avdotya v kolkhoz zapisalas (How Granny Avdotya Joined the Kolkhoz), was performed in 1930. Lyubimova continued to work in children's theater, writing pieces aimed at political education. Her Seryozha Streltsov (1936) and Snezhok (1948; The Snowball) became quite well known; Snezhok, a piece written in the spirit of the struggle against COSMOPOLITANISM, was awarded a Stalin Prize (1948, 2d class). Because of the very low artistic quality of her plays, Lyubimova, who lived in Moscow, received little attention after 1953 and is not usually mentioned in literary histories. Occasionally her hollow rhetoric and inability to present convincing motivation are cited. The general post-1956 conviction that Stalin Prizes were awarded to inferior works certainly applies in her case.

Works: Serëža Strel'cov (play), 1936; Snežok (play), 1948; P'esy (plays), 1955; P'esy (plays), 1965.

Secondary Lit.: S. Mikhalkov, Novye uspekhi sovetskoj lit., 1949; Anon., in Lit. gazeta No. 17, 1955; Z. Finickaja, in Družba narodov 1960:1; N. Putincev, in Teatral'naja žizn' 1969:4 and in Detskaja lit. 1971;7; M. Priležaeva, in Lit. gazeta Jan. 14, 1976, p. 8.

# M

**Makánin, Vladímir Semyónovich,** prose writer (b. March 13, 1937, Orsk). In 1960 Makanin graduated from Moscow University in mathematics; until the end of the 1960s he worked at the university. Concurrently, he attended the advanced courses for screenwriters and directors at the Film Institute. Makanin made his debut as a writer with the novel Pryamaya liniya (1965; The Straight Line), which appeared in the journal Moskva. The povest Bezottsovshchina (1971; Fatherlessness) was published in the same journal a while later. Both received a friendly reception from the critics. Since then, Makanin has published a new book almost every year, usually collections combining older and newer prose and including brief short stories. Soviet critics were especially divided in their view of the povest Predtecha (1982; The Precursor), published in the journal Sever, since Makanin's own attitude toward the difficult issue of natural healing remains unclear. As of 1985, Makanin had not yet been mentioned in Soviet histories of literature; he lives in Moscow.

Between 1967 and 1985, Makanin published 12 books through which he reveals his development into one of the noteworthy Russian prose writers in the USSR. Makanin's primary interest is the city dweller—at work, at home, and with his friends. As characters he prefers average people, never especially positive figures in an ethical sense, and depicts them in the critical, occasionally somewhat climactic, situations of daily life. L. Anninsky calls him a "born realist." Of chief importance for Makanin is the psychological exploration of his characters in their conflicts with themselves and their surroundings. His interest in and talent for constructing a plot are weak. In Pryamaya liniya he contrasts a materially oriented secondary-school graduate with a character who recognizes the value of ethical, spiritual dimensions. Using the example of the fate of a former "homeless waif" (bezprizorny), Bezottsovshchina reveals the enduring appreciation of goodness in life gained through the experience of a childhood filled with love. Starye knigi (1976; Old Books), a tensely structured povest, provides some insight into the Soviet black market for books, together with the development of a young girl's interpersonal relations. Portret i vokrug

(1978; A Portrait and Its Surroundings), a novel set in the film world, examines the issue of the portraitist's unconscious self-representation while depicting literary portraits. *Predtecha*, Makanin's povest the title of which is reminiscent of the Russian name for John the Baptist, concerns the serious spiritual and medical aspects of a therapy that is based on medicinal herbs and other natural powers and that is rooted in traditional culture, without ignoring the occasional ludicrous aspects of this topic.

*Works: Prjamaja linija* (novel), 1967; *Bezotcovščina, Soldat i soldatka* (pov.), 1971; *Povest' o Starom Posëlke* (pov. and short stories), 1974; *Na pervom dykhanii* (novel), 1976; *Starye knigi* (pov. and short stories), 1976; *Portret i vokrug* (novel), 1978; *Ključarëv i Alimuškin* (novel and short stories), 1979; *V bol'šom gorode* (pov.), 1980; *Na zimnej doroge* (pov., short stories, novel), 1980; *Golosa* (pov. and short stories), 1982; *Predteča* (pov.), 1983; *Reka s bystrym tečeniem* (pov. and short stories), 1983; *Gde skhodilos' nebo s kholmami* (pov.), 1984.

*Secondary Lit.:* I. Štokman, in *Lit. obozrenie* 1975:9; V. Kardin, in *Družba narodov* 1976:1; L. Anninskij, in *Lit. gazeta* Nov. 22, 1978, and in *Znamja* 1986:12; N. Podzorova, in *Lit. Rossija* Oct. 5, 1979, p. 15; V. Mordvinova, in *Oktjabr'* 1980:6; B. Pankin, in *Družba narodov* 1982:9; A. Kazincev and A. Latynina, in *Lit. obozrenie* 1983;10; A. Bočarov, in *Družba narodov* 1984:1; A. Lanščikov and V. Skuratovskij, in *Lit. gazeta* June 6, 1984, p. 5; I. Rodnjanskaja, in *Novyj mir* 1986:8.

**Makárenko, Antón Semyónovich,** pedagogue and prose writer (b. March 13 [March 1], 1888, Belopolye, prov. Kharkov—d. April 1, 1939, Moscow). Makarenko's father was a railway mechanic. Makarenko finished school in Kremenchuk and attended a one-year teachers college. He began work as a teacher in 1905. From 1914 to 1917 he studied at the Poltava Pedagogical Institute. After the Revolution, Makarenko initially worked as a school principal in Poltava; after 1920 he devoted himself to the education of juvenile delinquents. He built and directed a reform school (the Gorky Colony) near Poltava between 1920 and 1928 and the Dzerzhinsky Commune between 1927 and 1935. In 1925 he began writing his memoirs, and in 1937 he moved to Moscow and applied himself exclusively to writing literary and theoretical works.

Makarenko's major work, *Pedagogiches-* *kaya poema* (1925–35; A Pedagogical Poem; Eng. trs., *The Road to Life,* 1936, 1951), describes in autobiographical form the years of work that went into the enrollment of the many "homeless waifs" *(besprizornye).* Initially attacked for its "barrack-yard pedagogy," Makarenko's work, together with his principle of educating the child in a collective for the collective, has been considered a standard work for the training of Communist teachers since the establishment of an authoritarian system under Stalin. In *Flagi na bashnyakh* (1938; Flags on the Towers; Eng. tr., *Learning to Live,* 1953), based on his experience at the Dzerzhinsky Commune, Makarenko abandons the first-person form and submits more to the officially required principles of idealization and schematization in Communist education.

*Works: Pedagogičeskaja poèma* (novel), 1934–36 (see above); *Kniga dlja roditelej* (pedagogical theory), 1937 (Eng. tr., *A Book for Parents,* 1954; reprinted as *The Collective Family: A Handbook for Russian Parents,* 1967, 1973); *Flagi na bašnjakh* (pov.), 1939 (see above). —*Sobr. soč.,* 7 vols., 1950–52; 7 vols., 1957–58; 5 vols., 1971.

*Translations:* in German and Russian: *Gesammelte Werke: Marburger Ausgabe,* vols. 1– 5, 7, 9, 1976–82 (with detailed commentaries).

*Secondary Lit.:* N. A. Morozova, 2d ed., 1961; L. Adolphs, Bad Godesberg, 1962; G. Hillig and I. Rauch (bibliography), Wiesbaden, 1963; *RSPP* 3:1964; I. Rüttenauer, Freiburg, 1965.

**Makárov, Iván Ivánovich,** prose writer (b. Oct. 30 [Oct. 17], 1900, Saltyki, prov. Ryazan—d. 1940 [?], while imprisoned). Makarov was of peasant background; his father was a shoemaker. In 1919 Makarov completed his studies at a gymnasium in Ryazan, where he resided permanently from 1928 on. In 1920 he wrote an agitational play that was staged in the villages; that same year he became a member of the Communist Party. After writing several short stories, Makarov achieved recognition in 1929 for his novel *Stalnye ryobra* (Steel Ribs); the title symbolizes the electric power stations in the countryside. The objection was made that in his novel Makarov had elevated a hard-nosed, radical Party leader (who was attempting to carry out reforms in village life) too far above the masses. His short story *Ostrov* (1930; The Island), about an independent old farmer who seeks a way out

# MAKÓVSKY

through suicide, earned Makarov the abusive label "friend of the kulak." His later prose, such as the povest set in the Civil War period, *Reyd Chornogo Zhuka* (1931; The Raid of the Black Beetle), and *Na zemle mir* (1930; Peace on Earth), a first-person narrative told by a prison guard, was criticized for the psychological methods Makarov employed. In its presentation of the construction of an industrial complex in the Urals over the objections of both the urban and the rural population, Makarov's Five-Year Plan novel, *Misha Kurbatov* (1936), deviated so far from the official Party position that Makarov was branded a dangerous enemy of the people. He was arrested and liquidated; his name was no longer mentioned in literary studies. A commission (chaired by A. Perventsev; *Lit. gazeta* Sept. 8, 1956) was formed to review his literary estate; it recommended Makarov's REHABILITATION. Since 1957 several of his works have once again appeared in print.

*Works: Stal'nye rëbra* (novel), 1930, 1964; *Ostrov* (short story), in *Novyj mir* 1930:1; *Na zemle mir* (short story), 1931; *Rejd Černogo Žuka* (pov.), 1932, 1966; *Miša Kurbatov* (novel), 1936; *Černaja šal'* (novel), in *Oktjabr'* 1933:5–7, 2d ed., 1970.

*Secondary Lit.:* A. Glagolev, in *Novyj mir* 1930:3; V. Aleksandrova (1937), in her *Lit. i žizn'*, 1969, and in *Ost-Probleme* (1952:47; I. Kozlov, in *Moskva* 1959:6; *RSPP* 7(1):1971.

**Makóvsky, Sergéy Konstantínovich,** poet, art historian, publisher (b. Aug. 27 [Aug. 15], 1877, St. Petersburg—d. May 13, 1962, Paris). Makovsky's father, Konstantin Yegorovich (1839–1915), was a famous painter. Makovsky, however, only lived with him until 1893. Makovsky began his extensive published career as an art historian in 1898; his first book in the literary field was *Sobraniye stikhov* (1905; Collected Poems). Until he emigrated through the Crimea (around 1920), he was an important promoter and organizer in the fields of fine arts and literature. From 1908 to 1914 he organized world-famous expositions (or accompanied the Russian section at expositions abroad) in St. Petersburg, Brussels, Paris, and Leipzig; published his scientific essays on art in the three-volume work *Stranitsy khudozhestvennoy kritiki* (1906–13; Pages of Art Criticism); was cofounder and editor of the journals *Starye gody* (1907–17) and *Russkaya ikona* (1913); and made a lasting name for himself as founder and editor of a journal that united modern literature and art, *Apollon*

(1909–17). In emigration, at first in Prague and then in Paris, he continued this career. Four books about Russian art appeared between 1921 and 1925 in Berlin and Prague; from 1926 to 1932 he was a member of the editorial staff of the newspaper *Vozrozhdeniye*. From 1939 to 1944 he was an active board member of Obyedineniye russkikh pisateley (Union of Russian Writers) in Paris; between 1949 and 1959 he edited numerous volumes of poetry for the Parisian publisher Rifma. Starting in 1921, Makovsky began publishing poems regularly in various journals of the EMIGRATION; only after two decades did he return to publishing in book form with *Vecher* (1941; Evening). He included a large portion of these poems in their revised form in his second volume after *Vecher*, *God v usadbe* (1949; A Year on the Country Estate). *Requiem*, his ninth and last volume of poetry, which he prepared himself, was published in 1963 after his death. Makovsky's essays are important for the history of Russian literature. After first publishing some of them in journals, Makovsky collected these essays in the volume *Portrety sovremennikov* (1955; Portraits of Contemporaries—these included V. Ivanov, M. Voloshin, and N. Gumilyov) and in *Na Parnase "Serebryanogo veka"* (1962; On the Parnassus of the Silver Age).

Makovsky's poems reflect more than his profound knowledge of the essence of poetry and art; increasingly over the course of the years they became a linguistic avowal of the sacred origin of being. Nature is experienced in her beauty and her immediacy to creation; the word guided by reason is questioned as a valid form of expression. Poems describing Italian art in *Na puti zemnom* (1953; On Earthly Paths) become reflections on mankind and the world. Man is depicted as an eternal mystery. The form of his poems, which were praised by Yu. Terapiano, is conservative and clear, less narrative than confessional and reflective.

*Works:* (In the field of literature): *Sobranie stikhov* (poems), 1905; *Večer* (poems), Paris, 1941; *Somnium breve* (poems), Paris, 1948; *God v usad'be* (poems), Paris, 1949; *Krug i teni* (poems), Paris, 1951; *Na puti zemnom* (poems), Paris, 1953; *Portrety sovremennikov* (*essays*), New York, 1955; *V lesu* (poems), Munich, 1956; *Eščë stranica* (poems), Paris, 1957; *Na Parnase "Serebrjanogo veka"* (essays), Munich, 1962; *Requiem* (poems), Paris, 1963.

(In the field of literary scholarship): *Stranicy khudožestvennoj kritiki*, 3 vols., 1906–13; V. A. Serov, 1915; *Siluèty russkikh khu-*

*dožnikov*, Prague, 1922; *Poslednie itogi živopisi*, Berlin, 1922; *Grafica M. V. Dobužinskogo*, Berlin, 1922; *Narodnoe iskusstvo Podkarpatskoj Rusi*, Prague, 1922 (also in Czech and English, *Peasant Art in Subcarpathian Russia*, 1926).
*Secondary Lit.*: A. Nejmirok, in *Grani*, Frankfurt am Main, 12:1951 and 30:1956; Ju. Ivask, in *Novyj žurnal*, New York, 25:1951 and 35:1953 and in *Opyty*, New York, 9:1958; I. Činnov, in *Opyty* 1:1953; Ju. Terapiano, in *Opyty* 2:1953 and in *Sovremennik*, Toronto, 6:1962 and 7:1963; D. Klenovskij, in *Opyty* 5:1955; V. Zlobin, in *Vozroždenie*, Paris, 79:1958; Ju. Annenkov, in *Vozroždenie* 126:1962; K. Pomerancev, in *Mosty*, Munich, 9:1962; G. Mejer, in *Grani* 54:1963 and *Vozroždenie* 139:1963.

**Maksímov, Sergéy Sergéyevich**, prose writer, playwright (b. July 14 [July 1], 1916, Chernopenye on the Volga—d. March 11, 1967, Los Angeles). Maksimov's father was a village schoolteacher. Maksimov grew up in Moscow after 1923. As a 15-year-old, he was already publishing short pieces in Soviet journals such as *Murzylka* and *Smena;* in 1934 he was accepted into the Gorky Literary Institute. In 1936 he was sentenced to five years in a concentration camp. In 1941 he was exiled to the provinces and came to Smolensk, which was occupied by the Germans. There he was able to publish a volume of poetry and the povest *Sumerki* (Twilight) under the pseudonym of Sergey Shirokov. After being imprisoned by the Gestapo for six months, Maksimov came to Berlin in 1943 wshere he worked for "Vineta" (Eastern Section of the Ministry of Propaganda) and for the established émigré newspaper *Novoye slovo* (ed. by V. M. Despotuli). The stock of *Aly sneg* (The Red Snow), a volume of his works printed in Leipzig, was destroyed by bombs after its printing. By the end of World War II, Maksimov was living in Hamburg and was able to escape forced repatriation. He then moved to Camberg/Taunus and from there became a member of the editorial staff of the journal *Grani* in 1946. Maksimov wrote the novel *Denis Bushuyev* (1949; Denis Bushuyev; Eng. tr., *The Restless Heart*, 1951), the publication of which was considered a significant literary event not only in émigré circles but also—through translations into German (1949), English (1951), and Spanish—among a larger reading public. In June 1949 Maksimov moved to the United States where he was able to publish *Tayga* (1952; The Taiga), 16 short stories written during the war about his experiences in the camps. In *Goluboye molchaniye* (1953; The Blue Silence), Maksimov collected short stories, poems, and plays. He ended his publishing activity with *Bunt Denisa Bushuyeva* (1956; Denis Bushuyeva's Rebellion), which was written between 1953 and 1956 and formed the second and concluding volume of his novel. In the United States, where he lived in California, he did not find another profession.

Maksimov is one of the most talented writers of the second EMIGRATION. In his short stories he portrays the fates of individuals who become victims of oppression in Soviet concentration camps in a tense and gripping style. These stories earned the same respect that was later paid to V. Shalamov's short stories about camp life. *Denis Bushuyev* takes the form of a novel about a family set in the Stalin period; here Maksimov depicts both the interpersonal problems of his characters' private lives as well as the threats to and, in the end, the destruction of private life through the power of the state and its camps. In comparison to the first volume, the second volume is markedly less well executed. Maksimov has the ability to present people's unusual fates vividly in isolated episodes and in broad strokes. *Semya Shirokovykh* (The Shirokovykh Family) shows him to be a talented playwright. This play depicts the destruction of the family of a Soviet general as a consequence of the Soviet system; the trial of the general and of his future son-in-law on fabricated charges of spying forms the focal point of the plot. With *V restorane* (In a Restaurant), Maksimov wrote a very good one-act play with a surprising ending that takes an ironic look at the position of émigrés.

*Works: Denis Bušuev* (novel), Limburg, 1949, 2d ed., 1974 (see above); *Tajga* (short stories), New York, 1952; *Goluboe molčanie* (short stories, poems, plays), New York, 1953 (also contains the plays *V restorane* and *Sem'ja Širokovykh*); *Bunt Denisa Bušueva* (novel), New York, 1956.
*Secondary Lit.*: P. Stepanova, in *Vozroždenie*, Paris, 11:1950; I. Saburova, in *Lit. sovremennik*, Munich, 4:1952; V. Zavališin, in *Novyj žurnal*, New York, 30:1952; M. Korjakov, in *Novyj žurnal* 45:1956,; V. Rudinskij, in *Vozroždenie* 61:1957; V. Samarin, in *Vozroždenie* 207:1969.

**Maksímov, Vladímir Yemelyánovich** (pseud. of Lev Alekséyevich Samsónov), prose writer (b. Nov. 27, 1930, Moscow). Maksimov comes from a peasant family; his father was a worker who was in custody after 1933. From 1945 to 1950 Maksimov lived in children's homes and institutions for young criminals. For several years Maksimov worked in various regions of the Soviet Union on kolkhozes and construction projects. He initiated his work as a writer in 1952 by writing poems for a provincial newspaper in the Kuban region. In 1954 his first volume of poetry was destroyed at the direction of the Communist Party after it had already been set into type. His second volume, *Pokoleniye na chasakh* (1956; A Generation on Guard), found little recognition. Maksimov moved to Moscow, struggled along working at odd literary jobs until K. Paustovsky included his povest *My obzhivayem zemlyu* (1961; We Make the Earth Inhabitable) in his liberal anthology *Tarusskiye stranitsy*. *Zhiv chelovek* (1962; Eng. tr., *A Man Survives*, 1963), which appeared in the journal *Oktyabr* and was also adapted as a drama and successfully performed in 1965, won even greater recognition. After becoming a member of the Writers Union in 1963, Maksimov published a play (1964) and short stories in *Oktyabr* (1964, 1967), and belonged to the editorial staff of that journal from October 1967 to August 1968. Maksimov's first novel, *Sem dney tvoreniya* (1971; Eng. tr., *The Seven Days of Creation*, 1975), could not be published in the Soviet Union because of its unsparing exposition of Soviet reality and its profession of Christianity. After the publication of his works in the West in Russian and in translation had led to greater acclaim and his second novel, *Karantin* (1973; The Quarantine), had also circulated in SAMIZDAT, Maksimov was expelled from the Writers Union on June 26, 1973. Owing to the attention of the world public, Maksimov was allowed to emigrate at the end of February 1974, after having twice been forced to submit to treatment in a psychiatric institution. Maksimov lives in Paris; he is the editor in chief of the journal *Kontinent* and plays a highly regarded cultural-political role within the third emigration. In Paris he has written several additional novels.

Maksimov's early prose works published and recognized in the Soviet Union trace the destinies of people broken by fate; for example, in *Zhiv chelovek* he follows a youth who responds to society's ostracism after his father's arrest by becoming a thief and growing even more alienated, and in *Iskusheniye* (1964; The Temptation) he traces the fate of a war invalid deserted by his wife who flees into a cloister to escape from his shattered world. *Sem dney tvoreniya* is "the most radical re-jection of the Revolution that has been available in Russian since Stalin's death . . . a kind of sacred, anti-ideological epic" (von Ssachno). Through the initial enthusiasm and persistent disappointment of individual members of a worker's family during the 50-year period of the Soviet system, Maksimov depicts the neglected and deceived proletariat. The hope of a renewal through Christianity forms the conclusion here as it does in *Karantin*, although in the latter it appears out of the blue, for Maksimov primarily depicts people involves in drunken bouts, sex, cruelty, and violence. *Saga o Savve* (1975; The Ballad about Savva), the tale of an escaped prisoner in Russia, was published in parts in the Soviet Union. In *Proshchaniye iz niotkuda* (1973, 1982; Eng. tr., *Farewell from Nowhere*, 1979), Maksimov provides a poetic autobiography whose first part comprises childhood and youth and whose second, written entirely in emigration, also includes sketches about literary life in the Soviet Union and comes to terms with his own past. *Kovcheg dlya nezvanykh* (1976; An Ark for the Uninvited) takes place in the Soviet Far East at the end of World War II. Maksimov, who is to a certain extent influenced by F. Dostoyevsky, writes in a hard, unbalanced style. The scene of action, the time, and the perspective change frequently, and this universality lends Maksimov's prose the quality of being epically all-embracing. His persuasive power derives from the force of an elemental, scarcely refined talent for giving verbal expression to the painful experience of reality of the lower stratum of Soviet society and from his highly ethical, patriotic awareness of responsibility. Maksimov's novel *Zaglyanut v bezdnu* (1986; Staring into the Abyss), following the fate of Admiral Kolchak by blending history, politics with personal affairs, and Kolchak's love story, asks the question why the White Army failed.

*Works: Pokolenie na časakh* (poems), 1956; *My obživaem zemlju* (pov.), in *Tarusskie stranicy*, 1961; *Pozyvnye tvoikh parallelej* (play), in *Oktjabr'* 1964:2; *Živ čelovek* (pov.), 1964 (see above); *Iskušenie* (short story), in *Oktjabr'* 1964:9; *Šagi k gorizontu* (short stories), in *Oktjabr'* 1964:9; *Stan' za čertu* (pov.), in *Oktjabr'* 1967:2; *Sem' denej tvorenija* (novel), Frankfurt am Main, 1971 (see above); *Karantin* (novel), Frankfurt am Main, 1973; *Proščanie iz niotkuda* (autobiographical pov.), Frankfurt am Main, 1974, 2 vols., 1982 (vol. 1: *Pamjatnoe vino grekha*; vol. 2: *Čaša jarosti*) (see above); *Stan' za čertu* (play), in *Novyj žurnal*, New York, 116–17:1974; *Saga o Savve* (novel), Frankfurt am Main, 1975; *Kovčeg dlja nezvanykh* (novel), Frankfurt am Main, 1979; *Živ čelovek* (play), Frankfurt am Main, 1979; *Saga o nosorogakh* (essay), Frankfurt am Main, 1981; *Zagljanut' v bezdnu*, Paris, 1986.—*Sobr. soč.*, 6 vols., Frankfurt am Main, 1973–79.

Secondary Lit.: F. Levin, in *Lit. gazeta* Dec. 1, 1962; A. Berzer, in *Novyj mir* 1963:4; L. Anninskij, in *Teatr* 1965:10; H. v. Ssachno, in *Die Zeit* Dec. 1, 1972; L. Rževskij, in *Novyj žurnal* 119:1975; V. Iverni, in *Vestnik RKhD* 126:1978 and in *Grani*, Frankfurt am Main, 116:1980; G. Hosking, in his *Beyond Socialist Realism*, New York, 1980; *V literaturnom zerkale. O tvorčestve V. M.*, Paris–New York, 1986.

**Maláshkin, Sergéy Ivánovich**, prose writer (b. July 16 [July 4], 1888, Khomyakovo, prov. Tula). Malashkin's father was a peasant. Malashkin worked from the time he was 13; he was employed as an unskilled factory hand in Moscow (from 1904 on) and in many other parts of Russia (1908–14). From 1906 to 1915 he was a member of the RSDRP (Social Democrats), becoming a Communist Party member in 1917. Malashkin began writing poetry in 1916; his volume of poems *Muskuly* (1918; Muscles) was published after the Revolution. His position in literature, however, is based on his prose. Malashkin's povest *Luna s pravoy storony* (1926; The Moon from the Right), in its depiction of a Komsomol group in which 22 men share one woman, reflect the contemporary disintegration of moral values and the alienation of a privileged Party leadership class from the people at large and from the ideals of the Revolution; this much-printed and often-translated book evoked sharp criticism. In imitation of F. Dostoyevsky's *The Double*, Malashkin's *Bolnoy chelovek* (1927; The Sick Man) describes the process by which a commissar becomes conscious of the inhumanity and injustice of the wholesale executions carried out during the Revolution. Malashkin, who belonged to the PEREVAL group, remained active in literature until 1931. He participated in the First Congress of the Writers Union of the USSR, then vanished from literature for more than 20 years; he was probably expelled temporarily from the Party. After 1956 he published several little-noted novels, among them *Devushki* (1956; The Girls), about World War II, *Krylom po zemle* (1963; Winging over the Earth), which deals with the orthodox theme of postwar reconstruction, and *Gorod na kholmakh* (1973; The City on the Hills),

about the life of industrial workers during the years of revolution. Malashkin lives in Moscow; he holds no official posts and does not participate in the Writers Union congresses; in 1969, however, his name appeared among the signers of an accusation charging *Novy mir* with assuming a too liberal editorial policy (*Ogonyok* 1969:30).

Works: *Muskuly* (poems), 1918; *Luna s pravoj storony* (pov.), 1927; *Bol'noj čelovek* (pov.), 1928; *Zapiski Ananija Žmurkina* (novel), 1928, 2 vols., 1968–69; *Pokhod kolonn* (novel), 1931; *Devuški* (novel), 1956, 1972; *Krylom po zemle* (novel), 1963; *Strada na poljakh Moskovii* (novel), 1972; *Gorod na kholmakh* (novel), 1973.

Secondary Lit.: V. Poljanskij, in *Pečat' i revoljucija* 1927:2; M. Genina, in *Znamja* 1964:6; A. Elkin, in *Lit. gazeta* Feb. 19, 1975, p. 5; O. Mikhajlov, in *Lit. Rossija* July 14, 1978, p. 10.

**Máltsev, Elizár Yúryevich** (pseud. of E. Yu. Pupkó), prose writer (b. Jan. 4, 1917 [Dec. 22, 1916] Khonkholoy, Transbaikal). Maltsev was of peasant descent. In 1938–39 he studied at the Moscow Institute of Library Science; from 1939 to 1944 he studied by correspondence at the Gorky Literary Institute. Maltsev spent World War II in the hinterlands; his jobs included being a radio reporter in the Altai region. His first novel, *Goryachiye klyuchi* (1945; Hot Springs), about kolkhoz work in the Altai during the war, was recognized as artistically inadequate. Struve called his next thematically similar novel, *Ot vsego serdtsa* (1948; Eng. tr., *Heart and Soul*, 1953), one of the "typical examples of SOCIALIST REALISM in its worst forms" (Stalin Prize for 1948, 2d class). After 1953 Maltsev was exposed for his application of the THEORY OF CONFLICTLESSNESS, his concealment of genuine problems, and his "varnishing of reality." He became a member of the Communist Party in 1949. In *Voydi v kazhdy dom* (1960; Enter Every House) Maltsev presents in novel form the effects of the 1953 Party resolution on agriculture. He lives in Moscow. In 1967 Maltsev wrote a second part to *Voydi v kazhdy dom*.

Maltsev's prose of the Stalin period is characterized by superfluous information, fatuous adjectives, psychologically false and artificially folksy dialogue, a lack of compositional connection between parts, reduction to cheap black-and-white terms, and didacticism. *Voydi v kazhdy dom* corresponds to the liberal position of the THAW and is inspired by genuine concern for the fate of the Russian village. *Posledneye svidaniye* (1978; The Last Encounter) is a rather trivial detective story set in a Soviet village.

Works: *Gorjačie ključi* (novel), 1947 (under the title *Zerna v raspakhannom nebe*, 1981); *Ot vsego serdca* (novel), 1949 (see above); *Vojdi v každyj dom* (novel), 1961; *Poslednee svidanie* (pov.), in *Sever* 1978:2–3, separate ed., 1981.—*Izbr. proizv.*, 2 vols., 1972; *Sobr. soč.*, 3 vols., 1985–86.

Secondary Lit.: A. Drozdov. in *Novyj mir* 1946:12; A. Gaev, in *Lit. sovremennik*, Munich, 1951:2; Ju. Burtin, in *Novyj mir* 1962:1; *RSPP* 3:1964; V. Kardin, in *Družba narodov* 1980:5.

**Máltsev, Orést Mikháylovich,** prose writer (b. March 8 [Feb. 23], 1906, Skorodnoye, prov. Kursk—d. May 26, 1972, Moscow). Maltsev completed his studies at the Bryusov Institute of Literature and Art in 1933. He became a member of the Communist Party in 1944. Maltsev began his literary career with *Gory tronulis* (1929; The Mountains Moved), a novel about the suppression of the struggle for autonomy in Central Asia between 1921 and 1924; he rewrote the work in 1962. His novel *Yugoslavskaya tragediya* (1951; A Yugoslavian Tragedy), set in 1943–44, is a literarily weak transposition of the Party policies of the time, branding Tito as a traitor. Maltsev attempts to lend support to the accuracy of his depiction, which received a Stalin Prize (for 1951, 2d class) but was later reviled, by presenting it as a purported diary. A further war book, *Pokhod za Dunay* (1960; Campaign beyond the Danube), depicts the Germans as cowardly, disorganized, and stupid, thereby disparaging the achievements of the Soviet Army. Despite his constant efforts on behalf of the principle of PARTY SPIRIT, Maltsev, who lived in Moscow, was very little regarded.

Works: *Gory tronulis'* (novel), 1929, rev. ed. entitled *Gissarskij khrebet*, 1962; *Jugoslavskaja tragedija* (novel), 1951; *Rasskazy o pisateljakh Azii i Afriki* (short stories), 1960; *Pokhod za Dunaj* (novel), 1960; *Bliki na more* (novel), 1967; *Ljudi odnogo kolkhoza* (pov.), 1972.

Secondary Lit.: A. Jugov, in *Lit. gazeta* Feb. 9, 1952; P. Savin, in *Lit. Azerbajdžan* 1961:3; G. Radov, in *Lit. gazeta* Aug. 19, 1970, p. 6.

**Malýshkin, Aleksándr Geórgiyevich,** prose writer (b. March 21 [March 9], 1892, Bogorod-

skoe, prov. Penza—d. Aug. 3, 1938, Moscow). Malyshkin's father, though a peasant, made it possible for his son to attend a gymnasium in Mokshansk. In 1916 Malyshkin completed his philological studies at Petrograd University; he subsequently served with the Black Sea fleet. During the Civil War he participated in the battle for the Crimea on the side of the Bolsheviks. Malyshkin began writing short stories in 1912 while still a student. His povest *Padeniye Daira* (1923; The Fall of Dair) attracted a great deal of attention; the povest presents in abstract form the conquest of the Perekop isthmus in the Crimea and the suppression of the last center of anti-Bolshevik resistance. Wishing to raise the masses to the level of sole effectual historical factor, Malyshkin dispensed with individual characters. Written under B. Pilnyak's influence, the work is an expressive and poetic attempt to show the nameless masses, acting spontaneously, as heroic. After writing a few short stories, Malyshkin published *Sevastopol* (1929–30), a povest about the emotional perplexities of a sailor who, between February and December 1917, gradually opts for the Revolution. Malyshkin, who had briefly belonged to the writers' group PEREVAL, was severely attacked by RAPP officials (primarily A. Fadeyev) because of *Sevastopol*. From 1929 until his death Malyshkin belonged to the editorial board of *Novy mir*; from 1934 on, he served on the board of the Writers Union. In his novel *Lyudi iz zakholustya* (1937–38; People from the Backcountry), only half-completed at the time of his early death, Malyshkin treats the officially promoted theme of the first Five-Year Plan and reeducation; he consciously focused his attention, however, not on machines and manufacturing plants but on people. "He had been given a writer's vision and that inner scrupulousness that determines true talent" (Lidin).

Works: *Padenie Daira* (pov.), 1926; *Fevral'-skij sneg* (short stories), 1928; *Sevastopol* (pov.), 1931; *Ljudi iz zakholust'ja* (novel), 1938.—*Sobr. soč.*, 3 vols., 1940–47; *Soč.*, 2 vols., 1956, 1965; *Izbr. proizv.*, 2 vols., 1978.

Secondary Lit.: B. Guber, in *Novyj mir* 1926:4; K. Paustovskij (1938), in his *Sobr. soč.*, vol. 8, 1970; V. Lidin, in his *Ljudi i vstreči*, 1957; A. Khvatov, 1959, and in *Lit. učěba* 1981:6; *RSPP* 3:1964; I. Kramov, 1965, and in *Novy mir* 1967:11.

**Malyúgin, Leoníd Antónovich,** playwright (b. March 4 [Feb. 19], 1909, St. Petersburg—d. Jan. 20, 1968, Moscow). Malyugin completed a library course at a vocational school in Leningrad and in 1931 graduated from the Institute of Theater and Music. In 1943 he was put in charge of organizing a drama studio at the Leningrad Bolshoy Theater. For this studio he wrote his first drama, Starye druzya (1945; Old Friends), which, after some initial difficulties, was frequently performed and which received a Stalin Prize (1945, 2d class). Within the context of the subsequent Party campaign against COSMOPOLITANISM, Malyugin (like A. Borshchagovsky and others) was attacked as an "unpatriotic critic" and a "slanderer." His kolkhoz drama Rodnye mesta (1950; Familiar Places) suffered from its conformity to the new official THEORY OF CONFLICTLESSNESS. At first Malyugin had problems staging the plays he wrote afterward: Novye igrushki (1954; New Toys), Puteshestvie v blizhniye strany (1956; Journey to Nearby Lands), and Devochki—malchiki (1959; Girls and Boys). A result of his enduring interest in and work on Anton Chekhov is the play Nasmeshlivoye moyo schastye (1966; My Mocking Fortune), which is composed exclusively of original statements made by Chekhov and his contemporaries between 1884 and 1904, particularly the correspondence with his brothers and sisters and with Maksim Gorky. His last play, Zhizn Sent Ekzyuperi (1966; The Life of Saint-Exupéry), was frequently performed. Malyugin, who lived in Moscow from 1947 on and who taught at the Institute for Theater Arts until 1948, was never a delegate to a congress of the Writers Union. He is hardly ever mentioned in Soviet literary histories.

Malyugin is not a particularly gifted dramatist; nevertheless, his Starye druzya belongs to the group of frequently performed postwar plays and was staged again in 1969 and 1970 (198 performances in 1970). His plays feature the younger generation of his own time or are devoted to writers. Still, Malyugin was not always successful in completely realizing his ideas. His theoretical articles, several of which he brought together in Teatr nachinayetsya s literatury (1967; Theater Begins with Literature), reveal broad knowledge, a sense of responsibility, and good judgment.

Works: Starye druz'ja (play), 1946; Khmelëv (biography), 1948; Putešestvie v bližnie strany (play), Teatr 1956:11; Novye igruški. Putešestvie v bližnie strany (plays), 1957; Devočki—mal'čiki (play), in Teatr 1959:11; Starye druzja (dramatic selections), 1961; Putešestvie na kraj sveta, in Zvezda 1966:6–7; Nasmešlivoe moë sčast'e, in Don 1966:7; Teatr načinaetsja s literatury (critical essays), 1967;

Sjuzet dlja nebol'šogo rasskaza (film script), in Iskusstvo kino 1967:12; Žizn' Sent Ekzjuperi (play), in Don 1968:7; Čekhov, povest'-khronika, in Don 1969:1–3.

Secondary Lit.: M. Stroeva, in Teatr 1966:4; S. Cimbal, in Teatr 1968:5; I. Ganelina, in Teatr 1968:6; Ju. Vinogradov, in Teatr 1969:11; E. Surkov, in Iskusstvo kino 1970:1; L. Levin, in Lit. gazeta May 16, 1979, p. 8.

**Mamléyev, Yúry Vitályevich,** prose writer (b. Dec. 11, 1931, Moscow). Mamleyev's father was a professor of psychiatry. As early as his graduation from secondary school, Mamleyev clearly understood that, in the Soviet Union, a life dedicated to truth could not be combined with one's public activity. For this reason, he studied at the Technical Institute for Forestry (graduated in 1955) and taught mathematics at schools for workers' children (until 1974). He lived his true life underground. After 1953 he occupied himself with Indian philosophy, theosophy, esoteric and occult writings, and wrote his own prose based on these spiritual teachings. After 1958, his room in Moscow became the center for like-minded writers and artists. At the same time, an occult SAMIZDAT came into being in the Soviet Union. Between 1953 and 1973, Mamleyev wrote approximately 100 short stories that he knew could not be published in the Soviet Union, although they were unpolitical and not socially critical in content. Texts and tapes of his readings circulated through samizdat. After approximately 20 years of underground activity, Mamleyev applied to emigrate and decided to try to publish his works in the West. In the summer of 1974 he received permission to emigrate; until 1983 he lived in the United States, since then in Paris. Mamleyev was first introduced to the public in 1976 through the journals Novy zhurnal and Tretya volna; then several of his short stories were included in M. Shemyakin's anthology Apollon '77. Publications in the journals Gnosis and Ekho followed. The publication in the United States of a work bearing the title of one of his short stories, The Sky above Hell (1980; Nebo nad adom), led to his admission into the PEN Club. With Iznanka Gogena (1982; Gauguin's Other Side), Mamleyev combined nine of his short stories into his first collection in Russian.

The spiritual principle underlying Mamleyev's entire literary work is the conviction that earthly life is but a single phase of the frequent reincarnation of a noncorporeal being and that death signifies the liberation of the immortal "I" from the body. However, Mam-

MANDELSHTÁM **238**

leyev does not portray the man of faith, who by virtue of this knowledge is able to create a more secure and freer life for himself. On the contrary, he depicts people enmeshed in the grip of satanic powers, who murder, torture, assault, and are consumed by material and sexual desires. The central theme of his novel written between 1970 and 1971, *Poslednyaya komediya* (The Last Comedy), which is in fact composed of individual short stories, is the influence that supernatural powers have over people; this theme recurs in many of his short stories. The theme of the novel *Shatuny* (Vagrants), written between 1966 and 1968, is murder undertaken to discern the secrets of the soul of the murder victim and thereby the secret of the life to come; the novel reveals the penetrating depths of his gruesome, often tormented, prose, that shocks even him when he rereads it. But Mamleyev's intent is positive: to make the light of the human spirit visible through the darkness, to contribute to man's growth.

*Works:* Short stories, in *Novyj žurnal*, New York, 120:1975, 122:1976; 125:1976; *Tret'ja volna*, Montgeron, 1:1976, 5:1979, 7–8:1979, 9:1980; *Russian Literature Triquarterly* 14:1976; *Apollon*, Paris, 77:1977; *NRL: Neue russische Literatur*, Salzburg, 1978; *Gnosis*, New York, 1:1978, 5–6:1979; *Russica*, New York, 1981; *Strelec*, Paris, 1984:3, 1984:11, 1985:3, 1985:11, 1986:4; *Čast' reči*, New York, 4–5:1984; *Ėkho*, Paris, 13:1984; *Kontinent*, Paris, 47:1986. Interviews, in *Gnosis* 7–8:1979; *Russkaja mysl'*, Paris, Feb. 23, 1984; *Ėkho*, 13:1984; *Strelec* 6:1985. *Iznanka Gogena* (short stories), Paris–New York, 1982; *Dukhovnoe vozroždenie Rossii* (essays), in *Kontinent* 39:1984; *Živaja voda*, Paris–New York, 1986; *Živaja smert'* (short stories), Paris–Jersey City, 1987.

*Secondary Lit.:* J. McConkey, in *Ėpoch* 1980:1; G. Gibian, in *New Leader* Dec. 15, 1980; P. Lewis, in *Times Literary Supplement* May 15, 1981; D. Makkonki, in *Tret'ja volna*, New York, 12:1982; T. Goričeva, in *Kontinent* 36:1983; H. von Ssachno, in *Süddeutsche Zeitung* Sept. 8, 1984; J. Catteau, in *Magazin littéraire* July–Aug. 1986; G. Nivat, in *L'Express* May 2, 1986.

**Mandelshtám, Ósip Emílyevich,** poet, prose writer (b. Jan. 15 [Jan. 3], 1891, Warsaw—d. Dec. 27, 1938[?], in a labor camp, near Vladivostok). Mandelshtam's father was a merchant, and his mother was from the intelligentsia. He spent his youth in St. Petersburg

(where he attended business school and wrote his first poems) and Pavlovsk. In 1907 he went to Paris, where he developed an enthusiasm for the French symbolists. Mandelshtam's first poems were published in the journal *Apollon*. During this time he first met N. Gumilyov. Mandelshtam spent 1911 studying in Heidelberg; he then transferred to St. Petersburg University but never completed his studies. He became a member of the ACMEIST group "TSEKH POETOV" (Guild of Poets), which differentiated itself from the symbolists and futurists (see FUTURISM); his association with the Tsekh poetov led to his close friendship with Gumilyov and especially with Anna Akhmatova, a friendship that survived intact over a period of troubles and privations. *Kamen* (Stone), Mandelshtam's first book of poems, came out in 1913, at which time he also began publishing various essays. After the Revolution (toward which Mandelshtam initially held positive and mystical views), he traveled to Kiev, the Crimea (1919), and Georgia (1920), returning from Georgia to Moscow in the fall with I. Erenburg. His second book of poetry, *Tristia*, was published in 1922 (2d ed., 1923). In 1922 Mandelshtam married Nadezhda Yakovlevna Khazin, who later went with him into exile. Mandelshtam's first volume of prose, *Shum vremeni* (Eng. tr., The Noise of Time, 1965), was published in 1925. In 1928 he published an enlarged edition of this book, a volume of collected poems written before 1925, and a collection of essays on literature. An edition of his collected works was prepared in the fall of 1933, but as Mandelshtam refused to approve deletions demanded by the censors, the edition was never published. After 1928 the political campaign against him intensified; nevertheless, he was allowed to travel to Armenia in 1930 and to publish, in 1933, essays about his journey. Mandelshtam was arrested on May 13, 1934, and sentenced to three years in exile; he spent these three years partly in Cherdynsk (near Solikansk) and partly in Voronezh, living in the most degrading conditions. When he and his wife returned to Moscow in May 1937, they were helped primarily by V. Shklovsky. Mandelshtam was arrested for the second time on May 2, 1938. During his deportation to a Siberian labor camp, he very probably suffered from hallucinations; he is thought to have perished on Dec. 27, 1938, under as yet obscure circumstances. As a writer, Mandelshtam had already been prohibited from publishing since 1933. A strictly limited REHABILITATION ensued in 1956. From the 1960s on, Mandelshtam's name has been mentioned in memoirs and literary essays, while isolated poems and prose pieces have appeared from time to time, mostly in out-of-the-way journals. A volume in the "Biblioteka poeta" (Poet's Library) series, announced originally for 1959, was published only in 1973 and in a very limited printing (2d ed., 1974). The most complete edition of Mandelshtam's works that it has been possible to compile to date was prepared in the United States by G. Struve and B. Filippov (1955 and subsequently). Mandelshtam's wife provides an account of his fate in her memoirs (1970–72).

The tragic fate of Mandelshtam, one of the greatest of all Russian poets, affected both his own literary development and all modern Russian poetry, insofar as it has been deprived of his example. His veneration of the exacting severity of classical poetry (K. Batyushkov, A. Pushkin), also shared by Akhmatova and Gumilyov, reveals itself in all of Mandelshtam's work, which is characterized at the same time by his continually astonishing use of metaphors that are strained to the utmost. A. Blok noted that "his poetry arises from dreams—very original, and confined to the spheres of art alone." Having arisen from a visionary view of being, his poems are informed by that view and unveil themselves to the reader only gradually. Only "a few can be paraphrased" (C. Brown); primary meaning, secondary meaning, play with meaning, play with sound, metaphor, and association depend too heavily on their unique positioning in the poem. In Mandelshtam's early poems the romantic metaphor of divine inspiration has already been replaced by the demythicized power of the creative mind to comprehend the Logos in the word and the real in the unreal, and to present, in the poem, the world as a harmonious, supratemporal structure. The architectural theme (Paris, Athens, Byzantium) is woven into the poems in various ways; "for Mandelshtam, the sacred edifice is an important symbol not only for religion but just as much for art, so that it can free itself of the burden that hinders the objectivization of beauty" (Holthusen). European literature is likewise integrated into his work, so that Viktor Zhirmunsky was able to apply Schlegel's Poesie der Poesie to Mandelshtam. Many of his poems, especially the later ones that only hint at a terribly hard life, can be deciphered more easily by comparing frequently used images, such as stars, salt, and swallows, in their changing contexts. Mandelshtam's prose has similar characteristics; it cannot be assigned to conventional

categories: Puteshestviye v Armeniyu (1933; Journey to Armenia) is "a journey through grammatical forms, libraries, words, and quotations" (Shklovsky); in Yegipetskaya marka (1928; The Egyptian Stamp), surrealistic methods are taken beyond V. Khlebnikov's use, and poetry, autobiography, literary criticism, urban and human imagery, cultural philosophy, and puns are fused together into a new unity. In the terse suggestiveness of individual statements, Mandelshtam's studies in literary criticism cross beyond the boundaries of criticism into poetry.

Works: Kamen' (poems), 1913, greatly enl. ed., 1916; Tristia (poems), 1922 (reprinted, Ann Arbor, 1972); Šum vremeni (lyrical prose and essays), 1925 (see above), enl. ed. Egipetskaja marka, 1928 (reprinted, Ann Arbor, 1976); Stikhotvorenija (poems), 1928; O poèzii (essays), 1928; Putešestvie v Armeniju (lyrical prose), in Zvezda 1933:5; Zapisnye knižki: Zametki, in Voprosy lit. 1968:4; Stikhotvorenija (poems), 1973, 2d ed., 1974; Voronežskie tetradi (poems), Ann Arbor, 1980.—Sobr. soč. New York, 1955; Sobr. soč., 3 vols., Washington: vol. 1, 1964, 2d ed., 1967; vol. 2, 1966, 2d ed., 1971; vol. 3, 1966; vol. 4 (supplementary vol.), Paris, 1981 (with comprehensive bibliography).

Translations: The Prose of Osip Mandelstam: The Noise of Time, Theodosia, The Egyptian Stamp, trans. C. Brown, 1965; Selected Poems, trans. D. McDuff, 1973, 1975; Selected Poems, trans. C. Brown and W. S. Merwin, 1973, 1974; The Goldfinch and Other Poems, trans. D. Rayfield, 1973; Mandelshtam's Octets, trans. J. Riley, 1976; Fifty Poems, trans. B. Meares, 1977; Selected Essays, trans. S. Monas, 1977; Osip Mandelstam: Poems, trans. J. Greene, 1978; The Complete Critical Prose and Letters, ed. J. G. Harris, 1979; Osip Mandelstam's "Stone," trans. R. Tracy, 1980.

Secondary Lit.: V. Vejdle, in Vozdušnye puti, New York, 2:1961 and in his O poètakh i poèzii, 1973; N. A. Nilsson, in Scando-Slavica 1963; I. Bušman, Munich, 1964; A. Akhmatova, in Vozdušnye puti 4:1965; Vladimir Orlov, in Voprosy lit. 1966:10; E. Mindlin, in his Neobyknovennye sobesedniki, 1968; N. Mandel'štam, Vospominanija, New York, 1970 (Eng. tr., Hope Against Hope, 1970), and Vospominanija: Vtoraja kniga, Paris, 1972 (Eng. tr., Hope Abandoned, 1974); C. Brown, Cambridge, 1973; D. J. Koubourlis, Ithaca, N.Y., 1974; S. Broyde, Cambridge, 1975; G. Struve, in California Slavic Studies 1975, in Vestnik RKhD 1977:120, and in his O četyrëkh poè-

*takh*, London, 1981; J. Baines, Cambridge, 1976; *Russian Literature* 1977:2–3; A. A. Cohen, Ann Arbor, 1975; K. Taranovsky, Cambridge (Mass.), London, 1976; M. H. Gray, Diss., Ohio State Univ., 1977; D. M. West, Birmingham, 1980; W. Schlott, Frankfurt am Main–Bern, 1981, and Frankfurt am Main, 1984; N. Struve, Paris, 1982; O. Ronen, Jerusalem, 1983; I. Semenko, in *Wiener Slawistischer Almanach* 15:1985; P. Zeeman, in *Russian Literature* 1985:3.

**Mandelshtám, Yúry Vladímirovich,** poet (b. Sept. 25, 1908, Moscow—d. second half of 1943 [?] in prison in Germany). Mandelshtam left Russia with his parents in 1920; in Paris he attended the Russian secondary school until 1925 and completed his study of philology at the Sorbonne in 1929. He quickly became a part of the literary circles in Paris, made friends with V. Khodasevich, and worked as a critic for *Vozrozhdeniye*, *Chisla*, *Krug*, and other journals. As a poet, Mandelshtam made his debut in journals in 1929 and then with two collections published in Paris—*Ostrov* (1930; The Island) and *Vernost* (1932; Faithfulness). These were followed by *Tretiy chas* (1935; The Third Hour), a volume with 26 poems published in Berlin. *Iskateli* (1938; The Seekers), a collection of essays that reveal his thorough knowledge of European culture, was published in Shanghai. In this book, Mandelshtam writes about Dante, Pascal, Goethe, Swift, Mozart, Beethoven, Balzac. In 1938 Mandelshtam lost his wife; during the German occupation, on March 10, 1942, he was arrested as a Jew and was taken to Germany at the end of July 1943. A fourth volume with poems written between 1937 and 1941 that he compiled himself was published posthumously: *Gody* (1950; Years).

Mandelshtam's poems are characterized by a fundamental religious attitude that recognizes that earthly existence is embedded in a higher order of being and that physical existence forms a contrast with the incorporeal. The motifs of suffering caused by the world and by loneliness frequently penetrate even his numerous love poems. Despair, searching, and the sense of being pulled in many directions can oppose a positive acceptance of life. Mandelshtam often directs his poems to another person: to a beloved woman or to friends such as Vl. Smolensky or Yu. Terapiano. His poetry is austere and preserves the classical acemist tradition.

*Works: Ostrov* (poems), Paris, 1930; *Vernost'* (poems), Paris, 1932; *Tretij čas* (poems),

Berlin, 1935; *Iskateli* (essays), Shanghai, 1938; *Gody* (poems), Paris, 1950.

*Secondary Lit.:* L. Kel'berin, in *Čisla*, Paris, 2:1930; G. Struve, in *Rossija i slavjanstvo*, Paris, Aug. 2, 1930; Ju. Ivask, in *Novyj žurnal*, New York, 25:1951; Ju. Terapiano, in his *Vstreči*, New York, 1953.

**MAPP** (Moskóvskaya assotsiátsiya proletárskikh pisáteley [Moscow Association of Proletarian Writers]). Founded by the writers' group OKTYABR in March 1923, this radical Communist union included Oktyabr, MOLODAYA GVARDIYA, and "Rabochaya vesna." Its members opposed the group KUZNITSA as well as VAPP, which was influenced by Kuznitsa, and managed to transform VAPP to their liking in April 1924. MAPP remained the Moscow Section of VAPP—of RAPP after 1928— and was disbanded together with the latter by the Party Resolution of 1932 (see PARTY RESOLUTIONS ON LITERATURE).

**Maramzín, Vladímir Rafaílovich,** prose writer (b. Aug. 5, 1934, Leningrad). Maramzin's father was a factory foreman; his mother, a geography teacher. Maramzin spent his childhood in a rural provincial town and returned to Leningrad in 1945. Between 1952 and 1957 he studied electrical engineering; then he worked as an engineer and the head of the department of scientific inquiry in a factory from 1958 to 1965. His first prose work was written after 1958 and published in 1962. Since 1965 he has completely dedicated himself to literature and has published short stories in numerous newspapers and journals as well as the children's books *Tut my rabotayem* (1966; We Work Here) and *Kto razvozit gorozhan* (1969; Those Who Move the Citizens). Maramzim wrote screenplays for a good dozen films and television plays, including the one for a production of A. Chekhov's *Three Years* in 1965. The drama *Obyasnite mne kto-nibud—ya skazhu vam spasibo* (1963; If Someone Explains It to Me, I Will Thank You) was banned after its premiere. Maramzin was not a member of the Writers Union of the USSR, but from February 1966 to March 1975 he was a member of the "Professional Group" of Authors" of the Leningrad branch of the Writers Union of the RSFSR. From 1971 to 1974 he collected I. Brodsky's poems and translations and compiled a five-volume SAMIZDAT edition (about 2,000 pages). Some of his own stories also circulated in samizdat. When Maramzin was arrested on July 24, 1974, V. Maksimov published Maramzin's first long prose work, *Istoriya zhenitby Ivana Petrovicha* (1964; Eng. tr., "The Story of the Marriage of Ivan Petrovich," 1976), in *Kontinent* (2:1975; Paris). After confessing his guilt (*Le Monde* Feb. 13, 1975), Maramzin was given a suspended sentence of five years' imprisonment on Feb. 21, 1975. He left the USSR on July 12, 1975, and lives in Paris. After his emigration Maramzin first published the surrealistic prose work *Blondin obeyego tsveta* (1975; A Blond of Both Colors), then short stories, most of which had also been written in the Soviet Union, in the collections *Smeshneye chem prezhde* (1979; More Ridiculous Than Before) and *Tyanitolkay* (1981; The Push-Me-Pull-You), whose title story was written in 1966. Since 1978 he has been the publisher of the literary journal *Ekho* in Paris (with A. Khvostenko).

Both Maramzin's longer and briefer short stories evince an extraordinary stylistic diversity. They range from being purely realistic through the fantastic-satirical to the surrealistic-linguistic experimental, and they demonstrate A. Platonov's influence; "an interesting and original stylist, fond of puns and colorful, pungent, off-beat expressions" (D. Brown). Using the example of a girl in financial straits who sell herself for 30 rubles, *Istoriya zhenitby Ivana Petrovicha* provides realistic insight into spheres of urban daily life in the Soviet Union that would ordinarily be avoided. Only five stories from the cycle *Sekrety* (1966–67) appeared in the Soviet Union; this cycle depicts episodes from everyday Soviet life by using unexpected resolutions and occasionally unrealistic alienation. The short story *Tyanitolkay* is a masterful satire on the KGB that is reminiscent of Franz Kafka in its fantastic realism. *Blondin obeyego tsveta* is a surrealistic diary of a conforming artist who suffers failure in both his art and his private life. Here, as in many of his short stories, Maramzin examines the small inconsistencies of life.

*Works: Ogromnaja sila vospitatel'nogo značenija* (short story), in *Zvezda* 1964:9; *Inžener ob inženerakh* (feature articles), in *Zvezda* 1966:6; *Sekrety* (short stories), in journals including *Moskovskij komsomolec* Aug. 17, Sept. 7, Sept. 21, 1966, and *Russkaja mysl'*, Paris, Nov. 20, Dec. 25, 1975, Jan. 1, Jan. 15, Jan. 29, March 11, March 25, April 8, May 13, 1976; *Tut my rabotaem* (children's short stories), 1966, 2d ed., 1973; *My i naši vešči* (short stories), in *Junost'* 1968:8; *Kto razvozit gorožan* (children's short stories), 1969; *Istorija ženit'by Ivana Petroviča* (pov.), in *Kontinent*, Paris, 2:1975 (see above); *Blondin obeego cveta* (pov.), Ann Arbor, 1975; *Tjanitolkaj* (short story), in *Kontinent* 8:1976; *Smešnee čem prežde* (short stories and pov.), Paris, 1979; *Tjanitolkaj* (pov. and short stories), Ann Arbor, 1981.

*Secondary Lit.:* T. Khmel'nickaja, in *Lit. gazeta* May 19, 1966; A. Krestinskij, in *Zvezda* 1967:9; Ja. Gordin, in *Zvezda* 1970:6; Ju. Mal'cev, in *Grani*, Frankfurt am Main, 98:1975; N. Rubinštejn, in *Grani* 100:1976; L. Lifšic, in *Kontinent* 10:1977.

**Maríya, Mat** (real name Yelizavéta Yúryevna Skobtsóva, née Pilénko, in her first marriage Kuzminá-Karaváyeva), poet, playwright (b. Dec. 20 [Dec. 8], 1891, Riga—d. March 31, 1945 [?], Ravensbrück, Germany, while imprisoned). Mat Mariya's father was the mayor of Anapa. From 1906 to 1913 she lived in St. Petersburg, where she studied (Bestuzhev courses), was briefly married to a Bolshevik, and came into contact with A. Blok, V. Ivanov, and M. Voloshin. She collected her early poems in the volumes *Skifskiye cherepki* (1912; Scythian Crockery) and *Ruf* (1916; Ruth). In 1919 she emigrated as a member of the Socialist Revolutionary Party via Constantinople and Belgrade and arrived in Paris at the beginning of 1923 with her second husband. With the YMCA publishing house, she published (under the name of E. Skobtsova) *Zhatva dukha* (1927; Harvest of the Spirit) in two small volumes each containing four holy legends. The same publisher enlisted her, together with N. Berdyayev, V. Zenkovsky, and others, to contribute to a series of short monographs on Russian religious thinkers and also published her short books about F. Dostoyevsky, Vl. Solovyov, and A. Khomyakov in 1929. From this point on, her poems also appeared in journals and anthologies. Mat Mariya (Mother Maria) became a nun in the spring of 1932 and received the name Mariya after St. Mary of Egypt. She fulfilled her duty as a nun in active works of charity, especially in service to the poor. In Berlin she published a collection of poems, *Stikhi* (1937; Poems), under the name of "Monakhinya Mariya" (Nun Mariya). Mat Mariya was socially active in many cities throughout France and established in Paris, probably in the mid-1930s, a small social center called "Pravoslavnoe delo" (Orthodox Cause)—a meeting place for many writers and philosophers—from which she also looked after persecuted Jews during the occupation. On Feb. 9, 1943, she was arrested. In the German concentration camps she continued dedicating her life to others and was killed shortly before the end of World War II.

Her husband D. E. Skobtsov edited the first posthumous collection and published it under the name Mat Mariya, since this was the name by which she had become famous in France. With the help of her mother, Sofiya Pilenko, the second volume, Stikhotvoreniya (1947; Poems), was published by the society "Obshchestvo druzey Materi Marii" that had since been established in Paris. This volume also contains memoirs and a foreword by G. Rayevsky.

Mat Mariya is a poetically talented, intelligent, divinely blessed woman. From childhood on, she knew that she would die by a stranger's hand; in Paris she wrote of her willingness to accept "Solovki," that is, imprisonment in the concentration camps, as her place of residence "where the angels always sing." Her poetry, which she never rewrote, is most powerful aesthetically when she writes about her personal experiences. She does not preach, but instead describes her internal and external experiences and reveals her own struggle to find the true path chosen by God, her knowledge of human imperfection, her struggle for divine grace, the necessity of accepting fate, and man's responsibility before God for his every behavior, every action, every thought, "every undeciphered meeting," every flicker of pettiness. In the mystère in verse Anna (1947), Mat Mariya describes her own decision as a nun not to live in a cloister but to serve in the world, and in a continuation of the Faust story, discusses the deliverance from a pact with the devil through an offering of complete faith. Her mystère in verse Soldaty (1947; The Soldiers) raises the issue of the persecution of Jews and Communists by the Germans in France to a fundamental and religious level.

Works: Skifskie čerepki (poems), 1912; Ruf' (poems), 1916; Žatva dukha. Žitija svjatykh (short stories), 2 vols., Paris, 1927; Dostoevskij i sovremennost' (scholarly articles), Paris, 1929; Mirosozercanie VI. Solov'ëva (scholarly articles), Paris, 1929; A. S. Khomjakov (scholarly articles), Paris, 1929; Stikhi (poems), Berlin, 1937; Vstreči s Blokom (memoirs), in Sovremennye zapiski, Paris, 62:1936; Stikhotvorenija (poems), Paris, 1947 (also contains mystères in verse Anna and Soldaty; Stikhi (poems), Paris, 1949.

Secondary Lit.: G. Fedotov, in Sovremennye zapiski 35:1928; M. Cetlin, in Sovremennye zapiski 66:1938; K. Močul'skij, in Tretij čas, New York, 1:1946; G. Raevskij, in Mat' Marija's Stikhi, 1949; Ju. Terapiano, in his Vstreči, Paris, 1953; T. I. Manukhina, in Novyj žurnal, New York, 41:1955; V. Zander, in Vestnik

RKhD, Paris, 36:1955; N. Berdjaev, in Vestnik RKhD 78:1965; S. Gakkel', Paris, 1980; E. D. Klepinina-Aržakovskaja, in Vestnik RKhD 138:1983; E. Bogat, in Lit. gazeta June 26 1985, p. 13.

**Mariyengóf, Anatóly Borísovich,** poet, playwright (b. July 6 [June 24], 1897, Nizhny Novgorod—d. June 24, 1962, Leningrad). Mariyengof was of noble descent. He attended the gymnasium in Penza, where his first poems were also published. He was initially influenced by ego-futurism (see FUTURISM), but soon became one of the most important representatives of IMAGISM in Moscow. Mariyengof's brief enthusiasm for the Revolution because of its chaotic elements gave way to horror at the bloodshed. V. Markov calls him "perhaps the most original of all the Russian Imaginist poets" and emphasizes, in reference to his poetic and rhythmic experiments, that "he takes more poetical risks than does his friend Esenin." Between 1918 and 1922 Mariyengof had nine books—poems, poetic cycles, and a tragedy—published by the imagist publishing house; the subject matter included variations on the themes of the city, eroticism, disillusionment, and consciousness of the author's mission. In his theoretical and programmatic article about imagism, Buyan-ostrov (1920; The Island Buyan), Mariyengof proclaims that "Art is form. Content is one of the parts of form. . . . Profundity in content is a synonym for the beautiful. Beauty is a synonym for severity." After S. Yesenin's death Mariyengof described the bohemian life they shared in Roman bez vranya (1927; A Novel without Lies); his controversial exposition was strongly criticized. Postoronnyaya zhenshchina (1929; A Strange Woman), a film based on his own play and written in collaboration with N. Erdman, was banned. Mariyengof later tried to conform to the Party line in his dramas. His Shut Balakirev (Balakirev the Fool) was performed in Leningrad in 1941 and Zolotoy obruch (The Golden Hoop) was staged in Moscow in 1946. A play against COSMOPOLITANISM, Sud zhizni (1948; Life's Trial), was viewed with disfavor for being clichéridden. After 1955, the exclusively negative assessment of Mariyengof as "decadent" diminished somewhat; two small collections containing his later dramas were published, but his works from the 1920s were never reprinted. After Mariyengof's death, two journals published his memoirs, temperate versions, so to speak, of the 1927 autobiography.

Works: Vitrina serdca (poems), 1918; Mag-
dalina (poems), 1919; Konditerskaja solnc
'poems), 1919; Bujan-ostrov (essay), 1920, excerpted in Literaturnye manifesty, 1929 (reprinted, Munich, 1969); Stikhami čvanstvuju
(poems), 1921; Tučelët (poems), 1921; Zagovor durakov (play), 1922; Razočarovanie
'poems), 1922; Dvunogie (play), 1925; Stikhi
i poèmy 1922–26 (Novyj Mariengof) (poems),
1926; Roman bez vran'ja (novel), 1927, 2d
ed., 1928 (reprinted, Oxford, 1979); Ciniki
(novel), Berlin, 1928 (reprinted, Tel Aviv, 1978
[Eng. tr., Cynics, 1930); Brityj čelovek (novel),
Berlin, 1929 (reprinted, Berlin, 1968); Poemy
vojny (narrative poems), Kirov, 1942; Strannyj
kharakter (pov.), 1954; Malen'kie komedii
(plays), 1957; Roždenie poèta, Šut Balakirev
(plays), 1959; Roman s druz'jami (novel), in
Oktjabr' 1965:10–11.
    Secondary Lit.: V. Varšavskij, in Čisla, Paris,
7–8,:1933; V. Zavalishin, Early Soviet Writers, New York, 1958; V. Markov, Russian Imagism 1919–1924, Giessen, 1980; J. Graffy, in
Slavonic Review 1981:4.


**Márkish, Davíd Péretsovich,** prose writer (b.
Sept. 24, 1938, Moscow). Markish is the son
of Perets Markish, a Jewish writer who was
killed in 1952. After his father was imprisoned, Markish and his family were exiled to
Kazakhstan; after his father's REHABILITATION
in 1955, they were allowed to return to Moscow. There Markish completed his studies at
the Gorky Literary Institute (1957–62), as well
as the Advanced Courses for Scriptwriters and
Directors (1967–68). In the late 1950s Markish
began working primarily as a translator of
poetry and occasionally published his own
prose and poetry. In 1972 he received permission to emigrate to Israel. Between 1975
and 1983 Markish published six novels and a
volume of short stories in Israel and received
various literary prizes for his work (Israeli
prizes in 1977 and 1980, a British prize in
1978). His first novel, Priskazka (1978; A
Storyteller's Introduction; Eng. tr., A New
World for Simon Ashkenazy, 1976), was published in Portuguese in 1975, in modern Hebrew and English in 1976, in Swedish in 1977,
in French in 1981, and in German in 1982. Of
his other novels, Vershina utinoy polyanki
(1980; The Summit of Duck Meadow), Shuty
(1983; The Fools), and Pyos (1984; The Dog)
have been published in Russian to date. Chisto
pole (1978; The Open Field) and Kadam,
ubivshiy soroku (1982; Kadam, Killer of the
Magpie) have been published in modern Hebrew translations. Markish lives in Tel Aviv
and has been the chairman of the Russian

section of the Israeli Writers Union since 1978.
    Priskazka depicts his own experiences dur-
ing the years of exile in Kazakhstan; here the
degrading external living conditions only set
the stage for the young man's human experiences. His further life is described in Chisto
pole where, after an unsuccessful attempt to
escape illegally from the USSR in 1960, he—
now being a writer—travels all around the
Soviet Union; the novel provides a colorful,
unflattering image of Soviet society. A third
volume is planned that will unite these two
works into a trilogy entitled Lyogkaya zhizn
Simona Ashkanazy (The Easy Life of Simon
Ashkanazy). In Vershina utinoy polyanki,
Markish uses the example of a young poet
who is sent to Moscow to study at the Gorky
Literary Institute and there degenerates into
profligacy, thus providing a perceptive description of Soviet youth oriented entirely
toward material satisfactions. Through the figure of a Kirghiz hunter, Kadam, ubivshiy soroku portrays the risk involved in the cultural
subjugation of this Central Asian people. The
title of the novel Pyos symbolizes the Russian
émigré, who, like a stray dog, seeks shelter
and grows disillusioned with the unexercised
freedom in the free world. Shuty is a historical
novel concerning the court of Peter the Great.
Markish has the talent of an epic narrator who
unites relatively independent segments into a
novel through the use of a central hero.

    Works: Pjatero u samogo sebja (pov.), Len-
ingrad, 1966; Priskazka (novel), Tel Aviv, 1978
(see above); Zdes' i tam (short stories), in
Hebrew, Tel Aviv, 1978; Čisto pole (novel),
in Hebrew, Tel Aviv, 1978, in Swedish, 1980;
Veršina Utinoj poljanki (novel), in Dvadcat'
dva, Tel Aviv, 12–14:1980, separate ed. under
the title Petušok, Tel Aviv, 1986; Kadam,
ubivšij soroku (novel), in Hebrew, Tel Aviv,
1982, in Russian under the title V teni bol'-
šogo kamnja, Tel Aviv, 1986; Šuty (novel),
Tel Aviv, 1983; Pës (novel), Tel Aviv, 1984;
Za mnoj (notes), Tel Aviv, 1984; Granatovyj
kolodec (novel), Tel Aviv, 1986.
    Secondary Lit.: H. P. Klausenitzer, in
Frankfurter Allgemeine Zeitung Feb. 8, 1982;
W. Kasack, in Osteuropa 1984:1, p. 14, and
in Rheinischer Merkur March 2, 1984; E.
Wolffheim, in Neue Züricher Zeitung Nov.
22, 1985.


**Márkov, Geórgy Mokéyevich,** prose writer and
literary official (b. April 19 [April 6], 1911,
Novo-Kuskovo, oblast Tomsk). Markov's father was a peasant. Markov spent his youth
as a shepherd boy in Siberia; in 1924 he was

accepted into the Party-run Komsomol school; he worked as a journalist and as a youth official. Starting in 1930 he attended evening courses at Tomsk University; in the mid-1930s he moved to Irkutsk and began work as a writer; during World War II he served as a correspondent at the front. Since 1946 he has been a member of the Communist Party. Markov has belonged to the board of the Writers Union of the USSR since 1954 and to the secretariat since 1959; he held the position of first secretary from 1971 to 1986, making him the most influential literary official in the Soviet Union. In 1986 he became president of the Writers Union of the USSR. His speeches at all congresses of the Writers Union since 1954 have set the course for this organization. He has also belonged to the secretariat of the board of the Writers Union of the RSFSR since 1965 and was a delegate to the 26th Congress of the Communist Party in 1981. He lives in Moscow.

Markov's works are set in Siberia. His two-part first novel, Strogovy (1939–46; The Strogovs), portrays the history and background of the partisan movement in Siberia during the Revolution and traces the life of a family of beekeepers over three generations. It was awarded a Stalin Prize (for 1951, 3d class) and has frequently been reprinted. The continuation of this first work, the two-part novel Sol zemli (Salt of the Earth), followed in 1955 and 1960. Again historical, broadly epic in form, and rich with autobiographical material is the novel set in the early post-Revolutionary period, Otets i syn (1963–64; Father and Son). The same scene of action and the conservative structure of a long-winded family saga are also apparent in Sibir (1971–73; Eng. tr., Siberia, 1972); here Markov brings together the period of Bolshevik political activity and that in which the exiled Decembrists were active—the second quarter of the 19th century. This novel was awarded the Lenin Prize in 1976. In the novel Gryadushcheye tvoritsya segodnya (1981; The Future Is Created Today), Markov depicts Siberia's topical economic problems in his usual long-winded and hackneyed way, using the example—as he always does—of a Party official as protagonist.

Works: Strogovy (novel), 1939; Soldat pekhoty (short story), 1948; Pis'mo k Mareevku (short stories), 1952; Sol' zemli (novel), 1955–60; Otec i syn (novel), 1965; Orly nad Khiuganom (pov.), 1967; Žizn'. Literatura. Pisatel' (essays and articles), 1971; Sibir' (novel), 2 vols., 1973 (see above); (with E. Šim) Vysov

(play), in Teatr 1980:5; Grjaduščemu veku (novel), 1983.—Sobr. soč., 5 vols., 1972–74, and 1981–82.

Secondary Lit.: G. Kolesnikova, in Oktjabr' 1959:1; L. Fomenko, in Zvezda 1959:3; RSPP 3:1964; S. Smoljanickij, in Neva 1972:11, and foreword to Sobr. soč., 1972–74; P. Proskurin, in Novyj mir 1974:2; I. Bogatko, in Voprosy lit. 1981:4; I. Motjašov, in Lit. obozrenie 1983:4; V. Nekrasov, in Novoe russkoe slovo, New York, Oct. 6, 1985, p. 5.

**Márkov, Sergéy Nikoláyevich,** prose writer and poet (b. Sept. 12 [Aug. 30], 1906, Parfentyev, prov. Kostroma—d. April 4, 1979, Moscow). Markov's father was a land surveyor. Markov spent his youth in northern Kazakhstan; his jobs included clerking in Akhmolinsk. In 1924, after several individual poems had appeared in Siberian newspapers, Krasnaya niva was the first journal to accept one of Markov's poems for publication. Markov made several attempts at writing prose, after which Sibirskie ogni printed his first mature short story, Golubaya yashcheritsa (1928; The Blue Lizard); his first collection appeared under that title in 1929. Markov was interested in great discoverers and travelers; he himself had lived in different parts of the Soviet Union and combined archival studies with travels around his native land; he achieved academic recognition in 1943 when he was elected an ordinary member of the Geographical Society of the USSR. Markov lived in Moscow.

Markov occupies a special place in Soviet literature. He is a self-taught historian, geographer, and ethnologist. His intense absorption in the early discoverers, such as the first Russians to set foot in Alaska or to reach North Africa, is reflected in his poetry as well as in his prose. His works are set in deserts, at the polar icecap, and in the mountains of Tibet. Markov writes about events that range in time from the 9th to the 19th century. His prose style is dry and factual, but vivid. His verse, collected and published for the first time in 1946, reveals a similar compactness; it adheres to traditional forms and a strict aesthetic norm in its choice of rhyme and meter. Markov's verse reveals his intellectual view of remote cultures.

Works: Golubaja jaščerica (short stories), 1929 (1973); Solënyj kolodec (short stories), 1933; Raduga-reka (poems), 1946; Jukonskij voron (novel), 1946, 1977; Russkie ljudi na Kuril'skikh ostrovakh, 1946; Zolotaja pčela (poems), 1959; Arabskie časy (short stories),

1959; *Zemnye korni* (poems), 1961; *Zemnoj krug* (short stories), 1966; *Idušče k veršinam* (historical-biographical pov.), 1968; *Stikhotvorenija* (poems), 1971 (with autobiography); *Tamo-rus Maklaj* (pov.), 1975; *Serebrjanyj prostor* (poems), 1978—*Izbr. proizv.*, 2 vols., 1980.

*Secondary Lit.:* V. Maljugin, in *Molodaja gvardija* 1960:5; P. Železnov, in *Lit. Rossija* Sept. 20, 1963, pp. 14–15; M. Skuratov, in *Naš sovremennik* 1964:4; V. Voronov, in *Izvestija* Sept. 11, 1966; A. Urban, in *Prostor* 1973:1; A. Jugov, in *Lit. gazeta* Feb. 7, 1973, p. 5; I. Fonjakov, in *Lit. gazeta* Nov. 24, 1976, and in *Znamja* 1981:6.

**Marshák, Samuíl Yákovlevich,** poet (b. Nov. 3 [Oct. 22], 1887, Voronezh—d. July 4, 1964, Moscow). Marshak's father was an engineer in a chemical plant. The poems Marshak wrote during his years at the gymnasium led to his residing with M. Gorky's family in Yalta from 1904 to 1906. His first publication came in 1907. Between 1912 and 1914 Marshak studied in England and began translating English poetry into Russian. From 1914 to 1922 he was employed in child welfare (from 1917 to 1922 in Yekaterinodar). In 1922 he moved to Petrograd, where he worked in children's theater and where, beginning with *Detki v kletke* (1923; Children in a Cage), he wrote a whole series of books in verse for children. In 1924–25 he edited the journal *Novy Robinson*. After 1924 Marshak headed the children's literature section of the State Publishing House in Leningrad, actively sponsored avant-garde trends, such as the OBERIU (D. Kharms, A. Vvedensky), and supported authors such as Ye. Shvarts, B. Zhitkov, M. Ilyin, and V. Bianki, who became children's writers under his editorial direction. In 1934 Marshak delivered the speech on children's literature at the First Congress of the Writers Union; he was a member of the board of the Writers Union of the USSR until the end of his life. Marshak's Leningrad group was broken up around 1937 during the period of repression; some of its members were arrested. Marshak moved to Moscow in 1938. During World War II he wrote (in addition to children's poetry) poster texts for pictures by the satirical group "Kukryniksy"; his satirical verses often appeared in *Pravda*. Marshak was awarded a Stalin Prize four times (for 1941, 2d class; for 1943–44, 2d class; for 1948, 2d class; for 1950, 1st class). He visited England again in 1955, 1957, and 1959. After 1960 he also published autobiographical prose, essays on literature, and

*Izbrannaya lirika* (1962), a collection of verse, not intended for children, for which Marshak received the Lenin Prize in 1963.

Marshak is highly regarded as a translator of English poetry, particularly of Shakespeare's sonnets and the poems of Blake, Burns, Shelley, and Keats. His books for children and his narrative poems of varying length, such as *Bagazh* (1926; Baggage), *Mister Tvister* (1933; Eng. tr., *Mister Twister*, 1936), and *Blits-fritsy* (1942; The Blitz-Fritzes), are thematically and formally rich; they try to comprehend all aspects of a child's life and adhere in every case to contemporary subject matter. Marshak's plays for children, such as *Dvenadtsat mesyatsev* (1943; Eng. tr., *Twelve Months*, 1967) or *Umnye veshchi* (1964; Clever Things), also found a wide audience. Marshak's poems for adults are based on a sense of responsibility for one's life and are characterized by their simplicity, concreteness, and brevity. "Marshak's poetic style is conservative and classical in the manner of Pushkin, and his diction is conversational and clear" (D. Brown). In his literary criticism, Marshak proves to be highly sensitive to quality and naturalness in literature.

*Works: Detki v kletke* (children's poetry), 1923; *Bagaž* (children's poetry), 1926; *Mister Tvister* (children's poetry), 1933 (see above); *Blicfricy* (children's poetry), 1942; *Dvenadcat' mesjacev* (children's play), 1943 (see above); *V načale žizni* (autobiographical pov.), 1962 (Eng. tr., *At Life's Beginning*, 1964); *Izbr. lirika* (poems), 1962; *Umnye vešči* (children's play), 1964; *Liričeskie èpigrammy* (poems), 1965; *Stikhotvorenija i poèmy* (lyric and narrative poems), 1973.—*Soč.*, 4 vols., 1958–60; *Sobr. soč.*, 8 vols., 1968–72.

*Secondary Lit.:* B. Galanov, 1956, 1965; L. Čukovskaja, *V laboratorii redaktora*, 1960; V. Lakšin, in *Novyj mir* 1962:4; K. Čukovskij, in *Novyj mir* 1962:11; N. Koržavin, in *Novyj mir* 1963:3; L. Panteleev, in *Novyj mir* 1966:10; B. M. Sarnov, 1968; A. Ivič, in his *Vospitanie pokolenij*, 1969; A. Tvardovskij, in his *Stat'i i zametki o literature*, 3d ed., 1972; I. S. Maršak, in *Neva* 1975:7; *Žizn' i tvorčestvo Maršaka*, 1975; I. Kramov, in *Novyj mir* 1977:10; L. Druskin, in his *Spasënnaja kniga*, London, 1984.

**Martýnov, Leoníd Nikoláyevich,** poet (b. May 22 [May 9], 1905, Omsk—d. June 21, 1980, Moscow). Martynov's father was a railroad engineer. The Revolution prevented Martynov from completing a higher education; in the

1920s he worked at various professions. He began publishing poetry in Siberian journals in 1921. His travels around Siberia and Turkestan as a journalist in the late 1920s and early 1930s were reflected in a collection of articles, *Gruby korm* (1930; Rough Fodder); he later traveled in northern Russia. Martynov's narrative and lyric poems, collected in book form for the first time in 1939, attracted little attention. Conservative literary politics of the postwar period condemned his poetry as apolitical and nontopical, and so none of Martynov's earlier poems appeared in print after 1947. After 1955, when a volume of his poetry was once again published, Martynov became a popular representative of Soviet contemplative verse. His poems, standing outside the politics of the day, were always positively received and were regularly published in journals and in separate volumes. Martynov described his encounters with writers and books in *Vozdushnye fregaty* (1973; Frigates of the Air). He regularly attended the congresses of the Writers Union as a delegate; in 1966 he received the Gorky Prize for his volume *Pervorodstvo* (1965; Primogeniture) and in 1974 was awarded the State Prize of the USSR. He was elected to the board of the Writers Union of the USSR in 1971. Martynov was among the signers of a letter against A. Solzhenitsyn and A. Sakharov (*Lit. gazeta* Sept. 5, 1973). He lived in Moscow.

Early in his career Martynov was close to the Siberian futurists (see FUTURISM). V. Mayakovsky, N. Aseyev, and B. Pasternak are among those poets who left their mark on him. Before 1945 he wrote a series of historical epics in verse, set principally in a Siberian milieu, at the center of which he likes to place a dreamy seeker of truth. The high point of the first phase in Martynov's career is *Lukomorye* (1945; Cove), a group of poems connected by the image of a symbolic wonderland that he adapted from the Novgorodian epics. He relates this nostalgic fantasy world to contemporary reality. The themes of Martynov's highly regarded verse from his post-1955 phase span a broad range between the fantastic and the scientific, between the world of Greek mythology and modern civilization. Martynov's affirmation of the present, of the severance from yesterday by means of the perpetually new, dominates his poetry. Aesthetically speaking, this affirmation can signify a refusal to look back to one's own earlier work; politically speaking, it can signify the asseveration of the Communist faith in progress. Martynov writes narrative, descriptive poems, but his *oeuvre* is dominated by poems in which the concrete observation provides the impetus that leads to either direct or figurative philosophical meditation. Martynov is searching for the essential; in his best poems he frees "the subject matter, so to speak, from its shell" (Urban). His poetry is often proselike, with abundant use of enjambment; nevertheless, it is "always very intentionally controlled, and continues the symbolist tradition as much as it perpetuates the achievements of its successors" (Holthusen); "it contains an element of verbal magic, a richly developed subtext, allusions, the expressible, the play of associations freed from the demands of elementary logic" (Drawicz). Martynov's rich imagery relates modern civilization to nature; he achieves his sound effects by the use of alliteration and verbal parallelism.

*Works: Grubyj korm* (publicistic prose), 1930; *Stikhi i poèmy* (lyric and narrative poems), 1939; *Lukomor'e* (poems), 1945; *Stikhi* (poems), 1955; *Novaja kniga* (poems), 1962; *Pervorodstvo* (poems), 1965; *Stikhotvorenija i poèmy* (lyric and narrative poems), 2 vols., 1965; *Izbr. lirika* (poems), 1973; *Vozdušnye fregaty* (memoirs), in *Naš sovremennik* 1973:10–11, separate ed., 1974; *Giperboly* (poems), 1973; *Zemnaja noša* (poems), 1976; *Licom k solncu* (poems), 1977; *Uzel bur'* (poems), 1979; *Zolotoj zapas: Kniga stikhov* (poems), 1981; *Čerty skhodstva* (pov.), 1982.—*Sobr. soč.*, 3 vols., 1976–77.

*Translation: A Book of Poems*, 1979.

*Secondary Lit.:* V. Inber, in *Lit. gazeta* Dec. 7, 1946; Z. Papernyj, in *Oktjabr'* 1956:7 and in *Den' poèzii*, Moscow, 1962; A. Kaempfe, in *Grani*, Frankfurt am Main, 31:1956; A. Urban, in *Zvezda* 1964:10 and 1966–7; V. Dement'ev, 1971 and 1986; E. Vinokurov, in Martynov's *Izbr. lirika*, 1973; A. Mikhajlov, in *Moskva* 1975:5; P. Kosenko, in *Prostor* 1978:1; M. Čislov, in *Znamja* 1980:5; A. Marčenko, *Lit. obozrenie* 1983:6; S. Povarcov, in *Voprosy lit.* 1984:3; S. Zalygin, in *Lit. obozrenie* 1984:7; N. Staršinov, in *Lit. Rossija* Jan. 16, 1987, p. 9.

**Matvéyeva, Novélla Nikoláyevna**, poet (b. Oct. 7, 1934, Pushkin, near Leningrad). Matveyeva studied at the Gorky Literary Institute (correspondence courses because of her physical handicaps). Her first poems, published starting in 1958, were already acclaimed for their originality. After her first volume of poetry was published in 1961, others followed at certain intervals. Matveyeva's work is published in the journals *Yunost* and *Novyj mir*, among others. Like B. Okudzhava, she also writes songs that she sets to music and sings, accompanying herself on the guitar. She lives in Moscow.

Matveyeva is a very serious poet whose constantly noticeable concern is to avoid the familiar and the timeworn. She "tends to an allegorical art, in which an abstract, often fantastic, transformation of reality . . . facilitates a deeper understanding of her characteristic distinctiveness" (Levitsky). Soviet critics have occasionally perceived suggestions of the romantic, dreamlike world of A. Grin; these are most clearly recognizable in her playful songs. "In her modest, low-keyed verse she has a way of 'poeticizing' routine, mundane details, of finding unusual connections between ordinary objects and transforming them into images of heightened aesthetic, moral, and even social significance" (D. Brown). Matveyeva's metaphorical lyric poetry reveals that which has been concealed: in the contrast of surprising images, in the association of opposing powers, in the supersession of a static outlook for a dynamic one. The paradox of her point of view, the flight into humor and irony, and the joy in resonance that is reminiscent of M. Tsvetayeva are only some of her various ways of looking behind perceptible reality: "I search for the spirit behind the visible" (*Dusha veshchey* [1963; The Soul of Things]).

*Works: Lirika* (poems), 1961; *Korablik* (poems), 1963; *Duša veščej* (poems), 1966; *Lastočkina škola* (lyric and narrative poems), 1973; *Reka* (poems), 1978; *Kak složilas' pesnja . . .* (interview), in *Lit. Rossija* Nov. 5, 1982, pp. 16–17; *Zakon pesen* (poems), 1983; *Strana priboja* (poems), 1983; *Krolič'ja derevnja* (poems), 1984.

*Secondary Lit.:* B. Runin, in *Novyj mir* 1964:5; G. Medynskij, in *Junost'* 1966:7; V. Percov, in *Lit. Rossija* Dec. 16, 1966, pp. 8–9; L. Levickij, in *Novyj mir* 1967:6; L. Mikhajlova and G. Krasukhin, in *Lit. gazeta* Feb. 19, 1975, p. 6; I. Vinokurova, in *Novyj mir* 1979:4 and in *Lit. obozrenie* 1984:7; S. Čuprinin, in *Novyj mir* 1984:10.

**Mayakóvsky, Vladímir Vladímirovich,** poet and playwright (b. July 19 [July 7], 1893, Bagdadi, near Kutaisi, Georgia—d. April 14, 1930, Moscow). Mayakovsky's father was an impoverished nobleman employed as a forester in the Caucasus. After 1906 Mayakovsky lived in Moscow and was intermittently involved in revolutionary activities. He began study at an art school in Moscow in 1911. In 1912 he published his first poems in the futurist miscellany *Poshchochina obshchestvennomu vkusu* (A Slap in the Face of Public Taste) (see FUTURISM). Mayakovsky belonged to the cubo-futurists, a group that provocatively advocated rejection of all earlier art and searched for the new and nonbourgeois at any price. His first book of poems, *Ya* (I), was published in 1913, his first narrative poem, *Oblako v shtanakh* (A Cloud in Trousers), in 1915. Between 1915 and 1919 Mayakovsky shared an apartment in Petrograd and Moscow with Lilya Brik, to whom he was tied by a strong love, and with Osip Brik. In the futurists he saw the avant-garde of Communist culture, and, in himself, the "drummer" of the Revolution. In declamatory poems, such as "Levy marsh" (1918; Left March), he turned to the broad masses. With *Misteriya buff* (1918; rev. ed., 1921; Eng. tr., *Mystery Bouffe*, 1933), he created an allegorical theater piece about revolutionary events, which V. Meyerhold staged in Petrograd. Mayakovsky began his collaboration with the central press agency ROSTA in 1919; he wrote numerous captions and agitational poetry about current events. At the same time he wrote long political and propagandistic poems, such as *150,000,000* (1920) and *Vladimir Ilyich Lenin* (1924; Eng. tr., 1970), which overshadowed his more personal lyrics, such as "Lyublyu" (1922; I Love). Between 1923 and 1925 Mayakovsky edited the futurist journal *LEF*. He traveled all over Russia to recite his poetry; after 1922 he traveled abroad nine times (to Latvia, Germany, France, the United States, Czechoslovakia, and Poland). The gradual consolidation of the Soviet system, with its encouragement of proletarian writers and its hostility toward all experimental art, led to increasing attacks on Mayakovsky, particularly by RAPP. In the comedies *Klop* (1928; Eng. tr., *The Bedbug*, 1931) and *Banya* (1929; Eng. tr., *The Bathhouse*, 1963), Mayakovsky's satire was directed at the deterioration of revolutionary ideals and at the growing bourgeois inclinations of officials in his own country. In the course of transition to the Stalinist system of totalitarian rule, Mayakovsky himself joined RAPP in 1930; his friends viewed this as a betrayal, while RAPP officials continued to oppose him as an alien presence. *Banya*, also staged by Meyerhold, was closed down, Mayakovsky was deprived of his visa to travel abroad, and the exhibition "Twenty Years of Work" was boycotted. Shaken in addition by an unhappy love affair in Paris, he took his own life. Through more than 200 articles, O. Brik fought for Mayakovsky's recognition. In 1935, after both Briks had written a letter to Stalin, the assessment of Mayakovsky changed abruptly following Stalin's declaration that he was "the best and the most talented poet of our Soviet era"; nevertheless, his works with a critical edge, particularly Klop and Banya, remained banned until after Stalin's death. Of Mayakovsky's literary estate, almost all of his correspondence and an unknown number of works (such as Plokho [unpublished; Bad], the companion piece to the narrative poem Khorosho [1927; Good]) are not accessible; as a result, an objective description of his literary output cannot be made. In 1958 in the series "Literaturnoye nasledstvo," some supplemental material appeared (for example, part of his correspondence with Lilya Brik); however, the second volume has yet to be published. In Sweden in 1982, B. Jangfeldt published this correspondence in its entirety.

Mayakovsky possessed a great lyric and dramatic talent that, under the influence of futurism, strove to make a new poetic statement, one freed of all tradition and actively opposed to it. Mayakovsky's rebellion against bourgeois culture and the existing order found its ideological objective under the influence of the Revolution. In his declamatory verse his own concerns fuse with political duty; colloquial speech, bordering on slang, unites with rhetorical pathos; lyrical sensitivity blends with poetic journalism; loneliness, longing, and inner turmoil combine with limitless egocentric pretensions to leadership and an arrogance that despises humility. Innovations in Russian verse style, such as vers libre (whose cadence, measured only by stresses and meant for oral recitation, is visually emphasized by staggered lines cascading down the printed page), elliptical syntax, and great freedom of rhyme (which often depends only on assonance), all became, because of Mayakovsky, accepted stylistic features of Russian prosody. The nonrealistic element in Mayakovsky's provocative poetic imagery has its parallel in his dramas: in the pseudobiblical, symbolically lush scenes of the decline of capitalism and the paradise of communism in Misteriya buff, and in the satiric exaggeration of contemporary reality in Klop and Banya. Mayakovsky, who had described his own style as "tendentious realism," was an idealist who, with his "powerful rather than profound" (Slonim) writing, wanted to break through into reality. When this possibility was denied him, he abandoned life.

Works: Ja (poems), 1913; Oblako v štanakh (narrative poem), 1915; Prostoe kak myčanie

(poems), 1916; Misterija buff (play), 1921 (see above); 150,000,000 (narrative poem), 1920; Pro èto (narrative poem), 1923; Vladimir Il'ič Lenin (narrative poem), 1924 (see above); Khorošo (narrative poem), 1927; Klop (play), 1929 (see above); Banja (play), 1929 (see above); Perepiska 1915–1930 (correspondence of Mayakovsky and L. Brik), ed. B. Jangfel'dt, Stockholm, 1982; V mire Majakovskogo, ed. A. A. Mikhajlov and S. S. Lesnevskij, 2 vols., 1984.—Polnoe sobr. soč., 12 vols., 1934–38; 12 vols., 1939–49; 13 vols., 1955–61.

Translations: Mayakovsky and His Poetry, 1945; The Bedbug and Selected Poetry, 1960; Selected Poetry, 1960; The Complete Plays of Vladimir Mayakovsky, 1968; How Are Verses Made? 1970; Timothy's Horse, 1970; Electric Iron, 1971; Poems, 1972; Prologue Spoken by Mayakovsky, Vladimir Mayakovsky, a Tragedy, 1972.

Secondary Lit.: R. Jakobson, in Slav. Rundschau 1930; V. Šklovskij, 1940 and 1966; B. M. Èjkhenbaum, 1940; M. Nag, in Scando-Slavica 1958:4; Lit. nasledstvo 65:1958; A. M. Ripellino, Turin, 1959; C. Frioux, Paris, 1961; V. Katanjan, 4th ed., 1961; H. Uhlig, 1962; L. Stahlberger, The Hague, 1965; G. O. Vinokur, 2d ed., 1967; W. Storch, 1969; W. Woroszylski, London, 1972; E. J. Brown, Princeton, 1973; S. Everts-Grigat, Munich, 1975; B. Jangfeldt, Stockholm, 1976; V. D. Barooshian, The Hague, 1978.

**Mayórov, Nikoláy Petróvich,** poet (b. May 20, 1919, Durovka, prov. Simbrisk—d. Feb. 8, 1942, Barantsevo, oblast Smolensk). Mayorov was the son of peasants who evidently had become factory workers. From 1929 on, Mayorov lived in Ivanovo; he began studying history at Moscow University in 1937; in 1939 he started attending seminars with P. Antokolsky at the Gorky Literary Institute. Mayorov wrote his first poems while still in grammar school; several of his student poems appeared in hectographed university publications. Two narrative poems written in 1939 and 1940 were not preserved. Most of Mayorov's manuscripts, put away in a trunk at the beginning of World War II, were apparently lost. A part of the material that did survive was published in 1962 in My (We).

His fellow students testify to the fact that immediately before the war Mayorov was acknowledged as being among the most talented poets. His poems are characterized by their great passion and commitment to living intensely. His portrayal of N. Gogol burning a manuscript invites conjecture about Mayorov's own early ambivalence toward his work;

the themes of unhappiness about things not to be experienced and the soldier's early death reveal his premonition of his own fate. Mayorov's poetry is concrete, his language is mostly austere, terse, but already, in the few surviving items, varied and diversified.

Works: My (poems), 1962, 1972; poems, in Sovetskie poèty, pavšie na Velikoj Otečestvennoj vojne, 1965.
Secondary Lit.: B. Sluckij, in Lit. gazeta June 26, 1962; V. Prikhod'ko, in Znamja 1963:10; S. Narovčatov, in Lit. gazeta April 8, 1970, p. 7, and in Lit. i sovremennost' 10:1970.

**Medýnsky, Grigóry Aleksándrovich,** (pseud. of G. A. Pokróvsky), prose writer (b. Feb. 11 [Jan. 30], 1899, Kozelsk, prov. Kaluga—d. Feb. 22, 1984, Moscow). Medynsky's father was a village priest. From 1918 on, Medynsky served in various Soviet institutions, first as a teacher, then from 1922 to 1928 as a worker in the problem area of "homeless waifs" (bezprizornye); in 1928–29 he was especially active in the antireligious movement. Medynsky began his literary career by writing short stories for the purpose of anti-Christian propaganda, for example, Myod (1925; Honey), and treatises about the relationship of writers to religion, for example, Yesenin—yeseninshchina—religiya (1929; Yesenin—Yeseninism—Religion). Medynsky's contribution to the Party-promoted representations of industrial construction during the first Five-Year Plan was his didactically construed novel Samstroy (1930; Self-Construction). Medynsky spent the years of World War II doing propaganda work in the hinterlands. With Marya (1945–48) he wrote a typical novel of SOCIALIST REALISM of the lowest order, in which the lives of kolkhoz workers during the war are divested of their actual difficulties and idealized. It received a Stalin Prize (for 1949, 3d class), but was subsequently exposed as lacking any real conflict situation. The bulk of Medynsky's work is devoted to the subject of education, primarily of juvenile delinquents, for example, Povest o yunosti (1954; A Story about Youth) or Chest (1959; Honor). Medynsky assembled additional new works on the basis of the correspondence occasioned by these books. . . . Takovo eto "ya" (1967; . . . Such Is This "I") sketches a portrait of Felix Dzerzhinsky. Medynsky describes his own childhood in the short story Stupeni zhizni (1981; The Stages of Life). He lived in Moscow.

Works: Mëd (short story), in Molodaja gvardija 1925:6; Esenin—eseninščina—religija

(treatise), 1929; Samstroj (novel), 1931; Devjatyj "A" (pov.), 1940; Mar'ja (novel), 1949; Povest' o junosti (pov.), 1954; Čest', 1960; Trudnaja kniga (short stories), . . . Takovo eto "ja," in Junost' 1967:4; Puti i poiski, 1970; Stupeni žizni (short story), 1981.—Izbr. proizv., 2 vols., 1973; Sobr. soč., 3 vols., 1981–.
Secondary Lit.: A. Makarenko (1939), in his Sobr. soč., vol. 7, 1958, pp. 281–83; F. Abramov, in Novyj mir 1954:4; RSPP 3:1964; V. Eliseeva, in Novyj mir 1974:7 and 1981:8; E. Sidorov, in Oktjabr' 1980:6; Vl. Amlinskij, in Lit. Rossija March 16, 1984, p. 14; S. Pokrovskaja, in Lit. obozrenie 1986:7.

**Merezhkóvsky, Dmítry Sergéyevich,** prose writer (b. Aug. 14 [Aug. 2], 1865, St. Petersburg—d. Dec. 9, 1941, Paris). Merezhkovsky's father was a court official and a member of the Ukrainian aristocracy. From 1884 to 1889 Merezhkovsky studied history at the universities of Moscow and St. Petersburg. His first poem was published in 1881; it was followed by several volumes of verse (1888–1904). In 1889 he married Zinaida Gippius. Merezhkovsky translated Greek tragedies and traveled to Greece in the 1890s. He started work on an extensive religiophilosophical work in novel form, which developed into the historical novel-trilogy Khristos i Antikhrist (1896–1905; Christ and Antichrist). The volume of essays Vechnye sputniki (1896; Eternal Companions) and the lengthy treatise Tolstoy i Dostoyevsky (1901; Tolstoy and Dostoyevsky) attracted considerable attention. The second part of the trilogy, Voskresshiye bogi: Leonardo da Vinchi (1901; Eng. trs., The Romance of Leonardo da Vinci, 1901; The Forerunner, 1902), made Merezhkovsky's reputation as a writer in Western Europe. From 1905 to 1912 he lived in Paris, although his books continued to be published in Russia. His collected works were published in editions of 17 volumes (1911–13) and 24 volumes (1914). As an opponent of the October Revolution, Merezhkovsky fled to Paris by way of Warsaw in 1919. Convinced that Bolshevism was the absolute metaphysical Evil, he actively spoke out against Soviet power. In 1921 he wrote: "Our Russian troubles are only a part of the whole world's troubles." "We are the first, but not the last." Merezhkovsky continued to publish historical novels up to 1925, after which he published ten volumes of more philosophical writings, such as Iisus neizvestny (1932; Eng. tr., Jesus the Unknown, 1933) and—in German only—Tod und Auferstehung (1935; Death and Resurrection), an expression of Merezhkovsky's continuous search for divine truth. Merezhkovsky held firmly to his belief in the mission of the Russian emigration; in his hatred of the Communist system he even hoped that Hitler's attack on the Soviet Union would succeed. The first step in returning Merezhkovksy to Russian literature and making his works accessible to the Soviet reader was taken in 1986; the 24-volume edition of his works has been reprinted in the West (1973).

Merezhkovsky's literary work is influenced by his singular attitude toward religion, which led him continually to raise anew the basic questions of the realization of Christianity. His first poems reveal the influence of Semyon Nadson, while in his later poems he is a precursor of the symbolists. In his novels Merezhkovsky (influenced in part by Friedrich Nietzsche, V. Solovyov, and V. Rozanov) expresses a historical and religiophilosophical perspective that views the development of European culture as a struggle between paganism and Christianity, between the flesh and the spirit; the central concern of his novels is primarily philosophical, not historical. His depiction of the Decembrist uprising of 1825, *14 Dekabrya* (1918; Eng. tr., *December the Fourteenth*, 1923), is based on his experience of the horror of the October Revolution. Merezhkovsky's novels are all constructed in a relatively unchanging manner. The development of his thought finds expression through the use of strongly marked antitheses; his narrative technique consists of juxtaposing a major historical central character and a second, minor one; the latter is then used as the means of communicating the author's thoughts. For all their length, the novels are fluidly written and engrossing; they have also been successful in translation.

*Works: Stikhotvorenija* (poems), 1888; *Simvoly* (poems), 1892; *O pričinakh upadka i o novykh tečenijakh sovremennoj russkoj lit.* (essays), 1893; *Khristos i Antikhrist* (novel-trilogy; [1] *Otveržennyj*, 1896, 2d ed. under the title *Smert' bogov. Julian Otstupnik.* 1902; [2] *Voskresšie bogi. Leonardo da Vinči*, 1902; [3] *Antikhrist. Pëtr i Aleksej*, 1905); *Novye stikhotvorenija* (poems), 1896; *Večnye sputniki* (essays), 1897, 3d abridged ed., 1906 (reprinted, Letchworth, 1971); *Tolstoj i Dostoevskij* (essay), 1901–2; *Gogol' i čort* (essays), 1906; trilogy: (1) *Pavel I* (play), 1908, (2) *Aleksandr I* (novel), 1913, (3)*14 Dekabrja* (novel), 1918, Paris, 1921; *Sobr. stikhov* (poems), 1910 (reprinted, Letchworth, 1969); *Nevoennyj dnevnik 1914–16* (diary), 1917; *Carstvo Antikhrista* (essays), Munich, 1921 (with Z. Gip-

pius et al.); *Roždenie bogov (Tutankamon na Krite)* (novel), Prague, 1925; *Messija* (novel), in *Sovremennye zapiski*, Paris, 1926–27:27–32; *Tajna Zapada. Atlantida-Evropa*, Belgrade, 1930; *Iisus neizvestnyj* (novel), Belgrade, 1932(?); *Jesus der Kommende* (novel in German only), Frauenfeld, 1934; *Tod und Auferstehung* (novel in German only), Frauenfeld, 1935; *Dante* (novel), 2 vols., Brussels–Paris, 1939.—*Polnoe sobr. soč.*, 17 vols., 1911–13; 24 vols., 1914 (reprinted, Hildesheim, 1973.

*Translations: Julian the Apostate*, trans. C. Johnson, 1899, trans. B. Guerney, 1929; *The Death of the Gods*, trans. H. Trench, 1901; *The Romance of Leonardo da Vinci*, trans. H. Trench, 1901, trans. B. Guerney, 1928; *The Forerunner: The Romance of Leonardo da Vinci*, trans. H. Trench, 1902; *Peter and Alexis*, trans. H. Trench, 1905, trans. B. Guerney, 1931; *December the Fourteenth*, trans. N. Duddington, 1923; *Jesus the Unknown*, trans. H. Matheson, 1933; *Jesus Manifest*, trans. E. Gellibrand, 1935; *Atlantis/Europe: The Secret of the West*, no translator cited, 1971.

*Secondary Lit.:* A. Belyi, in his *Arabeski*, 1911 (reprinted, Munich, 1969; E. Lundberg, 1914; B. Poplavskij, in *Čisla*, Paris, 4:1930–31; Ju. Terapiano, in *Čisla* 9:1933; Z. Gippius, Paris, 1951; C. H. Bedford, in *Canadian Slavonic Papers* 1958, and separate ed., Lawrence, Kansas, 1975; B. G. Rosenthal, Diss., Berkeley, 1970, and The Hague, 1975; U. Spengler, Diss., Lucerne, 1972; H. Stammler, in *California Slavic Studies*, 1976; O. Holovaty, Diss., Vanderbilt Univ., 1977; S. Povarcov, in *Voprosy lit.* 1986:11.

***Metrópol*** (Metropole), literary almanac, Moscow, 1979, publishers: V. Aksyonov, A. Bitov, F. Iskander, Ye. Popov, and V. Yerofeyev. The publishers asked the Writers Union of the USSR for permission to publish this journal without censorship. After the request was denied, they presented the volume published in eight copies to the literary public and acquainted them with the case history on Jan. 23, 1979, in a café in Moscow. With this, *Metropol* was relegated to SAMIZDAT. Ardis in Ann Arbor, Michigan, made a photomechanical reprint (763 pages). The volume, its publishers and its authors were sharply criticized by the officials in the Writers Union and were affected by a number of restrictive measures. V. Aksyonov's emigration in 1980 can be seen as a result.

As a liberal, literary almanac, *Metropol* stands in the tradition of the almanacs *Lite-*

raturnaya Moskva, published in 1956 by M. Aliger, A. Bek, V. Kaverin, Ye. Kazakevich, A. Kotov, K. Paustovsky, V. Rudny, and V. Tendryakov, and Tarusskiye stranisty, published in 1961 by K. Paustovsky and four lesser known authors. Both almanacs were attacked following their publication in the Soviet Union because a few texts did not fully correspond to the general Party line. Twenty-three Soviet authors made texts available to Metropol that previously had generally been submitted in vain to various editiorial boards for publication. Among the best-known authors are: A. Aksyonov (with a nonrealistic drama), Yuz Aleshkovsky (with three songs from prison camps), B. Akhmadulina (with a surrealistic prose work), A. Bitov (with four prose texts not published since 1970–71), F. Gorenshteyn (with a 100-page povest), F. Iskander (with two especially good satires), S. Lipkin (with a few poems), I. Lisnyanskaya (with six mostly religious poems), A. Voznesensky (with a few poems previously published in the Soviet Union), V. Vysotsky (with 25 pages of poems and lyrics to songs). Yevgeny Popov (b. 1946) found special acclaim with his "Devil's Dozen Short Stories" that provide tragicomic insight into everyday Soviet life in pointed brevity. From his numerous publications in émigré journals, Genrich Sapgir (b. 1928) was known as one of the nonrealistic poets. His 11 poems in Metropol reveal a wealth of form—from the perfect, conservative sonnet to experimental, modernistic verse. From the physicist V. Trostnikov (b. 1928), a text was included that reflects the metaphysical dissatisfaction of the Soviet intelligentsia during the 1970s. For him the immortality of the soul is just as well proven as the origin of material existence in the spiritual realm. Criticism of Soviet society, which could have provided the grounds for prohibition within the Soviet Union, cannot be found in this volume. Nonetheless it breaks away from what is common in the Soviet Union through its form (nonrealistic texts), partially through its religious attitude, and through its foreword that speaks of the "nauseating," uniform routine in the journals and publishing houses" of the Soviet Union; it demands "nonstandardized literature" as a counterweight.

Works: Metropol': Literaturnyj al'manakh, Ann Arbor, 1979 (Eng. tr., Metropol: A Literary Almanac New York, 1982).
Secondary Lit.: R. Meier,in Neue Zürcher Zeitung Jan. 29, 1979; M. Geller, in Russkaja mysl', Paris, June 21, 1979; F. Kuznecov, in Lit. gazeta Sept. 19, 1979, p. 9; W. Kasack, in Osteuropa 1980:11; Ju. Aleškovskij, N. Koržavin, et al., in Grani, Frankfurt am Main, 118:1980; H. Muchnic, in New York Times Book Review Feb. 27, 1983; C. Proffer, Ann Arbor, 1985.

**Métter, Izraíl Moiséyevich,** prose writer (b. Oct. 5 [Sept. 22], 1909, Kharkov). Metter's father was in government administration. Metter worked as a mechanic after completing a seven-year school. From 1926 to 1929 he studied math in a technical institute in Kharkov but did not complete the program. In 1929 he moved to Leningrad and taught mathematics in various places. His occasional short stories began appearing in journals in 1928; Metter's first povest was published in 1936. During World War II, Metter initially worked for Leningrad radio; in 1942 he was evacuated to Perm, where he was active as a dramatist. Tovarishchi 1952; Eng. tr., "Comrades," in Soviet Literature 1955:3), based on the life of vocational students in Moscow, was quite well received, but after 1960 Metter himself no longer included it in his collections, maybe because its idealizations were too closely bound to a particular time. Metter lives in Leningrad; he has not participated in any congresses of the Writers Union. He is amicably regarded by post-Stalinist critics but has not yet received mention in literary histories.

Metter writes short stories and povesti; he focuses his carefully observing eye on daily life in the Soviet Union, primarily on the milieus of the school and the militia; he strives for an objective presentation free of newspaper heroism. Mukhtar (1960), Metter's povest about a police dog, attracted particular attention, both in book form and in its film version; it is a poetic creation about man's relationship to everything that lives in the world. Metter contrasts concrete respect for one's neighbor with abstract ties to people in general. He pursues a moral point, calls for life without the usual or comfortable lies but according to conscience alone. His language is clear, his psychology consistent, his conflicts unexaggerated. The point Metter wants to make is now and then plainly unambiguous, now and then subliminally hinted at through gentle humor or easily remembered imagery.

Works: Konec detstva (pov.), 1936; Tovarišči (pov.), 1952 (see above); Učitel' (short stories), 1954; Pervyj urok (short stories), 1956; Vstreča (short stories), 1957; Obida (short stories), 1960, includes Mukhtar (pov.); Po sovesti (short stories), 1965; Ljudi (short stories), 1968; Raznye sud'by (short stories), 1973; Puti žitejskie (short stories), 1974; Sredi ljudej (pov. and short stories), 1979; Svidanie (pov. and short stories), 1982; Vstreči i rasstavanija, 1984. Secondary Lit.: A. Vasil'ev, in Zvezda 1952:7; I. Vinogradov, in Novyj mir 1960:12; L. Lazarev, in Lit. gazeta March 2, 1961; I. Travkina, in Lit. gazeta Aug. 28, 1968, p. 5; RSPP 7(1):1971; St. Rassadin, in Neva 1981:5; P. Spivak, in Družba narodov 1984:12.

**Mezhdunaródnaya kníga** (The International Book), a Soviet foreign trade organization exercising a monopoly over the export and import of printed materials. Founded in 1923 as a "stock company," Mezhdunarodnaya kniga has had the legal status of an all-union foreign trade association since 1930. Five divisions existed in 1984: Sovinperiodika, Soviskusstvo (records, films, graphic arts, slides, and so on), Sovinfilateliya, Sovinkniga, and Soyuzkniga. Sovinkniga is further subdivided into the sections for capitalist countries (that is, the Western industrial nations), socialist countries, and the third world. Soyuzkniga is responsible for supplying Soviet bookstores with Western literature. Mezhdunarodnaya kniga has its own representatives in many countries. Until VAAP was established, Mezhdunarodnaya kniga was also responsible for buying and selling translation rights. Mezhdunarodnaya kniga is among the sponsors of the Moscow International Book Fair that has been held biennially since 1977. Mezhdunarodnaya kniga is headquartered in Moscow.

**Mézhirov, Aleksándr Petróvich,** poet (b. Sept. 6, 1923, Moscow). Mezhirov's father, who completed degrees in both law and medicine, provided his son with a comprehensive education in addition to traditional schooling. From 1941 to 1943 Mezhirov served as a soldier at the front, in part near Leningrad, then was invalided out of the army. In 1943 he was admitted to the Communist Party. Mezhirov began writing poetry while at school; he began publishing his verse in 1941. From 1943 to 1948 he studied at the Gorky Literary Institute. In 1947 he made a lengthy stay in Georgia. His first volume of verse, Doroga daleka (1947; A Far Road), was criticized for its too personal view of the events of the war. Subsequent volumes have appeared on a regular basis: Mezhirov's tenth book, Vetrovoye steklo (Wind-Glass), came out in 1961. Mezhirov lives in Moscow and has been a delegate to

congresses of the Writers Union only since 1970.

Mezhirov's verse found its thematic expression initially in the experience of war. With an eye toward the tragic, Mezhirov depicts day-to-day life at the front, avoiding both abstract confessions and the use of poetry as a weapon. He often makes a mental association to life during peacetime, as in his later poems he makes an association back to the war, describing, for instance, a view of nature changed by this experience. His visit to Georgia is reflected in his own work and in numerous, methodical translations. His more recent poems respond to the negative phenomena of the modern world, to soulless civilization and its uniformity, the helpless product of which is destructive or alienated young people. Not overtly didactic, but in search of the meaning of life, Mezhirov observes and structures the external forms of everyday life. He sees the world around him and himself from a distance; he has an ear for sorrow and injury but does not become pessimistic. His poetic language is syntactically condensed and clear; it has freed itself from many clichés and found new forms without having become extravagant.

*Works: Doroga daleka* (poems), 1947; *Novye vstreči* (poems), 1949; *Vozvraščenie* (poems), 1955; *Raznye gody* (poems), 1956; *Vetrovoe steklo* (poems), 1961; *Proščanie so snegom* (poems), 1964; *Ladožskij lëd* (poems), 1965; *Lebjažij pereulok* (poems), 1968; *Stikhotvorenija* (poems), 1969; *Nevskaja Dubrovka* (lyric poems and narrative poem; contains "Na rubežakh"), 1970; *Pozdnie stikhi* (poems), 1971; *Nedolgaja vstreča* (poems), 1975; *Vremena* (poems), 1976; *Pod starym nebom* (poems), 1977; *Očertan'ja veščej* (poems), 1977; *Proza v stikhakh*, 1982; *Tysjača meločej*, 1984; *Zakrytyj povorot* (poems), 1985.—*Izbr. proizv.*, 2 vols., 1981.

*Secondary Lit.:* A. Urban, in *Neva* 1962:6 and in *Zvezda* 1972:5; L. Anninskij, in *Moskva* 1963:12; M. Lapšin, in his *Ličnost' v literature*, 1973; E. Evtušenko, in *Družba narodov* 1972:4; T. Gluškova, in *Lit. obozrenie* 1976:1; N. Sotnikov, in *Moskva* 1977:9; E. Vinokurov, in *Lit. gazeta* Aug. 17, 1983, p. 4; M. P'janykh, in *Voprosy lit.* 1983:11 and 1985; S. Čuprinin, in *Novyj mir* 1984:3.

**Mikhalkóv, Sergéy Vladímirovich,** poet, playwright, literary official (b. March 12 [Feb. 27], 1913, Moscow). Mikhalkov's father was an agronomist. Mikhalkov published his first poem in 1928 while in school in Pyatigorsk. In 1930 he moved to Moscow. In 1935–37 he studied at the Gorky Literary Institute. In 1936 he published his first volume of children's poems, whose high educational value "in the spirit of the Soviet nation and Soviet power" A. Fadeyev highlighted in *Pravda*. He was a war correspondent during the occupation of eastern Poland in 1939 and during World War II. Mikhalkov received a Stalin Prize for children's poetry (for 1935–41, 2d class) and for the film script *Frontovye podrugi* (Girl Friends from the Front) (for 1941, 2d class). In 1943, together with G. El-Registan, Mikhalkov wrote the new national anthem for the USSR. Mikhalkov, who wrote his first drama for adolescents in 1938, continued to create dramas to further the political education of young people after the war. For *Ya khochy domoy* (1949; I Want to Go Home), a "crudely sentimental play" (Struve) directed against England, and for the anti-American propagandistic play *Ilya Golovin* (1949; Ilya Golovin), he received a third Stalin Prize (for 1949, 2d class). In 1950 he was admitted into the Communist Party. During de-Stalinization, Mikhalkov adapted himself somewhat to the liberalizing efforts but quickly became one of the most active dogmatic literary officials, one who often represented the Soviet Union during his trips abroad and who played a leading role in the defamation of A. Solzhenitsyn (for example, *Komsomolskaya pravda* Dec. 14, 1969). At the time when the Soviet intelligentsia was increasingly interested in F. Dostoyevsky, Mikhalkov wrote a stage play based on Dostoyevsky's story "Krokodil" called *Passazh v Passazhe* (1977; The Night's Lodging in the Passage). Since 1954 he has been a member of the board of the Writers Union of the USSR; since 1958 (its founding), a member of the board of the Writers Union of the RSFSR; since 1965 and 1967, respectively, a member of the secretariats of each organization. Since 1954 he has delivered a speech at every congress. In 1970 he became the chairman of the Writers Union of the RSFSR and was awarded the Lenin Prize, which was followed by other awards. In 1981 he was a delegate to the 26th Congress of the Communist Party. He lives in Moscow.

As a writer of children's stories, Mikhalkov is the epigone of S. Marshak and K. Chukovsky. He owes his advancement to his timely assimiliation of the Party line into children's verse, whose primitive black-and-white outlines (anti-COSMOPOLITANISM, anti-NATO, anti-Yugoslavian-revisionism, etc.) can scarcely be surpassed. Owing to their artistic failings (ex-cessive length, predictable denouements, obtrusive didacticism, and the artificiality of the issues), Mikhalkov's plays are even unable to attain their goal of short-lived political effect.

*Works: Stikhi* (poems), 1936; *Il'ja Golovin* (play), 1949; (with M. Rosenberg) *Frontovye podrugi* (film script), in *Izbr. scenarii sovetskogo kino* 3:1949; *Ja khoču domoj* (play), 1949; *Teatr dlja vzroslykh* (plays), 1979.— *Sobr. soč.*, 4 vols., 1963–64; 3 vols., 1970–71; 6 vols., 1981–83.

*Secondary Lit.:* L. Kassil', 1954; V. Tel'pugov and G. Eršov, 1956; K. Simonov, in *Pravda* June 4, 1964; B. Galanov, 2d ed., 1972; V. Bavina, 1976; I. Višnevskaja, in *Teatr* 1983:3.

**Mikháylov, Nikoláy Nikoláyevich,** prose writer (b. Dec. 23 [Dec. 10], 1905, Moscow—d. March 5, 1982, Moscow). Mikhaylov's father worked for the civil service. In 1930 Mikhaylov completed his studies in geography at the technical college for trade and industry in Moscow and went to work in Tashkent. Throughout his life, Mikhaylov made numerous expeditions and trips into every region of the USSR. Starting in 1927 he regularly published popular scientific essays and books about the Soviet Union. In 1933 M. Gorky engaged him to work on the journal *Nashi dostizheniya*. For his book *Nad kartoy Rodiny* (1947; Eng. tr., *Across the Map of the U.S.S.R.*, 1949), Mikhaylov received a Stalin Prize (for 1947, 3d class). *Idu po meridianu* (1957; Eng. tr., "I Follow the Meridian," in *Soviet Literature* 1958:5), a travel sketch that led him across the frontiers of his own country for the first time, received widespread attention. Mikhaylov regularly enlarged and rewrote his descriptions of all geographical regions of the Soviet Union. The version prepared for the 50th anniversary of the Revolution, *Moya Rossiya* (1966; My Russia), was awarded the Gorky Prize in 1968. An autobiographical povest, *Cherstvye imeniny* (1974; Difficult Name Day), presents scenes from his entire life. He combined these with old travel sketches in *Krug zemnoy* (1976; Around the World). Mikhaylov lived in Moscow and was a member of the review commission of the Writers Union of the USSR from 1954 to 1976.

Mikhaylov's books are smoothly written works of popular science with interpolated reflections or sketches from his personal experiences. Mikhaylov praises his homeland, especially for the progress achieved in the spirit of the Party, and offers statistics, not so that the reader can form his own opinion, but in order to underscore the positive image that conceals all uncertainties.

Works: *Khan-Tengri*, 1933; *Lico strany menjaetsja*, 1937; *Naša strana*, 1945; *Zemlja russkaja*, 1946; *Nad kartoj Rodiny*, 1947 (see above); *Idu po meridianu*, 1957 (see above); *Moja Rossija*, 1966; *Putešestvie k sebe*, in *Novyj mir* 1967:5; *Respublika jantarnaja*, 1970; *Čerstvye imeniny* (pov.), in *Novyj mir* 1974:2–3, separate ed., 1974; *Krug zemnoj* (pov.), 1976.

Secondary Lit.: N. Atarov, in *Novyj mir* 1948:2; S. Maršak, in *Novyj mir* 1958:9; L. Kudrevatykh, in *Lit. gazeta* Jan. 30, 1964; A. Zjabrev, in *Moskva* 1969:7; S. Baruzdin, in his *Ljudi i knigi*, 1978; obituary, in *Lit. gazeta* March 17, 1982, p. 6; E. Murzaev, in *Naš sovremennik* 1985:12.

**Mínsky, Nikoláy Maksímovich** (pseud. of N. M. Vilénkin), poet (b. Jan. 27 [Jan. 15], 1855, Glubokoye, prov. Vilna—d. July 2, 1937, Paris). Minsky attended secondary school in Minsk, studied law at St. Petersburg University from 1875 to 1879, then combined his work as a lawyer with that of a poet and philosophically inclined publicist. His first book, *Stikhotvoreniya* (1887; Poems), contains both short and long poems and the drama *Smert Kaya Grakkha* (Death of Kay Grakkh). In the treatise *Pri svete sovesti* (1890; In the Light of Conscience), he develops his teaching on "meonism" (from the Greek mē on, "nonbeing"), in which he sees the future religion replacing the existing religion, which is dying out in a crisis of faith. Minsky's ideas were rejected by both V. Solovyov and G. Plekhanov. In order to establish a newspaper, *Novaya zhizn*, he entered a short-lived union with the Social Democrats in 1905. He was forced to emigrate and lived in Paris until 1913; there he characterized "the interests of the Social Democrats as incompatible with the interests of culture." He returned to Russia, but a renewed visit to Paris caused by World War I in 1914 led to his final emigration. At the beginning of the 1920s, Minsky lived first in Berlin; later he became a member of the Soviet political mission in London. From 1927 to 1937 he lived in Paris.

Minsky's poems reflect the vacillations and contradictions of his life. In his well-written poems, Minsky—under the influence of Semyon Nadson and Maurice Maeterlink—reveals a profound search for the meaning of life and for a mainstay in God. Because of these poems, he is considered a precursor of the symbolists. Social poems stand next to philosophic ones. Coexisting as objectives are affirmative faith and melancholy, the recognition of being and of nonbeing. Minsky has also translated extensively (Homer's *Iliad*, Byron, Verlaine, Shelley, and others).

Works: *Stikhotvorenija* (poems), 1887 (reprinted, Letchworth, 1977); *Pri svete sovesti* (scholarly articles), 1890; *Religija buduščego* (scholarly articles), 1905; *Polnoe sobr. stikhotvorenij* (poems), 4 vols., 1970; *Iz mraka k svetu* (poems), Berlin, 1922; *Ot Dante k Bloku* (scholarly articles), 31 poems in *Poèty 1880–1890-kh godov*, 1972.

Secondary Lit.: V. Brjusov, in *Vesy* 1980:7 and in his *Sobr. soč.*, vol. 6, 1975; A. Blok, "Pis'ma o poèzii," in *Zolotoe runo* 1908:7–10, and in his *Sobr. soč.*, vol. 5, 1962; Ju. Ajkhenval'd, in *Istorija russkoj lit. 19 veka*, ed. D. Ovsjaniko-Kulikovskij, vol. 5, 1910, pp. 280–86; S. A. Vengerov, G. Polonskij, E. Radlov, in *Russkaja lit. XX veka*, ed. S. A. Vengerov, vol. 1, 1914, pp. 357–409, vol. 2, 1915, pp. 190–92 (reprinted, Munich, 1972); A. Luther, *Geschichte der russischen Lit.*, 1924; E. Mil'ton, in *Novyj žurnal*, New York, 91:1968; L. Dolgopolov and L. Nikolaev, in *Poèty 1880–1890-kh godov*, 1972; G. Wytrzens, in *Korrespondenzen: Festschrift für D. Gerhardt*, Giessen, 1977.

**Míntslov, Sergéy Rudólfovich,** prose writer (b. Jan. 13 [Jan. 1], 1870, Ryazan—d. Dec. 18, 1933, Riga). Mintslov's grandfather moved from Königsberg to St. Petersburg and became an important librarian and the tutor of the young Tsar Aleksandr III. Mintslov received his education at the cadet institute in Nizhniy Novgorod and at the Aleksandr School in Moscow. He studied archaeology. For his military service, he chose the country of his ancestors, Lithuania, and, after 1892, the Caucasus. Simultaneously, Mintslov was developing into one of the most important Russian collectors of, and experts on, rare books; he earned an enduring name for himself as a bibliophile and bibliographer. After Mintslov abandoned the career of officer, he combined the activity of a bibliographer with that of an archaeologist and writer. In addition, he established a large trade academy in St. Petersburg in 1900 and directed it until 1914. In 1916–17 Mintslov appears to have been active in Trebizond as an officer and an archaeologist. After the Bolshevik seizure of power, he remained in the West, lived for a while in Yugoslavia (Zemun), and moved in the mid-1920s to Riga. Mintslov first published in *Sovremennye za-*

piski (Paris) and in the publishing houses of
the Russian emigration in Berlin and, after
1927, in Riga. His historical novels enjoyed
great popularity among the Parisian émigrés—
in N. Knorring's poll of 1933, Mintslov's books
held first place with 251 loans from the Turgenev Library (I. Turgenev 92, I. Shmelyov
44, Yu. Felzen 24; see *Vstrechi*, 1934, p. 177).

From 1888 on, Mintslov published numerous historical short stories and novels, especially concerning the medieval history of Russia, Lithuania, and Western Europe, such as
*V grozu* (1902; By Thunder), *Pod shum dubov*
(1919; Under the Noise of the Oaks), *Priklyucheniya studentov* (1928; Adventure of the
Students), *Orliny vzlyot* (1931; Eagle's Flight).
Other works dealt with Siberia and the Far
East, such as *Ognenny put* (1905; The Fiery
Path) and *Sekretnoye porucheniye* (1915; Secret Agreement), and he published numerous
volumes of memoirs. His prose is distinguished by its comprehensive ethnographic
and historical knowledge and stands in the
tradition of Sir Walter Scott and P. I. Melnikov-Pechersky. Mintslov has a strong relationship to medieval mysticism and to nature and
its world of spirits: "The forest is the place
where submerged powers appear; therefore it
is horrible and mysterious for men who have
long since lost their connection to these powers."

Works: *Volki* (novel), 1899, 5th ed., Riga,
1927; *V grozu* (novel), 1902, 4th ed., Riga,
1927; *Ognennyj put'* (novel), 1905, Riga, 1929;
*Obzor zapisok, dnevnikov, vospominanij, pi-
sem i putešestvij, otnosjaščikhsja k istorii Rossii
. . .* (annotated bibliography), Novgorod,
1911–12 (reprinted, Leipzig, 1976); *Sekretnoe
poručenie*, Berlin, 1915; *Istoričeskie dramy*,
Trebizond, 1917; *Pod šum dubov* (novel), 1919,
Berlin, 1924; *Za mërtvymi dušami* (travel articles), Berlin, 1921 (reprinted, Paris, 1978,
also in *Sovremennye zapiski*, Paris, 5, 6, 8,
10, 15–17:1921–23); *Sny zemli* (novel), excerpts in *Sovremennye zapiski* 19–21:1924,
separate ed., Berlin, 1925; *To, čego my ne
znaem* (short stories), Sofia, 1926; *Zakat*
(novel), Berlin, 1926; *Svjatye ozëra. Nedav-
nee*, Riga, 1927; *Priključenija studentov* (novel),
Riga, 1928; *Mističeskie večera* (short stories),
Riga, 1930; *Orlinyj vzlët* (novel), Riga, 1931;
*Peterburg v 1903–1910 gg* (memoirs), Riga,
1931.

Secondary Lit.: A. Amov, in *Istoričeskij
vestnik* 134:1913; A. Izjumov, in *Na čužoj
storone*, Prague, 12:1925; E. Jakuševa, in *Vol'-
naja Sibir'*, Prague, 5:1929; P. Pil'skij, in Min-
clov's *Mističeskie večera*, 1930, pp. 5–43.

**Molodáya gvárdiya** (Young Guard), a union
of young Communist writers established in
October 1922 at the initiative of the Central
Committee of the Communist youth movement and composed primarily of the first
Komsomol writers. The most famous members included A. Bezymensky, A. Zharov, M.
Svetlov, M. Golodny; other members were I.
Doronin, V. Gerasimova, N. Bogdanov. A
number of writers who could not identify
with the aggressive politics of the Molodaya
gvardiya, such as Golodny and Svetlov, were
among the founders of the group PEREVAL in
early 1924. Molodaya gvardiya adopted the
same intolerant oppositional stance toward
KUZNITSA and the FELLOW TRAVELERS as did
the Communist Party group OKTYABR, with
which it was connected through double membership. In March 1923, Molodaya gvardiya
was incorporated into MAPP, the association
created by Oktyabr, and through this association later became part of RAPP. A publishing
house by the name of Molodaya gvardiya was
established in 1922 and still exists today.
Through its union with RAPP, Molodaya
gvardiya lost its reason for being and was
disbanded, at the very latest, together with
RAPP in 1932.

Secondary Lit.: Molodogvardeec. *Trëkhletie
gruppy pisatelej "Molodaja gvardija,"* 1926;
see also RAPP.

**Molodáya gvárdiya** (The Young Guard), a
literary and political journal of the Central
Committee of the Communist youth organization (Komsomol). *Molodaya gvardiya* was
founded in 1922 by the political-literary group
of the same name and was published in Moscow until 1941. In 1948 publication was resumed as an almanac (17 volumes); in 1956
it was reinstated as a monthly journal. Among
the editors of the first period are the writers
S. Gusev (1926–28) and A. Karavayeva (1931–
38); since 1972 control has been in the hands
of A. Ivanov (a member of the editorial staff
since 1969). Since 1956 the number of well-
known writers who have belonged to the editorial staff for more than a couple of years is
not large: A, Kalinin (1958–62), S. Sartakov
(1958–62), V. Fyodorov (1959–84), V. Tsybin
(1961–66), Yu. Kazakov (1963–66), A. Rekemchuk (1962–66, with interruptions), V.
Soloukhin (1964–81), P. Proskurin (1970–).
*Molodaya gvardiya* published the Komsomol
poets of the 1920s and 1930s, such as E.
Bagritsky, A. Bezymensky, M. Golodny, M.
Svetlov, I. Utkin, A. Zharov; the works of M.

Chumandrin, V. Mayakovsky (Klop), A. Neverov, N. Ostrovsky, I. Selvinsky, and A. Tarasov-Rodionov also appeared there. During the Stalin period, propagandists such as Ye. Dolmatovsky and V. Lebedev-Kumach published verse in its pages. In its second phase, the journal retained its emphatically political orientation and became the stronghold of nationalist Russian tendencies. In addition to the members of the editorial staff, writers who have published in Molodaya gvardiya include V. Aksyonov, Yu. Bondarev, M. Bubennov, N. Matveyeva, V. Nekrasov, V. Pikul, V. Roslyakov, B. Slutsky, A. Sobolev, A. Sofronov, I. Stadnyuk, V. Tendryakov, Yu. Trifonov, Ye. Vinokurov, and Ye. Yevtushenko. Molodaya gvardiya has also published poems by poets who died in World War II: P. Kogan, M. Kulchitsky, N. Mayorov. In 1975 the circulation was 590,000; in 1983, 790,000; in 1986, 650,000.

Secondary Lit.: A. Karavaeva, in Molodaja gvardija 1932:8–9 and 1962:5; Očerki istorii russkoj sovetskoj žurnalistiki, 1966; B. Filippov, in Russkaja mysl', Paris, April 20, 1978, pp. 10–11.

**Mórits, Yúnna Petróvna** (originally Pínkhusovna), poet (b. June 2, 1937, Kiev). Morits's first poems appeared in 1954; her first volume, Razgovor o schastye (Conversation about Happiness), followed in 1957. She finished her studies at the Gorky Literary Institute in 1961. The experiences of her journey across the Arctic Ocean were reflected in the lyric collection Mys Zhelaniya (1961; Cape of Desire), which attracted considerable attention with its unaffected combination of sensitive, intelligent sketches and descriptions of the rough reality of the sailor's life. Morits's verse, distant from the politics of the day, appears from time to time in Yunost. She was able to collect the poems of 1962–69 in Loza (1970; The Vine), which was followed by Surovoy nityu (1974; With Coarse Thread). A volume of poems by the Jewish poet M. Toif appeared in Morits's translation in 1964. She won a prize for her translation of poems by the Lithuanian poet Salomeya Neris (Novy mir 1968:5). Malinovaya koshka (1976; The Raspberry Cat) brings together 16 short narrative poems for children. The poems of Pri svete zhizni (1977; By the Light of Life) and Tretiy glaz (1980; The Third Eye) revolve around the questions of life, death, and art, and give fresh evidence of Morits's literary artistry. She lives in Moscow.

Morits consciously belongs to the tradition of M. Tsvetayeva; nevertheless, her talent is strong enough to speak for itself. Without playing experimental games, Morits continues the awareness of the word that is characteristic of pre-Revolutionary poetry. Many of her poems, arising from profound sadness, confront death and the problem of mortality. Her images, based on real and visionary elements, are always naturally expressed and never stoop to false pathos; many of them revolve around the pain of the soul, fate, loneliness, and the immediacy of childhood. An abundance of colors and a mixture of rhyme and assonance charcterize Morits's verse, as do often incantationlike repetitions and metaphors; new possibilities of interpretation of her verses, which grapple with the very essence of being, suggest themselves again and again.

Works: Razgovor o sčast'e (poems), 1957; Mys Želanija (poems), 1961; Pjat' stikhotvorenij o bolezni moej materi (poems), in Den' poèzii, Moscow, 1968; Sčastlivyj žuk (children's verse), 1969; Loza (poems), 1970; Surovoj nit'ju (poems), 1974; Malinovaja koška (poems), 1976; Pri svete žizni (poems), 1977; Tretij glaz (poems), 1980.—Izbr., 1982.

Secondary Lit.: A. Isbakh, in Oktjabr' 1962:8; E. Naumov, in Zvezda 1963:5; A. Kireeva, in Junost' 1971:5; S. Čuprinin, in Lit. obozrenie 1979:6; E. Ermilova and V. Novikov, in Lit. gazeta Aug. 5, 1981, p. 5; S. Lominadze, in Naš sovremennik 1983:11.

**Mórshen, Nikoláy Nikoláyevich** (pseud. of N. N. Márchenko), poet (b. Nov. 8, 1917, Kiev). Morshen's father wrote under the pseudonym N. V. Narókov. Morshen finished his studies in physics at Kiev University in 1941. In 1944 he went to Germany; he lived in Hamburg after World War II. Morshen, who began writing poetry in 1935, had his work first published in the emigration (in Grani from 1948 on and in Novy zhurnal from 1949 on). In 1950 Morshen moved to the United States, where he worked as a Russian language instructor in California until 1977. Apart from the regular publication of poems in Russian journals and an occasional inclusion in anthologies, three volumes of Morshen's verse were publsihed: Tyulen (1959; The Seal), in Germany; Dvoyetochie (1967; Colon) and Ekho i zerkalo (1979; Echo and Mirror) in the United States. Morshen lives with his family in Monterey, California.

Morshen's approximately 150 published poems show strong development. His early verse is shaped by the loss of his homeland and by his revolt against the anxiety and the lack of freedom in the Soviet Union. Relatively soon this temporal reference in his thematics becomes secondary and is retained for the most part only through his choice of imagery. Morshen writes reflective verse in which the world is comprehended in all its contradictoriness. The "colon" that in the title poem of the second volume replaces the "full stop" usually expected after the word "death" emphasizes his candor in respect to all essential questions of being. Primarily in his third volume, the word itself often becomes the subject of the poem; through neologisms and through play with the meaning of a word, as well as with parts of words and letters, the word becomes the point of departure for the analysis of meaning. The paradox and the irony of Morshen's message reveal his distance from world events and conceal his own position, forcing the reader to think further. Occasionally highly unusual rhymes give Morshen's verse an especial charm.

*Works:* Poems, in *Na Zapade: Antologija,* ed. Ju. Ivask, New York, 1953, and in *Literaturnoe zarubež'e,* Munich, 1958; *Tjulen'* (poems), Frankfurt am Main, 1959; *Dvoetočie* (poems), Washington, 1967; *Ėkho i zerkalo* (poems), Berkeley, 1979.

*Secondary Lit.:* I. Odoevceva, in *Novyj žurnal,* New York, 58:1958; V. Markov, foreword to Moršen's *Tjulen',* 1959; G. Struve, in *Novoe russkoe slovo,* New York, Oct. 1, 1959; L. Alekseeva, in *Grani,* Frankfurt am Main, 41:1959; S. Karlinsky, in *Novyj žurnal* 88:1967 and in *Slavic Review* 1982:1; B. Narcissov, in *Novyj žurnal* 125:1976; W. Kasack, in *Osteuropa* 1981:1; L. Flejšman, in *Odna ili dve russkikh literatury,* Lausanne, 1981; V. Setschkareff, in *Die Welt der Slaven* 1982:2; J. P. Hinrichs, epilogue in I. Elagin and N. Morjen, *Gedichten,* Maastricht, 1985; B. Filippov, in NRL: *Neue russische Literatur* 1985.

*Moskvá* (Moscow), a literary journal, published monthly in Moscow since 1957; since 1959 it has been the journal of the Writers Union of the RSFSR and of the Moscow branch of the Writers Union. The first editor in chief was N. Atarov, and his coworkers on the editorial staff included K. Chukovsky (1957–59), Ye. Dorosh (1957–58), and V. Lugovskoy (1957). In 1958 he was replaced by Ye. Popovkin; the following writers worked on the editorial staff under his direction: M. Sholokhov (1958–84), L. Nikulin (1958–67), Ye.

Maltsev (1961–64), S. V. Smirnov (1964–), and V. Roslyakov (1966–69). Since Ye. Popovkin's death in 1968, M. Alekseyev has been the editorial director. *Moskva* publishes literary works of all genres but gives preference to those that concern the capital. In this journal, works with a conservative character predominate, for example those by S. Babayevsky, G. Beryozko, Ye. Isayev, A. Ivanov, G. Medynsky, L. Nikulin, Ye. Permitin, Ye. Permyak, and A. Sofronov. However, *Moskva* has also published the prose of V. Belov, V. Nekrasov, K. Paustovsky, V. Syomin, Yu. Tendryakov, and F. Vigdorova. The journal earned considerable merit when Popovkin's advisers won approval for the publication of M. Bulgakov's novel *Master i Margarita,* which had been suppressed for 25 years (1966:11, 1967:1); his film script *Mertvye dushi* followed (1978:1). The publication of chapters from B. Pilnyak's *Solyanoy ambar* (1964:5), nine poems by O. Mandelshtam (1964:8), and five poems by M. Voloshin (1977:5) was exceptional and commendable. The circulation has always been quite high: 160,000 in 1964, 275,000 in 1975, 610,000 in 1984, and 450,000 in 1987.

*Secondary Lit.:* E. Popovkin, in *Nedelja* July 12–18, 1964; V. Voronov, in *Lit. Rossija* Dec. 24, 1965, p. 22; M. Alekseev, in *Lit. Rossija* Jan. 28, 1977, p. 3; interview, in *Lit. Rossija* April 2, 1982, p. 9.

*Mostý* (Bridges), an almanac for literature, art, and politics. A total of 15 volumes appeared between 1958 and 1970; volumes 1 to 10 were published in Munich by TsOPE (Tsentralnoye obyedineniye politicheskikh emigrantov iz SSSR [Central Association of Political Émigrés from the USSR]). After this organization was disbanded, volumes 11 to 15 were issued under the institutional name of Tovarishchestvo zarubezhnykh pisateley (Partnership of Foreign Writers) and under the personal responsibility of the editor G. Andreyev (pseudonym of G. A. Khomyakov), who later moved to the United States (no. 13/14, 1968, and no. 15, 1970). In its sections on literature, *Mosty* published poems and short prose works, usually written by émigré writers; memoirs (for example, Yu. Annenkov, B. Pilnyak, I. Babel, and M. Zoshchenko in 9:1962); and several articles on the history of literature and literary criticism by G. Adamovich, B. Filippov, Yu. Ivask, L. Rzhevsky, F. Stepun, G. Struve (including one on the newspaper *Vozrozhdeniye* in 3:1959), V. Veydle, V. Zavalishin (about A. Grin in 1:1958).

Secondary Lit.: V. Zlobin, in Vozroždenie, Paris, 100:1960; G. Andreev, in Russkaja literatura v èmigracii, ed. N. Poltorackij, Pittsburgh, 1972.

**Mozháyev, Borís Andréyevich,** prose writer (b. June 1, 1923, Pitelino, oblast Ryazan). In 1948 Mozhayev completed his studies in engineering at the military college in Leningrad and subsequently went to the Far East and China as a naval officer. During his 12 years of military service, he began working as a journalist. In 1954 his first short story appeared in a provincial newspaper; starting in 1956 his journalistic prose was published in supraregional journals. During his work in Siberia he collected and published folk poetry, as in Udegeyskiye skazki (1955; Udeheskian Tales). For the first time in Vlast taygi (1958; The Power of the Taiga), he collected his own prose, which deals with the changes and the conservative Stalinist traditions of his time, especially in the village, from a liberal point of view. With Polyushko-pole (1965; Field, My Field), Mozhayev switched to longer prose works. The povest that A. Tvardovsky published in Novy mir, Iz zhizni Fyodora Kuzkina (1966: From the Life of Fyodor Kuzkin), was attacked for its overly critical outlook and was first cleared for publication in book form in 1973 in the collection Lesnaya doroga (The Forest Path) under the title Zhivoy (The Living). In 1969 Mozhayev advocated an objective discussion of the "planned expulsion" of A. Solzhenitsyn from the Writers Union. After 1970, Mozhayev's books began appearing again. Mozhayev is seldom a delegate to the congresses of the Writers Union. He lives in Moscow.

Hunters, raftsmen, kolkhoz peasants, agronomists, artists, militiamen, and many other contemporary individuals are the figures in his vividly and excitingly written prose. Mozhayev favors strong personalities, just as he positions his creative activity clearly in support of the renunciation of undemocratic forms of government and the confirmation of action, both interpersonal and political, that is ruled by one's conscience. Zhivoy is an important literary contribution in praise of the Russian peasant who adapts to his difficult fate patiently and capably. The novel Muzhiki i baby (1976: Peasant Men and Women) describes the exploitation of the village in the early 1920s. The povest Poltora kvadratnych metra (1982; One and a Half Square Meters) presents the basic problems of legal inequality in the Soviet system and their human consequences in an amusingly ironic form by using the example of a renters' dispute.

Works: Udegejskie skazki (folk tales), 1955; Zori nad okeanom (poems), 1955; Vlast' tajgi (short stories), 1958; Sanja (short stories), 1961; V amurskoj dal'nej storone (publicistic prose), 1963; Poljuško-pole (pov.), 1965; Iz žizni Fëdora Kuz'kina (pov.), in Novyj mir 1966:7, and under the title Živoj, 1973; Dal'nevostočnye povesti, 1970; Dal'nie dorogi (short stories), 1970; Samostojatel'nost' (essay), 1972; Lesnaja doroga (short stories), 1973; Mužiki i baby (novel), 1976; Starye istorii (pov. and short stories), 1978; Poltora kvadratnykh metra (pov.), in Družba narodov 1982:4; Tonkomer (pov.), 1984; Kak zemlja vertitsja (play), in Teatr 1986:1.—Izbr. proizv., 2 vols., 1982.

Secondary Lit.: V. Anikin, in Lit. gazeta July 31, 1956; I. Zolotusskij, in Oktjabr' 1962:4; R. Agišev, in Lit. gazeta Nov. 12, 1966; G. Brovman, in Don 1967:7; F. Kuznecov, in Lit. Rossija July 12, 1974, p. 10; E. Isaev, S. Zalygin, A. Borščagovskij, Vl. Souloukhin, et al., in Russkaja mysl', Paris, Dec. 4, 1975, pp. 6–7; V. Khmara, in Lit. Rossija Aug. 15, 1980, p. 9; A. Kondratovič, in Lit. Rossija May 27, 1983, p. 11; K. Sapgir, in Grani, Frankfurt am Main, 131:1984.

**Mstislávsky, Sergéy Dmítriyevich** (pseud. of S. D. Maslóvsky), prose writer (b. Sept. 4 [Aug. 23], 1876, Moscow—d. April 22, 1943, Irkutsk). Mstislavsky's father was a professor. Mstislavsky studied natural science at St. Petersburg University (1895–1901) and took part in an anthropological and ethnological expedition to Tadzhikistan in 1896. From 1901 to 1912 he worked as a bibliographer and collaborator on various encyclopedias and published numerous journalistic pieces. Beginning in 1904 Mstislavsky, as a member of the Socialist Revolutionary Party and of the Central Committee of the All-Russian Officers' League, participated actively in the revolutionary movement; at the time of the October Revolution he was assigned to help in the arrest of the royal family. From 1921 on, Mstislavsky, who did not join the Communist Party, held various prominent cultural and political posts, such as acting editor in chief of the Great Soviet Encyclopedia (1925–30). Between 1925 and 1940 Mstislavsky wrote seven novels, based largely on his personal experiences during the Revolution. He held posts in the Writers Union of the USSR and taught at the Gorky Literary Institute in Moscow.

Mstislavsky's first novel, *Krysha mira* (1925; The Roof of the World), is based on experiences on expeditions during his student days. His presentations of the Revolution, such as *Na krovi* (1928; On the Blood), were criticized for insufficiently emphasizing the role of the Bolsheviks. After his death, Mstislavksy was represented in literary histories as the author of a single book (the only work of his to be reprinted), *Grach, ptitsa vesennyaya* (1937; Eng. tr., *Rook—Herald of Spring*, 1955), a book for young people about the revolutionary N. Bauman; Mstislavsky also adapted the book for the stage.

*Works: Kryša mira* (novel), 1925, 3d ed., 1930; *Na krovi* (novel), 1928; *Sojuz tjažëloj kavalerii* (novel), 1929; *Bez sebja* (novel), 1930; *Partioncy* (novel), 1933; *Grač, ptica vesennjaja* (pov.), 1937, 5th ed., 1963 (see above); *Nakanune: 1917 god* (novel), 1940.
*Secondary Lit.:* A. E., in *Novyj mir* 1928:7; S. Fenina, in *Teatr* 1956:4; *RSPP* 3:1964.

**Musátov, Alekséy Ivánovich,** prose writer (b. March 25 [March 12], 1911, Lizunovo, prov. Vladimir—d. Jan. 3, 1977, Moscow). Musatov was the son of a peasant. Musatov completed his studies at the Moscow Institute for Editing and Publishing in 1935. In 1930 he published some prose pieces based on the adventures of village children; the povest *Stozhary* (1948; Eng. tr., *Stozhary Village*, 1954) was awarded a Stalin Prize (1949, 3d class). Musatov was admitted to the Communist Party in 1952. He lived in Moscow and last attended a Writers Congress in 1959. Musatov's work has been extensively reprinted (ten books in 1970–71 alone).

Musatov's early prose unfolds in the village before collectivization, then shifts to the theme of the class struggle in the village; *Stozhary* tells of the mobilization of a children's brigade in the reconstruction of a postwar village. His themes, inspired by the latest Party position, often serve a pedagogical purpose, while the artistic value of his prose is of a low level. The schematic black-or-white portrayal of the characters is consistent with Musatov's inability to present events vividly. "Most often, the author replaces the artistic exposition of characters with illustrations of one or another of the heroes' successful achievements" (Braynina).

*Works: Šankhajka* (pov.), 1930; *Šekamjatka* (pov.), 1931; *Stožary* (pov.), 1948 (see above); *Dom na gore* (pov.), 1951; *Klava Nazarova* (pov.), 1958; *Višnëvyj sad* (pov., with M. Ljašenko), 1966; *Medunica* (pov. and short stories), 1967; *Čerëmukha* (pov.), 1970; *Nočnoj oboz* (pov.), 1971.
*Secondary Lit.:* V. Brajnina, in *Zvezda* 1954:6; G. Lenobl', in *Novyj mir* 1954:9; V. Nikolaev, 1962; M. Priležaeva, in *Lit. gazeta* July 2, 1964; E. Ivanova, in *Lit. Rossija* Sept. 29, 1972, p. 20; obituary, in *Lit. gazeta* Jan. 5, 1977, p. 2.

# N

**Nabókov, Vladímir Vladímirovich** (pseud. until 1940 was Vladímir Sírin), prose writer, poet (b. April 22 [April 10], 1899, St. Petersburg—d. July 2, 1977, Montreux). Nabokov's father was a jurist with a high position in the civil service. Nabokov emigrated in 1919. He studied French literature and entomology at Cambridge. From 1922 to 1937 he lived in Berlin and worked as a writer and translator. In St. Petersburg in 1916 and 1918 he compiled and privately published two small collections of his own poetry; some of these poems had appeared in journals. From 1921 to 1929 in *Rul* (Berlin), Nabokov regularly published poems that he collected into volumes of selected poems in 1923 and 1930. *Mashenka* (1926; Eng. tr., *Mary*, 1970), Nabokov's first novel, was followed by seven more by 1937. *Korol, dama, valet* (1928; Eng. tr., *King, Queen, Knave*, 1968) was published as a serial in the *Vossische Zeitung. Kamera obskura* (1932–33; Eng. tr., *Laughter in the Dark*, 1938) had been translated into 14 languages by 1963. In 1937 Nabokov emigrated to Paris where all of his novels had been published in *Sovremennye zapiski* since 1929. The last issue (70:1940) carried the beginning of *Solus Rex*; this novel was never completed. In Paris Nabokov worked as a translator and as a language and tennis instructor. The German invasion in 1940 forced him to move to the United States. From then on he wrote in American English and translated several important works of Russian literature (N. Gogol, A. Pushkin, M. Lermontov) into English. He was also active as an internationally recognized specialist on butterflies. From 1948 to 1959 he was a professor of literature at Cornell University; in 1960 he moved to Montreux (Switzerland) where he wrote new novels and translated many of his earlier works into English. None of Nabokov's works were published in the Soviet Union up to 1986, when several poems and the novel *Zashchita Luzhina* (1929–30; Eng. tr., *The Defense*, 1964) were printed.

Nabokov's poetry is characterized by a fundamental religiosity; it gives form to human existence rooted in the visible and invisible worlds. His verse is based on a nonrational awareness of man's destiny in the spiritual realm and of his repeated reincarnations. It is profound, concise, and clear. His conscious use of words forms one of the enduring characteristics of his numerous novels, in which the intellectual content is forced into the background by his zest for playing with the form of the novel, for breaking the action with ever new points of view, for parodying literary genres, for leading the reader through narrative labyrinths. His novels and short stories are characterized by paradoxical statements and the complexity that accompanies such paradoxes and by aesthetic pleasure in the artistic structure. Nabokov occupies a special position within the first emigration. His age at emigration makes it understandable why only a few of his early novels have a plot set entirely or partially in Russia. *Mashenka* provides insight into the onset of emigration; here the protagonist is a compound solely of ideal and remembered images. *Zashchita Luzhina,* a novel about chess that illuminates the border between genius and insanity, develops against a background of memories of Russia and criticism of the émigré life in Berlin. *Dar* (1937–38; Eng. tr., *The Gift*, 1963) combines the biography of a Russian author of the 19th century with a fictional story about the young biographer. Other Russian and American novels by Nabokov are dissociated from the world of experiences, especially *Lolita* (1955), which, with its unusual, erotic theme of the relationship between a 40-year-old man and a precocious 12-year-old girl, guaranteed Nabokov worldwide renown but perhaps kept him from receiving the Nobel Prize. (An earlier and much shorter version of this novel, under the title *Volshebnik* [written 1940], was first published in English in 1986 as *The Enchanter*.) *Ada or Ardor: A Family Chronicle* (1969) resumes the theme of lost Russian culture of the 19th century, as does *Pnin* (1957), and also reveals in the shifting levels of time one of Nabokov's essential concerns, that of the

continuity of the past and the significance of time. Nabokov's works are animated by the tension produced by combining scrupulous exactitude that is scientifically descriptive and realistic, a surrealistic, fantastic joy in creation, intellectual games of composition, and musical, spiritual intuition. "Not only his poetry but also his prose forges again and again into regions that one can scarcely err in designating mystical" (Setschkareff).

*Works: Stikhi* (poems), 1916; *Grozd'* (poems), Berlin, 1923; *Gornyj put'* (poems), Berlin, 1923; *Mašen'ka* (novel), Berlin, 1926 (reprinted, Ann Arbor, 1974) (see above); *Korol', dama, valet* (novel), Berlin, 1928 (reprinted, Ann Arbor, 1975) (see above); *Zaščita Lužina* (novel), Berlin, 1930 (reprinted, Ann Arbor, 1979), and in *Moskva* 1986:12 (see above); *Vozvraščenie Čorba* (short stories and poems), Berlin, 1930 (reprinted Ann Arbor, 1976) (Eng. tr., *The Return of Chorb*, 1976); *Sogljadataj* (novel), in *Sovremennye zapiski*, Paris, 44:1930 (reprinted, Ann Arbor, 1978) (Eng. tr., *The Eye*, 1965); *Kamera obskura* (novel), Paris, 1932 (reprinted, Ann Arbor, 1978) (see above); *Podvig* (novel), Berlin, 1932 (reprinted, Ann Arbor, 1974) (Eng. tr., *Glory*, 1971); *Otčajanie* (novel), Berlin, 1936 (reprinted, Ann Arbor, 1978) (Eng. tr., *Despair*, 1937); *Dar* (novel), in *Sovremennye zapiski* 63:1937 to 67:1938, separate ed., New York, 1952, 2d ed., Ann Arbor, 1975 (see above); *Izobretenie Val'sa* (play), in *Russkie zapiski*, Paris, Nov. 1938 (Eng. tr., *The Waltz Invention*, 1966); *Priglašenie na kazn'* (novel), Paris, 1938 (reprinted, Ann Arbor, 1979 and 1984) (Eng. tr., *Invitation to a Beheading*, 1959); *Sobytie* (play), in *Russkie zapiski* April 1938 (Eng. tr., *The Event*, 1984); *Solus Rex* (fragment of a novel), in *Sovremennye zapiski* 70:1940 (Eng. tr., 1973); *The Real Life of Sebastian Knight.* (novel), Norfolk, Conn., 1941; *Nikolai Gogol,* New York, 1944 (reprinted, London, 1973), Russian tr., in *Novyj mir* 1987:4; *Bend Sinister* (novel), New York, 1947; *Stikhotvorenija 1929–51* (poems), Paris, 1952; *Drugie berega* (memoirs), New York, 1954, 2d ed., Ann Arbor, 1978 (originally in English as *Conclusive Evidence,* 1951; Eng. tr., with revisions, *Speak, Memory,* 1967); *Lolita* (novel), Paris, 1955, Russian ed., New York, 1967 (reprinted, Ann Arbor, 1986); *Vesna v Fial'te* (short stories), New York, 1956 (reprinted, Ann Arbor, 1984); *Pnin* (novel), New York, 1957, Russian tr., 1983; *Pale Fire* (novel), New York, 1962, Russian tr., *Blednyj ogon',* 1984; *Ada or Ardor: A Family Chronicle* (novel), New York–Toronto, 1969; *Poems and Problems,* New York,

1971; *Transparent Things*, New York, 1972; *Look at the Harlequins!* (novel), New York, 1974; *Stikhi* (poems), Ann Arbor, 1979; *The Nabokov-Wilson Letters 1940–1971*, ed. S. Karlinsky, London, 1979.

*Secondary Lit.*: Bibliographies: A. Field, New York, 1973; S. Schuman, Boston, 1979; M. Juliar, New York, 1986.—N. Berberova, in *Novyj žurnal*, New York, 57:1959; P. Stegner, New York, 1966; A. Field, London, 1967, and New York, 1977; *Nabokov: The Man and His Work*, ed. L. S. Dembo, Madison, Wisc., 1967; C. R. Proffer, Bloomington, Ind., 1968; J. Moynahan, Minneapolis, Minn., 1971; W. W. Rowe, New York, 1971, and Ann Arbor, 1981; O. Mikhajlov, in *Naš sovremennik* 1974:1; D. E. Morton, New York, 1974; A. Appel, in *The Bitter Air of Exile: Russian Writers in the West 1922–1972*, ed. S. Karlinsky and A. Appel, Berkeley, 1977; J. Grayson, London, 1977; Z. Šakhovskaja, Paris, 1979; E. Pifer, Cambridge, 1980; V. Setschkareff, in *Die Welt der Slaven* 1980:1; D. Barton Johnson, in *Russian Literature* 1981:2 and Ann Arbor, 1985; *Nabokov: The Critical Heritage*, ed. N. Page, Boston, 1982; S. Davydov, Munich, 1982; R. Hof, Munich, 1984; D. Rampton, Cambridge, 1984; B. Boyd, Ann Arbor, 1985.

**Nagíbin, Yúry Márkovich**, prose writer and scriptwriter (b. April 3, 1920, Moscow). Starting in 1938, Nagibin studied medicine first and then studied at the Moscow Institute of Cinematography. At his literary debut in 1939, Yu. Olesha and V. Katayev expressed their encouragement; his first short story appeared in 1940. His first books appeared during World War II, while he worked first as a political official and then as a correspondent for the newspaper *Trud*. Since the war he has considered himself a professional writer. Nagibin has stayed with two forms of poetic expression: the short story, which seldom expands to a longer form, and the film script, which is often based on his own prose (by 1973 he had written about 30 film scripts). Nagibin is prolific and is widely read. As the author of two short stories that appeared in the liberal *Literaturnaya Moskva* (1956:2)—*Kharzarsky ornament* (Eng. tr., "The Khazar Ornament," in *Year of Protest, 1956*, 1960) and *Svet v okne* (Eng. tr., "A Light in the Window" in *Year of Protest, 1956*, 1960)—Nagibin briefly encountered difficulties with the conservative critics. From 1955 to 1965 he belonged to the editorial staff of the journal *Znamya*, thereafter, until 1981, to that of the journal *Nash sovremennik*. In 1966 he joined the signatories of

the petition for A. Sinyavsky and Yu Daniel, but his prose does not generally involve social criticism. Nagibin gained a seat on the board of the Writers Union of the RSFSR only in 1975 and on that of the Writers Union of the USSR only in 1981. He lives in Moscow.

Nagibin is an author who writes consciously; his short stories are well-thought-out and have a fixed plan before he commits them to paper. Once they are written down, they receive only stylistic corrections. He models episodes, not fates, and clarifies the essential in the insignificant and the commonplace. In this respect, as well as in his close relationship to the forests and marshes of the Meshchora in central Russia, his prose demonstrates its ties to that of K. Paustovsky. But the latter experiences nature primarily as a wanderer, Nagibin as a hunter (see *Kogda utki v pore* [1963; When It Is Duck Season]). The content of Nagibin's short stories is very wide-ranging, dominated by the themes of war, nature, love, and children. The characters include people of all classes, professions, and ages, and the stories take place in the various landscapes of the Soviet Union. They are united by a focus on interpersonal relationships, a belief in the goodness in people, superior psychological motivations, and purity of conscience, honor, and duty. Nagibin once described the central theme of his creative work as the "awakening of man," that is, a new perception of the environment, a more conscious relationship—one that has been altered in a positive way—to the next person and thereby to oneself. In the short story *Zimniy dub* (1953; Eng. tr., "The Winter Oak," in *The Pipe*, 1955), this awakening of an adult and a child in and through nature is delicately and convincingly portrayed. From 1967 to 1971 Nagibin wrote a series of autobiographical short stories based on his childhood that more openly reveal his attitude than is typical for him. This series was followed by a cycle about musicians and writers, poetic studies of the creative process, so to speak. *Zastupnitsa* (1980; The Patroness) is a play about the death of M. Lermontov.

*Works*: *Zerno žizni* (short stories), 1948; *Zimnij dub* (short stories), 1956 (see above for Eng. tr. of title story); *Trudnoe sčast'e* (pov.), 1956 (Eng. tr., "Happiness Hard-Won," in *Soviet Literature* (1957:4); *Khazarskij ornament* and *Svet v okne* (short stories), in *Lit. Moskva* 1956:2 (see above); *Skalistyj porog* (short stories), 1958; *Čistye prudy* (pov. and short stories), 1962; *Na tikhom ozere* (short stories), 1966; *Pereulki moego detstva* (short stories),

1971; *V aprel'skom lesu* (pov. and short stories), 1974; *Pik udači* (pov.), 1975; *Berendeev les* (short stories and essays), 1978 (Eng. tr. of title story, "Berendey's Forest," in *Soviet Literature* 1980:2); *Kinoscenarii* (film scripts), 1980; *Zastupnica* (play), in *Teatr* 1980:6; *Blestjaščaja i gorestnaja žizn' Imre Kal'mana* (pov.), in *Oktjabr'* 1984:4; *Sil'nee vsekh inykh velenij* (pov.), in *Naš sovremennik* 1984:12; *Poezdka na ostrova* (pov.), in *Neva* 1986:1.— *Izbr. proizv.*, 2 vols., 1973; *Sobr. soč.*, 4 vols., 1980–81.

*Translations: Each for All* (short stories), 1945; *The Pipe: Stories*, 1955; *Dreams: Stories*, 1958; *Selected Short Stories*, 1963; *Island of Love* (short stories), 1982; *The Peak of Success and Other Stories*, 1985.

*Secondary Lit.*: E. Vorob'ev, in *Novyj mir* 1955:11; N. Vasil'eva, in *Oktjabr'* 1958:12; *RSPP* 3:1964; I. Ajzenštok, in *Zvezda* 1961:6; N. Atarov, in *Lit. gazeta* Oct. 13, 1960, and foreword to *Izbr. proizv.*, 1973; V. Sakharov, in *Naš sovremennik* 1975:1; M. Bojko, in *Lit. obozrenie* 1976:1; E. J. Cochrum, Diss., Michigan State Univ., 1977, and bibliography in *Russian Language Journal* 115:1979; I. Bogatko, 1980; P. Gusev, in *Lit. gazeta* April 3, 1985, p. 4; R. Mustafin, in *Lit. obozrenie* 1985:10; V. Čajkovskaja, in *Lit. obozrenie* 1986:12.

**Nárbut, Vladímir Ivánovich,** poet (b. April 14 [April 2], 1888, Narbutovka, prov. Chernigov—d. Nov. 15, 1944 [?], while imprisoned). Narbut was the son of a landowner. He studied philology at St. Petersburg University. He published his first poem in 1909 and his first volume of verse, *Stikhi* (Poems), in 1910; he joined the ACMEISTS in 1912. After the Revolution, Narbut became a member of the Communist Party and was assigned to a series of political and cultural organizational posts, combining these duties with his own literary career until 1921. In Voronezh in 1918–19 Narbut edited the biweekly publication *Sirena*, which, unlike the PROLETKULT, advocated the preservation of cultural tradition. He lived in the Ukraine from 1920 to 1922, where he held, among other positions, the post of director of the YugROSTA. In 1922 he moved to Moscow, where he served in the press section of the Central Committee of the Communist Party; he founded and headed the publishing house Zemlya i fabrika (ZIF), which specialized in complete editions. Narbut was expelled from the Party in 1928 and relieved of his position. Only a few of his poems were later published in journals. In 1937 he became a victim of the government purges. After his

REHABILITATION (around 1956), Narbut's name was once again occasionally mentioned, but his work was not reprinted in the Soviet Union.

Narbut began by writing pure nature lyrics, which earned the respect of V. Bryusov and N. Gumilyov, although they objected to the lack of personal expression. The second cycle, *Alliluiya* (1912; Hallelujah), provoked a divided critical response because it prominently featured repulsive material. Narbut's poetry is very concrete and colorful, favoring a descriptive, rhythmic prose language that incorporates Ukrainian lexical elements. Among Soviet writers, E. Bagritsky was the strongest admirer of Narbut's lyrics. The leading Soviet critics give a negative assessment of Narbut's poems, even the later ones about "Razin's and Lenin's Revolution."

*Works: Stikhi* (poems), 1910; *Na okhote* (short stories), 1912; *Allilujja* (poems), 1912, 2d ed., 1922; *Vij* (poems), 1915; *Ognennyj stolb* (poems), 1920; *Stikhi o vojne* (poems), 1920; *Sovetskaja zemlja* (poems), 1921; poems, in *Novyj mir* 1933:6 and *Antologija Peterburgskoj poèzii akmeizma*, Munich, 1973.— *Izbr. stikhi* (selected poems), Paris, 1983.

*Secondary Lit.*: N. Gumilëv, in *Apollon* 1911:6, 1912:6, and in his *Sobr. soč.*, 4 vols., Washington, 1968; D. Klenovskij, in *Grani*, Frankfurt am Main, 23:1954; M. Zenkevič, in *Den' poèzii*, 1967; R. D. B. Thomson, in *Russian Literature* 1981:4; L. V. Berlovskaja, in *Russkaja lit.* 1982:3; V. Betaki, in *Russkaja mysl'*, Paris, Nov. 24, 1983, p. 10; A. Krjukov, in *Neva* 1984:2.

**Náritsa, Mikhaíl Aleksándrovich,** prose writer (b. 1909 [exact date unknown], in village near Pskov). Naritsa was of peasant descent. He completed his studies at a technical school for the fine arts in Leningrad and subsequently worked as a teacher there. In 1933–34 he spent a year in Arkhangelsk, then returned to Leningrad. From 1935 to 1940 Naritsa was interned in a forced labor camp; his wife and child were also exiled. They lived on a kolkhoz near Arkhangelsk from 1941 to 1948, then were exiled first to Luga and then in 1949, after another year in custody, to Karaganda. After his REHABILITATION in 1957, Naritsa was permitted to return to Leningrad and to work as a sculptor under the supervision of the Academy of Arts. In late 1960 he allowed the manuscript of *Nespetaya pesnya* (1960; The Unsung Song), a prose work written between 1949 and 1959 and based on his fate from childhood to 1941, to be taken out to the West. Naritsa applied for permission to leave the

USSR. He was arrested on Oct. 13, 1961, and incarcerated in a psychiatric institution from 1962 to 1965. His application for permission to emigrate in 1965 was refused. Naritsa's short, autobiographical account, *Prestuplenie i nakazaniye* (1970; Crime and Punishment), relates the details of his life between 1960 and 1965.

In contrast to the writings of A. Solzhenitsyn, A. Amalrik, or L. Chukovskaya, the significance of Naritsa's prose lies not in linking personal fate and artistic creation. Unassuming and largely limited to an account of the facts, it affords an insight into a life of tragedy and persecution.

*Works: Nespetaja pesnja* (pov.), in *Grani*, Frankfurt am Main, 48:1960, under the pseudonym M. Narymov, separate ed., Frankfurt am Main, 1964; *Prestuplenie i nakazanie* (autobiographical account), in *Posev*, Frankfurt am Main, 1971:8, from chapter 5 on also in *Kaznimye sumasšestviem*, Frankfurt am Main, 1971, pp. 371–80; *Moë zaveščanie* (autobiographical commentary), in *Russkaja mysl'*, Paris, June 24, 1976, p. 5; *Posle reabilitacii: Memuary* (memoirs), Frankfurt am Main, 1981.

*Secondary Lit.:* In *Grani* 51:1961; C. Gerstenmaier, *Die Stimme der Stummen*, Stuttgart, 1971; *Abuse of Psychiatry for Political Repression in the Soviet Union*, Washington, 1972.

**Narókov, Nikoláy Vladimírovich** (pseud. of N. V. Márchenko), prose writer (b. June 26, 1887, Bessarabia—d. Oct. 3, 1969, Monterey, California). Narokov studied at the polytechnic institute in Kiev and lived in Kazan. During the Revolution he was an officer in the Denikin army, but he managed to escape after being imprisoned by the Bolsheviks. Narokov became a mathematics teacher in the provinces; in 1935 he began teaching in Kiev. In 1932 he was briefly imprisoned. In addition to his work as a teacher, Narokov led various groups of amateur actors. Narokov left Kiev as part of the second EMIGRATION and lived in Germany from 1944 to 1950. In 1951 he began to publish short stories and novels in the West. His novel written in 1937 and set in the Soviet provinces, *Mnimye velichiny* (1952; Eng. tr., *The Chains of Fear*, 1958), brought him international fame through its translation into German, English, French, Spanish, and several Asian languages. In 1950 Narokov moved to Monterey, California, together with his son, the writer N. Morshen, and lived there until his death. His novel set in the period before the Revolution, *Nikuda*

(1961; Going Nowhere), was published in Russian only in the journal *Vozrozhdeniye*; his next novel, *"Mogu!"* (1965; "I Can"), was published in Buenos Aires. From 1957 to 1963, Narokov also published a few essays on Russian literature of the 19th century.

With *Mnimye velichiny*, Narokov proved himself a competent storyteller and a master of the longer form of the novel. Through two separate plot lines that come together at the end, this book attributes the falseness of human and political relationships in the USSR to the Communist system. It provides multiple glimpses into the work of the NKVD—into the cruelty, arbitrariness, self-deception, dishonesty, dependence, and only apparent power of its agents. Even after A. Solzhenitsyn's thorough treatment of these issues, Narokov's novel deserves to be acknowledged for its contribution to our understanding of the people of the USSR. In *Nikuda*, Narokov deals with the problem of true versus specious values within the framework of a relationship between a man and a married woman. In *"Mogu!"* he exposes the type of Soviet man who strives for power for power's sake.

*Works: Mnimye veličiny* (novel), New York, 1952 (see above); *Čekhov—obščestvennik* (essays), in *Novyj žurnal*, New York, 48:1957; *Nikuda* (novel), in *Vozroždenie*, Paris, 110–18:1961; *"Mogu!"* (novel), Buenos Aires, 1965.

*Secondary Lit.:* A. Slizskoj, in *Vozroždenie* 26:1953; R. Gul', in *Novyj žurnal* 33:1953; V. Turgaev, in *Sovremennik*, Toronto, 12:1965; Ja. Gorbov, in *Vozroždenie* 168:1965; Ju. Samarin, in *Novoe russkoe slovo*, New York, Oct. 20, 1974; L. Filonov, in *Poiski*, New York, 4:1982.

**Narovchátov, Sergéy Sergéyevich,** poet (b. Oct. 3, 1919, Khvalynsk, prov. Saratov—d. July 22, 1981, Koktebel). Narovchatov spent his youth partly along the Volga and partly in Moscow. In 1933–37 he lived with his parents in Kolyma (eastern Siberia). From 1937 to 1941 he studied humanities at the Moscow Institute for Philosophy, Literature, and History and at the Gorky Literary Institute; his studies were interrupted in 1940 by his participation in the Finnish-Russian War. He served as a soldier in World War II. He joined the Communist Party in 1943. As a poet, Narovchatov belongs to the war generation; his first volume of poetry, *Kostyor* (1948; The Campfire), comprises his war poems. Narovchatov wrote other poems and became active as a critic and literary historian. From 1965 until his death, he belonged to the administrative committees of the Writers Unions of the RSFSR and of the USSR and was a member of the secretariat of the Writers Union of the USSR from 1971 to 1981. From the end of 1974 until his death, Narovchatov served as editor in chief of *Novy mir*. He lived in Moscow.

Even in his volumes of poetry that appeared more than 20 years after the end of the war, more than half of the poems concern the war. The best are such poems as "Volchonok" (1945; The Small Wolf), where he gives compelling form to heartrending personal experience. Narovchatov later excluded many of the patriotic, rhetorical poems reflecting the spirit of that time. In the cycle *Razgovor s dochkoy* (1955; Conversation with Daughter), Narovchatov achieved only a limited transition to personal ethical themes. His writing is politically aware; he does not lapse into exaggerated patriotic pathos or anti-Western propaganda, but he also does not probe into essential human problems. His poems are mostly narrative in form and often lengthy. In the narrative poem *Vasily Buslayev* (1957–60), he searches for a new method by picking up the thread of folkloric elements in the history of Novgorod. Many of the poems written during his time as an official describe his travels. His essays unite the personal and the political.

Works: *Kostër* (poems), 1948; *Soldaty svobody* (poems), 1952; *Razgovor s dočkoj* (narrative poem), in *Znamja* 1955:6; *Gor'kaja ljubov'* (poems), 1957; *Četvert' veka* (poems), 1965; *Poèzija v dviženii* (essays), 1966; *Polden'* (poems), 1969; *Vasilij Buslaev* (narrative poem), in *Novyj mir* 1973:2; *Znamja nad vysotoj* (lyric and narrative poems), 1974; *My vykhodim v žizni: Kniga molodosti* (memoirs), 1978; *Neobyčnoe literaturovedenie*, 1981; *Stikhotvorenija i poèmy* (lyric and narrative poems), 1985.—*Izbr. proizv.*, 2 vols., 1972; *Sobr. soč.*, 3 vols., 1977–78.

Translation: *Selected Verse*, 1979.

Secondary Lit.: G. Levin, in *Lit. gazeta* Dec. 1, 1955, and in *Oktjabr'* 1958:9; N. Koržavin, in *Lit. gazeta* June 19, 1962; M. Lukonin, in *Lit. Rossija* Aug. 16, 1963, p. 10; P. Antokol'skij, in *Lit. gazeta* Aug. 18, 1964; O. Grudcova, 1971; V. Roždestvenskij, in *Lit. obozrenie* 1973:6; V. Rymaševskij, in *Lit. obozrenie* 1975:5; M. Sobol', in *Lit. obozrenie* 1979:9; A. Mednikov, in *Voprosy lit.* 1984:5.

**Nartsíssov, Borís Anatólyevich**, poet (b. Aug. [?] 1906, near Saratov—d. Nov. 27, 1982, Washington, D.C.). Nartsissov grew up in Jam-

burg as the son of a country doctor and completed secondary school in Dorpat (Tartu) in 1924. After completing a course of study in chemistry there from 1924 to 1930, he worked as a chemist. As a result of World War II, he went from Estonia to Tübingen and ended up in a camp for displaced persons near Munich after the war. He emigrated via Australia (1951–53) to the United States. He worked as a researcher for the Battelle Memorial Institute—until 1959 in Columbus, Ohio, and then until 1972 in Washington, D.C. Nartsissov, who had written poems since he was in secondary school and who had belonged to groups of poets while living in the Baltic States, published six volumes of poetry from 1958 to 1978. The last volume, *Zvyozdnaya ptitsa* (1978; The Starry Bird), includes all the poems from previously published volumes. He was also active as a critic and a translator from the Estonian.

Nartsissov's polarity as both scientist and poet gives his work a persuasive tension but his awareness of the danger of a rational knowledge of the world is not affected. A strong attachment to the numinous world provides the original source of his poetry, and he can present the demonic in a grotesque union with the real. Motifs such as the doppelgänger, mirrors, spirits, and dreamlike faces appear together with images of cities, landscapes, and objects he has experienced. "With his creativity, he opens slightly the door to a world existing close to us but concealed from us" (O. Anstey). Nartsissov, who believed in the reality of reincarnation, seldom found the path into a brighter world through his poetry. "He wrote vigorously and clearly, like H. Bosch, descriptively and discerningly" (B. Filippov). His vocabulary is broad—from Old Church Slavonic through expressions in dialect to mathematical terminology.

Works: *Stikhi* (poems), New York, 1958; *Golosa* (poems), Frankfurt am Main, 1961; *Pamjat'* (poems), Washington, 1965; *Pod''ëm* (poems), Louvain, 1969; *Šakhmaty* (poems), Washington, 1979; *Zvëzdnaja ptica* (poems), Washington, 1978.

Secondary Lit.: B. Filippov, in Nartsissov's *Zvëzdnaja ptica*, 1978, and in *Novoe russkoe slovo*, New York, March 13, 1983, p. 5; T. Pakhmuss, in *Novyj žurnal*, New York, 148:1982; F. Fesenko, O. Anstej, in *Novyj žurnal* 151:1983.

*Nash sovreménnik* (Our Contemporary), a literary journal published monthly in Moscow since 1964; until 1958 it was an organ of the Writers Union of the USSR, since then of the Writers Union of the RSFSR. This journal replaced an almanac that had been published between four and six times a year from 1956 to 1963, which itself had replaced the almanac *God . . . (The Year . . .)* that had appeared between one and four times a year from 1933 to 1937 and from 1949 to 1955 with a different title every year (*God XVI* = 1933, *God XXXVIII* = 1955, counting from the Revolution). Until 1957, editorial responsibility lay in the hands of V. Poltoratsky; he remained a member of the editorial staff until 1973 but was replaced as editor by B. Zubavin from 1958 to 1967. In response to sharp ideological criticism (see *Lit. Rossija* Jan. 12, 1968, p. 8), the journal was not allowed to publish throughout 1968. After the publication of V. Krupin's *Sorokovoy den* (1981:11), Yu. Seleznev was dismissed as deputy editor in chief and other changes in staff were undertaken. In the period before 1967, well-known writers who were members of the editorial staff included Vs. Ivanov (until 1963), V. Ovechkin (1955–58), and S. Nikitin (1962–67) in addition to Yu. Nagibin (1965–81), the only one to be retained in 1969. Since 1969 the editorial director has been S. Vikulov, previously an author of idyllic kolkhoz literature. Widely known authors who have subsequently been members of the editorial staff include Ye. Nosov (1969–), A. Astafyev (1969–81), V. Shukshin (1973–74), V. Rasputin (1975–), G. Troyepolsky (1976–), V. Belov (1978–), Yu. Bondarev (1978–), N. Shundik (1982–), M. Lukonin (1984–). *Nash sovremennik* conforms to the tradition of journalistic prose and has increasingly become an organ of the village-oriented, Russophile authors (see VILLAGE PROSE). The majority of writers on the editorial staff belong to this circle. The writers whose works are published there include F. Abramov, V. Belov, V. Bykov, F. Iskander, Yu. Kazakov, V. Krupin, V. Likhonosov, V. Makanin, V. Rasputin, V. Soloukhin, G. Troyepolsky. *Nash sovremennik* includes prose, poetry, and dramas, as well as occasionally literary remains (A. Averchenko, I. Babel, I. Bunin, Ye. Kazakevich, N. Teffi, A. Yashin, N. Yevdokimov, and others), literary criticism, and memoirs. In 1987 the circulation was 220,000.

*Secondary Lit.:* V. Litvinov, in *Lit. gazeta* Feb. 19, 1957; O. Vojtinskaja, in *Lit. i žizn'* March 20, 1959; P. Šebunin, in *Lit. i žizn'* June 29, 1962; L. Žak, in *Lit. Rossija* Sept. 18, 1964, p. 14; V. Surganov, in *Lit. gazeta* Oct.

13, 1971, p. 4; Anon., in *Lit. Rossija* Dec. 25, 1981, p. 4.

**Necháyev, Yegór Yefímovich,** poet (b. April 25 [April 13], 1859, Kharitonovo, prov. Tver—d. Nov. 23, 1925, Pavlovsky Posad, near Moscow). Nechayev was the son of a glassblower. Up until the Revolution, Nechayev worked at a glassworks. From 1880 on, he wrote poems based on his working environment; these poems were published and achieved some recognition. The first collections of his poetry were published in 1911 and 1914. The Revolution deprived Nechayev of his livelihood; in poems and letters he declared that he would rather starve than become a beggar. In 1919 he returned to Moscow, where he won recognition in the proletarian writers' group KUZNITSA, which printed some of his poems. Nechayev did not accept the PROLETKULT position of breaking with tradition but managed to remain aloof from literary and political altercations. The most complete collection of his poems up to that time, *Iz pesen starogo rabochego* (From the Songs of an Old Worker), appeared in 1922. Nechayev published his memoirs in 1924; he became a member of the Communist Party shortly before his death. N. Lyashko and S. Obradovich prepared a complete edition of his poetry in 1928; nevertheless, it is no more complete than the next edition, which appeared in 1955 after several decades of silence.

In simple, sober stanzas Nechayev's poems depict the hard labor at the glassworks and the misery of the workers but at the same time reveal the author's love for this trade and for nature.

*Works: Trudovye pesni* (poems), 1911; *Večernie pesni* (poems), 1914; *Pesni stekljanščika* (poems), 1922; *Iz pesen starogo rabočego* (poems), 1922; *Gutari* (selected poems), 1947.—*Polnoe sobr. soč.*, 1928; *Izbr.*, 1955; *U istokov russkoj proletarskoj poèzii* (also contains poems by F. S. Škulev and A. M. Gmyrev), 1965.

*Secondary Lit.:* A. Glagolev, in *Novyj mir* 1929:6; V. Bakhmet'ev, in *Lit. gazeta* Nov. 22, 1955; A. Kulinič, in his *Očerki po istorii russkoj sovetskoj poèzii 20-kh godov,* Kiev, 1958.

**Nedogónov, Alekséy Ivánovich,** poet (b. Nov. 1 [Oct. 19], 1914, Grushevsk, near Rostov-on-Don—d. March 13, 1948, Moscow, in a traffic accident). Nedogonov's father was a miner. Nedogonov began working as a carpenter in the mining industry when he was 15. In 1932 he went to work in an armaments factory in Moscow and at the same time pursued his studies, initially in a program for workers, and after 1935, at the Gorky Literary Institute. His first poems appeared in 1934. In 1939 Nedogonov completed his studies at the Gorky Literary Institute and was called up for military service. He saw action in the Finnish-Russian War and worked as a frontline reporter during World War II. His poems began appearing in the journals *Zvezda* and *Novy mir* in 1938, but no collections of Nedogonov's poetry were printed in his lifetime. His narrative poem *Flag nad selsovetom* (1947; Flag over the Village Soviet) attracted a great deal of attention as one of the first major works of literature about the return of soldiers from the front to their native land (it received a Stalin Prize for 1947, 1st class). The joyful atmosphere of the work corresponds to Nedogonov's own feelings; the problem it poses between two returnees—whether to rest on one's wartime laurels or to work on the reconstruction effort—is a standard one for the period; the second part of the work was subsequently criticized for conforming to the THEORY OF CONFLICTLESSNESS. Nedogonov skillfully emulates the folk-song style found in the works of N. Nekrasov and A. Tvardovsky and utilizes a variety of meters. His wartime and prewar poetry, which appeared in several collections after 1948, is actually unmusical and unprepossessing in its rhyme technique, but it is infused with human warmth, a closeness to nature, and modesty. Nodogonov handles a subject such as separation in wartime or elects to use the end of a yearlong attack of insomnia as a symbol for the end of the war.

*Works: Flag nad sel'sovetom* (narrative poem), 1947; *Prostye ljudi* (poems), 1948; *Izbr.,* 1949; *Izbr.,* 1958; *Lirika* (poems), 1964; *V otkrytom boju. Flag nad sel'sovetom* (lyric and narrative poems), 1971; *Vstrečnoe dykhanie* (poems), 1974.

*Secondary Lit.:* D. Danin, in *Novyj mir* 1948:10; M. Borisova, in *Zvezda* 1955:12; K. Pozdnjaev, in *Neva* 1957:11 and in *Lit. Rossija* June 24, 1966, pp. 10–11, Aug. 4, 1972, pp. 18–20, Nov. 24, 1972, pp. 16–18, and separate study, 1973; V. Tel'pugov, 1958; V. Dement'ev, in his *Ognennyj most,* 1970; A. Vasil'ev, in *Naš sovremennik* 1975:5; L. Judin, in *Don* 1984:10.

**Nekrásov, Víktor Platónovich,** prose writer (b. June 17 [June 4], 1911, Kiev—d. Sept. 3,

1987, Paris). Nekrasov's father was a doctor. Nekrasov studied architecture at the Institute of Civil Engineering in Kiev (graduated in 1936) and attended the acting academy (graduated in 1937). Nekrasov worked as an architect for a year and then as an actor and stage designer. From 1941 to 1944 he was at the front and fought in the battle of Stalingrad; at the end of World War II he was a deputy commander of an engineering battalion. In 1944 he became a member of the Communist Party. With his first literary work, the *povest V okopakh Stalingrada* (1946; Eng. tr., *Front-Line Stalingrad,* 1962), Nekrasov scored an extraordinarily great success (Stalin Prize for 1946, 2d class). By 1974 there were 120 editions in 30 languages. After Stalin's death, Nekrasov published, together with several short stories, two povesti in *Novy mir: V rodnom gorode* (1954; In the Home Town) and *Kira Georgiyevna* (1961; Eng. tr., 1962); these were sharply criticized because of their candid exposition of essential problems in contemporary Soviet society. Nekrasov was in Italy in April 1957 and in the United States in November 1960. His unprejudiced account of his trip to the United States, *Po obe storony okeana* (1962; Eng. tr., *Both Sides of the Ocean,* 1964), was even personally criticized by Khrushchev (*Pravda* March 10, 1963). After Khrushchev's fall, Nekrasov's travel sketches were expanded to include *Mesyats vo Frantsii* (1965; A Month in France) and were scarcely altered when published as a book in 1967. From 1957 to 1965 Nekrasov was also active as a scriptwriter. He published a number of well-received memoirs and articles about architecture, painting, film, and literature. Because of his liberal comments, Nekrasov was reprimanded by the Party in 1969 and expelled in 1973. When his house was searched on Jan. 17, 1974, all his manuscripts were confiscated, including one about Babiy Yar. In September 1974, Nekrasov was granted permission to emigrate with his wife. He traveled extensively and regularly published new works. He lived in Paris and was acting editor in chief of the journal *Kontinent* from 1975 to 1982.

Nekrasov was a prominent representative of the literature of candor. His book about Stalingrad portrays the war without the heroizing that had previously been customary, and it won lasting recognition for that "truth from the trenches" that concealed neither inconsiderate and improperly behaving officers nor the painful daily routine at the front. This spirit pervaded the best war literature after 1956 (G. Baklanov, B. Okudzhava, among others). In *V rodnom gorode* Nekrasov was the first to envision the soldiers' homecoming from the front not as an idyll or as a displacement of the battle to the front of socialist development but realistically as a problem involving the partner who has become a stranger, the mistrustful Party official, the trials of everyday life. In Kira Georgiyevna, Nekrasov combines an issue that was new in Soviet literature in 1961, that of the innocent person returning from 20 years in a prison camp, with the fate of a character who is not a "positive hero," Kira, "a woman, avoiding personal responsibility, and refusing to recognize the unpleasant" (D. Brown). Nekrasov also published some shorter stories, such as Sluchay na Mamayevom Kurgane (1965; Incident at the Mamay Hill), in which he blends the real and the fantastic, wartime experiences and the present day. He maintained this narrative style in emigration. His six major works—Zapiski zevaki (1975; Notes of an Idler), Vzglyad i nechto (1977; Views and Something More), Po obe storony steny . . . (1978; On Both Sides of the [Berlin] Wall . . .), Iz dalnikh stranstviy vozvratyas (1979–81; On Returning from Foreign Lands), Saperlipopet (1983), and Malenkaya pechalnaya povest (1986; A Sad Little Story)—combine through loose associations his new impressions of, and reflections on, the West with his remembrances, as well as with a critical view of himself and his opinions on Soviet policy. As both factual and human documents, these hold an important place in uncensored Russian literature.

Works: V okopakh Stalingrada (pov.), 1947 (see above); V rodnom gorode (pov.) 1955; Pervoe znakomstvo (report), 1958; Vasja Konakov (short stories), 1961; Kira Georgievna (pov.), 1961 (see above); Po obe storony okeana (travel notes), in Novyj mir 1962:11 and New York, 1984 (see above); Vtoraja noč' (short stories), 1965; Slučaj na Mamaevom Kurgane (short story), in Novyj mir 1965:12; Putešestvija v raznykh izmerenijakh (reports), 1967; Dom Turbinykh (short story), in Novyj mir 1967:8; Deduška i vnuček (short story), in Novyj mir 1968:9; O vul'kanakh, otšel'nikakh i pročem (short story), in Grani, Frankfurt am Main, 74:1970; V žizni i v pis'makh (essays), 1971; Komu èto nužno? (autobiographical report), in Novoe russkoe slovo, New York, April 17, 1974; Zapiski zevaki, in Kontinent, Paris, 4:1975; Vzgljad i nečto, in Kontinent 10, 12–13:1977; Po obe storony steny . . . , in Kontinent 18–19:1978–79; Iz dal'nikh stranstvij vozvratjas' . . . , in Vremja i my, Jerusalem, 48–49, 61:1979–81; Stalingrad (novel and short stories), Frankfurt am Main, 1981; Saperli-

popet, ili Esli by da kaby, da vo rtu rosli griby (memoirs), London, 1983; Malen'kaja pečal'naja povest' (pov.), in Grani 135:1985, separate ed., London, 1986.

Secondary Lit.: M. Ščeglov (1954), in his Literaturnaja kritika, 1971; K. Simonov, in Lit. gazeta April 26, 1955; Ju. Bondarev, in Lit. gazeta June 17, 1961; RSPP 3:1964; I. Vinogradov, in Novyj mir 1968:3; A. P. Reilly, America in Contemporary Soviet Literature, New York, 1971; W. Kasack, in Osteuropa 1975:3; V. Poltoratzky, Diss., Vanderbilt Univ., 1977; E. Brejtbart, in Grani 107:1978; K. Pomerancev, in Russkaja mysl', Paris, July 5, 1984, p. 10.

Nevá (Neva, for the river on which St. Petersburg was built), a literary journal published monthly in Leningrad since 1955; since 1959 it has been the journal of the Writers Union of the RSFSR and of the Leningrad branch of the Writers Union of the USSR. The editors in chief have been A. Chernenko (1955–57), S. Voronin (1957–64), the film-script writer A. F. Popov (1964–79), the critic and literary scholar D. T. Khrenkov (1979–84), and the writer B. N. Nikolsky (1985–). Well-known authors who have been members of the editorial staff for extended periods of time include only V. Rozhdestvensky (1967–77), G. Gor (1967–81), D. Granin (1967–), and M. Dudin (1980–). Neva publishes prose, poetry, journalism, and literary criticism as well as translations from other socialist countries on a relatively regular basis. In addition, since 1981 Neva has included a section entitled "Sedmaya tetrad" (The Seventh Notebook) that offers numerous short articles on the history of Leningrad (previously St. Petersburg and Petrograd). Neva publishes literary works by Leningrad writers such as O. Berggolts, N. Braun, L. Druskin, M. Dudin, G. Gor, G. Gorbovsky, G. Goryshin, D. Granin, A. Kushner, V. Panova, G. Semyonov, V. Shefner, S. Voronin. In 1963 the circulation was 200,000; in 1984, 320,000; in 1987, 290,000.

Secondary Lit.: L. Kostin, in Lit. gazeta May 5, 1955; D. Tevekeljan, in Lit. obozrenie 1985:11.

**Nevérov, Aleksándr Sergéyevich** (pseud. of A. S. Skóbelev), prose writer, playwright (b. Dec. 24 [Dec. 12], 1886, Novikovka, prov. Samara—d. Dec. 24, 1923, Moscow). Neverov was the son of a peasant. In 1906 he began teaching in a village school after completing a two-year teachers college. In 1915, at the time of World War I, he became an army surgeon's assistant. During the Revolution, Neverov was affiliated with the Socialist Revolutionaries but went over to the Bolsheviks in 1919; he occupied various posts in governmental and cultural institutions in Samara. Neverov, who had started publishing occasional short stories in journals in 1906, was cofounder of a people's theater for which he wrote plays after 1919; one of these plays, Baby (1920; Womenfolk), received first prize in a Moscow competition in 1920. In the famine of 1920–21 Neverov fled with the starving masses from the Volga region to Tashkent. In the spring of 1922 he moved to Moscow and joined the proletarian writers' group KUZNITSA even though he himself was of peasant descent and was associated with the theme of the village. Neverov wrote prose that appeared frequently in Krasnaya nov, Krokodil, Krestyanka, and other periodicals. Interest in this talented provincial writer increased after his unexpected early death from heart failure. The 1926 edition of Neverov's collected works went through five printings by 1930; his most important prose work, Tashkent—gorod khlebny (1923; Eng. trs., A City of Bread, 1927; Tashkent, 1930), was one of the most popular books for young people during the 1920s and remained on the schools' required reading lists until the mid-1930s. Neverov received little attention after 1937; since 1953 his works have again been reissued and he has become the subject of scholarly articles.

Neverov's drama Baby shows the brutality of peasant life much in the manner of A. Chekhov's "V ovrage" (In the Ravine). Zakharova smert (1920; Zakhar's Death) brings together family conflicts and ideological antagonisms. Golod (1921; Famine), a dramatic presentation of the terrible famines of catastrophic proportions that occurred after the Revolution, was not approved by official authorities because of its merciless candor. In Tashkent—gorod khlebny Neverov explored the same incredibly shocking scenes from the perspective of a 12-year-old who, with a child's anxious gravity, moves through scenes of death, poverty, violence, and suffering. The hopeful conclusion ensured the book's distribution. Neverov presents the themes of famine, woman in the Revolution, and the contrast between old and new forces in the village in other works as well, including Andron Neputyovy (1922; Good-for-Nothing Andron) and Gusilebedi (1923; Geese and Swans), a posthumously published novel that Neverov began in 1918 and that he originally planned as a far more ambitious work than the final version would indicate.

Works: Baby (play), 1920; Zakharova smert (play), 1922; Smekh i gore (play), 1922; Lico žizni (short stories), 1923; Taškent—gorod khlebnyj (pov.), 1923 (see above); P'esy (plays), 1923; Gusi-lebedi (novel), 1924, 1973; Andron Neputëvyj (pov.), 1925; Golod (play), 1927.– Polnoe sobr. soč., 7 vols., 1926, 5th ed., 1930; 2 supplementary vols., 1926–27; Sobr. soč., 4 vols., 1957–58; Izbr., 1971, 1977.

Secondary Lit.: N. Fatov, 1926; N. Strakhov in Oktjabr' 1958:2 and separate 2d ed., 1972; L. A. Tamašin, in Russkaja lit. 1960:3; V. P. Skobelev, 1964; RSPP 3:1964; E. Poljakova, in Novyj mir 1967:4; A. Vanjukov, 1972, in Volgo 1976:12, and in Russkaja lit. 1986:4; A. N. Iz archiva pisatelja: Issledovanija, vospomina nija, 1972; V. Čalmaev, in Pod"ëm 1980:4 and 5 and 1982; Ju. Galkin, in Lit. Rossija May 15 1981, p. 20.

**Nikándrov, Nikoláy Nikándrovich** (pseud. of N. N. Shevtsóv), prose writer (b. Dec. 19 [Dec 7], 1878, Petrovsko-Razumovskoye, near Moscow—d. Nov. 18, 1964, Moscow). Nikandrov's father was a postal clerk. Nikandrov grew up in Sevastopol and after a short period of study became a village schoolteacher. He was intermittently in internal exile or under arrest for taking part in revolutionary activities; he lived in exile from 1910 to 1914. Nikandrov was in Sevastopol during the Civil War; he lived in Moscow from 1922 on. Nikandrov began publishing occasional prose in 1903. His bestknown story, Beregovoy veter (1909; The Coast Wind), furnished the title for several prose collections published between 1915 and 1964. After the Revolution, Nikandrov chose to write on topical subjects that were distinctly tendentious. His Lyubov Ksenii Dmitriyevny (1926; The Love of Kseniya Dmitriyevna), for instance, tells the story of a member of what was once the upper class who goes to work for her erstwhile domestic servant and who is once again accepted by her husband after she learns how to type. In 1926 the critic L. Voytolovsky reproached Nikandrov, not without justification, for "writing in an intolerably lengthy and slovenly manner." Nikandrov's ability to render the direct speech of simple Russians naturalistically and with humor—and his pleasure in doing so—is not informed by any larger power of organization that would have enabled him to develop a plot situation or to produce a work of art.

Works: Beregovoj veter (short stories), 1915 Rybolovy (short story), 1925; Ljubov' Kseni Dmitrievny (short stories), 1926; Morskie prostory (short stories), 1935; Beregovoj veter (short stories), 1964.—*Sobr. soč.*, 5 vols., 1929. *Secondary Lit.*: L. Vojtolovskij, in *Novyj mir* 1926:3; I. Sac, in *Lit. kritik* 1934:10; B. Val'be, in *Zvezda* 1965:8; *RSPP* 7(1):1971: A. Peregudov, in *Novyj mir* 1980:1.

**Nikíforov, Geórgy Konstantínovich,** prose writer (b. June 7 [May 26], 1884, Saratov—d. 1937 or 1939, while imprisoned.) Nikiforov was the son of a paperhanger. Before the Revolution, he worked as a turner; he moved to the Urals in 1914. He joined the Communist Party in 1917, and worked in public education. In 1923 he moved to Moscow. Nikiforov's first poems appeared in 1918–20; he switched to prose in 1924. He belonged to the writers' groups KUZNITSA and OKTYABR. Nikiforov published numerous short stories up to 1937 and also began publishing longer prose works in 1926. The best known was his novel *U fonarya* (1927; By the Lantern), which had gone through 18 printings by 1936.

Nikiforov's major theme is the conversion of those who had originally regarded the Revolution with apathy or hostility. He was constantly attacked because he criticized the NEP in what is probably his best short story, *Ivan Brynda* (1925; Nikiforov's only work to be published in *Krasnaya nov*); he denounced the growth of a Soviet bureaucracy and a technological intelligentsia that gave only lip service to maintaining contact with the working class. Nikiforov's prose is uneven, his dialogue too long; his control of the plot lacks a central focus. The exceptions to these faults may well be due to good editing. At the end of the 1930s Nikiforov fell victim to the government purges. After his REHABILITATION in 1956, a commission was formed to reevaluate his literary estate (*Lit. gazeta* Sept. 8, 1956), but nothing was reprinted.

*Works: Ivan Brynda* (short story) in *Krasnaja nov'* 1925:1; *Stepanida* (short stories), 1927; *U fonarja* (novel), 1929; *Ženščina* (novel), 1930; *Edinstvo* (novel), 1933; *Mastera* (novel), 1936–37.—*Sobr. soč.*, 5 vols., 1927–28; *Sobr. soč.*, 7 vols. (of which only vols. 1, 2, 6, and 7 were published), 1928–31. *Secondary Lit.*: I. Evdokimov, in *Na postu* 1925:1; A. Ležnev, in *Novyj mir* 1928:5; V. Aleksandrova (1933), in her *Lit. i žizn'*, New York, 1969; L. Fedorov, in *Lit. kritik* 1937:9; *RSPP* 3:1964.

**Nikítin, Nikoláy Nikoláyevich,** prose writer (b. Aug. 8 [July 27], 1895, St. Petersburg—d. March 26, 1963, Leningrad). Nikitin's father was a railway administration employee. Nikitin grew up in northern Russian. Between 1915 and 1917 he studied philology in St. Petersburg; in 1918 he joined the Red Army as a volunteer. Nikitin, who had once published a short story in 1916, joined the SERAPION BROTHERS in 1921 and embarked on a regular literary career in 1922. For a long time Nikitin was criticized as a writer whose background was not proletarian; coincident with his increasing conformity to the Party line, he achieved recognition when he received a Stalin Prize (for 1950, 2d class) for his novel *Severnaya Avrora* (1950; Northern Lights). Nikitin dramatized the novel in 1952; he had written several dramas before and he wrote several after as well. Nikitin, who lived in Leningrad, belonged to the editorial board of the journal *Zvezda* from 1951 until his death and was a member of the board of the Writers Union of the USSR.

Nikitin's early prose depicts specific incidents from the period during and after the Revolution, stressing the elemental nature of events while remaining politically neutral or else viewing the Reds and the Whites in an equally negative light, as in *Kamni* (1923; Stones). *Polyot* (1923–24; Flight) describes this period in all its chaos as expressed in interpersonal and sexual terms; it also reveals Nikitin's consciousness of form in his experiments with fragmentary narrative structure under the influence of Ye. Zamyatin and B. Pilnyak. G. Struve points out that "in a highly concentrated form, nearly all the characteristics of the Russian prose fiction of this period are to be found in Nikitin." In the late 1920s Nikitin's works became weaker. *Eto nachalos v Kokande* (1939; It Began in Kokand) is a novel, subsequently revised, about the beginning of the Soviet regime in Uzbekistan. Nikitin's depiction of the struggle against interventionist troops in 1918–19 in his Stalin Prize-winning novel *Severnaya Avrora* constitutes his contribution to the anti-Western campaign of the 1950s and to the cult of Stalin. The novel was reprinted in 1971.

*Works: Rvotnyj fort* (short stories), 1923; *Kamni* (short story), 1923; *Sejčas na Zapade* (feature articles), 1924; *Polët* (short stories), 1925; *Prestuplenie Kirika Rudenko* (novel), 1928; *Špion* (novel), 1930; *Èto načalos' v Kokande* (novel), 1940; *Severnaja Avrora* (novel), 1950, 1971; *Pogovorim o zvëzdakh* (short stories), 1959.—*Sobr. soč.*, 6 vols. (only vols. 1, 2, 6 published), 1928–29; *Izbr.*, 2 vols., 1959; *Izbr. proizv.*, 2 vols., 1968. *Translation: Night and Other Stories*, 1978. *Secondary Lit.*: V. Volin, in *Na postu* 1923:1;

B. Guber, in *Novyj mir* 1926:6; B. Kosteljanec, in *Zvezda* 1951:4; L. Plotkin, in *Zvezda* 1963:12; *RSPP* 3:1964; M. Smirnov, in *Zvezda* 1975:8; B. Plaskacz, in *Russian Language Journal* 109:1977.

**Nikítin, Sergéy Konstantínovich,** prose writer (b. Oct. 10, 1926, Kovrov, oblast Vladimir—d. Dec. 18, 1973, Vladimir). From 1944 to 1947 Nikitin studied at the Institute for International Relations in Moscow; in 1948 he transferred to the Gorky Literary Institute, from which he completed his studies in 1952 by a correspondence course. Beginning in 1948 he worked as a journalist for the provincial papers of his native region; in 1952 he joined the staff of *Ogonyok*. In 1952 he published his first volume of short stories, revised and edited by Ye. Kazakevich. In 1956 he joined the Communist Party. In the early 1960s Nikitin moved to Vladimir, where he assumed the position of directing secretary of the local section of the Writers Union. He did not, however, take part in any Writers Congresses. Besides his largely autobiographical povest, *Paduchaya zvezda* (1964; Falling Star), Nikitin wrote primarily short stories that appeared in journals, general anthologies, and collections of his work.

Nikitin belongs to that group of writers who, in the tradition of I. Turgenev, I. Bunin, and K. Paustovsky, are closely tied to their homeland and to nature. His attention is focused on interpersonal relationships, the emotions of simple people, and the everyday events that influence people's lives. His prose is apolitical; while it is neither propaganda nor social criticism, it is nevertheless representative of its time. Nikitin's plots are not original, but they are psychologically tidy; without avoiding evil and suffering, they are oriented toward good. Even in his shorter prose Nikitin strives to capture the vicissitudes of a whole lifetime in a calm narrative flow.

*Works: Vozvraščenie* (short stories), 1952; *V bessonnuju noč'* (short stories), 1959; *Golubaja planeta* (short stories), 1962; *Vesennim utrom* (short stories), 1966; *Padučaja zvezda* (pov.), 1967; *Dom pod lipami* (short stories), 1969; *Večernjaja zarja* (short stories and pov.), 1970; *Živaja voda* (short stories and pov.), 1973; *Snežnye polja* (short stories), 1976.

*Secondary Lit.:* O. Mikhajlov, in *Novyj mir* 1959:10; M. Lapšin, in *Naš sovremennik* 1961:6, in a separate study, 1971, and in his *Ličnost' v literature,* 1973; *RSPP* 3:1964; V. Šišok, in *Moskva* 1965:10; B. Sprov, in *Moskva* 1978:1.

**Nikoláyeva, Galína Yevgényevna** (pseud. of G. Ye. Volyánskaya), prose writer (b. Feb. 18 [Feb. 5], 1911, Usmanka, prov. Tomsk—d. Oct. 18, 1963, Moscow). Nikolayeva was the daughter of a teacher. She studied medicine in Gorky (1929–35), then worked in higher education there; from 1942 to 1945 she served as a military doctor in the Volga region and North Caucasia. Nikolayeva, who had published her first poems in 1939, left medicine for a career in journalistic and literary work in 1945 and lived in Moscow. Her first novel, *Zhatva* (1950; Eng. tr. *Harvest*, 1952), received a Stalin Prize (1st class, 1950). Her second novel, *Bitva v puti* (1957; The Battle en Route), reflected the altered Party line and moderately criticized the Stalinist period; it, too, was highly regarded. From 1954 to the time of her death, Nikolayeva belonged to the boards of the Writers Unions of the USSR and the RSFSR.

Nikolayeva's first prose piece was the short story *Gibel komandarma* (1945; Death of the Commander), which presumably was taken from her own experience of the sinking of a hospital ship on the Volga. *Zhatva* is dedicated to a standard theme of postwar literature, the transformation of a backward, war-ravaged kolkhoz into a model establishment under the guidance of the Party. Allusions to existing grievances and abuses and a tone of genuine humanity raise this novel above the majority of works of SOCIALIST REALISM. These features are even more important in *Bitva v puti,* in which Nikolayeva does not rely simply on optimism but uses psychologically heightened love relationships and a more true-to-life presentation of production problems attributable to dogmatic Party officials in her portrayal of the "battle en route" to true communism as it was propagandized in the immediate post-Stalinist period. The novel became a standard work in its 1959 revised version. In addition to her prose, Nikolayeva also wrote two dramas in collaboration with S. Radzinsky: *Vasily Bortnikov (Vysokaya volna)* (1952; Vasily Bortnikov [The High Wave]) and *Pervaya vesna* (1955; The First Spring).

*Works: Gibel' komandarma* (short story), in *Znamja* 1945:10, separate ed., 1953; *Žatva* (novel), 1951 (see above); (jointly with S. Radzinskij) *Vasilij Bortnikov (Vysokaja volna)* (play), 1952; *Povest' o direktore MTS i glavnom agronome,* 1954 (Eng. tr., The Newcomer, 1955); (jointly with S. Radzinskij) *Pervaja vesna* (play), in *V rodnom kraju* 1955; *Bitva v puti* (novel), 1958, 2d ed., 1959.—*Sobr. soč.,* 3 vols., 1972–73.

*Secondary Lit.*: B. Brajnina, in *Novyj mir* 1946:6; A. Tarasenkov, in *Novyj mir* 1950:10; I. Gusev, in *Grani*, Frankfurt am Main, 41:1959; G. Lenobl', in *Voprosy lit.* 1959:7; V. Čalmaev, in *Znamja* 1961:2; *RSPP* 3:1964; L. F. Pičurin, 1970; A. Janov., in *Lit. i sovremennost'* 11:1972; M. Aliger, in *Lit. gazeta* March 4, 1981, p. 11; *Vospominanija o G. N.*, Moscow, 1984; A. Aleksandrova, in *Znamja* 1984:5.

**Nikúlin, Lev Veniamínovich** (pseud. of Lev Vladímirovich Olkonítsky), prose writer (b. May 20 [May 8], 1891, Zhitomir—d. March 9, 1967, Moscow). Nikulin's father was an actor. Nikulin attended business schools in Odessa and Moscow, finishing in 1918; he began publishing poems and stories in 1910. He served as cultural officer in the Red Army; in 1921–22 he was assigned to the diplomatic mission in Afghanistan; from 1922 on, he worked as a journalist, traveling abroad frequently. After producing some pieces about his experiences in Afghanistan, Nikulin turned first to writing adventure novels with revolutionary motifs, such as *Nikakikh sluchaynostey* (1924; Not a Matter of Chance), and then moved on to historical themes, as in *Golye koroli* (1926; The Naked Kings). In addition, he wrote some fiction based on his personal experiences, the most ambitious of which is *Vremya, prostranstvo, dvizheniye* (1933; Time, Space, and Motion). Nikulin joined the Communist Party in 1940. In pseudoheroic war stories Nikulin makes light of the serious truth of his time. His novel about Napoleon's defeat in 1813–14, *Rossii vernye syny* (1950; Russia's Loyal Sons; Stalin Prize, 3d class, 1951), is sharply anti-Western (see COSMOPOLITANISM). Over 1,000 pages long, *Moskovskiye zori* (1954–57; Moscow Dawns) blends personal experiences with documented history. Before 1951 Nikulin also wrote dramas and was active as a literary critic. He owes his place in literature entirely to his official career, which included posts on commissions of the Writers Union.

Nikulin's prose is unfocused, on the level of individual sentences, of scenes, and of the work as a whole; he never succeeded in writing a compact, consistent work. Too many digressions obscure any line of development. His lack of originality (for example, compare his *Moskovskiye zori* to V. Gilyarovsky's *Moskva i Moskvichi*) and his inability to fashion fictional material were often criticized. Very few of the many books he wrote ever came out in a second edition.

*Works: Nikakikh sluchajnostej: Kinematografičeskij roman* (novel), 1924; *Khmel'* (novel),

Berlin, 1924; *Golye koroli* (novel), 1926; *Vremja, prostranstvo, dviženie* (novel), 2 vols., 1933; *Rossii vernye syny* (novel), 1950; *Moskovskie zori* (novel), 2 vols., 1954–58; *Trus* (novel), 1961; *Mërtvaja zyb'* (novel-chronicle), 1965 (Eng. tr., *The Swell of the Sea*, 1972).—*Soč.*, 3 vols., 1956.

*Secondary Lit.*: F. Levin, in *Lit. kritik* 1938:2; L. Lazarev, in *Novyj mir* 1955:2; I. Kramov, in *Lit. gazeta* Feb. 6, 1962; *RSPP* 3:1964.

**Nílin, Pável Filíppovich**, prose writer (b. Jan. 16 [Jan. 3], 1908, Irkutsk—d. Oct. 2, 1981, Moscow). Nilin's father was an exiled settler. Nilin held several jobs in his youth; in 1937 he became a journalist. This career took him from Siberia through the Volga region and the Ukraine to Moscow. His literary ability was recognized by S. Gekht on the basis of Nilin's first short stories, *Zolotye ruki* (Golden Hands) and *Matvey Kuzmich*, both published in *Novy mir* in 1937. In 1939 Nilin adapted his first novel, *Chelovek idyot v goru* (1936; Man Goes Uphill), about the miners of the Donbas, for the film *Bolshaya zhizn* (Big Life). The script for the film received a Stalin Prize (for 1935–40, 2d class). During World War II, Nilin was a frontline reporter; in 1944 he was admitted to the Communist Party. As a consequence of Zhdanov's restrictive cultural policies, the second part of Nilin's film was banned by the Party Resolution of Sept. 4, 1946 (see PARTY RESOLUTIONS ON LITERATURE). It was shown in revised form in 1958. Nilin was first generally acknowledged as a writer in the post-Stalinist period, primarily for his best povest, *Zhestokost* (1956; Eng. trs., *Cruelty*, 1958; *Comrade Venka*, 1959), based on a short story published in 1940 about the fight against crime in the 1920s. Set in Siberia, the plot of this exciting work revolves around a young policemen who is concerned about humane interrogation methods and resocialization, but who ultimately takes his own life, horrified by the pervasive cruelty. Using two young secret policemen, whom he compares to make his point, Nilin also condemns fundamental distrust and the use of violence justified by pretended obedience in *Ispytatelny srok* (1956; Probationary Period). Nilin's *Cherez kladbishche* (1962; Across the Cemetery), a povest set in 1942, is characterized not by highlighted events of war but by psychological penetration into human contradictions and a renewed warning against biased justice; like both of the other major prose works of these years, it was also filmed. Nilin became a member of the boards of the Writers Unions of the USSR and the RSFSR in 1970–71 but did not engage in cultural politics. He lived in Moscow.

Works: Matvej Kuz'mič (short story), 1938; Zolotye ruki (short stories), 1939; Čelovek idët v gory (novel), 1939; Bol'šaja žizn' (film script), 1945; Poezdka v Moskvu (novel), 1954; Žestokost'. Ispytatel'nyj srok (pov.), 1957 (see above); Znamenityj Pavljuk (pov. and short stories), 1957 (also contains the short story Bližajšij rodstvennik); Čerez kladbišče (pov.), 1962; Četyre povesti (pov.), 1970; Znakomoe lico (pov. and short stories), 1975; Vpervye zamužem (short story), in Novyj mir 1978:1; Iz afrikanskogo dnevnika (short story), in Družba narodov 1979;4 (Eng. tr., "Pages from an African Diary," in Soviet Literature 1980:8); Interesnaja žizn' (pov. and short stories), 1982.

Secondary Lit.: S. Gecht, in Lit. kritik 1938:4; N. Pijašev, 1962; V. Lakšin, in Novyj mir 1962:11 (reprinted in Lit. i sovremennost' 4:1963); V, Kardin, 1964, in Lit. gazeta Aug. 30, 1962, and in Voprosy lit. 1963:5, 1984:7; RSPP 3:1964; L. Kolobaeva, 1969; P. Antokol'skij, in Oktjabr' 1975:10; O. Smirnov, in Lit. obozrenie 1977:1; V. Rosljakov, in Lit gazeta Nov. 12, 1986, p. 5.

**Nizovóy, Pável Geórgiyevich** (pseud. of P. G. Tupikóv), prose writer (b. Oct. 30 [Oct. 18], 1877, or 1882, Novosyolki, prov. Kostroma—d. Oct. 4, 1940, Moscow). Nizovoy's father was a soldier. Nizovoy spent his youth in the country; at the age of 13 he became a painter's apprentice in Moscow. He traveled through Russia between 1903 and 1907. During World War I, Nizovoy worked as a hospital orderly; he went to the Altai after the Revolution. Nizovoy moved to Moscow in 1920; there he became a member of the proletarian writers' group KUZNITSA (1921–23). Nizovoy first began experimenting with writing in 1907, and by 1915–16 he had published nonscholarly books on cultural history, astronomy, and other topics. From 1921 on, he dedicated himself exclusively to literature, writing short stories and novels that dealt with current topics. None of his work was reprinted after his death.

Nizovoy's early work, such as Yazychniki (1922; The Pagans), was influenced by Knut Hamsun; this povest portrays people who find happiness in their association with nature. Short stories set in areas of Siberia that saw partisan activity contain autobiographical elements. Following the standard model for depicting the class struggle in his povest Chernozemye (1923; The Black Earth Region), Nizovoy describes the village before and dur-

ing the Revolution. In his novel Okean (1929; Eng. tr., The Ocean, 1936), which takes place in the polar sea region, he returns to the theme of transformation through the Revolution. His contributions to the literature of the Five-Year Plan, such as his novel Stal (1932; Steel), are particularly weak. Nizovoy has little literary instinct, as his excessive use of epithets (among other things) reveals.

Works: Jazyčniki (pov.), 1922; Černozem'e (pov.), 1923; Teni (short stories), 1924; Krylo pticy (pov. and short stories), 1926; Stal' (novel), 1932; Okean (novel), 1933 (see above).—Sobr. soč., 6 vols., 1927–31.

Secondary Lit.: Derevenskij (pseud. of A. Neverov), in Na postu 1923:4; N. Smirnov, in Novyj mir 1929:1; B. Agapov, in Lit. kritik 1934:4; RSPP 7(1):1971.

**Nósov, Nikoláy Nikoláyevich**, prose writer (b. Nov. 23 [Nov. 10], 1908, Kiev—d. July 26, 1976, Moscow). Nosov's father was an actor. Nosov finished school in 1923. From 1927 to 1932 he studied in Kiev and in Moscow at the Institute of Cinematography. He worked as a film director between 1932 and 1951. After 1938 Nosov published stories for children; his first collection, Tuk-tuk-tuk (Knock-Knock-Knock), appeared in 1945. His somewhat longer story, Vitya Maleyev v shkole i doma (1951; Vitya Maleyev in School and at Home; Eng. tr., Schoolboys, 1954), was very widely read (Stalin Prize for 1951, 3d class). In 1954 Nosov wrote Priklyucheniya Neznayki i ego druzey (Eng. tr., The Adventures of Dunno and His Friends, 1958), the first volume in a series of stories set in a fairy-tale land of Russian children no bigger than a thumb and connected by the character of Neznayka ("Dunno," or "Know-nothing"). Nosov reworked many of the stories into theater pieces. He lived in Moscow, was elected to the board of the Writers Union of the RSFSR in 1958 and 1970, and received the Krupskaya Prize in 1969.

Nosov's stories are part of every Soviet child's customary reading. Short episodes, occasionally contrived and always fully detailed, teach honesty, comradeship, open-mindedness, willingness to work, etc., and illustrate the reprehensibility of envy, vanity and rudeness. Some have a first-person narrative structure using a child narrator; others particularly the Neznayka stories, are pure fiction. The simplification of real life in the Neznayka stories—for example, of modern technology and medicine, and also of psychology—to fit a form supposedly appropriate for children, sometimes produces an exaggerated effect and underestimates a child's ability to think.

Works: *Tuk-tuk-tuk* (short stories), 1945; *Vesëlaja semejka* (pov.), 1949 (Eng. tr., *Jolly Family*, 1954); *Vitja Maleev v škole i doma* (pov.), 1952 (see above); *Priključenija Neznajki i ego druzej* (short stories), 1954 (see above); *Neznajka v Solnečnom gorode* (short stories), 1958; *Neznajka na Lune* (novel), 1967; *Povest' o moëm druge Igore* (pov.), 1972; *Povesti*, (pov.), 1978.—*Sobr. soč.*, 3 vols., 1968–69; 4 vols., 1979–82.

Secondary Lit.: Ju. Oleša, in *Lit. gazeta* July 28, 1955; Ju. Pukhov, in *Zvezda* 1955:10 and in his *Pisatel' i žizn'*, 1963; S. Rassadin, 1961; S. Baruzdin, in *Neva* 1961:12; G. Savčenko, in *Detskaja lit.* 1970:6; B. Dubin, in *Lit. obozrenie* 1973:10; A. Aleksin, in *Lit. gazeta* Aug. 4, 1976, p. 3.

**Nósov, Yevgény Ivánovich,** prose writer (b. Jan. 15, 1925, Tolmachevo, oblast Kursk). Nosov's father was a metalworker. During World War II, Nosov was assigned to an antitank unit; he completed school afterward and worked as a journalist. His first publications, some with his own drawings, began to appear in 1947. Nosov writes short stories and longer tales (see POVEST) that were published for the first time in his native city of Kursk in *Na rybachyey trope* (1958; On the Fisherman's Beat). His collection *Tridtsat zyoren* (1961; Thirty Seeds), published in Moscow, gave Nosov entry to acknowledged Soviet literature, in which he is considered a writer of village prose. In 1962 Nosov completed his studies at the Gorky Literary Institute. His short stories appear in the journal *Nash sovremennik* and are collected and published in book form on a regular basis. In the povest *Usvyatskiye shlemonostsy* (1977; The Helmetwearers of Usvyaty) he portrays the effects of the beginning of the war (1941) in the village. In 1970 Nosov became a member of the board of the Writers Union of the RSFSR; he lives in Kursk.

Nosov's narration and descriptions are balanced and natural. His subject is the contemporary village inhabitants in the central Russian landscape, with occasional flashbacks to the war years. The people in his prose most often derive from simple circles and have a close relationship to nature. He depicts everyday situations that hint at human destinies; above all he knows how to elucidate the gradual transformation of a person's character or

to reveal it gradually in the course of an unobtrusive plot. "Nosov's plots have an open-ended, almost accidental quality, consisting of events that in themselves, as a rule, have no unusual importance" (D. Brown). His dialogue is lively and is marked by the language of country people.

Works: *Na rybač'ej trope* (short stories), 1958; *Tridcat' zëren* (short stories), 1961; *Gde prosypaetsja solnce* (pov. and short stories), 1965; *V čistom pole za prosëlkom* (pov. and short stories), 1967; *Berega* (short stories), 1971; *Krasnoe vino pobedy* (pov. and short stories), 1971; *Most* (pov. and short stories), 1974; *Usvjatskie šlemonoscy* (pov. and short stories), 1977; *Izbr. proizv.*, 2 vols., 1983.

Secondary Lit.: D. Golubkov, in *Lit. gazeta* Feb. 28, 1968, p. 4; V. Čalmaev, *Khram Afrodity*, 1972; F. Čapčakhov, in *Lit. gazeta* June 6, 1973, p. 6; Ju. Seleznev, in *Oktjabr'* 1975:1; I. Dedkov, in *Naš sovremennik* 1976:7; I. Solov'ëva, in *Lit. obozrenie* 1979:1; A. Kondratovič, in *Naš sovremennik* 1982:1; V. Vasil'ev, in *Naš sovremennik* 1985:1, 1986:10.

**Nóvgorod-Séversky, Iván Ivánovich** (pseud. of Yan Plyashkévich), poet, prose writer (b. Nov. 13, 1893, Alekseyevsk, Amur region, Siberia—d. July 10, 1969, near Paris). Novgorod-Seversky spent his childhood in the Amur region, lived later in Mariinsk (prov. Tomsk), attended the Mechanical-Technical Institute in Omsk, and completed the officer candidate school in Irkutsk. In his youth, he explored all of Siberia during his journeys by horse and mail coach. In approximately 1913 he also began to work as a writer. During World War I he was an officer, then he fought in the volunteer army against the Bolsheviks. Probably in 1920, Novgorod-Seversky emigrated via Constantinople and Bulgaria to Paris, where he studied at the theological institute in 1926–27. He married Yu. A. Kutyrina, I. Shmelyov's niece. By the time he was living in Constantinople, Novgorod-Seversky had already developed a rich, religiously grounded writing style for both poetry and prose. In the foreword to Novgorod-Seversky's collection of poems *Zapolyarye* (1939; Behind the Polar Circle), Shmelyov called him the "singer of the frigid region." His published works seem to be extensive, but bibliographically the list is partially unverifiable. At the time of his death, he claimed a total of 31 works of poetry and 5 of prose. The first posthumously published volume of short stories, *Khristos u morya Galileyskogo—videniye Petra* (1970; Christ at the Sea of Galilee—a Vision of Peter's), also contains numerous reprints of articles about him. *Moya Sibir* (1973; My Siberia), the second such volume—the publication of which was also overseen by his wife—provides a good selection with its 100 short stories. Novgorod-Seversky is a talented, religiously inspired Russian writer who is unjustly ignored in histories of literature. His poetry as well as his prose offers something original and unique in Russian literature. Among his poetic works, those poems in the volume *Mater Bozhiya Derzhavnaya* (1966; The Mother of God—the Queen of Heaven) that are directed to various icons of the Mother of God stand out; these are essentially prayers rather than descriptive representations. He also composed many poems about nature in which he depicts the beauty of Siberia—the taiga, the steppes, the trees, the animals and plants, the farms and estates. Fairy-tale poems recall A. Pushkin; children's verses reveal his great love for children. His short stories contain both his own experiences and historical elements. His *Skazki sibirskiye* (1964; Siberian Fairy Tales) combines Christian and mythical elements derived from Siberian folklore. Novgorod-Seversky is just as comfortable in the world of the Bible as in that of the age-old wisdom of the Siberian shamans. His fairy tales told in lively dialect stem from the traditions of both Russian and non-Russian peoples. Biblical and apocryphal events are supported by divine truth, just as his fairy-tale world is. Yu Terapiano comments: "According to Novgorod-Seversky's perception, the world is penetrated by the spiritual rays of a higher order."

*Works: Kak rastut kresty* (poems), Constantinople, 1921; *Zapoljar'e* (poems), Paris, 1939; *Ajsbergi* (poems), Paris, 1942; *Ave Marija* (poems), Paris, 1958; *Čudny Liki Tvoi, Presvjataja* (poems), Paris, 1958; *Skazki sibirskie, Legendy o Bož'ej materi* (fairy tales), Munich, 1960 (title also *Skazki Mikheiča*); *Stepnye ogni* (poems), Munich, 1964; *Mater' Božija Deržavnaja: Čudny Liki Tvoi, Presvjataja* (poems), Paris, 1966; *Severnoe poslanie* (poems), Paris, 1968; *Khristos u morja Galilejskogo—videnie Petra* (short stories), Paris, 1970; *Moja Sibir'* (short stories), Paris, 1973.

*Secondary Lit.:* I. Šmelëv, in Novgorod-Severskij's *Zapoljar'e*, 1939, and *Severnoe poslanie*, 1968; Ja. Gorbov, in *Vozroždenie*, Paris, 114:1961; K. D., in *Mosty*, Munich, 9:1962; E. Latyševa, in *Rossija*, New York, May 21, 1969, and Oct. 15, 1969; Z. Šakhovskaja, in *Russkaja mysl'*, Paris, Aug. 11, 1969; P. Kovalevskij, in

*Russkaja mysl'* Sept. 11, 1969; O. Možajskaja, in *Russkaja mysl'* Sept. 11, 1969; Ju. Terapiano, in *Russkaja mysl'* Oct. 30, 1969.

**Nóvikov, Iván Alekséyevich,** prose writer (b. Jan. 13 [Jan. 1], 1877, Ilkovo, prov. Orlov—d. Jan. 10, 1959, Moscow). Novikov's father was a landowner. Novikov studied agricultural science in Moscow; from 1901 to 1909 he worked as a scientist in Kiev and also edited the journal *Zemledeliye* (1906–9). Novikov first began to combine his work with a literary career in 1899. His poems, short stories, and articles appeared in various newspapers and journals; his first volume of selected works came out in 1904. Between 1905 and 1910 Novikov made several journeys to Western Europe. The best known of his numerous prose works was *Mezhdu dvukh zor* (1915; Between Dusk and Dawn), a novel written in the realistic manner of I. Turgenev and I. Bunin that presents the problems of the younger generation at the beginning of the 20th century. In 1917 Novikov moved to Moscow; he continued his literary career after the Revolution. In 1925 he objected to the political regimentation of literature: "Every literary work lives a full life only when it has been organically born, without taking a premediated and purely rational tendentious course." In the 1930s Novikov turned his attention to the genre of the historical novel and achieved recognition for his diffusely written novels *Pushkin v Mikhaylovskom* (1936; Pushkin at Mikhaylovskoye) and *Pushkin na yuge* (1943; Pushkin in the South), which he combined under the title *Pushkin v izgnanii* (1947; Pushkin in Exile). His Pushkin research also inspired children's stories, a theater piece, a film, and an operatic libretto. Modern versions of earlier Russian literary monuments were also a part of Novikov's extensive literary activity.

*Works: Iskanija* (short stories), 1904; *Meždu dvukh zor'* (novel), 1915; *Višni* (short stories), 1927; *Gorod, more, derevnja* (pov.), 1931; *Puškin v Michajlovskom* (novel), 1936; *Puškin na juge* (novel), 1943; *Puškin v izgnanii* (novel), 1947; *Pod rodnym nebom* (poems), 1956.—*Izbr. soč.*, 3 vols., 1955; *Sobr. soč.*, 4 vols., 1966–67.

*Secondary Lit.:* V. Lidin, in *Naš sovremennik* 1959:3; Ja. Volkov, 1961, and in *Lit. Rossija* Jan. 14, 1977, pp. 6–7; *RSPP* 7(1):1971.

**Nóvikov-Pribóy, Alekséy Sílych** (pseud. of A. S. Nóvikov), prose writer (b. March 24 [March

12], 1877, Matveyevskoye, prov. Tambov—d. April 29, 1944, Moscow). Novikov-Priboy's father was a peasant. Novikov-Priboy served in the navy from 1899 to 1906. In the Russo-Japanese War (1904–5) he worked as supply officer aboard the armored cruiser *Oryol* during the voyage of the Second Pacific Squadron from the Baltic Sea to the Sea of Japan, where the squadron was destroyed in the battle of Tsushima; Novikov-Priboy was taken prisoner. Two brochures on the subject of the battle, which he published in 1907 under the pseudonym "A. Zatyorty (former sailor)," were confiscated. From 1907 to 1913 he lived abroad as an émigré. After the Revolution, Novikov-Priboy devoted himself to his literary career, writing prose about the life of sailors. His major work was the novel *Tsusima* (1932–35; Eng. tr., *Tsushima*, 1936); the second part of the novel received a Stalin prize, 2d class, for 1935–41. Novikov-Priboy was a member of the board of the Writers Union of the USSR from 1934 until his death in 1944.

Novikov-Priboy's early stories about sailors, such as *Podvodniki* (1923; The Submariners) or *V bukhte Otrada* (1924; In the Bay of Delight), deal with extraordinary events and received A. Voronsky's full approval as eyewitness, firsthand accounts. Part 1 of *Tsusima* realistically describes daily life on board a ship; Part 2 presents material drawn from the author's personal experiences of the battle, contemporary accounts by other participants, and the plentiful literature on the subject. New research (Westwood) has revealed that, in the course of the novel's constant expansion and revision in later editions, the negative picture of the tsarist fleet was altered so that numerous details no longer agreed with historical documents, nor even with Novikov-Priboy's own reports of 1906–7. Their limited pretensions to stylistic form notwithstanding, Novikov-Priboy's sailors' stories are thrilling to read and are frequently reprinted.

*Works:* Morskie rasskazy (short stories), 1917; V bukhte Otrada (short story), in *Prožektor* 1924:16–17; Solënaja kupel' (novel), 1929; Cusima (novel), 1932–35 (see above); Kapitan pervogo ranga (novel), 1943–45 (Eng. tr., *The Captain*, 1946).—Sobr. soč., 5 vols., 1926–27; 1927–28; 6 vols., 1929; 1929–31; 5 vols., 1949–50; 1963.

*Secondary Lit.:* V. Krasil'nikov, in *Novyj mir* 1927:5, 1937:3, and in a separate study, 1966; *RSPP* 3:1964; J. N. Westwood, in *Slavic Review* 1969:2; Vospominanija o N.-P., 1969; I. Novikov, in *Oktjabr'* 1977:2; A. S. Novikov-Priboj v vospominanijakh sovremennikov,

1980; L. Lekhtina, in *Lit. Rossija* Nov. 13, 1981, p. 20.

*Nóvy mir* (New World), a literary journal published in Moscow since 1925 by the publisher of the newspaper *Isvestiya*; since 1947 it has been an organ of the Writers Union of the USSR. Initially editorial responsibility belonged to A. Lunacharsky (a member of the editorial staff until 1931) and Yu. Steklov, then to I. Skvortsov-Stepanov until 1926 when it was given to the critic V. Polonsky (pseud. of V. P. Gusin), who held this position until 1931. He was replaced by the editor in chief of *Isvestiya*, I. Gronsky, who was also made the director of the organizing committee of the new WRITERS UNION. Following sharp Party criticism of the journal's promotion of B. Pilnyak (*Novy mir* 1936:9), Gronsky was arrested in 1937 and replaced by V. Stavsky, who was replaced in turn by V. Shcherbina in 1941. The Party Resolution of 1946 (see PARTY RESOLUTIONS ON LITERATURE) also led to an almost completely new editorial staff at *Novy mir*. K. Simonov became the editor in chief; in 1950 he was replaced by A. Tvardovsky. The actively liberal literary course Tvardovsky adopted after Stalin's death, and especially the inclusion of contributions by the writers V. Pomerantsev and F. Abramov and by the critics M. Shcheglov and V. Lifshits, led to the editorial staff's condemnation by the board of the Writers Union of the USSR in October 1954. Tvardovsky was replaced by Simonov who, however, continued to follow a liberal course for the most part. Special controversies arose over the publication of V. Dudintsev's novel *Ne khlebom yedinym*. In 1958 the editorship was again given to Tvardovsky; under his leadership *Novy mir* became the focal point for quality literature devoted to truthful representation and stood in opposition to the journal OKTYABR. One of the greatest events of his years as editor was the publication of A. Solzhenitsyn's povest *Odin den Ivana Denisovicha* (1962). The change in literary policy from the middle of the 1960s became apparent in March 1967 through officious criticism of *Novy mir*'s publication of works by B. Mozhayev, V. Syomin, and others, as well as through a major attack in *Ogonyok* (1969:30; see *Novy mir* 1969:7). This ultimately led to Tvardovsky's dismissal in 1970 and thus to the considerable and permanent decline in the journal's quality. V. Kosolapov was the editor in chief from 1970 to 1974; he was followed by S. Narovchatov, also a writer, from 1974 to 1981, then by the publicist colonel V. Karpov. In 1986 S. Zalygin became editor in chief. Apart from A. Lunacharsky, K. Simonov, A. Tvardovsky, and S. Narovchatov, members of the editorial staff during the 50-year-long life of the journal have included the following writers: A. Malyshkin (1929–39), F. Gladkov (1932–40), L. Leonov (1932–41), M. Sholokhov (1939–54, then moved to *Oktyabr*), K. Fedin (1941–77), V. Katayev (1946–54), B. Lavrenyov (1954–59), V. Ovechkin (1958–68), Ye. Dorosh (1967–70), Ch. Aytmatov (1967–), A. Rekemchuk (1970–), F. Taurin (1970–75), Ye. Vinokurov (1971–87), O. Chukhontsev (1987–). *Novy mir* published works by all of these authors. In the 1920s the forefront was held by the works of FELLOW TRAVELERS such as I. Babel, S. Yesenin, S. Klychkov, L. Leonov, P. Oreshin, B. Pasternak, B. Pilnyak, M. Prishvin, M. Shaginyan, I. Selvinsky, and A. Vesyoly. In the 1930s, E. Bagritsky, M. Isakovsky, M. Koltsov, A. Novikov-Priboy, M. Sholokhov, Vs. Vishnevsky, and others were published there; during World War II, P. Bazhov and V. Inber also joined the ranks. Numerous essential works of Soviet literature appeared after the war, especially starting in 1953, such as those by F. Abramov, A. Akhmatova, V. Aksyonov, G. Baklanov, O. Berggolts, Yu. Bondarev, Yu. Dombrovsky, Ye. Dorosh, I. Drutse, I. Erenburg, V. Fomenko, V. Grossman, F. Iskander, V. Katayev, V. Kaverin, Ye. Kazakevich, V. Kornilov, N. Korzhavin, V. Krupin, S. Marshak, N. Matveyeva, B. Mozhayev, V. Nekrasov, V. Ovechkin, V. Panova, K. Paustovsky, D. Samoylov, V. Syomin, Ya. Smelyakov, M. Svetlov, V. Tendryakov, M. Tsvetayeva, A. Tvardovsky, Ye. Yevtushenko, N. Zabolotsky, and S. Zalygin. *Novy mir* was the first to publish writers such as Ch. Aytmatov, I. Grekova, V. Lipatov, A. Solzhenitsyn, G. Troyepolsky, G. Vladimov, V. Voynovich. In 1927 the circulation was already 28,000 (the highest of all literary journals); in 1975, 172,000; in 1980, 320,000; and in 1987 it climbed to 490,000.

Secondary Lit.: I. Gronskij, in *Novyj mir* 1934:12; *Ob ošibkakh žurnala Novyj mir*, in *Lit. gazeta* Aug. 17, 1954; *Iz lit. arkhivov*, in *Novyj mir* 1964:5; A. Tvardovskij, in *Novyj mir* 1965:1; N. Dikušina, in *Novyj mir* 1965:1; *V Sekretariate Pravlenija Sojuza Pisatelej SSSR*, in *Lit. gazeta* March 29, 1967, p. 2; S. Medwedjew, *Zehn Jahre im Leben des Alexander Solschenizyn*, 1974, chaps. 2 and 19; *Sekretariat Pravlenija Sojuza Pisatelej SSSR . . .* , in *Novyj mir* 1975:1; A. Solženicyn,

*Bodalsja telënok s dubom*, Paris, 1975; E. B. Rogovin, Diss., Columbia Univ., 1974; T. Miller, Diss., Vanderbilt Univ., 1976, and Ann Arbor, 1983; E. R. Frankel, Cambridge, 1981; A. Gladilin, in *Russkaja mysl'*, Paris, Jan. 7, 1982; D. Spechler, New York, 1982; S. Abramov, in *Novyj mir* 1985:1; "*Novomu miru*"—*60 let*, in *Lit. gazeta* Jan. 1, 1985, p. 5; V. Nekrasov, in *Novoe russkoe slovo*, New York, Jan. 27, 1985, p. 4; S. Zalygin, in *Lit. gazeta* Aug. 26, 1987, p. 7.

*Nóvy zhurnál* (New Journal), a journal for literature, culture, and politics established in New York in 1942 by M. Aldanov and M. Tsetlin, representatives of the first emigration. Four issues have usually been published each year; no. 165 appeared in 1986. After M. Tsetlin's death (1945), M. Karpovich assumed the position of editior in chief; after his death (1959), Roman Gul took over, the first writer to hold this position. Since 1977 various contributors have shared in the editing. Initially, *Novy zhurnal* filled the gap remaining after the journal *Sovremennye zapiski* was forced to cease publication in 1940 and it published prose by such authors as M. Aldanov, I. Bunin, V. Nabokov, M. Osorgin, B. Zaytsev. After 1945, the authors associated with *Novy zhurnal* were those who had emigrated from France to the United States during World War II or those who had left the Soviet Union with the German troops. In this way I. Yelagin became a regular contributor to *Novy zhurnal*. With an excerpt from B. Pasternak's *Doktor Zhivago* (54:1958), *Novy zhurnal* began publishing works that were not allowed to appear in the Soviet Union because of censorship. The prose of L. Chukovskaya, V. Shalamov, and the émigré authors A. Kuznetsov and M. Dyomin followed. *Novy zhurnal* also published a series of previously unpublished literary works and of letters by deceased Russian writers, including M. Bulgakov, I. Bunin, N. Erdman, Z. Gippius, V. Khodasevich, N. Klyuyev, L. Lunts, D. Merezhkovsky, M. Tsvetayeva, M. Voloshin, and Ye. Zamyatin. In addition to the literature of the emigration, the journal includes a wealth of literary criticism, with contributions by G. Adamovich, A. Bakhrakh, A. Belinkov, Ye. Etkind, R. Gul, Yu. Ivask, V. Markov, R. Pletnev, L. Rzhevsky, M. Slonim, G. Struve, V. Veydle, and V. Zavalishin. Much otherwise inaccessible material on literature and history can be found in the memoirs that *Novy zhurnal* has regularly included since its inception. The reputation this journal enjoys within the Soviet Union, even unofficially, is confirmed by the fact that, before she emigrated to the West, Stalin's daughter Svetlana Alliluyeva gave *Novy zhurnal* $5,000 from the advance for her first book. During the 1970s the average circulation was 1,600; the circulation in 1986 was 1,300.

*Secondary Lit.:* Index in nos. 101, 113, 135, and 157; R. Gul', in *Novyj žurnal* 87:1967, 100:1970, 149:1982, and 162:1986 and in *Russkaja literatura v èmigracii,* ed. N. Poltorackij, Pittsburgh, 1972; G. Andreev, in *Russkaja mysl',* Paris, Nov. 1, 1984, p. 12, and May 9, 1985, p. 10.

# O

**Oberiú** (Obyedineniye Realnogo Iskusstva [Assocation for Real Art]), an association of writers and other artists in Leningrad between 1926 and 1930 that sought to renew art by breaking away from realism when it was becoming canonical. The last sound in the name *Oberiu* (-u-) parodies the usual -ism (Russian -izm) and alludes to the comic element in their artistic statement. In 1926 this group was formed by the young poets Daniil Kharms, Aleksandr Vvedensky, and Nikolay Zabolotsky; other members include a lesser known playwright and poet, Igor Bakhterev, the playwright Aleksandr Razumovsky, the poet Yury Vladimirov, and the prose writer Doyvber (Boris) Levin; Konstantin Vaginov was a member for a while; Nikolay Oleynikov was artistically close to the Oberiuts, as was Yevgeny Shvarts. Among painters, Kazimir Malevich was an active member; Pavel Filonov was artistically close. Since literary works by the Oberiuts were rarely published, their primary activity between the end of 1926 and April 1930 lay in staging theatrical performances at, among other places, Inkhuk (the House for Artistic Culture), which was under Malevich's direction until it was closed in 1928. Plans for their own theater, to be called Radiks, could not be realized. The *Oberiu Manifesto,* composed primarily by Zabolotsky, appeared in January 1928; it demanded the authorization of diverse artistic movements in the Soviet Union, clearly defined the Oberiu's own goals in poetry, film, and theater, and characterized their primary representatives. In their goal of pursuing an artistic revolution parallel to the political one, the Oberiuts were influenced by the futurists (see FUTURISM), especially V. Khlebnikov and V. Khodasevich, but they spoke out against *zaum* poetry, that is, against a metalanguage in art. Their approach to depicting and having an effect on reality was the art of the absurd, the suspension of the conventional division of time and of logic in the poetic message, the unusual confrontation between elements that were in themselves realistic. To a great extent, the plays by Kharms and Vvedensky reject a consistent plot and identity of character and dissociate the elements kaleidoscopically to the point of making individual lines of dialogue independent. People's estrangement, the despiritualization of existence, is reflected in the characters' marionettelike actions. In the few examples that have been preserved, concrete topical criticism comes occasionally to the fore; a tragic perception of the world that is alienated, concise, and depersonalized in varying degrees always lies behind the message. The Oberiuts' activities met with the sharp protest of the leading literary officials. Publications (for example, an almanac in 1927) were halted, performances criticized. The deathblow came in an article by L. Nilvich in *Smena* (April 9, 1930) in which he accused the Oberiuts of protesting against the dictatorship of the proletariat. From 1933 to 1934 a few members still met at L. Lipavsky's (also known as L. Savelyev, author of children's books). With the help of Marshak and Oleynikov, Kharms and Vvedensky made a living by writing children's books after 1927. In 1931 the arrests began that led to the deaths of Oleynikov, Kharms, and Vvedensky and to Zabolotsky's lengthy detention in a camp. L. Chukovskaya first drew attention to the group of Oberiuts in 1960; during the following decade her contemporaries and philologists at home and abroad gradually began to reconstruct fragmentarily the creative work of the members of this group. About 1970, their absurdist art found successors in Andrey Amalrik and Vladimir Kazakov. With Mikhail Levitin's performance of a collage based on Kharms's works and biography in the Teatr minyatyur in Moscow, in 1986–87, the absurdist art of the Oberiu returned to literary life.

*Works:* See KHARMS, D.; LEVIN, D.; VAGINOV, K.; VVEDENSKIJ, A.; ZABOLOCKIJ, N.;

"Manifest Oberiu," in *Afiši Doma pečati* 2:1928, reprinted in Milner-Gulland, see below.

*Secondary Lit.:* L. Čukovskaja, *V laboratorii redaktora,* 1960, 2d ed., 1963: A. Aleksandrov, in *Světova literatura,* Prague, 1968:6, in *Československá rusistika* 1968:5, in *Russkaja lit.* 1966:3 and 1970:3, and in *Zvezda* 1966:10; A. Wołodźko, in *Slavia Orientalis* 1967:3; R. R. Milner-Gulland, in *Oxford Slavonic Papers,* 1970; G. Gibian, ed., *Russia's Lost Literature of the Absurd,* Ithaca, N.Y., 1971; M. Arndt, in *Grani,* Frankfurt am Main, 81:1971; V. Kaverin, in *Zvezda* 1971:10, p. 144; A. Drawicz, *Zaproszenie do podróży,* Kraków, 1974, pp. 118–40; W. Kasack, in *Forschung und Lehre: Abschiedsschrift zu Joh. Schröpfers Emeritierung und Festgruss zu seinem 65. Geburtstag,* Hamburg, 1975; I. Bakhterev, *Vospominanija o Zabolockom,* 1977; M. Mejlakh, in his *A. Vvedenskij, Polnoe sobr. soč.,* vol. 1, Ann Arbor, 1980; S. Sigov, in *Russian Literature* 20–21:1986; A. Vishevsky, in *Slavic and East European Journal* 1986:3.

**Oboldúyev, Geórgy Nikoláyevich,** poet (b. May 19 [May 7], 1896, Moscow—d. Aug. 27, 1954, Golytsino, oblast Moscow). From his youth, Oboldúyev exhibited a great love of music; he later played the piano with distinction. His study of humanities, initiated in 1916 at Moscow University, had to be discontinued because of the Revolution. In 1919 Oboldúyev was drafted into the Red Army. In the 1920s he began to write poetry, worked for various publishing houses, and concurrently attended the Bryusov Institute of Literature and Art (graduating in 1924). At the beginning of the 1930s, Oboldúyev worked in Karelia as a conductor and traveled on concert tours with youth orchestras. From 1933 to 1939, probably with brief interruptions, Oboldúyev was held in prison and internal exile. During World War II he served at the front. From 1945 to 1954 Oboldúyev lived in Golytsino and came only rarely and almost secretly to Moscow. As a poet Oboldúyev led an underground existence and was known to only a few insiders. During his lifetime, only a single poem (1929) and one short story (1943) were published. Anna Akhmatova's presence at his funeral testifies to his unofficial recognition. Oboldúyev left behind two typescript volumes of his poetry that were ready for publication and a third volume consisting of a major novel in verse, *Ya videl* (I Saw). Out of all this material, his widow was able to publish only six poems in the Soviet Union (1967–78). However, a representative selection from the volumes of poetry, *Ustoychivoye neravnovesye* (1979; Stable Disequilibrium), was published in the Cologne series "Arbeiten und Texte zur Slavistik."

The experimental spirit of the 1920s is reflected in Oboldúyev's early work, in which he took a special interest in the movements of FUTURISM and CONSTRUCTIVISM. A certain proximity to the OBERIU association is observable, but he was not a member of this group either. His theme "is the theme of preserving human, civic, and artistic dignity in the face of omnipotent totalitarianism" (A. Terezin). Musical motifs and imagery play a role in his poems, and not only in those dedicated to Sergey Prokofyev, his close friend. The keynote of his creative work is a profound despair at the brutality and the hostility toward spirituality present in his surroundings.

*Works:* Poems, in *Novyj mir* 1929:5; in *Moskovskij komsomolec* April 7, 1967; in *Den' poèzii 1968,* Moscow, 1968; in the journal *Kolobok* 1969:2; and in *Den' poèzii 1978,* Moscow, 1978; *Teatr* (short story), in *Volga* 1943:1; *Ustojčivoe neravnoves'e* (poems from 1923 to 1949), Munich, 1979.

*Secondary Lit.:* E. Blaginina, *Okna v sad,* 1966, pp. 65–82; V. Portugalov, in *Den' poèzii 1968,* Moscow, 1968; Vl. Glocer, in *Kratkaja literaturnaja ènciklopedija* 5:1968; L. Ozerov, in *Den' poèzii 1978,* Moscow, 1978; A. Terezin and W. Kasack, in Oboldúev's *Ustojčivoe neravnoves'e,* 1979; I. Burikhin, in *Grani,* Frankfurt am Main, 118:1980; R. Ziegler, in *NRL: Neue russische Literatur,* Salzburg, 5–6:1983.

**Obradóvich, Sergéy Aleksándrovich,** poet (b. Sept. 14 [Sept. 2], 1892, Moscow—d. Oct. 25, 1956, Moscow). Obradovich's father was an artisan with an interest in literature. In 1907 Obradovich went to work in a printing shop; he published his first poems in 1912. He served as a soldier during World War I (1914–18). In 1918 he worked in a Moscow printing shop and joined the PROLETKULT; his poetry was published in Proletkult periodicals and Red Army publications. In 1920 Obradovich, together with M. Gerasimov, V. Aleksandrovsky, V. Kazin, and V. Kirillov, among others, left the Proletkult to form KUZNITSA, an association of writers that continued to advocate independent (that is, not subservient to the Party) proletarian poetry. In the 1920s Obradovich was secretary of the VAPP leadership; he published numerous volumes of verse after

1921; between 1922 and 1927 he was head of the literary section of *Pravda*. Like other proletarian writers, Obradovich stopped producing new works of literature around 1935. He was admitted to the Communist Party in 1941. In the final years of his life Obradovich was predominantly occupied with translations and editions of poetry from non-Russian Soviet republics.

As a proletarian poet Obradovich sang the praises of the October Revolution and the liberation of the factory workers of the world ("The Revolution's fiery wheel/ Will not stop halfway!"); several of his poems from 1921 are closely related to the Russian situation: "Four years of famine and anguish/ To the sound of hooting and whistling and howling," "Oktyabr. 1917–21" (October 1917–21).

*Works: Vzmakh* (poems), 1921; *Sdvig* (poems), 1921; *Oktjabr'* (poems), 1922; *Vintovka i ljubov': Stikhi 1921–23* (poems), 1924; *Rabočij front* (poems), 1933; *Stikhotvorenija* (poems), 1936; *Dorogi* (poems), 1947; *Izbr.* (poems), 1954; *Stikhi* (poems), 1958.
*Secondary Lit.:* A. Voronskij, in his *Lit. portrety*, vol. 2, 1929; S. Kir'janov, in *Oktjabr'* 1947:8; R. A. Šaceva, in *Proletarskie poèty pervykh let sovetskoj èpokhi*, 1959.

**Óbruchev, Vladímir Afanásyevich,** geologist, prose writer (b. Oct. 10 [Sept. 28], 1863, Klepenino, prov. Tver—d. June 19, 1956, Zvenigorod, oblast Moscow). Obruchev's father was an officer. Obruchev finished his studies at the St. Petersburg Institute of Mining in 1886; as a geologist he took part in numerous expeditions to Central Asia, Siberia, Mongolia, and northern China. As a university professor Obruchev taught in Simferopol (1918–19), Tomsk (1919–21), and Moscow (1921–29); in 1929 he became a member of the Academy of Sciences of the USSR and in 1939 the director of the Academy's Institute of Arctic Soil Science. The focal point of his scientific work, reflected in over 700 books and articles and some 3,000 scholarly papers, was loess formation, glaciation, permafrost, and Siberian tectonics, as well as the geology of gold deposits. Obruchev first became involved in literary activity while a student. In the course of his long life he converted his knowledge and experience as a scientist into works of literature.

Obruchev's first work of any stature is *Plutoniya* (written in 1915, published in 1924; Eng. trs., *Plutonia*, 1957, 1961), a science-fiction novel influenced by Jules Verne's *Voy-*

*age au centre de la terre* (1864); using the hollow earth theory, the novel presents scientifically based information about prehistoric conditions in an engaging and vivid manner. A similar type of novel is *Zemlya Sannikova* (1926; Eng. tr., *Sannikov Land*, 1955), which takes place in Siberia near the Arctic Ocean at the beginning of the 19th century. The adventure of expeditions, experienced by Obruchev himself or described by other scientists (such as Nikolay Przhevalsky), is reflected in the *povesti Zolotoiskateli v pustyne* (1928; Gold Prospectors in the Desert) and *V debryakh Tsentralnoy Azii* (1951; In the Wilds of Central Asia; Eng. tr., *Kukushkin: A Geographer's Tales*, 1961).

*Works: Plutonija* (novel), 1924, 1958 (with the following) (see above); *Zemlja Sannikova* (novel), 1926 (see above); *Zolotoiskateli v pustyne* (pov.), 1928; *Istorija geologičeskikh issledovanij Sibiri* (scholarly articles), 5 vols., 1931–38; *Geologija Sibiri* (scholarly articles), 3 vols., 1935–38; *V debrjakh Central'noj Azii* (pov.), 1951 (see above); *V staroj Sibiri* (memoirs and letters), 1958; *Putešestvija v prošloe i buduščee*, 1961, 2d ed., 1965.
*Secondary Lit.:* E. Murzaev, in *Novyj mir* 1953:10; E. Murzaev, V. V. Obručev, G. Rjabukhin, 1959; M. Postupal'skaja, S. Ardašnikova, 1963; V. A. Obručev (omnibus volume), 1965.

**Odárchenko, Yúry Pávlovich,** poet (b. Aug. 21 [Aug. 8], 1903—d. June [?], 1960, Paris). Odarchenko grew up in the Ukraine and lived as an émigré in Paris. He owned a tailoring shop where he made women's clothing from silk that he hand-painted himself. In the 1930s Odarchenko lived apart from the Parisian literary émigré community; he was a friend of Vladimir Smolensky. In 1947 he published the almanac *Orion*, which included works by I. Bunin, B. Zaytsev, A. Remizov, and G. Ivanov. Starting in 1948, isolated poems of his appeared in *Novy zhurnal* and *Vozrozhdeniye*. He published a single slender collection of 46 poems, *Denyok* (1949; A Small Day). Odarchenko took his own life. Vasily Betaki collected his poems and some of his prose works and republished them in 1983.

Odarchenko's poetry consciously bears the stamp of parable and depicts everyday occurrences as well as surrealistic events. His message, which is often produced or substantiated by a surprising denouement, alludes to the abyss of human existence. Moreover, his creative imagination is permeated wth a sense of divine justice. "Odarchenko draws for us, as it were, a three-tiered model of human psychology: at the lowest level—faith, conscience, spirituality. Above these—the layer of everything sordid, the subliminal. At the very top—a thin coating of respectability, purity" (Betaki). Odarchenko's close ties to the demonic world are especially strongly expressed in his prose fragments. *Nochnoye svidaniye* (1956; The Nocturnal Encounter) may be considered autobiographical: the depiction of a seemingly routine visit from Vladimir (Smolensky) in which the latter expounds on the equivalence between a poet's creativity and human conduct in the eyes of the divine tribunal. The visit turns out to be a vision of one who has just passed away. On the surface, Odarchenko's texts often appear innocent, but on deeper examination they reveal a strong spiritual incisiveness.

Works: *Denëk* (poems), Paris, 1949; *Nočnoe svidanie* (short story), in *Vozroždenie*, Paris, 67:1956; *Stikhi i proza* (poems and prose), Paris, 1983.
Secondary Lit.: Ju. Terapiano, in *Russkaja mysl'*, Paris, May 24, 1975; K. Pomerancev, in *Mosty*, New York, 12:1982, in Odarchenko's *Stikhi i proza*, 1983, and in *Russkaja mysl'* April 25, 1985, pp. 8–9; V. Betaki, in Odarchenko's *Stikhi i proza*, 1983; B. Filippov, in *Novoe russkoe slovo*, New York, Sept. 18, 1983, p. 5; I. Odoevceva, in *Russkaja mysl'* Nov. 8, 1984, p. 11.

**Odóyevtseva, Irína Vladímirovna** (pseud. of Iraída Gustávovna Ivánova, née Heinicke), poet, prose writer (b. Nov. 23, 1901, Riga). Odoyevtseva's father was an attorney. In Petrograd, after the Revolution, she studied at Dom iskusstv (The House of the Arts) and became N. Gumilyov's favorite pupil. She published her first poem in *Mir Iskusstva* (2:1920). Her first volume of poetry, *Dvor chudes* (1922; The Court of Wonders), appeared shortly before she emigrated to Paris via Berlin with her husband, the poet Georgy Ivanov, in 1922. In Paris she sporadically published poems in various journals but dedicated herself at first to prose. Her novels *Angel smerti* (1927; Angel of Death), *Izolda* (1931; Isolde), *Zerkalo* (1939; The Mirror), and *Ostav nadezhdu navsegda* (1954; Eng. tr., *All Hope Abandon*, 1949) were successful, and some of them were translated. Only after World War II did she again publish smaller volumes of poetry, such as *Kontrapunkt* (1950; Counterpoint), *Desyat let* (1961; Ten Years), *Zlataya tsep* (1975; The

Golden Chain), in which she included some poems from her early period, occasionally lightly reworked. In her memoirs, *Na beregakh Nevy* (1967; On the Shores of the Neva), she concentrated exclusively on the years 1918–22 and depicted especially her meetings with N. Gumilyov and, in addition, with G. Ivanov, O. Mandelshtam, and M. Kuzmin. Starting in 1978 she began publishing a supplement, *Na beregakh Seny* (On the Shores of the Seine), that covers her time in Paris only to a limited extent. Odoyevtseva occasionally wrote reviews. She lived in Paris before returning to the USSR in 1987 in the Gorbachev *glasnost* period.

Odoyevtseva's early poems show ACMEIST discipline. Corresponding to the spirit of the time, she wrote some ballads on contemporary themes (like N. Tikhonov). Many verses distinguish themselves through the inclusion of suprarational elements, such as a vision of Gumilyov after his execution. This union of unreal and real, of dream and reality, generally characterizes Odoyevtseva's many poems. At an advanced age, she also characterized parapsychological experiences as the source of individual poems. Her verses are very personal; many are directed toward her writer friends; often they are arguments with herself: her poetic being, her past life, her basically positive attitude toward life. Odoyevtseva's prose is fluid and conversational; the first three novels, which take place in France, start with the problem of precocious young girls, although *Zerkalo* is partially a description of the French film world. The fourth, *Ostav nadezhdu navsegda*, deals with the end of the 1930s in the Soviet Union. She has been reproached for giving an erroneous reflection of Soviet life, especially in this novel, whereas her exposition of the problems (one's relationship to inner freedom and outer freedom; the disappointment with bolshevism) has been recognized as being new in Russian literature. In addition to their poetic elaboration, Odoyevtseva's remembrances of her years in Petrograd are of historical value.

Works: *Dvor čudes* (poems), 1922; *Angel smerti* (novel), Paris, 1927, 2d ed., 1938; *Izol'da* (novel), Berlin, 1931; *Zerkalo* (novel), Paris, 1939; *Kontrapunkt* (poems), Paris, 1950; *Stikhi napisannye vo vremja bolezni* (poems), Paris, 1952; *Ostav' nadeždu navsegda* (novel), New York, 1954 (see above); *God žizni* (novel), in *Vozroždenie*, Paris, 63–68:1957; *Desjat' let* (poems), Paris, 1961; *Odinočestvo* (poems), Washington, 1965; *Na beregakh Nevy* (memoirs), Washington, 1967; *Na beregakh Seny* (memoirs), in *Russkaja mysl'*, Paris, 1978–81, separate ed., Paris, 1983; *Zlataja cep'* (poems), Paris, 1975; *Portret v rifmovannoj rame* (poems), Paris, 1976; *Ja slovno by i ne uezžala iz Rossii . . .* (interview), in *Russkaja mysl'* March 3, 1983, p. 8.

Secondary *Lit.*: I. Èrenburg, in *Novaja russkaja kniga* 3:1922; V. Mirnyj, in *Sovremennye zapiski*, Paris, 69:1939; G. Adamovič, in *Novyj žurnal*, New York, 61:1960; A. Bakhrakh, in *Mosty*, Munich, 7:1961 and *Grani*, Frankfurt am Main, 130:1983; R. Gul', in *Novyj žurnal* 92:1968; Z. Šakhovskaja, in *Vozroždenie* 196:1968; E. Bobrova, in *Novyj žurnal* 146:1982; T. Fesenko, in *Novyj žurnal* 155:1984.

**Ognyóv, Nikoláy** (pseud. of Mikhaíl Grigóryevich Rózanov), prose writer (b. June 26 [June 14], 1888, Moscow—d. June 22, 1938, Moscow). Ognyov's father was a lawyer. Ognyov was arrested in 1906 for illegal activities; from 1910 on, he was a juvenile welfare worker in the Butyrka section of Moscow. He fought at the front in World War I. After the Revolution, Ognyov continued to work with young people. He founded the first children's theater in Moscow and wrote numerous pieces for it that were later performed in other cities as well; from 1921 to 1924 he worked in the children's colonies of Moscow. Ognyov, who had been publishing short stories in various newspapers since 1906, collected the most significant of them in an anthology, published in 1925; he devoted himself completely to his writing from then on. He became a member of the constructivists (see CONSTRUCTIVISM) and, later, of PEREVAL. Ognyov's fictional diary, *Dnevnik Kosti Ryabtseva* (1926–27; *The Diary of Kostya Ryabtsev*; Eng. tr., *The Diary of a Communist Schoolboy*, 1928), was known both in the Soviet Union and abroad. He wrote two sequels to *Dnevnik*: *Iskhod Nikpetozha* (1928; *Nikpetozh's End*; Eng. tr., *The Diary of a Communist Undergraduate*, 1929) and *Tri izmereniya* (1929–32; *Three Dimensions*). In 1937 Ognyov taught at the Gorky Literary Institute. After the posthumous publication of his *Rasskazy* (1938; *Short Stories*), Ognyov's work was not reprinted in the Soviet Union until a new edition of *Dnevnik Kosti Ryabtseva* came out in 1966. Although his death was officially announced, an enforced silence concerning him was imposed after 1939; the first significant article about his work (by L. Kassil) did not appear until 1963.

According to A. Voronsky, Ognyov's "interesting, profoundly meaningful" short stories (influenced by L. Andreyev, F. Sologub, and A. Bely), deserved to be as well known as *Dnevnik Kosti Ryabtseva*. In *Dnevnik*, Ognyov provides, through the prism of a less-than-perfect 15-year-old pupil, a bird's-eye view of the reform measures attempted in Soviet high schools (1923–24), such as student participation in administrative management, the disbanding of classes, independent study, and the practice of political activism. The candor of this first novel is diminished in the subsequent volumes; their artistic merit is further weakened by an authorial commentary that, bowing to the wishes of the critics, attempts to force the partial point of view of the diary form into ideological agreement with the Party line.

Works: *Rasskazy* (short stories), 1925; *Dnevnik Kosti Rjabceva* (novel), 1927, 2d enl. ed., 1929 (reprinted, 1966) (see above); *Iskhod Nikpetoža* (under the title *Kostja Rjabcev v vuze*; novel), 1929 (see above); *Krušenie antenny* (short stories), 1933; *Tri izmerenija* (novel), 1933; *Rasskazy* (short stories), 1938; *Iz literaturnykh arkhivov* (letters from 1926–31), in *Novyj mir* 1964:10.—*Sobr. soč.*, 5 vols. (of which only vols. 1, 3, and 4 were published), 1928–29.

Secondary *Lit.*: A. Voronskij, in his *Lit. portrety*, vol. 2, 1929; A. Selivanovskij, in *Novyj mir* 1933:1; L. Kassil', in *Lit. Rossija* June 28, 1963, pp. 20–21; *RSPP* 3:1964; V. Ivaščenko, in *Lit. gazeta* Feb. 15, 1967.

**Oktyábr** (October), a union of intolerant Communist writers. Oktyabr was established in Moscow on Dec. 7, 1922, as an organization of young Communist Party members opposed to KUZNITSA and to the PROLETKULT, which was just passing away. Its leaders were G. Lelevich, S. Rodov, and I. Vardin; its writer members included A. Bezymensky, I. Doronin, Yu. Libedinsky, A. Tarasov-Rodionov, A. Vesyoly, and A. Zharov. Later D. Furmanov and the militant critic L. Averbakh joined. Oktyabr described itself as "proletarian"; in contrast to Kuznitsa, this designation was purely ideological, however, since 80 percent of its members belonged to the pre-Revolutionary intelligentsia. Oktyabr accepted complete submission to the Party line, including the shift toward private ownership inherent in NEP, and rejected apolitical belles lettres and experiments with form (see FUTURISM; IMAGISM; FORMALIST SCHOOL) as well as Kuznitsa's abstract world revolutionary idealization of workers and machines. Oktyabr's first journal, Na postu, published between 1923 and 1925, gave its members the name napostovtsy ("onguardists"); the second journal, Oktyabr, which began publication in 1924, has retained its name to this day. Oktyabr espoused an extraordinarily dogmatic, demagogic, intolerant, and self-righteous literary policy, claiming to be the overseers of the true Communist ideology. For Oktyabr, literature was only a means of combining Bolshevik propaganda with topical themes. In March 1923, the Moscow Association of Proletarian Writers (MAPP) was founded with Oktyabr's help, and, as a result, in April 1924 the Kuznitsa-affiliated VAPP was transformed into a new Oktyabr-oriented VAPP. In 1924 several members who disagreed with Oktyabr's crude practices, Vesyoly for example, formed PEREVAL. Sharp internal disputes arose over the suppression or inclusion of non-Communist writers—the FELLOW TRAVELERS, who (especially in A. Voronsky's Krasnaya nov) were most responsible for the high reputation enjoyed by Soviet literature—and over the Party Resolution of June 18, 1925 (see PARTY RESOLUTIONS ON LITERATURE). Oktyabr fell apart at the end of 1925. The main officials perpetuated their militant policy within the framework of RAPP.

Secondary Lit.: H. Ermolayev, Soviet Literary Theories 1917–1934, Berkeley, 1963; Lit. manifesty, 2d ed., 1929 (reprinted, Munich, 1969).

Oktyábr (October), a literary journal that has been published monthly in Moscow since 1924, at first as an organ of the intolerant Party-affiliated MAPP, in 1925 of VAPP, from 1926 to 1932 of VAPP and MAPP, in 1933–34 of the Organizing Committee of the Writers Union of the RSFSR, from 1934 to 1959 of the Writers Union of the USSR, from 1959 to 1968 of the Writers Union of the RSFSR, since then of the Writers Union of the USSR. In the first few years, the position of editor in chief rotated among various VAPP officials (S. Rodov, G. Lelevich, A. Fadeyev); from 1926 to 1929, A. Serafimovich was the editorial director. F. Panfyorov, a member of the editorial staff since 1928, except for a brief interruption in 1930 when the entire editorial staff was dismissed, became the editor in chief in 1931 and held this position until 1954. After the journal published an announcement by P. Vershigora that encouraged truthfulness in depictions of the partisan struggle (1954:4), Panfyorov was replaced by M. Khrapchenko

(from 1954 to 1957), but in 1957 he regained his position and retained it until his death. His successor from 1961 to 1973 was V. Kochetov who, in an unremitting struggle against the liberal tendencies of the journal Novy mir, made Oktyabr into a bulwark of conservatism. Under his successor, A. Ananyev, the journal regained some of its literary value. Writers who have been members of the editorial staff for several years include A. Bezymensky (1924–25, 1932–37), M. Sholokhov (1928–30, 1931–41, 1954–58), A. Surkov (1931–41), V. Ilyenkov (1931–51), A. Afinogenov (1932–37), P. Pavlenko (1941–45), St. Shchipachov (1941–45, 1954–57), A. Perventsev (1946–81), B. Polevoy (1946–50), S. Babayevsky (1951–54, 1957–), M. Bubennov (1960–67), A. Prokofyev (1967–71), P. Proskurin (1974–78), G. Baklanov (1974–), A. Prokhanov (1982–). In the 1920s, the most significant literary works appeared in the journals Krasnaya nov and Novy mir, which were attacked by Oktyabr. In the 1930s, Oktyabr published works by A. Chapygin, V. Kaverin, Vya. Shishkov, and A. Tolstoy, among others. During World War II, the authors Oktyabr published included A. Chakovsky, B. Gorbatov, and V. Vasilevskaya. After the war, many of the works shaped by the THEORY OF CONFLICTLESSNESS and by the Stalin cult of personality were published in Oktyabr. Even during the THAW and its aftermath, Oktyabr remained faithful to the principle that literature should reflect the prevailing Party policy. Authors such as S. Babayevsky, Ye. Dolmatovsky, B. Polevoy, A. Sofronov, and V. Zakrutkin, whose works frequently appeared in Oktyabr around 1980, confirm the perpetuation of this canon. In 1927 the circulation was 10,000; in 1987, 185,000.

Secondary Lit.: V Sojuze Sovetskikh Pisatelej, in Lit. gazeta June 3, 1954; V. Revič, in Voprosy lit. 1960:3; V Sekretariate Pravlenija Sojuza Pisatelej SSSR, in Lit. gazeta April 12, 1967, p. 3; Očerki istorii russkoj sovetskoj žurnalistiki, 1968; A. Egorunin, in Lit. Rossija Dec. 23, 1977, p. 3.

Okudzháva, Bulát Shálvovich, poet, prose writer (b. May 9, 1924, Moscow). Okudzhava is of Caucasian descent; he grew up in Moscow in the Arbat and writes only in Russian. Okudzhava's father (a Georgian) was a high-level Party official who was executed in 1937, a victim of Stalin's purges. His mother (an Armenian) was sent to a prison camp; she was rehabilitated in 1955. In 1942, before graduating from school, Okudzhava volunteered to join the military and was sent to the front. From 1945 to 1950 he studied Russian philology at the University of Tiflis; after graduating he worked as a village schoolteacher near Kaluga until 1955; *Lirika* (Lyric Poetry), his first volume of poetry, appeared there in 1956. His mother's REHABILITATION enabled them to return to Moscow, and Okudzhava considers this period the beginning of his literary career. In 1955 he joined the Communist Party. Sometime in 1957 Okudzhava began to recite his poems accompanying himself on the guitar, at first privately and after 1960 publicly; this quickly led to his popularity and renown. After a second volume of poetry, *Ostrova* (1959; Islands), Okudzhava published his first work of prose, *Bud zdorov shkolyar* (1961; Eng. tr., "Lots of Luck, Kid!" in *Pages from Tarusa*, 1964), in K. Paustovsky's *Tarusskiye stranitsy;* this is a candid autobiographical depiction of his experiences at the front that was sharply criticized for its pacifism and that was not published again until Gorbachev's *glasnost* period in 1987. Okudzhava's poetry appeared in journals and circulated through SAMIZDAT and tape recordings. From 1964 to 1967 three shorter volumes were published. After a short novel for children, *Front prikhodit k nam* (1965; The Front Comes to Us), Okudzhava published one historical novel, *Bedny Avrosimov* (1969; Poor Avrosimov), and then a second, *Mersi, ili pokhozhdeniya Shipova* (1971; Merci; or, The Adventures of Shipov; Eng. tr., *The Extraordinary Adventures of Secret Agent Shipov in Pursuit of Count Leo Tolstoy in the Year 1862*, 1973). In 1974 Okudzhava resumed writing poetry. Okudzhava, who signed the petitions for A. Sinyavsky and Yu. Daniel (1966) and for A. Solzhenitsyn (1969), was threatened with expulsion from the Party in connection with the reprinting of his works in the West (1965), but the explanation he was forced to write (*Lit. gazeta* Nov. 18, 1972) kept this threat from being realized. After a long pause, Okudzhava again published his poems and songs in *Arbat, moy Arbat* (1976; Arbat, My Arbat). In *Puteshestviye diletantov* (1976–78; The Travels of Dilettantes; Eng. tr., *Nocturne: From the Notes of Lt. Amiran Amilakhvari, Retired*, 1978), Okudzhava unfolds a more entertaining than historical tale of the upper class in Petersburg during the middle of the 19th century. He lives in Moscow.

Okudzhava is primarily a poet who describes his youthful experiences in the war and denounces the senselessness of war. His poetry preserves his never tranquil relationship to his surroundings; it is personal and often characterized by sadness. Themes of loneliness, of the vacillation between hope and hopelessness, and of the flight from responsibility into obedience alternate with occasional religious elements and often with his wartime experiences, which are sometimes presented with satiric alienation. (For example, *Odin soldat na svete zhil* [Once There Was a Paper Soldier]). His exposition, which makes use of rhyme and meter in a traditional way, is sometimes narrative in form and contains elements of repetition and components reminiscent of folk songs. Metaphorical language and irony mask some contemporary criticism; his message is not limited to the present day. Okudzhava does not generally stipulate how his poems are to be sung; their presentation arises from his improvisation. Despite their strong appeal when he sings them with guitar accompaniment, Okudzhava's poems are not song texts but primarily lyrical expressions governed by words. With his first prose work, *Bud zdorov, shkolyar*, Okudzhava produced, just as V. Nekrasov and G. Baklanov did, his own contribution to the candid depiction of war: war that is capable of destroying one's last illusions through the cold, hunger, dampness, danger of death, meanness, and helplessness one is forced to endure. In the novel *Bedny Avrosimov*, which was republished as a separate book under the title *Glotok svobody* (A Draught of Freedom; Eng. tr., *A Taste of Liberty [Poor Avrosimov]*, 1986), Okudzhava takes the fate of the Decembrists as a point of departure and, through the use of a fictitious narrator from the second half of the 19th century and the constricted perspective of a clerk to the court, allegorically condemns the practice of informing on people and presents the fateful relativity of the interchangeable roles of accuser and accused in politics.

*Works: Lirika* (poems), 1956; *Ostrova* (poems), 1957; *Bud' zdorov, školjar* (pov.), in *Tarusskie stranicy*, 1961, first separate ed., 1987 (see above); *Vesëlyj barabanščik* (poems), 1964; *Po doroge k Tinatin* (poems), 1964; *Front prikhodit k nam* (pov.), 1965; *Promoksis* (short story), in *Junost'* 1966:1; *Mart velikodušnyj* (poems), 1967; *Vremja idët*, in *Voprosy lit.* 1967:8; (autobiography) in *Polen*, Warsaw, 1967:10; *Proza i poèzija*, 3d ed. enl. and corrected, Frankfurt am Main, 1968 (contains *Bud' zdorov, školjar* and *Promoksis*); *Dva romana* (novels), Frankfurt am Main, 1970 (*Bednyj Avrosimov* and *Fotograf Žora*); *Glotok svobody: Povest' o Pavle Pestele* (= *Bednyj*

*Avrosimov)* (novel), 1971 (see above); *Mersi, ili pokhoždenija Šipova: Starinnyj vodevil'* (novel), in *Družba narodov* 1971:12, separate ed., 1975 (see above); *Putešestvie diletantov: Iz zapisok otstavnogo poručika Amirana Amilakhvari* (novel), in *Družba narodov* 1976:8–9 and 1978:9–10, separate ed., 1979 (see above); *Arbat, moj Arbat* (poems and songs), 1976; *Minuvšee menja ob"emlet živo . . .* (discussion), in *Voprosy lit.* 1980:8; *Stikhotvorenija* (poems), 1984; *Svidanie s Bonapartom* (novel), 1985.—*Izbr. proza,* 1979.

*Translation:* Sixty-five Songs. 65 pesen (score with English and Russian lyrics), Ann Arbor, 1982.

*Secondary Lit.:* A. Sinjavskij, A. Menšutin, in *Novyj mir* 1961:1; A. Kondratovič, in *Novyj mir* 1962:6; A. Kireeva, in *Junost'* 1965:2; A. Kon, in *Teatr* 1967:9; G. Krasukhin, in *Voprosy lit.* 1968:9; K.-D. van Ackern, Munich, 1976; V. Iverni, in *Kontinent,* Paris, 12:1977; I. H. Corten, in *Russian Language Journal* 117:1980; A. Baženova, in *Oktjabr'* 1984:9; S. Čuprinin, in *Novyj mir* 1985:6; D. Boss, Munich, 1985.

**Olésha, Yúry Kárlovich,** prose writer, playwright (b. March 3 [Feb. 19], 1899, Yelizavetgrad—d. May 10, 1960, Moscow). Olesha's father was an impoverished Polish nobleman. From 1902 on, Olesha lived in Odessa; he completed his studies at a local gymnasium in 1917 and studied law in Odessa for two years. In 1919 he joined the Red Army as a volunteer. Olesha's first poems date from 1916. He wrote Communist agitational poems in Odessa (1921), Kharkov (1922), and Moscow (1923); in Moscow he wrote primarily for the railroad newspaper *Gudok* under the pseudonym "Zubilo" (a volume of selections from *Gudok* appeared in 1924). In 1927 Olesha published his novel *Zavist* (Eng. trs., *Envy,* 1936, 1947, 1975) in *Krasnaya nov;* the work generated a polemical discussion and established Olesha's position in Russian literature. His subsequent works were all of lesser artistic merit. Olesha first wrote, in addition to the children's book *Tri tolstyaka* (1928; Eng. tr., *The Three Fat Men,* 1964) and some short stories, two dramas: *Zagovor chuvstv* (1929; Eng. tr., *The Conspiracy of Feelings,* 1969), which was based on *Zavist,* and *Spisok blagodeyaniy* (1931; Eng. tr., *A List of Assets,* 1963). These were followed only by short stories and screenplays. *Zavist* was included in the 1935 and 1936 volumes of Olesha's selected works but was not published again for 20 years. During World War II, Olesha was evacuated with the Odessa film studio to Ash-

khabad, where he worked in press and radio and translated from Turkmen into Russian. From 1945 on, he eked out a miserable existence in Moscow without a residence permit. After the 20th Party Congress, Olesha, about whom nothing could be written between 1941 and 1956, was allowed to return to the literary scene. Entries from his diary appeared in *Literaturnaya Moskva,* vol. 2, in 1956; several of his earlier works were reprinted this same year. His stage adaptation of F. Dostoyevsky's *The Idiot* for the Vakhtangov Theater in 1958 was the final result of decades-long critical preoccupations. His book of autobiographical literary aphorisms, *Ni dnya bez strochki* (Eng. tr., *No Day without a Line,* 1979), published posthumously in 1965 with the assistance of V. Shklovsky, no longer bears the stamp of creative power.

Olesha's more than 1,000 agitational poems, written in the course of six years, reached millions of readers in the 1920s; the poems have not been reprinted since that time. His short but highly significant novel *Zavist* is the first literary attempt to depict communism as a moral problem. In the inner conflict of Kavalerov, who strives for recognition by the new society but who revolts against its exclusive utilitarianism, Olesha investigates the psychological dilemma faced by a large segment of the intelligentsia at the time of the book's writing (1922–27). He pits Kavalerov against a Communist managerial type, a success-oriented, strong physical specimen who is totally lacking in sensibility, and centers the conflict within Kavalerov alone. The work's unusual structure corresponds to its psychological motivation: one part is a first-person narrative, the other is third-person, with minimal external plot. The depiction of Soviet reality is ironically exaggerated; the work as a whole is laconically concentrated and consciously formulated to the last. Since the problem Olesha poses lies in the soul, it is not represented as powerfully in the drama *Zagovor chuvstv,* although Olesha's refined dialogue technique, reminiscent of I. Turgenev and A. Chekhov, establishes him as a gifted dramatist.

*Works: Zubilo* (poems), 1924; *Tri tolstjaka* (novel), 1928 (see above); *Zavist'* (novel), 1928 (see above); *Zagovor čuvstv* (play), in *Oktjabr'* 1929:1 (see above); *Spisok blagodejanij* (play), 1931 (see above); *Višnëvaja kostočka* (short stories), 1931; *Igra v plakhu* (play), in *30 dnej* 1934:5; *Valter* (film script), in *Zvezda* 1937:4; *O lise* (children's verse), 1948; *Ni dnja bez stročki* (diary), 1965 (see above).—*Izbr.,* 1935; 1936; 1974; *Izbr. soč.,* 1956; *P'esy,* 1968.

Translations: Love and Other Stories, 1967; Complete Short Stories and Three Fat Men, 1979; The Complete Plays, 1983.

Secondary Lit.: N. A. Nilsson, in Scando-Slavica 1965; A. Drawicz, in Cahiers du monde russe et soviétique 1967:3; E. K. Beaujour, New York, 1970; D. G. B. Piper, in Slavonic and East European Review 110:1970; M. Čudakova, 1972; S. Appel, Munich, 1973; V. B. Šklovskij, foreword to Oleša's Izbr., 1974; Vospominanija o Ju. Oleše, 1975; B. Jampol'-skij, in Kontinent, Paris, 6:1976; V. Percov, 1976; A. Belinkov, Madrid, 1976; P. M. Johnson, Diss., Cornell Univ., 1976; M. Numano, in Novyj žurnal, New York, 45:1981; K. Ingdahl, Diss., Univ. of Stockholm, 1984, and in Slavonic and East European Review 1985:4.

**Oléynikov, Nikoláy Makárovich,** poet, prose writer (b. Aug. 1898, Kamenskaya, the Don—d. May 5, 1942 [?], while imprisoned). Oleynikov came from a well-to-do Cossack family; he served as a Red Army officer in the Civil War and became a member of the Communist Party in 1920. He worked as a journalist in Rostov-on-Don; in 1925 he went to Leningrad, where he worked with S. Marshak and Ye. L. Shvarts in the State Publishing House's department of children's books. Oleynikov was associated with the group OBERIU, particularly with D. Kharms and A. Vvedensky. Like them, he could publish only children's literature. He edited the journals Yozh (The Hedgehog) in 1928–29 and Chizh (The Siskin) in 1934 and 1937. In addition to his numerous journal contributions, Oleynikov also published many children's books in the period 1926–37, some under the pseudonym he used at Yozh, Makar Svirepy. Of his serious work, only three poems were published (in Tridtsat dney 1934:10). Oleynikov was arrested (probably in 1938) and purged; his name was banned from literary studies. After his REHABILITA-TION, a few of his poems, preserved in copy, were printed in various Soviet periodicals (after 1964); a volume of his selected poems was published in the West in 1975.

V. Kaverin, who considered Oleynikov to be "one of the most intelligent people I have ever met in my life," said: "For him, irony . . . was one of the means of existence." The few known poems demonstrate this view of life from an ironic, often mocking distance. Oleynikov is supposed to have written numerous parodies of contemporary and classical writers as well as of literary genres. "He was an original, and in a manner perhaps rare in Soviet cultural life: a brilliant, biting, sometimes destructive wit, perpetrator of absurd or anarchic practical jokes, master of verbal repartee" (Milner-Gulland). Oleynikov incorporated a racy eroticism into his poems. Behind his comic mask stand a tragic perception of the world and a despair about his own epoch that are expressed, not, as with the members of Oberiu, by absurdist defamiliarization techniques, but by occasional outbursts: "Orlov is gone, Kozlov is gone, dear friends, won't you please pray for us!" ("Peremena familii," A Change in the Family Name). In his poems for children, Oleynikov depicts events of Soviet history and of the present in a concise and vivid manner. In 1935–36 Oleynikov, working with Shvarts, wrote several film scripts.

Works: Pervyj sovet (short story), 1926; Boevye dni (short story), 1927; Tanki i sanki (short story), 1928; three poems, in Tridcat' dnej 1934:10; "Tarakan," "Peremena familii," two poems, in Den' poèzii, Leningrad, 1966; poems, in Voprosy lit. 1969:3 and 1970:7; Stikhotvorenija (poems), Bremen, 1975; Ironičeskie stikhi, New York, 1982.

Secondary Lit.: I. Rakhtanov, in Detskaja lit. 1962:2; I. Bakhterev and A. Razumovskij, in Den' poèzii, Leningrad, 1964; A. Dymšic, in Voprosy lit. 1969:3; A. Aleksandrov, in Russkaja lit. 1970:3; V. Kaverin, in Zvezda 1971:10; R. R. Milner-Gulland, in Russian and Slavic Literature, 1976; S. Poljanina, in NRL: Neue russische Literatur 2–3, Salzburg, 1979–80; A. Losev, in Russkaja mysl', Paris, Nov. 25, 1982; see OBERIU.

**Ópyty** (Experiments), journal for literature published in New York between 1953 and 1957 in nine issues. Issues 1 to 3 were edited by R. N. Grinberg and V. L. Pastukhov; M. E. Tsetlina is named as publisher of issues 1 to 6. Yu. Ivask took over as editor starting with issue 4. Opyty is a discriminating literary journal with an emphasis in the field of literary criticism and the history of émigré literature. Thus, Opyty published extensive excerpts from B. Poplavsky's prose and from the letters of M. Tsvetayeva to A. Shteyger, the reminiscences of V. Nabokov, and numerous essays and reviews by G. Adamovich, Yu. Ivask, V. Markov, F. Stepun, G. Struve, Yu. Terapiano, and V. Veydle. A poetry section at the beginning of each issue offered the works of N. Berberova, I. Chinnov, G. Ivanov, D. Klenovsky, S. Makovsky, I. Odoyevtseva, and V. Smolensky. The contributors also included G. Gazdanov, A. Remizov, V. Varshavsky, and B. Zaytsev.

Secondary Lit.: V. Zlobin, in Vozroždenie, Paris, 80:1959.

Oréshin, Pyotr Vasílyevich, poet, prose writer (b. July 28 [July 16], 1887, Saratov—d. March 15, 1938[?], while imprisoned). Oreshin's father was an estate agent. Oreshin began publishing his verse in 1911. The poems he wrote as a soldier in World War I were directed against the horrors of war; they depict a sense of isolation and emptiness. After the Revolution, Oreshin belonged to the group of "peasant poets" (with S. Yesenin, N. Klyuyev, and S. Klychkov); this group came under increasing attack by the representatives of RAPP. Oreshin published over 50 books, including a four-volume collection of poems (1923–28) that contained only a part of the more than 1,000 poems he had written. Some, like "Garmonist" (The Accordion Player), became popular songs. In addition to his shorter verse, Oreshin also wrote a series of narrative poems and some mostly autobiographical prose. He was arrested in 1937, a victim of the Stalinist purges, and for a long time it was assumed that he had died in 1943. Since Oreshin's REHABILITATION, which in 1958 led to the publication of a new volume of his verse after 20 years of silence, 1938 has been considered to be the year of his death.

Oreshin's poetry is completely devoted to peasant life. In the tradition of A. Koltsov, N. Nekrasov, and I. Nikitin, his verse makes frequent use of folk-song elements. "He has enriched every line of his poems with village scenery, life, and the dialogue of the muzhik" (Krasilnikov). In addition to his nature lyrics, Oreshin wrote many narrative poems that express the day-to-day concerns of the peasant during the Revolution, NEP, and collectivization, and that represent his attempt to adapt to new times. Militsioner Lyuksha (1927; Militiaman Lyuksha) "is the best of Oreshin's 'everyday life' poems" (Zavalishin); it paints an ironic portrait of bribery and corruption during the NEP period. Oreshin was ideologically condemned by the official critics; nevertheless, he had considerable influence on Soviet peasant literature (for example, A. Tvardovsky, M. Isakovsky).

Works: Zarevo (poems), 1918; Alyj khram (poems), 1922; Sobr. soč., 4 vols. (Ržanoe solnce, 1923; Solomennaja plakha, 1925; Rodnik [contains Milicioner Ljukša, narrative poem], 1927; Otkrovennaja lira, 1928); Ničego ne bylo (pov.), 1926; Zlaja žizn' (pov.), 1931, 2d ed., 1964; Pod sčastlivym nebom (poems), 1937; Stikhotvorenija i poèmy (lyric and narrative poems), 1958; Povesti i rasskazy (short stories), 1960; Stikhi (poems), 1964; Izbr. (selected writings), 1968.

Secondary Lit.: V. Krasil'nikov, in Novyj mir 1925:7; D. Gorbov, in Novyj mir 1927:10; V. Zavalishin, Early Soviet Writers, New York, 1958; A. I. Mikhajlov, in Russkaja lit. 1973:1 and 1974:3.

Orlóv, Sergéy Sergéyevich, poet (b. Aug. 22, 1921, Megra, near Belozersk, oblast Vologda—d. Oct. 7, 1977, Leningrad). Orlov's father was a teacher. In 1940–41 Orlov studied history at Petrozavodsk University. From 1941 to 1944 he was a soldier; eventually he became the commander of a tank; he was demobilized after being severely wounded. Orlov, who published his first literary efforts in provincial newspapers in 1940, belongs to the generation of war poets. His first collection, Front, appeared in Chelyabinsk in 1942; he attracted attention with Tretya skorost (1946; Third Gear). In 1954 Orlov graduated from the Gorky Literary Institute. He attended all congresses of the Writers Union held from 1954 on; in 1958 he became a member of the board of the Writers Union of the RSFSR and served on its secretariat from 1970 on. Orlov lived in Leningrad.

One of Orlov's best-known poems, "Yego zaryli v shar zemnoy" (1944; They Buried Him in the Terrestrial Sphere), directs the consciousness to those killed in action by using clear, vivid, and unassuming language. In 1946 Orlov was attacked for his pessimism (Lit. gazeta Oct. 20). Years after the war, Orlov's verse was still inspired by frontline experiences and the memory of the dead. His poems of the late Stalinist period that were written in accordance with the Party line to depict the reconstruction of the country are without aesthetic value, but his portraits of simple people and their destiny and his lyrics about the tranquillity of his northern Russian homeland remain worthwhile. Orlov likes to use imagery taken from the prosaic objects of everyday life. In the mid-1960s he devoted many poems to the situation of human beings throughout history. His love lyrics, such as the narrative poem Odna lyubov (1961; Love Alone), are dominated by the theme of estrangement caused by forced separation in wartime and the renunciation of a beloved woman for the sake of her happiness. Later poems, such as those found in the slender volume Vernost (1973; Loyalty), revolve around day-to-day experiences and travels; they penetrate little into human depths. For this collection the poet received the Gorky prize in 1979.

Works: Front (poems), 1942; Tret'ja skorost' (poems), 1946; Pokhod prodolžaetsja (poems),

1948; *Stikhotvorenija* (poems), 1956; *Stikho-tvorenija 1938–1958* (poems), 1959; *Odna lju-bov'* (narrative poem), 1961; *Koleso* (poems), 1964; *Sozvezdie* (poems), 1964; *Vernost'* (poems), 1975; *Beloe ozero* (lyric and narra-tive poems), 1975; *Kostry* (poems), 1978; *V lëgkoj pesne berëz*, 1983.—*Izbr.*, 2 vols., 1971; *Sobr. soč.*, 3 vols., 1979–80.
    *Secondary Lit.:* Ju. Oleša, in *Novyj mir* 1952:12; V. Dement'ev, in *Oktjabr'* 1955:5 and in *Moskva* 1960:6 and 1966:9; D. Moldavskij, in *Zvezda* 1959:5 and in *Oktjabr'* 1962:3; D. Khrenkov, 1964; A. Èl'jaševič, in his *Poèty. Stikhi. Poèzija*, 1966; S. Narovčatov, foreword to Orlov's *Izbr.*, 1971; N. Kondakova, in *Oktjabr'* 1975:1; A. Pikač, in *Zvezda* 1980:1; S. O., *Vospominanija sovremennikov*, 1980; A. Ur-ban, in *Zvezda* 1981:8; V. Kočetkov, in *Lit. obozrenie* 1984:8.

**Oshánin, Lev Ivánovich,** poet (b. May 30 [May 17], 1912, Rybinsk, prov. Yaroslavl). Osha-nin's father was a jurist. Oshanin was active in industry until 1935. He attended the Gorky Literary Institute (1936–39); in 1930 he began his literary activity by writing prose and po-etry. In 1937 he began to write lyrics for songs in which he illustrated topical political themes. Some songs written during World War II be-came popular. In 1944 he joined the Com-munist Party. After the war, he turned espe-cially to the theme of the Communist youth movement in the Eastern blok, and his *Gimn demokraticheskoy molodyozhi mira* (1947; Hymns to the Democratic Youth of the World) became well known. Several collections ap-peared after 1948. For songs and poems about the film *Yunost mira* (The Youth of the World), Oshanin received a Stalin Prize (for 1949, 1st class). His later discovery that at times "many didactic, quickly rhymed slogans from lead-ing articles in the provincial newspapers" were written under the guise of songs is essentially a comment upon his own work. In dramas (written with E. B. Uspenskaya) and poetic tales, Oshanin also failed to attain artistic depth; the didactic intention remains on the surface. He lives in Moscow and has belonged to the board of the Writers Union of the RSFSR since 1958 and to that of the Writers Union of the USSR since 1976.

    *Works: Vsegda v puti* (poems), 1948; *Moskva majskaja* (songs), 1949; *Stikhi o ljubvi* (poems), 1957; *Sto pesen* (songs), 1966; *Kak sozdava-las' pesnja* (essays), 1967; *"Tekstoviki" ili poèty?* (essay), in *Voprosy lit.* 1967:8; *Èto budet vot tak* (songs and poems), 1969; *Ostrovitjane* (songs and poems), 1972; *Izdaleka-dolgo . . .*

*(poems), 1977; Samolëty i solov'i: Kniga liriki,* 1982.—*Sobr. soč.*, 3 vols., 1980–81.
    *Secondary Lit.:* D. Moldavskij, in *Zvezda* 1950:7; Ju. Surovcev, in *Lit. gazeta* Nov. 19, 1955; A. Kovalenkov, in *Moskva* 1965:3; V. V. Tjurin, 1972; A. P'janov, in *Lit. gazeta* March 22, 1978, p. 5, and in *Oktjabr'* 1982:5.

**Osorgín, Mikhaíl Andréyevich,** (pseud. of M. A. Ilyín), prose writer (b. Oct. 19 [Oct. 7], 1878, Perm—d. Nov. 27, 1942, Chabris, France). Osorgin was of noble Russian descent. In 1902 Osorgin completed his studies at Moscow University and began a career as a lawyer. After joining the Socialist Revolutionary party in 1904, he was arrested in 1905 and was allowed to emigrate in 1906. He lived in Italy until 1916; in Russia he won recognition as a foreign correspondent for *Russkie vedomosti;* moreover, his work was published in Russian literary journals. He returned in 1916. After the October Revolution, Osorgin was involved in organizing unions of journalists and writ-ers, as well as the Writers Bookstore (Knizh-naya lavka pisateley). Arrested several times in 1919 and 1921, Osorgin was one of a group of intellectuals expelled to Germany in 1922. In 1923 he succeeded in making his way to Paris via Berlin and Italy; he retained his Soviet passport until 1937. In Paris he worked again as a journalist. Osorgin became known as a writer of literature with his first novel, *Sivtsev Vrazhek* (1928; Eng. tr., *Quiet Street,* 1930), an unvarnished presentation of revo-lutionary events, the English translation of which was enormously successful in the United States. Osorgin wrote more novels and various short stories. During the German invasion in 1940 he remained in unoccupied territory and courageously published in the United States articles directed against National Socialism and Bolshevism as forces inimical to democ-racy.
    Osorgin, the author of 20 books, among them five novels, belongs to the tradition of I. Goncharov, I. Turgenev, and L. Tolstoy. This basic orientation is combined with a modest experimentation with narrative technique; in *Sivtsev Vrazhek,* for instance, Osorgin juxta-poses separate chapters about very different people, even animals. *Svidetel istorii* (1932; History's Witness) deals with the terrorist acts of 1905–6 by achieving, to some extent, a sense of ironic estrangement through the use of a fictional observer. *Volny kamenshchik* (1937; The Freemason)—"a wise book that reflects an outstanding gift of observation as well as a firm command of style" (Setchkar-eff)—is set among Russian émigrés. Osorgin

also published a series of autobiographical books that profit from his unpretentious and decent attitudes.

*Works:* Očerki sovremennoj Italii (essays), 1913; Prizraki (pov.), 1917; Skazki i neskazki (short stories), 1918; Iz malen'kogo domika (publicistic prose), Riga, 1921; Sivcev Vražek (novel), Paris, 1928 (see above); Povest' o sestre (pov.), Paris, 1931 (Eng. tr., *My Sister's Story*, 1931); Čudo na ozere (short stories), Paris, 1931; Svidetel' istorii (novel), Paris, 1932; Kniga o koncakh (novel), Paris, 1935; Vol'nyj kamenščik (novel), Paris, 1937; Povest' o nekoej device (short stories), Tallinn, 1938; V tikhom mestečke Francii (June–Dec. 1940) (memoirs), Paris, 1946; Pis'ma o neznačitel'nom: 1940–42 (publicistic prose), New York, 1952; Vremena (memoirs), Paris, 1955; Dnevnik Galiny Benislavskoj. Protivorečija, in Glagol, Ann Arbor, 3:1981.

*Translation:* Selected Stories, Reminiscences, and Essays, 1982.

*Secondary Lit.:* V. Janovskij, in Čisla, Paris, 1933:7–8; G. Garvič, in Novyj žurnal, New York, 4:1943; M. Aldanov, foreword to Osorgin's Pis'ma . . ., 1952; G. Struve, Russkaja literatura v izgnanii, New York, 1956; M. Barmache, D. M. Fiene, and T. Ossorguine, Bibliography, Paris, 1973; D. M. Fiene, Diss., Indiana Univ., 1974, and in Russian Literature Triquarterly 16:1979; V. Setchkareff, in Text, Symbol, Weltmodell, Munich, 1984.

**Ostróvsky, Nikoláy Alekséyevich,** prose writer (b. Sept. 29 [Sept. 16], 1904, Viliya, prov. Volhynia—d. Dec. 22, 1936, Moscow). Ostrovsky's father was a laborer. Ostrovsky joined the Komsomol in 1919 and was severely wounded fighting with the Red Army in 1920. In 1921–22 he worked as an assistant electrician; in 1923 he became a Komsomol official. He became a member of the Communist Party in 1924. Ostrovsky was bedridden and blinded by progressive paralysis after 1927. Driven to be of further service to the Communist idea, he began writing literature. Under the influence of M. Gorky's Mother he wrote the novel Kak zakalyalas stal (1932–34; Eng. trs., *The Making of a Hero*, 1937; How the Steel Was Tempered, 1952) from his own experience; in revised form (1935), the novel became one of the most widespread works of Soviet literature. In the central character of Pavel Korchagin, Ostrovsky's own life is elevated into a work of literature: a laborer's child, living through the destitution and fighting of the Civil War, commendably serving in positions

of leadership during the first phase of socialist construction, becoming a martyr who, destined to die young, places all his strength at the service of the Party. The work, which owes its effect not to artistic quality but to the author's political passion and sympathy with the central character, was intensively propagandized by A. Fadeyev and other officials because of its pro-Party political and pedagogical purpose. Pavel Korchagin became the prototype of the "positive hero" in the theory of SOCIALIST REALISM. "The popularity of Pavel Korchaghin before, during, and even a few years after World War II took on the proportions of a cult" (Slonim). Ostrovsky's unfinished second novel, Rozhdyonnye burey (1936; Eng. tr., *Born of the Storm*, 1939), no longer based on material from personal experience, is cliché-ridden and very weak.

*Works:* Kak zakaljalas' stal' (novel), in Molodaja gvardija 1932 and 1934, rev. ed., 1935 (see above); Rožděnnye burej (novel), 1936 (see above).—Soč., 2 vols, 1953; Sobr. soč., 3 vols., 155–56; 3 vols., 1967–68; Soč., 3 vols., 1969; Sobr. soč., 3 vols., 1974.

*Secondary Lit.:* E. Balbanovič, 2d ed., 1946; L. Timofeev, 2d ed., 1956, in Moskva 1979:9, in Don 1982:1, and in Novyj mir 1984:9; RSPP 3:1964; S. Tregub, 1964, 2d ed., 1973; L. Anninskij, 1971; V. Timofeev, in Moskva 1979:9 and in Don 1982:11; A. Guski, in Zeitschrift für slavische Philologie 1981:1.

**Otsup, Georgy Avdeyevich.** See RAYEVSKY, GEORGY AVDEYEVICH.

**Otsúp, Nikoláy Avdéyevich,** poet (b. Oct. 23, 1894, Tsarkoye Selo—d. Dec. 28, 1958, Paris). Otsup's father was court photographer in St. Petersburg. Otsup graduated from secondary school in Tsarskoye Selo in 1913 and began his studies at the Faculty of History and Philology of St. Petersburg University; in 1913–14 he studied at the Sorbonne and then returned to St. Petersburg. He was one of N. Gumilyov's followers and belonged to his union of poets, TSEKH POETOV; in 1920, after serving in World War I, Otsup participated in its reestablishment. The publishing house Tsekh poetov issued his first volume of poetry, Grad (1921; The City). He emigrated in 1922, going first to Berlin, where he reissued his first collection, and then settling in Paris. There Otsup wrote for numerous journals and published two volumes of poems written between 1922 and 1926: V dymu (1926; In Smoke) nd *Vstrecha* (1928; Meeting), which included a narrative poem written in Berlin. In 1930 the Osteuropa Institute in Breslau published his essay "The Latest Russian Poetry." Otsup, who had set himself the goal of transmitting the culture of his Petersburg period to the generation growing up in emigration, founded in the same year the journal *Chisla*, which, under his editorship, became the stronghold for the publication of, above all, these younger writers (10 issues by 1934). His great reverence for and knowledge of Dante found expression in the novel set in the Parisian émigré milieu, *Beatriche v adu* (1939; Beatrice in Hell). As a volunteer in the French Army in World War II, Otsup was captured in Italy for antifascist activity; his first escape attempt was unsuccessful; his second attempt—from a concentration camp in 1942—succeeded. Otsup fought in the Italian resistance movement. During the war he began a voluminous poem (12,000 verses) called *Dnevnik v stikhakh* *(1935–1950)* (1950; Diary in Poems [1935–1950]). After the war Otsup earned a doctorate in France with a dissertation on N. Gumilyov (1951) and then taught at the Ecole Normale Supérieur. With *Tri tsarya* (1958; The Three Kings), he published a biblical drama. Before his sudden death, Otsup edited editions of F. Tyutchev (1957) and Gumilyov (1958). A two-volume collection of his poetry written between 1918 and 1958 was published posthumously with a foreword by André Mazon and K. Pomerantsev: *Zhizn i smert* (1961; Life and Death). In the same year, his essays on literature were published in two volumes.

Otsup is a significant literary personality of the Parisian emigration and a talented poet. He succeeded in making the meeting between Russian émigrés and new cultural spheres (Italy, France) a profitable experience for his poetry. His poetry has a fundamental life-affirming tone that cautiously refrains from denying the physical even in love. Death is viewed with a firm religious conviction. His poems progress from description to reflection; they can be broadly narrative, especially in his narrative poems and in his diary in verse. Russian literature is always present as object or as comparison. Dante's Beatrice, who appears in poems, in a novel, and in essays, is for him "the boldest synthesis of philosophy, religion, and the most real earthly, human love" (*Literaturnye ocherki*, p. 136). His drama *Tri tsarya* illustrates the power of faith by using the example of David and events in the Old Testament. *Sovremenniki* (1961; Contemporaries) combines articles about N. Gumi-

lyov, A. Bely, S. Yesenin, K. Chukovsky, and Ye. Zamyatin and more general essays about contemporary literature. The edited volume *Literaturnye ocherki* (1961; Literary Contributions), which unfortunately does not provide bibliographic information, contains twelve essays about authors such as F. Tyutchev, M. Lermontov, N. Gumilyov, A. Blok, and V. Mayakovsky (an unmasking of Soviet literary propaganda) and about Otsup's concept of "personalism," which embraces the Christian ideal of "ora et labora" and which he advocated as a positive alternative to communism and as the renunciation of individualism and capitalism. Otsup's poems stem from Gumilyov's ACMEIST approach and in his best work have preserved this heritage.

*Works: Grad* (poems), 1921, 2d ed., Berlin, 1922 (reprinted, Letchworth, 1976); *V dymu* (poems), Paris, 1926; *Vstreča* (narrative poem), Paris, 1926; *Die neueste russische Dichtung*, Breslau, 1930; *Beatriče v adu* (novel), Paris, 1939; *Dvevnik v stikhakh* (poetic diary), 1950; *Tri carja* (play), Paris, 1958; *Žizn' i smert'* (poems), 2 vols., Paris, 1961; *Sovremenniki* (essays), Paris, 1961; *Literaturnye očerki* (essays), Paris, 1961.

*Secondary Lit.:* P. Bicilli, in *Sovremennye zapiski*, Paris, 35:1928 and in *Russkie zapiski*, Paris, 19:1939; Z. Gippius, in *Čisla*, Paris, 2–3:1930; B. Poplavskij, in *Čisla* 4:1930–31; P. Tverskoj, in *Grani*, Frankfurt am Main, 11:1951; N. Tarasova, in *Grani* 39:1958; V. Zlobin, in *Vozroždenie*, Paris, 86:1959; Ja. Gorbov, in *Vozroždenie* 120:1961; V. Il'in, in *Vozroždenie* 161:1965.

**Ovéchkin, Valentín Vladímirovich,** prose writer (b. June 22 [June 9], 1904, Taganrog—d. Jan. 27, 1968, Tashkent). Ovechkin's father was a bookkeeper. The turmoil of revolution forced Ovechkin to find a job immediately in 1919; until 1923 he worked as a cobbler, then as a teacher and Komsomol official in the countryside. From 1925 to 1931 he was director of a peasant commune. He was admitted to the Communist Party in 1919. In 1934 Ovechkin exchanged his Party job in agricultural administration for a career in journalism; in 1935 he published his first volume of short stories in Rostov. In 1937 he was expelled from the Communist Party for interceding for an accused friend. After 1939 he published in Moscow literary journals. During World War II, Ovechkin served as a political officer in frontline units; he was later transferred to the press section. In 1943 he was reinstated in the Communist Party. He attracted critical attention with his povest *S frontovym privetom* (1945; Eng. tr., *Greetings from the Front*, 1947). From 1948 on, Ovechkin lived in Lgov (Kursk). The publication of Ovechkin's *Rayonnye budni* (1952; District Weekdays) was one of the most significant events in the development of kolkhoz literature because of its revelation of serious problems in attitude affecting the management class; Ovechkin had added four more stories to the volume by 1956. Ovechkin, who sharply criticized the official literary establishment and idyllic, falsified kolkhoz literature at the Second Congress of the Writers Union in 1954, exerted a positive influence on literature candidly portraying Soviet agriculture. Between 1958 and 1961, during which time he lived in Kursk, Ovechkin increasingly applied himself to dramatic writing (as he had already done between 1947 and 1951). In despair over the disregard of his well-meant criticism, Ovechkin once attempted suicide during this period. After 1963 he lived in Tashkent and worked on an extensive documentary prose work about the kolkhoz; financial considerations prevented him from returning to central Russia during his lifetime. From July 1958 until his death, Ovechkin belonged to the editiorial board of *Novy mir*; from 1954 on, he was a member of the board of the Writers Union of the USSR.

Ovechkin's most important contribution to Soviet literature is his kolkhoz prose (the antecedent of VILLAGE PROSE), which he saw as a polemical, literary means of narrowing the gap separating Party leadership in agriculture from objective reality. He spotlights the unwise and degrading use of false promises and political blackmail to fulfill norms, and he points out the contrast between technically and psychologically sound practices based on interest in the well-being of the population and dogmatic management based only on furthering personal careers within the Party. Ovechkin's talent lies in his ability to write lively and at times humorous dialogue, spoken most often by middle-level officials; he uses this dialogue, rather than plot development, to bring profound problems into the open. For this reason Ovechkin's dramas are not effective on stage. His own life experience imbues his dialogue with a persuasive power. In general, the critics accepted Ovechkin's portrayals as conforming to the Party line; nevertheless, they attributed his criticism of the present as applying to the past only. During Gorbachev's campaign for *glasnost* (openness) in 1986, Aleksandr Buravsky, in his play *Govori!* (Speak), used Ovechkin's prose and his biography to depict the actuality of his annihilating criticism of Party functionaries.

*Works: Kolkhoznye rasskazy* (short stories), 1935; *Rasskazy* (short stories), 1939; *S frontovym privetom* (pov.), 1946, 1973; *Povesti i rasskazy* (pov. and short stories), 1948; *Na perednem krae* (short stories), 1953; *Očerki o kolkhoznoj žizni* (documentary prose), 1953, 2d ed., 1954; *Rajonnye budni* (pov.), 1956; *Trudnaja vesna* (pov.), 1956; *Pust' èto sbudetsja* (plays), 1962 (contains *Bab'e leto; Nastja Kolosova; Letnie doždi; Vremja požinat' plody*); *Dorogi, nami razvedannye* (pov. and short stories), 1967; *Stat'i, dnevniki, pis'ma* (essays, diaries, letters), 1972; *Gosti v stukačakh* (short stories and essays), 1972, 2d ed., 1978; *Zametki na poljakh* (essays), 1973; *Perepiska A. T. Tvardovskogo i V. V. Ovečkin* (letters), in *Sever* 1979:10 and 1980:2.—*Izbr. proizv.*, 2 vols., 1963.

*Secondary Lit.:* B. Agapov, in *Novyj mir* 1949:8 and 1957:2; M. Privalenko, 1955; M. Lapšin, in *Naš sovremennik* 1959:3 and 1984:9 and in *Neva* 1961:4; *RSPP* 3:1964; A. Tvardovskij, in *Novyj mir* 1968:1; S. Zalygin and G. Troepol'skij, in *Novyj mir* 1968:9; N. Atarov, in *Novyj mir* 1973:9; V. Kantorovič, in *Voprosy lit.* 1974:6; B. Fedorov, in *Zvezda* 1976:1; P. Carden, in *Russian and Slavic Literature*, ed. R. Freeborn, Ann Arbor, 1976; L. Vil'ček, 1977; S. Babënyševa, in *SSSR: Vnutrennie protivorečija*, New York, 2:1981; *Vospominanija o V. Ovečkine*, 1982; M. Kolosov, in *Lit. gazeta* June 27, 1984, p. 6.

# P

**Panfyórov, Fyódor Ivánovich,** prose writer (b. Oct. 2 [Sept. 20], 1896, Pavlovka, prov. Simbirsk—d. Sept. 10, 1960, Moscow). Panfyorov's father was a peasant. Panfyorov attended but did not complete a teachers college; he began his literary career in 1918 by writing short prose and insignificant plays on rural themes. He became a member of the Communist Party in 1926. Between 1924 and 1931 Panfyorov served as editor of *Krestyansky zhurnal* (Peasant Journal); between 1931 and 1960 he edited, with brief interruptions, the journal *Oktyabr*. Panfyorov was appointed to the board of the Writers Union in 1934. His most frequently printed novel, *Bruski* (1928–37; Eng. trs., *Bruski: A Story of Peasant Life in Soviet Russia*, 1930; *And Then the Harvest*, 1939), is a long and tedious attempt to propagandize the kolkhoz system; its literary inadequacies, principally in parts three and four, are considerable. M. Gorky characterized Panfyorov as an example of "a writer who is poorly acquainted with the literary language and who generally writes in an unreasoned, slipshod manner" (*Lit. gazeta* Feb. 6, 1934); K. Simonov denounced his idealizing tendentiousness in 1954. During World War II, Panfyorov began writing a trilogy that depicts the immediate present in a manner contrived to accord with the Party line; Part 1, *Borba za mir* (1945–47; The Struggle for Peace), received a Stalin Prize (for 1947, 2d class), as did Part 2, *V strane poverzhennykh* (1948; In the Land of the Vanquished) (for 1948, 3d class). In Part 3, *Bolshoye iskusstvo* (1949; Big Art), the "positive hero" of the trilogy is primitively exalted to such a degree that he was rejected even by the orthodox critics. Panfyorov then wrote another trilogy, *Volga matushka-reka* (1953–60; Mother Volga), which wavers between honest criticism of the Stalinist past and its defense.

*Works: Bruski* (novel), 1928–37 (see above); Trilogy: (1) *Bor'ba za mir* (novel), 1945, (2) *V strane poveržennykh* (novel), 1948, (3) *Bol'šoe iskusstvo* (novel), in *Oktjabr'* 1949:11, 2d rev. ed., 1954; *Volga matuška-reka*, trilogy: (1) *Udar* (novel), 1953, (2) *Razdum'e* (novel), 1958, (3) *Vo imja molodogo* (novel), 1960.—*Sobr. soč.*, 6 vols., 1958–59.

*Secondary Lit.: RSPP* 3:1964; V. A. Surganov, in *Moskva* 1966:9 and 1967; B. Brajnina, in *Oktjabr'* 1976:9; *Fëdor Panfërov: Vospominanija druzej*, 2d ed., 1977; A. *Panfërov*, 1980.

**Panóva, Véra Fyódorovna**, prose writer, playwright (b. March 20 [March 7], 1905, Rostovon-Don—d. March 3, 1973, Leningrad). Panova did not complete her gymnasium education; from 1922 to 1946 she worked as a journalist for local newspapers. She wrote her first drama in 1933. In 1940 she moved to Leningrad, where she lived permanently. In 1944–45 Panova did newspaper and radio work in Perm; from there she traveled on assignment with a hospital train, an experience that led to her first major prose work, *Sputniki* (1946; Eng. trs., *The Train*, 1949; *Sputniki*, 1965). For *Sputniki* and for both of her following works,

*Kruzhilikha* (1947; Eng. trs., *The Factory*, 1950; *Looking Ahead*, 1955) and *Yasny bereg* (1949; The Bright Shore), Panova received three Stalin prizes (for 1946, 1st class; for 1947, 2d class; and for 1949, 3d class). Her novel *Vremena goda* (1953; Eng. tr., *Span of the Year*, 1957) remained one of the most criticized works in the Soviet Union until 1955. Panova belonged to the boards of the Writers Unions of the USSR and the RSFSR from 1954 and 1958 on, respectively. In addition to further prose works, Panova wrote dramas and film scripts based on her own fiction.

Panova's novel *Sputniki* appeared before the cultural-political petrification that followed the Party Resolution of Aug. 14, 1946 (see PARTY RESOLUTIONS ON LITERATURE). "*The Train*, a deceptively simple narrative about the routine life of a hospital train, is notable for the absence of heroics, preaching, or obvious propaganda" (D. Brown). Her following novels are associated with the Party-dictated literature about industrial and agricultural progress, but they stand well above other representatives of this genre. The accusation of objectivity and too little emphasis on the principle of PARTY SPIRIT, already made with respect to Panova's previous novels, is the basis of the attacks by such dogmatic critics as V. Kochetov and K. Simonov on *Vremena goda*, really the first major post-Stalinist novel. In this work Panova attempts to portray the life of the Communist elite from the year 1950 on, showing the coexistence of the high and the low, the positive and the negative, with as little "lacquering" as possible and without expressing personal opinions. Her interest in child psychology led to the narrative cycle *Seryozha* (1955). Panova's strongly autobiographical work, *Sentimentalny roman* (1958; Sentimental Novel), uses the device of double perspective provided by a character's current and remembered experiences; the novel's portrayal of the 1920s generated considerable controversy. A new element was added to Panova's work after 1965 by her deliberately simple prose pieces, often mosaiclike in their stylization, based on material from Old Russian history: *Liki na zare* (1966; Images at Daybreak); this work's positive description of Christianity in Russia evoked the censure of atheist critics. In her drama *Tredyakovsky i Volynsky* (1968), Panova allegorically illustrates the relationship between the artist and the state.

*Works: Sputniki* (novel), 1946 (see above); *Kružilikha* (novel), 1947 (see above); *Jasnyj bereg* (pov.), 1949; *Vremena goda* (novel), 1954, rev. ed., 1956 (see above); *Serëža* (short stories), 1955; *Sentimental'nyj roman* (novel), 1958; *Rabočij posëlok. Saša. Rano utrom* (pov.), 1966; *Pogovorim o strannostjakh ljubvi* (play), 1968; *Tred'jakovskij i Volynskij* (play), in *Neva* 1968:6; *Liki na zare* (historical pov.), 1969; *Zametki literatora* (essays), 1972; *Svad'ba kak svad'ba* (play), in *Teatr* 1973:1; *O moej žizni, knigakh i čitateljakh* (memoirs), 1975; *Kotoryj čas? Son v zimnjuju noč'* (novel), in *Novyj mir* 1981:9; *Bessonnica* (play), in *Neva* 1985:4.—*Izbr. soč.*, 2 vols., 1956; *Sobr. soč.*, 5 vols., 1969–70; *Izbr.*, 1972, 2 vols., 1980.

*Translations: Time Walked*, 1959; *Serezha and Valya*, 1964; *A Summer to Remember*, 1965; *On Faraway Streets*, 1968; *Selected Works*, 1976 (contains *The Train; Valya; Volodya; Seryozha*).

*Secondary Lit.:* L. Skorino, in *Znamja* 1959:5; L. Plotkin, 1962; Z. Boguslavskaja, 1963; *RSPP* 3:1964; A. Ninov, 1964, in *Zvezda* 1975:3 and 1979:6, and in *Lit. gazeta* Jan. 7, 1981, p. 4; E. Starikova, in *Novyj mir* 1965:3; L. Kopelev, in *Lit. gazeta* April 15, 1967, p. 6; N. S. Gornickaja, 1970; A. Kondratovič, in *Družba narodov* 1976:1; "Vospominanija Very Panovoj," in *SSSR: Vnutrennie protivorečija* 3:1982; R. Hinkle Kreuzer, in *Slavic and East European Journal* 1983:4.

**Pantelèyev, L.** (pseud. of Aleksèy Ivánovich Yeremèyev), prose writer (b. Aug. 22 [Aug. 9], 1908, St. Petersburg—d. July 1987). His father was in the tsarist army. Owing to the death of his parents during the Revolution, Panteleyev became a "homeless waif" (besprizornye) and was sent to the home for juvenile delinquents, Shkid (Shkola sotsialno-individualnogo vospitaniya im. F. Dostoyevskogo [Dostoyevsky School for Social-Individual Education]) in 1921 for three years. There he became friends with G. Belykh; after their release they settled down together in Leningrad as journalists. The book they coauthored, *Respublika Shkid* (1927; The Shkid Republic), found wide circulation at home and abroad. Until the early 1930s; Panteleyev published other short stories. After Belykh became a victim of the state's arbitrary force in 1938, Panteleyev almost lost his position in literature. Thanks to the efforts of K. Chukovsky and S. Marshak, he returned to the ranks of Russian literature in 1954. A large volume of selected works (1954) was followed by several new, slightly reworked editions of *Respublika Shkid* after 1961. His experiences as a reporter at the front during World War II found an echo in short stories about the fate of children in Leningrad and in the documentary prose work *V osazh-*

*dyonnom gorode* (1964; In the Besieged City) Panteleyev's remembrances of Ye. Shvarts, S Marshak, D. Kharms, and K. Chukovsky ar also artistically and historically valuable. I *Priotkryvaya dver* (1980; The Slightly Openeι Door), Panteleyev published, among othe things, excerpts from his notebooks datin from 1924 to 1947 ranging from aphorisms t brief observations to short stories. Panteleye lived in Leningrad; he participated in the con gresses of the Writers Union of the USSI (except in 1959 and 1967) and of the Writer Union of the RSFSR, but he never held officiɑ positions.

Panteleyev's creative work is always baseι on his personal experiences. The work writteι together with G. Belykh, *Respublika Shkid* belongs among the most important testimon ials to the children who were the victims o the Revolution and to post-Revolutionary ed ucational experiments at integrating the ne glected children into the new system. Froɯ the same sphere of experiences came othe short stories, including *Chasy* (1928; Th Watch), which concerns the problem of man' responsibility for his own life. The union be tween self-evident revolutionary heroism anι humor made the short story *Paket* (1933; Th Dispatch) widely known. As is all of Pante leyev's early prose, this story is distinguisheι by the preservation of the linguistic peculiar ities of the fictitious young narrator who tell the story in the first person. In his later shor stories for children, Panteleyev proves hiɯ self a good psychologist who avoids politicɑ didacticism as well as "childlike" simplifi cation and who writes succinctly, excitingly and in a humanly moving way. Panteleyeʋ demonstrates in his notebooks and memoir the same talent for vivid, episodic presentɑ tion that is faithful to the truth.

*Works:* (with G. Belykh) *Respublika Škiι* (pov.), 1927; *Časy* (short story), 1928; *Pakɛ* (short story), 1933; *Povesti i rasskazy* (shor stories), 1939; *Lën'ka Panteleev* (novel), 1939 new ed., 1952; *Na jalike* (short stories), 1948 *Rasskazy i povesti* (short stories), 1952; ʋ *osaždënnom gorode* (memoirs, short story) 1964; *Iz Leningradskikh zapisej* (diary), iɪ *Novyj mir* 1965:5; *Živye pamjatniki* (shor stories, diary, memoirs), 1966; *Priotkryvajɛ dver'* . . . (short stories, essays, sketches) 1980.—*Izbr.*, 1967; *Sobr. soč.*, 4 vols., 1970– 72; 4 vols., 1983–85.

*Secondary Lit.:* N. Zamoškin, in *Novyj mi* 1927:6; L. Zukerman, in *Molodaja gvardijι* 1933:12; K. Čukovskij, in *Lit. gazeta* Dec. 4 1954, and in Panteleev's *Sobr. soč.*, 1970–72

L. Čukovskaja, in *Voprosy lit.* 1958:2; B. Sarnov, in *Lit. i žizn'* Sept. 7, 1960, and 1959; S. Maršak (1961), in his *Sobr. soč.*, vol. 7; A. Rubaškin, in *Zvezda* 1963:11; E. Putilova, in *Neva* 1964:7, and 1969, and in *Avrora* 1982:2; N. Bank, in *Neva*, 1967:10; I. Andreeva, in *Lit. obozrenie* 1981:3.

**Párnok, Sofíya Yákovlevna** (pseud. of S. Ya. Parnókh), poet (b. Aug. 12 [July 30], 1885, Taganrog—d. Aug. 26, 1933, Karinskoye, near Moscow). Parnok's father was a pharmacist; her mother, a doctor. In Taganrog, Parnok graduated from a secondary school specializing in the classics, briefly attended the conservatory in Geneva in 1904, and then studied law in Moscow, probably under the influence of V. M. Volkenshteyn, to whom she was married from 1907 to 1909. The poems she included in her first volume, *Stikhotvoreniya* (1916; Poems), were written between 1912 and 1915; her friendship with M. Tsvetayeva and M. Voloshin also dates from this period. She experienced the Bolshevik Revolution in Sudak in the Crimea. In 1922 she returned to Moscow from there. In the volume *Rozy Pierii* (1922; The Roses of Pieria), she compiled her poems from this period, which do not describe political events. In Moscow, Parnok led an impoverished existence as a translator; during NEP, private publishers issued two small collections of her poems: *Muzyka* (1926; Music) and *Vpolgolosa* (1928; In a Quiet Voice). From 1926 to 1928 she worked in a kind of legal SAMIZDAT organization, a publication society of 30 poets called Uzel (The Knot). *Almast*, an opera libretto, written in 1917–18 in cooperation with the composer A. A. Spendiarov (published in the United States in 1979) and based on Armenian epic tradition, was performed in 1930. The increasing political pressure in 1929–30 silenced Parnok. Before her death she again found blissful happiness in her love for N. E. Vedeneyeva, which also found expression in many poems. After 1922, Soviet literary critics paid little attention to Parnok; after her death, she was completely ignored; in the United States in 1979, Sofiya Polyakova published all of her 261 poems with an extensive introduction, facilitating Parnok's reappearance on the Russian literary scene.

Parnok first won recognition as a poet from M. Voloshin, V. Khodasevich, and V. Bryusov; she consciously follows in the tradition of Karolina Pavlova, E. Baratynsky, and F. Tyutchev. She was critical of symbolism, but also rejected the path of ACMEISM. Her precise poetry, which is close to prose yet conscious of words and rhymes, is filled with motifs from Classical Greece (especially Sappho) and dedicated to themes of artistic creativity (also to music). Her conversion from the Jewish faith to Russian Orthodoxy after 1907 was reflected in the religious spirit of her work throughout her life. In addition to exceptional love poetry, she wrote poems during her late period that make guarded political references and bear witness to the loneliness of the political independent and to his or her inner struggle against spiritual violation.

*Works: Stikhotvorenija* (poems), 1916; *Rozy Pierii* (poems), 1922; *Loza* (poems), 1923; *Muzyka* (poems), 1926; *Vpolgolosa* (poems), 1928; *Sobr. stikhotvorenij* (also contains *Almast*) (poems), Ann Arbor, 1979.

*Secondary Lit.:* M. Vološin, in *Reč'* 1917:129; A. Berkova, in *Pečat' i revoljucija* 1923:2; V. Brjusov, in *Pečat' i revoljucija* 1923:4; V. Khodasevič, in *Vozroždenie*, Paris, Sept. 14, 1933; S. Poljakova, in Parnok's *Sobr. stikhotvorenij*, 1979, and Ann Arbor, 1983; Ju. Ivask, in *Russkaja mysl'*, Paris, Sept. 10, 1981, p. 10; T. Nikol'skaja, in *NRL: Neue russische Literatur*, Salzburg, 2–3:1979–80; A. Bakhrakh, in *Novoe russkoe slovo*, New York, March 31, 1985, p. 5.

**Parnóv, Yereméy Iúdovich,** prose writer (b. Oct. 20, 1935, Kharkov). Parnov completed his course of study in chemistry at the Peat Institute in Moscow in 1958; he worked as a scientist and attained the degree of candidate. Together with **Mikhaíl Tíkhonovich Yémtsev** (b. July 11, 1930, in Kherson), Parnov began writing science fiction in 1961. Their first stories, such as the povest *Uravneniye s Blednogo Neptuna* (1963; The Equation from Pale Neptune), appeared in various collections and series. Early on, Parnov demonstrated a special interest in Far Eastern, especially Indian and Tibetan, religions. Since the 1970s he has published on his own and has turned from science fiction more toward history. The thematic range of his numerous longer and shorter novels is wide and combines entertainment with information on popular scientific topics. Parnov, who remains unmentioned in Soviet histories of literature, represented the Soviet Union in international science-fiction organizations and has been on the board of the Writers Union of the RSFSR since 1985. He lives in Moscow.

Parnov's works show a true interest in spiritual as well as esoteric and mystical questions. *Uravneniye s Blednogo Neptuna* is based on the theory that the scientific knowledge of a dead person can be accessed via the preserved radiation. *Dusha mira* (1964; The Soul of the World) discusses the influence of thoughts on plants. *Vozvratite lyubov* (1966; Return the Love) uses the viewpoint of a mortally ill physicist to contrast today's critical view of science and civilization with the renewal he experiences through inner enlightenment. *Klochya tmy na igle vremeni* (1970; Wisps of Darkness on the Needle of Time) is a trip through time that illustrates the almost mystical experiences of total unity—and the dangers attendant in them. *Tretiy glaz Shivy* (1975; Shiva's Third Eye) reveals in its very title Parnov's candid acceptance of Hindu wisdom and esoteric knowledge (third eye = eye of spiritual vision). With *Bogi lotosa* (1980; The Gods of Lotos) Parnov achieved a mixture of travel sketches and philosophical essays in popular form; he delves deep into Tibet's past and present and takes a critical view of the occult in the West. *Tron Lyutsifera* (1985; Lucifer's Throne) contains critical essays full of information on contemporary, historical, and esoteric movements and on those based on Eastern wisdom in Europe and the United States. Set partly in a Buddhist cloister, partly in the mythological land of Shambala where time does not exist in the physical, earthly sense, *Prosnis v Famaguste* (1983; Awakening in Famagusta) is a work that, like all of Parnov's works in this genre, illuminates the enigmatic aspects of existence.

*Works* (with M. Emcev): *uravnenie s Blednogo Neptuna* (pov.), in *Fantastika*, 1963, separate ed., 1964 (also contains *Duša mira* [pov.]); *Vosstanie tridcati trillionov* (pov.), in *Al'manakh naučnoj fantastiki* 1:1964; *Vozvratite ljubov'* (pov.), in *Fantastika*, 1966; *Kloč'ja t'my na igle vremeni* (novel), 1970.
*Works* (Parnov alone): *Sekretny uznik* (pov.), 1972; *Larec Marii Mediči* (novel), 1972; *Tretij glaz Šivy* (novel), 1975; *Šest' dnej do Genui* (pov.), in *Oktjabr'* 1979:11; *Bogi lotosa*, 1980; *Drakony groma, Rasskazy i povesti* (short stories and pov.), 1981; *Prosnis' v Famaguste* (pov.), in *Oktjabr'* 1983:2; *Pylajuščie skaly* (pov.), in *Oktjabr'* 1984:8; *Tron Ljucifera* (essays), 1985.
*Secondary Lit.*: R. Nudel'man, in *Lit. Rossija* April 23, 1965; D. Srednyj, in *Lit. gazeta* July 8, 1980; M. Lathouwers, in *Irénikon*, Chevetogne (Belgium), 1975:2; B. Gafurov, in *Lit. gazeta* Jan. 21, 1976; V. Povoljaev, in *Lit. Rossija* June 13, 1980; V. Suteev, in *Lit. obozrenie* 1982:5; G. Gordeeva, in *Novyj mir*

1983:10; N. Ivanova, in *Lit. gazeta* Dec. 19, 1984; L. Tokarev, in *Lit. gazeta* Sept. 25, 1985.

**Partiynost.** See PARTY SPIRIT.

**Party Resolutions on Literature,** resolutions of the Central Committee of the Communist Party of the Soviet Union on issues concerning Soviet literature and literary criticism. To maintain a consistent orientation within the entire cultural sphere of activity in the Soviet Union, the Communist Party uses special resolutions as a complement to the continual influence it exercises through positioning Party members—selected by using the system of *nomenclatura*—in key positions in the apparat, through the system of CENSORSHIP of all intellectual output, through the Central Committee's appointment of the editors in chief of literary journals and newspapers, through theses of Party congresses and the greetings delivered to the WRITERS CONGRESSES, and through editorials in *Pravda*. Some party resolutions have had the nature of general directives (1925, 1932, 1946); others are more limited in nature; many changes in principles, such as the repressions around 1937 (see GULAG AND LITERATURE) or the REHABILITATIONS after 1956, are not attributable to a Party resolution. Only some of the resolutions are published in full.

Dec. 1, 1920, *O "Proletkultakh"* (On the Proletkult). This resolution suppressed the PROLETKULT movement by placing it under the control of the People's Commissariat for Education; this movement was pursuing an independent path not subordinate to the Party in building up a proletarian culture including literature.

June 18, 1925, *O politike partii v oblasti khudozhestvennoy literatury* (On Party policy in the field of belles lettres). With this resolution, a modus vivendi was established between the diverse "proletarian" and non-Marxist literary groups in accord with Bukharin's ideas. In line with the principle of class struggle on the "literary front" and the rejection of a "neutral art," several tendencies were allowed to coexist for a time. This concept was linked with the plan to bring the FELLOW TRAVELERS and peasant writers gradually to the side of the proletariat and to promote proletarian writers in order to enable them to take over the leadership. The resolution remained in effect until approximately 1927; then VAPP (All-Union Association of Proletarian Writers) was promoted as spokesman by the Central Committee, and A. Voronsky was repressed.

Dec. 28, 1928, *Ob obsluzhivanii knigoy massovogo chitatelya* (On providing the mass public with books). This resolution proclaimed that belles lettres should enjoy rights equal to those of political and popular scientific literature and that the sole function of literature is Communist education.

Dec. 25, 1929, *O vystuplenii chasti sibirskikh literatorov i literaturnykh organizatsiy protiv Maksima Gorkogo* (On the statement of a part of Siberian writers and writers' organizations against Maksim Gorky). The Novosibirsk Proletkult group "Nastoyashcheye" (The Present), which had accused Gorky of becoming "increasingly the mouthpiece and cloak for the entire reactionary portion of Soviet literature" and of protecting "the entire Soviet Pilnyak clique," was sharply condemned in this resolution. The resolution illustrates the severity of political disagreements about literature. In this instance the Party defended Gorky against excessively coarse attacks; as a rule, however, RAPP was supported with reference to the liquidation of modern and experimental movements such as the FORMALIST SCHOOL or OBERIU, or renegades such as PEREVAL.

April 23, 1932, *O perestroyke literaturno-khudozhestvennykh organizatsiy* (On the reorganization of literary-artistic organizations). This resolution mandated the dissolution of RAPP and all the still-existing literary associations and ordered the formation of a single WRITERS UNION of the USSR and analogous organizations in other fields of art. The resolution became the basis for the attempt to unify intellectual life in the Soviet Union. The general loyalty formula—the Writers Union should unite "all writers who support the foundations of Soviet power and who aspire to participate in the building of socialism"—provided for the exclusion of nonconformists. In 1934 this formulation was expanded in the charter of the Writers Union of the USSR through the addition of the concept of SOCIALIST REALISM.

Dec. 2, 1940, *O literaturnoy kritike i bibliografii* (On literary criticism and bibliography). The resolution states: "At present, literary criticism is an especially weak link." It orders the dissolution of the section of critics in the Writers Union of the USSR, forbids publication of the journal *Literaturny kritik* (last issue 1940:11–12), and instructs the editorial staffs of literary journals to form their own departments of criticism and bibliography.

Aug. 14, 1946, *O zhurnalakh "Zvezda" i "Leningrad"* (On the journals *Zvezda* and *Leningrad*). The sharpest attack on the two Leningrad journals for their publication of ideologically damaging works, especially those by M. Zoshchenko and A. Akhmatova, is contained in this resolution. Nonpolitical literature of any kind was almost fully prohibited. Every inclusion or acknowledgment of non-Russian intellectual accomplishment was proscribed as "kowtowing to the contemporary bourgeois culture of the West." The resolution led not only to the expulsion from the Writers Union of Akhmatova and Zoshchenko, who were selected as victims without prevailing cause, but also to the considerable ossification of literary policy following the somewhat more relaxed approach during World War II. Literature became "material illustrating the directives of the Politburo" (Steininger). The Leningrad Party secretary, Politburo member Andrey Zhdanov, had a considerable influence on the new cultural policy.

Aug. 26, 1946, *O repertuare dramaticheskikh teatrov i merakh po ego uluchsheniyu* (On the repertoire of dramatic theaters and measures for its improvement). This resolution condemned the inclusion of foreign bourgeois plays, as well as the inadequate number of performances in general, and propagandized for new Soviet plays. It also included an order to playwrights to write artistically valuable dramas about Soviet man and to the theater committee "to stage annually in every theater no less than two or three new, ideologically and artistically high quality plays on contemporary Soviet themes." The resolution accentuated the decline of Soviet dramaturgy and promoted the development of the THEORY OF CONFLICTLESSNESS.

1953–58. Stalin's death on March 5, 1953, and the 20th Party Congress in 1956 led to a change in literary policy, to the so-called THAW. The Party Resolution of Feb. 10, 1948, on questions of music—which condemned V. Muradeli, D. Shostakovich, S. Prokofyev, A. Khachaturyan, and others for their historical falsification, cacophony, decadence, separation from the folk song, and formalism that was inimical to the people—was rescinded by a resolution dated May 28, 1958. The literary resolutions, however, remained in effect despite numerous authors' efforts to appeal. Nevertheless, Akhmatova and Zoshchenko were readmitted to the Writers Union, and the condemned film by P. Nilin, *Bolshaya zhizn,* was released.

April 5, 1958, *Ob ustranenii nedostatkov v izdanii i retsenzirovanii inostrannoy khudo-*

*zhestvennoy literatury* (On overcoming the deficiencies in the publication and reviewing of foreign belles lettres). Cautious restraint was placed on the translation of foreign literature readmitted during the Thaw and on its treatment in criticism and scholarship. Demands were made for politically conscious selections as well as for prefaces providing the correct ideological slant.

1972, *O literaturno-khudozhestvennoy kritike* (On literary criticism). This apparently unpublished resolution is mentioned, among other places, in the *Literaturnaya gazeta* of Jan. 26, 1972. The commentaries contain only a call for intensified critical activity. The support for conformist critics can be seen in the simultaneous quotation of Brezhnev's pronouncement at the 24th Party Congress (March 1971)—the congress at which Stalin''s reputation was partially restored—that "literary criticism should more actively promote the Party line."

Oct. 12, 1976, *O rabote s tvorcheskoy molodyozhyu* (On work with creative youth). This resolution refers directly to Brezhnev's speech at the 25th Party Congress and reflects a concern for the political indoctrination and professional development of young writers and artists. The Writers Union of the USSR and its counterparts are encouraged to form commissions for working with youth. The reestablishment of the journal *Literaturnaya uchoba* (Literary Training) is endorsed.

April 26, 1979, *O dalneyshem uluchshenii ideologicheskoy politiko-vospitatelnoy raboty* (On the further improvement of ideological political-educational work). This unusually verbose resolution, which was only published in excerpts, appeals to VAAP and the Writers Union, in addition to many other institutions that are active in the field of ideology, and demands general improvement in their work. Express reference is made to Brezhnev's war memoirs, which had been awarded the Lenin Prize (see LITERARY PRIZES) just a few days before.

Summer 1982, *O tvorcheskikh svyazyakh literaturno-khudozhestvennykh zhurnalov c praktikoy kommunisticheskogo stroitelstva* (On the creative connections between literary journals and the practice of Communist construction). This apparently incompletely published resolution contains, in addition to the usual ideological demands, an allusion to literary works "with serious deviation from the truth of life" *(s seryoznym otstupleniyem ot zhiznennoy pravdy)*—that is, from valid Party opinion—in their depiction of "Russian history" *(otechestvennoy istorii)*, of "socialist

revolution, and of collectivization." It appears to be especially directed against authors of VILLAGE PROSE, with their objective depiction of forced collectivization and of the peasants' more humane life in preceding centuries, as well as against chauvinist tendencies within the "Russianists." The old demand for a "positive hero" with an educative function is renewed. In no Party resolution is the board of censors (Glavlit) named as the addressee, although the practical implementation of most of the regulations lies in its hands.

*Secondary Lit.*: KPSS o kul'ture, prosveščenii i nauke: Sbornik dokumentov, 1963; Dokumente zur sowjetischen Lit. Politik, ed. K. Eimermacher, 1972; Kulturpolitik der SU, ed. O. Anweiler and K.-H. Ruffmann, 1973; KPSS v rezoljucijakh i rešenijakh s''ezdov konferencij i plenumov CK, 8th ed., 14 vols., Moscow, 1970–82.

**Party spirit** *(partíynost;* other translations: Party discipline, conformity to the Party line), one of the central terms of Soviet literature and of SOCIALIST REALISM: the principle that the writer is expected to subordinate himself to the current outlook of the Communist Party. In accordance with this principle, the writer should not portray empirical truth in his works but truth as defined by the Party. This term became prevalent in literature during the second half of the 1940s. Since the context of Lenin's article "Partiynaya organizatsiya i partiynaya literatura" (1905; Party Organization and Party Literature) is ignored, reference to it is construed to mean that belles lettres should be subordinated to the Party line. In 1920 Lenin applied the principle of Party spirit to literature in eliminating the PROLETKULT; from them on, this principle became the guideline of literary groups such as OKTYABR, MAPP, and RAPP and became, although not at first explicitly, the highest principle of the single Writers Union of the USSR established by decree of the Central Committee of the Communist Party. Since the Party Resolution of 1946 (see PARTY RESOLUTIONS ON LITERATURE), appeals to Party spirit have formed an essential component of all official comments. Consequences of the application of this principle in literature are the frequent rewriting of even recognized works (for example, by A. Fadeyev, M. Sholokhov, L. Leonov) to accord with changes in the Party line and the lack of complete editions of the collected works of Soviet authors. To provide information on the Party line, the Central

Committee uses the system of Party Resolutions, the press, and internal instructions; to enforce adherence to the Party line, it relies on the secretariat of the Writers Union with its "buro," CENSORSHIP, and editors.

*Secondary Lit.*: R. Messer, in *Zvezda* 1948:11; G. A. Wetter, *Der dialektische Materialismus*, Freiburg, 1952; H. Ermolaev, *Soviet Literary Theories 1917–1934*, Berkeley, 1963 (reprinted, New York, 1977); B. Küppers, *Die Theorie vom Typischen in der Lit.*, Munich, 966; A. Dubrovin, in *Kommunist* 1975:6, and separate study, 1977; A. Dremov, 1980.

**Pasternák, Borís Leonídovich,** poet, prose writer (b. Feb. 10 [Jan. 29], 1890, Moscow—d. May 30, 1960, Peredelkino, near Moscow). Pasternak's father was an impressionist painter; his mother, a pianist. Pasternak studied music and, starting in 1909, philosophy at Moscow University and at Marburg in 1912; in 1913 he graduated from Moscow University. His first poems appeared in 1913. Pasternak joined "Tsentrifuga" (Centrifuge), a literary group within FUTURISM. N. Aseyev and S. Bobrov published his first volume of poetry, *Bliznets v tuchakh* (1914; Twins in Clouds); Pasternak included most of these poems in his second volume of poetry, *Poverkh baryerov* (1917; Beyond the Barriers). The publication of his third volume, *Sestra moya zhizn* (1922; Eng. tr., *My Sister—Life*, 1982), received great acclaim; these poems were written during the summer of 1917 but were inspired not by political events but rather by his experience of nature and love. After the next volume, *Temy i variatsii* (1923; Themes and Variations), Pasternak "was recognized as the outstanding younger poet of post-Revolutionary Russia" (Struve). In the shorter verse epics *Devyatsot pyaty god* (1925–26; The Year 1905), *Leytenant Shmidt* (1926–27; Lieutenant Schmidt), and *Spektorsky* (1931), Pasternak included some revolutionary events as seen from his own changing perspective but refused in principle to write poetry as a "social mission." Starting in 1922 Pasternak also published prose; the first collection, *Rasskazy* 1925; Short Stories), contained *Detstvo Lyuvers* (Eng. tr., "Childhood of Luvers," 1945), *Apellesova Cherta* (Eng. tr., "Il tratto di Apelle," 1945), *Pisma iz Tuly* (Eng. tr., "Leters from Tula," 1945), *Vozdushnye puti* (Eng. tr., "Aerial Ways," 1945). In 1929 this collection was followed by *Okhrannaya gramota* 1931; Eng. tr., in *Safe Conduct*, 1945), his first autobiographical short story and one ded-

icated to the memory of Rainer Maria Rilke; in this work, Pasternak's view of art, which is rooted in Western European thought, stands in direct contradiction to the reactionary ideas of the ruling RAPP officials. After the publication of *Vtoroye rozhdeniye* (1932; The Second Birth), a volume with new poetry, several volumes of selections from earlier poetry appeared before 1937. In 1934 Pasternak was even elected to the board of the new Writers Union. After 1936 he was forced to restrict himself to translation work, especially the translation of Shakespeare's tragedies. "'His versions of poets from Soviet Georgia won Stalin's approval and probably saved him from being 'repressed' during the era of the purges" (Slonim). During the somewhat relaxed cultural policy of World War II, Pasternak was allowed to publish two smalller volumes of new, original poetry: *Na rannikh poezdakh* (1943; On the Early Trains) and *Zemnoy prostor* (1945; Earthly Openness). After the war, Pasternak published primarily translations including the now famous one of Goethe's *Faust* (1953). During the THAW, Pasternak was allowed to publish ten poems from the novel *Doktor Zhivago* in the journal *Zvezda* (1954:4); however, his hope of publishing the novel itself (Eng. tr., *Doctor Zhivago*, 1958) in the Soviet Union was not realized. The novel was published in Italy in 1957; translations into all the major languages of the world followed, making Pasternak the best-known contemporary Russian writer. Not until 1987 was a publication in the journal *Novyj mir* announced for 1988. In 1958 he was awarded the Nobel Prize (primarily for his poetry); this set off such a hue and cry among the literary functionaries in the USSR that Pasternak was forced to refuse to accept it. He was expelled from the Writers Union and remained ostracized until his death. Whereas his collected works appeared in the United States, his REHABILITATION occurred in the Soviet Union only after 1961 and was limited to his lyrics. It was only in February 1987 that his expulsion from the Writers Union was rescinded. The collection *Stikhotvoreniya i poemy* (1965; Lyric and Narrative Poems), for which A. Sinyavsky wrote the introduction, also contains the volume *Kogda razgulyayetsya* (1956–59; Eng. tr., *When the Skies Clear*, 1962), which was planned as Pasternak's last.

Pasternak's early poetry grows out of the symbolist tradition of A. Blok and "strongly emphasizes the musical principle of composition" (Holthusen). Unusual and increasingly concise metaphors lend multifaceted depth to his poetic message, which is closely tied to nature, but they make comprehension more difficult. Reflecting the tendency throughout Europe, Pasternak's poetry became simpler over the years; elements of the classical tradition grew stronger, making more easily accessible the uppermost, occasionally narrative, level from behind which a religious image of the world held in the grip of goodness is revealed through recurrent glimpses. "Physical and spiritual levels, nature and history, everyday occurrences and imaginative flights are considered as mere aspects of one and the same unity" (Slonim). The novel *Doktor Zhivago*, which Pasternak considered his most important work, finds its climax in its lyrical passages and in the poems at the close of the book; its interwoven composition and multilayered message become evident only after several readings. It is a historical novel that comprehends and interprets, in its own cogent way, the Revolution, the suppression of creative energy around 1929, and—in the epilogue—World War II without actually becoming political; it is also a poetic representation of the fateful interdependency of human existence in general.

*Works: Bliznec v tučakh* (poems), 1914; *Poverkh bar'erov* (poems), 1917, enl. ed., 1929, 2d ed., 1931; *Sestra moja žizn'* (poems), 1922, 2d ed., 1923 (reprinted, Ann Arbor, 1976) (see above); *Temy i variacii* (poems), 1923 (reprinted, Ann Arbor, 1972); *Rasskazy* (short stories), 1925; *Devjat'sot pjatyj god* (includes *Lejtenant Šmidt*) (narrative poems), 1927, 2d ed., 1930, 3d ed., 1932, 45h ed., 1937; *Spektorskij* (narrative poem), 1931; *Okhrannaja gramota* (autobiography), 1931 (see above); *Vtoroe roždenie* (poems), 1932, 2d ed., 1934; *Stikhotvorenija v odnom tome* (lyric and narrative poems), 1933, 2d ed., 1935, 3d ed., 1936; *Vozdušnye puti* (short stories), 1933 (reprinted, Ann Arbor, 1976); *Povest'*, 1934; *Na rannikh poezdakh* (poems), 1943; *Zemnoj prostor* (poems), 1945; *Izbr.*, 1948; *Doktor Živago* (novel), Milan, 1957 (see above); *Stikhotvorenija i poèmy* (lyric and narrative poems), 1961; *Stikhotvorenija i poèmy* (lyric and narrative poems), 1964; *Stikhi* (poems), 1966; *Ljudi i položenija* (autobiography, in *Novyj mir* 1967:1; *Slepaja krasavica* (play), London, 1969 (Eng. tr., *The Blind Beauty*, 1969); *Stikhotvorenija i poèmy* (lyric and narrative poems), 1976; *Perepiska s Ol'goj Frejdenberg* (letters), New York, London, 1981 (Eng. tr., *The Correspondence of Boris Pasternak and Olga Freidenberg*, 1982); *Vozdušnye puti* (collection), 1982 (contains 17 works of prose from various years).—*Soč.*, 3 vols., Ann Arbor, 1961 (with bibliography); *Izbr.*, 2 vols., 1985.

*Translations: Poems*, 1959, 2d ed., 1964; *The Poetry of Boris Pasternak 1917–1959*, 1959; *In the Interlude: Poems 1945–1960*, 1962; *Collected Short Prose*, 1977; *Selected Poems*, 1983.

*Secondary Lit.*: Various articles in *Grani*, Frankfurt am Main, 40:1958; G. Struve, in *Vozdušnye puti*, New York, 1:1960; A. Sinjavskij, in *Novyj mir* 1962:3; M. Aucouturier, Hamburg, 1965; D. L. Plank, The Hague, 1966; B. P. i Sojuz pisatelej, in *Novyj žurnal*, New York, 83:1966; S. d'Angelio, in *Osteuropa* 1968:7; H. Gaumnitz, Diss., Tübingen, 1969; N. A. Troickij, Ithaca, N.Y., 1969; J. W. Dyck, New York, 1972; J. Döring, Munich, 1973; O. R. Hughes, Princeton, 1974; H. Birnbaum, Ghent, 1976; P. A. Bodin, Stockholm, 1976; M. Sendič, in *Russian Language Journal* 105:1976 (bibliography); H.Gifford, Cambridge, 1977; G. de Mallac, Norman, Okla., 1981; L. Flejšman, Munich, 1981, and Jerusalem, 1984; M. Kreps, Ann Arbor, 1984.

**Paustóvsky, Konstantín Geórgiyevich**, prose writer (b. May 31 [May 19], 1892, Moscow—d. July 14, 1968, Moscow). Paustovsky's father was a railway administrator. Paustovsky was first published in 1912. His philological studies were interrupted in 1914; during World War I he worked as a medical orderly. During the revolutionary years he worked as a journalist in Kiev, Odessa, the Caucasus, and (after 1923) in Moscow. Paustovsky first achieved major recognition as a writer with *Kara-Bugaz* (1932; Eng. tr., "The Gulf of Kara-Bugas," in *Selected Stories*, 1949), a part-historical, part-journalistic, part-literary povest associated with socialist construction. After 1934, the year in which SOCIALIST REALISM became the official doctrine, Paustovsky retreated to writing predominantly descriptions of nature and portraits of artists (Isaak Levitan, Orest Kiprensky, Taras Shevchenko). During World War II he did not contribute to the emotionally charged patriotic literature being officially promoted; instead, he wrote short stories about people with exceptional lives. After the war he began his major work, the autobiographical *Povest o zhizni* (1945–63; Eng. tr., *The Story of a Life*, 1964), which he was unable to continue until the beginning of the THAW in 1954. From this time on, Paustovsky advocated giving thought to the true value of literature and actively worked for the REHABILITATION of persecuted writers (I. Babel, Yu. Olesha, M. Bulgakov, A. Grin, N. Zabolotsky, among others) and the rights of writers under political attack (V. Dudintsev, A. Sinyavsky, Yu. Daniel). He was coeditor of the two most important liberal anthologies, *Literaturnaya Moskva* (1956) and *Tarusskiye stranitsy* (1961; Eng. tr., *Pages from Tarusa*, 1964). Beginning in the second half of the 1950s Paustovsky achieved an international reputation with the six-volume *Povest o zhizni*, which was translated into many languages. In the Soviet Union he was highly respected as a "symbol of integrity" and as a master of "poetry in prose." Up until his death, he divided his time between Tarusa and Moscow, where he taught at the Gorky Literary Institute. Paustovsky's literary talent lies in his ability to present situations in a detailed and vivid manner. This talent first became apparent in the 1930s, when he turned to writing nature descriptions of the Meshchora forests, lakes, and swamps south of Moscow without strong plot lines. It found a second form of expression in his portrayal of interpersonal encounters, seen as fateful, in which Paustovsky's view is focused on what is good and beautiful in man and nature. His narrative structure, irrespective of length, is mostly additive, stringing together episode after episode. The first-person narrative form predominates, with the first-person narrator acting as observer. Complicated hypotactic narrative structures with multiple plot lines are foreign to Paustovsky's work. His plays carry a secondary meaning. His essays about contemporary writers and his travel descriptions are a mixture of personal reminiscence, lyrical nature imagery, and reflection. Through the example of his own lyrical prose and his theoretical contributions on the work of other writers, such as *Zolotaya roza* (1955; Eng. tr., *The Golden Rose*, 1957), Paustovsky has exerted a positive influence on many Russian writers, including Yu. Bondarev, Yu. Kazakov, Yu. Nagibin, and V. Soloukhin.

*Works:* Morskie nabroski (short stories), 1925; Kara-Bugaz (pov.), 1932 (see above); Kolkhida (pov.), 1934 (Eng. tr., "Colchia," in *Selected Stories*, 1949); Zolotaja roza (essays), 1955 (see above); *Povest' o žizni* (memoirs), 2 vols., 1966 (see above); Naedine s osen'ju (short stories), 1967; Blizkie i dalëkie (literary portraits), 1967.— Sobr. soč., 6 vols., 1957–58; 8 vols., 1967–70; 9 vols., 1981– (vol. 7 appeared in 1983).

*Translations:* The Black Gulf (short stories), 1946; Selected Stories, 1949, 1974; The Flight of Time: New Stories, 1955; A Book about Artists, 1978.

*Secondary Lit.:* L. Levickij, 1963; RSPP 3:1964; E. Aleksanjan, 1969; W. Kasack, Cologne, 1971 (with extensive bibliography); A. Drawicz, Warsaw, 1972; E. N. Dihbahl, Diss., Univ. of Colorado, 1974; D. W. Lumpkins,

Diss., Vanderbilt Univ., 1974; *Vospominanija o K. P.*, 1975; D. Carik, 1979; G. Trefilova, 1983.

**Pavlénko, Pyotr Andréyevich,** prose writer (b. July 11 [June 29], 1899, St. Petersburg—d. June 16, 1951, Moscow). Pavlenko was the son of an artisan; he grew up in Tiflis, where he finished school in 1917. In 1920 he joined the Communist Party and worked as a political instructor and commissar in the Red Army. Pavlenko was sent first to Turkey and then to Western Europe as a trade representative (1924–27). When he returned to Moscow, he became one of the leading officials in the literary field. On his own initiative he traveled to Turkmenistan in 1930 with a group of leading writers (N. Tikhonov, V. Lugovskoy, L. Leonov, G. Sannikov, Vs. Ivanov), subsequently publicizing the Soviet system through his work. Pavlenko's major works, the novels *Na Vostoke* (1936–37; Eng. tr., *Red Planes Fly East*, 1938) and *Schastye* (1947; Eng. tr., *Happiness*, 1950), are presentations of current topics in the service of the principle of PARTY SPIRIT. Pavlenko received a Stalin Prize (1947, 1st class) for *Schastye*. Three more Stalin Prizes followed (1st class) for propagandistic film scripts. Pavlenko was assigned as a journalist to report on the Finnish-Russian War, the Polish campaign, and World War II. Because of his health he lived in the Crimea (1945–51), where he was entrusted with the leadership of the local writers' organization. As a typical representative of SOCIALIST REALISM, Pavlenko also belongs to the small group of writers who were permitted to travel abroad (the United States, Italy) during this time and to write about their travels.

Pavlenko is a little-read pseudorealist writer. In *Puteshestviye v Turkmenistan* (1931–32; Journey to Turkmenistan), he indulged an inclination to pile up facts. After his novel *Barrikady* (1932; The Barricades), about the Paris Commune of 1870, he developed the then-encouraged topic, the threat of war, in his novel *Na Vostoke*. *Schastye*, about postwar reconstruction in the Crimea, attracted attention as a contribution to the cult of Stalin; the novel describes the resettlement of the Kuban Cossacks without specifying the reason behind it, that is, the deportation of the Crimean Tatars. It is a crude contribution to the Party's campaign against COSMOPOLITANISM.

*Works:* Aziatskie rasskazy (short stories), 1929; Putešestvie v Turkmenistan (journalistic articles), 1932; Barrikady (novel), 1932; Na Vostoke (novel), 1937 (see above); Alek-

*sandr Nevskij* (film script, in collaboration with S. Eisenstein), 1938; *Sčast'e* (novel), 1947 (see above); *Padenie Berlina* (film script, in collaboration with M. Čiaureli), in *Znamja* 1948:11; *Amerikanskie vpečatlenija* (journalistic articles), 1949; *Ital'janskie vpečatlenija* (journalistic articles), 1951; *Molodaja Germanija* (journalistic articles), 1951.—*Sobr. soč.*, 6 vols., 1953–55.

*Secondary Lit.*: L. Skorino, in *Novyj mir* 1948:5, 1949:8, and the foreword to Pavlenko's *Sobr. soč.*, 1953; L. Levin, 1953, 2d ed., 1956; *RSPP* 3:1964; R. Fatuev, in *Lit. Rossija* July 11, 1969, pp. 16–17; N. Tikhonov, in *Lit. gazeta* July 11, 1979, p. 6.

*Pechát i revolyútsiya* (Press and Revolution), "journal for literature, art, criticism, and bibliography" that appeared in Moscow as an organ of the State Publishing House from 1921 to 1930. From 1921 to 1924, six lengthy issues were published annually; thereafter usually eight appeared each year. The editorial board consisted of active Party members such as A. Lunacharsky; for the issues from 1921 to 1929:4, leadership was in the hands of the Marxist critic V. P. Polonsky (pseudonym of V. P. Gusin). The Party's increasing insistence on a totalitarian orientation for intellectual life contradicted the relative breadth of this Marxist organ. For this reason, Polonsky was dismissed at the beginning of 1929, and the editorial board was newly constituted. Leadership came into the hands of V. M. Friche (1929:5–9). After his death, he was followed by I. Bespalov; V. Pereverzev played a significant role in the editorial board during his tenure. During RAPP's struggle to control intellectual life completely, the journal positioned itself on the side of the group "Litfront" in 1930; this led to its prohibition after 1930:6 with the victory of RAPP. *Pechat i revolyutsiya* reflected in articles, reviews, and regular chronicles the cultural life at home and abroad from a Marxist viewpoint. Discussions about literary-political and methodological questions found ample room: for example, those about the FORMALIST SCHOOL (1924:5); the "social mandate" with its insistence on certain themes (1929:1 and 2–3, with contributions by F. Gladkov, L. Leonov, B. Pilnyak, I. Selvinsky, A. Karavayeva, K. Fedin); or RAPP (1929:10, which was attacked for its "practical opportunism"). The review portion, on which N. Aseyev, V. Bryusov, and A. Voronsky cooperated, was comprehensive and, as was the case with the entire journal, not limited to Russian works.

*Works*: Reprint of the journal, Nendeln, Liechtenstein, 1970.

*Secondary Lit.*: A. Voronskij, in *Krasnaja nov'* 1921:3; D. Gorbov, in *Novyj mir* 1927:12; G. Belaja, in *Očerki istorii russkoj sovetskoj žurnalistiki 1917–1932*, 1966; E. Gol'ceva, in *Voprosy lit.* 1970:3 and Diss., Moscow 1970.

**Pereléshin, Valéry Frántsevich** (pseud. of V. F. Salátko-Petríshche), poet (b. July 20 [July 7], 1913, Irkutsk). Pereleshin's father was a railroad engineer and was descended from Polish–White Russian nobility. Pereleshin emigrated to Harbin with his mother in 1920; he completed his studies there at the faculties of law (1935) and theology (1943). From 1938 to 1945 he was a monk. Early on, Pereleshin became a respected poet in Harbin. From 1939 to 1943 he lived in Peking, then in Shanghai. Pereleshin published his first collection of poetry, *V puti* (1937; On the Way), in Harbin, and by 1944 three other collections had followed. At the end of 1952 he and his mother moved to Rio de Janeiro, Brazil. An unsuccessful attempt to interest *Novy zhurnal* in his work led to his withdrawal from literature. He worked at many professions; from 1957 to 1961 he was a librarian at the British Council. With the publication of the sonnets "Krestny put" (Stations of the Cross) in *Vozrozhdeniye* in Paris in 1967, Pereleshin returned to the literary scene. His poems and reviews began appearing in such journals as *Vozrozhdeniye*, *Novy zhurnal*, and *Grani*, and volumes of his own poetry began to be published. His profound understanding of Chinese language, literature, and culture became apparent in his translations of Chinese poetry, the publication of which begins with *Stikhi na veyere* (1970 Poems on a Fan), a small collection with an excellent introduction. On the basis of a correspondence with a young Moscow poet and translator, he wrote a great number of sonnets between 1971 and 1974 from which he selected 153 (one less than Shakespeare had written and corresponding to the number of fishes caught in the net [see John 21:1–11] for the volume *Ariel* (1976). In *Yuzhny kres* (1978; The Southern Cross), Pereleshin introduces poets of his third homeland, Brazil, in translation. In *Nos odros volhos* (1983) he combined his own poems in Portuguese with his translations of English, Russian, and Chinese poetry.

In his youth, Pereleshin was impressed by M. Lermontov, then later by N. Gumilyov. Their religious attitude and acmeist linguistic clarity, respectively, have characterized hi own poetry throughout his life. "The harmony and regularity of Pereleshin's poems have as their basis the spiritual source that gives form to substance" (Rannit). In addition, his poems are often the expression of an ennui, a melancholy, and they voice inner doubt to the point of embodying the tension between light and darkness, despair and faith, accusation and prayer. Special themes in Pereleshin's poetry are his rejection of love for a woman and his critical examination of the joy and pain of passion for young men. In *Poema bez predmeta* (1977–80; Poem without a Subject) he created an autobiography in verse. Pereleshin enjoys molding the individual poem around a leading motif, a comprehensive image, which he then deepens and varies. He does not narrate, nor does he draw on his direct experience, but he always explores fundamental issues. "Zveno," a cycle of sonnets at the end of the volume *Ariel*, depicts by way of its content and form the experience of recurring earthly lives through reincarnation.

*Works: V puti* (poems), Harbin, 1937; *Dobryj ulej* (poems), Harbin, 1939; *Zvezda nad morem* (poems), Harbin, 1941; *Žertva* (poems), Harbin, 1944; *Južnyj dom* (poems), Munich, 1968; *Stikhi na veere* (poems, translations from the Chinese), Frankfurt am Main, 1970; *Kačel'* (poems), Frankfurt am Main, 1971; *Zapovednik* (poems), Frankfurt am Main, 1972; *S gory Nevo* (poems), Frankfurt am Main, 1975; *Arièl'* (poems), Frankfurt am Main, 1976; *Poèma bez predmeta*, in *Sovremennik*, Toronto, 35–42, 45–46:1977–80 (the last two songs were not printed because the journal ceased publication); *Južnyj krest* (poems, translations from the Portuguese), 1978; *Russian Poetry and Literary Life in Harbin and Shanghai 1930–1950* (memoirs in Russian), Amsterdam, 1987.

*Secondary Lit.:* Ju. Ivask, in *Novyj žurnal*, New York, 92:1968 and foreword to *Arièl*, S. Karlinsky, in *Novoe russkoe slovo*, New York, Feb. 9, 1969, and in *Christopher Street* December 1977; A. Rannit, in *Novyj žurnal* 107:1972 and in *Russian Language Journal* 106:1976 and 113:1978; L. Lifšic-Losev, in *Russian Language Journal* 111:1978; B. Narcissov, in *Novyj žurnal* 138:1980; J. P. Hinrichs, in *Cahier van De Lantaarn*, Leiden, 23:1983 and in Perelešin's memoirs, 1987.

**Perevál** (Mountain Pass), a Marxist literary association of the 1920s. Pereval arose in Moscow at the end of 1923 and the beginning of 1924 and was composed of young Communist writers who had left the groups MOLODAYA

GVARDIYA or OKTYABR because of their intolerant orthodox Party course and had joined the ranks of the *Krasnaya nov* authors who, for their part, considered the futurists (see FUTURISM) and constructivists (see CONSTRUCTIVISM) too rational and formalist. The designation *Pereval* derives from "Na perevale," an article by A. Voronsky that appeared in his journal *Krasnaya nov* (1923:6, Oct.–Nov.) and that discussed the transition from the inadequate literature of the present to the expected rich literature of the era of communism. At first, Pereval had only a few members such as M. Golodny, M. Svetlov, A. Vesyoly; Voronsky never formally joined. Starting in 1924, Pereval published anthologies of the works of its authors with the title *Pereval* (until 6:1928); E. Bagritsky, G. Guber, and A. Platonov were among its authors then. In 1925, 70 percent of Pereval's members were also members of the Communist Party or the Komsomol. In 1926 the number of members began to increase. In 1927 the Pereval manifesto was signed by 56 members, including (in addition to those already named) N. Dementyev, A. Karavayeva, I. Kasatkin, I. Katayev, D. Kedrin, S. Malyshkin, N. Ognyov, M. Prishvin, I. Yevdokimov, and N. Zarudin. Pereval accepted the need to fulfill the "social mandate" but demanded that the writer have the right to select his theme according to his own discretion and insisted on the realistic representation of "immediate impressions" and the "candor" of the writer (as opposed to Party obedience). Pereval embraced literary tradition and the Party Resolution of 1925 (see PARTY RESOLUTIONS ON LITERATURE), that is, the principle of the coexistence of different literary groups. These clear definitions, proposed especially by the Pereval theoreticians D. Gorbov and A. Lezhnev, led to continual controversies with the VAPP officials, who were first and foremost exclusively politically minded and not guided by literary principles. In 1927 P. Slyotov and G. Glinka joined Pereval, but this year also marked the beginning of a persistent withdrawal of members, or rather a transfer to VAPP (including Dementyev, Golodny, Karavayeva, Ognyov, Yevdokimov) and to the constructivists (Bagritsky). By early 1930, when RAPP's pressure on all other literary groups intensified, membership had already been greatly reduced. Pereval continued to publish anthologies under the title *Rovesniki* (Contemporaries; nos. 7 and 8 of *Pereval*, 1930 and 1932), in which the prose of I. Katayev, Slyotov, and Zarudin deserves literary and political recognition. In 1930 Pereval also published an anthology, *Perevaltsy*, that included the contributions of Guber, Prishvin, and Voronsky. This and vol. 7 of *Rovesniki* triggered RAPP's final offensive. To the article "Nepogrebyonnye mertvetsy" (The Unburied Dead) in *Komsomolskaya pravda* (March 8, 1930), authorized by the Central Committee of the Party, Pereval was still allowed to reply, but two "discussions" between Pereval and RAPP officials had only a condemnatory character (*Lit. gazeta* May 19, 1930). P. Pavlenko, A. Novikov, A. Malyshkin, and M. Prishvin were among those who then withdrew from Pereval. Pereval was finally disbanded only by the Party Resolution of April 23, 1932. Zarudin, the chairman of Pereval from 1924 to 1932, and I. Katayev, Lezhnev, and Vesyoly are some of Pereval's most important authors who, like Voronsky, became victims of the purges after 1937.

*Secondary Lit.:* Pereval (anthology), vols. 1–6, 1924–28, continued under the title *Rovesniki*, vols. 7–8, 1930, 1932; D. Gorbov, *Poiski Galatei*, 1929; A. Glagolev, in *Novyj mir* 1930:5; G. Glinka, *Na perevale*, New York, 1954; *Lit. manifesty*, 2d ed., 1929 (reprinted, Munich, 1969); P. Scherber, in *Von der Revolution zum Schriftstellerkongress*, Berlin, 1979.

**Permítin, Yefím Nikoláyevich,** prose writer (b. Jan. 8, 1896 [Dec. 27, 1895], Unst-Kamenogorsk, prov. Semipalatinsk—d. April 18, 1971, Moscow). Permitin's father was a cabinetmaker. Permitin took his examinations for teaching in 1913. After taking part in World War I and in the Civil War in Siberia, he was employed in the area of national education in his native region. In the early 1930s he moved to Moscow and wrote several novels about the class struggle in a village in the Altai. In revised form they became raw material for the five-part novel *Gornye orly* (1951; Mountain Eagles). His next novel, *Ruchyi vesenniye* (1955; Spring Streams), was written in order to popularize land reclamation policy in accordance with the Party line. Permitin's *Ranneye utro* (1958; Early Morning) heralded the beginning of an autobiographical tetralogy about the development of the Soviet village; the dogmatists greeted the work's first two parts, which were combined under the title *Pervaya lyubov* (1962; First Love), as a conservative corrective to critical depictions of the Stalinist period. *Poema o lesakh* (1970; A Poem of the Forests) completed the work as a trilogy; Permitin united the series under the title *Zhizn Alekseya Rokotova* (1972; The Life

of Aleksey Rokotov). He received the Gorky Prize for the work. From 1965 on, Permitin occupied various official posts in the Writers Unions of the USSR and the RSFSR. In terms of form and content, Permitin's works are schematic and overly diffuse, even in the briefest passages. Even Soviet critics reproached him with making use of historical facts in an arbitrary manner.

*Works: Kogti* (novel), 1931; *Gornye orly* (novel), 1951; *Ruč'i vesennie* (novel), 1955; *Rannee utro* (novel), 1958; *Pervaja ljubov'* (novel), 2 vols. (vol. 1: *Rannee utro*), 1962; *Poèma o lesakh* (novel), 1970; *Žizn' Alekseja Rokotova* (novel-trilogy composed of the three preceding novels), 1972; *Strast'* (short stories), 1973.—*Sobr. soč.*, 4 vols., 1978–80.

*Secondary Lit.:* E. Starikova, in *Znamja* 1952:7; V. Nazarenko, in *Zvezda* 1956:4; G. Serebrjakova, in *Naš sovremennik* 1963:4; *RSPP* 3:1964; G. Mantorov, 1966; M. P. Škerin, 1971; A. Koptelov, in *Sibirskie ogni* 1975:3.

**Permyák, Yevgény Andréyevich,** prose writer (b. Oct. 31 [Oct. 18], 1902, Perm—d. Aug. 17, 1982, Moscow). Permyak's father was a postal clerk. Permyak studied pedagogy at Perm University from 1924 to 1930. In the mid-1930s he began writing numerous dramas that were not much in demand because of their artistic weaknesses. About that time he wrote *Yermakovy lebedi* (1942; Yermak's Swans), inspired by motifs from P. Bazhov's folktales from the Urals, a continuing influence on Permyak's work. With *Kem byt?* (1946; Whom Should I Be?), Permyak turned to writing numerous popular science and didactic books for children, propagandizing the following theme: "Only work brings happiness, honor, and joy . . . and makes small men great." Permyak turned to an adult audience by writing a few "small novels" after 1960. He lived in Moscow; from 1959 to his death he was a delegate to all congresses of both Writers Unions and served as chairman of the Appeals Commission of the Writers Union of the RSFSR from 1970 to 1980.

Permyak's *Skazka o serom volke* (1960; Eng. tr., *The Tale of the Grey Wolf*, 1960) describes the visit of a Russian emigrant, a farmer living in the United States, who learns about the superiority of the kolkhoz system from his brother; even the dogmatic critics considered *Staraya vedma* (1961; The Old Witch) insufficiently convincing in its depiction of the perniciousness of private property; *Schastlivoye krusheniye* (1964; The Fortunate Misfortune) is just as uncompact and incompetent in its attempt to portray the relative unimportance of the physical element in a socialist marriage. *Razgovor bez obinyakov* (1977; Plain Speaking) consists of 12 primitive propaganda articles about happiness in the Soviet state.

*Works: Kem byt'?*, 1946; *Geroj grjaduščikh dnej* (documentary pov.), 1951; *Ot kostra do kotla* (short story), 1959; *Na vse cveta radugi* (short stories), 1959; *Skazka o serom volke* (novel), 1960 (see above); *Staraja ved'ma* (novel), 1961; *Sčastlivoe krušenie* (novel), in *Naš sovremennik* 1964:3; *Gorbatyj medved'* (novel), 2 vols., 1965–67; *Detstvo Mavrika* (pov.), 1969; *Moj kraj* (short stories and articles), 1970; *Poslednie zamorozki* (novel), 1972; *Razgovor bez obinjakov* (short stories), 1977.—*Izbr. proizv.*, 2 vols., 1973; *Sobr. soč.*, 4 vols., 1977–80.

*Secondary Lit.*: V. Gura, in *Moskva* 1962:10 and separate studies, 1972, 1982; S. Baruzdin, in *Lit. gazeta* Oct. 3, 1964; Ju. Rjurikov, in *Novyj mir* 1965:8; G. Drobot, in *Lit. gazeta* April 17, 1974, p. 6; V. Starikov, in *Lit. Rossija* Sept. 20, 1974, p. 7; S. Soloženkina, in *Lit. Rossija* July 11, 1980, p. 11; obituary, in *Lit. Rossija* Aug. 27, 1982, p. 17.

**Pérventsev, Arkády Alekséyevich**, prose writer (b. Jan. 26 [Jan. 13], 1905, Nagut, prov. Stavropol—d. Nov. 2, 1981, Moscow). Perventsev's father was a teacher. Perventsev was active in politics and journalism until 1929; he subsequently attended the Baumann Institute of Technology in Moscow and worked in mechanical engineering. His first short stories and a novel, *Kochubey*, appeared in 1937. During World War II, Perventsev was initially employed in the rear; in 1942 he became a war correspondent for *Izvestiya*. He received two Stalin Prizes (both for 1948, 2d class) for one of his books about the war, *Chest smolodu* (1948; Honor from Youth), and for his participation on the film *Tretiy udar* (The Third Blow). In 1950 he was admitted to the Communist Party. As a recognized writer during the Stalinist period, Perventsev was frequently included in delegations traveling abroad. As a prose writer and dramatist, he continued to write on Party-encouraged topics; his works achieved high circulation figures. He belonged to the board of the Writers Union of the RSFSR from 1958 on and to the Writers Union of the USSR from 1971 on. Perventsev lived in Moscow.

Artistically, Perventsev's works are so bad that in spite of the fact that they adhere to the Party's propaganda line of the time, they met with limited recognition even from the dogmatic critics. The majority are set in the Kuban. *Kochubey* and *Nad Kubanyu* (1938–40; Over the Kuban) are Civil War novels; *Ispytaniye* (1942; Eng. tr., *The Ordeal*, 1944), *Ognennaya zemlya* (1945; The Burning Land), and *Chest smolodu* are books written in the heroic mold about World War II; *Mladshiy partnyor* (1951; Junior Partner) is an anti-American, agitational piece, his contribution to the campaign against COSMOPOLITANISM. Perventsev is among those writers "who glorified Stalin in a most subservient way" (Slonim). *Matrosy* (1953–61; Sailors) and many of his short stories are set in a navy milieu. *Chornaya burya* (1974; Black Storm) glorifies the Party's and the State's aid in overcoming storm damage in 1969. The problems in Perventsev's works are contrived, his style is skewed, his imagery is inconsistent, and his characters are trite.

*Works: Kočubej* (novel), 1937; *Nad Kuban'ju* (novel), 1939; *Ispytanie* (novel), 1942 (see above); *Ognennaja zemlja* (novel), 1946; *Čest' smolodu* (novel), 1949; *Mladšij partnër* (play), 1951; *V Islandii* (travel notes), 1952; *Razgovor o kul'turnom čeloveke* (on etiquette), 1959; *Matrosy* (novel), 1961; *Gamajun—ptica veščaja* (novel), 1963; *Olivkovaja vetv'* (novel), 1966; *Ostrov nadeždy* (novel), 1968; *Sekretnyj front* (novel), 1972; *Černaja burja* (novel), 1974.—*Izbr. proizv.*, 2 vols., 1950; *Sobr. soč.*, 6 vols., 1977–80.

*Secondary Lit.*: L. Skorino, in *Oktjabr'* 1940:4–5; V. Zalesskij, in *Novyj mir* 1952:11; Z. Papernyj, in *Novyj mir* 1962:9; *RSPP* 3:1964; P. Insakov, 1973; M. Zarudnyj, in *Lit. gazeta* May 23, 1973, p. 4; L. Usenko, in *Lit. obozrenie* 1974:2; A. Sofronov, in *Lit. gazeta* Jan. 29, 1975, p. 3; V. Evpatov, in *Oktjabr'* 1980:1.

**Peskóv, Geórgy** (pseud. of Yeléna Albértovna Déysha-Sionítskaya), prose writer (b. 1898 [?]—d. Dec. 22, 1977, near Paris). Details of her biography are not known and were not obtainable through correspondence with Slavicists who knew her. Peskov corrected the assumption that her pseudonym was a translation into Russian of the name George Sand; she chose her son's first name and adopted the family name of her estate Pesochin (prov. Kharkov). Peskov wrote a total of 230 short stories and povesti, most of them after she emigrated to Paris. These were published in many journals and newspapers (*Illyustrirovannaya Rossiya, Zveno, Sovremennye za-*

*piski, Posledniye novosti).* Only two collections were published in Paris: *Pamyati tvoyey* (1930; To Your Memory) and *V rasseyanii sushchiye* (1959; Those Who Live in the Diaspora). In emigration Peskov did not belong to any group and remained less recognized than her talent deserved. In 1974 Margaret Dalton paid her proper tribute.

Peskov's short stories are sustained by a strong connection to the transcendental in that they exhibit an impartial understanding of the effect of good and evil spiritual powers on earthly activities (in the sense of M. Lermontov's "Demon"), of visionary perception of spiritual powers, of telepathy, and so on. She imagines and describes such an effect in social and interpersonal life after the Revolution. "Nearly all of Peskov's 'magic' tales are of a uniformly high caliber, not only as far as plot development, characterization, and suspense are concerned, but also because of a certain contagious 'spark' of irrationality" (Dalton). In *Gonets* (The Messenger), when Peskov reports on a communication delivered during the Civil War by a messenger who dies at the same moment in a distant location, she manages to relate such an unusual event with realistic persuasiveness. The lead story *Pamyati tvoyey* exhibits similar sobriety; in this tale a priest shot by the Bolsheviks appears to a young nonreligious man in a vision and asks him to pray for the murderers. Next to Peskov's "magic" short stories are those whose motives are purely psychological and ethical; these predominate in her second volume and often concern the theme of adapting to a foreign culture.

*Works: Pamjati tvoej* (short stories), Paris, 1930; *Zlaja večnost'* (pov.), in *Sovremennye zapiski* 48–49:1932; *Meduza* (short story), in *Pëstrye rasskazy*, New York, 1953; *V rassejanii sušcie* (short stories), Paris, 1959; *My i oni* (excerpt from *Razgovor s soboj*), in *Ekho*, Paris, 1978:1.

*Secondary Lit.:* F. Stepun, in *Sovremennye zapiski* 42:1930; G. Struve, in his *Russkaja literatura v izgnanii*, New York, 1956, pp. 301–4; M. Dalton, in *Mnemozina: Studia litteraria russica in honorem Vsevolod Setchkarev*, Munich, 1974.

**Peskóv, Vasíly Mikháylovich,** prose writer (b. March 14, 1930, Orlovo, oblast Voronezh). Peskov became a member of the Communist Party in 1951. He initially worked as a Pioneer leader and film technician; in 1953 he became a photojournalist for the Voronezh Komsomol newspaper. In 1956 Peskov joined the staff of *Komsomolskaya pravda* as a correspondent. The articles he wrote for this newspaper were collected for the first time in *Zapiski fotoreportyora* (1960; Notes of a Photojournalist). In 1964 Peskov received the Lenin Prize for his next collection, *Shagi po rose* (1963; Steps on the Dew). He lives in Moscow.

Peskov uses only one genre, the short journalistic essay. He selects politically approved, prominent events as his subject matter. His professional honors enabled him to travel abroad as far as the Antarctic; his impressions of this major trip appear in the individual sketches of *Belye sny* (1965; White Dreams). Peskov's journey to Kamchatka is reflected in his book *Kray sveta* (1967; The World's Edge). His consciously concise style, often eschewing verbs, makes but a temporary impression and proves itself, by constant repetition, to be of minor artistic merit. Peskov is a propagandist and sees the world around him "through the Party's eyes" (Permyak).

*Works: Zapiski fotoreportëra* (articles), 1960; *Šagi po rose* (articles), 1963; *Belye sny* (articles), 1965; *Kraj sveta* (articles), 1967; *Putešestvie s molodym mesjacem* (articles), 1969; *Otečestvo* (articles), 1970; *Po dorogam Ameriki* (in collaboration with B. Strel'nikov) (articles), 1973; *Vojna i ljudi* (articles), 1979; *Pticy na provodakh*, 1982.

*Secondary Lit.:* E. Permjak, in *Lit. gazeta* Dec. 7, 1963; S. Tregub, in *Moskva* 1964:1; Ju. Apečenko, in *Pravda* March 3, 1968; S. Vysockij, in *Naš sovremennik* 1973:5; V. Revič, in *Lit. obozrenie* 1984:11.

**Pétnikov, Grigóry Nikoláyevich,** poet (b. Feb. 6 [Jan. 25], 1894, St. Petersburg—d. May 11, 1971, Stary Krym). Petnikov studied law (as well as music and Slavic philology) at Moscow University; he completed his studies in Kharkov. In 1914 N. Aseyev and Petnikov founded the small publishing house Liren, one of the centers of FUTURISM, in Kharkov. In the foreword to their first volume, *Letorey* (1915), which contains poems by both authors, Petnikov asserts the superiority of the world of words to the world of things. Petnikov became an admirer and disciple of V. Khlebnikov, who also published with Liren and, together with Petnikov, signed the "Mandate of the Chairmen of the Globe" in 1917. In 1918–19 Khlebnikov wrote of Petnikov's next two volumes of verse: "In *Byt pobegov* [1918; The Escape Milieu] and *Porosl solntsa* [1918; Sun Shoots], Petnikov weaves, persistently, exactingly, with strong pressure of will, his 'pattern book of wind phenomena,' and his writing's clear coldness of will and his intellect's sharp sword, guided by the word, where there is 'in a raw former existence a damp Mnestr [a splice of *mne* ("me") and *Dnestr*]' and the 'reflected glory of the all-impossible heights,' clearly distinguish him from his contemporary Aseyev" (*Werke*, vol. 2, pp. 319–20). Petnikov, who also translated Novalis, opposed the notion that life must adapt to the heated tempo of industry. His poetry, free of meter, rhyme, syntax, and often of grammatical forms as well, containing abundant archaisms and neologisms, stands rather close to nature. Between 1918 and 1920 Petnikov held cultural-political posts in Kharkov and Kiev, edited various journals, including *Puti tvorchestva*, and even wrote revolutionary poetry. Collections of his work were published in 1928, 1934, and 1936; these, however, had broken away considerably from the experimental impetus of futurism. Petnikov subsequently disappeared from literature; by no later than the late 1950s he was making his living as a translator in Stary Krym. In 1961 his *Zavetnaya kniga* (The Yearned-for Book) once again brought him to the attention of Soviet readers. Between 1963 and 1972, four more volumes of Soviet readers. Between 1963 and 1972, four more volumes of his verse were published, also in Simferopol. Very little of Petnikov's original poetic power is visible in his late poems.

*Works: Letorej* (poems, written in collaboration with N. Aseev), 1915; *Byt pobegov* (poems), 1918; *Porosl' solnca* (poems), 1918, 2d ed., 1920; *Kniga Marii—Zažgi Snega* (poems), 1920; *Nočnye molnii* (poems), 1928; *Molodost' mira* (poems), 1934; *Izbr. stikhi* (poems), 1936; *Zavetnaja kniga* (poems), 1961; *Otkrytye stranicy* (poems), 1963; *Utrennij svet* (poems), 1967; *Lirika* (poems), Simferopol', 1969; *Pust' trudjatsja stikhi* (poems), Simferopol', 1972.
*Secondary Lit.*: E. Kagarow, in *Der Sturm* 1926:7–8; Ju. Terapiano, in *Russkaja mysl'*, Paris, June 10, 1961; L. Levickij, in *Novyj mir* 1962:7; V. Markov, *Russian Futurism*, Berkeley, 1968; Ju. Kotljar, in *Oktjabr'* 1968:10; N. Stepanov, in *Lit. gazeta* Jan. 21, 1970, p. 6; V. Sakharov, in *Družba narodov* 1974:2.

**Petróv, Yevgény** (pseud. of Yevgény Petróvich Katáyev), prose writer, whose major works were written in collaboration with Ilya Ilf (b. Dec. 13 [Nov. 30], 1903, Odessa—d. July 2, 1942, in an airplane crash during a flight between Sevastopol and Moscow). Petrov was the son of a teacher; he completed his studies at a classical gymnasium in 1920, then worked as a journalist and criminal investigator. In 1923 he moved to Moscow, where as a contributor to various journals (for example, *Krasny perets*) he published satirical commentaries and humorous short stories. He first met Ilf in 1925 at the editorial offices of *Gudok*. After completing military service, Petrov began his collaborative literary career with Ilf on the initiative of Valentin Katayev (Petrov's brother). Together Ilf and Petrov wrote the novels *Dvenadtsat stulyev* (1928; Eng. trs., *Diamonds to Sit On*, 1930; *The Twelve Chairs*, 1961) and *Zolotoy telyonok* (1931; Eng. trs., *The Little Golden Calf*, 1932; *The Golden Calf*, 1962, 1964), which are among the best-known satirical works of early Soviet literature (see ILF). Short satirical articles written by Ilf and Petrov appeared in *Pravda*, *Ogonyok*, and *Chudak*. Between 1926 and 1930 Petrov also published several slender collections of his own humorous short stories. At the end of 1933 and the beginning of 1934, both writers traveled in Italy and other European countries; they spent six months in the United States (1935–36). They wrote their journalistic account of the trip, *Odnoetazhnaya Amerika* (1936; Eng. tr., *Little Golden America*, 1937), together; each wrote 20 chapters and they collaborated on seven more. After Ilf's death, Petrov published part of his notebooks, wrote several film scripts, and worked as a journalist during World War II. He joined the Communist Party in 1939. Parts of an unfinished futuristic novel, *Puteshestviye v stranu kommunizma* (1939–42; Journey to the Land of Communism), were published after Petrov's death; the novel, without resorting to fantastic devices, sketched a picture of the Soviet Union as it was expected to be in 25 years' time (that is, in 1963). Petrov's depiction of the USSR of the future, a country that has surpassed the war-weakened capitalist countries in every way (from fashion to transportation), is in many respects suggestive of his American experience.

*Works and Secondary Lit.*: see ILF, I.
*Petrov's Works: Radosti Megasa* (short stories), 1926; *Bez doklada* (short stories), 1927; *Frontovyj dnevnik* (diary), 1942; *Vozdušnyj izvozčik . . .* (film scripts), 1943; *Ostrov mira* (play), 1947; *Neokončennyj roman "Putešestvie v stranu kommunizma"* (novel), in *Lit. nasledstvo* 74:1965.
*Secondary Lit. on Petrov*: M. Čarnyj, in his

Ušedšie gody, 1967; A. V. Dunkel, Diss., New York Univ., 1972; L. Slavin, in Lit. gazeta Dec. 6, 1978, p. 6; Ju. Ščeglov, in Wiener Slawistischer Almamach 15:1985, pp. 169–209.

**Petróv-Vódkin, Kuzmá Sergéyevich,** painter, prose writer (b. Nov. 5 [Oct. 24], 1878, Khvalynsk, prov. Saratov—d. Feb. 15, 1939, Leningrad). Petrov-Vodkin's father was a shoemaker. Petrov-Vodkin early revealed a double talent for painting and writing and received his first lessons at Baron von Stieglitz's Academy of Technical Design in St. Petersburg between 1895 and 1897. From this time on he also wrote short stories on a regular basis, but they were never published; supposedly they were written under the influence of Maurice Maeterlinck. Petrov-Vodkin continued his studies in Moscow between 1897 and 1905 and made lengthy journeys to Western Europe, particularly to Munich. Between 1905 and 1908 he lived in Italy and France, visited North Africa, then settled in St. Petersburg. After the Revolution, Petrov-Vodkin became a professor at the Art Institute in Leningrad; in 1932 he became chairman of the Leningrad Artists Union. In 1923, 1930, and 1932 he published some autobiographical literature and, in 1938, a small book for children. A silence was imposed concerning Petrov-Vodkin's work for almost three decades after his death. An exhibit of his work took place in the Russian Museum in Leningrad in 1966; that same year saw the publication of the first monograph about him. His autobiographical works were not reprinted until 1970.

Poyezdka v Afriku (1910; Journey to Africa) was Petrov-Vodkin's first book of travel notes; it was followed by Samarkandiya (1923; Samarkandia), which tells of his encounter with the art of the Middle East. Khlynovsk is devoted to his childhood and school years and the account is continued in Prostranstvo Evklida (1932; Euclidean Space). Petrov-Vodkin describes his first journeys to Europe, providing insight into the process of aesthetic formation through the artist's encounters with different countries and various kinds of art; he combines a vividly and humorously related personal element with fundamental ideas about art. From his work emerges the portrait of a significant artist and scholar.

Works: Poezdka v Afriku (travel reminiscences), in Na rassvete, vol. 1, Kazan', 1910; Aojja. Priključenija Andrjuši i Kati v vozdukhe, pod zemlëj i na zemle, 1914; Samarkandija (travel reminiscences), 1923; Moja povest': (1) Khlynovsk, 1930, (2) Prostranstvo Èvklida, 1932; reprint of Samarkandija and Moja povest', 1970.

Secondary Lit.: V. Kostin, 1966; Ju. Rusakov, foreword to Petrov-Vodkin's Khlynovsk, 1970; G. Filippov, in Zvezda 1970:8; V. Solov'ëv, in Novyj mir 1971:1; E. Klimov, in Novyj žurnal, New York, 105:1971; G. Curikova and I. Kuz'mičev, in Neva 1974:6; A. Pistunova, in Moskva 1978:11.

**Petrovýkh, Maríya Sergéyevna,** poet (b. March 26 [March 13], 1908, Norsky Posad, prov. Yaroslavl—d. June 1, 1979, Moscow [?]). Petrovykh wrote her first poems as a child and became aware of an inner attraction to Armenia during her school years. After graduating from school, she attended the Advanced Literature Course in Moscow and completed the requirements for the Faculty of Literature at Moscow University through correspondence courses. Petrovykh possesses a great poetic talent; she began publishing in 1926 but was able to publish isolated poems only extremely rarely. She became well known solely as a highly gifted translator (after 1935), especially from the Armenian but also from other languages including Yiddish (Perets Markish, among others) and Lithuanian. Her love for Armenia found its highest expression in a journey there in 1944. As an editor of volumes of poetry by Armenian poets, Petrovykh also promoted the dissemination of Armenian poetry (including Geram Saryan in 1947, Avetik Isaakyan in 1956, Ovanes Tumanyan in 1969). Thanks solely to the Armenians, a single small collection of her own poetry (together with her translations) was published in Yerevan during her lifetime: Dalneye derevo (1968; The Distant Tree). Petrovykh lived in Moscow. A representative selection of the poetry of this poet, who was especially admired by A. Akhmatova, was published only after her death. A. Tarkovsky wrote the foreword to this volume, Prednaznacheniye (1983; Predestination).

Petrovykh was an extraordinarily gifted poet who was hindered throughout her life in developing her talent and in reaching her audience. Her poems grew out of an understanding of human fate that is attentive to the spiritual and that is grounded in the intellectual. The delicacy of her interpretation of nature contrasts with the clear precision of her comprehension of injustice, of cruelty, of the absence of freedom among the people she observes. War poems express a rejection of war as such and pain at separation and at the use of force.

They are above any sort of nationalism. The avowal of man's communion with nature offers solace. Nature also provides the source of her metaphorically rich language and expresses spirituality as well as circumspectly intimated opposition toward political subjugation. "Iz nenapisannoy poemy" (From an Unwritten Poem) provides a brief glimpse of her agreeable vision of her own passage from death into the life after death without even a hint of a death wish—despite her interminable anguish over a poetic life lived in a void. The high praise A. Akhmatova and B. Pasternak paid her creativity affords a slender ray of light on this suppressed poetic existence.

*Works: Dal'nee derevo* (poems), 1968; *Prednaznačenie* (poems), 1983; *Stikhi i perevody* (poems and translations), 1986.
*Secondary Lit.:* S. Maršak, in *Lit. gazeta* May 31, 1962; A. Akhmatova, in *Voprosy lit.* 1965:4; L. Mkrtčjan, in *Lit. Rossija* Dec. 17, 1965, p. 15, and foreword to Petrovykh's *Dal'- nee derevo*, 1966; A. Saakjanc, in *Kratkaja literaturnaja ènciklopedija* 5:1968; A. Tarkovskij, foreword to Petrovykh's *Prednaznačenie*, 1983; G. Levin, in *Lit. gazeta* July 18, 1984, p. 5; A. Lavrin, in *Novyj mir* 1984:8; B. Sarnov, in *Lit. obozrenie* 1985:8; M. Ptuškina, in *Družba narodov* 1985:8.

**Petrushévskaya, Lyudmíla Stefánovna,** playwright, prose writer (b. May 26, 1938, Moscow). Petrushevskaya's father was an administrator. Petrushevskaya completed her studies at Moscow University and began writing short stories in the mid-1960s. In 1972 she worked as an editor for the central television studio. She published her first two short stories in *Avrora* in 1972. After the mid-1970s, Petrushevskaya also made her name as a playwright, but performances of her works were limited to small, semiprofessional stages. The one-act *Lyubov* (Love) appeared in the journal *Teatr* in 1979; Yu. Lyubimov included it in a performance of three short plays at the Taganka Theater in 1981–82. The plays *Stakan vody* (A Glass of Water) and *Uroki muzyki* (Music Lessons) were performed on little-known Moscow stages in 1983. The considerable recognition Petrushevskaya received in theater circles stands in marked contrast to the number of her works that were published or performed. In 1985 her works were first performed on a larger stage (Sovremennik Theater): *Kvartira Kolumbiny* (Columbine's Apartment), together with two other plays. She lives in Moscow.

Petrushevskaya's attention focuses on the depressing interpersonal relationships of daily life. With unsparing openness, she depicts primarily women who are faced with incomprehensible harshness, lovelessness, and baseness. She hints that misunderstandings, unspoken feelings, and conditions of life in the Soviet Union—especially cramped living quarters—contribute to this situation; generally, however, she neither explains nor provides a way of escaping from the brutality, which she observes and depicts by using consciously contemporary slang. In *Lyubov*, Petrushevskaya depicts a married couple without affection for one another, from their return from the marriage registry office through their decision to divorce and to their resolution to remain together nevertheless. In *Stakan vody* she counterposes two women of different generations who cannot shed their terrible loneliness. In the play *Tri devushki v golubom* (1983; Three Girls in Blue), she uses an argument about a dacha to contrast good and bad behavior in order to illustrate the relativity of human action through the complete ethical reversal of the characters. Petrushevskaya's hope of publishing a volume of collected works—*Bessmertnaya lyubov* (Undying Love) that would have included such short stories as *Skripka* (The Violin), *Smotrovaya ploshchadka* (The Parade Square), and *Manya* (Manya)—still remained unfulfilled in 1985. Her writing provides a release from deeply empathic suffering, a cry of protest without an echo.

*Works: Rasskazčica; Istorija Klarissy* (short stories), in *Avrora* 1972:7; *Seti i lovuški* (short story), in *Avrora* 1974:4; *Dva okoška* (play), 1975 (VAAP stage manuscript); *Bystro khorošo ne byvaet, ili Čemodan čepukhi* (play), in *Odnoaktnye p'esy*, 1978; *Prokhodite v kukhnju* (play), in *Odnoaktnye p'esy*, 1979; *Ljubov'* (play), in *Teatr* 1979:3; *Vsë ne kak u ljudej* (play), in *Odnoaktnye p'esy*, 1979; *Ozelenenie* (play), in *Odnoaktnye p'esy*, 1980:2; *Smotrovaja ploščadka* (short story), in *Družba narodov* 1982:1; *Tri devuški v golubom* (play), in *Sovremennaja dramaturgija* 1983:3; *Bessmertnaja ljubov'* (interview), in *Lit. gazeta* Nov. 23, 1983, p. 6; *Čerez polja* (short story), in *Avrora* 1983:5; *Uroki muzyki*, *Lestničnaja kletka* (play), in V. Slavkin, L. Petruševskaja, *P'esy*, 1983, pp. 76–155.
*Secondary Lit.:* A. Arbuzov, in *Teatr* 1979:3; E. Gessen, in *Vremja i my*, Tel Aviv, 81:1984; A. Smeljanskij, in *Sovremennaja dramaturgija* 1985:4; M. Turovskaja, in *Novyj mir* 1985:12; M. Stroeva, N. Klado, in *Sovremen-*

*naja dramaturgija* 1986:2; R. Doktor, A. Plavinskij, in *Lit. obozrenie* 1986:12.

**Píkul, Valentín Sávvich,** prose writer (b. July 13, 1928, Leningrad). At the end of World War II, Pikul was drafted into the navy. Barring his earliest literary efforts, he began his activity as a writer with the novel *Okeansky patrul* (1954; Ocean Patrol). By 1983 Pikul had written more than a dozen novels, including some two-part historical novels, that are beloved among a wide circle of readers. Probably because of the poor literary quality of his works, Pikul is not mentioned in histories of literature nor had he been a delegate to Writers Congresses as of 1981. He lives in Riga.

Pikul is an experienced writer who knows how to captivate the reader with his novels, which tend toward the trivial. He is accused of handling history somewhat too freely; he conceals or falsifies the role of the church. The setting of his novels ranges from the 17th to the 20th century. *Bayazet* (1961) concerns the Russo-Turkish War of 1877–78; *Iz tupika* (1968; Out of the Dead End), the Revolution in Murmansk; *Moonzund* (1973; Moon Strait), World War I in the Baltic. *Perom i shpagoy* (1972; With Feather and Sword) is an attack on Frederick the Great; *Bitva zheleznykh kantslerov* (1977; The Battle of the Iron Chancellors), on Bismarck. *Rekviyem karavanu RQ–17* (1979; Requiem for Convoy RQ–17) describes the destruction of British ships in 1942 and is based on David Irving's book (London, 1968). The novel *U posledney cherty* (1979; At the Last Line), concerning the last years of the Romanov dynasty and Grigory Rasputin, touched off deep resentment, since Pikul not only portrayed the private life of the tsar's family in unusual detail but, with an excess of Russian patriotism, depicted the role of the Jews in an exclusively negative light. With his historical novels, Pikul pursues clearly topical goals: the support of a Russian patriotism that borders on chauvinism; anti-Semitism; and hostility toward religion.

*Works:* Okeanskij patrul' (novel), 1954; *Bajazet* (novel), 1961; *Iz tupika* (novel), 1968; *Perom i špagoj* (novel), 1972; *Moonzund* (novel), 1973; *Mal'čiki s bantikami* (autobiographical pov.), 1974; *Slovo i delo* (novel), 2 vols., 1974–75; *Iz staroj škatulki* (novel), 1976; *Bitva železnykh kanclerov* (novel), 2 vols., 1977; *Rekviem karavanu RQ–17* (novel), 1979; *U poslednej čerty* (novel), in *Naš sovremennik* 1979:4–7; *Tri vozrasta Okini-san* (novel), in *Neva* 1981:9–11; *Favorit* (novel), 2 vols., 1984;

*Istoričeskie miniatjury* (short stories), in *Avrora*, 1985:8–10; *Pod šelest znamën* (novels), 1986.

*Secondary Lit.:* M. Čekhanovec, in *Zvezda* 1973:4; Ju. Petrovskij, in *Zvezda* 1975:7 and 1978:7; V. Mavrodin, in *Avrora* 1978:3; L. Gerasimova, Ju. Gordin, Ju. Osipov, in *Lit. obozrenie* 1978:8; A. Šagalov, in *Znamja* 1979:2; I. Puškarëva, in *Lit. Rossija* July 27, 1979; K. Mehnert, *The Russians and Their Favorite Books*, Stanford, 1983; D. Urnov, in *Lit. gazeta* March 20, 1985, p. 5; A. Gulyga, in *Moskva* 1985:7; A. Marčenko, V. Oskockij, A. Kazincev, in *Lit. obozrenie* 1986:7.

**Pilnyák, Borís Andréyevich** (pseud. of B. A. Vógau), prose writer (b. Oct. 11 [Sept. 29], 1894, Mozhaysk—d. Sept. 9, 1941 [or possibly 1938], while imprisoned). Pilnyak's father was a Volga German veterinarian; his mother, a Russian Tatar. Pilnyak began publishing short stories in various journals in 1915 and collections of his work by 1918. In 1920 he completed business school in Moscow. With his novel *Goly god* (1922; Eng. trs., *The Naked Year*, 1928, 1975), Pilnyak became known as one of the first writers to depict the Revolution in its inner tension between elemental and rational forces and as an active experimenter with form; "his 'novel' *Goly god* . . . placed him at the head of a whole school, or movement, in Soviet literature" (Struve). In 1922–23 he traveled to Germany and England. After several volumes of his prose had been published, his *Povest nepogashennoy luny* (1926; Eng. tr., in *The Tale of the Unextinguished Moon and Other Stories*, 1967) drew sharp official condemnation because Pilnyak had taken as the subject of his work the rumor that the revolutionary general Mikhail Frunze had been disposed of in 1924 when orders from the highest authority forced him to submit to an operation. *Novy mir*, the journal in which the povest appeared, printed a retraction in its next issue. He was allowed to continue publishing and traveling abroad (to China, Japan, the United States, and the Near East). Although Pilnyak submitted his povest *Krasnoye derevo* (1929; Eng. tr., *Mahogany*, 1965) to a Berlin publisher through the regular channels of the All-Union Society for Cultural Relations with Foreign Countries, or VOKS (see Hayward), its publication in Berlin led to Pilnyak's expulsion from RAPP, his removal as chairman of the All-Russian Writers Association, and an anti-Pilnyak campaign of such virulence that M. Gorky protested that it "somehow destroys all of the services he has rendered to the field of Soviet literature" (1930).

Pilnyak apologized and conformed to approved methods of presentation. *Volga vpadayet v Kaspiyskoye more* (1930); Eng. tr., *The Volga Falls to the Caspian Sea*, 1931) is his contribution to the literature of the Five-Year Plan; he revised and annotated *Kamni i korni* (1927; Stones and Roots), his book on traveling in China and Japan, to correspond to the official position. At the First Congress of the Writers Union of the USSR, Pilnyak was elected to the board of that body. His last novel, *Sozrevaniye plodov* (1936; Ripening of the Fruit), conforms to official ideology. In 1937 Pilnyak was one of the first victims of the government purges. His REHABILITATION took place on Dec. 6, 1956, but not until 1976 was a volume of his selected works reprinted in the Soviet Union. Up to 1986 Pilnyak was hardly ever mentioned in literary histories, and then he was usually presented in a negative light.

Pilnyak depicted revolutionary events as being something primal, a national uprising of the peasant masses in the spirit of past centuries. He continues the old search for an understanding of Russia's position between Europe and Asia. His works are set chiefly in the Russian provinces. Pilnyak recognized early the conflict inherent in the Revolution itself between the anarchic element and the Bolshevik obsession with organization, between the real revolutionary heroes and the center of power; he finally depicted disillusioned revolutionaries in *Krasnoye derevo*. The chaos of revolutionary events found formal expression in his brittle, episodic, experimental narrative structure, which, under the influence of A. Bely and supported by the example of A. Remizov and Ye. Zamyatin, freed itself from traditional realistic narrative form and its self-contained plot. Individual events are isolated, fragmented, and temporally displaced; they are held together by symbolic imagery and repetition. Like *Goly god*, which it complements chronologically and thematically, *Mashiny i volki* (1925; Machines and Wolves) exhibits all the characteristic features of this montage technique. *Povest nepogashennoy luny* is, in comparison to Pilnyak's earlier works, full of action and self-contained. Even later, Pilnyak continued to employ the mosaiclike compositional technique that permits him to cite extensively from his own work and from that of others and to incorporate material from newspapers and documents—to use, for instance, a politically purified version of *Krasnoye derevo* in *Volga vpadayet v Kaspiyskoye more*. Pilnyak's ornamental style, which exerted a considerable influence on other writers, is visible in the textual microstructure, even in the syntax itself.

*Works: Byl'ë* (short stories), 1919, 2d ed., 1922 (reprinted, Munich, 1970); *Golyj god* (novel), 1922 (reprinted, Letchworth, 1966) (see above); *Povest' peterburgskaja* (pov.), Berlin, 1922; *Tret'ja stolica* (pov.), 1923, in *Sobr. soč.*, vol. 4, under the title *Mat'-mačekha*; *Anglijskie rasskazy* (short stories), 1924; *Mašiny i volki* (novel), 1925 (reprinted, Munich, 1971); *Povest' nepogašennoj luny* (pov.), in *Novyj mir* 1926:5 (reprinted, in G. Glinka, *Na perevale*, New York, 1954; reprinted under the title *Ubijstvo komandarma*, London, 1965 (see above); *Očerednye povesti* (pov.), 1927; *Kitajskij dnevnik* (pov.), 1927; *Rasplesnutoe vremja* (short stories), 1927 (reprinted, Chicago, 1966); *Kamni i korni* (novel), 1927 (reprinted, Chicago, 1966); *Krasnoe derevo* (pov.), Berlin, 1929 (reprinted, Chicago, 1968) (see above); *Volga vpadaet v Kaspijskoe more* (novel), 1930 (see above); *O-kej* (novel), 1933 (reprinted, London, 1972); *Sozrevanie plodov* (novel), 1936; "Soljanoj ambar" (chapter of novel), in *Moskva* 1964:5; *Dvojniki* (novel), London, 1983; *Zaštat* (short story), in *Znamja* 1987:5.—*Sobr. soč.*, 8 vols., 1929–30; *Izbr. proizv.*, 1976.

*Translations: Tale of the Wilderness*, 1925; *Ivan Moscow*, 1935; *The Tales of the Unextinguished Moon and Other Stories*, 1967; *Mother Earth and Other Stories*, 1968.

*Secondary Lit.:* Boris Pilnjak, 1928 (reprinted, with bibliography, Letchworth, 1973); M. Gorkij (1930), in his *O literature*, 1937; M. Hayward, in *Survey* 36:1961; P. Palievskij, in *Voprosy lit.* 1966:8; L. Kuzmich, Diss., New York Univ., 1967; V. Novotný, "Pilňakovy literární montáže," Diss., Prague, 1969; A. P. Reilly, *America in Contemporary Soviet Literature*, New York, 1971; K. N. Brostrom, in *Slavonic and East European Journal* 1974:3; V. Reck, Montreal–London, 1975; R. Damerau, Giessen, 1976; A. Schramm, Munich, 1976; T. R. N. Edwards, Diss., Bristol, 1977, and 1982; M. C. Smith, Diss., Univ. of Pennsylvania, 1978; special issue of *Russian Literature* 1984:1; G. Browning, Ann Arbor, 1985.

**Piotrovsky, Vladimir Lvovich.** See KORVIN-PIOTROVSKY, VLADIMIR LVOVICH.

**Pisákhov, Stepán Grigóryevich,** prose writer (b. Oct. 24 [Oct. 12], 1879, Arkhangelsk—d. May 3, 1960, Arkhangelsk). Pisakhov's father was a jeweler and engraver. Pisakhov attended art school in St. Petersburg, leaving because of the Revolution of 1905. After studying in Paris, he continued his education under the direction of the painter Ya. S. Goldblat in St. Petersburg. Pisakhov traveled to many countries, including Italy, France, North Africa, Turkey, and Palestine. His major interest, however, lay in the Russian North. As an ethnographer, painter, and folklorist, he participated in various expeditions and traversed large areas on his own. In 1924 and after 1932 Pisakhov wrote down and sporadically published a number of prose pieces based on peasant life; these were brought together in his first collection, Skazki (1938; Folktales), first published in Arkhangelsk and printed in Moscow only in 1957. Pisakhov was profoundly drawn to nature and to phenomena of primitive life not comprehensible to logic. Among his friends in Moscow, where he rarely visited, was V. Lidin. Pisakhov was a member of the Writers Union but is not mentioned in literary histories.

Lidin called Pisakhov "the poetic soul of the North"; saying that he had the same importance for the North that P. Bazhov had for the Urals. In his prose Pisakhov maintains the effect of the anonymous narrators (skazitelifantasty) of the North, embodied in his Senya Malina from the village of Uyma near Arkhangelsk. His prose is rich in the fantastic and the improbable, the everyday and the fabulous; above all it preserves the linguistic characteristics of the White Sea region. Yu. Kazakov has described the folktales written by Pisakhov (who was intimately familiar with the tradition) as being on a par with orally transmitted folktales.

Works: Skazki (folktales), 1938, 1940, 1949, 1957, 1959, 1978, and in B. Šergin, S. Pisakhov, Skazy i skazki, 1985.
Secondary Lit.: A. Mikhajlov, in Voprosy lit. 1958:6; Ju. Kazakov, in Lit. i žizn' June 10, 1959; V. Lidin, in Naš sovremennik 1960:5 and in his Ljudi i vstreči, 1961; RSPP 3:1964.

**Pisménny, Aleksándr Grigóryevich**, prose writer (b. Sept. 4 [Aug. 22], 1909, Bakhmut, prov. Yekaterinoslav—d. Aug. 22, 1971, Moscow). Pismenny's father was an engineer. Pismenny studied philology at Moscow University. He began publishing publicistic prose and short stories in Nashi dostizheniya, Krasnaya nov, and other journals in 1928. He made a name for himself with V malenkom gorode (1938; In a Small Town), a novel that depicts the transformation of the provinces by industrialization and that shows the inadequate recognition of the importance of the

provinces in comparison to Moscow and Leningrad. The first collection of Pismenny's short stories, Cherez tri goda (1939; In Three Years), is also devoted to a realistic depiction of the time. Pismenny, who possessed no extraordinary talent but who was able "to communicate the spirit of the present in a simple and unassuming manner" (V. Aleksandrova), was sharply attacked; only after Stalin's death did he again attract the critics' attention and manage to see V malenkom gorode and other works reprinted. His novel Prigovor (The Verdict), written in 1952, deals with hostile elements who were exposed as saboteurs of industrial construction in the 1930s; even in its revised version of 1955 the subject matter seems trite, but the work shows, as do the povest Dve tysyachi metrov nad urovnem morya (1958; Two Thousand Meters Above Sea Level) and the novel Bolshiye mosty (1965; Big Bridges), a consistently humane position and an ability to depict "the subtlest nuances of spiritual dynamics" (L. Slavin). Pismenny was never delegated to any of the Congresses of the Writers Union and lived in Moscow. His volume of memoirs, Fart (1980; Happiness), which makes explicit his awareness of being responsible for his own publications, was published posthumously.

Works: V malen'kom gorode (novel), 1938, 2d ed., 1956; Čerez tri goda (short stories), 1939; Kraj zemli (pov.), 1943; Prigovor (novel), 1952, 2d ed., 1955; Dve tysjači metrov nad urovnem morja (pov.), 1960; Bol'šie mosty (novel), 1965; Rukotvornoe more (short stories and pov.), 1978; Fart (memoirs, letters, short stories), 1980; Izbr., 1982.
Secondary Lit.: V. Aleksandrova (1939), in her Lit. i žizn' 1969; M. Sčeglov, in Novyj mir 1955:7; L. Slavin, in Novyj mir 1956:8; N. Asanov, in Lit. gazeta Sept. 18, 1956; L. Levickij, foreword to Pis'mennyj's V malen'kom gorode. Pokhod k Bosforu, 1966; L. Druskin, in Zvezda 1966:12; I. Varlamova, in Lit. obozrenie 1975:3; L. Meškova, in Lit. obozrenie 1981:8.

**Platónov, Andréy Platónovich** (pseud of A. P. Kliméntov), prose writer, playwright (b. Sept. 1 [Aug. 20], 1899, Voronezh—d. Jan. 5, 1951, Moscow). Platonov's father was a locomotive mechanic. Platonov began working in 1913 at jobs that included unskilled laborer, mechanic, and foundry worker; in 1919–20 he served in the Red Army. He completed his studies at the Polytechnic Institute in Voronezh in 1924 and went to work as a specialist in land reclamation and in electrification. By

1918 he was regularly publishing poetry and prose in local publications; his first volume of poetry appeared in 1922 and his first collection of short stories in 1927. That latter year he moved to Moscow to work as an engineer in central management; he soon left this position to work exclusively as a writer. After publishing numerous books and articles for journals, Platonov was sharply criticized in 1929 for his short story *Usomnivshiysya Makar* (Doubting Makar); the attack was also connected with Platonov's brief membership in the PEREVAL group. In 1929 his novel *Chevengur* (Eng. tr., 1978), already set in galleys, was not allowed to be published. His povest *Kotlovan* (Eng. trs., *The Foundation Pit*, 1974, 1975), written in 1929–30, was allowed to appear in the Soviet Union only in 1987. His short story *Vprok* (At an Advantage), which also made no effort to tone down the negative aspects of forced collectivization, led in 1931 to the suppression of Platonov's creative career, and probably to his internal exile. Heading the campaign against him was A. Fadeyev, who had initially published *Vprok* in *Krasnaya nov*. Platonov's short stories appeared occasionally between 1934 and 1937, and a volume of collected stories was published in 1937; in the following years Platonov published mostly articles of literary criticism (on A. Pushkin, Ernest Hemingway, Karel Čapek, A. Grin, K. Paustovsky, among others) under the pseudonyms F. Chelovekov (1937–41) and A. Firsov (1938–40). In October 1942 he became a frontline reporter for *Krasnaya zvezda*, and subsequently published numerous short stories and six small volumes of collected works. The increasing virulence of literary politics initiated by the Party Resolution of Aug. 14, 1946 (see PARTY RESOLUTIONS ON LITERATURE) produced V. Yermilov's shattering criticism of Platonov's short story *Semya Ivanova* (The Ivanov Family; later renamed *Vozvrashcheniye*, The Return). Excluded from literature, Platonov died in 1951 of tuberculosis contracted from his son, who had died in 1940 after returning from internal exile. Apart from four short texts that still managed to appear after 1946, Platonov's short stories again became available to Soviet readers only after the 20th Party Congress, but then relatively often. With the aid of his wife, M. A. Platonova, many texts were published for the first time from Platonov's own manuscripts. Most of his dramas are still unpublished. Platonov's main works, such as *Chevengur* and *Kotlovan*, had appeared only in the West up to 1986.

All of Platonov's work is governed by the principle of absolute honesty. His early prose is still close to the ornamental style, but over the years it became compact and solid. His powerful short stories of the 1920s combine lyricism and irony; their effectiveness is frequently due to their contrast between the lofty and the lowly, the heroic and the ridiculous. *Gorod Gradov* (1926; Gradov City) is a biting and profound satire on Soviet bureaucracy. The motif of the industriousness of the railway workers, which Platonov depicts free of any imposed pattern and with genuine sympathy, dominated his work in the 1930s. His povest *Dzhan* (1933–35), first published in 1964, interweaves the realistic and the fabulous; it is a parable, universally valid, in which an idealistic and faithful Party member fails to impose communism on his own impoverished desert people. *Kotlovan* depicts in a parabolic manner the gap between the leading figures of the socialist bourgeoisie and the proletarian masses living like slaves. Platonov's war stories combine a patriotic consciousness with a merciless presentation of the horror that war can bring to a family. The human being always stands at the center of his prose, which is permeated by a sound sense of psychology. "His sentences have the slow, liturgical, and precisely measured rhythm characteristic of writers of village prose" (Drawicz).

*Works: Golubaja glubina* (poems), 1922; *Epifanskie šljuzy* (pov. and short stories), 1927; *Sokrovennyj čelovek* (pov.), 1928; *Gorod Gradov* (short story), in *Krasnaja panorama* Sept.– Oct. 1928; *Proisxoždenie mastera* (pov.), 1929; *Usomnivšijsja Makar* (short story), in *Oktjabr'* 1929:6; *Vprok* (short story), in *Krasnaja nov'* 1931:3 and in *Opal'nye povesti*, New York, 1955; *Reka Portudan'* (short stories), 1937; *Bronja* (short stories), 1943; *V storonu zakata solnca* (short stories), 1945; *Soldatskoe serdce* (short stories), 1946; *Sem'ja Ivanova* (short story), in *Novyj mir* 1946:10–11; *Volšebnoe kol'co i drugie skazki* (fairy tales), 1954; *Džan* (pov.), in *Prostor* 1964:9; *V prekrasnom i jarostnom mire* (pov. and short stories), 1965, 2d ed., 1979; *Kotlovan* (pov.), London, 1969, and in *Novyj mir* 1987:6 (see above); *Smerti net!* (short stories), 1970; *Tečenie vremeni* (pov. and short stories), 1971; *Čevengur* (novel), Paris, 1972 (see above); *Četyrnadcat' krasnykh izbušek* (play), in *Grani*, Frankfurt am Main, 86:1972; *Potomki solnca* (pov. and short stories), 1974; *Juvenil'noe more*, in *Ékho*, Paris, 1979:4 and in *Znamja* 1986:6; *Razmyšlenija čitatelja*, 1980; *Potaënnyj Platonov*, Paris–New York, 1983; *Starik i staruxa. Poterjannaja proza*, Munich, 1984; *Svežaja voda iz kolodca* (short stories and pov.), 1984.—*Izbr. rasskazy,*

1958; *Rasskazy*, 1962; *Izbr.*, 1966; 1977; 2 vols., 1978; *Sobr. soč.*, 3 vols., 1984–85.

*Translations: The Fierce and Beautiful World*, 1970; *Finist, the Falcon Prince*, 1973; *Fro and Other Stories*, 1975; *Collected Works*, 1978.

*Secondary Lit.*: A. Fadeev, in *Krasnaja nov'* 1931:5–6; V. Ermilov, in *Lit. gazeta* Sept. 11, 1948; L. Slavin, in his *Portrety i zapiski*, 1965; E. Landau, in *Novyj mir* 1965:6; A. Kiselëv, extensive bibliography in *Novyj žurnal*, New York, 97:1969; I. Kramov, in *Novyj mir* 1969:8; V. Nekrasov, in his *V žizni i v pis'makh*, 1971; *RSPP* 7(2):1972; M. Geller, foreword to Platonov's *Čevengur*, 1972, and Paris, 1982; P. Šveikauskas, Diss., Brown Univ., 1972 (with extensive bibliography); M. Jordan, Letchworth, 1973, A. Olcott, Diss., Stanford Univ., 1976; V. Varšavskij, in *Novyj žurnal* 122:1976; V. Čalmaev, 1978; V. Maramzin, bibliography, in *Ėkho*, Paris, beginning 1979:4; A. Teskey, M. A. Diss., Belfast, 1979; N. Poltavceva, 1982; V. Vasil'ev, 1982; L. Šubin, in *Voprosy lit.* 1984:1.

**Podyáchev, Semyón Pávlovich,** prose writer (b. Feb. 8 [Jan. 27], 1866, Obolyanovo-Nikolskoye, prov. Moscow—d. Feb. 17, 1934, Obolyanovo-Nikolskoye [now Podyachevo]). Podyachev was of peasant descent. He finished the village school in 1880, then studied for a while at a technical school in Cherepovets. For years he moved around Russia, earning a scanty living by doing odd jobs. From 1888 to 1890 he was editorial secretary for the journal *Rossiya*, in which his first short stories were published. At the end of the 1890s Podyachev returned to his native village and engaged in farming; at the same time he recorded his experiences. In 1901 V. Korolenko discovered Podyachev's talent; he edited his work and published it in *Russkoye bogatstvo* between 1902 and 1909. They continued to correspond until 1917. In 1916 Podyachev became chairman of the Union of Peasant Writers. In 1918 he joined the Communist Party and received a cultural-political post. He continued to write. A 6-volume edition of his works appeared between 1911 and 1914. It was followed between 1927 and 1930 by an 11-volume edition, and later by occasional volumes of selected prose.

Podyachev is a genuine peasant writer not only by birth but also in his thematics. *Mytarstva* (1902; Ordeals), the title of his first major book, sets the tenor for his entire oeuvre: the personally witnessed or experienced suffering of the peasant in all its cruelty, poverty, drunkenness, crudity, and dependence. In a similar manner *Sredi rabochikh* (1904; Among the Workers) and *Zabytye* (1909; The Forgotten) depict the different manifestations of the hard life of the rural poor without differentiating the characters from each other. Podyachev does not have the power to raise autobiographical elements to the level of self-contained literary forms by manipulating plot to achieve coherence, but he can render individual scenes vividly and with feeling. After the Revolution, Podyachev's short stories assumed an agitational character. The last thing he wrote was his autobiography, *Moya zhizn* (1929–31; My Life).

*Works: Mytarstva* (publicistic prose), 1903; *Po ètapu* (publicistic prose), 1905; *Sredi rabočikh* (publicistic prose), 1905; *Zabytye* (short story), 1914; *Na spokoe* (short stories), 1918; *Žizn' mužickaja*, 1923; *Derevnja* (short stories), 1929; *Moja žizn'*, 1930–31; *Povesti i rasskazy* (pov. and short stories), 1951.—*Sobr. soč.*, 6 vols., 1911–14; *Polnoe sobr. soč.*, 11 vols., 1927–30; *Izbr.*, 1955; *Izbr. proizv.*, 1966.

*Secondary Lit.*: B. Anibal, in *Novyj mir* 1925:10; M. Gorkij, in Pod''jačev's *Polnoe sobr. soč.*, vol. 1, 1927; G. Jakubovskij, in *Novyj mir* 1928:9; *RSPP* 3:1964; *S. P. P. 1866–1934*, 1968; M. Makina, 1981.

**Pogódin, Nikoláy Fyódorovich** (pseud of N. F. Stukálov), playwright (b. Nov. 16 [Nov. 3], 1900, Gundorovskaya, near Rostov-on-Don—d. Sept. 19, 1962, Moscow). Pogodin's father was a peasant. Pogodin began working as a journalist in 1920; he started in the provinces, then from 1922 to 1929 wrote for *Pravda* (he contributed over 200 articles). His first drama, *Temp* (1929; Eng. tr., *Tempo*, in *Six Soviet Plays*, 1934), was inspired by a journalistic assignment that took him to the Stalingrad tractor works. Pogodin became one of the best-known Soviet dramatists and wrote more than 40 plays. From 1934 until his death he belonged to the board of the Writers Union of the USSR; from 1951 to 1960 he was editor in chief of the journal *Teatr*. In 1959 he received the Lenin Prize for his trilogy about Lenin, *Chelovek s ruzhyom* (1937; Eng. tr., *The Man with the Gun*, in *International Literature* 1938:7), *Kremlyovskiye kuranty* (1941, rev. ed., 1956; Eng. tr., *The Chimes of the Kremlin*, in *Soviet Scene*, 1946), and *Tretya, pateticheskaya* (1958; The Third Pathétique); he had previously received a Stalin Prize in 1941 (for 1935–41, 1st class) for the first part of the trilogy, written for the 20th anniversary of the October Revolution.

Pogodin's subject matter has always responded to the topical problems encountered in the various stages of the Soviet Union's development; his plays reveal genuine dramatic talent but vary considerably in terms of quality. During the period of the first Five-Year Plan, he wrote Temp and Poema o topore (1930; Poem about an Axe), loosely connected series of scenes with numerous characters and barely existent plot, intended to serve, so to speak, as documentary records of the socialist construction of that particular period. Pogodin's play Aristokraty (1934; Eng. tr., Aristocrats, 1937, and in Four Soviet Plays, 1937), successful in spite of its psychological weakness, is devoted to the theme of the reeducation of adherents of the old regime by means of forced labor on the White Sea Canal; the play is structured more functionally than his earlier work. Both Chelovek s ruzhyom and the first version of Kremlyovskiye kuranty brought Stalin onto the stage, thus conforming to the growing cult of personality. For reasons of health, Pogodin was not called upon to serve as a correspondent during World War II. His war plays, constructed not on the basis of personal experience but according to suggested outlines, were weak for this very reason, even in Pogodin's own opinion. Written in accordance with the Party line, his plays of the late Stalin period, such as his contribution to the struggle against COSMOPOLITANISM and parody of President Truman, Missuriysky vals (1949; The Missouri Waltz), deserve just as little attention. Pogodin, who was attacked at the Second Congress of the Writers Union by an official dramatist of A. Korneychuk's status, in 1955 wrote Sonet Petrarki (1956; A Petrarchan Sonnet), a dramatic contribution to liberal literature that recognizes the individual independently of his social or professional function, demands that the Party acknowledge the existence of a private sphere, and demonstrates the loathsomeness of those who denounced others. Using as his example a high official's experience of platonic love, Pogodin attempts—as Yu. Olesha did 30 years before in his Zavist—to justify the spiritual element in literature and the everyday life of a system based on materialism. Pogodin turned his attention to the problems of the younger generation in several subsequent dramas, such as Malenkaya studentka (1959; The Little Coed) and Golubaya rapsodiya (1961; Rhapsody in Blue). His last drama, Albert Eynshteyn (Albert Einstein), on which he began work in 1960, was completed after Pogodin's death by his secretary, A. Volgar.

Works: Krasnye rostki (publicistic prose), 1926; Temp (play), 1931 (see above); Poèma

o topore (play), 1932; Aristokraty (play), in Krasnaja nov' 1935:4 (see above); Čelovek s ruž'ëm (play), in Oktjabr' 1937:12 (see above); Kremlëvskie kuranty (play), 1941, rev. ed., in Teatr 1955:4 (see above); P'esy (plays), 1948 (contains Temp; Poèma o topore; Posle bala; Moj drug; Aristokraty; Čelovek s ruž'ëm; Sotvorenie mira; Minuvšie gody); P'esy (plays), 1952 (contains Moj drug; Aristokraty; Čelovek s ruž'ëm; Missurijskij val's); Sonet Petrarki (play), in Lit. Moskva 1956:2; Tret'ja, patetičeskaja (play), in Teatr 1958:9; Malen'kaja studentka (play), in Sovremennaja dramaturgija 6:1959; Cvety živye (play), in Teatr 1960:7; Jantarnoe ožerel'e (novel), 1960; Golubaja rapsodija (comedy), in Teatr 1961:3; Tren'bren' (play), in Teatr 1966:11; Al'bert Èjnstejn (tragedy), in Teatr 1968:9; S čego načinaetsja p'esa (essays), 1969.—Sobr. dramatičeskikh proizv., 5 vols., 1960–61; Neizdannoe, 2 vols., 1969; Sobr. soč., 4 vols., 1972–73.

Secondary Lit.: A. Gurvič, Tri dramaturga, 1936; N. Zajcev, 1958; A. Anastas'ev, 1964; B. Kholodov, 1967; Slovo o Pogodine: Vospominanija, 1968; A. Volgar', in Pogodin's Sobr. soč., 1972–73; E. Kornilov, Ju. Nemirov, in Don 1978:1; A. Minkin, in Teatr 1981:2.

**Poletáyev, Nikoláy Gavrílovich,** poet (b. Aug. 5 [July 24], 1889, Odoyev, prov. Tula—d. March 16, 1935, Moscow). Poletayev spent his childhood in Odoyev with his grandmother; later he lived with his mother in Moscow in conditions of poverty. He completed business school and from 1905 on worked as a bookkeeper for the railroad in Bryansk. His first poem was printed in the newspaper Izvestiya on the first anniversary of the October Revolution. In the same year (1918) Poletayev joined the literary studio of the Moscow PROLETKULT, which published his first volume of verse, Stikhi (1919; Poems). In 1920 he became a member of KUZNITSA, which printed individual poems of his in its journals and published his books Pesnya o solovyakh (1921; A Song of Nightingales) and Slomannye zabory (1923; Broken Fences). Poletayev's brief writing career ended with the small volume of short stories Zheleznodorozhniki (1925; The Railway Workers) and Rezky svet (1926; Harsh Light), a collection of poems written between 1918 and 1925. In 1927–28 Poletayev worked on the editorial staff of the journal Oktyabr. He was very ill the last years of his life.

Poletayev occupies a special position among the proletarian writers. He quickly freed himself from the pathos associated with the Kuznitsa poets and wrote pessimistic poems recalling his childhood in the city and the loneliness that comes with being poor; this he contrasted with more soothing images of the village and nature. Although formally weak, his poetry discloses an inner concern. The poem "Siniye tetradi" (1925; The Blue Notebooks) combines a retrospective glance at his personal disappointments with the hope and promise of youth.

Works: Stikhi (poems), 1919; Pesnja o solov'jakh (poems), 1921; Slomannye zabory (poems), 1923; Železnodorožniki (short stories), 1925; Rezkij svet (poems), 1926; Stikhi (poems), 1930; O solov'jakh, kotorykh ne slykhal (poems), 1932; Izbr. stikhi (poems), 1935, 1938; Stikhotvorenija (poems), 1957.
Secondary Lit.: A. Voronskij, in Lit. portrety, vol. 2, 1929; K. Zelinskij, in Oktjabr' 1947:11 and in his Na rubeže dvukh epokh, 1960, pp. 84–88.


**Polevóy, Borís Nikoláyevich** (pseud. of B. N. Kámpov), prose writer (b. March 17 [March 4], 1908, Moscow—d. July 12, 1981, Moscow). Polevoy's father was a lawyer; his mother, a doctor. Polevoy grew up in Tver after 1913. He began working as a journalist while still at school. After graduating from a technical vocational school, Polevoy worked in the textile industry; following the appearance of his first collection of publicistic prose (in 1927), he became a professional journalist in 1928. His first major prose work, Goryachiy tsekh (1939; The Hot Guild), was received as a contribution to the literature of industrial construction. Polevoy became a member of the Communist Party in 1940. In 1941 he moved to Moscow, becoming a war correspondent for Pravda and a political instructor with the Red Army. Polevoy's story of an unusual war hero, Povest o nastoyashchem cheloveke (1946; Eng. tr., A Story about a Real Man, 1949), became his best-known work; it received a Stalin Prize (for 1946, 2d class) and in 1948 Sergey Prokofyev reworked it into operatic form. Polevoy's war experiences were further reflected in his collection of short prose, My—sovetskiye lyudi (1948; Eng. tr., We Are Soviet People, 1949), for which he received another Stalin Prize (for 1948, 2d class); in the novels Zoloto (1949–50; Gold), Gluboky tyl (1958; Far in the Rear), and Doktor Vera (1966; Doctor Vera); and in the diary excerpts V bolshom nastuplenii (1967; In the Major Offensive) and Do Berlina—896 kilometrov (1973; 896 Kilometers to Berlin). Polevoy also published numerous publicistic articles about his travels, which included trips to the United States and China. Polevoy published his memoirs in the last years of his life: Siluety (1978; Silhouettes), 35 portraits of cultural functionaries, and Samye pamyatnye (1980; Most Memorable), a history of his career as a reporter. From 1946 to 1958 Polevoy was a deputy of the Supreme Soviet of the RSFSR; he belonged to the boards of the Writers Unions of the USSR (from 1954 on) and the RSFSR (from 1958 on); in 1967 he became one of the executive secretaries of the Writers Union of the USSR. He lived in Moscow and was editor in chief of the journal Yunost from 1962 on.

In his highly touted war book, Povest o nastoyashchem cheloveke (2.34 million copies had been printed by 1954), Polevoy wants to create an image of the ideal Soviet hero. As the basis of the work, written in 19 days during the Nuremberg trials, he selects an actual event, the story of a Soviet pilot who was wounded, rescued, had both legs amputated, and then was reassigned. The book is written in the tradition of N. Ostrovsky and makes its point by means of its tendentiousness, not its literary quality. Polevoy's other works are also based on diary entries; he simply reworked these for his travel notes. Historical facts are often incorrect, character sketches inconsistent, and plots contradictory. His didacticism, in terms of the principle of PARTY SPIRIT, remains superficial.

Works: Memuary všivogo čeloveka (publicistic prose), 1927; Gorjačij cekh (pov.), 1940; Povest' o nastojaščem čeloveke (pov.), 1947 (see above); My—sovetskie ljudi (publicistic prose), 1948 (see above); Zoloto (novel), 1950; Sovremenniki (short stories), 1952; Amerikanskie dnevniki (diary), 1956; Glubokij tyl (novel), 1959; Naš Lenin (short stories), 1961; Na dikom brege (novel), 1962; Doktor Vera (novel), 1967; V bol'šom nastuplenii (diary), 1967; Do Berlina—896 kilometrov (diary), 1973; Èti četyre goda (articles), 2 vols., 1974; Siluèty (publicistic prose), 1978; Samye pamjatnye (publicistic prose), 1980.—Izbr. proizv., 2 vols., 1969; Sobr. soč., 9 vols., 1981– (vol. 6 appeared in 1983).
Translations: To the Last Breath, 1945; From a Soviet War Correspondent's Notebook, 1945; From Belgorod to the Carpathians, 1947; Shores of a New Sea: Short Stories, 1954; He Came Back, 1956; "The Girl from Moscow," in The Girl from Moscow and Other Stories, 1966; The Final Reckoning: Nuremberg Diaries, 1978.
Secondary Lit.: B. Galanov, 1957; N. Želtova, in Voprosy sovetskoj lit. 6:1957; A. Alek-

sandrov, in *Zvezda* 1963:8; *RSPP* 3:1964; A. Kondratovič, in *Novyj mir* 1968:8; Ju. Žukov, in *Lit. obozrenie* 1975:3; V. Ozerov, in *Oktjabr'* 1980:2; S. Baruzdin, in *Družba narodov* 1982:10; V. Karpov, in *Oktjabr'* 1982:5.

**Polónskaya, Yelizavéta Grigóryevna** (pseud. of Y. G. Movshensón), poet (b. June 26 [June 14], 1890, Warsaw—d. Jan. 11, 1969, Leningrad). Polonskaya's father was an engineer. Polonskaya graduated from a gymnasium in St. Petersburg in 1907 and went on to study medicine at the Sorbonne in Paris (1907–14). Her first poems date from 1913. In 1915 Polonskaya returned to Russia, where she worked as a doctor, first at the front, later in Petrograd-Leningrad (until 1931). During that time she studied with N. Gumilyov and K. Chukovsky at the Studio for Literature. Her poetry, collected for the first time in *Znamenya* (1921; Banners), bears the stamp of the ACMEISTS. Through the Studio, Polonskaya became the only female member of the SERAPION BROTHERS, a literary group that acknowledged the primacy of art over politics. Meanwhile she turned to translating poetry from English and French; her translations promptly won recognition. Between 1923 and 1933 Polonskaya published 11 small books for children, consisting of poems, fairy tales, and short stories. After 1931, writing became her main career; she traveled for a while through the Soviet Union for *Leningradskaya pravda*, an experience reflected in such works as her collection of feature articles, *Lyudi sovetskikh budney* (1934; Everyday Soviet People). Additional volumes of her poetry came out in 1935, 1937, and 1940. During World War II she once again worked as a doctor. After the war Polonskaya returned to live in Leningrad. She expanded the number of languages from which she translated (Slavic languages and languages spoken in the Caucasus; she translated, for instance, the Armenian epic *David of Sassoon*) and published her memoirs (particularly of M. Zoshchenko) in addition to her own poetry.

Polonskaya's poetry is clear and beautiful. It sounds much like prose, an impression reinforced by the frequent use of enjambment; it abjures emotionalism and makes an impact solely on the basis of its humanity and its profundity of thought. It arises directly out of actual experiences, such as S. Yesenin's death, a mother's wartime farewell to her son, or the removal of street barriers in liberated Leningrad. At times she narrates, at times she reflects; but her statement always carries implications that go beyond the specific. Polonskaya,

who never stooped to propaganda, is seldom published (1960, 1966), certainly less than she deserves, but she is regarded benignly by official critics.

*Works: Znamen'ja* (poems), 1921; *Pod kamennym doždëm* (poems), 1923; *Zajčata* (children's lit.), 1923; *Časy* (children's lit.), 1925; *Uprjamyj kalendar'* (poems), 1929; *Ljudi sovetskikh budnej* (feature articles), 1934; *Goda* (poems), 1935; *Novye stikhi* (poems), 1937; *Vremena mužestva* (poems), 1940; *Kamskaja tetrad'* (poems), 1945 (part of the obviously unpublished manuscript *Poterjanyj i vozvraščennyj dom; Na svoikh plečakh* (poems), 1948; *Stikhotvorenija i poèma* (lyric and narrative poems), 1960; *Izbr.* (selected works), 1966; memoirs, in *Trudy po russkoj i slavjanskoj filologii*, Tartu, 1963:6, in *Prostor* 1964:4, in *Zvezda* 1965:7, and in *Neva* 1966:1.

*Secondary Lit.*: E. Minc, in *Zvezda* 1960:11; A. Anatol'ev, in *Zvezda* 1966:10.

**Pomeróntsev, Vladímir Mikháylovich,** prose writer (b. July 22 [July 9], 1907, Irkutsk—d. March 26, 1971, Moscow). In 1928 Pomerantsev completed his law studies at Irkutsk University. He served as a judge in the Volga region. During World War II he fought as a soldier at the front; subsequently he became an officer assigned to enemy propaganda. In the postwar period Pomerantsev worked for the *Tägliche Rundschau*, a Soviet newspaper published in the Soviet occupation zone of Germany; his first articles appeared there. Pomerantsev's first novel, *Doch bukinista* (1951; The Secondhand Bookseller's Daughter), is set in Germany during this period. His essay *Ob iskrennosti v literature* (1953; On Sincerity in Literature), which, as one of the most important contributions to the THAW, was published by A. Tvardovsky in *Novy mir*, led to a literary scandal. In the essay, Pomerantsev exposed the principal reasons for the decline of Russian literature under Stalin and pointed primarily to the contradiction between personally discovered, objective truth and purported pseudotruth in accord with the principle of PARTY SPIRIT. Pomerantsev's contribution was officially condemned and K. Simonov replaced Tvardovsky at *Novy mir* (*Lit. gazeta* Aug. 17, 1954). After 1957 Pomerantsev appeared regularly in print as the author of novellas, collected in *Neumolimy notarius* (1960; The Implacable Notary) and *Nespeshny razgovor* (1965; A Leisurely Conversation). He lived in Moscow; he was not a delegate to the congresses of the Writers Union of the USSR or the Writers Union of the RSFSR. Pomerantsev, who had already formulated several genuine conflicts of his period (in contrast to the THEORY OF CONFLICTLESSNESS) in *Ob iskrennosti v literature*, writes action-packed, dramatically gripping prose. His subject matter is often taken from the sphere of legal violations; he takes a look at the psychological bases of criminal behavior and affords, as in *Pervy potseluy* (1959; First Kiss), relevant glimpses into everyday Soviet life.

Works: *Doč' bukinista* (novel), 1951; *Ob iskrennosti v literature* (essay), in *Novyj mir* 1953:12; *Zrelost' prišla* (pov.), 1957; *Pervyj poceluj* (pov.), in *Moskva* 1959:6; *Neumolimyj notarius* (short stories), 1960; *Nespešnyj razgovor* (pov. and short stories), 1965; *Čudodei* (pov. and short stories), 1968; *Zrelost' prišla* (pov., short stories, novel), 1976; *Doktor Èske* (novel), 1980.

Secondary Lit.: S. Štut, in *Oktjabr'* 1952:5; L. Skorino, in *Znamja* 1954:2; B. Privalov, in *Lit. i žizn'* Jan. 27, 1961; F. Svetov, in *Voprosy lit.* 1962:12; N. Atarov, in *Lit. gazeta* Sept. 18, 1965; A. Marčenko, in *Lit. gazeta* Sept. 11, 1968, p. 5; A. Ninov, in *Neva* 1976:1.

**Poplávsky, Borís Yuliánovich,** poet (b. June 7 [May 24], 1903, Moscow—d. Oct. 9, 1935, Paris). In 1919 Poplavsky emigrated with his parents via Constantinople to Paris. After 1928, Poplavsky occasionally published poems (barely 60 during his lifetime) in journals, especially in *Volya Rossii* before 1930 and in *Sovremennye zapiski* between 1929 and 1935. Only once did he succeed in finding someone to finance a volume of his selected verse: *Flagi* (1931; Flags). In addition to lyric poems, he also wrote a few fragmentary prose works and literary criticism that appeared in Nikolay Otsup's *Chisla* in 1930–31. Poplavsky's living conditions were extraordinarily difficult; he lived in poverty, often in need. He died of an overdose of heroin, probably more of an accident resulting from his search for mystical ecstasy than a conscious desire for death. Immediately after his death, Poplavsky was described as one of the most significant literary talents in emigration by renowned critics such as D. Merezhkovsky and V. Khodasevich. Shortly afterward two collections appeared: *Snezhny chas* (1936; The Snowy Hour), with poems from 1931 to 1935, and *V venke iz voska* (1938; In a Wreath of Wax). A compilation of the poems discovered after his death followed in 1965. In 1980–81 S. Karlinsky

published a three-volume edition of Poplavsky's works in Berkeley.

Poplavsky's creative work is shaped by Charles Baudelaire, Guillaume Apollinaire, the French surrealists, James Joyce, and, on the Russian side, by A. Blok and M. Lermontov. His early lyric poems have a surrealist quality in which all objects, seasons of the year, and times of day seem animate. The later lyric poems are more mystical, are set on the border between antiquity and Christianity, and remind one of V. Rozanov. They are steeped in religious searching in the spirit of F. Dostoyevsky and exist by form rather than by logic. Images are united in multilayered symbolic significance, and a frequently appearing "you" may be God, a beloved one, or love itself. Many poems arise from a deep loneliness; everything is musical; the protracted reworking of numerous versions cannot be detected in the final form, which almost seems improvised. *Apollon Bezobrazov* (1930–35), his longest prose work, mixes personal confessions with thoughts about poetry and poets; other works are more plot intensive, reflect his experiences in France, and, as lyrical prose, often resemble his poetry.

Works: *Flagi* (poems), Paris, 1931; "Apollon Bezobrazov" (chapter from a novel), in *Čisla*, Paris, 2–3:1930, 5:1931, and *Opyty*, New York, 1, 5, 6, 1953–56; *Snežnyj čas* (poems), Paris, 1936; "Domoj s nebes" (chapter from a novel), in *Krug*, Paris, 1–3:1936–38, and in *Russkaja mysl'*, Paris, Jan. 14, 21, and 28, and Feb. 5, 1982; *V venke iz voska* (poems), Paris, 1938; *Iz dnevnikov, 1928–1935* (diaries), Paris, 1938; *Dirižabl' neizvestnogo napravlenija* (poems), Paris, 1965.—*Sobr. soč.*, 3 vols., 1980–81 (reprints of editions from 1931, 1939, and 1965).

Secondary Lit.: S. Osokin, in *Russkie zapiski* 11:1938; N. Tatiščev, in *Krug* 3:1938, in *Novyj žurnal*, New York, 15:1947, in *Vozrož-denie*, Paris, 165:1965, Paris, 1972, and in *Russkaja mysl'* April 18, 1986, p. 8; V. Khodasevič, in his *Literaturnye stat'i i vospominanija*, New York, 1954; G. Adamovič, in his *Odinočestvo i svoboda*, New York, 1955; S. Karlinsky, in *Slavic Review* 1967:4, in *Triquarterly* 27:1973, and in *The Bitter Air of Exile*, Berkeley, 1973; A. Olcott, in *Triquarterly* 27:1973; Ju. Ivask, in *Russkaja literatura v èmigracii*, ed. N. Poltorackij, Pittsburgh, 1972, and in *Russkaja mysl'* Aug. 28, 1980; N. Berberova, in her *Kursiv moj*, Munich, 1972; E. Rajs, in *Grani*, Frankfurt am Main, 114:1979; M. Menegaldo, in *Revue des Études slaves* 1981:4; R. Thompson, in *Slavic and East Eu-*

*ropean Journal* 1984:3; I. Ždanevič, in *Sintaksis*, Paris, 16:1986.

**Popóv, Vladímir Fyódorovich,** prose writer (b. July 28 [July 15], 1907, Kharkov). Popov worked in various steel mills; in 1938 he completed a correspondence course in metallurgical engineering. During World War II he was evacuated with his factory from the Ukraine to the Urals. Based on his own experiences, Popov's novel *Stal i shlak* (1948; Eng. tr., *Steel and Slag*, 1951) describes the evacuation of a steel operation and the partisan activity of those who remain behind; the work strives to affirm the Party's goals and to stress the beneficent role of its functionaries in overcoming all difficulties and in forming capable and efficient collectives. Stalin himself becomes a symbolic figure: a steel foundryman who fuses the Soviet peoples together. Popov received a Stalin Prize (for 1948, 2d class). In subsequent prose works Popov continued to write about industry, workers, and engineers. In his second novel, *Razorvanny krug* (1966; The Broken Circle), the Party solves a contrived conflict between experienced experts at a Siberian tire factory and backward research workers at an institute. Popov's novel *Tihkaya zavod* (1980; Still Waters), the title of which he took from Teffi, is a historical production novel based on the usual trite pattern and set in the Urals. Popov's works, the weaknesses of which include schematic construction and characterization by means of direct exposition, quite rightly attracted minimal attention. Popov lives in Moscow.

*Works:* Stal' i šlak (novel), 1948 (see above); *Razorvannyj krug* (novel), 1966; *Obretěš' v boju* (novel), 2 vols., 1970; *I èto nazyvaetsja budni . . .* (novel), in *Zvezda* 1973:8–10; *Tikhaja zavod'* (novel), in *Novyj mir* 1980:6–7, separate ed., 1981.—*Sobr. soč.*, 3 vols., 1973–74.

*Secondary Lit.:* A. Tarasenkov, in *Novyj mir* 1949:2; V. Koževnikov, in *Novyj mir* 1949:5; A. Gorlovskij, in *Družba narodov* 1966:8; I. Nen'ko, in *Oktjabr'* 1974:7; T. Gamzaeva, in *Moskva* 1979:3; V. Novikov, in *Lit. gazeta* Nov. 3, 1982, p. 5.

**Popóv, Yevgény Anatólyevich,** prose writer (b. Jan. 5, 1946, Krasnoyarsk). From 1963 to 1968 Popov studied geology in Moscow; in 1972 he applied to both the Gorky Literary Institute and the All-Union Film Institute

(VGIK) but was admitted to neither. From 1968 to 1975 Popov worked as a geologist near Krasnoyarsk and thereafter moved to Moscow. Popov began writing short stories at a young age; the first were published in 1962 in a local newspaper. Between 1970 and 1976 he participated in conferences of young writers; since 1971 his short stories have also occasionally appeared in Moscow publications, including once in *Novy mir* (1976) with a foreword by V. Shukshin. On Oct. 3, 1978, Popov became a member of the Writers Union of the USSR. From 1968 to 1978 Popov submitted five volumes of short stories to various publishers, but not one was accepted for publication. He earns a living by translating and doing odd jobs. Persistent publication difficulties and attempts to make him, as well as other young authors, produce literature in conformity with the Party line preceded Popov's participation in the almanac METROPOL (1979) as copublisher and author of 13 short stories. The consequence for him was a complete ban on publishing his works and expulsion from the Writers Union of the USSR (on May 16, 1979) as well as from the Litfond (Dec. 1980). In Moscow in May 1980, Popov joined the unofficial Club of Belletrists whose publication *Katalog*, like *Metropol*, appeared in TAMIZDAT. In 1986 he was once again able to publish a short story in the journal *Yunost*. Popov lives in Moscow.

By 1980 Popov had written more than 200 short stories, 10 short dramas, and 2 plays of several acts. In his short stories he depicts people in the reality of Soviet life; his attention is drawn toward those whose external living conditions are difficult. Rather than an unusual situation in a cleverly constructed plot, what makes his short stories distinctive is the examination of daily life and the disclosure of human depth in the commonplace. He depicts the Russian who is prepared to endure the unchanging, dehumanizing state of affairs. "About frightful things he speaks casually and even monotonously" (V. Iverni). In his short stories Popov reveals a refreshing breadth, in the characters and their fates he chooses to depict as well as in his representational style, which ranges from staid realism through tragicomic irony to a point of view diffracted through interpolated narrators.

*Works:* Short stories, in *Sibirskie ogni* 1971:5; in *Lit. gazeta* 1972:42, 1973:33; in *Lit. Rossija* 1974:29, 1975:7, 1976:4; in *Družba narodov* 1977:3 *Čërtova djužina rasskazov* (short story), in *Metropol'* 1979; *Veselie Rusi* (short stories),

Ann Arbor, 1981; six short stories, in Katalog, Ann Arbor, 1982; Tikhij Evstaf'ev i gomo futurum (short story), in Junost' 1986:11. Secondary Lit.: G. Semënov, in Avrora 1974:2; V. Šukšin, in Novyj mir 1976:4; V. Osockij, in Lit. obozrenie 1976:10; V. Bondarenko, in Lit. Rossija Aug. 18, 1976; W. Kasack, in Osteuropa 1980:11; N. Gorbanevskaja, in Russkaja mysl', Paris, Nov. 5, 1981; autobiography and bibliography, in Katalog, Ann Arbor, 1982; V. Iverni, in Russkaya mysl' Feb. 10, 1983; G. Hosking, in Index on Censorship, Nov. 1983.

**Póvest** (story, tale), Russian genre term for a prose form that differs from the short story (rasskaz) through its greater length and from the novel (roman) through its generally more epically additive structure. Povest is sometimes translated as short story, at other times as short novel or novel, and even occasionally as novella. These terms may be applicable in individual cases, although novella may be defended in only exceptional atypical cases because povest corresponds to a nonhypotactic narrative and does not exhibit a dramatic structure but rather a greater independence of its parts. Just as the term povest in ancient Russian literature is used to designate a chronicling of events, that is, an originally oral epic narration, so its basis in the literature of the 19th and 20th centuries is a paratactic, episodically rich narrative with a single plot line. The term is frequently applied to prose that seems too long for a short story and too short for a novel; in such cases the translation short novel may be applicable, since the term novel is not limited to longer prose works with multiple plot lines and the degree of independence of the parts varies. On the other hand, the essentially epically additive character of the povest can lead to its becoming quite lengthy (for example, the six-volume Povest o zhizni [The Story of a Life] by K. Paustovsky). Much Russian prose is variously described as both povest and novel in Russian secondary literature; I. Turgenev, for example, called his novel Dvoryanskoye gnezdo (A Nest of Gentlefolk) a povest as well as a novel. In this dictionary the term remains untranslated.

**Pravdúkhin, Valerián Pávlovich,** prose writer and critic (b. Feb. 2 [Jan. 21], 1892, Tanalykskaya, prov. Orenburg—d. July 15, 1939 [?], while imprisoned). After Pravdukhin graduated from a gymnasium with a certificate al-

lowing him to teach in rural schools, he went to Moscow; there he studied in the Department of History and Philology at the Shanyavsky People's University from 1914 to 1917. After the Revolution he and his wife, L. Seyfullina, worked together in Chelyabinsk in the field of public education. In Novosibirsk in 1921 he was one of the founders and editors of the journal Sibirskiye ogni, in which he published some of his own literary criticism between 1922 and 1925, including Literatura o revolyutsii i revolyutsionnaya literatura (1923; Literature about Revolution and Revolutionary Literature), a discussion of I. Erenburg, B. Pilnyak, A. Malyshkin, and other writers. In 1923 Pravdukhin moved to Moscow and worked as a critic for Krasnaya nov and Krasnaya niva, where he headed the criticism section. Because he was associated with A. Voronsky and because in the interest of depicting genuine human experience he condemned the "pseudoclassicism of modern poetic art" and its hollow zeal concerning the class struggle (as well as because of his earlier membership in the Socialist Revolutionary Party), Pravdukhin was attacked by the VAPP critics (such as I. Vardin) in 1924. That same year saw the final appearance of a book of his literary criticism, Literaturnaya sovremennost (1924; The Literary Present). Pravdukhin wrote several dramas in collaboration with L. Seyfullina, including Virineya (1924) and Chorny yar (1931; The Black Ravine) After 1926 he published stories about hunting and traveling. After he was branded as a Trotskyite, the last work Pravdukhin was able to publish was a novel based on the history of the Ural Cossacks, Yaik ukhodit v more (1936; The Yaik Flows to the Sea). It exhibits Pravdukhin's ability to write vivid folkloric descriptions in the tradition of early Gogol. Pravdukhin, who stood up in support of M. Bulgakov, became a victim of the government purges sometime around 1937. He won REHABILITATION after 1956, but he and his work are very seldom mentioned in the Soviet literary press.

Works: Literatura o revoljucii i revoljucionnaja literatura, (essay), in Sibirskie ogni 1923:1–2; Tvorec. Obščestvo. Iskusstvo (essays), 1923; Literaturnaja sovremennost' 1920–24 (essays), 1924; Virineja (play), 1925, written in collaboration with L. Sejfullina; Po izlučinam Urala (short stories), 1929; Gody, tropy, ruž'ë (short stories), 1930, 2d ed., 1968; Čërnyj jar (play), 1931, written in collaboration with L. Sejfullina; Okhotnič'ja junost' (short stories), 1933; V stepi i gornoj tajge (children's stories), 1933; *Jaik ukhodit v more* (novel), in *Krasnaja nov'* 1936:2–4, separate ed., 1937, 2d ed., 1968.

*Secondary Lit.:* I. Vardin (1924), in *Dokumente zur sowjet. Lit. Politik*, ed. K. Eimermacher, Stuttgart, 1972; L. Sejfullina, in her *O literature*, 1958; E. Permitin, in his *Okhotnič'e serdce*, 1962; A. Šmakov, in his *Naše lit. včera*, 1962; A. Karpov, in *Lit. Rossija* March 17, 1967, p. 18, and in *Prostor* 1968:12.

**Prilezháyeva, Maríya Pávlovna,** prose writer (b. June 22 [June 9], 1903, Yaroslavl). Prilezhayeva completed her studies at the Faculty of Pedagogy of Moscow University in 1929, then worked as a teacher and educator in children's homes. In 1937 she began her literary career with the intention of contributing in this manner to the Communist education of youth. She was admitted to the Communist Party in 1952. Prilezhayeva lives in Moscow; she has been a member of the board of the Writers Union of the USSR since 1967.

In her prose, Prilezhayeva attempts to realize the principles of SOCIALIST REALISM; in particular, she focuses on education in accordance with the Party line and the depiction of positive heroes. Her work is structured according to a preconceived model based on a primitive and unrealistic view of life from the end of the previous century to the present; it is diffuse in its triviality and its conflicts are contrived. Her choice of acknowledged giants of the Party (Lenin, Krupskaya, Kalinin) as her subject matter and her development of a reliable writing pattern assure Prilezhayeva of minor successes such as *Udivitelny god* (1966; Eng. tr., *A Remarkable Year*, 1980), the winner of a 1966 competition for the best book about Lenin for young readers, or *Zhizn Lenina* (1970; *Life of Lenin*), which received the Krupskaya Prize in 1971. In *Zelyonaya vetka maja* 1978; The Green Branch of May), Prilezhayeva uses autobiographical materials to describe the October Revolution.

*Works: Junost' Maši Strogovoj* (pov.), 1948; *S toboj tovarišči* (pov.), 1949; *S beregov Medvedicy* (pov.), 1956; *Puškinskij val's* (pov.), 1961; *Udivitel'nyj god* (pov.), 1966 (see above); *Žizn' Lenina* (biography), 1970; *Zelënaja vetka maja. Tret'ja Varja* (pov.), 1978.—*Sobr. soč.*, 3 vols., 1973–75.

*Secondary Lit.:* B. Galanov, in *Novyj mir* 1948:10; S. Narovčatov, in *Novyj mir* 1957:11; V. Osipov, in *Molodaja gvardija* 1967:4; S. Mikhalkov, in *Komsomol'skaja pravda* Feb.

7, 1967; A. Aleksin, in *Lit. gazeta* Sept. 3, 1975, p. 5; Vl. Razumnevič, in *Novyj mir* 1976:2.

**Príshvin, Mikhaíl Mikháylovich,** prose writer (b. Feb. 4 [Jan. 23], 1873, Khrushchovo, Yelets region, prov. Oryol—d. Jan. 16, 1954, Moscow). Prishvin's father was a merchant. Prishvin grew up in the countryside, attended school in Yelets and Tyumen (Siberia) until 1893, studied at the technical institute in Riga, and then went on to study agronomy at Leipzig University; in 1902 he received his degree as a soil science engineer, then worked as an agronomist in Russia until 1905. In 1905 he traveled to Karelia, an experience that was reflected in the semiscientific, semiliterary publication *V krayu nepuganykh ptits* (1907; In the Land of Unfrightened Birds). Prishvin subsequently traveled to northern Russia and Norway (1907), to the settlements of the Old Believers in the Volga region (1908), and to Central Asia. From 1908 to 1912 he was associated with the literary circles around A. Remizov and D. Merezhkovsky in St. Petersburg. After the Revolution, which Prishvin opposed, he lived mostly in rural areas and described his hunting and nature experiences in short prose. Prishvin enjoyed a reputation that was established, if somewhat diminished because of his nonpolitical attitude, especially as a children's writer, despite several attacks during the RAPP period. His povest *Zhen-shen* (1933; Eng. tr., *Jen Sheng: The Root of Life*, 1936) was inspired by his trip to the Urals and the Soviet Far East in 1931. Prishvin continued to write until his death at an advanced age.

K. Paustovsky correctly characterized Prishvin as the "bard of Russian nature." His work is devoted almost exclusively to the depiction of personal experiences in the primeval Russian countryside. His first books combine factual information and personal experience with the replication of folk poetry and dialect-colored folk speech. Prishvin achieves the highest degree of synthesis "between travelogue and legendlike tone" (Lampl), between the temporal and the timeless, the real and the symbolic, in his povest *U sten grada nevidimogo* (1909; At the Walls of the Invisible City) as well as in his novella *Chorny arab* (1910; Eng. tr., in *The Black Arab and Other Stories*, 1947), which he enhances by the use of the doppelgänger motif. His autobiographical novel *Kashcheyeva tsep* (1923–54; Kashchey's Chain), *Zhen-shen*, the "prose poems" in *Fatseliya* (1940), and his many publications from the Soviet period are more realistically and episodically composed, non-fictional, and often of great verbal beauty in their depiction of nature. "The significant detail, the significant part synecdochically represents the whole; microcosmic phenomena express and define the macrocosmic whole" (Parrot).

*Works: V kraju nepuganykh ptic* (travel sketches), 1907; *Za volšebnym kolobkom* (travel sketches), 1908; *U sten grada nevidimogo* (pov.), 1909; *Čërnyj arab* (short stories), 1923 (see above); *Kaščeeva cep'* (novel), 1927, enl. ed., 1960; *Žen-šen* (pov.), first published under the title *Koren' žizni*, in *Krasnaja nov'* 1933:3 (see above); *Facelija*, in *Novyj mir* 1940:9; *Kladovaja solnca* (short stories), 1946 (Eng. trs., *Treasure Trove of the Sun*, 1952; *The Sun's Storehouse*, 1956); *Korabel'naja čašča* (pov.), 1955 (Eng. tr., *Shiptimber Grove*, 1957); *Osudareva doroga* (novel), 1958; *Skazka o pravde*, 1973; *Iz dnevnika 1947–48*, in *Sever* 1982:8.—*Sobr. soč.*, 3 vols., 1912–14; 7 vols., 1927–30; 6 vols., 1929–31; 4 vols., 1935–39; 6 vols., 1956–57; 8 vols., 1983– (vol. 6 appeared in 1983); *Izbr. proizv.*, 2 vols., 1972; *Izbr.*, 1979.

*Translations: The Lake and the Woods; or Nature's Calendar*, 1952; *Nature's Diary*, 1958.

*Secondary Lit.:* T. Khmel'nickaja, 1959; *RSPP* 3:1964; I. Motjašov, 1965; H. Lampl, Diss., Vienna, 1967; M. F. Pakhomova, 1970; G. Eršov, 1973; G. Goryšin, in *Avrora* 1973:2; D. Hannaway, Diss., Syracuse Univ., 1975; R. J. Parrot, in *Slavic Review* 1977:3 and in *Russian Language Journal* 109:1977; *Prišvin i sovremennost'*, 1978; P. Vykhodcev, in *Russkaja lit.* 1980:1 and 1984:4; L. Golovanov, in *Moskva* 1984:8.

**Prísmanova, Ánna Semyónovna,** poet (b. 1898—d. Nov. 5, 1960, Paris [?]). Prismanova belongs to the second generation of the first wave of EMIGRATION and must have come to Paris in the mid-1920s. The poems in her first volume, *Ten i telo* (1937; Shadows and Body), were written from 1929 to 1936; the first is a poem on the death of B. Poplavsky (1935); two others are dedicated to her husband, A. Ginger. Both remained in Paris under German occupation. In 1946 they were among the Russian émigrés who accepted Soviet passports with patriotic hopefulness. In the early postwar years, Prismanova published the collections *Bliznetsy* (1946; Twins) and *Sol* (1949; Salt). In the year of her death came *Vera*

(1960; Vera Figner), a historical, lyrical narrative poem. Her literary estate was donated to the Soviet authorities.

Prismanova's poems always convey the quality of searching. In the spiritual realm it is a search for the genuine, the true; in the human sphere, for oneself; in the linguistic, for the proper form. The tension resulting from this search finds expression in unusual images, in provocative expressions, in introspection and self-irony. Her themes concern personal and interpersonal events, which she often presents in a narrative style, though in a setting that is outside the realm of daily life. For her last book, *Vera*, she depicted a heroine of the Revolution of 1905, whom she dislikes, as a means of self-discovery.

*Works: Ten' i telo* (poems), Paris, 1937; *Bliznecy* (poems), Paris, 1946; *Sol'* (poems), Paris, 1949; *Vera* (narrative poem), Paris, 1960; *O gorode i ogorode* (short story), in *Mosty*, Munich, 12;1966.

*Secondary Lit.:* V. Vejdle, in *Sovremennye zapiski*, Paris, 63:1937; A. Gorskaja, in *Vozroždenie*, Paris, 108:1960; E. Tauber, in *Novyj žurnal*, New York, 64:1961.

**Pristávkin, Anatóly Ignátyevich,** prose writer (b. Oct. 17, 1931, Lyubertsy, oblast Moscow). A war orphan, Pristavkin grew up in children's homes; in 1954 he began his work as a writer. While studying at the Gorky Literary Institute, from which he graduated in 1959, he worked for a while as a construction worker on the Bratsk High Dam. This experience had a great impact on much of his later literary work, which is devoted to the task of opening up Siberia. From 1963 to 1966, Pristavkin belonged to the editorial staff of the journal *Molodaya gvardiya*; in 1965 he joined the Communist Party of the Soviet Union. For the book *Na Angare* (1975; On the Angara), a "work about the heroic accomplishments through labor of our contemporaries," he was awarded the annual prize of the Writers Union of the USSR in 1978. In addition to documentary prose about Siberia, which Pristavkin has continued to write in *Angara-reka* (1977; The Angara River) and *Angara* (1981), Pristavkin writes lyrical, autobiographical prose about his intimate relationship to the land in central Russia, such as *Seliger Seligerovich* (1964) or *Vozdelay pole svoye* (1981; Till Your Field). In a different vein is the povest *Soldat i malchik* (1977; The Soldier and the Youth), in which he recounts a central ethical experience from his childhood in an orphanage.

Pristavkin's greatest contribution to Russian literature is probably *Gorodok* (1983; The Little City), a novel about Siberia completed in the mid-1970s that remained unpublished for a long time because of its genuine insights into labor discipline and the black market in construction that contradicted socialist propaganda. Pristavkin lives in Moscow.

Pristavkin writes documentary prose based on his own experiences and observations. His works about Siberia date from his frequent trips to Bratsk; they penetrate interpersonal relationships depicted in individual situations but do not transform them into fictional events. *Gorodok* recounts the activities of workers who are building their own private homes next to the state-run construction site and who develop their own self-administered community. The workers are very fond of this well-run community built from materials obtained on the black market (actual title: Vorgorodok [The Stolen City]), but the homes were not provided for in the plan and must be torn down. In *Soldat i malchik*, orphans rob a sleeping soldier, yet one of the boys, plagued by his conscience, feels obliged to restore the soldier's possessions, in spite of being persecuted by the other children. Although not poetically inspired, Pristavkin's prose is interesting for its ethical point of view, and parts are factually and sociologically revealing.

*Works:* Malen'kie rasskazy (short stories), 1959; Moi sovremenniki (pov.), 1959; Seliger Seligerovič (pov.), 1965; Golubka (novel), in Znamja 1967:3–6; Na Angare, 1975; Soldat i mal'čik (pov.), 1977; Angara-reka, 1977; Angara, 1981; Vozdelaj pole svoe (pov. and short stories), 1981; Bol'šaja Angara (pov.), in Znamja 1981:1–2; Gorodok (novel), in Novyj mir 1983:1–2; Nočevala tučka zolotaja (pov.), in Znamja 1987:3–4.

*Secondary Lit.:* A. Klitko, in Naš sovremennik 1965:3; A. Bučis, in Družba narodov 1969:2; E. Moroz, in Lit. obozrenie 1975:12; V. Il'in, in Znamja 1978:7; I. Duèl', in Znamja 1982:4 and in Družba narodov, 1985:1; R. Sagabaljan, in Lit. Rossija April 29, 1983, p. 14; L. Korobkov, in Lit. obozrenie 1983:12.

**Prize of the Leninist Komsomol.** See LITERARY PRIZES.

**Prokhánov, Aleksándr Andréyevich,** prose writer (b. Feb. 26, 1938, Tiflis). Prokhanov graduated from the aeronautics institute in

1960. Since 1967 he has published journalistic prose. From 1982 to 1985 he published four novels with the political purpose of propagandizing, in accordance with the Party line, the Soviet policy of enlarging the sphere of influence of communism in strategic areas around the world. In 1985 he attained an influential position in the hierarchy as a member of the secretariat of the board of the Writers Union of the RSFSR. He lives in Moscow.

With *Derevo v tsentre Kabula* (1982; A Tree in the Center of Kabul), Prokhanov wrote the first Soviet novel about Afghanistan; it falsely portrays the USSR's aggression as fraternal assistance and degradingly describes the Afghans as underdeveloped people incapable of running their own lives. *V ostrovakh okhotnik . . .* (1983; On the Islands, a Hunter . . . ) is set in Cambodia; *Afrikanist* (1984; The Africanist), in Mozambique; and *I vot prikhodit veter* (1984; And a Gale Blows Up), in Nicaragua. His trivial, fulsome, shamelessly untruthful descriptive style, with an oversupply of cheap, colorful epithets and pathos-laden adverbs, links these potboilers of SOCIALIST REALISM, which cannot portray what is desired as though it were reality. Prokhanov appeals primarily to the tear ducts and to Russian national pride. The publication of such conscious falsification and agitation contradicts every move toward international understanding.

*Works:* Neopalimyj cvet (documentary essays), 1972; Derevo v centre Kabula (novel), in Oktjabr' 1982:1, separate ed., 1982; V ostrovakh okhotnik . . . (pov.), in Novyj mir 1983:5; Afrikanist (novel), in Znamja 1984:3–4; I vot prikhodit veter (novel), in Znamja 1984:9–10; Seryj soldat (short story), in Znamja 1985:2; Risunki Batalista (novel), in Moskva 1986:9–10.

*Secondary Lit.:* I. Grinberg, in Moskva 1970:2; H. von Ssachno, in Süddeutsche Zeitung March 20, 1982, and May 11–12, 1985; M. Geller, in Obozrenie, Paris, 6:1983; V. Ganičev, in Družba narodov 1985:1; G. Viren, in Oktjabr' 1985:4; A. Barkhatov, in Lit. Rossija Aug. 1, 1986, pp. 8–9.

**Prokófyev, Aleksándr Andréyevich,** poet (b. Dec. 2 [Nov. 19], 1900, Kobona, on Lake Ladoga—d. Sept. 18, 1971, Leningrad). Prokofyev's father was a fisherman. Prokofyev became a Communist Party member in 1919. He served in the Red Army during the Civil War. His first volumes of verse, such as *Polden* (1931; Noon) and *Pobeda* (1932; Victory), contain grandiloquent hymns to the proletarian revolution and combine Communist self-assertiveness with robust motifs from the Lake Ladoga region. In subsequent collections, such as *Doroga cherez most* (1933; The Way across the Bridge), Prokofyev switches more to writing poems, conforming in vocabulary and syntax to folk poetry, about his native region. Several of his poems were set to music. During the Finnish-Russian War and World War II (in Leningrad) Prokofyev worked for the army press and wrote hymnic poems about the invincible army. The lengthiest work of this kind, *Rossiya* (1944; Russia), was awarded a Stalin Prize (for 1943–44, 2d class). From 1945 to 1948 and again from 1955 to 1965, Prokofyev was managing secretary of the Leningrad chapter of the Writers Union of the USSR. In 1961 he received the Lenin Prize for *Priglasheniye k puteshestviyu* (1960; Invitation to Travel), one of the collections that he published on a yearly basis. As a member of the secretariats of the Writers Union of the USSR from 1954 on and of the Writers Union of the RSFSR from 1958 on, Prokofyev was among those Soviet writers who frequently traveled abroad; this travel is reflected in volumes such as *Stikhi s dorogi* (1963; On the Road: Poems).

Prokofyev prefers to base his poems on self-confident, generally patriotic, strongly emphatic declamation rather than on a concrete event. His poems incorporate the classic style of G. Derzhavin's odes; they have but one level of meaning, often employ grammatical rhyme, and are concerned not with compact utterance but with the accumulation of epithets and striking expressions.

*Works: Polden'* (poems), 1931; *Ulica Krasnykh Zor'* (poems), 1931; *Pobeda* (poems), 1931; *Doroga čerez most* (poems), 1933; *Vremennik* (poems), 1934; *Stikhotvorenija* (poems), 1938; *Rossija* (narrative poem), 1944; *Stikhotvorenija* (poems), 1947; *Zareč'e* (poems), 1955; *Priznanija* (poems), 1956; *Priglašenie k putešestviju* (poems), 1960; *Stikhi s dorogi* (poems), 1963; *Grozd'ja* (poems), 1967; *Bessmertie* (poems), 1970; *Stikhotvorenija i poèmy* (lyric and narrative poems), 1976.—*Sobr. soč.*, 2 vols., 1961; 4 vols., 1965–66; 4 vols., 1978–80; *Izbr.*, 2 vols., 1972; *Sobr. soč.*, 4 vols., 1978–80.

*Secondary Lit.:* V. Bakhtin, 2d ed., 1963, and in *Den' poèzii*, Leningrad, 1973; I. Grinberg and E. Dobin, 1966; S. Baruzdin, in *Neva* 1975:6; V. Dement'ev, in *Naš sovremennik* 1978:6; V. Bazanov, in *Russkaja lit.* 1979:4; A. Nesterov, in *Moskva* 1984:10; D. Moldav-

skij, 1985; I. Vinokurova, in *Oktjabr'* 1985:11; B. Kežun, in *Zvezda* 1986:1.

**Proletkúlt** (Proletarskiye kulturno-prosvetitelskiye organizatsii [proletarian cultural and educational organizations]), proletarian cultural organizations that came into being in February 1917 and were merged into the All-Russian Proletkult at the first conference organized by A. Lunacharsky, the People's Commissar for Education in the Kerensky government. Using G. Plekhanov's concept of "class culture," the Proletkult theoreticians such as A. Bogdanov sought to promote, as the superstructure over the industrial base, the formation of a proletarian culture whose representatives were to be the working class led by the industrial proletariat. This cultural development, envisioned as a replacement for bourgeois class culture together with the rejection of the intelligentsia and the peasantry, should occur independently of, but parallel to, political and economic changes. The attitude toward their cultural inheritance was sharply divided. After the October Revolution, the Proletkult quickly developed into a mass organization with 100 centers (studios) (1919), 80,000 apprentices (1920), and about 20 journals, in addition to anthologies of proletarian poetry. Among the most famous Proletkult writers are V. Aleksandrovsky, M. Gerasimov, V. Kazin, V. Kirillov, S. Obradovich, N. Poletayev; they praised world revolution, the glory of work, and the collective in abstract, emotion-laden verses that were eclectic in form. The Communist Party leadership was split in their view of the Proletkult: Lunacharsky held a positive view; Trotsky considered "proletarian culture" out of the question; Lenin sharply rejected the Proletkult. After the Bolshevik faction was unable to win the majority at the First All-Russian Congress of the Proletkult (Oct. 3–12, 1920), the Proletkult was legally attached to the People's Commissariat for Education through a resolution of the Central Committee dated Nov. 10, 1920, and a writ of the Central Committee dated Dec. 1, 1920 (see PARTY RESOLUTIONS ON LITERATURE). Autonomy was proper before the October Revolution; now all cultural work must be under the direction of the Communist Party. The above-mentioned writers withdrew in February 1920 and formed the independent organizations KUZNITSA (Moscow) and KOSMIST (Petrograd). The Proletkult gradually faded away; formally the last studios were disbanded only by the Party Resolution of 1932. With the formation of the literary association OKTYABR (1922), which was composed solely of Party members, the term proletarian experienced a progressive modification; working-class origin was replaced by a Party-line-oriented consciousness. The leadership of the associations of "proletarian" writers (VAPP) was transferred into the hands of representatives of the intelligentsia. The "dictatorship of the proletariat" behaved with increasing antagonism toward supporters of the Proletkult; for two decades following 1937, their names could not be found in Soviet literature; Gerasimov, Kirillov, and others became victims of government repression. The Proletkult's literary significance is minimal.

Works: Proletarskie poèty pervykh let sovetskoj èpochi, 1959.
Secondary Lit.: Lit. manifesty, 2d ed., 1929 (reprinted, Munich, 1969); V. Khodasevič, in his Literaturnye stat'i i vospominanija, New York, 1954; K.-D. Seemann, in Jahrbücher für Geschichte Osteuropas 1961:2; H. Ermolaev, Soviet Literary Theories 1917–1934, Berkeley, 1963 (reprinted, New York, 1977); L. Denisova, in Voprosy filosofii 1964:4; Proletar. Kulturrevolution in Sowjetrussland, Munich, 1969; Dokumente zur sowjetischen Literaturpolitik 1917–1932, ed. K. Eimermacher, Stuttgart, 1972; P. Hübner, in Kulturpolitik der Sowjetunion, Stuttgart, 1973; H. Günther, in Aesthetik und Kommunikation 12:1973; P. Gorsen, E. Knödler-Bunte, Proletkult, 2 vols., Stuttgart–Bad Cannstatt, 1974–75; B. Dejdar, in Československá rusistika 24:1979; G. Gorzka, Diss., Marburg, 1979.

**Proskúrin, Pyotr Lukích,** prose writer (b. Jan. 22, 1928, Kositsy, oblast Bryansk). Proskurin was of peasant descent. He grew up in his native village, which was occupied by German troops between 1941 and 1943. He worked on the kolkhoz until 1950. After completing military service (1950–53), Proskurin remained in the Soviet Far East, where he worked as a lumberjack and raftsman and began his literary career. He lived in Khabarovsk (1957–62), in Moscow (1962–64; there he took continuing education courses at the Gorky Literary Institute), and in Oryol (1964–68). Since 1968 he has lived in Moscow. Proskurin has published major prose works regularly since 1960. In 1969 he took part in the attack on

Novy mir (see Novy mir 1969:7); in 1970 he joined the editorial staff of the journal Molodaya gvardiya. Since that time he has participated in the congresses of the Writers Unions of the RSFSR and USSR and is a member of the board of both organizations. In 1974 he received the State Prize of the USSR.

Proskurin's writing career began with descriptions of life under German occupation and partisan activity (the novels Glubokiye rany [1960; Deep Wounds] and Iskhod [1966; The Exodus]) and depictions of postwar village life (Gorkiye travy [1964; Bitter Grasses]). His Kamen serdolik (1968; Cornelian) deals, in a psychologically consistent manner, with the fate of an artist who cannot find his niche in life. With Sudba (1972; Fate) and Imya tvoyo (1977; Thy Name), Proskurin has written an extensive, monumental work encompassing several decades of Soviet history (part 1: 1929–44; part 2: to the present); it describes village life and space flights, fictionally depicts characters from all social classes, and presents Stalin himself: it spans the unusually wide range between social criticism and the assertion of Russian might. In his work Proskurin not only makes his own experiences conform to a conventional picture of Soviet history but also emphasizes the leadership's responsibility and the role of the Party. His writing style is diffuse, revealing no particular interest in form.

Works: Glubokie rany (novel), 1960; Korni obnažajutsja v burju (novel), 1962; Gor'kie travy (novel), 1964; Iskhod (novel), 1967; Kamen' serdolik (novel), 1968; Čerta (pov. and short stories), 1972; Sud'ba (novel), 1973; Imja tvoë (novel), 1978; Slovom ne ubij. Glavy iz avtobiograf. knigi (memoirs), in Naš sovremennik 1983:6; Čërnye pticy (pov.), in Roman-gazeta 1983:1; Porog ljubvi. Povest' vstreč i dorog (pov.), in Moskva 1985:3–4; Poludennye sny (pov.), 1985.—Izbr. proizv., 2 vols., 1976; Sobr. soč., 5 vols., 1981–83.
Secondary Lit.: V. Šisov, in Moskva 1967:3; M. Kolesnikova, in Znamja 1969:3; RSPP 7(2):1972; D. Dyčko, in Zvezda 1973:9; F. Kuznecov, in Lit. obozrenie 1977:12; V. Tarsis, in ZeitBild March 12, 1980 and April 9, 1980; A. Ovčarenko, in Naš sovremennik 1983:2; V. Calmaev, 1983, and Lit. gazeta July 18, 1984; A. Lanščikov, in Lit. gazeta June 12, 1985, p. 5.

# R

Radzínsky, Edvárd Stanislávovich, playwright (b. Sept. 23, 1936, Moscow). In 1959 Radzinsky graduated from the Moscow Institute for Historian-Archivists. Radzinsky, whose father—Stanislav Adolfovich Radzinsky—was also a playwright and a member of the Writers Union, was allowed to stage his first play, Mechta moya . . . Indiya (My Dream . . . India), at the Moscow Youth Theater in 1960. It remained unpublished, as did his following play, Vam 22, stariki (1962; You Are 22, You Old Ones). Radzinsky became famous for 104 stranitsy pro lyubov (1964; 104 Pages about Love), a frequently performed (3,106 times in 103 theaters in the Soviet Union in 1965) and keenly controversial play that was staged in Leningrad under the title Yeshcho raz pro lyubov (Once Again about Love). It was published in 1974, his first drama in book form. Equally controversial because of their depiction of the artist's conflict with society were his two following plays: Snimayetsya kino . . . (1966; A Film Is Shot . . . ) and Obolstitel Kolobashkin (1968; The Seducer Kolobashkin), which tended toward the fantastic. In the following years, Radzinsky turned increasingly toward film and wrote screenplays. The play Monolog o brake (Monologue about Marriage) was staged in Leningrad in 1973; Besedy s Sokratom (Conversations with Socrates), a play completed in 1973, was performed in Moscow in 1975. In the play Lunin, ili smert Zhaka, zapisannaya v prisutstvii Khozyaina (1979; Lunin; or, The Death of Jacques, Recorded in the Presence of the Landlord; Eng. tr., I, Mikhail Sergeevich Lunin, 1982), Radzinsky focused on the historically unclarified particulars of the death of a Decembrist and portrayed the problems of imprisoning political opponents through the unusual form of a dramatized report by the murdered man. In the histories of literature written up through 1980, Radzinsky is scarcely mentioned. He lives in Moscow.

Radzinsky writes entertaining plays expressing a serious concern about interpersonal relationships among young people. His plays are typical of the artistic protest against the dramas with answers characteristic of the SOCIALIST REALISM of the Stalin period; they portray people who doubt themselves, they never depict ideal types, and they seldom allow the conclusion to be anticipated. Their structure is perhaps somewhat too loose, but it provides the opportunity for topically critical allusions that through comedy gain audience appeal.

Works: 104 stranicy pro ljubov (play), in Teatr 1964:12, separate ed., 1965; Snimaetsja kino (play), in Teatr 1966:1; Obol'stitel' Kolobaškin (fantastic comedy), in Teatr 1968:1; 104 stranicy pro ljubov'. P'esy (plays), 1974 (contains also Čut'-čut' o ženščine; Snimaetsja kino); Lunin, ili smert' Žaka, zapisannaja v prisutstvii Khozjaina (play), in Teatr 1979:3 (see above); Besedy s Sokratom (plays), 1982 (contains also Obol'stitel' Kolobaškin; Ona v otsutstvii ljubvi i smerti; Prodolženie Don Žuana; Pejzaž s rekoj i krepostnymi stanami; Lunin . . . ); Teatr vremën Nerona i Seneki (play), in Sovremennaja dramaturgija 1982:1; Prijatnaja ženščina s cvetkom i oknami na sever (play), in Teatr 1983:7; Staraja aktrisa na rol' ženy Dostoevskogo (play), in Sovremennaja dramaturgija 1984:1; Sportivnye sceny 1981 goda (play), in Sovremennaja dramaturgija 1986:4.

Secondary Lit.: I. Višnevskaja, in Teatr 1965:2; L. Anninskij, in Teatr 1965:10; N. Abalkin, in Lit. Rossija Nov. 22, 1968, pp. 8–9; E. Kalmanovskij, in Zvezda 1969:1; E. Gorfunkel', in Teatr 1974:1; M. Voronenko, in Teatr 1975:8; A. Demidov, in Teatr 1975:11; N. Paleeva, in Lit. obozrenie 1981:6; A. Štejn, in Teatr 1982:11.

Rafálsky, Sergéy Mílich, prose writer, poet, journalist (b. Sept. 2 [Aug. 19], 1896, Kholonevo, prov. Volhynia—d. Nov. 13, 1981, Paris). Rafalsky's father was a clergyman. Rafalsky completed secondary school in Ostrog in June 1914 and began studying law in St. Petersburg. In the spring of 1917 he transferred to Kiev University, joined the People's Freedom party (Narodnaya svoboda), and fought under General Wrangel against the Bolsheviks. From Poland, where he worked as a teacher in Ostrog, he moved to Prague in 1922. He completed his studies at the faculty of Russian jurisprudence there in December 1924 and worked at the Institute for the Study of Russia until 1927. In Prague he began his lifelong work as a writer and journalist. He was among the organizers of the group "Poets' Cell" (Skit poetov) and published poems in journals such as Volya Rossii, Spolokhi, and Perezvony. His

article *Klass tvorcheskoy mysli* (1922; The
Class of Creative Thoughts) stimulated especially intense controversy. During these years,
Rafalsky was closely identified with the Smenovekhovtsy movement with its hope for
"normalization" in Soviet Russia. In 1925 he
married Tatyana Nikolayevna Ungerman, lived
with her in Ostrog at his father's house from
1927 to 1929, and then moved to Paris where
he finally settled. In Paris he worked in the
silk-painting studio of the poet Dovid Knut.
After World War II he turned more strongly
toward journalistic and literary work. He published poems in *Grani* and his first short story,
*Iskusheniye ottsa Afanasiya* (1956; The
Temptation of Father Afanasy), in *Vozrozhdeniye*. In 1958 he became a permanent contributor to the New York newspaper *Novoye
russkoye slovo*, and in 1967 to the Parisian
newspaper *Russkaya mysl*. He published some
of his articles under pseudonyms ("Rafail,"
"Sergey Raganov," "———Sky"). Three books
appeared only after his death: memoirs edited
by B. Filippov, *Chto bylo i chego ne bylo*
(1984; What Was and What Was Not); a selection of his poems, *Za chertoy* (1983; Beyond
the Border), the publication of which was
supervised by R. Guerra; as well as a volume
of prose, *Nikolin bor* (1984; Nikolin Bor). Each
work makes a valuable contribution to Russian literature.

Rafalsky was well known as a journalist.
His own opinions, which he presented in his
articles, not infrequently touched off discussions. Of lasting significance are his literary
works. In *Iskusheniye ottsa Afanasiya* he depicts the cracking of the Marxist exterior and
the beginning of change in an agent who is
commanded to conduct atheistic subversion
while working as a priest. His concern to
present inner truth rather than the external
documentary truth is well realized through
changes in perspectives. In the short story *Vo
yediny iz subbot* (Once on a Saturday), he
uses the experience of Judas between Good
Friday and Easter Sunday as a means of illustrating the concept of resurrection. The sur-
realistically or parapsychologically explicable
encounter between the resurrected Jesus and
Judas provides the point of departure for deep
spiritual interpretation. Both this work and
Rafalsky's longest short story, *Nikolin bor*—
an attempt to depict life in emigration—benefit from several plot lines that occasionally
break off and are enriched by fantasy. Among
the high points of the plot, which is set partly
in the Soviet Union, is the rescue in approximately 1946 of a naïve individual who is
willing to return. In *Chto bylo i chego ne bylo*,

Rafalsky shares with the reader his last years
in Russia: "We feel the pulse of the epoch
itself, its true, lively life" (B. Filippov). A
consciousness of language and a linguistic
playfulness characterize Rafalsky's work. Bold
is his inclusion of contemporary terminology
in his poetic paraphrase of an ancient text
concerning the extinction of Atlantis, *Posledny vecher* (1966; The Last Evening). Rafalsky's poetry distinguishes itself from Russian
poetry of his time through the frequent use of
free verse; his poetry ranges from political to
religious perceptions.

*Works:* Lyric and narrative poems, in *Grani*,
Frankfurt am Main, 34–35:1957, 37:1958,
41:1959, 43:1959, 44:1959, 48:1960, 60:1966;
in *Novyj žurnal*, New York, 143:1981; *Klass
tvorčeskoj mysli* (article), in the collection *Za
čertoj*, Prague, Nov. 1922 (reprinted in *Novyj
žurnal* 149:1982); *Iskušenie otca Afanasija*
(short story), in *Vozroždenie*, Paris, 59:1956;
*Bolezn' veka* (essays), in *Kontinent*, Paris,
11:1977 (cf. *Kontinent* 15:1978); *Za čertoj*
(poems), Paris, 1983; *Čto bylo i čego ne bylo*
(memoirs), London, 1984; *Nikolin bor* (short
stories), Paris, 1984

*Secondary Lit.:* K. Pomerancev, in *Russkaja
mysl'*, Paris, Dec. 17, 1981, p. 9; V. Rybakov,
in *Russkaja mysl'* April 22, 1982; R. Guerra,
in Rafal'skij's *Za čertoj*, Paris, 1983; E. Rajs,
in Rafal'skij's *Za čertoj*, Paris, 1983; B. Filippov, in Rafal'skij's *Čto bylo i čego ne bylo*,
1984, and in *Novoe russkoe slovo*, New York,
Dec. 15, 1985; V. Blinov, in *Novyj žurnal*
160:1985.

**Rakhmánov, Leoníd Nikoláyevich,** prose
writer and playwright (b. Feb. 28 [Feb. 15],
1908, Kotelnich, prov. Vyatka). From 1926 to
1928 Rakhmanov studied at the Leningrad
Electrotechnical Institute. He began his writing career in the late 1920s with short stories
based on student life. *Bazil* (1933; Basil) depicts the tragic fate of a serf who is an architect of churches in the early 19th century in
St. Petersburg; Rakhmanov describes a long
trip to the north in *Umny malchik* (1934; A
Bright Boy). Rakhmanov made a name for
himself with a play about Lenin, *Bespokoy-
naya starost* (1937; Eng. tr., *Restless Old Age*,
1958), written for the 20th anniversary of the
Revolution; the film version, *Deputat Baltiki*
(1937; Deputy of the Baltic), was popular as
well. In the biologist Polezhayev, who is to a
large extent meant to represent K. A. Temi-
ryazev, Rakhmanov portrays an old scholar
who immediately joins the Bolsheviks. The

play, set in 1916–17, contains lively dialogue, but the plot is insufficiently concentrated. It was revised for a new production in Leningrad in 1970. During World War II, Rakhmanov was temporarily a frontline reporter, an experience reflected in several dramatic and narrative works, the last being the play *Kamen, kinuty v tikhiy prud* (1963; A Stone Cast into a Quiet Pond). After the war Rakhmanov again took up the theme of the scientist and wrote two film scripts about Mikhail Lomonosov. A volume of memoirs, *Lyudi—narod interesny* (1978; People Are an Interesting Folk), praised by V. Kaverin in his review, mentions such well-known authors as O. Forsh, K. Paustovsky, Yu. Tynyanov, M. Zoshchenko, and many others. Rakhmanov lives in Leningrad. He has taken part in the congresses of the Writers Union (with the exception of the 1967 Congress), but holds no offices.

*Works: Bazil'* (pov.), 1933; *Umnyj mal'čik* (pov.), 1934; *Deputat Baltiki* (film script), 1937, in collaboration with D. Del', A. Zarkhi, I. Khejfic, in *Izbrannye scenarii sovetskogo kino* 1:1949; *Bespokojnaja starost'* (play), 1937, in *P'esy sovetskikh pisatelej* 5:1954 (see above); *P'esy i scenarii* (plays and film scripts), 1956; *Kamen', kinutyj v tikhij prud* (play), in *Zvezda* 1963:1; *Očen' raznye povesti*, 1965; *P'esy, povesti, vospominanija*, 1972; *Čët-nečet* (dramatic pov.), in *Teatr* 1974:7; *Ljudi—narod interesnyj* (memoirs), 1978, 2d ed., 1981.

*Secondary Lit.:* O. Grudcova, in *Teatr* 1963:11; A. Bitov, in *Lit. gazeta* July 2, 1966; A. Akimova, in *Znamja* 1966:10; G. Gor, in *Neva* 1968:5; I. Štok, in *Lit. gazeta* June 17, 1970, p. 8; A. Svobodin, in *Teatr* 1970:8; V. Kaverin, in *Lit. gazeta* Sept. 27, 1978, p. 4; A. Makedonov, in *Neva* 1983:2.

**Rakhmánova, Álya**, also **Alexándra** (pseud, of Galína Nikoláyevna), prose writer (b. June 27, 1898, the Urals [Perm?]). Rakhmanova's father was a physician. During the Civil War, Rakhmanova fled to Irkutsk and completed her studies in the humanities there. In 1921 she married Arnulf von Hoyer, a former Austrian prisoner of war, and was expelled from the USSR together with him in 1925. After a difficult struggle for existence, she attained rapid international fame with her first diary, *Studenten, Liebe, Tscheka und Tod* (1931; Students, Love, Cheka, and Death; Eng. tr., *Flight from Terror*, 1933), which described her life from 1916 to 1920. In rapid succession she published two sequels, *Ehen im roten*

*Sturm* (1932; Marriages in the Red Storm) and *Milchfrau in Ottakring* (1933; Milkmaid in Ottakring), and drew upon her childhood diaries (written before 1916) in *Geheimnisse um Tataren und Götzen* (1933; Secrets about Tatars and Idols). None of these nor any of her following books were ever published in Russian. Her husband translated her books from the Russian manuscript and edited them slightly (for example, he changed names). All the translations into the other 21 languages are derived from the German version. In the 1930s Rakhmanova was one of the most frequently read Russian authors; in 1936 she received first prize in a competition for "the best contemporary anti-Bolshevik novel" sponsored by the Académie d'Education et d'Entraide Social in Paris for her novel *Die Fabrik des neuen Menschen* (1935; The Factory of the New Man). After 1937 Rakhmanova wrote nine biographical novels about famous figures in Russian literature and history and five more autobiographical works. In 1945 she fled to Switzerland to evade the Soviet troops; since 1949 she has lived in Ettenhausen in Thurgau.

Rakhmanova writes in a style that is ethically oriented, descriptive, and entertaining, and she is probably the only Russian author to have no works published in Russian. Altogether more than 2 million copies of her books have been issued. Her autobiographical works and diaries transmit, on the one hand, a vivid image of a life filled with suffering during the Revolution, Civil War, and the first phase of emigration, and, on the other, a humanely convincing religious attitude, a positive acceptance of fate that goes beyond concrete events. Her novels about L. Tolstoy, F. Dostoyevsky, A. Pushkin, and I. Turgenev reveal a special understanding for the fate of the women who lived with these authors; some of her other novels are dedicated entirely to women famous in Russian culture, such as the actress and theater director Vera Fyodorovna Komisarzhevskaya and the mathematician Sonya Kovalevskaya. In every case the works are the product of historical study undertaken together with her husband and reveal the historical figures from a sympathic, subjectively feminine point of view.

*Works: Studenten, Liebe, Tscheka und Tod* (diary), Salzburg, 1931 (see above); *Ehen im roten Sturm* (diary), Salzburg, 1932; *Milchfrau in Ottakring* (diary), Salzburg, 1933; these three diaries were compiled and published under the titles *Symphonie des Lebens*, Salzburg, 1935, and *Meine russischen Tagebücher*, Graz—

Vienna–Cologne, 1960; *Geheimnisse um Ta-taren und Götzen* (novel), Salzburg, 1933; *Die Fabrik des neuen Menschen* (novel), Salzburg, 1935; *Tragödie einer Liebe* (novel), Berlin, 1937; *Wera Fedorowna* (novel), Graz, 1939; *Einer von vielen* (biography), 2 vols., Zurich, 1946; *Das Leben eines grossen Sünders* (novel about Dostoyevsky), 2 vols., Zurich, 1947; *Ssonja Kowalewski* (novel), Zurich, 1950; *Jurka erlebt Wien* (diary), Zurich, 1951; *Die Liebe eines Lebens* (novel about Turgenev), Frauenfeld, 1952; *Die falsche Zarin* (novel), Frauenfeld, 1954; *Im Schatten des Zarenhofes* (novel about Pushkin), Frauenfeld, 1957; *Ein kurzer Tag* (biography of Chekhov), Frauenfeld, 1961; *Tiere begleiten mein Leben* (memoirs), Frauenfeld, 1963; *Die Verbannten* (novel), Frauenfeld, 1964; *Tschaikovskij* (biography), 1972.

*Secondary Lit.:* L. J., in *Osteuropa*, Königsberg, 1931:1; E. S., in *Osteuropa* 1932:1; various reviews, in *Der Gral*, Munich, 1931:1, 1932:1, 1933:1, 1935:1; P. Thun-Hohenstein, in *Wort und Wahrheit* 1948:6; R. Herle, in *Die Furche*, Vienna, May 19, 1956, and Oct. 22, 1960; G. Leech-Anspach, in *Der Tagesspiegel*, Berlin, Aug. 19, 1979; W. Kasack, in *Osteuropa*, Stuttgart, 1980:12.

**RAPP** (Rossíyskaya assotsiátsiya proletárskikh pisáteley [Russian Association of Proletarian Writers]), the leading Communist organization of writers in the Soviet Union prior to the Party Resolution of 1932 concerning the formation of the WRITERS UNION of the USSR (see PARTY RESOLUTIONS ON LITERATURE). RAPP was established in 1928 at the First All-Union Congress of Proletarian Writers when VAPP was renamed; for its part, VAPP was removed from the influence of KUZNITSA in 1924 by officials of the OKTYABR group. Within the VOAPP (Vsesoyuznoye obyedineniye assotsiatsiy proleatarskikh pisateley), also founded in 1928, RAPP was the largest and the dominant union. RAPP replaced VAPP as the publisher of the journal *Na literaturnom postu*, which followed in the tradition of the militantly Communist journal published by Oktyabr, *Na postu*, but which replaced the principle of condemning the cultural inheritance with that of "learning from the classics." With the critic L. Averbakh as general secretary and the writers A. Fadeyev, Yu. Libedinsky, and V. Kirshon as the leading officials, RAPP conducted an unrelenting campaign against all other literary associations or movements such as PEREVAL, CONSTRUCTIVISM, LEF, OBERIU, and especially

against the FELLOW TRAVELERS. The Party considered RAPP the standard-bearer (*provodnik*) of its literary policy and, with RAPP's help, strove to attain a standardized ideological orientation in literature. In early 1930 the other groups were virtually dissolved; RAPP's militantly imperative tone increased. For example, the Resolution of May 4, 1931, ordered every proletarian writer "to represent the heroes of the Five-Year Plan" and "to announce their progress in complying with this regulation in two weeks." Within RAPP, power struggles and ideological controversies sharpened whereby the decisive theoretical positions adopted by RAPP did not meet with the approval of the Party leadership. The Party Resolution of April 23, 1932, dissolved RAPP and ordered the establishment of an official and united Writers Union. The leading RAPP officials, Averbakh, Fadeyev, Kirshon, M. Chumandrin, and A. Afinogenov, became members of the Organizing Committee of the Writers Union of the USSR. Soviet historiography's attitude toward RAPP's activities has fluctuated markedly since its dissolution.

*Secondary Lit.: Lit. manifesty*, 2d ed., 1929 (reprinted, Munich, 1969); E. I. Brown, *The Proletarian Episode in Russian Literature*, New York, 1953; H. Ermolaev, *Soviet Literary Theories 1917–1934*, Berkeley, 1963; L. K. Švecova, "Lit. gazeta," in *Očerki istorii russkoj sovetskoj žurnalistiki*, 1968; S. Šešukov, *Neistovye revniteli*, 1970; *Dokumente zur sowjetischen Literaturpolitik 1917–1932*, ed. K. Eimermacher, Stuttgart, 1972; *Kulturpolitik der Sowjetunion*, Stuttgart, 1973.

**Ráskin, Aleksándr Borísovich**, prose writer (b. Oct. 8 [Sept. 25], 1914, Vitebsk—d. Feb. 4, 1971, Moscow). Raskin was first published in 1937; in 1938 he completed his studies at the Gorky Literary Institute. His satirical talent was initially influenced by E. Petrov (in his capacity as editor). Up until 1945 Raskin wrote prose works, such as *Vosklitsatelny znak* (1939; Exclamation Point), and plays in collaboration with M. R. Slobodsky. The first collection of his own parodies and epigrams, *Momentalnye biografii* (1959; Momentary Biographies), brought him recognition for his particular gift. Many of his unpublished epigrams circulated publicly. Raskin was known abroad as well as at home for his series of children's short stories about "Papa" as a small boy: *Kak papa byl malenkim* (1961; Eng. tr., *When Daddy Was a Little Boy*, 1966) and *Kak malenky papa uchilsya v shkole* (1963; How

Little Papa Attended School). Raskin was married to F. Vigdorova and lived in Moscow.

Raskin writes short prose and dramatic scenes that concentrate on a single experience and point to one denouement. Their humor may be found in situations that often move in parallels, as well as in the conclusions. Raskin's satire, limited by censorship, is directed at harmless abuses in Soviet society; his children's stories make their pedagogical impact through their admission of Little Papa's errors and weaknesses. Raskin's parodies and epigrams on contemporary writers, biting and to the point, reveal his brilliant command of the language.

Works: Momental'nye biografii (parodies and epigrams), 1959; Očerki i počerki (satiric commentary and parodies), 1959, 2d ed., 1962; Kak papa byl malen'kim (children's stories), 1961, 2d ed., 1965 (see above); Kak malen'kij papa učilsja v škole (children's stories), 1963; Èto ja? (epigrams; illustrated by Kukryniksy), 1968.

Secondary Lit.: G. Vladimov, in Novyj mir 1960:4; Ju. Mann, in Lit. gazeta March 23, 1961; S. Rassadin, in Novyj mir 1962:4; V. Smirnova, in Znamja 1963:12.

Raspútin, Valentín Grigóryevich, prose writer (b. March 15, 1937, Ust-Úda, oblast Irkutsk). In 1959 Rasputin graduated from the Faculty of History and Philosophy at Irkutsk University and then worked as a journalist in Siberia. His first collection of short stories, Ya zabyl sprosit u Leshki (1961; I Forgot to Ask Leshka), was followed by others in regular succession after 1965. The longer povest published in Nash sovremennik, Posledniy srok (1970; Eng. tr., Borrowed Time, 1981), won Rasputin high regard and gave him a name as one of the best prose writers of his generation, as did his two following novels, Zhivi i pomni (1974; Eng. tr., Live and Remember, 1978) and Proshchaniye s Matyoroy (1976; Eng. tr., Farewell to Matyora, 1979). He lives in Irkutsk and became a member of the board of the Writers Union of the RSFSR in 1975 and a member of the board of the Writers Union of the USSR in 1981. Since 1975 he has been a member of the editorial staff of Nash sovremennik and was awarded the State Prize of the USSR in 1977.

Rasputin belongs to those Russian writers whose special attention focuses on the Russian village, pristine and little damaged by civilization. The essence of his prose is the simple countryman rooted in the earth, with his naturalness, his wisdom about life that is independent of his intellect, and his unspoiled, respectable character. Dengi dlya Marii (1967; Eng. tr., Money for Maria, 1981) analyzes the dissimilarities in human nature and the insignificance of material values as compared to moral values of character, using the issue of one's willingness to help in a financial crisis. In Posledniy srok, four siblings are confronted with the death of their 80-year-old mother, and their characters are exposed in the brief period between her expected and her actual death. In Zhivi i pomni Rasputin chooses the period at the end of World War II and the meeting between a woman and her husband the deserter to portray meticulously and touchingly the psychological aspects of the most serious questions, including self-trial by suicide and complicity through love. Proshchaniye s Matyoroy takes place in Siberia, like all Rasputin's novels, where, using the example of people in a village earmarked for inundation when an artificial reservoir is created, the true values of tradition and religion confront the superficiality and hustle and bustle brought on by civilization. His povest Pozhar (1985) serves more or less as a sequel; its story takes place in a settlement built where the flooded village stood. In his novels, Rasputin joins together episodes from the daily routine of the village and of life, episodes that he joins into an organically unified novel through unusual circumstances. With its predominant concern for the spiritual, Rasputin's prose also offers insight into current and former problems of daily life in the Soviet Union.

Works: Ja zabyl sprosit' u Leški (short stories), 1961; Kraj vozle samogo neba (short stories), 1966; Čelovek s ètogo sveta (short stories), 1967; Den'gi dlja Marii (pov. and short stories), 1968 (see above); Poslednij srok (pov. and short stories), 1970 (see above); Vniz i vverkh po tečeniju (pov.), 1972; Živi i pomni (pov.), 1975 (see above); Proščanie s Materoj (pov.), in Naš sovremennik 1976:10–11, separate ed., 1976 (see above); Povesti, 1980; Vek živi—vek ljubi (short stories), 1982; Požar (pov.), in Naš sovremennik 1985:7.—Izbr. proizv., 2 vols., 1984.

Secondary Lit.: V. Šišov, in Moskva 1967:9; V. Gejdeko, in Moskva 1971:6; Ju. Seleznev, in Molodaja gvardija 1973:10; F. Kuznecov, in Lit. obozrenie 1975:3; A. Bočarov, in Oktjabr' 1975:6; W. Kasack, in Osteuropa 1975:7; V. Baranov, in Lit. obozrenie 1975:12; V. Vasil'ev, in Naš sovremennik 1976:6; O. Salynskij, V. Oskockij, Ju. Seleznev, A. Ovčarenko, E. Starikova, in Voprosy lit. 1977:2; S. Smirnov, in *Lit. Rossija* Oct. 6, 1978, p. 11; V. Iverni, in *Kontinent*, Paris, 15:1978; N. Tenditnik, 1978; I. Corten, in *Russian Language Journal* 114:1979; G. Hosking, in his *Beyond Socialist Realism*, New York, 1980; R.-D. Kluge, in *Die russische Novelle*, Düsseldorf, 1982; C. Link, Diss., Indiana Univ., 1983; I. Dedkov, in *Novyj mir* 1984:7; R. Schäper, Munich, 1985; E. Starikova, in *Novyj mir* 1985:12; D. Gillespie, London, 1986; S. Semëneva, in *Znamja* 1987:2.

**Rayévsky, Geórgy Avdéyevich** (pseud. of G. A. Otsúp), poet (b. Dec. 29, 1897, Tsarskoye Selo—d. Feb. 19, 1963, Stuttgart). Rayevsky's father, Avdey Otsup, was court photographer in St. Petersburg. In contrast to his brother Nikolay Otsup, Rayevsky did not belong to the group TSEKH POETOV after World War I. Rayevsky emigrated to Paris at the beginning of the 1920s; there he joined the group "Perekryostki" established in 1926 (whose members included Yu. Terapiano, V. Smolensky, D. Knut, and Yu. Mandelshtam). After 1928, Rayevsky's poems appeared regularly in such journals as *Sovremennye zapiski* and *Chisla*; he published three books of poetry: *Strofy* (1928; Strophes), with 46 poems written between 1923 and 1927; *Novye stikhotvoreniya* (1946; New Poems), with 77 poems; and *Tretya kniga* (1953; The Third Book), in which 34 poems were collected. He lived in Orly; he died on a trip to Germany.

Rayevsky writes serious contemplative poetry that always allows his fundamentally religious attitude to be felt. It pains him that people squander their brief earthly existence in haste and dissension when God has given them the prerequisites for leading good and highly important lives. It also pains him that he experiences of the horror of war are so quickly repressed. He recalls the wealth of childhood observations, the purity and lightheartedness of children's acceptance of being. Yet despite his distress at the world disfigured by men—a world he can strikingly create through images of nature—he retains the certainty of his knowledge of the bright world of God's design.

*Works:* Strofy (poems), Paris, 1928; Novye stikhotvorenija (poems), Paris, 1946; Tret'ja kniga (poems), Paris, 1953.
*Secondary Lit.:* Ju. Terapiano, in *Novyj kobl'*, Paris, 4:1928; M. Slonim, in *Volja Rossii*, Paris, 7:1928; G. Adamovič, in *Sovremennye zapiski*, Paris, 38:1929; E. Tauber, in *Grani*, Frankfurt am Main, 21:1954; Ju. Ivask, in *Opyy*, New York, 4:1955.

**Rehabilitation** (*reabilitátsiya*), the legal act of annulling a conviction and reinstating previous rights. With writers it is necessary to distinguish between rehabilitation as a citizen by an act of the court and rehabilitation as an artist by an act of the Writers Union. During the THAW, rehabilitation occurred frequently, especially after the 20th Party Congress in 1956 and the Party Resolution "On the Defeat of the Cult of Personality and of Its Consequences" (*Pravda* July 2, 1956). In this Party document it was acknowledged that "serious infractions of Soviet legal norms and massive repressive measures have occurred"; "many honest Communists and non-Party Soviet citizens have suffered who were not guilty." In form, these "repressive measures" range from public insult (for example, being called a Trotskyist, a Cosmopolitan) to a ban on the publication or performance of an author's works, loss of job or apartment, internal exile, imprisonment in a camp, and up to execution. As an example, O. Mandelshtam and A. Voronsky were sentenced to internal exile; they died following a second term of imprisonment. P. Slyotov survived imprisonment in a camp; N. Zabolotsky was held in a camp for several years, then in internal exile, and eventually returned to Moscow; after serving his term of internal exile. N. Korzhavin was not allowed to return to Moscow. The writers discussed in this work who became victims of the purges are. A. Ya. Arosev, I. E. Babel, G. G. Belykh, S. F. Budantsev, A. K. Gastev. M. P. Gerasimov, B. A. Guber, N. St. Gumilyov, I. M. Kasatkin, I. I. Katayev, D. Kharms, V. P. Kin, V. T. Kirillov, V. M. Kirshon, S. A. Klychkov, N. A. Klyuyev, V. V. Knyazev, S. A. Kolbasyev, M. E. Koltsov, B. P. Kornilov, M. P. Loskutov, I. I. Makarov, O. E. Mandelshtam, V. I. Narbut, G. K. Nikiforov, N. M. Oleynikov, P. V. Oreshin, B. A. Pilnyak, V. P. Pravdukhin, V. Ropshin, A. I. Tarasov-Rodionov, S. M. Tretyakov, P. N. Vasilyev, A. Vesyoly, A. I. Vvedensky, B. Ya. Yasensky, N. Zarudin, and V. Ya. Zazubrin.

Imprisonment was always followed by expulsion from the Writers Union in addition to systematic elimination from the literary scene. The works of a persecuted writer were no longer published, his books were removed from libraries, his name was no longer mentioned in secondary literature. The practice in effect at the beginning of the 1920s differs from that followed from the 1930s on in that Gumilyov's poems continued to be published after his execution. A few individuals were rehabilitated even during the Stalin period (A. Afinogenov, O. Berggolts), but generally writers returned neither to their normal life nor to the literary scene after their imprisonment or internal exile. All these measures remained a secret. After Stalin's death, one could occasionally glean some information about rehabilitations through information in *Literaturnaya gazeta* where one could read that a commission for a literary estate had been established; in addition, the KRATKAYA LITERATURNAYA ENTSIKLOPEDIYA (1962–75, up to vol. 8), when discussing these authors, included the remark that an author "was illegally repressed and posthumously rehabilitated." Generally notification of an author's rehabilitation coincided with the first official announcement of his death; rehabilitation could have economic consequences (payment of pensions). Among writers, rehabilitation formed the prerequisite for a return to the literary scene. For many writers who were eliminated from literature without regard for legal or administrative procedures—for example, M. Tsvetayeva, M. Bulgakov, or Yu. Olesha—their return was the result of a decision made by the editor in possession of their manuscripts (probably in consultation with the Central Committee of the Communist Party) and the permission of the censor. The extent of their reappearance varied quite radically. Some writers, such as P. Vasilyev, have been regularly reprinted since their rehabilitation; for others, only a single volume of their selected works was published at the end of the 1950s (for example, I. Babel, M. Gerasimov). Some are only represented by a single facet of their work (for example, for D. Kharms and V. Vvedensky, only their children's stories were published); some only appear in anthologies (for example, N. Oleynikov). After a break of several decades, volumes of the selected works of a number of important authors have been published since 1973, usually once in relatively small print runs aimed primarily at the audience abroad: O. Mandelshtam (1973), I. Severyanin (1975), F. Sologub (1975), Vyacheslav Ivanov (1976), B. Pilnyak (1976), N. Klyuyev (1977 and 1981), M. Voloshin (1977), A. Remizov (1978), S. Klychkov (1985). In 1986 a new wave of such publications began (V. Nabokov, Ye. Zamyatin, N. Gumilyov). None of the works of D. Merezhkovsky and L. Lunts, among others, were reprinted. In the same way, the inclusion of these authors in the secondary literature differs greatly from author to author. While M. Koltsov was given his own chapter in the history of literature published by the Academy of Sciences, Pilnyak was only occasionally mentioned and then disparagingly. Only

seldom, and with decreasing frequency since 1965, is the fact of rehabilitation and of the injustices suffered mentioned in Soviet publications. The third edition of *Bolshaya sovetskaya entsiklopediya* (1970–78) remains silent on both issues for all victims. Among writers who have been expelled from the Writers Union since Stalin's death, or who have withdrawn, such as G. Vladimov, S. Lipkin, and I. Lisnyanskaya, only B. Pasternak has been reaccorded partial literary recognition (as a poet, not as a prose writer) so far as is known. The sentences against I. Brodsky, A. Amalrik, A. Sinyavsky and Yu. Daniel, Yu. Galanskov, and others remain in force. In Soviet publications, these writers have been eliminated from the literary scene, as have all the writers of the second and third emigrations. A certain change can be seen since the end of 1986: for example, S. Lipkin was reinstated in the Writers Union, and short texts by METROPOL authors Ye. Popov and Viktor Yerofeyev were printed.

1. *Legal Documents:* "Ob amnistii: Ukaz ot 27.3.1953g.," in *Sbornik zakonov SSSR 1938–1967*, 1968, pp. 627–28; "O preodolenii kul'ta ličnosti i ego posledstvij: Postanovlenie CK KPSS, 30.6.56," in *Pravda* July 2, 1956; text of a legal decree, in Z. Medvedev, *Desjat' let posle "Odnogo dnja Ivana Denisoviča,"* London, 1973, pp. 38–40.
2. *Secondary Lit.:* S. Štut, in *Novyj mir* 1956:9; A. Makarov, in *Znamja* 1958:4; H. McLean, in *Problems of Communism* 1970:3–4.
3. *Literary Representations:* Of life in the camps: A. Aldan-Semënov, E. Ginzburg, V. Grossman, V. Šalamov, A. Solženicyn. Of one's fate in internal exile: A. Solženicyn, *Rakovyj korpus*, Paris, 1968; A. Amal'rik, *Neželannoe putešestvie v Sibir'*, New York, 1970; N. Mandel'štam, *Vospominanija*, New York, 1970. Of the problems of those who were released: V. Kaverin, V. Nekrasov, G. Vladimov.

**Rekemchúk, Aleksándr Yevséyevich,** prose writer (b. Dec. 25, 1927, Odessa). Rekemchuk's father worked for the civil service. In 1943–46 Rekemchuk attended the artillery academy; in 1946–47 he studied at the Gorky Literary Institute in Moscow, graduating in 1952 after taking correspondence courses. In 1948 he joined the Communist Party. From 1947 to 1959 he worked as a journalist in the northern European part of the Soviet Union. After a collection of his short stories was published in 1956 for the first time, Rekemchuk turned, in 1959, to longer prose works with *Vremya letnikh otpuskov* (Summer Vacation) and to the writing of film scripts. In 1963 Rekemchuk moved to Moscow and was given positions on the editorial staffs of various journals. Since 1970 he has been a member of the board of the Writers Union of the RSFSR and since 1971 of that of the Writers Union of the USSR.

Part of Rekemchuk's prose recalls his observations of northern Russia; another, his childhood experiences. He focuses on his childhood in *Tovarishch Gans* (1965; Comrade Hans), an autobiographical *povest* about a boy in Kharkov and his stepfather, an Austrian, who entered the Soviet Union in the 1930s. He expands upon the theme of socialist development and human relations and contrasts them to the clichés of the Stalin period; he includes, for example, the private sphere of the characters in the industrial novel *Skudny materik* (1968; The Meagre Continent); he depicts people in a not exaggeratedly idealistic fashion. In the novel *Nezhny vozrast* (1979; Tender Age), he illustrates, using his own experiences, a boy's maturation during World War II, from his evacuation and work in industry to his military training at the novel's conclusion. Rekemchuk writes fluidly; the vividness of the individual scenes may be attributable to his work in film; various plot lines are loosely connected. Behind the unoriginal nature of the problems he deals with, no deeper message can be found.

*Works: Stuža* (short stories), 1956; *Vremja letnikh otpuskov* (pov. and short stories), 1959; *Molodo-zeleno* (pov.), 1962; *Tovarišč Gans* (pov.), 1965; *Skudnyj materik* (novel), 1968; *Mal'čiki* (pov.), 1970 (Eng. tr., *Boys Who Did A-Singing Go*, 1972; *Dočkina svad'ba* (short stories), 1971; *Khlopoty* (pov. and short stories), 1976; *Istok i ust'e* (short stories and novel), 1977; *Nežnyj vozrast* (novel), 1979; *Tridcat' šest' i šest'* (novel), in *Novyj mir* 1982:11–12 and 1986:10–12.—*Izbr. proizv.*, 2 vols., 1977.
*Secondary Lit.:* A. Makarov, in *Znamja* 1966:2; V. Gejdeko, in *Voprosy lit.* 1970:6 and in *Znamja* 1972:1; *RSPP* 7(2):1972; Ju. Leonov, in *Naš sovremennik* 1975:7; N. Avčinnikova, in *Znamja* 1979:9.

**Rémizov, Alekséy Mikháylovich**, prose writer (b. July 6 [June 24], 1877, Moscow—d. Nov. 26, 1957, Paris). Remizov's father was a merchant. After graduating from a commercial school, Remizov studied at Moscow University (Faculty of Physics and Mathematics). Remizov unintentionally participated in a student demonstration and was exiled. He spent six years in Penza, Vologda, Ust-Sysolsk (Komi). His experience of northern Russia, its monasteries and folklore, left its mark upon the future poet. After 1905 Remizov was allowed to live in St. Petersburg. By 1897 Remizov had already begun to publish a considerable number of short stories, essays, translations, reviews, and other works in journals. *Posolon* (1907; With the Sun), his first collection of 25 adpated fairy tales, was the first of a total of 83 books, only some of which include duplicated material. His third book, *Limonar* (1907; Limonarium), ushered in an equally large number of writings from the religious sphere, especially from religious folklore and the Apocrypha. His fictional prose begins with the novel *Prud* (1908; The Pond). *Besovskoye deystvo* (1907; Devilry) was the first of three dramas that combine medieval miracle plays with folklore (see Segel). With more than 2,000 pages, an eight-volume edition of his works was published as early as 1910 to 1912 and included both previously published and new material. In the revolutionary events of 1917, Remizov saw the tragic destruction of ancient, religious Russia, an event comparable to the Tatar invasion of the 13th century. His *Slovo o pogibeli zemli Russkoy* (1918; Lay of the Destruction of the Land of Russia), written before October 1917, is a dire vision of the historic incursion that was soon compared to A. Blok's "The Twelve." Remizov was able to emigrate to Berlin in August 1921; at the end of 1923 he settled in Paris. In emigration he remained a productive writer to an advanced age. Remizov published a total of 45 books in emigration, but no books were published between 1931 and 1949. Until the end of the 1920s, Remizov—who had been acquainted with all the leading writers in Russia—exercised a great influence on younger prose writers and left his mark to a large degree upon the ornamental style of writers such as I. Babel, Vs. Ivanov, L. Leonov, Yu. Olesha, B. Pilnyak, and Ye. Zamyatin. The first and only volume of his selected works to be published in the USSR after 1921 appeared in 1978. Remizov's work is bibliographically well documented in the West (H. Sinany and H. Lampl) and extensively reprinted.

Remizov is an extremely prolific and influential Russian writer. Not only did he create highly original works of prose lexically, syntactically, and structurally, but he was also very talented as a painter. Under the influence of his wife, the archaeologist Serafima Pavlovna Remizova-Dovgello (1880/83–1943), with whom he discussed all of his works, he also became well known as a Russian paleocalligrapher. His original and adapted works, which he always wrote concurrently, are united through his great sense of the transcendental, of religion, myth, and mysticism, as well as through his linguistically oriented consciousness to which content is subordinated. His adaptations include popular fairy tales and legends (Russian, Georgian, Armenian, Tibetan, Siberian), sagas, parables, apocryphal and canonical legends of saints, and mythological transmissions. In addition to the novel *Prud*, his fictional texts include the novel *Chasy* (1908; Eng. tr., *The Clock*, 1924), in which clocks become the symbol of senseless and painfully unrelenting life, and the povest *Krestovye syostry* (1910; Sisters of the Cross), which depicts the fate of deeply troubled people on the fringe of society and is thus reminiscent of F. Dostoyevsky (in a religious and social sense). In this short novel in particular and in Remizov's life and work in general, dreams play a significant role. "He believed that dreams and reality were firmly bound, interpenetrating one another, and that dreams, not being subject to conventional causal or temporal relations, were the sole means of communicating with the dead and penetrating the souls of the living" (Shane). He published collections of his own dreams, for example, "Bedovaya dolya" (1909; Deplorable Fate), and combined dreams with reality in works such as *Vzvikhryonnaya Rus* (1927; Russia in the Whirlwind) or *Ogon veshchey* (1954; The Fire of Things), subtitled *Sny i predsonye* (Dreams and Preliminary Dreams), where he discusses Russian authors and themes from Russian literature. *V pole blakitnom* (1922; Eng. tr., *On a Field Azure*, 1946), *Olya* (1927), and *V rozovom bleske* (1952; In a Rosy Luster) are interrelated works devoted to the life of his wife in which the degree of fiction varies. *Shumy goroda* (1921; Noises of the City), scenes from revolutionary events, reveals his compassion for human suffering and his ability to view his experiences intellectually. In his thematically extremely diverse prose there exist elements of symbolist concentration as well as expressionist excess. In addition to the artistic means of folk poetry, such as repetition and the pervasion of strong rhythm, Remizov also occasionally uses alienation achieved through a stylistic device, such as oral narration by a fictional character (SKAZ). His language reveals the interweaving of a strong attachment to traditional Russian with a striving toward the renewal of poetry and includes Russian literary language of the 17th century as well as dialectic and vernacula vocabulary characterized by strict avoidanc of Western word derivatives.

Works: (Owing to Remizov's stylistic idio syncrasies, most genre designations have beer omitted.) *Posolon'*, 1907, Paris, 1930; *L* *monar'*, 1907; *Prud*, 1908; *Časy*, 1908 (se above); *Krestovye sёstry*, 1910; *Pjataja jazvo* in *Lit.-khudozestvennyj al'manakh izdo* *tel'stva "Šipovnik"* 18:1912 (reprinted, Letch worth, 1970) (Eng. tr., in *The Fifth Pestilence* 1927); *Besovskoe dejstvo* (play), 1919; *Šum* *goroda*, Revel', 1921; *Ognennaja Rossija*, Re vel', 1921 (also contains *Slovo o pogibeli zeml* *Russkoj)*; *Rossija v pis'menakh*, Berlin, 1922 *V pole blakitnom*, Berlin, 1922 (see above) *Skazki russkogo naroda*, Berlin, 1923; *Kuk* *kha. Rozanovo pis'ma*, Berlin, 1923 (re printed, New York, 1978); *Vzvikhrёnnaja Rus* Paris, 1927 (reprinted London, 1979); *Olja* Paris, 1927; *Zvezda nadzvёzdnaja*, Paris, 192ε *Po karnizam*, Belgrade, 1929; *Moskovskie lju* *bimye legendy. Tri serpa*, 2 vols., Paris, 192ς *Pljašuščij demon*, Paris, 1949; *Podstrižen nymi glazami*, Paris, 1951; *Besnovatye: Savv* *Grudcyn i Solomonija*, Paris, 1951; *V rozovor bleske*, New York, 1952 (reprinted, Letch worth, 1969); *Meljuzina*, Paris, 1952; *Myškin dudočka*, Paris, 1953; *Martyn Zadeka*, Pari 1954; *Ogon' veščej*, Paris, 1954; *Krug sčast'j* Paris, 1957; *Vstreči. Peterburgskij buerak*, Pari 1981; *Učitel' muzyki* (pov.), Paris, 1983.– *Sobr. soč.*, 8 vols., 1910–12 (reprinted, Mu nich, 1971); *Izbr.*, 1978.

*Translation: Selected Prose*, 1985.

*Secondary Lit.*: A. Rystenko, Odessa, 191: K. Čukovskij, in his *Kniga o sovremennyk* *pisateljakh*, 1914; M. Gorlin, in *Osteurop* 1934; N. Andreev, in *Grani*, Frankfurt ar Main, 34–35:1957; N. Kodrjanskaja, Paris, 195ς and Paris, 1977; S. Burke, Diss., Univ. of Texa 1966; K. Geib, Munich, 1970; A. Shane, i *Russian Literature Triquarterly* 4:1972; H Lampl, in *Wiener Slavistisches Jahrbuc* 17:1972, 24:1978, and in *Wiener Slawistische Almanach* 2:1978 (bibliographical notice) an 10:1982; Ju. Andreev, in *Voprosy lit.* 1977:ε bibliography, ed. H. Sinany, Paris, 1978; J. A H. Bailey, Diss., Univ. of Washington, 197ε G. Nachtailer Slobin, Diss., Yale Univ., 197ε and Ann Arbor 1981; C. Rosenthal, Diss Stanford Univ., 1980, and Ann Arbor, 198<sup></sup> N. V. Reznikova, Berkeley, 1980; *Russian Lit* *erature Triquarterly* 18–19:1985–86 (specia issues).

**Réysner, Larísa Mikháylovna**, prose write (b. May 13 [May 1], 1895, Lublin, Poland—d

Feb. 9, 1926, Moscow). Reysner's father was a professor of constitutional law. Reysner spent her early childhood in Tomsk and lived in Germany from 1903 to 1907; she completed her schooling and went on to study neurology and philology in St. Petersburg. Her literary career began in 1913. Reysner (whose father belonged to the Revolutionary intelligentsia and published the literary journal Rudin with his daughter in 1915–16) joined the Bolsheviks after the Revolution, became a member of the Communist Party in 1918, and was the first woman commissar on the general staff of the navy. V. Vishnevsky chose to make her the key figure in his Optimisticheskaya tragediya. From 1921 to 1923 she lived with her husband, F. Raskolnikov, in Afghanistan, where he had been dispatched as Soviet ambassador. In 1923–24 Reysner traveled twice to Germany. Afterward she worked in Moscow in the editorial offices of Izvestiya and traveled around the Soviet Union. She died of typhoid fever. After 1928 she was scarcely ever mentioned in print; after 1936 silence was imposed on her works for 20 years.

Reysner's literary career began with Atlantida (1913; Atlantis), a drama influenced by L. Andreyev that mythologically depicts the salvation of humanity by the sacrificial death of a young man. In Rudin she published symbolist and ACMEIST poems, as well as literary criticism. Her post-Revolutionary works are closely associated with the places where she lived and with the Revolutionary idea. Front (1918–22), Afganistan (1922–25), Gamburg na barrikadakh (1924; Eng. tr., Hamburg at the Barricades, 1977), and V strane Gindenburga (1925; In the Land of Hindenburg) are examples of poetic reportage from the period when she served as commissar and journeyed abroad. The expressionistic style, rich in metaphor, with which she sought to capture the excitement of the age encountered opposition from the proletarian critics, but it raised her associative pictures of the times from simple journalism into the sphere of the literary.

Works: Atlantida (play), in Lit.-khudožestvennyj al'manakh izdatel'stva "Šipovnik" 21:1913; Afganistan (feature articles), 1925; Gamburg na barrikadakh (feature articles), 1925 (see above); V strane Gindenburga (feature articles), 1926; Front (feature articles), 1928.—Sobr. soč., 2 vols., 1928; Izbr., 1958, 1965, 1980.
Secondary Lit.: N. Smirnov, in Novyj mir 1926:3 and 1929:2; I. Kramov, in Moskva 1957:4 and foreword to Rejsner's Izbr., 1980; N. Takaševa, in Moskva 1965:9; M. Roščin, in Novyj mir 1966:2; E. Landau, in Prostor 1967:8; L.

R. v vospominanijakh sovremennikov, ed. I. Naumova, 1969; RSPP 7(2):1972; S. Žitomirskaja, in Lit. gazeta May 21, 1975, p. 6; E. Solovej, 1985.

**Románov, Pantelêymon Sergêyevich,** prose writer (b. Aug. 5 [July 24], 1884, Petrovskoye, prov. Tula—d. April 8, 1938, Moscow). Romanov's father was probably a priest. Romanov studied law at Moscow University until 1908, then worked in a bank and as a civil servant. He commenced an epic work, Rus (Russia), in 1907–8 and published his first short story in the journal Russkaya mysl in 1911. Parts of Rus were among his first book-length publications, which appeared beginning in 1924. Romanov was popular with readers; on the basis of his short stories about life in the Soviet Union of the 1920s, however, the critics treated him with reserve. His novel Tovarishch Kislyakov (1930; Comrade Kislyakov; Eng. tr., Three Pairs of Silk Stockings, 1931), which was also successful abroad, triggered very harsh criticism from V. Kirshon and A. Bek, among others. Although a 7-volume edition of his works appeared in 1925–27 and a 12-volume edition came out in 1928–29 and was even reprinted in 1929–30, Romanov more and more found himself being excluded from literature in the following years. Isolated works appeared until 1936; among them was a feature story about the Stakhanovite workers, Novye lyudi (New People), printed in Novy mir; nevertheless, after the publication of a volume of selected works in 1939, a year after his death, Romanov's literary existence in the Soviet Union came to an end. No more of his books appeared; he is sporadically represented in the literary histories.

Five parts of Rus appeared during Romanov's lifetime; the unfinished novel describes the life of the Russian landowners and peasants up to the period of World War I. It is loosely constructed and relatively lacking in plot. It met with initial approval from A. Lunacharsky, but it was soon viewed with disfavor because it deviated from the accepted image of the peasant as a revolutionary-to-be. Romanov's prose about the Soviet period is gripping and vivid; it achieves its effect primarily by its realistic rendering of dialogue and scene and deals with ethical problems in the area of love and sexuality, which, within the framework of early Soviet morality, were viewed only as being physiological and as imposing no matrimonial obligations (for example, in Bez cheryomukhi [1926; Eng. tr., Without Cherry Blossom, 1930] and Novaya

skrizhal [1928; Eng. tr., The New Commandment, 1933]). Tovarishch Kislyakov presents
the problem of the intelligentsia's position at
the end of the 1920s: its shaken belief in the
ideals of the Revolution, its fear of the threat
posed by informers in view of mounting suspicion, its concern about a declining approval
of actual objective results and the growing
success of unscrupulous opportunists. Romanov writes that this "second assault of the
Revolution, its class war, appeared to many
to be more horrible than all the storms and
tempests of the first."

Works: Rus', 5 vols., 1923–36; Zemletrja-
senie (play), 1924: Voprosy pola (short stories), 1926; Bez čerëmukhi (short stories), 1927
(see above); Khorošie mesta (short stories),
1927; Novaja skrižal' (novel), 4th ed., 1930
(see above); Tovarišč Kisljakov (novel), in
Nedra 18:1930, (reprinted, New York, 1952)
(see above); Sobstvennost' (novel), 1933; Rasskazy (short stories), 1935; Novye ljudi (feature articles), in Novyj mir 1936:3.—Sobr. soč.,
7 vols., 1925–27; Polnoe sobr. soč., 12 vols.,
1928–29, 2d ed., 1929–30 (without vol. 9);
Izbr., 1939.
  Secondary Lit.: V. Korolenko (1909), in Voprosy lit. 1962:4; E. Mustangov, in Zvezda
1926:4; N. Zamoškin, in Novyj mir 1926:6 and
1926:12; D. Gorbov, in his Lit. očerki, 1928,
pp. 149ff. and 174–79; V. Aleksandrova (1930),
in her Lit. i žizn', New York, 1969; RSPP
7(2):1972.

**Romashóv, Borís Sergéyevich,** playwright (b.
June 30 [June 18], 1895, St. Petersburg—d.
May 6, 1958, Moscow). Romashov's parents
were actors. He finished school in Kiev in
1915, worked in the theater until 1921, and
moved to Moscow in 1922. There he earned
his living as a journalist and theater critic and
made his first attempts at writing drama. Romashov's play Fedka-yesaul (1924), based on
his Civil War experiences, marked the beginning of what was to become an extensive
series of dramatic works that always conformed to whatever themes were current at
the time. Among Romashov's most important
dramas is Vozdushny pirog (1925; Meringue),
a grotesque comedy about skulduggery during
NEP. In Ognenny most (1929; Bridge of Fire),
a play addressing the problem of the intelligentsia during the Revolution, Romashov
paints an idealized picture of the role of leading Communists in the building of industry.
In an unpleasant manner he supports mutual
mistrust as necessary "vigilance" in Rodnoy

dom (1937; The Family House). Romashov's
war plays attracted little attention. Velikaya
sila (1947; A Great Force), a play conforming
to the Party's struggle against COSMOPOLITAN
ISM (which in the play is revealed in a respec
for foreign science or in the wearing of foreign
clothing), received a Stalin Prize (for 1947
1st class). Romashov later wrote about the
theater, but books such as Dramaturg i teat
(1953; The Playwright and the Theater), lack
ing a theoretical foundation and assuming a
one-sidedly ideological standpoint (as he doe
in support of the dramatist A. Surov), are o
little value. Romashov's last play, Nabat v
gorakh (1958–64; Alarm in the Mountains)
in which he returns to the subject of the Civi
War, was completed by A. Romashova.

  Works: P'esy (plays), 1935, 1948, 1951 (con
tains Velikaja sila; Ognennyj most; Bojcy
Znatnaja familija), 1954; Dramaturg i teatr
1953; Vozdušnyj pirog (1925; comedy), in P'esy
sovetskikh pisatelej 1:1953; Vmeste s vam
(biography), 1964; Zvëzdy ne mogut pogas
nut' (play), 1966 (also contains Nabat v go
rakh).
  Secondary Lit.: V. Lakšin, in Novyj mi
1954:4; L. Višnevskaja, in Teatr 1960:7; V
Pimenov, in Teatr 1965:8, in Naš sovremen
nik 1966:11, and in Ogonëk 1970:26, p. 12.

**Rópshin, V.** (pseud. of Borís Víktorovich Sá
vinkov, prose writer (b. Jan. 31 [Jan. 19], 1879
Kharkov—d. May 7, 1925 [?], Moscow, while
imprisoned). His father was a public prose
cutor. After studying law for two years, he
was expelled from St. Petersburg University
in 1899 because of his political activities; he
completed his studies in Berlin and Heidel
berg. He was a leading member of the Socialis
Revolutionary Party and as a terrorist wa
involved in assassination attempts against the
most highly-placed members of governmen
between 1903 and 1905. After 1909, while i
emigration in Paris, he wrote (under his pseu
donym) a literary account of his political anc
terrorist experiences. After the February Rev
olution of 1917 he played a leading role ir
the government; after the October Revolutior
he continued to resist the Bolsheviks for som
time and in 1918 went to Paris by way o
Shanghai. In Warsaw in 1920 he took over the
leadership of the Russian Political Committee
for the struggle against the Bolsheviks and
participated in the fighting on the Dnepr River
In August 1924 he returned to the Sovie
Union and was immediately arrested; afte
several days he was sentenced to death bu

was reprieved and the sentence commuted to 10 years' imprisonment. According to the official version, his death occurred by suicide; according to A. Solzhenitsyn's research, he was forcibly pushed from a window into the inner courtyard of Lubyanka Prison. As a writer, Ropshin did not limit himself to memoirs; on the contrary, in Kon bledny (1909; Eng. tr., The Pale Horse, 1917) he explored various psychological motivations (fanaticism, cynicism, personal revenge, self-sacrifice, dependence) from the point of view of a terrorist in an impressionistic and absorbing manner. Z. Gippius, who remained in contact with Ropshin for a long time, supposedly revised the work stylistically. Under her influence Ropshin also wrote poetry. In To, chego ne bylo (1911; Eng. tr., What Never Happened, 1917), he expressed his disappointment with the Revolution of 1905. Ropshin's memoirs appeared in print in the Soviet Union until 1928.

Works: Kon' blednyj (novel), 1909 (reprinted, Munich, 1974) (see above); To, čego ne bylo (novel), 1911 (see above); Vo Francii vo vremja vojny, 2 vols., 1916–17; Kon' voronoj (novel), 1924 (Eng. tr., The Black Horse, 1924); Poslednie pomeščiki, 1925; Vospominanija terrorista (memoirs), in Byloe 1917:1–3, 1918:1–3, 6, separate ed., 1926, 3d ed., 1928 (Eng. tr., Memoirs of a Terrorist, 1931); Avtobiografija (1921), in Vozdušnye puti, New York, 5:1967; Posmertnye stat'i i pis'ma (essays and letters), 1926.

Secondary Lit.: B. Pares, in Slavonic Review 1925–26; R. Gul', 1930; F. Stepun, Paris, 1950; Z. Gippius, Dmitrij Merežkovskij, Paris, 1951; A. Šamaro, in Nauka i religija 1966:4; A. Solženicyn, Arkhipelag GULag, vol. 1, Paris, 1973, pp. 371–74.

Róshchin, Mikhaíl Mikháilovich (pseud. of M. M. Gibelmán), prose writer, playwright (b. Feb. 10, 1933, Kazan). Roshchin grew up in Sevastopol and came to Moscow after World War II. He worked in a factory and as a journalist; in 1958 he completed a correspondence course at the Gorky Literary Institute. In 1958 he joined the Communist Party. His short stories began appearing in 1952; he first collected these in V malenkom gorode (1956; In a Small Town). By the second collection, Kakikh-nibud dvadtsat minut (1965; Any Old Twenty Minutes), his lucid treatment of topical everyday problems was recognized. Roshchin's play Valentin i Valentina (1971; Eng. tr., Valentin and Valentina, in Nine Modern

Soviet Plays, 1977) scored an unusual success with the public; it was among the most frequently performed plays in the Soviet Union, with 2,060 performances in 1972 and 2,552 performances in 1973. Roshchin has continued to work in both genres. He lives in Moscow.

Roshchin's works concern the normal course of everyday life and expose its problematic nature. His prose works move slowly and dwell on details. In Moy uchitel Grisha Panin (1965; My Teacher Grisha Panin) he brings a young factory worker who is interested in continuing his studies face to face with an older group of obscurantist workers but also introduces their direct opposite who is prepared to include workers in higher education. Through a journey on a freighter, a symbol of the uniformity with which life passes by, the povest Reka (1973; The River) makes its appeal clear: recognize the special in the commonplace and enrich life through conscious observation. Roshchin's plays reveal a remarkable talent for setting up a scene. In Valentin i Valentina he successfully depicts the special difficulties of love as perceived by the youth of his generation. He adroitly combines dialogue about love with a presentation of the scenes the dialogue recalls. In this play, as in the one written in 1967, Stary Novy god (The Old New Year), he avoids providing answers. In the latter piece, Roshchin presents the problems people face in an affluent society; how one can be spiritually suffocated by material possessions, yet how freedom from possessions does not lead to the desired goal either. Grotesque exaggeration gives the play the character of a comedy, without masking his serious concern. In Eshelon (1972; The Transport Train), Roshchin harkens back to his experiences during the wartime evacuation. Considering its epic features, this play is an interesting example of "Roshchin's skill at using stage effects to lend a facade of greater substance to characters" (Segel). In Speshite delat dobro (1979; Hurry to Do Good), he opens the story with the rescue of a 15-year-old girl who has attempted suicide. The rescuer's attempt then to help free her from her problems within his own family quickly provokes his mistrust of the environment and triggers profound new dilemmas.

Works: V malen'kom gorode (short stories), 1956; Kakikh-nibud' dvadcat' minut (short stories), 1965 (contains Moj učitel' Griša Panin); S utra do noči (pov. and short stories), 1968; Bunin v Jalte (pov.), in Družba narodov 1970:11; 24 dnja v raju (pov. and short sto-

ries), 1971; *Valentin i Valentina* (play), in *Teatr* 1971:12 (see above); *Reka* (pov.), in *Družba narodov* 1973:5; *Staryj Novyj god* (play), in *Teatr* 1974:2; *Reka* (pov. and short stories), 1978; *Spešite delat' dobro* (play), in *Teatr* 1979:4; *P'esy* (plays), 1980 (contains *Devočka, gde ty živёš'?*; *Staryj Novyj god; Posle duèli; Valentin i Valentina; Remont; Èšelon; Muž i žena snimut komnatu; Galoši sčast'ja*); *Rasskazy s dorogi* (short stories), 1981.
*Secondary Lit.:* L. Anninskij, in *Lit. gazeta* Nov. 13, 1965; F. Čapčakhov, in *Lit. gazeta* Dec. 16, 1970, p. 4; D. Tevekeljan, in *Moskva* 1973:7; K. Mehnert, in *Osteuropa* 1974:4; F. Svetov, in *Lit. obozrenie* 1974:4; B. Stanilov, in *Teatr* 1981:4; V. Klimenko, in *Lit. obozrenie* 1982:7.

**Roslyakóv, Vasíly Petróvich,** prose writer (b. March 17, 1921, Prikumsk, Stavropol territory). From 1939 to 1941 Roslyakov studied at the Moscow Institute of Philosophy, Literature, and History (MIFLI); then he served as a soldier, and in 1950 he graduated from Moscow University. Since 1945 he has been a member of the Communist Party. During World War II, Roslyakov was already working as a journalist for partisan papers; starting in 1950, his first short stories appeared. In 1953 he defended his candidate's dissertation, *Sovetsky poslevoyenny ocherk* (1956; Soviet Journalistic Postwar Prose), and has continued to work as a critic since that time. Roslyakov became well known through his contribution to the new candid literature about the war: *Odin iz nas* (1962; One of Us). Roslyakov has published much in *Novy mir, Yunost,* and other journals. He lives in Moscow and has participated in the congresses of the Writers Unions only since 1965.

*Odin iz nas* depicts humanities students at MIFLI during the prewar period and their action at the front during the period of Soviet defeat. This short novel is autobiographical and describes, among other things, the fate of the fallen poets P. Kogan, M. Kulchitsky, and N. Mayorov (Roslyakov himself provides the information about the models for his characters). *Obyknovennaya istoriya* (1962; A Common Story) illustrates young people's tragic love through parts of a correspondence and through a short frame story; it demonstrates Roslyakov's fine psychological sense and his concise expressive style. Together with short stories and journalistic prose about, for example, the construction of a motorworks factory on the Kama—*Pervaya vstrecha* (1972;

The First Meeting)—Roslyakov also writes novels. *Poslednyaya voyna* The Last War) continues the events described in *Odin iz nas* and, using a largely autobiographical protagonist ("my brother, my shadow, my bright spirit"), depicts a flight after being taken prisoner and working for the partisans. The novel *Vitenka* (1981; Vitenka) illustrates human concerns: a child's spiritual development and the parents' love.

*Works: Sovetskij poslevoennyj očerk* (scholarly articles), 1956, excerpt in *God tridcat' sed'moj,* 1954; *Odin iz nas* (pov.), 1962; *Obyknovennaja istorija* (pov.), 1963; *Nedavnie vstreči,* in *Oktjabr'* 1964:8; *Krasnye berёzy* (pov.), 1966; *Ot vesny do vesny* (novel), 1967; *Pervaja vstreča* (feature articles), in *Novyj mir* 1972:1; *Poslednjaja vojna* (novel), 1974; *Dobraja osen',* in *Novyj mir* 1974:7; *Poslednjaja vojna* (pov. and novel), 1978; *Viten'ka* (novel and short stories), 1981; *Čužoe i svoe* (essay), in *Novyj mir* 1984:1.
*Secondary Lit.:* L. Lazarev, in *Lit. gazeta* April 12, 1962; I. Velembovskaja, in *Znamja* 1964:11; I. Kozlov, in *Lit. obozrenie* 1974:8; B. Možaev, in *Lit. obozrenie* 1978:5; A Prokhanov, in *Lit. Rossija* Aug. 21, 1981, p. 9.

**Rozhdéstvensky, Róbert Ivánovich,** poet (b. June 20, 1932, Kosikha, Altai Territory). Rozhdestvensky's father was a career officer; his mother, a military physician. He studied humanities at Petrozavodsk University (1950–51) and at the Gorky Literary Institute (1951–56). Rozhdestvensky began to publish poems in 1950; his first volume, *Flagi vesny* (1955; Banners of Spring), appeared in Petrozavodsk. The next volume, *Ispytaniye* (1956; Trial), was published in Moscow under the editorship of V. Lugovskoy. Rozhdestvensky's journalistic poetry, the declamatory aspect of which is reminiscent of V. Mayakovsky, found swift dissemination, and Rozhdestvensky was permitted to take numerous trips abroad. The verse epic *Rekviyem* (1961; Requiem) made an essential contribution to his recognition as a poet; this solemn heroic visualization of sorrow and heroism in war was set to music by B. Kabalevsky. Since 1965 Rozhdestvensky has been on the board of the Writers Union of the RSFSR; since 1971, on the board and secretariat of the Writers Union of the USSR. In 1972 he received the Prize of the Leninist Komsomol (see LITERARY PRIZES); in 1979, the State Prize of the USSR. K. Simonov wrote the foreword to the first comprehensive collection of his poems, *Za dvadtsat let* (1973;

For Twenty Years). Rozhdestvensky lives in Moscow.

Rozhdestvensky's poems are journalistic. He loves to address his listeners with entreaty and rhetorical questions, which lend a suggestive force to his verse. In the period of anti-Stalinism, his lyrical journalism showed liberal tendencies; later it was carried along by the solemn expression of the utopian world of communism. Rozhdestvensky assimilates the headline-making events of his day such as space exploration and visits from Paris and New York, because for him "the morning newspaper is like heroin for the addict" ("Golod," in Vseryoz). His verses are defined by rhythm and vivacity, not restrained and compressed by meter or rhyme. Anaphora and other parallel constructions distinguish his verse from prose but do not replace the lack of depth and complexity.

Works: Flagi vesny (poems), 1955; Ispytanie (poems), 1956; Moja ljubov' (narrative poem and lyric poems), 1956; Drejfujuščij prospekt (poems), 1959; Rekviem (narrative poem), in Junost' 1961:2, separate ed., 1970; Rovesniku (poems), 1962; Neobitaemye ostrova (poems), 1962; Radius dejstvija (poems), 1965; Syn very (poems), 1966; Vser'ëz (poems), 1970; Posvjaščenie (poems), 1970; Radar serdca (poems), 1971; Za dvadcat' let (poems), 1973; Pered prazdnikom (lyric and narrative poems), 1974; Golos goroda (poems), 1977; Semidesjatye (poems), 1980; Èto vremja (poems), 1983.—Izbr. proizv., 2 vols., 1979; Sobr. soč., 3 vols, 1985–.

Translations: A Poem on Various Points of View, and Other Poems, 1968; Everyday Miracles: Selected Poetry 1956–1980, 1983.

Secondary Lit.: V. Nazarenko, in Zvezda 1955:5; L. Anninskij, in Znamja 1961:9 and in Don 1966:11; T. Dimitrovna, in Godišnjak na Sofijskija universitet . . . , 63:2, 1970; I. Mežakov-Korjakin, in Melbourne Slavonic Studies 5–6:1971; V. Korotič, in Novyj mir 1975:7; A. Isaev, in Oktjabr' 1980:4; A. Mal'gin, in Lit. obozrenie 1983:8.

**Rozhdéstvensky, Vsévolod Aleksándrovich,** poet (b. April 10 [March 29], 1895, Tsarskoye Selo, near St. Petersburg—d. Aug. 31, 1977, Leningrad). Rozhdestvensky began writing poetry while in school; he published his first volume of poems, Gimnazicheskiye gody (1914; Gymnasium Years), at the same time that he began his studies in the Department of History and Philology at St. Petersburg University. World War I interrupted his studies, during which he had become acquainted with N. Gumilyov and O. Mandelshtam. His volumes Leto (1920; Summer) and Zolotoye vereteno (1921; The Golden Spindle) belong to the poetry of ACMEISM; up to that time Rozhdestvensky was also a member of the TSEKH POETOV (Guild of Poets). He worked as a translator for the publishing house Vsemirnaya literatura. Beginning in the mid-1920s, Rozhdestvensky conformed more and more to the demands for topical subject matter. Zemnoye serdtse (1933; Heart of Earth) was conceived as a contribution to the literature of socialist construction. During World War II, Rozhdestvensky was a war correspondent; he wrote song lyrics, among other things. At an advanced age he wrote Stranitsy zhizni (1962; Life's Pages), reminiscences (of the writers M. Gorky, N. Tikhonov, S. Yesenin, O. Forsh, among others) that had little to add to an already familiar picture. A second book of memoirs, Shkatulka pamyati (1972; The Memory Box), combines personal experiences with stories from the lives of Russian and French writers. Rozhdestvensky belonged to the editorial staff of the journal Zvezda in 1939 and from 1956 to 1967 and to the editorial staff of Neva from 1967 until his death. He took part regularly in the congresses of the Writers Union of the RSFSR between 1958 and 1975, although he never read a speech; he lived in Leningrad.

After his acmeist phase, Rozhdestvensky became a conformist, but not a propagandistic poet. His use of the theme of socialist construction during the first Five-Year Plan and after the war (primarily concerning Leningrad) is complemented by his lyrical portraits of writers (for example, A. Pushkin, A. Fet, Byron, D. Kedrin) and musicians (Chopin, Tchaikovsky). The structure of his verse is classical, at times narrative (in the historical sphere as well), and often descriptive (even becoming pure nature poetry). His easy-to-read verses contain no surprises.

Works: Gimnaziceskie gody (poems), 1914; Leto (poems), 1921; Zolotoe vereteno (poems), 1921; Bol'šaja medvedica (poems), 1926; Granitnyj sad (poems), 1929; Zemnoe serdce (poems), 1933; Rodnye dorogi (poems), 1947; Stikhotvorenija (poems), 1956; Russkie zori (poems), 1962; Stranicy žizni (memoirs), 1962, 2d ed., 1974; Čitaja Puškina (essays), 1962, 2d ed., 1966; Zolotaja osen' (poems), 1969; Škatulka pamjati (memoirs), 1972; Dobryj den' (poems), 1973; Žizn' slova (poems), 1977.— Izbr., 1965; 2 vols., 1974.

Secondary Lit.: I. Vasil'eva, in Zvezda 1960:6, 1971:3, and 1975:4 and 1983; V. Ditc, in Neva

1963:7, and *Avrora* 1975:4, and in *Zvezda* 1985:4; A. Amsterdam, 1965, and in *Neva* 1970:12; V. Šefner, in *Lit. gazeta* Dec. 9, 1970, p. 4. Nov. 21, 1972, and Sept. 7, 1977; A. Urban, in *Lit. obozrenie* 1975:10; N. Tikhonov, in *Neva* 1977:12; V. Azarov, in *Zvezda* 1985:4.

**Rózov, Víktor Sergéyevich,** playwright (b. Aug. 21 [Aug. 8], 1913, Yaroslavl). Starting in 1934, Rozov attended an acting school in Moscow. A soldier in World War II, he was severely wounded in 1941. Then he worked as an actor in theaters at the front and, in the postwar period, as a director in Alma-Ata and later in Moscow. In 1949 the performance of his drama *Yeyo druzya* (Her Friends) was well received. In 1952 he completed his studies at the Gorky Literary Institute. After Stalin's death, Rozov became one of the leading Soviet dramatists with a play that was translated into ten languages, *V dobry chas* (1954; Eng. trs., *Good Luck!* in *Soviet Literature* 1955:9; *The Young Graduates*, in *Russian Plays for Young Audiences*, 1977), and other truthful depictions of the problems of youth that broke with previous portrayals. In 1956 he published the drama he wrote during the war, *Vechno zhivye* (Eng. tr., *Alive Forever*, in *Contemporary Russian Drama*, 1968); his film adaptation, *Letyat zhuravli* (The Cranes Are Flying), was awarded a prize in Cannes in 1958. *V poiskakh radosti* (Eng. tr., *In Search of Happiness*, 1961) set a record of 4,662 performances at 98 theaters in the Soviet Union in the winter of 1957–58. The film script *A, B, V, G, D . . .* (1961; Eng. tr., *A, B, C,* in *The New Writing in Russia*, 1964) was criticized, just as V. Aksyonov's *Zvyozdny bilet* had been, for emphasizing the negative aspects of youth and was not released for filming. Among his dramas of the 1960s, *Pered uzhinom* (1961; Before Supper) and *Zateynik* (1966; The Social Director) grapple with the problems of the Stalin period in a very clear way. Apart from dramas (18 by 1986), Rozov also wrote essays about an author's work and about ethical problems. Since 1977 he has occasionally published parts of an autobiographical work, *Puteshestviya v raznye storony* (1977–82; Trips in Different Directions). From 1955 to 1969, and again from 1987, he belonged to the editorial staff of the journal *Yunost,* and since 1982 he has belonged to that of the new journal *Sovremennaya dramaturgiya.* He lives in Moscow.

Rozov's versatile dramatic talent, which developed fully after 1953, grows out of a great humanistic ethical concern. His first drama, *Vechno zhivye,* could be neither published nor performed when it was written in 1943. It distinguished itself from propagandistic war drama by having a weak woman as its protagonist rather than an exemplary "positive hero" of SOCIALIST REALISM. This is the only one of Rozov's plays to be revised several times, for the first performance in 1956 at the Sovremennik Theater in Moscow as well as for the new published version in 1973. In his first successful dramas, Rozov depicts the problems of youth between secondary school and college; the novelty he introduced to the post-Stalin period lay in his selecting as the protagonist a skeptical, immature person *(V dobry chas* or *V poiskakh radosti)* or even a nihilist *(V doroge* [1961; On the Way, the dramatized version of *A, B, V, G, D . . .*]). In *V doroge* Rozov shifts to the atectonic form of drama with an epic arrangement of 37 scenes, a form that creates the prerequisite for a credible representation of the principal character's transformation through privation, danger, guilt, and love in ever new situations and that corresponds especially well to the open-ended conclusion for which Rozov always strives. In *Pered uzhinom,* Rozov deals with the problems of behavior toward parvenus of the Stalin period and distinguishes between the brutal, rationalist Stalinist and the opportunist of weak character. *Zateynik* is one of the best Soviet dramas of all time and also one of the best in the unusual style of analytic dramas. Rozov unites a gradual comprehension of the horror of the past with a demonstration of the effects of despotic power in the private sphere, using the example of the meeting—after 14 years—of two school comrades, one of whom used political and psychological pressure to take away the other's beloved wife during the Stalin period. Rozov's dramas are, on the whole, individually very differently structured, from typical hypotactic works such as *Neravny boy* (1960; The Unfair Fight) to typical paratactic ones such as *Traditsionny sbor* (1967; The Reunion). He prefers the two-act play with little change of scene. The span of time is usually brief, distinguishing him from A. Arbuzov, for example. The two dramatic adaptations that do encompass a broad expanse of time, however, I. Goncharov's *Obyknovennaya istoriya* (1966; A Common Story) and F. Dostoyevsky's *Bratya Karamazovy,* called *Malchiki* (1971; The Young Boys), equally demonstrate Rozov's own ethical concern and his great dramatic talent for finding ever new scenic solutions. Contemporary social problems are also accented in *Gnezdo* glukharya (1979; The Nest of the Wood Grouse), in which both the philistine older man who holds a leadership position and the inconsiderate cynic struggling to improve his position are satirically depicted; both are embodiments of the nonideological, materialistically oriented plot. The play has an allegorical power that extends beyond the plot line, concise dialogue from which the characters' individuality emerges, everyday speech patterns that are true to life, good psychology (including child psychology), constant resonance of the inexpressible qualities in the human soul, rejection of direct delineation of character (judgments are to be made by the reader and/or audience), ample use of stage directions, and a plot involving the family, in which the mother plays an important role. The deepest reaches of interpersonal problems are explored. The central figure of Kabanchik (1986; The Little Boar), which was not allowed to be staged between 1981 and 1986, is the son of a high-ranking nomenclatura functionary who was sentenced for criminal machinations.

Works: Eë druz'ja (play), 1951; Tvoj put' (Stranica žizni) (play), 1953; V dobryj čas (comedy), 1955 (see above); Večno živye (play), 1956 (see above); Letjat' žuravli (film script), 1959; P'esy (plays), 1959 (contains V poiskakh radosti [see above]; Stranica žizni; V dobryj čas; Večno živye); Neravnyj boj (comedy), 1960; A, B, V, G, D (film script), in Junost' 1961:9 (see above), and, as play, V doroge, 1962; Pered užinom (comedy), 1963; V poiskakh radosti (comedy), 1963 (see above); V den' svad'by (play), 1964; Zatejnik (play), 1966; Obyknovennaja istorija (play), 1966 (dramatization of I. Gončarov's novel); Tradicionnyj sbor (play), in Teatr 1967:3; Moi šestidesjatye (plays), 1969 (contains V doroge; V den' svad'by; Zatejnik; Tradicionnyj sbor); S večera do poludnja (play), 1970 (Eng. tr., From Night till Noon, in Nine Modern Soviet Plays, 1977); Iz besed s molodymi literatorami (essays), 1970; Mal'čiki (play), 1971; Situacija (comedy), 1973; V dobryj čas (plays), 1973 (contains also Neravnyj boj; V poiskakh radosti; Stranica žizni; V doroge; V den' svad'by; S večera do poludnja; Tradicionnyj sbor; Večno živye); Četyre kapli (comedy), in Teatr 1974:7; Prikosnovenie k vojne (autobiographical short story), in Smena 1975:20; Der Kulturleiter. Zatejnik (play; Russian-German ed.), Stuttgart, 1977; Gnezdo glukharja (play), in Teatr 1979:2; Putešestvija v raznye storony (autobiography), extracts in Avrora 1977:7, Neva 1980:2 and 1982:11, and Junost' 1980:2; Khozjain (play), in Sovremennaja dramatur-

gija 1982:1; Kabančik (play), in Sovremennaja dramaturgija 1987:1.—Izbr. (plays), 1983 (contains Večno živye; V dobryj čas; V poiskakh radosti; V doroge; V den' svad'by; Zatejnik; Tradicionnyj sbor; S večera do poludnja; Četyre kapli; Gnezdo glukharja).
Secondary Lit.: A. Kron, in Teatr 1955:5; I. Solov'ëva, in Novyj mir 1960:8; I. Višnevskaja, in Teatr 1963:6; I. Meister, Diss., Bonn, 1965; V. Anastas'ev, 1966, and in Teatr 1973:8; M. Turovskaja, in Moskva teatral'naja, 1966, p. 266; W. Kasack, in Neusprachl. Mitteilungen aus Wissenschaft u. Praxis 1970:3, in Zeitschrift für slavische Philologie 1975:1, and in Kritisches Lexikon zur fremdsprachigen Gegenwartslit., Göttingen, 1985; B. Ljubimov, in Teatr 1981:10; A. Smeljanskij, in Sovremennaja dramaturgija 1982:1; B. Ezerskaja, in Novoe russkoe slovo, New York, July 22, 1984, p. 6.

**Rubtsóv, Nikoláy Mikháylovich,** poet (b. Jan. 3, 1936, Yemetsk, oblast Arkhangelsk—d. Jan. 19, 1971, Vologda). Rubtsov grew up in a village; he was placed in an orphanage following the early death of his parents. After completing forestry school in Totma (Vologda Oblast) in 1952, he went to work as a stoker on fishing boats in the North Sea; beginning in 1955 he fulfilled his military service with the North Sea fleet. From 1959 to 1962 Rubtsov worked as a mechanic in a factory in Leningrad; while working there, he applied to and was accepted as a student by, the Gorky Literary Institute in 1962 on the basis of his early poems. He was expelled in 1964 and was able to complete his studies at the institute by correspondence only in 1969. A small collection of his poems appeared in 1965; before his premature death (he was allegedly strangled by a woman), Rubtsov published three more volumes of verse, the titles of which reflect his poetic message: Zvezda poley (1967; Star of the Fields), Dusha khranit (1969; The Soul Preserves), and Sosen shum (1970; Murmur of the Pines). Rubtsov, who lived in Vologda, was recognized by both native and émigré Russians as a poet of Russian nature, Russian soil, and tradition. Numerous collections of his poetry have appeared since his early death.
     A. Urban said of Rubtsov: "He began from a point most poets reach only after long seeking." Rubtsov's unaffected and somewhat elegiac poems express his deep tie to the Russian village and its churches; the world of technology, the city, and soulless civilization are so foreign to him that he never once contrasts

it to his own world of stars, water, and birch trees, of stillness and space. Rubtsov builds on the strength of his own convictions, rejecting any writing that does not stem from his own joy or his own sorrow. His poetry records universal situations and seldom mentions individual experiences; it reveals "the naked and defenseless human soul, which finds itself in a complicated, colorful world not easily accessible to thought" (Akatkin).

Works: Lirika (poems), 1965; Zvezda polej (poems), 1967; Duša khranit (poems), 1969; Sosen šum (poems), 1970; Zelënye cvety (poems), 1971; Poslednij parokhod (poems), 1973; Podorožniki (poems), 1976; Stikhotvorenija (1953–1971), 1977; Izbr., 1982.
Secondary Lit.: V. Dement'ev, in Moskva 1970:9 and 1973:3; A. Urban, in Voprosy lit. 1971:4; V. Akatkin, in Voprosy lit. 1974:3; I. Nikiforova, in Lit. obozrenie 1974:6; V. Kožinov, in Naš sovremennik 1975:9 and separate study, 1976; E. Evtušenko, in Lit. gazeta Aug. 18, 1976, p. 7; A. Pikač, in Voprosy lit. 1977:9; V. Volkov, in Kontinent, Paris, 15:1978; S. Vikulov, in Naš sovremennik 1981:12; Vospominanija o R., 1983; N. Konjaev, in Neva 1986:1.

**Ruchyóv, Borís Aleksándrovich** (pseud. of B. A. Krivoshchókov), poet (b. June 15 [June 2], 1913, Troitski, prov. Orenburg—d. Oct. 24, 1973, Magnitogorsk). Ruchyov completed a nine-year school in 1930, then worked voluntarily as a mixer of concrete and carpenter on the construction of the city of Magnitogorsk; he was employed as a journalist for the Komsomol newspaper at the same time. His first volume of verse, Vtoraya rodina (Second Homeland; edited by E. Bagritsky and A. Surkov), appeared in 1933. Ruchyov was one of the youngest participants in the First Congress of the Writers Union of the USSR. Beginning in 1935 he studied at the Gorky Literary Institute by correspondence. Ruchyov spent the years from 1937 to 1957 in forced labor camps (Kolyma) and in exile (in Kirghizia). After his REHABILITATION, he lived in Magnitogorsk, wrote down the poetry he had composed mentally while imprisoned, and became well known primarily for his verse epics such as Lyubava (1962; this work received the Gorky Prize in 1967), which continue the tradition of Komsomol construction poetry of the 1930s. Beginning in 1958 Ruchyov participated regularly in the congresses of the Writers Union; in 1970 he became a member of the Commu-

nist Party and was elected to the board of the Writers Union of the RSFSR.
The theme of genuine enthusiasm for labor (set by the example of Magnitogorsk), which motivated Ruchyov's early poems, continued to be a dominant factor after his release from custody. At the same time, Ruchyov was able convincingly to express readiness for action and sacrifice and the strengthening of the individual through inner identification with his work. He presented his years in camp as being an isolated case of injustice, never as typifying the fate of many; the motif of the misfortune of not being permitted to defend the fatherland as a soldier during World War II appears frequently. The depiction of the war in the narrative poem Nevidimka (1942–57; The Invisible One) was abstract, rich in hyperbole, and oriented toward folk poetry. Ruchyov's lyric poetry is narrative; he prefers longer epic poems, which in form are somewhat monotonous but exact and natural.

Works: Vtoraja rodina (poems), 1933; Lirika (poems), 1958 (also contains the narrative poem Nevidimka); Krasnoe solnyško (poems), 1960; Ljubava (narrative poem), 1963; Magnit-gora (lyric and narrative poems), 1964; Poèmy (narrative poetry), 1967; Stikhotvorenija i poèmy (lyric and narrative poems), 1976.— Izbr., 1969; Sobr. soč., 2 vols., 1978–79.
Secondary Lit.: K. Vanšenkin, in Novyj mir 1959:6 and in his Lica i golosa, 1978; A. Vlasenko, in Molodaja gvardija 1961:12; D. Starikov, 1969; V. Sorokin, in Moskva 1973:6; L. Gal'ceva, 1973, and foreword to Ruč'ëv's Sobr. soč., 1978–79; Ju. Boldyrev, in Novyj mir 1981:1.

**Rússkiye zapíski** (Russian Annals), a cultural-political and literary journal that was published in Paris from 1937 to 1939 in a total of 21 issues. This journal was originally foreseen as the sequel to Sovremennye zapiski, and the editors of Sovremennye zapiski—N. D. Avsentyev, I. I. Bunakov, M. V. Vishnyak, V. V. Rudnev—were the editors of Russkiye zapiski for issues 1 to 3 (1937–38). As it turned out, however, the journals followed more of a parallel course. Russkiye zapiski was established at the initiative of the émigré group in Shanghai (see EMIGRATION); the first three issues also contain special material relevant to its founders. P. N. Milyukov served as the editor in chief from 1938 (issue no. 4) until the beginning of World War II. Russkiye zapiski contains, together with the regular appearance of Milyukov's reminiscences of the years 1905 and 1906, the valuable first publications of numerous authors from the first emigration: for example, poems by I. Knorring, D. Knut, A. Ladinsky, G. Rayevsky, A. Shteyger, Yu. Terapiano, and M. Tsvetayeva, and prose by I. Bunin, G. Gazdanov, Z. Gippius, D. Merezhkovsky, V. Nabokov, M. Osorgin, A. Remizov, Teffi, and B. Zaytsev.

Secondary Lit.: G. Struve, Russkaja literatura v izgnanii, New York, 1956, pp. 239–41.

**Ryazanov, Eldar Aleksandrovich.** See BRAGINSKY, EMIL VENIAMINOVICH.

**Rybakóv, Anatóly Naúmovich** (pseud. of A. N. Arónov), prose writer (b. Jan. 14 [Jan. 1], 1911, Chernigov). Rybakov's father was an engineer. Rybakov grew up in Moscow after 1918. In 1934 he completed his studies in transport engineering. From 1934 to 1946 Rybakov worked as an engineer for motor vehicle transport companies in Ufa, Kalinin, Ryazan, and in the military. After World War II, Rybakov devoted himself to literature; his novels are often reprinted and filmed. He lives in Moscow.

Rybakov began with an adventure story for children, Kortik (1948; Eng. tr., The Dirk, 1954); which he continued with Bronzovaya ptitsa (1956; Eng. tr., The Bronze Bird, 1958). As a contribution to the required industrial novels, Rybakov wrote Voditeli (1950; The Drivers), which was awarded a Stalin Prize (for 1950, 2d class) but was later criticized, in accordance with Party doctrine of that time, because of his limitation to the strictly professional sphere. In Yekaterina Voronina (1955; Catherine Voronin), Rybakov also fell back on his own realm of experiences in "vehicle transportation." Rybakov proves himself an expert in child psychology in three short novels that are connected by the same (also linguistically identifiable) narrator who tells the story in the first person: Priklyucheniya Krosha (1960; Krosh's Adventure), Kanikuly Krosha (1966; Krosh's Vacation), Neizvestny soldat (1970; The Unknown Soldier). In the first two, the boy is 15 and 16, respectively, a character similar to the young people V. Rozov creates; the boy's development during a time of stress is depicted and he ascertains that "there is not a bad time; there are bad people," in view

of the subterfuges engaged in by an informer during the Stalin period, for example. The third povest combines a contemporary account by the now 18-year-old with a tragic plot line taken from the war and reveals Rybakov's solid development in the mastery of form and his gift of incorporating serious ethical problems into fluidly narrated contemporary events. Tyazholy pesok (1978; Eng. tr., Heavy Sand, 1981) is a vast novel that describes the fate of a Jewish family at home and abroad between 1910 and 1943. The theme, which is unusual for Soviet literature, gains contemporary significance, through Rybakov's one-sided view, because of the widespread desire among Soviet Jews to emigrate to Israel.

Works: Kortik (pov.), 1948 (see above); Voditeli (novel), 1950; Ekaterina Voronina (novel), 1955, rev. eds., 1958, 1960, and 1970; Bronzovaja ptica (pov.), 1956 (see above); Priključenija Kroša (pov.), 1960; Leto v Sosnjakakh (novel), 1965; Kanikuly Kroša (pov.), 1966; Neizvestnyj soldat (pov.), 1971; Celinnyj semestr (pov.), in Oktjabr' 1973:12; Tjaželyj pesok (novel), 1979 (see above); Deti Arbata (novel), in Družba narodov 1987:4–6.—Izbr. proizv., 2 vols., 1978; Sobr. soč., 4 vols., 1981–82.

Secondary Lit.: Z. Papernyj, in Znamja 1950:6 and 1961:3; RSPP 4:1966; L. Belaja, in Znamja 1966:8; A. Bek, in Novyj mir 1970:12; Ju. Trifonov, in Lit. Rossija Feb. 5, 1971, p. 5; Ju. Krutogorov, in Lit. obozrenie 1974:6; E. Starikova, 1977, and in Oktjabr' 1981:1; Marran, in Vremja i my, Tel Aviv, 41:1979; Ju. Boldyrev, in Oktjabr' 1983:2.

**Rybakóv, Vladímir Mechislávovich,** prose writer (b. Sept. 29, 1947, Alès, prov. Gard, France). Rybakov's father, a Pole, and his mother, a Russian, were both doctors and painters; as Communists they returned to the USSR in 1956. Rybakov worked in various regions of the USSR. At the age of 15 he wrote his first short stories. In 1964 he began studying history in Chernovitsy; in 1966 he was expelled from the university for his critical statement and was inducted into the military. Two of his three and one-half years of military service were spent on the Russian-Chinese border (1967–68). After his discharge in 1969, Rybakov worked as a porter, welder, and locksmith; in addition, although he had no prospect of being published, he resumed his writing. At the end of 1972 Rybakov managed to return to France. Until 1984 he worked on the editorial staff of the newspaper *Russkaya mysl*, where his literary and political articles appeared regularly. He also publishes in *Grani*, *Kontinent*, *Vremya i my*, and *Ekho*. Through his two novels, *Tyazhest* (1977; Eng. tr., *The Burden*, 1984) and *Tavro* (1981; Brand), he won recognition as a serious writer. In 1984 he moved to Frankfurt am Main.

In *Tyazhest* Rybakov was the first and until now the only Russian author to provide a truthful picture of the daily life of Soviet soldiers on the Chinese front. The exceedingly harsh discipline, the ranking by classes and even by years of induction, the quantitative and qualitative lack of rations, the escape into drugs, and the constant fear are described by examining their effect on human lives. Ideological and spiritual problems are even more prominent in *Tavro*, a novel depicting the first period of adjustment of a Russian émigré to France. Against a background of material and interpersonal problems, Rybakov probes the essential question of how a Soviet émigré can come to terms with his Soviet education in totalitarianism; this "brand" of his hinders his normal integration. The unvarnished truth of daily life for a Soviet soldier is clearly revealed in the 68 short stories that Rybakov collected in *Tiski* (1985; Vise). The image chosen for the title reflects the physical and psychic pressure to which both the troops and the officers are subjected. Rybakov related typical events that he himself experienced as a soldier and that he observed in the war between the Soviet Union and Afghanistan during the 1980s. His sober reports of scenes from daily life of degradation, demagogy, brutality, willingness to conform, and Russian chauvinism are ultimately an appeal to safeguard human dignity. Rybakov is currently writing a third novel, *Ten topora* (The Shadow of the Axe), that illustrates the evolution of an unusual relationship to authority and the necessity of deciding about right and wrong, life and death, using the example of an isolated group of people at a Siberian drilling rig. Another novel that is half science fiction and half history will use Mongolian and other examples to depict the state's tendency to abolish private property.

*Works: Sovetskaja armija bez oreola* (essay), in *Russkaja mysl'*, Paris, Nov. 11, 1976; *Tjažest'* (novel), Frankfurt am Main, 1977; *Tavro* (novel), Frankfurt am Main, 1981; *Ten' topora* (novel fragment), in *Russkaja mysl'* Feb. 9 and 16, 1984, p. 8; *Tiski* (short stories), Frankfurt am Main, 1985.

*Secondary Lit.*: E. Kanak, in *Russkaja mysl'* Feb. 3, 1977; V. Sinkevič, in *Novoe russkoe slovo*, New York, Oct. 17, 1982; Anon., in *Kontinent*, Paris, 33:1982; G. Vladimov, in Rybakov's *Tiski*, Frankfurt am Main, 1985; K. Pomerancev, in *Russkaja mysl'* Oct. 25, 1985, p. 10; W. Kasack, in *Neue Zürcher Zeitung* Sept. 20–21, 1986.

**Rylénkov, Nikoláy Ivánovich**, poet (b. Feb. 15 [Feb. 2], 1909, Alekseyevka, prov. Smolensk—d. June 23, 1969, Smolensk). Rylenkov's father was a peasant. Rylenkov completed his schooling in Roslavl in 1926; he then worked as a village schoolteacher. In 1933 he graduated from the Smolensk Pedagogical Institute (Department of Language and Literature) and went on to a career in editing. Rylenkov began writing poetry while still in school; his first poem was published in 1926. His first volume of verse, *Moi geroi* (My Heroes), appeared in 1933; it was, like the publications that followed it, ignored by the critics because Rylenkov wrote only apolitical nature poems. During World War II, Rylenkov served initially as a frontline officer for an engineering unit; in February 1942 he became a correspondent. He joined the Communist Party in 1945. Rylenkov continued to publish during the Stalin period, but only after 1954 did he find critical recognition (which came not only for his poetry but also for his lyrical prose, which he was developing at the same time). Rylenkov took up residence in Smolensk again in 1943. From 1954 on, he participated in all of the congresses of the Writers Unions of the USSR and the RSFSR; he belonged to the board (from 1958 on) and to the secretariat (from 1965 on) of the Writers Union of the RSFSR.

The entire body of Rylenkov's poetry consists of variations on the theme of his native Smolensk landscape, with his love of its plants and animals, its waters and soil. He observes its manifestations and integrates these with his thoughts about human beings. When the state ideology returned to an emphasis on historical consciousness, historical themes entered his work, occasionally in ballad form. Rylenkov's narrative poems—such as *Aprel* (1942; April), about reunion with his family during the war—and his prose are autobiographical in nature; thus his *Koktebelskaya elegiya* (written in 1967–68 but published for the first time posthumously in 1976; Koktebel Elegy) contains his recollections of M. Voloshin. Poetic contemplation, the depiction of particular situations, and reflection dominate his work, while conflict, plot, and political interpretation are avoided. It is not profound thought or multileveled meaning that characterizes Rylenkov's poems (especially the shorter ones), but naturalness, simplicity, and unassuming moderation.

*Works: Moi geroi* (poems), 1933; *Dykhanie* (poems), 1938; *Zelënyj cekh* (poems), 1949; *Stikhotvorenija i poèmy* (lyric and narrative poems), 1956, reissued in 2 vols., 1959; *Korni i list'ja* (poems), 1960; *Na ozere Sapšo* (short stories), 1966; *Kniga vremeni* (poems), 1969; *Koktebel'skaja èlegija* (memoirs), in *Zvezda* 1976:6.—*Izbr. proizv.,* 2 vols., 1974.
    *Secondary Lit.:* L. Levickij, in *Novyj mir* 1959:7; E. Osetrov, in *Molodaja gvardija* 1959:2, n *Lit. Rossija* Jan. 12, 1968, pp. 16–17, and in separate study, 1974; L. Anninskij, in *Lit. gazeta* Feb. 8, 1962; V. Dement'ev, in *Voprosy lit.* 1967:12; V. Zvezdaeva, in *Zvezda* 1977:10 and in *Don* 1979:3; A. Turkov, in *Naš sovremennik* 1985:7.

**Rzhévsky, Leoníd Denísovich** (until 1969 his real name was L. D. Surazhévsky), prose writer, literary scholar (b. Aug. 21 [Aug. 8], 1905, Moscow—d. Nov. 13, 1986, New York). Until 1930 Rzhevsky studied philology in Moscow; in 1941 he passed his candidate's exam. Between 1928 and 1941 he taught at various institutes, as a lecturer after 1938. In 1941 Rzhevsky was taken prisoner by the Germans. After 1944 he lived near Munich and adopted the pseudonym of Rzhevsky. From 1950 to 1953 he lived in the area around Frankfurt, where he worked as an editor for the journal *Grani.* From 1953 to 1963 he was a university lecturer in Lund, Sweden. In 1963 he accepted a position as a professor in the United States and moved there. Rzhevsky combined literary creativity with literary scholarship in numerous books and essays). His first larger work of prose, *Devushka iz bunkera* (1950–1; The Girl from the Bunker), had been followed, by 1984, by four novels and numerous short stories (in *Grani, Mosty, Novy zhurnal,* and other journals); he collected some of his short stories and published them in three volumes. In Munich in 1958, Rzhevsky compiled an anthology of the second EMIGRATION, *Literaturnoye zarubezhye* (The Literary Abroad). Rzhevsky lived in New York, worked as a professor of Slavic literatures, and was a member of the American PEN Club.
    In most of his works, Rzhevsky combines the events of emigration with experiences in his homeland or encounters with later émigrés.

He is one of the few authors of the second emigration also to depict interaction with Germans in the postwar period. Rzhevsky favors the first-person structure and enjoys incorporating reflections on writing the prose work into the work itself. In its expanded and reworked version, his first novel, *Devushka iz bunkera,* bears the title *Mezhdu dvukh zvyozd* (1951–53; Between Two Stars); this work depicts Soviet citizens caught between Soviet and American constellations. (An abbreviated version was translated into Spanish.) In *Sentimentalnaya povest* (1954; A Sentimental Tale), which was translated into German, a love story—a frequent element in Rzhevsky's prose—is interwoven with a public meeting in the Soviet Union in 1940–41 to defame a university instructor (that is, V. V. Vinogradov, Rzhevsky's teacher). The short story *Dve nedeli* (1959: Two Weeks) portrays the fear and the quest for solace of a deathly ill first-person narrator who, without any serious reflection, has rejected the idea of life after death. For the novel *Dina* (1979), Rzhevsky chose the theme of a young Soviet woman who marries a foreigner yet remains dependent on the KGB. *Bunt podsolnechnika* (1981; The Mutiny of the Sunflowers) attempts to depict the topic "creative work and freedom" illustrated by referring to the encounter of writers of the second and third emigration. Rzhevsky's descriptive prose is distinguished by detailed delineation of character and lengthy dialogue, both of which develop from a simple plot line that often preserves the independence of episodes. In addition to his books on F. Dostoyevsky, B. Pasternak, and A. Solzhenitsyn, Rzhevsky's works of literary criticism have honored the second emigration.

*Works: Devuška iz bunkera* (novel), in *Grani,* Frankfurt am Main, 8–9:1950, 11:1951, later expanded under the title *Meždu dvukh zvëzd,* New York, 1953; *Nagrada* (play), in *Grani* 12:1951; *Sentimental'naja povest',* in *Grani* 21:1954; *Dve nedeli: Zapiski iz bol'ničnoj kojki* (short story), in *Grani* 42:1959; *Dvoe na kamne* (pov. and short stories), Munich, 1960; . . . *pokazavšemu nam svet: Optimističeskaja povest',* Frankfurt am Main, 1961; *Čerez proliv* (pov. and short stories), Munich, 1966; *Sputnica: Zapiski khudožnika* (novel), in *Mosty,* New York, 13–14:1968, 15:1970; *Tvorec i podvig: Očerki po tvorčestvu Aleksandra Solženicyna* (essays), Frankfurt am Main, 1975 (Eng. tr., *Solzhenitsyn: Creator and Heroic Deed,* University, Alabama, 1978); *Dve stročki vremeni* (novel), Frankfurt am Main, 1976; *Dina: Zapiski khudožnika* (novel), New York,

1979; *Bunt podsolnečnika* (novel), Ann Arbor, 1981; *Zvezdopad* (pov.), Ann Arbor, 1984. *Secondary Lit.*: R. Gul', in *Novyj žurnal*, New York, 34:1953, and in his *Odvukon'*, New York, 1973; V. Zavališin, in *Novyj žurnal* 62:1960; G. Adamovič, in *Novoe russkoe slovo*, New York, April 2, 1961; F. Stepun, in *Mosty*, Munich, 7:1961; T. Fesenko, in *Novyj žurnal* 145:1981; N. Andreev, in *Novyj žurnal* 147:1982; V. Iverni, in *Kontinent*, Paris, 34:1982; K. Sapgir, in *Russkaja mysl'*, Paris, Feb. 17, 1983; J. Baer, in *Russian Language Journal* 131:1984; R. Dneprov, in *Russkaja mysl'* Jan. 24, 1986, p. 12.

# S

**Salýnsky, Afanásy Dmítriyevich,** playwright (b. Sept. 9, 1920, Smolensk). After completing school, Salynsky worked in a factory and a mine and became a journalist in 1939. As a soldier in World War II, he became a member of the Communist Party in 1942. After the war Salynsky lived in Sverdlovsk where his first drama, *Bratya* (1947; The Brothers), was performed in 1949 under the title *Doroga pervykh* (The Path of the First). This drama, as well as the next one, *Opasny sputnik* (1952; The Dangerous Companion), belongs to the style of industrial drama that was widespread at that time. From 1956 to 1972, Salynsky, who moved to Moscow at the beginning of this period, staged seven dramas whose themes conformed to the contemporary concerns of the Party. *Barabanshchitsa* (1958; The Female Drummer) was performed most often, with 4,325 performances at 176 theaters in the Soviet Union in 1960. In 1971 there were still more than 100 performances. Since the Third Congress of the Writers Union of the USSR in 1959, Salynsky has been among the leading literary officials and is especially responsible for drama. He is a member of the secretariat of the Writers Union of the USSR and has given a speech at every congress. He was one of those awarded the Stanislavsky Prize in 1972. He is editor in chief of the journal *Teatr*.

*Zabyty drug* (1955; The Forgotten Friend), a play written in accordance with Party doctrine about the problems of a discharged, unjustly condemned prisoner in a labor camp, received little acclaim, and neither did *Khleb i rozy* (1958; Bread and Roses), which was written for the 40th anniversary of the October Revolution and concerns the establishment of Soviet power in the Altai. In *Barabanshchitsa* Salynsky describes a former Soviet female agent who, in 1943 in a liberated city, struggles to overcome people's mistrust because of her "collaboration" with the Germans. The war theme is a factor in still other plays. *Mariya* (1969; Eng. tr., *Maria*, in *Nine Modern Soviet Plays*, 1977) was well received; here

Salynsky chose the theme of conflict between humane Party leadership and reckless industrial development, using the example of the construction of a power station in Siberia. He combines ethical and political problems in *Molva* (1980; The Rumor), whose story is set in the NEP period with its questioning of revolutionary ideals. Salynsky's plays stem mainly from his own experiences, but they contain much that is constructed for the sake of the political idea, resulting in conflicts as unnatural as the dialogue.

*Works: Opasnyj sputnik* (play), 1953; *Zabytyj drug* (play), in *Teatr* 1955:11; *Khleb i rozy* (play), 1958; *Barabanščica* (play), in *Teatr* 1959:1, 1960; *Lož' dlja uzkogo kruga* (comedy), 1964; *Kameški na ladoni* (play), in *Teatr* 1965:4, separate ed., 1966; *P'esy* (plays), 1966 (contains the six plays cited); *Mužskie besedy* (play), in *Teatr* 1967:9, 1969; *Marija* (play), in *Teatr* 1969:12; *Letnie progulki* (play), in *Novyj mir* 1973:10; *Dolgoždannyj* (play), in *Teatr* 1975:9; *Dramy i komedii* (plays), 1977 (contains the ten plays cited); *Molva* (play), in *Teatr* 1980:9; *Sladkaja sobačka, ili Ošibka velikogo Vasi Osokina* (play), in *Teatr* 1982:2; *O žizni, dramaturgii, teatre* (articles, essays), 1982; *Perekhod na letnee vremja* (play), in *Teatr* 1983:12; *Vozdušnyj poceluj* (comedy), in *Sovremennaja dramaturgija* 1985:1; *Spasenie* (play), in *Teatr* 1985:5.

*Secondary Lit.*: N. Ignat'eva, in *Lit. gazeta* June 17, 1954; N. Gromov, in *Lit. gazeta* Sept. 2, 1961, and in *Teatr* 1965:6; A. Radiščeva, in *Teatr* 1972:9; A. Belkin, in *Lit. obozrenie* 1974:6; Ja. S. Fel'dman, 1976; A. Smeljanskij, in *Lit. gazeta* May 19, 1982, p. 8; I. Ungurjanu, in *Teatr* 1984:8.

**Samizdát** (self-publishing), an acronym analogous to official abbreviations such as Gosizdat (Gosudarstvennoye izdatelstvo [State Publishing House]) or Detizdat (Children's Publishing House). This term was developed in early 1966 to denote private literary and journalistic production and distribution in the Soviet Union as a replacement for book publication subject to state censorship. Historically the distribution in Russia of literary works that were not allowed by the censor dates back to at least the end of the 18th century when A. Radishchev's "Journey from St. Petersburg to Moscow" circulated in transcribed copies. After the Revolution, this tradition was continued, for example with M. Bulgakov's dramas or the OBERIU poems of D. Kharms and A. Vvedensky. Only starting in 1959 did this form of private reproduction and transmission of literary works acquire a greater scope and thereby become a substitute for printed works, a feature that distinguishes samizdat from the private and personal transmission of information in transcribed copies. Since duplicating machines are not allowed in private hands in the Soviet Union, the text is typed in numerous copies or photographed. The number of copies increases rapidly through the transcription of transcriptions. Especially with poetry and songs (B. Okudzhava, A. Galich, V. Vysotsky), tape recordings and copies of these tapes constitute an additional aspect of samizdat. Dissemination in the West contributes greatly to circulation since numerous samizdat works are published and read over the radio and thus return to the Soviet Union (this process is known as TAMIZDAT [there-publishing]). In terms of content, samizdat includes pure literature as well as political documentation, both published and unpublished material, and works written in the original as well as translations. Publication in samizdat occurs both with and without the author's consent. Since 1959 a series of samizdat journals have appeared, such as Sintaksis (published by A. Ginzburg), Bumerang (published by V. Osipov), Feniks (Phoenix; published by Yu. Galanskov), Poiski (Searches; no. 1, 1978), as well as almanacs such as Metropol (1979) and Katalog (1980). O. Mandelshtam's, B. Pasternak's, and N. Korzhavin's poems were circulated through samizdat, as were the novels of A. Solzhenitsyn, V. Grossman, and V. Maksimov, the autobiographical and journalistic writings of A. Amalrik, the reports on the trials of I. Brodsky and Sinyavsky-Daniel, and other writings. These trials, as well as the distribution of the unofficial court records, also reveal the controversies between the government and samizdat. Since in many respects samizdat legally corresponds to the widespread system of wall newspapers and does not, in principle, run counter to the existing laws, the state organs

try to proceed against samizdat by using Article 70 of the penal code of the RSFSR, which imposes harsh penalties for "anti-Soviet agitation and propaganda." Numerous samizdat publishers and authors were sentenced to long terms in camps or to internal exile; some were permitted to emigrate. Outside the Soviet Union, samizdat publications are collected by several institutions (for example, the Library of Congress, Slavic and East European Division, Washington, D.C., and the Bodleian Library, Slavonic Section, Oxford), and they are also published, especially by Radio Liberty, Munich (Arkhiv Samizdata, 1972–75; Materialy Samizdata, since 1973); by Posev Publishing House, Frankfurt am Main (Volnoye slovo); by Kuratorium Geistige Freiheit, Bern (Russ. Samizdat); and by the Alexander Herzen Foundation, Amsterdam (Biblioteka Samizdata).

*Secondary Lit.*: K. van het Reve, in *Die Zeit* April 10, 1970; A. Boiter, in *Osteuropa* 1972:9 and in *Russian Review* 1972; D. A. Loeber, in *Rabels Zeitschrift für ausländisches und internationales Privatrecht* 1973:2–3; A. Terc (A. Sinjavskij), in *Kontinent*, Paris, 1:1974; F. J. M. Feldbrugge, Leiden, 1975; Ju. Mal'cev, *Vol'naja russkaja lit.*, Frankfurt am Main, 1976; Ju. Višnevskaja, in *Russkaya mysl'*, Paris, Jan. 27, 1977, p. 5; *Samizdat tridcatykh godov*, in *Russkaja mysl'* April 7, 1977, pp. 4–5; D. Pospielovsky, in *Canadian Slavonic Papers*, 1978:1; G. Svirskij, *Na lobnom meste*, London, 1979; V. P., in *Kontinent* 52:1986.

**Samóylov, Davíd Samuílovich** (pseud. of D. S. Káufman), poet (b. June 1, 1920, Moscow). Samoylov studied humanities in Moscow (1938–41). He served as a soldier in World War II. Samoylov, who had written poems since his youth, first concentrated on translating from Polish, Czech, Hungarian, and other languages. His first volume of poetry appeared in 1958. Samoylov was represented in K. Paustovsky's *Tarusskiye stranitsy* published in 1961 with six poems and the narrative poem *Chaynaya* (The Tea Room). His own volumes followed: *Vtoroy pereval* (1963; The Second [Mountain] Pass), *Dni* (1970; Days), *Ravnodenstviye* (1972; Equinox), and *Volna i kamen* (1974; Wave and Stone). With *Kniga o russkoy rifme* (1973, 2d ed., 1982; A Book on Russian Rhyme), Samoylov proved himself an excellent authority on Russian verse technique, which he deals with from *byliny* (traditional Russian epic poetry) up to the present. Samoylov lives in Moscow and in Parnu,

Estonian SSR, has not participated in the congresses of the Writers Unions, and does not hold any positions.

As a member of the war generation and a highly talented poet, Samoylov made a late appearance on the literary scene and thus his wartime experiences have never played a dominant role in his creative work. Samoylov often turns to history. His condemnation of Ivan the Terrible's cruelty, which the Tsar justified for national and political reasons, aims beyond the idealization of historic personalities under Stalin. Almost half of *Vtoroy pereval* consists of the section "Sukhoye plamya" (The Dry Flames), which Samoylov calls "historical scenes"; in them, using the example of Aleksandr Menshikov, he exposes the senselessness of destroying other people's lives as a national-historical expedient. *Chaynaya*, which is written more like a ballad, symbolically formulates, by using a contemporary situation, the poet's right to portray the pain and suffering of the people. Dream, vision, and a jumbled mixture of historical epochs and the present day (in *Posledniye kanikuly* [1973; The Last Vacation]) offer him the possibility of a multilevel message. The frequent use of dialogue strengthens the polarity of the poetry, which never depends on the unusual. Behind the "clarity of view, of thought, of image" that V. Kardin praises and behind the form that is semantically and syntactically simple and oriented toward Russian classicism stand a tragic perception of the world and an aspiration toward justice and human freedom.

*Works: Bližnie strany* (poems), 1958; *Čajnaja* (narrative poem), in *Tarusskie stranicy*, 1961; *Vtoroj pereval* (poems), 1963; *Dni* (poems), 1970; *Ravnodenstvie* (lyric and narrative poems), 1972; *Kniga o russkoj rifme* (poems), 1973, 2d ed., 1982; *Poslednie kanikuly* (narrative poem), in *Den' poèzii*, Moscow, 1973; *Volna i kamen'* (poems), 1974; *Vest'* (poems), 1978; *Izbr.* (lyric and narrative poems), 1980; *Zaliv* (poems), 1981; *Vremena* (poems), 1983; *Stikhotvorenija* (poems), 1985.

*Secondary Lit.:* V. Kardin, in *Družba narodov* 1960:3; B. Sarnov, in *Novyj mir* 1964:3; A. Drawicz, *Zaproszenie do podróży*, Kraków, 1974, pp. 273–76; P. Vegin, in *Oktjabr'* 1974:12; Ju. Mineralov, in *Moskva* 1975:2; L. Anninskij, in *Družba narodov* 1979:9; V. Baevskij, in *Voprosy lit.* 1981:5 and 1986; N. Gubenko, S. Čuprinin, in *Lit. gazeta* Dec. 3, 1986, p. 4.

**Sapgír, Génrich Veniamínovich,** poet (b. Nov. 20, 1928, Biysk, Altai). Sapgir's father was a

shoemaker. Sapgir became independent of his family at the age of 14. Arseny Alvig (a disciple of I. Annensky), and later Yevgeny Kropivnitsky, concerned themselves with his literary education. Sapgir lives in Moscow, publishes poetry for children (approximately 40 books from 1960 to 1984), wrote scripts for children's theater and cartoon films, and translated the Jewish poet Ovsey Driz. In the 1960s he led the unofficial avant-garde group of poets called "Konkret" (which included such poets as V. Bakhchanyan, I. Kholin, V. Levin, E. Limonov, and V. Nekrasov) and organized exhibitions of nonconformist artists in his apartment. In 1973, in the journal *Priroda*, he was able for the first time to publish one of his serious poems. Since 1975 he has published these poems in the West in such journals as *Tretya volna* (since 2:1976), *Kontinent* (16:1978), and *Vremya i my* (since 62:1978), as well as in the anthologies *Apollon-77* and METROPOL. As his first book, the publishing house Tretya volna (Paris, New York) issued *Sonety na rubashkakh* (1978; Sonnets on Shirts); the title alludes to two sonnets that he wrote on his own shirts for a 1975 exhibition of avant-garde artists as "examples of visual poetry" (these exhibits were disallowed by the censor).

Sapgir is a very talented poet with a distinctive, multifaceted linguistic power of expression. From his first unpublished collections "Golosa" (1963; Voices), "Psalmy" (1965; Psalms), and "Elegii" (1968; Elegies), only a few isolated poems became known. The published volume of sonnets combines the seriousness of his concern and his playfulness with language. Sapgir is able to pursue philosophic issues, such as spirit and body, death and life, friendship and love; by identifying the poetic "I" with an object, he allows a suitcase, a shirt, a signature, even a part of the body, to speak. His range of available forms extends from classical narrative means of expression, through multiple lexical and syntactical experiments, up to stringing together nouns that serve only as signals. His imagery is bold and strongly alienating. The parallel positioning of very different kinds of linguistic information creates a broad field for the fantasy of the recipient. Sapgir generally avoids using punctuation.

*Works:* Poems, in *Freiheit ist Freiheit*, Zurich, 1975; in *Tret'ja volna*, Paris, since 2:1976; in *Vremja i my*, Tel Aviv, since 62:1978; in *Kontinent*, Paris, 16:1978; in *Apollon-77*, Paris, 1977; in *NRL: Neue russische Literatur*, Salzburg, 1978; in *Metropol'*, Ann Arbor, 1979; in *Čast' reči*, New York, 1980; in *The Blue La-*

goon: *Anthology of Modern Russian Poetry*, vol. 1, Newtonville, Mass., 1980; *Sonety na rubaškakh* (poems), Paris, 1978; *Iz sbornika "Psalmy Davida"* (poems), in *Tret'ja volna* 6:1979; *Skladen'* (cycle of poems), in NRL: *Neue russische Literatur* 4–5:1983; *Golosa* (poems), in Ёkho, Paris, 14:1986.

*Secondary Lit.:* Anon., in *Kontinent* 17:1978; P. Vajl, in *Tret'ja volna* 6:1979; W. Kasack, in *Osteuropa* 1980:11; R. Ziegler, in *Russische Lyrik heute*, Mainz, 1983; K. Sapgir, in *Novoe russkoe slovo*, New York, March 31, 1985, p. 5.

**Sartakóv, Sergéy Venedíktovich,** literary official, prose writer (b. March 26 [March 13], 1908, Omsk). Sartakov's father was a railroad employee. Sartakov completed school in 1924; he worked as a carpenter and bookkeeper; in 1931–34 he served in the Red Army. In 1938 his first short story appeared. Sartakov's activity during World War II has not been disclosed. After the war, collections of his short stories appeared in Krasnoyarsk. For a three-part novel, *Khrebty Sayanskiye* (1948–55; The Sayan Mountains), Sartakov chose the theme of the origin of revolutionary thought in Siberia before 1905. Since 1951 he has been a member of the Communist Party. In 1954 Sartakov was accepted on the staff of the Writers Union of the USSR; in 1957 he became the deputy chairman of the organizing committee of the Writers Union of the RSFSR, and, as a member of the board, was given the chairmanship of the Litfond. In 1958 he moved to Moscow; until 1962 he was a delegate to the Supreme Soviet of the RSFSR and a member of the editorial staff of the journal *Molodaya gvardiya*. In 1967 Sartakov became one of the secretaries of the Writers Union of the USSR; in 1971, chairman of the statutory commission and deputy chairman of the secretariat of the board of the Writers Union of the USSR. *Barbinskiye povesti* (1957–67; Eng. tr., *Siberian Stories*, 1979), which is composed of three short stories, won the State Prize in 1970.

Sartakov's distinction is based solely on his work as an official. The literary quality of his books, which always involve Siberia, is so insignificant that he is seldom mentioned in the comprehensive Soviet histories of literature, despite the fact that his adherence to the principle of PARTY SPIRIT is unquestioned. The same old pattern of the capitalist exploitation of the worker in whom the Bolsheviks instill a revolutionary consciousness appears in *Khrebty Sayanskiye*. In *Pervaya vstrecha* 1967; First Meeting) and *Zharky letniy den*

(1969; A Hot Summer Day), Sartakov also published short stories about Lenin. In *Svintsovy monument* (1980; Leaden Monument) he traces a Siberian worker's development into a painter who conforms to Party dogma. Sartakov's style is awkward and not at all precise; he lacks a visual imagination and compositional ability.

*Works: Aleksej Khudonogov* (short stories), 1946; *Po Čunskim dorogam* (pov.), 1946; *Khrebty Sajanskie* (novel), 3 vols., 1948–55; *Pervaja vstreča* (short stories), 1967; *Barbinskie povesti* (short stories), 1968 (see above); *Žarkij letnij den'* (short stories), 1969; *Filosofskij kamen'* (novel), 2 vols., 1971 (Eng. tr., *The Philosopher's Stone*, 1975); *A ty gori, zvezda* (novel), in *Oktjabr'* 1974:4–6 and 1975:1–3, separate ed., 1976; *Svincovyj monument* (novel), 1981; *Voskrešenie listvennicy*, Paris, 1985.—*Izbr.*, 2 vols., 1975; *Sobr. soč.*, 6 vols., 1978–80.

*Secondary Lit.:* B. Beljaev, in *Novyj mir* 1951:8; A. Pavlovskij, in *Zvezda* 1958:12; RSPP 4:1966; L. Kaljarskaja, in *Znamja* 1968:3; G. Eršov, 1969; G. Brovman, in *Lit. gazeta* April 23, 1975, p. 4; A. Dremov, 1975; I. Kučakov, in *Oktjabr'* 1978:4; B. Brajnina, in *Moskva* 1983:1; A. Dremov, I. Dremova, in *Znamja* 1984:11.

**Sávich, Ovády Gértsovich,** prose writer (b. July 17, 1896, Warsaw—d. July 19, 1967, Moscow). Savich came from a well-educated family and wrote his first poems while still a schoolboy; in 1915 he began studying law at Moscow University. He worked as an actor from 1917 to 1923. Savich allegedly lived for some time in Paris (not, however, as an émigré). He published short stories in (among other journals) *Krasnaya nov* and brought out two collections, *Korotkoye zamykaniye* (1927; Short Circuit) and *Plavuchiy ostrov* (1927; The Floating Island). These were followed by his most important published work, *Voobrazhayemy sobesednik* (1928; The Imaginary Interlocutor). "It is one of the very few Soviet novels dealing almost entirely with personal problems and without political implications" (Struve). From 1932 to 1936 Savich was in Paris as a correspondent for *Komsomolskaya pravda*. I. Erenburg, who had become a friend of Savich's in the early 1920s, took him to Spain in 1937; Savich remained there until 1939 as a correspondent for TASS. His participation in the Spanish Civil War inspired such works as *Lyudi internatsionalnykh brigad* (1938; People of the International Brigades) and *Dva goda v Ispanii* (1961; Two

Years in Spain). Savich worked as a journalist during World War II, at first for the Central Committee of the Komsomol, then for Informbyuro. After the war he worked primarily as a translator; together he and Erenburg translated J.-P. Sartre's *Nekrassov* (*Tolko pravda in Znamya* 1955:8), but Savich translated mostly Spanish and Latin American poets (several books beginning in 1959). In retirement he lived in Moscow and at his death left unpublished prose, poetry, and literary essays. Savich is not mentioned in Soviet literary histories.

"In Savich's life there were three patches of happiness—*Voobrazhayemy sobesednik*, his defense of Spain, and his translations" (Kaverin). Savich's prose has its source in the ornamental and fragmentary style of the Pilnyakian school. A short story such as *Konokrady* (1927; The Horse Thieves) reveals an artistically high level in creating a suspenseful narrative whose plot line is often broken off to increase tension. *Voobrazhayemy sobesednik* is the story, rich in symbols, of a little man who after 50 years of a banal existence comes suddenly to reflect on the possibilities of a self-realization that he has never achieved (the narrative is intensified by the introduction of an imaginary alter ego); overwhelmed by his reflections, he gradually goes to ruin.

*Works: V gorakh* (pov.), in *Krasnaja nov'* 1925:9; *Korotkoe zamykanie* (short stories), 1927; *Plavučij ostrov* (short stories), 1927; *Voobražaemyj sobesednik* (novel), 1928, Berlin, 1929; *Van'ka-vstan'ka* (pov.), 1928; *Ljudi internacional'nykh brigad* (essays), 1938; *Sčast'e Kartakheny* (short stories), 1947; *Dva goda v Ispanii* (memoirs), 1961, 3d ed., 1975. (A selective bibliography of Savich's translations into Russian appears in *Kratkaja literaturnaya enciklopedija*, vol. 6, 1971.)
*Secondary Lit.*: Ju. Fel'zen, in *Čisla*, Paris, 1:1930; R. Zernova, in *Novyj mir* 1961:11; H. Pross-Weerth, in *Kindlers Lit. Lexikon*, vol. 7, 1965; B. Sluckij, in *Inostrannaja lit.* 1967:2; V. Ognëv, in *Den' poèzii*, Moscow, 1971; V. Kaverin, *Sobesednik* 1973, pp. 173–86.

**Sayánov, Vissarión Mikháylovich** (pseud. of V. M. Makhlín), poet, prose writer (b. June 16 [June 3], 1903, Geneva—d. Jan. 22, 1959, Leningrad). Sayanov's father emigrated to Europe for political reasons. From the time he was four, Sayanov lived in Siberia (prov. Irkutsk), where his parents were exiled after their return; he later took his pseudonym from the

name of the local mountain range. He did not participate in the Civil War. Sayanov attended Leningrad University (1922–25). He began his literary career as a poet; in 1923 he became a member of LAPP, then later joined "Smena" (1926–29). His first volume of verse appeared in 1926, and other volumes followed on a regular basis. In the late 1920s Sayanov decided to depict, in a series of novels, the events that transformed Russia between the end of the last century and the present. His plan was interrupted by World War II, in which Sayanov participated as a correspondent. The second part of the series, *Nebo i zemlya* (1935–54; Heaven and Earth), a novel about the first Russian pilots, received a Stalin Prize in 1948 (3d class), even though Sayanov had been personally attacked in the Party Resolution of 1946 (see PARTY RESOLUTIONS ON LITERATURE). The first novel in the series, *Lena* (1953–54; The Lena River), about revolutionaries during the tsarist period, and the third part, *Strana rodnaya* (1953–56; Native Land), which deals with the period 1928–46, attracted less attention. Sayanov continued his activities as a literary critic and as an editor; he held, among others, a post on the editorial board of the "Biblioteka poeta" (Poet's Library) series. He was a member of the board of the Leningrad section of the Writers Union of the USSR (from 1941 on); he was also a member of the boards of the Writers Unions of the USSR (from 1954 on) and of the RSFSR (from 1958 on).

Sayanov's trilogy remains, in terms of its content, within the framework of much of the literature of his time. Chronology, rather than character or plot line, unites its various parts; the narration is leisurely but not without suspense; nevertheless, the author adds his own comments to the work's underlying psychological disclosures instead of letting the work speak for itself. The center of gravity of Sayanov's work lies in his poetry, in which the influence of various modernist tendencies was initially discernible. Sayanov's *Komsomolskiye stikhi* (1928; Komsomol Poems) is burdened with the usual internationalistic and ascetic enthusiasm of the time; in Sayanov's later verse, G. Struve missed "the attractive personal accent of his more youthful poetry." "In his overworked style the flavor of the period became lost" (Azarov). The strongest personal note is sounded in the narrative poem *Zolotaya Olyokma* (1934; Golden Olyokma), a portrayal of the old and the new Siberia.

*Works: Fartovye goda* (poems), 1926; *Komsomol'skie stikhi* (poems), 1928; *Zolotaja*

*Olëkma* (narrative poem), 1934; *Nebo i zemlja* (novel), 1935–54; *Lukomor'e* (narrative poem), 1939; *Iva* (narrative poem), 1939; *V bojakh za Leningrad* (articles), 1943; *Njurnbergskij dnevnik* (poems), 1946; *Lena* (novel), 1954–55; *Strana rodnaja* (novel), 1953–56; *Kolobovy* (novel in verse), 1956; *Stikhotvorenija i poèmy* (lyric and narrative poems), 1966; *Stikhotvorenija* (poems), 1970.—*Izbr. soč.*, 2 vols., 1955; *Soč.*, 2 vols., 1959.

*Secondary Lit.*: M. Zen'kevič, in *Novyj mir* 1929:6; V. Azarov, in *Zvezda* 1953:9 and in *Neva* 1973:3; V. Abramkin and A. Lur'e, 1958, 1959; *RSPP* 7(2):1972; D. Khrenkov, 1972; A. Volkov, in *Zvezda* 1980:7.

**Sedýkh, Andréy** (pseud. of Yákov Moiséyevich Tsvíbak), prose writer (b. Aug. 14 [Aug. 1], 1902, Feodosiya). Sedykh's father was a journalist. Sedykh completed secondary school in Feodosiya and emigrated via Constantinople to Paris in 1920. There he graduated from the Ecole des Sciences politiques in 1925. From 1922 on, Sedykh worked regularly as a journalist and was a frequent contributor to P. Milyukov's newspaper *Posledniye novosti* and, after he completed his studies, correspondent for this newspaper in parliament. He was also a correspondent for *Segodnya* (Riga) and *Novoye russkoye slovo* (New York). With *Stary Parizh* (1925; Old Paris), Sedykh began compiling his commentary and literary sketches into books. A. Kuprin wrote the foreword for *Parizh nochyu* (1928; Paris by Night). Around 1930 Sedykh adopted his pseudonym. After I. Bunin was awarded the Nobel Prize, he asked Sedykh to work as his secretary. Before the Germans invaded in 1941, Sedykh was forced to flee Paris. He arrived in New York on Feb. 20, 1942, and was immediately given a position on the editorial staff of the journal *Novoye russkoye slovo*. During the first few years, Sedykh earned his living working for an insurance company. By 1984, Sedykh had published 16 books of his short stories and commentary, some of which were reprinted several times, and he had won wide recognition among the Russian émigré community both within the United States and abroad as editor in chief of the journal *Novoye russkoye slovo*, which he took over in 1973, and as a writer and social activist.

Sedykh has the ability to transpose his observations and experiences of everyday life into clear and vivid works of short prose. Through numerous exchanges of dialogue in which he attempts to preserve the linguistic individuality of non-Russian peoples (for ex-ample, the Tatars in the Crimea) he lends life and local color to his prose. His themes are partly contemporary, partly reminiscent, and they reveal the people, nature, and atmosphere of the time being depicted. *Doroga cherez okean* (1942; The Trip over the Ocean) describes the experiences of his second flight; in *Dalyokiye blizkiye* (1962; Distant People, Near People), whose fourth edition is planned, he collected literary portraits, remembrances, and quotes from letters and transformed them into striking essays about writers such as M. Aldanov, D. Aminado, K. Balmont, I. Bunin, D. Knut, A. Remizov, and other important figures of Russian cultural life. His work *Zemlya Obetovannaya* (1962) was translated into English as *This Land of Israel* (New York, London, 1967). *Puti-dorogi* (1980; Many Kinds of Travels) combines writings about his trips to Italy and Spain with extracts from books dating from 1931 and 1942.

*Works* (1925–28 under the name of Cvibak, from 1930 under the name of Sedykh): *Staryj Pariž* (short stories), Paris, 1925; *Monmartr* (short stories), Paris, 1927; *Pariž noč'ju* (short stories), Paris, 1928; *Tam, gde žili koroli* (short stories), Paris, 1928; *Tam, gde byla Rossija* (short stories), Paris, 1931; *Lyudi za bortom* (short stories), Paris, 1933; *Doroga čerez okean* (short stories), New York, 1942; *Zvezdočěty s Bosfora* (short stories), New York, 1948; *Sumasšedšij šarmanščik* (short stories), New York, 1951; *Tol'ko o ljudjakh* (short stories), New York, 1955; *Dalëkie, blizkie* (literary portraits), New York, 1962, 3d ed., 1979; *Zemlja Obetovannaja* (short stories), New York, 1962 (see above); *Zamelo tebja snegom, Rossija* (short stories), New York, 1964; *Ierusalim, imja radostnoe* (short stories), New York, 1969; *Krymskie rasskazy* (short stories), New York, 1977; *Puti-dorogi* (short stories), New York, 1980.

*Secondary Lit.*: P. Stepanova, in *Golos minuvšego*, Paris, 3:1926; A. S., in *Volja Rossii*, Prague, 5–6:1927; G. Adamovič, in *Sovremennye zapiski*, Paris, 38:1929; E. Bakunina, in *Čisla*, Paris, 9:1933; M. Cetlin, in *Novyj žurnal*, New York, 3:1942; G. Aronson, in *Novyj žurnal* 19:1948; R. Gul', in *Novyj žurnal* 41:1955 and 76:1964; V. Zavališin, in *Novyj žurnal* 69:1962; V. Samarin, in *Grani*, Frankfurt am Main, 54:1963; Ju. Terapiano, in *Sovremennik*, Toronto, 10:1964; N. Andreev, in *Russkaja mysl'*, Paris, March, 4, 1982, p. 11; *Tri jubileja Andreja Sedýkh*, New York, 1982 (with contributions from V. Sinkevič, I. Bunin, L. Rževskij, and others); N. Gorbanevskaja, in *Kontinent*, Paris, 35:1983.

**Sedýkh, Konstantín Fyódorovich,** prose writer, poet (b. Jan. 21 [Jan. 8], 1908, Poperechny Zerentuy, Transbaikal region—d. Nov. 21, 1979, Irkutsk). Sedykh's parents were considered Transbaikal Cossacks. After attending school for three years, Sedykh began working as a rural correspondent for the Komsomol in 1925 and graduated from a pedagogical technical school in Chita. He finally settled in Irkutsk in 1931 where he worked as a journalist. From 1933 to 1950 he published eight volumes of poetry with Siberian provincial publishers. During World War II he was a reporter at the front. After 1934 he worked on a single, monumental work about the Transbaikal Cossacks: his two-volume first novel, *Dauriya* (1942–48; Daurian), which was awarded a Stalin Prize (for 1949, 2d class). This work, together with *Otchiy kray* (1958; The Native Circle) and another novel, was intended as a trilogy. Sedykh seldom participated in Writers Congresses and is little noticed.

Sedykh's poetry is an emotional, abstract glorification of his homeland and socialism. *Dauriya* represents an attempt to depict the history of the Transbaikal Cossacks after 1854 in accordance with the Party line, with emphasis on the class antagonism and on the leading role of the Bolsheviks. The characters in this long-drawn-out family saga, which by the appearance of *Otchiy kray* had reached the Civil War, are invented and are complemented by few historical personalities. Artificial dialogue and interpretive epithets demonstrate the weaknesses of this work, which is not praised for its "artistry" even in the Soviet Union, although it was reprinted in 1973 and 1982.

*Works: Daurija* (novel), 2 vols., 1942–48; *Otčij kraj* (novel), 1958; *Stepnye maki* (poems), 1969.
*Secondary Lit.:* Ju. Konstantinov, in *Zvezda* 1950:9; A. Sakhaltuev, in *Moskva* 1958:9; *RSPP* 4:1966; A. Merkulov, in *Lit. Rossija* Jan. 26, 1968, p. 11; V. Truškin, in *Sibir'* 1983:1.

**Selvínsky, Ilyá** (orig. Karl) **Lvóvich,** poet, playwright (b. Oct. 24 [Oct. 12], 1899, Simferopol—d. March 22, 1968, Moscow). Selvinsky's father was a furrier. Selvinsky grew up in Yevpatoriya; he completed his law studies at Moscow University in 1923. The various occupations at which Selvinsky was employed included instructor of fur farming in Kirghizia (1929). Selvinsky, who began writing poetry in 1915, published his first volume

of poems, *Rekordy* (Records), in 1926. The most gifted and most consistent representative of the group of poets associated with CONSTRUCTIVISM, he undertook an experimental search for new forms of linguistic expression with V. Mayakovsky. Initially Selvinsky concentrated on long epics in verse, among which *Zapiski poeta* (1927; Notes of a Poet) stands out from the point of view of experimentation and poetics. In the first part Selvinsky presents himself as Evgeny Neye, while the second part contains the latter's poem, "Sholkovaya luna" (The Silken Moon). In the early 1930s Selvinsky went on to write avant-garde dramas in verse. *Komandarm 2* (1928; Commander of the Second Army) was produced by V. Meyerhold; *Umka—Bely Medved* (1933; Umka the Polar Bear) generated a great deal of discussion and was also performed abroad. In the early 1930s Selvinsky was able to travel to all the major capitals of Western Europe; his experiences abroad were reflected in his narrative verse. In 1937 he turned to verse dramas. During World War II he saw active service as a frontline officer in the Crimea, the Caucasus, and the Baltic. He became a member of the Communist Party in 1941. Selvinsky's work, which stands aloof from political themes of the day and which continually strives, within set limits, toward formal experimentation, always made its way into print but received little critical attention (see *Lit. gazeta* Oct. 19, 1954). Between 1955 and 1960 Selvinsky completely recast his important works written around 1930. He collected his attempts at verse theory in *Studiya stikha* (1962; Studio of Verse). After a drama on Lenin, *Chelovek vyshe svoyey sudby* (1962; A Man above His Destiny), Selvinsky also wrote an autobiographical novel, *O, yunost moya!* (Oh, My Youth!), which first appeared in *Oktyabr* (1966:6–7).

Selvinsky assumes a special position in Soviet literature on the basis of his long epics and tragedies in verse, which serve as a specific expression of his search for new possibilities in the area of versification. From Selvinsky's affiliation with the constructivists comes his championing of "local rhyme," which attaches particular importance to the function of rhyme words in relation to content. *Ulyalayevshchina* (1924; Ulyalayevism), an epic in verse about partisans and guerrilla warfare in the steppes that makes use of strong linguistic local color, was completely rewritten in 1956 with Lenin as the central figure. The novel in verse *Pushtorg* (1927; The Fur Trade), which raises the problem of the intelligentsia under the dictatorship of the proletariat and many other cultural and historical questions, was attacked because the main character commits suicide and the interpretation of events is not in accordance with the Party line. In the cycle of poems *Davayte pomechtayem o bessmertye* (1964–66; Let's Dream of Immortality), Selvinsky acknowledges both the continuation of individual spiritual existence after the death of the physical body and reincarnation, basing his conclusions on the latest findings of physics. Of his avant-garde dramas in verse, the satire *Pao-Pao* (1931), about an orangutan that under Communist influence is liberated from his brutish and bourgeois tendencies and becomes human, lies on the borderline of the absurd. Thematically Selvinsky's tragedies in verse span a broad range. *Babek* (1941), later called *Orla na pleche nosyashchiy*, takes place in 9th-century Armenia; *Livonskaya voyna* (1944; The Livonian War) conforms to the then-conventional theme of Ivan the Terrible; *Chitaya Fausta* (1947; Reading Faust), a drama structured in the Brechtian manner, depicts the 20th-century German intelligentsia. *Arktika* (1960; The Arctic), a novel that harks back to Selvinsky's participation in an expedition by ship in 1933 and to the narrative poem *Chelyuskiniana* (1937–38), is only one example of how Selvinsky never tired of seeking fresh linguistic expression, even in his later years.

*Works: Rekordy* (poems), 1926; *Uljalaevščina* (narrative poem), 1927, 2d rev. ed., 1956; *Zapiski poèta* (narrative poem), 1928; *Puštorg* (novel in verse), 1929; *Komandarm 2* (play), 1930; *Pao-Pao* (play), 1932; *Umka—Belyj Medved'* (play), 1935; *Rycar' Ioann* (play), 1937; *Babek* (play), 1941 (title later changed to *Orla na pleče nosjaščij*); *Rossija*, drama-trilogy: (1) *Livonskaja vojna*, 1944, (2) *Ot Poltavy do Ganguta*, 1951, (3) *Bol'shoj Kirill*, 1957; *Čitaja Fausta* (play), 1952; *Arktika* (novel), 1960; *Čelovek vyše svoej sud'by* (play), 1962; *Studija stikha* (articles), 1962; *O, junost' moja!* (novel), 1967; *Carevna-Lebed'* (play), in *Oktjabr'* 1968:5.—*Izbr. proizv.*, 2 vols., 1956, 1960; *Sobr. soč.*, 6 vols., 1971–74; *Izbr. proizv.*, 1972.

*Secondary Lit.*: A. Selivanovskij, in *Lit. kritik* 1935:2; O. Reznik, in *Moskva* 1958:2, in *Oktjabr'* 1967:2, and 1967, 2d ed., 1972; D. Moldavskij, in *Oktjabr'* 1962:1; I. Szymak, Warsaw, 1965; I. Mikhajlov, in *Neva* 1973:12, p. 190, and in *Zvezda* 1979:10; R. Grübel, in *Wiener Slawistischer Almanach* 6:1980; *O Selvinskom. Vospominanija*, 1982; S. Anisimova, in *Novyj mir* 1983:7.

**Semyónov, Geórgy Vitályevich,** prose writer (b. Jan. 12, 1931, Moscow). In 1949 Semyonov graduated from the industrial institute in Moscow and began working as a sculptor (including embellishing facades in Moscow). In 1960 he completed his second course of study at the Gorky Literary Institute. Semyonov enjoys traveling and has spent much time in the Volga region and in the north of Russia. He has been publishing short stories in journals and in collections since 1961. Semyonov lives in Moscow, first participated in a congress of the Writers Union in 1970, and has belonged to the boards of the Writers Unions of the RSFSR and of the USSR since 1980 and 1981, respectively. Since 1979 he has been a member of the editorial staff of *Nash sovremennik*.

By using not completely ordinary but by no means extraordinary events, especially meetings between individuals, Semyonov paints portraits of simple people, with a special eye for emotional experiences. The often tragic entanglement with one's counterpart and the conflict with one's self, rather than external events, constitute the essential aspect of his work. The development of the plot, which he enjoys embedding within the traditional framework of a journey, is of epic tranquillity. Much is only impressionistically hinted at; no solutions are offered to the problems presented. Semyonov's prose distinguishes itself through a careful, descriptive style that is bound up with nature. Various critics have given him a friendly reception; in 1981 he received the Gorky Prize for Literature from the RSFSR. In histories of literature, however, he has not yet been discussed.

*Works: Na Volge* (short story), in *Znamja* 1961:3; *Sorok četyre noči* (short stories), 1964 (Eng. tr. of title story, "Forty-four Nights," in *Soviet Literature* 1965:2); *Lebedi i sneg* (short stories), 1964; *Raspakhnutye okna* (short stories), 1966; *Kto on i otkuda* (short stories), 1968; *Luna zvenit* (short stories), 1968; *Večerom, posle doždja* (short stories), 1969; *K zime minuja osen'* (pov. and short stories), 1972; *Dnej čereda* (short stories and pov.), 1973; *Uličnye fonari* (pov.), 1976; *Vol'naja nataska* (novel), 1978; *Frigijskie vasil'ki* (pov.), 1980; *Utrennie slëzy*, 1982; *Zemnye puti*, in *Novyj mir* 1985:7.

*Secondary Lit.*: V. Kožinov, in *Lit. gazeta* July 11, 1961; I. Grinberg, in *Moskva* 1961:12; M. Blinkova, in *Novyj mir* 1964:7; S. Georgievskaja, in *Lit. gazeta* July 24, 1965; G. Lebedev, in *Neva* 1967:12 and in *Zvezda* 1969:1; V. Cybin, in *Znamja* 1971:6; I. Štokman, in *Znamja* 1974:8; V. Kurbatov, in *Naš sovre-*

mennik 1976:7; L. Bežin, A. Bragin, in Naš sovremennik 1980:7; A. Mikhajlov, in Novyj mir 1984:2.

**Semyónov, Gleb Sergéyevich,** poet (b. April 18, 1918, Petrograd—d. Jan. 23, 1982, Leningrad). Semyonov's father was a writer (Sergey Aleksandrovich, 1893–1942). Semyonov's first poems appeared in 1935; his first collection was Svet v oknakh (1947; A Light in the Window); another was Plechom k plechu (1952; Shoulder to Shoulder), which was followed by the slender volume Otpusk v sentyabre (1964; Vacation in September), for a long time his only available collection. Only the fourth volume, the selection Stikhotvoreniya (1979; Poems), provided a chronologically well-organized profile of his remarkable creative work. Semyonov was occasionally included in anthologies. He also translated poetry written by the people living in the extreme north of the Soviet Union. At the beginning of the 1960s, Semyonov moved from Leningrad to Moscow. He was not a delegate to congresses of the Writers Unions and was overlooked in histories of literature.

Semyonov writes careful, precise, and metaphorically dense poetry. The allusions of limited images and brief intimations about interpersonal relationships give rise to profound messages. A thread of nature, of the living, illuminatingly penetrates the images of the city and of the lifeless people of technology, regardless of whether this thread evokes the experience of the Leningrad blockade or a more current experience. His often wistful poetry seeks freedom from the external, the ugly, the automated. In its allegorical force, the concrete individual image or the experience that is alluded to presses forward to essential questions.

Works: Svet v oknakh (poems), 1947; Plečom k pleču (poems), 1952; Otpusk v sentjabre (poems), 1964; Sosny (poems), 1972; Stikhotvorenija (poems), 1979; Po tëmnym ulicam razluki (poems), in Vremja i my, Tel Aviv, 70:1983.
Secondary Lit.: I. Andreeva, in Znamja 1965:8; T. Khmel'nickaja, in Zvezda 1965:8 and 1973:9, and in Neva 1979:12; N. Bank, in Lit. obozrenie 1980:11; E. Ètkind, in Vremja i my, Tel Aviv 70:1983.

**Semyónov, Sergéy Aleksándrovich,** prose writer (b. Oct. 19 [Oct. 7], 1893, Naumovo-

Pochinok, prov. Kostroma—d. Jan. 12, 1942, in a military hospital on the Leningrad front). Semyonov's father was a metal worker. During his childhood Semyonov moved to St. Petersburg; there he worked as a laborer, a postal worker, and an employee of an insurance agency. In 1918 he was admitted to the Communist Party and saw action with the Red Army in Mongolia and in the Arctic. From 1921 to 1939 Semyonov held various cultural and political posts in Leningrad, including positions as head of the literature section of the Leningrad state publishing house and editor of the literary almanac Kovsh. Semyonov's own prose was first published in 1921. His moving documentary novel, Golod (1922; Eng. tr., Hunger, in Flying Osip, 1925), had gone through nine editions by 1936. After several collections of short stories, his novel Natalya Tarpova (1927–28), also set in the post-Revolutionary period, received considerable attention. Between 1932 and 1936 Semyonov participated in three Arctic expeditions, later incorporating his experiences into his literary work. He was elected to the board of the Writers Union of the USSR in 1934. After the Finnish-Russian War, Semyonov also saw action as a battalion commissar in World War II. He has received little attention since his death. Semyonov's last book to be published in the Soviet Union appeared in 1936.

Golod portrays the effects of the catastrophic famine of 1919 (during which Semyonov's father died) from the point of view of a 15-year-old girl. Semyonov's rendering of thoughts and dialogue, diarylike and often impressionistic, reveals his great gift for psychology and his innate talent. His presentation of spiritual petrification and alienation within a family during the famine is more than a candid contemporary document. His short stories also often have a first-person narrative structure and reproduce a person's stream of consciousness (such as Tif [1922, Typhus]). His longest work, Natalya Tarpova, is an attempt at comprehending a post-Revolutionary reality split between Party organizations, day-to-day life at the factory, and family life. The novel's weak plot development reveals the limitations of Semyonov's concern to describe moderately his characters' experiences in imitation of the FELLOW TRAVELERS.

Works: Tif (short story), in Krasnaja nov' 1922:1; Golod (novel), 1922 (see above); Edinica v millione (short stories), 1922; Kopejki (short stories), 1924; Natal'ja Tarpova (novel),

2 vols., 1927–30; *Odnotomnik* (novel and short stories), 1936.—*Soč.*, 2 vols., 1925–27; *Sobr. soč.*, 4 vols., 1928–31.

*Secondary Lit.*: A. Palej, in *Novyj mir* 1927:4; S. Pakentrejger, in *Novyj mir* 1927:10; *RSPP* 4:1966.

**Semyónov, Yulián Semyónovich,** prose writer (b. Oct. 8, 1931, Moscow). In 1935 Semyonov completed his studies in the history and economy of the Near East. Semyonov was then a teaching assistant at Moscow University, worked in Kabul, and translated from Afghan. As a writer and journalist with a special interest in questions of state security, he saw his works published in mass media such as *Ogonyok* and *Smena*. He belonged to the editorial staff of *Moskva* (1962:11 to 1967:10). He lives in Moscow and works from time to time as a correspondent for *Literaturnaya gazeta* in the West.

Semyonov writes many long, plot-intensive short stories with adventurous themes. As protagonists he chooses bold polar aviators, courageous geologists, strong and noble militiamen. *Petrovka 38* (1963; Eng. tr., 1965) is a trite, lengthy detective story, filled with improbable occurrences from which, using a conventional plan, an exciting story is constructed. *Major Vikhr* (1967) is a light novel concerning the military and espionage. Soviet critics have often censured the simplified contrasts between Semyonov's characters and the superficiality of conflicts. The novel *Semnadtsat mgnoveniy vesny* (1970; Eng. trs., *Seventeen Moments of Spring*, 1973; *The Himmler Ploy*, 1978) takes place in Hitler's headquarters in 1945; *Brillianty dlya diktatury proletariata* (1971; Diamonds for the Dictatorship of the Proletariat) is a detective story set in the post-Revolutionary period. Under the title *Alternativa* (1975–78; The Alternative), Semyonov collected his earlier novels and arranged them chronologically according to the time frame of the plot. Semyonov's prose has been made into movies.

*Works: 49 časov 25 minut* (pov.), 1960; *Ukhodjat, čtoby vernut'sja* (pov. and short stories), 1961; *Pri ispolnenii služebnykh objazannostej* (pov.), 1962 (Eng. tr., *In the Performance of Duty*, 1963); *Petrovka 38* (pov.), 1964 (see above); *Parol' ne nužen* (pov.), 1966; *Major Vichr'* (novel), 1967; *Semnadcat' mgnovenij vesny* (novel), 1970 (see above); *Brillianty dlja diktatury proletariata* (novel), in *Oktjabr'* 1971:1–2; *Al'ternativa* (political

chronicles), 4 vols., 1975–78; *Gorenie* (novel), 1977; *TASS upolnomočen zajavit'* . . . (pov.), in *Družba narodov* 1979:7–8, separate ed., 1979; *Prikazano vyžit'* (novel), in *Moskva* 1983:7–8; *Press-centr* (novel), in *Družba narodov* 1984:3–5; *Psevdonim* (pov.), in *Znamja* 1984:11–12; *Akcion* (novel), in *Družba narodov* 1985:8–9; *Èkspansija* (novel), in *Znamja* 1985:7–11 and 1986:8–10.—*Sobr. soč.*, 5 vols., 1983–.

*Secondary Lit.*: L. Anninskij, in *Lit. gazeta* Oct. 20, 1959; F. Svetov, in *Novyj mir* 1964:1; A. Beljaev, in *Oktjabr'* 1972:6; V. Beljaev, in *Lit. gazeta* June 28, 1972, p. 5; Ju. Idaškin, in *Oktjabr'* 1973:2, in *Neva* 1983:9, and in *Lit. Rossija* Nov. 29, 1985, p. 20; A. Gladilin, in *Russkaja mysl'*, Paris, Oct. 25, 1979, p. 13; K. Mehnert, in *Die Zeit*, Hamburg, March 6, 1981, p. 67.

**Serafimóvich, Aleksándr Serafímovich** (pseud. of A. S. Popóv), prose writer (b. Jan. 19 [Jan. 7], 1863, Stanitsa Nizhnekurmoyarskaya [Don District]—d. Jan. 19, 1949, Moscow). Serafimovich's father was a Cossack officer. Serafimovich studied in the Department of Physics and Mathematics at St. Petersburg University between 1883 and 1887, at which time he was exiled to the Arkhangelsk region for three years because of his political contacts. His short story *Na ldine* (On the Ice Floe) was first published in 1889; his first collection of short stories, reviewed positively by V. Korolenko, came out in 1901. Serafimovich, who had taken up residence in the Don region again in 1890, moved to Moscow in 1902, became a member of the literary group "Sreda," and worked as M. Gorky's protégé for the publishing house Znaniye. Serafimovich's first novel, *Gorod v stepi* (1912; City in the Steppe), takes a Marxist point of view in its discussion of the development of capitalism in connection with the construction of the first Russian railroads. After the Revolution, Serafimovich became a member of the Communist Party (1918), and served as director of the literature section of *Izvestiya* and as a correspondent for *Pravda*. In 1922 he began writing his only novel to be completed in the Soviet period, *Zhelezny potok* (1924; Eng. tr., *The Iron Flood*, 1935), which is considered a classic work of Soviet literature. Serafimovich describes the retreat of a Bolshevik army, accompanied by women and children, from the Caucasus to the north; by de-emphasizing individual characters, he attempts, in accordance with the trend at that time, to show the masses as an active force. Serafimovich emphasizes the heroic by means of an epic, emotional style, with epic cataloging and rhetorical questions. From November 1926 until August 1929, Serafimovich served as editor in chief of the journal *Oktyabr*; in 1934 he was appointed to the board of the Writers Union of the USSR. In his 80th year, together with V. Veresayev, Serafimovich was awarded a Stalin Prize (for 1942, 1st class) "for many years of achievements in the field of literature."

*Works: Na l'dine* (short story), in *Russkie vedomosti* Feb. 26 and March 1, 1889; *Očerki i rasskazy* (short stories), 1901; *Na Presne* (short story), in *Sbornik tovariščestva "Znanie"* za 1906 g., 1906:10; *Peski* (short story), in *Lit.-khudožestvennye al'manakhi izdatel'stva "Šipovnik"* 1908:3 (Eng. tr., "Sand," in *Sand and Other Stories*, 1955); *Gorod v stepi* (novel), in *Sovremennyj mir* 1912:1–5; *Železnyj potok* (novel), 1924 (see above); *Sbornik neopublikovannykh proizv. i materialov* (unpublished materials), 1958.—*Sobr. soč.*, 4 vols., 1903–10; 15 vols., 1928–30; 11 vols., 1931–33; 10 vols., 1940–48; 7 vols., 1959–60.

*Secondary Lit.:* N. Fatov, 1927; V. Kurilenko, 1950; W. Beitz, Halle, 1961; R. Khigerovič, 3d ed., 1963; RSPP 4:1966; A. Volkov, 1969; V. Lafferty, in *Canadian Slavonic Papers* 1974:2 and Diss., London, 1974; *Vospominanija sovremennikov ob A. S.*, 1977; A. Sofronov, in *Oktjabr'* 1983:1.

**Serapion Brothers** (Serapiónovy brátya), a group of young writers in Petrograd at the beginning of the 1920s who championed the renewal of literature and the primacy of art over ideology. The Serapion Brothers came together through the literary studio of the House of Arts, where they met as the pupils of Ye. Zamyatin, V. Shklovsky, K. Chukovsky, N. Gumilyov, and B. Eykhenbaum; there they held their first official meeting on Feb. 1, 1921, and met regularly every week thereafter. After a short while, the membership consisted of K. Fedin, I. Gruzdyov, Vs. Ivanov, V. Kaverin, L. Lunts, N. Nikitin, Ye. Polonskaya, V. Pozner, M. Slonimsky, N. Tikhonov, and M. Zoshchenko. M. Gorky, who helped establish the group, and V. Shklovsky, who had promoted it, emigrated to Germany in 1922; Pozner (b. 1905) went to Paris in the same year; Lunts, the driving force of the group, went to Germany in 1923. Nikitin and Ivanov had joined Moscow literary circles by 1924 at the latest. The designation *Serapion Brothers*, which probably came from Lunts, refers to E.

T. A. Hoffmann's collection of short stories with this title (4 vols., 1819–21); these short stories are presented as the work of a group of imaginary authors who are friends and who meet regularly. A planned almanac, *1921 god*, did not come to pass, but in the following year the first and only joint publication appeared in Berlin: *Serapionovy bratya* (1922). With conscious political and artistic pleasure, the Serapion Brothers expressed their search for new narrative forms partly (the so-called Westerners) by experimenting with often adventurous plots (Lunts, Kaverin) and partly (the so-called Orientalists) by cultivating an ornamental style with confused syntax, rhythmic effects, and an episodic structure influenced by A. Remizov (Nikitin, Ivanov); others, such as Zoshchenko and Slonimsky, went their own separate ways. Because they rejected literature that had been degraded into a propaganda instrument and demanded that "literary work be organic, realistic, live its own separate life . . . not be a copy of nature but live on a level with nature," a demand clearly formulated by Lunts in *Pochemu my Serapionovy bratya* (Eng. tr., "Why We Are Serapion Brothers," in *The Serapion Borthers*, 1975), the group was tolerated as an organization of FELLOW TRAVELERS in accordance with the Party Resolution of 1925 (see PARTY RESOLUTIONS ON LITERATURE) but was increasingly attacked by Marxist Party critics; no regular meetings of the remaining Serapion Brothers occurred after 1927. The greeting of the Serapion Brothers, "Zdravstvuy, brat, pisat ochen trudno" (Greetings, brother, writing is very difficult), was heard no longer. Earlier membership was viewed in a negative light (see the Party Resolution of 1946 and the fate of Zoshchenko) or considered a sin of one's youth (for example, for the conformists Fedin and Tikhonov). Kaverin actively championed the group's REHABILITATION in the 1960s; the avant-garde prose of the Serapion Brothers written between 1921 and 1924 is reprinted infrequently and only after being revised.

*Secondary Lit.:* Serapionovy brat'ja (anthology), 1922 (reprinted, Munich, 1973), preface by F. Scholz; L. Lunc, "Počemu my Serapionovy brat'ja," in *Lit. zapiski* 1922:3 (see above); V. Kaverin, in *Novyj mir* 1965:9; G. Kern, in *Novyj žurnal*, New York, 81–84:1965–66; H. Oulanov, *The Serapion Brothers*, The Hague, 1966; M. Minokin, in *Russkaja lit.* 1971:1; *The Serapion Brothers: A Critical Anthology* (stories and essays), eds. G. Kern and C. Collins, Ann Arbor, 1975; B. Kosanović, in *Russian Literature* 1985:2.

**Serebryakóva, Galína Iósifovna,** prose writer (b. Dec. 20 [Dec. 7], 1905, Kiev—d. June 30, 1980, Moscow). Serebryakova's father was a country doctor. Serebryakova became a member of the Communist Party in 1919; she was politically active during the Civil War. Between 1920 and 1925 she studied medicine at Moscow University, then worked as a journalist. Representing *Komsomolskaya pravda,* she traveled to China (1927), Geneva and Paris (1927–28), and England (1930–32); her travels and experiences inspired several volumes of journalistic prose. As part of her preparation for writing a comprehensive work on Karl Marx, she received authorization to visit numerous West European countries. The first part of the work, *Yunost Marksa* (1934–35; Marx's Youth), was variously received; its proper Party position could not hide the novel's serious artistic flaws. Serebryakova's husband had fallen victim to the Stalinist terror, and in 1936 she herself was arrested (see *Oktyabr* 1936:9). After 20 years she underwent REHABILITATION and returned to Moscow, where she actively continued to support the consolidation of conservative forces in the Writers Union. She completed her trilogy on Marx (titled *Prometey* [Prometheus]) with the parts *Pokhishcheniye ognya* (1961; The Theft of Fire) and *Vershiny zhizni* (1962; The Summits of Life). In December 1963 Serebryakova occasioned some comment with her overt attack on I. Erenburg at a reception for writers held by Khrushchev. A Polish translation of her description of her camp years, *Smerch* (Maelstrom), which could not appear in the Soviet Union because the theme had been banned, was printed in Paris, an action she protested (*Lit. gazeta* Dec. 27, 1967, p. 5). In a novel about Friedrich Engels, *Predshestviye* (1966; Preparing the Way), and in further novels about Lenin, S. Kirov, D. Furmanov, and other Communists, she adhered to her traditional theme.

Serebryakova's works receive attention only because of their themes and their Party-line treatment of material. She is incapable of structuring her abundant material into novel form; even Johann Stock, a fictional character in her Marx trilogy, is unconvincing: he remains nothing more than a "representative of the proletariat as a whole, an oversimplified mouthpiece" (F. Levin). The essence of her work is stifled by peripheral characters and superfluous detail.

*Works: Ženščiny èpokhi francuzskoj revoljucii,* 1929 (Eng. tr., *Nine Women,* 1932); *Junost' Marksa* (novel), 1934–35; *Pokhišcenie* *ognja* (novel), 1961; *Veršiny žizni* (novel), 1962; *Prometej* (trilogy composed of previous three novels), 1963; *Stranstvija po minuvšim godam* (short stories), 1963; *Predšestvie* (novel), 1966; *Smiercz* (in Polish), in *Kultura,* Paris, 1967:7–8; *Iz pokolenija v pokolenie* (novel), 1973.—*Sobr. soč.,* 5 vols., 1967–69; *Izbr.,* in 2 vols., 1975; *Sobr. soč.,* 6 vols., 1977–80.

*Secondary Lit.:* F. Levin, in *Lit. kritik* 1935:12; V. Goffenšefer, in *Novyj mir* 1960:5; V. Povoljaev, in *Lit. gazeta* Feb. 4, 1970, p. 3; *RSPP* 7(2):1972; A. Rothberg, *The Heirs of Stalin,* Ithaca, N.Y., 1972; N. Starosel'skaja, in *Lit. obozrenie* 1974:8; A. Manfred, foreword to Serebryakova's *Sobr. soč.,* 1977–80; obituary, in *Lit. gazeta* July 9, 1980, p. 3; M. Lapšin, in *Oktjabr'* 1981:2.

**Sergéyev-Tsénsky, Sergéy Nikoláyevich,** (pseud. of S. N. Sergeyev), prose writer (b. Sept. 30 [Sept. 18], 1875, Preobrazhenskoye, prov. Tambov—d. Dec. 3, 1958, Alushta, in the Crimea). Sergeyev-Tsensky's father was an officer, later a teacher. In 1895 Sergeyev-Tsensky completed teachers college in Glukhov and worked as a teacher until 1904. He served in the military in 1904–5 and 1914–15. He started writing early and was first published in 1898. In 1907 he turned to writing large-scale, for the most part historical, novels; he continued to write many such novels until his death at an advanced age. He lived in the Crimea from the end of World War I. In 1919, during the Civil War, Sergeyev-Tsensky contributed to the publications of the propaganda section of General Anton Denikin's "Osvag." Several of his short stories from the early 1920s, such as *Zhestokost* (1926; Cruelty), indicate that he associated the Revolution above all with the horror, privation, and hunger that it brought to Russia for many years. In the late 1920s and early 1930s, Sergeyev-Tsensky was persecuted by the RAPP critics. His historical novel *Sevastopolskaya strada* (1936–38; The Ordeal of Sevastopol) received a Stalin Prize in 1941 (for 1935–41, 1st class). In 1943 he received a doctorate for his work in literary criticism and became a member of the Academy of Sciences of the USSR. In 1946 his novel *Brusilovsky proryv* (1943; Eng. tr., *Brusilov's Breakthrough,* 1945) was branded "ideologically harmful" because of its objective depiction of World War I. The collected works of the historical novelist, who had since become completely acceptable, appeared for the first time in 1955–56; Sergeyev-Tsensky revised several of his earlier novels for this edition.

Sergeyev-Tsensky's early prose is saturated with a pessimism reminiscent of L. Andreyev. With the novel *Valya* (1914; Eng. tr., *Transfiguration*, 1926), he began the cycle *Preobrazheniye Rossii* (The Transfiguration of Russia), which focuses, in 12 novels, 3 povesti, and 2 fragments (with 3 more novels planned), on the period from the beginning of World War I to the February Revolution; the novels are given continuity by the regular appearance of several fictional characters. The five novels of the cycle that deal with the events of the war (written between 1934 and 1944) are distinguished by their attempt at objectivity; they make abundant use of documents, newspaper reports, and historical commentary. Sergeyev-Tsensky rarely turned to topical subjects, although he did so in his contribution to the novels of the Five-Year Plan, *Iskat, vsegda iskat* (1935; To Search, Always to Search), where he historically expands on the subject of the building of Dnepropetrovsk. The 1,600-page *Sevastopolskaya strada* begins with the subject of the Crimean War (1854–55) and develops into an anti-British panorama on a world-historical scale. Around 1930 Sergeyev-Tsensky wrote several works (prose and drama) about classical writers (A. Pushkin, N. Gogol, M. Lermontov). His style is one of vividness and clarity; his characterization, nature imagery, and descriptions of battle are rich in similes and metaphorical expressions.

*Works: Sad* (short story), 1906; *Babaev* (novel), 1908; *Žestokost'* (short story), in *Novyj mir* 1926:2–3; *Preobraženie Rossii*, novel series: *Valja*, 1914 (under the title *Preobraženie;* see above), *Obrečënnye na gibel'*, 1927, 2d ed., 1955, *Zaurjad-polk*, 1934, *Iskat', vsegda iskat'*, 1935, *Ljutaja zima* (also under the title *Massy, mašiny, stikhii*), 1936, *Brusilovskij proryv*, 1943 (see above), *Puški vydvigajut*, 1944, *Puški zagovorili*, 1956 (written in 1944), *Utrennij vzryv*, 1952; *Preobraženie čeloveka*, 1955, *Lenin v avguste 1914 goda* (fragment), 1957; *Sevastopol'skaja strada* (novel), 3 vols., 1936–39; *Rodnaja zemlja* (poems), 1958; *Radost' tvorčestva* (articles, memoirs, letters), 1969.—*Sobr. soč.*, 10 vols., 1955–56; 12 vols., 1967; *Izbr. proizv.*, 2 vols., 1975.
*Secondary Lit.:* G. S. Makarenko, 1957; *RSPP* 4:1966; P. I. Plukš, 1968, 1975; Ju. D. Anipkin, 1974; M. Ševcov, 2d ed., 1976.

**Sevéla, Éfraim Yévelevich,** prose writer (b. March 8, 1928, Bobruysk, Belorussia). Sevela's father was a wrestling trainer. By 1943 Sevela had already joined the Red Army. He studied Russian literature and journalism at the University of Minsk (1945–48) and then worked as a journalist in Vilnius until 1956. After 1956 Sevela became active in the motion picture industry and moved to Moscow. He wrote screenplays for eight films; he also occasionally participated in their filming as director and actor. After Sevela organized, on Feb. 24, 1971, the first demonstration by Russian Jews to protest Soviet anti-Semitism and to demand permission to emigrate, he himself was allowed to emigrate to Paris on May 4, 1971. In the autumn of 1971, Sevela moved to Israel where he served nine months in the army, including during the Yom Kippur war. In Paris in 1971, Sevela began writing; by the time he left Israel in 1975 he had written six books, some of which first appeared in translation and most of which were first published after 1976. In 1976 he settled in the United States; by 1985 he had written ten additional novels and povesti and had published a collection of short stories, *Popugay, govoryashchiy na idish* (1982; The Parrot Who Could Speak Yiddish), that synthesizes the unusual breadth of his narrative talent. In 1987 Sevela moved from New York to Berlin.

In *Legendy Invalidnoy ulitsy* (1975; Eng. tr., *Legends from Invalid Street*, 1974), written in 1971, Sevela compiled several of his short stories about Jewish life in Belorussia and Vilnius. His second work, the novel *Viking* (1982; Eng. tr., *Truth Is for Strangers*, 1976), was written in 1973 and first appeared in English; it discusses the issue of a Soviet writer living in Lithuania in 1948–49 who sells himself to the system. *Monya Tsatskes—Znamenosets* (1977; *Monya Tsatskes—*the Flagbearer; Eng. tr., *The Standard Bearer*, 1983) presents the life of a Jewish soldier from Lithuania during World War II, often using ironic exaggeration. In *Ostanovite samolyot, ya slezu* (1977; Stop the Plane, I'm Getting Off), Sevela displays with special variety his talent for creating fantasy and comedy as well as the seriousness with which he views politically and humanely the issue of Jewish emigration. In *Farewell, Israel* (1975; Russian unpublished: Proshchay, Izrail) he records in a documentary style the difficulties confronting Russian Jews in Israel and explains why he left. *Pochemu net raya na zemle* (1981; Eng. tr., *Why There Is No Heaven on Earth*, 1983) recounts in a delightfully unsentimental way the childhood of a Jewish boy in Belorussia who ends up becoming a victim of the SS. The antithesis between the Communist system and the free, democratic world as seen by a 13-year-old girl defines the novel written concurrently (1978–79), Zub mudrosti (1981; The Wisdom Tooth). The novel Proday svoyu mat (1982; Sell Your Mother) is satirically aimed at Jews in Berlin who are addicted to commerce. The themes of luck in misfortune and mortal danger unite the scenes from the life of a Lithuanian Jew in the short novel whose plot Sevela first developed as a screenplay, Mama (1982). The same positive attitude is revealed in the novel Vsyo ne kak u lyudey (1984; Nothing as It Should Be), the odyssey of a 13- to 17-year-old Russian Jew who makes it all the way to Berlin with the soldiers. From 1976 to 1983 Sevela worked on another novel—Toyota-korolla (1984; Toyota Corolla)—in which a journey by car from Los Angeles to New York serves as the narrative scaffolding for illustrating the contrasting views of life held by an older, anti-Communist Russian émigré and a young, leftist-oriented American woman. Sevela has a talent for depicting the life experiences of Jews in Belorussia, Lithuania, Israel, Germany, and the United States in an entertaining, descriptive, and imaginative way and for addressing essential political and human concerns.

Works: Legendy Invalidnoj ulicy (short stories), Jerusalem, 1977 (see above); Ostanovite samolët—ja slezu! (novel), 1977, 2d ed., 1980; Monja Cackes—znamenosec (novel), Jerusalem, 1978 (see above); Mužskoj razgovor v russkoj bane (novel), Jerusalem, 1980; Počemu net raja na zemle? (novel), Jerusalem, 1981 (see above); Zub mudrosti (novel), Jerusalem, 1981; Viking (novel), New York, 1982 (see above); Prodaj svoju mat' (dramatic pov.), Jerusalem, 1982; Popugaj, govorjaščij na idiš (short stories), Jerusalem, 1982; Mama (film script), Jerusalem, 1982; Vsë ne kak u ljudej (novel), New York, 1984; Tojota-korolla (novel), New York, 1984.
Secondary Lit.: C. Leviant, in Midstream Oct. 1975; G. Laub, in Die Zeit Nov. 16, 1979; B. Nielson-Stockeby, in Die Weltwoche, Zurich, Nov. 21, 1979; T. Nowakowski, in Frankfurter Allgemeine Zeitung Dec. 12, 1979; W. Kasack, in Neue Zürcher Zeitung Nov. 8, 1983, p. 25.

**Severyánin, Ígor** (pseud. of Ígor Vasílyevich Lotaryóv), poet (b. May 16 [May 4], 1887, St. Petersburg—d. Dec. 20, 1941, Tallinn [Reval]). Severyanin was from an aristocratic background; his father was an officer. Severyanin did not attend university; his first poem was published in 1905 and marked the beginning of an extensive poetic output that initially reflected the influence of Konstantin Fofanov and Mirra Lokhvitskaya. In October 1911 Severyanin heralded ego-futurism (see FUTURISM) as a new innovative trend (he later allied himself briefly with the cubo-futurists). Severyanin's Gromokipyashchiy kubok (1913; The Thunder-seething Goblet), a volume of poetry with an introduction written by F. Sologub, attracted a good deal of attention; it went through seven printings in two years. In mid-1918 Severyanin emigrated to Estonia. A successful declaimer of his own verse, he organized occasional "poezovechera" (poetry evenings) in Helsinki, Danzig, Berlin, Paris, and (in 1930–31) in Yugoslavia and Bulgaria; nevertheless, he kept aloof from émigré groups and lived in the Estonian fishing village of Toila. As a poet, Severyanin had largely lost his audience by the 1920s; he was still able, however, to publish several volumes in Berlin before 1923, then in Tartu, and later in Belgrade and Bucharest in the early 1930s. Severyanin translated many Estonian poets. He lived in increasing poverty. After the annexation of the Baltic states by the Soviet Union in 1940, he adjusted to the changed political situation by writing conformist poetry.

Severyanin has a remarkable literary talent, which because of its provocative verbal style generated not only enthusiasm but also sharp disapproval during the period of ego-futurism. With other futurists he shared the rejection of tradition (A. Pushkin), the demand for innovation in every field, a delight in public scenes, and an inclination to a bohemian lifestyle. N. Gumilyov said, "Of course, nine tenths of his writings can be interpreted in no other way than as a desire to cause scandal." His Gromokipyashchiy kubok was initially successful among intellectuals; it quickly made Severyanin into a widely and extraordinarily popular poet. His poetry is inspired mostly by his own experience, which is then narratively or descriptively structured. It revolves around the theme of love, reaches into everyday experiences, and preserves a lifelong closeness to nature. Its innate musicality, together with Severyanin's often unusual metrics, unites with a delight in neologisms. Severyanin's bold verbal creations inform his individual style. In them, much of his ironic distance (which veils the true attitude that stands behind an exaggerated neologism) is discernible. After the revolutionary futurist verse of his youth, Severyanin's poetry in the period of his emigration developed a simple, more traditional naturalness.

Works: Gromokipjaščij kubok (poems), 1913; Zlatolira (poems), 1914; Ananasy v šampanskom (poems), 1915; Victoria regia (poems), 1916 (these 4 vols. later together as Sobr. poèz reprint [see below]); Poèzoantrakt (poems), 1915; Poèzokoncert (poems), 1918; Crème de violettes (poems), Jur'ev, 1919; Menestrel' (poems), Berlin, 1921; Padučaja stremnina (novel in verse), 2 vols., Berlin, 1922; Solovej (poems), Berlin, 1923; Rosa oranževogo časa (poems), Jur'ev, 1925; Adriatika (poems), Narva, 1932; Medal'ony, sonety i variacii o poètakh, pisateljakh i kompozitorakh, Belgrade, 1934; poems, in Novyj žurnal, New York, 44:1956, 73:1963, 83:1966; Solnečnyj dikar', in Trudy po russkoj i slavjanskoj filologii, Tartu, 9:1966; Stikhotvorenija (poems), 1975, 2d ed., 1978.—Sobr. poèz, 4 vols., 1915–16 (reprinted, Washington, 1966–70); 4 vols., 1918.

Secondary Lit.: N. Gumilëv, in Apollon 1911:4 and 1914:1–2 (reprinted in his Sobr. soč., vol. 4, Washington 1968); V. Brjusov (1915), in his Sobr. soč., vol. 2, 1955; Ju. Šumakov, in Zvezda 1965:3; Ju. Ivask, in Novyj žurnal 91:1968; V. Markov, Russian Futurism, Berkeley, 1968; V. Roždestvenskij, foreword to Stikhotvorenija, 1975; A. Urban, in Zvezda 1975:9; I. Odoevceva, in Russkaja mysl', Paris, March 16 and 30, 1978; E. Boronowski, Diss., Münster, 1978; N. Khardžiev, in Russian Literature 1978:4.

**Seyfúllina, Lídiya Nikoláyevna,** prose writer (b. April 3 [March 22], 1889, Varlamovo, prov. Orenburg—d. April 25, 1954, Moscow). Seyfullina's father was an Orthodox priest of Tatar extraction. Before the Revolution, Seyfullina worked as a teacher, librarian, actress, and staff member of the local cultural agency. She was a member of the Socialist Revolutionary Party between 1917 and 1919. From 1919 to 1921 she was a librarian in Chelyabinsk and wrote for a children's theater that she herself organized; from 1921 to 1923 she worked in the editorial offices of the state publishing house in Novosibirsk. Seyfullina published her first short stories in Sibirskiye ogni; one of these, Pravonarushiteli (Eng. tr., "The Lawbreakers," in Flying Osip, 1925), made her famous both in Russia and abroad. After 1923 she lived in Moscow and Leningrad; in the 1920s she was one of the writers who received both recognition (above all by

A. Voronsky and N. Aseyev) and criticism (by V. Shklovsky, for example). In 1925 she and her husband, V. P. Pravdukhin, staged her povest Virineya (1924); it became her most frequently performed play. She wrote several newspaper articles on the basis of her journeys to Turkey (1924) and Europe (1927). Seyfullina received less critical attention from the 1930s on; she was nevertheless elected to the board of the Writers Union of the USSR in 1934. She published her work infrequently because of her "inner physical aversion to any lie" (Shaginyan).

Her experience of the Revolution in the provinces, particularly in its exposure of the elemental in human beings, turned Seyfullina into a writer. She is one of the first authors to depict their observations of this time in literature: her Pravonarushiteli deals with the theme of young people uprooted by the Revolution; Peregnoy (1922; Humus) depicts the transformation of a good-for-nothing peasant in a ruined, devastated village; while Virineya portrays the growth and tragic death of a countrywoman in the confusion of the post-Revolutionary period. Seyfullina's attention is focused on the natural man; her later works, written and set in the city, are weak. Her manner of presentation is naturalistic. Because of her disinclination to use idealized revolutionary clichés, Seyfullina came under critical attack but was defended by (among others) the writer L. Reysner.

Works: Pravonarušiteli (short story), 1922 (see above); Četyre glavy (pov.), 1922; Peregnoj (pov.), 1923; Virineja (pov.), 1925; O literature (essays and memoirs), 1958.—Sobr. soč., 3 vols., 1925; 5 vols., 1926–27; 5 vols., 1927–28; 6 vols., 1929–31; 4 vols., 1968–70; Soč., 2 vols., 1980.

Secondary Lit.: Lidija Sejfullina, ed. E. Nikitina, 1928, 2d ed., 1930; V. Aleksandrova, in Socialističeskij vestnik 1939:4–5 (reprinted in her Lit. i žizn', New York, 1969); Sejfullina v vospominanijakh sovremennikov, 1961; RSPP 4:1966; Z. Sejfullina, 1970; N. N. Janovskij, 2d ed., 1972; V. Kardin, 1976.

**Shaginyán, Mariétta Sergéyevna,** prose writer (b. April 2 [March 21] 1888, Moscow—d. March 21, 1982, Moscow). Shaginyan was the daughter of an Armenian doctor and a university teacher. In Moscow she studied humanities from 1908 to 1912 and mineralogy from 1912 to 1914. World War I interrupted the continuation of her studies in Heidelberg. During the war and the Revolution, Shaginyan lived in Rostov-on-Don; in 1921 she moved to Petrograd, in 1927 to Armenia, and in 1931 to Moscow. Shaginyan was already active as a writer before the Revolution, which she greeted as a mystical Christian event, and she continued to write until her death at an advanced age. During World War II she was evacuated to the Urals. From 1942 on, she was a member of the Communist Party. In 1944 she received her doctorate for a book about Taras Shevchenko. In 1950 she was awarded a Stalin Prize (3d class) for a journalistic prose piece, *Puteshestviye po Sovetskoy Armenii* (1946–50; Eng. tr., *Journey through Soviet Armenia*, 1954), and in 1972 the Lenin Prize for four books about Lenin. Shaginyan was on the board of the Writers Union of the USSR from 1934 until her death and was in the presidia of all congresses of the Writers Unions of the RSFSR and the USSR from 1965 until her death.

Shaginyan began writing symbolist lyric poems in 1903; the second volume in this style, *Orientalia* (1913), was issued in seven editions from 1913 to 1922, some of which were published in Berlin. *Svoya sudba* (1923; One's Own Fate), a novel written in 1916, together with various stories, and set in a mental clinic, was substantially reworked in 1954. Some accounts of the early Soviet period such as *Peremena* (1922–23; The Change) or *Priklyucheniya damy iz obshchestva* (1923; The Adventure of a Lady from Society) present her personal endeavors to adjust to the new system; these were attacked in *Na postu*. Under the ironic pseudonym "Jim (Dzhim) Dollar," Shaginyan published the adventure story *Mess-Mend, ili Janki v Petrograde* (1924); Eng. tr., *Mess-Mend: The Yankees in Petrograd*, 1987), an agitational satire that, among other things, was supposed to divert interest from foreign detective stories. The new editions that appeared after 1956 were repeatedly reworked. Two other works in the same genre written in the 1920s had less success. In the novel *K i k* (1929; abbreviation for Koldunya i kommunist [Witch and Communist]), Shaginyan tried to unite political agitation with experiments in narrative technique (the same event from four perspectives). The main achievement of her four-year stay in Armenia, *Gidrotsentral* (1930–31; The Hydroelectric Power Station), is a Five-Year Plan novel whose purpose is to propagate the planned economy, not human concerns. This novel also exists in multiple reworked versions. Until 1957, Shaginyan had published essentially journal-

istic prose and library treatises, such as *Ural v oborone* (1943–44; Urals in Defense); *Dnevnik pisatelya* (1953; Diary of a Writer), in which serious substantive errors and banalities were proven to exist in 1954; and *G. T. Shevchenko* (1941), *I. A. Krylov* (1944), *I. V. Gyote* (1950; J. W. Goethe), and *Nizami* (1955). At the end of the 1950s, Shaginyan returned to the project involving various novels about Lenin. The first part dealt with the 1860s and appeared in 1938 under the title *Bilet po Rossii* (Ticket through Russia); after being criticized, it was not returned. Reworked, it formed the basis for the novel *Semya Ulyanovich* (1958; The Ulyanov Family), which she continued with *Pervaya Vserossiyskaya* (1965; The First All-Russian), dealing with Lenin's father and the 1870s, and with *Bilet po istorii* (1970; Ticket through History). Her trips to England, Italy, and Czechoslovakia also found an echo in her journalistic prose. At an advanced age Shaginyan wrote her memoirs, *Chelovek i vremya* (1972–78; Man and Time).

*Works:* Pervye vstreči (poems), 1909; Orientalia (poems), 1913, 2d ed., 1922; Uzkie vrata (short stories), 1914; Putešestvie v Vejmar (articles), 1923; Svoja sud'ba (novel), 1923; Mess-Mend, ili Janki v Petrograde (novel), 1924 (see above); Peremena (novel), 1924; Priključenija damy iz obščestva (novel), 1924; K i k (novel), 1929; Gidrocentral' (novel), 1931; Bilet po Rossii (novel), 1938, rev. ed., 1970; G. T. Ševčenko (biography), 1941; I. A. Krylov (biography), 1944; Ural v oborone (sketches), 1944; Putešestvie po Sovetskoj Armenii (sketches), 1950 (see above); I. V. Gёte (biography), 1950; Dnevnik pisatelja (sketches), 1953; Nizami (biography), 1955; Sem'ja Ul' janovykh (novel), 1959; Pervaja Vserossijskaja (novel), 1965; Četyre uroka u Lenina (sketch), 1970; Čelovek i vremja (memoirs), in Novyj mir 1971:4, 1972:1–2, 1973:4, 1975:3, 1977:1, 1978:4, 9, 11, separate ed., 1980; Očerki raznykh let (essays), 1977; 50 pisem D. D. Šostakoviča, Novyj mir 1982:12; Ural'skij dnevnik (diary), in Novyj mir 1985:4–5.—Sobr. soč., 7 vols., 1929–30 (vols. 2–4 appeared); 4 vols., 1935; 6 vols., 1956–58; 9 vols., 1971–75; Izbr. proizv. 2 vols., 1978.

*Secondary Lit.:* N. Zamoškin, in Novyj mir 1929:12; L. Skorino, in Oktjabr' 1947:8, in Znamja 1955:9, in Lit. i sovremennost' 11:1972, and separate study, 1975; M. Lifšic, in Novyj mir 1954:2; L. Žak, in Lit. Rossija Jan. 14, 1966, p. 8, and in Lit. i sovremennost' 7:1966; RSPP 6(1):1969; M. Agurskij, in Russkaja mysl',

Paris, Feb. 1, 1979, p. 7; A. Rubaškin, in Zvezda 1983:3; K. Serebrjakov, in Lit. gazeta Jan. 16, 1985, p. 5.

**Shalámov, Varlám Tíkhonovich,** prose writer, poet (b. July 1 [June 18], 1907, Vologda—d. Jan. 18, 1982, Moscow). Shalamov's study of law at Moscow University from 1926 to 1929 was interrupted by his first conviction and sentencing to three years in a prison camp. From 1932 to 1937 Shalamov published a few poems and little prose. After 1937 he spent 17 years in prison camps around Kolyma. After his REHABILITATION he began to write poems again; from 1957 on, these appeared in journals such as Moskva, Znamya, and Yunost and were also collected and published in books: the first was Ognivo (1961; The Flint); the fourth, Moskovskiye oblaka (1972; Moscow Clouds). In addition, Shalamov wrote short documentary sketches concerning his prison-camp experiences; these were distributed through SAMIZDAT and, after 1966, frequently appeared in Novy zhurnal (New York) under the collective title Kolymskiye rasskazy (Eng. trs., Kolyma Tales, 1980; Graphite, 1981) (see his letter on this subject in Lit. gazeta Feb. 23, 1972, p. 9). A complete edition was published in London in 1978. Following his rehabilitation, Shalamov lived in Moscow; he was accepted into the Writers Union of the USSR on Feb. 15, 1973. Shalamov has not yet been included in histories of literature.

Shalamov's poems reflect in a simple, not especially concise, manner the bitterness of his experience of life. This bitterness is manifested in a certain detachment toward the evil in man, in a yearning for humanity, but especially in the images of snow and frost that are contrasted to the deceitful consolation of fire. The effect of his prison-camp sketches, which have received high praise from authors such as G. Aygi and A. Sinyavsky, rests on the concreteness of the individual cases he reports and on a suspenseful style of transmitting information. These sketches are limited to realistic, autobiographical exposition; each recounts a single experience; they reject any sort of narrative or technical refinements and create their effect through the horror of the brutality that occurred.

Works: Poetry: Ognivo, 1961; Šelest list'ev, 1964; Doroga i sud'ba, 1967; Moskovskie oblaka, 1972; Točka kipenija, 1977. Prose: Tri smerti d-ra Austino (pov.), in Oktjabr' 1936:1; Kolymskie rasskazy (short stories), London, 1978 (see above).

Secondary Lit.: B. Sluckij, in Lit. gazeta Oct. 5, 1961; V. Prikhod'ko, in Znamja 1962:4; V. Inber, in Lit. gazeta June 23, 1964; L. Levickij, in Novyj mir 1964:8; E. Kalmanovskij, in Zvezda 1965:2; S. Kirsanov, in Grani, Frankfurt am Main, 79:1971; A. Rostovceva, in Moskva 1973:9; G. Hosking, in New Universities Quarterly, Spring 1980; V. Perelešin, in Russian Language Journal 117:1980; A. Sinjavskij, in Sintaksis, Paris, 8:1980; V. S. Dunham, in Slavic Review 1982:3; G. Ajgi, V. Jakubov, L. Kornev, A. Jakobson, in Vestnik RKhD, Paris, 137:1982; A. L'vov, in Novoe russkoe slovo, New York, March 13, 1983, p. 4; A. Šor, in Novyj žurnal, New York, 155:1984.

**Shapíro, Borís Izraílevich,** poet (b. April 21, 1944, Moscow). Shapiro's father was a professor of economics. From 1961 to 1968 Shapiro studied at Moscow University, primarily physics, but also logic and Russian stylistics. In 1964, together with fellow students, he established a working circle for poetry called "Klenovy list" (The Maple Leaf); at Moscow University this group organized two poetry festivals lasting several days and held four performances of "Poetic Theater." Attempts to publish his own poetry in the Soviet Union failed, in part because Shapiro refused to add some topical political poetry to his own unpolitical poems. In December 1975, Shapiro was allowed to emigrate to the Federal Republic of Germany. In 1979 he was awarded the degree of Doctor of Natural Science in physics at the University of Tübingen. Since 1981 he has worked as a physicist at the University of Regensberg where he combines work in the field of theoretical physics with research on the "mathematical theory of language dynamics." Shapiro was first introduced to the public with a volume in German, Metamorphosenkorn (1981; Grain of Metamorphosis). In addition to translated poems, this book also contains poems that Shapiro wrote in German after emigrating to Germany. In 1983 he completed a new volume of poetry written in German, Ein Tropfen Wort (A Drop of Word), as yet unpublished. For Solo na fleyte (1984; Flute Solo), Shapiro collected his most important Russian poems from more than two decades.

For Shapiro, sound is the primary element in poetic creation. The diversity of form in Solo na fleyte is attributable to the richness of the realm of sounds seeking verbal expression. Shapiro himself speaks of "musical presemantics" in the sense of a context-free semantics of musical organization in poetry.

This semantics is recognizable in his preference for parallelism, assonance, and unusual rhymes, whereby concordant sounds are often selected in order to intensify a semantic dissonance. In the forefront stand the themes of nature, poetry, music, love, and death; in the background lies a search for security in earthly life that springs from a cautiously intimated belief in a divine order. The clarity of form reflects a discipline in spiritual matters that allows the recognition of evil in this world to withdraw indiscreetly. His verse structure reveals multiplicity: from elliptical brevity to proselike narration that masters rhythm. Since moving to Germany, Shapiro has become a bilingual poet who explores the phonetic source of his poetry even in German.

*Works: Metamorphosenkorn* (poems), Tübingen, 1981; *Solo na flejte* (poems), Munich, 1984; *Speši* (poems), in *Vstreči*, Philadelphia, 1986.

*Secondary Lit.*: K. Borowsky, in *Šapiro's Metamorphosenkorn*, 1981; W. Kasack, in *Osteuropa* 1982:12, p. 987, and in *Šapiro's Solo na flejte*, 1984.

**Shatróv, Mikhaíl Filíppovich** (pseud. of M. F. Marshák), playwright (b. April 3, 1932, Moscow). In 1956 he completed his study of mining engineering in Moscow. Shatrov's first drama, *Chistye ruki* (1955; Clean Hands), was performed at the Moscow Youth Theater. His third play, *Imenem revolyutsii* (1957; In the Name of the Revolution), which depicts Lenin with two fatherless children, won acclaim as the best drama written in honor of the 40th anniversary of the October Revolution and continued to be performed frequently for many years. In 1961 Shatrov joined the Communist Party; in 1962 he was accepted into the Writers Union. In 1970 he was a delegate to a congress of the Writers Union of the RSFSR for the first time; in 1974 his twelfth drama was performed. He lives in Moscow.

Shatrov began his literary career by writing plays about the Komsomol; among these, *Mesto v zhizni* (1956; A Place in Life) was influenced by V. Rosov's *V dobry chas*. *Yesli kazhdy iz nas* (1958; If Every One of Us) was criticized for its primitive didacticism. Soviet critics mention Shatrov's plays about Lenin most frequently: *Imenem revolyutsii*; *Shestoye iyulya* (1964; July 6th), concerning the defeat of the Socialist Revolutionaries in 1918; *Tridtsatoye avgusta (Bolsheviki)* (1968; Eng. tr., *The Bolsheviks*, in *Nine Soviet Plays*, 1977), which features the attempt on Lenin's life;

*Revolyutsionny etyud* (1979; A Revolutionary Etude), which attempts to connect different generations; *Tak pobedim* (1982; Thus We Will Succeed), featuring Lenin before his death. *Loshad Przhevalskogo* (1972; Przewalski's Horse) concerns students on a construction project in the Virgin Lands; *Pogoda na zavtra* (1974; Weather Forecast for Tomorrow) takes place in an automobile factory; *Moi Nadezhdy* (1977; My Three Nadezhdas) is set among three generations of weavers. Shatrov's dramatic art is journalistic, occasionally too simplistic and contrived, but always concerned with combining political or social problems and human ones. Together with the historian V. Loginov, Shatrov composed *Fevral* (1979; February), a "novel-chronicle" about the February Revolution of 1917 in monologues and documents.

*Works: Imenem revoljucii* (play), in *Sovremennaja dramaturgija* 3:1957; *Šestoe ijulja* (play), in *Naš sovremennik* 1964:4, separate ed., 1966; *Tridcatoe avgusta* (play), in *Teatr* 1968:7 (see above); *Lošad' Prževal'skogo* (play), in *Teatr*, 1972:11; *18-j god* (play), 1974; *Pogoda na zavtra* (play), in *Teatr* 1974:3; *Moi Nadeždy* (play), in *Teatr* 1977:10; *Revoljucionnyj ètjud* (play), in *Teatr* 1979:6; (jointly with V. Loginov) *Fevral'* (novel-chronicle), in *Junost'* 1979:9–11; *Izbr.* (plays), 1982 (contains *Imenem revoljucii*; *Gleb Kosmačev*; *Šestoe ijulja*; *Bol'ševiki*; *Lošad' Prževal'skogo*; *Pogoda na zavtra*; *Konec*; *Moi Nadeždy*; *Sinie koni na krasnoj trave [Revoljucionnyj ètjud]*; *Tak pobedim!*); *Diktatura sovesti* (play), in *Teatr* 1986:6.

*Secondary Lit.*: E. Jupaševskaja, in *Zvezda* 1958:11; Ju. Babuškin, in *Teatr* 1960:11; V. Pimenov, in *Teatr* 1965:4; V. Lakšin, in *Novyj mir* 1968:9; K. Ščerbakov, in *Teatr* 1973:1; A. Mednikov, in *Lit. Rossija* Feb. 15, 1974, p. 15; N. Potapov, in *Teatr* 1980:2; M. Stroeva, in *Lit. gazeta* Jan. 20, 1982, p. 8; O. Efremov, in *Sovremennaja dramaturgija* 1982:1. V. Potëmkin, in *Neva* 1986:1; T. Landa, in *Novyj mir* 1986:11.

**Shchipachóv, Stepán Petróvich**, poet (b. Jan. 7, 1899 [Dec. 26, 1898], Shchipachi, prov. Perm—d. Jan. 2, 1980, Moscow). Shchipachov's father was a peasant. From 1914 on, Shchipachov worked in a bookstore; in 1917 he was drafted into the army and in 1919 became a Red Army volunteer and a member of the Communist Party. Shchipachov's first poems were published in a local newspaper in 1919; his first volume of poetry came out

SHÉFNER 362

in 1923. In 1922 he attended classes in pedagogy in Moscow; from 1922 to 1929 he
taught political subjects in the army, after
1926 in Moscow. Between 1929 and 1931
Shchipachov was assistant editor of the newspaper *Krasnoarmeyets*. In 1930 he became one
of the founders of the literary association of
the Red Army and Navy (LOKAF). From 1931
to 1934 he studied literature at the Institute
of Red Professors. Shchipachov was not among
the participants of the First Congress of the
Writers Union in 1934; in 1935 he turned to
a purely literary career and became one of
those widely recognized poets who are represented in all the anthologies. During World
War II, Shchipachov was in the service of
*Pravda* and army newspapers. He received a
Stalin Prize twice (for 1948, 2d class, and for
1950, 1st class). Shchipachov participated in
all congresses of the Writers Union held since
1954; he belonged to the boards of the Writers
Unions of the USSR (from 1954 on) and the
RSFSR (from 1958 on). He lived in Moscow.

Shchipachov's lyrical talent is somewhat
limited. In his youth he conformed to the
cosmic-hyperbolic writing style of KUZNITSA;
later, it is rather the avoidance of loud dec-
lamations and hollow enthusiasm that causes
his poetry to stand out. Thematically his work
remains well within the framework of conventional confessional poems that address
communism, fatherland, and the happy future, but it combines these programmatic
principles with the motifs of nature and love,
and later of age, without becoming deeply
personal. In the later Stalin period he stood
out all the more positively because of this
innately lyrical element. His poetry is most
often confined to the presentation of one simple thought; its observations have a slightly
banal effect. Shchipachov's short poems and,
to a lesser degree, his narrative poems, achieved
some recognition, since his inferior musical
ability and narrow vocabulary are less evident
in them.

*Works: Po kurganam vekov* (poems), 1923;
*Odna šestaja* (poems), 1931; *Stroki ljubvi*
(poems), 1944; *Pavlik Morozov* (narrative
poem), 1950; *Berëzovyj sok* (autobiography),
1956; *Ladon'* (poems), 1964; *Krasnye list'ja*
(poems), 1967; *Tovariščam po žizni* (poems),
1972; *Sineva Rossii* (poems), 1976: *Poèmy*
(narrative poems), 1978.—*Izbr. proizv.*, 2 vols.,
1965, 1970; *Sobr. soč.*, 3 vols., 1976–77.
*Secondary Lit.:* B. Grossman, in *Novyj mir*
1940:10; V. Percov, in *Novyj mir* 1949:4; V.
Dement'ev, 1956, 1970, 1975; S. Babënyševa,

1957; K. Vanšenkin, in *Lit. obozrenie* 1973:3;
A. Surkov, in *Lit. gazeta* Jan. 9, 1974, p. 2;
Kh. Mar, in *Lit. gazeta* Oct. 15, 1980, p. 6; E.
Dolmatovskij, in *Voprosy lit.* 1984:5; L. Obu-
khova, in *Lit. Rossija* Jan. 11, 1985, p. 15.

**Shéfner, Vadím Sergéyevich**, poet, prose writer
(b. Jan. 12, 1915 [Dec. 30, 1914], Petrograd).
After the early death of his father, Shefner
was one of the "homeless waifs" (*besprizornye*) for a while. In 1931 he graduated from
secondary school. In 1937 he graduated from
the worker faculty of Leningrad University.
He worked in factories in Leningrad as a stoker and draftsman. After 1936 he published
poems that he first collected in *Svetly bereg*
(1940; Bright Shore). His first short story also
appeared in 1940. During World War II, Shefner was a soldier, then later a correspondent
at the front in Leningrad. He joined the Communist Party in 1945. During the 1950s, Shefner traveled within the USSR—Siberia, Caucasus, Central Asia, Belorussia—and in
Czechoslovakia. By 1982 he had published
about 20 volumes of his remarkable contemplative poetry and about 6 volumes of short
stories. Shefner is too little noticed by critics
and literary historians. Since 1970 he has
been a member of only the board of the Writers Union of the RSFSR; he lives in Leningrad.

Shefner is one of the most important exponents of contemplative poetry, of the poets
who carry on the tradition of F. Tyutchev and
are closely associated with that of L. Martynov, N. Zabolotsky, and E. Vinokurov. What
most distinguishes Shefner's lyric poetry from
other Russian lyric is its temporal breadth:
man in the cave-dwelling period is viewed
together with man in the skyscraper; in autumn man also experiences the coming spring;
the mirror in a bomb-shattered house is the
point of reference for a glimpse into the un-
disturbed past; the horror of war at present
and in the future with its vaulted air-raid
shelters is united with the vaults of the monk's
cell of Nestor, the early Russian chronicler,
and with the " 'vault' of heaven, steeped in
worlds for a billion years." The world of technology merges with the world of nature, and
Shefner has a strong relationship to both
("Goroda—prodolzheniye prirody" [1962;
Cities Are the Continuation of Nature]). Images of nature serve as allegory for him and,
in their simplicity, as an ideal of beauty ("Bez
ukrasheniy" [1959; Without Jewelry]). He ascribes positive value to suffering in people's
lives ("Tvoyo neschastye v tom, chto ty ne
znal bedy"[1958; Your Misfortune Is That You

Did Not Know Sorrow]). Shefner's poetry is not dedicated to political themes. Formally it is characterized by great conciseness, imagery, neologisms, unusual epithets; it is generally rhymed. In prose, to which he turned also after 1952, Shefner especially treasures documentarily precise texts and science fiction that essentially deals with ethical and psychological questions. Together with short stories and longer stories (povesti) of an autobiographical nature (for example, vagabond children or the Leningrad blockade as in *Sestra pechali* [1970; The Sister of Sorrow]) can be found his memoirs of childhood: *Imya dlya ptitsy, ili Chayepitiye na zholtoy verande* (1976; A Name for a Bird; or, Teatime on the Yellow Veranda). His science fiction takes pleasure in speaking in playful seriousness about apparent nonsense or jocularly about serious matters; his poetic imagination also uses fairy-tale elements as its source.

*Works: Svetlyj bereg* (poems), 1940; *Prigorod* (poems), 1946; *Moskovskoe šosse* (poems), 1951; *Vzmor'e* (poems), 1955; *Oblaka i dorogi* (short stories), 1957; *Neždannyj den'* (poems), 1958; *Stikhi* (poems), 1960; *Znak zemli* (poems), 1961; *Nynče, večno, i nikogda* (short stories), 1963; *Stikhotvorenija* (poems), 1965; *Sestra pečali* (pov. and short stories), 1970; *Stikhotvorenija* (poems), 1972; *Skromnyj genij* (science fiction), 1974 (Eng. tr. of title story, "A Modest Genius: A Fairy-Tale for Grownups," in *Russian Science Fiction*, 1969, ed. R. Magidoff); *Cvetnye stëkla* (poems), 1975; *Pereulok pamjati* (poems), 1976; *Imja dlja pticy* (pov.), 1977; *Storona otpravlenija* (poems), 1979; *Vtoraja pamjat'* (poems), 1981; *Gody i migi* (poems), 1983; *Lačuga dolžnika* (novel), 1983; *Skazki dlja umnykh* (poems), 1985.— *Izbr. proizv.*, 2 vols., 1975, 1982.

*Secondary Lit.*: A. Makedonov, in *Novyj mir* 1964:6; S. E. Arro, in *Literatura v škole* 1965:6; A. Èl'jaševič, *Poèty, stikhi, poèzija*, 1966, pp. 116–93; I. Kuz'mičev, 1968; W. Kasack, in *Neue Zürcher Zeitung* Feb. 4, 1973; T. Gluškova, in *Lit. obozrenie* 1973:9; Vs. Roždestvenskij, in *Lit. gazeta* Jan. 22, 1975, p. 4; M. Sobol', in *Lit. obozrenie* 1977:12; I. Kuz'mičev, in *Neva* 1981:7; A. Mikhajlov, in *Lit. obozrenie* 1982:10; A. Pikač, in *Lit. obozrenie* 1983:5; G. Filippov, in *Zvezda* 1985:1.

**Shershenévich, Vadím Gabriélevich,** poet (b. Feb. 6 [Jan. 25], 1893, Kazan—d. May 18, 1942, Barnaul). Shershenevich's father was a famous professor of jurisprudence. Shershenevich's first volumes of verse (published in

Moscow, 1911, and subsequently) reveal the influence of the symbolists, particularly of K. Balmont; in 1913 N. Gumilyov praised his poetic language. Shershenevich was then a member of the ego-futurists (see FUTURISM). In 1918 he became one of the founders and leader of the IMAGISM group, to which he was bound by ties of friendship, especially with A. Kusikov. Influenced by Russian writers and literary critics and by Filippo Marinetti, he became the leading theoretician of imagism. Dismayed by the bleakness of the literary products coming from the groups OKTYABR and KUZNITSA, Shershenevich, in protest against the poetry of the past, sought poetic expression beyond the "drive for agit-output." Under increasing political pressure, Shershenevich fell back on doing stage adaptations and translations (Shakespeare, Baudelaire, Corneille, Parny). His own poetry was not reprinted.

Love poems and metapoetry predominate in Shershenevich's verse. His "protagonist is an antihero who struggles to fence himself off from an unbearable social reality" (Markov). Gumilyov points out that Shershenevich's poetry is characterized by "an unassuming but well-regulated style and interesting constructions" and by "refined rhymes [that] do not overbalance his lines." In terms of content, Shershenevich occasionally shocks the reader by introducing something completely unexpected, even disgusting. As he freed himself from futurism, he formulated the following: "Poetry is the art of combining autonomous words, word-images" (*Zelyonaya ulitsa*). In $2 \times 2 = 5$ Shershenevich found himself in conflict with the critics of his theories of imagism; he called for, among other things, the "breakup of grammar"; his demands exceeded his own ability to realize them.

*Works: Vesennie protalinki* (poems), 1911; *Carmina* (poems), 1913; *Romantičeskaja pudra* (poems), 1913; *Zelënaja ulica* (essays), 1916; *Avtomobil'ja postup'* (poems), 1916; *Večnyj žid* (play), 1919; *Lošad' kak lošad'* (poems), 1920; $2 \times 2 = 5$ (essays), 1920; *Kooperativy vesel'ja* (poems), 1921; *Russkaja poèzija i revoljucija* (essays), 1942; in *Cahiers du monde russe et soviétique* 1974:1–2.

*Secondary Lit.*: N. Gumilëv, in *Apollon* 1913:3 (reprinted, in his *Sobr. soč.*, vol. 4, Washington, 1968, pp. 314–18); V. Markov, *Russian Futurism*, Berkeley, 1968, and *Russian Imaginism*, Giessen, 1980; N. A. Nilsson, *The Russian Imaginists*, Stockholm, 1970; A. Lawton, in *Russian Literature Triquarterly* 12:1975, Diss., Univ. of California, Los Angeles, 1976, in *Slavic and East European Journal* 23:1979, and Ann Arbor, 1981.

**Shéynin, Lev Románovich**, prose writer, playwright (b. March 25 [March 12], 1906, Brusovanka, prov. Vitebsk—d. May 11, 1967, Moscow). Sheynin studied at the Bryusov Institute of Literature and Art in Moscow from 1921 to 1923. After a six-month special training program, he worked as research leader on behalf of the public prosecutor's office and the militia from 1923 to 1950. Sheynin, a member of the Communist Party since 1929, combined his literary activity with his other work after 1928, at first as a writer of prose, and later, after 1936 and partly with the Tur brothers, also as a playwright. After World War II, Sheynin served as a delegate to the Nuremberg trials. He received a Stalin Prize (for 1949, 1st class) for the screenplay he wrote with the Tur brothers for the film *Vstrecha na Elbe* (1947; Meeting at the Elbe). After 1950, Sheynin devoted himself entirely to writing. He lived in Moscow.

Sheyhnin is a typical exponent of light fiction that follows the Party line. Based on his knowledge of court proceedings, he wrote numerous novels, short stories, plays, and films about detectives. They are schematically developed, constructed to build tension, and never pass up the opportunity to fulfill the educational mission of the Party and the Cheka (NKVD, MVD). Among his supporters are L. Nikulin, N. Pogodin, A. Perventsev. Soviet histories of literature do not mention Sheynin, despite his many books.

*Works: Zapiski sledovatelja* (short stories), 1938, enl. ed., 1968 (Eng. tr., *Diary of a Criminologist*, 195–); *Voennaja tajna* (novel-trilogy), 1943–59; (together with the Tur brothers) *Vstreča na El'be* (film script), in *Izbr. kinoscenarii 1949–50*, 1951; *Pomilovanie* (pov.), in *Moskva* 1965:1; *Volki v gorode* (play), in *Oktjabr'* 1965:1; *P'esy* (plays), 1969.

*Secondary Lit.*: L. Nikulin, in *Znamja* 1956:4; S. Larin, in *Moskva* 1958:1; A. Dymšic, in *Lit. gazeta* May 17, 1967, p. 11.

**Shim, Eduárd Yúryevich** (pseud. of E. Yu. Shmidt), prose writer (b. Aug. 23, 1930, Leningrad). Shim was evacuated from Leningrad during World War II and was raised in an orphanage. Following his return and temporary work in a factory, he studied architecture at a technical school and worked in a con-

struction firm after 1950. Starting in 1949, his first short stories began appearing in, among others, the children's magazine *Murzilka*. The children's book publisher also published his short book *Leto na Korbe* (Summer on Korba) in 1951. Shim served in the army from 1952 to 1955. Since 1956 his works have regularly appeared in journals. Following the publication of the collection *Neslyshnye golosa* (1957; Inaudible Voices), his stories have occasionally been collected in books. Since 1959 Shim has been a member of the Writers Union of the USSR; he moved to Moscow probably at the beginning of the 1960s. Only in 1965 was he a delegate to the Second Congress of the Writers Union of the RSFSR. He has gradually shifted to the longer prose form of the *povest*; *Malchik v lesu* (1967; Eng. tr., *The Boy in the Forest*, 1979) was especially noted. Together with Georgy Markov, Shim composed the play *Vyzov* (1980; The Summons), which concerns the topical problem of environmental protection in Siberia.

Shim is a good storyteller with a deep attachment to nature. He has a close relationship to children, who are often the protagonists in his short prose and whose relationship to the world of adults he depicts with psychological perception. From observation of the concerns and sorrows of daily life, Shim chooses events that stand out or whose distinctiveness he can make evident. He enjoys depicting people who let themselves be moved, who can be amazed and filled with enthusiasm, whose spirits soar, who believe in goodness. This has sometimes led to the criticism that his stories are somewhat contrived. Shim's prose is concise in form and grounded in conscious compositional ability, yet Shim himself admits that the depth and truth of his message, the "spiritual temperature of the author," are more important to him than technical perfection (*Voprosy lit.* 1969:7).

*Works: Leto na Korbe* (short stories), 1951; *Neslyšnye golosa* (short stories), 1957; *Belye berëzy* (short stories), 1959; *Derevjannaja kniga* (short stories), 1960, 1965; *Martovskij sneg* (short stories), 1962; . . . *A deti ne slušajutsja roditelej* (play in one act), 1966; *Mal'čik v lesu* (pov.), in *Znamja* 1967:7 (see above); *Vanja pesenki poët* (short stories), 1969; *Voda na kameškakh* (pov.), 1970; *Skazki, najdennye v trave* (short stories), 1972; *Perekrëstok* (short stories), 1975; *Dvojnoj svet* (pov. and short stories), 1980; (with G. Markov) *Vyzov* (play), in *Teatr* 1980:5.

*Secondary Lit.*: V. Bušin, in *Znamja* 1960:5;

M. Roščin, in *Novyj mir* 1962:11; I. Grinberg, in *Moskva* 1968:1; S. Obrazcov, in *Lit. obozrenie* 1973:2; E. Ol'khovič, in *Lit. obozrenie* 1976:2; N. Savickij, in *Teatr* 1981:2; S. Klimovič, in *Lit. Rossija* Aug. 28, 1981, p. 11.

**Shiryáyev, Borís Nikoláyevich,** prose writer (b. Nov. 7 [Oct. 27], 1889, Moscow—d. April 17, 1959, San Remo, Italy). Shiryayev's father was owner of a large estate. Shiryayev completed his studies in the Faculty of History and Philology at Moscow University. He then studied in Germany and graduated from a military academy in Russia. After serving as an officer in World War I, he hid in the Caucasus from 1917 to 1920. He was arrested in 1920; in 1922 his death sentence was commuted to a sentence of ten years' imprisonment in a newly created concentration camp on the island of Solovki, formerly a monastery. In addition to working as a forester and raft builder, Shiryayev was active in the camp theater. In 1929, owing to overcrowding at the camp, his sentence was commuted to three years of internal exile in Central Asia, where he was able to work relatively freely as a journalist. After returning to Moscow in 1932, Shiryayev was again arrested and exiled to Rososh (central Russia) under indecent conditions, again for three years (no housing was provided, no contacts were allowed). From 1932 to 1942 Shiryayev lived in Stavropol and taught at teachers colleges in Stavropol and Cherkassk as a professor of Russian literature and language. After this region was occupied by the Germans in 1942, Shiryayev became the first editor of the free Russian newspaper there. As a result of the German defeat, Shiryayev came via Berlin to Belgrade, where he edited a Russian newspaper for the Cossack units in the German armed forces. On Feb. 12, 1945, Shiryayev was posted to Italy to establish a Russian newspaper. He remained there after the war—at first in a displaced persons camp—and, in addition to various jobs undertaken to earn his living, worked as a writer and literary scholar for journals such as *Vozrozhdeniye* (starting in 1950) and *Grani* (starting in 1952). His first three books were published in Buenos Aires; these included two collections of short stories from Italy and the Soviet Union—*Di-Pi v Italii* (1952; DP in Italy) and *Ya chelovek russky* (1953; I Am a Russian)—as well as *Svetilniki russkoy zemli* (1953; Radiant Spiritual Personalities of the Russian Soil). His later works were published in New York, Munich, Frankfurt, and Brussels. Shiryayev did not receive a religious education but found his way to a Christian faith on Solovki; he converted to Catholicism in Italy.

Shiryayev is a realistic writer who primarily reworks for his prose what he has himself experienced or heard. His greatest merit lies in his depiction of World War II from the perspective of a patriotic Russian who rejects the totalitarian Soviet system and who is prepared to cooperate with the Germans out of national conviction. The novel *Kudeyarov dub* (1957–58; Kudeyar's Oak), which points out the problematic ethical and political dimensions of this theme, provides a fundamental counterpoint to A. Fadeyev's novel *Molodaya gvardiya*, which was not a product of his experience and was adulterated to conform to the Party line. The povest *Ovechya luzha* (1952; The Lamb's Pool) is set in somewhat the same time frame and illustrates the fate of a persecuted Russian clergyman. Russian literature owes a literary debt to Shiryayev who, as one of the first prisoners on Solovki and one of the few survivors, has written a depiction of the life of the prisoners held there from 1922 to 1927 that is marked by the religious spirit of the monastery and the monks despite the murders and material destruction. In his book *Neugasimaya lampada* (1954; The Inextinguishable Icon Lamp), he adapted previously published tales, such as the story of a small city-state that resisted the Reds in the Civil War. *Urensky tsar* (1950; The Tsar of Ureni) and *Gorka Golgofa* (1953; The Mount of Golgotha) are short stories of the great deeds of the martyrs of Solovki, sainted by the Russian Orthodox Church Outside of Russia in 1981. A short essay published posthumously, *Religioznye motivy v russkoy poezii* (1960; Religious Motifs in Russian Poetry), is a valuable supplement to the usual histories of literature. His attempts to portray the pre-Soviet period in *Posledniy barin* (1954; The Last Baron) and in the tale of a horse thief, *Vanka-Vyuga* (1955), are eclipsed to a great extent by the short stories and novels about the Soviet period.

*Works: Stavropol'—Berlin* (essays), in *Časovoj*, Brussels, 287, 293, 303:1949–50; *Raba politiki: Vospominanija podsovetskogo žurnalista* (essays), in *Vozroždenie*, Paris, 8:1950; *Urenskij car'* (short story), in *Vozroždenie* 11–13:1950; *Oveč'ja luža* (pov.), in *Grani*, Frankfurt am Main, 16:1952; *Di-Pi v Italii* (short stories), Buenos Aires, 1952; *Gorka Golgofa* (short stories), in *Grani* 20:1953; *Ja čelovek russkij!* (short stories), Buenos Aires, 1953; *Svetil'niki Russkoj Zemli* (short stories), Buenos Aires, 1953; *Neugasimaja lampada* (short stories), New York, 1954; *Poslednij barin* (pov.), in *Vozroždenie* 33–36:1954; *Van'ka-V'juga* (pov.), in *Vozroždenie* 37–41:1955; *Sovremennaja rossijskaja intelligencija* (essays), Munich, 1955; *Kudejarov dub* (pov.), Frankfurt am Main, 1958; (continuation) *Khorunžij Vakulenko*, in *Grani* 42:1959; *Religioznye motivy v russkoj poèzii* (scholarly articles), Brussels, 1960.

*Secondary Lit.:* V. Zeeler, in *Russkaja mysl'*, Paris, Dec. 12, 1950, and March 20, 1953; L. Rževskij, in *Grani* 18:1953 and in *Russkaja literatura v èmigracii*, ed. N. Poltorackij, Pittsburgh, 1972; V. Krylova, in *Lit. sovremennik*, Munich, 1954; V. Arsen'ev, in *Grani* 24:1955; A. P., in *Grani* 27–28:1955; N. Čukhov, in *Znamja Rossii*, New York, 306:1969.

**Shishkóv, Vyacheslav Yákovlevich,** prose writer (b. Oct. 3 [Sept. 21], 1873, Bezhetsk, prov. Tver—d. March 6, 1945, Moscow). Shishkov's father was a commercial employee. In 1881 Shishkov graduated from the civil engineering school in Vyshnevolotsk. Until the Revolution, Shishkov worked at his profession, initially in European Russia and after 1894 for 20 years in Siberia, where, after passing supplemental exams, he conducted expeditions for the technical investigation of rivers. After 1915 he worked in the Ministry of Transport in Petrograd. From 1908 on, Shishkov occasionally worked as a writer; his first collection from his wealth of experiences during his professional travels, *Sibirsky skaz* (1916; Siberian Stories), was published in Petrograd. From 1917 on, his primary occupation was that of writer, and he shifted gradually to longer prose forms. In 1924 he belonged to the FELLOW TRAVELERS who protested against the militant proceedings of the Party functionaries in the OKTYABR group. From 1926 to 1929 the most comprehensive collection of his work, in 12 volumes, was published. His two-volume historical novel about Siberia, *Ugryum-reka* (1933; Gloomy River), was published beginning in 1928. During World War II, Shishkov lived in besieged Leningrad until 1942 and worked on a novel about the 18th century, *Yemelyan Pugachov* (1941–45). He died shortly before completing it and was posthumously awarded a Stalin Prize (for 1943–44, 1st class).

Shishkov is a good, realistic storyteller whose profound knowledge of various regions of Siberia and whose interest in the language of its people have found diverse literary expression in his prose. In *Vataga* (1924; The Gang), he depicts the Revolution in its hideous disinhibition that touched off robbery, murder, and chaos. This criticized novel has not been reprinted since 1927. His second novel about the Civil War, however, *Peypus-ozero* (1925; Lake Peypus), remained acceptable. With *Stranniki* (1931; Eng. tr., *Children of Darkness*, 1931) Shishkov made his contribution to the exposition of the problem of the "homeless waifs" *(besprizornye)*. *Ugryum-reka* describes the decline of a merchant's family in Siberia from the end of the last century until World War I. *Yemelyan Pugachov* develops a broad historical panorama by using the peasant uprising of 1773–75 and the evolution of the Cossack rebel into the alleged Tsar Peter III. Shishkov avoids "the false tone . . . and did not unduly idealize the peasants or denigrate the aristocrats" (Slonim).

*Works: Sibirskij skaz* (short stories), 1916; *Tajga* (pov.), 1916; *Medvežač'e carstvo* (fairy tale), in *Severnoe sijanie* 1919:1–2; *Vataga* (novel), 1925; *Pejpus-ozero* (pov.), 1925; *Stranniki* (novel), 1931 (see above); *Ugrjum-reka* (novel), 2 vols., 1933; *Emel'jan Pugačёv* (novel), 3 vols., 1946–47.—*Polnoe sobr. soč.,* 12 vols., 1926–29; *Izbr. soč.,* 6 vols., 1946–48; 4 vols., 1958; *Sobr. soč.,* 8 vols., 1960–62.

*Secondary Lit.:* M. Majzel', 1935; V. Bakhmet'ev, 1947, and in *Lit. gazeta* Dec. 25, 1965; A. Bogdanova, 1953; I. Izotov, 1956; G. Markov, in Shishkov's *Sobr. soč.,* 1960–62; *RSPP* 6(1):1969; V. A. Čalmaev, 1969; N. Eselev, 1973, 2d ed., 1976; *Vospominanija o V. Š.,* 1979; Vl. Kočetov, 1981; S. Sartakov, in *Lit. gazeta* Sept. 28, 1983, p. 5,; N. Janovskij, 1984.

**Shkápskaya, María Mikháylovna** (née Andréyevskaya), poet (b. Oct. 15 [Oct. 3], 1891, St. Petersburg—d. Sept. 7, 1952, Moscow). Shkapskaya's father was a civil servant. She completed her study of philology at Toulouse University in 1914 and returned to Russia. Shkapskaya published her first poems in 1910; her first volume of poetry was *Mater dolorosa* (1921), which was given extraordinarily high praise by P. Florensky, among others. This was followed by *Chas vecherny* (1922; Evening Hour) and, in Berlin, by *Baraban Strogogo Gospodina* (1922; The Drum of the Strict Lord)—labeled "counterrevolutionary" by V. Bryusov—and *Krov-ruda* (1922; Blood Ore). Then three shorter books were published in Moscow: *Yav* (1923; Reality), *Kniga o Lukavom Seyatele* (1923; Book of the Cunning

Sower), *Zemnye remyosla* (1925; Earthly Handicrafts). Shkapskaya, who wrote religious poetry, was forced into silence by Communist pressure. She apparently not only published no further poetry but also wrote no more poems. She became a journalist for the *Vechernyaya krasnaya gazeta* in Leningrad and published five books of documentary prose (1930–32 and 1942). By publishing an anthology of Shkapskaya's poems in 1979, B. Filippov rescued her from obscurity.

Shkapskaya is a talented poet whose creativity stems from her religious conviction. In the center of her creative work stands the woman as lover and mother. She sees women in their earthly—physical and spiritual—happiness and misfortune, in their turning toward and away from God. Love, pregnancy, birth, abortion, joy in children, sense of loss at their death—all are frequent themes. B. Filippov points out that the literary youth of Leningrad in the mid-1920s labeled Shkapskaya the 'Three V's"—*vedma, vakkhanka, volchitsa* (witch, bacchante, she-wolf); to this image he opposes that of the "Vasilisa Rozanova of Russian poetry," since she tries to find a worthy place for the physical that will not offend the holy. *Yav* is a brief verse epic written in 1919 that vividly and almost expressionistically describes a man's execution at the gallows and the tension among the victim, the mother, and the bystanders, involving also the religious view of the event. Shkapskaya uses rhyme and assonance, but she often publishes her verse without line breaks.

*Works: Mater dolorosa* (poems), 1921; *Čas večernyj* (poems), 1922; *Baraban Strogogo Gospodina* (poems), Berlin, 1922; *Krov'-ruda* (poems), Berlin, 1922; *Jav'* (narrative poem), 1923; *Ca-Ca-Ca: Kitajskaja poèma* (narrative poem), Berlin, 1923; *Kniga o Lukavom Sejaele* (poems), 1923; *Zemnye remësla* (poems), 1925; *Stikhi* (poems), London, 1979.

*Secondary Lit.:* V. Brjusov, in *Pečat' i revoljucija* 1923:1; G. Lelevič, in *Krasnaja nov'* 1925:1; B. Filippov, in *Novoe russkoe slovo*, New York, May 1, 1973, and in Škapskaja's *Stikhi*, London, 1979; E. Žiglevič, in Škapskaja's *Stikhi*, London, 1979; A. Bakhrakh, in *Novoe russkoe slovo* Dec. 9, 1979, p. 5; Z. Sakhovskaja, in *Russkaja mysl'*, Paris, Dec. 13, 1979, p. 8; V. Sinkevič, in *Novoe russkoe slovo* Jan. 27, 1980; Anon., in *Kontinent*, Paris, 23:1980.

**Shklóvsky, Víktor Borísovich,** prose writer, literary critic (b. Feb. 6 [Jan. 25], 1893,

St. Petersburg—d. Dec. 5, 1984, Moscow). Shklovsky's father was a mathematics teacher of Jewish-Russian ancestry. Shklovsky studied humanities at Petrograd University. His first works were published in 1908. From 1916 on, Shklovsky was among the active members of OPOYAZ (Society for the Study of Poetic Language) and became one of the leading theoreticians of the FORMALIST SCHOOL. In 1917 Shklovsky joined the Socialist Revolutionaries and fought against the Whites and against the Bolsheviks. In 1920 he returned to Petrograd, worked as a professor at the Russian Institute for Art History, and supported the SERAPION BROTHERS and LEF. In 1922 he was forced to emigrate, going via Finland to Berlin where his first two belletristic works were published: *Sentimentalnoye puteshestviye* (1923; Eng. tr., *Sentimental Journey*, 1970) and *ZOO, ili pisma ne o lyubvi* (1923; Eng. tr., *ZOO; or, Letters Not about Love*, 1971). Given amnesty, Shklovsky returned to the Soviet Union in 1923 and continued his literary and literary-theoretical activity in connection with modern trends until, in the face of pressure from a cultural policy that was becoming increasingly more one-sided ideologically, he put a stop to his experimental efforts with *Pamyatnik nauchnoy oshibke* (Monument to a Scientific Error; in *Lit. gazeta* Jan. 27, 1930). As early as 1926, Shklovsky became active in films and children's literature. These areas remained accessible to him in a limited way. His book *O Mayakovskom* (1940; Eng. tr., *Mayakovsky and His Circle*, 1972) was attacked because it overvalued FUTURISM. After 1953 he again found recognition as a theoretician; another autobiographical work, *Zhili-byli* (1961; Once Upon a Time), deals especially with the period before 1917. His biography *Lev Tolstoy* (1963; Eng. tr., 1978) is subjective and provocative but also contains numerous factual errors. For his book *Eyzenshteyn* (1976; Eisenstein), he received the State Prize of the USSR for 1979. From 1934 on, Shklovsky participated in all congresses of the Writers Union of the USSR (except that held in 1959) and of the Writers Union of the RSFSR; he lived in Moscow.

Shklovsky is an extraordinarily dynamic personality, thanks more to his being an originator of new literary methods than to his consistent research work. His belletristic works convert his theoretical considerations into practice and attempt to break apart the usual framework of the novel, but in their plotless, autobiographical, discursive structure they also correspond to Shklovsky's impulsive nature. The title of a book about the catastrophes of

the Revolution, *Sentimentalnoye puteshest-*
*viye,* ironically refers to Laurence Sterne and
to his "journey." *ZOO,* a compilation of 30
letters to Alia (=Elsa Triolet), brilliantly and
paradoxically depicts Berlin in the years 1922–
23 from an emigrant's point of view and is as
permeated with literary-historical and literary-theoretical reflections and as unclassifia-
ble by genre as is everything Shklovsky has
written.

Works: *Sentimental'noe putešestvie* (novel),
1923 (see above); *ZOO, ili pis'ma ne o ljubvi*
(novel), Berlin, 1923 (see above); *O teorii prozy*
(essays), 1925; *Tret'ja fabrika,* 1926 (Eng. tr.,
*Third Factory,* 1977); other theoretical articles
in *Literatura fakta,* ed. N. Čužak, 1929 (reprinted, Munich, 1977); *Marko Polo razvedčik*
(children's book), 1931; *O Majakovskom*
(memoirs), 1940 (see above); *Khudožestven-*
*naja proza* (essays), 1959; *Žili-byli* (memoirs),
1964; *Tetiva. O neskhodstve skhodnogo* (essays), 1970; *Ejzenštejn* (biography), 2d ed.,
1976.—*Sobr. soč.,* 3 vols. 1973–74; *Izbr.*
*proizv.,* 2 vols., 1983.
    Secondary Lit.: L. Timofeev, in *Novyj mir*
1941:1; L. Anninskij, in *Moskva* 1961:1; *Lit.*
*gazeta* Jan. 24, 1963; *RSPP* 6:1969; L. Alekseev, in *Voprosy lit.* 1971:1; I. Andronikov, in
*Lit. gazeta* Jan. 17, 1973, p. 3, and foreword
to *Sobr. soč.,* 1973; R. Sheldon, in *Slavic*
*Review* 34:1975 and in V. Š.: *An International*
*Bibliography,* Ann Arbor, 1977; V. Erlich, R.
Sheldon, in *Slavic Review* 35:1976; M. C.
Smith, Diss., Univ. of Pennsylvania, 1978; A.
Peskov, in *Lit. obozrenie* 1984:9; L. Rubin-
štejn, in *Novoe russkoe slovo,* New York, Dec.
14, 1984, p. 9; I. Serman, in *Russkaja mysl',*
Paris, Dec. 27, 1984, p. 10.

**Shkvárkin, Vasíly Vasílyevich,** playwright (b.
May 16 [May 4], 1894, Tver—d. Nov. 14, 1967,
Moscow). Shkvarkin, who wrote his first drama
in 1924, previously worked in the leather
trade and in a bank; he served in the Red
Army and was able to study philology for
only one year. In a competition for historical
dramas, his *V glukhoye tsarstvovaniye* (1924;
In the Dark Domination of the Tsars), also
known under the title *Predatelstvo Degayeva*
(Degayev's Betrayal), was acknowledged to be
the best. With *Vredny element* (1927; The
Dangerous Element), Shkvarkin switched to
the genre in which he had great and prolonged
success with the public—the topical light
comedy with musical interludes. By 1940 approximately nine such plays were famous,

some of which were also performed in foreign
countries; by far the most successful was *Chu-*
*zhoy rebyonok* (1933; Eng. tr., *Father Un-*
*known,* in *Soviet Scene,* 1946); the 500th performance occurred in 1939. Shkvarkin's last
two plays, whose theme is World War II, were
performed in 1945 without particular success.
In the period 1925–45 the critics paid little
attention to Shkvarkin despite his occasional
exceptional stage successes; after 1946 he was
temporarily removed from the literary scene.
A single collection of his works appeared in
1954 during the period of the THAW. Since
then, his plays have again been performed
occasionally. *Chuzhoy rebyonok* remained
constantly on numerous stages in the Soviet
Union from 1959 to 1971, with an average of
300 performances per year. Shkvarkin played
no role whatsoever in literary-political life
and lived in Moscow.
    Shkvarkin is a talented author of light com-
edies with a sense for scenic effectiveness but
without a message extending beyond the depiction of unusual events. In *Vokrug sveta na*
*samom sebe* (1927; Around the World of Itself) he brings an unemployed actor among
tricksters in Butyrka prison; also in *Shuler*
(1929; The Cardsharper) much of the comedy
derives from the confusion and ridicule of the
"old-timers." An attempt to accommodate
himself to contemporary Komsomol themes,
in *Kto idyot?* (1931; Who Goes There?), was
unsuccessful. Following a successful play about
an apparent pregnancy, *Chuzhoy rebyonok,*
came *Prostaya devushka* (1937; The Simple
Girl) and *Vesenniy smotr* (1937; Spring Show),
also with innocent plots. Somewhat more satirical was *Strashny sud* (1939; The Last Judgment), which was constructed from well-
known elements such as theft, divorce, confusion, and a happy ending. Of the wartime
plays *Posledniy den* (1945; The Last Day), also
known as *Proklyatoye kafe* (The Accursed
Café), and *Mirnye lyudi* (1945; Peaceful People), the second was again produced in 1957.
Shkvarkin's plays are qualitatively quite distinct, united by good-natured mockery of the
bourgeoisie and by decent, humane attitudes.

Works: *Predatel'stvo Degaeva* (play), 1926;
*Vokrug sveta na samom sebe* (comedy), 1927;
*Šuler* (comedy), 1929; *Kto idët?* (comedy), 1932;
*Čužoj rebënok* (comedy), in *P'esy sovetskikh*
*pisatelej* 4:1954 (see above); *Prostaja devuška*
(comedy), 1940; *Komedii,* 1954 (contains *Ču-*
*žoj rebënok; Vesennij smotr; Prostaja de-*
*vuška; Strašnyj sud); Komedii,* 1966.
    Secondary Lit.: V. Frolov, in his *O sovetsko*

komedii, 1954, and in Oktjabr' 1958:3; I. Štok, in Teatr 1958:8; L. Klimova, in Očerki istorii sovetskoj dramaturgii, 1966.

**Shmelyóv, Iván Sergéyevich,** prose writer (b. Oct. 3 [Sept. 21], 1873, Moscow—d. June 24, 1950, Paris). Shmelyov came from a merchant's family of Old Believers. From 1894 to 1898 he studied law at Moscow University; until 1907 he worked in the provincial government. His literary activity began in 1895. Around 1900 he joined the "Znaniye" circle. The novel Chelovek iz restorana (1911; The Waiter) made him quite famous. In 1912 Shmelyov, together with I. Bunin, B. Zaytsev, N. Teleshov, and V. Veresayev, among others, was one of the partners in the "Publisher of the Authors" in Moscow, the firm that published an eight-volume edition of his works. Before the Revolution he fled to the Crimea, to Alushta, where he withstood the horrors of the Civil War and the famine. At the end of 1922 he succeeded in leaving the country via Moscow. He lived briefly in Berlin and then settled in Paris. One of the first books he wrote in emigration was Solntse myortvykh (1923; Eng. tr., The Sun of the Dead, 1927), a gripping autobiographical depiction of the devastation of the Revolution, a work that, through its many translations, shocked people. Shmelyov wrote much in the following decades and became one of the most influential and regularly translated émigré writers.

Shmelyov is strongly influenced by Russian tradition and Christian belief. His early works continue the literature of social compassion and show, as in Pod gorami (1910; At the Foot of the Mountains), his capacity for uniting the spiritual with a description of nature. The povest written in the Crimea, Neupivayemaya chasha (1921; Eng. tr., Inexhaustible Cup, 1928), which tells of the love of an icon-painting serf for his mistress, has mystical overtones. Next to the documentary work Solntse myortvykh, which was highly praised by Thomas Mann and Gerhart Hauptmann, stand numerous stories from his years of tribulation in the Crimea, such as Svet razuma (1928; The Light of the Spirit). There is also prose written during his life as an émigré. Later, Shmelyov turned to the depiction of more distant remembrances and themes of old, pious, and tradition-bound Russia. Leto Gospodne (1933; The Year of Our Lord) describes the importance of the great Orthodox holidays; his last novel, Puti nebesnye II (1937–48; Paths to Heaven, parts 1 and 2), described

the gradual purification of an atheist under the influence of an Orthodox novice. Part 3 was not completed and remained unpublished. Shmelyov's style can be too lyrical and overly emphatic. Masterly is his grasp of the skaz style—interrupting the action of the plot by switching to a fictitious narrator. Here, N. Leskov's influence can be seen; Leskov's writings, together with those of F. Dostoyevsky, had an effect on Shmelyov.

Works: Pod gorami (short story), 1910; Raspad. Graždanin Ulejkin (short stories), 1910; Čelovek iz restorana (novel), 1911; Neupivaemaja čaša (pov.), Paris, 1921, Moscow, 1922 (see above); Sladkij mužik (short stories), Berlin, 1921; Eto bylo (short stories), Berlin, 1923 (Eng. tr., That Which Happened, 1924); Na pen'kakh (short story), in Sovremennye zapiski, Paris, 26:1925; Solnce mërtvykh (memoirs), Paris, 1926 (see above); Pro odnu starukhu (short story), Paris, 1927; Svet razuma (short stories), 1928; Istorija ljubovnaja (novel), Paris, 1929 (Eng. tr., The Story of a Love, 1931); Leto Gospodne (memoirs), Belgrade, 1933, Paris, 1948; Bogomol'e (memoirs), Belgrade, 1935, Paris, 1948; Njanja iz Moskvy (novel), Paris, 1936; Puti nebesnye (novel), 2 vols., Paris, 1937–48; Izbrannye rasskazy (short stories), New York, 1955; Kulikovo pole. Staryj Varlaam (short stories), Paris, 1958; Povesti i rasskazy (short stories), Moscow, 1960, 1966; Soldaty, Paris, 1962; Inostranec (fragments of a novel), Paris, 1963; Duša Rodiny (essays), Paris, 1967; Svet večnyj (short stories), Paris, 1968.—Rasskazy (works), 8 vols., 1910–16.

Secondary Lit.: J. Legras, in Le Monde Slave 1935:3; M. Aschenbrenner, Königsberg, 1937; Ju. A. Kutyrina, Paris, 1960; O. Sorokin, Diss., Univ. of California, Berkeley, 1965; T. Ozkaya, Diss., New York Univ., 1976; A. Černikov, in Russkaja lit. 1980:1; Bibliographie des oeuvres d. I. Chmelev, Paris, 1980; W. Schriek, Munich, 1986.

**Shólokhov, Mikhaíl Aleksándrovich,** prose writer, literary official (b. May 24 [May 11], 1905, Kruzhilin, Don region—d. Feb. 21, 1984, Stanitsa Veshenskaya, prov. Rostov). Sholokhov's father worked for the civil service; his mother was of half-Cossack ancestry. Until 1918 Sholokhov attended secondary school. From the end of 1922 until May 1924 he worked at odd jobs in Moscow; his first pieces were published in newspapers. Then he returned to the Don region; from 1926 until his death he lived in Veshenskaya. In 1926 his first two collections of short stories appeared. In 1932 he was accepted into the Communist Party. From 1934 on, he was a member of the leading group in the Writers Union of the USSR; from 1967 on, he was also one of the secretaries of the board and was a member of the presidia of all the congresses of the Writers Union. The four-volume novel that was awarded a Stalin Prize (for 1935–41, 1st class) and became the most frequently printed novel in the Soviet Union—*Tikhiy Don* (Eng. abridged tr., *And Quiet Flows the Don*, 1934, and *The Don Flows Home to the Sea*, 1940, and a more complete tr. in 4 vols., *And Quiet Flows the Don*, 1960)—was published under Sholokhov's name from 1928 to 1940. In 1974 A. Solzhenitsyn renewed the rumors that had existed since the end of the 1920s that the real author was Fedor Kryukov, a Cossack leader who died in 1920 and who could not be published because he belonged to the "White Guard." Only 5 percent of the first two parts and 30 percent of the last two parts were said to have been written by Sholokhov. In 1932 Sholokhov interrupted publication of *Tikhiy Don* to describe collectivization in *Podnyataya tselina* (1932; Eng. tr., *Seeds of Tomorrow*, 1935, and *Harvest on the Don*, 1960) but did not immediately complete this novel. In 1936 Sholokhov was appointed a delegate to the Supreme Soviet and served in this capacity until his death. During World War II, Sholokhov was a correspondent for *Pravda*; in 1959 he began to publish part of his third novel, *Oni srazhalis za Rodinu* (Eng. tr., "They Fought for Their Country," in *Soviet Literature* 1959:7). At the end of the Stalin period, Sholokhov was forced to rewrite *Tikhiy Don* in accordance with Party doctrine, especially to eliminate all the sections that report on the Cossacks' efforts to attain autonomy. The edition published in 1953 was again partially altered in 1965. From the 18th Party Congress in 1939 on, Sholokhov was regularly appointed a delegate. Since the founding of the Writers Union of the RSFSR in 1958, Sholokhov was a member of the board. In 1959, after 27 years, he completed the second part of *Podnyataya tselina* and was awarded the Lenin Prize in 1960. At the 22d Party Congress Sholokhov was elected to the Central Committee. In 1965 he was awarded the Nobel Prize and was allowed to travel to Stockholm to receive it in contrast to B. Pasternak and Solzhenitsyn. At the 23d Party Congress in 1966, to the horror of world public opinion, Sholokhov defamed the writers Yu. Daniel and A. Sinyavsky, who had been condemned

to long terms of imprisonment, as well as the large number of respectable writers and critics who had worked to bring about their release. L. Chukovskaya responded in an open (SAM-IZDAT) letter: "The business of writers is not to prosecute but to care. . . . One must confront ideas with ideas, not with camps and prisons." Sholokhov, however, called the unlawful judgment not stiff enough.

In the 55 years he worked as a writer, Sholokhov published several short stories but only two novels. *Tikhiy Don* is a combination of a historical epic about the Cossacks from before World War I until 1922 and a family saga that is reminiscent of the 19th-century novel tradition, but the novel is historically adulterated. Sholokhov avoids a primitive division into good and bad corresponding to the political division between Red and White, but the composition as a whole is weak. The strongest quality of his work lies in the meticulous rendering of detail. "The novel has unquestionably been overpraised and many defects of its language and composition overlooked" (Struve). *Podnyataya tselina* publicizes with the same careful inclusion of tragic elements the collectivization and class struggle in the countryside. Sholokhov "loses his sense of proportion" (Slonim) and reveals his inability to master the material. S. Zalygin, who once again took up this theme in *Na Irtyshe*, provides an objective representation in contrast to Sholokhov's disingenuous propaganda about the annihilation of the kulaks.

*Works: Tikhij Don* (novel), 1928–40, 2d rev. ed., 1953 (see above); *Podnjataja celina* (novel), 1932–59 (see above); *Oni srazalis' za Rodinu* (novel), 1959 (see above).—*Sobr. soč.*, 8 vols., 1956–60; 8 vols., 1968–69; 8 vols., 1975, 1980.

*Secondary Lit.:* J. Rühle, in *Der Monat* 90:1956; D. Stewart, in *American Slavic and East European Review*, 1959, and separate study, Ann Arbor, 1967; A. Britikov, 1964; L. Čukovskaja (1966), in her *Otkrytoe slovo*, New York, 1976; *RSPP* 6(2):1969; G. Ermolaev, in *Mosty*, New York, 15:1970; L. Jakimenko, 2d ed., 1970; D*, *Stremja "Tikhogo Dona,"* Paris, 1974; V. Petelin, 1974; A. B. Murphy and others, in *New Zealand Slavonic Journal* 1975–77; V. Gura, 1980; *Velikij khudožnik sovremennosti*, 1983.

**Shtéyger, Anatóly Sergéyevich,** poet (b. July 7, 1907, Nikolayevka, prov. Kiev—d. Oct. 24, 1944, Leysin, Switzerland). Shtéyger was descended from a long-established Bernese lineage and bore the title of baron. His ancestors emigrated to Russia at the beginning of the 19th century. Soon after the Revolution, Shteyger fled first to Constantinople with his parents and siblings; from there he went via Prague to Paris where he published his first slender volume of poetry, Etot den (1928; This Day); from then on he occasionally published poems in journals. Shteyger belonged to the younger generation of the first emigration; his reception was cautiously positive, and he was gratified by the encouragement his friendship with Georgy Adamovich provided. He lived primarily in Nice and frequently traveled around Europe. Shteyger, who was seriously ill with tuberculosis, published two more volumes of poetry during his lifetime: Eta zhizn (1931; This Life) and Neblagodarnost (1936; Ungratefulness). Thereafter he published only in the journals Sovremennye zapiski (64–70:1937–40) and Russkiye zapiski (1937–38). He spent World War II in a sanatorium in Switzerland and spoke out against National Socialism in his journalistic articles. The volume $2 \times 2 = 4$ (1950), for which he himself had selected poems from the years 1929 to 1939, appeared posthumously.

Shteyger's poetry has its roots in the "silver age" of Russian poetry, especially in the works of I. Annensky and the acmeists. In his poetry he expresses the fundamental issues of human existence, such as loneliness, suffering, death, hope. For these qualities, as well as for the simplicity and modesty of his never extravagant or modern form, he is considered the purest representative of the "Parisian Note," of which G. Adamovich is an exponent. Thematically, sorrow at the state of the world and a yearning for tenderness predominate; pessimistic, like many who suffer from tuberculosis, he can only accept the present—this day, this hour; he perceives every encounter as a potentially final meeting. An ironic detachment, often expressed parenthetically, underscores his painful perception of the world, one not far removed from the transcendental yet one not counterbalanced by faith.

Works: Ètot den' (poems), Paris, 1928; Èta žizn' (poems), 1931; Neblagodarnost' (poems), Paris, 1936; $2 \times 2 = 4$ (poems), Paris, 1950, 2d ed., New York, 1982; Samoubijstvo (short story), in Russkaja mysl', Paris, May 24, 1984, p. 8, and June 7, 1984, pp. 8–9; Detstvo (memoirs), in Novyj žurnal, New York, 154:1984.

Secondary Lit.: L. Červinskaja, in Krug, Paris, 1:1936; Ju. Ivask, in Novyj žurnal 25:1951 and in Štejger's $2 \times 2 = 4$, New York, 1984; Ju. Terapiano, in his Vstreči, New York, 1953; G.

Adamovič, in his Odinočestvo i svoboda, New York, 1955; Z. Šakhovskaja, in Vozroždenie, Paris, 195:1968; M. Dal'ton, in Novyj žurnal 156:1984; T. Pachmuss, in Cahiers du monde russe et soviétique 1985:3.

**Shteyn, Aleksándr Petróvich** (pseud. of A. P. Rubinshtéyn), playwright (b. Sept. 28 [Sept. 15], 1906, Samarkand). Shteyn studied at Leningrad University. In 1930 he was accepted into the Communist Party. Shteyn, who first worked as a journalist, began working as a dramatist in 1929 by writing two plays together with the Tur brothers and Ya. Gorevich. The first dramas he wrote by himself, Vesna dvadtsat pervogo (1939–40; Spring 1921) and Prolog (1939)—whose inserted scene involving Stalin was dropped when it was adapted in 1955—met with little success. His drama Zakon chesti (1948; The Law of Honor), which concerns the accusation and condemnation of a supranational-thinking scientist as an inimical cosmopolitan (see COSMOPOLITANISM), forms an especially embarrassing document of the times, particularly since the author was reproached for similar behavior (Novy mir 1964:12, p. 209). For the film version, Sud chesti (1948; Disciplinary Committee), Shteyn was awarded a Stalin Prize (for 1948, 1st class); for Flag admirala (1946–50; The Admiral's Flag), a play about the period of Catherine II with a clear connection to the present day, he received another Stalin Prize (for 1950, 2d class). Because of its negative exposition of a Party functionary, Personalnoye delo (1954; A Personal Matter) received much attention; however, M. Shcheglov proved as early as 1956 that this drama about the end of the Stalin period avoided the actual problems. Among the other ten dramas and comedies (written by 1973), Mezhdu livnyami (1964; Between the Thunderstorms) brought on a semiofficial Party condemnation (Pravda July 12, 1964) because Lenin was portrayed as too much of a dictator. Polemic also developed around the frequently performed play Vdovets (1965; The Widower), while Aplodismenty (1967; Applause), a play linking the contemporary world of the theater to the father-son conflict, was well received. Compiled extensively from V. Vishnevsky's Pervaya konnaya and Optimisticheskaya tragediya is U vremeni v plenu (1970; In the Grip of Time), a portrait of Vishnevsky with a nonchronological description of the wars between 1914 and 1945 that uses a fictional narrator. His Italyanskaya tragediya (Italian Tragedy) became a success in 1971. Through

SHTOK

partial use of original quotes, he presented A. Blok and other writers in a play about Revolutionary events, *Versiya* (1976; The Version). Shteyn lives in Moscow.

Shteyn has an unquestionable dramatic talent; his plays are performed regularly, yet there is something artificial about the conflicts he describes; they do not go deep enough. His willingness to adapt to the required subject matter was evident in the Stalin period and during the earlier part of the THAW and has remained so up to the present day. He has never held official positions, but he has belonged to the editorial staff of the journal *Teatr* since 1957 without interruption. His memoirs, *Povest o tom, kak voznikayut syuzhety* (1964; A Tale of How Subjects Arise), were criticized for their one-sidedness and distortion. He continued his memoirs with *Vtoroy antrakt* (1975; The Second Pause) and later also collected autobiographical texts, for example, in *Nayedine so zritelem* (1982; Alone with the Audience).

Works: *Talant* (play), 1936; *Vesna dvadcat' pervogo* (play), 1940; *Zakon česti* (play), 1948; *Flag admirala* (play), 1950; *Kinoscenarii: Sud česti. Podvodnaja lodka. "T-9." Baltijcy* (film scripts), 1950; *P'esy* (plays), 1953 (contains *Vesna dvadcat' pervogo; Zakon česti; Flag admirala); Personal'noe delo* (play), 1955; *P'esy* (plays), 1956 (contains *Vesna dvadcat' pervogo; Flag admirala; Personal'noe delo; Prolog); Gostinica "Astorija"* (play), 1957; *Vesennie skripki* (play), in *Teatr* 1959:8; *Okean* (play), 1962; *P'esy* (plays), 1962 (contains *Vesna dvadcat' pervogo; Flag admirala; Gostinica "Astorija"; Vesennie skripki; Okean); Povest' o tom, kak voznikajut sjužety* (memoirs), 1965; *Vdovec* (play), in *Teatr* 1965:9; *Meždu livnjami* (play), 1966; *Dramy* (plays), 1966 (contains *Flag admirala; Prolog; Meždu livnjami; Personal'noe delo; Gostinica "Astorija"; Okean); Aplodismenty* (play), in *Teatr* 1967:3; *Poslednij parad* (comedy), 1969; *U vremeni v plenu* (play), in *Teatr* 1970:1; *P'esy* (plays), 1972 (contains *Okean; Meždu livnjami; Vdovec; Gostinica "Astorija"; Aplodismenty; U vremeni v plenu); Noč'ju bez zvëzd* (play), in *Teatr* 1973:9; *Vtoroj antrakt* (memoirs), in *Teatr* 1975:1–4, separate ed., 1976; *Okean* (plays), 1976 (contains *Okean; Flag admirala; Prolog; Meždu livnjami; Personal'noe delo; Vdovec; Aplodismenty; Noč'ju bez zvëzd; Gostinica "Astorija"); Nebo v almazakh* (short stories), 1976; *P'esy* (plays), 2 vols., 1978 (contains *Meždu livnjami; Prolog; Flag admirala; Talant; Aplodismenty; U vremeni v plenu; Pojuščie peski; Versija; Vesennie*

skripki; *Poslednij parad; Personal'noe delo; Gostinica "Astorija"; Okean; Vdovec; Noč'ju bez zvëzd; Žil-byl ja); Naedine so zritelem* (essays), 1982; *Potop-82* (play), in *Sovremennaja dramaturgija* 1982:2; *On i ona* (play), in *Teatr* 1984:8.

Secondary Lit.: D. Zolotnickij, in *Teatr* 1955:7; M. Ščeglov, in *Lit. Moskva* 1956:2; L. Maljugin, in *Novyj mir* 1964:12; *Otvetstvennost' khudožnika*, in *Teatr* 1964:9; M. Korallov, in *Teatr* 1967:1; K. Ščerbakov, in *Teatr* 1967:9; M. Švydkoj, in *Teatr* 1974:10; N. Zajcev, in *Neva* 1980:5; V. Pimenov, in *Teatr* 1980:12; E. Kameneckij, in *Lit. obozrenie* 1983:6; A. Salynskij, L. Viv'en, in *Teatr* 1986:9.

**Shtok, Isídor Vladímirovich,** playwright (b. March 19 [March 6], 1908, St. Petersburg—d. Sept. 17, 1960, Moscow). Shtok's father was an orchestra conductor; his mother, an opera singer. After he completed school in Kharkov in 1925, Shtok attended an acting school associated with the Moscow Theater of the Revolution and worked as an actor with the touring theater company of the PROLETKULT. Shtok became a playwright with *Komsomol kak takovoy* (1927; The Komsomol Such as It Is), his first play. At the beginning of the 1930s, Shtok worked as a journalist in Magnitogorsk, where *Zemlya derzhit* (1931; The Earth Holds), a play about current development problems, was performed. Shtok had written at least 24 dramas and comedies by 1971 (Tolchenova says 40); many of these have been performed in Moscow and Leningrad. He achieved success with satirical fairy-tale plays such as *Chortova melnitsa* (1953; The Devil's Mill) that were performed in the Moscow Puppet Theater. During World War II, Shtok served with the fleet in the Arctic Ocean, among other places. In 1953 he joined the Communist Party. At the Second Congress of the Writers Union, Shtok was a participant without voting rights. From 1958 on, he was regularly appointed a delegate to the congresses of the Writers Union of the RSFSR and belonged to its board from 1965 to 1970. He lived in Moscow.

Shtok's dramas are mostly topical and patriotic with a prevailing ethical concern. During the battle against COSMOPOLITANISM, he made his contribution with anti-American plays such as *Pobediteli nochi* (1950; Victors of the Night; earlier called *Russky svet* [Russian Lights]). Numerous plays concern the navy. To the frequently translated belong *Yakornaya ploshchad* (1960; The Anchoring Place), where in unusual situations he develops interpersonal problems linked with military limitations. Concentrating entirely on the family sphere and ethical questions is the often performed play *Leningradsky prospekt* (1961). *Eto ya—vash sekretar* (1982; It Is I— Your Secretary), a play about Soviet dissidents that does not suppress the arguments of the defenders of human rights, was published posthumously. Shtok's dialogue is lively, but in order to accommodate the intended difficulties, the plot is often too artificial and part of the character development is left to the direct statements of the figures. Shtok has also written a lot about playwrights and the theater.

*Works: Karavan* (play), in *Teatr* 1957:5; *Večnoe pero* (play), 1958; *Dramy* (plays), 1960; *akornaja ploščad'* (play), in *Teatr* 1960:2, separate ed., 1961; *Leningradskij prospekt* (play), in *Sovremennaja dramaturgija* 1961:1, separate ed., 1964; *Ob"jasnenie v nenavisti* (play), in *Teatr* 1964:2; *Rasskazy o dramaturgakh* (short stories), 1965; *Tri drami i dve komedii* (plays), 1965; *Leningradskij prospekt* (plays), 1969; *Zemlja Zamoskvoreckaja* (play), in *Teatr* 1970:6; *Aleksandra Vasnecova* (plays), 1971; *Prem'era* (short stories), 1975; *P'esy* (plays), 1977; *Èto ja—vaš sekretar'!* (play), in *Teatr* 1982:1; *Rejs* (play), in *Sovremennaja dramaturgija* 1982:3.

*Secondary Lit.:* I. Višnevskaja, in *Voprosy lit.* 1960:2; K. Ščerbakov, in *Molodaja gvardija* 1964:12; Ju. Zubkov, in *Lit. Rossija* Oct. 24, 1969, p. 16, and in *Oktjabr'* 1972:2; N. Tolenova, in *Ogonëk* 1968:15; N. Lejkin, in *Lit. obozrenie* 1978:6; L. Donatov, in *Russkaja mysl'*, Paris, Oct. 21, 1982, p. 6.

**Shtorm, Geórgy Petróvich,** prose writer (b. Sept. 24 [Sept. 12], 1898, Rostov-on-Don—d. April 27, 1978, Moscow). Shtorm's father was a civil servant. Shtorm spent his early years in St. Petersburg; from 1910 on, he lived in the south of Russia. From 1919 to 1921 he studied at the Don University (Rostov) in the Department of History and Philology. Shtorm's first narrative poem, *Karma ioga* (1921; The Yogi's Karma), appeared in Rostov the same year he moved to Moscow. At the end of the 1920s, Shtorm published several historical novels that won recognition because of their authenticity and verbal style. In the 1930s Shtorm, like V. Grossman, was on the periphery of the circle around K. Paustovsky and R. Frayerman. Between 1939 and 1947 he worked in various publishing houses. During World War II he was in Alma-Ata, working in film and radio; he returned to Moscow in 1943.

His best-known book was *Flotovodets Ushakov* (1946; Admiral Ushakov), about the late-18th-century tsarist admiral of the Black Sea fleet who was held in official esteem during World War II. After 1954 Shtorm made a name for himself with his research into the fate of Aleksandr Radishchev's manuscripts. Occasionally he commented upon historical publications, pointing out, for instance, a gross falsification by G. Serebryakova (*Lit. gazeta* April 16, 1957, p. 3). Shtorm did not enter into literary politics and did not participate in any congresses of the Writers Union except the first one in 1934.

Shtorm's first major prose work, *Povest o Bolotnikove* (1930; The Tale of Bolotnikov), deals with a peasant uprising during the Time of Troubles in the 17th century. "History and fiction are skillfully blended" (Struve); the style is concise and impressionistic. The work went through numerous editions. *Trudy i dni Mikhaila Lomonosova* (1932; The Works and Times of Mikhail Lomonosov) portrays the Russian scholar and poet coherently and consistently. Shtorm published his book about Ushakov (1752–1817) in several variants with differing titles, finally incorporating it into *Stranitsy morskoy slavy* (1954; Pages of Naval Glory), in which Radishchev's fate also plays a part.

*Works: Karma ioga* (poems), 1921; *Povest' o Bolotnikove* (pov.), 1930; *Trudy i dni Mikhaila Lomonosova* (biography), 1933; *Flotovodec Ušakov* (novel), 1946; *Podvigi Svjatoslava* (short story), 1947; *Stranicy morskoj slavy* (short stories), 1954; *Deti dobroj nadeždy* (short stories), 1959; *Potaënnyj Radiščev* (scholarly study), 1965, 3d ed., 1974.

*Secondary Lit.:* N. Bogoslovskij, in *Novyj mir* 1933:7–8; A. Zapadov, in *Znamja* 1956:1; G. Makogonenko, in *Lit. gazeta* Feb. 11, 1965; *RSPP* 6(2):1969; I. Andronikov, in his *Ja khoču rasskazat' vam . . .*, 1971; M. Koz'min, in *Lit. gazeta* Oct. 4, 1978, p. 5.

**Shúbin, Pável Nikoláyevich,** poet (b. March 27 [March 14], 1914, Chernavsk, Yelets District, prov. Oryol—d. April 11, 1951, Moscow). Shubin's father was a worker. From 1929 to 1933 Shubin was a worker in the Stalin Steelworks in Leningrad. Taking evening courses, he completed a technical engineering school in 1932. From 1933 to 1936 he studied philology at the Leningrad Pedagogical Institute. Shubin began writing poetry around 1930 and was soon able to publish his first collection, *Nachalo* (1931; The Beginning). His more mature work begins with the collections Veter v litso (1937; Wind in the Face) and Parus (1940; The Sail). As a soldier and war correspondent during World War II, Shubin was assigned to Volkhov, Karelia, the Arctic area, Norway, and Manchuria. Altogether he wrote some 10,000 lines of poetry and about 50 songs. Part of this output was printed in his collections, such as Vo imya zhizni (1943; In the Name of Life). Shubin lived in Moscow and published two more volumes of verse before his early death. A small circle of friends has attempted to ensure him a place in Soviet literature.

The central point of Shubin's literary work lies in his war poetry. He depicts real experiences at the front in all their difficulty and their urgency; his heroism is not empty enthusiasm but a vital act. Shubin's poetry consists of description and report; reflection moves into the background. His stanzas are metrically variable, his rhyme schemes simple, but his poetry is fluid and not particularly dense. The poems written before and after the war, such as "Osen" (1946; Autumn), which Shubin dedicated to M. Prishvin, express his intense relationship with nature.

Works: Načalo (poems), 1931; Veter v lico (poems), 1937; Parus (poems), 1940; Vo imja žizni (poems), 1943; Soldaty (poems), 1948; Dorogi, gody, goroda (poems), 1949; Izbr., 1952; Stikhotvorenija (poems), 1952; Stikhotvorenija i poèmy (lyric and narrative poems), 1959; Izbr. lirika, 1966; Stikhotvorenija (poems), 1971; Stikhotvorenija (poems), 1982.

Secondary Lit.: A. Kovalenkov, foreword in Šubin's Izbr., 1952, and in Znamja 1957:5; V. Lifšic, in Den' poèzii, Moscow, 1957; A. Abramov, in Pod''ëm 1964:5 and in Sever 1970:5; A. Dymšic, in Neva 1974:12; A. Kogan, 1974; I. Vinokurova, in Novyj mir 1975:5; B. Runin, in Novyj mir 1983:12.

Shukshín, Vasíly Makárovich, prose writer, movie director, movie actor (b. July 25, 1929, Srostki, Altai—d. Oct. 2, 1974, Stanitsa Kletskaya, oblast Volgograd). At the age of 16 Shukshin began working in his native kolkhoz, later in factories in central Russia. From 1949 to 1952 he was with the fleet; in 1953–54 he was director of an evening school for village youth; from 1954 to 1960 he studied at a union institute for the motion-picture industry in Moscow where he graduated from the faculty for directors. In 1955 he was admitted into the Communist Party. In 1957 he

began appearing in numerous films as an actor; in 1958 his first short story appeared in the journal Smena (no. 15); the collection Selskiye zhiteli (Village Dwellers) appeared in 1963. His film script Zhivyot takoy paren (1964; Such a Fellow Does Live) enjoyed international success as a film directed by him ("Golden Lion" at the 16th Film Festival in Venice). Until his early death, Shukshin combined the three professions of director, actor, and author. Many a discussion developed around his usually short prose works, which were highly praised by renowned critics. Shukshin received official recognition as a prizewinner (with others) of the State Prizes of the RSFSR (The Brothers Vasilyev Prize, 1967) and of the USSR (1971). In 1976 he was posthumously awarded the Lenin Prize for his film making.

In his numerous short stories, Shukshin depicts unusual situations of everyday life with a sense for the comic and the tragic. Somewhat odd individuals from among the masses stimulate his descriptive talents; usually these are restless people captured at the moment of departure or arrival, or people who must grapple with a problem that interrupts the normal course of events. His partially captivating, partially exciting, always lively and expressive portrayal evolves from the problematic nature of a man who has changed his milieu, usually from the village to the city, but also from a penal camp to freedom (Kalina krasnaya [1973; Eng. tr., Snowball Berry Red, 1979]). His novel about Stepan Razin, Ya prishol dat vam volyu (1971; I Came to Bring You Freedom), for whose filming Shukshin fought in vain, is a richly colored image of the life of the Russian people and a visualization of the tragedy of insurgents struggling against the power of the state. Shukshin's sympathy goes to the impulsive people, not to the ones who act judiciously according to plan, and to those with religious ties. Shukshin launches right into the plot, writes economically, creates lively dialogue, and lets the concrete situation take on symbolic significance through its open-ended resolution.

Works: Sel'skie žiteli (short stories), 1963; Živët takoj paren' (film script), 1964; Ljuba viny (novel), part 1, 1965; Tam, vdali (short stories), 1968; Ja prišël, dat' vam volju (novel) in Iskusstvo kino 1968:6, Sibirskie ogni 1971:1-2, separate ed., 1974, 1982; Zemljaki (short stories), 1970; Kharaktery (short stories), 1973; Kalina krasnaja (film-pov.), in Naš sovremennik 1973:4 (see above); Besedy pri jasnoj luni (short stories), 1974; *Brat moj* (short stories and pov.), 1975; *Okhota žit'* (short stories), 1977 (Eng. tr., *I Want to Live*, 1973); *Nravstvennost' est' pravda* (essays), 1979; *Voprosy samomu sebe* (articles, essays, letters), 1981; *Ljubaviny* (novel), part 2 in *Družba narodov* 1987:1–2.—*Izbr. proizv.*, 2 vols., 1975; *Sobr. soč.*, 3 vols., 1984–85.

*Secondary Lit.*: M. Alekseev, in *Moskva* 1964:1; V. Čalmaev, in *Sever* 1972:10; S. Zalygin, in *Lit. gazeta* June 11, 1973, p. 6; L. Anninskij, in *Lit. obozrenie* 1974:1 and in *Novyj mir* 1975:12; A. Urban, in *Zvezda* 1974:4; obituary, in *Lit. gazeta* Oct. 9, 1974, p. 4; G. Goryšin, in *Avrora* 1975:6; V. Korobov, 1977; M. Geller, in *Vestnik RKhD* 120:1977; N. Tolčenova, 1978; *Èkran i žizn'*, 1979; G. Mitin, V. Serdjučenko, in *Novyj mir* 1980:9; G. Hosking, in his *Beyond Socialist Realism*, New York, 1980; V. Gorn, 1981; L. Emel'janov, 1983; Ju. Tjurin, 1984; H. Wüst, Munich, 1984; V. Bystrov, in *Russkaja lit.* 1984:4; M. Šneerson, in *Novoe russkoe slovo*, New York, May 19, 1985, p. 5.

**Shúndik, Nikoláy Yeliséyevich,** prose writer (b. July 30, 1920, Mikhaylovka, Khabarovsky Territory). Of peasant descent, Shundik grew up in Siberia. After he attended a pedagogical professional school, the Komsomol sent Shundik to work as a teacher among the Chukchi from 1939 to 1946. He became a member of the Communist Party in 1946. From 1947 to 1952 he studied at the pedagogical institute in Khabarovsk. After 1947, Shundik became known for his journalistic writings. He lived in Ryazan (1957–65), then he moved to Saratov and was appointed editor in chief of the journal *Volga* (until 1976). Since 1958 he has belonged to the board of the Writers Union of the RSFSR; in 1975 he was given a place in the secretariat. He has belonged to the board of the Writers Union of the USSR since 1967, and since the 1970s he has lived in Moscow. In 1979 he was awarded the State Prize of the RSFSR.

Shundik's first works, such as *Na zemle Chukotskoy* (1949; In Chukchi Country), concern his experiences as a teacher. *Na Severe dalnem* (1952; In the Far North) contrasts the happy life of Chukchi children under the Soviet regime with their dismal, melancholy American counterparts (see COSMOPOLITAN-SM). Everything Shundik writes, even the novel that does not concern the Chukchi theme, *V strane sineokoy* (1968–70; In the Blue-eyed Land), is formed in accordance with the cheap scheme of the hardworking Party functionary who proves himself in a struggle against internal and external enemies. The novel *Bely shaman* (1977; The White Shaman) returns to the theme of political and cultural reform among the Chukchi people. With *Drevniy znak* (1982; The Old Sign), Shundik even switches to combining a fairy-tale-style novel with topical anti-American politics (the neutron bomb). Shundik writes ponderously and unexpressively. His much too long prose is artificially enriched with pathos and pseudofolkloric elements. He has also ventured into the dramatic sphere.

*Works: Na zemle Čukotskoj* (publicistic prose), 1949; *Na Severe dal'nem* (pov.), 1952; *Bystronogij olen'* (novel), in *Oktjabr'* 1952:9–10, separate ed., 1953; *Oderžimaja* (play), in *Neva* 1963:5; *Rodnik u berëzy* (novel), 1964; *V strane sineokoj* (novel), 1973; *Belyj šaman* (novel), 1979; *Drevnij znak* (novel), 1982.— *Sobr. soč.*, 4 vols., 1983–84.

*Secondary Lit.*: V. Šišov, in *Neva* 1965:8; RSPP 6(2):1969; L. Fink, in *Moskva* 1970:9; V. Surganov, in *Moskva* 1974:1; Ju. Lukin, in *Lit. gazeta* Feb. 15, 1978, p. 4; I. Bogatko, in *Lit. obozrenie* 1979:6; S. Alieva, in *Lit. Rossija* June 11, 1982, p. 14; V. Vasil'ev, in *Naš sovremennik* 1983:4.

**Shvarts, Yeléna Andréyevna,** poet (b. May 17, 1948, Leningrad). Shvarts's father, Andrey Dzhedzhula, was of Tatar-Ukrainian descent, studied history, became a Party official at Kiev University, and probably died in 1948. Her mother was the director of the literary section of the Leningrad Dramatic Theater for many years. The Egyptian sculptures decorating the house in Leningrad (on Ul. Kalyayeva) in which Shvarts lived until 1962 made a lasting impression on her. In 1971 she completed a correspondence course of study in English language and literature at the Leningrad Theatrical Institute. Shvarts began writing inspired religious poetry as a child. Since the end of the 1960s, these poems have circulated in SAMIZDAT and have been included in samizdat journals. Occasionally Shvarts has been officially permitted to recite her poetry, but apparently only twice have isolated poems of hers appeared in Soviet periodicals. Between 1976 and 1978, four collections of poetry became well known through samizdat; the titles of the cycles *Prostye stikhi dlya sebya i dlya Boga* (1976; Simple Poems for Myself and for God) and *Grubymi sredstvami ne dostich bla-*

zhenstva (1978; Salvation Cannot Be Attained through Vulgar Means) reveal the content of these collections. Shvarts's poems are regularly published in various periodicals in the West. Publication in the United States of a volume not compiled by Shvarts herself called Tantsuyushchiy David (1984; The Dancing David) occurred in 1985. Shvarts also writes essays and works as a translator; she lives in Leningrad.

Shvarts writes religious poetry that is based on Christian concepts and seeks to establish man's place in a world governed by evil. Free will affords man the option of conquering the satanic elements within himself. Many of her poems are characterized by visions: in the cycle "Kinfiya" a Roman poetess tells of her deeds that brought affliction to herself and others; in "Plavaniye" (Swimming) Shvarts describes an extracorporeal experience; "Videniye tserkvi na vodakh" (Vision of a Church on the Water) blends grotesque, unearthly horror with angelic piety. Even when Shvarts portrays man's sinfulness and vulnerability, a quest for the key to the meaning of life remains discernible. Shvarts's profound poems bear witness to an unbroken spiritual and religious vitality amidst a materialistic and politicized world.

Works: Poems, in Èkho, Paris, 1978:2, 1979:1; in Gnosis, New York, 5–6:1979; in Kovčeg, Paris, 5:1980; in Glagol, Ann Arbor, 3:1981; in Tret'ja volna, Montgeron, 12:1982; in Vestnik RKhD, Paris, 140:1983. Vid na suščestvovanie ili put' čerez kol'co, in Muleta, Paris, 1:1984; Iz novoj knigi stikhov: "Korabl' " (poems), in Russkaja mysl', Paris, Dec. 27, 1985 (Lit. priloženie), pp. iv–v; Tancujuščij David (poems), New York, 1985; poems, in Strelec, Montgeron–Jersey City, N.J., 1986:3.

Secondary Lit.: I. Burikhin, in Kovčeg 6:1981 and in Muleta 1:1984; T. Goričeva, in Grani, Frankfurt am Main, 120:1981.

**Shvarts, Yevgény Lvóvich,** playwright (b. Oct. 21 [Oct. 9], 1896, Kazan—d. Jan. 15, 1958, Leningrad). Shvarts's father was a doctor. Shvarts grew up in Maykop. He did not complete his study of law at Moscow University because he was concurrently working as an actor in Rostov-on-Don and, after 1921, in Petrograd, among other places. From his base in Rostov he also worked as a journalist in the Don Basin in 1923 and 1924. In 1924 Shvarts became S. Marshak's coworker in the children's book department of the State Pub-

lishing House where he wrote journal articles and books in verse and prose. He was close to the OBERIU group. In 1928 Shvarts discovered the true outlet for his talent: the play with fairy-tale elements. In Undervud (1929; The Underwood), his first drama, and in Klad (1933; The Treasure) fairy-tale elements are heavily incorporated into contemporary reality. Shvarts's plays seldom reflected official policy; most of them were performed but received little official attention. Ten (1940; Eng. tr., The Shadow, 1975), in which the fairy-tale element approaches political satire, was swiftly removed from the repertory after its premiere. Drakon (1943–44; Eng. trs., The Dragon, 1963, and in Three Soviet Plays, 1966; and The Naked King, The Shadow, and The Dragon, 1975), which Shvarts wrote in Kirov and Stalinabad (Tadzhikistan) during the evacuation from besieged Leningrad, remained banned after its premiere until 1962. In vain L. Malyugin attempted to stage Odna noch (1942; A Night), a drama about the blockade that is free from fairy-tale elements; it was inconsistent with the required heroic pathos. After the war, Shvarts scraped by in Leningrad with odd jobs. At the Second Writers Congress in 1954, O. Berggolts demanded that this "independent and humane talent" be returned to the Soviet stage. The first collection of his dramas appeared in 1956. Gradually his plays began to be performed again including, in 1957, Povest o molodykh suprugakh (Tale of the Newlyweds), which was written at the end of the 1940s, and, only in 1960, Goly korol (1934; Eng. tr., The Naked King, 1972), his earliest political fairy-tale play. Gustaf Gründgens, who produced Ten in Berlin in 1947, was probably the first to stage his works abroad. After 1956 Shvarts's works were often translated and performed at home and abroad. In the Soviet Union his fairy tales have been among the most frequently performed works for many years. His memoirs written in the years after 1949 and absolutely dedicated to the truth, were published by Lev Losev in Paris in 1982.

The majority of Shvarts's approximately 2½ plays, only some of whose texts were published, use existing fairy-tale motifs, especially from Hans Christian Andersen. Only part of these are addressed to children, most particularly his plays for puppet theater, but also Krasnaya shapochka (1936; Eng. tr., Little Red Riding Hood, 1972), Snezhnaya koroleva (1938; The Snow Queen), and the film script Zolushka (1946; Cinderella). Shvarts contrasts the good characters (with their fidelity, valor helpfulness) with the bad (with their egoism, treachery, cruelty) without obtrusive didacticism. Next to these plays for children stand the political-allegorical fairy-tale plays directed more toward adults. *Goly korol,* after Andersen's "Swineherd," "The Emperor's New Clothes," and "The Princess and the Pea," is linked to *Ten* and *Drakon* through its criticism of tyrants. "Shvarts' most political and philosophical plays are at the same time his most Aesopian" (Segel). The long-standing prohibition against these plays in which evil temporarily gains the upper hand affirms that contemporary criticism was not limited to Hitler. *Drakon,* the more political piece, also exposes the danger of patiently accepting force.

Works: *Rasskaz staroj balalajki* (short story), 1925; *Skazka o poterjannom vremeni* (puppet play), 1948 (Eng. tr., *A Tale of Stolen Time,* 1966); *Pervoklassnica* (pov.), 1949; *Ten' i drugie p'esy* (plays), 1956 (contains *Dva klёna* [Eng. tr., *The Two Maples,* 1976]; *Snežnaja koroleva; Ten* [see above]; *Odna noč'; Obyknovennoe čudo; Zoluška); Kukol'nyj gorod* (puppet play), 1959; *P'esy* (plays), 1960 (contains the same works as the 1956 ed., except *Odna noč',* and also includes *Klad; Golyj korol'* [see above]; *Drakon* [see above]; *Povest' o molodykh suprugakh; Don Kikhot); P'esy* (plays), 1962 (contains the same plays as the 1960 ed.); *Skazki, povesti, p'esy* (fairy tales, pov., plays), 1969; *P'esy* (plays), 1972 (contains the same pieces as the 1960 ed., except *ng Golyj korol'* and with the addition of *Krasnaja šapočka); Izbr.,* Chicago, 1973; *Belyj volk* (memoirs), in *Pamjat',* Paris, 3:1980; *Iz vospominanij* (memoirs), in *Russkaja mysl',* Paris, May 13, 20, and 27, and June 3, 1982; *Menuary* (autobiography), Paris, 1982; *Klad; Snežnaja koroleva; Golyj korol'; Ten'; Drakon; Dva klёna; Obyknovennoe čudo; Povest' o molodykh suprugakh; Zoluška; Don Kikhot,* 1982.

Secondary Lit.: S. Cimbal, in several editions, and in *Teatr* 1972:4; V. Kaverin, in his *Zdravstvuj, brat! Pisat' očen' trudno . . .,* 1965; .. Maljugin, in *Teatr* 1966:6; *My znali E. Š.,* 1966; E. Kalmanovskij, in *Zvezda* 1967:9; L. R. Simard, Diss., Cornell Univ., 1970; E. Š. *Mensch und Schatten,* ed. L. Debüser, Berlin, 1972; I. H. S. Corten, Diss., Berkeley, 1972, nd in *Russian Literature Triquarterly* 16:1979; .. Rakhmanov, in his *P'esy, povesti, vospominanija,* 1972; J. D. Clayton, in *Etudes slaves t est-européennes,* 1974; I. Lipelis, in *Russian Language Journal* 112:1978 and 114:1979; A. J. Metcalf, Birmingham, 1979; L. Loseff, in

his *On the Beneficence of Censorship,* Munich, 1984.

**Simáshko, Morís** (Maurice) **Davídovich** (pseud. of M. D. Shámis), prose writer (b. March 18, 1924, Odessa). Simashko's father was a microbiologist; his mother, a Volga-German. Simashko served in World War II as a fighter pilot and flight instructor. In 1950 he graduated in journalism from Kazakhstan University and was admitted into the Communist Party. Simashko made his appearance as a writer in 1948, using a pseudonym produced by reversing the letters of his Jewish name. He selected Kazakh history as his theme and lived in Alma-Ata. Until 1974 he belonged to the editorial staff of the Russian-language literary journal in Kazakhstan—*Prostor*—and published in Moscow and Alma-Ata. Simashko is little noticed in the Soviet Union, but his historical fiction has been translated into English, French, Portuguese, Polish, Hungarian, German, and various Asian languages.

Simashko became well known with V *Chornykh Peskakh* (1958; In the Black Desert), a long story about the Civil War that illustrates the collision between the principle of class struggle with its national particularities and the traditional blood feud. His later creative activity goes back to far-distant centuries in which Simashko chooses events from the Near East and Central Asia that have remained unnoticed by historiographers. Simashko's frequently reprinted novel about a religious reformer, *Mazdak* (1971), takes place on the border between the 5th and 6th centuries and in its fundamental opposition to tyrannical rulership contains many generally human and political parallels to later times. In the novel *Kommissar Dzhangildin* (1978; Commissar Dzhangildin), Simashko turns his attention to a Kazakh revolutionary hero and even brings in Lenin to make a personal appearance. His novel *Iskupleniye dabira* (1979; The Atonement of the Scribe) concerns the Persian poet and philosopher Omar Khayyam (11th and 12th centuries). Simashko writes in a succinct style that is rich in reportage and marked by the noticeable predominance of independent clauses.

Works: *V Čёrnykh Peskakh* (pov.), in *Novyj mir* 1958:10, separate ed., 1965; *Povesti Krasnykh Peskov,* 1960, 1966; *Novaja zemlja* (scenario), in *Prostor* 1963:8; *Khronika carja Kavada* (pov.), 1968; *Mazdak* (novel), 1971, 1974,

1975; *Kommissar Džangil'din* (novel), 1978; *Iskuplenie dabira* (historical novel), 1979; *Kolokol* (novel), in *Prostor* 1982:1–3.
*Secondary Lit.*: V. Kardin, in *Družba narodov* 1959:2; A. Stil', in *Prostor* 1974:3; M. Karataev, in *Lit. gazeta* June 25, 1975, p. 5; B. Khotimskij, in *Družba narodov* 1979:11; V. Varžapetjan, in *Družba narodov* 1980:8; S. Aksënova, in *Lit. obozrenie* 1984:1.

**Símonov, Konstantín** (Kiríll) **Mikháylovich,** poet, prose writer, playwright (b. Nov. 28 [Nov. 15], 1915, Petrograd—d. Aug. 28, 1979, Moscow). Simonov's father served in the tsarist army. After completing his studies at a factory school in Saratov, Simonov worked as a turner until 1935. His first poem was published in 1934. From 1935 to 1938 Simonov attended the Gorky Literary Institute. He began by writing love lyrics, but became famous for narrative poems with political themes. In 1939 he wrote his first drama, *Istoriya odnoy lyubvi* (The Story of One Love); ten more followed. During World War II, Simonov was a correspondent for *Krasnaya zvezda*. His imploring love poem, "Zhdi menya" (1941; Wait for Me), circulated in millions of copies. In 1942 Simonov became a member of the Communist Party. He received three Stalin Prizes in the course of the war: for his drama *Paren iz nashego goroda* (1941; The Fellow from Our Town; for 1941, 1st class); for a drama published in *Pravda, Russkiye lyudi* (1942; Eng. tr., *The Russians*, in *Four Soviet War Plays*, 1943; for 1942, 2d class); and for his first major prose work, a povest about Stalingrad, *Dni i nochi* (1943–44; Eng. tr., *Days and Nights*, 1945; for 1943–44, 2d class). In response to the Party Resolution of Aug. 26, 1946, calling for more Soviet plays on topical subjects (see PARTY RESOLUTIONS ON LITERATURE), Simonov wrote a propaganda play, *Russky vopros* (1946; Eng. tr., *The Russian Question*, in *Soviet Literature* 1947:2), to comply with the policies of anti-Americanism and anti-COSMOPOLITANISM; he received a Stalin Prize for the work (for 1946, 1st class). A Stalin Prize for 1948 (1st class) followed, awarded for a poetry cycle written in a similar spirit, *Druzya i vragi* (1948; Eng. tr., *Friends and Foes*, 1952). Simonov received a sixth Stalin Prize (for 1949, 2d class) for his drama *Chuzhaya ten* (1949; Someone Else's Shadow). From 1946 to 1954 Simonov was vice general secretary of the Writers Union of the USSR and at the same time (until 1950) editor in chief of *Novy mir*; in addition, he was a candidate member of the Central Committee of the Communist

Party from 1952 to 1956 and thereafter (until 1961) a member of the Central Committee's Appeals Commission. In 1954 the Central Committee took the editorship of *Novy mir* away from A. Tvardovsky and returned it to Simonov, but Simonov, like Tvardovsky, maintained a relatively liberal literary-political course. In the years of de-Stalinization Simonov was among those who pressed for a revision of the Central Committee decree of 1946 and who cautiously questioned the rigid dogmas of SOCIALIST REALISM. In 1958 he was obliged to return *Novy mir* to Tvardovsky. That same year he did not take part in the establishment of the conservative Writers Union of the RSFSR; nor did he participate in the Third Congress of the Writers Union of the USSR in 1959. Simonov returned to the subject of the war in his *Zhivye i myortvye* (1959; Eng. tr., *The Living and the Dead*, 1962; Lenin Prize, 1974), and except for his publicistic work, stayed with that subject. After 1965 Simonov participated in all Writers Congresses; he was a member of the boards of both Writers Unions; he became one of the secretaries of the Writers Union of the USSR again in 1967. In 1967 Simonov still favored publication of A. Solzhenitsyn's short stories and *Rakovy korpus*, but by 1973 he was among those who signed the letter of condemnation (*Pravda* Aug. 31). Simonov, while living in Moscow, frequently traveled abroad.

The emotionalism of Simonov's unpretentious verses about love, friendship, nostalgia, and ties to the fatherland contributed to their widespread recognition and circulation. Typical of his poetry is the combination of a concrete narrative element that serves a political function and an intimate personal element, as, for example, in "Ty pomnish, Alyosha, dorogi Smolenshchiny . . ." (1941; You Remember, Alyosha, the Roads of Smolensk . . .). Simonov's dramas from the Stalinist period are didactic propaganda plays on the themes of the day. *Chetvyorty* (1961; Eng. tr., *The Fourth*, in *Soviet Literature* 1961:9) is a conscience-probing drama that depicts a survivor's confrontation with the dead whom he has conjured up out of his memory and who appear onstage. Simonov's prose grew out of the war and remains almost entirely limited to that subject. He continues *Tovarishchi po oruzhiyu* (1952; Comrades in Arms), his first novel about the battle of Mongolia in 1939, in several other works by retaining some of the same major characters: *Zhivye i myortvye*, in which personal experiences at the front are mixed with criticism of Stalin's erroneous policies, depicts for the first time the defeat of the Red Army in June–November 1941; Soldatami ne rozhdayutsya (1964; Soldiers Are Made, Not Born), in which it even becomes possible, at the time of writing, to include the motif of the abuse of power by security officers, revives the battle for Stalingrad. Posledneye leto (1970–71; The Last Summer) describes the crushing of German troops by Operation Bagration in June 1944; in standard novel procedure, love and the events of war are fused together, Stalin once again appears as the wise commander-in-chief, and nothing more is said about the camps. "All Simonov's novels could be classed as satisfactory second-rate literature which in all countries has a considerable appeal among mass readers" (Slonim). His novels are a poitical barometer measuring the lower liberal limits of the Party line. In the 1970s Simonov compiled and published, with present-day commentaries, the war diaries that were the source of his novels.

Works: Nastojaščie ljudi (poems), 1938; Paren' iz našego goroda (play), 1941; Russkie judi (play), 1942 (see above); Dni i noči (pov.). 1944 (see above); Russkij vopros (play), 1946 see above); Dym otečestva (pov.), 1947; Druz'ja vragi (poems), 1948 (see above); Čužaja ten' play), 1949; Tovarišči po oružiju (novel), 1952; Živye i mërtvye (novel), 1959 (see above); Četvërtyj (play), 1961 (see above); Soldatami ne roždajutsja (novel), 1964; Poslednee leto novel), 1971; Nezadolgo do tišiny (diary), 1974; Raznye dni vojny (diary), in Družba narodov 1974:4–6; Japonija 46 (diary and short stories), 1977; Stikhotvorenija i poèmy (lyric and narrative poems), 1982; Sofija Leonidovna (pov.), in Družba narodov 1985:2.— Soč., 3 vols., 1952–53; Sobr. soč., 6 vols., 1966–70; 10 vols., 1979–85.

Secondary Lit.: I. Višnevskaja, 1966; RSPP 4:1966; S. Ja. Fradkina, 1968; L. Plotkin, in Lit. i sovremennost' 11:1972 and in Avrora 1975:2; L. I. Lazarev, 1974; V. Poltoratzky, Diss., Vanderbilt Univ., 1977; L. Fink, 1979; K. Vanšenkin, in Oktjabr' 1984:11; K. S. v rospominanijakh sovremennikov, 1984; G. Gordeev, A. Rubaškin, K. Griščinskij, in Zvezda 1985:10.

**Sinkévich, Valentína Alekséyevna**, poet (b. Sept. 29, 1926, Kiev). Sinkevich grew up in the small provincial city of Oster where her parents had moved at the end of the 1920s to escape repression. Her father, a lawyer, worked there as a mathematics teacher. Her parents' library provided the cornerstone of her edu-

cation. In 1942 she was brought to Germany as a forced laborer. After World War II she lived in displaced persons camps in Flensburg and Hamburg. In 1950 Sinkevich moved to the United States; since 1960 she has worked in Philadelphia as a bibliographer. Sinkevich has written poetry since her childhood, but she made her first public appearance as a poet when she was more than 40 years old with a book that was welcomed by I. Odoyevtseva and Yu. Terapiano: Ogni (1973; Fire). Since 1983 Sinkevich has been editor of the poetry almanac Vstrechi, which provides an annual forum for poets and artists, and she was one of the publishers of its predecessor, Perekrestki (1977–82). Since 1983 Sinkevich has published poems in this almanac and in journals of the EMIGRATION and has published both her second book, Nastupleniye dnya (1978; Daybreak), and her third book, Tsvetenye trav (1985; The Blooming of Grass), which combines new poems with poems previously published in various journals.

Sinkevich writes poetry characterized by a conscious acceptance of the spiritual dimensions of life and of their material manifestations, especially in art. She reveals people's loneliness and their inner turmoil and describes the relativity of their perceptions. In doing this, she occasionally crosses the border between dream and vision. Consciousness raising is also accomplished through linguistic techniques; she illuminates the differences in meaning between similarly sounding words through parallel structure. She owes her underlying religious attitude to her parents, an attitude that finds expression in her reverence for nature and her veneration of people such as St. Francis of Assisi and Albert Schweitzer. In her poetry marked by musical rhythm, Sinkevich can renounce rhyme or incorporate both assonance and rhyme. She also writes poetry in English.

Works: Ogni (poems), New York, 1973; Nastuplenie dnja (poems), Philadelphia, 1978; Cveten'e trav (poems), Philadelphia, 1985; poems, in Perekrëstki, Philadelphia, 1–6:1977–82, and in Vstreči, Philadelphia, since 1983.

Secondary Lit.: I. Odoevceva, in Novoe russkoe slovo, New York, Dec. 19, 1973; L. Rževskij, in Novoe russkoe slovo Oct. 13, 1985, p. 5.

**Síntaksis** (Syntax), a journal for "publicistic prose, criticism, and polemics." Published since 1978 in Paris and edited by A. Sinyavsky (until issue no. 11 in 1983) and his wife,

M. Rozanova, Sintaksis appears in two or three issues a year (no. 17 in 1987). The title was taken from the SAMIZDAT journal Sintaksis that was published in Moscow in 1959–60. The first four issues of the new journal were dedicated to the editor of this precursor, A. Ginzburg. Sintaksis comments on topical problems in literature and emphatically distances itself from Kontinent under the editorship of V. Maksimov. The majority of articles are written by M. Rozanova and by A. Sinyavsky, who occasionally also uses his literary pseudonym, A. Terts. Among the more frequent contributors are Ye. Etkind, L. Kopelev, and I. Pomerantsev; articles are also contributed by G. Nivat, S. Dovlatov, and A. Zinovyev. Issue no. 7, edited by A. Terts and closely resembling his ironic, surrealistic style, is unusual in that it is a collection by one N. Lepin entitled "Parafrazy i pamyatvovaniya, Moscow, 1979" (Paraphrases and Remembrances), Moscow, 1979). This collection consists of short, polemical, literary essays as well as parodies of the spiritual and religious works of world literature. Occasionally individual contributions from conferences among Russian émigré writers are published; for example, issue no. 10 (1982) reported on a conference held in May 1981 in Los Angeles.

Translation: Syntaxis—Russische Intellektuelle in der Opposition, in Neue Rundschau (special issue), Frankfurt am Main, 93:1982.
Secondary Lit.: K. Pomerancev, in Russkaja mysl', Paris, July 20, 1978, p. 4; V. Rybakov, in Russkaja mysl' April 5, 1979, p. 8; I. Burikhin, in Tret'ja volna, Montgeron, 11:1981; G. Andreev, in Russkaja mysl' Jan. 13, 1983, Nov. 3, 1983, p. 10, June 14, 1984, p. 12, June 28, 1985, p. 12; V. Aksënov, in Russkaja mysl' April 25, 1986, p. 10.

**Sinyavsky, Andrey Donatovich.** See TERTS. ABRAM.

**Sirin, Vladimir.** See NABOKOV, VLADIMIR VLADIMIROVICH.

**Skaz,** a Russian literary term—formed from skazat (to tell)—lacking a precise English equivalent and designating a special narrative style where the narrator's voice is different from that of the author. The narrative style of the skaz contrasts with the norms for written language. The contrast is generally accomplished through the use of a fictitious first-person narrator from a different social stratum than that of the expected reader, usually from less educated circles. The deviation from the literary norm is usually intensified through an oral narrative style that is primarily expressed syntactically. In the 19th century the skaz technique was first used by N. Gogol and then especially by N. Leskov; in their attempts to revive Russian prose, writers such as A. Bely, A. Remizov, Ye. Zamyatin, B. Pilnyak I. Babel, M. Zoshchenko, L. Leonov, and L Panteleyev turned to the skaz around 1920 At the same time, theoreticians such as Yu. Tynyanov, B. Eykhenbaum, and V. Vinogradov occupied themselves with the skaz. The structure of the skaz can vary. Generally, it is prose written in the first person, often framed by an impersonal, fictional tale or by a second tale also written in the first person. However, the primary skaz tale can also be fictional, and the narrator composing this tale may allow himself to be recognized only through word choice, syntax, and rhythms of speech.

Secondary Lit.: B. Èjkhenbaum, Illjuzija skaza, in his Skvoz' lit., 1924; Ju. Tynjanov Lit. segodnja, in Lit. sovremennik 1924:1; V. Vinogradov, Problema skaza v stilistike, in Poètika 1:1926; M. Bakhtin, Problemy poètiki Dostoevskogo, 2d ed., 1963; K. Hamburger, Die Logik der Dichtung, 2d ed., Stuttgart, 1968: Ju. Striedter, introduction to Texte der russischen Formalisten, Munich, 1969 (also contains translations of the articles by B. Èjkhenbaum and V. Vinogradov).

**Skitálets, Stepán Gavrílovich** (pseud. of S. G Petróv), prose writer and poet (b. Nov. 9 [Oct. 28], 1869, Obsharovka, prov. Samara—d. June 25, 1941, Moscow). Skitalets's father was a cabinetmaker and gusli performer. Skitalets attended teachers college in Samara until his expulsion for political reasons; he was politically active until 1905. He began his literary career between 1897 and 1903 as a contributor to newspapers; in 1898 he became acquainted with M. Gorky, who influenced his literary work considerably. After 1902 both his short and longer prose pieces were printed by Gorky's publishing house Znaniye. Shortly after 1908 Skitalets broke with the Bolsheviks and Gorky, who had criticized his novel Etapy (1908; Stages) for its pessimism. The most extensive collection of his works appeared in eight volumes during World War I. Skitalets's attitude toward the October Revolution was one of disapproval. In 1921 he emigrated to Harbin in Manchuria after a futile attempt to lead the cause of the starving peasants in his own Volga region. After 1928 he was able to publish in *Novy mir* and *Krasnaya nov*, and in 1934 was induced to return. He participated in the First Congress of the Writers Union in 1934, but without voting rights. He lived in Moscow until his death, after which his works were practically ignored; his last novel, *Kandaly* (Kandaly [a village on the Volga]), which appeared in *Oktyabr* in 1940, was not published in book form until 1956.

Skitalets is a realistic narrator with particular interest in the sorrow of the common people and their striving for beauty and freedom. He often depicts artistically gifted or enlightened simple people (as in his short story *Lyubov dekoratora* [1901; The Scene Painter's Love]). His poetry is formally unpretentious and primarily narrative.

*Works: Skvoz' stroj* (autobiographical pov.), 1901 (Eng. tr., *Publican and Serf*, 1905); *Povoj sud* (short story), 1905; *Etapy* (pov.), 1908, rev. ed., 1937; *Dom Černovykh* (novel), 1935, 1983; *Kandaly* (novel), in *Oktjabr'* 1940:1–10, separate ed., 1956; *V lit. bojakh* (essays), 1959.—*Polnoe sobr. soč.*, 8 vols., 1916–18; *Izbr. rasskazy*, 1939; *Izbr. proizv.*, 1955; *Povesti i rasskazy. Vospominanija* (pov., short stories, memoirs), 1960; *Izbr.*, 1977.

*Secondary Lit.*: A. Tregubov, in Skitalec's *Izbr. proizv.*, 1955, *Kandaly*, 1956, and *Izbr.*, 1977; E. Petrov-Skitalec, in *Novyj žurnal*, New York, 63:1961; L. K. Korol'kova, 1964.

**Skobtsova, Yelizaveta Yuryevna.** See MA-RIYA, MAT.

**Slávin, Lev Isáyevich,** prose writer (b. Oct. 27 [Oct. 15], 1896, Odessa—d. Sept. 7, 1984, Moscow). Slavin's father worked for the civil service. In 1916 Slavin began studying at Odessa University, but in the same year he was inducted into the army as a soldier at the front. From 1918 to 1920 he served in the Red Army. After 1920 he worked as a journalist in Odessa; there he became a member of literary circles together with I. Babel, E. Bagritsky, S. Gekht, I. Ilf, Yu. Olesha, and others. In 1922 his first story appeared. In April 1923 he moved to Moscow and became a correspondent for the newspapers *Gudok* and *Vechernyaya Moskva*. His first larger work, *Naslednik* (1930; The Heir), a novel about the problems of the intelligentsia before the Revolution, was reissued in its fourth edition in 1936, then disappeared and reappeared after

1957. Slavin's drama *Interventsiya* (1932; The Intervention), which deals with the Civil War in Odessa in 1918–19, has remained on the stage almost without interruption. The 600th performance took place in the Vakhtangov Theater in Moscow in 1971. In the 1930s, alongside his regular journalistic work, he was quite active in film. In 1934 he made a trip to Mongolia with B. Lapin and Z. Khatsrevin. Short stories that he wrote during World War II as a correspondent at the front, such as *Dva boytsa* (1942; Two Warriors), were guardedly criticized but also filmed. Reports from the occupied lands, such as *Poyezdka v Tserbst* (1945; Journey to Zerbst), demonstrate his pleasure in attaching comic trimmings to serious statements. In his works written after World War II, Slavin recounted his experiences during his trips to Poland and Belgium and chose historicobiographical materials, as in *Neistovy* (1973; The Raging One), a short novel about V. Belinsky in experimental form. The novel *Ardennskiye strasti* (1977; Passion in the Ardennes) concerns the German troops' attack on the western front near the end of World War II. In *Portrety i zapiski* (1965; Portraits and Notes), he captured memories of the writer friends of his youth in Odessa and of others, concisely, lively, and vividly. Slavin was among the signatories of the petition for A. Sinyavsky and Yu. Daniel in 1966. He lived in Moscow.

*Works: Naslednik* (novel), 1931; *Intervencija* (play), 1933; *Moi zemljaki* (later, *Dva bojca*) (pov.), 1942; *Poezdka v Cerbst* (short story), 1947; *Po tu storonu kholma* (pov.), 1960; *Portrety i zapiski* (memoirs and notes), 1965; *Predvestie istiny* (short stories), 1968; *Moj čuvstvitel'nyj drug* (short stories and memoirs), 1973; *Neistovyj* (pov.), 1973; *Ardennskie strasti* (novel), 1977.—*Izbr.*, 1957; 1970; *Izbr. proizv.*, 2 vols., 1981.

*Secondary Lit.*: A. Glagolev, in *Novyj mir* 1931:2; R. Pikel', in *Novyj mir* 1933:12; S. Bondarin, in *Novyj mir* 1967:1; *RSPP* 7(2):1972; M. Radeckaja, in *Lit. obozrenie* 1974:8; obituary, in *Lit. gazeta* Sept. 19, 1984, p. 6.

**Slávkin, Víktor Iósifovich,** playwright (b. Aug. 1, 1935, Moscow). Slavkin completed his studies at the Institute for Rail Transport Engineers in Moscow in 1958 and worked as a civil engineer. In the early 1960s, his first one-act plays, such as *Plokhaya kvartira* (The Poor Apartment), written in 1966, were staged at the Variety Studio Theater of Moscow University. In the journal *Yunost*, where from

1967 to 1984 he was in charge of the section on satire and humor, he published, after several journalistic contributions, the short story *Sosedi po vertikali* (1977; Neighbors in a Vertical Line); this tale revealed the true vicissitudes of life by using grotesque, comic depiction. *Vzroslaya doch molodogo cheloveka* (1979; The Adult Daughter of a Young Man) was the first of his longer plays to be performed at the Stanislavsky Theater in Moscow. His first plays to be published were the one-acts *Kartina* (1982; The Picture) and *Orkestr* (1982; The Orchestra). These were followed by a joint publication with L. Petrushevskaya, *Pyesy* (1983; Plays), which includes four of his one-act plays. In the 1985–86 season, the studio of the Taganka Theater staged his play written in 1979–80, *Serso* (Cerceau), to wide acclaim. He lives in Moscow.

Slavkin's plays are set in the immediate present. His early one-acts differ considerably from his later, multiple-act plays that fill an entire evening. In a satiric, grotesque style, filled with events and tensions, *Plokhaya kvartira* illustrates the housing situation in the Soviet Union; a family lives in a shooting gallery; their home is being used for target practice, and not only in a figurative sense. *Orkestr* is a successful dramatic parable that brings loneliness, egotism, and cheerful self-deception to the stage in an absurd form that recalls M. Bulgakov and D. Kharms. *Kartina* is a play with two characters that concerns a painter who feels compelled regularly to view his only picture in a hotel room. Verbal visualization of the picture is the high point of the dialogue, which transcends the unusual situation to penetrate to the very depths of art. By contrast, Slavkin's two later plays depict situations that scarcely distinguish themselves from normal life and in which Soviet social problems are only cautiously hinted at. In *Vzroslaya doch molodogo cheloveka*, Slavkin confronts his generation of 40-year-olds with, on the one hand, the period of their youth, which idealized forbidden American jazz, and, on the other hand, contemporary youth, that is, their own children. The play *Serso*, the title of which refers to the old French circle game called "cerceau," brings six people together for a chance friendly encounter. Loneliness, nostalgic longing for lost love, and the inability to begin anew set the tone. Slavkin's last plays are analytically structured and attempt to make present-day problems, especially people's solitude, comprehensible by illuminating the past. The external events are primarily limited to encounters between people who have never met before

or who have not seen each other in a long time. The emphasis lies in finely polished dialogue in the tradition of A. Chekhov. The viewer is able to identify with the characters, each of whom is equal in importance, and is led to consider essential questions about life.

*Works: Vzroslaja doč' molodogo čeloveka* (play), 1979 (VAAP acting copy); *Kartina* (play), in *Sovremennaja dramaturgija* 1982:2; *Orkestr* (play), in *Odnoaktnye p'esy*, 1982; *P'esy* (with L. Petruševskaja) (plays), 1983 (contains *Plokhaja kvartira*; *Kartina*; and others). *Serso* (play), in *Sovremennaja dramaturgija* 1986:4; *Černo-beloe kino* (film script), in *Iskusstvo kino* 1986:6.

*Secondary Lit.*: G. Gorin, in *Sovremennaja dramaturgija* 1982:2; A. Smeljanskij, in *Sovremennaja dramaturgija* 1985:4; O. Kučkina, in *Lit. gazeta* April 16, 1986, p. 8.

**Slonímsky, Mikhaíl Leonídovich,** prose writer (b. Aug. 1 [July 20], 1897, St. Petersburg—d. Oct. 8, 1972, Leningrad). Slonimsky's father was a regular contributor on the staff of *Vestnik Evropy*; the literary historian S. A. Vengerov was his maternal uncle. After completing his studies at a gymnasium, Slonimsky enlisted as a wartime volunteer. For two years he studied in the Department of History and Philology at Petrograd University. In 1920 he became the secretary of Dom iskusstv (The House of the Arts), where the Studio for Literature produced the germ cell that grew into the SERAPION BROTHERS. Slonimsky belonged to this literary group from its inception. He published his first collection of short stories, *Shestoy strelkovy* (The Sixth Rifle Regiment), in 1922. After 1923 Slonimsky worked on the editorial staffs of various journals and publishing houses. In 1926 he turned to the novel genre, writing *Lavrovy* (The Lavrovs), which he continued thematically in the novel *Foma Kleshnyov* in 1931. After two trips abroad (in 1927 and 1932), Slonimsky wrote *Povest o Levine* (1935; The Tale of Leviné), a frequently reprinted history of the Bavarian republic of 1919. During World War II, Slonimsky published several war stories, then revised *Lavrovy* to fit the ideological demands of the period, changing the title to *Pervye gody* (1949; The First Years). Slonimsky devoted a trilogy to the development of the technological intelligentsia: *Inzhenery* (1950; The Engineers), *Druzya* (1954; Friends), and *Rovesniki veka* (1959; Contemporaries of the Century); the trilogy attracted little attention. The obligatory criticism of Stalin's cult of personality in his *Sem let spustya* (1963; Seven Years Later) was in keeping with the Party line at that time. Toward the end of his life Slonimsky wrote memoirs of his literary contemporaries. From 1934 to 1954 he was a member of the board of the Writers Union of the USSR; although he held no office after that time, he continued to participate in all congresses of the Writers Unions of the USSR and the RSFSR. Slonimsky lived in Leningrad.

Slonimsky "first wrote impressionistic stories, which had a freshness and promise" (Slonim) and which "show a very strong influence of Zamyatin's manner and style" (Struve). His novels center on the problem of the integration of the intelligentsia into Communist society. *Lavrovy* manages to derive its power from its depiction of the experience of war; the composition of Slonimsky's subsequent work lacks the force of artistic conviction.

*Works: Šestoj strelkovyj* (short stories), 1922; *Mašina Èmeri* (short stories), 1924; *Lavrovy* (novel), 1927, substantially revised as *Pervye gody*, 1949, subsequently under its original title; *Foma Klešněv* (novel), 1931; *Povest' o Levině* (pov.), 1935; *Pograničniki* (short stories), 1937; *Inženery* (novel), 1950; *Druz'ja* (novel), 1954; *Rovesniki veka* (novel), 1959; *Sem' let spustja* (novel), 1963; *Kniga vospominanij* (memoirs), 1966.—*Soč.*, 4 vols., 1928–29; 4 vols., 1931–32; *Sobr. soč.*, 4 vols., 1969–70; *Izbr.*, 2 vols., 1980.

*Secondary Lit.: RSPP* 4:1966; N. Lugovcov, 1966; G. Filippov, in *Zvezda* 1973:8; F. Scholz, foreword to *Serapionovy brat'ja*, 1922 (reprinted, Munich, 1973); V. Zamkovoj, in *Neva* 1975:9; V. Sažin, in *Zvezda* 1977:8.

**Slútsky, Borís Abrámovich,** poet (b. May 7, 1919, Slavyansk, Don Basin—d. Feb. 22, 1986, Moscow). Slutsky's father was a white-collar worker; his mother, a teacher. Slutsky attended school in Kharkov; he studied in Moscow starting in 1937, first law and then at the Gorky Literary Institute (graduated 1941). During World War II he was a soldier; after being seriously wounded he became a *politruk* (political instructor). In 1943 he joined the Communist Party. Slutsky, who had published his first poems in 1941, did not publish his next poems until 1953. In 1956 I. Erenburg publicly demanded that a collection of his poetry be published, and this was accomplished with the publication of *Pamyat* (1957; Memory). *Vremya* (1959; Time), *Segodnya i*

*vchera* (1963; Today and Yesterday), and *Rabota* (1964; Work) followed; from these Slutsky compiled two volumes of selected works in 1965. In 1963 he edited a volume of Jewish poems. Slutsky's poems about his memories of the war are inimical to pathos and have assured him a recognized position, although one that is not without antagonists (Dymshits). His works appeared regularly in journals, and he had published 13 collections of poetry by 1981. Slutsky first participated in a congress of the Writers Union (RSFSR) in 1970 and lived in Moscow.

For a long time, Slutsky's poetry was defined by the theme of war, whose dead forced him to ever new expression. He recounted people's individual fates, put himself in the victim's place, honored the fallen poet M. Kulchitsky in a short cycle, comprehended the tragedy of everyday life at the front, and avoided sentimentality and rhetoric. The critical examination of the poet's task also occupies a central place in Slutsky's poetry; also important are portraits of individual writers and artists. Observations, thoughts, and reminiscences are mixed together; occasionally an experience narrated like a ballad provides the impetus. With the passing years, questions about departing youth and about death have increased; he sees his own life implanted within a larger context. His message is sometimes too unidimensional but is always upheld by a great sense of responsibility. In addition to his published poetry, he wrote very good political verse, criticizing phenomena of the Soviet system; these verses were published in the Soviet Union only in 1987. "Despite his straight-from-the-shoulder pundit's manner, Slutsky is clearly a troubled and contradictory poet" (D. Brown). Formally Slutsky strives for a syntactically simple, proselike structure with semantics that seem natural yet are enriched by historical and colloquial elements. He consistently uses the trick of juxtaposing homonyms to the point of creating a rhyme scheme based on similar roots. Repetition and assonance give shape to his poetry, sometimes embracing entire stanzas; his poetry is kept laconically concise but is always oriented toward a prose style.

*Works: Pamjat'* (poems), 1957; *Vremja* (poems), 1959; *Segodnja i včera* (poems), 1963; *Rabota* (poems), 1964; *Izbr. lirika* (poems), 1965; *Pamjat'* (selection), 1965; *Sovremennye istorii* (poems), 1969; *Godovaja strelka* (poems), 1971; *Dobrota dnja* (poems), 1973; *Prodlënnyj polden'* (poems), 1975; *Vremja moikh rovesnikov* (poems), 1977; *Neokončennye spory* (poems), 1978; Izbr., 1980; Sroki (poems), 1984. Secondary Lit.: I. Èrenburg, in Lit. gazeta July 28, 1956; A. Dymšic, in Zvezda 1958:6 and in Moskva 1965:5; A. Urban, in Zvezda 1965:1; L. Lazarev, in Voprosy lit. 1967:1 and in Lit. obozrenie 1974:10; V. Solov'ëv, in Neva 1973:2; E. Evtušenko, in Lit. Rossija July 6, 1973, pp. 14–15; V. Sokolov, in Lit. obozrenie 1982:4; O. Khlebnikov, in Lit. obozrenie 1985:6.

**Slyótov, Pyotr Vladímirovich,** prose writer (b. May 3 [April 21], 1897, Włocławsk, prov. Warsaw—d. after 1981). Slyotov participated in the Civil War; he began to publish in 1919 and studied in Saratov and Moscow. When he joined the Pereval group in 1927, he already had a certain reputation as a writer. His first book, Proryv (1928; The Breakthrough), harkened back to the theme of the Civil War. Much noticed was his povest Masterstvo (1930; Artistry), a representation of the old conflict between the artist of genius and the assiduous one with talent. Slyotov had selected an Italian violin maker from around 1800 as an example (he made violins himself) and tried to expand the theme A. Pushkin dealt with in Mozart and Salieri by using a politicorevolutionary line that allows the genius to become a revolutionary and an atheist at the same time. In Pereval, Slyotov was primarily in contact with A. Lezhnev and I. Katayev and defended them in their opposition to RAPP until Pereval was forced to disband. After that, Slyotov was only allowed to publish for a few years: biographies of Dmitri Mendeleyev (1933), Modest Mussorgsky (1934), and Mikhail Glinka (1935) and insignificant contributions to the literature of the Five-Year Plan. In 1945 he was admitted into the Communist Party. In 1948 he was probably sent to a forced labor camp. In 1956 he achieved REHABILITATION. In 1958 two volumes of his selected works appeared; thereafter his name was mentioned only in connection with his translations, except for a positive reference to Masterstvo made by Yu. Dombrovsky (Voprosy lit. 1967:6) and scanty good wishes for his 70th and 75th birthdays. In 1977 and 1980 his works were again reprinted. He lived in Moscow and did not participate in the congresses of the Writers Union.

Works: Proryv (pov.), 1928; List'ja (pov.), in Novyj mir 1929:2 (reprinted in G. Glinka, Na perevale, 1954); Perevozčik, in Novyj mir 1929:11; Masterstvo (pov.), 1930; Zaštatnaja respublika (novel;), 1930; Reč' P. Slëtova (speech), in Novyj mir 1931:10; Povesti i ras-

skazy (short stories), 1934; Šagi vremeni (contains Zaštatnaja respublika; Masterstvo; Smelyj argonavt; Okurok), 1958; Besedy s načinajuščimi pisateljami (essays), 2d ed., 1958; Zaštatnaja respublika (contains Smelyj argonavt; Masterstvo; Zaštatnaja respublika), 1977; Ravnodenstvie (novel), 1980; foreword to S. Borodin, Dmitrij Donskoj, 1980.
Secondary Lit.: A. Ležnev, in Novyj mir 1928:8; N. Zamoškin, in Novyj mir 1930:1; A. Glagolev, in Novyj mir 1931:2; G. Glinka, Na perevale, 1954; Anon., in Lit. Rossija May 5, 1967, p. 15, and May 5, 1972, p. 7.

**Smelyakóv, Yarosláv Vasílyevich,** poet (b. Jan. 8, 1913 [Dec. 26, 1912], Lutsk, prov. Volhynia—d. Nov. 27, 1972, Moscow). His father was a railway worker of peasant origin. In 1931 Smelyakov completed his apprenticeship as a printer in Moscow. The first of his poems, inspired by an enthusiasm for Komsomol ideals, attracted the attention of M. Svetlov and E. Bagritsky. Smelyakov himself set the type for his first volume of poems, Rabota i lyubov (1932; Eng. tr., Work and Love, 1976). He was in a prison camp from 1934 to 1937; between 1941 and 1944 he was a prisoner of war in Finland. After the war Smelyakov received a residence permit for Moscow. He published an anthology of patriotic poetry, Kremlyovskiye yeli (1948; The Kremlin Spruces), which "was distinguished above all by the maturity and broad reach of its emotion from the superficial and essentially unfeeling emotionality" (Korzhavin) that characterized the poetry of that period. According to Korzhavin, an attack by S. Lvov against the alleged pessimism in this book was the reason why Smelyakov, who in the meantime had published a primitive propagandistic verse epic, Lampa shakhtyora (1949; The Miner's Lamp), was once again arrested. His REHABILITATION probably did not take place until 1956. Smelyakov's verse epic Strogaya lyubov (1956; A Stern Love), written at least in part in the labor camp, met with extensive approval, as did the collection Razgovor o glavnom (1959; A Conversation about the Main Thing). Smelyakov, who participated in Writers Union congresses beginning in 1958, was elected to the boards of the Writers Unions of the USSR (1967) and the RSFSR (1970). For his cycle Den Rossii (1966; Russia's Day), he received the State Prize in 1967; he was entrusted with the leadership of the poetry section of the Writers Union of the USSR, and took an active part in the campaign against A. Solzhenitsyn. Smelyakov lived in

Moscow and belonged to the editorial boards of *Druzhba narodov* (from 1958 on) and *Soviet Literature* (from 1963 on). The representation of his experience as a worker, influenced by a Komsomol enthusiasm for revolutionary ideals, was the source of Smelyakov's work. The themes of the younger generation and of the working class are also often met with in his later work; they are combined with Soviet patriotism in its many various forms. In *Strogaya lyubov* Smelyakov portrays the younger generation of the 1920s and 1930s; he never completed this verse epic, however. His later poems often focus on the immediate present in its relationships to more recent or more distant history. The quality of Smelyakov's depth and form of expression is very inconsistent; it reveals (as such good judges of literature as Ye. Vinokurov, N. Korzhavin, and Z. Paperny have pointed out) genuine talent but also the weak over-all style of this poet, who was pummeled by fate and ruined by alcohol. Smelyakov's good poems are characterized by strong imagery, his poorer poems by a cheap, rhymed declamatory style.

*Works: Rabota i ljubov'* (poems), 1932, 2d ed., enl., 1960 (see above); *Kremlëvskie eli* (poems), 1948; *Lampa šakhtera* (narrative poem), 1949; *Strogaja ljubov'* (narrative poem), 1956; *Razgovor o glavnom* (poems), 1959; *Zolotoj zapas* (poems), 1962; *Den' Rossii* (poems), 1967; *Svjaznoj Lenina* (poems), 1970; *Dekabr'* (poems), 1970; *Služba vremeni* (poems), 1975; *Stikhotvorenija i poèmy* (lyric and narrative poems), 1979.—*Izbr. proizv.*, 2 vols., 1967, 1970; *Sobr. soč.*, 3 vols., 1977–78.

*Secondary Lit.:* A. Mikhajlov, in *Novyj mir* 1960:6 and in *Lit. gazeta* Oct. 14, 1970, p. 7; Z. Papernyj, in *Novyj mir* 1961:10; E. Vinokurov, in *Lit. Rossija* March 8, 1963, pp. 4–5 (reprinted, in his *Poèzija mysli*, 1966), and in *Lit. gazeta* Jan. 26, 1983, p. 5; L. Lavlinskij, in *Oktjabr'* 1966:4; V. Dement'ev, 1967; S. B. Rassadin, 1971; N. Koržavin, in *Grani*, Frankfurt am Main, 91:1974; Zaleščik, in *Lit. gazeta* May 21, 1975, p. 7; E. Evtušenko, in *Lit. gazeta* May 18, 1977, p. 6; A. Pikač, in *Zvezda* 1981:2.

**Smirnóv, Sergéy Sergéyevich,** prose writer (b. Sept. 26 [Sept. 13], 1915, Petrograd—d. March 22, 1976, Moscow). Smirnov's father was an electrical engineer. Smirnov attended school in Kharkov. He studied at the Moscow Institute of Energetics between 1932 and 1937 but left without completing the degree. Beginning in 1937 he worked as a journalist and studied at the Gorky Literary Institute (until 1941). During World War II, Smirnov initially served at the front; he became a war correspondent in 1943. He joined the Communist Party in 1946. For several years he worked for a military publishing house, then from March 1950 until October 1954 he was on the editorial staff of *Novy mir*, where he held the post of deputy editor in chief from November 1953 on. In 1951 he was admitted to the Writers Union of the USSR. The experiences of these years inspired several journalistic books about the war, such as *V boyakh za Budapesht* (1947; The Battle for Budapest). From 1954 until 1964 Smirnov conducted an investigation into the fate of the Brest fortress and its defenders, who held out for over a month in an area occupied by the Germans. He later expanded his first small book on this subject, *Krepost na granitse* (1956; The Border Fortress), into a more comprehensive account, *Brestskaya krepost* (1964; The Brest Fortress). Smirnov described his research and his meetings with survivors and recorded reminiscences of separate incidents, integrating the whole into a war narrative that conformed to the Party line. Smirnov's account did not achieve journalistic consistency, nor did it aspire to being a historical, documentary novel. For this work he received the Lenin Prize in 1965. Smirnov, who in 1958 had led the anti-Pasternak debate of board members from the Writers Unions of the USSR and the RSFSR (see *Novy zhurnal*, New York, 83:1966), held active posts in both organizations: in 1959–60 he was editor in chief of *Literaturnaya gazeta;* from 1958 on, he belonged to the boards of both Writers Unions and sat on the commissions of their congresses; in 1975–76 he was secretary of the Writers Union of the USSR. His literary career was based on an output limited to journalistic accounts from World War II, such as *Rasskazy o neizvestnykh geroyakh* (1963; Tales of Unknown Heroes), two episodically structured dramas, and reportage of his travels abroad (he visited 50 countries between 1958 and 1970). Smirnov lived in Moscow.

*Works: V bojakh za Budapešt* (reportage), 1947; *Na poljakh Vengrii* (reportage), 1954; *Krepost' na granice* (reportage), 1956; *Krepost' nad Bugom* (play), 1956; *Ljudi, kotorykh ja videl* (play), 1958; *Poezdka na Kubu* (reportage), 1962; *Rasskazy o neizvestnykh gerojakh* (reportage), 1963, 3d enl. ed., 1968; *Brestskaja krepost'* (reportage), 1964.—*Sobr. soč.*, 3 vols., 1973.

*Secondary Lit.:* I. Andronikov, in *Novyj mir* 1958:2, in *Lit. gazeta* July 22, 1961, and in

Smirnov's *Sobr. soč.*, 1973; *RSPP* 4:1966; V. Sokolov, in *Novyj mir* 1975:8; M. Lapšin, in *Moskva* 1975:9; A. Mednikov, in *Voprosy lit.* 1978:5; V. Kosolapov, in *Voprosy lit.* 1982:9.

**Smirnóv, Sergéy Vasílyevich**, poet (b. Dec. 28 [Dec. 15], 1913, Yalta). Smirnov's father was a photographer. Smirnov grew up in a village near Yaroslavl in his parents' homeland. In 1932 he moved to Moscow, worked after 1934 in a Komsomol brigade building the Metro, and attended evening classes at the Gorky Literary Institute from 1935 to 1940. His first volume of poetry was published in 1939. He was admitted to the Communist Party in 1941 and served as a soldier in World War II. Thereafter, Smirnov worked for a time for *Pravda*. In 1947 he was accepted into the Writers Union of the USSR and has published regularly since then. Since 1954 he has been a member of the board of the Writers Union of the USSR; since 1958, of the board of the Writers Union of the RSFSR. He lives in Moscow and was awarded the Gorky Prize in 1969.

Smirnov writes patriotic confessional verses in accordance with SOCIALIST REALISM and pseudophilosophic truisms. A lack of musical perception may account for the absence of metrical arrangement; division into lines and primitive rhymes distinguish what he writes from prose. The content is simple and remains journalistic. An autobiographical verse epic, *Svidetelstvuyu sam* (1967; I Testify Myself), harkens back to the old Stalin worship: "This picture/ is deeply implanted in the soul,/ where it glows/ and burns like fire." His ability to translate patriotism, optimism, and political perception into poetry is so minimal that a Soviet critic commented on the danger of unintentional humor in 1953.

Works: *Druz'jam* (poems), 1939; *Otkrovennyj razgovor* (poems), 1951; *Moi vstreči* (poems), 1955; *Stikhotvorenija i korotkie basni* (poems), 1960; *Svidetel'stvuju sam* (narrative poem), in *Moskva* 1967:10; *Rossija—Rodina moja* (poems), 1967; *Moë i naše* (poems), 1973; *Neizvestnyj—izvesten* (narrative poem), 1974; *Svetoči moi* (poems), 1977; *Tebe odnoj* (poems), 1980.—*Izbr. stikhotvorenija i poèmy*, 2 vols., 1974.

Secondary Lit.: Z. Papernyj, in *Novyj mir* 1953:2; L. Eršov, in *Neva* 1963:5; A. Mikhajlov, in *Lit. gazeta* Oct. 31, 1963; A. Migunov, 1970; E. Ševeleva, in *Lit. obozrenie* 1973:5; A. Parpara, in *Lit. Rossija* Feb. 15, 1980, p. 7.

**Smirnóv, Vasíly Aleksándrovich**, prose writer (b. Jan. 13, 1905 [Dec. 31, 1904], Sinitsyno, prov. Yaroslavl—d. Oct. 19, 1979, Moscow). Smirnov's father was a peasant. Smirnov completed the Party school in Rybinsk in 1924; in 1925 he joined the Communist Party; also in 1925 he became a correspondent for the Komsomol. Smirnov published his first novel, *Gar* (Scorched), in *Oktyabr* in 1927. In 1930 the Communist Party dispatched him to Ivanovo Oblast, where he became secretary of the local RAPP group. He moved back to Yaroslavl in 1935 and in 1939–40 took correspondence courses from the Gorky Literary Institute, although he did not complete the degree. A second novel, *Synovya* (1940; Eng. tr., *Sons*, 1947), was published before World War II; during the war Smirnov served as a frontline correspondent. Four parts of Smirnov's major work, *Otkrytiye mira* (1947–73; The Discovery of the World), were published; he continued to work on it up until his death. In 1949 Smirnov moved to Moscow, where he was appointed to various positions in the Writers Union of the USSR. He became a member of the board of the Writers Union of the USSR in 1954; from 1954 to 1959 he was one of the board's secretaries; and from 1959 to 1965 he held the post of editor in chief of the journal *Druzhba narodov*.

Smirnov's literary work consists of two novels in addition to several minor works. *Synovya* deals with the fate of a village woman from the time of the Civil War to the period of the second Five-Year Plan. Based more or less on autobiographical material, *Otkrytiye mira* describes a village youth's growing awareness of the world in the decade before the Revolution. The first part of the novel, published as an independent povest, received the greatest attention; subsequent parts did not preserve the child's point of view, allowing the novel's artificial structure to become too obvious. Smirnov writes with extraordinarily broad strokes and a lack of action; he likes to interpolate pointed authorial intrusions into the text and enjoys using colloquial peasant speech.

Works: *Gar'* (novel), 1930; *Synov'ja* (novel), 1940 (see above); *Otkrytie mira* (novel), part 1, 1948, part 2, 1957, parts 1–3, 1972, part 4, in *Znamja* 1973:10–12.

Secondary Lit.: K. Paustovskij, in *Novyj mir* 1948:3; M. Ščeglov, in *Oktjabr'* 1956:3 and in his *Lit. kritika*, 1971; *RSPP* 4:1966; M. Lapšin, in *Moskva* 1968:12, 1975:1, and in his *Ličnost' v literature*, 1973; L. Terakopjan, in *Lit.*

*obozrenie* 1974:7; V. Vikhrov, in *Lit. gazeta* Jan. 22, 1975, p. 5.

**Smolénsky, Vladímir Alekséyevich,** poet (b. Aug. 6 [July 24], 1901, Lugansk, prov. Yekaterinoslavsk—d. Nov. 8, 1961, Paris). Smolensky's father was a colonel and a landowner; in 1920 he was shot by the Bolsheviks; Smolensky fought with the Whites and emigrated to Paris in 1920. There he completed Russian secondary school and studied economics (Vysshaya kommercheskaya shkola). His first poems were published in 1929. His first book, *Zakat* (1931; Sunset), contains 40 poems. The second, *Nayedine* (1938; Alone), was issued by the publisher of the journal *Sovremennye zapiski* where Smolensky regularly published poems. Smolensky spent World War II in Paris and published in *Vozrozhdeniye* and *Novy zhurnal*. His third publication, *Sobraniye stikhotvoreniy* (1957; Collected Poetic Works), comprises both the third book containing new poems, "Schastye" (Happiness), and the first two. He especially esteemed the poetry of M. Lermontov, A. Blok, and V. Khodasevich and was a friend of Yu. Odarchenko; the last-named wrote a short story about him. His last book of 41 poems appeared posthumously.

Smolensky wrote contemplative poetry of a profound seriousness that belongs spiritually and linguistically among the most significant expressions of émigré poetry. Fundamental themes are human loneliness, love, earthly suffering, and death. His message is not confined to the negative but expresses a solemn appeal, derived from a strong religious faith, to see, accept, and cherish the good in spite of the vicissitudes of earthly existence. A few poems, such as "Moyemu ottsu" (To My Father) and "Angel smerti" (Angel of Death), depict true visionary experiences. A definite belief in angels and the conviction that man lives after death are threads that run through his entire creative work. Smolensky wrote only a few political poems; their message, however, always has a general significance; thus he places Stalin's "Trotskyist" murders in the context of betrayed friends and of eventual heavenly revenge, and he envisions Soviet gulag crimes in the light of the obligation of a poet who lives in freedom to speak out for the imprisoned and the murdered—"Stikhi o Solovkakh" (Poems about Solovki). Linguistically Smolensky's poems are distinguished by their conscious sound patterns (his recitations were very popular in Paris), by their diverse repetitions, and by their clar-

ity. Smolensky looks for new word combinations (not neologisms) in order to touch people emotionally in a positive way.

*Works: Zakat* (poems), Paris, 1931; *Naedine* (poems), Paris, 1938; *Mistika A. Bloka* (essay), in *Vozroždenie*, Paris, 37–38:1955; *Mysli o Khodaseviče* (essay), in *Vozroždenie* 41:1955; *Sobranie stikhotvorenij* (poems), Paris, 1957; *Vospominanija* (memoirs), in *Vozroždenie* 98:1960; *Stikhi* (poems), Paris, 1963.

*Secondary Lit.:* P. Bicilli, in *Sovremennye zapiski*, Paris, 49:1932; V. Zlobin, in *Vozroždenie* 70:1957; G. Struve, in *Novyj žurnal*, New York, 53:1958; S. Rafal'skij, in *Grani*, Frankfurt am Main, 38:1958; Ju. Terapiano, in *Opyty*, New York, 9:1958; K. Pomerancev, in *Vestnik RSKhD*, Paris, 65:1962, in *Mosty*, Munich, 12:1966, and in *Russkaja mysl'*, Paris, Nov. 27, Dec. 11, and Dec. 18, 1980; T. Veličkovskaja, in *Vozroždenie* 142:1963.

**Sóbol, Andréy** (pseud. of Yúly Mikháylovich Sóbol), prose writer (b. May 25 [May 13], 1888, Saratov—d. May 12, 1926, Moscow, a suicide). Sobol was born into a poor Jewish family; he left his parents at the age of 14 and from then on never settled permanently anywhere. In 1906 he was sentenced to four years of forced labor in Siberia for his political activities; in 1909 he successfully escaped to Switzerland. As an emigrant, Sobol was in many European countries; he eventually fought in Serbia during World War I, then returned to Russia under a false name. Sobol, who began writing prose fiction in 1913, published his first collection of short stories and a much-discussed novel, *Pyl* (Dust; first printed in the journal *Russkaya mysl*), in 1915. As a Socialist Revolutionary, Sobol became commissar of the 12th Army after the February Revolution of 1917. After the October Revolution he left for Kiev with I. Erenburg; in 1921 he lived for a while in Koktebel, apparently with M. Voloshin. In 1922 Sobol settled in Moscow and pursued his literary career. Between 1923 and 1925 he published four collections of short stories and completed a four-volume edition of his collected works. None of his work has been reprinted since 1928.

The central problem presented in Sobol's realistic, psychological prose is that of the intellectual who is searching for a correct attitude to adopt toward revolutionary events. He describes disillusioned revolutionaries and counterrevolutionaries in *Oblomki* (1923; The Wreckage). In *Salon-vagon* (1922; The Pullman Car), a long short-story in an impressionistic manner set at the time of the provisional government, "Sobol succeeds in conveying both the fantastic nature of events and the inner drama of the commissar, who sees his long-desired Revolution turn into a grim and cruel reality" (Struve). Sobol is a good stylist; he knows how to combine the possibilities of the realistic with those of the fantastic and understands well how to take on the speech mannerisms of a fictional character, (as in Memuary vesnushchatogo cheloveka (1922; Memoirs of a Freckled Man).

Works: Rasskazy (short stories), 1915; Pyl' (novel), 1916; Salon-vagon. Bred (short stories), 1922; Ljudi prokhožie (short stories), 1923; Oblomki (short stories), 1923; Otkrytoe pis'mo, in Na postu 1923:2–3; Kniga malen'kikh rasskazov (short stories), 1925; Panoptikum (short stories), 1925 (Eng. tr., Freak Show, 1930); Ljubov' na Arbate (short stories), 1925 (reprinted, Ann Arbor, 1979); Memuary vesnuščatogo čeloveka, in Novyj mir 1926:1.— Sobr. soč., 4 vols., 1926; 3 vols., 1928.

Secondary Lit.: D. Gorbov, in Krasnaja nov' 1926:8 and in his U nas i za rubežom, 1928; Z. Štejnman, in Zvezda 1927:1 and separate study, 1927.

Sóbolev, Leoníd Sergéyevich, prose writer, literary official (b. July 21 [July 9] 1898, Irkutsk—d. Feb. 17, 1971, Moscow). Sobolev's father was an officer from the lesser nobility. Sobolev began his education in the cadet corps of the navy in St. Petersburg in 1910. In 1918 he switched to the Red Fleet and served there as an officer until 1931. In 1926 his first short story appeared. In 1930 Sobolev became a member of the military writers' union LOKAF; in 1931 he became the organizational secretary of the Leningrad branch and published his first novel, Kapitalny remont (1932; Eng. trs., Romanoff, 1935; The Big Refit, 1965), in their journal Znamya. A trip to Central Asia in 1935 aroused his interest in Kazakhstan; he wrote a book with M. Auezov, Epos i folklor kazakhskogo naroda (1939; Epic and Folklore of the Kazakh Peoples), and translated Kazakh literature. In 1938 Sobolev moved to Moscow. In World War II he was a correspondent for Pravda; he received a Stalin Prize (for 1942, 2d class) for Morskaya dusha (1942; Eng. tr., Soul of the Sea, 1946), a collection of heroic war stories. From the wartime events also comes Sobolev's last literary work, Zelyony luch (1954; Eng. tr., The Green Light, 1955). Sobolev, who belonged to the

board of the Writers Union of the USSR from 1934 on, was active almost solely as a functionary after 1954. He retained his position on the board of the Writers Union of the USSR when the organization (in 1957) and the leadership (from 1958 until his death) of the Writers Union of the RSFSR were transferred to him. As early as 1954 he demanded that the position of first chairman of the Writers Union of the USSR be filled by a Party functionary (instead of a writer), and he remained one of the main critics of efforts at liberalization, demanding in 1970, among other times, "ideological war." From 1958 to 1971 he was a member of the Supreme Soviet of the USSR, and he became a member of the presidium of this organization in 1970.

Sobolev's not extensive literary work is limited to an exposition, in accordance with Party doctrine, of life in the navy, especially among the officers. Kapitalny remont concerns the tsarist fleet before the Revolution and was criticized for its exclusively negative outlook. In 1961 Sobolev added four chapters to this work. The povest Zelyony luch reveals Sobolev's talent for exciting exposition. His stories do not derive from daily life at the front but strive to propagate superhuman heroism in unusual situations with pedagogic intent. Painstakingly included tragic elements are intended to strengthen the effect of the triumphal denouement.

Works: Kapital'nyj remont (novel), 1933, rev. ed., 1961 (see above); (with Auèzov) Èpos i fol'klor kazakhskogo naroda (essay), in Lit. kritik 1939:10–11, 1940:1; Morskaja duša (short stories), 1942 (see above); Zelënyj luč (pov.), 1955 (see above).—Izbr. proizv., 3 vols., 1962; Sobr. soč., 6 vols., 1972–74.

Secondary Lit.: L. Ščerbina, in Novyj mir 1944:4–5; M. Ščeglov, in Novyj mir 1955:4, and in his Literaturnaja kritika, 1971; V. Surganov, 1962, in Oktjabr' 1958:7, in Sobolev's Sobr. soč., 1972, and in Lit. obozrenie 1986:9; RSPP 4:1966; V. Pimenov, in Moskva 1980:12.

Socialist realism (Sotsialistíchesky realízm), a Communist, exclusively political theory of art that has been generally mandatory in the Soviet Union since 1934 in literature, literary criticism, and literary scholarship, as indeed in all fields of art. The limitation placed on the literary term realism by the ideological term socialist separates socialist realism from poetics. The term socialist realism was first mentioned on May 20, 1932, by I. Gronsky, chairman of the Organizing Committee for the

Establishment of the Writers Union of the USSR (according to the Party Resolution of April 23, 1932 [see PARTY RESOLUTIONS ON LITERATURE]; see *Lit. gazeta* May 23, 1932) and intensively promoted in 1932–33 by Gronsky and by V. Kirpotin, the head of the literary section of the Central Committee of the Communist Party. The concept was applied retroactively; earlier works by Soviet authors recognized by Party critics and written since M. Gorky's novel *Mat* (Mother) was published in 1907 were considered examples of socialist realism. The definition of socialist realism given in the first statute of the Writers Union of the USSR in 1934 has remained the point of departure for all interpretations despite its ambiguity: "Socialist realism, the fundamental method of Soviet literature and literary criticism, demands of the artist a truthful, historically concrete depiction of reality in its revolutionary development. The truthfulness and historical concreteness of the artistic depiction of reality must be combined with the ideological remolding and reeducating of the working people in the spirit of socialism." The corresponding passage in the statute of 1971 reads: "Socialist realism is a well-tested creative method of Soviet literature that is based on the principles of Party spirit and of closeness to the people; [it is] the method of truthful, historically concrete depiction of reality in its revolutionary development. Socialist realism has provided Soviet literature with distinguished achievements; in possession of an inexhaustible wealth of artistic means and styles, it opens up all possible avenues for developing the individual features of talent and of innovation in all genres of creative literary work." The basis of socialist realism is thus the understanding of literature as an ideological instrument of influence for the Communist Party, of literature as limited to political propaganda. Literature should support the Party in the struggle for the victory of communism. In a statement attributed to Stalin for the period 1934 to 1953, writers were described as "engineers of human minds." The principle of PARTY SPIRIT *(partiynost)* demanded that authors, critics, and literary scholars dispense with empirically recognized truth and replace this with the Party's truth; that is, they could not depict what they subjectively experienced and recognized but what the Communist Party had previously labeled typical. The statement "historically concrete depiction of reality in its revolutionary development" demanded that all historical, current, and future phenomena be integrated into the theory and doctrine of historical materialism according to the current interpretation favored by the Party. For example, A. Fadeyev had to rewrite his novel *Molodaya gvardiya* (The Young Guard), which was awarded a Stalin Prize, because the Party subsequently wanted its ostensible leading role in the partisan struggle to be given more emphasis for pedagogical and propagandistic purposes. In terms of the present day, the depiction of reality "in its revolutionary development" means that, rather than depicting the existing imperfect reality, the anticipated ideal condition (the workers' paradise) should be imaginatively portrayed. L. Timofeyev, one of the main theoreticians of socialist realism, stated in 1952: "The future is depicted as the tomorrow that has already been born and brightens today with its light." From this representation that is divorced from reality arose the term "positive hero" *(polozhitelny geroy)*, one who should be a paragon, a builder of a new life, a person capable of leadership, a man without any inner doubts, that is, a model Communist and the focal point of works of socialist realism. Accordingly, socialist realism demands from each work a basic "optimism" that is designed to reflect the Communist belief in progress as well as to prevent a depressed or unhappy mood. The depiction of military defects in World War II or general human suffering is inconsistent with the principles of socialist realism and must at least be outweighed by positive elements. A characteristic title for this inner discrepancy is V. Vishnevsky's *Optimisticheskaya tragediya* (Optimistic Tragedy). The term *revolutionary romanticism* is frequently applied to socialist realism's flight from reality. In the mid-1930s a closeness to the people *(narodnost)* was included among the requirements of socialist realism. This term refers back to the tendencies prevalent among a part of the Russian intelligentsia during the second half of the 19th century and concerns the understandability of literature among simple people as well as the inclusion of popular idioms and proverbs. The principle of closeness to the people also served to suppress experimental art. Although socialist realism is viewed as supranational and was exported to the countries within the Soviet sphere of influence after World War II as part of the messianic belief in the conquest of the world through communism, patriotism also belongs among its principles, that is, the action of the plot is generally limited to the Soviet Union and emphasis is given to the superiority of everything Soviet and especially Russian. When the term *socialist realism* is applied to writers in the West or in developing countries, it refers to a positive appraisal of a Communist, pro-Soviet attitude. In general the concept *socialist realism* refers to the content of a linguistic work of art rather than to its form and has thus contributed to the considerable neglect Soviet writers, critics, and literary scholars exhibit toward form.

The principles of socialist realism have been interpreted, promoted, an observed with varying consistency since 1934. Deviation can lead to loss of the title "Soviet writer," to exclusion from the Writers Union, even to prison camp (see GULAG AND LITERATURE) and death if the author's depiction of reality is viewed as falling outside "the revolutionary development," that is, as exhibiting a critical attitude toward reality, and thus as being antagonistic and prejudicial toward the Soviet Union. Topical criticism, especially in the form of irony and satire, is foreign to socialist realism, and use of it led to the persecution of M. Zoshchenko and M. Bulgakov as well as to the conviction of A. Sinyavsky, for example. After Stalin's death, the principles of socialist realism (and thus socialist realism itself indirectly) were sharply attacked and were made responsible for the decline of Soviet literature. The demands raised by distinguished authorities for sincerity, for conflicts that were true-to-life, for people in doubt and suffering, and for works without clearly forseeable endings confirmed socialist realism's alienation from reality. The more individual works fulfilled these demands during the period of the THAW, the more they were attacked by conservative critics who repeatedly took offense primarily at the objective depiction of the negative aspects of Soviet reality. In his essay about socialist realism distributed abroad and in SAMIZDAT, Sinyavsky justifiably highlighted how socialist realism found its parallels not in the realism of the 19th century but in the classicism of the 18th. The vagueness of the concept made it feasible to conduct pseudodiscussions from time to time and to develop a vastly exaggerated literature. Thus at the beginning of the 1970s the terms "socialist realism," "socialist art," and "democratic art" were weighed against one another. The "discussions" could not hide the fact that the concept of socialist realism is bound up with politics and thus, like the leading role of the Party, admits to no discussion, even within the Party's own sphere of influence.

*Secondary Lit.:* V. Kirpotin, in *Lit. kritik* 1931:3; K. E. Harper, *Controversy on Soviet* *Literary Criticism on the Doctrine of Socialist Realism*, Diss., Columbia Univ., 1950; L. Timofeev, in *Oktjabr'* 1952:4; G. A. Wetter, *Der dialektische Materialismus*, Freiberg, 1952; H. Ermolaev, *Soviet Literary Theories 1917–1934: The Genesis of Socialist Realism*, Berkeley, 1963 (reprinted, New York, 1977), further in *Sowjetsystem und demokratische Gesellschaft*, vol. 5, Freiburg, 1972; A. Bušmin, in *Russkaja lit.* 1963:4, 1964:4; A. Terc (A. Sinjavskij), *Čto takoe socialističeskij realizm*, in *Fantastičeskij mir Abrama Terca*, New York, 1967 (Eng. tr., *On Socialist Realism*, New York, 1960); C. V. James, *Soviet Socialist Realism: Origins and Theory*, London, 1973; J.-U. Peters, in *Zeitschrift für slavische Philologie* 1974:2; A. Ovčarenko, *Socialističeskij realizm*, 1977; E. Možejko *Der sozialistische Realismus—Theorie, Entwicklung und Versagen einer Literatur-Methode*, Bonn, 1977; D. F. Markov, *Problemy teorii socialističeskogo realizma*, 1978, and in *Voprosy lit.* 1983:1; H. Günther, Stuttgart, 1984.

**Sofrónov, Anatóly Vladímirovich,** playwright, poet (b. Jan. 19 [Jan. 6] 1911, Minsk). Sofronov's father was the chief of police in Kharkov. Between 1921 and 1941 Sofronov lived in Rostov-on-Don where he was employed in the factory for agricultural machinery for six years. There he worked as the secretary for the factory newspaper and also wrote poems that were published in book form in 1934. In 1937 Sofronov graduated from the Faculty of Literature at the teachers college in Rostov. In 1940 he was accepted into the Communist Party. During World War II he worked as a correspondent for *Izvestiya*. In 1946 he wrote his first drama, V *odnom gorode* (In a City), which premiered in 1947. This propagandistic work written in accordance with the Party line was awarded a Stalin Prize (for 1947, 2d class), as was his following play, *Moskovsky kharakter* (Eng. tr., *The Moscow Character*, in *Soviet Literature* 1949:8), which premiered in 1948 (for 1948, 1st class). The next drama, *Karyera Beketova* (1948; Beketov's Career), which aided the campaign against COSMOPOLITANISM, belonged, after its initial acclaim, among the works that were subjected to the Party's criticism in 1951 despite their PARTY SPIRIT; Sofronov himself was the author of the Party-authorized criticism that was directed against himself and A. Fadeyev, I. Katayev, and K. Simonov (*Lit. gazeta*, Aug. 14, 1951). From 1953 to 1986 Sofronov was the editorial director of the mass circulation journal *Ogonyok*, which remained conservative even during the THAW. Since 1954 Sofronov has belonged to the board of the Writers Union of the USSR, and he became one of the secretaries of the board in 1975; since 1958 he has also belonged to the Writers Union of the RSFSR. Regular trips abroad to all parts of the world as a delegate of the Writers Union found an echo in his propagandistic prose and poetry. By 1982 Sofronov had published about 40 dramas, among which the light comedies were extremely successful with the public. In 1960 *Million za ulybku* (1958; A Million for a Smile) was his most frequently performed play, with 6,015 performances in 154 theaters. He lives in Moscow.

Sofronov's political dramas, each of which depicts a contemporary theme according to the Party line, are cheap propaganda. The Soviets point to *V nashi dni* (1952; In Our Days) as an example of the negative consequences of the THEORY OF CONFLICTLESSNESS; *Chelovek v otstavke* (1956; The Retired Man) was supposed to help stem the tide of de-Stalinization; *Beregite zhivykh synovey* (1963; Protect the Living Sons) defends the functionaries of the Stalin period who were under attack; *Demidovy* (1964; The Demidovs) publicizes the liberality of post-Stalinist Party policy regarding renegades; *Emigranty* (1967; The Emigrants), with its negative portrait of the United States and its one-sided treatment of Russians living abroad, constitutes one aspect of the Party's ideological war; *Labirint* (1968; The Labyrinth) is pure political agitation on the theme of the Vietnam War. In contrast to his comedies, these tendentious Party dramas seldom appear on the stages of the Soviet Union. After his success with *Stryapukha* (1959; The Female Cook), which was performed 4,637 times in 1960, he continued to use this theme in three comedies: *Stryapukha zamuzhem* (1961; The Female Cook as Married Woman), *Pavlina* (1964), and *Stryapukha—babushka* (1978; The Female Cook as Grandmother); to be sure, these plays are criticized for their cheap repetition, but they are nevertheless frequently performed. *Operatsiya na serdtse* (1981; The Heart Operation), a play concerned with medical ethics, is characterized by a trite black-and-white plan. Sofronov writes routinely and superficially, uses simple clichés, limits the plot to a few elements, never attempts to penetrate the depths by exploring the gray areas. His poetry does not transmit an image of concrete experience but limits itself to a broad and banally pre-

sented harangue in support of peace, friendship, and a happy Soviet Union.

*Works: Solnečnye dni* (poems), 1934; *Pered znamenem* (poems), 1948; *P'esy* (plays), 1953 (contains *V odnom gorode; Moskovskij kharakter* [see above]; *V naši dni; Inače žit' nel'zja*); *Ot vsekh širot* (play), 1958; *Dramy* (plays), 1959; *Tri komedii: Strijapukha, Strjapukha zamužem, Pavlina* (plays), 1967; *Na bližnem i dal'nem zapade* (feature articles), 1968; *Lëd zeleneet po vesne* (poems), 1970; *Labirint* (plays), 1971 (contains *Cemesskaja bukhta; Deti moi, deti; Sny; Èmigranty; Labirint; Letjat ženikhi; Nakazanie bez prestuplenija; Ne ver'te mužčinam*); *Vlast'* (play), in *Moskva* 1974:7; *Giganty* (play), in *Moskva* 1976:2; *Vremja proščanij i vstreč* (travel articles, portraits, thoughts), 1977; *Pesnja žizni* (play), in *Moskva* 1977:4; *Zemnoe pritjaženie* (play), in *Moskva* 1978:2; *Strjapukha-babuška* (play), in *Oktjabr'* 1978:12; *V glub' vremeni* (novel in verse), 2 vols., 1980, 1984; *Srok davnosti* (play), in *Oktjabr'* 1981:2; *Operacija na serdce* (play), in *Moskva* 1981:8.—*Izbr. proizv.*, 2 vols., 1955; 2 vols., 1961; *Sobr. soč.*, 5 vols., 1971–72; *Soč.*, 6 vols., 1984.

*Secondary Lit.:* A. Sinjavskij, in *Novyj mir* 1959:8; A. Vlasenko, in *Teatr* 1963:11; Ju. Idaškin, in *Oktjabr'* 1971:1; N. Tolčenova, *Velenie vremeni*, 1972; L. Nikolaeva, in *Lit. obozrenie* 1974:6; D. Kholendro, in *Teatr* 1981:1; I. Savel'ev, in *Novyj mir* 1985:11; Ju. Zubkov, 1985.

**Sokolóv, Mikhaíl Dmítriyevich**, prose writer (b. Jan. 24 [Jan. 11], 1904, Sulin, prov. Rostov). Sokolov's father was a factory worker. In 1921 Sokolov was admitted into the Communist Party and then received his education at the Communist Sverdlov University in Moscow. Since 1924 Sokolov has lived in Rostov-on-Don; he graduated from the economics institute there in 1931 and has worked as a Party and industrial official. In 1939 he published the first part of the novel *Iskry* (Sparks), which he completed three decades later with the fourth part. This history of the 1905 Revolution in the Don region, formulated according to the standards of the Stalin period, was interwoven into the pattern of class struggles and commonplace family quarrels (the son of the poor peasant who had been beaten becomes a revolutionary) and met with constant criticism because of its length, inconsistency of character, and inadequate realization of ideological concerns, yet received a Stalin Prize (for 1950, 2d class). Including Lenin in the third part did not alter the critics' views. Sokolov, who demanded some restructuring and the decentralization of the theater at the Second Congress of the Writers Union of the USSR in 1954, was the editor in chief of the journal *Don* from 1956 to 1975.

*Works: Mečta Varvary* (play), in *Don* 1955:1; *Iskry* (novel), 4 vols., 1939–70; *Groznoe leto* (novel), 1982.
*Secondary Lit.:* M. Koz'min, in *Novyj mir* 1950:11; L. Žak, in *Lit. Rossija* Dec. 27, 1963, p. 10; G. Kondrašev, in *Zvezda* 1968:4 and 1971:3; N. Gluškov, in *Oktjabr'* 1974:1; G. Brovman, in *Don* 1979:1; G. Dmitrienko, in *Znamja* 1984:3.

**Sokolóv, Sásha** (pseud. of Aleksándr Vsévolodovich Sokolóv), prose writer (b. Nov. 6, 1943, Ottawa). Sokolov's father was in the diplomatic service. In December 1947, his father, deputy military attaché at the Soviet Embassy, was expelled from Canada; thereafter Sokolov grew up in Moscow. In 1962 he began his studies at the military institute for foreign languages; he left this institute in 1965 and began studying journalism at Moscow University in 1967. In order to work concurrently as a journalist, he transferred to the evening division from 1969 to 1971; during this period he worked for the newspaper *Literaturnaya Rossiya* under his own name. After completing his education he lived partially in Moscow, partially in the provinces (especially along the Volga where he worked as a gamekeeper). As a reporter from the capital working in the area around Yoshkar Ola, he enjoyed a certain freedom that he took advantage of to create images of people in rhythmic prose. His most important longer prose work, *Shkola dlya durakov* (Eng. tr., *A School for Fools*, 1977), could not be considered for publication in the Soviet Union because of its surrealistic character; it was published in the United States after he emigrated (October 1975). Sokolov settled in Canada, but lives part of the year in the United States. A second novel, *Mezhdu sobakoy i volkom* (1980; Between Dog and Wolf [that is, at twilight]), met with less appreciation because of its greater surrealism, but it was honored as the "best prose of 1981" by the Leningrad SAMIZDAT journal *Chasy*.

In its day, *Shkola dlya durakov* was the most surrealistic work of modern Russian literature. Written intuitively in one sitting, it

was reworked about five times with great attention being paid to word choice, as has been the case with Sokolov's other prose works. Correlations between individual parts and changes in the stylistic levels characterize the structure. Not only is a consistent plot lacking, the characters also change their identity. Time in the physical sense is suspended, as is the boundary between life and death. Sokolov's linguistic experiments reflect a spiritual search and an intuitive recognition of essential connections, together with many concrete references to Soviet reality and to Russian history. The book was translated into English, German, Italian, Dutch, and French. The one poetic and two prose sections of *Mezhdu sobakoy i volkom* were written concurrently; this work reveals an even stronger intermingling of the real and the imaginary, of fantasy, reminiscences, and daydreams. Since it is even more difficult to comprehend, it has remained untranslated to date (1986). Set in the beginning of the 21st century, within the framework of a fictitious biography of a grandnephew of Lavrentiy Beria, Sokolov's third novel, *Palisandriya* (1984; Palisandriya), offers surrealistic, occasionally grotesque, sequences depicting a captive individual in a privileged position. The multiple layers of ironic exposition lend the novel an extraordinary literary quality.

*Works: Škola dlja durakov* (novel), Ann Arbor, 1976 (see above), 2d corrected ed., Ann Arbor, 1983; *Meždu sobakoj i volkom* (novel), Ann Arbor, 1980; interview, in *Russkaja mysl'* Paris, Nov. 12, 1981; *Palisandrija* (novel), Ann Arbor, 1984; *Trevožnaja kukolka* (essay), in *Kontinent*, Paris, 49:1986.
*Secondary Lit.:* Ph. Ingold, in *Wiener Slawistischer Almanach* 3:1979; F. Moody, in *Russian Literature Triquarterly* 16:1979; D. B. Johnson, in *Fiction and Drama in Eastern and Southeastern Europe*, Columbus, Ohio, 1980, and in *Vremja i my*, Jerusalem, 64:1982; I. Burikhin, in *Grani*, Frankfurt am Main, 118:1980; E. Ternovskij, in *Russkaja mysl'* June 26, 1980; V. Aksënov, in *Russkaja mysl'* June 16, 1983; O. Matič, in *Sintaksis*, Paris, 15:1986; M. Ziolkowski, in *World Literature Today* 1986:2.

**Sokolóv, Vladímir Nikoláyevich,** poet (b. April 18, 1928, Likhoslavl, oblast Kalinin). Sokolov's father was an engineer. In 1952 Sokolov graduated from the Gorky Literary Institute. Sokolov has been publishing poems since 1948;

his first volume, *Utro v puti* (1953; The Morning on Its Way), which concerns his World War II experiences as a child during the evacuation, appeared in Moscow. During this period, Ye. Yevtushenko and other Gorky Literary Institute students had high regard for Sokolov as the one "who taught us to have a serious relationship to poetry." Sokolov was represented with a poem in the liberal anthology *Literaturnaya Moskva* (1956:2). Additional volumes of poetry, *Trava pod snegom* (1958; Grass under the Snow) and *Na solnechnoy storone* (1961; On the Sunny Side), led to his general acclaim as a good nonjournalistic poet, a reputation that was secured by frequent publications from 1965 on. Sokolov also translated Georgian poetry. He lives in Moscow, participated in a congress of the Writers Union of the USSR for the first time in 1971, and was given a position on the board of the Writers Union of the RSFSR in 1975 and on that of the Writers Union of the USSR in 1980.

Owing to his age, Sokolov belongs to the oldest of those writers who did not experience the war at the front and thus this theme plays a minimal and variable role in his writing. Sokolov is considered a "traditionalist" in Soviet parlance; he is a poet of spiritual experiences, of deeply perceived incidents that he conscientiously holds on to, keeps from disappearing, and raises above the level of a unique experience. He does not create verses about the daily political routine. Economy and modesty of expression, a firm grounding in tradition, and strong, metaphorically grounded succinctness reveal a conscious opposition between his own literary work and propagandistic pathos. Sokolov gives form to the fragility of existence and to the peril existing in a world that appears to be secure. He loves images of clear autumn, of snow, of a delicate landscape, and of the city and lends these an intricate expressiveness that belies their external simplicity.

*Works: Utro v puti* (poems) 1953; *Trava pod snegom* (poems), 1958; *Na solnečnoj storone* (poems), 1961; *Smena dnej* (poems), 1965; *Raznye gody* (poems), 1966; *Izbr. lirika* (poems), 1967; *Sneg v sentjabre* (poems), 1968; *Stikhotvorenija* (poems), 1970; *Četvert' veka* (poems), 1975; *Gorodskie stikhi* (poems), 1976; *Pozdnee utro* (poems), 1977; *Spasibo, myzyka* (lyric and narrative poems), 1978; *Sjužet* (lyric and narrative poems), 1980; *Dolina* (lyric and narrative poems), 1981.—*Izbr. proizv.*, 2 vols., 1981; *Stikhotvorenija*, 1983.

*Secondary Lit.:* E. Evtušenko, in *Lit. gazeta* Jan. 25, 1955, and Dec. 28, 1965; L. Anninskij, in *Molodaja gvardija* 1964:2; A. Mikhajlov, in *Znamja* 1968:9 (reprinted in *Lit. i sovremennost'* 9:1969) and in *Družba narodov* 1969:6 and 1975:12; Ju. Ajkhenval'd, in *Novyj mir* 1969:5; I. Volgin, in *Lit. gazeta* June 9, 1971, p. 5; V. Kožinov, in *Naš sovremennik* 1974:1; P. Košel', in *Lit. obozrenie* 1978:4; D. Černis, in *Voprosy lit.* 1979:9 and in *Novyj mir* 1985:2; S. Čuprinin, in *Oktjabr'* 1985:9

**Sokolóv-Mikitóv, Iván Sergéyevich,** prose writer (b. May 30 [May 18], 1892, Oseki, prov. Kaluga—d. Feb. 20, 1975, Moscow). Sokolov-Mikitov's father was an administrator in the timber trade. Sokolov-Mikitov grew up in the region around Smolensk, went to St. Petersburg in 1910 to study agriculture, gave this up in 1911 and became a journalist in Reval. Between 1912 and 1914 Sokolov-Mikitov became acquainted with many of the harbors of Europe and Africa as a sailor with the merchant marine. In World War I he was a medic and an aviator. In 1920, after the Revolution, he continued his sailor's life in the Crimea; he lived in Berlin in 1921–22 and published *Kuzovok* (1922; The Little Basket), his first collection of eight short stories, as well as other short books. From 1922 to 1930 he lived in the Smolensk region and regularly published short prose works that appeared in a three-volume collection in 1929. In the 1930s and in the second half of the 1940s, Sokolov-Mikitov took part in expeditions into the outlying regions of Soviet Asia and northern Russia, and these trips found an echo in his writings. He participated in the congresses of the Writers Unions of the USSR and the RSFSR from 1954 to 1967, but always lived a withdrawn life—after 1933 in Leningrad or in a wooden house in Karacharovo.

Sokolov-Mikitov is often praised for his attachment to nature and his human decency. Influenced by I. Bunin, he has much in common with M. Prishvin and K. Paustovsky— the hunters and observers of the forest, the fields, and the lakes. From the reports of his excursions into Soviet Asia, parallels with V. Arsenyev emerge. His prose is especially vivid and expressive when he captures his own experiences, weaker when he recounts what he has been told. Occasional criticism because of insufficient political interpretation appears, but this is outweighed by regular friendly response to his prose (for example, from Yu. Trifonov, A. Tvardovsky, and V.

Nekrasov); the attention paid him in histories of literature, however, is minimal.

Works: Kuzovok (short stories), 1922; Čižikova lavra (short stories), 1927; Na rečke Nevestnice (short stories), 1928; Lenkoran' (short stories), 1934; Łetjat lebedi (short stories), 1936; Rasskazy okhotnika (short stories), 1946; Na tëploj zemle (short stories), 1954; Zvuki vesny (short stories), 1962; U svetlykh istokov (short stories), 1969; Zvuki zemli (short stories), 1972.—Sobr. soč., 3 vols., 1929; Soč., 2 vols., 1959; Sobr. soč., 4 vols., 1965–66; Izbr. proizv., 2 vols., 1972; 1 vol., 1981; Sobr. soč., 3 vols., 1985–.

Secondary Lit.: A. Tvardovskij, in Sokolov-Mikitov's Soč., 1959; V. Nekrasov, in Novyj mir 1962:5 and in Novoe russkoe slovo, New York, March 28, 1982, p. 5; RSPP 4:1966; P. Dudočkin, in Russkaja lit., 1972:3; Ju. Trifonov, in Novyj mir 1972:4; M. Smirnov, 1974; V. Lazarev, in Naš sovremennik 1976:1; V. Lakšin, in Oktjabr' 1981:7; V. Smirnov, 1983; Tvorčestvo S.-M., 1983; Vospominanija ob I.S. S.-M., 1984; G. Goryšin, in Naš sovremennik 1985:8.

**Sologúb, Fyódor** (pseud. of Fyódor Kuzmích Tetérnikov), poet, prose writer (b. March 1 [Feb. 17], 1863, St. Petersburg—d. Dec. 5, 1927, Leningrad). Sologub's father was a tailor, Sologub graduated from a teachers college in 1882; he taught mathematics, at first in the provinces (until 1892), then in St. Petersburg (until 1907). Sologub began publishing poetry in the symbolist style in 1884 and novels in 1896; he became famous for his novel Melky bes (1907; Eng. tr., The Little Demon, 1916). Sologub himself viewed the trilogy Navyi chary (Deadly Spells), originally published 1907–9 and best known in its reworked form Tvorimaya legenda (1914; Eng. tr., The Created Legend, 1916), as his best work. A 12-volume edition of his works (1909–12) was followed by a second edition in 1913, planned for 20 volumes. After the Revolution, his recognition and opportunities to create declined sharply. In 1921 Sologub asked Lenin for permission to go abroad; the denial of Sologub's request drove his wife to suicide. Sologub managed to publish eight slender volumes of poetry before 1923; after that, he existed by doing translations. His literary estate is almost inaccessible. Melky bes was reprinted in 1933 and 1958. After Sologub's death, two volumes of his selected poems appeared in 1939 and 1975 in the series "Biblioteka poeta" (Poet's Library).

Sologub was one of the most important of the Russian symbolists. His work is characterized by a skeptical idealism and is pervaded by melancholy; it combines the fantastic-demonic with a retreat into the beauties of nature; again and again it lays bare the discrepancy between reality and illusion. The motif of death, which reveals itself in manifold, often gruesome ways, is common. A death wish, even the glorification of "sweet death," proves to be, in the greater context, a disguise, a mask that protects against a very real fear of death (which intermittently overcomes Sologub in visions of his dead wife). His patriotic poems from the period of the Russo-Japanese War and World War I are thematically isolated from the rest of his work. Sologub's poetic language is simple and clear, yet (not least important) it is conjured up out of musical elements. In 1921 I. Erenburg compared its effect to that of narcotics. Melky bes, which tells the story of the life and ruin of a morally degenerate, spiritually bankrupt, and covetous provincial schoolteacher toward the end of the 19th century, is intended as a representation of the evil in man; the novel's artistically interwoven plot lines effectively convey the oppressive atmosphere of baseness and wickedness in everyday life. Tvorimaya legenda, Sologub's major symbolist work, merges the real and the transreal, attempts to convey a solipsistic vision of the world, and incorporates satirical allusions to contemporary society into the larger mystical-symbolic plot. The themes of his 100 short stories (traced by A. Leitner for the period 1894 to 1921) range from demonism and satanism, through death and sexuality, to biblical content. "Sologub's prose style is totally unpretentious and detached; the style is often calculatedly (and ironically) naïve, and even the most gruesome and absurd matters are narrated in a straightforward and sententious tone" (Holthusen). "He was the first to discover the riches of the Russian language, unused until his time, that lay in its sound structure and in the richness of its syntactic and stylistic possibilities" (Selegen). Sologub also wrote symbolist dramas in which he communicates, through emphasis on masks and puppetlike elements, a sense of doubt about things seemingly real.

Works: Stikhi (poems), 1896; Teni (short stories), 1896; Tjažëlye sny (novel), 1896; Žalo smerti (short stories), 1904; Rodine (poems), 1906; Melkij bes (novel), 1907 (reprint of 1933 ed., Letchworth, 1966); Pobeda smerti (play), 1907; Plamennyj krug (poems), 1908; Tvorimaja legenda (novel), 3 vols., 1914, vols. 18–

20 in *Sobr. soč.*, 1913–14 (reprinted, Munich, 1972); *Fimiamy* (poems), 1921 (reprinted, Letchworth, 1972); *Nebo goluboe* (poems), 1921 (reprinted, Letchworth, 1972); *Sobornyj blagovest* (poems), 1921; *Čarodejnaja čaša* (poems), 1922 (reprinted, Letchworth, 1970); *Koster dorožnyj* (poems), 1922 (reprinted, Letchworth, 1980); *Stikhi* (poems), 1923; *Stikhotvorenija* (poems), 1939; *Izbr.*, Chicago, 1965; *Stikhotvorenija* (poems), 1975 *Rasskazy* (short stories), Berkeley, 1979.—*Sobr. soč.*, 12 vols., 1909–12; 20 vols., 1913–14 (vols. 1, 3, 5, 6, 9, 11–20 published).

*Translations:* The Sweet-Scented Name and Other Fairy Tales, Fables, and Stories, ed. S. Graham, 1915; The Old House and Other Tales, trans. J. Cournos, 1916; The Little Demon, trans. J. Cournos and R. Aldington, 1916, trans. J. Wilks, 1962; The Created Legend, trans. J. Cournos, 1916, trans. S. Cioran, 1979; Little Tales, trans. J. Cournos, 1917; The Petty Demon, trans. A. Field, 1962; The Kiss of the Unborn and Other Stories, trans. M. Barker, 1977; Bad Dreams, trans. V. W. Smith, 1978.

*Secondary Lit.:* A. Blok, in *Pereval* 1907:10 and in his *Sobr. soč.*, vol. 5, 1962; I. Èrenburg, *Portrety russkikh poètov*, 1922; G. Struve, in *Novyj žurnal*, New York, 16–17:1947; J. Holthusen, The Hague, 1960; G. Selegen, Washington, 1968; E. Bristol, in *Russian Review* 1971; P. P. Brodsky, Berkeley, 1972; C. Hansson, Stockholm, 1975; K. L. Robbins, Washington, 1975; A. Leitner, Munich, 1976; V. Černjavskij, in *Grani*, Frankfurt am Main, 108:1978; H. Baran, in *NRL: Neue Russische Literatur*, Almanach 2–3, 1979–80; S. Rabinowitz, Columbus, 1980; *O Fedore Sologube*, St. Petersburg, 1911 (reprint, Ann Arbor, 1983); V. Erofeev, in *Voprosy lit.* 1985:2; L. Klejman, Ann Arbor, 1983.

**Soloúkhin, Vladímir Alekséyevich,** poet, prose writer (b. June 14, 1924, Alepino, oblast Vladimir). Soloukhin is of peasant descent. From 1938 to 1942 he studied at the Engineering Institute in Vladimir (tool mechanics); during World War II he served as a soldier in the Kremlin special unit. He began publishing poetry in 1946; from 1946 to 1951 he attended the Gorky Literary Institute; since 1952 he has been a member of the Communist Party. His first volume of poetry, *Dozhd v stepi* (1953; Rain in the Steppes), named after a poem written in 1947, was praised for its independence and "delicate magic of imagery" (Shcheglov). Within the framework of his journalistic work for *Ogonyok*, Soloukhin wrote sketches of his trips at home and abroad start-

ing in 1951. His first independent publication of such documentary prose was *Rozhdeniye Zernograda* (1955; The Birth of Zernograd), a report about the Virgin Lands. With *Vladimirskiye prosyolki* (1957; Eng. tr., *A Walk in Rural Russia*, 1966), Soloukhin developed a lyrical, topical, and, at the same time, tradition-conscious prose form that brought him great acclaim. This form also influenced the autobiographical novel *Mat-machekha* (1964; Mother-Stepmother; also the plant coltsfoot). At the beginning of the 1960s, Soloukhin acquired an interest in Russian icons; he began to champion their preservation and consideration, becoming a collector and an expert with respect to both content and technique. His publications on this topic, *Pisma iz Russkogo muzeya* (1966; Letters from the Russian Museum) and *Chornye doski* (1969; Black Boards; Eng. tr., *Searching for Icons in Russia*, 1971) met with both strong consideration and criticism. Soloukhin, who participated in the campaign against B. Pasternak in 1958, was a member of the board of the Writers Union of the RSFSR from 1958 to 1975 and has belonged to that of the Writers Union of the USSR since 1959; from 1964 to 1981 he belonged to the editorial staff of MOLODAYA GVARDIYA. In 1979 he was awarded the State Prize of the RSFSR. He lives in Moscow but spends much time in the woodland area around his home town.

Soloukhin is one of the writers favorably disposed toward Russian tradition, rural life, and religious aspects. "He is the most prominent contemporary writer of nationalist orientation, but he carefully dissociates himself from extreme reactionary positions" (D. Brown). In his poetry, Soloukhin has developed from poems bound up with tradition to an expressive form that is close to prose, forgoes rhyme and meter, and structures the verse through syntactic parallels and repetitions of words and parts of sentences. In a volume of essays in 1965, *S liricheskikh pozitsiy* (From Lyrical Points of View), he spoke out in favor of freedom of verse structure, while at the same time spurning modern endeavors in the visual arts. Soloukhin's prose, which in its associative structure and in the often strong recession of the plot closely resembles that of K. Paustovsky (fittingly Soloukhin has written about Paustovsky's work), combines documentary elements of journalistic prose with a mood of poetry about nature; the earthy rusticity of his own observations among kolkhoz peasants with art-historical and religious-philosophic reflections; a national Russian enthusiasm for the native land and cultural tradition with a concrete depiction of his time and criticism of contemporary issues. *Kaplya rosy* (1960; A Drop of Dew) portrays the story of his native village and its people. His own experience also characterizes the novel *Matmachekha*, for which Soloukhin selected the true fictional form (third-person structure) instead of his usual first-person structure and in which he opposes the Stalin period and the consequences its repressive measures had on people to a belief in the power of nature. Soloukhin's *Pisma iz Russkogo muzeya* and *Chornye doski* extend beyond art-historical reflections to a positive representation of Christianity. In *Olepinskiye prudy* (1973; The Ponds of Olepino), Soloukhin combines humorous sketches of trips at home and abroad with the lyrical prose work "Trava" (Grasses) that, using fundamentals of botanical knowledge, a visualization of nature, and personal experiences, offers prudent, economical deliberations on journalistic topics of current interest. *Poseshcheniye Zvanki* (1975; Visit to Zvanka) recalls G. Derzhavin's manor house, which has been destroyed since the war, and analyzes the religious element in Derzhavin's ode "Bog" (God). *Prigovor* (1975; The Judgment), a story about a complaint against death, stands somewhat apart among Soloukhin's literary works. His sympathetic title essay in *Vremya sobirat kamni* (1980; A Time to Gather Stones Together) concerns the famous cloister destroyed in the Soviet period, Optina Pustyn.

*Works: Dožd' v stepi* (poems), 1953; *Roždenie Zernograda* (feature articles), 1955; *Za sin'-morjami* (prose), 1956; *Razryv-trava* (poems), 1956; *Vladimirskie prosëlki* (prose), 1958 (see above); *Žuravlikha* (poems), 1959; *Kaplja rosy* (prose), 1960; *Otkrytki iz V'etnama* (prose), 1961; *Imejuščij v rukakh cvety* (poems), 1962; *Liričeskie povesti* (short stories and prose), 1964; *Svidanie v Vjaznikakh* (prose), 1964; *S liričeskikh pozicij* (essays), 1965; *Mat'-mačekha* (novel), 1966; *Pis'ma iz Russkogo muzeja* (prose), in *Molodaja gvardija* 1966:9–10, Frankfurt am Main, 1968, abridged ed., Moscow, 1967; *Sorok zvonkikh kapelej* (poems), 1968; *Čёrnye doski* (prose), in *Moskva* 1969:1 (see above); *Slavjanskaja tetrad'* (prose), 1972; *Olepinskie prudy* (prose), 1973; *Poseščenie Zvanki* (prose), in *Moskva* 1975:7; *Prigovor* (lyric reportage), in *Moskva* 1975:1; *Sedina* (poems), 1977; *Kameški na ladoni* (essays), 1977; *Med na khlebe* (pov. and short stories), 1978 (Eng. tr., *Honey on Bread*, 1982); *Vremja sobirat' kamni* (essays), 1980; *Kolokol, Pervoe poručenie* (short stories), in *Grani*, Frankfurt am Main, 118:1980;

*Prodolženie vremeni, Pis'ma iz raznykh mest* (prose), in *Naš sovremennik* 1982:1; *Stikhotvorenija* (poems), 1982; *Volšebnaja paločka* (essays), 1983; *Bedstvie s golubjami* (short stories and essays), 1984; *Kameški na ladoni*, in *Novyj mir* 1986:8.—*Izbr. proizv.*, 2 vols., 1974; *Sobr. soč.*, 4 vols., 1983–84.

*Translations: White Grass* (short stories), 1971; *Sentenced and Other Stories*, 1983.

*Secondary Lit.:* M. Ščeglov, in *Lit. gazeta* Oct. 16, 1954; I. Sokolov-Mikitov, in *Novyj mir* 1959:1; Ju. Burtin, in *Novyj mir* 1960:7; L. Ljubimov, in *Naš sovremennik* 1969:9; *RSPP* 7(2):1972; E. Morozova, G. Cvetov, in *Russkaja reč'* 1975:2; N. G. Kosačeva, in *Russian Language Journal* 121–22:1981; S. Rybak, in *Družba narodov* 1981:3; V. Dement'ev, in *Moskva* 1984:5; A. Voznesenskij, in *Lit. gazeta* June 13, 1984; p. 4; A. Georgievskij, in *Oktjabr'* 1984:10; M. Grossen, in *Grani*, Frankfurt am Main, 130:1984; A. Ovčarenko, in *Novyj mir* 1985:7.

**Solovyóv, Leoníd Vasílyevich,** prose writer (b. Aug. 19 [Aug. 6], 1906, Tripoli, Lebanon— d. April 9, 1962, Leningrad). Solovyov's father was in the diplomatic service. Solovyov's family returned to Russia in 1909 and lived in the province of Samarkand until 1920. He remained in Central Asia until 1931, earning his living in various ways, including as teacher of Russia and journalist. In 1924–25 he collected folklore of the Fergana Valley. He completed his studies at the State Institute of Cinematography (Department of Film Scripts) in 1932, and between 1932 and 1935 published five books and pamphlets. Solovyov attracted attention with his book *Vozmutitel spokoystviya* (1940; Disturber of the Peace; Eng. tr., *Adventures in Bukhara*, 1956), which he based on the Central Asian folkloric tradition of Hoça Nasrettin. During World War II he served as a war correspondent with the navy. His short novel, *Ivan Nikulin—russky matros* (1943; Ivan Nikulin—Russian Sailor), went through numerous editions. Solovyov spent the years from 1946 to 1954 in prison camp or exile. Afterward he took up residence in Leningrad; two years later he published a sequel to his book about Hoça Nasrettin, *Ocharovanny prints* (Eng. tr., *The Enchanted Prince*, 1957), which was published together with the first part (*Vozmutitel spokoystviya*) under the title *Povest o Khodzhe Nazreddine* (1956; The Tale of Hoça Nasrettin). Thematically, the two parts had already been incorporated into two film scripts written in 1945. Parts of a book about Solovyov's experiences in Central Asia, *Iz "Knigi yunosti"* (1963; From "The Book of Youth"), were published posthumously.

Solovyov's place in Russian literature is based on *Vozmutitel spokoystviya*, which had been inspired by the tradition of some 300 humorous episodes from the life of the 13th-century semilegendary Turkish folk sage, Hoça Nasrettin. The character in Solovyov's novel preserves the traditional mixture of knavery and magnanimity with sympathy for the oppressed, and of poetic wisdom with love of adventure, which moderates the amusing element of fantasy in the second part. Stylistically, Solovyov's eloquence and expressiveness have effectively kept his loose adaptations of traditional episodes in harmony with the Oriental spirit of the original.

*Works: Kočev'e* (pov.), 1932; *Vysokoe davlenie* (novel), 1938; *Vozmutitel' spokojstvija* (pov.), 1940 (see above); *Ivan Nikulin—russkij matros* (novel), 1943; *Khodža Nazreddin: 2 lit. scenarija* (film scripts), 1945; *Povest' o Khodže Nazreddine (Vozmutitel' spokojstvija; Očarovannyj princ)*, 1956 (see above); *Sevastopol'skij kamen'* (short stories), 1959; *Iz "Knigi junosti"* (short stories), 1963.—*Izbr.*, 3 vols., 1964.

*Secondary Lit.:* Ju. Karasev, in *Moskva* 1957:4; L. Anninskij, in *Družba narodov* 1958:1; E. Solov'ëva, in *Neva* 1964:2; *RSPP* 4:1966; D. Moldavskij, in his *Tovarišč smekh*, 1981.

**Solovyóv, Vladímir Aleksándrovich**, playwright (b. April 8 [March 26], 1907, Sumy, prov. Kharkov—d. Jan. 30, 1978, Moscow). Solovyov first wrote poetry and satirical verse but shifted to drama with *My olonetskiye* (1932; We from Olonets) and the polemical topical drama *Lichnaya zhizn* (1934; The Private Life), which was published in *Krasnaya nov*. Following the play *Chuzhoy* (1938; The Stranger) on the timely theme of industrial sabotage, Solovyov became especially famous through *Feldmarshal Kutuzov* (1940; published in 1939 under the title *1812 god* and reworked again later on; Eng. tr., *Field Marshal Kutuzov*, in *Seven Soviet Plays*, 1946). In this play, in the spirit of effective patriotic propaganda but in historically very simplified form, he emphasized the people as the decisive factor. With respect to form, he modeled himself after A. Pushkin's *Boris Godunov* with its changing scene of action. Solovyov was awarded a Stalin prize for this play (1935–41, 2d class) and for his next play, *Veliky gosudar* (1944; The

Great Sovereign) (for 1945, 2d class). This drama, dedicated to the reevaluation of Ivan the Terrible according to the Party line—a farsighted ruler who was forced to use strongarm methods with his people out of patriotic motives—is a typical example of the propagation of the Stalin cult of personality with direct political relevance for the time, especially in the Party's thesis that mass sacrifices are justifiable by historical necessity. The 1955 revised version accommodated itself to the changed Party line; now Ivan acknowledged that he caused innocent blood to be spilled. With *Izmena natsii* (1952; The Betrayal of the Nation), which concerns the 1871 uprising of the Paris commune, Solovyov remained with historical themes; in *Tsar Yury* (1966), which deals with the mythical tsar who the Russian people hoped would bring salvation during the Time of Troubles, he offered a sequel to *Veliky gosudar* (later given the title *Tsar Ivan*). Solovyov also wrote plays about World War II: *Doroga pobedy* (1946; The Way of Victory) and *Opasnaya professiya* (1958; Dangerous Profession), about the adventurous life of underground fighters struggling against the German occupation. Solovyov dealt with topical themes again in the satire *Myortvy kapital [Chameleon]* (1956; The Dead Capital [Chameleon]), in the antireligious film script *Malenkoye kolyosiki istorii* (1963; A Little Wheel of History), and in *Myslyashchiye, lyubyashchiye i oderzhimye* (1968; The Thinking, Loving, and Obsessed). With *Gibel poeta* (1961; The Death of the Poet), Solovyov wrote a play about Pushkin; with *Denis Davydov* (1963), he wrote a "heroic comedy" about the Hussar poet of the same time, whose material he had used for an opera libretto in 1957. Solovyov writes blank verse as a rule. His plays show experience but no depth. Solovyov, who lived in Moscow, played no role in the literary-political life of the Soviet Union.

*Works: Ličnaja žizn'* (comedy), in *Krasnaja nov'* 1934:8; *1812 god* (play), in *Novyj mir* 1939:10–11; *Fel'dmaršal Kutuzov* (play), 1940 (see above); *Velikij gosudar'* (play), 1945; *Chameleony* (play), 1957; *Malen'koe kolësiko istorii* (film script), in *Iskusstvo kino* 1963:8; *P'esy* (plays), 1948, 1950; *Istoričeskie dramy* (plays), 1956, 1960; *Velikij gosudar'. Car' Jurij; Puškin* (plays), 1972; *Vek nynešnij i vek minuvšij* (plays), 1975.—*Izbr.*, 2 vols., 1982 (contains *Car' Ivan; Car' Jurij; Kutuzov; Denis Davydov; Puškin pri dvore ego veličestva; Prizrak v Pariže; Mysljaščie, ljubjaščie i oderžimye; Pereprava; Jabloki, kotorye ne prodajutsa . . . ; Opasnaja professija).*

Secondary Lit.: B. Mejlakh, in Lit. gazeta
Aug. 29, 1961; O. Dzjubinskaja, in Teatr
1963:11; Ju. Ajkhenval'd, in Teatr 1968:8; T.
Steblecova, 1980.

Solzhenítsyn, Aleksándr Isáyevich, prose
writer (b. Dec. 11, 1918, Kislovodsk). Solzhenitsyn graduated from Rostov University with
distinction (Faculty of Physics and Mathematics); concurrently he was enrolled in correspondence courses at the Moscow Institute
of Philosophy, Literature, and History. Starting in 1941 he served as a soldier in World
War II; after having attained the rank of captain, he was imprisoned in 1945; until 1953
he was held in prison and special camps; until
1956 he remained in "perpetual exile" in Central Asia. During this period Solzhenitsyn began to write. In 1957 he won REHABILITATION
and was sent to Ryazan as a teacher. With the
express permission of Khrushchev, A. Tvardovsky published Solzhenitsyn's long short-
story Odin den Ivana Denisovicha (Eng. tr.,
One Day in the Life of Ivan Denisovich, 1963,
rev. tr., 1971) in Novy mir in 1962. This first
depiction of Soviet forced labor camps became the greatest literary success in the Soviet
Union of the postwar period (see GULAG AND
LITERATURE). In 1963 three more short stories
were published in Novy mir. Solzhenitsyn
was recommended for the Lenin Prize in 1964,
but he did not receive it owing to a political
change of direction. In 1966 he published a
short story in the Soviet Union for the last
time. His letter to the delegates at the Fourth
Congress of the Writers Union of the USSR in
May 1967 created an international furor; in
this letter he discussed the harm that censorship inflicts on Soviet literature as well as the
suppression of his own works. Rakovy korpus
(1968; Eng. tr., The Cancer Ward, 1968) and
V kruge pervom (1968; Eng. tr., The First
Circle, 1968), two great novels written between 1955 and 1967 concerning his experiences in exile and in the camps, circulated in
SAMIZDAT and were published in the West,
making him world famous. These were followed by the less highly acclaimed publication of two of the four dramas written between
1951 and 1960: Svecha na vetru (1968; Eng.
tr., Candle in the Wind, 1973); later published
under the title Svet, kotory v tebe [The Light
within You]) and Olen i shalashovka (1968;
Eng. tr., The Love-Girl and the Innocent, 1969;
later published under the title Respublika truda
[The Republic of Work]). Solzhenitsyn's uncompromising attitude toward the Writers
Union's demands for conformity led to his
exclusion on November 5, 1969. In 1970 he

was awarded the Nobel Prize but was unable
to accept it in person. The campaign against
Solzhenitsyn in the Soviet Union intensified.
In the same year he allowed Avgust chetyrnadtsatogo (1971; Eng. tr., August 1914, 1972),
the first volume of his planned multipart
("knots") epic work on World War I and the
Russian Revolution, Krasnoye koleso (The Red
Wheel), to be published in Paris. Later this
book was enlarged by doubling its size (1983).
After the authorities tracked down the manuscript of Arkhipelag GULag (1973–75; Eng.
tr., The Gulag Archipelago, 3 vols., 1974–78),
a documentary-literary treatment of repression in the Soviet Union since 1918 that Solzhenitsyn had been keeping secret, he decided to publish it in Paris. Solzhenitsyn was
expelled from the Soviet Union in February
1974 and settled in Zurich with his family.
From there he first published previously written works: Pismo vozhdyam Sovetskogo So-
yuza (1974; Eng. tr., Letter to the Soviet Leaders, 1974), an admonition and exhortation
concerning the future of Russia; Prusskiye
nochi (1974; Eng. tr., Prussian Nights, 1977),
a narrative poem concerning the Red Army's
march into East Prussia in 1945 that was written in 1950 while he was being held in a
camp; and Bodalsya telyonok s dubom (1975;
Eng. tr., The Oak and the Calf, 1980), an
autobiographical treatment of Soviet literary
policy between 1961 and 1974. Solzhenitsyn
published 11 chapters of his historical novels
separately in Lenin v Tsyurikhe (1975; Eng.
tr., Lenin in Zurich, 1976). In August 1976 he
moved to Cavendish, Vermont. There he revised all his earlier prose for an edition of his
collected works and, after studying the history
of the period, wrote additional "knots" to
Krasnoye koleso: Oktjabr 16-go (October 1916)
consists of two volumes and Mart 17-go (March
1917) is planned for publication in four volumes, the first two of which appeared in December 1986. He also occasionally voiced his
opinion on the world political situation.
    Solzhenitsyn is, as was originally acknowl-
edged publicly in the Soviet Union, one of
the most significant epic talents of modern
Russian literature. Committed solely to truthful representation, he chose to depict life during the Stalin period, especially in forced
labor camps and special camps for intellectuals, in his first three great prose works; the
defeat of the tsarist army in the battle of Tan-
nenberg in Avgust chetyrnadtsatogo; and the
dangers—not limited to the Soviet Union—of
misapplying science in the spiritual sphere in
Svet, kotory v tebe. Arkhipelag GULag is the
most comprehensive portrayal of the organized system of injustice (camps, trials, ad-

ministrative measures) of the entire Soviet period. It combines documentary material with personal experiences or events reported by former prisoners. *Bodalsya telyonok s dubom* provides a vivid account of Solzhenitsyn's fate up to his second period of imprisonment and exile and is at one and the same time poetically structured and a documentation of the political history of his time. Solzhenitsyn's works, including his dramas, are epically, additively composed with a great independence of chapters and scenes and with many characters. In his prose works, the central action is limited to a period of a few days (in *Rakovy korpus* to a few weeks). In his works that attempt to come to terms with the Stalin period, flashbacks make it possible to encompass the entire epoch. The primary plot contains the dramatic, suspenseful elements that guarantee the unity of a work of art. Objectivity is maximized through frequently shifting points of view, through the complete rejection of commentary, and—in *Krasnoye koleso*—through several structural levels (fiction, historical reports, documents, lyrical impressionistic parts). A conscious linguistic succinctness that favors ellipses and neologisms created from old Russian roots distinguishes his poetry and his journalistic works.

*Works: Odin den' Ivana Denisoviča* (pov.), 1963 (see above); *Matrënin dvor* (short story), in *Novyj mir* 1963:1 (Eng. trs., "Matryona's Home," in *We Never Make Mistakes*, 1963, and in *Stories and Prose Poems, 1971*); *Zakhar-Kalita* (short story), in *Novyj mir* 1966:1 (Eng. tr., "Zakhar-the-Pouch," in *Stories and Prose Poems*, 1971); *Rakovyj korpus* (novel), 2 vols., Frankfurt am Main, 1968 (see above); *V kruge pervom* (novel), Frankfurt am Main, 1968 (see above), rev. ed., Paris, 1978; *Olen' i šalašovka* (play), London, 1968 (see above); *Sveča na vetru* (play), in *Student*, London, 11–12, 1968, and in *Grani*, Frankfurt am Main, 71:1969 (see above); *Avgust Četyrnadcatogo* (novel), Paris, 1971 (see above), rev. ed., Paris, 1983; *Arkhipelag GULag* (literary documentation), 3 vols., Paris, 1973–75 (see above); *Pis'mo voždjam Sovetskogo Sojuza* (essay), Paris, 1974 (see above); *Na vozvrate dykhanija i soznanija* (essay), together with two others, in *Iz-pod glyb*, Paris, 1974 (Eng. tr., "As Breathing and Consciousness Return," in *From Under the Rubble*, 1975, reprinted, 1981); *Prusskie noči* (narrative poem), Paris, 1974 (see above); *Bodalsja telënok s dubom* (autobiography and documentary prose), Paris, 1975 (see above); *Lenin v Cjurikhe* (chapters from novel), Paris, 1975; *Izbr.*, Pullman, Mich., 1976; *Rasskazy* (short stories), Frankfurt am Main,

1976; *Pesni i kinoscenarii*, Paris, 1981 (contains trilogy *1945 god; Pir pobeditelej* [Eng. tr., *Victory Celebrations*, 1983]; *Plenniki* [Eng. tr., *Prisoners*, 1983]; and *Respublika truda* [see above]; also *Svet, kotoryj v tebe* [see above]; *Znajut istiny tanki*, and *Tunejadec); Publitsistika: Stat'i i reči* (articles and speeches), Paris, 1981; *Krasnoe koleso* (novels), Paris, 1983– (contains, up to 1986: knot 1: *Avgust Četyrnadcatogo*, rev. ed., 1983; knot 2: *Oktjabr' Šestnadcatogo*, 1984; knot 3: *Mart Semnadcatogo*, 1986).—*Sobr. soč.*, 6 vols., Paris, 1969– 70, and 1978– (16 vols. appeared through 1986).

*Translations: Stories and Prose Poems*, 1971 (later under the title *Matryona's House and Other Stories*, 1975); *Six Etudes*, 1971; *East and West*, 1980.

*Secondary Lit.:* G. Lukács, Neuwied, 1970; A. Rothberg, Ithaca, 1971; L. Rževskij, *Tvorec i podvig*, Frankfurt am Main, 1972; R. Pletnev, Paris, 2d ed., 1973; P. Daix, Paris, 1974; H. Björkegren, Nuffield, 1973; *Über Solschenizyn*, Darmstadt, 1973 (with bibliography); J. B. Dunlop, Diss., Yale Univ., 1973; V. Carpovich, New York, 1976; F. Barker, New York, 1977; R. Brackman, Diss., New York Univ., 1980; G. Nivat, Paris, 1980 (in Russian, London, 1984); M. Šneerson, Frankfurt am Main, 1984; M. Scammell, London, 1985; *Solzhenitsyn in Exile*, ed. J. B. Dunlop and others, Stanford, 1985.

**Sosnóra, Víktor Aleksándrovich,** poet (b. April 28, 1936, Alupka, Crimea). During World War II, Sosnora was in Leningrad at the beginning of the blockade and was later moved to Kuban territory; he was with the partisans for a while. He completed secondary school in Lvov. From 1955 to 1958 he served in the military. He worked as a locksmith in a Leningrad engineering works (1958–63) while studying philology by correspondence at the same time. As a poet, Sosnora was discovered by N. Aseyev in 1958. Aseyev wrote the foreword to Sosnora's first volume of poetry, *Yanvarsky liven* (1962; January Shower), which was published two years after some of the poems first appeared in journals. Sosnora dedicated *Triptikh* (1965), his next volume of poetry, to Aseyev; this work was praised by B. Slutsky. Because of his headstrong, good-natured, ironic relationship to early Russian history and because of the illogical composition of his contemporary poems, opinions about Sosnora's poetry are contradictory. Some older poems reappeared in the volumes *Vsadniki* (1969; Riders), *Aist* (1972; The Stork), *Stikhotvoreniya* (1977; Poems), and *Kristall* (1977; Crystal); Sosnora also published in almanacs and journals. A volume of short stories (1965–73), Letuchiy Gollandets (1979; The Flying Dutchman), was published in Frankfurt am Main. Up through 1982, Sosnora was not selected as a delegate to congresses of the Writers Union. He lives in Leningrad.

In Sosnora's lyric verse, poems with motifs from the Primary Chronicle, The Lay of Igor's Campaign, and Kievan heroic poetry stand out strongly. These poems constitute half of the fiirst volume, a third of the second, and all of the third. Sosnora imitates these epic works neither in meter nor in content but transplants the figures of heroic poetry into an unheroic, merry, or warlike—also erotic—but always human everyday situation. Often he uses figures from Western European, ancient Greek, and Russian literature to produce poems rich in associations. In his unhistorical poems, images of the modern industrial world stand next to those of nature; they derive their power from the union between distant notions that usually also have a tonal germaneness. Plays on words and phonetic associations that reflect V. Khlebnikov's influence and that of the futurists (see FUTURISM) form an essential characteristic of his entire creative output. Often the meaning is difficult to discern; sometimes the lack of purpose seems to be the principle; at other times sorrow forces its way through the armor of poetic buffoonery. His prose not published in the Soviet Union is lyrical and impressionistic, an attempt at surrealism.

Works: Janvarskij liven' (poems), 1962; Triptikh (poems), 1965; Vsadniki (poems), 1969; Aist (poems), 1972; Kristall (poems), 1977; Stikhotvorenija (poems), 1977; Letučij Gollandec (short stories), Frankfurt am Main, 1979; Pesn' lunnaja (poems), 1982; Spasitel'-nica otečestva (pov.), in Neva 1984:12.
Secondary Lit.: N. Aseev, in Izvestija Jan. 8, 1962; V. Zajcev and G. Krasukhin, in Oktjabr' 1963:2; V. Portnov, in Novyj mir 1963:2; B. Sluckij, in Lit. gazeta Dec. 9, 1965; A. Prokof'ev, in Lit. Rossija July 10, 1970, p. 16; V. Solov'ëv, in Junost' 1971:2; A. Prijma and S. Čuprinin, in Lit. obozrenie 1973:8; Vl. Novikov and A. Pikač, in Lit. obozrenie 1979:1; K. Sapgir, in Russkaja mysl', Paris, Jan. 31, 1980, p. 13; V. Novikov, in Novyj mir 1984:4.

Sovreménnye zapíski (Contemporary Annals), a cultural-political and literary journal published in Paris between 1920 and 1940. Although originally envisioned as a monthly journal in keeping with the "thick" Russian journals, a maximum of six issues per year were published (1921); after 1931 only two or three appeared each year; when publication was completely stopped as a result of the German occupation, a total of 70 volumes had been published. Sovremennye zapiski was always jointly managed by a group of editors from the first emigration: N. D. Aksentyev, I. I. Bunakov, M. V. Vishnyak, A. I. Gukovsky (died 1925), V. V. Rudnev. Sovremennye zapiski enjoyed a good reputation as the first comprehensive cultural journal of the emigration. When the 50th volume was published in 1933, V. Khodasevich observed that the editors were able, "without themselves being artists or literary scholars, to compile in the sections for poetry and belles lettres everything or almost everything truly outstanding that was written abroad during these years" (Sovremennye zapiski 51, p. 440). For the literary section the editors accepted F. Stepun's advice; this section included works by G. Adamovich, M. Aldanov, K. Balmont, N. Berberova, I. Bunin, Yu. Felzen, G. Gazdanov, Z. Gippius, G. Ivanov, Vyach. Ivanov, V. Khodasevich, D. Merezhkovsky, V. Nabokov (Sirin), M. Osorgin, G. Peskov, B. Poplavsky, A. Remizov, I. Shmelyov, A. Shteyger, Yu. Terapiano, A. Tolstoy (vol. 1 was initiated with his Khozhdeniye po mukam), M. Tsvetayeva (in 36 issues), B. Zaytsev.

Secondary Lit.: Index to issues 1–65 (1920–37); V. Rudnev, in Sovremennye zapiski 51:1933; M. Višnjak, in Russkaja literatura v èmigracii, ed. N. Poltorackij, Pittsburgh, 1972, and in Novyj žurnal, New York, 20:1948; R. Johnston, in Canadian Slavonic Papers 1982:1.

Stadnyúk, Iván Fótiyevich, prose writer (b. March 8, 1920, Kordyshevka, oblast Vinnitsa). Stadnyuk's father was a peasant. From 1939 to 1958 Stadnyuk served in the military. In 1940 he was accepted into the Communist Party; in 1957 he graduated from the Moscow institute for the printing trade (Faculty of Editors). Stadnyuk, who first published in 1940, served in World War II as a reporter at the front and, in the postwar period, published numerous collections of short stories about the lives of soldiers. Maksim Perepelitsa (1952), a collection of 13 short stories about daily life in the military, is carried along by the artificially optimistic spirit of the THEORY OF CONFLICTLESSNESS. His novel Lyudi ne angeli (1962; Eng. tr., People Are Not Angels, 1963), which takes into account the dark side of

Stalinist agricultural policy, won a certain regard. A second part (1965) served as a positive counterweight. Stadnyuk, who has been active on the board of the Writers Union of the RSFSR since 1965 and on that of the Writers Union of the USSR since 1971, willingly participates in the maneuvers of the Warsaw Pact and is considered a military author conditioned by Party policy. A planned monumental work about World War II, *Voyna* (1970–80; War), presents, in accordance with the present Party line, Stalin and the main figures of his rule, such as Molotov, in a positive light again, in contrast to the 20th and 22d Party Congresses; the first three parts (third part published in 1980) only cover events up through July 1941. Stadnyuk is little noticed, owing to his modest artistic ability. He lives in Moscow.

*Works: Èto ne zabudetsja* (short stories), 1951; *Maksim Perepelica* (short stories), 1952; *Ljudi s oružiem* (short stories), 1956; *Ljudi ne angeli* (novel), 1963 (see above), vols. 1–2, 1966; *Vojna* (novel), vol. 1, 1971, vol. 2, in *Molodaja gvardija* 1974:5, separate ed., 1974, and vol. 3, in *Molodaja gvardija* 1980:5–6, separate ed., 1980; *Khleb istiny* (novel, play), 1975.—*Sobr. soč.*, 4 vols., 1982–85.

*Secondary Lit.:* V. Utarov, in *Znamja* 1953:5; M. Alekseev, in *Moskva* 1963:4; V. Khmara, in *Moskva* 1966:5; V. Poltorackij, in *Moskva* 1971:5; S. Voronin, in *Zvezda* 1975:5; M. Tanfil'ev, in *Zvezda* 1981:9; V. Nekrasov, in *Novoe russkoe slovo*, New York, Dec. 12, 1982, p. 2; S. Borzunov, in *Lit. gazeta* Oct. 2, 1985, p. 4.

**Stalin Prize.** See LITERARY PRIZES.

**State Prize of the RSFSR.** See LITERARY PRIZES.

**State Prize of the USSR.** See LITERARY PRIZES.

**Stávsky, Vladímir Petróvich** (pseud. of V. P. Kirpíchnikov), literary official (b. Aug. 12 [July 30], 1900, Penza—d. Nov. 14, 1943, near Nevelya). Stavsky's father was a worker. Stavsky became a Communist Party member in 1918. During the revolutionary fighting he served as a political commissar. In 1922–23 he worked as a freight handler in Rostov. In 1926 Stavsky became chairman of SKAPP, the proletarian writers' group in the northern Caucasus; he became secretary of RAPP in Moscow in 1928.

Stavsky was actively involved in forced collectivization and wrote falsified, literarily worthless *povesti* on the subject, such as *Stanitsa* (1926; The Cossack Village) and *Razbeg* (1930; A Running Start). In the early 1930s the Communist Party also put Stavsky in charge of organizing the Writers Union; he was a member of the Board of the Writers Union and was largely responsible for Party control of this organization. After M. Gorky's death in 1936 Stavsky became general secretary of the Writers Union (until 1941), was named a deputy of the Supreme Soviet in 1937, and served as editor in chief of *Novy mir* from 1937 to 1940. Beginning with the Polish campaign in 1939, Stavsky was a correspondent for *Pravda*. Because he occupied a leading position during the period of mass persecutions, the illegality of which was admitted after 1956 (see REHABILITATION), Stavsky is liable for a considerable share of the responsibility for the purges.

*Works: Stanica* (pov.), 1928; *Razbeg* (pov.), 1932; *Frontovye zapiski* (articles), 1942.

*Secondary Lit.:* RSPP 4:1966; A. Surkov, in *Lit. gazeta* Aug. 13, 1980, p. 6.

**Stepánov, Aleksándr Nikoláyevich,** prose writer (b. Feb. 2 [Jan. 21], 1892, Odessa—d. Oct. 30, 1965, Moscow). Stepanov's father was a career officer. Stepanov was trained at the cadet corps in Polotsk (1901–3); he lived with his father in besieged Port Arthur during the Russo-Japanese War. In 1913 he completed his studies at the St. Petersburg Institute of Technology. Stepanov fought at the front during World War I and with the Red Army during the Civil War; from 1921 on, he worked as an engineer in Krasnodar. He made his initial attempt at writing in the beginning of 1932. His first book, the historical novel *Port Artur* (1940–41; Eng. tr., *Port Arthur*, 1947), brought him recognition; it was awarded a Stalin Prize (for 1943–44, 1st class). The novel was frequently reprinted in perpetually revised and expanded editions; this novel remained Stepanov's one recognized work. The attempt to write a sequel dealing with the period 1905–17, *Semya Zvonaryovykh* (1959–63; The Zvonaryov Family), did not meet with approval and remained unfinished. Stepanov became a member of the Communist Party in 1947; in 1954 he took part in a congress of the Writers Union of the USSR for the only time in his life. He lived in Moscow from 1957 until his death.

*Port Artur* is a voluminous historical novel,

based in part on documents, in part on the current political interpretations. Stepanov's ability to present events aesthetically is limited, his descriptions are not very vivid, and his dialogue is incapable of conveying more than a single level of meaning.

Works: *Port Artur* (novel), 2 vols., 1940–41 (see above); *Sem'ja Zvonarëvykh* (novel), 2 vols., 1959–63.
Secondary Lit.: K. Osipov, in *Novyj mir* 1941:4; V. Kurganov, in *Zvezda* 1961:8 and in *Russkaja lit.* 1967:1; *RSPP* 4:1966.

**Streléts** (The Archer), a literary journal of the third wave of EMIGRATION published monthly since January 1984 in Montgeron, France, and Jersey City, New Jersey. The founder is Aleksandr Glezer, who became well known for his active support for nonconformist modern Russian art; the journal is published by his publishing house, Tretya volna (The Third Wave). The journal has a large format made lively through the inclusion of black-and-white photographs and a clever layout; each issue contains 48 pages. *Strelets* is a cultural journal whose form and content are diverse, contemporary yet conscious of tradition, pluralistic, and consciously antitotalitarian. In almost every issue *Strelets* offers poetry, short stories, a serialized novel, reprints of older Russian texts, reviews, an interview, and essays on literature and modern art, especially on exhibitions by Russian artists in the West. The basic principle of the unity of Russian literature and art, independent of place of origin (Russia or emigration), leads to a broad representation. Articles, especially those by S. Yuryenen on literary developments in the USSR, complement the primary works, which tend to be works written in emigration. The breadth of the offerings is clear from the fact that 104 authors are represented in 1,000 pages of text from the years 1984 and 1985. Among the authors whose works have been reprinted in the "literary archive" are A. Averchenko, A. Bely, G. Gazdanov, Z. Gippius, A. Mariyengof, A. Platonov, A. Remizov, Yu. Terapiano; among the poets published in the journal are V. Betaki, D. Bobyshev, N. Gorbanevskaya, V. Iverni, V. Krivulin, Yu. Kublanovsky, L. Losev, V. Lyon, K. Pomerantsev, I. Ratushinskaya, G. Sapgir, Ye. Shvarts, V. Sinkevich, Ye. Ternovsky, A. Tsvetkov; among the prose writers are Yu. Aleshkovsky, Yu. Galperin, V. Maksimov, Yu. Mamleyev, Yu. Miloslavsky, V. Nekrasov, D. Savitsky, and S. Yuryenen. The last issue of each year contains brief biographical notes

about the authors. The journal has been very favorably reviewed.

Secondary Lit.: Anon., in *Russkaja mysl'*, Paris, Dec. 29, 1983; Ju. Mamleev, in *Russkaja mysl'* March 1, 1984; G. Andreev, in *Russkaja mysl'* May 10, 1984; Aug. 16, 1984; March 14, 1985; and Nov. 22, 1985; A. Kopejkin, in *Novoe russkoe slovo*, New York, April 29, 1984; S. Jur'enen, in *Novoe russkoe slovo* Aug. 10, 1984; K. Sapgir, in *Kontinent*, Paris, 40:1984.

**Strugátsky, Arkády Natánovich, and Borís Natánovich**, prose writers who share authorship (Arkady Natanovich b. Aug. 28, 1925, Batum; Boris Natanovich b. April 15, 1933, Leningrad). The Strugatskys' father was an art historian; their mother, a teacher. Arkady Natanovich specialized in Japanese studies at the Military Institute for Foreign Languages in Moscow (1943–49); he worked at various scholarly institutes after his discharge from the military in 1955. He lives in Moscow. Boris Natanovich studied astronomy from 1950 to 1955 and worked at the Pulkovo Observatory until 1965. He lives in Leningrad. Since 1956 the brothers have coauthored works of nonrealistic prose. As long as they stuck to science fiction they were fully recognized; their transition to a surrealistic presentation of contemporary problems evoked the censure of the dogmatic critics. "The 'gulf' between the ill-will of the critics and the attitude of the readers is especially wide here" (*Molodaya gvardiya* 1965:4, p. 289). Some of their 20 povesti that became famous between 1959 and 1983 appeared in regional journals. *Strana bagrovykh tuch* (1959; The Land of the Red Clouds) and *Put na Amalteyu* (1960; Eng. tr., *Destination: Amaltheia*, 1962), their first books, belong to the tradition of outer-space-oriented fiction. After 1962 they turned more toward social or philosophical science fiction. *Ponedelnik nachinayetsya v subbotu* (1965; Eng. tr., *Monday Begins on Saturday*, 1977) deals ironically with, among other things, materialistically oriented thought and also recalls the traditional time machine. *Khishchnye veshchi veka* (1965; Eng. tr., *The Final Circle of Paradise*, 1976) is a satire concerning a materially satiated society that lacks spiritual goals. *Ulitka na sklone* (1966; Eng. tr., *The Snail on the Slope*, 1980), a story within a story whose two parts were published separately only a single time in the USSR, depicts people who are dependent on the inscrutable, illogical measures of a bureaucratic totalitarian system. *Gadkiye lebedi* (1972; Eng. tr., *The Ugly Swans*, 1979) circulated in the Soviet Union only through SAMIZDAT but was published in the West. *Piknik na obochine* (1972; Eng. tr., *Roadside Picnic and Tale of the Troika*, 1977) has been highly acclaimed by Stanislaw Lem as a classic of science fiction and concerns the remnants of a possible previous invasion by extraterrestrial beings found in mysterious restricted areas. *Za milliard let do kontsa sveta* (1976; A Million Years to the End of the World; Eng. tr., *Definitely Maybe*, 1978) reveals people confronting the universe's enigmatic reactions to research that could interfere with its own structure. *Zhuk v muraveynike* (1979; Eng. tr., *The Beetle in the Anthill*, 1980) takes place in a unitary state of the future in which the mystery of an emissary from an extraterrestrial civilization is never entirely solved. The brothers Strugatsky became two of the most beloved writers of nonrealistic prose in the USSR during the 1960s; their prose combines suspense, vividness, clever use of details, and grotesque alienation of the realistic particulars of everyday Soviet life, with a clear psychological understanding and a serious human and social message. Unexceptionable artistic accomplishments, their works follow in the tradition of Ye. Zamyatin by using the form of social satire widely permitted in the Soviet Union but without attempting his comprehensive critique of the system.

*Works:* Strana bagrovykh tuč (pov.), 1959; Put' na Amal'teju (pov.), 1960 (see above); Popytka k begstvu (pov.), in Fantastika 1962 g., 1962 (Eng. tr., *Escape Attempt*, 1982); Vozvraščenie (pov.), 1962 (new ed., Polden', XXII vek, 1967 [Eng. tr., *Noon, 22nd Century*, 1978]; Stažëry (pov.), 1962; Dalëkaja raduga (pov.), 1964 (Eng. trs., *Far Rainbow*, 1967 and 1979; also contains Trudno byt' bogom [Eng. tr., *Hard to Be a God*, 1973]); Sueta vokrug divana (short story), in Fantastika 1964 g., 1964; Khiščnye vešči veka (fantastic pov.), 1965 (see above); Ponedel'nik načinaetsja v subbotu (pov.), 1965 (see above); Ulitka na sklone (pov.), vol. 1 in Èllinskij sekret, 1966, and vol. 2 in Bajkal 1968:1–2 (see above), and Skazka o trojke (pov.), in Angara 1968:4–5 (Eng. tr., *Tale of the Troika*, 1977), both published together, Frankfurt am Main, 1972; Vtoroe našestvie marsian (pov.), in Bajkal 1967:1 (Eng. tr., *The Second Invasion from Mars*, 1979); Otel' "U pogibšego alpinista" (pov.), in Junost' 1970:9–11, separate ed., 1982; Obitaemyj ostrov (pov.), 1971 (Eng. tr., *Prisoners of Power*, 1977); Malyš (pov.), in Avrora 1971:8–

11; Gadkie lebedi (pov.), Frankfurt am Main, 1972 (see above); Piknik na obočine (fantastic pov.), in Avrora 1972:7–10 (see above); Paren' iz preispodnej (fantastic pov.), in Avrora 1974:11–12 (Eng. tr., "The Kid from Hell," in *Escape Attempt*, 1982]; Za milliard let do konca sveta. Rukopis', obnaružennaja pri strannykh obstojatel'stvakh (fantastic pov.), in Znanie—sila 1976:9–12, 1977:1, separate ed., 1980 (see above); Žuk v muravejnike (fantastic pov.), in Znanie—sila 1979:9–12, 1980:1–3, 5, 6 (see above); Nenaznačennye vstreči (contains three pov.: Izvne, Piknik, na obočine, and Malyš), 1980; Zona, New York, 1983; Khromaja sud'ba (fantastic pov.), in Neva 1986:8–9.

*Secondary Lit.:* A. Gromova, in Lit. Rossija March 26, 1965, p. 11; V. Revič, in Molodaja gvardija 1965:4, in Lit. gazeta June 4, 1975, and in Lit. obozrenie 1980:12; V. Saparin, in Kommunist 1967:12; G. Gor, in Lit. gazeta Oct. 22, 1969, p. 6; D. Rudnev, in Grani, Frankfurt am Main, 78–79:1970–71; RSPP 7(2):1972; D. Suvin, in Canadian-American Slavic Studies 6:1972 and 8:1974; H. Földeak, Neue Tendenzen der sowj. Science Fiction, 1975; W. Kasack, in Osteuropa 1976:1; Ju. Smelkov, in Lit. obozrenie 1981:10.

**Suleyménov, Olzhás Omárovich** poet (b. May 18, 1936, Alma-Ata). Suleymenov is a Kazakh who writes in Russian. In 1959 he graduated in geology from Alma-Ata University and began a supplementary course of study at the Gorky Literary Institute in Moscow (graduated 1961). L. Martynov first introduced his poetry in *Literaturnaya gazeta* in 1959. His first collection, *Argamaki*, followed in 1961. In the same year Suleymenov published a verse epic dedicated to the cosmonaut Yury Gagarin, *Zemlya, poklonis cheloveku* (Earth, Bow Down before Man), that was awarded the prize of the Kazakhstan Komsomol in 1966. Suleymenov's poetry quickly attracted considerable attention but was primarily published by the Kazakhstan State Publishing House rather than in Moscow. He was allowed to make several trips abroad. *Glinyanaya kniga* (1969; The Clay Book) sparked much discussion because of its experimental character. In *Nad belymi rekami* (1970; Above the White Rivers), Suleymenov combined poetry and prose. He also wrote philological articles about Slavic and Turkish languages and literatures; he especially questions *The Lay of Igor's Campaign* (in an article sharply criticized by D. Likhachov). Suleymenov lives in Alma-Ata and is one of the secretaries of the Writers Union of the Kazakhstan SSR. In 1981 he was a delegate to the 26th Party Congress of the Communist Party.

Suleymenov began as a quite talented poet whose poems derive their effectiveness primarily from their imagery. The friendly reception from Russian poets and critics may be initially attributable to the Asiatic motifs (steppes, horses, nomads, yurts), but the symbolic power of his imagery is also an essential aspect. These images are often assembled from such diverse realms that interpretations vary widely. Many critics have detected elements reminiscent of V. Khlebnikov. Suleymenov loves paradoxes, searches for occasional neologisms, sees the word not only as a means for creating a poetic image but also as the object of linguistic interest. His poetry is close to prose and rich in alliterations and musical elements that can perhaps be traced to the harmony of vowels in the Turkish languages. Glinyanaya kniga recounts centuries of Kazakh history as a symbol for the present day and reveals Suleymenov's continual endeavor to gain self-knowledge through his poetic statement.

Works: Argamaki (poems), 1961, 1976; Solnečnye noči (poems), 1962; Noč'-parižanka (poems), 1963; Dobroe vremja voskhoda (poems), 1964; God obez'jany (poems), 1967; Sinjaja mgla i sinie molnii (scholarly article on the Igor tale), in Prostor 1968:9; Glinjanaja kniga (poems.), 1969; Nad belymi rekami (poems and prose), 1970; Povtorjaja v polden' (poems), 1973; Kruglaja zvezda (poems), 1975; Az i Ja: Kniga blagonamerennogo čitatelja (scholarly articles), 1975; Opredelenie berega (lyric and narrative poems), 1976, 1979; Prostaja kruglaja zevzda (interview), in Lit. obozrenie 1985:4.

Secondary Lit.: L. Martynov, in Lit. gazeta June 13, 1959; V. Portnov, in Novyj mir 1963:9; O. Mikhajlov, in Lit. gazeta June 20, 1964; Kh. Makhmudov, in Prostor 1969:6; A. Marčenko, in Voprosy lit. 1970:9; G. Averin, in Zvezda 1974:7; D. S. Likhačëv, in Zvezda 1976:6; V. Vladimirov, in Prostor 1980:6.

**Surkóv, Alekséy Aleksándrovich,** poet, literary official (b. Oct. 13 [Oct. 1], 1899, Serednevo, prov. Yaroslavl—d. June 14, 1983, Moscow). Surkov's father was a peasant. Surkov fought in the Civil War, then worked for the Party, at first in the provinces. In 1925 he joined the Communist Party. After moving to Moscow, Surkov worked as one of the RAPP officials in 1928, and in 1934 he graduated

from the Department of Literature of the Institute of Red Professors. Surkov made his first literary attempts in 1918, and his first collection of poetry about the Civil War, Zapev (1930; Solo Part), appeared in 1930; several military songs based on his texts became well known in the mid-1930s. From 1939 to 1945 Surkov was a correspondent at the front during the Polish campaign, the Finnish-Russian War, and World War II. He composed many patriotic lyrics to songs that reflected the soldiers' perceptions, and he became one of the most popular war poets. Some of his poems, with their natural engagement and masculine harshness and borne by hatred, wrath, and pain, provide a contrast to the typical hollow pathos of the time. He was awarded a Stalin Prize for his war poetry (for 1943–44, 1st class). From 1944 to 1946 he was the editor in chief of Literaturnaya gazeta; from 1945 to 1953, of Ogonyok. In 1949 Surkov became a member of the secretariat of the board of the Writers Union of the USSR; in 1951 he received a second Stalin Prize for his collection of old and new poetry, Mirumir (1950; Peace to the World) (for 1950, 2d class). After having advanced through the Party hierarchy in 1952, he replaced A. Fadeyev and assumed the leadership of the Writers Union as first secretary in 1953. He retained this position until 1959, that is, throughout the period of most of the REHABILITATIONS but also during the persecution of B. Pasternak. Surkov led many delegations to all corners of the world. In 1966 he lost his position as a candidate of the Central Committee of the Communist Party but remained a member of the Supreme Soviet, a position he held from 1954 on. From 1967 on, Surkov was regularly confirmed as one of the secretaries of the Writers Union. In addition he was on the board of the Writers Union of the RSFSR from 1958 on. Surkov, whose own creativity spent itself on his war poetry, also translated from the languages of countries within the Soviet sphere of influence. From 1962 to 1975 he was editor in chief of KRATKAYA LITERATURNAYA ENTSIKLOPEDIYA (Short Encyclopedia of Literature, vols. 1–8). He lived in Moscow.

Works: Zapev (poems), 1930; Nastuplenie (poems), 1932; Tak my rosli (poems), 1940; Dekabr' pod Moskvoj (poems), 1942; Soldatskoe serdce (poems), 1943; Miru-mir (poems), 1950; Vostok i Zapad (poems), 1957; Golosa vremeni. Zametki na poljakh istorii lit. 1934–65 (essays and talks), 1965; Posle vojny: Stikhi 1945–70 (poems), 1972—Sobr. soč., 4 vols., 1965–66; Izbr., 2 vols., 1974.

Secondary Lit.: A. S. Kulinič, 1953; O. Reznik, in Oktjabr' 1954:2, 2d ed., 1969, 3d ed., 1979; S. V. Vladimirov, D. M. Moldavskij, 1956; I. Grinberg, in Znamja 1958:3, separate study, 1958, and in Naš sovremennik 1974:10; M. Sobol', in Izbr., 1974; S. Baruzdin, in his Ljudi i knigi, 1978; B. Leonov, in Moskva 1984:10.

**Svetlóv, Mikhaíl Arkádyevich,** poet (b. June 17, [June 4], 1903, Yekaterinoslav—d. Sept. 28, 1964, Moscow). Svetlov came from a family of Jewish artisans. In 1919 he was one of the first members of the Komsomol; in 1920 he volunteered to fight in the Civil War. After 1922 he was in Moscow, where he published his first volume of verse, Relsy (Rails), in 1923. He studied at Moscow University in 1927–28. Svetlov became well known and popular with his romantic, revolutionary balladlike poem "Grenada" (1926; Granada). His skepticism regarding the departure from the ideals of the Revolution represented by NEP and by upstart, "unsmiling" officials and his inclination toward the helpless ("Starushka" [1947; The Old Woman]) led to constant attacks on his work by the official critics. Svetlov, who made no contributions to the theme of the Five-Year Plan at the beginning of the 1930s, wrote "Kakhovka" (1935), a song based on revolutionary experiences that was very popular before World War II. He turned to dramatic writing, but even his first play, Glubokaya provintsiya (1935; The Distant Province), in which he draws attention to the lack of personal happiness of the peasants on the kolkhoz, was attacked in Pravda (April 10, 1936) and taken off the stage. Mys Zhelaniya (1940; The Cape of Desire) and other dramas remained unprinted and unperformed. During World War II, Svetlov was a correspondent for Krasnaya zvezda in Leningrad. He wrote Dvadtsat vosem (1942; Twenty-eight) and Liza Chaykina (1942), the only two of his poetic cycles in which the characters are the same, and achieved the recognition he deserved for his poem "Italyanets" (1943; The Italian). After the war Svetlov was actually able to publish two volumes of selected works, but his name was almost never mentioned by reviewers or critics. At the Second Congress of the Writers Union of the USSR in 1954, in which Svetlov participated without the right to speak, S. Kirsanov and O. Berggolts spoke on his behalf. Svetlov resumed literary activity. His volume of new poems, Gorizont (1959; The Horizon), was welcomed positively. Full recognition came to Svetlov only after his death; in an

unusual departure from convention, he was posthumously awarded the Lenin Prize in 1967.

Svetlov's verse, particularly his early poems, derives from a concrete situation, most often narrated, which is almost always contrasted to another, spatially or temporally distanced situation. In such a manner Svetlov connects the image of a student, starved for education, with Joan of Arc in "Rabfakovke" (1926; To a Coed from the Workers' Department). The second level is often of a romantic, unreal nature. As in the inner monologue of the soldier in front of the enemy he has killed ("Italyanets"), Svetlov often dealt with the problem of death. His poetry is always multilayered; it leaves much unsaid and consequently lives on in the imagination. It is predominantly concrete; the subject matter generates symbols that express spiritual and humane intent. Svetlov is an independent writer who "loved to soften pathos with a gentle irony" (Smelyakov).

Works: Rel'sy (poems), 1923; Kniga stikhov (poems), 1929; Skazka (play), 1939; Dvadcat' let spust'ja (play), 1940; Izbr. stikhi (poems), 1948; Izbr. stikhi i p'esy (poems and plays), 1950; Stikhi i p'esy (poems and plays), 1957; Gorizont (poems), 1959; Sorok let moej liriki (poems), 1965; Stikhotvorenija i poèmy (lyric and narrative poems), 1966; Stikhi poslednikh let (poems), 1970; P'esy (plays), 1970—Izbr. proizv., 2 vols., 1965; Sobr. soč., 3 vols., 1974–75.

Secondary Lit.: E. Ljubarёva, 1960; Z. Papernyj, in Oktjabr' 1961:1, in Novyj mir 1963:6, and in a separate study, 1967; E. Vinokurov, in Smena 1963:11; Ja. Smeljakov, in Svetlov's Izbr. proizv., 1965; F. G. Svetov, 1967; Ty pomniš', tovarišč (memoirs), 1973; L. Ozerov, in Lit. gazeta June 28, 1978, p. 7; M. Aliger, in her Tropinka vo rži, 1980; Ja. Khelemskij, in Lit. gazeta July 6, 1983, p. 6.

**Syómin, Vitály Nikoláyevich,** prose writer (b. June 12, 1927, Rostov-on-Don—d. May 10, 1978, Koktebel). From 1942 to 1945 Syomin was a German prisoner of war. He passed his high-school graduation examination in 1948 after working in a factory and attending a technical school. Between 1948 and 1953 he studied at the Rostov Pedagogical Institute in the Department of Literature. In January 1953 Syomin was expelled from the institute for having been a prisoner of war; he worked in a penal camp in the Kubyshev area. In 1954 he was permitted to exchange his work at physical labor for a post as a teacher in a small village school in a remote province.

There Syomin succeeded in completing his studies at the Taganrog Pedagogical Institute by correspondence in 1956, in which year he was allowed to reside once again in Rostov. From this time on, he began publishing short stories, collected for the first time in the volume *Shtorm na Tsimle* (1960; Storm on the Tsimla Reservoir). From 1958 to 1962 Syomin worked as a journalist for a local newspaper, then for television. With his povest *Semero v odnom dome* (1965; Eng. tr., Seven in One House, 1968), Syomin began to publish in *Novy mir*. Because of the story's mercilessly revealing portrayal of life in the area around Rostov, Syomin was criticized, even in *Pravda* (Aug. 11, 1965); the case generated widespread discussion. Syomin was never appointed a delegate to the congresses of the Writers Union of the Soviet Union.

Syomin's talent received its initial impulse from the injustice that he suffered at the hands of suspicious Soviet authorities who penalized him for the misfortune of being taken prisoner as a child. He depicted the fate of the 15-year-olds who matured quickly under the influence of World War II and the German occupation in *Lastochka-zvyozdochka* (1963; Little Swallow–Little Star). In *Sto dvadtsat kilometrov do zheleznoy dorogi* (1964; 120 Kilometers to the Railroad), Syomin elected to use a first-person narrative structure in order to render more documentarily his observations of people in a village lying far from any civilization, without electricity or medical aid, where the people are closer to belief in sorcery than to any knowledge of modern cities. The work's optimistic epilogue, obedient to the demands of SOCIALIST REALISM, is so artificial that it can only be explained as the result of intervention on the part of the editorial board and the censors. *Semero v odnom dome*, in which Syomin paints an undistorted portrait of the sorely-tried, simple Russian woman, also owes its effect to the author's love of truth and to his gift for comprehending the kind of life lived by those who vegetate on the outskirts of a city, leading a precarious material existence, and whose life is determined by the needs that arise as the result of war, supply problems, the housing shortage, crime, and narrow-minded philistinism. Syomin's *Nagrudny znak "Ost"* (1976; The "Ost" Order) reflects his experiences in a German concentration camp; however, it also becomes an indictment of totalitarian oppression in his own country in its depiction of the human being at the mercy of wickedness and baseness. In a way, Syomin's prose forges an autobiographical chain. His narra-

tion rambles and abounds in details and characters, but it is nevertheless compelling in its vividness and sincerity.

*Works: Štorm na Cimle* (short stories), 1960; *Lastočka-zvëzdočka* (pov.), 1965; *Povest'*, *Rasskazy* (pov. and short stories), 1965 (contains *Sto dvadcat' kilometrov do železnoj dorogi*); *Semero v odnom dome* (pov.), in *Novyj mir* 1965:6 (see above); *Asja Aleksandrovna* (short story), in *Novyj mir* 1965:11; *V sorok vtorom* (memoirs), in *Novyj mir* 1968:5; *Ženja i Valentina* (novel), in *Novyj mir* 1972:11, separate ed., 1974; *Sem'sot šest'desjat tretij* (novel and pov.), 1977; *Nagrudnyj znak "Ost"* (novel, pov., and short stories), 1978; *Plotina* (novel), in *Družba narodov* 1981:5; *Rabočie zametki* (essays), 1984.

*Secondary Lit.:* A. Makarov, in *Znamja* 1966:3; V. Lakšin, in *Novyj mir* 1966:8; RSPP 7(2):1972; V. Razumnevič, in *Oktjabr'* 1974:5; L. Lavlinskij, in *Novyj mir* 1979:4; V. Kamjanov, in *Novyj mir* 1982:1; E. Džičoeva, in *Znamja* 1986:3.

**Syómushkin, Tíkhon Zakhárovich,** prose writer (b. June 26 [June 13], 1900, Staraya Kutlya, prov. Penza—d. May 6, 1970, Moscow). Syomushkin's father was a peasant. Syomushkin worked as a teacher after the Revolution; he was at the same time (1922–24) a student at the Second Moscow University. Beginning in 1924 Syomushkin participated in several expeditions to the northeastern Siberian peninsula of Chukotka, held various cultural and political posts, and contributed to the creation and recording of the Chukchi literary language under the supervision of V. G. Bogoraz; in 1928 he directed the first boarding school for Chukchi children. After 1932 Syomushkin wrote two books about the Chukchi and the Eskimos. *Chukotka* (1939) relates his personal experiences; it was popular as a children's book despite its lack of clarity and its psychological weakness (most obvious in the dialogue). Written in the spirit of anti-COSMOPOLITANISM that characterized postwar ideology, Syomushkin's *Alitet ukhodit v gory* (1947–49; Eng. tr., Alitet Goes to the Hills, 1948), reflects the life of the Chukchi from their exploitation by Americans and kulaks to their deliverance by the Bolsheviks; the novel was awarded a Stalin Prize (for 1948, 2d class) and disseminated by Moscow in translation. Syomushkin wrote hardly anything afterward. In 1952 he was admitted to the Communist Party; in 1955 he visited the North Polar Station and wrote a short story about it, *Polyot v Arktiku* (1956; Flight to the Arctic). The aesthetic imperfections of Syomushkin's prose considerably weaken the potential that lies in the folkloristic novelty of his material.

Works: *Na Čukotke*, 1938 (early draft of the following); *Čukotka* (pov.), 1939; *Alitet ukhodit v gory* (novel), 2 vols., 1947–49 (see above);

*Polët v Arktiku* (short story), 1956; *Priključenija Ajvama* (pov.), 1956; *Ugrjum-Sever* (short stories and memoirs), 1968.—*Izbr. proiz.*, 2 vols., 1970.
Secondary Lit.: Ja. Černjak, in *Novyj mir.* 1948:5; A. Markuša, in *Znamja* 1956:1; *RSPP* 4:1966; "Pevec severa," in *Dal'nij vostok* 1970:6.

# T

**Tamizdát** (there-publishing), a linguistic formation analogous to SAMIZDAT (self-publishing) and Gosizdat (State Publishing House) that refers to publication abroad of the works of authors living in the USSR. Tamizdat is a product of Soviet censorship, which forbids the state publishing houses to publish works that run counter to the prevailing view of the Communist Party. The term *tamizdat* came into being in 1957 and is connected with the publication of B. Pasternak's novel *Doktor Zhivago* in Milan. As in this case, publication abroad, that is, tamizdat, generally follows years of attempting to get a work published at home. At the beginning of the Soviet period, works by authors still living in the Soviet Union were frequently published abroad, especially by émigré publishers in Berlin. In 1929, however, B. Pilnyak was sharply criticized for allowing *Krasnoye derevo* to be published in Berlin, although he had used VOKS (All-Union Society for Cultural Relations with Foreign Countries) as an intermediary. Since then, publication abroad has been impossible. Whereas Pasternak's behavior was condemned by many otherwise liberal writers, in the following case—Terts/Arzhak, which became known in 1965—and in all subsequent cases, only support for tamizdat authors has been expressed (signatures collected, and so forth). In 1966 A. Sinyavsky and Yu. Daniel were convicted for their works written using pseudonyms that were published in tamizdat after 1959 and 1962, respectively. The worldwide protest has compelled the authorities to find other ways of harassing tamizdat authors since that time. In most cases they have been expelled from the Writers Union. At the beginning of the 1970s, the authorities made the effort to persuade tamizdat authors such as B. Okudzhava, V. Voynovich, A. Gladilin, V. Shalamov, and the brothers Strugatsky to denounce publication abroad and to keep them as Soviet writers. Only in a few cases is it known whether an author voluntarily submitted his work to the West for publication or whether samizdat copies made their way to the West and were published without the author's consent.

Tamizdat includes publication in the numerous émigré journals such as *Ekho, Grani, Kontinent, Novy zhurnal, Strelets, Vestnik RKhD*, or *Vremya i my*, as well as works issued by publishing houses, especially those in the United States, France, the Federal Republic of Germany, and England. Before VAAP was founded in 1973, important tamizdat authors were the following (the year refers to the publication of a book, which was preceded by an ever increasing number of publications in journals): 1957 B. Pasternak; 1959 A. Terts; 1962 V. Tarsis; 1965 N. Arzhak (Daniel), L. Chukovskaya; 1966 (only in journals) V. Shalamov; 1967 Ye. Ginzburg; 1968 A. Solzhenitsyn; 1969 A. Amalrik, A. Galich; 1972 V. Kazakov, V. Maksimov, N. Gorbanevskaya, A. and B. Strugatsky, A. Gladilin. By creating VAAP the Soviet government attempted to halt the growth of tamizdat, yet only the content of the works published abroad and regulations concerning foreign currency provide a legal framework for harassing the authors. Among the important authors who published in tamizdat after 1973 and who later emigrated are: 1975 G. Vladimov, V. Voynovich, L. Kopelev (in German since 1971); 1978 F. Gorenshteyn (in German), S. Dovlatov; 1981 Yu. Kublanovsky. In this time frame those whose opportunities for publication were either nonexistent or severely restricted included: 1974 V. Kornilov; 1975 G. Aygi (in Czech since 1967), L. Borodin, V. Yerofeyev; 1981 S. Lipkin; 1983 I. Lisnyanskaya.

Group tamizdat came into being in 1979 with the almanac METROPOL; at the time of publication, some of the authors participating published both at home and abroad (V. Aksyonov, A. Bitov, F. Iskander, F. Gorenshteyn); some maintained a distance from tamizdat (A. Voznesensky); others withdrew from the Writers Union and became tamizdat authors (S. Lipkin, I. Lisnyanskaya). The *Katalog* (1982) of the independent Russian Club of Belletrists that was compiled in Moscow in 1980 and also submitted for publication in the Soviet Union was a second publication of group tamizdat. In addition to the publisher F. Berman, the seven authors who are represented with excerpts from their works and tabular résumés include the *Metropol* author Ye. Popov and the writer who previously published in the Viennese almanac *Neue russische Literatur* (1979–80), Ye. Kharitonov.

Together with the tamizdat of living authors, to whom the term is generally applied, there is the tamizdat of deceased authors whose works are entirely or partially suppressed in the Soviet Union. Important posthumous, usually scholarly, editions (collected or individual works) of the works of Russian authors who did not emigrate, whose possiblities for publication were held in check, and who often became victims of the purges appeared in the years mentioned or from that year on: 1954 N. Klyuyev; 1955 O. Mandelshtam; 1962–68 N. Gumilyov; 1966 B. Pilnyak; 1967–68 A. Akhmatova; 1968 M. Bulgakov; 1968–71 V. Khlebnikov; 1969 A. Platonov; 1970 V. Grossman; 1971 Vyach. Ivanov; 1974 D. Kharms, A. Vvedensky; 1975 N. Oleynikov; 1976 N. Erdman; 1977 M. Kuzmin; 1978 G. Obolduyev; 1979 M. Shkapskaya, S. Parnok; 1980 V. Grossman; 1981 V. Vysotsky; 1982 K. Vaginov, B. Vakhtin, M. Voloshin; 1983 V. Narbut.

The third aspect of tamizdat concerns the publications of authors in EMIGRATION. The new books by representatives of the third emigration who were once a part of "Soviet literature" come closest to the tamizdat of authors still living in the Soviet Union. These are followed by works of authors of the first emigration whose output has generally been sanctioned (such as M. Gorky), who have been endorsed anew after experiencing a temporary ban (such as M. Tsvetayeva, A. Kuprin, I. Bunin), or who, after being excluded for a long time, are now tolerated except for a few works (such as I. Shmelyov, A. Remizov, V. Nabokov). Finally, tamizdat includes the works of writers from the first and second emigration none of whose works have yet been published at home (such as D. Merezhkovsky, Yu. Felzen, or N. Morshen).

Tamizdat primarily serves the natural function of facilitating publication that is free from censorship and of rescuing from oblivion the published and unpublished material of deceased authors. Since tamizdat publications are brought into the Soviet Union, not in large numbers to be sure but not only in individua copies, and are acquired by a few centra libraries for restricted collections, tamizda reaches the strata of scholarly specialists a well as the especially interested reader, primarily writers. Thus tamizdat exercises an influence, however limited, on literature written in the Soviet Union. Moreover, tamizda has an effect on Soviet publication policy many living authors attained the long-denied permission to publish at home after publication through tamizdat (for example, G. Vladimov, V. Aksyonov). The fundamental certainty of tamizdat also offers an escape from the absolute despair over the impossibility of publishing one's own works that, for example completely silenced D. Klenovsky from 1926 to 1945 and largely silenced K. Paustovsky from 1946 to 1953. The censors allow some authors to depict events with greater veracity in order to counter a drop in the quality of literature published in the Soviet Union as compared to that published abroad and to keep writers from publishing in tamizdat (for example, Yu. Trifonov). For some deceased authors, publication at home, usually in a very small print run, occurred after one or more works were published abroad; this ha been the case for O. Mandelshtam, B. Pilnyak Vyach. Ivanov, N. Gumilyov, Ye. Zamyatin As an unfortunate, politically conditioned emergency measure, tamizdat serves as an important link between "Soviet literature" sanctioned in the Soviet Union and the literature of emigration. Tamizdat accentuates the unity of contemporary Russian literature, independent of its point of origin.

*Secondary Lit.*: See CENSORSHIP: EMIGRATION; LITERARY JOURNALS; METROPOL; SAMIZDAT; VAAP. In addition, nearly all journal published in emigration fulfill the role of tamizdat, including the almanacs *Apollon '77* Paris, 1977; *NRL: Neue russische Literatu* (Russian and German), Salzburg, 1978, 1979-80, 1981–82; *Katalog*, Ann Arbor, 1982.

**Tan, V. G.** (also N. A. Tan; pseud. of Vladími Gérmanovich Bogoráz), ethnographer and pros writer (b. April 27 [April 15], 1865, Ovruch prov. Volhynia—d. May 10, 1936, on his wa to Rostov-on-Don). Bogoraz came to St. Pe tersburg in 1880; while a student at St. Pe tersburg University he joined the revolution ary populists. After a three-year incarceratio in the Peter-Paul Fortress, he was exiled t Kolyma (in northeastern Siberia) for ten years There he devoted himself to intensive scho

arly research in the disciplines of ethnography, folklore, and linguistics, with the result
that the Imperial Academy of Sciences included him in an expedition in 1894–96 to
study the Chukchi, secured his return to St.
Petersburg, and sent him off again in 1900–1.
In addition to his scholarly studies, Bogoraz
also published poetry and prose under his
pseudonyn Tan; he made his literary debut in
*Russkaya mysl* and *Russkoye bogatstvo* in
1896. Tan attracted attention with his *Chu-
kotskiye rasskazy* (1899; Tales from Chukotka). His first novel, *Vosem plemyon* (1902;
Eight Tribes), was followed by *Zhertva drakona* (1909; The Dragon's Sacrifice) and *Na
ozere Loche* (1914; On Lake Loch), fictional
events set in paleolithic times. Tan became
known in Western Europe in translation. An
edition of his works published in 1910–11
consisted of ten volumes. After the Revolution, Tan initially worked as a consultant for
the Museum of Anthropology and Ethnography in Leningrad, then taught as a professor
in local institutes and founded the Institute
of Northern Peoples. He was attacked politically because of his non-Bolshevik past. In
1932 he founded the Academy of Science's
Museum of the History of Religion and became its director. In the early 1930s he began
publishing new literary works: *Kolymskiye
rasskazy* (1931; Tales from Kolyma) and *Vos-
kressheye plemya* (1935; The Resurrected
Tribe), a novel about the post-Revolutionary
development of the Chukchi. After his death,
Tan's works were suppressed for more than
20 years; with the cooperation of his earlier
colleagues, however, some of his prose was
reprinted after 1958.

*Works:* Čukotskie rasskazy (short stories),
1899, 1962; *Vosem' plemën* (novel), 1902, 1962;
Žertva drakona (novel), 1909; *Na ozere Loče*
(pov.), 1914; *Sojuz molodykh* (novel), 1928,
3d ed., 1963; *Kolymskie rasskazy* (short stories), 1931; *Čukči* (scholarly study), 2 vols.,
1934–39; *Voskressee plemja* (novel), 1935;
Severnye rasskazy (short stories), 1958.—Sobr.
soč., 10 vols., 1910–11; 4 vols., 1928–29.
*Secondary Lit.:* Pamjati V. G. Bogoraza, 1937;
T. Z. Sëmuškin, in Tan's Severnye rasskazy,
1958; B. L. Komanovskij, in Tan's Severnye
rasskazy, 1958, and in Lit. Rossija April 16,
1965, p. 14; B. I. Kartašev, Po strane olennykh
ljudej, 1959; M. Voskobojnikov, in Družba
narodov 1965:4.

**Tarásov-Rodiónov, Aleksándr Ignátyevich,**
prose writer (b. Oct. 7 [Sept. 25], 1885, Astrakhan—d. Sept. 3, 1938 [?], while impris-

oned). Tarasov-Rodionov's father was a surveyor. Tarasov-Rodionov joined the RSDRP
(Social Democrats) in 1905 as a member of a
Bolshevik combat team. In 1908 he completed
his law studies at Kazan University. During
the Revolution and Civil War, Tarasov-Rodionov rose to the rank of company commander in the Red Army. Between 1921 and
1924 he held the post of examining magistrate
in the Supreme Court. Tarasov-Rodionov belonged initially to the literary group KUZ-
NITSA; in 1922 he was one of the founders of
the militantly dogmatic association OKTYABR.
His novel *Shokolad* (1922; Eng. tr., Chocolate,
1932), first published in *Molodaya gvardiya*
and soon translated into many languages, generated sharp discussion. In the novel, Tarasov-Rodionov defended the death sentence
passed on an established Bolshevik and head
of the secret police in a provincial town in
spite of the fact that his misdeed was a minor
one (the acceptance, through his wife, of a
counterrevolutionary gift of some chocolate
bars) and that the judges were aware that the
punishment exceeded the crime. Tarasov-Rodionov even compels the condemned man
himself to recognize the necessity of his personal disgrace and execution for the greater
good of Communist politics. Tarasov-Rodionov's presentation of the miscarriage of justice
based on popular sentiment as determined by
the Party encountered the opposition of various critics; A. Voronsky emphasized the considerable aesthetic defects of his prose. Tarasov-Rodionov's intolerant literary-political
position is also expressed in "Klassiches-
koye" i klassovoye (1923; "Classical" and
Class), his most important contribution to the
journal *Na postu*; the article crudely attacks
Voronsky (among others). A later, never-com-
pleted trilogy, *Tyazholye shagi* (A Heavy
Tread), which in the novels *Fevral* (1927; Eng.
tr., February 1917, 1931) and *Iyul* (1930; July)
describes the Revolution in memoiristic style,
was aesthetically and ideologically condemned. Tarasov-Rodionov participated in the
First Congress of the Writers Union of the
USSR in 1934, but without the right to vote.
In 1937 he was once again attacked for *Shokolad*, branded "an enemy of the people,"
and, as if following the plot of his novel,
probably shot. Tarasov-Rodionov underwent
REHABILITATION beginning in 1956. His works,
however, have not been reprinted and are
criticized for presenting the Party point of
view incorrectly.

*Works:* Šokolad (pov.), in Molodaja gvardija 1922:6–7 (reprinted, in Opal'nye povesti,
New York 1955 (see above); "Klassičeskoe" i

*klassovoe*, in *Na postu* 1923:2–3; *Fevral'* (novel), 1927 (see above); *Ijul'* (novel), 1930.
*Secondary Lit.*: A. Voronskij, in *Krasnaja nov'* 1923:1 and in his *Lit. portrety*, vol. 2, 1929, pp. 262–66; L. Averbakh, in *Molodaja gvardija* 1925:10–11; V. Aleksandrova (1939), in her *Lit. i žizn'*, New York, 1969, pp. 324–25, and in *Ostprobleme* 1952:47.

**Tarkóvsky, Arsény Aleksándrovich** poet (b. June 25 [June 12], 1907, Yelizavetgrad). Tarkovsky studied at the Academy of Literature (Advanced State Courses in Literary Studies) from 1925 to 1929. He worked on the editorial staff of the newspaper *Gudok* from 1924 to 1929 and on that of the army newspaper *Boyevaya trevoga* from 1941 to 1943. Since 1932 Tarkovsky has been active as a translator, particularly of the Oriental classics. Tarkovsky was more than 50 years old when he made his first public appearance with his own poetry, which had remained unpublished for decades. Together with a few poems in almanacs and journals, six volumes of his poetry appeared over the next 20 years: *Pered snegom* (1962; Before the Snow), *Zemle zemnoye* (1966; To the Earth, the Earthly), *Vestnik* (1969; Messenger), *Stikhotvoreniya* (1974; Poems), *Zimniy den* (1980; Winter's Day), and the comprehensive collection *Izbrannoye* (1982; Selected Works). He also published a collection of his translations from the Georgian, *Volshebnye gory* (1978; Magic Mountains). Experts quickly classed Tarkovsky among the leading poets in the Soviet Union. He lives in Moscow, is not part of the literary establishment, and only participated in the congresses of the Writers Union in 1954 and 1965; however, he did sign the petition for A. Sinyavsky and Yu. Daniel in 1966. For his translations he was awarded the State Prize of the Kara-Kalpak ASSR (1967) and of the Turkmen SSR (1971). Tarkovsky also writes theoretical contributions and reviews.

Tarkovsky's philosophical lyric poetry stands in the tradition of F. Tyutchev, A. Fet, and especially that of the ACMEISTS, including B. Pasternak and M. Tsvetayeva. Not avant-garde experiments but far-reaching and exhaustive use of the possibilities of the classical tradition determines the form of his verse. His concern is to contribute to the harmony of the external world through poetry, as A. Blok did. The vast wealth of images and metaphors makes his poetry complex and occasionally provides the opportunity for time-specific interpretation of the generally timeless themes of art, love, humanity, death. Tarkovsky can

start with specific situations, but they will span space and time as with everything he uses and reveal the poet as the mediator between the past and the present, between cultures (for Tarkovsky, often Roman poetry). Tarkovsky believes in the magic of words; for him "the word in prose is proportional to the word in poetry as a physical experiment is to a miracle" (1967), and thus he suffers from the imperfectibility of linguistic expression, from the incompatibility of opposites that are united in a higher sense, and from disjunctive appearances, but he is far along in achieving their synthesis in poetry. Tarkovsky's poems are laconic and measured; the discipline of form reflects the discipline of thought.

*Works: Pered snegom* (poems), 1962; *Povest' o prekrasnoj Gulaim*, 1958, 2d ed.; 1965; *Zemle zemnoe* (poems), 1966; *Vestnik* (poems), 1969; articles, in *Voprosy lit.* 1967:5–6, 1969:1, 1972:2, in *Lit. gazeta* Aug. 2, 1967, p. 7, Nov. 22, 1967, p. 5, Dec. 13, 1967, p. 6; *Stikhotvorenija* (poems), 1974; *Volšebnye gory: Poèzija Gruzii* (poems), 1978; *Ja polon nadežd i very v buduščee russkoj poèzii* (interview), in *Voprosy lit.* 1979:6; *Zimnij den'* (poems), 1980.—*Izbr.*, 1982.
*Secondary Lit.*: A. Urban, in *Zvezda* 1964:5, 1966:11, and 1975:9; V. Portnov, in *Novyj mir* 1967:1; B. Runin, in *Voprosy lit.* 1967:5; A. Mikhajlov, in *Znamja* 1968:9; S. Arro, in *Zvezda* 1972:3; W. Kasack, in *Osteuropa* 1975:4; S. Čuprinin, in *Lit. obozrenie* 1980:8; A. Lavrin, in *Družba narodov* 1983:7.

**Társis, Valéry Yákovlevich**, prose writer (b. Sept. 23 [Sept. 10], 1906, Kiev—d. March 3, 1983, Bern). Tarsis's father was of Greek ancestry; he worked as a groom and later as a stock clerk and died in prison in 1942. His mother was a Ukrainian. Tarsis studied at the University of Rostov-on-Don from 1924 to 1929 and received his doctorate for a study of the poetry of the Italian Renaissance. He published a small reference book, *Sovremennye russkiye pisateli* (1930; Contemporary Russian Authors), among other things, and worked in Moscow until 1937 in the State Publishing House for Literature. Two of his own short stories appeared in *Novy mir: Noch v Kharachoye* (1937; A Night in Kharachoye) and *Dezdemona* (1938). Tarsis earned a living as a translator. As a war correspondent at the front during World War II, he was seriously wounded three times. After the war, he again earned his living as a translator in Moscow and wrote numerous novels, only some of which were published many years later in the West. He managed to bring all the manuscripts to England in 1961. The first to be published was the short story *Skazaniye o siney mukhe* (1962; Eng. tr., *The Bluebottle*, 1962), a biting satire about Soviet life in his time. On Aug. 23, 1962, Tarsis was arrested and sent to a penal psychiatric institution; in March 1963, after worldwide protest, he was released. He announced his withdrawal from the Communist Party and the Writers Union in 1963. His time in prison was reflected in the povest *Palata No. 7* (1963; Eng. tr., *Ward 7*, 1965). Numerous translations awakened an international interest in Tarsis's fate. In 1965 Tarsis served as the editor of the SAMIZDAT journal *Sfinsky*. In 1966 he was granted an exit permit to visit England as he requested (Feb. 7); the return journey, however, was denied him, thus causing his expatriation (Feb. 18). From 1967 to 1970 he lived in Germany; then he moved to Switzerland where he completed a collection of novels, dramas, and poems. He regularly wrote about newly published Russian literature in the journal *Zeit-Bild*.

Among the works Tarsis wrote in the Soviet Union, the trilogy *Kombinat naslazhdeniy* (1967; Eng. trs., vol. 1, *The Gay Life*, 1968; vol. 2, *The Pleasure Factory*, 1967; vol. 3, *A Thousand Illusions*, 1969) and an autobiographical povest, *Sedaya yunost* (1968; Gray Youth), were published in addition to *Stolknoveniye s zerkalom* (1970; Collision with the Mirror), the first volume of a planned ten-volume novel *Riskovannaya zhizn Valentina Almazova* (The Dangerous Life of Valentin Almazov). The manuscript of this great prose work conceived as an encyclopedia of daily life in the Soviet Union from the 1930s to the present day was completed in Switzerland with volumes 6 through 9. Volume 8, *Nedaleko ot Moskvy* (1981; Near Moscow), appeared on the occasion of his 75th birthday. Tarsis's prose is consciously influenced by F. Dostoyevsky. The uncertain individual who is searching for stability makes a frequent appearance. The narrative is rich with reflections. The work is shaped by religion and seeks to expose the misuse of power and the absence of spiritual freedom in the Soviet Union through satiric expression, and thereby to illustrate how conditions have worsened, on the whole, owing to the Revolution. Much that originated in emigration, including the novel *Moi bratya Karamazovy* (My Brothers Karamazov) and the poetic tragedy *Faust v adu* (Faust in Hell), remained unpublished at his death.

*Works: Sovremennye russkie pisateli* (literary handbook), 1930; *Noč' v Kharačoe* (short story), in *Novyj mir* 1937:5; *Dezdemona* (pov.), in *Novyj mir* 1938:9; *Skazanie o sinej mukhe*. *Krasnoe i čërnoe* (short story), Frankfurt am Main, 1963, 2d ed., 1966 (see above); *Palata No. 7* (pov.), Frankfurt am Main, 1966, 2d ed., 1974 (see above); *Kombinat naslaždenij* (novel-trilogy), Frankfurt am Main, 1967 (see above); *Sedaja junost'* (autobiography), Frankfurt am Main, 1968; *Riskovannaja žizn' Valentina Almazova* (novel sequence), vol. 1: *Stolknovenie s zerkalom*, Frankfurt am Main, 1970–; vol. 8, *Nedaleko ot Moskvy*, Frankfurt am Main, 1981.—*Sobr. soč.*, 12 vols., Frankfurt am Main, 1967–(vols., 1, 4, 8, and 12 have appeared).

*Secondary Lit.:* Biography, in *Grani*, Frankfurt am Main, 57:1965; deprivation of his citizenship, in *Lit. gazeta* Feb. 22, 1966; Z. Maurina, *Porträts russ. Schriftsteller*, 1968; P. Hübner, in *Berichte des Bundesinstituts für ostwissenschaftl. und internationale Studien* 1969:63; M. Bogojavlenskij, in *Grani* 70:1969; B. Skryl'nikov, in *Russkaja mysl'*, Paris, May 18, 1978, p. 14; P. Sager, in *ZeitBild*, Bern, 1981:19; W. Kasack, in *Neue Zürcher Zeitung* March 8, 1983; S. Juren'en, in *Russkaja mysl'* March 31, 1983, p. 13.

**Tatyánicheva, Lyudmíla Konstantínovna,** poet (b. Dec. 19, [Dec. 6], 1915, Ardatov, prov. Simbirsk, the Urals—d. April 9, 1980, Moscow). Tatyanicheva attended school in Sverdlovsk; beginning in 1930 she worked as a turner while at the same time taking evening courses at the Sverdlovsk Institute of Nonferrous Metals (1932–34). In 1934 she moved to the industrial city of Magnitogorsk, then under construction, where she remained until 1944, working as a newspaper editor. In 1941 she graduated from the Gorky Literary Institute by correspondence and joined the Communist Party. From 1944 to 1946 she was director of the regional publishing house in Chelyabinsk, where her first volume of poetry, *Vernost* (1944; Loyalty), was published. From then on, she was published partly in Moscow, for example, *Rodnoy Ural* (1950; Native Urals), partly in the publishing houses in the Urals, for example, *Vishnyovy sad* (1954; Cherry Orchard) and a selection of her poems from the period 1940–55 (Sverdlovsk, 1965). Beginning in 1958 Tatyanicheva occupied various positions as a literary official; she belonged to the board of the Writers Union of the RSFSR (serving as one of the secretaries from 1965 to 1975) and to the board of the

Writers Union of the USSR (from 1967 on). Around 1970 Tatyanicheva moved from Chelyabinsk to Moscow. A volume of her poems, Zoryanka (1970), received the Gorky Prize in 1971.

Tatyanicheva felt herself to be the poet of the Urals, which, as industrial center and homeland, became the major theme of her verse. Her patriotism and her stand in support of factory workers and of building the Soviet Union mark her work as belonging to SOCIALIST REALISM. Tatyanicheva's often-printed poetry is declamatory and primitive.

Works: Vernost' (poems), 1944; Rodnoj Ural (poems), 1950; Sinegor'e (poems), 1958; Malakhit (poems), 1960; Carevny (poems), 1968; Zorjanka (poems), 1970; Vysokij moj bereg (poems), 1971; Pora medosbora (poems), 1974; Khvojnyj mëd (poems), 1978.—Izbr., lirika 1940–65, 1965.

Secondary Lit.: B. Solov'ëv, in Moskva 1963:10; A. Mikhajlov, in Novyj mir 1966:3 and in Lit. gazeta Oct. 6, 1971, p. 5; T. Lebedeva, in Ural 1972:10; V. Razumnevič, in Pravda July 5, 1974; I. Grinberg, in Lit. obozrenie 1974:10; S. Soloženkina, in Lit. gazeta Dec. 19, 1979, p. 6; V. Fëdorov, in Naš sovremennik 1982:10.

Táuber, Yekaterína Leonídovna, Poet (b. Dec. 3 [Nov. 20], 1903, Kharkov). Tauber's father was a professor of criminal and commercial law at Kharkov University. Tauber emigrated with her parents to Belgrade in 1920, studied French language and literature at the university there, and graduated in 1928. She taught French for four years in a school. In Belgrade in 1933 she served as translator and copublisher of an anthology of new Yugoslavian poetry published by the Union of Russian Authors and Journalists in Yugoslavia. Her own poetry, which she had begun writing at the age of seven, appeared in journals after 1927. In 1936 she married Konstantin Starov and moved to the French Riviera. While her first volume of poetry, Odinochestvo (1935; Loneliness), is entirely shaped by suffering— "You don't write poems out of happiness"— more confident tones permeate the second, Pod senyu olivy (1948; In the Shadow of the Olive Tree), and especially the third, Plecho s plechom (1955; Shoulder to Shoulder), making evident her acceptance of a God-given fate and her grateful appreciation of nature. After World War II, Tauber taught Russian in Cannes for 16 years and was in close contact with B. Zaytsev, I. Bunin, D. Klenovsky, and G. Iva-

nov. Even at her advanced age, Tauber has remained active in literature; she published a fourth volume, Nezdeshniy dom (1973; The Not-Here House), works regularly on the almanac Perekryostki (see VSTRECHI), and compiled her most important poems in Vernost (1984; Faithfulness). Tauber lives in Mougins, France.

Tauber's poems reveal a ceaseless, painstaking search for the proper word. She is aware of the divine grace, the burden, and the duty of poetic talent. Her point of departure is always her inner experience and her wrestling with the necessity of accepting fate. Tauber has an alert eye for nature and the gift of capturing its harmony in language. By these means, her Christian convictions are allowed cautious expression. Tauber understands interpersonal scenes. As with scenes of nature, which she poetically shapes, or a unique spiritual experience, these scenes are vested with the allegorical quality of the universally valid. A few contemporary poems, such as those concerning departure at the beginning of the war or the remembrance of Russian village landscape (Pod senyu, nos. 16 and 27), belong to the lasting treasures of Russian literature.

Works: Antologija novoj jugoslavskoj liriki, Belgrade, 1933 (coeditor and contranslator); Odinočestvo (poems), Berlin, 1935; Pod sen'ju olivy (poems), Paris, 1948; Plečo s plečom (poems), Paris, 1955; Nezdešnij dom (poems), Paris, 1973; Vernost' (poems), Paris, 1984.

Secondary Lit.: A. Nejmirok, in Grani, Frankfurt am Main, 24:1955; G. Zabežinskij, in Novyj žurnal, New York, 42:1955; A. Radaškevič, in Russkaja mysl', Paris, April 4, 1985, p. 10; Ju. Kublanovskij, in Grani 136:1985; T. Fesenko, in Novyj žurnal 158:1985; V. Sinkevič, in Strelec 1987:7.

Taúrin, Frants Nikoláyevich, prose writer (b. Jan. 27 [Jan. 14], 1911, Petrovskoye, prov. Tula). Taurin's father was a worker. In 1930 Taurin graduated from an industrial-technical school in Kazan; thereafter he worked as an engineer in leatherworking plants in Siberia. In 1939 he joined the Communist Party and temporarily worked as a Party secretary in Yakutsk. After 1952 he worked on the project to construct a hydroelectric power plant in Irkutsk. Taurin began his career as a writer with an industrial novel that takes place during World War II, K odnoy tseli (1950; Toward a Single Goal); its plot adheres to a familiar scheme (thanks to the Party leaders, the increased norms are successfully fulfilled). Crit-

icism of its artistic weakness led to a new
version entitled *Na Lene-reke* (1954; On the
Lena). The theme of *Angara* 1956–57) is the
construction of hydroelectric power plants in
Siberia. In the trilogy *Daleko v strane irkut-
skoy* (1961–63; Far Away in Irkutsk Country),
Taurin tries to cover the 100 years of Siberia's
development from a tsarist *Katorga* (peniten-
tiary) to a Soviet industrial region. Contrived
plots with artificial problems predictably resolved in accordance with the Party line and
the lack of persuasiveness of each individual
scene prompted the critics' very unenthusias-
tic response. Historical-biographical works
such as *Bez strakha i upryoka* (1977; Without
Fear and Reproach) and *Kamenshchik revolyutsii* (1980; Mason of the Revolution) focus
on lesser known revolutionaries. *U vremeni v
plenu* (1980; Under the Spell of Time) describes a life (1914–33) divided between village and city and devoted to the Soviet system. Taurin was a member of the secretariat
of the Writers Union of the RSFSR from 1965
to 1970 and moved from Irkutsk to Moscow.
In 1970, after the dissolution of the editorial
staff of *Novyj mir* headed by A. Tvardovsky,
Taurin was given the position of director of
the prose section (until 1975).

*Works:* K *odnoj celi* (novel), 1950; *Na Lene-
reke* (novel), 1954; *Angara* (novel), 2 vols., in
*Dal'nii Vostok* 1956:1–2 and 1957:4–5;
*Gremjaščij porog* (novel), in *Znamja* 1961:3–
5, separate ed., 1962; *Katoržnyj zavod* (novel),
in *Sibirskie ogni* 1963:1–2, separate ed., 1968;
*Partizanskaja bogorodica* (novel), in *Angara*
1963:3–4, separate ed., 1968; *Put' k sebe*
(novel), in *Neva* 1966:8–9, separate ed., 1967;
*Bajkal'skie krutye berega* (novel), in *Sibirskie
ogni* 1969:9–10, separate ed., 1969; *Bez strakha
i uprëka* (pov.), 1977; *U vremeni v plenu*
(novel), 1980; *Kamenščik revoljucii* (pov.),
1981.—*Izbr. proizv.*, 2 vols., 1983.

*Secondary Lit.:* L. Aramilev, in *Oktjabr'*
1951:5; N. Janovskij, in *Zvezda* 1956:12; P.
Nilin, in *Novyj mir* 1957:1; E. Jazovickaja, in
*Sibirskie ogni* 1970:11; I. Gerasimov, in *Novyj
mir* 1982:3.

**Teátr** (Theater), a monthly journal for the
dramatic arts and theater criticism that has
been published in Moscow since 1937. *Teatr*
replaced the journal *Teatr i dramaturgiya*
(1933–36; Theater and Dramaturgy). Publication was suspended from June 1941 to August
1945. The first editor was I. Altman. Starting
with 1941:4, he was replaced by V. Mochalin,
and the journal was placed under the control

of the Committee for Artistic Affairs of the
Council of People's Commissars of the USSR.
In 1946 Yu. Kalashnikov was appointed editor. In early 1949 the editorial staff was extensively reorganized as a result of the policy
against COSMOPOLITANISM. A. Solodovnikov
was appointed editor; the playwrights B. Romashov and A. Sofronov joined the staff; the
journal became the organ of the Writers Union
of the USSR and of the Committee for Artistic
Affairs of the Council of Ministers of the USSR
(in 1957 it became the organ of the Writers
Union of the USSR and of the Ministry of
Culture of the USSR). In 1951 editorial responsibility was placed in the hands of the
playwright N. Pogodin; a member of the editorial staff from 1946 to 1949, he retained his
position on the editorial staff until his death
even after being replaced as editor by V. Pimenov in 1960. Since then the editors in chief
has been Yu. Rybakov (1965–69) and the
playwrights V. Lavrentyev (1969–72), A. Salynsky (1972–82), and G. Borovyk (1982–).
*Teatr* regularly publishes new plays, reviews
of dramas and performances, and articles on
theory, on the history of the Russian theater,
and—within narrow limits—on foreign theater. The circulation in 1987 was 40,000.

**Téffi** (pseud. of Nadézhda Aleksándrovna
Buchínskaya, née Lókhvitskaya), prose writer
(b. May 21 [May 9], 1872 St. Petersburg—d.
Oct. 6, 1952, Paris). Teffi was of aristocratic
background; her father was a professor of crim-
inology. She began publishing in 1901, at
first poetry, then short stories and newspaper
commentaries that (in connection with the
Revolution of 1905) tended toward a position
critical of the established regime. From 1908
on, Teffi was a regular contributor to the journal *Satirikon* (founded by A. Averchenko) and
then to *Novy Satirikon*, until it was banned.
When her first collection appeared in book
form in 1910, Teffi was already known to a
broad stratum of readers. (Her name was so
popular that there was even a Teffi Perfume.)
Her attitude toward the February Revolution
(1917) was positive; the October Revolution
forced her to flee first to the Crimea and then,
in 1919, through Constantinople to Paris. There
she continued to contribute regularly to the
feuilleton sections of Russian newspapers. Her
first books in emigration, *Chorny iris* (1921;
The Black Iris) and *Tak zhili* (1922; That's the
Way We Lived), were published in Stockholm; they revealed the tragic core that existed alongside Teffi's talent for satire and
irony. For reasons of illness, Teffi (who adopted

a clear anti-Nazi position) was forced to remain in Paris during the German occupation in World War II. Occasional articles continued to appear in Russian émigré newspapers in America after the war. Altogether Teffi published some 30 books during her lifetime, almost half of them before she emigrated. In the 1970s some individual short stories were printed in Paris and Moscow.

Teffi's short stories reveal her considerable talent; the literary value of the prose written to meet newspaper specifications varies. Teffi's instant popularity with a broad readership is in accordance with the topicality of her subject matter, which in the Paris period concentrated on experiences from émigré life. Sympathy for the suffering of poor and simple people endows many of her short stories with a certain profundity. The contrast between appearance and reality is typical of Teffi's vision. In the volume *Vedma* (1936; The Witch), which I. Bunin, A. Kuprin, and D. Merezhkovsky valued highly, the lore of Russian mythology and legend blends with themes from everyday life.

*Works:* Sem' ognej (poems), 1910; Jumoristiceskie rasskazy (short stories), 2 vols., 1910; Karusel' (short stories), 1913; I stalo tak . . . (short stories), 1913; Dym bez ognja (short stories), 1914; Neživoj zver' (short stories), 1916; Tikhaja zavod' (short stories), Paris, 1921; Cërnyj iris (short stories), Stockholm, 1921; Tak žili (short stories), Stockholm, 1922; Passiflora (short stories), Paris, 1923; Večernij den' (short stories), Prague, 1924; Gorodok (short stories), Paris, 1927, New York, 1982; Kniga Ijun' (short stories), Belgrade, 1931; Avantjurnyj roman (novel), Paris, 1931; Vospominanija (memoirs), Paris, 1932, 2d ed., enl., 1980; P'esy (plays), Berlin, 1934; Ved'ma (short stories), Berlin, 1936; O nežnosti (short stories), n.p., 1938; Zigzag (short stories), Paris, 1939; Vsë o ljubvi (short stories), Paris, n.d. (1946?) (Eng. tr., All About Love, 1985); Zemnaja raduga (short stories), New York, 1952; poems, in Poety "Satirikona," Moscow, 1966; Rasskazy (short stories), Moscow, 1971.

*Secondary Lit.:* M. Cetlin, in Novyj žurnal, New York, 6:1943; G. Aleksinskij, in Grani, Frankfurt am Main, 16:1952; A. Sedykh, in Vozdušnye puti, New York, 3:1963; E. Haber, Diss., Harvard Univ., 1971, in Russian Literature Triquarterly 9:1974, and in Mnemozina, Munich, 1974; E. B. Neatrour, Diss., Indiana Univ., 1972, and in Russkaja mysl', Paris, Aug. 13, 1981, pp. 12, 14; Z. Šachovskaja, in her Otraženija, Paris, 1975; L. Evstigneeva, in Voprosy lit. 1976:6; A. Bakhrakh, in Russkaja mysl' June 14, 1979, p. 11.

**Teleshóv, Nikoláy Dmítriyevich**, prose writer (b. Nov. 10 [Oct. 29], 1867, Moscow—d. March 14, 1957, Moscow), Teleshov's father was a merchant. Teleshov completed his studies at the Moscow School of Applied Business in 1884; his first poems were published in the same year. In 1899 Teleshov organized the writers' group "Sreda," whose members included L. Andreyev, I. Bunin, M. Gorky, A. Kuprin, A. Serafimovich, and V. Veresayev. He contributed to the miscellanies issued by the publishing house Znaniye. Between 1895 and 1917 Teleshov published a series of books, mostly of shorter realistic prose pieces. After the Revolution he worked, among other places, in the Commissariat for Education, and after 1926, as director of the Museum of the Moscow Art Theater. In the main, he worked on his frequently reprinted memoirs, *Zapiski pisatelya* (1943; Eng. tr., *A Writer Remembers*, 1946).

The most important part of Teleshov's literary career lies in the pre-Soviet period. His journeys to the Urals and to Siberia provide the local color for a portion of his short stories and articles, which endeavor to depict everyday life realistically and with an element of social criticism. A series of legends and fairy tales reveal Teleshov's rich sense of fantasy. In his memoirs, Teleshov describes primarily his meetings with famous authors, such as A. Chekhov, M. Gorky, and L. Andreyev.

*Works:* Na trojkakh (short stories), 1895; Za Ural (journalistic prose), 1897; Rasskazy (short stories), 2 vols., 1903–8; Meždu dvukh beregov (short stories), 1910; Rasskazy (short stories), 4 vols., 1913–17; Černoju noč'ju (short stories), 1919; Pereselency (short stories), 1929; Lit. vospominanija (memoirs), 1931; Zapiski pisatelja (memoirs), 1943 (see above).—Izbr. soč., 3 vols., 1956.

*Secondary Lit.:* A. Volkov, in Novyj mir 1944:11–12; V. Lidin, in Naš sovremennik 1959:3 and in his Ljudi i vstreči, 1965; V. Borisova, foreword to Teleshov's Izbr. soč., 1956.

**Tendryakóv, Vladímir Fyódorovich**, prose writer (b. Dec. 5, 1923, Makarovskaya, oblast Vologda—d. Aug. 3, 1984, Moscow). Tendryakov's father was a judge and later a public prosecutor. After being wounded in World War II, Tendryakov worked as a teacher and a Komsomol official. In 1945 he studied at the Institute of Cinematography in Moscow; in 1946 he transferred to the Gorky Literary Institute, graduating from there in 1951. From 1948 on, he was a member of the Communist

Party. Tendryakov published several short stories from 1947 to 1953, mostly in *Ogonyok*, but he first "became a writer during the years 1953–56" and "was one of the characteristic figures in the literary proceedings of these years" (Solovyova). After 1954 a volume of his prose, which grapples with social and ethical concerns, appeared almost every year: short stories and povesti, as well as the novels *Za begushchim dnyom* (1959; Day by Day) and *Svidaniye s Nefertiti* (1964; A Rendezvous with Nefertiti). Some of Tendryakov's short stories were filmed. Together with G. Baklanov and Yu. Bondarev, Tendryakov wrote the screenplay for the film *49 dney* (1962; 49 Days). Tendryakov was a member of the board of the Writers Union of the USSR and that of the Writers Union of the RSFSR. He lived in Moscow.

Tendryakov's creative work was first acclaimed as a reaction against the artificial conflicts and the so-called THEORY OF CONFLICTLESSNESS of the Stalin period. In the center of his prose stands the individual who is culpable or who has been thrown out of the normal course of his life by tragic circumstances and who recognizes that the conventional or standard conceptions of right and wrong, of guilt and vindication, have failed the test of reality. In an unconventional way, Tendryakov seized upon the issues of one's behavior in the face of death, the meaning of insincere marriage bonds, the existence of various trends in art (including the abstract), and one's attitude toward religious young Christians in the atheistic Communist society; in his exploration of these issues, the never optimistic "solution" is less important than the multidimensionality of the study. The closing sentence of the povest *Sud* (1961; The Court)—"There is no harsher court than the court of one's own conscience"—sums up the plot line in most of his prose. Tendryakov has only occasionally been censured by the orthodox critics, but especially for *Troyka, semyorka, tuz* (1960; Eng. tr., *Three, Seven, Ace and Other Stories*, 1973). *Apostolskaya komandirovka* (1969; Apostolic Mission) represents one of the attempts within Soviet literature to resolve the problem of Christian belief atheistically according to the Party line, in that a Soviet citizen inquiring about the meaning of life is confronted with primitive, shallow Christianity. In *Noch posle vypuska* (1974; The Night after the Discharge), Tendryakov attacks the practice, prevalent in the Communist sphere of influence, of using skillful clichés to educate youth to hold the most uniform conceptions instead of preparing them for independent, critical thought; he com-

bines this attack as a story within the story of his central concern: man being put to the test in a special situation that is set apart from daily routine. In *Zatmeniye* (1977; Eclipse), Tendryakov has a woman who is choosing between two men decide in favor of the materially insecure but religiously seeking one. In *Rasplata* (1979; Atonement) he portrays the complicity of all men in the parricide committed by a 15-year-old. For more than a decade *Shestdesyat svechey* (1980; Sixty Candles) could not be published; in this povest, a school director brings before his conscience the false, also Party-inspired, decisions made during the course of his 60-year-long life. The frequent and distinctive pattern of rendering thoughts by using a specifically Russian style of "substitutionary narration" reflects Tendryakov's deep psychological interest.

*Works: Padenie Ivana Čuprova* (short story), 1954; *Sredi lesov* (short stories), 1954; *Tugoj uzel* (novel), 1956; *Čudotvornaja* (pov.) 1958; *Za gušćim dněm* (novel), in *Molodaja gvardija* 1959:10–12 and in *Povesti*, 1961; *Trojka, semërka, tuz* (pov.), in *Novyj mir* 1960:3 (see above); *Sud* (pov.), 1961; *Črezvyčajnoe* (pov.), 1961; *Povesti*, 1961; *Korotkoe zamykanie* (pov.), 1962; *Ne ko dvoru* (pov.), 1965; *Putešestvie dlinoj v vek* (science fiction), 1965; *Svidanie s Nefertiti* (novel), 1965; *Končina* (pov.), in *Moskva* (1968:3; *Apostol'skaja komandirovka* (pov.), in *Nauka i religija* 1969:8–10; *Noč' posle vypuska* (pov.), in *Novyj mir* 1974:9; *Perevertyši* (pov.), 1974; *Zatmenie* (pov.), in *Družba narodov* 1977:5; *Rasplata* (pov.), in *Novyj mir* 1979:3; *Šest'desjat svečej* (pov.), in *Družba narodov* 1980:9; *Den'*, vytesnivšij žizn'* (memoirs), in *Družba narodov* 1985:1; *Požar* (play), in *Sovremennaja dramaturgija* 1985:2; *Čistye vody Kiteža* (pov.), in *Družba narodov* 1986:8.—*Izbr.*, 2 vols., 1963; *Izbr.*, 1972; *Izbr.*, 1973; *Sobr. soč.*, 4 vols., 1978–80.

*Translation: A Topsy-Turvy Spring: Stories*, 1978.

*Secondary Lit.:* I. Vinogradov, in *Novyj mir* 1958:9; V. Litvinov, in *Oktjabr'* 1961;6; I. Solov'ëva, in *Novyj mir* 1962:7; *RSPP* 5:1968; L. Antopol'skij, in *Družba narodov* 1971:1; N. Podzorova, in *Oktjabr'* 1974:10; T. Peresun'ko and others, in *Lit. obozrenie* 1975:1; L. S. Parcira, Diss., Michigan State Univ., 1975; L. H. Wangler, Diss., Univ. of Pittsburgh, 1977; V. Dudincev, in *Lit. obozrenie* 1977:12; G. Hosking, in his *Beyond Socialist Realism*, New York, 1980; A. Èl'jaševič, in *Novyj mir* 1982:7; V. Serdjučenko, in *Oktjabr'* 1983:11; V. Rosljakov, in *Lit. gazeta* Aug. 15, 1984, p. 7; V. Kardin, in *Novyj mir* 1985:9.

Terapiáno, Yúry Konstantínovich, poet, literary critic (b. Oct. 21 [Oct. 9], 1892, Kerch— d. July 3, 1980, Gagny, France). Terapiano graduated from the secondary school for classical languages in Kerch in 1911 and completed his study of law in Kiev in 1916. He was inducted into the military in 1917 and was registered in the volunteer army in the Crimea in 1919. The Bolshevik victory necessitated his emigration. In Paris in 1925 he became cofounder and first chairman of the Union of Young Poets. His first volume of poetry, Luchshiy zvuk (1926; The Best Sound), appeared in Munich; the next, Bessonnitsa (1935; Sleeplessness), in Berlin; and the next two, Na vetru (1938; In the Wind) and Stranstviye zemnoye (1950; Earthly Wandering), in Paris. Terapiano found definite acclaim as a wide-ranging religious poet but became especially known as a literary critic. From 1945 to 1955 he wrote regularly for the New York newspaper Novoye russkoye slovo, thereafter for more than 25 years for the Paris newspaper Russkaya mysl. A volume of memoirs, Vstrechi (1953; Meetings), describes the intellectual atmosphere of Paris from 1925 to 1939 and contains, among other things, portraits of K. Balmont, Yu. Felzen, Z. Gippius, V. Khodasevich, D. Merezhkovsky, and B. Poplavsky. A collection of 67 poems, Izbrannye stikhi (1963; Selected Poems), is so strongly defined by Terapiano's philosophy of life at the time of publication that his development is not evident. Terapiano published one additional volume, Parusa (1965; Sails). The volume of Russian émigré poetry he collected, Muza diaspory (1960; Muse of the Diaspora), provides through its informative preface an introduction to the trends within Russian poetry written abroad.

Terapiano, who has concerned himself with Egyptology, ancient history, and theosophy and who feels himself especially drawn to Zoroastrianism, the ancient Persian religion, began to publish poems about Islam, gnosticism, and the wisdom of Egypt in Luchshiy zvuk. In the volume Bessonnitsa he had already released himself from this specific theme and had shifted to the theme that continued to define his poetry: questions about the accommodation of earthly events to the divine plan, about addressing and searching for God, about solitude and security in faith, about poetry as drudgery and joy. Paris and nature are often factors in his poetry; his yearning for his lost Crimea is only implied; political poems are rare and generally weak. Of visionary power is his poem about death, "Byl angel poslan . . ." (An Angel Was Sent . . .), which

constitutes a view of death, limbo, and the world to come. Terapiano's last volume, Parusa, is borne along by the same steadfast religious faith as his earlier volumes. Formally, Terapiano adheres to the classical or the ACMEIST discipline and to a large extent lets his "I" take second place. Terapiano's only well-known povest, Puteshestviye v neizvestny kray (1946; Journey to an Unknown Land), is a short, significant, partially surrealistic presentation of prehistoric human conditions that are still determined by the union with the divine cosmic presence. This depiction is based on Terapiano's extensive knowledge of Asian religious wisdom and on his deep appreciation for the spiritual bases of earthly existence.

Works: Lučšij zvuk (poems), Munich, 1926; Bessonnica (poems), Berlin, 1935; Na vetru (poems), Paris, 1938; Putešestvie v neizvestnyj kraj (short story), Paris, 1946; Stranstvie zemnoe (poems), Paris, 1950; Vstreči (memoirs), New York, 1953; introduction to Muza diaspory, Frankfurt am Main, 1960; Parusa (poems), Washington, 1965; Ob odnoj lit. vojne [Khodasevic: G. Ivanov] (essay), in Mosty, Munich, 12:1966; Literaturnaja zizn' russkogo Pariža za polveka (essays), Paris–Jersey City, 1987.—Izbr. stikhi, Washington, 1963.

Secondary Lit.: G. Struve, in Russkaja mysl', Paris, 1:1927, and Russkaja literatura v izgnanii, New York, 1956; K. Močul'skij, in Sovremennye zapiski, Paris, 58:1935; I. Odoevceva, in Novyj žurnal, New York, 76:1964, 82:1966, in Russkaja mysl' July 17, 1980 and Jan. 29, 1981, and in Novoe russkoe slovo, New York, Aug. 24, 1980; Ja. Gorbov, in Vozroždenie, Paris, 186:1967; Ju. Ivask, in Novyj žurnal 144:1981.

Ternóvsky, Yevgény Samóylovich, prose writer (b. Aug. 2, 1941, Ramenskoye, oblast Moscow). Ternovsky's father was an engineer. Ternovsky studied at the Institute for Foreign Languages in Moscow via correspondence courses (1960–61). Thereafter he worked as a cargo carrier, male nurse, and translator, especially of romantic poetry. Works of literary criticism and translations appeared in Moscow journals in the 1960s. Ternovsky discovered Christianity and began to publish in émigré journals in 1973. In 1974 he left the Soviet Union to live in Paris. He studied at the University of Cologne and taught there and at the University of Lille, where a Ph.D. degree was conferred upon him in 1985. He regularly wrote for Russkaya mysl. Together with Z. Shakhovskaya and R. Guerra he published the Russky Almanakh (Paris, 1981), an anthology of the works of writers from the three emigrations. His first novel, written in Moscow in 1973, Strannaya istoriya (1976; A Peculiar Story), identifies him as an independent writer.

Ternovsky became inspired to undertake creative writing by reading F. Dostoyevsky. In Strannaya istoriya he recounts a period of continual vicissitudes in the life of an office employee from the perspective of a first-person narrator. This period coincides with a phase in the spiritual search of one who understands the meaninglessness of a life determined by materialism in the Soviet Union. Ingenious symbols (for example, a snowstorm) and a cautiously proposed solution within the religious sphere enhance the artistic value of this novel written from internal necessity. Ternovsky's second novel, Priyomnoye otdeleniye (1979; Admissions), provides insight into the flagrant social inequalities of the Soviet system, using the example of two patients and their husbands. The compositional harmony, especially the gradual unfolding of the past, and the character of the dramatis personae demonstrate a good storytelling ability.

Works: Živoj jazyk prosnuvšejsja prirody (essay), in Voprosy lit. 1967:7; (under pseudonym N. Antonov) Gody bezvremenščiny (review), in Grani, Frankfurt am Main, 89–90:1973; Krest i kamen'. O romane V. Maksimova "Karantin" (review), in Grani 92–93:1973; (under his own name) Soimennik i imjarek (essay), in Grani 100:1976; Ten' nad Rossiej (short story), in Russkaja mysl', Paris, Sept. 23, 1976; Strannaja istorija (novel), Frankfurt am Main, 1977; Priëmnoe otdelenie (pov.), Frankfurt am Main, 1979.

Secondary Lit.: W. Kasack, in Neue Zürcher Zeitung Nov. 25, 1976, p. 57, and Sept. 26, 1979, p. 27; V. Vejdle, in Russkaja mysl' June 9, 1977, p. 8.

**Terts, Abrám** (pseud. of Andréy Donátovich Sinyávsky), prose writer, literary scholar (b. Oct. 8, 1925, Moscow). Sinyavsky's father was a Party official (arrested 1951). Sinyavsky served as a soldier in World War II, then studied humanities (Russian and Soviet literature) at Moscow University, graduating in 1949; in 1952 he defended his candidate's dissertation (on M. Gorky), then worked as a lecturer at Moscow University and as a research assistant at the Institute for World Literature of the Academy of Sciences. Through essays, articles in handbooks, and criticism of A. Akhmatova, E. Bagritsky, I. Babel, O. Berggolts, M. Gorky, B. Pasternak, and others, Sinyavsky became well known as a fine literary scholar. In 1955 he wrote his first work of fictional prose, the fantastic short story V tsirke (At the Circus). After the 20th Party Congress and without any consideration for censorship regulations, Sinyavsky wrote the essay Chto takoye sotsialistichesky realizm (1956; Eng. tr., On Socialist Realism, 1960), an ironic, knowledgeable analysis of this artistic dogma that refutes the official interpretation and thus proves the relationship between the dogma and classicism (see SOCIALIST REALISM). At the same time he wrote a longer story, Sud idyot (1956; Eng. tr., The Trial Begins, 1960). At the end of 1956 Sinyavsky sent these works to France. They appeared after 1959 under the pseudonym of Terts, partially in translation at first. Further fantastic fictional prose followed: the short stories Ty i ya (1959; You and I); Kvartiranty (1959; The Renters); Grafomany (1960; The Graphomaniacs); Gololeditsa (1961; Ice-covered Ground); Pkhents (1965); and the novel Lyubimov (1961–62; Eng. tr., The Makepeace Experiment, 1965). A collection of notes, Mysli vrasplokh (1965; Eng. trs., Thought Unaware, 1965; Unguarded Thoughts, 1972), only appeared after Sinyavsky had been identified as Terts and arrested on Sept. 8, 1965. Together with Yuly Daniel (N. Arzhak), Sinyavsky was sentenced to seven years at hard labor because of his satires. K. Paustovsky's petition to testify on behalf of the accused in court was denied. The critic Z. Kedrina and the official A. Vasilyev, as members of the Writers Union, were willing to speak in support of the accusation. A. Ginzburg composed a white paper concerning the trial that was distributed through SAMIZDAT and published in the West. Worldwide protests from writers in the Soviet Union and all civilized nations and from Communist parties in other countries resulted from this sentence. Sinyavsky and Daniel became the most famous prisoners in the Soviet Union. M. Sholokhov, however, slandered the condemned and their defenders at the 23d Party Congress (1966) and hinted at the death penalty allowable "according to a revolutionary understanding of the law." In a dispassionate letter of protest, Lidiya Chukovskaya emphasized the monstrosity of these proceedings as self-defamation of Sholokhov personally. Sinyavsky served out his sentence in Potma and was released on June 8, 1971. Through his letters to his wife he was able to remain active as a writer; he published excerpts in *Golos iz khora* (1973; Eng. tr., *A Voice from the Chorus*, 1976) in London. In 1973 he received permission to emigrate with his wife and son. Sinyavsky works as a professor of Russian literature in Paris and has retained the pseudonym Terts for his prose works.

Terts's literary work is an argument against the coercion and deceit of Soviet reality. The image of this stratum of reality is refracted through various narrative and technical means; it is especially grotesquely distorted through the inclusion of the fantastic, the supernatural, and the world of dreams, madness, and hallucinations. Reality is rendered as pseudoreality, the fantastic as true to life. Terts's satire is leveled at chauvinism, at the atmosphere of mistrust and fear, at the inhuman system of surveillance—using the time frame of the end of the Stalin period—as well as at the Communist principle that the end sanctifies the means *(Sud idyot)* and at the Moscow literary establishment *(Grafomany)*. Lyubimov mixes political satire and a timeless antiutopia with the philosophical issue of a right to the irrational instead of to rationally guided "good fortune" (Dalton). *Pkhents* creates the grotesque by transplanting a being from another planet into the everyday world of Moscow and is typical in its frequent inclusion of sexual and doppelgänger motifs. Terts's works have a fragmentary structure; their multidimensionality often arises through a change in narrative perspective; their tension through the nonchronological sequencing of particulars. Terts's religiosity was already apparent in *Mysli vrasplokh*. *Golos iz khora* offered insights into the essence of man, insights that have arisen from the suffering of a mature man who looks on life from the distance of one who has been disenfranchised and forcibly isolated. Interspersed are charming observations of ordinary Russia made by fellow prisoners, observations that reveal the linguistically sensitive scholar and poet. During the first decade of his emigration, Terts published numerous essays and some books dedicated to authors; together with a strangely provocative book, *Progulki s Pushkinym* (1975; Walks with Pushkin), comes the comprehensive poetic view of his predecessor who is esteemed for his satire and religiosity: *V teni Gogolya* (1975; In Gogol's Shadow). Focusing on the paradoxical is *"Opavshiye listya" V. V. Rozanova* (1982; V. V. Rozanov's "Fallen Leaves"); like everything Terts wrote, this is marked by his linguistic joy of creation. *Kroshka Tsores* (1980; Little Tsores) refers back to early grotesqueries and telescopes

components that are autobiographical, reminiscent of E. T. A. Hoffmann, evocative of Soviet reality, and fairy-tale-like. In the novel *Spokoynoy nochi* (1984; Good Night) he depicts a few tragic situations of his own life, giving insight into the inhuman work of the KGB.

*Works:* (with I. Golomštok) *Pikasso*, 1960; *Davajte govorit' professional'no*, in *Novyj mir* 1961:8; (with A. Menšutin) *Poèzija pervykh let revoljucii 1917–20*, 1964; *Fantastičeskie povesti*, *Sud idët* (see above), *Lyubimov* (see above), *Čto takoe socialističeskij realizm* (see above) (contains also *V cirke*, *Ty i ja*, *Grafomany*, *Pchenc*; title on jacket *Fantastičeskij mir A. T.*), New York, 1967 (Eng. tr., *Fantastic Stories*, 1963); *Mysli vrasplokh*, New York, 1966 (see above); *Golos iz khora*, London, 1973 (see above); *Plaidoyer pour la liberté de l'imagination* (articles of literary criticism), Paris, 1973 (Eng. tr., *For Freedom of Imagination*, (1971); *Literaturnyj process v Rossii*, in *Kontinent*, Paris, 1:1974; *V teni Gogolja*, London, 1975; *Progulki s Puškinym*, London, 1976; articles, in *Sintaksis*, Paris, 1 and 2:1978, 3:1979, 6 and 8:1980, 9:1982, 10:1983, 12:1984; *Kroška Cores*, Paris, 1980; *"Opavšie list'ja" V. V. Rozanova*, Paris, 1982; *Spokojnoj noči* (novel), Paris, 1984.

*Secondary Lit.:* See ARZHAK, NIKOLAY. B. Filippov, in *Grani*, Frankfurt am Main, 60:1966; R. Gul', in *Novyj žurnal*, New York, 84:1966; M. Mihajlov, *Russische Themen*, Bern, 1969; D. Brown, in *Slavic Review* 1970:4; R. Lourie, Ithaca, N.Y., 1975; M. Dalton, New York, 1975; V. Levin, Munich, 1975; M. Slonim, in *Russkaja mysl'*, Paris, March 18, 1976, p. 6; N. Rubinštejn, in *Vremja i my*, Jerusalem, 9:1976; A. Durkin, in *Slavic and East European Journal* 1980:2; R. Podruzskij, in *Russkaja mysl'* May 27, 1982, p. 13; A. Woronzoff, in *Russian Language Journal* 126–27:1983; V. E. Alexandrov, in *Slavonic and East European Review* 1984:2; G. Nivat, in *Russkaja mysl'* Dec. 6, 1984, p. 10.

**Thaw** *(Óttepel)*. Taken from a short novel with this title by I. Erenburg, this designation, especially well established in Western secondary literature, covers the period after Stalin's death (March 5, 1953) in which a certain relaxation in cultural policy occurred. After the repressive literary policy of the Stalin period, which led to a sharp drop in the standard for published works of literature, to the suppression of essential works, and to the death of a great number of writers (see REHA-

BILITATION), the first decade thereafter was a period of hope for the creative intelligentsia and was coupled with a great artistic revival. In literary policy, the Party and the state searched for a new means of maintaining control over literature and for ensuring that the insistence on the need for critical and free expression of opinion could not turn into criticism of the Party and the system itself, while on the other hand seeking to avoid continuing the Stalinist policy of tyranny. The conservative and liberal tendencies in the Party and state leadership existed side by side and were reflected in the variable course in literary policy. On the basis of political events, the Thaw can be divided into three periods, each of which was followed by a more repressive phase. The first period (1953–54) is characterized especially by the literary and theoretical contributions of I. Erenburg, K. Paustovsky, V. Pomerantsev, and F. Abramov, who rejected the political phrases connected with SOCIALIST REALISM. In October 1953, the title of a poem by N. Zabolotsky (in Novy mir) mentioned the term ottepel for the first time; Erenburg's prose work of the same title followed in May 1954 (in Znamya). The reaction against this period led to A. Tvardovsky's dismissal from his position as editor in chief of the journal Novy mir (1954:9). The Second WRITERS CONGRESS reflected these diverse tendencies. The second period began following the 20th Party Congress in 1956, at which Khrushchev's "secret speech" concerning Stalin's crimes made it possible to criticize the effects of his policies. Especially well known are V. Dudintsev's novel Ne khlebom yedinym (1956; Not by Bread Alone) and the almanac Literaturnaya Moskva (1956:2), whose editors included K. Paustovsky, V. Kaverin, and V. Tendryakov. The rebellion against Soviet domination in Hungary in the autumn of 1956, the suppression of which left its imprint on poets of the younger generation such as I. Brodsky, led to a restrictive policy in the Soviet Union as well, and thereby to the harsher condemnation of the above-mentioned publications. The coexistence of nonconformist and conservative literature and literary criticism persisted. During the period of strong conservative pressure (1959–60) the first SAM-IZDAT journal was published. More liberal tendencies received their endorsement at the 22d Party Congress (1961) with the official condemnation of Stalin. Among the most significant literary works of the third period are Yu. Bondarev's novel Tishina (Silence), which attempts to depict candidly the postwar period; V. Rozov's drama Zateynik (The Social

Director), with its portrayal of the effects power and fear have on people's private lives; S. Zlobin's Propavshiye bez vesti (Missing in Action), with its indictment of the persecution of Soviet prisoners of war by their own authorities; and A. Solzhenitsyn's Odin den Ivana Denisovicha (Eng. tr., One Day in the Life of Ivan Denisovich, 1963), the first candid depiction of the horror of the camps in the Soviet Union. To restrain the further growth of literature concerned with the negative events of the Stalin period and their perpetuation in the present, the Party met with various writers during the winter of 1962–63. The Thaw ended in 1963. A clear sign of the end was the court's conviction of the apolitical poet I. Brodsky in March 1964; his activity as a translator was not recognized as work. After Khrushchev's fall in October 1964, the conservative powers gained control, but the fate of writers such as V. Aksyonov, L. Chukovskaya, Yu. Daniel, A. Galich, V. Nekrasov, A. Sinyavsky, A. Solzhenitsyn, G. Vladimov, and V. Voynovich reveals that the spirit of the Thaw continues to characterize true literature in the Soviet Union. See EMIGRATION.

*Secondary Lit.:* G. Gibian, Minneapolis, 1960; A. Steininger, Wiesbaden, 1965; H. Segall, in HRL 1985.

**Theater October** (Teatrálny oktyábr), a term created by V. Meyerhold in September 1920 for the purpose of revolutionizing and politicizing the theater in the Soviet Union in the sense of combining a Bolshevik agitational stage with leftist views on art. Artists such as the director Vsevolod Yemilyevich Meyerhold (1874–1939), a student of Constantin Stanislavsky, and futurists such as V. Mayakovsky (see FUTURISM) found in the October Revolution the possibility for realizing their revolutionary, experimental views on art. To be sure, in the world of the theater, this signified a politically one-sided and spiritually weak phase of Russian theater life, but it was an extraordinarily fruitful phase in terms of form, a phase that affected the development of the entire European theater. On political holidays, mass demonstrations with thousands of participants were staged that, in their external form, borrowed from medieval mystery plays (see V. Mayakovsky, Misteriya buff, and N, Yevreinov, Vzyatiye Zimnego dvortsa). In 1920, after A. Lunacharsky appointed Meyerhold director of the theatrical department of the People's Commissariat for Education, the principles of political mass theater were applied to the stage as well: sovereign control by the director; preference given to adaptation and improvisation over the words of the playwright, which were denigrated as raw material; engagement of anonymous groups; dissolution of the boundaries between the stage and the house, between the performers and the audience; preference given to pantomime, dance, music, acrobatics, and clowning instead of to dramatic dialogue; complete rejection of realism in favor of abstract artistic constructions, even in the creation of the scenery. On the one hand, Meyerhold strove, together with the new political powerholders, to use the theater like the military for the political reeducation of the masses; on the other hand, theatrical practice revealed an experimental diversity. In his own theater, Meyerhold combined "biomechanics" (the rational transformation of spirituality into physical forms of expression), CONSTRUCTIVISM of space (dissolution of the picture-frame stage, curtain, and wings through the technical design of movable terraces, revolving stages, and escalators), and medieval buffoonery (for efficacy with the masses). In his "unfettered theater," A. Tairov (1885–1950) created a kind of theatrical artistry that is close to expressive dance and that was supposed to be free from all literary, psychological, representational, and technical ambitions. Ye. Vakhtangov (1883–1922), also a student of Stanislavsky, developed a theater of improvisation, of theatrical vision, a "theater of complete freedom, color and musicality that stood in sharp contrast to the living conditions in Russia at that time" (J. Rühle). Among the numerous avant-garde theaters, both the Hebrew studio "Habima," established by Vakhtangov with Marc Chagall as set designer, and the PROLETKULT Theater, with Sergei Eisenstein as director, distinguished themselves. Together with other Soviet directors such as Vsevolod Pudovkin and Aleksandr Dovzhenko, Eisenstein carried this artistic impetus into the new art form of the film and established a worldwide reputation for early Soviet film.

All of these internationally recognized accomplishments were short-lived. The Communist ideologues in RAPP enforced their primitive ideas and closed these theaters; they suppressed not only the revolutionary and the experimental but every true form of art. Meyerhold's execution in a GULAG has symbolic meaning. Only in very circumspect fashion were Soviet theaters able to build on these traditions during the period of the THAW, as a result of Meyerhold's REHABILITATION. Experiment and improvisation stand in opposi-

tion to the principles of SOCIALIST REALISM and PARTY SPIRIT.

Secondary Lit.: A. Tairov, Zapiski režissëra, 1921; E. Znosko-Borovskij, Russkij teatr načala 20 veka, Prague, 1925; R. Fülop-Miller, Geist und Gesicht des Bolschewismus, Zurich, 1926, pp. 157–81; J. Gregor, R. Fülop-Miller, Das russische Theater, Vienna, 1927; Habima, Hebräisches Theater, Berlin, 1928; Le théâtre dans l'URSS, Moscow, 1933; Istorija sovetskogo teatra, vol. 1, 1933; E. Vakhtangov, Zapiski, pis'ma, stat'i, 1939; Ju. Elagin Taming of the Art, New York, 1951, and Tëmnyj genij [Vsevolod Mejerkhol'd], New York, 1955, 2d ed., London, 1982; E. Lo Gatto, Storia del teatro russo, 2 vols., Florence, 1952; N. Gorčakov, Istorija sovetskogo teatra, New York, 1956; V. Mejerkhol'd, in Teatr 1957:3 and in his Stat'i, pis'ma, reči, besedy, 2 vols., 1968; J. Rühle, Das gefesselte Theater, Cologne, 1957 (new ed. under the title Theater und Revolution, Munich, 1963), and in Sowjetsystem und demokratische Gesellschaft, entry Theater, Freiburg, 1972; H. Segel, Twentieth-Century Russian Drama, New York, 1979; M. Hoover, in HRL 1985; N. Morjanak-Bamburac, in Russian Literature 16(1):1986.

**Theory of Conflictlessness** (Teóriya beskonflíktnosti), a theory frequently discussed at the beginning of the 1950s, in which the principles of SOCIALIST REALISM were seen as excluding the representation of conflicts and of negative features in general from contemporary literature. In the second half of the 1930s, Marxist theorists developed the idea that, in view of humanity's continual progress from capitalism to ideal communism, in the phase of socialism neither "antagonistic nor nonantagonistic contradictions could exist," that even "the possibility of contradictions and conflicts is excluded" (see Pod znamenem marksizma 1940:8). Whereas the Party had expected literature in the 1920s to depict conflicts between "old and new," between the pre-Revolutionary and the Revolutionary, and had considered all negative phenomena to be "remnants of capitalism," according to the theory these conflicts must gradually diminish. The dogma of socialist realism—the "representation of reality in its revolutionary development," that is, the ideally awaited condition—supported the birth of a literature without conflicts. To be sure, there was nominally no such thing as a theory of conflictlessness, but the measures taken by the censor and the pronouncements of leading critics had that effect. Forbidden, for example, was the depiction of any conflicts between the individual and state authorities such as arose around the issues of forced collectivizaton, administrative deportation, the arbitrariness of sentences to forced labor and the consequences these sentences had on families; forbidden also was the description of privation after the war; excluded were death (except heroic death in battle), doubt, human weaknesses. In view of the increasingly monotonous and alienated literature in which these tendencies increased after the Party Resolutions of 1946 (see PARTY RESOLUTIONS ON LITERATURE), demands for the representation "of the encounter between 'the good and the better' and later between 'the better and the excellent' " (B. Lavrenyov) were only an inadequate attempt to make artistic legitimacy conform to the nonsensical ideological system. Many works that were awarded Stalin Prizes were written according to this scheme. The term as such was probably developed in 1952 to provide an explanation for the decline of Soviet literature during the Stalin period (Pravda April 7, 1952). Since the attack on the perniciousness of the theory of conflictlessness was not accompanied by a liberal attitude toward more truthful representations of the authentic conflicts in life, nothing was changed. However, during the THAW the theory of conflictlessness and its consequences were selected as the dialectical starting point for the demand for the liberalization of literature. Since many conflicts have remained taboo—that is, were ruled off limits again after 1965 (such as the theme of the suffering endured by Soviet citizens during the Stalin period)—the theory of conflictlessness continues to form an appreciable element of Soviet literary policy.

*Secondary Lit.: Preodolet' otstavanie dramaturgii, in Pravda April 7, 1952; V. Pomerancev, in Novyj mir 1953:12; A. Kron, in Lit. Moskva, vol. 2, 1956; E. Ètkind, Sovetskie tabu, in Sintaksis, Paris, 9:1981.*

**Tíkhonov, Nikoláy Semyónovich,** poet, literary official (b. Dec. 4 [Nov. 22], 1896, St. Petersburg—d. Feb 8, 1979, Moscow). Tikhonov's father was a hairdresser. Tikhonov finished business school in 1911. He served as a hussar in World War I and fought with the Red Army from 1918 to 1921. Tikhonov, who began writing poetry in the military, published his first poems together with K. Vaginov and S. Kolbasyev in the almanac Ostro-

vityane (vol. 1, 1921), put out by the Petrograd literary group of the same name. In 1922 he became a member of the SERAPION BROTHERS. Tikhonov became popular for his revolutionary ballads, such as "Ballada o sinem pakete" (1922; Ballad of the Blue Packet). In the 1920s and 1930s Tikhonov undertook numerous journeys, particularly to Central Asia and the Caucasus and devoted himself more and more to his career as a literary official. He was elected to the board of the Writers Union at its first congress in 1934; thereafter he always held leading positions. For his Leningrad war epic in verse, Kirov s nami (1941; Kirov Is with Us), he was awarded a Stalin Prize (for 1941, 1st class); he received additional Stalin Prizes for 1948 (1st class) and for 1951 (1st class). As a result of the Party Resolution of 1946 (see PARTY RESOLUTIONS ON LITERATURE), Tikhonov had to resign the chairmanship of the Writers Union of the USSR to A. Fadeyev, but he remained in the administration as one of the secretaries. After World War II, Tikhonov was active in the world peace movement; he was a deputy of the Supreme Soviet of the USSR from 1946 on. He received the Lenin Prize in 1970 for a collection of his prose works. Tikhonov lived in Moscow.

Tikhonov's "poetic beginnings in the early twenties were auspicious" (E. Brown). His revolutionary poetry is inspired by the romantic enthusiasm for the heroic and the extraordinary; it is austere in its selection of words and images and has "a strong, metallic ring" (Struve). In its concreteness and its conciseness (reminiscent of ACMEISM), Tikhonov's poetry found justifiable approval and gained him a reputation as a poet of the new period. The revolutionary theme was later changed into cheap, idealized war poetry. A parallel development is discernible in the transformation of his early exotic verses with Asian motifs into journalistic, tendentious poems—at first about Soviet Asia and the Caucasus, later about the Communist world peace movement—which Tikhonov supplemented by writing additional propagandistic verse of topical Party interest.

*Works: Orda (poems), 1922; Kirov s nami (narrative poem), 1941; Stikhi o Jugoslavii (poems), 1947; Na Vtorom Vsemirnom Kongresse mira (poems), 1951; Ustnaja kniga (memoirs), in Voprosy lit. 1980:6–8; Stikhotvorenija i poèmy (lyric and narrative poems), 1981.—Sobr. soč., 6 vols., 1958–59; 7 vols., 1973–76.*
*Secondary Lit.: P. Antokol'skij, in Lit. i sovremennost' 7:1967; I. Grinberg, 2d ed., 1972;*

D. F. K. Norman, Diss., Univ. of Colorado, 1974; *Bibliografičeskij ukazatel'*, ed. V. A. Šošin, 1975 and 1981; S. Šunjaeva, in *Vestnik Moskovskogo universiteta: Serija Filologija* 1977:6; M. Dudin, in *Avrora* 1983:11.

**Tolstóy, Alekséy Nikoláyevich**, prose writer, playwright (b. Jan. 10, 1883 [Dec. 29, 1882], Nikolayevsk, prov. Samara—d. Feb. 23, 1945, Moscow). Tolstoy's father was an aristocrat and landowner. From 1901 to 1908 Tolstoy studied at the St. Petersburg Institute of Technology (1906 in Dresden), without completing a degree. He began publishing symbolist poetry in 1905, short stories in 1908. Tolstoy had been acknowledged as a prose writer before World War I for his novels and short stories; he had also written seven plays before the Revolution. He took an anti-Bolshevik position in 1917, working in General Anton Denikin's propaganda section. In 1918 he emigrated, first to France, then in 1921 to Berlin. In emigration he wrote, among other works, an autobiographical *povest*, *Detstvo Nikity* (1920–22; Eng. tr., *Nikita's Childhood*, 1945), and a portrayal of the Revolution, *Khozhdeniye po mukam* (1920; Eng. tr., *The Road to Calvary*, 1923), which was later revised and expanded as *Syostry* (The Sisters), and became Part 1 of his major work, the trilogy *Khozhdeniye po mukam* (1920–41; Eng. tr., *Road to Calvary*, 1946). Tolstoy joined the small émigré movement of the "Smenovekhovtsy," who accepted Bolshevism as the present form of Russian government. In 1923 Tolstoy received permission to return to the Soviet Union. There he became engaged in extensive literary activity, and "with his usual opportunistic flair, chose the right Party protectors and the safest way to write what he wanted" (Slonim). Tolstoy was attacked as a FELLOW TRAVELER in the 1920s (even though, for example, his utopian novel *Aelita* [1922–23; Eng. tr., 1985], written in emigration, is dedicated to a proletarian revolution on Mars); nevertheless, he soon managed to reach an unusually high and respected position. After M. Gorky's death he became chairman of the Writers Union of the USSR, in 1937 a deputy to the Supreme Soviet of the USSR, in 1939 a member of the Academy of Sciences. In 1937 Tolstoy made his contribution to the cult of Stalin with his novel *Khleb* (Eng. tr., *Bread*, 1937), which, based on a "fallacious conception" (Alpatov), glorifies Stalin's role in the defense of Tsaritsyn. During the period of historical revisionism, Tolstoy turned to the historical novel as well. His *Pyotr Pervy* (1929–45; Eng. trs., *Peter the Great*, 1932; *Peter the*

*First*, 1959) is one of the most important works of Soviet literature; it received the first Stalin Prize (for 1935–41, 1st class). Another Stalin Prize followed for the completed trilogy, *Khozhdeniye po mukam* (for 1942, 1st class). Along with other writers, Tolstoy conformed to the new interpretation of Ivan the Terrible, of whom Stalin thought highly. Burdened though it was with considerable historical falsifications, Tolstoy's two-part drama, *Ivan Grozny* (1941–43; Ivan the Terrible), won him his next Stalin Prize (for 1943–44, 1st class; awarded posthumously) and remained the best known of his 30-odd dramas. A period of national mourning was officially designated following his death.

Tolstoy's pre-Revolutionary works, which are set in the sphere of the provincial aristocracy, are based primarily on unusual, even grotesque incidents. They are humorous, erotic, rich in observation, and imaginative. A. Blok recorded in his diary: "Tolstoy is full-blooded and stout and sensuous and has the elegant affectations of the aristocrat, but he spoils everything by his rowdiness and his immature philosophy of life." After his return to the Soviet Union, Tolstoy remained aloof not only from literary groupings but also from the attempt to renew the Russian prose style. His own style remains a part of the realist tradition and is marked by particularly great vividness and clarity. His novel *Aelita*, influenced by H. G. Wells, begins the tradition of Soviet utopian literature. It was followed by numerous "entertaining novels with a sufficient amount of social stuffing" (Slonim). Tolstoy was made famous through his two most voluminous works, written over a period of decades: *Pyotr Pervy* and *Khozhdeniye po mukam*. The historical work describes Peter's life from his childhood to 1701; it is distinguished primarily by its broad panorama of secondary characters drawn from all classes; all the subjectivity of its presentation is coordinated with historical materials. The gradual conversion of the intelligentsia to Bolshevism constitutes the theme of Tolstoy's trilogy about the Revolution. In its original version, the first part is a remarkable novel about the spiritual guest of the Russian intelligentsia before the Revolution. Taken as a whole, the trilogy developed, after repeated revisions, the tendentiousness that led to its designation as a "classic" work of Soviet literature.

*Works: Khromoj barin* (novel), 1915 (Eng. tr., *The Lame Prince*, 1958); *Detstvo Nikity* (pov.), 1922 (see above): *Khoždenie po mukam* (novel), 3 vols., 1920–41; *Aèlita* (novel), 1923 (see above); *Pëtr Pervyj* (novel), 3 vols.,

1930–45 (see above); *Khleb* (novel), 1937; *Ivan Groznyj* (play, in two parts), 1942–43; *Zapisnye knižki* (notebooks), in *Lit. nasledstvo* 74:1965; *Rubaška Blans* (play, in collaboration with I. Èrenburg), in *Sovremennaja dramaturgija* 1982:4.—*Sobr. soč.*, 15 vols., 1927–31; 15 vols., 1929–30; 8 vols., 1934–36; *Polnoe sobr. soč.*, 15 vols., 1946–53; *Sobr. soč.*, 10 vols., 1958–61; 8 vols., 1972.
Secondary *Lit.*: I. Veksler, 1948; A. Alpatov, 1958; Ju. Krestinskij, 1960; G. Nivat, in *Cahiers du monde russe et soviétique* 1961; K. Čukovskij, in *Moskva* 1964:4; L. Poljak, 1964; V. Baranov, *Revoljucija i sud'ba khudožnika*, 1967; *RSPP* 5:1968; G. Smirnova, 1969; *Vospominanija ob A. N. T.*, 1973; N. Arsen'ev, in *Novyj žurnal*, New York, 122:1976; N. S. Tyrras, Diss., Univ. of British Columbia, 1978; L. I. Zvereva, 1982; S. Borovikov, 1984.

**Trenyóv, Konstantín Andréyevich,** playwright (b. June 2 [May 21], 1876, Romashovo, prov. Kharkov—d. May 19, 1945, Moscow). Trenyov's father was a peasant. In 1903 Trenyov completed his studies at the St. Petersburg Archaeological Institute and the Theological Academy. He worked as a teacher. Trenyov embarked on his literary career in 1898; he published his first drama in 1910 and a collection of short stories in 1915. In 1924 he wrote a historical drama, *Pugachovshchina* (Pugachovism), which was presented by the Moscow Art Theater. In Soviet literary histories Trenyov is acknowledged as one of the founders of Soviet dramatic art primarily on the basis of his drama *Lyubov Yarovaya* (1926; Stalin Prize for 1935–41, 1st class; Eng. tr., in *In a Cossack Village*, 1946). In this openly propagandistic play, Trenyov illustrates the revolutionary conflict between the Reds and the Whites, using a married couple as his example: the wife, fighting on the side of the Bolsheviks, abandons her husband, who is with the Whites, to his death. This play of epic construction is impaired primarily by lack of action and generally schematic characterization; it owes its reputation to its tendentious subordination of all things personal to the will of the Party. As with his other works, Trenyov revised the play several times. Of his later plays, only *Na beregu Nevy* (1937; On the Banks of the Neva), which looks back to the events of 1917, elicited a positive response, and only after Trenyov had expanded his portrayal of Lenin in compliance with the demands of the critics.

Works: *Vladyka* (short stories), 1915; *Pugačëvščina* (play), 1924; *Ljubov' Jarovaja* (play),

1927, rev. ed., 1937; *P'esy* (plays), 1935; *Na beregu Nevy* (play), 1937; *Zabytye rasskazy* (short stories), 1959; *P'esy, stat'i, reči* (plays, essays, and speeches), 1980.—*Sobr. soč.*, 2 vols., 1927–28; *Izbr. proizv.*, 2 vols., 1947–49, 1955.
Secondary *Lit.*: E. Surkov, 1953; V. A. Diev, 1960; R. Fajnberg, 1962; D. Ustjužanin, 1972; *Živoj Trenëv* (memoirs), 2d ed., 1976.

**Trétya volná** (The Third Wave), "almanac for literature and the fine arts," whose title alludes to the "third wave" of EMIGRATION, which reached its peak in the 1970s. *Tretya volna* was established in France in 1976 by Aleksandr Glezer, first as a journal and after issue no. 2 in 1977 as an almanac. With issue no. 10 in 1980, the editorial offices were moved to the United States. The use of "Paris–New York" in the masthead (starting with issue no. 12, 1982) reveals the preference given these two cities by the émigré community. In 1986, issue no. 19 was published. *Tretya volna* is an organ for nonconformist art in words and images. Each issue contains poetry, prose, and reviews as well as illustrations, reports of exhibitions, and other texts concerning newest Russian art. Through the publisher A. Glezer, *Tretya volna* is linked to his Russian Museum in Exile (Russky muzey v izgnanii) in Montgeron. *Tretya volna* makes an effort to provide a forum for nonconformist artists in the USSR by offering them the possibility of publishing in TAMIZDAT. Among the authors whose works have been published in *Tretya volna* are V. Aksyonov, G. Aygi, D. Bobyshev, N. Bokov, S. Dovlatov, A. Galich, Yu. Galperin, Ye. Kozlovksy, V. Lyon, L. Losev, V. Maksimov, Yu. Mamleyev, V. Maramzin, V. Nechayev, V. Rybakov, G. Sapgir, B. Vakhtin, A. Volokhonsky, Yu. Voznesenskaya, V. Vysotsky, S. Yuryenen.

Secondary *Lit.*: V. Malašin, in *Russkaja mysl'*, Paris, June 8, 1978, p. 12; conference report, in *Tret'ja volna* 7–8:1979; A. Danilovič, in *Russkaja mysl'* Jan. 20, 1983, p. 11; S. Jur'enen, in *Russkaja mysl'* April 21, 1983, p. 12; M. Muravnik, in *Russkaja mysl'* Sept. 15, 1983, p. 10; Ju. Mamleev, in *Russkaja mysl'* Nov. 17, 1983, p. 10; A. Dranov, in *Novoe russkoe slovo*, New York, Sept. 6, 1985, pp. 3–4.

**Tretyakóv, Sergéy Mikháylovich,** playwright (b. June 20 [June 8], 1892, Goldingen, prov. Kurland—d. Aug. 9, 1939 [?], while imprisoned). Tretyakov's father was a teacher. Tretyakov attended school in Riga, then studied law at Moscow University, finishing in 1916. He joined the ego-futurists (see FUTURISM) and spent the years from 1919 to 1922 in the Soviet Far East and Siberia working in cultural administration; with N. Aseyev and D. Burlyuk he belonged to the futurist circle around the journal *Tvorchestvo*. His first volume of verse, *Zheleznaya pauza* (1919; The Iron Pause), was published in Vladivostok. In 1922 Tretyakov returned to Moscow and continued to fight for revolutionary experimentation in art; he belonged to the LEF group. He worked with S. Eisenstein in the Theater of the Proletkult (from 1923 to 1926) and with V. Meyerhold in the latter's theater (from 1922 to 1926). After freely adapting materials by M. Martinet and A. Ostrovsky for stage production, Tretyakov was able to see his own plays performed; *Neporochnoye zachatiye* (1923; Immaculate Conception), *Slyshish, Moskva?!* (1923; Are You Listening, Moscow?!), and—set in the assembly hall of a factory—*Protivogazy* (1924; Gas Masks). In 1924–25 Tretyakov lectured on Russian literature at Peking University. His drama *Rychi, Kitay!* (1926; Eng. tr., *Roar, China!*, 1931) was well received. At the same time Tretyakov published articles in *Pravda*; a collection of journalism, *Chzhungo* (1927; Jong-guo); and a novel in the form of an interview, *Den Shikhua* (1930; Eng. tr., *Chinese Testament: The Autobiography of Tan Shih-hua as Told to Tretyakov*, 1934). Tretyakov wrote numerous articles in an effort to contribute to Communist construction; such, for instance, are his two books on collectivization, *Vyzov* (1930; The Challenge) and *Tysyacha i odin trudoden* (1934; A Thousand and One Workdays). Tretyakov edited the last five issues of *Novy LEF* after V. Mayakovsky left the journal. In 1930–31 Tretyakov traveled to Germany, Denmark, and Austria, where he came into close contact with Erwin Piscator and Bertolt Brecht, among others. In 1934 he was the first to acquaint the Russian reader with Brecht's work in his translation of three of the German writer's dramas *(Epicheskiye dramy)*. *Lyudi odnogo kostra* (1936; People of a Single Bonfire) tells the story of writers, including Brecht, F. Wolf, J. R. Becher, H. Eisler, T. Plivier, whose works were burned by the Nazis. Tretyakov's stay in Czechoslovakia in 1935 was reflected in *Strana–perekryostok* (1937; A Crossroads Country). He was arrested in the fall of 1937; his REHABILITATION occurred in 1956.

For Tretyakov, poems were "smelting laboratories for words, workplaces in which verbal materials are flexed, cut, riveted, welded, and assembled" (1922) and the writer was "a

Communist verbal functionary." *Slyshish, Moskva?!* is set in the Germany of 1923; it dispenses with any attempt to individualize its part-real, part-grotesque characters; posterlike, they represent the exploiters and the exploited and demonstrate the theses of the class struggle in schematic dialogue. *Rychi, Kitay!* is a Communist propaganda play with strong anti-American tendencies; it is set in the milieu of Chinese dock workers, with characters to some extent individualistically drawn. In Germany alone it has been staged more than a hundred times; it was presented by the Theater Guild in New York in 1930.

*Works: Železnaja pauza* (poems), 1919; *Jasnyš* (poems), 1919; *Slyšiš', Moskva?!* (play), 1924, 2d ed., 1966, with the two plays following; *Protivogazy* (play), 1924; *Čžungo* (publicistic prose), 1927; *Ryči, Kitaj* (play), 1930 (see above); *Vyzov* (publicistic prose), 1930; *Den Ši-khua: Bio-interv'ju* (novel), 1930 (see above); *Mesjac v derevne* (publicistic prose), 1931; *Tysjača i odin trudoden'* (publicistic prose), 1934; *Ljudi odnogo kostra* (literary portraits), 1936; *Strana-perekrëstok* (publicistic prose), 1937; *Den Ši-khua. Ljudi odnogo kostra. Strana-perekrëstok* (publicistic prose), 1962.

*Secondary Lit.:* S. Margolin, *Pervyj rabočij teatr Proletkul'ta*, 1930; A. M. Ripellino, *Majakovskij und das russische Theater der Avantgarde*, 1964; RSPP 7(2):1972; L. Az'muko, Irkutsk, 1972; F. Mierau, in *Zeitschrift für Slawistik* 1975 and 1976; L. Kleberg, in *Scando-Slavica* 23;1977.

**Trífonov, Yúry Valentínovich,** prose writer (b. Aug. 28, 1925, Moscow—d. March 28, 1981, Moscow). Trifonov's father was a Party official who joined the revolutionary movement in 1905 and organized the Red Guards in Petrograd; in 1937 he became a victim of the purges. Trifonov completed school in Tashkent in 1942 and then worked in Moscow airplane factories. From 1944 to 1949 he studied at the Gorky Literary Institute. His first short stories appeared in 1947; Trifonov's povest *Studenty* (1950; Eng. tr., *Students*, 1953) gained recognition with a Stalin Prize (for 1950, 3d class). Trifonov won rapid national and international acclaim in the 1970s. With *Obmen* (1969; Eng. tr., *The Exchange*, 1975), *Predvaritelnye itogi* (1970; Eng. tr., *Taking Stock*, 1978), and *Dolgoye proshchaniye* (1971; Eng. tr., *The Long Goodbye*, 1978), Trifonov created three short novels about daily life in contemporary Moscow; in *Dom na naberezhnoy* (1976; Eng. tr., *The House on the Embankment*, 1983) and

Starik (1978; Old Man) he added a historical perspective. For the series "Ardent Revolutionaries," he wrote the purely historical novel Neterpeniye (1973; Eng. tr., The Impatient Ones, 1978). Despite his role as one of the leading Soviet writers of his time, Trifonov never held leading positions; he was only on the board of the Writers Union of the RSFSR from 1965 to 1970. He lived in Moscow.

In all his works, Trifonov attempts to depict truthfully the life of the upper classes in the Soviet Union. His social criticism, especially of thinking focused on material prosperity, of the class structure of Soviet society, and of the lack of spiritual reference points, goes deeper than that of other authors who are less well known abroad, but his criticism conveys only a "partial truth" (Shenfeld). Utoleniye zhazhdy (1963; The Quenching of Thirst) draws upon his trips to Turkmenistan (1956–63) and reflects the hopes prevalent following the 20th and 22d Party Congresses. Otblesk kostra (1965; The Reflection of Fire) is a half-documentary report about his father's fate; misleadingly, only 2 percent of the text is devoted to the years 1921–37, however. The topical issue of interpersonal relationships within Soviet extended families distinguishes his three Moscow povesti; the novel Soviet critics most frequently object to, Dom na naberezhnoy, alludes to the purges of 1937 and 1949, to class privileges, and to the success of unprincipled opportunists; furthermore, it best reveals Trifonov's conscious work with multilevel narrative structure. Starik is an attempt to rehabilitate the Cossack victims of the early Soviet period and to contrast the alienated youth to the idealized revolutionaries who are their grandfathers. In Neterpeniye, a novel about the terrorists who assassinated the tsar in 1881, Trifonov attempts to break some taboos, although he does accept the Party's inclusion of the anarchists among the Marxist-Leninist precursors of the Revolution. Trifonov's narrative style is convoluted and slow-moving but rich in flashbacks, changes of perspective, and reflections; with psychological realism he places emphasis on people and their errors and doubts, and he rejects any kind of social and political classification or assessment. Trifonov's last novel, Vremja i mesto (1981; Time and Place), whose Russian-language version bears the marks of the censor (differing from the German one), offers a wealth of details from the life of a writer in the Soviet Union from the 1930s to the 1970s.

Works: Studenty (pov.), 1951 (see above); Pod solncem (short stories), 1959; Utolenie žaždy (novel), 1963; Fakely na Flaminio (short stories and sketches), 1965; Otblesk kostra (pov.), in Znamja 1965:2, rev. ed., 1966; Kepka s bol'šim kozyr'kom (short stories), 1969; Obmen (pov.), in Novyj mir 1969:12 (see above); Predvaritel'nye itogi (pov.), in Novyj mir 1970:12; Dolgoe proščanie (pov.), 1973 (see above); Neterpenie (novel), 1973 (see above); interview, in Voprosy lit. 1974:8; Drugaja žizn' (pov.), in Novyj mir 1975:8, separate ed., 1976 (Eng. tr., Another Life, 1983); Dom na naberežnoj (pov.), in Družba narodov 1976:1, separate ed., Ann Arbor, 1983 (see above); Starik (novel), in Družba narodov 1978:3, separate ed., 1979; Vremja i mesto (novel), in Družba narodov 1981:9–10, separate ed., 1981; Večnye temy (essays), 1984; Isčeznovenie (novel), in Družba narodov 1987:1.—Izbr. proizv., 2 vols., 1978; Sobr. soč., 4 vols., 1985–.

Secondary Lit.: V. Rosljakov, in Moskva 1963:10; I. Kramov, in Novyj mir 1967:3; Ju. Andreev, in Lit. gazeta March 3, 1971, p. 5; V. Sokolov et al., in Voprosy lit. 1972:2; G. Brovman, in Lit. gazeta March 8, 1972, p. 5; RSPP 7 (2):1972; A. Bočarov, in Oktjabr' 1975:8; V. Dudincev, in Lit. obozrenie 1976:4–5; E. Reissner, in Osteuropa 1979:2; G. Hosking, in his Beyond Socialist Realism, New York, 1980; I. Šenfel'd, in Grani, Frankfurt am Main, 121:1981; S. Erëmina, V. Piskunov, in Voprosy lit. 1982:5; T. Patera, Diss., McGill Univ., 1982; G. Ermolaev, V. Golovskoj, in Russian Language Journal 1983:3; Natalja Ivanova, 1984; E. Èl'jaševic, in Zvezda 1984:12; L. Anninskij, in Družba narodov 1985:3; Jurij Trifonov. 1925–1981 gg. (bibliography), 1985.

**Troyepólsky, Gavriíl Nikoláyevich,** prose writer (b. Nov. 29 [Nov. 16], 1905, Novospasovka, prov. Tambov). Troyepolsky's father was an Orthodox clergyman. In 1924 Troyepolsky graduated from the agricultural institute in Borisoglebsk. Until 1930 he worked as a teacher; from 1930 to 1954, as an agronomist in kolkhozes. Troyepolsky, who had once published a short story in 1937, became known as a writer in 1953 with the publication in Novy mir of his journalistic satirical short stories, Iz zapisok agronoma (From the Notes of an Agronomist). From then on, he only worked as a writer; in 1954 he moved to Voronezh where he still lives today. In 1958–61 his first novel about agriculture, Chernozyom (Black Earth), was published in parts. From his journalistic prose, O rekakh, pochvakh i prochem (1965; About Rivers, Ground, and Other Things), a sharp indictment of the catastrophic water policy in central Russia that A. Tvardovsky printed in Novy mir, met with great acclaim. Troyepolsky has participated in all the congresses of the Writers Union of the USSR and that of the RSFSR since 1958. He has been a member of the board of the Writers Union of the USSR since 1967 and of that of the Writers Union of the RSFSR since 1975. He was awarded the State Prize of the USSR in 1975 and joined the editorial staff of *Nash sovremennik* in 1976.

In the second half of the 1950s, Troyepolsky made a name for himself as one of the best representatives of journalistic prose concerning agriculture. In this he follows V. Ovechkin, sharing with him the expertise gained from his own practical experience and a tendency toward frankness in negative descriptions. *Kandidat nauk* (1958; The Candidate in [Agricultural] Science) continues the satirical *Iz zapisok agronoma* in its critique of the pseudosciences. *Chernozyom* records agricultural development from the Revolution to collectivization, also depicting the unjust measures involved in the latter campaign. (The edition published in 1972 has been reworked.) The novel translated into more than 20 languages, *Bely Bim Chornoye ukho* (1971; White Bim, Black Ear; Eng. tr., *Beem*, 1978), the story of a dog in which many see a roman à clef about Tvardovsky, is tied to Troyepolsky's central realm of experience through descriptions of nature and hunts. Through its allegorical power and reflections, this novel reveals general human concerns especially clearly.

*Works: Iz zapisok agronoma* (short stories), 1954; *Prokhor semnadcatyj i drugie* (short stories), 1954; *U krutogo jara* (short stories), 1956; *Kandidat nauk* (pov.), 1959; *Zapiski agronoma* (short stories), 1961 (enl. ed. of *Iz zapisok agronoma*, 1954); *Černozëm* (novel), 1962; *V kamyšakh* (short stories), 1964; *O rekakh, počvakh i pročem* (memoirs), in *Novyj mir* 1965:1; *Belyj Bim Čërnoe ukho* (pov.), 1972 (see above); *Zdravyj smysl* (short stories and pov.), 1975.—*Soč.*, 3 vols., 1977–78.

*Secondary Lit.*: V. Ognëv, in *Znamja* 1954:1; V. Ovečkin, in *Lit. gazeta* Oct. 29, 1955; V. Sultanov, in *Lit. Rossija* Nov. 26, 1965, p. 5; *RSPP* 5:1968; V. Skobolev, 1969; I. Borisova, in *Novyj mir* 1971:8; V. Kanaškin, in *Lit. Rossija* July 26, 1974, p. 5; B. Možaev, in *Lit. Rossija* Sept. 3, 1976, p. 6; V. Lakšin, in *Lit. Rossija* Nov. 28, 1980, pp. 14–15; N. Gorbačëv, Ju. Gribov, in *Naš sovremennik* 1985:11.

**Tsekh poétov** (Guild of Poets), a group of ACMEIST poets that was established in 1911 in St. Petersburg as a counterweight to the symbolists. With N. Gumilyov as the leading

figure, the group existed until 1914; it was renewed in 1920 with a somewhat different makeup and lasted until 1923. A large number of the members emigrated. The membership included, above all, G. Adamovich, A. Akhmatova, S. Gorodetsky, G. Ivanov, V. Lozinsky, O. Mandelshtam, V. Narbut, S. Neldikhen, I. Odoyevtseva, N. Otsup, V. Rozhdestvensky, K. Vaginov, M. Zenkevich. Through the initiative of N. Otsup, Tsekh poetov was revived once in exile in Berlin, and S. Gorodetsky revived it once briefly in Moscow in 1925. As the name Tsekh poetov indicates, the members were especially concerned with emphasizing craftsmanship and conscious work on linguistic creation. Their opposition to symbolism was especially directed against the overemphasis given to the magical character of language and led to A. Blok's accusation that they would "drown themselves in the cold swamp of soulless theories and every possible kind of formalism." Tsekh poetov published the journal *Giperborey* in 1912 and 1913, as well as volumes of poetry by individual authors. With *Drakon* (1921; The Dragon), Tsekh poetov began publishing almanacs of poetry; two more volumes were published in Petrograd, each with a different title. In Berlin in 1923, these volumes were reprinted with few alterations and a fourth volume was added. The first volume of poetry issued by the Moscow Tsekh poetov was *Styk* (1925), with prefaces by A. Lunacharsky and S. Gorodetsky and poems by A. Bely, B. Pasternak, G. Shengeli, and many others.

*Secondary Lit.*: N. Gumilëv, *Nasledie simvolizma i akmeizm* (essays), in *Apollon* 1913:1 and in his *Sobr. soč.*, vol. 4, Washington, 1968; A. Blok, *Bez božestva, bez vdokhnoven'ja (Cekh akmeistov)* (essays), 1921, and in his *Sobr. soč.*, vol. 6, 1962, pp. 174–84; A. Akhmatova, in *Vozdušnye puti*, New York, 4:1965, pp. 35–45, and in her *Sočinenija*, vol. 2, Washington, 1968, pp. 173f.

**Tsvetáyeva, Marína Ivánovna**, poet (b. Oct. 8 [Sept. 26], 1892, Moscow—d. Aug. 31, 1941, Yelabuga). Tsvetayeva's father (the son of a village clergyman) was a professor at Moscow University and the founder of the museum of fine arts there; her mother (of German-Polish ancestry) was a pianist, a student of A. Rubinstein. During her secondary-school years, Tsvetayeva spent some time in Italy, Switzerland, Germany, and France on various occasions and witnessed the publication of her first collection of poetry, *Vecherniy albom*

(1910; Evening Album), which attracted the attention of M. Voloshin, V. Bryusov, and N. Gumilyov. In 1915 she met O. Mandelshtam, and a brief friendship ensued. She belonged to none of the literary groups, such as the symbolists, ACMEISTS, or futurists (see FUTURISM). She opposed the October Revolution; her husband, Sergey Efron, fought with the Whites. Before she followed him into emigration in 1922, she published several volumes of poetry in Moscow. After three years in Prague, she moved to Paris at the end of 1925. Early recognition was followed by increasingly strained relations with the leading circles of emigration, as reflected in the negative reviews of her only book of poetry to appear in Paris, *Posle Rossii* (1928; After Russia). Loneliness, poverty, homesickness for the country of her mother tongue, and concern for her son led her to return to the USSR in 1939. After becoming entangled in a secret service operation, her husband had already returned to the USSR, been imprisoned, and possibly already been shot before Tsvetayeva's arrival. Their daughter, Alya, also repatriated in 1937, was in a prison camp (REHABILITATION probably 1955). Tsvetayeva was not given an apartment in Moscow and made a living by translating. Of her own works, only a single poem from her days in Prague was reprinted. At the beginning of World War II she was evacuated. After vain attempts to establish a position through writers such as N. Aseyev, she put an end to her tragic life. With the help of I. Erenburg, V. Orlov, and her daughter, Tsvetayeva has gradually been accepted into Soviet literature again since the Second Writers Congress. K. Paustovsky published 7 of her poems in *Literaturnaya Moskva* (1956:2) and 42 in *Tarusskiye stranitsy*. Volumes of her selected poems have frequently appeared since 1961. In the West, since 1953, more of her prose and poetry has been published. Poems to or about her written by A. Akhmatova, A. Bely, O. Mandelshtam, S. Marshak, B. Pasternak, Rainer Maria Rilke, and M. Voloshin, among others, express high acclaim for her.

Tsvetayeva's early work developed during the high point of Russian lyricism at the beginning of the 20th century. Her poems, which attained their first great height of expression in the volume *Remeslo* (1923; Handicraft), are marked by great conciseness, a wealth of imagery, and frequent parallelisms in meaning and sound. Like other lyricists of her time, she compresses her verse by omitting the verbs (usually the verbs of motion) and unites vernacular and ancient Russian elements with the literary language of the 20th century.

"Tsvetayeva's language is characterized by lofty rhetoric but at the same time is completely turned toward the rhythmic life of the word and the verse" (Holthusen). Next to much personal poetry stand poems that draw on Greek mythology, verse epics dealing with Russian fairy-tale motifs, and political poetry. In this connection, she portrays the White Army's struggle against the Bolsheviks in the cycle *Lebediny stan* (Eng. tr., *The Demesne of the Swans*, 1980), written from 1917 to 1921 and first published in Munich in 1957, and in the narrative poem *Perekop*, written in 1928 and 1929 and first published in 1967. In *Krysolov* (1925–26; The Pied Piper), she created a lyrical, social, and political satire that denounced the bourgeoisification of the revolutionaries. In personal recollections and thoughts about contemporary poets (Bryusov, Pasternak, Voloshin), Tsvetayeva's prose captures the essential aspects of these artistic personalities, using an impressionist narrative style. Of the short dramas she wrote, the first four, written from 1918 to 1921, come under the influence of neoromanticism; two from the 1920s reflect her preoccupation with Greek mythology.

*Works: Večernij al'bom* (poems), 1910; *Volšebnyj fonar'* (poems), 1912; *Vërsty I* (poems), 1922 (reprinted, Ann Arbor, 1972); *Car'-devica: Poèma-skazka* (narrative poem), 1922 (reprinted, Letchworth, 1971); *Stikhi k Bloku* (poems), Berlin, 1922 (reprinted, Letchworth, 1978); *Razluka* (poems), Berlin, 1922; *Remeslo* (poems), Berlin, 1923; *Psikheja* (poems), Berlin, 1923; *Molodec* (narrative poem), Prague, 1924; *Krysolov* (narrative poem), Paris, 1925 (reprinted, Letchworth, 1978, and Vienna, 1982); *Posle Rossii 1922–1925* (poems), Paris, 1928 (reprinted, Paris, 1976); *Povest' o Sonečke*: part 1, in *Russkie zapiski* 1938:3 (reprinted in *Novyj mir* 1976:3); part 2, in *Neizdannoe*, Paris, 1976 (reprinted in *Novyj mir* 1979:12); *Proza*, New York, 1953; *Lebedinyj stan* (poems), Munich, 1957 (see above); *Izbr.* (selection), Moscow, 1961; *Izbr. proizv.*, Moscow, 1965; *Moj Puškin* (essays), Moscow, 1967; *Perekop* (narrative poem), in *Vozdušnye puti*, New York, 5:1967; *Pis'ma k Anne Teskovoj* (letters), Prague, 1969; *Proza*, Letchworth, 1969; *Stikhotvorenija* (poems), Letchworth, 1969; *Nesobrannye proizv.*, Munich, 1971 (with bibliography 1966–70); *Neizdannye pis'ma* (letters), Paris, 1972; *Neizdannoe* (poems, plays, prose), Paris, 1976; *Metel'. Priključenie. Ariadna* (plays), Letchworth, 1978; *Stikhotvorenija i poèmy* (lyric and narrative poems), 1979.—*Izbr. proza*, 2 vols., New York, 1979; *Soč.*, 2 vols., 1980; *Stikho-*

*tvorenija i poèmy,* 5 vols., New York, 1980–. *Translations: Selected Poems,* 1971; *A Captive Spirit: Selected Prose,* 1980. Secondary Lit.: I. Èrenburg, in Lit. Moskva, vol. 2, 1956; Vl. Orlov, in Izbr. proizv., 1965; S. Karlinsky, Berkeley, 1966, 2d rev. and enl. ed., 1985 (with a thorough bibliography); M. Slonim, in Novyj žurnal, New York, 100:1970 and 104:1971; A. Cvetaeva, Vospominanija, Moscow, 1971; G. Smith, in Slavonic and East European Review 1975: A. Livingstone, in Russian Literature Triquarterly 11:1975; A. M. Kroth, Diss., Univ. of Michigan, 1977; A. Èfron, Paris, 1979; S. El'nickaja, in Wiener Slawistischer Almanach 3, 4, 7, 11, 15:1979–85; O. P. Hasty, Diss., Yale Univ., 1980; M. Razumovsky, Vienna, 1981; M. C. Studien und Materialien, Vienna, 1981; A. Saakjanc, in Moskva 1982:10; M. Razumovskaja, London, 1983; S. Poljakova, Ann Arbor, 1983; M.-L. Bott, Frankfurt am Main, 1984; J. Faryno, Vienna, 1985.

**Tsvetkóv, Alekséy Petróvich,** poet (b. Feb. 2, 1947, Ivano-Frankovsk, Ukraine [formerly Stanisław, Poland]). Tsvetkov's father was an officer. Tsvetkov grew up in Zaporozhye. He studied chemistry at Odessa University in 1964–65, then history at Moscow University until 1968, and journalism there from 1971 to 1974. He lived in Siberia and Kazakhstan for a while and earned a living in Moscow through odd jobs as a newspaper correspondent, watchman, proofreader. Tsvetkov was occasionally able to recite his poetry publicly, but it was published infrequently. In 1975 he emigrated to the United States. In 1976–77 he was copublisher of the newspaper Russkaya zhizn (San Francisco). He continued his studies at the University of Michigan and was awarded the doctoral degree in 1983 for a dissertation entitled "The Language of Andrey Platonov." Tsvetkov's poems appear in journals such as Kontinent, Ekho, Vremya i my, Strelets. A selection of his poetry written between 1968 and 1975 was published in Russian and German in the almanac NRL: Neue russische Literatur (Salzburg), no. 4–5 in 1983. The titles of both of his collections of poetry, Sbornik pyes dlya zhizni solo (1978; Collection of Plays for Solo Life) and Sostoyaniye sna (1981; Dream Condition), point to the avant-garde form of his philosophical poetry. He lives in Washington, D.C.

Tsvetkov's early poems examine the spiritual dimensions of a concrete situation, for example, a shooting or a trip across the steppes. Gradually the degree of abstraction of his metaphysically well-grounded poetry increased, the punctuation disappeared, and the result is a metaphorically rich, ambiguous, philosophical poetry that is constantly seeking to understand its own fate. In his imagery, the fields of history, music, and nature predominate. His relationship to the world preserves an ironic distance and frames his seriousness with playful effortlessness; the maxim from 1977 remains true: "I am in favor of the unity of moral striving in the actions and work of an artist."

Works: Poems, in, among others, Kontinent, Paris, 13:1977, 20:1979, 24:1980; in Èkho, Paris, 1979:2–3; in Vremja i my, Tel Aviv, 30:1978, 76:1984; in Strelec, Montgeron–Jersey City, N.J. 1985:6; Autobiography and experimental prose, in Apollon '77, Paris, 1977. Sbornik p'es dlja žizni solo (poems), Ann Arbor, 1978; Sostojanie sna (poems), Ann Arbor, 1981; Ontologičeskie napevy: Stikhi 1968–1975 (poems, in Russian and German), in NRL: Neue russische Literatur 4–5:1981–82, Salzburg, 1983; Èdem (poems), Ann Arbor, 1985.

**Tsýbin, Vladímir Dmítriyevich,** poet, prose writer (b. March 11, 1932, Samsonovskaya, oblast Frunze). Tsybin was of peasant descent. In his youth Tsybin worked as a miner and a factory hand; he took part in geological expeditions. Tsybin published his first poem in 1952; he subsequently studied at the Gorky Literary Institute, graduating in 1958. Tsybin became known as a poet with a close relation to nature by using his Cossack homeland as his subject through his early volume of verse, Roditelnitsa step (1959; Mother Steppe). It was followed by other volumes, including Puls (1963; Pulse). Vspleski (1967; Splashes) was Tsybin's first volume of short stories; he supplemented it with Kapeli (1972; Droplets), while continuing to publish additional collections of verse. From late 1961 to early 1966 he was affiliated with the journal Molodaya gvardiya as a member of its editorial board; from 1973 to 1979 he was with the journal Znamya. Tsybin became a member of the board of the Writers Union of the RSFSR in 1965 and of that of the Writers Union of the USSR in 1981. He lives in Moscow.

Tsybin's early verse, inspired by Cossack life, vividly combines highly colored nature imagery with scenes occasionally taken from the Civil War. His depiction of nature often symbolizes the individual's relationship to his destiny or to his fellowmen. Tsybin's verse preserves its ties to the earth and its closeness to his native land even as it gradually turns more and more toward contemplation, to the poet's conflict with himself, to his scrutiny of his own being. Tsybin's verse is not rhetorical or politically tendentious; neither is it characterized by any particular density. Tsybin tends toward the concrete element, which can become an intensely expressive metaphor, now and then heightened by contrast. "Tsybin's poetry is a mixture of contemporary standard Russian, archaisms, and rural dialect" (D. Brown). His verse is determined more by rhythm than by meter; it often approaches prose, as in his short stories, which, frequently based on the world of his own childhood, have quite a lyrical character.

*Works: Roditel'nica step'* (poems), 1959; *Medovukha* (poems), 1960; *Pul's* (poems), 1963; *Au!* (poems), 1967; *Vspleski* (short stories), 1967; *Glagol* (poems), 1970; *Izby* (poems), 1971; *Kapeli* (pov. and short stories), 1972; *Vspleski. Kapeli* (short stories), 1973; *Izbr. Stichotvorenija, Poèmy,* 1979.

*Secondary Lit.:* L. Lavinskij, in *Družba narodov* 1964:5; L. Anninskij, in *Moskva* 1964:5; V. Čalmaev, in *Lit. gazeta* July 31, 1968, p. 4; S. Ostrovoj, in *Lit. Rossija* Sept. 24, 1971, p. 20; V. Primerov, in *Don* 1980:3; I. Denisova, in *Lit. Rossija* Dec. 12, 1983, p. 8.

**Tur,** bratya (Tur Brothers), playwrights (pseuds. of Leoníd Davýdovich Tubélsky, b. April 11 [March 29], 1905, Tagancha, prov. Kiev—d. Feb. 14, 1961, Moscow; and Pyotr Lvóvich Rýzhey, b. Jan. 24 [Jan. 11], 1908, Kiev—d. Oct. 2, 1978, Moscow). Tubelsky attended the Leningrad Institute of Oriental Studies, Ryzhey studied at the Leningrad Institute for Theater Arts. They began their collaborative career in 1923 as journalists; in 1925 they selected the pseudonym "Tur Brothers," and in the early 1930s began their work in theater and film. They wrote numerous plays (frequently with other authors, such as L. Sheynin) that went over well with the public. They served as war correspondents during World War II. Their film script *Vstrecha na Elbe* (1947; Meeting at the Elbe), written with Sheynin and based on the Turs' play *Gubernator provintsii* (1947; The Provincial Governor), presented the Red Army as an ideal liberator; it was awarded a Stalin Prize (for 1949, 1st class). The Turs' trite plays, such as *Pobeg iz nochi* (1958; Escape from Out of the Night), for instance, or *Severnaya madonna* (1961; Northern Madonna), were performed frequently. After the death of Tubelsky-Tur,

Ryzhey-Tur, who lived in Moscow, wrote plays with his wife, Ariadna. Their play about A. Kollontay, *Chrezvychayny posol* (1966; Ambassador Extraordinary), has attracted the most attention.

The Turs' first public success was *Ochnaya stavka* (1937; Eng. tr., *Showdown,* 1938), a play that propagandized the Soviet secret police and called for vigilance against spies. Journalistic and criminological themes in accord with the political status quo continued to exercise a determining influence over a portion of their copious dramatic output. Their war play, *Dym otechestva* (1943; Eng. tr., *Smoke of the Fatherland,* in *Seven Soviet Plays,* 1946), "because of its pervasive melodramatic rhythm . . . [is] really a very theatrical play and not without interest despite its many familiar ingredients" (Segel). In addition there are biographical plays, for example, *Sofya Kovalevskaya* (1943); plays that typically illustrate the THEORY OF CONFLICT-LESSNESS, such as *Tretya molodost* (1952; Third Childhood); and dramas with conventional interpersonal problems, such as *Koleso schastya* (1955; The Wheel of Fortune). The Turs' plays are primitive and schematic, their political or moral lesson is obvious, their theme is inadequately realized. Soviet criticism has always pointed out these defects; literary histories ignore the Tur Brothers entirely. The number of performances of their plays, however, attest to the success of the plays with the public and their effectiveness in staging.

*Works: Očnaja stavka* (play), in *Oktjabr'* 1937:9 (see above); *Vstreča na El'be* (film-script written in collaboration with L. Šejnin), in *Izbr. kinoscenarii* 1949–50, 1951; *Gubernator provincii* (play), in *P'esy sovetskikh pisatelej* 1955:9; *Posle razluki* (play), 1957; *Pobeg iz noči* (play), 1959; *Dramy* (plays), 1962; *Sredi bela dnja* (short stories), 1964; Ariadna and Petr Tur: *Črezvyčajnyj posol* (play), 1968; *P'esy* (plays), 1975 (contains *Edinstvennyj svidetel'*; *Črezvyčajnyj posol; Perebežčik; Sverstnicy; Lunnaja sonata).*

*Secondary Lit.:* N. Abalkin, in *Novyj mir* 1953:5; M. Turovskaja, in *Lit. gazeta* April 7, 1956; V. Pimenov, in *Pravda* March 10, 1964, and in *Teatr* 1967:12; G. Kožukhova, in *Pravda* Feb. 22, 1971.

**Tvardóvsky, Aleksándr Trífonovich,** poet (b. June 21 [June 8], 1910, Zagorye, prov. Smolensk—d. Dec. 18, 1971, Krasnaya Pakhra, near Moscow). Tvardovsky's father was a peasant and blacksmith who was persecuted as a kulak. Tvardovsky wrote his first poems as a child; he began his career as writer and journalist while a student at the Smolensk Pedagogical Institute and the Moscow Institute of Philosophy, Literature, and History (from which he graduated in 1939). In 1931 he found in Put k sotsializmu (The Path to Socialism) the narrative verse form that is the distinctive characteristic of his work. Tvardovsky became famous for his narrative poem about the collectivization of agriculture, Strana Muraviya (1936; The Land of Muravia), which received a Stalin Prize (for 1935–41, 2d class) in 1941. He joined the Communist Party in 1940. Tvardovsky served as a war correspondent during the Polish campaign (1939), the Finnish-Russian War (1940), and World War II. His Vasily Tyorkin (1941–45; Eng. tr., Vassili Tyorkin, 1975), an extensive narrative poem, became one of the most popular literary works of the war period and even aroused the enthusiasm of I. Bunin; the poem (which received a Stalin Prize for 1943–44, 1st class) describes with great humor the joys and the suffering of simple soldiers. A more tragic note is sounded in Dom u dorogi (1946; The House by the Road), for which Tvardovsky was awarded a Stalin Prize for 1946, 2d class. In 1950 he was named editor in chief of Novy mir but lost the position in 1954 in connection with the attacks directed against the journal's liberal tendencies in the period following Stalin's death. He was reinstated in 1958 and made Novy mir into the nucleus of those forces of literature that strove to portray candidly Soviet reality. Of his own narrative poems (which look upon the period of Stalinist oppression in a new spirit), Za dalyu-dal (1950–60; Far, Far Away) was officially recognized and received the Lenin Prize in 1961; Tyorkin na tom svete (1954–63; Tyorkin in the Other World) continued his war poem as a parody; while Po pravu pamyati (1967–69; By Right of Memory), which contained (among other things) the truth about his father's fate as a victim of collectivization, was banned by the censor. (It was published only in 1987.) A. Solzhenitsyn was one of the many talented writers whom Tvardovsky encouraged and protected from conservative reactions. In 1970 Tvardovsky was forced to resign as editor of Novy mir. His death, about a year and a half later, was described by Solzhenitsyn in his obituary as being directly related to the destruction of Tvardovsky's efforts on behalf of Russian literature. Tvardovsky long held responsible positions in the area of literature as a member of the boards of the Writers Unions of the

USSR (from 1950 on) and of the RSFSR (from 1958 on), and in particular as a secretary of the board of the Writers Union of the USSR (1950–54, 1959–71); he also served four terms as representative to the Supreme Soviet; and under Khrushchev he even became a candidate for the Central Committee of the Communist Party. After 1965 he was exposed to increasing attacks by conservative forces; nevertheless, he was awarded another State Prize in 1971. "Tvardovsky's death was the turning point of an entire period in the country's cultural life" (Zh. Medvedev).

Stylistically, Tvardovsky's work forms a relatively solid whole through his use of narrative verse forms (ballads, verse epics), which, harking back to N. Nekrasov and A. Pushkin, employ folklore elements, are easily understood, and appeal to a large public. While his early work consistently adheres to the principles of SOCIALIST REALISM, his works of the post-Stalin period belong more and more to the literature of accusation grappling with the problems of overcoming the past and democratizing the present. He uses, furthermore, the epic plot device of the journey and often incorporates reflections of social and political events. Death interrupted Tvardovsky's attempt to present the whole truth about the horrors of the times he lived through.

Works: Put' k socializmu (narrative poem), 1931; Strana Muravija (narrative poem), 1936; Vasilij Tërkin (narrative poem), 1945 (see above); Dom u dorogi (narrative poem), 1948; Za dal'ju-dal' (narrative poem), 1960; Tërkin na tom svete (narrative poem), 1963; Kniga liriki (poems), 1967; O literature (essays), 1973; V seredine veka: Perepiska A. T. Tvardovskogo i V. V. Ovečkina, 1946–68 (correspondence between Tvardovsky and V. V. Ovechkin), in Sever 1979:10, 1980:2; Pis'ma o literature, 1985; Stikhotvorenija i poèmy (lyric and narrative poems), 1986; Po pravu pamjati (narrative poem), in Znamja 1987:2.—Sobr. soč., 4 vols., 1959–60; 5 vols., 1966–71; 6 vols., 1976–83.

Translations: Tyorkin and the Stovemakers: Poetry and Prose, 1974; Selected Poetry, 1981.

Secondary Lit.: P. F. Roščin, 1966; A. Turkov, 2d ed., 1970; Z. Medvedev, Desjat' let posle "Odnogo dnja Ivana Denisoviča," London, 1973; V. Lakšin, in Družba narodov 1974:7 and in Oktjabr' 1980:9; K. Vanšenkin, in Voprosy lit. 1975:1; V. Nekrasov, in Rossija, Turin, 3:1977; A. Kondratovič, 1978, 1984; A. Makedonov, 1981; N. D. Kotovčikhina, in Russkaja lit. 1985:4; V. Aksënov, in Russkaja mysl', Paris, Sept. 6, 1985, p. 9.

**Tynyánov, Yúry Nikoláyevich,** prose writer, literary critic (b. Oct. 18 [Oct. 6], 1894, Rezhitsa, prov. Vitebsk—d. Dec. 20, 1943, Moscow). Tynyanov was the son of a doctor. He completed his studies in the Department of History and Philology at Petrograd University in 1918. Between 1918 and 1921 he worked as a translator (French) for the Comintern. From 1921 to 1930 he was professor of literary history at the Russian Institute of Art History in Leningrad. Tynyanov was one of the most important theoreticians of the FORMALIST SCHOOL; his publications include many fundamental studies on the styles of A. Pushkin, F. Tyutchev, N. Nekrasov, F. Dostoyevsky, V. Bryusov, A. Blok, and V. Khlebnikov, as well as on the development of period styles. Repression of the formalist school motivated Tynyanov to embark on a growing literary career in addition to his work in philology. He wrote three historical novels based on his research, several historical short stories, and film scripts based on literary materials. Tynyanov supervised the scholarly preparation of the most distinguished Soviet series of editions of Russian poets, "Biblioteka poeta" (Poet's Library). He also worked as a translator (particularly of Heinrich Heine's poetry). In 1934 he was elected to the board of the Writers Union of the USSR. During World War II, Tynyanov, gravely ill for a long time, was evacuated to Perm. In the late Stalin period Tynyanov received little attention; V. Kaverin initiated his return to literature at the Second Congress of the Writers Union in 1954.

Tynyanov is not only one of the most eminent Russian literary critics but also one of the most important historical novelists. Kyukhlya (1925) helped the poet Vilkhelm Kyukhelbeker, exiled to Siberia as a Decembrist in 1825, to take his legitimate place in Russian literature; the novel provides, in addition to a faithful picture of the period, "an interesting psychological study of a literary and political Don Quixote" (Struve). Smert Vazir-Mukhtara (1927–28; Eng. tr., Death and Diplomacy in Persia, 1938) deals with the fate of Aleksandr Griboyedov, the playwright and diplomat who was murdered in Tehran in 1829; modeled on the work of Ye. Zamyatin and A. Bely, the novel has a structure that is fragmentary and rich in symbols. Part 3 of Pushkin (1935–43), Tynyanov's third novel about a writer, remained uncompleted. Less experimental in form, the novel illustrates with historical accuracy the first two decades of the 19th century and presents "a fascinating description of the poet's childhood and adolescence" (Slonim) up to 1820. Tynyanov's considerable talent for plot construction, satire, and the grotesque is expressed in short stories such as Podporuchik Kizhe (1928; Eng. tr., "Second Lieutenant Asfor," 1965). A. Belinkov sees a problem of the present, which Tynyanov addresses in his historical novels, in the conflict of an extraordinary personality with the masses and society.

*Works: Problema stikhotvornogo jazyka* (articles), 1924, enl. ed., 1965 (Eng. tr., The Problem of Verse Language, 1981); Kjukhlja (novel), 1925; Smert' Vazir-Mukhtara (novel), 1929 (see above); Arkhaisty i novatory (articles), 1929 (reprinted, Munich, 1967, extracts reprinted in Texte der russ. Formalisten, Munich, 1969); Podporučik Kiže (short story), 1930 (see above); Puškin (novel), parts 1 and 2, 1936, part 3 in Znamja 1943:7–8, parts 1–3 in Soč., vol. 3, 1959, 1-vol. ed., 1974; Puškin i ego sovremenniki (articles), 1969; Poètika. Istorija literatury. Kino (articles), 1977; Tynjanovskij sbornik, 1984.—Sobr. soč., 2 vols, 1931; Soč., 1941; Soč., 3 vols., 1959; Soč., 2 vols., 1985.

*Secondary Lit.:* L. Cyrlin, 1935; A. Belinkov, 1960, 2d ed., 1965; V. Kaverin, in Novyj mir 1964:10, in his Sobr. soc., vol. 6, 1966, in Novyj mir 1966:8, and in his Sobesednik, 1973; Jurij Tynjanov: Pisatel' i učёnyj, 1966; RSPP 5:1968; B. Èjkhenbaum, in his O proze, 1969; E. Korpala-Kirzak, Wroclaw, 1974; T. Khmel'nickaja, in Zvezda 1974:9; E. J. Harden, in Mnemozina, Munich, 1974; S. Rosengrant, Diss., Stanford Univ., 1976; R. Jakobson, in Rossija, Turin; 3:1977; Z. A. Breschinsky, Diss., Vanderbilt Univ., 1978; D. and Z. A. Breschinsky, in Slavic and East European Journal 1985:1; V. Mil'čina in Lit. obozrenie 1985:12.

# U

Union of Soviet Writers. See WRITERS UNION.

Ushakóv, Nikoláy Nikoláyevich, poet (b. June 6 [May 25], 1899, Rostov-Yaroslavsky—d. Nov. 17, 1973, Kiev). Ushakov's father was in the military service. Ushakov completed his degree in the School of Law at the Institute of Political Economy in Kiev in 1924 but never actually practiced law. He published his first poem in Kiev in 1923. Ushakov spent most of his life in Kiev; nevertheless, his first volume of verse, Vesna respubliki (1927; Spring of the Republic), appeared in Moscow. For a while Ushakov belonged to the constructivists (see CONSTRUCTIVISM); with them he found a means of expression that brought him limited but serious and abiding recognition and shielded him from literary and political altercations. For over four decades Ushakov also did an estimable job as translator, particularly of works of Ukrainian literature. In his later years Ushakov went beyond the confines of poetry: he wrote a lyrical prose work about Kiev, Povest bystrotekushchikh let (1960; The Chronicle of Fleeting Years), a novel, Vdol goryachego asfalta (1965; Along the Hot Asphalt), and essays of literary criticism. He lived in Kiev and in 1973 received the Shevchenko State Prize of the Ukrainian SSR.

The influence of B. Pasternak and N. Aseyev is apparent in Ushakov's poetry, which is characterized as much by an interest in modern technique as by an openness to nature; he handles these two spheres, however, not as conflicting elements but as complements of each other. His work further includes material based on his travels to the farthest reaches of his own country, from the Amur to the Carpathians, from the Arctic Circle to Kerch. His material is not at all publicistically importuning but is directed inward, toward people, and is distinguished, according to Ye. Vinokurov, by its "unobtrusiveness" and its "lifelong individual course." Ushakov's work has multiple layers of meaning and avoids the superfluous word. His techniques of rhyme and assonance are so diverse and varied that they offer the possibility of a "detailed classification of rhyme" (Urban).

Works: Vesna respubliki (poems), 1927; Gorjačij cekh (poems), 1933; Putešestvija (poems), 1940; Svežij večer (poems), 1955; Povest' bystrotekuščikh let (pov.), 1950; Vdol' gorjačego asfal'ta (novel), 1965; Teodolit (poems), 1967; "75" (poems), 1971; Moi glaza (poems), 1972; Moj vek (poems), 1973; Jakorja zemli (poems), 1974; Stikhotvorenija i poèmy (lyric and narrative poems), 1980.—Soč., 2 vols, 1979.

Secondary Lit.: V. Tel'gunov, 1961; A. Urban, in Zvezda 1962:7, 1963:6, 1974:7, and 1979:10; E. Vinokurov, in Lit. gazeta Oct. 1, 1969, p. 5; M. Novikova, Mir, na obraz množimyj, 1970; N. Šatylov, in Lit. obozrenie 1973:5.

Útkin, Iósif Pávlovich, poet (b. May 28 [May 15], 1903, Hsingan, northern China—d. Nov. 13, 1944, near Moscow). Utkin's father worked for the railroad. Utkin grew up in Irkutsk, served in the Red Army from 1920 to 1922, then worked as a journalist. In 1924 he was sent by the Party and the Komsomol to Moscow to study at the State Institute of Journalism (he graduated in 1927). His first literary success, promoted by V. Mayakovsky, was a lasting one; it came with a narrative poem taken from his own Jewish milieu: Povest o ryzhem Motele, gospodine inspektore, ravvine Isaye, i komissare Blokh (1925; The Tale of Redheaded Motele, Mr. Inspector, the Rabbi Isaiah, and Commissar Blokh). Pervaya kniga stikhov (1927; A First Volume of Poems), a collection of Utkin's revolutionary poetry written between 1923 and 1926, won recognition, with A. Lunacharsky's support; nevertheless, Utkin was subsequently more and more often attacked by the critics of RAPP for promoting an abstract humanism without considering the point of view of the class struggle (he had spoken out in principle against killing) and for being petit bourgeois. In 1930–31 Utkin wrote publicistic poetry for Pravda. He later returned to the theme of the Civil War, striking a pessimistic and despairing note, especially in his unpublished material. After being wounded during World War II, he became a frontline reporter. Utkin lost his life in an airplane accident.

Like M. Svetlov, Utkin was one of the most beloved Komsomol poets of the 1920s. A. Voronsky's observation, that Utkin endeavored to unite the heroic element present in the Civil War experience with tender human sensations and perceptions, remains valid for

Utkin's poems from World War II. His best poems are distinguished by their sympathy for the lonely, for the powerless and the unprotected, and, above all, for women. Like the narrative poems about Motele and *Miloye detstvo* (1933; Beloved Childhood), his lyric poetry is often narrative or descriptive and owes its effect to somewhat romanticized, exceptional situations that arouse the reader's compassion.

*Works: Povest' o ryžem Motele.* . . (narrative poem), 1926; *Pervaja kniga stikhov* (poems), 1927; *Miloe detstvo* (narrative poem), 1933; *Stikhi* (poems), 1935, 1937, 1939; *Lirika*

(poems), 1939; *O rodine, o družbe, o ljubvi* (poems), 1944; *Stikhi i poèmy* (lyric and narrative poems), 1956; *Stikhotvorenija i poèmy* (lyric and narrative poems), 1966; *Lirika—žanr ètičeskij* (essay), in *Lit. Rossija* May 11, 1973, p. 17.—*Izbr.*, 1975.

*Secondary Lit.:* A. Lunačarskij, in *Komsomol'skaja pravda* Feb. 20, 1927 (reprinted in his *Stat'i o sovetskoj lit.*, 1971); E. Garnevskaja, in *Novyj mir* 1937:10; D. Fiks, in *Lit. Rossija* May 10, 1963, p. 21; A. Saakjanc, 1969; V. Koržev, 1971; A. Žarov, in *Lit. gazeta* June 14, 1978, p. 5; B. Efimov, in *Lit. Rossija* May 20, 1983, p. 17; L. Lenč, in *Lit. gazeta* Aug. 28, 1985, p. 5.

# V

**VAÁP** (Vsesoyúznoye agéntstvo po ávtorskim pravám [All-Union Agency for Authors' Rights, the Copyright Agency of the USSR]). VAAP was established in 1973 in connection with the Soviet Union's accession to the world copyright convention (the 1952 Geneva version, not the expanded 1971 Paris version); the agreement was signed on Feb. 27, 1973, and came into effect on May 27, 1973. A summary of the unpublished decree of the Council of Ministers of the USSR dated Aug. 16, 1973, was published in *Izvestiya* on Dec. 27, 1973. The statutes of VAAP were passed on Sept. 20, 1973. The founders of VAAP, who form the "Conference"—the governing body of VAAP that must meet at least once every five years—include the Writers Union of the USSR as well as the Unions of Fine Arts, of Composers, of Journalists, of Filmmakers, of Architects; the Academy of Sciences; some state committees; the Ministries of Culture and Foreign Trade; and the news service Novosti. Authors themselves are not allowed to be members of VAAP. VAAP is a "societal" organization vested with the rights of a legal person. VAAP claims and exercises monopoly rights vis-à-vis the Soviet originator of literary, artistic, scientific, and journalistic works. (VAAP exercises these rights in both domestic and foreign transactions.) It represents the rights of Soviet and foreign authors when their works are being used in the USSR as well as the rights of Soviet authors and their legal successors when their works are used abroad. A Soviet author is not at liberty to transfer independently the right to use his work to a foreigner; VAAP must make these arrangements. A Soviet publishing

company is not legally entitled to acquire independently the rights to use a foreign work from the author or the publisher; VAAP must make these arrangements. After decades of protests by American and other Western official and private institutions against the Soviet use of foreign copyrighted property without any license whatsoever, VAAP was established at a time when authors living in the USSR were increasingly publishing abroad their works that ran counter to the views of the censors and when, in addition, the number of Soviet scientific publications being translated in the West was so great as to make the continued license-free use of this copyrighted material appear no longer financially advantageous to the Soviets. The creation of VAAP has not changed anything with regard to the migration of manuscripts to the West (from SAMIZDAT to TAMIZDAT, that is, from "self-publishing" to "there publishing"). VAAP practices censorship in connection with the dispensation of translation rights, however. The establishment of VAAP preceded a change in Soviet copyright law. Since 1974, VAAP has been a member of CISAC, the International Union of Authors and Composers. VAAP is one of the three founders and sponsors of the Moscow International Book Fair, which has been held in September every two years since 1977. Since 1975 VAAP has systematically built up foreign representation. VAAP has developed a wealth of activity around the promotion of selected Soviet works to foreign publishers. VAAP is located in Moscow (K 104, 6a Bolshaya Bronnaya Street); it has opened branches in all republics and territories of the Soviet Union and is represented at international book fairs. VAAP makes a special effort to sell rights at the Moscow International Book Fair. From 1973 to 1981 the chairman of VAAP was B. Pankin; K. Dolgov, who previously had been head of the Literature Section in the Cultural Department of the Central Committee of the Communist Party, succeeded him. In April 1986 N. Chetverikov took over the position; he too has belonged to the staff of the Central Committee of the Communist Party.

Secondary Lit.: M. M. Boguslavskij, Voprosy avtorskogo prava v meždunarodnykh otnošenijakh, 1973, and in Sovetskoe gosudarstvo i pravo 1975:6; A. Dietz, in Jahrbuch für Ostrecht 1973; B. Pankin, in Lit. gazeta Sept. 26, 1973; Anon., in Der Spiegel 1973:10; VAAP, The Illustrated Information Bulletin of the Copyright Agency of the USSR, 1974–; V. Vojnovič, in his Putëm vzaimnoj perepiski, Paris, 1979, pp. 245–48; Normativnye akty po avtorskomu pravu, 1979; D. A. Loeber, "VAAP," in University of Illinois Law Forum 1979:2 and "Urheberrecht der Sowjetunion," in Quellen des Urheberrechts, Frankfurt am Main, 1981 (unbound collection); "Kontakty i kontrakty VAAP," in Lit. gazeta Sept. 12, 1979; A. Vvedenskij, "Kontaktam krepnut'," in Lit. Rossija Sept. 26, 1980, p. 5; F. Majoros, Die Rechte ausländischer Urheber in der UdSSR seit dem Beitritt zur Genfer Konvention, vol. 2 of Berichte des Bundesinstitutes für Ostwissenschaftliche und Internationale Studien, Cologne, 1981; "Zasedanie soveta učreditelej VAAP," in Lit. Rossija Sept. 24, 1982, p. 15.

Váginov, Konstantín Konstantínovich (pseud. of K. K. Vagingejm), poet, prose writer (b. April 16 [April 4], 1899, St. Petersburg—d. April 26, 1934, Leningrad). Vaginov's study of law (1917–21) was considerably hindered by his induction into the Red Army (1918–22). Vaginov lived in Petrograd, belonged to the acmeists (Tsekh poetov) for a while, and published one short collection of poems, Puteshestviye v khaos (1921; Trip into Chaos), and another (untitled) one in 1926. With N. Tikhonov he belonged to the group "Ostrovityane." In the middle of 1927 he joined the last literary union of modernist writers in the USSR, OBERIU. Close to the spirit of Oberiu are his novel Kozlinaya pesn (1928; The Goat Song) and the novel about this novel, Trudy i dni Svistonova (1929; The Works and Days of Svistonov), as well as Bambachada (1931), all of which the official critics failed to understand or rejected as they did everything Vaginov wrote. The title of Vaginov's last published volume of poetry, Opyty soyedineniya slov posredstvom ritma (1931; Experiments in the Union of Words through Rhythm), reveals that his form-conscious, experimental attitude was in force until the end. In his novel Garpagoniada (Harpogoniad), which was written from 1932 to 1933 and was published in 1983 in the United States, Vaginov depicts a grotesque portrait of the early Soviet Leningrad full of cranks and unlucky fellows. His last volume of poetry before his early death (probably of tuberculosis), Zvukopodobiye (The Likeness of Sounds), remained unpublished. In the Soviet Union, his work was not reprinted; his name was not mentioned in histories of literature. The discovery of the Oberiuts did, however, focus attention also on Vaginov after 1961. In Cologne in 1982, Leonid Chertkov oversaw the first edition of his collected poems.

In Vaginov's early poems, which won recognition from G. Adamovich, V. Bryusov, V. Khodasevich, and N. Gumilyov, among others, images of the ancient world, reminiscences of M. Voloshin and O. Mandelshtam, exceptionally unusual epithets, and a fundamental pantheistic disposition can be found. The Oberiu Manifesto (1928) speaks of his phantasmagory of the world, clothed in both fog and shivers at the same time, and of his breath, which is capable of warming things up. Vaginov's novels, created with a consciousness of language that includes rhythmic prose, are satiric and present, in a grotesque way, eccentric people from the previous century in present-day Soviet life.

Works: Putešestvie v khaos (poems), 1921 (also contains the cycle "Ostrova," 1919) (reprinted, Ann Arbor, 1972); [Stikhotvorenija] (poems), 1926 (reprinted, Ann Arbor, 1978); Kozlinaja pesn' (novel), 1928 (reprinted, Ann Arbor, 1978); Trudy i dni Svistonova (novel), 1929 (reprinted, New York, 1982); Bambačada (novel), 1931; Opyty soedinenija slov posredstvom ritma (poems), 1931; Sobr. stikhotvorenij (poems), Munich, 1982; Garpagoniada (novel), Ann Arbor, 1983.
Secondary Lit.: R. Messer, in Zvezda 1930:4; I. Oksenov, in Novyj mir 1933:7–8; T. Nikol'skaja and L. Čertkov, in Den' poèzii, Leningrad, 1967; L. Čertkov and W. Kasack, in Vaginov's Sobr. stikhotvorenij, 1982; G. Volkov, in Novoe russkoe slovo, New York, April 22, 1984, p. 6; V. Zavališin, in Novyj žurnal, New York, 157:1984; I. Zaborova, in Russkaja mysl', Paris, Jan. 31, 1986, p. 10.—See OBERIU.

Vakhtín, Borís Borísovich, prose writer (b. Nov. 3, 1930, Rostov-on-Don—d. Nov. 12, 1981, Leningrad). Vakhtin was the son of the writer Vera Panova and of a journalist who died in the camps. Vahktin grew up in a Ukrainian village and studied sinology at Leningrad University (1949–54). He passed his candi-date's examinations and in 1952 began work-ing at the Leningrad Branch of the Institute for the Peoples of Asia of the Academy of Sciences of the USSR; in 1975 he was not allowed to defend his completed doctoral dis-sertation. Vakhtin had been writing short sto-ries since the beginning of the 1950s but had been able to publish only three in the Soviet Union (in 1965 and 1970); most circulated through SAMIZDAT. Vakhtin had repeatedly and actively advocated the free exercise of literary talent (including at the proceedings against I. Brodsky in 1964, A. Sinyavsky and Yu. Daniel in 1966, I. Ogurtsov in 1968, and V. Maramzin in 1975; and by founding the literary association "Gorozhane" [The Towns-people] in 1964). His povest written in 1965, Odna absolyutno schastlivaya derevnya (Eng. tr., An Absolutely Happy Village, 1984), at-tained special popularity through samizdat. After 1978, Vakhtin's friend V. Maramzin published this story and three others in Paris. In 1979 Vakhtin submitted the povest Dub-lyonka (Eng. tr., The Sheep-skin Coat, 1984) to the almanac METROPOL, the publication of which in the USSR was forbidden. Even Gibel Dzhonstauna (1982; The Ruin of Jonestown), a journalistic work concerning the mass sui-cide committed by an American religious sect in 1978, was only published posthumously. The last two works mentioned, probably the best of Vakhtin's prose known to date, were published in book form in the United States as Dve povesti (1982; Two Povesti). The change in the literary policy of the Soviet Union made it possible for a first book by Vakhtin to appear there in 1986 with the publication of Gibel Dzhonstauna; the volume also included five short stories.

The few known examples of Vakhtin's nar-rative prose reveal an exceptional talent; their content—scenes from everyday Soviet Rus-sian life—contributes less to a great aesthetic pleasure than does their linguistically con-scious narrative form with varying stylistic levels. In 26 scenes from the life of a Russian peasant woman whose husband was killed in the war, Odna absolyutno schastlivaya de-revnya portrays the thoughts of simple people. In this portrayal, naturalistic comic dialogue alternates with the surrealistic reproduction of the thoughts of objects (for example, a foun-tain) and the first-person narrator changes, thereby shifting the narrative perspective even within a single scene. Ironic distancing does not diminish the tragedy. Dublyonka is a trav-esty of N. Gogol's The Overcoat set among the Soviet black-market upper class that also ex-poses the world of literature and censorship. Russian literature during Vakhtin's brief cre-ative period has few authors who exhibit a similar joy in verbal expression (others in-clude A. Bitov and S. Sokolov).

Works: Eë ličnoe delo (abridged), Nožnicy v more (short stories), in Molodoj Leningrad, 1965; Portret neznakomca (short story), in Avrora 1970:12; Van'ka Kain (short story), in Vremja i my, Tel Aviv, 14:1977; Odna abso-ljutno sčastlivaja derevnja (pov.), in Ėkho, Paris, 1978:2 (see above); Seržant i frau (short story), in Ėkho 1978:3; U pivnogo lar'ka (short story), in Ėkho 1978:4; Lëtčik Tjutčev, ispy-tatel', (short story), in Ėkho 1979:4; Eë ličnoe delo (complete), Paporotnik i landyš and Tak složilas' žizn' moja (short stories), in Tret'ja volna, Montgeron, 5:1979; Dublënka (pov.), in Metropol', Ann Arbor, 1979 (see above); Abakasov—udivlënnye glaza (excerpt from the pov.), in Russkaja mysl', Paris, Dec. 3, 1981, pp. 8–9; Gibel' Džonstauna (feature articles), in Novyj mir 1982:2; Dve povesti (contains Odna absoljutno sčastlivaja derevnja and Dublënka), Ann Arbor, 1982; Gibel' Džon-stauna (feature articles and short stories), 1986.

Secondary Lit.: W. Kasack, in Osteuropa 1980:11; I. Efimov, in Novoe russkoe slovo, New York, Nov. 20, 1981, and in Ėkho 13:1984; V. Maramzin, in Russkaja mysl' Nov. 26, 1981, p. 10; Ja. Vin'koveckij, in Kontinent, Paris, 35:1983.

Vampílov, Aleksándr Valentínovich, play-wright (b. Aug. 19, 1937, Kutulik, oblast Ir-kutsk—d. Aug. 17, 1972, on Lake Baikal). Vampilov grew up in Siberia; in 1960 he com-pleted his studies in philology at Irkutsk Uni-versity; he then worked in Irkutsk as a jour-nalist and he lived there until his early death. In 1959 and 1960 Vampilov published short one-act plays in two collections; in 1961, un-der the pseudonym A. Sanin, he published a small collection of humorous short stories as they had originally appeared in the journal Angara beginning in 1958. His third one-act play, Dom oknami v pole (1964; The House with Windows Overlooking a Field), was pub-lished in the journal Teatr. During this period Vampilov attended classes at the Gorky Literary Institute in Moscow; the manuscript of his first full-scale drama, Proshchaniye v iyune (1965; Farewell in June), attracted the attention of V. Rozov and A. Arbuzov. Its publication in Teatr in 1966 made Vampilov famous in the Soviet Union; by 1970 the number of performances had exceeded 100 per year, even though the Moscow and Leningrad theaters did not begin performing Vampilov's plays until relatively late. In addition to the three early one-act plays, Vampilov wrote five dramas, of which Utinaya okhota (1970; Eng. tr., Duck Hunting, 1980) was particularly highly regarded. Provintsialnye anekdoty (1971; Provincial Anecdotes) created a great sensation at a seminar of young dramatists of the RSFSR held in Dubulty on the Baltic Sea in 1971. Vampilov did not live to see the premieres of his two last pieces; he drowned while out rowing.

Vampilov had an unusual dramatic talent for portraying ethical problems, in particular those that dealt with honesty vis-à-vis oneself and others, in the form of comedy. He stands "in the forefront of Russian dramatists of the generation that came to prominence after the death of Stalin" (H. Segel). Dom oknami v pole already shows Vampilov's predilection for paradoxical situations; in this play, two people first recognize their affection for each other as they part after three years. Proshchaniye v iyune revolves around forms of corruption in the university milieu. Starshiy syn (1968; The Elder Son), which earlier bore the titles Nravoucheniye s gitaroy (Moral Lesson with Guitar), Svidaniye v predmestye (Suburban Rendezvous), and Predmestye (The Suburb), selects the problem of human deception; the deceiver probes the consequences of deceiving a person whose trust he has gained. Utinaya okhota is about a weak-willed, well-off person, insincere in his everyday life, who is temporarily brought to take stock of himself by a powerful external impetus but who then falls back into the same old rut. In Proshlym letom v Chulimske (1971; Eng. tr., Last Summer in Chulimsk, in Nine Modern Soviet Plays, 1977), Vampilov combines the recurring problem of compromise with conscience and of weakness of character with a love story. Provintsialnye anekdoty, also called Dva anekdota (Two Anecdotes), consists of two independent satires connected by the scene of action, a provincial inn: Istoriya s metranpazhem (1971; History with a Make-up Man) is a modern comedy of errors reminiscent of N. Gogol's Revizor, and Dvadtsat minut s "angelom" (1970; Twenty Minutes with an "Angel") is a grotesque satire illustrating the inability of

many people to accept an unselfish willingness to help, or even to consider it possible. Vampilov's plays are compact and contain numerous levels of meaning; his characters develop slowly and with psychological conviction. His attention is directed to contemporary human weaknesses, the moral consequences of which he exposes in the often comic, pointed situations of daily life.

Works: Sčast'e Kati Kozlovoj (play), in Odnoaktnye p'esy, 1959; Tikhaja zavod' (play), in Volžskij almanakh 13:1960; Stečenie obstojatel'stv (short stories), 1961; Dom oknami v pole (comedy in one act), in Teatr 1964:11; Proščanie v ijune (play), in Teatr 1966:8, separate ed., 1966; Predmest'e (comedy), in Angara 1968:2, and under the title Staršyj syn, 1970; Dvadcat' minut s "angelom" (comedy), in Angara 1970:4, and excerpt in Smena 1973:12; Utinaja okhota (play), in Angara 1970:6 (see above); Istorija s metranpažem (comedy), 1971; Prošlym letom v Čulimske (play), in Sibir' 1973:3, separate ed., 1974 (see above); Izbr., 1975, 2d ed., 1984; Belye goroda (short stories and journalistic prose), 1979; Dom oknami v pole (plays), 1982; Voron'ja rošča; Uspekh (plays), in Sovremennaja dramaturgija 1986:1.

Secondary Lit.: B. Privalov, in Moskva 1962:9; A. Bulgak, in Teatr 1972:5; V. Rozov, in Teatr 1972:10; A. Demidov, in Teatr 1973:1; and 1974:3; T. Čebotarevskaja, in Lit. gazeta May 22, 1974, p. 8; V. Solov'ëv, in Avrora 1975:1; Ju. Smelkov, in Lit. obozrenie 1975:3; W. Kasack, in Osteuropa 1975:6; V. Sakharov, in Naš sovremennik 1976:3; Ju. Solomeina, in Teatr 1977:12; A. Vasilevskij, in Novyj mir 1980:7; J. E. Bernhardt, Diss., Univ. of Pittsburgh, 1980; V. Lakšin, in Oktjabr' 1981:3; V. Klimenko, in Naš sovremennik 1983:6; M. Doyé, in Kritisches Lexikon für fremdsprachige Gegenwartsliteratur, Göttingen, 1985; J. Breitenegger, Diss., Klagenfurt, 1986; A. Germ-Wilkiewcz, Mainz, 1986.

Vanshénkin, Konstantín Yákovlevich, poet (b. Dec. 17, 1925, Moscow). Vanshenkin's father was an engineer. Vanshenkin served in World War II as a parachutist (sergeant). He studied geology in Moscow in 1947–48, then changed to the Gorky Literary Institute where he graduated in 1953. Vanshenkin, who wrote his first poems in 1946, received only muted positive reviews for his first volume of poetry, Pesnya o chasovykh (1951; Song of the Sentry), because his war poems lacked close ties to the period. His narrative poem Serdtse ma-

*teri* (1954; Mother's Heart), which portrays without pathos a mother's inability to believe in the death of her son, won greater acclaim. Since then, Vanshenkin has published much in journals and anthologies and almost annually publishes collections of works of various lengths. In 1954 Vanshenkin became a member of the board of the Writers Union of the USSR but was again chosen only in 1976. Following occasional prose based on his wartime experiences, Vanshenkin planned to write an autobiographical novel at the beginning of the 1970s but left it as a collection of remembrances of writers (A. Tvardovsky, among others), composers, and actors and essaylike observations on literature: *Nabroski k romanu* (1973; Sketches for a Novel), whose sequel is *Litsa i golosa* (1975; People and Voices). Apart from this he wrote various short stories. He lives in Moscow.

Vanshenkin is one of the fine Russian poets. In 1957 Tvardovsky described him as the most talented of his contemporaries but, at the same time, warned him against reacting to all appearances of life in a similar way (*Voprosy lit.* 1972:6, pp. 132–33). Vanshenkin's poetry is unpolitical, usually describes experiences of daily life, and is seldom narrative. Ye. Vinokurov sees the typical element of his lyrical statement in the "plastic and picturesque." In his concreteness, Vanshenkin captures moments of life, often painful ones, in a valid poetic form. Detail contains the universally valid; as an impulse or a simile, nature becomes the organic component of his contemplative lyric poetry. His poetry is carried along by a belief that the unmediated power of a poetic talent triumphs independently of the passing praise or curse of the critics. ("Nizprovergayut nezaslushenno. . ." [1961; Undeservedly one is dragged through the mud . . .]). The form of his poetry is modest and natural, just as his statement also discretely leads toward simplicity and naturalness.

*Works: Pesnja o časovykh* (poems), 1951; *Portret druga* (poems), 1954; *Serdce materi* (narrative poem), in *Novyj mir* 1954:12; *Vesna* (poems), 1955; *Okna* (poems), 1962; *Povoroty sveta* (poems), 1965; *Solov'inyj koridor* (poems), 1967; *Izbr.*, 1969; *Stancija* (poems), 1970; *Poezdka k drugu* (poems), 1971; *Prikosnovenie* (poems), 1972; *Kharakter* (poems), 1973; *Nabroski k romanu* (essays), 1973; *Lica i golosa*, in *Voprosy lit.* 1975:1, separate ed., 1978; *Povesti i rasskazy* (pov. and short stories), 1976; *Dorožnyj znak* (poems), 1977; *Desjatilet'e* (poems), 1980; *Pozdnie jabloki*

(poems), 1980; *Rodnja* (poems), 1983; *Žizn' čeloveka* (poems), 1983; *Poiski sebja* (memoirs), 1985; *Dalëkij svet* (poems), 1985—*Izbr. proizv.*, 2 vols., 1975; *Sobr. soč.*, 3 vols., 1983–84.

*Secondary Lit.:* L. Lazarev, in *Lit. gazeta* March 31, 1956; E. Vinokurov, in *Lit. gazeta* Dec. 10, 1959; L. Levickij, in *Novyj mir* 1965:9; A. Urban, in *Lit. gazeta* Nov. 28, 1973, and in *Novyj mir* 1981:5; S. Zalin, in *Lit. gazeta* Oct. 15, 1975, p. 5; I. Rostovceva, in *Oktjabr'* 1976:2; A. Mikhajlov, 1979; P. Ul'jašov, in *Lit. gazeta* Feb. 4, 1981, p. 6; *RSPPo* 4:1981; I. Fonjakov, in *Zvezda* 1985:2; P. Sirkes, in *Novyj mir* 1985:8.

**VAPP** (Vserossíyskaya assotsiátsiya proletárskikh pisáteley [All-Russian Association of Proletarian Writers]), a literary organization embracing many groups that was founded in October 1920 at a conference of proletarian writers organized by the literary association KUZNITSA and that was sanctioned by the People's Commissariat for Education in 1921. Leadership was in the hands of V. Kirillov, who had transferred from the PROLETKULT to Kuznitsa. After April 1924, with the help of MAPP, VAPP came under the exclusive influence of the dogmatic Party officials who were members of OKTYABR, and by 1928 it had become the leading writers' organization in the Soviet Union. In February 1926 sharp controversies arose among the leaders: I. Vardin, S. Rodov, and G. Lelevich were relieved of their positions; power lay in the hands of L. Averbakh, Yu. Libedinsky, V. Kirshon, V. Yermilov, and M. Luzgin. Later, in addition to several other critics, A. Fadeyev appeared on the scene. After 1926 VAPP published the journal *Na literaturnom postu*, which recalled Oktyabr's militant, orthodox journal *Na postu*, and fought against PEREVAL, adherents of the FORMALIST SCHOOL, CONSTRUCTIVISM, and all FELLOW TRAVELERS. With the formation of an All-Union Organization of Associations of Proletarian Writers (VOAPP) in 1928, VAPP was renamed RAPP (Russian Association of Proletarian Writers).

*Secondary Lit.:* See RAPP.

**Varshávsky, Vladímir Sergéyevich,** prose writer (b. Oct. 24 [Oct. 11], 1906, Moscow— d. Feb. 22, 1978, Geneva). Varshavsky's father was an attorney; his mother, Olga Norova, was an actress; his godfather was K. Stanislavsky. Varshavsky spent a happy childhood in Moscow and in 1920 emigrated with his parents through Kiev, the Crimea, and Constantinople to Prague where he completed school and the study of law at the university. His father, who was a monarchist, remained there working as an influential journalist, was arrested in 1945, and died in Soviet custody. In 1928 Varshavsky himself moved to Paris where he graduated from the Sorbonne. He first won recognition with the short story *Shum shagov Frantsua Vilona* (1929; The Sound of the Steps of François Villon). His fundamental religious attitude made possible his association with the circle around the journal *Novy grad*, founded in 1931 and edited by I. I. Fondaminsky, F. A. Stepun, and G. P. Fedotov. His philosophical interests—especially in Henri Bergson—also helped him gain a good position in other Parisian circles (for example, with D. Merezhkovsky and Z. Gippius). Varshavsky occasionally published reviews, essays, and autobiographical prose in the open journal of the younger generation, *Chisla*, among others. At the beginning of World War II, Varshavsky volunteered for the French army, distinguished himself through his great spirit of sacrifice in battle (he was awarded the Croix de Guerre), and spent the years until 1945 in Pomerania as a prisoner of war. He described the experiences of these years in *Pervy boy* (1946; The First Battle) and in *Sem let* (1950; Seven Years). Varshavsky became especially well known for his book *Nezamechennoye pokoleniye* (1956; The Unnoticed Generation) describing the attempt to take a census of the generation composed of the sons and daughters of the first emigration, including his good friend B. Poplavsky. Varshavsky, who had found work in French film shortly before the war, scraped through after the war working as a night watchman and at other jobs. From 1950 to 1968 he lived in the United States. For *Ozhidaniye* (1972; Waiting), Varshavsky compiled diverse autobiographical prose works, including the revised version of *Sem let*. During his lifetime, parts of *Rodoslovnaya bolshevizma* (1982; The Family Tree of Bolshevism), a contemporary religious treatise, appeared in *Novy zhurnal*.

Varshavsky's prose is poetically structured autobiography. He chooses fictitious names for himself and the people close to him and is thus beholden only to generalities, especially to a spiritual grasp of events, rather than to details. In *Pervy boy* he comes to terms with how a person who is prepared to sacrifice his life in the secure knowledge of the permanence of personal existence can conquer the fear of death. *Nezamechennoye po-* *koleniye* contains chapters on the life of the Parisian émigré community—the Montparnasse group, the YMCA, Russian resistance fighters in France—and the attempt to ascertain the spiritual position of his generation, which is oriented around Christianity and democracy. *Ozhidaniye*, a book that he himself wanted to call "Rasseyannost" (Diaspora), combines his childhood reminiscences with the experience of the war and, last but not least, his attempt at self-discovery revealed through accounts of dreams. His enthusiasm for Marcel Proust may have found its literary expression in the occasional psychological tendency in his writings. Generally his style is unpretentious and unassuming. *Rodoslovnaya bolshevizma* combines a critical analysis of the attempts to trace the development of Soviet totalitarianism to Russian history and Russian character with a depiction of the fate of the church in history. Varshavsky's entire creative work aims at influencing society through the concept of Christian love.

*Works:* Šum šagov Francua Vil'ona (short story), in *Volja Rossii*, Paris, 1929:7; *Pervyj boj* (short story), in *Novyj žurnal*, New York, 14:1946; *Sem' let* (pov.), Paris, 1950; *Nezamečennoe pokolenie*, New York, 1956; *Oži-danie* (pov.), Paris, 1972; *Rodoslovnaja bol'-ševizma* (scholarly articles), Paris, 1982.
*Secondary Lit.:* Ju. Denike, in *Novyj žurnal* 44:1956; K. Fotiev, in *Novyj žurnal* 131:1978 and in *Novoe russkoe slovo*, New York, May 15, 1983; A. Šmeman, in *Kontinent*, Paris, 118:1978; E. Valin, in *Novyj žurnal* 150:1983; D. Bobyšev, in *Russkaja mysl'*, Paris, Feb. 9, 1984, p. 11.

**Vasilévskaya, Vánda Lvóvna** (original Polish: Wanda Wasilewska), prose writer (b. Jan. 21, 1905, Kraków—d. July 29, 1964, Kiev). Vasilevskaya's father was an ethnographer, publicist, and official in the Polish Socialist Party. Vasilevskaya studied philology at Kraków University from 1923 to 1927. She was actively involved in politics and in the 1930s turned also to journalism, writing for leftist journals and newspapers. Her novel *Ojczyzna* (1935; The Homeland) and short story *Ziemia w jarzmie* (1938; A Country under the Yoke), both in Polish, were devoted to the theme of the exploited peasantry. During the Polish campaign of 1939 Vasilevskaya fled to the Soviet Union; she became a Soviet citizen and a member of the Communist Party (1941) and served as a deputy of the Supreme Soviet until 1962. The works she had originally written in

Polish appeared in Russian. She described the resistance and the misfortunes of Ukrainian women under German occupation in *Raduga* 1942; Eng. tr., *The Rainbow*, 1943). For this she received a Stalin Prize (1942, 1st class). She was awarded additional Stalin Prizes (for 1943–44, 2d class) for her much-remarked povest *Prosto lyubov* (1944; Eng. tr., *Just Love*, 1945), which evoked criticism for its departure from the accepted model of the positive hero, and (for 1951, 2d class) for the trilogy *Pesn nad vodami* (Song over the Waters), begun in 1933, in which she depicts in accordance with the Party line the fate of the Polish-Ukrainian border area annexed by the Soviets in 1939. Vasilevskaya lived in Kiev; she was married to the playwright A. Korneychuk.

*Works:* *Raduga* (pov.), 1942 (see above); *Prosto ljubov'* (pov.), 1944 (see above); *Kogda zagoritsja svet* (pov.), 1946; *Pesn' nad vodami* (novel-trilogy): (1) *Plamja na bolotakh*, 1940, (2) *Zvëzdy v ozere*, 1945–46, (3) *Reki gorjat*, 1951.—*Sobr. soč.*, 6 vols., 1954–55.

*Secondary Lit.:* M. Markuševič, in *Novyj mir* 1939:12; E. Usievič, 1953; L. Vengerov, 1955; A. Salynskij et al., in *Lit. gazeta* July 30, 1964; Anon., in *Lit. gazeta* Jan. 15, 1975, p. 7, and Jan. 29, 1975, p. 1; K. Grigor'ev, in *Lit. gazeta* Jan. 23, 1980, and Jan. 23, 1985, p. 3.

**Vasílyev, Borís Lvóvich,** prose writer (b. May 21, 1924, Smolensk). Vasilyev comes from an old family of officers; he fought in World War II as a sergeant in the paratrooppers and graduated from the military academy in 1948. From 1948 to 1953 he worked as a transportation-equipment engineer in the Urals. In 1952 he joined the Communist Party. He began his career as a writer with the play *Ofitser* (1955; The Officer), which was followed by several other plays and film scripts. Vasilyev became famous overnight for a brief war novel, *A zori zdes tikhiye . . .* (1969; Eng. tr., *The Dawns Are Quiet Here*, 1975), which has been frequently reprinted and was made into a film. Yu. Lyubimov's impressive staging at the Taganka Theater was one of 17 different stage versions. In 1975 Vasilyev was awarded the State Prize of the USSR for the prose version and the film script. In *V spiskakh ne znachilya* (1974; Eng. tr., *His Name Was Not Listed*, 1978), Vasilyev again addressed the theme of war. Vasilyev's later prose works—such as his novel set in a village, *Ne strelyayte v belykh lebedey* (1973; Don't Shoot the White Swans), and his historical novel, *Byli i nebyli* (1977–

80; True and Imaginary Tales)—were also well received by a wide circle of readers. In 1981 Vasilyev was a delegate to a congress of the Writers Union for the first time. He lives in Moscow.

Vasilyev is an eloquent writer who also owes his popularity in the Soviet Union to his work in film and television. For his novels and short stories, he enjoys selecting tragic fates and portraying them at their culminating moment. *A zori zdes tikhiye* depicts the combat mission and death of five women soldiers. *V spiskakh ne znachilsya* reveals the hopeless struggle, love, and death of a young soldier in the fortress at Brest-Litovsk; *Ne strelyayte v belykh lebedey*, probably his strongest book about the human condition, describes the sufferings of a simple village dweller of good intentions and virtuous deeds. *Byli i nebyli* broadly draws the fates of officers in the Russo-Turkish War in Bulgaria in 1877–78. With *Letyat moi koni* (1982; Fly My Horses), Vasilyev wrote an autobiographical povest concerning his youth that, with its reflections about art and life, is characterized by respect for his father and his forefathers.

*Works:* *A zori zdes' tikhie . . .* (pov.), in *Junost'* 1969:8, separate ed., 1971 (see above); *Ivanov kater* (pov.), in *Novyj mir* 1970:8–9; *Ne streljajte v belykh lebedej* (novel), in *Junost'* 1973:6–7, separate ed., 1975; *V spiskakh ne značilsja* (novel), in *Junost'* 1974:2–4, separate ed., 1975 (see above); *Byli i nebyli* (novel), in *Novyj mir* 1977:8–9, 1978:3–4, 1980:9–10; *Vstrečnyj boj* (pov.), in *Junost'* 1979:5; *Kažetsja, so mnoj pojdut v razvedku* (pov.), in *Junost'* 1980:2; *Letjat moi koni . . .* (pov. and short stories; 1984; *Neopalimaja kupina* (pov.), in *Znamja* 1986:2.

*Secondary Lit.:* F. Levin, in *Družba narodov* 1970:1; V. Zeleščuk, in *Lit. Rossija* Jan. 22, 1971, p. 7; L. Uvarova and V. Baranova, in *Lit. obozrenie* 1973:12; A. Bočarov, in *Pravda* July 22, 1974; A. Danina, in *Neva* 1975:10; B. Khotimskij, in *Znamja* 1981:2; K. Mehnert, *The Russians and Their Favorite Books*, Stanford, 1983; I. Sokolova, in *Lit. gazeta* March 26, 1986, p. 4.

**Vasílyev, Pável Nikoláyevich,** poet (b. Dec. 25 [Dec. 12], 1910, Zaysan, in northeastern Kazakhstan—d. 1937 [?], while imprisoned). Vasilyev's father was an instructor at Omsk Pedagogical Institute; both parents were descended from Siberian Cossacks. Vasilyev attended school in Pavlodar from 1919 to 1926. After spending only a few months at Vladivostok University in 1926, he left to lead the unsettled life of a wanderer; by 1929 he had roamed through all parts of Siberia and also spent some time with the fishing fleet in Vladivostok (1929). Vasilyev started writing poetry as a child; it began appearing in periodicals in 1927. In 1929 he settled in Moscow and studied at the Bryusov Institute of Literature and Art. His years of roving inspired two volumes of feature articles, *V zolotoy razvedke* (1930; Prospecting for Gold) and *Lyudi v tayge* (1931; People of the Taiga). The attitude of the RAPP officials toward Vasilyev's poetry, which was antiurban, erotic, and associated with the free life of the Cossacks, was crudely critical. His first epic in verse, the 18-part *Pesnya o gibeli kazachyego voyska* (1928–32; Song of the Destruction of the Cossack Host), was disseminated in duplicated copies. He was a friend of N. Klyuyev and S. Klychkov. Vasilyev very quickly wrote ten folkloric-historical epics in verse, only one of which, *Solyanoy bunt* (1934; The Salt Riot), ever appeared in print. Vasilyev was arrested for the first time in 1932; in 1934 a campaign was launched against him, accusing him of alcoholism, rowdiness, White Guardist sympathies, and defending the kulaks. After M. Gorky joined in the persecution campaign and hinted at the expediency of "quarantining" Vasilyev, Vasilyev's subsequent attempts to conform were useless. A plenum of the board of the Writers Union, meeting Feb. 22–25, 1937, branded him "an infamous enemy of the people"; shortly afterward he was arrested and, presumably, soon executed. Vasilyev's name was absent from Soviet literature until his REHABILITATION around 1956, which was followed by the publication of materials from his manuscripts. The controversy regarding his political position was sparked anew, but this time S. Zalygin deservedly defended the poet murdered at the age of 26. Vasilyev's poetry is characterized by an earthy, graphic power. Fairy-tale elements mingle with Cossack history and a revolutionary present. Strong characters, powerful animals, fierce action, and the colorful landscape of the steppes are expressively combined in scenes that create great forward momentum with varied rhythms. Bloody revolutionary events experienced in Vasilyev's childhood are presented without reference to historical persons or incidents. Vasilyev's high opinion of Cossacks and capable peasants and his departure from the approved pattern of Civil War poetry may have been the major causes of his persecution.

*Works: V zolotoj razvedke* (articles), 1930; *Ljudi v tajge* (articles), 1931; *Soljanoj bunt*

(narrative poem), 1934; *Izbr. stikhotvorenija i poèmy* (selected verse), 1957; *Stikhotvorenija i poèmy* (lyric and narrative poems), 1968; *Stikhotvorenija* (poems), 1975.

*Secondary Lit.:* K. Zelinskij, in *Oktjabr'* 1957:4 (revised version in Vasil'ev's *Izbr. stikhotvorenija i poèmy*, 1968); A. Makarov, in *Znamja* 1958:4; S. Zalygin, in *Sibirskie ogni* 1966:6 (reprinted in Vasil'ev's *Izbr. stikhotvorenija i poèmy*, 1968); A. A. Mikhajlov, *Stepnaja pesn'*, 1971; P. Vykhodcev, 1972; T. Madzigon, in *Prostor* 1981:1; *RSSPo* 4:1981; D. Mečik, in *Novoe russkoe slovo*, New York, Feb. 21, 1982.

**Vasílyev, Sergéy Aleksándrovich,** poet (b. July 30 [July 17], 1911, Kurgan, prov. Tobolsk—d. July 2, 1975, Moscow). Vasilyev was the son of a civil servant. In 1927 he moved to Moscow and began working in a printing shop in 1928. In 1931 he started publishing the poems that were later published in the collection *Vozrast* (1933; Age); he completed his studies at the Gorky Literary Institute in 1938. During World War II, Vasilyev worked as a war correspondent (in the service of *Pravda*, in particular). In the postwar period he wrote the officially desired patriotic verse; his song lyrics about Moscow and Stalin, *Moskva sovetskaya* (1947; Soviet Moscow), and *Pervyj v mire* (1950; The First in the World), his verse epic about A. F. Mazhaysky, the Russian who was claimed to be the inventor of the airplane, became quite popular. From 1954 on, Vasilyev participated in every congress of the Writers Union of the USSR and RFSFR; he belonged to the board of the Writers Union of the RSFSR from 1965 on. His poetry was regularly published. His narrative poem *Dostoinstvo* (1972; Virtue), about the heroic conduct of a Soviet general taken prisoner and finally murdered by the Germans, received the Gorky Prize in 1973. Vasilyev lived in Moscow.

Vasilyev's work is superficial and diffuse; to meet the demands of meter and rhyme, he fills in his lines with superfluous words. Every subject, from current political headlines to ephemeral day-to-day events, is to be found in Vasilyev's narrative or descriptive poems; nevertheless, even his war poems lack conviction. His parodies are parodies in name only, and even his nationalistic and didactic pathos rings hollow.

*Works: Vozrast* (poems), 1933; *Portret partizana* (verse trilogy), 1944, 1956; *Moskva sovetskaja* (poems), 1947 *also partially re printed in Oktjabr'* 1947:9); *Pervyj v mir*

(narrative poem), 1950; *Satiričeskie stikhi* (poems), 1957; *Ostorožno! Golubi!* (poems), 1960; *Stikhi. Poèmy. Parodii* (lyric and narrative poems), 1964; *Dostoinstvo* (narrative poem), in *Lit. Rossija* May 26, 1972, pp. 6–9; *Pod nebom Rossii* (poems), 1972.—*Izbr. proizv.*, 2 vols., 1966; *Izbr. proizv.*, 2 vols., 1970; *Izbr.*, 1977; *Sobr. soč.*, 3 vols., 1977–79.
*Secondary Lit.*: V. Dement'ev, in *Pravda* June 18, 1958; V. Sajanov, in *Znamja* 1958:6; A. Dymšic, in *Neva* 1963:8; B. Leonov, in *Oktjabr'* 1974:2; M. Sobol', in *Lit. gazeta* March 26, 1975, p. 5; Ju. Prokušev, in *Moskva* 1977:7; V. Evpatov, in *Oktjabr'* 1981:8.

**Váyner, Arkády Aleksándrovich,** and **Geórgy Aleksándrovich,** coauthors of detective novels (Arkady Aleksandrovich b. Jan. 13, 1931, Moscow; Georgy Aleksandrovich b. Feb. 10, 1938, Moscow). Both brothers studied law; Arkady Aleksandrovich completed his studies in 1953; Georgy Aleksandrovich, in 1961. Arkady Aleksandrovich worked as a detective with the militia; Georgy Aleksandrovich, as a journalist. Their first novel, *Chasy dlja mistera Kelli* (1970; A Clock for Mr. Kelly), was the story of a crime they experienced firsthand. The detective story *Oshchupyu v polden* (1968; Groping at Noon) brought them a wide circle of readers through its publication in the journal *Ogonyok* with its circulation of 2 million. Through their additional eight detective novels written since 1980, they have become the most frequently read authors of this genre in the Soviet Union. Their novels are often filmed and translated. *Era miloserdiya* (1976; The Era of Sympathy) is considered their best novel; in 1979 it was aired as a five-part television film with V. Vysotsky in the leading role. They live in Moscow.

The brothers Vayner coauthor books by sketching out a subject and plot together and then dividing up the chapters. Their psychological penetration of their characters is good; their rendition of life in the USSR and their favorable depiction of the Soviet militia reveal their concessions to the image favored by the censor. The reappearance of a detective who serves as narrator connects many of their novels. What distinguishes their detective novels is excellent composition, often with multiple levels and multiple perspectives, increasing tension, adroit deception of the reader, well-positioned passages that retard the denouement, and a suprising resolution. In *Vizit k Minotavru* (1972; A Visit to the Minotaur), they incorporate the story of Antonio Stradivari into a criminal case concerning a violin; in *Lekarstvo dlya Nesmeyany* (1978; Medi-

cine against Fear) they integrate the tale of Paracelsus in 16th-century Germany. *Era miloserdiya* depicts a criminal manhunt in 1945 in which humanism, impartiality, and the will to sacrifice lead to success.

*Works: Časy dlja mistera Margulajsa* (pov.), in *Naš sovremennik* 1967:10 and 12, separate ed. under the title *Časy dlja mistera Kelli*, 1970; *Ošćup'ju v polden'* (pov.), in *Ogonëk* 1968:8–13, separate ed., 1969; *Vizit k Minotavru* (novel), 1972; *Ja, sledovatel'* . . . (pov.), 1972; *Dvoe sredi ljudej* (pov.), 1973; *Gonki po vertikali* (novel), 1974, 1978; *Èra miloserdija* (novel), 1976; *Ne poterjat' čeloveka*, 1978; *Lekarstvo dlja Nesmejany* (novel), 1978; *Gorod prinjal!* . . . (pov.), 1980; *Kurskij rejd* (film script), 1982; *Ob"ezžajte na dorogakh sbitykh košek i sobak* (pov.), in *Družba narodov* 1986:7.
*Secondary Lit.*: N. Naumova, in *Neva* 1971:7; Ju. Lopusov, in *Oktjabr'* 1975:8; O. Dmitriev, in *Lit. obozrenie* 1977:2; A. Smulevič, in *Lit. gazeta* Jan. 17, 1979, p. 4; I. Medvedeva, in *Znamja* 1981:1; K. Mehnert, *The Russians and Their Favorite Books*, Stanford, 1983; B. Göbler, Munich, 1987.

**Végin, Pyotr Víktorovich,** poet (b. July 21, 1939, Rostov-on-Don). Vegin published his first poems in the journal *Yunost* in 1962; in 1964 S. Narovchatov introduced him, together with six other young poets, through the anthology *Prityazhenye* (Attraction). His own books, *Vintovaya lestnitsa* (1968; The Winding Staircase) and *Pereplyvi Letu* (1973; Swim across the Lethe), regularly followed the publication of his works in *Yunost* and numerous other journals. *Let lebediny* (1974: Swan Flight), *Zimnyaya pochta* (1978; Winter Post), *Nad kryshami* (1979; Above the Roofs), and *Sozvezdiye Ottsa i Materi* (1981; Constellation of Father and Mother) are additional volumes of poetry encompassing a good 100 pages that are seldom—but generously—treated by the critics. Vegin also translated poetry from many languages. He lives in Moscow.

The point of departure for Vegin's poetry is generally the observable world of his surroundings: commonplace occurrences, nature, art, but not politics. His poems reveal an international field of vision and are connected by a wealth of imagery evoking ephemeral experience. Many poems demonstrate a strong relationship with his parents, especially with his mother. From among many purely descriptive poems appear the deeply spiritual ones as well, such as "Raskopki" (*Yunost* 1980:5), which figuratively warns against meddling with evil. Vegin recognizes the power of suprarational forces, the often unappreciated value of acting in accordance with one's instinct. For him, the significance of beauty is not material ("Smysl krasoty ne materialen"). Occasionally he lets his preference for the poetry of the Oberiuts (see OBERIU), especially that of N. Oleynikov, be seen through ironical expression. Vegin writes diffusely, often narratively, chooses assonance instead of rhyme, combines many lines in a proselike fashion through enjambment, even inserts brief prose passages between verses. The imagery of his poems can lapse into the intellectually contrived, but it is always pertinent.

*Works:* Poems, in *Pritjažen'e*, 1964; *Vintovaja lestnica* (poems), 1968; *Pereplyvi Letu* (poems), 1973; *Let lebedinyj* (poems), 1974; *Zimnjaja počta* (poems), 1978; *Nad kryšami* (poems), 1979; *Sozvezdie Otca i Materi* (poems), 1981; interview, in *Lit. gazeta* Feb. 3, 1982, p. 16; *Val's derevenskoj luny: Kniga liriki* (poems), 1983; *Serebro* (poems), 1984.

*Secondary Lit.:* K. Lapin, in *Lit. gazeta* Aug. 4, 1964; E. Nesterova, in *Don* 1980:3; V. Klimov, in *Junost'* 1980:8 and in *Družba narodov* 1984:5; Ju. Ivanov, in *Lit. obozrenie* 1984:2; A. Kazincev, in *Naš sovremennik* 1985:10.

**Velichkóvsky, Anatóly Yevgényevich,** poet, prose writer (b. Dec. 14 [Dec. 1], 1901, Warsaw—d. Jan. 2, 1981, Paris). Velichkovsky spent his youth in the south of Russia—in the summer on his father's estate, in the winter in Elizavetgrad where his father taught at the school for young members of the gentry. Velichkovsky fought as an officer in the volunteer army and emigrated through Poland to France. There he was first a laborer in the steel mill in Cannes, then a taxi driver in Lyons. During World War II, Velichkovsky settled in Paris and remained there. His poems appeared in anthologies and journals starting in 1947. His first collection with 37 poems, *Litsom k litsu* (1952; Face to Face), was published by S. Makovsky in the Rifma publishing house; the next volume, *S boru po sosenke* (1974; A Few Trees from the Forest), followed his longest prose work, the povest *Bogaty* (1972; The Wealthy One). The third volume of poetry, *O postoronnem* (1979; On Irrelevancies), was followed after his death by a volume he had prepared, *Nerukotvorny svet* (1981; The World Not Made by Human Hands).

Velichkovsky belongs to those writers in the first wave of EMIGRATION who only began to write in the West, but he occupies a special position since he was not a participant in Parisian literary life before the war. His poetry has a religious basis and is close to nature. In his work, nature, which he depicts in complete detail, always forms the point of departure for his spiritual understanding of human nature. Velichkovsky opposes the world of rationality and technology created by man to the world created by God in which nature is most clearly recognizable. Velichkovsky has a prudent view of daily life, whose legitimacy he does not dispute, but he protests against a world in which power, breach of promise, and cunning promote success. The narrative poem *Son* (1965; Dream) illustrates the apocalyptic vision of an atomic war as a cosmic event in the imagery of the Bible. Velichkovsky's poems maintain a clear language rich with imagery, sometimes reveal ironic distance, and enjoy letting their spiritual depth be recognized in their closing lines. In a cautiously ironic style, his novel *Bogaty* depicts the present with its dangers of civilization (which he occasionally fantastically overstates) and its last strongholds in nature and love.

*Works:* Licom k licu (poems), Paris, 1952; Son (narrative poem), in *Novyj žurnal*, New York, 81:1965; *Bogatyj* (pov.), Paris, 1972; *S boru po sosenke* (poems), Paris, 1974; *O postoronnem* (poems), Paris, 1979; poems, in *Perekrëstki*, Philadelphia, 4:1980; *Nerukotvornyj svet* (poems), Paris, 1981.

*Secondary Lit.:* Ju. Ivask, in *Opyty*, New York, 1:1953, and with R. Guerra, in Veličkovskij's *Nerukotvornyj svet*, 1981; A. Nejmirok, in *Grani*, Frankfurt am Main, 18:1953; V. Perelešin, in *Novyj žurnal* 144:1981.

**Veresáyev, Vikénty Vikéntyevich** (pseud. of V. V. Smidóvich, prose writer (b. Jan. 16 [Jan. 4], 1867, Tula—d. June 3, 1945, Moscow). Veresayev's father was a doctor. In 1888 Veresayev completed his studies in history at St. Petersburg University; in 1894 he received a medical degree from Dorpat University. He subsequently practiced medicine, initially in Tula, then in St. Petersburg. Veresayev began his literary career in his student days. Of the prose works he published in Marxist journals in the 1890s, his *Bez dorogi* (1895; Without a Road) attracted the most attention. His *Zapiski vracha* (1901; Eng. tr., *Memoirs of a Physician*, 1916) led to great popularity. After being denied a residence permit for St. Petersburg for a two-year period as a result of his political activities, Veresayev settled in

Moscow in 1903, where, as a realist, he belonged to the literary group "Sreda." During the Russo-Japanese War he was employed as a military doctor. In the povest K zhizni (1909; Toward Life), a fictionalized diary, Veresayev formulated his break with his previous positions and his inclination toward Friedrich Nietzsche and Henri Bergson. In 1909 the first five-volume edition of his works was completed; another appeared in 1913. In 1910 Veresayev made a journey to Greece, which led to a lifelong occupation with classical literature and to numerous translations (of Sappho and Hesiod, among others). Zhivaya zhizn (1911 and 1915; Living Life) is a work about L. Tolstoy and F. Dostoyevsky, written in the manner of an essay, in which Veresayev's sympathy lies with Tolstoy; in the second part he comes to terms with Nietzsche. Veresayev spent the post-Revolutionary period in the Crimea. His novel V tupike (1922; Eng. tr., The Deadlock, 1927), which first appeared in Krasnaya nov, reflects his negative attitude toward the terrorism of the period. Veresayev retreated into his work in the field of literary criticism; his endeavors found expression in the major collections of documents Pushkin v zhizni (1926–27; Pushkin in Life) and Gogol v zhizni (1933; Gogol in Life). Veresayev's recognition as a writer is demonstrated by the publication of two editions of his complete works (in 12 volumes in 1928–29 and in 16 volumes in 1929–31), as well as by his election to the board of the Writers Union of the USSR in 1934, although his most recent novel, Syostry (1933; Eng. tr., The Sisters, 1934), had been criticized in the Komsomol for its realistic presentation of negative points of view. After this, Veresayev wrote basically memoirs and, in the last years of his life, made translations of Homer's Iliad and Odyssey that were published posthumously. His complete works were awarded a Stalin Prize in 1943 (for 1942, 1st class).

The central theme of Veresayev's prose fiction is the position of the intellectual in his time. His work is always connected with its respective present; it is realistic and often autobiographical. Veresayev is furthermore "a scrupulous and observant witness of the social and psychological processes of his time" (Struve). Bez dorogi depicts the difficulties of the Russian populists (narodniki) in the realization of their social and ideological ideas. V tupike illustrates the hopelessness in which a liberal intellectual who rejects all use of force finds himself when faced with the bloody terrorism of the October Revolution. Syostry takes a look at forced collectivization from the

point of view of the intelligentsia. Stylistically, Veresayev always remained within the tradition of critical realism, which concentrates on describing the contemporary milieu; he was criticized for his efforts at objectivity, and abstained from any formalistic experimentation.

Works: Bez dorogi (pov.), 1895; Zapiski vrača (publicistic prose), 1901 (see above); Na vojne (publicistic prose), 1908 (Eng. tr., In the War, 1917); K žizni (pov.), in Sovremennyj mir 1909:1–3; Živaja žizn' (essays), 2 vols., 1911, 1915; V tupike (novel), 1924 (reprinted, Chicago, 1966) (see above); Puškin v žizni (literary criticism), 4 vols., 1926–27, substantially rev. 6th ed., 1936 (reprinted, The Hague, 1969, and Chicago, 1970); Gogol v žizni (literary criticism), 1933; Sëstry (novel), 1933 (see above); Sputniki Puškina, 2 vols., 1934 (reprinted, The Hague, 1970), 2d ed., 1973; Vospominanija (memoirs), 1936; Aleksandr Sergeevič Puškin (biography), 1945; Nevydumannye rasskazy o prošlom (memoirs), 1963, 1968; V svjaščennom lesu (play), in Sovremennaja dramaturgija 1984:1.—Soč., 5 vols., 1898–1909; Polnoe sobr. soč., 4 vols., 1913; 12 vols., 1928–29; 16 vols., 1929–31; Sobr. soč., 5 vols., 1961.

Secondary Lit.: G. N. Ferster, in Čisla, Paris, 1:1930; S. Vržosek, 1930; G. Brovman, 1959; Ju. Babuškin, 1966; RSPP 7(1):1971.

**Vershígora** (also Vershigorá), **Pyotr Petróvich,** prose writer (b. May 16 [May 3], 1905, Severinovka, Moldavia—d. March 27, 1963, Moscow). Vershigora's father was a village schoolteacher. From 1927 to 1930 Vershigora studied at the Odessa Conservatory (Division of Stage Direction); after completing his studies, he worked as a manager in various theaters; in 1938 he completed his studies at the Film Academy and began working as a film director in Kiev. During World War II, Vershigora was employed in a reconnaissance unit. In 1943 he became commander of the first Ukrainian Partisan Division and a member of the Communist Party; as general he received the honorary title "Hero of the Soviet Union." Vershigora, who had begun his literary career before the war with several unpublished and now lost short stories, published in 1945–46 the documentary povest Lyudi s chistoy sovestyu (Eng. tr., Men with a Clear Conscience, 1949), which was awarded a Stalin Prize (for 1946, 2d class), but which, under pressure from orthodox critics, had to conform to the official representation of the war. In the late

Stalin period, Vershigora actively pleaded on behalf of persecuted partisans (such as P. Voronko). In 1954 he took a position against the presentation of the war in an academic work (in *Oktyabr* 1954:4), which led to the dismissal of the editors F. Panfyorov and I. Paderin. In *Reyd na San i Vislu* (1959; Drive to the San and Vistula), Vershigora reworks the partisan theme, while in *Dom rodnoy* (1962; The Ancestral Home), he depicts the people of the postwar period, revealing the inconsistency between the propaganda image of society and reality.

The book *Lyudi s chistoy sovestyu*, repeatedly praised by V. Kaverin, offers, in its original version, "an interesting and patently truthful account of the raids made behind enemy lines" (Struve). The *povest*, which uses the first-person narrative structure, was very popular at one time; it is gripping and clearly written and belongs to the war literature with a serious purpose. Because of pressure from the censors, many statements were changed in later editions, particularly about the aimlessness of partisan activity.

*Works:* Ljudi s čistoj sovest'ju (parts 1 and 2; pov.), 1946 (parts 3 and 4 later published under the title *Karpatskij rejd*, 1950), rev. and enl. ed., 1951; *Rejd na San i Vislu* (pov.), 1960 (appears in later eds. as concluding part of Ljudi s čistoj sovest'ju); *Nevydumannye priključenija* (short stories), 1960; *Voennoe tvorčestvo narodnykh mass* (historical report), 1961; *Dom rodnoj* (novel), 1962; V Pol'še v sorok četvërtom . . . (memoirs), in *Russkaja mysl'*, Paris, Dec. 1, 8, and 15, 1983.

*Secondary Lit.:* P. Trofimenko, in *Novyj mir* 1952:7; *RSPP* 1:1959; P. Voron'ko, in *Novyj mir* 1963:4; V. Timofeeva, in *Zvezda* 1963:11, pp. 187–88; H. J. Dreyer, Munich, 1976.

**Véstnik Rússkogo Khristiánskogo Dvizhéniya** (Herald of the Russian Christian Movement), a religious, philosophical, and literary journal of the EMIGRATION. Vestnik has been published in Paris since 1925 and bore the title *Vestnik Russkogo Studencheskogo Khristianskogo Dvizheniya* (Herald of the Russian Christian Students Movement) until 1974 (issue number 111). In 1925 the Russian Christian Students Movement commissioned its secretary in Paris, Nikolay Zernov, who had completed his theological studies in Belgrade, to publish a bulletin to foster ties among the young émigré students spread across Europe. The monthly journal was jointly published by Zernov and I. Lagovsky; when Zernov moved to England in 1930, he was supported by G. Fedotov in the years 1930–31. After 1932 the journal could only be published sporadically. From 1937 to 1939 Professor V. Zenkovsky assumed the duties of publication (5–6 issues per year, 50–60 pages per issue). After publication was interrupted because of World War II, the journal was reestablished in Munich in 1949 by A. Kiselyov, a pupil and friend of I. Lagovsky, the publisher for many years who probably died in 1941. In 1950 the editorial staff returned to Paris, where I. V. Morozov, secretary of the Russian Christian Students Movement, agreed to assume publication of the journal. In addition to editorial staffs in Paris and New York, Morozov was joined by N. A. Struve, who has exercised editorial responsibility since 1970. Since 1955 the journal has been published about four times a year, and its size has increased tremendously since the early 1970s. In 1953 with issue number 26, continuous numeration was introduced (starting from 1949). Issue number 148 was published in 1986.

In its first period of publication, this journal primarily addressed organizational issues within the Russian Christian Students Movement, church-related matters, and religious questions. In those days, the important religious and philosophical journals *Put* and *Novy grad* were being published in Paris. In its second—postwar—period, Vestnik developed into a significant religious journal that also addressed literary, cultural, and social issues on a regular basis. In the section on religion, texts from previous centuries were reprinted, in addition to articles by N. Berdyayev, S. Bulgakov, S. Frank, V. Ilyin, N. Lossky, L. Shestov, and other leading religious thinkers. Also regularly included are reports on the life of the church and on antireligious policy in the USSR as well as some texts from SAMIZDAT, documenting the addition of Moscow to Paris and New York as places of publication since 1974. In the section on literature, A. Solzhenitsyn has been accorded ample space since the 1970s. Generally those Russian writers are included who are open-minded about religious or spiritual issues, such as A. Akhmatova, G. Aygi, A. Blok, I. Brodsky, Yu. Kublanovsky, O. Mandelshtam, B. Pasternak, F. Sologub, V. Tendryakov, M. Tsvetayeva, and M. Voloshin; sometimes their original texts are included, sometimes articles about these authors are published. Even in the review section, literature is regularly included alongside religious, church, and cultural matters.

In 1925 the circulation was 300; in 1927, 1,350; and in 1970, 1,700. As of 1986 there was still no index.

Secondary Lit.: N. Struve, in Vestnik RSKhD 100:1971 and 112–13:1974; N. Zernov, in Vestnik RSKhD 100:1971; A. Kiselëv, in Vestnik RSKhD 100:1971; V. Maramzin, in Ėkho 1978:2, p. 156; K. Fotiev, in Novoe russkoe slovo, New York, Nov. 16, 1980, p. 5, and Aug. 8, 1982, p. 9; Ju. K[ublanovskij], in Russkaja mysl', Paris, Jan. 27, 1983, p. 10, Sept. 8, 1983, p. 10, June 21, 1985, p. 10, and Jan. 3, 1986, p. 12; E. Khorvat, in Russkaja mysl' May 5, 1983, p. 10, and June 6, 1984, p. 12.

**Vesyóly, Artyóm** (pseud. of Nikoláy Ivánovich Kochkúrov), prose writer (b. Sept. 29 [Sept. 17], 1899, Samara—d. Dec. 2, 1939 [?], while imprisoned). Vesyoly's father was a Volga stevedore. Vesyoly began working at odd jobs when he was 15. He joined the Communist Party in March 1917. During the Civil War, Vesyoly fought with the Red Army in the Volga region and in Siberia; he was also a sailor with the Black Sea fleet. Beginning in 1922 he studied at the Bryusov Institute of Literature and Art, then at Moscow University, but did not complete the degree. In 1919 and 1921 he wrote dramas and became known for his bold prose works (influenced by A. Bely and B. Pilnyak), such as Reki ognennye (1924; Rivers of Fire) and Strana rodnaya (1926; Native Land). Up to 1926 Vesyoly belonged to the group PEREVAL, and after 1929, to RAPP. Rossiya, krovyu omytaya (1924–32; Russia Washed in Blood), a novel about the Revolution and Civil War, is considered to be his major work. In 1929 he was attacked by RAPP for alluding to the lack of sufficient respect given the fighters of the Revolution and for pointing out the excessive growth of Party bureaucracy. In Gulyay, Volga! (1932; Surge, Volga!) he depicts the Siberian campaign of the 16th-century Cossack leader Yermak. In 1937 Vesyoly became a victim of the government purges; his name was passed over in silence until his REHABILITATION in 1956.

Vesyoly's is an original literary talent. Thematically, his work keeps to Revolutionary events; stylistically, it preserves the expressive and ornamental mode of Pilnyak's school. His prose consists of numerous individual scenes and episodes related to each other only by mood; even the syntax is fragmentary. Vesyoly wants to express the instinctive and elemental action of the masses, not of the individual person; accordingly, he was reproached for insufficiently emphasizing the organizational achievements of the Party. His language is rich in colloquial expressions and regionalisms. Occasionally its rhythmic, musical structure is graphically emphasized.

Works: My (play), in Krasnaja nov' 1921:3; Reki ognennye (short stories), 1924; Dikoe serdce (short story), in Krasnaja nov' 1924:1, separate ed., 1926; Strana rodnaja (novel), 1926 (part in LEF 1925:3); Gor'kaja krov' (short stories), 1926; Bol'šoj zapev (short stories), 1927; Pirujuščaja vesna (short stories), 1929; Rossija, krov'ju omytaja (novel), 1932, 3d enl. ed., 1935; Guljaj, Volga! (novel), 1932; Čapany (short stories), 1935.—Izbr. proizv., 1958, 1970; Rossija, krov'ju omytaja. Guljaj, Volga! (selected novels), 1970.

Secondary Lit.: D. Gorbov, in Novyj mir 1925:12; A. V. Sbornik statej, ed. E. Nikitina, 1931; M. Čarnyj, in Lit. kritik 1933:2, in Oktyabr' 1957:9, and separate study, 1960; M. Serebrjanskij, in Novyj mir 1934:11; Ju. Libedinskij, in Novyj mir 1957:10; RSPP 1:1959; Z. A. Vesëlaja, in Lit. nasledstvo 74:1965 and in Vesëlyj's Izbr. proizv., 1970; I. Šenfel'd, in Russkaja mysl', Paris, March 28, 1985, p. 13.

**Vígdorova, Frída Abrámovna,** prose writer (b. March 16 [March 3], 1915, Orsha, prov. Mogilyov—d. Aug. 7, 1965, Moscow). Vigdorova's father was a teacher. In 1938 she completed her studies at the Moscow Pedagogical Institute, then worked as a teacher of Russian literature and language. From 1938 until her death she pursued a career as a journalist and writer. From her first separately published book, Moy klass (1949; Eng. tr., Diary of a Russian Schoolteacher, 1960), her work was devoted to the theme of proper academic instruction. In 1961 K. Paustovsky included a contribution by Vigdorova in his liberal volume, Tarusskiye stranitsy (Eng. tr., Pages from Tarusa, 1964): her Glaza pustye i glaza volshebnye (Blank Eyes and Magic Eyes) illustrates, using specific examples, her bold advocacy of non-stereotyped education and of educating children to discriminate and to think for themselves. Vigdorova took down a record of I. Brodsky's trial in Leningrad in 1964; this transcript was the first document of its kind to circulate in SAMIZDAT; it appeared in New York in 1965. Consequently, A. Ginzburg dedicated his record of the Sinyavsky-Daniel trial to her. Vigdorova was married to A. Raskin; her friends included E. Etkind, L. Kopelev, and Lidiya Chukovskaya, who wrote some important but as yet unpublished memoirs about her. Chukovskaya characterized Vigdorova as one of the few people who would never have been capable of self-deception. Vigdorova lived in Moscow.

Vigdorova's work is permeated with a love of justice, excellent child psychology, and warm, sympathetic understanding. She wrote documentary reports, such as those collected in Dorogaya redaktsiya (1963: Dear Editor), and works of fiction, such as Doroga v zhizn (1954; Road to Life), about the development of the Makarenko schoolchildren. Concise, colloquial dialogue set within an everyday situation that has been elevated to the noteworthy makes Vigdorova's characters individual and distinct.

Works: Moj klass (pov.), 1949; Doroga v žizn' (pov.), 1954; Černigovka (pov.), 1959; Glaza pustye i glaza volšebnye, in Tarusskie stranicy, 1961 (see above); Semejnoe sčast'e (novel), 1962; Dorogaja redakcija (articles), 1963; Ljubimaja ulica (pov.), 1964; Zasedanie suda . . . nad Iosifom Brodskim (documentary paper), in Vozdušnye puti, New York, 4:1965; Èto moj dom. Černigovka. Semejnoe sčast'e (pov.), 1966; Minuty tišiny (essays), 1967; Kem vy emu prokhodites' (essays and articles), 1969.

Secondary Lit.: A. Bruštejn, in Novyj mir 1958:5; M. Blinkova, in Novyj mir 1962:2; E. Maksimova, in Novyj mir 1964:5; L. Čukovskaja, foreword to Vigdorova's Èto moj dom . . . , 1966, and in Russian Literature Triquarterly 5:1973; N. Dolinina, in Detskaja lit., 1966, 1967; L. Lazarev, in Novyj mir 1970:1; R. Orlova, in SSSR: Vnutrennie protivorečija, vol. 3, 1982, and in her Vospominanija o neprošedšem vremeni, Ann Arbor, 1983; R. Zernova, in Russkaja mysl', Paris, Sept. 20 and 27, 1985.

**Víkulov, Sergéy Vasílyevich,** poet (b. Sept. 13, 1922, Yemelyanovskaya, oblast Vologda). Vikulov's father was a farmhand and soldier. Vikulov spent his youth in a north Russian village among peasants, carpenters, and hunters. During World War II he was a soldier; he joined the Communist Party in 1942. In 1951 he graduated from the Vologda Pedagogical Institute (Faculty of Literature). Vikulov's first volumes of poetry, such as Zavoyovannoye schastye (1949; Happiness Earned), are idyllic adulterations of the true condition of agriculture. Vikulov stayed with his theme of the Soviet village; he describes the conditions of

life there and recounts isolated incidents. After 1956 he also included the past, and during the period of de-Stalinization he took a critical view of many things, for example, in the narrative poem Okna na zaryu (1964; Window to Dawn). Vikulov participated without voting rights in the congress establishing the Writers Union of the RSFSR in 1958. In 1964 he was awarded the Gorky Prize; since 1965 he has attended all congresses, and since 1975 he has belonged to the secretariat, of the Writers Union of the RSFSR. At the end of the 1960s Vikulov moved to Moscow; in 1969 the editorship of the journal Nash sovremennik was turned over to him. In 1969 Vikulov was among the conservative signatories of the attack on Novy mir in Ogonyok (see Novy mir 1969:7, p. 285). Vikulov publishes often, especially narrative poems.

As a poet, Vikulov has little talent. His poems lack rhythm, meter, and musicality. They can be distinguished from prose only through their division into lines and their occasionally primitive rhyme scheme; they are long and diffuse. The theme revolves solely around the village—the source of Russian life; he often deals with topical journalistic issues (for example, he criticizes the organization of large kolkhozes or the promotion of rabbit breeding). In addition to a lack of technical ability, he is reproached by Soviet critics for the inconsistent solutions he provides to the problems he presents.

Works: Zavoëvannoe sčast'e (poems), 1949; Zaozer'e (poems), 1956; Preodolenie (narrative poem), in Neva 1962:5; Okna na zaryu (narrative poem), in Oktjabr' 1964:1; Okolica (poems), 1966; Izbr., 1967; Izbr., 1972; Plug i borozda (poems), 1972; Ot krylečka (poems), 1973; Rodovoe derevo (lyric and narrative poems), 1975; Izbr., 1979; Vskhody (poems), 1982; Razgovory-razgovory . . . (poems), 1985.

Secondary Lit.: A. Urban, in Zvezda 1963:2; editorial in Lit. Rossija Oct. 4, 1963, p. 15; V. Dement'ev, in Naš sovremennik 1966:7 and in Moskva 1979:9; V. Vigiljanskij, in Znamja 1973:4; Vl. Soloukhin, in Lit. Rossija Aug. 24, 1973, p. 11; D. Kovalëv, in Lit. obozrenie 1976:2; V. Korobov, 1980; Ju. Lukin, in Znamja 1982:9; V. Černikov, in Lit. gazeta Dec. 11, 1985, p. 5.

**Village prose** (Derevénskaya próza), a term that came into use in the 1960s to describe Russian prose that is set in the village and is especially conscious of the traditional human and ethical values that form an integral part of the centuries-old Russian village. Under Stalin, life in the Russian village was only seldom depicted and then adulterated when it was; in particular, the forced establishment of the kolkhozes was idealized (M. Sholokhov) and the reconstruction of villages after World War II was inaccurately portrayed (S. Babayevsky); in 1952 V. Ovechkin began writing documentary kolkhoz prose that pointed out the damage caused by state control of agriculture when central decision-making power lies in the hands of nonfarmers. An economically oriented prose of indictment (for example, Ye. Dorosh) flourished under Khrushchev, who—from the Party's and the state's perspective—concerned himself with agriculture to a considerably greater extent than his predecessors had. The more fictionalized the accounts, the more prominence was given to the human consequences of the state's mismanagement (for example, V. Tendryakov, A. Yashin, S. Antonov). After A. Solzhenitsyn's *Matryonin dvor* (1963; Eng. tr., "Matryona's House," in *Stories and Prose Poems,* 1971) focused attention on the human and especially the Christian religious values preserved in the central Russian village despite the conditions of poverty, Russian village prose gained momentum and generated many of the best works in Russian literature over the succeeding decades. In a series of novels, F. Abramov depicted village life in the Arkhangelsk region in detail; V. Belov highlighted the virtues of the peasant community before collectivization in the traditionalist region of Vologda; S. Zalygin condemned the destruction of the village tradition in Siberia; in his short stories, V. Shukshin gave new life to whimsical peasant characters and contrasted them to the dehumanized city dwellers; A. Astafyev warned against the ecological dangers of modern civilization. In addition, the following made names for themselves as writers of village prose: V. Afonin (Siberia), S. Bagrov, I. Drutse (Moldavia), F. Iskander (Abkhazia), V. Krupin, S. Krutilin, V. Lichutin, V. Likhonosov, V. Lipatov, B. Mozhayev, Ye. Nosov, M. Roshchin, G. Semyonov, V. Syomin, G. Troyepolsky, M. Vorfolomeyev, S. Voronin. V. Rasputin achieved the highest national and international fame with his novels set in a Siberian village that convincingly defend the religious and universal human norms of tradition. Authors such as V. Soloukhin who include cultural treasures—churches, monasteries, icons, noblemen's residences—in addition to the village in their defense of Russian tradition have occasionally been criticized. In general, however, village prose, which is at variance with the principles of the 1917 Revolution and which often appears in the journal *Nash sovremennik,* enjoys sympathetic official tolerance, since the political forces tending toward Russian patriotism in the USSR feel themselves essentially supported by this genre.

*Secondary Lit.:* Žizn' kolkhoznoj derevni i literatura, ed. K. I. Bukovskij, Moscow, 1956; F. Kuznecov, in *Novyj mir* 1973:6; Y. Perret-Gentil, in *Osteuropa* 1978:9; G. Hosking, *Beyond Socialist Realism,* London, 1980; V. Akimov, in *Neva* 1982:1; G. Witte, *Die sowjetische Kolchos- und Dorfprosa der fünfziger und sechziger Jahre,* Munich, 1983; V. Calmaev, L. Vil'ček, in *Voprosy lit.* 1985:6.

**Vinográdov, Anatóly Kornéliyevich,** prose writer (b. April 9 [March 28], 1888, Polotnyanye Zavody, prov. Smolensk—d. Nov. 26, 1946, Moscow). Vinogradov's father was a teacher. In 1912 Vinogradov completed his studies in the Departments of History and Philology and of Physics and Mathematics at Moscow University. From 1921 to 1925 he was director of the Lenin Library in Moscow (the Rumyantsev Museum previous to its annexation). In the literary field Vinogradov worked initially as a scholar, particularly in the area of French literature; after 1931 he published several historical novels. In *Tri tsveta vremeni* (1931; Eng. tr., *Three Colours of Time,* 1946), his first novel, he relates the life of the French writer Stendhal to Napoleon's Russian campaign. *Povest o bratyakh Turgenevykh* (1932; A Tale of the Brothers Turgenev) depicts the relationship of Nikolay and Aleksandr Turgenev to Russian Freemasonry. *Chorny konsul* (1932; Eng. tr., *The Black Consul,* 1935) takes place in 1791 in the French part of Haiti during the French Revolution. In *Osuzhdeniye Paganini* (1936; Eng. tr., *The Condemnation of Paganini,* 1946), he selects the life of a musician as his subject; in *Khronika Malevinskikh* (1943; Chronicle of the Malevinskys), his topic becomes the biography of the chemist D. Mendeleyev.

Vinogradov's novels are fluently and vividly written, with lively dialogue; his frequent use of quotations from letters and diaries, however, often has a cumbersome effect. Historically his works are rather unreliable. Only a portion of the errors has been eliminated from posthumous editions of his work.

*Works: Tri cveta vremeni* (novel), 1931, rev. ed., 1957 (see above); *Povest' o brat'jakh Tur-*

genevykh, 1932; Čërnyj konsul (pov.), 1933, rev. ed., 1957 (see above); Osuždenie Paganini (novel), 1936 (see above); Bajron (biography), 1936; Stendal' i ego vremja (biography), 1938, 1960; Khronika Malevinskikh (novel), 1943.— Izbr. proizv., 3 vols., 1960.

Secondary Lit.: K. Loks, in Novyj mir 1931:12; I. Ležnev, in Novyj mir 1944:8–9; Anon., in Zvezda 1958:7; RSPP 1:1959.

Vinokúrov, Yevgény Mikháylovich, poet (b. Oct. 22, 1925, Bryansk). From 1943 on, Vinokurov was a soldier, then an officer, in World War II. As a child he began writing poems. The first were published in 1948; in 1951 he graduated from the Gorky Literary Institute, where he himself has taught since 1966. His first volume of poetry, Stikhi o dolge (1951; Poems about Duty), was followed by the second only in 1956—Sineva (The Blue). In 1952 he joined the Communist Party. Since the changed atmosphere following the 20th Party Congress, Vinokurov has written much and his works have been collected into numerous, mostly slender, volumes. They are great favorites, out of print only days after they are published, and are well received by the critics although they are never concerned with topical political themes. Vinokurov, who has never enjoyed reading his poems in public as Ye. Yevtushenko does, has never stood in the spotlight; he does not kindle polemics or scandal. In 1968 he was allowed to publish his 18th volume of poetry, a long (500-page) collection. In 1976 a two-volume selection of his works was published. Selected translations have appeared in Poland, Czechoslovakia, and Hungary. Noteworthy is the anthology he edited, Russkaya poeziya XIX veka (1974; Russian Lyric of the 19th Century). He lives in Moscow and has belonged to the board of the Writers Union of the USSR since 1967.

Vinokurov stands consciously in the tradition of F. Tyutchev and Ye. Baratynsky and writes contemplative poetry. The point of departure for his poetry was his experience in the war, not experience of false heroism but of the witnessing of death and loneliness; usually these poems were written only later on from his memories. Vinokurov goes to the depth of inconspicuous things. Without telling a story, he selects extreme situations involving the senses, as well as images of technology and of the city, seldom of nature, to penetrate to the depth of human existence. Daily life and a civilization that is threatening

spirituality provide his impulse to create. His lyric poetry is born of inspiration (one poem begins: "I will not give up the word 'inspiration' "); he trusts his lyric sense and seldom alters what he has written down. Contrast, ambivalence, and occasional paradoxes help him expose the truth. Man is revealed as searcher, doubter. Vinokurov does not proclaim; he hints, he strives for the poem that "ends with many periods, not just with one," that only reveals itself after repeated readings. As he restores original meaning to apparently worn-out words in unusual contexts, so does he seek to strengthen the effective force of the poem through rhyme. "There is an air of modesty, candor, and artlessness in Vinokurov's poetry that has obviously been carefully cultivated" (D. Brown). Vinokurov's best lyric poetry has a density that does not permit even one word to be deleted or moved. Vinokurov has written numerous essays about writers (F. Tyutchev, A. Fet, A. Pushkin, among others) and about the essential questions of poetry. In 1966 these essays were collected for the first time and published with a title that is most typical of his own work, Poeziya i mysl (Poetry and Thought).

Works: Stikhi o dolge (poems), 1951; Sineva (poems), 1956; Voennaja lirika (poems), 1956; Priznan'ja (poems), 1958; Lico čelovečeskoe (poems), 1960; Muzyka (poems), 1964; Stikhotvorenija (poems), 1964, 1974; Kharaktery (poems), 1965; Zemnye predely (poems), 1965; Poèzija i mysl' (essays), 1966; Ritm (poems), 1967; Serëžka s Maloj Bronnoj (poems), 1968, 1974; Zreliščа (poems), 1968; Izbr. iz devjati knig (poems), 1968; Žest (poems), 1969; Metafory (poems), 1972; V silu veščej (poems), 1973; Kontrasty (poems), 1975; Prostranstvo (poems), 1976; Ostaetsja v sile (essays), 1979; (with N. Arsen'ev) Po zakonam voennogo vremeni (pov.), in Oktjabr' 1980:11–12, separate ed., 1982; Bytie (lyric and narrative poems), 1982; Argumenty (poems), 1984; Ipostas' (poems), 1984.—Izbr. proizv., 2 vols., 1976; Sobr soč., 3 vols., 1983–84.

Translations: poems in Three New Soviet Poets, 1967; The War Is Over, 1976; Selected Poems (parallel Russian-English text), 1979.

Secondary Lit.: St. Rassadin, in Novyj mir 1962:1; È. Rajs, in Grani, Frankfurt am Main, 55:1964; Ju. Arkadskij, in Volga 1968:3; W. Kasack, in Neue Zürcher Zeitung Jan. 16, 1972; A. Turkov, in Lit. obozrenie 1974:5; I. Rodnjanskaja, in Oktjabr' 1975:9; E. M. V., in Lit. gazeta Nov. 5, 1975, p. 4; S. Čuprinin, in Lit. obozrenie 1978:3; N. Matveeva, in Avrora

1979:4; V. Soloukhin, in *Lit. gazeta* Sept. 10, 1980, p. 5; G. Levin, in *Inostrannaja Lit.* 1983:6; I. Volgin, in *Novyj mir* 1985:10.

**Virtá, Nikoláy Yevgényevich** (pseud. of N. Ye. Karélsky), prose writer, playwright (b. Dec. 19 [Dec. 6], 1906, Bolshaya Lazovka, prov. Tambov—d. Jan. 3, 1976, Moscow). Virta's father was a village priest; both parents were executed, probably in 1921. Beginning in 1923 Virta worked as a journalist; he was later associated with the Theater of Young Workers (TRAM) in Moscow from 1930 on. Virta became well known for his novel on the Antonov rebellion, *Odinochestvo* (1935; Eng. tr., *Alone*, 1958; Stalin Prize for 1935–41, 2d class), which he adapted for the stage as *Zemlya* (1937; The Earth). Virta's second novel, *Zakonomernost* (1937; Lawfulness), describes the struggle against Trotskyite opposition for the first time. During the Finnish-Russian War (1939–40) and World War II, Virta was a war correspondent. in the postwar period he received three more Stalin Prizes: for the drama *Khleb nash nasushchny* (1947; Our Daily Bread), an idealized kolkhoz play (Stalin Prize for 1947, 2d class); for *Zagovor obrechonnykh* (1948; Conspiracy of the Doomed), an anti-Western propaganda play against COSMOPOLITANISM (Stalin Prize for 1948, 1st class); and for the film script *Stalingradskaya bitva* (1947; The Battle of Stalingrad; Stalin Prize for 1949, 1st class), which was criticized after 1953 for deferring to the cult of personality. Virta is considered to be one of the exponents of the THEORY OF CONFLICTLESSNESS chiefly on account of his article in *Sovetskoye iskusstvo* Jan. 16, 1952). On April 28, 1954, Virta, who was near Moscow, was expelled from the Writers Union along with A. Surov and A. Voloshin. It is probable that he was allowed to rejoin in 1956. A novel was published, *Krutye gory* (1956; Steep Mountains), that addressed the new agricultural policy. Virta adapted it for the stage as *Dali-dalniye, neoglyadnye* (1957; The Remote, Unsurveyable Distance). His novel *Step da step krugom* (1960; The Steppe, the Steppe on All Sides) is dedicated to the theme of the Virgin Lands. Virta was a delegate only to the First Congress of the Writers Union of the RSFSR (1958) and the Third Congress of the Writers Union of the USSR (1959); he lived in Moscow.

Virta is a weak writer who briefly attracted attention by accommodating himself to the demands of Stalinist propaganda. His early plans to write a trilogy as the first part of a cycle of six novels fell through. In terms of content, the original versions of *Odinochestvo* and *Zakonomernost* have a certain interest because of the perspective they provide on anti-Soviet tendencies (Struve). Later Virta always selected themes that conformed to the Party line; in *Dali-dalniye, neoglyadnye* he used the technique of the author who comments on and takes part in the action.

*Works:* Odinočestvo (novel), 1937, rev. ed., 1957 (see above); Zemlja (tragedy), 1937; Zakonomernost' (novel), 1938; Khleb naš nasuščnyj (play), 1947; Stalingradskaja bitva (film script), 1947; V odnoj strane (play), 1949 (also under the title Zagovor obrečënnykh); P'esy (plays), 1949 (contains Zagovor obrečënnykh; Khleb naš nasuščnyj); P'esy (plays), 1950 (contains Zemlja; Velikie dni; Khleb naš nasuščnyj; Zagovor obrečënnykh); Večernij zvon (novel), 1951, rev. ed., 1961; Gibel' Pompeeva (comedy), 1954; Krutye gory (novel), 1956; Dali-dal'nie, neogljadnye (play), 1960; Step' da step' krugom (novel), 1960; Bystrobeguščie dni (novel), 1965; Kol'co Luizy (pov.), 1971; Pobeg (pov.), 1973.—Izbr. proizv., 2 vols., 1973; Sobr. soč., 4 vols., 1980–82.

*Secondary Lit.:* V. Kin, Novyj mir 1936:7; E. Usievič, in Lit. kritik 1937:7; F. Gladkov, in Lit. gazeta April 6, 1954 (see Komsomol'skaja pravda March 17, 1954); I. Terent'ev, in Grani, Frankfurt am Main, 32:1956; RSPP 1:1959; T. Napolova, in Zvezda 1960:10; B. Emel'janov, in Teatr 1962:5; K. Stratilatova, in Lit. gazeta Dec. 22, 1976, p. 7.

**Vishnévsky, Vsévolod Vitályevich,** playwright (b. Dec. 21 [Dec. 8], 1900, St. Petersburg—d. Feb. 28, 1951, Moscow). Vishnevsky's father was a geodesist. Vishnevsky left the gymnasium at the age of 14 to volunteer for the front; at 17 he joined the Bolsheviks and participated in the insurrection in Petrograd. During the Civil War he served with the First Cavalry and as a political officer and fleet commander. In 1920–21 Vishnevsky published several frontline reports in military newspapers. In Novorossiysk in 1921 he organized a revolutionary theater production of an eight-hour, outdoor play with a huge cast about the Kronstadt rebellion. Vishnevsky continued to be a political agitator, partly in his role as literary official (initially under the auspices of RAPP) and partly in his role as writer. He was among those who actively opposed M. Bulgakov. In the mid-1920s he brought out a collection of his Civil War articles; in 1929 he wrote *Pervaya Konnaya* (The First Cavalry), a turn to a controversial form of epic-dramatic theatrical production. In 1937 he was admitted to the Communist Party. In 1941–42 Vishnevsky was a war correspondent in Leningrad. After 1944 he lived in Moscow, where he was editor in chief of the journal *Znamya* and published, among other things, V. Nekrasov's novel about Stalingrad. Late in 1946, at a time of increasing control over the course of literary politics, Vishnevsky became assistant general secretary of the Writers Union of the USSR.

Of Vishnevsky's six propagandistic plays, only *Optimisticheskaya tragediya* (1932; Eng. tr., *An Optimistic Tragedy*, in *Four Soviet Plays*, 1937) has entered the repertoire, even in Communist countries. In this play Vishnevsky depicts the disciplinary action taken against an anarchistic unit of sailors by a woman commissar and the death of a regiment for the Bolshevik idea. He underscores the political purpose of his weakly plotted and dramatically ineffective piece by introducing authorial commentaries spoken by a chorus. Soviet critics declared his antifascist piece *Na Zapade boy* (1931; Battle in the West) cliché-ridden, unfit to be a part of "standard instruction in political indoctrination." *Nezabyvayemy 1919-y* (1949; Unforgettable 1919), a play about Stalin's putative role in the Revolution written for Stalin's 70th birthday, is not only as artistically weak as Vishnevsky's other works but is, moreover, based on an embarrassing falsification of history; the work, which received a Stalin Prize for 1949, 1st class, reveals Vishnevsky's political idealism as a faithful Stalinist.

*Works: Za vlast' Sovetov* (short stories), 1924; *Na Zapade boj* (play), 1933; *Optimističeskaja tragedija* (play), in *Novyj mir* 1933:2 (see above); *My iz Kronštadta* (film script), in *Izbr. scenarii sovetskogo kino* 1:1949; *Stat'i, dnevniki, pis'ma o literature i iskusstve* (articles, diaries, letters), 1961; *Izbr.*, 1966 (contents include: *Pervaja Konnaja; Optimističeskaja tragedija; U sten Leningrada; My iz Kronštadta; My, russkij narod); Vperëd smotrjaščij* (articles, essays, speeches), 1971; *Dnevniki voennykh let* (diaries), 1974.—*Sobr. soč.* 6 vols., 1954–61.

*Secondary Lit.:* O. K. Borodina, 1958; A. N. Anastas'ev, 1962; A. M. Mar'jamov, 1963, and in *Teatr* 1970:12; V. B. Azarov, 1966, 2d ed., 1970; V. O. Percov, 1967; A. Grebenščikov, 1970; G. Ambernadi, in *Lit. obozrenie* 1975:8; V. Percov, in his *Ot svidetelja sčastlivogo . . .* , 1977; V. Khelemendik, 1980.

**Vladímirova, Líya** (pseud. of Yúliya Vladímirovna Khrómchenko, née Dubróvkina), poet, prose writer (b. Aug. 18, 1938, Moscow). Vladimirova's father was a geologist; her mother was a geographer and a writer of children's books; her maternal grandfather (Ye. A. Ganeyzer) was a writer. Vladimirova was able to study at the All-Union Film Institute (VGIK) from 1956 to 1961 on the basis of a few of her scripts having been broadcast as radio plays and television films. Vladimirova's first published work was the short story *Pervy potseluy* (1957; The First Kiss) in the journal *Yunost;* after that she had to wait thirteen years until she was able to publish seven poems (*Moskovsky komsomolets* Feb. 15, 1970). These were followed by only another ten poems in *Yunost* and *Smena.* Vladimirova, who was only able to read her poetry aloud in private circles, came under suspicion by the KGB and was allowed to emigrate to Israel on April 1, 1973. There she has regularly published poems in numerous journals and almanacs and has also published the volumes of poetry that include poems from her Moscow period: *Svyaz vremyon* (1975; Connection of Times), *Pora predchuvstviy* (1978; Time of Foreboding), and *Sneg i pesok* (1982; Snow and Sand). A volume of selected poems was published in Hebrew in 1984. Her first book of prose, *Pismo k sebe* (1985; A Letter to Myself), contains a second povest, *Strakh* (Fear). She lives in Netanya.

Vladimirova's poems are marked by a great internal tension that also finds expression in the frequent naming of contrasts. She presents opposites such as movement and stillness, honesty and falsehood, being and appearance, dream and reality, secrecy and revelation, accident and predetermination, an instant and eternity, earthly loneliness and cosmic inclusion, in many variations. In her presentation these extremes approach one another but leave tension and melancholy behind. Vladimirova's poetry is unpolitical, occasionally close to nature, descriptive, and—even when she chooses the title "Ballade"—not narrative. Armed with a fundamentally religious attitude and prepared for suffering, she is engaged in a continual search for man's place in life.

*Works: Svjaz' vremën* (poems), Tel Aviv, 1975; *Pora predčuvstvij* (poems), Tel Aviv, 1978; *Sneg i pesok* (poems), Tel Aviv, 1982; *Pis'mo k sebe* (pov.), Tel Aviv, 1985.

*Secondary Lit.:* V. Betaki, in *Grani,* Frankfurt am Main, 97:1975; D. Markiš, in *Zion,* Jerusalem, 1975:12; Anon., in *Kontinent,* Paris,

6:1976 and 19:1979; I. Odoevceva, in *Russkaja mysl'*, Paris, Aug. 9, 1976; P. Akar', in *Novoe russkoe slovo*, New York, July 9, 1978, p. 5; V. Sinkevič, in *Novoe russkoe slovo* Aug. 29, 1982, p. 5; D. Šturman, in *Novoe russkoe slovo* March 27, 1983, p. 5.

**Vladímov, Geórgy Nikoláyevich,** prose writer (b. Feb. 19, 1931, Kharkov). Vladimov's parents were teachers. In 1953 Vladimov graduated in law from Leningrad University; in 1954 he began working as a literary critic. He worked as an editor in the prose section of *Novy mir* (1956–59). His first original work of prose appeared in 1960. His harshly realistic novella about open-pit mining, *Bolshaya ruda* (1961; Eng. tr., *Striking It Rich*, 1963), was highly regarded. In a document dated May 26, 1967, addressed to the Fourth Congress of the Writers Union of the USSR, Vladimov demanded the public discussion of A. Solzhenitsyn's letter about the board of censors: "Without the freedom to engage in creative work, without the freedom to comment on all the social and moral problems pervading the life of the people, Soviet literature cannot exist." In his letter Vladimov, in reference to the lot of his own work, pointed out that the barriers of censorship themselves served to push works into SAMIZDAT. He had in mind his novel *Verny Ruslan* (Eng. tr., *Faithful Ruslan*, 1979), which on the advice of A. Tvardovsky had been enlarged but later was not published by *Novy mir*. Vladimov later revised the novel once more for publication in the West in Frankfurt am Main. Vladimov's novel *Tri minuty molchaniya* (1969; Three Minutes of Silence), which Tvardovsky published in *Novy mir*, was sharply attacked by semi-official critics and was authorized to appear as a book only in 1976. (A reworked version that restored the censor's deletions was published in Frankfurt in 1982.) In 1977 Vladimov withdrew from the Writers Union and soon thereafter assumed the leadership of the Moscow chapter of Amnesty International. Under the threat of prosecution, Vladimov was forced to emigrate to the Federal Republic of Germany on May 26, 1983. He lives near Frankfurt. From 1984 to 1986 he was editor in chief of the review *Grani*.

*Bolshaya ruda* describes the wretched fate of a truck driver who wants to fulfill the same quota with his little truck that the larger trucks are required to fulfill; he is the only one of his brigade to drive in the rain and is killed in an accident. The traditional conflict in Soviet literature between the collective and the individual is freed from the usual schematic treatment. Theme, protagonist, the plot's resolution, and numerous details consciously deviate from the cliché of the idealized industrial novels that were supposed to depict socialist development. Through its multilevel account, *Verny Ruslan* illustrates the compulsion plaguing a former camp dog after the camp is disbanded, the tragedy of a freed man who is made rootless by a long period of imprisonment, and the hopelessness of the prisoners in the camp. The alienation created by telling the story from the dog's point of view lends the tale allegorical power in depicting the consequences of demagogy and of "training" people to think as the state desires. Against an unsparingly depicted background of the harsh working conditions on board a fishing boat, where people are locked into the ceaseless treadmill of breadwinning and given no time for necessary self-reflection, *Tri minuty molchaniya* illustrates a man's transformation and his growing appreciation of the seriousness of life through his experience of deadly peril and love. Vladimov writes quite vividly, lets the narrated time period advance slowly, and lends the events a barely endurable tension. The comedy *Shestoy soldat* (1981; The Sixth Soldier) combines interpersonal concerns with the problem of political suspicion manipulated to personal advantage. *Ne obrashchayte vnimanya, maestro* (1982; Pay No Attention, Maestro), a realistic-satirical short story about the KGB's tailing of an author, was published shortly before his emigration.

*Works: Bol'šaja ruda* (pov.), in *Novyj mir* 1961:7, separate ed., 1962, 1971 (see above); *Tri minuty molčanija* (pov.), in *Novyj mir* 1969:7–9, separate ed., 1976, and complete ed., Frankfurt am Main, 1982; *Vernyj Ruslan* (novel), Frankfurt am Main, 1975 (see above); *Dialog o proze* (with F. Kuznecov), in *Lit. gazeta* Feb. 18, 1976, p. 6; *Šestoj soldat* (play), in *Grani*, Frankfurt am Main, 121:1981; *Ne obraščajte vniman'ja, maèstro* (short story), in *Grani* 125:1982, separate ed., expanded by a documentary text, Frankfurt am Main, 1983 (contains letter to the Fourth Congress of the Union of Soviet Writers, 1967); interview, in *Russkaja mysl'*, Paris, July 7, 1983, p. 13.

*Secondary Lit.:* E. Starikova, in *Znamja* 1962:1; S. Rassadin, in *Junost'* 1962:4; D. Tevekeljan, in *Moskva* 1970:1 and in *Lit. i sovremennost'* 10:1970; L. Anninskij, in *Junost'* 1970:6; W. Kasack, in *Neue Zürcher Zeitung* Dec. 6–7, 1975 and May 28–29, 1983; V. Černjavskij, in *Grani* 106:1977; G. Hosking, in his

*Beyond Socialist Realism*, New York, 1980; M. Popovskij, in *Russkaja mysl'* July 14, 1983, p. 12; B. Borisoglebskij, in *Vremja i my* 90:1986; A. Gladilin, in *Novoe russkoe slovo*, New York, March 2, 1986, pp. 5–6.

**VOAPP.** See VAPP.

**Volnóv, Iván Yegórovich** (pseud. of I. Ye. Vladímirov), prose writer (b. Jan. 15 [Jan. 3], 1885, Bogoroditskoye, prov. Oryol—d. Jan. 9, 1931, Bogoroditskoye). Volnov 's father was a peasant. In 1900 Volnov attended the teachers college in Kursk. From 1903 on, he was a member of the Socialist Revolutionary Party and took part in political and terrorist activities. He was imprisoned from 1908 to 1910, then fled abroad. Volnov became acquainted with M. Gorky in Capri; under Gorky's influence he began to write autobiographical prose beginning in 1911. After the February Revolution in 1917 Volnov returned to Russia, where he became a delegate to the Constituent Assembly. Not even Gorky, who in 1931 wrote the foreword to the second edition of Volnov's collected works (discontinued after his death), knew much about Volnov's life between 1917 and 1920, except that Volnov broke with the Socialist Revolutionaries. Volnov lived in a rural village and published occasionally. From 1937 to 1956 an enforced silence was imposed on his works.

Volnov's most important book, *Povest o dnyakh moyey zhizni* (1912; A Tale of the Days of My Life), with its parts *Detstvo* (Childhood) and *Otrochestvo* (Adolescence), and its continuation, *Yunost* (1913; Youth), is a chroniclelike report of village life with a one-sided emphasis on the suffering and oppression of the poor. Its further continuation, *Vozvrashcheniye* (Return), written in 1928, did not appear until 1956. Volnov's differences with the Socialist Revolutionaries are reflected in *Vstrecha* (1927; The Meeting). His narrative style overflows with long-winded dialogue; he would no longer attract attention at all but for Gorky's past recommendation.

*Works: Povest' o dnjakh moej žizni* (pov.), 1914, 2d ed., 1931, 1976; *Junost'* (pov.), 1917; *Na otdykhe* (pov.), 1926; *Vstreča* (pov.), 1928.— *Sobr. soč.*, 4 vols., 1927–28; 2 vols., 1928–30, 1931 (only vol. 1 published); *Izbr.*, 1956.
*Secondary Lit.*: B. Guber, in *Novyj mir* 1926:5; M. Gor'kij (1931) et al., in Volnov's *Izbr.*, 1956; *RSPP* 1:1959; S. Ljandes, in *Lit.*

*Rossija* May 31, 1963, p. 4; M. Minokin, 1966; V. Surganov, in *Voprosy lit.* 1975:3.

**Volódin, Aleksándr Moiséyevich** (pseud. of A. M. Lífshits), playwright (b. Feb. 10, 1919, Minsk). Volodin worked as a village schoolteacher before being sent to the front as a soldier. In 1949 he completed his studies at the Film Institute (Department of Film Scripts). Later he became an editor at the Leningrad studio for popular scientific films. Volodin's activity as a writer began in 1954 with a volume of short stories. His first drama, *Fabrichnaya devchonka* (1956; The Girl from the Factory), sparked a long-lived discussion because of its denunciation of mendacious Communist ethics and Party practices in daily life. By 1983 a total of 14 plays were well known, but only two collections had been published: *Dlya teatra i kino* (1967; For Theater and Kino) and *Portret s dozhdem* (1977; Portrait with Rain). Volodin, who lives in Leningrad, also writes filmscripts and occasionally shorter prose works. For the film *Osenniy marafon* (1979; Autumn Marathon) he was awarded the State Prize of the RSFSR in 1981.

Volodin is one of the best Russian dramatists, although also frequently criticized. Although he is mentioned either not at all or disparagingly in histories of literature, his second play, *Pyat vecherov* (1959; Eng. tr., Five Evenings, 1966) belongs to the permanent repertoire of several Soviet theaters and was performed between 110 and 407 times a year between 1959 and 1973. In *Fabrichnaya devchonka* he stirs up sympathy for a girl who is persecuted by the secretary of the Komsomol and discharged from a factory. In *Pyat vecherov* he exposes interpersonal relationships in daily life, contrasting these to the heroic farce perpetuated by the press. *V gostyakh i doma* (1960; As a Guest and at Home), an unpublished play, concerns the conflicts between a mother, who is looking for new attachments after the death of her husband, and her grown-up children. *Moya starshaya sestra* (1961; My Older Sister)—called *Starshaya sestra* in its later version, reworked after being frequently criticized—illustrates the danger of letting one's loving care for another evolve into the assertion of one's own will; it is considered one of his best plays (1963: 342 performances in 14 theaters). *Naznacheniye* (1963; The Appointment), about a man who is not prepared to assume a position of leadership, led to an official reprimand from the Ministry of Culture of the USSR (*Teatr* 1963:10) and to considerable modifications. *Attraktsiony* (1967; Attractions) is a staging of the film scripts *Pokhozhdeniya zubnogo vracha* (The Adventures of a Dentist), a tragicomedy concerning the difficulties talented people encounter in society, and *Pokhozhdeniya fokusnika* (The Adventures of the Magician), a mixture of clownery and smirking grotesquerie (previously appearing under the title *Zagadochny indus* [The Mysterious Hindu]). *Dultsinea Tobosskaya* (1971; Dulcinea from Toboso) is an inversion of the Don Quixote adventure set in the prudent world of the present. *S lyubimymi ne rasstavaytes* (1969; Don't Separate Yourselves from Your Loved Ones) places interpersonal relationships in the forefront and contains fairy-tale elements, as does the still unpublished drama *Petruchcho* (1972; Petruchio). Volodin's dramatic art arises from the search for an honest representation of essential human concerns in contrast to the heroic clichés found in the dramas of SOCIALIST REALISM of the Stalin period. The man with a weak will who is more likely to sacrifice himself than to attain his goal, the little-noticed or even the persecuted, the man whom fate has broken—these are the title characters he depicts. Using an episodic structure, he exposes but does not solve problems. He addresses the danger the collective poses for the individual and the difficulties the especially talented encounter in their environment, as well as the issues of sexuality and morality. His receding plot has been compared to A. Chekhov and his emerging fairy-tale symbolic quality to Ye. L. Shvarts. Conservative critics note the absence of ideological professions, recognize, to be sure, his true-to-life realism, but do not accept this reality as typical of society. Volodin's short story *Stydno byt neschastlivym* (1971; Shameful to Be Unhappy) reveals his positive attitude toward life linked with a bitter smile. The film *Osenniy marafon* concerns the problem of loneliness and the limits of goodness. *Portret s dozhdem* depicts the eventful life of a woman in whom "the divine instinct of motherly love lives" (Klimenko) and who finds her life fulfilled in existing for others.

Works: *Rasskazy* (short stories), 1954; *Fabričnaja devčonka* (play), in *Teatr* 1956:9, separate ed., 1957; *Pjat' večerov* (play), in *Teatr* 1959:7 (see above); *(Moja) staršaja sestra* (play), 1961; *Dlja teatra i kino* (plays, film scripts, and essays), 1967 (contains *Pjat' večerov; Staršaja sestra; Naznačenie; Idealistka;*

*Proisšestvie kotorogo nikto ne zametil; Pokhoždenija zubnogo vrača; Zagadočnyj indus; Optimističeskie zapiski); S lyubimymi ne rasstavajtes'* (pov.), in *Avrora* 1969:1; *Stydno byt' nesčastlivym* (short story), in *Avrora* 1971:4; *Portret s doždem* (plays), 1980 (contains *Dul'sineja Tobosskaja; S ljubimymi ne rasstavajtes'; Osennij marafon; Portret s doždem; Dve strely*); *Blondinka* (play), in *Teatr* 1984:8; *Grafoman* (play), in *Sovremennaja dramaturgija* 1985:2.

Secondary Lit.: M. Alekseev, in *Novyj mir* 1956:11; V. Smirnova, in *Teatr* 1957:4; E. Surkov, in *Znamja* 1958:3; G. Dubasov, in *Lit. i žizn'* Oct. 12, 1960; Ju. Zubkov, in *Teatr* 1963:10; V. Gaevskij, in *Teatr* 1967:4; K. Rudnickij, in *Novyj mir* 1968:1; Ju. Andreev, in *Zvezda* 1973:9; V. Solov'ëv, in *Novyj mir* 1974:8; V. Klimenko, in *Lit. obozrenie* 1980:10; S. Aksënova, in *Lit. obozrenie* 1983:6; I. Solov'ëva, in *Teatr* 1985:2.

**Volokhónsky, Anrí,** poet, prose writer (b. March 19, 1936, Leningrad). Volokhonsky grew up in Leningrad. After completing his studies at the Chemical-Pharmaceutical Institute, Volokhonsky worked in the field of ecology for many years. Privately, he studied the literature of the Cabals and, from the 1950s on, wrote poems, songs, and plays (occasionally with A. Khvostenko, his friend for many years). He was able to publish only a few poems in the Soviet Union. At the end of 1973 he was allowed to emigrate; in January 1974 he moved to Israel and in the autumn of 1985 to Munich, West Germany. He publishes poems, especially in *Ekho, Kontinent,* and *Dvadtsat dva.* Volokhonsky compiled his poetry written before 1982 into his book *Stikhotvoreniya* (1983; Poems). His newer poems and the short drama *Molchaniye veka* (The Silence of the Century) are contained in the collection *Tetrad Igreyny* (1984; Igreyna's Notebook). Volokhonsky publishes philosophical essays in the journals *Gnosis* and *Vestnik RKhD.* His religious attitude has also found expression in his study *Bytiye i Apokalipsis* (1984; Genesis and Revelation), which is set up as a commentary on the Bible—Genesis and Revelation. Together with poems and essays Volokhonsky has written longer works of prose, for example, the novel *Roman—pokoynichek* (1982; A Novel—The Pretty Little Corpse).

Volokhonsky belongs to the Lenigrad modernist movement in Russian poetry. V. Betaki points out that the roots of his creativity can be found in V. Khlebnikov and D. Kharms.

His poems are marked by parody, irony, and the grotesque and have their origin as much in philosophy as in daily life. They enjoy posing questions and hint at answers only by using abundant imagery. His poems gain their aesthetic value entirely from the effect of bold combinations of words, neologisms, their music, and their provocative rhymes.

*Works:* Poems, in *Kontinent,* Paris, 9:1976, 22:1980, 43:1985; in *Ėkho,* Paris, 1979:1 and 4, 1980:2 and 4, 13:1984; in *Dvadcat' dva,* Tel Aviv, 16:1980. Essays in *Ėkho* 1978:1, in *Gnosis,* New York, 3–4:1978, in *Vestnik RKhD,* Paris, 133:1981; (with A. Khvostenko) *Labirint, ili Ostrov Ižecov* (play), in *Ėkho* 1980:2; *Roman—pokojniček* (novel), New York, 1982; *Stikhotvorenija* (poems), Ann Arbor, 1983; *Tetrad' Igrejny* (poems and play), Jerusalem, 1984; *Bytie i Apokalipsis: Kommentarij k knigam Bytija, Tvorenija i Otkrovenija Ioanna* (scholarly articles), Jerusalem, 1984; (with A. Khvostenko) *Basni A. Ch. V.* (poems), Paris, 1984; *Škura Bubna* (poems), Jerusalem, 1986; *Foma* (narrative poem with commentaries), Hamburg, 1986.

*Secondary Lit.:* G. Janeček, in *Slavic and East European Journal* 1982:4; M. Kaganskaja, in *Dvadcat' dva* 31:1983; V. Betaki, in *Kontinent* 43:1985.

**Volóshin, Aleksándr Nikítich,** prose writer (b. Sept. 12 [Aug. 31] 1912, St. Petersburg—d. May 28, 1978, Kemerovo). Voloshin's father was a stoker. Voloshin spent his childhood in Siberia; in 1929 he began work as a construction laborer near Kuznetsk. During his period of military service he took courses by correspondence from the Leningrad Communist Institute of Journalism (beginning in 1934), then worked for provincial newspapers. Voloshin returned to Siberia after seeing frontline action in World War II. His first attempt at a longer prose piece, *Zemlya Kuznetskaya* (1949; Eng. tr., *Kuznetsk Land,* 1953), a typical "production novel," received a Stalin Prize (for 1949, 2d class). In 1954 Voloshin was charged with drunkenness and disorderly conduct and was expelled from the Communist Party. *Dalniye gory* (1951; Far Mountains), his novel about the miners of the Dalnegorsk region, went almost unnoticed in spite of its propagandizing of the Stakhanovite movement. Voloshin lived in Kemerovo; not until 1970 did he participate in a congress of the Writers Union of the RSFSR as a member with full rights.

Voloshin is mentioned in the literary his-tories only because he received a Stalin Prize. His 1949 novel served as one of the examples to which post-1953 critics pointed when they maintained that Stalin Prizes were bestowed on works of inferior literary value. Plot development and scenes are artificially presented; the purported technical innovations, which should constitute a positive picture of the cheaply idealized central character, never materialize; problems become subject to the THEORY OF CONFLICTLESSNESS; the language is affected and mannered.

*Works:* Zemlja Kuzneckaja (novel), 1949 (see above); Dal'nie gory (novel), in *Sibirskie ogni* 1951:4–6; Ispytanie (play), 1955; Vsë pro Natašku (novel), 1967.

*Secondary Lit.:* B. Agapov, in *Novyj mir* 1949:12; B. Isaev, in *Zvezda* 1950:10; F. Gladkov, in *Lit. gazeta* April 6, 1954 (see VIRTA, N.) RSPP 1:1959; A. Vlasenko, in *Oktjabr'* 1964:9; L. Latynin, in *Lit. gazeta* Dec. 27, 1967, p. 4.

**Volóshin, Maksimilián Aleksándrovich** (pseud. of M. A. Kiriyénko-Volóshin), poet (b. May 28 [May 16], 1877, Kiev—d. Aug. 11, 1932, Koktebel, in the Crimea). Voloshin came from an aristocratic family and was descended from Zaporozhye Cossacks and Germans who were russified in the 17th century. In 1897 he completed his studies at the gymnasium in Feodosiya. In 1898 he was forced to cut short his law studies at Moscow University because of his participation in student demonstrations. Disregarding his early endeavors, by 1900 he was pursuing a steady career as a writer and painter. In 1900 his article on K. Balmont's translation of Gerhart Hauptmann appeared in *Russkaya mysl.* From 1903 to 1917 he lived mostly in Paris and acquired a broad education; he traveled a great deal in Europe (taking extensive walking tours) and regularly visited Russia. He contributed to the symbolist journals *Vesy* and *Zolotoye runo,* and was a friend of M. Tsvetayeva. At this time Voloshin became an anthroposophist. *Stikhotvoreniya* (1910; Poems), a volume influenced by the French symbolists, was very positively reviewed by V. Bryusov. A second volume followed, *Anno mundi ardentis 1915* (1916), with poems about World War I. Voloshin's verse became more austere, now approaching that of the ACMEISTS, and he published in *Apollon.* Shortly before the 1917 February Revolution he returned to Russia and thereafter lived uninterruptedly in Koktebel in a villa on the coast of the eastern

Crimea acquired by his mother in 1903. He experienced the Revolution as an act of destruction and demonic force. At first two more volumes of verse were published in Kharkov: Iverni (1918) and Demony glukhonemye (1919; Deaf and Dumb Demons). During the battles in the Crimea, Voloshin witnessed the worst kind of terrorism; he tried in a small way to check the murders and to alleviate distress, both practically and through prayer. The "Red Leader" Bela Kun lived with him, and he gave refuge to White officers; he was himself on the list of those to be liquidated. His experience was reflected in his poetry (see "Dom poeta" [The Poet's House]). The volume Stikhi (1922; Poems) was published in Moscow. From the collection Plamena (Flames), which was published abroad in 1920, the poems Stikhi o terrore (1923; Poems of the Terror) were published in Berlin, where Voloshin's Demony glukhonemye was also brought out in a second edition. In his subsequent work Voloshin remained a consistent opponent of the Communist system. The press hounded him, but patrons in high places preserved his life and freedom. For a short time Voloshin received a pension (courtesy of A. Lunacharsky), the rest of the time he lived in great material need; he painted watercolors and wrote poems; as a person who emanated humanity, he gave comfort to many distressed individuals (for example, to S. Yesenin's wife after his suicide) and kept an open house for countless numbers of writers and members of the intelligentsia in the Soviet Union. In summer his home became a vacation spot for numerous writers and acquaintances; at one point over 100 persons were guests there simultaneously. Voloshin, whose work was not published in the Soviet Union between 1922 and his death, died of natural causes in 1932; he had bequeathed his house to the Literary Fund (Litfond) of the Writers Union of the USSR shortly before. Since then it has served as a holiday site and workplace for members of the Union. For decades an enforced silence was imposed concerning Voloshin. Since 1960 he has occasionally been mentioned in the Soviet Union. The first collection of his verse in the Soviet Union since 1922 appeared in 1977.

Voloshin's early work was influenced by the French; it combined mysticism with classical antiquity and revealed his love of Greek culture. His contact with the acmeists imparted clarity, firmness, and compactness to his poetry; the individual word gained in weight. His poetry is inspired by a profound religiousness, a commitment to history, and a quest for an understanding and conquest of sorrow. In the Revolution he saw bloody terrorism, in the Bolsheviks he saw those who, possessed by the devil, plunged Russia into chaos, but he believed in the divinely ordained necessity of this destruction as the purification preceding a new creation. Frequently his poems seek understanding in history, in the lives of the saints—for example, Svyatoy Serafim (1919; St. Serafim)—or above all in the Russian peasant revolts and the French Revolution. He illustrates horror by historical analogy, and speaks of it from the perspective of the victim. "Dom poeta" connects his own fate with a view of the history of the Crimea; it reflects the inner freedom, acquired through sorrow and faith, of this little-noted poet—this "Frenchman in culture, Russian in soul and word, and German in spirit and blood" (M. Tsvetayeva).

Works: Čajka i Solomeja (poems), Kiev, 1909; Stikhotvorenija 1900–1910 (poems), 1910; Liki tvorčestva (essays), 1914; Anno mundi ardentis 1915 (poems), 1916; Iverni (poems), 1918; Demony glukhonemye (poems), 1919, 2d ed., Berlin, 1923 (reprinted, London, 1965); Svjatoj Serafim (narrative poem, written 1919), in Novyj žurnal, New York, 72:1963; Stikhi (poems), 1922; Stikhi o terrore (poems), Berlin, 1923; Stikhi i perevody (poems and translations), Berlin, 1923; "Dom poèta" (poem, written 1926), in Novyj žurnal 31:1952, abridged in Raduga 1965:9; Skazanie ob inoke Èpifanii (short story, written 1929), in Trudy Otdelenija drevnej russkoj lit. AN SSSR 17:1961; five poems, in Novyj žurnal 39:1954; Puti Rossii (poems), Paris, 1969; four poems, in Den' poèzii, Moscow, 1971; Stikhotvorenija (poems), 1977; Pis'ma (letters), in Vremja i my, Tel Aviv, 28:1978; Stikhotvorenija i poèmy (lyric and narrative poems), 2 vols., Paris, 1982–84; Surikov (essays), 1985.

Secondary Lit.: V. Brjusov, in Dalëkie i blizkie, 1912 (reprinted, Letchworth, 1973); E. Lann, 1927; M. Cvetaeva, Živoe o živom, in Sovremennye zapiski 52–53:1933 (reprinted in her Proza, New York, 1953); V. Karalin, in Grani, Frankfurt am Main, 4:1948; S. Makovskij, in Vozroždenie, New York, 1949:2 and in Novyj žurnal 39:1954; L. Dadina, in Novyj žurnal 39:1954; V. Orlov, in Voprosy lit. 1966:10, pp. 125–26; E. Mindlin, in his Neobyknovennye sobesedniki, 1968; V. Pavlov, in Grani 87–88:1973; D. White, in Slavic and East European Journal 1975:3; M. V.—Khudožnik, 1976; B. Filippov, in Vestnik RKhD, Paris, 120:1977; M. P. Reese-Antsaklis, Diss., Brown Univ., 1977; I. Kuprijanov, 1978; S.

Schwartz Smernov, Diss., Syracuse Univ., 1978; C. E. A. Marsh, Diss., London, 1979; L. Fejnberg, in *Don* 1980:7; C. Wallrafen, Munich, 1982; A. Vasilevskij, in *Novyj mir* 1987:2.

*Vólya Rossíi* (The Will of Russia), a journal for politics and culture that was created by the circles of Socialist Revolutionaries around Kerensky as a daily newspaper in Prague in 1922 and was published as a monthly journal from 1924 to 1932. After 1927 the editorial staff was located in Paris. *Volya Rossii* espoused the "defense of democratic socialism against the Bolshevik dictatorship." Mark Slonim was the editor of the literary section. *Volya Rossii*'s most important literary contributors were A. Remizov and M. Tsvetayeva; among the older émigrés who contributed to *Volya Rossii* were K. Balmont, V. Khodasevich, M. Osorgin, and B. Zaytsev; among temporary émigrés were A. Bely and V. Shklovsky. *Volya Rossii* also championed the literature being written in the Soviet Union and took the position that literature "lives and will develop regardless of the blows of the Communist dictatorship, the constraints of the censors, and the stupid attempts to cultivate flowers of proletarian art [PROLETKULT] in the orangeries of VAPP and *Na postu* [OKTYABR]" (Slonim). Authors published in *Volya Rossii* included N. Aseyev, I. Babel, S. Chorny, O. Forsh, L. Leonov, V. Mayakovksy, I. Novikov, B. Pasternak, B. Pilnyak, K. Trenyov, and Ye. Zamyatin. The journal engaged in polemic controversies with I. Bunin, Z. Gippius, A. Kuprin, D. Merezhkovsky, and I. Shmelyov. After 1926 *Volya Rossii* also included the works of young émigré writers such as G. Gazdanov, B. Poplavsky, Yu. Terapiano, or V. Varshavsky. In addition to original works in Russian and literary criticism, *Volya Rossii* also published translations of the works of Western European authors such as Karel Čapek, Thomas Mann, Marcel Proust, Romain Rolland, and Jiři Wolker.

*Secondary Lit.*: M. Slonim, in *Volja Rossii* 1924:4 and in *Russkaja literatura v èmigracii*, ed. N. Poltorackij, Pittsburgh, 1972.

*Voprósy literatúry* (Questions of Literature), a journal dealing with questions of literature and the history and theory of literature that has been published in Moscow since 1957 by the Writers Union of the USSR and the Institute for World Literature of the Academy of Sciences. The first editor in chief was A. G.

Dementyev; he was succeeded from 1959 to 1979 by V. M. Ozerov; since then the position has been held by M. Kozmin. The editorial collective is primarily composed of critics and literary scholars, including N. Gudzy (1957–65), V. Pertsov (1957–80), L. Lazarev (1961–), V. Kosolapov (1963–71), A. Dymshits (1963–75). The only writer to be a member of the editorial staff was G. Beryozko (1960–82). *Voprosy literatury* publishes mainly secondary literature, rarely publications from literary bequests. Especially interesting are polls conducted by the journal concerning the work patterns of living writers and their relationship to their own work. In 1975 the circulation was 25,000; in 1987, 15,000.

**Vorfoloméyev, Mikhaíl Alekséyevich**, playwright (b. Oct. 9, 1947, Cheremkhovo, oblast Irkutsk). Vorfolomeyev spent his childhood in his birthplace and the nearby village and worked in a factory after completing school. His first play, *Polyn* (1975; Wormwood), premiered in Cheremkhovo and made him famous by winning a competition as the best play about World War II. In 1978–79 he made a successful debut in Moscow—where he had moved by that time—with *Zanaveski* (1977; Curtains). *Svyatoy i greshny* (1978; Holy and Sinful) is his first published play (1979). However, by 1985 he seems to have written a total of 17 plays. The skimpy secondary literature views him as a noteworthy dramatic talent.

Vorfolomeyev, who is essentially of peasant descent, has written some plays that belong to the so-called VILLAGE PROSE. In *Zanaveski* he contrasts a tradition-bound groom and a virtuous but egotistical and cynical kolkhoz chairman who adapts himself to the system. In *Leto krasnoye* (1978; Beautiful Summer), Vorfolomeyev penetrates to the spiritual foundations of the power of the village and of its people. *Svyatoy i greshny* takes place in the city; here a plumber confronts, on the one hand, the familiar pressure to attain a higher standard of living through additional unofficial work and through the common theft of state property and, on the other hand, ethical principles such as "Thou shalt not steal." Vorfolomeyev puts both God and the devil onstage and in this way lifts the problem out of Soviet daily life into the realm of principle. Vorfolomeyev has also written a historical drama, *Khabarov* (1982), as well as the plays *Rasskazhu vam—ne poverite* (1977; You Won't Believe What I Tell You), *Ministr yeyo velichestva* (1981; Her Majesty's Minister), *Derevenskaya komediya* (1982; The Village Comedy), *Ya podaryu tebe lyubov* (1982; I Give You Love), and *Osen* (1982; Autumn). Vorfolomeyev knows how to use the swift presentation of conflicts to make his plays exciting and effective onstage. The topicality of his concerns combines well with his underlying spiritual message.

Works: *Polyn'* (play), 1975 (VAAP acting copy); *Zanaveski. Sceny sel'skoj žizni* (play), 1977 (VAAP acting copy); *Rasskažu vam—ne poverite!* (play), 1977 (VAAP acting copy); *Leto krasnoe* (play), 1978 (VAAP acting copy); *Svjatoj i grešnyj* (tragicomedy), 1978 (VAAP acting copy), and in *Teatr* 1979:5; *Letela ptica rozovaja* (one-act play), 1981; *Osen'* (play), in *Sovremennaja dramaturgija* 1983:2; *Khabarov* (play), in *Sovremennaja dramaturgiya* 1986:3.

Secondary Lit.: N. Savickij, in *Teatr* 1979:5; V. Bondarenko, in *Sovremennaja dramaturgija* 1983:2.

**Vorónin, Sergéy Alekséyevich**, prose writer (b. July 13 [June 30], 1913, Lyubim, prov. Yaroslavl). Voronin's father worked for the civil service. In 1928 Voronin completed his training as a lathe operator in a factory professional school in Leningrad; he then worked in a factory and studied geology (without graduating). From 1937 to 1945 he participated in expeditions to the Far Eastern Republic, to the Urals, to the Volga region, and to the Caucasus to plan new railroad lines. His attempt to create a novel from his diary notes was unsuccessful. Voronin's first short story, *Tayozhnik* (1944; The Man of the Taiga), tries to clarify various ideas of property and acquisition by using the example of a Siberian gold prospector. In 1947 he was admitted into the Communist Party. In the same year, Voronin's first collection of short stories was published. Voronin worked as a journalist; in 1951–52 he was entrusted with the administration of the Leningrad branch of *Literaturnaya gazeta*. In the novel *Na svoyey zemle* (1948; On My Own Ground), Voronin describes the fate of the Russian settlement and the kolkhoz organization in the territory of Finnish West Karelia, annexed in 1940 after the Finnish-Russian War and again incorporated into the Soviet Union in 1947. Voronin became well known through the short story that takes place in a kolkhoz during the war, *Nenuzhnaya slava* (1956; Eng. tr., "Limelight," in *Soviet Literature* 1957:10). From 1957 to 1964 he was editor in chief of the journal *Neva*; at this time he also seized on

themes involving coming to grips with the Stalinist past, like that of the attitude toward the survivors of the Vlasov army (*V rodnykh mestakh* [1959; In the Homeland]) or the fear of denunciation (*Nochnye strakhi* [1963; Nighttime Fear]). From the diaries written during his stay in Siberia comes the novel *Dve zhizni* (1962; Two Lives). Voronin collected individual short stories into volumes such as *Roman bez lyubvi* (1968; Novel without Love) or *Vstrecha na derevenskoy ulitse* (1980; Meeting in the Village Street). He has belonged to the board of the Writers Union of the RSFSR since 1965 and joined the conservative group that attacked *Novy mir* (see *Novy mir* 1969:7). In 1976 he was awarded the State Prize of the RSFSR. He lives in Leningrad.

Voronin has called his desire to force people out of their indifference the main concern of his works. He describes mostly isolated situations and episodes; he does not have the gift for creating more complex plots. Voronin's prose is quite varied. Occasionally disturbing are his ponderousness and an excess of colloquial semantics and syntax, even apart from direct speech; from time to time, what he recounts can be humanely moving.

Works: *Vstreči* (also contains *Taëžnik*) (short stories), 1947; *Na svoej zemle* (novel) 2 vols., 1948–52; *Nenužnaja slava* (short stories), 1956 (see above); *V rodnykh mestakh* (short story), in *Neva* 1959:9; *Dve žizni* (novel), 1962; *Roman bez ljubvi* (short stories), 1968; *Stuk v polnoč'* (short stories), 1972; *Derevenskie povesti i rasskazy*, 1974; *Roditel'skij dom* (pov. and short stories), 1974; *Kamen' Marii* (pov. and short stories), 1977; *Vstreća na derevenskoj ulice* (short stories), 1980; *Žizneopisanie Ivana Petroviča Pavlova* (pov.), 1984.—*Izbr.*, 2 vols., 1973; *Sobr. soč.*, 3 vols., 1981–82.

Secondary Lit.: RSPP 1:1959; S. S. Smirnov, in *Lit. gazeta* Oct. 27, 1959 (see also Nov. 10, 1959); L. Fomenko, in *Zvezda* 1968:1; A. Pyl'nev, in *Neva* 1973:7; Vl. Soloukhin, in *Lit. Rossija* July 13, 1973, p. 7; S. Kozlova, in *Naš sovremennik* 1974:7; L. Emel'janov, 1975; V. Tunimanov, in *Zvezda* 1981:6; Ju. Petrovskij, in *Zvezda* 1983:7; V. Sukhner, in *Lit. gazeta* April 17, 1985, p. 5.

**Vorónsky, Aleksándr Konstantínovich**, critic, prose writer (b. Aug. 31 [Aug. 19], 1884 Dobrinka, prov. Tambov—d. Oct. 13, 1943 [?], while imprisoned). Voronsky's father was an Orthodox priest. Voronsky was a student at the seminary in Tambov until his expulsion.

In 1904 he joined the Communist Party and was active in Bolshevik Party work up to the Revolution. In the post-Revolutionary period Voronsky became a leading figure in the sphere of Marxist literary politics; like Trotsky, he rejected the idea of the PROLETKULT and worked for a gradual reeducation of the intelligentsia. Around the journal Krasnaya nov (which he edited from 1921 to 1927), Voronsky gathered a core group of writers who did not share the narrow ideological Party orientation of the OKTYABR group, but were seen as FELLOW TRAVELERS. The group PEREVAL grew out of theoretical conceptions based on Voronsky's literary insights. The transition to totalitarianism in literature under the direction of RAPP led in 1927 to Voronsky's first arrest as a Trotskyite, expulsion from the Party, and, presumably, exile in Siberia. Important works of literary criticism, including his Iskusstvo videt mir (1928; The Art of Seeing the World) and Literaturnye portrety (2 vols., 1928–29; Literary Portraits), nevertheless continued to appear. During this time Voronsky turned to writing autobiographical prose. In 1930 a contrite recantation enabled him to return to Moscow and to a politically neutral, supervised job as an editor in the State Publishing House's section on classical literature. The politicians of RAPP continued to use the word "Voronskyism" (Voronshchina) as a term of abuse. According to G. Glinka, Voronsky was arrested early in 1935; according to Soviet encyclopedias, he was subjected to unjust reprisals in 1937 and achieved REHABILITATION after 1956.

The bulk of Voronsky's work lies in literary politics and literary criticism. A few works were reprinted in 1963 and in 1982. A short excerpt from Voronsky's book Gogol, confiscated in 1935, appeared in 1964. Voronsky's autobiographical prose reveals his writing talent and recounts personal experiences from his youth long before the Revolution. Za zhivoy i myortvoy vodoy (1928–29; Eng. tr., Waters of Life and Death, 1936) is set during the period Voronsky spent in custody; Bursa (1933; The Seminary) describes his school days and his underground political work. Both works were reprinted after Voronsky's rehabilitation.

Works: Iskusstvo i žizn' (essays), 1924; Lit. tipy (essays), 1925 (reprinted, Leipzig, 1985); Iskusstvo videt' mir (essays), 1928; Lit. portrety (essays), 2 vols., 1928–29; Za živoj i mërtvoj vodoj (memoirs), in Novyj mir 1928:9–12 and 1929:1, 2d ed., 1970, 3d ed., 1971 (see above); Bursa (memoirs), 1933, 3d ed., 1966;

Gogol' (literary criticism), [1935], excerpt in Novyj mir 1964:8; Lit. kritičeskie stat'i (essays), 1963; Izbr. 1976; Stat'i (essays), Ann Arbor, 1980; Izbr. stat'i o literature (essays), 1982.

Secondary Lit.: H. McLean, in American Slavic and East European Review 1949:3; G. Glinka, Na Perevale, New York, 1954; G. Porębina, Warsaw, 1964; I. Mašbic-Verov, in Lit. gazeta Sept. 1, 1964; R. A. Maguire, Red Virgin Soil: Soviet Literature in the 1920's, Princeton, 1968; I. Masing-Delic, in Scando-Slavica 1976; V. Akimov, in Neva 1977:5; G. Belaja, in Voprosy lit. 1983:10; E. Sidorov, in Lit. gazeta Sept. 5, 1984, p. 7; Anon., in Voprosy lit. 1985:2.

Voynóvich, Vladímir Nikoláyevich, prose writer (b. Sept. 26, 1932, Stalinabad). Voynovich's father was a journalist; his mother, a teacher. Voynovich spent his childhood in a village, then learned the carpenter's trade. From 1951 to 1955 he served in the army. His first attempts at writing poetry date from this period. Voynovich completed his secondary-school education at night school. Permission to study at the Gorky Literary Institute was denied him in 1956 and 1957. During this time he worked as a carpenter in Moscow. After one and one-half years at the Moscow Pedagogical Institute, Voynovich went to the Virgin Lands in Kazakhstan where he wrote his first works of prose. In 1960 he was given a position in radio broadcasting in Moscow. His song about the cosmonauts was given wide official distribution. Voynovich's first short story, My zdes zhivyom (1961; We Live Here), which A. Tvardovsky published in Novy mir, was enthusiastically welcomed by V. Tendryakov and immediately placed Voynovich among "the most gifted young prose writers" (Kardin). Because of Voynovich's objective exposition of the shortcomings in the present-day Soviet Union, a violent quarrel broke out among the critics. His two following short stories were criticized for the same reason. One of them, Kem ya mog by stat (He Whom I Could Have Become), whose title Tvardovsky changed to Khochu byt chestnym (1963; Eng. tr., "I'd Be Honest If They'd Let Me," 1965), was also successful as a drama in 1967 and 1968 (157 performances in 1968). He also adapted his next prose work, Dva tovarishcha (1967; Two Comrades), as a drama. After a temporary prohibition against his dramas was lifted, this work was performed a great number of times. A novel that he began writing in 1963, Zhizn i neobychaynye pri-

*klyucheniya soldata Ivana Chonkina* (Eng. tr., *The Life and Extraordinary Adventures of Private Ivan Chonkin,* 1977), circulated in SAMIZDAT. The beginning was published in Frankfurt am Main in 1969, the entire book in Paris in 1975. In 1972, Voynovich, who had repeatedly found himself in difficulties because of this book and because of his having earlier signed the petitions for Sinyavsky-Daniel and Yu. Galanskov, was allowed to publish two books. In 1973, when the VAAP was formed, Voynovich protested in an open letter against this institution with whose assistance Soviet authors would be robbed of even their foreign rights. In February 1974 Voynovich was expelled from the Writers Union of the USSR and was accepted into the PEN Club of France. In the documentary short novel *Ivankiada* (1976; Eng. tr., *The Ivankiad,* 1977), Voynovich exposes the attempt by the nomenclatural functionary S. S. Ivanko to take for himself a room promised to Voynovich. In December 1980 Voynovich was allowed to emigrate to the Federal Republic of Germany; he lives near Munich. He regularly publishes satirical essays and short stories on current events of Soviet and émigré literary life; 43 of them he collected in the book *Antisovetsky Sovetsky Sojuz* (1985; Eng. tr., *The Anti-Soviet Soviet Union,* 1986).

Through his Chonkin novel and *Ivankiada,* Voynovich has become one of the leading Russian satirists of his time. His early short stories run counter to the propaganda of the media—for example, the idealization of the work conducted in the Virgin Lands *(My zdes zhivyom)* or the Soviet construction industry *(Khochu byt chestnym)*—but they are not yet satirical. *Zhizn i neobychaynye priklyucheniya soldata Ivana Chonkina* paratactically develops the topos of the soldier senselessly standing guard and presents an antithesis to the usual heroic emotionalism. Voynovich's satire, directed against the military, the militia, and the Party, is in essence a critique of the entire Soviet system. The figure of Chonkin, who becomes entangled in comically depicted situations, gradually assumes a tragic dimension. The sequel, *Pretendent na prestol* (1979; Eng. tr., *Pretender to the Throne,* 1981), does not retain the structure of a picaresque novel composed of unconnected adventures. This sharpened satire, which is more pointedly directed at the doublethink and doublespeak existing in the Soviet Union, culminates with a twofold misconception: Chonkin as political criminal and as folk hero. In *Putyom vzaimnoy perepiski* (1979; Eng. tr., *In Plain Russian,* 1979) Voynovich collected his

older prose works and journalistic pieces. From the beginning Voynovich has proven himself an excellent, realistic interpreter of human character through short exchanges of dialogue and a writer with a special gift for the lively arrangement of details. The novel *Moskva 2042* (1986; Eng. tr., *Moscow 2042,* 1987) combines experiences of emigration in Europe and the United States with a utopian depiction of life in Moscow after 20 years as a city where socialism has been realized.

*Works: My zdes' živëm* (short story), in *Novyj mir* 1961:1; *Khoču byt' čestnym* (short story), in *Novyj mir* 1963:2; *Dva tovarisšča* (pov.), in *Novyj mir* 1967:1; *Povesti,* 1972; *Stepen' doverija,* 1972; *Otkrytoe pis'mo predsedatelju VAAP* (letter), Oct. 2, 1973; *Putëm vzaimnoj perepiski* (pov.), in *Grani,* Frankfurt am Main, 87–88:1973; *Žizn' i neobyčajnye priključenija soldata Ivana Čonkina* (novel), vols. 1 and 2, Paris, 1975 (partial reprint in *Grani* 72:1969) (see above); *Proisšestvie v Metropole* (autobiographical short story), in *Kontinent,* Paris, 5:1975 (Eng. tr., "Incident at the Metropole," 1977); *Ivankiada: Rasskaz o vselenii pisatelja Vojnoviča v novuju kvartiru* (short novel), Ann Arbor, 1976; *Pretendent na prestol* (novel), Paris, 1979 (see above); *Putëm vzaimnoj perepiski* (pov., short stories, letters), Paris, 1979 (see above); *Vojna protiv pisatelej* (letter dated Oct. 23, 1980), in *Ekho,* Paris, 1980:3; *Fiktivnyj brak* (play), in *Vremja i my,* Jerusalem, 72:1983: *Tribunal* (play), London, 1985; *Antisovetskij Sovetskij Sojuz* (essays), Ann Arbor, 1985 (see above); *Moskva—2042* (novel), Ann Arbor, 1986 (see above).

*Secondary Lit.:* V. Tendrjakov, in *Lit. gazeta* Feb. 25, 1961; V. Kardin, in *Voprosy lit.* 1961:3; S. Rassadin, in *Junost'* 1962:4; G. Brovman, in *Moskva* 1963:6; interview, in *Die Zeit* Jan. 17, 1975, pp. 19–20; Ju. Višnevskaja, in *Russkaja mysl',* Paris, July 17, 1975; R. R., in *Grani* 97:1975; Ju. Terapiano, in *Russkaja mysl'* May 13, 1976; M. A. Szorluk, in *Russian Literature Triquarterly* 14:1976; D. Štok, in *Grani* 104:1977; W. Kasack, in *Fiction and Drama in Eastern and Southeastern Europe,* Columbus, Ohio, 1980; G. Hosking, in his *Beyond Socialist Realism,* New York, 1980; N. Koržavin, in *Novoe russkoe slovo,* New York, Oct. 3, 1982, p. 5; M. Sendich and S. Lubenskij, in *Russian Language Journal* 131:1984.

*Vozdúshnye putí* (Aerial Paths), a literary almanac whose five issues were published in

New York between 1960 and 1967 under the editorship of R. N. Grinberg. The title's reference to B. Pasternak reflects the content of the first almanac, which commemorated his 70th birthday and appeared during the deplorable censure of the poet in his homeland. The title is also intended to illustrate the speciousness of artificial boundaries on earth. Each issue of *Vozdushnye puti* contains significant works of modern Russian literature and contributions by renowned critics and Slavicists such as G. Adamovich, B. Filippov, V. Markov, L. Rzhevsky, F. Stepun, G. Struve, V. Veydle. The works published in *Vozdushnye puti* have included A. Akhmatova's *Poema bez geroya* (1, 2), 57 poems by O. Mandelshtam (2), I. Babel's short stories and letters (3), B. Khodasevich, M. Tsvetayeva, and B. Savinkov (4, 5), the record of I. Brodsky's trial recorded by F. Vigdorova (4), M. Tsvetayeva's narrative poem *Perekop* (5), and a detailed letter written by A. Bely to his first wife, Anna A. Turgeneva, about languishing in physical and spiritual deprivation after the Revolution (5).

Secondary Lit.: V. Zlobin, in *Vozroždenie*, Paris, 98:1960.

**Voznesénsky, Andréy Andréyevich,** poet (b. May 12, 1933, Moscow). Voznesensky's father was a hydraulics engineer. In 1957 Voznesensky graduated from the Moscow Institute of Architecture. In 1962 Voznesensky, whose poetry harkens back to the tradition of the 1920s, named B. Pasternak as the older poet whose advice he considered most valuable. Voznesensky combines his talent as a poet with that of a painter. His poems began appearing in newspapers and journals in 1958. His first volumes of poetry, *Parabola* and *Mozaika*, were published in 1960. Their bold form caused a great sensation at home and abroad, and in no time gave Voznesenksy a reputation that helped him win many trips abroad. A sojourn in the United States in 1961 found an echo in the cycle *Sorok liricheskikh otstupleniy iz poemy Treugolnaya grusha* (1962; Forty Lyrical Digressions from the Poem Triangular Pear). In 1963 Voznesensky read his poetry in Paris; in 1967, in Munich; in the same year there was an outcry in the world press when the authorities in Moscow prevented him from reading in New York. At the Fourth Congress of the Writers Union a few months later, Voznesensky was given a position on the board of the Writers Union of the USSR, a position he still retains. In performance as a series of songs and sketches at the Taganka Theater in Moscow, the avant-garde theater in the tradition of the 1920s, *Antimiry* (1964; Eng. tr., *Antiworlds*, 1966), a frequently discussed cycle of poems, was well attended for several years. Voznesensky's poems and verse epics (also cycles) appear regularly in journals and almanacs and are collected into books in which he also always includes earlier poems. These are scarcely objects of controversy any more. In 1978 he was awarded the State Prize of the USSR. In 1979 he contributed to the nonconformist almanac ME-TROPOL but provided only material already published in the Soviet Union. He lives in Moscow.

What brought Voznesensky swift worldwide acclaim is his own poetic style, the extravagance of which at first provided a marked contrast to the officially propagated poetry of the Stalin period. Voznesensky writes his poems in one sitting and leaves the first draft unaltered. His poetry grows out of his experience of the city and of civilization as worldwide phenomena, and in its geographic breadth and emphatic connection to the technology of the 20th century it stands in contrast to Russian poetry that is closely tied to nature. Through the years his concern over the scientific-technical revolution has found expression in his work; next to love poems stand political ones that encourage freedom for poets. A title such as *Vzglyad* (1972; View) emphasizes the visual-descriptive aspect; the title *Akhillesovo serdtse* (1966; Achilles' Heart), his message: man's most valuable features are his heart and soul. Technology and civilization are, above all, components of Voznesensky's extremely bold and wide-ranging metaphorical language. Voznesensky's metaphors are sometimes selected not to serve the chosen goal—to shed light on interrelationships and to connect opposites through their mutually metamorphic relativity—but to become a game of the unusual for the sake of the unusual. In his early work he is above all an opponent of traditional rhyme. Sound, rhythm, assonance, and internal rhyme characterize his poetry. His word games are equal to his sound games; he uses the phonetic structure to develop his local semantics and his metaphors, both of which derive from CONSTRUCTIVISM (Holthusen). Searching for the irreplaceable word and struggling for maximum succinctness are foreign to Voznesensky; his goal is to achieve journalistic effect through novelty, even through the provocatively exceptional in content and sound.

*Works:* Parabola (poems), 1960; Mozaika (poems), 1960; Sorok liričeskikh otstuplenij iz poèmy Treugol'naja gruša (poems), 1962; Antimiry (poems), 1964 (see above); Akhillesovo serdce (poems), 1966; Ten' zvuka (poems), 1970 (Eng. tr., *The Shadow of Sound*, 1975); Vzgljad (poems), 1972; Vypusti pticy! (poems), 1974; Dubovyj list violončel'nyj (selection of lyric and narrative poems), 1975; Vitražnykh del master (poems), 1976; Soblazn' (poems), 1979; Izbr. lirika, 1979; Bezotčëtnoe (poems), 1981; O (pov.), in Novyj mir 1982:11; Proraby ducha (poems and essays), 1984.—Sobr. soč., 3 vols., 1983–84.

*Secondary Lit.:* A. Sinjavskij and A. Men'-šutin, in Novyj mir 1961:1; N. Koržavin, in Novyj mir 1961:3; P. Forgues, in Survey 49:1963: N. A. Nilsson, in Scando-Slavica 1964; E. Rajs, in Grani, Frankfurt am Main, 55:1964; W. G. Jones, in Slavonic and East European Review 1968; A. Mikhajlov, 1970; V. Pankov et al., in Lit. obozrenie 1973:2; J. Bailey, in Slavic and East European Journal 1973: V. Solov'ëv, in Avrora 1975:3; A. E. Hudspeth, Diss., Univ. of North Carolina at Chapel Hill, 1975; A Maršenko, in Voprosy lit. 1978:9; N. P. Condee, Ann Arbor, 1981; A. Urban, I. Šajtanov, in Lit. obozrenie 1982:9; V. Betaki, in Grani 136:1985.

*Vozrozhdéniye* (Renaissance), a literary and political journal published in Paris from 1949 to 1974. The journal's predecessor was the newspaper Vozrozhdeniye, which appeared as a daily from 1924 to 1935, as a weekly from 1936 to 1940, and was financed by the same Armenian patron, A. O. Gukasov (d. 1969), who later funded the journal. The first editor of the newspaper was P. B. Struve; he was followed by I. F. Semyonov in 1927. In 1949 the literary scholar I. I. Tkhorzhevsky assumed the editorship of the journal; after his death in 1950, this task was assumed by the historian S. P. Melgunov. Editors changed frequently until 1958, when Prince S. S. Obolensky took over the editorship, first together with V. A. Zlobin, then in 1960 with I. N. Gorbov. A total of 243 issues were published between 1949 and 1974. Vozrozhdeniye was considered a Russian nationalist publication that was closely affiliated with the Russian Orthodox Church and that had sprung from the soil of the volunteer White Army during the Civil War. The journal preserved its anti-Communist orientation throughout its life. It competed with the newspaper Posledniye novosti and the journal Sovremennye zapiski. In addition to political articles, Vozrozhdeniye focused on literature and literary criticism. Among the important writers who contributed to this journal are I. Bunin, Z. Gippius, D. Merezhkovsky, A. Remizov, V. Smolensky, and B. Zaytsev. In addition, contributing authors in the fields of religion and philosophy included N. Arsenyev, V. N. Ilyin, and V. V. Zenkovsky. In his dissertation, Jaroslaw Tomasziwskyj describes Vozrozhdeniye's history, its editors, and its most important authors and provides a list of the contents through August 1973.

*Secondary Lit.:* G. Meier, in Vozroždenie 42–44:1955; Ja. Tomasziwskyj, Diss., Vanderbilt Univ., 1974.

*Vrémya i my* (The Time and We), a literary journal of the third Russian emigration, published since 1976, at first monthly and then, since 1980, every two months. Tel Aviv is listed as the place of publication for volumes 1–4; New York and Paris were added from issue 49 in 1980 to issue 57 in 1981. Since issue 58, the places of publication have been given as "Jerusalem, Paris." In 1986, issue 92 was published. The editor in chief is Viktor Perelman in Jerusalem; since 1980 he has been supported by Dora Shturman in Israel and Yefim Etkind in France. Vremya i my sees itself as a literary and sociopolitical journal that frequently takes note of Jewish questions, since its focal point is Israel, without concentrating on these alone. In each issue, this jounal publishes original works of poetry and prose, mostly from the emigration but also from the Soviet Union (SAMIZDAT; TAMIZDAT). A comprehensive topical section contains articles in the fields of journalism, sociology, philosophy, religion, and literary criticism, among others. In additon, an illustrated article on modern art is enclosed with each issue. Among the authors who frequently publish in Vremya i my are poets such as D. Bobyshev, I. Burikhin, A. Khvostenko, N. Korzhavin, I. Lisnyanskaya, and L. Vladimirova and prose writers such as Yu. Aleshkovsky, S. Dovlatov, F. Gorenshteyn, F. Kandel, B. Khazanov, A. Lvov, V. Nekrasov, V. Rybakov, B. Vakhtin, I. Yefimov, and Z. Zinik.

*Secondary Lit.:* V. Maramzin, in Èkho, Paris, 1978:3; editorial in Vremja i my 50:1980; G.

Andreev, in Russkaja mysl', Paris, July 8, 1982, p. 10, Dec. 2, 1982, p. 12, March 3, 1983, p. 10, Oct. 13, 1983, p. 12, July 12, 1984, p. 12, Nov. 29, 1984, p. 12.

**Vstréchi** (Encounters), 1. A monthly journal published in Paris by the editors G. V. Adamovich and M. L. Kantor from January to June 1934 (issues 1 to 6, 286 pages total). This journal emphasized modern Russian literature; in addition, regular contributions included essays and shorter articles on the fine arts, film, and theater, as well as on German, French, and English literature and on current economic and political events. Similar to the journal Chisla, Vstrechi was a forum especially open to the second generation of the first emigration. The contributors to Vstrechi included N. Berberova, R. Blokh, Yu. Felzen, G. Gazdanov, G. Ivanov, D. Knut, Yu. Mandelshtam, I. Odoyevtseva, N. Otsup, B. Poplavsky, A. Shteyger, M. Tsvetayeva, V. Varshavsky, and V. Zlobin. In addition to the two editors, frequent contributors to the critical section were P. Bitsilli and V. Veydle; articles by I. Shmelyov, Z. Gippius, and D. Merezhkovsky can also be found. An index to the six issues provides a guide to the contents.

**Vstréchi** (Encounters), 2. An annual literary almanac dedicated exclusively to new poetry and containing several illustrations of modern Russian art. Vstrechi has been published in Philadelphia, Pennsylvania, since 1983. Vstrechi's immediate predecessor had the title Perekryostki (Crossroads) and recalls—without directly referring to it—the group of poets that arose in Paris in 1926 and included D. Knut, Yu. Mandelshtam, G. Rayevsky, V. Smolensky, and Yu. Terapiano. Perekryostki, six issues of which were published between 1977 and 1982, also in Philadelphia, had a publishing committee (announced in issue no. 2, 1978) whose members are not all named in every issue. It included I. Burkin (1919), S. Gollerbakh (1923), I. Lyogkaya (1932), B. Pushkaryov, V. Shatalov (1918), V. Sinkevich (1926). Vstrechi is edited by the poet V. Sinkevich who is supported by an editorial staff composed (as of 1984) of S. Gollerbakh, Ye. Dubrovina (1946), M. Kreps (1940), and V. Shatalov. As both titles imply, Vstrechi, like Perekryostki before it, brings together poets of all generations and the three waves of EMIGRATION: in addition, poetry translated from other languages is included whenever possible. The approximately 25 authors who are included

in each issue of the approximately 80-page almanac live chiefly in the United States; some live in other Western countries. Material submitted from the USSR constitutes a rare exception. The poems, selected for their aesthetic qualities yet in an attempt to get a broad representation, occasionally include the first published poems of young talents. In addition to the members of the editorial staff, the more frequently appearing authors include L. Alekseyeva, O. Anstey, I. Chinnov, B. Filippov, N. Korzhavin, N. Morshen, B. Nartsissov, V. Pereleshin, Strannik, L. Vladimirova, and I. Yelagin. Vstrechi has been well received and has sold quite well.

*Secondary Lit.:* E. Dubrovina, in Novoe russkoe slovo, New York, Oct. 7, 1984.

**Vvedénsky, Aleksándr Ivánovich,** poet, playwright, prose writer (b. Dec. 6 [Nov. 23], 1904, St. Petersburg—d. Dec. 20, 1941 [?], while imprisoned). Vvedensky's father worked for the civil service. In 1921 Vvedensky began studying humanities at Petrograd University but did not graduate. His earliest existing poem was written in 1920; in 1923 he was favorably referred to as a futurist poet. At the end of 1925 Vvedensky began appearing with D. Kharms at literary performances of the group "Levy flang." In both 1926 and 1927 a poem appeared in the almanacs of the Leningrad Union of Poets; otherwise his poetic statement remained limited to the dissemination of manuscript copies of his works and to readings given at literary performances. These performances were organized first by various "left" groups of artists, later by the association Vvedensky formed with Kharms and N. Zabolotsky in 1927, OBERIU, which, through absurd surrealist works, protested against the ruling literary establishment and its opposition to experimentation. The play Minin i Pozharsky (1926; Minin and Pozharsky) remains from Vvedensky's early period. Whether this play was ever performed is not known. Public readings by Oberiu were stopped in April 1930 when its activities were characterized as a "protest against the dictatorship of the proletariat" (Smena April 9, 1930). Like Kharms, Vvedensky was offered the opportunity of working in the children's book department of the "House of the Press" by S. Marshak in the spring of 1927. Between 1928 and 1941 he published at least 32 children's books between 12 and 16 pages in length, mostly in verse form with pictures. In 1932 Vvedensky was arrested and imprisoned. Between 1936 and 1941 Vvedensky lived in Kharkov, where he wrote the absurd play *Yolka u Ivanovykh* (1938; The Christmas Tree at the Ivanovs), the first work to make him famous in the West 40 years later. On Sept. 27, 1941, he was arrested, and then in connection with the evacuation he became a victim of the purges. Until the 20th Party Congress no mention was made of Vvedensky. After his RE-HABILITATION a new edition of his frequently reprinted children's book *Kto?* (1930; Who?) appeared together with his only children's povest, *O devochke Mashe, o sobake Petushke, i o koshke Nitochke* (1937; About the Girl Masha, the Dog Petushka, and the Cat Nitochka). Since then Vvedensky has occasionally been mentioned and quoted. The first selection of his own poetry drawn from random samizdat discoveries was compiled in Cologne in 1974; this was followed by the publication of his collected works in the United States in 1980 in an edition overseen by M. Meylakh and based on the archive salvaged by Ya. S. Druskin.

The Oberiu Manifesto (1928) describes Vvedensky as the most leftist of the group, that is, the greatest experimenter; I. Rakhtanov characterized him as the "most Oberiut of the Oberiuts." The degree of alienation fluctuates widely in the works that have come down to us. The less absurd reveal his awe of the dark powers (demons) and the cruelty of man. An essential point of departure for his surrealistic exposition of the concrete is his understanding of time, which diverges from the mechanical division of time and leads to dissolution into isolated moments. In *Minin i Pozharsky* he grotesquely unites historical figures from various epochs; in *Yolka u Ivanovykh* he presents "children" from one to 82 years of age who are eventually left by their "parents" in the room with the Christmas tree and who abruptly die. Death and sexuality, both despiritualized into mechanical processes, form frequent themes together with loneliness. In Vvedensky's poetry for children only the playfulness of his absurd poetry remains, but in theme, meter, and logical organization the poems are much more "normal" than those of Kharms.

*Works: Mnogo zverej* (children's verse), 1928; *Kto?* (children's verse), 1930 (reprint of the 20th rev. ed., 1956); *Ščenok i kotenok* (children's verse), 1937 (reprinted, 1976); *O devočke Maše, o sobake Petuške i o koške Nitočke* (pov.), 1937, 1956; *Doždik, doždik* (children's verse), 1962; *Ëlka u Ivanovykh* (play), in *Grani*, Frankfurt am Main, 81:1971;

*Izbr.*, Munich, 1974; *Potec* (dramatic scenes), in *Russian Literature Triquarterly* 11:1975; *Sny* (children's verse), 1977; *Minin i Požarskij* (play), Munich, 1978.—*Polnoe sobr. soč.*, Ann Arbor, 1980– (vol. 2 appeared in 1984).

*Secondary Lit.*: See OBERIU. W. Kasack, foreword to *Izbr.*, 1974 (with bibliography); O. G. Revzina, in *Russian Literature* 1978:4; M. Mejlakh, in *Ėkho*, Paris, 1978:2, and foreword to *Polnoe sobr. soč.*, 1980; A. Stone-Nakhimovskij, Vienna, 1982.

**Vysótsky, Vladímir Semyónovich,** poet, songwriter, actor (b. Jan. 15, 1938, Moscow—d. July 25, 1980, Moscow). Vysotsky's father was a colonel in the intelligence forces; his mother was a translator of German technical literature. From 1947 to 1949 Vysotsky lived with his parents in Eberswalde (GDR). Vysotsky studied at the Acting Academy of the Moscow Art Theater (1956–60) and thereafter worked as a stage actor. From 1964 until his death, he was the leading actor at the Taganka Theater, Moscow's most avant-garde theater under the direction of Yury Lyubimov. On the stage, where his roles included Hamlet, as well as in 26 films, where he also sang to guitar accompaniment, Vysotsky quickly became exceptionally popular. He appeared privately and publicly singing songs he composed himself, but the lyrics to his songs were not published. The uncensored almanac METROPOL included 25 pages of his songs. Millions of copies of tape recordings of these songs have circulated in the Soviet Union. In 1966 Vysotsky was married to the Russian actress from Paris Marina Vladimirovna Poljakova (stage name: Marina Vlady). Owing to her procurement (she worked in the Central Committee of the French Communist Party), he regularly received exit permits (visas) to France. In 1979 he went on a concert tour through the United States. His early death, attributable in part to excessive alcohol consumption, was not officially reported but led to a spontaneous nighttime demonstration of national mourning by tens of thousands of people from all levels of society in front of the Taganka Theater, an event that is scarcely imaginable in the Soviet Union and only occurs once in decades. His grave in the Vagankovskoye cemetery is visited year after year by thousands of admirers. After his death, *Nerv* (1981; The Nerve), a volume of selected works with some 130 poems chosen by Robert Rozhdestvensky, was approved. Many famous songs are entirely absent; others such as "Ballada o volchyey gibeli" (Ballade of a Wolf's Death) and "Ochi chornye" (Black Eyes) have been cut in half. A three-volume edition overseen by Boris Berest and Arkady Lvov in New York, *Pesni i stikhi* (1981–83; Songs and Poems), includes approximately 600 songs, some prose, Vysotsky's comments on his work, and secondary literature; up to 1987 only two volumes had appeared.

As a singer of ballads in the tradition of B. Okudzhava and A. Galich, Vysotsky became the idol of millions of Soviet citizens; he owes his popularity to his ability to assimilate the life of the people in his country and his time with its joy and sorrow, its fear and hope; to present it in complete truth; and to sing of it with an inner resourcefulness bordering on self-abandonment. His spiritual sensitivity toward his chosen theme is completely conveyed to the Russian listener. Vysotsky is also able to empathize with a fate he has not himself experienced, especially the horrors of war and the torments of the camps. His fundamental attitude is religious, pacifistic, helpful; his style of expression is multidimensional: descriptive, accusing, humorous, amusing, ironic, entreating. His delivery was rough, almost husky, filled with pathos, variable, and always well suited to the text. "In him the outskirts of the city, the back alleys, the topsy-turvy asphalted Russia can be found" (A. Voznesensky in *Novy mir* 1982:11, pp. 116f.). "He created, as it were, a synthesis of poetry and the garbage of the commonplace, of music and the platitudes of Soviet daily life, of theater and the half-drunken power of street voices" (L. Krugly).

*Works:* Poems, in *Metropol'*, Ann Arbor, 1979 (Eng. tr., 1982); *Tret'ja volna*, Montgeron, 1979:7–8; *Nerv* (poems), 1981; *Pesni i stikhi*, 3 vols. (vols. 1 and 2, New York, 1981, 1983, have appeared); *Poètičeskaja sjuita* (poems), in *Avrora* 1986:6.

*Secondary Lit.:* V. Delone, in *Kontinent*, Paris, 26:1980; L. Kruglyj, in *Russkaja mysl'*, Paris, Aug. 14, 1980; numerous contributions in Vysotsky's *Pesni i stikhi*, New York, 1981–83; V. Alloj, in *Russkaja mysl'* Aug. 5, 1982; L. Žukhovickij, in *Oktjabr'* 1982:10; H. Pfandl, in *Wiener Slawistischer Almanach* 9:1982; A. Demidova, in *Lit. obozrenie* 1983:1; S. Kormilov, in *Russkaja reč'* 1983:3; P. Leonidov, New York, 1983; L. Kuperštejn, in *Novoe russkoe slovo*, New York, July 1, 1984, p. 8; A. Gerškovič, in *Russkaja mysl'* Feb. 7, 1985, p. 11; D. Boss, Munich, 1985; V. Smekhov, in *Avrora* 1986:6; A. Demidova, in *Lit. obozrenie* 1987:1.

# W

**Writers Congresses** (Sézdy pisáteley SSSR), congresses of the WRITERS UNION of the USSR in Moscow and of the Writers Unions of individual union republics in the respective capital cities. These congresses form the highest governing body of the Writers Union according to the statute of the Writers Union of the USSR. Not every member of the Writers Union may attend the Writers Congresses, only a small percentage (approximately 7 percent); these are usually members of the Communist Party. Only a select group of delegates has the right to deliver a speech. The First Writers Congress was held between Aug. 17 and Sept. 1, 1934, after the dissolution of all the literary organizations prevalent during the 1920s and the establishment of a single union had been decreed by the Party Resolution of 1932 (see PARTY RESOLUTIONS ON LITERATURE). Excessively long reportorial and self-congratulatory lectures on particular genres within Soviet literature set the tone. Another essential theme was the newly created concept of SOCIALIST REALISM (M. Gorky, A. Fadeyev); in addition, the position of creative talents within Party-minded literature (I. Babel, I. Erenburg, and others) was discussed. Contrary to the statute, which called for Writers Congresses to be held every three years, the Second Writers Congress was not convened under Stalin. (However, local second writers congresses were held in the majority of republics in 1939 or 1946–48.) The Second Writers Congress of the Writers Union of the USSR in 1954 bore the mark of the THAW following Stalin's death. This congress was preceded by congresses of local writers unions in all of the republics except the RSFSR between April and October 1954. Among other reasons, this practice was retained to facilitate the appointment of delegates to the central congress. Condemnation of the editorial staff of *Novy mir* for publishing the article by V. Pomerantsev urging sincerity in literature left its mark on the Second Writers Congress. This congress demonstrated hope for liberalization (V. Kaverin, Erenburg), showed its limitations (A. Surkov, Fadeyev), and paved the way for a series of REHABILI-

TATIONS. The Third Writers Congress in 1959 followed the first and founding congress (in 1958) of the Writers Union of the RSFSR, which was established to strengthen conservative tendencies. In response to a series of measures perpetuating the literary policy of the Stalin period, distinguished delegates did not attend. The establishment of a secretariat of the board as the most important governing body of the Writers Union was announced at this congress. Envisioned as a manifestation of unity among Soviet writers under the new leadership of Brezhnev and Kosygin on the occasion of the 50th anniversary of the Soviet Union and carefully orchestrated by the Party's censorship of all speeches, the Fourth Writers Congress in 1967 acquired a surprising accent from A. Solzhenitsyn's letter to the delegates demanding the discussion of the issue of censorship and other restrictions on freedom in literature in the Soviet Union as well as the responsibility borne by leaders of the Writers Union with regard to persecutions. Although reading or discussing the letter was forbidden, in unofficial talks this letter remained the center of attention. At the Fifth Writers Congress in 1971, the officials directed special attention

toward literary criticism as a mechanism of political control. This position was already evident at the 24th Party Congress, and indeed the Party congresses preceding each Writers Congress generally provide the topical focus. Through confidential meetings with Party members among the delegates preceding every Writers Congress, the Party imparts it concrete instructions. At the Sixth Writers Congress in 1976, which stood under the cloud of the Party Resolution of 1972 "On Artistic Literary Criticism," G. Markov stressed the "harmonious relationship between the Party and the creative intelligentsia" as well as the necessity of entrusting younger members in the Writers Union with positions in the Union. The Seventh Writers Congress in 1981 was characterized by the cult of Brezhnev as "writer" and by the inclusion of Soviet writers in the international Communist struggle for peace; in addition, the decline of elements of civic pride (grazhdanstvennost) in poetry was criticized. The Eighth Writers Congress (June 24–28, 1986) was marked by the call—supported by M. Gorbachev—for greater openness (glasnost) and was enlivened by several speeches. A. Voznesensky, M. Likhachov, and Ye. Yevtushenko urged the pub-

Participants in the Congresses of the Writers Union of the USSR 1934–1986

| Date | Members of the Writers Union | Of These, CP Members | Delegates* | Of These, CP Members |
|---|---|---|---|---|
| 1. Aug. 14–Sept. 1, 1934 | 1,500 | | 597 | 356 |
| 2. Dec. 15–26, 1954 | 3,695 | | 720 | 522 |
| 3. May 18–23, 1959 | 4,801 | | 471 | 377 |
| 4. May 22–27, 1967 | 6,608 | | 473 | 403 |
| 5. June 29–July 2, 1971 | 7,290 | 4,050 | 497 | 432 |
| 6. June 21–25, 1976 | 7,942 | 4,550 (as of March 1, 1976) | 542 | 464 |
| 7. June 30–July 3, 1981 | 8,773 | 5,157 (as of March 1, 1981) | 563 | 496 |
| 8. June 24–28, 1986 | 9,584 | | 543 | 474 |

*Includes only those who in fact participated in the Congress

Participants in the Congresses of the Writers Union of the RSFSR 1958–1985

| Date | Members of the Writers Union | Delegates* | Of These, CP Members |
|---|---|---|---|
| 1. Dec. 7–13, 1958 | | 397 | 295 |
| 2. March 3–7, 1965 | 3,138 | 429 | 321 |
| 3. March 24–27, 1970 | 3,605 | 488 | 397 |
| 4. Dec. 15–18, 1975 | 3,860 | 530 | 427 |
| 5. Dec. 9–12, 1980 | 4,318 | 523 | 428 |
| 6. Dec. 11–14, 1985 | | 516 | 451 |

*Includes only those who in fact participated in the Congress

lication of prohibited works by authors such as A. Akhmatova, A. Bely, V. Khlebnikov, V. Khodasevich, D. Merezhkovsky, B. Pasternak, A. Remizov, F. Sologub, Ye. Zamyatin. Voznesensky argued in favor of creating a cooperative publishing house and removing the restrictions of the Party Resolution of Aug. 14, 1946. V. Rozov advocated the ideals of truth and spirituality in literature.

The presence of leading Party officials and the exchange of reciprocal greetings substantiate the formal assertion of unity with the Communist Party. For the duration of each Writers Congress the following committees are formed: presidium, secretariat, referendum committee, and statutory committee. In keeping with the statute of the Writers Union, either the delegates or the board of the Writers Union elects members to the following governing bodies of the Writers Union: board, secretariat, auditing committee. The speeches delivered at a Writers Congress are first published in part in *Literaturnaya gazeta*, later in the reports of the Congress. The system of multiple controls that governs participation in the Congress, the opportunity to deliver a speech, and the content of all speeches ensure that the reports of the Congresses—aside from a few exceptions—provide only a homogeneous collection of comments on literature and politics reflecting the prevailing Party line and ranging from self-glorification to condemnation of nonconformist literary works.

*Secondary Lit. for Congresses of the Writers Union of the USSR:* 1. Pervyj Vsesojuznyj s"ezd sovetskikh pisatelej: Stenografičeskij otčët, 1934; "Plenum pravlenija Sojuza pisatelej SSSR," in Lit gazeta Sept. 4 and 11, 1974. 2. Vtoroj Vsesojuznyj s"ezd sovetskikh pisatelej . . . , 1956 (excerpts translated in Ost-Probleme 1955:4); W. Kasack, in Deutsche Rundschau 1955:5. 3. Tretij s"ezd sovetskikh pisatelej . . . , 1959; D. Burg, in Mosty, Munich, 2:1959; V. Ščerbina, in Voprosy lit. 1959:9. 4. Četvërtyj s"ezd pisatelej SSSR . . . , 1968; editorials in Voprosy lit. 1966:7; P. Hüber, in Berichte des Bundesinstituts für ostwissenschaftliche und internationale Studien 1967:46; V. Kaverin, in Posev, Frankfurt am Main, 1971:10; S. Medwedjew, Zehn Jahre im Leben des Aleksandr Solschenizyn, 1974, pp. 76–79; A. Solženicyn, in his Bodalsja telënok s dubom, Paris, 1975, pp. 486–92. 5. Pjatyj s"ezd pisatelej SSSR . . . , 1972; L. Donatov, in Posev 1971:8. 6. Šestoj s"ezd pisatelej SSSR . . . , 1978. 7. Sed'moj s"ezd pisatelej SSSR . . . , 1983. 8. Vos'moj s"ezd pisatelej SSSR, in Lit. gazeta July 2, 1986.

*Secondary Lit. for Congresses of the Writers Union of the RSFSR:* 1. Pervyj učreditel'nyj s"ezd pisatelej Rossijskoj Federacii . . . , 1959. 2. Vtoroj s"ezd pisatelej RSFSR . . . , 1966. 3. Tretij s"ezd pisatelej RSFSR . . . , 1972. 4. Četvërtyj s"ezd pisatelej RSFSR . . . , 1977. 5. Pjatyj s"ezd pisatelej RSFSR . . . , 1982. 6. Šestoj s"ezd pisatelej RSFSR, 1985, in Lit. gazeta Dec. 18, 1985.

**Writers Union of the USSR** (Soyúz pisáteley SSSR), the sole union of writers in the USSR, established in response to the Party Resolution of April 23, 1932 (see PARTY RESOLUTIONS ON LITERATURE), and existing since the First WRITERS CONGRESS (Aug. 17–Sept. 1, 1934). The Writers Union replaced RAPP and other literary groups that, after being initially tolerated, were either disbanded at the end of the 1920s with RAPP's help or integrated into RAPP (see PROLETKULT; KUZNITSA; OKTYABR; MOLODAYA GVARDIYA; LEF; PEREVAL; SERAPION BROTHERS; CONSTRUCTIVISM; OBERIU). The Writers Union is formally a voluntary association but in fact provides the sole basis for professional advancement and material security for anyone active in the field of literature in the Soviet Union.

When the Union was established in 1934 there were 1,500 members. The membership has grown as follows: 1954: 3,695; 1959: 4,801; 1967: 6,608; 1971: 7,290; 1976: 7,942; 1981: 8,773; 1986: 9,584. In 1981, the last year for which statistics are available, the membership consisted of the following groups (the numbers in parentheses are for 1967): prose writers, 3,211 (2,272); poets, 3,007 (2,185); playwrights, 412 (481); authors of children's books, 249 (180); critics and literary scholars, 1,151 (921); translators, 522 (380), essayists (ocherkisty), 104 (111); folklorists, 13 (37). In 1976, out of a total of 7,833 members (as of March 1, 1976), 3,665 wrote in Russian. The statute of the Writers Union, frequently altered since 1934, makes SOCIALIST REALISM the compulsory precept for the activity of all the members. The members are thus obliged to serve the Communist Party and the principle of PARTY SPIRIT; that is, their work should always be subordinated to the prevailing Party policy. The supreme governing body of the Writers Union of the USSR is the Writers Congress, to which a portion of the membership is delegated. In 1981, 563 members (496 being members of the Communist Party) participated in the Congress out of a total of 8,773 members (5,157 being members of the Party). In accordance with the statute passed on July

1, 1971, the Congress of the Writers Union elects the board (pravleniye), which consisted of 150 members in 1986 (235 in 1981). The board selects the secretariat of the board (sekretariat pravleniya), which was composed of 36 members in 1986 (58 in 1981), in addition to the chairman of the board (1959–77 Konstantin Fedin; no successor up to 1986; since 1986 Georgy Markov) and the first secretary (1971–86 Markov; since 1986 V. V. Karpov). The plenum of the board meets at least once a year. In addition beginning in 1971, the board elects the buro of the secretariat (byuro sekretariata), consisting of about ten people. In fact, however, the leadership is neither in the hands of the board nor in the hands of the secretariat or the buro of the secretariat; instead it is realized by a working secretariat (about ten employees, who are rather administrative workers than writers). In 1986 Yu. N. Verchenko was affirmed as the head of this group of secretaries. In 1934 M. Gorky was president of the Writers Union; after his death A. Tolstoy assumed this position, while the Party official V. Stavsky became general secretary. Contrary to the statute of 1934, the Second Congress was not held until 1954. The former RAPP official A. Fadeyev played a leading role in the Writers Union from its founding; following the Party Resolution of 1946, the leadership of the Union was transferred from N. Tikhonov to Fadeyev; from 1954 to 1958 A. Surkov was in charge. Each of the 15 republics has its own writers union; the decisions of the central governing bodies of the Writers Union of the USSR are binding on these unions. Established only in 1958 as a conservative counterweight to the then liberally oriented powers in the Writers Union of the USSR, the Writers Union of the RSFSR was headed by L. Sobolev from 1958 to 1971; after his death, S. Mikhalkov assumed leadership. The Writers Union of the RSFSR has numerous branches; in 1980 there were 20 branches in autonomous republics and regions and 55 in regions and provinces (for example, in Moscow or in the Vologda region).

Admission to the Writers Union is granted on the basis of an application that must be supported by three members; usually the applicant must have published two books and be able to provide reviews. Admission must be approved by two-thirds of the members of the local branch of the Writers Union of the USSR and by more than half of the members of the board or the secretariat of the Writers Union of the USSR. "Behavior that offends the honor and dignity of a Soviet writer, . . .

deviation . . . from the principles and duties defined in the statute of the Writers Union" can lead to a reprimand or punishment. These disciplinary measures correspond to those provided for within the Communist Party: first there is public criticism (obshchestvennoye poritsaniye), warning (preduprezhdeniye), and strict warning (strogoye preduprezhdeniye); these are followed by a series of actual penalties: comment (postavit na vid), reprimand (vygovor), reprimand entered in one's personal file (vygovor s zaneseniyem v lichnoye delo), severe reprimand, severe reprimand entered in one's personal file, severe reprimand with a warning entered in one's personal file, and exclusion—the supreme punishment. Well-known examples of exclusion from the Unions are all victims of Stalinism: A. Akhmatova and M. Zoshchenko in 1946; and, in the period since Stalin's death, A. Sinyavsky, Yu. Daniel, N. Korzhavin, L. Chukovskaya, A. Solzhenitsyn, V. Nekrasov, A. Galich, E. Etkind, V. Voynovich, L. Kopelev, Ye. Popov. Since 1977 some members have withdrawn in protest: G. Vladimov, V. Aksyonov, I. Lisnyanskaya, S. Lipkin (in connection with METROPOL). In special cases, exclusion from the Writers Union is accompanied by exclusion from the Literary Fund (Litfund), entailing considerable hardship in case of illness, for example.

Among the responsibilities of the Writers Union of the USSR belongs first and foremost the political leadership and supervision of the members. For this purpose, meetings are held with the leading governing bodies, sometimes with the secretary for ideological issues of the Central Commitee of the Communist Party. In addition, controversial works are discussed in the committees. These deliberations are generally secret, but the details of the discussions concerning the works of B. Pasternak, V. Dudintsev, and A. Solzhenitsyn have become known. All such deliberations are preceded by conferences of Party groups, that is, of all Party members among the proposed participants. They either decide on the procedure later made obligatory for everyone in accordance with the principle of Party discipline or receive instructions from the Central Committee. The Writers Union has its own buildings with numerous apartments in the cities as well as dachas (for example, in writers' colonies such as Peredelkino, Komarovo, Koktebel); residence in both is assigned by the Litfund. The Union also has its own houses for creativity (dom tvorchestva) outside the cities for temporary use by writers, a sanatorium, and its own medical facilities. Among the material incentives, whose bestowal is always tied to ideological conformity, are informational trips (tvorcheskiye komandirovki). All trips abroad taken by members are subject to the approval of the foreign commission of the Writers Union of the USSR. Under the direct control of the Writers Union are a series of institutions. One is the Gorky Literary Institute, established on Dec. 3, 1933, and located in Moscow in the house where A. Herzen was born, at Tverskoy bulvar 25. At this specialized institute, which is also under the control of the Ministry for Higher and Special Education of the USSR, handpicked secondary-school graduates interested in literature can study and attend lectures given by distinguished writers. The Gorky Literary Institute also offers a one-year course for members of the Writers Union who do not have a secondary-school diploma, the so-called Advanced Literature Courses. Other institutions controlled by the Writers Union include the Litfund, the social insurance institution of the Writers Union (Moscow, Begovaya ul. 17a); the All-Union Administration for Protection of Authors' Rights (Vsesoyuznoye upravleniye po okhrane avtorskikh prav pisateley [VUOAPP]), which oversees all authors' rights within the Soviet Union (individual authors' rights with respect to publication abroad are vested in the office of VAPP [Vsesoyuznoye agentstvo po avtorskim pravam (All-Union Agency for Authors' Rights)], which does not come under the authority of the Writers Union); the Central House of Literature (Tsentralny dom literatorov, Moscow, ul.

Gertsena 53), which includes a large lecture hall and a restaurant reserved exclusively for members and their guests. The Writers Union of the USSR administers a collection of journals and the newspaper Literaturnaya gazeta, as well as the publishing house Sovetsky pisatel (Soviet Writer). Since 1958 other publications have been placed under the control of the Writers Union of the RSFSR.

The power of the leading officials of the Writers Union of the USSR is quite extensive and ranges from granting permission to publish and deciding on the size of a print run, through assigning apartments, to granting or denying assistance to those in need. Criticism of misuse of power seldom appears in the press. The strongest criticism was voiced during the THAW and was aimed especially at the excessive bureaucracy, the shift from literary to administrative work and meetings, impropriety in criticism, and the right of the artistically weaker to judge the artistically more gifted.

Secondary Lit.: See also EMIGRATION; METROPOL'; SAMIZDAT; TAMIZDAT; WRITERS CONGRESSES. "Sojuz pisatelej SSSR," in Kratkaja sovetskaja ènciklopedija 7:1972; A. Rybakov, in Voprosy lit. 1969:4; A. Solženicyn, Bodalsja telënok s dubom, Paris, 1975; E. Ètkind, Zapiski nezagovorščika, London, 1977; L. Čukovskaja, Process isključenija, Paris, 1979; Vmeste s partiej, vmeste s narodom, 1981; diverse articles on the 50th anniversary of Writers Union, in Novyj mir 5–8:1984 and Lit. gazeta, Sept. 12, 1984, pp. 2–4.

# Y

Yákovlev, Aleksándr Stepánovich (pseud. of A. S. Trífonov-Yákovlev), prose writer (b. Dec. 5 [Nov. 23], 1886, Volsk, prov. Saratov—d. April 11, 1953, Moscow). Yakovlev's father was an illiterate housepainter of peasant descent. Yakovlev ran away to the forests near Perm to become a "holy hermit" when he was 12 years old; he returned after a trek of 1,000 kilometers. He completed the municipal school in 1901. Drawn into the revolutionary movements around 1905, the deeply religious Yakovlev became an atheistic member of the Socialist Revolutionary Party; he lived in various cities and was also a student in St. Petersburg. Up until World War I, in which he served for one year as an orderly, he was a teacher and journalist in Rostov-on-Don. From

1915 on, he lived in Moscow. His povest Povolniki (1923; The Freebooters), based on revolutionary experiences and first published in Berlin, attracted some attention. His collected works, with a foreword by A. Lunacharsky, were printed in 1926; seven volumes of a planned nine-volume edition came out in 1928–29. In 1928 Yakovlev participated in an Arctic expedition to search for Roald Amundsen; in 1929 he was on the first airplane flight from Moscow to Tashkent. Yakovlev continued to write publicistic and literary works.

Yakovlev, whom V. Lidin regarded in a positive light, wrote an unusually great deal, yet often did not finish what he started. Yearly month-long stays alone at his dacha near Moscow were consistent with his childhood urge to become a hermit. Even the structure of his prose, which describes the fate of individuals in contrast to that of the masses, is determined by the fate of the author himself, who had worked his way up by his own power. Yakovlev's works range from the period of the Revolution, as he depicts it in Oktyabr (1923; October) or Chelovek i pustynya (1926–29; Man and the Wilderness), to Velikiye stalinskiye stroyki (1953; Stalin's Great Constructions). His works are largely autobiographical, chronologically narrated, and qualitatively different from each other. In the beginning they combined elements from folk epics, Volga peasant dialect, and literary language (Shafir); they contain (as, for example, in Yakovlev's write-up of the Arctic expedition) vivid and humanely sympathetic observations of animals.

Works: Oktjabr' (pov.), 1923, 1965; Povol'niki (short stories), 1923; Čelovek i pustynja (novel), 1929, 3d ed., 1970; Velikie stalinskie strojki (articles, essays, and short stories), 1953; Bagul'nik (short stories), 1972.—Sobr. soč., 4 vols., 1926; Polnoe sobr. soč., 9 vols. (only vols. 1–7 published), 1928–29; Izbr., 1955; Izbr. proizv., 1957.
Secondary Lit.: A. Šafir, in Novyj mir 1928:8; A. Ja., ed. E. Nikitina, 1928, 2d ed., 1929; V. Lidin, in Jakovlev's Izbr., 1955, and in his Ljudi i vstreči, 1957; M. Belova, 1967; RSPP 7(2):1972; C. Solodar', in Lit. obozrenie 1973:3.

**Yan, Vasíly Grigóryevich** (pseud. of V. G. Yanchevétsky), prose writer (b. Jan. 4, 1875 [Dec. 23, 1874], Kiev—d. Aug. 5, 1954, Zvenigorod, near Moscow). Yan's father was a teacher of Greek and Latin in a gymnasium. Yan completed his studies in classical philology at St. Petersburg University in 1897; until 1899 he trekked extensively through central and northern Russia, then spent a year in England as a correspondent. Between 1900 and 1904 Yan traveled, mostly on horseback, through Central Asia; he was a frontline reporter during the Russo-Japanese War; his subsequent travels included Greece, Persia, and Egypt. Yan taught Latin in St. Petersburg between 1906 and 1912; in those years and during World War I (in the Balkans), he pursued a career in journalism. From 1918 to 1923 Yan lived in Minusinsk (Siberia) and thereafter resided in Moscow, except for the years 1926–28, when he worked as a journalist in Samarkand.

Yan has a place in Russian literature on the

basis of the historical prose he began preparing in 1923 and publishing in 1931. After writing a few short povesti, such as Finikiyskiy korabl (1931; The Phoenician Ship) or Spartak (1933; Spartacus), he began his major work, a trilogy about the Mongol invasion in the 13th century. The work's origin lies in an encounter with Genghis Khan in a dream in 1904. Part 1, Chingis-khan (Eng. tr., Jenghiz Khan, 1945), appeared in 1939; part 2, Baty (Eng. tr., Batu-Khan, 1945), came out in 1942; part 3, K "poslednemu moryu" (Toward the "Last Sea"), was published posthumously in 1955. The "amazing picture of the Tartar Empire and of Russia under the yoke of the Golden Horde" (Slonim) is based on years of source study and is responsibly written; the work, with its vivid and thrilling style, is fascinating, and was frequently reprinted. The trilogy's first part owes its Stalin Prize (for 1941, 1st class) to its subject matter (resistance against a superior adversary, occupation, battle for liberation), which was given relevance by the events of World War II.

Works: Zapiski pešekhoda (articles), 1901; Finikijskij korabl' (pov.), 1931; Spartak (pov.), 1933; Ogni na kurganakh (pov.), 1947; trilogy: Čingis-khan (pov.), 1939 (see above); Batyj (pov.), 1942 (see above), abridged version for children: Našestvie Batyja (pov.), 1941; K "poslednemu morju" (pov.), 1955; last three titles first published together as a trilogy in 1960; Junost' polkovodca: Istoričeskaja povest' iz žizni Aleksandra Nevskogo (pov.), 1952; Zagadka ozera Kara-nor (short stories), 1961; Putešestvie v prošloe (essays), in Voprosy lit. 1965:9; Istoričeskie povesti, 1969.
Secondary Lit.: L. Borisov, in Zvezda 1964:5; RSPP 6(2):1969; L. Razgon, 1969; M. V. Jančeveckij, in Russkaja lit. 1972:2 and in Lit. obozrenie 1985:5; A. Khvatov, in Zvezda 1975:1; T. K. Lobanova, 1979; V. Torin, in Neva 1985:1; I. Minc, in Lit. gazeta April 17, 1985, p. 7.

**Yasensky, Bruno.** See JASIEŃSKI, BRUNO.

**Yáshin, Aleksándr Yákovlevich** (pseud. of A. Ya. Popóv), poet, prose writer (b. March 27 [March 14], 1913, Bludnovo, prov. Vologda—d. July 11, 1968, Moscow). Yashin was of peasant descent. He first began publishing his poems in provincial newspapers in 1928; in 1932 he completed his studies at the Vologda Pedagogical Institute, after which he taught in a village school and became head of the organizational committee of the Vologda branch of the Writers Union of the USSR. Yashin moved to Moscow after the First Congress of the Writers Union of the USSR in 1934. From 1935 to 1941 he studied at the Gorky Literary Institute, working at the same time as assistant editor on a factory newspaper. Yashin, whose first volume of verse appeared in Arkhangelsk in 1934, published several collections of his lyrical and narrative poems in Moscow beginning in 1938. He joined the Communist Party in 1941. During World War II he was a soldier and a frontline reporter. His poetry of the postwar period is influenced by the THEORY OF CONFLICTLESS-NESS; his narrative poem Alyona Fomina (1949) received a Stalin Prize (for 1949, 2d class). At the Second Congress of the Writers Union of the USSR in 1954, Yashin confessed that because he lacked the courage of his convictions he was guilty of contributing to the insincerity that characterized the literature of the Stalinist period. He supported the return of S. Yesenin to Soviet literature. Yashin's own work reached a crucial turning point at this stage; he turned to writing prose in which he depicted life in the village with relentless candor and for which he was sharply criticized. In his verse he turned particularly to his northern Russian peasant homeland; his poems are informed by the same "uncompromising integrity" (Burtin) as his prose. The title of his collection Sovest (1961; Conscience) still refers to this new awareness; in Bosikom po zemle (1965; Barefoot over the Earth), he describes his bond to Yesenin. His verse was generally well accepted. In 1954 Yashin became a member of the board of the Writers Union of the USSR, but was not reelected after 1959; he remained a permanent delegate to the congresses.

Alyona Fomina idealizes postwar kolkhoz life in compliance with the demands of SO-CIALIST REALISM. In Rychagi (1956; Levers), a terse parable about the degradation of human beings by the Party during the Stalin era, Yashin made a significant contribution, with regard to content, composition, and language, to the clarification of the recent past. In the story Vologodskaya svadba (1962; Vologda Wedding), Yashin presents an unvarnished picture of his peasant homeland, against which conservative critics engaged in polemics. The first-person narrative structure found in most of his stories connects Yashin's prose and his poetry. In the poems written after 1953 he comes to terms in part with his own fate, "As if I were reborn" ("Po svoyey orbite," 1959; In One's Own Orbit), and in part with the difficult lot of the people from his native

region ("Zholtye listya," 1963; Yellow Leaves). "Very few of our writers have written with such penetration, with such understanding of the 'soul' of trees, moss, water, all the 'hidden beauty' of the forests," wrote F. Abramov of Yashin's nature poems, which include elements from folk songs as well as occasional reminiscences of the war.

Works: Pesni Severu (poems), 1934; Alëna Fomina (narrative poem), 1949; Ryčagi (short story), in Lit. Moskva 1956:2, separate ed., London, 1965; Svežij khleb (poems), 1957; Sovest' (poems), 1961; Bosikom po zemle (poems), 1965; Den' tvorenija (poems), 1968; Bessonnica (poems), 1968; Dnevniki 1941–1945 (diary), in Oktjabr' 1975:4, separate ed., 1977; Bobrišnyj Ugor: Iz dnevnikov poslednikh let (diary), in Oktjabr' 1980:1–2.—Izbr. proizv., 2 vols., 1972; Sobr. soč., 3 vols., 1984–86.

Secondary Lit.: N. Kalitin, in Novyj mir 1966:2; Ja. Smeljakov and Vas. Belov, in Lit. Rossija July 19, 1968, p. 14; Ju. Burtin, in Novyj mir 1969:10; K. Simonov, foreword to Jašin's Izbr. proizv., 1972; F. Abramov, in Novyj mir 1973:4 and in his Portrety, 1983; V. Soloukhin, in Den' poèzii, Moscow, 1973, and in Lit. gazeta March 30, 1983, p. 5; A. Mikhajlov, 1975, in Oktjabr' 1976:3, and in Lit. Rossija Nov. 25, 1983, pp. 12–14; N. Jašina, 1977; V. Oboturov, in Lit. gazeta July 23, 1980, p. 4.

**Yefrémov, Iván Antónovich** prose writer (b. April 22 [April 9], 1907, Vyritsa, prov. St. Petersburg—d. Oct. 5, 1972, Moscow). Yefremov was a sailor in 1923–24. From 1924 to 1935 he studied biology and paleontology and took part in expeditions to the Transcaucasus, Central Asia, and eastern Siberia; in 1935 he completed his studies at the Leningrad Geological Institute. With 65 scientific publications to his name, Yefremov received a doctorate in biology in 1940. He began writing utopian prose based on natural science and technology in 1944. His novel Tumannost Andromedy (1957; Eng. tr., Andromeda: A Space-Age Tale, 1960) became the most popular work of its kind in the Soviet Union after World War II and served as a sign that science fiction would again be tolerated. Yefremov lived in Moscow.

Yefremov's first utopian short stories are based on scientific hypotheses, some of which (for example, the existence of prehistoric rock drawings in Siberia) were subsequently confirmed. The setting of his fantastic novellas, collected in Velikaya Duga (1949–53; The

Great Arc), is historical Egypt and Greece. The highly successful *Tumannost Andromedy* sketches a futuristic picture of the cosmos in the year 2850, when the Communist ideal has been realized and bonds of friendship have been forged with people on other planets. In the "adventure novel" *Lezviye britvy* (1963; The Razor's Edge), which dispenses with continuous action, no artistic unity ensues from the novel's separate political-pedagogical, scientific, and fantastic elements; in its development of Freudian psychoanalytical thought and Hindu conceptions of the world, however, the work exhibits a remarkable independence with regard to official doctrine. "Yefremov created his system of viewing the world, based on moral and metaphysical concepts of self-perfectibility, the confrontation of good and evil, and set it against prevailing dogma" (Geller).

*Works: Vstreča nad Tuskaroroj* (short stories), 1944 (Eng. tr., *A Meeting over Tuscarora and Other Adventures*, 1946); *Belyj rog* (short stories), 1945; *Na kraju Ojkumeny* (pov.), 1949 (Eng. tr., *Land of Foam*, 1957, 1959); *Zvëzdnye korabli* (pov.), 1953; *Velikaja Duga* (short stories and pov.), 1956; *Tumannost' Andromedy* (novel), 1958 (see above); *Serdce Zmei* (pov.), in *Junost'* 1959:1 (Eng. tr., in *The Heart of the Serpent*, 1966); *Lezvie britvy* (novel), 1964; *Čas Byka* (novel), 1970.—*Soč.*, 3 vols., 1975; *Sobr. soč.*, 5 vols., 1986–.

*Secondary Lit.*: N. Cvetkova, in *Moskva* 1957:2; Ju. Rjurikov, in *Lit. i sovremennost'* 1:1960; V. Sytin, in *Moskva* 1961:5; E. Brandis and V. Dmitrevskij, *Čerez gory vremeni*, 1963, and in *Neva* 1972:4; A. Lebedev, in *Novyj mir* 1964:6; *RSPP* 7(1):1971; H. Földeak, *Neuere Tendenzen der sowj. Science Fiction*, Munich, 1975; G. Grebenschikov, in *Russian Language Journal* 106:1976; L. Geller, in *Vremja my*, Tel Aviv, 24:1977, 33:1978; A. Kazancev, in *Lit. gazeta* April 21, 1982, p. 5; H. Stephan, in *MERSL* 6:1982.

**Yelagin, Ivan Venediktovich.** See ELAGIN, IVAN VENEDIKTOVICH.

**Yemtsev, Mikhail Tikhonovich.** See PARNOV, YEREMEY IUDOVICH.

**Yeroféyev, Venedíkt,** prose writer (b. 1933 or 1939 near Moscow). Obtaining biographical information about Yerofeyev is nearly impossible. He is supposed to have studied history for a time at Moscow University and at the pedagogical institute in Vladimir, to be proficient in Latin, and to be a music lover. Early on he must have become an alcoholic and have earned his living as a part-time worker; it is rumored that he worked as a cable layer for eight years. As a student he began writing literature, but he was never able to publish anything in the Soviet Union. Several of his works were considered lost, such as *Zapiski psikhopata* (Notes of a Psychopath) written in 1956 and a novel about student life written in 1961. After appearing in SAMIZDAT, his povest written in 1968, *Moskva-Petushki* (1973; Eng. tr., *Moscow to the End of the Line*, 1980), came to be published in TAMIZDAT, first in Israel and then in Paris in 1977. His work and its many translations established Yerofeyev's name as a writer. A second book of his came belatedly into the public eye with the povest written in 1973, *Vasily Rozanov glazami eksentrika* (1982; Vasily Rozanov with the Eyes of an Eccentric.) Although additional novels are spoken of, for example, "Shostakovich," texts are not available. Yerofeyev lived in Petushki for a long time; his fate is unknown.

Yerofeyev is an educated, sensitive, linguistically talented man who despairs at Soviet reality yet who has the ability to create original poetic works of art out of his despair. With the help of the epic narrative structure of a train trip from Moscow to the dismal town of Petushki 120 kilometers away, *Moskva-Petushki* provides complex insights into Soviet reality, Russian alcoholism, and the mental and behavioral changes that result from the constant consumption of alcohol. Like his next work, this povest is written in the first person and is rich in reflections, "in exalted transcendent language with many literary allusions" (E. Brown). In *Vasily Rozanov glazami eksentrika*, Yerofeyev reveals himself even more strongly as a surrealist who blends grotesque unreality with reality; here he combines the reading of the works of V. Rozanov with a meeting with himself. His assessment of Soviet reality and its architects using the measuring rod of common sense and the maxims of great philosophers yields doubt, despair, deep sighs, horror, and religious searching. In *Valpurgiyeva noch* (1985; Walpurgis Night), Yerofeyev realistically depicts the situation of a mentally dependent Jewish alcoholic who is admitted to a Soviet psychiatric clinic and abandoned to the repressive measures of its personnel.

*Works: Moskva-Petuški* (pov.), in *AMI* 3:1973, separate ed., Paris, 1977 (see above); *Vasilij Rozanov glazami èksentrika* (pov.), in *NRL: Neue russische Literatur*, Salzburg, 1978

(Russian and German), separate ed. under the title Glazami èksentrika, New York, 1982; Val'purgieva noč' ili "Šagi komandora" (play), in Kontinent, Paris, 45:1985. Secondary Lit.: Anon., in Kontinent 14:1977; P. Vajl', A. Genis, in Ėkho, Paris, 1978:4, in Sovremennaja russkaja proza, Ann Arbor, 1982, and in Grani, Frankfurt am Main, 139:1986; V. S. Dunham, in Venedikt Erofeev: Moscow to the End of the Line, New York, 1980; M. Al'tsuller, in Novyj žurnal, New York, 146:1982; L. Kunin, in Novoe russkoe slovo, New York, March 6, 1983, p. 4; A. Drawicz, in Russkaja mysl', Paris, April 19, 1984, pp. 8–9.

Yesénin, Sergéy Aleksándrovich, poet (b. Oct. 3 [Sept. 21], 1895, Konstantinovo, prov. Ryazan—d. Dec. 28, 1925, Leningrad). Yesenin was of peasant descent. He was raised by his grandparents, who were Old Believers, in a strict religious environment. Between 1912 and 1915 he studied at the Shanyavsky People's University in Moscow and worked as a proofreader. His first poems were published in various journals in 1914. In 1915 Yesenin met A. Blok in Petrograd and was drawn into literary circles there. Under the influence of Blok and S. Gorodetsky he allied himself with the peasant poets, N. Klyuyev in particular. Yesenin's first volume of verse, Radunitsa (1919; Day of the Dead), was received positively. In 1917 he was associated with the left Socialist Revolutionaries. He welcomed the October Revolution in the sense that it was a spiritual revolt consistent with his messianic hopes for a peasant paradise. In 1919 Yesenin moved to Moscow and became associated with a literary group calling themselves imagists (see IMAGISM). From time to time he would embrace an unprincipled life-style in the company of drunkards, prostitutes, and drug addicts. His meeting with the American dancer Isadora Duncan resulted in an unfortunate marriage, a world tour (May 1922—August 1923), and scandals that made headlines around the world. Yesenin's temporary return to his native village in 1924 and his attempt to conform to Communist reality were unable to alleviate his sense of despair. He put an end to his life in a Leningrad hotel room. Yesenin, who at the time of his death was one of the most popular poets in Russia, was, over the years, virtually consigned to oblivion by conservative Party critics who turned "Yeseninism" (yeseninshchina) into a negative criterion. His works were reprinted after 1955.

Yesenin's natural lyrical talent as the mournful poet of the old Russian village, of the meadows, clouds, and huts, with their associations with religious imagery, was amplified by various symbolist influences (A. Bely, Blok) but was strong enough always to remain independent. His early poems, written back in the village following his first encounter with the city, include simple, emptionally charged ballads about animals, such as "Pesn o sobake" (1915; Song of a Dog). Like Bely and Blok, Yesenin deals with revolutionary events as they relate to the realm of Christian ideas; in his case the religious element revealed in the imagery or in the appearance of Christ in the poem "Tovarishch" (1917; Comrade), for example, is ambivalent to the point of blasphemy. In the narrative poem Inoniya (1918), the imagery of which is reminiscent of Marc Chagall, Yesenin paints a vision of the longed-for peasant paradise, free of the enslaving urban civilization. Seeking the revolutionary element in Russian history, he wrote a lyrical drama, Pugachov (1921), whose allegories can be deciphered only with difficulty because of the work's linguistic eccentricities. Yesenin's disappointment with Russia's development into an urban-oriented, proletarian, antipeasant state exacerbated his melancholy inclinations; his escape into a life of dissipation inspired another cycle of poems written after 1920 and collected in the volumes Ispoved khuligana (1921; The Confession of a Hooligan) and Moskva kabatskaya (1924; The Moscow of Taverns). Yesenin's attempt at poetic self-assertion ended in despair when he realized that, as a poet in Soviet Russia, he had had the ground cut out from under him. His verse, often narrative in form, rich in color, sound, and unusual verbal combinations, achieved simplicity and clarity in the last two years of his life. "The contradictions that had ruined his life and led him to his tragic end were close to thousands of young men and women who had also been uprooted and trampled under during the cataclysm: they read their own complaints into his poems of sorrow and discouragement" (Slonim).

Works: Radunica (poems), 1916, 1918, 1919, 1921; Preobraženie (poems), 1918, 1921; Sel'-skij časoslov (narrative poems), 1918; Inonija (poems), 1918; Goluben' (poems), 1920; Trerjadnica (poems), 1920, 1921; Ispoved' khuligana (poems), 1921; Pugačëv (narrative poem), 1922; Stikhi skandalista (poems), Berlin, 1923; Tovarišč. Inonija (narrative poems), Berlin, 1923; Moskva kabackaja (poems), 1924; Stikhi (poems), 1924; Rus' sovetskaja (poems)

Baku, 1925; *Berëzovyj sitec* (poems), 1925; *Persidskie motivy* (poems), 1925; *Izbr. stikhi* (selected poems), 1925.—*Sobr. soč.*, 4 vols., 1926–28; *Izbr.*, 1946; *Soč.*, 2 vols., 1955; 5 vols., 1961–62; 5 vols., 1966–68; 6 vols., 1977– 80.
*Translation: Confessions of a Hooligan: Fifty Poems*, 1973.
*Secondary Lit.:* I. Rozanov, 1926; F. de Graaff, Leiden, 1933, 2d ed., 1966; V. Markov, in *Grani*, Frankfurt am Main, 25:1955; E. Naumov, 1960, 2d ed., 1965, 1973; I. Èrenburg, *Ljudi, gody, žizn'*, 1961; J. Veyrenc, The Hague, 1968; G. McVay, Oxford, 1969, and Ann Arbor, 1976; L. V. Fisher, Diss., Harvard Univ., 1972; Ju. Prokušev, 1973, 2d ed., 1975; S. Košečkin, Tbilisi, 1977; *Sergej Esenin* (collection), 1978; C. V. Ponomareff, Boston, 1978; *Esenin: A Biography in Memoirs, Letters, and Documents*, Ann Arbor, 1982; *RSPPo* 8:1985; P. Tartakovskij, 1986; *V mire Esenina*, 1986.

**Yevdokímov, Iván Vasílyevich,** prose writer (b. Feb. 3 [Jan. 22], 1887, Kronstadt—d. Aug. 28, 1941, Moscow). From 1911 to 1915 Yevdokimov was a student in the Department of History and Philology at St. Petersburg University; he worked as librarian, teacher, and lecturer in Russian and West European art history at the Institute for National Education in Vologda. In 1922 he moved to Moscow, where he worked for the State Publishing House. Yevdokimov began publishing in 1915. For a short time he achieved recognition with his first novel, *Kolokola* (1926; The Bells), which describes the 1905 Revolution in an industrial city of the Moscow region with the greatest possible realism, thus sketching a broad picture of the Russian province in those years. The novel had been reprinted seven times by 1935. His novels of the following years are carelessly written and belong to the trivia of minor fiction. Yevdokimov also wrote books on the art history of northern Russia and biographical short stories about M. Vrubel (1925), V. Surikov (1933), I. Repin (1940), and I. Levitan (1940).

*Works: M. A. Vrubel'* (short story), 1925; *Kolokola* (novel), 1926, 7th ed., 1935; *Čistye prudy* (novel), 1927; *Zaozer'e* (novel), 1928–31 (as vols. 2–4 of the *Sobr. soč.*); *V. I. Surikov* (short story), 1933; *Žar-ptica* (novel), only in *Novyj mir* 1936:2–4; *Repin* (short story), 1940; *Levitan* (short story), 1940.—*Sobr. soč.*, only vols. 1–4 published, 1928–31.
*Secondary Lit.:* N. Smirnov, in *Novyj mir* 1926:12; N. Bogoslovskij, in *Novyj mir* 1929:7;

*RSPP* 1:1959; W. Schäfer, in Kindler's *Lit.-Lexikon*, vol. 4, 1968; A. Dymšic, in his *Problemy i portrety*, 1972.

**Yevdokímov, Nikoláy Semyónovich,** prose writer (b. Feb. 26, 1922, Bobr, in the later Krupki Rayon, oblast Minsk). Yevdokimov was a soldier in World War II; in 1948 he completed his studies at the Gorky Literary Institute in Moscow. Since then he has published short novels in *Znamya* and other journals, and these have occasionally been reissued in collections. Since 1970 Yevdokimov has been a delegate to the congresses of the Writers Union of the USSR. Yevdokimov lives in Moscow.

Yevdokimov's first *povest*, *Vysokaya dolzhnost* (1950; The High Post), is of necessity subordinated to the theme of production in force at that time, but it avoids the usual polarization into positive and negative figures. After Stalin's death, Yevdokimov was one of the authors who, with great seriousness, investigated the question of the meaning of life and whose work thus attained religious dimensions. *Greshnitsa* (1960; The Sinner), his first *povest* to be widely recognized and to be filmed as an antireligious work, depicts the fate of a young girl who grows up among the Baptists. Caught between the frantically depicted believers and the surrounding world of nonbelievers, she finds an escape only through suicide. His novel *U pamyati svoi zakony* (1966; Memory Knows Her Own Laws) is his most significant and most spiritually profound work. The protagonist, a factory director, sees the story of his life from a religious perspective, proceeding from the original light and progressing through guilt and suffering to the final inner illumination and resurrection. An excellent paraphrase of Genesis on the meaning of work and the depiction of a primal encounter with God deepen the message of this novel. Structurally this work attains an advantage through the transition among three first-person narrators. Man's search for inner justification in his life remains Yevdokimov's central theme. In *Neobkhodimy chelovek* (1967; A Necessary Man) the protagonist realizes that meaning is to be found not in the customary realm of external good fortune but in another, spiritual realm. In *Byla pokhoronka* (1973; There Was a Notification of Death) he depicts a war invalid who, out of a false sense of concern for his family, allows them to believe incorrectly in his death for many years. *Byla voyna kogda-to . . .* (1975; Once There Was a War . . . ), which also takes war as its starting point, is completely dedicated to the inner light that illuminates an individual. *Strastnaya ploshchad!* (1977; Passionate Square) reveals a man whose conscience will not let him rest because he failed to understand a fateful meaning—failed to accept a proffered friendship—thirty years previously. In a similar way, the protagonist in *Proisshestviye iz zhizni Vladimira Vasilyevicha Makhonina* (1981; An Event in the Life of V. V. Makhonin) is forced to examine his behavior of decades previously when he failed to recognize the depth of love of a nurse who was attending him. Unrealistic elements designed to deepen the spiritual meaning play a stronger role in *Vospominaniya o prekrasnoy Ungarii* (1983; Recollection of Beautiful Hungary), a memoir that also bridges decades.

*Works:* Vysokaja dolžnost' (pov.), in *Oktajabr'* 1950:9, separate ed., 1952; *Grešnica* (pov.), in *Znamja* 1960:12, separate ed., 1961; *U pamjati svoi zakony* (pov.), in *Znamja* 1966:6–7, separate ed., 1979; *Neobkhodimyj čelovek* (pov.), in *Znamja* 1967:6; *Skazanie o Njurke—gorodskoj žitel'nice* (pov.), in *Družba narodov* 1970:7; *Byla pokhoronka* (pov.), in *Naš sovremennik* 1973:5; *Byla vojna kogda-to . . .* (pov. and short stories), 1975; *Strastnaja ploščad'* (pov.), in *Naš sovremennik* 1977:6; *Obida* (pov.), in *Znamja* 1981:4; *Proizšestvie iz žizni Vladimira Vasil'eviča Makhonina* (pov.), in *Novyj mir* 1981:5; *Vospominanija o prekrasnoj Ungarii* (memoirs), in *Družba narodov* 1983:6; interview, in *Voprosy lit.* 1984:7.

*Secondary Lit.:* B. Brajnina, in *Znamja* 1951:3; Z. Krakhmal'nikova, in *Znamja* 1957:12; A. Bočarov, in *Lit. gazeta* Jan. 21, 1961, p. 3, and in *Znamja* 1982:2; M. Lathouwers, in *Irénikon*, Chevetogne (Belgium), 1970:1 and in *Glaube in der 2. Welt* 1978:7–8; V. Vasil'ev, in *Naš sovremennik* 1975:3; D. Tevekeljan, in *Lit. obozrenie* 1977:11 and in *Novyj mir* 1979:3; V. Turbin, in *Lit. Rossija* Feb. 26, 1982, p. 11; F. Koluncev, in *Lit. gazeta* March 3, 1982, p. 6; A. Andrianov, in *Lit. gazeta* Nov. 14, 1984, p. 5.

**Yevréinov, Nikoláy Nikoláyevich,** playwright, director, literary scholar (b. Feb. 26 [Feb. 13], 1879, Moscow—d. Feb. 7, 1953, Paris). Yevreinov's father was an engineer. Yevreinov grew up in Dorpat (Tartu), Yekaterinoslav, and Pskov and, after 1892, attended the Imperial School of Jurisprudence in St. Petersburg that was reserved for the nobility; he graduated in 1901 having completed his secondary education as a jurist. He displayed an early musical and dramatic talent, and he wrote his first dramatic and musical works at this time and directed their performance. His first play was published in 1900. From 1901 to 1910 he was a civil servant in the Ministry of Transportation. Simultaneously he completed his education as a composer, studying under N. Rimsky-Korsakov, among others, at the St. Petersburg Conservatory. From 1900 to 1908 he wrote numerous plays, including one that bears the influence of symbolism, *Fundament schastya* (1902; The Foundation of Happiness), and his most famous harlequinade, *Vesyolaya smert* (1908; Eng. tr., *A Merry Death*, 1916). His idea of renewing the theater by incorporating elements of ancient and medieval theatrical forms as well as "primitive art" was realized through the establishment of the Ancient Theater (Starinniy teatr) in St. Petersburg; he served with great success as the artistic director there in 1907–8 and 1911–12. In 1908 the first volume of his *Dramaticheskiye sochineniya* (Collected Dramatic Works) was published. Also in 1908 the best-known personality of the St. Petersburg avant-garde theater, V. Komissarzhevskaya, offered him the position of director after dismissing V. Meyerhold; he held this position until the theater closed in 1909 owing to financial pressure. From 1910 to 1917, Yevreinov directed the satiric theater "Krivoye zerkalo" (The Distorting Mirror) that he cofounded; here he staged approximately 100 plays, including 14 of his own, in 1910–14 and 1916–17. As an intimate theater it also had great success on tour. In 1912 the tsar allowed Yevreinov's most famous play from this period, named after Gogol's *Revizor* (The Inspector General), to be performed before the court in Tsarskoye Selo. During this period Yevreinov wrote numerous books about the oretical and historical questions concerning the theater, and he published the second volume of his collected plays in 1914. He spent the years from 1914 to 1917 in Kuokalla in Yu. Annenkov's house. After the Bolshevik takeover in 1917, Yevreinov lived in Sukhumi and Tiflis and staged a few plays in the south of Russia. After his return to Petrograd in 1920, he and Annenkov organized a mass theatrical event to celebrate the third anniversary of the Revolution—*Vzyatiye Zimnego dvortsa* (1920; The Conquest of the Winter Palace); thereafter, however, he rejected almost every offer to cooperate with the new system as Meyerhold was doing (see THEATER OKTOBER). A few of his plays were performed; in 1922–23 Yevreinov was allowed to travel to Western Europe. In January 1925 he moved to Warsaw with his wife owing to a deliberate transfer of the theater "Krivoye zerkalo." In May 1925 he emigrated further to Paris. In emigration, Yevreinov wrote nine plays (three of which were ballets), including the philosophical harlequinade *Samoye glavnoye* (1920; Eng. tr., *The Chief Thing*, 1926), which was translated into 27 languages and performed in 25 countries. He made this into the first part of a trilogy with the addition of *Korabl pravednykh* (1924; Eng. tr., *The Ship of the Righteous*, 1973) and *Teatr vechnoy voyny* (1928; The Theater of Eternal War). In its concluding section, his *Histoire du théâtre russe* (1947; Russ. *Istoriya russkogo teatra*, 1955) contained much that was personal. In occupied Paris in 1943, Yevreinov took over the direction of a Russian theater. His last books, such as *Pamyatnik mimolyotnomu* (1953; A Monument to the Transient), are dedicated to the theater in emigration.

Yevreinov is one of the most important personalities of the Russian theater in the first decades of the 20th century. As a theoretician, director, and author of approximately 30 plays he concerned himself with providing a new conception of the meaning of theater for man's self-experience and as a source of joy. In doing so, he linked up with the commedia dell'arte as well as with the ancient and medieval theater. The diversity of his talent led to his many parallel activities. In *Predstavleniye lyubvi* (Imagination of Love), which was not performed in Russia, he put into practice his theory of "monodrama," with a commanding hero who serves as a prism through whom the viewer perceives the world. In *Vesyolaya smert*, he illustrates the attitude of affirming life and taking advantage of each moment by using the figures of Harlequin, Pierrot, Columbine, and Death. In *Samoye glavnoye*, Yevreinov treats the question of the meaning of life in a more complex way by presenting the Paraclete (the Holy Spirit), the greatest mediating figure in the New Testament, in various masks. Even here, Yevreinov used elements of comedy. His *Revizor* is a parody of other views of the theater that were common in his time; thus it is directed against K. Stanislavsky. The diversity of Yevreinov's works, in which tragic farce predominates, remains formidable.

*Works: Dramatičeskie soč.* (collected plays), 3 vols., 1908–23; *Vvedenie v monodramu* (scholarly articles), 1912; *Teatr kak takovoj* (scholarly articles), 1912; *Teatr dlja sebja* (scholarly articles), 3 vols., 1915–17 (Eng. tr., *The Theatre in Life*, 1927); *Samoe glavnoe*

(play), 1921 (reprinted, Ann Arbor, 1980) (see above); *Proiskhoždenie dramy* (scholarly articles), 1921; *Pamjatnik mimolëtnomu* (scholarly articles), Paris, 1953; *Istorija russkogo teatra* (literary history), New York, 1955; *Šagi Nemezidy* (1939) (play), Paris, 1956; *Čemu net imeni* (1935–37) (play), Paris, 1965.

*Translation: Life as Theater: Five Modern Plays*, 1973.

*Secondary Lit.:* V. Kamenskij, 1917; A. Kašina-Evreinova, Paris, 1964; G. Kalbous, in *Russian Language Journal* 92:1971; C. Collins, in *Russian Literature Triquarterly* 2:1972; C. Moody, in *Russian Literature Triquarterly* 13:1975; S. Volkonskij, A. Evreinova, et al., in *Russkaja mysl'*, Paris, Feb. 22, 1979, pp. 8–9; G. Abensour, Paris, 1981; E. Kannak, in *Novyj žurnal*, New York, 142:1981; S. Golub, in *MERSL* 7:1984.

**Yevtushénko, Yevgény Aleksándrovich,** poet (b. July 18, 1933, Zima, oblast Irkutsk). Yevtushenko's father was a geologist; his mother, a musician. Yevtushenko grew up in Siberia until 1944, write his first poems in 1949, and published his first volume of poetry, *Razvedchiki gryadushchego* (1952; Scouts of the Future), while a student at the Gorky Literary Institute (1951–54). With the long autobiographical poem *Stantsiya Zima* (1953; Eng. tr., "Zima Junction," 1962), Yevtushenko became the most popular Soviet author at home and abroad and remained so for a decade. His topical poetry was regularly published in large print runs; public readings drew immense audiences; regular trips abroad allowed him to appear as the representative of the cultural policy of the THAW. Frequent contradictions between a conformist and a nonconformist attitude led to a rapid loss of regard. Yevtushenko protested against the Soviet Union's invasion of Czechoslovakia in 1968 but undertook self-criticism in a talk on the representation of the Stalin period during the 1950s at the Fifth Congress of the Writers Union. From 1962 to 1969 he was a member of the editorial staff of the journal *Yunost* and a member of the board of the Writers Union of the USSR from 1967 to 1981. In March 1974 he spoke out in defense of the exiled A. Solzhenitsyn, but in *Isvestiya* in August 1974 he published a poem in support of the ideological struggle. Yevtushenko lives in Moscow.

Yevtushenko was at first considered the Soviet poet who "more completely than other poets expressed the perception of the newly granted freedom" (Runin, 1960). The easy intelligibility of his poetry also contributed to his excessive success, as did the scandal that the critics often kindled. Aiming at a journalistic effect, Yevtushenko selected some themes relating to contemporary Party policy (for example, "Nasledniki Stalina" [1962; Eng. tr., "The Heirs of Stalin," 1963], Bratskaya GES [1965; Eng. tr., Bratsk Station, 1966]) and some themes of a less dogmatic nature (for example, "Babiy Yar" [1961; Eng. tr., 1962], "Ballada o brakonyerstve" [1965; Ballade about Poaching]). Yevtushenko's poems are usually narrative in form and rich in descriptive details. Many are long-winded, declamatory, and superficial. Seldom does his clearly evident poetic talent reveal itself in multilevel and substantive statements. Yevtushenko writes easily and loves word and sound play that tends toward affectation. His ambition of becoming, in the shadow of V. Mayakovsky, the tribune of the post-Stalin generation seems to have temporarily crippled his talent, as revealed in "Po yagody" (In Search of Berries), for example. His literary criticism, compiled in Talant yest chudo nesluchaynoye (1980; A Talent Is Not an Accidental Wonder), combines literary sensitivity with autobiographical elements. In a loose narrative sequence, the novel Yagodnye mesta (1981; Eng. tr., Wild Berries, 1984) links up anti-American reports, critical observations of contemporary Soviet life, confessional statements about Siberia, and images of the hereafter drawn from the scientist K. Tsiolkovsky. In 1984 he was awarded the State Prize of the USSR for the poem Mama i neytronnaja bomba (1982; Mother and the Neutron Bomb).

Works: Razvedčiki grjaduščego (poems), 1952; Tretij sneg (poems), 1955; Stancija Zima (narrative poem), in Oktjabr' 1956:10 and in Grani, Frankfurt am Main, 33:1957; Zima (poems), 1956; Obeščanie (poems), 1957; Luk i lira (poems), 1959; Četvërtaja Meščanskaja (short story), in Junost' 1959:2 and in Grani 43:1959; Jabloko (poems), 1960; Nežnost' (poems), 1962; Vzmakh ruki (poems), 1962; Avtobiografija (autobiography), London, 1964 (Eng. tr., Precocious Autobiography, 1963); Bratskaja GÈS (poems), 1965 (see above); Idut belye snegi (poems), 1969; Tret'ja pamjat': Das Dritte Gedächtnis (poems in Russian and German), Berlin, 1970; Pojuščaja damba (poems), 1972; Doroga nomer odin (poems), 1972; Poèt v Rossii—bol'še čem poèt (narrative poem), 1973; Intimnaja lirika (poems), 1973; V polnyj rost (lyric and narrative poems), 1977; Utrennij narod (poems), 1978; Talant est' čudo neslučajnoe (essays), 1980; Točka

opory (feature articles), 1981; Jagodnye mesta (novel), 1982 (see above); Mama i nejtronnaja bomba (narrative poem), in Novyj mir 1982:7; Počti naposledok (poems), 1985.—Izbr. proizv., 2 vols., 1975, 1980; Sobr. soč., 3 vols., 1983–84.

Translations: The Poetry of Yevgeny Yevtushenko 1953–1965, 1965; Poems, 1966; Stolen Apples, 1971; From Desire to Desire, 1976; Nostalgia for the Present, 1978.

Secondary Lit.: B. Runin, in Novyj mir 1960:11; A. Sinjavskij, in Grani 63:2967; E. Vinokurov, in Evtušenko's Idut belye snegi, 1969; I. Meshakov-Korjakin, in Melbourne Slavonic Studies 3:1969; I. Grinberg, in Lit. obozrenie 1973:4; A. Urban et al., in Lit. obozrenie 1975:8; N. P. Condee, Diss., Yale Univ., 1978; E. Sidorov, in Novyj mir 1980:12; Ju S. Nekhorošev, A. P. Šitov, bibliography, 1981; RSPPo 7:1984; R. Milner-Gulland, in MERSL 7:1984.

**Yúgov, Alekséy Kuzmích**, prose writer (b. March 23 [March 10], 1902, Kamenskoye, oblast Kurgan, Siberia—d. Feb. 13, 1979). Yugov received his medical degree in Odessa in 1927. He practiced medicine in Siberia until 1930, then moved to Moscow and devoted himself to journalism and writing. The narrative poem Lyotchiki (The Fliers) was his first publication in 1923. In Bessmertiye (1939–44; Eng. tr., Immortality, 1945), he selected as his theme the class struggle in the Siberian gold-prospecting milieu in the early days of Soviet rule. Afterward he turned, in his two-part novel Ratobortsy (1946–49; The Champions), to early Russian history (Aleksandr Nevsky), adopting a narrowly nationalistic point of view in accordance with the struggle against COSMOPOLITANISM. The construction of the Volga power station inspired some publicistic prose and the novel Na bolshoy reke (1956; On the Big River). From 1958 to 1975 Yugov belonged to the board of the Writers Union of the RSFSR; in 1972 he received the Gorky Prize for his two-part novel about the years of revolution, Strashny sud (1969–71; The Last Judgment), in which he presents Trotsky (among others) as a traitor during the Revolution and as responsible for Lenin's early death.

Yugov is a very conservative writer who, against considerable opposition, advocated the generous addition of archaic, dialectical, and colloquial elements to the Russian literary language. His attacks against literary specialists for their interpretation and translation of the Slovo o polku Igoreve (The Lay of Igor's

Campaign) produced a bad impression. Yugov's contemporary prose emphasizes the leading role of the Party; his historical works stress the superiority of Great Russianness. His plots are contrived and his style is cumbersome and mannered.

*Works: Lětčiki* (narrative poem), 1923; *Bessmertie* (novel), 1944 (see above); *Ratoborcy* (novel), 2 vols., 1949; *Na bol'šoj reke* (novel), 1960; *Šatrovy* (novel), 1967 (later the first volume of the following); *Strašnyj sud* (novel), 1969–71.—*Sobr. soč.*, 4 vols., 1984–.

*Secondary Lit.: V. Ditc, in Neva* 1961:4; A. Gorelov, in *Neva* 1962:8; R. Budagov, in *Voprosy lit.* 1963:2; Ju. Strekhnin, in *Lit. gazeta* June 24, 1970, p. 5; L. Dmitriev and O. Tvorogov, in *Russkaja lit.* 1972:1; N. Dalada, 1973; A. Khvatov, in *Naš sovremennik* 1977:3; S. Baruzdin, in *Družba narodov* 1982:5.

*Yúnost* (Youth), an illustrated literary journal that has been published monthly in Moscow since 1955 as an organ of the Writers Union of the USSR. This journal, which V. Katayev founded and edited until 1962, met with its first success with the publication of a translation of Thor Heyerdahl's *Kon Tiki;* later its unconventional expositions of the problems of youth (for example, by V. Aksyonov and V. Rozov) were especially well received. Contributing authors include A. Akhmadulina, S. Antonov, B. Balter, A. Bitov, V. Bykov, O. Chukhontsev, F. Iskander, A. Kuznetsov, Yu. Morits, Yu. Nagibin, A. Rekemchuk, B. Slutsky, A. Tvardovsky, B. Vasilyev, A. Voznesensky, and Ye. Yevtushenko. From 1962 to 1981, B. Polevoy was the editor in chief; his successor, A. Dementyev, is a poet. The editorial collective has included the following well-known writers: S. Marshak (1955–64), G. Medynsky (1955–79), N. Nosov (1955–62), M. Prilezhayeva (1955–79), V. Rozov (1955–69, and again since 1987), V. Aksyonov (1962–69), Ye. Yevtushenko (1964–69), A. Aleksin (1969–), V. Amlinsky (1976–), B. Vasilyev (1977–), R. Kazakova (1979–). The journal enjoys great popularity. In 1975 the circulation was 2.6 million; in 1986, 3.3 million.

*Secondary Lit.:* "Obsuždenie žurnala Junost'" in *Voprosy lit.* 1968:2; V. Khmara, in *Pravda* Oct. 11, 1970; A. Marčenko, in *Novyj mir* 1972:10; V. Kataev, in *Junost'* 1975:6; B. Polevoj, in *Lit. Rossija* June 6, 1980, p. 8; A. Gladilin, in *Novoe russkoe slovo*, New York, July 6, 1980, p. 5, and in *Russkaja mysl'*, Paris,

Jan. 7, 1982, p. 12; Anon., in *Lit. gazeta* April 18, 1983, pp. 1–2.

**Yurásov, Vladímir** (at first, S.) (pseud. of Vladímir Ivánovich Zhabínsky), prose writer (b. Oct. 15 [Oct. 2], 1914, Sibiu [Hermannstadt], Rumania). Zhabinsky grew up in Rostov-on-Don with his stepfather, who was a laborer. After he completed school in 1930, he worked as an electrician. In 1932 he went to Leningrad and became a foreman in ship construction. After 1934 he studied at the LIFLI (Leningrad Institute of Philosophy, Literature, and History, which became part of Leningrad University in 1936). Arrested in 1937, he was sentenced to eight years in a prison camp in 1938. Owing to the confusion during World War II, he was able to escape in 1941, to live in hiding for three years, and, starting in 1944, to serve in the Red Army by using a fabricated life history. He was sent to Eastern Europe as an engineer with a demolitions unit and ended up as a lieutenant colonel with the SVA (Soviet Military Administration) in East Berlin. After 1947 he held a similar position as a civilian. Facing the threat of renewed security checks, he fled to the West in the same year. He met with considerable difficulty in gaining recognition as a political refugee and managed to escape extradition to the Soviet Union by the Americans only by fleeing. In 1951 he obtained an entry visa into the United States; from 1952 to 1981 he worked at Radio Liberty in New York using the name Rudolf. As such he frequently was severely attacked by the Soviet press. In 1951 he first published his works written in the Soviet Union, for which R. Gul invented the pseudonym S. Yurasov. From his experiences in the Soviet Union and in Germany came his only novel, *Parallaks* (1972; Eng. tr., *Parallax*, 1966), which he began writing while in Germany. Chapters were published in various journals after 1951, and the first part, *Vrag naroda* (1952; Enemy of the People), appeared as a book written by "Vladimir Yurasov." A preprint of the novel appeared in the journal *Novoye russkoye slovo* (Dec. 1970–July 1971). Before the complete Russian book edition appeared, an abridged but well-received English translation was published without the author's consent in 1966. The THAW brought about a concern with the new cultural developments in the Soviet Union that led to the book *Prosvety* (1958; Glints of Light), which contains 18 articles about V. Dudintsev, S. Kirsanov, A. Surkov, emigration, piety, and other themes of Soviet spiritual life in 1956 and 1957. Yurasov has not returned to his literary activity since that time. He lives in Nyack near New York City.

Yurasov offers an important counterpoint to Soviet war literature in *Parallaks* in that he illustrates from his own experiences the spiritual situation of a high Soviet officer in the immediate postwar period. The settings—Moscow, a collective farm, East Berlin, Munich—become the focal points of the fates of Russians leading up to emigration. His experience of the popularity of A. Tvardovsky's narrative poem about Tyorkin led Yurasov to write his own continuation, *Vasily Tyorkin posle voyny* (1953; Vasily Tyorkin after the War), which shows this classic Russian soldier "at home" and as occupier. However, Yurasov only rarely approaches Tvardovsky's unique linguistic rhythm. Short stories such as *Gore tomu zhe kuvshinu* (1951; Woe for This Jug) reveal his gift for realistically enlivening a tragic fate, as here the fate of a Polish Jew taken by the Soviets.

*Works: Segežskaja noč'* (narrative poem) [1939], in *Novyj žurnal*, New York, 27:1951; *Iz perevodov samogo sebja* (poems) [1939–48], in *Grani*, Frankfurt am Main, 11:1951; *Gore tomu že kuvšinu* (short story), in *Lit. sovremennik*, Munich, 1:1951; *Vrag naroda* (novel), New York, 1952; *Vasilij Tërkin posle vojny* (narrative poem), New York, 1952; *Prosvety: Zametki o sovetskoj lit. 1956–57* (essays), Munich, 1958; *Parallaks* (novel), New York, 1972 (see above).

*Secondary Lit.:* R. Gul', in *Novyj žurnal* 30:1952; N. Stanjukovič, in *Vozroždenie*, Paris, 62:1957.

**Yuryenén, Sergéy Sergéyevich** (Latin spelling he used, Serge Iourienen), prose writer (b. Jan. 21, 1948, Frankfurt on the Oder, Germany). Yuryenen's father, who died a few days before Yuryenen was born, was a lieutenant engineer in the Soviet Army. Yuryenen studied Russian language and literature at the universities of Minsk and Moscow from 1966 to 1973 and then worked on the editorial staff of the journal *Druzhba narodov*. Yuryenen, an admirer of Yu. Kazakov, published short stories in the Soviet Union between 1974 and 1976, including *Kormilets* (1975; The Provider), which won the first prize in a competition for the best short story on contemporary student life. After Yuryenen collected some of his short stories in *Po puti k domu* (1977; On the Way Home), he became a member of the Writers Union. Yuryenen married a foreigner and was

allowed to emigrate and join her in Paris in November 1977. In order better to reach Western European readers, Yuryenen turned to the longer literary form of the novel. His first work in this genre, *Volny strelok* (1984; Free Gunner), appeared in a French translation in 1980; it was well received by French critics. This work was followed by *Narushitel granitsy* (1984; The Violator of the Border), which was published in the journal *Strelets*. Yuryenen completed his third novel in 1984: *Syn imperii, infantilny roman* (The Son of the Empire, an Infantile Novel). He moved from Paris to Munich in 1984, where he is working as an editor for the cultural program of the Russian Service of Radio Liberty.

The novel *Volny strelok*, to a large extent autobiographical, uses as its narrative structure the journey shared by an author and the KGB agent tailing him. It illustrates the internal disintegration and the duplicitous speech of the intelligentsia in the Soviet Union that is required by the system, as manifested in cynicism, sexual desire, a yearning for the West, and a search for meaning in philosophies other than Marxism (for example, in Indian philosophy). In *Narushitel granitsy* he depicts students of Moscow University in their attempt to remain true to their convictions even after the THAW.

*Works: Kormilec* (short story), in *My molodye*, 1976; *Po puti k domu* (short stories), 1977; *Okhota na svetljačkov* (short story), in *Ėkho*, Paris, 1978:2; *Pod znakom Bliznecov* (short story), in *Kontinent*, Paris, 17:1978; *Son Lomonosova* (short story), in *Tret'ja volna*, Paris, 5:1979; *Vol'nyj strelok* (novel), Paris–New York, 1984; interview, in *Strelec*, Montgeron–Jersey City, N.J., 1984:5; *Narusitel' granicy* (novel), in *Strelec* 1984:6–11, separate ed., Paris, 1986; *Syn imperii, infantil'nyj roman* (novel), Ann Arbor, 1986; *Ėmigrantka Ėmma* (short story), in *Strelec* 1986:1.

*Secondary Lit.:* S. Baruzdin, in *Komsomol'skaja pravda* Feb. 24, 1976; L. Levin, in *Junost'* 1977:4; N. Sand, in *Le Monde* Sept. 19, 1980, Russian translation in *Tret'ja volna*, New York, 14:1983; V. Rybakov, in *Kontinent* 27:1981; B. Nielsen-Stokkeby, in *Die Welt* April 20, 1984; A. Glezer, in *Novoe russkoe slovo*, New York, May 1, 1984; B. Paramonov, in *Russkaja mysl'*, Paris, Oct. 25, 1984, p. 10; M. Kasack, in *Osteuropa* 1984:11–12; A. Radaškevič, in *Russkaja mysl'* March 28, 1986, p. 10; C. Emerson, in *The New York Times Book Review* June 29, 1986; V. Aksënov, in *Obozrenie*, Paris, 21:1986.

# Z

**Zabolótsky, Nikoláy Alekséyevich,** poet (b.
May 7 [April 24], 1903, Kazan—d. Oct. 14,
1958, Moscow). Zabolotsky's father was an
agronomist. In 1910 Zabolotsky moved with
his parents to Sernur, in the district of Ur-
zhum, prov. Vyatka. From 1920 to 1925 he
studied philology, first in Moscow, then in
Petrograd, where he graduated from the Pedagogical Institute. In 1926–27 he served in the
army. He finally obtained a position in Leningrad in the Division of Children's Literature
of the State Publishing House, headed by S.
Marshak. Zabolotsky, who had already written many poems in his student days, first
began publishing his poems in 1927; his publications also included children's books and
contributions to the children's journals *Yozh*
and *Chizh*. Zabolotsky belonged to the group
of absurdist writers OBERIU; he formulated
their manifesto, published in 1928. His first,
largely surrealistic volume of verse, *Stolbtsy*
(1929; Eng. tr., *Scrolls*, 1971), was sharply
criticized by RAPP, but was highly regarded
by connoisseurs. A second volume, *Stikhotvoreniya 1926–1932* (Poems 1926–1932), was
not permitted to appear, even though the galley proofs had already been printed. Zabolotsky's epic in verse, *Torzhestvo zemledeliya*
(1929–32; The Triumph of Agriculture), generated such criticism from the Party that the
issue of the journal *Zvezda* in which it was
scheduled to appear (1933: 2–3) was seized,
lines were changed, and the issue was reprinted. After cooperating with the new Writers Union and making certain concessions to
the prevailing critics, Zabolotsky was able to
bring out a further collection, *Vtoraya kniga*
(1937; Second Book). On March 19, 1938,
however, he was arrested and sentenced to
five years in a concentration camp. From August 1944 to May 1946 Zabolotsky lived in
exile in the Altai and Karaganda; after 1946
he was permitted, as a member of the Writers
Union, to reside again in Moscow and even
to publish a volume of verse in 1948. As he
had before his arrest, Zabolotsky now lived
primarily on his translations, particularly from
Georgian; he also wrote a famous paraphrase
of The Lay of Igor's Campaign. Many of his
own poems from this period were first published following his complete REHABILITA-
TION after Stalin's death; thus, for example,
his "Lesnoye ozero" (1938; The Forest Lake)
appeared in *Novy mir* in 1956. Yet one more

collection of his poems was published in 1957,
the year before his early death, when Zabolotsky lived mostly in Tarusa and had his only
opportunity to go abroad as a delegate to a
European congress of writers in Italy. Not
until a decade later was Zabolotsky fully recognized as one of the most important Russian
poets of the Soviet period.

Zabolotsky's early work revolves around the
problem of the city and the masses; it is influenced by V. Khlebnikov, stamped with the
concreteness of FUTURISM, and characterized
by a farcical diversity of metaphors. The poet's
particular contrapositioning of words, with
the goal of "defamiliarizing" them, results in
new verbal references; nevertheless, the degree of absurdity in Zabolotsky's works is
below that of the other members of Oberiu.
Nature is comprehended as chaos and prison,
harmony as illusion. *Torzhestvo zemledeliya*
combines futurist experimentation with elements from the heroic-comic verse epics of
the 18th century. Problems of death and immortality characterize Zabolotsky's poetry
during the 1930s. Ironic exaggeration or ironic
simplification is used to indicate distance from
the object being depicted. His later poems are
connected by their philosophical intent, their
conflict with nature, and their naturalistic,
unimpassioned language; they are more emotional, musical, and stand closer to tradition
(A. Pushkin, Ye. Baratynsky, F. Tyutchev).
Allegorical features are combined with the
anthropomorphic treatment of nature that
characterized his earlier verse ("Groza" [1946;
The Storm]).

*Works: Stolbcy* (poems), 1929 (see above);
*Vtoraja kniga* (poems), 1937; *Stikhotvorenija*
(poems), 1948; *Stikhotvorenija* (poems), 1957;
*Stikhotvorenija* (poems), 1959; *Izbr.* (poems),
1960; *Stikhotvorenija* (poems), Washington,
1965; *Stikhotvorenija i poèmy* (lyric and narrative poems), 1965; *Izbr.* (poems), 1970
(foreword by E. Vinokurov).—*Izbr. proizv.,* 2
vols., 1972; *Sobr. soč.,* 3 vols., 1983–84.

*Secondary Lit.:* V. Zavališin, in *Novyj žurnal,* New York, 58:1959; A. Rannit, B. Filippov, and E. Rajs, in Zabolotsky's *Stikhotvorenija,* Washington, 1965; N. Čukovskij, in
*Neva* 1965:9; A. Turkov, 1966; S. Karlinsky,
in *Slavic Review* 1967; A. Makedonov, 1968;
F. Björling, Stockholm, 1973; E. Ètkind, in his
*Poètičeskij stroj russkoj liriki,* 1973; I. Masing-

Delic, in *Scando-Slavica* 1974; R. Milner-Gulland, in *Russian Literature Triquarterly* 8:1974; L. Ozerov, in *Moskva* 1974:9; E. Rajs, in *Grani*, Frankfurt am Main, 102:1976; I. Rostovceva, 1976 and 1984; *Vospominanija o Z.*, 1977, 2d ed., 1984; W. F. Jack, Diss., Univ. of Michigan, 1977; B. Filippov (1958), in his *Stat'i o literature*, London, 1981; S. Pratt, in *Slavic and East European Journal* 1983:2; G. Groman, in *Novyj mir* 1985:9; *RSPPo* 9:1986.

**Zadórnov, Nikoláy Pávlovich,** prose writer (b. Dec. 5 [Nov. 22], 1909, Penza). Zadornov's father was a veterinarian. Zadornov grew up in Siberia. After completing secondary school, he worked as an actor and director at theaters in Siberia and in the Urals from 1926 to 1935. In World War II he worked in radio broadcasting. At this time he wrote his first novel, *Amur-batyushka* (1944; Eng. tr., *Amur Saga*, 1971), which was dedicated to the theme of the Russian colonization of Siberia. In 1946, after Latvia was incorporated into the Soviet Union, Zadornov moved to Riga. He wrote sequels to his first novel with *Dalyoky kray* (1949; The Distant Land) and *K okeanu* (1950; To the Ocean) and was awarded a Stalin Prize (for 1951, 2d class) for the trilogy. *Kapitan Nevelskoy* (1956–58; Captain Nevelskoy) and *Voyna za okean* (1960–63; The War for the Sea), his later multivolume novels, are set in the same historical era. A trilogy consisting of *Tsunami* (1972), *Simoda* (1975), and *Kheda* (1979) is dedicated to Admiral Putyatin and Russo-Japanese relations in 1854–55. Zadornov lives in Riga.

Zadórnov's works revolve around the themes of the Russian settlement of Siberia and the history of the Far East. Their goal is to emphasize the Russians' cultural superiority over the Siberians or the Japanese. They are historically untrustworthy, show interest in folkloric details, and are long-winded without having any psychological depth. In *Zholtoye, zelyonoye, goluboye . . .* (1967; Yellow, Green, Blue . . .) he develops a hackneyed image of a writer who provides valuable assistance to a regional Party secretary. The straightforward, honeyed portrayal of character, together with an idealizing purpose, demonstrates the author's incompetence.

*Works:* Amur-batjuska (novel), 1944, rev. ed., 1958 (see above); Dalëkij kraj (novel), 1949; K okeanu (novel), 1950 (also under title K Tikhomu okeanu); Kapitan Nevel'skoj (novel), 2 vols., 1956–58; Vojna za okean (novel), 3 vols., 1963; Žëltoe, zelënoe, goluboe

. . . (novel), 1967; Zolotaja likhoradka (novel), 1971; Cunami (novel), 1972; Simoda (novel), in *Novyj mir* 1975:7–9, separate ed., 1975; Kheda (novel), in *Novyj mir* 1979:4–6, separate ed., 1979; Gonkong (novel), in *Novyj mir* 1982:1–2, separate ed., 1983.—*Sobr. soč.*, 6 vols., 1977–79.

*Secondary Lit.:* G. Gor, in *Zvezda* 1951:1; P. Proskurin, in *Lit. Rossija* Oct. 11, 1963, p. 10; *RSPP* 2:1964; V. Enišerlov, in *Novyj mir* 1968:1; N. Eselëv, in *Lit. gazeta* Oct. 22, 1969, p. 5; L. Bondina, in *Lit. Rossija* Jan. 18, 1974, p. 17; S. Krivšenko, in *Lit. gazeta* Feb. 4, 1976, p. 4; O. Novikova, in *Lit. gazeta* Oct. 31, 1979, p. 5; A. Gvozdeva, 1984.

**Zakrútkin, Vitály Aleksándrovich,** prose writer (b. March 27 [March 14], 1908, Feodosiya—d. Oct. 9, 1984, station Kochetovskaya, oblast Rostov). Zakrutkin's father was a teacher. Zakrutkin grew up in a village. In 1931 he began teaching in the Soviet Far East. In 1932 he completed his education at the Blagoveshchensk Pedagogical Institute by correspondence. In 1936 he wrote his candidate's dissertation on A. Pushkin in Leningrad and was appointed to the chair for Russian literature at the Rostov Pedagogical Institute. Zakrutkin's first prose work, *Akademik Plyushchov* (1940; Academy Member Plyushchov), a long povest, met with slight and very restrained recognition. In World War II, Zakrutkin was a correspondent at the front. In 1947 he settled in the village Kochetovskaya on the Don. After writing a novel about the Civil War period, *U morya Azovskogo* (1946; On the Sea of Azov), Zakrutkin wrote the novel *Plavuchaya stanitsa* (1950; Eng. tr., *Floating Stanitsa*, 1954), in which he idealized the daily life of Soviet fishermen in accordance with the style of the period; he received a Stalin Prize for this novel (for 1950, 3d class). With volume 1 of *Sotvoreniye mira* (1955–56; The Creation of the World), Zakrutkin undertook a comprehensive work depicting the fall of the bourgeois world after 1921 and the rise of the USSR as a world power before 1945. In the second part, which was published in *Oktyabr* in 1967, we find "a persistent effort to recall Stalin's services to his country again and again" (F. Svetov). The third part followed in 1975 and 1978. Through his participation in the formation of the conservative Writers Union of the RSFSR, Zakrutkin became an active literary official who opposed de-Stalinization and liberalization. He belonged to the board of the Writers Union of the RSFSR from 1958 on, to the secretariat of that organization from

1965 on, and to the editorial staff of the newspaper Literaturnaya Rossiya from 1963 on. For his povest set during World War II, Mater chelovecheskaya (1969; Mother Humanity), he received the Gorky Prize in 1970; for Sotvoreniye mira, the State Prize of the USSR in 1982. Zakrutkin has no literary talent. He chooses to include a pretentious number of historical particulars in his works but is unable to create a totality from them.

Works: Akademik Pljuščov (pov.), 1940; U morja Azovskogo (novel), 1946; Plavučaja stanica (novel), 1950 (see above); Sotvorenie mira (novel), 3 vols. (vol. 1, 1956; vol. 2, 1968; vol. 3, 1979); Mater' čeloveceskaja (pov.), 1969; Dorogami bol'šoj vojny, 1971; Na zolotykh peskakh (pov.), in Don 1986:5–6.—Sobr. soč., 4 vols., 1977–80; Izbr., 3 vols., 1986–87.

Secondary Lit.: G. Vladimov, in Novyj mir 1958:11; F. Svetov, in Novyj mir 1968:2; V. Petelin, 1969, and in Moskva 1979:11; A. Dymšic, in his Problemy i portrety, 1972; K. Prijma, in Don 1981:11; N. Lisovskaja, in Don 1984:11.

**Zalýgin, Sergéy Pávlovich,** prose writer (b. Dec. 6 [Nov. 23], 1913, Durasovka, prov. Ufa in Siberia). Zalygin's father was a librarian. In 1939 Zalygin completed his studies in hydrology in Omsk. He pursued a scientific career, participating as an engineering hydrologist in expeditions to Siberia along the northern Ob River during World War II. In 1948 he completed his dissertation and was offered a chair in agricultural irrigation in Omsk. Zalygin, who had begun publishing some literary works in 1940, moved to Novosibirsk in 1955 and became primarily a writer, although he also works with the Academy of Sciences of the USSR. From short prose works that appeared annually in collections, he switched to lengthier works in 1962; much discussion developed around these works since Zalygin tackles the genuine problems of the Soviet period. In spite of this, Zalygin knows how to be sufficiently acceptable; in 1968 he was awarded the State Prize for Solyonaya Pad (1967; Salt Hollow), Around that time he moved to Moscow; since 1970 he has belonged to the secretariat of the Writers Union of the RSFSR, and since 1986 to the buro of the secretariat of the Writers Union of the USSR. In August 1986 he was appointed editor in chief of the journal Novyj mir.

Zalygin's first novel, Tropy Altaya (1962; Paths in Altai), is set in the world of scientists and is an attempt to master the form of the novel. The povest Na Irtyshe (1964; On the Irtysch River) takes place in 1931 during collectivization in a Siberian village; at the same time that it provides a contrast with M. Sholokhov's Podnyataya tselina, it is the first work honestly to depict the injustice and inhumanity of strong-arm tactics as they were evidenced, for example, in the liability created for a family by the political crimes of one of its members. The novel Solyonaya Pad, in its description of the Civil War, also brought into the open for the first time the negative Communist leader, the inhumane fanatic who is contrasted with a true peasant leader. With his next novel, Yuzhnoamerikansky variant (1973; Eng. tr., The South American Variant, 1979), Zalygin shifts from historicopolitical problems to a question not usually dealt with in Soviet literature—that of extramarital relationships—using the contemporary example of a successful scientist who is dissatisfied with her marriage. Human problems stand in the forefront of the novel Komissiya (1975; The Commission), which is a sequel to Solyonaya Pad both spatially—Siberia—and chronologically—the Civil War. The chaos of the time and the narrow perspective of the peasants allow Zalygin to express some criticism of the Revolution, criticism that has been proven true by history, although it contradicts the Party line. The problem of condemning people, institutions, and ideas in the name of the Revolution, merely because they belong to "what has been," stands in the center of his seven-part novel Posle buri (1980–85; After the Storm), whose first four parts cover the period from 1921 to 1926. Zalygin has also made noteworthy contributions to the study of literature by writing about A. Chekhov and A. Platonov, among other authors.

Works: Rasskazy (short stories), 1941; Na Bol'šuju zemlju (short stories), 1952; Očerki i rasskazy (publicistic prose and short stories), 1955; Obyknovennye dni (short stories), 1957; Tropy Altaja (novel), 1962; Na Irtyše (pov.), 1965; Solënaja Pad' (novel), 1968; Čerty professii (essays), 1970; Literaturnye zaboty (essays), 1972, 2d ed. corrected and enl., 1979, and 3d ed. enl., 1982; Južnoamerikanskij variant (novel), 1973 (see above); Komissija (novel), 1976; Festival' (short stories), 1980; Posle buri (novel), in Družba narodov 1980:4–5, 1982:5 (separate ed., 1982), 1985:7–9; Sobesedovanija, 1982; Rasskazy ot pervogo lica (short stories), 1983.—Izbr. proizv., 2 vols., 1973; Sobr. soč., 4 vols., 1979–80.

Secondary Lit.: A. Berzer, in Znamja 1956:9;

RSPP 2:1964; Vs. Surganov, in Lit. Rossija May 29, 1964, p. 6, in Lit. gazeta Aug. 23, 1967, p. 4, and in Lit. i sovremennost' 8:1968; N. Janovskij, 1966; G. Kolesnikova, 1969; A. Elkin, in Moskva 1973:12; L. Terakopjan, 1973; V. Dement'ev, in Lit. gazeta Jan. 28, 1976, p. 4; N. N. Shneidman, in Russian Language Journal 106:1976; V. Tarsis, in ZeitBild Jan. 14, 1981; A. Njukin, in Lit. obozrenie 1982:12 and in Novyj mir 1983;12; I. Dedkov, 1985, and in Lit. gazeta Dec. 11, 1985, p. 4.

**Zamyátin, Yevgény Ivánovich,** prose writer, playwright (b. Feb. 1 [Jan. 20], 1884, Lebedyan, prov. Tambov—d. March 10, 1937, Paris). Zamyatin traveled considerably and was politically active in the Bolshevik faction of the Social Democratic Party while a student at St. Petersburg Polytechnic Institute. In 1908 he graduated with a degree in naval engineering. He began publishing literary works in 1908. His short story Uyezdnoye (1913; A District Tale) attracted an extraordinary amount of attention from both critics and readers. Until the Revolution, Zamyatin combined his two careers. His povest Na kulichkakh (1914; Out in the Sticks) resulted in judicial proceedings against him for antimilitarism; in 1916–17 he worked in England as a naval engineer, a fact reflected in his povest Ostrovityane (1918; Eng. tr., The Islanders, 1978. After the Revolution, Zamyatin became a leading figure in Petrograd; he founded journals, supervised literary classes, and exerted a strong influence on the literary group called the SERAPION BROTHERS. Zamyatin's own message in his prose and dramatic works and in his writings on literary theory was now directed against the pretensions of Communist officials who presumed to have access to an exclusive truth and who tried to enforce it by arbitrary means. Written in 1920–21, his major novel, My (Eng. tr., We, tr. by G. Zilboorg, 1924; tr. by M. Ginsburg, 1972; tr. by B. Guerney, 1972), describing a negative utopia, was first published in Czech, English, and French; it has yet to be approved for publication in the Soviet Union. Zamyatin's drama in defense of heretics, Ogni svyatogo Dominika (1922; The Fires of St. Dominic), was indeed published in Petrograd and Berlin but was not performed. His dramatic play Blokha (1925; The Flea), which thematically harks back to N. Leskov's "Levsha," was performed with great success at the Moscow Art Theater. From 1929 on, Zamyatin was increasingly persecuted by the RAPP critics to the point that he asked Stalin in June 1931 for authorization to leave the country:

"I know that I have the very unpleasant habit of saying not what is most advantageous at the given moment, but what I consider to be the truth instead." Amazingly, he was able to emigrate in 1931 and went to Paris in 1932, where he died five years later. In 1952 the first complete edition of My in Russian was published in New York. In 1986 O. Mikhaylov was able to publish a book with Zamyatin's prose in Voronezh (Povesti. Rasskazy).

As a brilliant stylist, Zamyatin exerted a considerable influence on many Russian writers. He further refined A. Remizov's "ornamental prose" into a satiric, often grotesque surrealism, which he himself designated neorealism. His attempt to achieve clear narrative structures and mathematical metaphors reveals the debt he owes to his engineering background. What made his work (the short stories of 1917–22) "a model of new literary technique, was not only its compactness and perfect composition, but also the device of significant details and symbolic central images" (Slonim). In Mamay (1921) and Peshchera (1922; The Cave), Zamyatin depicts the initial phase of Communist rule, which he sees as regression to a precivilized, troglodytic state. The novel My, which was composed after Zamyatin's own preoccupation with H. G. Wells's utopias, is an ingenious, visionary view of a totalitarian system with its belief that all events can be controlled by reason and its standardization of all its subjects. Zamyatin depicts the resistance of the irrational and the individual, as well as their repression by force. The work directly influenced Aldous Huxley (Brave New World) and George Orwell (1984). Ogni svyatogo Dominika takes place during the Inquisition and, in its depiction of the burning of a heretic, attacks allegorically the totalitarian ideology as well as the methods of the Soviet security organs. Blokha's importance lies primarily in its attempt to revive the Russian theater in the first quarter of the century. Zamyatin uses elements from the early period of Russian stage art, from Russian folk comedy, and from the commedia dell'arate.

Works: Uezdnoe (short story), 1916, 1923; Na kuličkakh (pov.), 1916; Ostrovitjane (pov.), 1922 (see above); Ogni svjatogo Dominika (play), 1922 (reprinted, Würzburg, 1973); Mamaj (short story), 1923; My (novel), Czech, French, English eds., 1924–29, excerpt in Russian in Volja Rossii, Prague, 1927, complete Russian ed., New York, 1952 (see above); Blokha (play), 1926; Obščestvo počětnykh zvonarej (play), 1926 (reprinted, Würzbug,

1973); *Nečestivye rasskazy* (short stories), 1927 (reprinted, Ann Arbor, 1978, and Letchworth, 1979); *Navodnenie* (short story), 1930 (reprinted, Ann Arbor, 1978); *Bič Božij* (novel), 1937; *Lica* (essays), New York, 1955; *Povesti i rasskazy* (pov. and short stories), Munich, 1963; *Povesti. Rasskazy*, 1986.—*Sobr. soč.*, 4 vols., 1929; *Soč.*, 2 vols., Munich, 1970, 1982.

*Translations: The Dragon: Fifteen Stories*, 1967; *A Soviet Heretic: Essays by Yevgeny Zamyatin*, 1970.

*Secondary Lit.:* T. Tamanin, in *Russkie zapiski*, Paris, 16:1939; D. J. Richards, London, 1962; P. Palievskij, in *Voprosy lit.* 1966:8; A. M. Shane, Berkeley, 1968; E. Lampl, Diss., Vienna, 1971; D. Hobzová, in *Cahiers du monde russe et soviétique* 1972; S. J. Layton, Diss., Yale Univ., 1972; R. Russel, in *Slavonic and East European Review* 1973:122; C. Collins, The Hague, 1973; G. Leech-Anspach, Wiesbaden, 1976; C. Barnard, Diss., Sheffield, 1978; R. Parrott, in *Russian Literature Triquarterly* 16:1979; N. Franz, Munich, 1980; J. J. van Baak, in *Russian Literature* 1981:4; A. Barrat, in *Slavonic and East European Review* 1984:3; L. Scheffler, 1984; L. B. Cooke, in *Russian Literature* 1985:4.

**Zarúdin, Nikoláy Nikoláyevich,** poet, prose writer (b. Oct. 13 [Oct. 1], 1899, Pyatigorsk— d. 1937 [?], while imprisoned). Zarudin came from a family of Russian Germans; his father, Nikolay Eduardovich Eykhelman, changed the family name in 1914. Zarudin attended the gymnasium in Nizhegorod. During the Civil War he served as a political commissar; afterward, he remained a follower of Trotsky. Zarudin was expelled from the Communist Party. His first volume of poetry appeared in 1923. Later he published short and longer prose pieces in *Krasnaya nov*, as well as in other places. He was considered to be an excellent speaker and oral storyteller. Zarudin was an active member of PEREVAL and for that reason was exposed to violent attacks by VAPP and RAPP at the end of the 1920s. In 1937 he became a victim of the government purges.

Zarudin considered F. Tyutchev, A. Grigoryev, and I. Bunin to be his literary models; he was, furthermore, greatly influenced by B. Pilnyak. His poetry and prose are written in an artificial, ornamental language overflowing with epithets and similes. His most important work is the novel *Tridtsat nochey na vinogradnike* (1932; Thirty Nights in a Vineyard), which in its eight parts, full of a "cosmic" spirit, provides a glimpse into the pre-Revolutionary patriarchal way of life of the ances-

tral home and contains numerous political allusions concealed in its intricate and elusive style.

*Works: Sneg višennyj* (poems), 1923; *Polem—junost'ju* (poems), 1928, 1970; *Drevnost'* (short story), in *Rovesniki* 7:1930 (reprinted, G. Glinka, *Na perevale*, New York, 1954, pp. 145–65); *Tridcat' nočej na vinogradnike* (novel), 1932, 1976; *Zakon jabloka* (short stories), 1966; publication of literary remains, in *Lit. Rossija* June 7, 1968, pp. 10–11.

*Secondary Lit.:* G. Glinka, *Na perevale*, pp. 137–44; P. Ul'jašov, in *V mire knig* 1971:12.

**Záytsev, Borís Konstantínovich,** prose writer (b. Feb. 10 [Jan. 29], 1881, Oryol—d. Jan. 28, 1972, Paris). Zaytsev was descended from a noble family. His father was a mining engineer. Beginning in 1898, Zaytsev studied at the Moscow Institute of Technology, the St. Petersburg Institute of Mining, and Moscow University (law), in each case without graduating. L. Andreyev published Zaytsev's first lyrical-impressionistic sketch, *V doroge* (On the Road), in the Moscow newspaper *Kuryer* in 1901 and introduced him to N. Teleshov's writers' circle, "Sreda." Between 1906 and 1911, three collections of short stories appeared; by 1919, there were seven. Zaytsev himself considered the short story *Golubaya zvezda* (1916; The Blue Star) to be the most expressive that he had written up to 1922. In 1921 he worked at the Writers Bookshop in Moscow; in 1922 he was elected chairman of the All-Russian Writers Association. In June 1922 Zaytsev received an exit visa on the grounds of illness; he lived at first in Germany and Italy, then after 1924 in Paris. In Berlin he achieved the rare distinction of having a seven-volume edition of his works published (1922–23). In Paris, Zaytsev continued to write novels and biographical works until an advanced age and was increasingly esteemed as the last link to the "Silver Age" of Russian literature in the early 20th century.

Zaytsev and his work belong to the tradition of I. Turgenev and A. Chekhov. In his work, content recedes in favor of an impressionistic, feeling-dominated atmosphere. The religious element, an aversion to all striving for material prosperity and easy security, and a sympathy for wanderers and the dispossessed form the connecting threads of his works. Almost all of his prose takes place in a Russian, some in an Italian, milieu. The novel *Zolotoy uzor* (1926; The Golden Pattern) covers the pre-Revolutionary period and the Revolution; *Dom* v *Passi* (1935; The House in Passy) provides, in Zaytsev's typically impressionistic manner, a glimpse into the day-to-day life of the first Soviet emigration in France. Zaytsev's most ambitious work is a four-volume autobiographical novel, which he began with *Puteshestviye Gleba* (1937; Gleb's Journey) and completed with *Drevo zhizni* (1953; The Tree of Life). Some works, such as *Afon* (1928; Mount Athos), a report about his own pilgrimage there, are completely devoted to the religious theme. His literary biographies of Turgenev, Chekhov, F. Tyutchev, and V. Zhukovsky stand apart from his other work. One of Zaytsev's most important achievements is his translation of Dante's *Divine Comedy*, which he had started in Russia and which he took up again around 1942 (published 1961).

*Works: Dal'nij kraj* (novel), 1915; *Tikhie zori* (short stories), 1916, Munich, 1961; *Ulica sv. Nikolaja* (short stories), Berlin, 1923; *Prepodobnyj Sergej Radonežskij* (short story), Paris, 1925; *Zolotoj uzor* (novel), Prague, 1926; *Afon* (travel notes), Paris, 1928; *Anna* (novel), Paris, 1929 (Eng. tr., *Anna*, 1937); *Žizn' Turgeneva* (biography), 1932; *Dom v Passi* (novel), Berlin, 1935; *Putešestvie Gleba* (novel-tetralogy): (1) *Zarja*, Berlin, 1937, (2) *Tišina*, Paris, 1948, (3) *Junost'*, Paris, 1950, (4) *Drevo žizni*, New York, 1953; *Moskva* (essays), Paris, 1939, Munich, 1960, 1973; *Žukovskij* (biography), Paris, 1951; *Čekhov* (biography), New York, 1954; *Dalëkoe* (essays), Washington, 1965; *Reka vremën* (pov. and short stories), New York, 1968; *Pis'ma I. i V. Buninym* (letters), in *Novyj žurnal*, New York, 139, 140:1980, 143:1981, 146, 149:1982, 150:1983.—*Sobr. soč.*, 7 vols., Berlin, 1922–23; *Izbr.*, New York, 1973.
*Secondary Lit.*: Èllis (pseud. of L. Kobylinskij), in *Vesy* 1908:2; Ju. Ajkhenval'd, in his *Siluèty russkikh pisatelej*, Berlin, 1923 (reprinted, The Hague, 1969); N. Ocup, in *Sovremennye zapiski*, Paris, 37:1928; G. Adamovič, in his *Odinočestvo i svoboda*, New York, 1955, and in *Russkaja mysl'*, Paris, Feb. 12, 19, and 26, 1981; E. Tauber, in *Grani*, Frankfurt am Main, 33:1957; F. Stepun, in *Mosty*, Munich, 7:1961; V. Zavališin, in *Novyj žurnal* 63:1961; A. Šiljaeva, New York, 1971, and in *Novyj žurnal* 106:1972; P. Gribanovskij, in *Russkaja literatura v èmigracii*, ed. N. Poltorackij, Pittsburgh, 1972; V. Grebenščikov, in *Russian Language Journal* 108:1977; Ju. Terapiano, in *Russkaja mysl'* March 10, 1977, p. 8; R. Guerra, Paris, 1982; V. Savva, in *Grani* 130:1983; O. Mikhajlov, in *Lit. Rossija* Aug. 14, 1986, pp. 16–17.

**Zazúbrin, Vladímir Yákovlevich** (pseud. of V. Y. Zubtsóv), prose writer (b. June 6 [May 25], 1895, Penza—d. July 6, 1938 [?], while imprisoned). Zazubrin's father was a railway official. In 1916 Zazubrin was arrested for illegal activities. From August 1918 to November 1919 he fought with Kolchak's army in Siberia, then went over to the Bolsheviks. In 1921 he joined the Communist Party (later he presumably left or was expelled). From his experiences during the Civil War and his own activity as an agitator came Zazubrin's novel *Dva mira* (1921; Two Worlds), which made him famous (it was even read to the troops). In the 1920s Zazubrin became the leading organizer of the literary and political life of western Siberia. From 1923 to 1928 he was chief editor of the journal *Sibirskiye ogni* in Novonikolayevsk (now Novosibirsk); from 1926 to 1928 he belonged to the leadership of the Siberian Writers Union, which he had helped found. Zazubrin's short story *Obshchezhitiye* (1923; The Dormitory) clearly showed his condemnation of NEP and was most sharply attacked by G. Lelevich, an official from OKTYABR ("We have not yet had such a shameful, disgusting, driveling, libelous work on the Revolution and the Communist Party"). M. Gorky, who had returned from emigration, called Zazubrin to Moscow in 1928. A second novel, *Gory* (1933; Mountains), on the topic of collectivization, remained unfinished. His speech on Gorky's death and a few memoirs about Gorky were the last things Zazubrin published, in 1936. After his arrest (1937?), an enforced silence was imposed concerning Zazubrin until his REHABILITATION (1956?). *Dva mira* was reprinted in 1959.

As a writer, Zazubrin is worth mentioning only for *Dva mira*. This novel, probably the first longer prose work of the Soviet period, is a mosaiclike chronicle of the Civil War in Siberia; it is not a poetically work of art, governed by continuous action. Zazubrin pursues definite Bolshevik goals in his naturalistic accounts of cruelty taken from the domain of the White Army; he loves sharp contrasts and symbolic scenes. After his rehabilitation, Zazubrin's presentation of this early period was characterized as ideologically correct in contrast to B. Pilnyak's; his condemnation of NEP was attributed to his lack of understanding of the methods involved in building socialism.

*Works: Dva mira* (novel), 1921, 10th ed., 1933, abridged ed., 1958, 1959; *Obščežitie* (short story), in *Sibirskie ogni* 1923:5–6; *Gory* (novel), 1935; *Khudožestvennye proizvede-*

nija, stat'i, doklady, reči, perepiska (selected works), 1972.

Secondary Lit.: G. Lelevič, in Na postu 1924:1; M. Kuznecov, in his Sovetskij roman, 1963, pp. 149–51; RSPP 2:1964; A. Zyrin, in Zvezda 1973:5; N. Janovskij, in his Istorija i sovremennost', 1974.

**Zenkévich, Mikhaíl Aleksándrovich,** poet (b. May 21 [May 9], 1891, Nikolayevsky gorodok, prov. Saratov—d. Sept. 16, 1973, Moscow). Zenkevich's first poem appeared in 1906; his first volume of verse, Dikaya porfira (1912; Wild Porphyry), was printed in St. Petersburg by Tsekh poetov, the publishing house of the ACMEISTS, to whom Zenkevich belonged. In 1915 he completed his law degree at St. Petersburg University; he also spent two years studying philology in Jena and Berlin. In 1923 he moved to Moscow and joined the staff of the publishing house Zemlya i fabrika. In his choice of themes Zenkevich conformed to the demands of the Party; eight volumes of his verse had been published by 1937. Zenkevich then shifted the main emphasis of his work to translation. He joined the Communist Party in 1947; 1954 was the only year in which he was delegated to attend a congress of the Writers Union. In Skvoz grozy let (1962; Through the Storm of Years), Zenkevich was able to publish a selection of his own works. He lived in Moscow.

The early poetry of Zenkevich's acmeist period is dominated by cumbersome poems on the subject of prehistoric existence. His juxtaposition of paleontological imagery with the theme of man's insignificance resulted in his being accused of pessimism after the Revolution. Zenkevich composed poems that presented war in all its horror and that expressed hope in things to come. His descriptions of Party meetings, his songs praising the use of machinery in agriculture, his narrative poems about pilots or the glorification of Stalin, such as Zenkevich published before 1939 (in, among other journals, Novy mir), remained superficial. His translations, on the other hand, achieved recognition.

Works: Dikaja porfira (poems), 1912; Četyrnadcat' stikhtvorenij (poems), 1918; Pašnja tankov (poems), 1921; Pod parakhodnym nosom (poems), 1926; Pozdnij polët (poems), 1928; Izbr. stikhi (selected poems), 1932; Izbr. stikhi (selected poems), 1933; Nabor vysoty (poems), 1937; Skvoz' grozy let (poems), 1962; Izbr., 1973.

Secondary Lit.: N. Gumilëv, in Apollon 1912:3–4 (reprinted, in his Sobr. soč., vol. 4, Washington, 1968, pp. 290ff.); V. Dynnik, in Krasnaja nov' 1936:1; I. Mikhajlov, in Neva 1964:3; I. Levidova, in Inostrannaja lit. 1966:1; RSPPo 9:1986.

**Zhárov, Aleksándr Alekséyevich,** poet (b. April 13 [March 31], 1904, Semyonovskaya, prov. Moscow—d. Sept. 7, 1984, Moscow). Zharov attended the nonclassical secondary school in Mozhaysk for a while and occupied various leading positions in the Komsomol from 1918 to 1925, at first in Mozhaysk and later in the Central Committee of the Komsomol in Moscow. In 1920 he joined the Communist Party. In 1921 he briefly studied at Moscow University; in the same year his first collection of poetry appeared. In October 1922 Zharov was among the founders of the MOLODAYA GVARDIYA. Zharov published numerous volumes of lyric poetry and narrative poems, including Garmon (1926; Harmonica), which was welcomed as a special achievement. During World War II he worked in a political capacity and as a correspondent with the Soviet fleet. During the postwar period, his lyrics for songs, including those for the "Hymn of the Young Pioneers," became well known. Zharov did not hold any positions within the Writers Unions. He lived in Moscow.

Zharov became famous as a member of the group of early Komsomol poets; he is quite a minor figure artistically. The glorification of Soviet youth is his central theme and PARTY SPIRIT his central commandment. Zharov's poor but political verses are hastily written and in spite of many expletives have neither rhythm nor meter. In 1928 V. Polansky called attention to the logical contradiction of his pathos-laden words; in 1930 V. Tarsis referred to the conventionality of his artistic means and imagery. Zharov's poems had no lasting propagandistic effect, but he is regularly featured in anthologies and histories of literature.

Works: Slovo o Povolž'e (poems), 1921; Lirika (poems), 1947; Znamenoscy junosti (poems), 1958; Strana junosti (poems), 1968; Stikhotvorenija. Pesni. Poèmy, 1973—Izbr. proizv., 2 vols., 1954; Sobr. soč., 3 vols., 1980–81.

Secondary Lit.: V. Polonskij, in Novyj mir 1928:11; V. Tarsis, in his Sovremennye russkie pisateli, 1930; S. Tregub, in Novyj mir 1941:2; E. Dolmatovskij, in Ogonëk 1954:15 and in Lit. gazeta April 18, 1979, p. 5; M. Škerin, 1980; RSPPo 9:1986.

Zhitkóv, Borís Stepánovich, prose writer (b.
Sept. 11 [Aug. 30], 1882, Novgorod—d. Oct.
19, 1938, Moscow). Zhitkov's father was a
mathematics instructor at a teachers college
in Novgorod. In 1906 Zhitkov completed his
studies in the Department of Natural Sciences
at Novorossiysk University. While a student,
he also trained as a helmsman and went to
sea numerous times. Zhitkov taught and was
involved in research for three years, then
worked for a second degree at St. Petersburg
Polytechnical Institute, graduating as a naval
engineer in 1916. He became harbor engineer
in Odessa in 1917; in 1923 he moved to Petrograd where, discovered by K. Chukovsky
and encouraged by S. Marshak, he began a
literary career as a children's writer. Between
1924 and 1938 Zhitkov published some 60
children's books that were highly regarded for
their sense of responsibility to the child, the
amount of factual information they contained,
and their clear language. Zhitkov died of lung
cancer in Moscow in 1938. In the obituary
notice, V. Shklovsky emphasized Zhitkov's
ability to write in an interesting manner about
the simplest things. Zhitkov's work attracted
less attention after 1940. His Viktor Vavich, a
novel about the Revolution of 1905 that Zhitkov himself regarded as his major work, was
published in 1941, but all copies were destroyed with the approval of A. Fadeyev. In
1955 L. Chukovskaya published a short monograph about Zhitkov and for the first time, a
selection of his works.

Zhitkov is one of the leading Russian children's writers. In addition to prose, he wrote
short plays and works of popular science. His
experiences at sea and his technical expertise
(reflected even in his small encyclopedia for
preschoolers, Chto ya videl [1939; What I
Saw]) greatly influenced his work from the
very first book, Zloye more (1924; The Wicked
Sea). Zhitkov's work is action-packed, frequently in conversational form, always vivid
and clear. His goal as a writer is to impart
knowledge properly and to educate his young
reader in genuine human qualities. "The basis
of Zhitkov's attitude toward children is in his
conviction that children's preferences, antip-
athies, sorrows, and joys are not trifles, not
playthings, but something every bit as serious
and important as the feelings of adults" (L.
Chukovskaya, p. 118).

Works (all children's books): Zloe more,
1924; Morskie istorii, 1925; Reka v uprjažke,
1927; Pro ètu knigu 1927; Telegramma, 1927;
Plotnik, 1928; Udav, 1928; Čudaki, 1931; Belyj domik, 1936; Čto byvalo, 1939, 1973; Čto

ja videl, 1939, 1978; Pomošč' idët, 1939; Rasskazy, 1940; Izbr., 1957, 1963, 1969, 1978.
    Secondary Lit.: V. Šklovskij, in Lit. kritik
1938:12; A. Ivič, in Lit. kritik 1939:3 and in
his Vospitanie pokolenij, 4th ed., 1969; L.
Čukovskaja, 1955, and in her Process isključenija, Paris, 1979, pp. 29–34; K. Čukovskij,
in his Iz vospominanij, 1958; L. Isarova, in
Komsomol'skaja pravda Sept. 10, 1967, p. 3;
G. Černenko, in Neva 1982:9.


Zinóvyev, Aleksándr Aleksándrovich, prose
writer (b. Oct. 29, 1922, Pakhtino, oblast Kostroma). Zinovyev's father was a painter; his
mother, a peasant. Zinovyev attended school
in Moscow from 1933 to 1939. During World
War II, Zinovyev was a fighter pilot. From
1946 to 1951 Zinovyev studied philosophy at
Moscow University; following completion of
the training for a university lectureship, he
was on the staff of the institute of philosophy
of the Academy of Sciences of the USSR from
1954 to 1977; in addition he taught at Moscow
University as a professor from 1967 to 1969.
Zinovyev specialized in the field of mathematical logic and won international recognition. During the 1970s, difficulties arose that
gradually led to his exclusion from research
and teaching. Zinovyev turned increasingly to
literary activity. The publication in the West
of his first work, which satirically and bitingly
exposed the Soviet system, Ziyayushchiye vysoty (1976; Eng. tr., The Yawning Heights,
1979), resulted in his expulsion from the
Communist Party, which he had joined after
Stalin's death, and from his scientific posts.
On Aug. 6, 1977, Zinovyev was allowed to
emigrate to the Federal Republic of Germany,
and he has lived in Munich since that time.
At brief intervals in Switzerland, he published first the books originally written in the
Soviet Union since 1973, and then those written later; they were well received.

Zinovyev, who according to his own account can write for as long as 20 hours at a
time and never revises his works, published
nine books between 1976 and 1982, some of
which are quite long. They all pursue the goal
of exposing the Communist system of government and its society in a satirical, sociologically analytic way. Ziyayushchiye vysoty is a
loose connection of several hundred short,
individual pieces in which all conceivable
realms of the intelligentsia's life are represented. The abstractly described, completely
schematic characters facilitate recognition of
the contemporaries he means to refer to. A
continuous, uninterrupted plot line is miss-

ing. Numerous obscenities have a repelling effect. From unpublished parts, Zinovyev subsequently developed the books *Svetloye budushcheye* (1978; Eng. tr., *The Radiant Future*, 1980) and *Zapiski nochnogo storozha* (1979; Notes of a Nightwatchman); in the first, the plot is carried by the figure of a staff member of a Soviet institute of philosophy who serves as storyteller. The title of *V preddverii raya* (1979; In the Atrium of Paradise) alludes to the "real socalism" that Brezhnev proclaimed to be the preliminary stage of communism. In *Zholty dom* (1980; The Madhouse), scenes in a mental institution alternate with descriptions of Party plans for improving political consciousness. *Gomo sovetikus* (1982; Homo Sovieticus) describes the third emigration—split internally and suspecting each other of belonging to the secret service. Zinovyev regards his stylistically very monotonous works as chapters of a larger book. His works are written without artistic talent in a quite consistent form of satiric condensation and abstraction that often requires commentary. In their individual segments, they form one of the sharpest and most pertinent sociological analyses of Soviet society, although they would gain considerably from elementary inclusion of Western analytic literature concerning communism and from respect for other "dissidents," at least for A. Sakharov and A. Solzhenitsyn.

*Works: Zijajuščie vysoty* (novel), Lausanne, 1976 (see above); autobiography, in *Posev*, Frankfurt am Main, 1978:8, and *Russkaya mysl'* Paris, May 25 1978; *Svetloe buduščee* (novel), Lausanne, 1978 (see above); *V preddverii raja* (novel), Lausanne, 1979; *Bez illjuzii* (essays), Lausanne, 1979; *Zapiski nočnogo storoža* (novel), Lausanne, 1979; *Žëltyj dom* (novel), 2 vols., Lausanne, 1980; *Kommunizm kak real'nost'* (essays), Lausanne, 1981 (Eng. tr., *The Reality of Communism*, 1984); *My i Zapad* (articles and interviews), Lausanne, 1981; *Gomo sovetikus* (short stories), Lausanne, 1982; *Moj dom—moja čužbina* (poems), Lausanne, 1982; *Našoj junosti polët* (documentary prose), Lausanne, 1983; *Ni svobody, ni ravenstva, ni bratstva* (articles), Lausanne, 1983; *Èvangelie dlja Ivana* (poems), Lausanne, 1984; *Ruka Kremlja* (play), in *Kontinent*, Paris, 47:1986.

*Secondary Lit.:* G. Andreev, Cologne, 1978; G. Hosking, in *The Times Literary Supplement* May 23, 1980; D. Šturman, in *Vremja i my* 62:1981; A. Abramov, in *Tret'ja volna*, New York, 12:1982; K. Pomerancev, in *Russkaja mysl'* Dec. 30, 1982, pp. 12–13; M. Ioffe, in *Novoe russkoe slovo*, New York, March 17,

1985, p. 4; E. Arkhipova, in *Russkaja mysl'* March 28, 1985, p. 13.

**Zlóbin, Stepán Pávlovich,** prose writer (b. Nov. 24 [Nov. 11], 1903, Moscow—d. Sept. 15, 1965, Moscow). Zlobin spent his childhood in Ufa and Ryazan. Between 1921 and 1924 he studied at the Bryusov Institute of Literature and Art in Moscow. Tuberculosis forced him to quit his teaching job in Ufa in 1925; afterward he worked in the area of economic management. Zlobin began his writing career in 1924 with a fairy tale in verse for children. Because of the aggravated literary and political situation, in 1929 Zlobin withdrew his novel *Dorogi* (Roads), then being set at the printer's, from publication; written between 1925 and 1927, the novel is set in the southern Urals and spans the period from the end of the 19th century to 1927. His first historical novel, *Salavat Yulayev* (1929), was successful. Zlobin then turned to the area of his own experiences among Soviet youth. The publishing house Molodaya gvardiya published his novel *Zdes dan start* (1931; Ready, Set, Go) but rejected a second novel because of its negative treatment of the Komsomol. At the end of the 1930s Zlobin again turned to writing novels about the peasant uprisings of the 17th century; he became chairman of the historical literature section of the Writers Union of the USSR. His work was interrupted by World War II, during which Zlobin was taken prisoner by the Germans. Freed in January 1945, he was able to serve as a frontline reporter until the end of the war. Zlobin began a novel about his imprisonment, but it proved to be unpublishable in 1946. He completed the historical novels *Ostrov Buyan* (1948; The Island of Buyan) and *Stepan Razin* (1951), and was awarded a Stalin Prize (for 1951, 1st class). After Stalin's death, Zlobin worked for liberalization in literature; he made a substantial contribution with his extensive novel *Propavshiye bez vesti* (1962; Missing in Action), which served to restore the honor of Soviet prisoners of war. Zlobin was able to complete only about half of the manuscript of *Utro veka* (The Morning of the Century), a novel about the revolutionary period of 1905, which he had started in 1950.

Zlobin was an extremely self-critical writer who spent decades revising his works in manuscript and even after each publication. Revised versions of *Salavat Yulayev*, for instance, appeared in 1941, 1953, and 1962. Zlobin takes pains to achieve historical accuracy and to moderate his use of folk-speech elements and historical color in his presentations of the peasant uprisings of the 17th and 18th centuries. *Propavshiye bez vesti,* the prisoner-of-war novel based on his own experiences, on the one hand shows the courage of Russian soldiers in the camp and, on the other, denounces the injustice with which former prisoners were persecuted and arrested by Soviet authorities.

*Works: Pereplokh* (fairy tale), 1924; *Salavat Julaev* (novel), 1930; *Ostrov Bujan* (novel), 1948; *Stepan Razin* (novel), 1951; *Propavšie bez vesti* (novel), 2 vols., 1962; *Po obryvistomu puti* (novel), 1967.—*Sobr. soč.,* 4 vols., 1980–81.
*Secondary Lit.:* V. Ivanov, in *Pravda* Feb. 19, 1952; S. Petrov, in *Znamja* 1952:1; I. Kozlov, in *Naš sovremennik* 1964:2; M. Korallov, in *Voprosy lit.* 1965:9; G. Baklanov, in *Lit. Rossija* Nov. 30, 1973, p. 9; I. Kozlov, foreword to Zlobin's *Sobr. soč.,* 1980–81.

**Zlóbin, Vladímir Anányevich,** poet (b. July 1894, St. Petersburg—d. Dec. 9, 1967, Paris). Zlobin's father was a rich merchant who left his family and wandered through Russia as a pilgrim. Zlobin began studying at St. Petersburg University before World War I and became known as the longtime friend and secretary of Z. Gippius and D. Merezhkovsky. N. Otsup introduced him to his future lifelong friends in 1916, and together with them, Zlobin left Russia on Dec. 24, 1919. After spending some time in Warsaw, Gippius, Merezhkovsky, and Zlobin moved to Paris in 1921 where they shared an apartment. Zlobin, who had begun writing poems as a student, published new poems in numerous journals starting in 1926. In 1927–28 he served as editor of the journal *Novy korabl* (for issues 1–4; Yu. Terapiano was also a member of the editorial staff); in 1927 he became secretary of "Zelyonaya lampa" (The Green Lamp), Gippius's literary salon. Only once did Zlobin compile his poetry into a book, and its title referred to Gippius: *Posle yeyo smerti* (1951; After Her Death). Zlobin also worked consistently as a critic and directed his attention, apart from his two lifelong partners, especially toward religious poets such as V. Smolensky, S. Makovsky, or G. Ivanov. Starting in 1950, Zlobin published poetry in *Vozrozhdeniye;* in issues 80–100, under the title *Literaturny dnevnik* (1958–60; Literary Diary), he published essays on events in Russian literature both in emigration and in the Soviet Union. He always fought against illusions

concerning the totalitarian and antireligious character of Soviet literary policy (on G. Ivanov in no. 82, B. Pasternak in no. 84, V. Nabokov in no. 85, N. Otsup in no. 86, Z. Gippius in no. 93). With *Tyazholaya dusha* (1970; Eng. tr., *A Difficult Soul,* 1980) he created a literary monument to Gippius.

Zlobin, who reveals an elevated artistic sensibility in his literary essays, is also a fine Russian poet. His poems derive from a direct life experience (even in dreams) and reveal his search for the spiritual connections that lie beneath the surface and reflect the will of God. Thus, motifs such as death, soul, angels, Satan, paradise, or hell appear often, and questions of spiritual or physical love are just as frequently addressed as are those concerning life after death and contact with the dead. The poem that Terapiano included in his anthology *Muza Diaspory,* "Ya sam sebya zakoldoval" (I Bewitched Myself), tells of an intense experience of meditation. Zlobin's imagery reveals its origins in symbolism; it also has a cosmic measure.

*Works: Posle eë smerti* (poems), Paris, 1951; *Literaturnyj dnevnik* (essays), in *Vozroždenie,* Paris, 80–100:1958–60; *Tjažëlaja duša* (scholarly articles and memoirs), Paris, 1970 (see above).
*Secondary Lit.:* Ju. Ivask, in *Opyty,* New York, 1:1953; N. Andreev, in *Grani,* Frankfurt am Main, 20:1953; M. Vega, in *Vozroždenie* 76:1958; T. Pachmuss, *Intellect and Ideas in Action* (correspondence with Z. Gippius), Munich, 1972.

**Známya** (The Banner), a literary journal published in Moscow since 1931, the first two years under the title *LOKAF. Znamya* was founded as a journal of LOKAF, the literary association of the Red Army and Navy, and has preserved its partiality toward military literature. From 1934 to 1948 Vs. Vishnevsky was entrusted with its direction; the majority of the editorial staff was dismissed in response to the sharp criticism of the Central Committee, an outgrowth of the Party Resolution of 1946 (in part because of their minimal exposure of COSMOPOLITANISM and of their publication of E. Kazakevich's story *Dvoye v stepi*) (see PARTY RESOLUTIONS ON LITERATURE). From 1948 to 1986 the editor in chief was V. Kozhevnikov, an opponent of liberalizing efforts; the like-minded critic L. Skorino was also a member of the editorial staff from 1949 to 1986. In 1986 G. Baklanov became editor in chief. The following writers were members of the editorial staff for periods of varying length: V. Lugovskoy (1931–44, with brief interruptions), A. Novikov-Priboy (1934–44), A. Sofronov (1949–53), Yu. Nagibin (1955–65), A. Ananyev (1967–73), V. Tsybin (1973–79), V. Makanin (1987–). *Znamya* published works with military themes by such authors as L. Sobolev, P. Pavlenko, V. Grossman, K. Simonov, A. Tvardovsky, G. Markov, and A. Chakovsky but also published works of general interest by such writers as L. Leonov, Yu. Trifonov, D. Granin, I. Erenburg, Vl. Lidin, and Yu. Nagibin. In 1986–87, in the Gorbachev *glasnost* period, *Znamya* published many good works of literature by talented contemporary writers and poets such as B. Akhmadulina, A. Bitov, I. Drutse, F. Iskander, A. Pristavkin, A. Tarkovsky, as well as works that had been banned for a long time, such as A. Tvardovsky's *Po pravu pamyati*, M. Bulgakov's *Sobachye serdtse*, and poems or prose works by N. Gumilyov, V. Khodasevich, V. Kornilov, B. Pilnyak, and A. Platonov. In 1975 the circulation was 170,000; in 1987 it was 277,000.

*Secondary Lit.*: "O žurnale 'Znamja,' " in *Kul'tura i žizn'* Jan. 11, 1949, and in *O partijnoj i sovetskoj pečati*, 1954; *Očerki istorii russkoj sovetskoj žurnalistiki*, 1968; V. Koževnikov, in *Lit. Rossija* Jan. 16, 1981, p. 8; I. Kozlov, in *Lit. gazeta* Jan. 28, 1981, p. 2.

**Zórin, Leoníd Génrikhovich,** playwright (b. Nov. 3, 1924, Baku). In 1946 Zorin graduated from Baku University, in 1947 from the Gorky Literary Institute. Zorin worked as a playwright in Baku and moved to Moscow in 1948 where his drama *Molodost* (Youth) was performed in 1949. In 1952 he joined the Communist Party. In 1954 he became well known at home and abroad for his play *Gosti* (Guests). By 1980 Zorin had written about 30 plays; of these, his 12 comedies especially enjoyed great popularity with the public. In Soviet histories of literature, Zorin is viewed critically for ideological reasons. In 1970 he was a delegate to a congress of the Writers Union of the RSFSR for the first time. In accordance with the striving for candor prevalent during the THAW, the existence of a "new upper class spoiled by power" (Steininger) is frankly conceded in *Gosti* and accounted for as the "consequence of the Soviet form of society." Zorin was sharply criticized, and the play was removed from the repertoire; after 1957, however, Zorin was again regularly permitted to publish and stage his plays: *Chuzhoy pasport*

(1957; Someone Else's Passport), *Svetly may* (1958; Bright May), *Dobryaki* (1959; The Goodnatured Ones). *Druzya i gody* (1962; Friends and Years), one of Zorin's best-known plays, reveals his commitment to a society free from Stalinist injustice and his talent as a playwright. In fourteen scenes set between 1934 and 1961, this play sets forth the fates of several friendships among youths and interposes the politically determined injustices of misuse of military office, defamation used to gain personal advantage, and the expulsion of someone's father from the Party in 1937 and the father's later death. The play bears the dedication: to the memory of my father. The chosen examples, however, are presented propitiously as rare exceptions to the Stalin period being depicted and only carefully hint at the true nature of the problems and their tragic consequences. Zorin, who was nevertheless reproached by the orthodox critics for "attributing everything to the cult of personality" (*Oktyabr* 1963:8, p. 183), turned toward interpersonal concerns in *Paluba* (1963; The Deck). *Dion* (1965), set in the time of the Roman Emperor Domitian, was banned in Leningrad, probably because of its symbolic contemporary criticism. In *Dekabristy* (1967; The Decembrists), Zorin created a historical tragedy that, together with A. Svobodin's *Narodovoltsy* and M. Shatrov's *Bolsheviki*, was well received at the 50th anniversary of the October Revolution as a depiction of three generations of the revolutionary intelligentsia. *Varshavskaya melodiya* (1967; Eng. tr., *A Warsaw Melody*, 1968), a play about the difficulties confronting a Soviet citizen who wants to marry a foreigner, was staged 150 times in ten years. *Tsarskaya okhota* (1974; Tsar's Hunt) concerns Count A. Orlov's tragic deception of a woman who pretended to be a daughter of Peter I at the end of the 18th century. The comedy *Izmena* (1979; Adultery) reveals Zorin's ability to make a traditional subject freshly amusing through ironic variations.

*Works: Gosti* (play), in *Teatr* 1954:2; *Alpatov* (play), 1957; *Proščanie* (play) in *Teatr* 1959:3; *Svetlyj maj. Dobrjaki, Uvidet' vovremja, Po moskovskomu vremeni* (plays), 1962; *Druz'ja i gody* (play), in *Teatr* 1962:8; *Dekabristy* (play), in *Teatr* 1967:12; *Tranzit* (play), in *Teatr* 1973:8; *Teatral'naja fantazija* (plays), 1974 (contains *Konec i načalo; Dekabristy; Dobrjaki; Ènciklopedisty; Teatral'naja fantazija; Paluba; Varšavskaja melodija* [see above]; *Tranzit; Serafim, ili tri glavy iz žizni Kramolnikova; Stress; Burnye dni Garunskogo); Carskaja okhota (play), 1977 (acting copy); Nez-*

*nakomec* (play), in *Teatr* 1977:1; *Izmena* (play), in *Teatr* 1979:1; *Pokrovskie vorota* (play), 1979; *Karnaval* (play), in *Teatr* 1981:1; *Staraja rukopis'* (novel), in *Sever* 1980:8–9; *Citata* (play), in *Teatr* 1986:8; *Izbr.* (plays), 2 vols., 1986.

*Secondary Lit.*: editorial, in *Lit. gazeta* May 27, 1954; K. Mehnert, in *Osteuropa* 1954:5; N. Ignat'eva, in *Voprosy lit.* 1963:3; Ju. Rybakov, in *Lit. gazeta* Dec. 4, 1963; I. Višnevskaja, in *Teatr* 1967:10; V. Lakšin, in *Novyj mir* 1968:9; I. Čerejskij, in *Teatr* 1971:8; A. Svobodin, in *Teatr* 1974:11; V. Klimenko, in *Lit. obozrenie* 1980:1; L. Anninskij, in *Novyj mir* 1981:7.

**Zóshchenko, Mikhaíl Mikháylovich,** prose writer (b. Aug. 10 [July 29], 1895, Poltava—d. July 22, 1958, Leningrad). Zoshchenko's father was an artist. Zoshchenko studied law in St. Petersburg from 1913 to 1915; in 1915 he enlisted as a volunteer in World War I; in 1918–19 he served as a volunteer in the Red Army. He frequently changed jobs until his sudden recognition as a writer in 1922; from 1921 on, he was a member of the SERAPION BROTHERS in Petrograd, a group that maintained that art must be free of political regimentation. His comic and satiric short stories made Zoshchenko a very popular Soviet writer; his works reached readers in many social strata. In spite of the difficulty in translating them, his stories were soon popular abroad. Between 1922, when his first collection, *Rasskazy Nazara Ilyicha gospodina Sinebryukhova* (The Stories of Nazar Ilyich, Mr. Sinebryukhov), was published, and 1946, there were 91 first editions and republications of his books. With the intensification of dogmatic criticism (RAPP), attacks on Zoshchenko increased; the critics—willfully ignoring the point that satire is an artificial device—accused Zoshchenko of exaggeration or of exposing social abuses and human weaknesses that are atypical or nonexistent. A performance in Moscow of Zoshchenko's comedy, *Uvazhayemy tovarishch* (Esteemed Comrade), planned in 1930–31 by V. Meyerhold in conjunction with V. Mayakovsky's *Klop*, was stopped; performances in Leningrad were at variance with Zoshchenko's own conception of the work. Between 1929 and 1931 Zoshchenko was still able to bring his short stories together in a six-volume edition, the most comprehensive up to that time. In the 1930s Zoshchenko's satire became less colorful. *Golubaya kniga* (1935; The Light-blue Book), which compositionally unites individual stories by means of cycles and narrative

frames, distinctly revives the novella-cycles of the Renaissance (D. Moldavsky); it contains several witty short stories of the early period that have been changed into rational, logical, and normalized form, and thus weakened artistically. "In his search for a way out, Zoshchenko turned to 'noncomic' genres" (Kaverin): he depicted the social reintegration of a criminal in a penal camp in *Istoriya odnoy zhizni* (1934; The History of One Life) and wrote a biography, *Taras Shevchenko*, in 1939 (Shevchenko's 125th jubilee year). This change was alien to his talent. During World War II, Zoshchenko was evacuated to Alma-Ata. A self-analytical *povest*, *Pered voskhodom solntsa* (1943; Eng. tr., *Before Sunrise*, 1974), was very sharply condemned (A. Fadeyev labeled it "unpatriotic," while N. Tikhonov claimed it was "totally alien to the character of Soviet literature"). It was one part of an autobiographical work that was to be called *Klyuchi schastya* (Keys of Happiness); the second part, *Povest o razume* (A Tale of Reason), appeared in *Zvezda* 1972:3). As the Communist Party intensified its administrative control of literature after the war, Zoshchenko was selected, along with Anna Akhmatova, as a major victim for attack in the Party Resolution of Aug. 14, 1946 (see PARTY RESOLUTIONS ON LITERATURE). The grounds (the reprinting of the children's story *Priklyucheniya obezyany* [1945; Adventures of a Monkey]) were so flimsy that Zoshchenko believed that there had been some misunderstanding and futilely turned to Stalin for justice. The Writers Union expelled him. As an outcast, he existed solely by doing translations. His return to the Writers Union in July 1953 did not lead to the publication of a volume of selected works until 1956; the broken talent could not be healed. Posthumous volumes of selected works offer very little of his early work. Soviet literary history remains divided on his merits.

The astonishing thing about Zoshchenko's style is his independence from such possible models as N. Gogol, N. Leskov, A. Chekhov, A. Remizov, and all other Soviet literature. His two- or three-page reflections on experiences taken from everyday Soviet life are comically refracted through the prism of a fictitious, half-educated narrator who is sincerely surprised by the awful circumstances around him (see SKAZ). In addition to the use of alogisms, hyperbole, and similar devices, Zoshchenko generates a good deal of humor by transplanting Soviet propaganda slogans into an inappropriately commonplace context. "The design of each story is clearly delineated and is almost on the verge of implausibility even though it is based on perfectly realistic incidents" (Slonim). In several longer tales, such as Strashnaya noch (A Terrible Night), humor serves to accentuate tragedy.

Works: Rasskazy Nazara Il'iča gospodina Sinebrjukhova (short stories), 1922; Jumoristiceskie rasskazy (short stories), 1923; Uvažaemye graždane (short stories), 1926; Uvažaemyi tovarišč (play), in 30 dnej 1930:9 (reprinted in Strelec, Montgeron–Jersey City, N.J., 1986:3); Istorija odnoj žizni (pov.), 1934; Vozvraščënnaja molodost' (pov.), 1934; Golubaja kniga (short stories), 1935; Taras Ševčenko (biography), in Lit. sovremennost' 1939:2–3; Izbr. rasskazy i povesti 1923–56 (short stories), 1956; Izbr., Ann Arbor, 1960; Rasskazy. Fel'etony. Komedii. Neizdannye proizvedenija (short stories and comedies), 1963; Pered voskhodom solnca, New York, 1967, 2d ed., 1973 (see above); Rasskazy (short stories), Frankfurt am Main, 1971; Povest' o razume, in Zvezda 1972:3; Povesti i rasskazy (short stories), 1983.—Sobr. soč., 6 vols., 1929–31; Izbr. proizv., 2 vols., 1946; 1968; 1978; 1982.

Translations: Russia Laughs, 1935; The Woman Who Could Not Read and Other Tales, 1940; The Wonderful Dog and Other Tales, 1942; Scenes from "The Bathhouse" and Other Stories of Communist Russia, 1961; Nervous People and Other Stories, 1963.

Secondary Lit.: M. Z. Stat'i i materialy, 1928 (reprinted, Letchworth, 1973); A. R. Domar, in Through the Glass of Soviet Literature, ed. E. Simmons, New York, 1953; RSPP 2:1964; V. Kaverin, in Novyj mir 1965:9; L. Daetz, "Studien zur sowjet-russischen Kurzgeschichte," Diss., Munich, 1969; D. M. Moldavskij, in Russkaja lit. 1970:4 and separate study, 1977; C. S. Katowitz, Diss., Univ. of Pennsylvania, 1972; A. Starkov, 1974; V. Zoščenko, in Voprosy lit. 1975:10; J. D. Cukierman, Diss., Univ. of Michigan, 1978; M. Čudakova, 1979; M. Z. v vospominanijakh sovremennikov, 1981; Ju. K. Ščeglov, in Wiener Slawistischer Almanach 7:1981; A. B. Murphy, 1981; Ju. Tomaševskij, in Lit. gazeta Aug. 8, 1984, p. 6; B. Semënov, in Neva 1984:8; A. Žolkovskij, in Sintaksis, Paris, 16:1986; M. Kreps, Benson, Vt., 1986.

**Zozúlya, Yefím Davýdovich,** prose writer (b. Dec. 10, 1891, Moscow—d. Nov. 3, 1941, Rybinsk). Zozulya's father was a commercial clerk. Zozulya spent his childhood in Lodz and Odessa. He worked as a journalist in Odessa

(beginning in 1911), then in Petrograd (1914–18). In 1919 Zozulya moved to Moscow, where in 1922 he founded the journal Ogonyok with M. Koltsov. He did not associate himself with any literary groups. Zozulya's short stories appeared regularly in small collections, as well as in a three-volume edition (1927–29). From 1937 on, what little he published was in journals. During World War II, Zozulya enlisted in the army, was taken ill at the front, and died in a military hospital. His work remained unpublished and unmentioned. No articles appeared about him until 1956; a single volume of his selected works was published in 1962.

Zozulya is a highly gifted master of the psychological short story; he initially patterned himself on A. Chekhov. He focuses his vision on the interpersonal situations of daily urban life, which he enlarges in almost microscopic detail and which he at times generalizes in a satirical manner. His astonishing gift of observation reveals the typical element in life's coincidences. He strives "to see in things and events, not their direct meaning, nor their mechanical relationship, but something difficult to distinguish, although quite fully distinct, something that hides between the lines" (Koltsov). Soon after the Revolution, Zozulya began to defamiliarize the short stories that were critical of his time by introducing fantastic and grotesque elements into them; the influence of Ye. Zamyatin in these stories—for example, in Rasskaz ob Ake i chelovechestve (1919; The Tale of Ak and Mankind)—is apparent. Two novels from around 1930 remained unfinished.

Works: Gibel' glavnogo goroda (short stories), 1918; Tom pervyj (short stories), 1923; Sobr. novell (short stories), 1930; Ja doma (short stories), 1962; Tysjača (short story), in Lit. Rossija Jan. 7, 1972, p. 17.—Sobr. soč., 3 vols., 1927–29.

Secondary Lit.: S. Olenov, in Na postu 1923:2–3; M. Kol'cov, foreword to Zozulya's Sobr. soč., 1927–29; K. Levin, in Naš sovremennik 1961:6; A. Dejč, foreword to Ja doma, 1962; RSPP 2:1964; M. Matusovskij, in Lit. gazeta Jan. 20, 1982, p. 5.

**Zvezdá** (The Star), a literary journal that has been published in Leningrad since 1924, every two months at first, then monthly since 1927. Zvezda was the first journal published in Leningrad whose role was to perpetuate the tradition of the "thick" Russian journals, in which, in addition to short prose, poetry, and criticism, many novels were published before they could appear in book form. The first editor in chief was I. M. Maysky (until 1925:1). Thereafter the editor changed frequently; authors who were members of the editorial staff included N. Tikhonov (1929–44), Yu. Libedinsky, occasionally as editor in chief (1929–37), V. Sayanov (1929–31, 1944–46, 1953–59), A. Tolstoy (1933–38), M. Slonimsky (1934–41, 1959–66), B. Lavrenyov (1937–41, 1946–47), V. Rozhdestvensky (1939, 1957–67). Continuously since 1957, the editor in chief has been G. Kholopov, who briefly held this position in 1939–40. Under his editorship, authors who are at all recognized have stopped joining the editorial staff. In the 1920s *Zvezda* was essentially a journal of the FELLOW TRAVELERS. Almost all the SERAPION BROTHERS, such as V. Kaverin, M. Slonimsky, M. Zoshchenko, N. Nikitin, N. Tikhonov, and K. Fedin, were published there. In addition to the authors on the editorial staff, the early contributing authors included O. Forsh, Yu. Tynyanov, A. Akhmatova, and N. Braun. In 1932 *Zvezda* became the organ of the Writers Union of the USSR. *Zvezda* continued publication during the blockade in World War II. The ideological obduracy of the postwar period found its expression in the Party Resolution of Aug. 14, 1946 (see PARTY RESOLUTIONS ON LITERATURE), which especially criticized *Zvezda* in a crass fashion and inveighed against A. Akhmatova and M. Zoshchenko in an embarrassingly obscene way. In more recent times *Zvezda* has continued to be essentially an organ of Leningrad writers and has published the works of V. Panova, D. Granin, E. Grin, Yu. German, V. Shefner, G. Gorbovsky, and S. Voronin. In 1927 the circulation was 5,000; in 1975, 113,000; and in 1987, 140,000.

*Secondary Lit.:* G. Kholopov, in *Zvezda* 1959:1, 1964:1, 1974:1 and in *Lit. gazeta* Dec. 21, 1983, p. 5; "O žurnalakh 'Zvezda' i 'Leningrad': Iz postanovlenija CK VKP(b) ot 14 avgusta 1946 goda," in *KPSS o kul'ture prosveščenii i nauke*, 1963; *Očerki istorii russkoj sovetskoj žurnalistiki*, 1968.

# Index of Names

# Index of Subjects